THE
CAMBRIDGE
MODERN HISTORY

CAMBRIDGE UNIVERSITY PRESS

C. F. CLAY, Manager

LONDON : FETTER LANE, E.C. 4

NEW YORK : THE MACMILLAN CO.
BOMBAY
CALCUTTA } MACMILLAN AND CO., Ltd.
MADRAS
TORONTO : THE MACMILLAN CO. OF
CANADA, Ltd.
TOKYO : MARUZEN-KABUSHIKI-KAISHA

THE
CAMBRIDGE
MODERN HISTORY

PLANNED BY

THE LATE LORD ACTON LL.D.
REGIUS PROFESSOR OF MODERN HISTORY

EDITED BY

A. W. WARD LITT.D.

G. W. PROTHERO LITT.D.

STANLEY LEATHES M.A.

VOLUME XII
THE LATEST AGE

New York
THE MACMILLAN COMPANY

First Edition **1910**

Reprinted **1917, 1920**

PRINTED IN GREAT BRITAIN

PREFACE.

OUR task is now approaching its conclusion. The first circular issued by the Syndics of the University Press, setting forth the plan and purpose of this *History*, is dated in March, 1898. The present editors assumed their conjoint duties in November, 1901. Our first volume appeared before the end of 1902. The last volume of our text should be published in the autumn of 1910. The volume of maps, and the general index, with genealogical and other tables, should be ready shortly after. We shall then have discharged our arduous undertaking, and given our work to the world, conscious of its imperfections, but grateful for the indulgent and sympathetic reception which it has met. Our cordial thanks must once more be expressed to all those who have generously afforded us assistance, and contributed their learning and wisdom to the common store.

The present volume has unfortunately been delayed by illness and serious accident affecting one of our contributors. The rest of the chapters have been for some months in their final shape. Hence it is to be feared that, in certain cases, the views on the immediate outlook expressed in our text refer to a situation which has since been more or less modified. No great revolution has, up to this date, occurred to confound our main conceptions of the trend of current events; but in Hungary the prospect of an enduring parliamentary settlement no longer seems immediate, and in Great Britain the financial question has been overshadowed by a graver constitutional issue. Above all, since these pages were printed off, this country and this empire have been profoundly affected by the lamented death of our wise, self-sacrificing, and beloved monarch, Edward VII, whose reign, though all too short, had done so much for the prosperity of his people and for the cause of peace and goodwill among nations. In the presence of national sorrow the violence of political passion has been abated, and a spirit of mutual conciliation has descended upon us. The reign of our new King thus begins amid happy auguries.

The period of history with which this volume deals presents many obvious difficulties to the historian. Living in a crowded and circumscribed fragment of a fraction of the world which he is attempting to describe, he must transport himself by imagination to some higher sphere whence the nations and their fortunes may be seen to range themselves in intelligible perspective. Writing under the influence of momentary and transitory impressions, he must free himself from their bondage and pay homage to the future and the past. He must endeavour to see this world, not as it affects the prejudices, interests, and limited outlook of his contemporaries, but as it might appear to one who should look back on it without any personal concern in its turmoil. Only partial success is possible; but he may console himself for partial failure with the belief that he is handing down to posterity one of those records of contemporary impressions which history is bound to respect if only they be sincere, impartial, and accurately informed.

Sources of information are not lacking. Secret history, such as is included in confidential papers and private correspondence, remains, for the most part, unrevealed. Rumours and false reports cannot yet be controlled or checked. But in the abundance of contemporary literature, solid as well as ephemeral, lies the answer to nine-tenths of all the historical problems relating to this age which will ever receive even an approximate solution. We are, in many ways, more amply instructed about our own time than we are in the affairs of any other age; the main difficulty lies in the fact that hardly a beginning has been made in the sorting, sifting, arranging, and summarising of the bewildering mass of accessible knowledge. With these difficulties we and our contributors have done our best to cope.

A chapter on the foreign relations of the United States during the great Civil War finds a place in this volume, since it was observed that these relations had been insufficiently explained in the American volume (Vol. vii.), and further elucidation was needed for the clear understanding of the *Alabama* question, which looms large in the opening years of our period. An introductory chapter deals with the larger aspects of world history in the period, and five chapters at the close of the volume treat of those movements that are most distinctive of the latter part of the nineteenth century: the development of an international code of law, and the establishment of standing international tribunals; the social movement in Europe and America; the advance of the knowledge of nature and of the surface of the globe on which we live; and the systematic study of the history of man from his earliest appearance upon this earth to the present time.

Our hearty thanks are due to all our contributors and helpers; and, in particular, Professor Pares, the author of two chapters on modern Russia, wishes us to put on record his obligations and our own to many distinguished publicists and statesmen in Russia who have placed at his disposal their intimate knowledge of Russian affairs and politics, and have thus enabled him to give an authoritative account of a most obscure and important section of modern history.

With feelings of regret, not untempered by relief, we take our formal, though not our final, leave of all our readers and critics. The support of the public, without which this history could not have been brought to its conclusion, is a remarkable proof of the serious and compelling interest taken by a large class in the results of historical study; that interest has been fostered and encouraged by our critics, whose comments have often been illuminating, and have never been hostile or malicious. Had the great student, who conceived the plan of this work, survived to see its completion, he would not, we think, have been disappointed with his audience.

A. W. W.

G. W. P.

S. L.

CAMBRIDGE,
July, 1910.

TABLE OF CONTENTS.

CHAPTER I.

MODERN EUROPE.

By STANLEY LEATHES, M.A., formerly Fellow of Trinity
College, First Civil Service Commissioner.

CHAPTER II.

FOREIGN RELATIONS OF THE UNITED STATES
DURING THE CIVIL WAR.

By J. WESTLAKE, K.C., LL.D., Trinity College, formerly
Whewell Professor of International Law.

CHAPTER III.

GREAT BRITAIN.

By Stanley Leathes, M.A.

CHAPTER IV.

IRELAND AND THE HOME RULE MOVEMENT.

By R. Dunlop, M.A., Victoria University.

CHAPTER V.

THE THIRD FRENCH REPUBLIC.

By Émile Bourgeois, Professor in the University of Paris.

CHAPTER VI.

THE GERMAN EMPIRE.

By HERMANN ONCKEN, Professor in the University of Heidelberg.

(1)

THE FIRST SEVEN YEARS OF THE EMPIRE.
(1871–7.)

Contents. xiii

(2)

The Triple Alliance and the culminating period of Bismarck's ascendancy.

(3)

Bismarck's Fall, and after.

(1888–1910.)

CHAPTER VII.

AUSTRIA-HUNGARY.

By Louis Eisenmann, Professor in the University of Dijon.

CHAPTER VIII.

UNITED ITALY.

By Thomas Okey.

CHAPTER IX.

THE LOW COUNTRIES.

By the Rev. George Edmundson, M.A., late Fellow and Tutor of Brasenose College, Oxford.

HOLLAND.

CHAPTER X.

THE IBERIAN PENINSULA.

By DAVID HANNAY, formerly H.M. Vice-Consul at Barcelona.

SPAIN.

PORTUGAL.

CHAPTER XI.

SCANDINAVIA.

By Ludvig Stavenow, Professor in the University of Göteborg.

SWEDEN.

CHAPTER XII.

REACTION AND REVOLUTION IN RUSSIA.

By Bernard Pares, M.A., Trinity College, Professor in the University of Liverpool.

CHAPTER XIII.

THE REFORM MOVEMENT IN RUSSIA.

By Bernard Pares, M.A.

CHAPTER XIV.

THE OTTOMAN EMPIRE AND THE BALKAN PENINSULA.

By WILLIAM MILLER, M.A., Corresponding Member of the Historical and Ethnological Society of Greece.

CHAPTER XV.

EGYPT AND THE EGYPTIAN SUDAN.

(1841–1907.)

By F. M. Sandwith, M.D., University of Durham, formerly Professor of Medicine, Egyptian Government School of Medicine.

CHAPTER XVI.

THE BRITISH EMPIRE IN INDIA.

By P. E. ROBERTS, B.A., late Scholar of Worcester College, Oxford.

CHAPTER XVII.

THE FAR EAST.

By Sir ROBERT KENNAWAY DOUGLAS, Professor of Chinese,
King's College, London; formerly Keeper of the Oriental
Printed Books and MSS. at the British Museum.

CHINA.

CHAPTER XVIII.

THE REGENERATION OF JAPAN.

By J. H. LONGFORD, Professor of Japanese in King's College, London; formerly H.M. Consul at Nagasaki.

CHAPTER XIX.

THE RUSSO-JAPANESE WAR.

By Major F. B. Maurice, General Staff Officer.

CHAPTER XX.

THE EUROPEAN COLONIES.

By E. A. Benians, M.A., Fellow of St John's College.

CHAPTER XXI.

THE REPUBLICS OF LATIN AMERICA.

(1)

HISTORICAL SKETCH TO 1896.

By F. A. KIRKPATRICK, M.A., formerly Scholar of Trinity College.

(2)

THE INTERNATIONAL POSITION OF THE LATIN AMERICAN RACES.

By SANTIAGO PEREZ TRIANA, Envoy Extraordinary and Minister Plenipotentiary for the Republic of Colombia.

CHAPTER XXII.

THE MODERN LAW OF NATIONS AND THE PREVENTION OF WAR.

By Sir FREDERICK POLLOCK, Bart., LL.D., D.C.L., formerly Fellow of Trinity College.

CHAPTER XXIII.

SOCIAL MOVEMENTS.

By Sidney Webb, LL.B., Barrister-at-Law.

CHAPTER XXIV.

THE SCIENTIFIC AGE.

By W. C. DAMPIER WHETHAM, M.A., F.R.S., Fellow
of Trinity College.

CHAPTER XXV.

MODERN EXPLORATIONS.

By J. D. ROGERS, M.A., formerly Stowell Fellow of
University College, Oxford.

ASIA.

CHAPTER XXVI.

THE GROWTH OF HISTORICAL SCIENCE.

By G. P. GOOCH, M.A., formerly Scholar of
Trinity College.

LIST OF BIBLIOGRAPHIES.

CHAPTER I.

MODERN EUROPE.

In this period the History of Europe becomes in a sense the History of the world. In the sixteenth century, when our continuous narrative begins, the European system embraced only a part of the European Continent. European culture and European political methods had pervaded little more than the countries of France, the Netherlands, Germany, Bohemia, Spain, Italy, England. Outlying countries such as Scotland, Ireland, Scandinavia, Poland, were more or less apart from the main current of European affairs. Russia had not entered the European circle. South-eastern Europe, including a large part of Hungary, had fallen or was shortly to fall under Ottoman rule. The great geographical discoveries of the fifteenth and sixteenth centuries prepared the way for the later spread of European civilisation and European principles of government; but the full effect of these discoveries was not felt until the nineteenth century. The establishment of Spanish and Portuguese rule in Central and Southern America brought about a real extension of European influence to the other hemisphere; but the advance then made was arrested, and the more complete assimilation of those areas to European standards begins with the revolt from Spain and the creation of independent Republics on a European model during the first half of the nineteenth century. It was carried further by the great immigrations which took place towards the end of the same century; and it received its seal and recognition, in 1907, when the Republics of South and Central America entered the European Congress of the Hague as equal members of the European confraternity. These communities may now be regarded as outlying members of the European brotherhood, ruled under the same forms of government, practising the same arts, pursuing the same commerce and industry by the same financial methods, in short, as States created and living after the European pattern. Thus, during the nineteenth century the whole of the South American Continent was added to the realm which is dominated by European political and industrial conditions.

In 1784 the existence of an independent federation of European communities in the North American Continent was formally recognised. But much remained to be done before the whole of that vast territory was conquered, and colonised, and reduced to the European pattern. During the first half of the nineteenth century European domination swept steadily forward—westward and northward and southward ; but the work of settlement and organisation was able to move more rapidly after railways and telegraphs had been introduced, and the period covered by this volume has witnessed the final consolidation all over the United States of a new and fairly homogeneous European race ; absorbing Anglo-Saxons, Celts, Germans, Spaniards, Italians, Slavs, accepting every European variety, but rejecting Mongolian intruders with resolute aversion ; dwelling in enforced proximity with multitudes of African negroes, but refusing to admit them to social or real political equality. Meanwhile the British and French community in Canada has been moving forward somewhat more slowly but on parallel paths, until the whole of the North American Continent has become subject to a transatlantic European stock, predominantly British in certain characteristics, but constituting, through the blending of races and the influence of surroundings, a novel European type or types.

Meanwhile, in the Far South-East other European semi-independent communities have been growing to political maturity. The Australian States have been consolidated and united in a great Federal Union. The British Dominion of New Zealand is firmly established. There also we see the same determination to preserve the European type uncontaminated and to forbid the intrusion of Mongols or other Asiatics.

At this moment in South Africa, after a great racial war of conservative Dutch and Huguenot settlers against more progressive newcomers from Europe, all nationalities and parties have agreed to unite into one State the several British and Dutch communities from the Cape of Good Hope to the Zambesi. Whatever may be the outcome of these changes, it is certain that the ideas and aims of modern European enterprise must ultimately prevail against the archaic traditions that were inherited from the isolated *vortrekkers* of the Veldt. In South Africa, again, we see an instinctive aversion from Asiatic immigration overpowering any imperial sympathy of common citizenship, and demanding unanimously that Europeans alone should be admitted as colonists. But, there, State-builders are also confronted with the more difficult problem of the political relations between the dominant European minority and the aboriginal inhabitants who form the greater part of the population. Whatever temporary expedients may be adopted, it is certain that the European inhabitants will demand and ultimately obtain political and social predominance.

Thus, over two continents and part of a third self-governing communities, organised and conducted on European lines, have established or brought to completion their ascendancy within the period covered by this volume. In Europe itself the European system has been extended by the creation of Bulgaria as an autonomous principality on the European model in 1878, and by the inclusion therein of Eastern Rumelia in 1885. The recent declaration of Bulgarian independence establishes a new independent European State. The occupation of Bosnia and the Herzegovina by the Austro-Hungarian monarchy in 1878 was another step in the same direction; and the annexation of these provinces in 1908 did little more than register an accomplished fact; but the inevitable absorption of the Turkish dominions in Europe into the European system has hitherto been delayed. The attempt initiated in 1908 to reorganise the Ottoman empire according to European political ideas is so recent that its results cannot yet be even guessed.

But the extension of the sphere of European influence during recent years is not fully set forth by the enumeration of autonomous communities which have been established, enlarged, developed, or consolidated in Europe or in other Continents. Almost the whole of Africa has been partitioned among the European Powers by the delimitation of their respective spheres of influence at the Conference of Berlin, 1884-5, and by subsequent Conventions. The French occupation of Tunis (1881-4) brought a fresh section of the Mediterranean littoral under European rule. From Algeria in the north to the Congo in the south and Senegal in the west, uninterrupted French supremacy is now recognised; and Timbuktu is no longer a city of mystery. The protectorate of Madagascar, asserted by France in 1883, led in 1896 to annexation of that island. British authority is established over all the valley of the lower Niger, where the governing powers of the Royal Niger Company were taken over in 1900. On the Congo the French have occupied since 1884 wide tracts of country, and the Congo Free State, set up by Europe about the same time under the rule of the King of the Belgians, has recently been annexed to the Belgian State. The old Portuguese possessions in Angola, Mozambique, on the Zambesi, and south of the Zambesi, have been delimited. The Germans have marked out great claims in the south-west, and on the east of Africa (1884); in the race for African possessions they started somewhat late, but they succeeded also in establishing themselves in the Cameroons and in Togoland. Somaliland is divided between the French, the Italians, and the British. The southern part of the African littoral on the Red Sea has fallen to Italy. The British occupation of Egypt, begun in 1882, appears likely to be permanent, and led in 1896-8 to the conquest of the vast provinces of the Sudan, thus linking up the territory in British possession from Mombasa to the Mediterranean. Bechuanaland was snatched from the Boers in 1885; and the enterprise of Cecil Rhodes and others has extended British dominion beyond the Zambesi, to join the province known as British Central Africa, which has been separately developed. Abyssinia and Morocco are almost the only native Powers in Africa which retain their independence, though Tripoli, as a dependency of the Ottoman empire, remains outside the European system.

Almost the whole of Africa has thus become an annex of Europe, and while the greater part of it has not been settled, and much of it is unsuitable for European settlement, the fortunes of its countless peoples and of its boundless tracts depend upon the policy, are controlled by the force, and are contingent on the jealousies, of the European Powers. This process of delimitation has been for the most part initiated and carried out within the last thirty years.

The Asiatic Powers present more obstinate resistance to European ideas and European conquest. The Ottoman empire in Asia Minor, Mesopotamia, Syria, and Arabia, has remained hitherto practically impervious to European influence. In Persia the rivalry of Russia and Great Britain has preserved the Shah's dominions intact in the midst of internal revolution; while the insecurity of the government and financial instability has retarded commercial penetration. Siberia has been opened up by the Great Siberian Railway begun in 1891; and colonisation has been rapidly proceeding. In Central Asia, Russian power has advanced steadily southwards till it impinges on the frontiers of Persia, Afghanistan, and Chinese Turkestan. Further east, Tibet has been the centre of irresolute but notable international rivalries, culminating in the British expedition of 1904 to Lhassa. But Tibet remains, except to isolated enterprise, the most impenetrable district of the inhabited world. China herself has presented an obstinate and gelatinous resistance to warlike or peaceful penetration. The Russian occupation of Manchuria was brought to an end by the Japanese War of 1904–5. But the occupation of Kiaochow and the neighbouring district by the Germans in 1897–8 involved a notable and permanent diminution of Chinese sovereignty; the Liao-Tung peninsula has changed hands more than once and now rests in Japanese possession; the wars of 1894 and 1904 finally destroyed Chinese pretensions to suzerainty over Korea, and substituted Japanese supremacy in that peninsula. The acquisition of Annam by the French, begun in 1858 by the conquest of Saigon, was completed in 1886 by the establishment of a French protectorate over the whole of the kingdom. Siam has probably been saved from European absorption by the mutual jealousy of Great Britain and France. British influence in the protected States of the Malay peninsula has been extended and recently consolidated by an agreement with Siam, the nominal suzerain. Upper Burma was conquered and annexed by Great Britain in 1886. But the most remarkable extension of the European system in the Far East has resulted from the adoption of western political methods by the Empire of Japan. That Empire has been admitted to alliance on equal terms by Great Britain; a Japanese representative has sat in the Congress of the Hague; Japan has waged successful war with one of the greatest of European Powers; she has annexed Formosa and dominates Korea; she has effectively claimed recognition as an equal from the members of the European confraternity; she is on the one hand the champion of Asiatic independence, on the other hand the pioneer in the introduction of European sciences, European political methods, and European commercial enterprise into some of the most impenetrable districts of the distant East. She is a bulwark against European conquest, but a missionary of the European propaganda. The institution of American rule in the Philippines since 1898 has established in the Far East yet another centre of vigorous competitive activity, and added one more to the tale of the rivals who jostle each other for commercial and political superiority on the coasts of China and in the western waters of the Pacific.

Thus, the work begun by the Spanish and the Portuguese in the sixteenth century, later taken up by the Dutch, and more rapidly carried forward by Clive, Warren Hastings, and their successors, has moved with ever increasing rapidity as the nineteenth century drew towards its close. Those Asiatic Powers and regions, which have maintained their independence hitherto, can only escape European rule by the establishment of strong and stable governments, and by the adoption at any rate of European military arts, together with such inventions as railways, telegraphs, and telephones, which are necessary to military efficiency. The whole world is now the sphere of European activity; and the compass of this *History* requires to be correspondingly enlarged.

It is idle to censure the inevitable or to pass judgment upon destiny; the European nations have resembled other conquering races in their brutality, violence, and rapacity; this exotic rule has been seen perhaps at its worst in the valley of the Congo, at its best in the recent government of India, and in Egypt; it has produced some unscrupulous pirates and many conscientious, laborious, self-sacrificing administrators; religious missions have been active, but on the whole the benefits conferred have been rather material than moral; wealth has increased in consequence of improved order and security; famine has been curbed, slavery has been put down, the desert has been reclaimed, communication has been accelerated, knowledge has been diffused; but it is perhaps too soon to cast the balance and to set the advantages against the evils of European rule. It is enough to note the fact that in the world-wide struggle for life, wealth, and power the Europeans have for the moment proved their indisputable predominance; three quarters of the world have come under their sway; and the independence of the remainder is held by a precarious tenure.

In Europe itself one of the most remarkable features of the most recent period has been the steady advance of democracy. In France, a democratic autocracy was replaced by a democratic Republic as a consequence of the great War with Germany. The German Empire was established about the same time on a democratic basis. The Italian kingdom has a democratic Constitution. The franchise has been considerably extended in Great Britain and the practical working of the Constitution has been rendered more democratic in municipal and local as well as in national affairs. Bulgaria, the latest addition to European States, is controlled by popular suffrage, as are also the other independent polities of the Balkan peninsula. Quite recently universal suffrage was adopted by Austria as an attempt to solve her racial difficulties. Its adoption in Hungary is under consideration. In Russia, in spite of periodic reactions, there seems to be an advance in the same direction. Even Turkey is making the democratic experiment. If it succeeds, every country in Europe, not even excepting Russia, will have recognised to some extent the democratic principle, and all the self-governing European communities beyond the seas have adopted democratic government.

Democracy, it is true, is capable of very varying interpretations. In Germany it has proved compatible with the existence of a powerful monarchy, which has, in the main, succeeded in expressing more accurately the aspirations of the nation as a whole than any representative assembly or popular press. In England, it is still tempered by a strong aristocratic bias. In many countries the resources of government are freely used to influence the elections. In the United States, the representative machinery is in great measure controlled by powerful interests and organisations, though their domination is largely due to popular indifference, and may at any time be swept away by the action of the people. In Southern and Central America, democracy has commonly led to the more or less precarious establishment of the autocratic rule of powerful Presidents ; of this the remarkable career of President Diaz in Mexico is the most striking example ; and personal ambitions, under these conditions, have brought about periodic revolutions in most of the Latin States of America. But even in these countries some homage must be paid to the popular will. In every country where the Constitution is democratic, representative institutions afford a means, however imperfect, for the expression of popular sentiments ; they act as a real check on the executive authorities and exercise a modifying influence upon older national institutions and customs.

Seeing that modern representative democracy was practically unknown in Europe before the French Revolution, the universal acceptance of the democratic principle among European nations constitutes a striking revolution, accomplished in many cases without any violent convulsion. In theory, democracy might naturally lead to the exercise of state authority in the sole interest of the most numerous, that is, the poorest, class of voters. In practice, though the interests of the masses are more carefully studied now than in any previous period, though the socialistic movement has obtained great hold in many countries, and many socialistic measures have been adopted, the introduction of democratic institutions has not as yet led to that political warfare of class against class, which theorists have prophesied. Democracy promotes civil strife; but it also affords a means for its speedy and peaceable settlement. Simultaneously with the general introduction of democracy, in all the principal countries of Europe the education of the people has been undertaken as a part of government duty; and this condition, together with the development of the popular press, and improvement of means of communication and transit, has facilitated the introduction of this constitutional method in European communities; some look forward to its adoption in British India and Egypt; it is being tried in Turkey; but few would assert with confidence that democracy was suited to Asiatics; in spite of the example of Hayti, none perhaps would venture to propose its general application to the communities of African negroes. It is a European invention, and perhaps only suited to the European race and European culture.

The period since 1871 has been, so far as western Europe is concerned, a period of peace. Such great wars as have been waged have been fought on the confines of the European system—in the Balkan peninsula and in Manchuria. But the peace has been an armed peace. Following the example of Prussia, almost all the Great and most of the minor Powers of Europe have organised their armies on a basis of universal compulsory military service. On a peace footing the armies of the five great continental Powers amount to over two million men and their annual expenditure reaches £158,000,000. On a war footing they are supposed to be able to muster over twenty millions of soldiers. When we remember that, in addition to defraying his share of the necessary expenditure, every man in these countries is bound if required to give up two or more years of his life to military training, the weight of this load becomes apparent. Yet, under democratic conditions, these sacrifices are made without serious complaint, in republican France as in autocratic Russia. The burden of naval expenditure and compulsory naval service has in addition to be sustained; and on the whole this burden is rapidly increasing. Proposals for limiting military and naval expenditure are made from time to time; but, even if it were possible to frame the principles of such limitation and enforce them, the attempt would involve the determination of relative national strength; no impartial authority exists to decide what relative military strength would represent the total force, actual and potential, of the several nations; no nation would acquiesce in a position of permanent inferiority which it felt able to remedy by its own efforts; moreover, conditions change, and any adjustment adopted today would cease in a short time to suit the actual facts. No alteration in the existing policy as regards armaments is in sight.

On the whole, the existence of this tremendous military equipment makes for peace. The consequences of war would be felt in every house-

CH. I.

hold; and statesmen, as well as nations, shrink from the thought of a conflict between forces so immense. Peace, it is true, obliterates the memories of war; but peace also creates habits of peace; security breeds the love of security; we are never safe from the outbreak of some great national passion; but the desire of war for war's sake, the hunger for military glory, the national impulses and traditions which influenced the career and policy of the third Napoleon, seem for the time at any rate to have lost their operative power; the nations appear to desire peace, and, if they desire it, they may perhaps retain it.

The preponderance on the Continent of Europe which came to the German Empire as a result of the Franco-Prussian War has during subsequent years been perceptibly increased. The German Constitution, with all its defects, has placed the whole resources of the German nation for war and defence at the disposal of the Federal Government. The organisation of the army has, so far as we know, been maintained at its traditional standard of efficiency; a strong navy is being built up; the population which in 1871 was about forty-one millions now amounts to sixty-five millions. The wealth of the country arising from commerce and industry has increased even beyond this proportion. The revenue, though insufficient for the Federal expenditure, has been supplemented by loans which the unpledged credit of the new unified State has been able to secure on moderate terms. While Germany has thus been growing in wealth and power, the advance of other countries has been relatively slow. French population has been stationary; and Russia, Germany's other great rival on the Continent of Europe, has been recently crippled by a disastrous war and internal disorder. This disturbance of the balance of power by natural growth and external accidents has created a certain uneasiness in Europe and in recent years has led France and Russia to enter into friendly understandings with Great Britain. But, beyond a certain disposition to influence the course of diplomatic negotiation by hints which have hardly amounted to threats, no overt act of aggression can be laid to the charge of the German Government; and the policy of deliberate and continued warlike expansion, of which Treitschke was for many years a chief exponent, has received no sanction or countenance from the responsible leaders of the German people.

In the years immediately following the establishment of the German Empire Bismarck thought it necessary to protect the new State by alliances tending to isolate or at any rate to neutralise France. The first attempt in this direction was seen in the *Dreikaiserbund* of 1872. This informal and elastic understanding between Germany, Russia, and Austria-Hungary was shaken during the Russo-Turkish War of 1877–8, when the interests of Austria and Russia were plainly seen to be divergent. From that date onwards, although the league of the three Emperors was ostensibly maintained, the bonds between Austria and Germany were drawn tighter. In 1879 Austria and Germany formed a defensive alliance against an attack by Russia on either Power. In 1884 a fresh agreement was contracted between the three Emperors; and about the same time Bismarck thought it well to conclude a reinsurance treaty with Russia, stipulating for neutrality in case either Power was attacked by a third. But the rivalry between Austria and Russia prevented any permanent accord between these two Powers; and Germany was forced to decide whether the Austrian or the Russian alliance was the more valuable. She decided in favour of Austria. In 1887 the treaty between Austria and Germany became public; but in the same year Bismarck appears to have again endeavoured to "reinsure" with Russia, and with this policy he coquetted until his fall.

The French expedition to Tunis in 1881 and the subsequent occupation of that country by France brought about for a time the complete alienation of Italy from France, and this led in 1882 to the accession of Italy to the Austro-German League. This triple alliance has been maintained to the present day; though friendly relations between Italy and France have been completely restored since 1898, and it is doubtful how far Germany and Austria could rely on the cordial cooperation of Italy in the event of war. On the Morocco question Italy showed herself more sympathetic to France than to Germany; the Italian people felt that their interests in the Balkans had not been sufficiently regarded by Austria in her recent annexation of Bosnia and the Herzegovina; and no united general policy is maintained by the Triple Alliance, similar to that pursued by Austria and Germany.

The league of the three Emperors was in effect determined in 1887. Overtures made on behalf of the Central Powers to Great Britain about that time alarmed both France and Russia; Russian loans were readily subscribed in Paris; in 1891 the French fleet visited Cronstadt; in 1893 a Russian fleet returned the visit at Toulon; and in 1895 a formal alliance between France and Russia was announced.

Since 1895 the European situation has been governed by the Dual Alliance of France and Russia and the Triple Alliance of Austria and Germany to which Italy is still formally attached. Both alliances are, so far as is known, purely defensive. Great Britain has throughout the period maintained a cordial understanding with Italy, and has recently established very sympathetic relations with France; and, more recently still, her differences with Russia have been composed. She has been accused of attempting to form a ring of all the Western Powers against Germany; but there seems no foundation for this charge. She has, however, departed to some extent from her policy of deliberate isolation; she has contracted more than one intimate friendship, and, since 1902, a definite alliance with Japan, renewed in 1905.

The alliance with Japan requires some explanation. Until about 1894, British predominance in the Far East was undisputed. But, after the close of the war between China and Japan, the activity of the other European Powers was increased; and France, Germany, and Russia took upon themselves to settle the outcome of that war without the cooperation of Great Britain. The result was that Great Britain took no part in robbing Japan of the spoils of war; on the other hand, she had allowed questions of the greatest moment in the Far East to be decided without any reference to her wishes or interests. For the time her prestige in the Far East was seriously impaired; and it seems improbable that her unique predominance in those quarters can ever be restored. Britain has no need for territorial expansion; her declared interest is the maintenance of the open door for commerce, and for this purpose the integrity of Chinese territory is required. After various moves and counter-moves, and minor annexations, the Anglo-Japanese Alliance was adopted as a means to this end, and has up to the present fully answered the purpose. So long as the Alliance continues, the predominance of the Allies in Chinese waters is sufficient for all probable contingencies.

If China has been one great storm-centre of European policy, the Balkan peninsula has been for a longer period a more serious point of danger. In the Near East, since the Russo-Turkish War, Servia, Bulgaria, Greece, Armenia, Crete, have each from time to time troubled the European atmosphere; but the effective balance of power between Austria and Russia has prevented up to the present any serious change in the *status quo*. How long this precarious equilibrium can be maintained is doubtful. In this district not only the rivalries of Austria and Russia have to be considered, but also the mutual jealousies of Servia, Bulgaria, and Greece, which make for war, and the emulous propaganda of Greeks and Bulgarians in Macedonia. The financial and administrative weakness of the Ottoman Power is another source of danger. The firm establishment of an honest and efficient government at Constantinople would do much to diminish the danger of war.

During the period following on the War of 1877–8, the influence of Great Britain with the Porte, at first considerable, afterwards declined. The sympathies of the English nation with unfortunate peoples such as the Armenians were found inconvenient at Stamboul; and the advice of English ministers as to reforms in methods of government, though ineffective, was resented. Germany for many years took the place of Great Britain as principal adviser to the Sultan, and reaped advantages in commercial ways. However, the desire imputed to Germany—the establishment of her industrial and commercial supremacy in Asia Minor —has not been achieved; and the recent revolution in Turkey has for the moment restored British influence at Constantinople.

Great Britain has, for the most part, remained outside the great European combinations, taking an independent line in each discussion that arose. The nature of her interests demands that she should oppose in turn every Power that from time to time threatens to disturb the existing equilibrium; and no alliance or bond that she may contract is likely to have any other end in view. Her military weakness precludes her from intervening with effect in any purely continental struggle; her naval predominance, so long as it is maintained, enables her to dispense, for the most part, with extrinsic aid in the defence of her possessions across the sea; no European alliance could assist her to protect her Indian frontier, or to coerce her African neighbours; it is likely, therefore, that she will continue to avoid all embarrassing ties, so long as the existing Balance of European Power seems secure. This policy has led her to protect the crumbling empires of Turkey and of China. Lord Salisbury declared, in a fit of characteristic pessimism, that Great Britain had backed the wrong horse in supporting Turkey; but, if internal regeneration results in either or both of these cases, the British policy will be justified; conquest is not a remedy for misgovernment, though it is its natural penalty.

While the mutual fears of the great European Powers, aided perhaps by a genuine desire for peace, have curbed their animosities for thirty years, the same forces have shielded by an almost spontaneous international guarantee the lesser States. Any attempt to conquer Holland or Belgium or Switzerland seems precluded by the existing state of European feeling; and Greece, though helpless, was delivered in 1897 from the vengeance of Turkey by the concerted action of the European conclave. It may be that with lapse of time the States of the Balkan peninsula will also come to be regarded as keystones of the European harmony, which it is dangerous and criminal to disturb.

The period prior to 1871 was a period of the formation of new States on a large scale. The subsequent period has witnessed a reaction. The minor nationalities have vigorously asserted their independent rights. Bohemia and Ireland have insistently proclaimed their national individuality. Finland has maintained a strenuous fight for independent existence. Polish nationality resists all efforts at absorption. While Hungary demands full recognition as an equal partner in the Dual Monarchy, she has herself to reckon with the several claims of her subordinate Slavonic peoples. Norway has split off from Sweden. Compared with these spontaneous manifestations of separatist feeling and national aspirations, the Pangermanic and Panslavonic movements seem pale and ineffective results of academic or interested propaganda. Either movement might serve as an excuse for the operations of dynastic ambition; neither seems likely to exercise an independent influence on history. Cosmopolitanism has been at a discount; and the almost universal adoption of a close protective system of tariffs by European nations, while inspired no doubt by other and more immediate political and economic motives, has fitted in appropriately with the general desire for completeness, variety, and self-sufficiency of national life.

CH. I.

As a symptom of the sincere desire for peace prevailing in Europe during this period, we may note the extended use of arbitration for the settlement of minor disputes.   Disputes between nations can be divided into disputes which turn on limited questions of right, capable of juridical solution, and disputes which result from the clash of irreconcilable national impulses.   No Arbitration Court could have ruled out the natural aspiration of Prussia to take her place as the chief unit in a consolidated German people.   No authority could suppress the right of France to regard such a development as a menace to her own security.   The rival and fixed desires of these two Powers could not both be satisfied; the arbitrament of force could alone decide the issue.   But such minor questions as the delimitation of doubtful boundaries, the adjudication of blame in accidental collisions, rights of fishing, rights of sealing, petty violations of neutrality, have often in the past separately or cumulatively led up to breaches of the world's peace.   Such questions have, again and again, been successfully adjusted by international arbitration in late years; arbitration treaties have been extensively concluded; and a permanent Arbitration Court has been set up at the Hague before which Germany and France have recently appeared, for the decision of a point of dignity as well as of a point of right.   The Casa Blanca arbitration is a marked step towards the peaceful consolidation of the European community and the recognition of a common and binding code of law.

In earlier volumes the attempt has been made to show the shifting from time to time of the centre of gravity of Europe.   From about 1660 to 1870 that centre of gravity was undoubtedly in Paris.   Since 1871 France, though still in the forefront of European culture, has lost something of her pride of place.   The centre of European politics proper has been at Berlin; the centre of world-politics, which are also European politics in the larger sense, has been in London.   And it is not by accident that the Hague, midway between London and Berlin and nearly equidistant from Paris, has been chosen as the meeting-ground of European councils.   Whether the coming generation sees the centre of world-politics transferred from London to Washington depends on various contingencies; among others, on the policy adopted by Great Britain towards her self-governing Colonies, and on the degree of interest which the United States may come to take in matters outside their own boundaries.   Up to the present, the United States have taken no share in European politics, little in world-politics; but the Spanish War and the annexation of the Philippines have introduced a change.

During this period of peace the population of Europe has rapidly increased; and its overflow has gone to replenish the North and South American Continents, and to a less degree, other quarters of the globe. Meanwhile wealth has increased beyond proportion; and the mechanical arts have advanced with great rapidity.   The knowledge of natural processes and laws has been progressively extended; and the application of science to the satisfaction of material wants has been more effective than in any other period of the world's history. Not only methods of production, but methods of finance, have been revolutionised. The development of the joint-stock company system has rendered capital more fluid, has multiplied the owners of property, has substituted the fictitious person with its soulless mechanism of managing directors and board for the human and individual owner or employer, has concentrated power without fixing responsibility, has diverted attention to stock exchange speculation and company promotion in lieu of personal enterprise, has given opportunity for new forms of fraud, sometimes on a prodigious scale, and by the establishment of gigantic combinations, especially in the United States of America, has threatened to stifle competition for the benefit of colossal monopolies. By these changes the spirit and general aspect of commerce and industry have been altered; the authority and economic importance of individuals have been not diminished but increased; but, in the eye of the world and of the law, the company has been substituted for the man. This process had, of course, begun before the last century, but its immense extension has taken place chiefly in the last forty years.

The concentration of thought and energy on the production and accumulation of wealth has infused the whole epoch with a materialistic tinge. The systematic and self-conscious study of the fine arts and the collection of artistic treasures have been carried further than before; but the artistic imagination has been sterile. A high general level has been maintained in the plastic and pictorial arts; but genius has been conspicuously absent. Engineering has made enormous strides; architecture has been uninspired. Fiction has flourished more than poetry; but the great mass of stories and romances seem designed rather to satisfy the general need for an anodyne, for temporary oblivion, than to realise an artistic ideal. Journalistic and fugitive literature of every description has been abundant. There have been great actors, and superb theatrical display, but no great dramatists. The most notable productions in drama have been critical and rebellious, like those of Ibsen, rather than enthusiastic in the worship and quest of beauty. After the robust optimism of Robert Browning and George Meredith a common note of pessimism becomes apparent in most of the few writers of acknowledged European eminence who have recently come to the front, in Anatole France, Tolstoi, Thomas Hardy, and Maxim Gorky; Maeterlinck withdraws himself into a mystical and melancholy land of faery, far removed from sordid contemporary struggles and the tyranny of the senses; while Gabriele d'Annunzio makes surrender, without reserve or scruple, to the poetry of animalism and creates a world of beauty in which thought and the higher emotions have no place. The chief efforts of constructive political thought have been devoted to the framing of the materialistic

CH. I.

utopias of social reformers. Even the Church has been infected; the modern priest is sometimes more concerned for the unemployed than for the unrepentant. Music alone among the creative arts has been alive and fruitful; and the production and popularity of the romantic musical dramas of Wagner have been perhaps the most noteworthy artistic events of the generation.

Since the fall of Bismarck, no statesman of unquestionable greatness has appeared in the European arena. It may be that some were great, but emergencies did not arise to test and prove their greatness. The career of William Ewart Gladstone fills a large part of our period, but as Prime Minister his influence in foreign policy was felt more by the action which he declined to take, or took unwillingly, than by any far-sighted course of conduct in affairs. The inscrutable Disraeli still moves the world by the imperialistic aspirations which he first aroused in the unimaginative souls of his fellow countrymen, but his actual achievements were small. Lord Salisbury steered a skilful course safely through troubled waters. Gambetta's dominant personality touched the imagination and won the affections of France, but his career was blighted and ineffectual. Of men still living it is too soon to speak, but we should look in vain for any whose actual achievements entitle him to rank with Cavour, or Lincoln, or Bismarck. Even the successes of Japan appear to have been won, not by the efforts and policy of one man, but by the harmonious energy of many inspired with a common purpose. In spite of democratic conditions, monarchs have played their full share in moulding the history of nations. Francis Joseph, Queen Victoria, Victor Emmanuel, William II, Edward VII, have been not the least important statesmen of the period; while Abd-ul-Hamid and Tz'ŭ Hsi deserve a separate sentence. But, on the whole, the conditions of the time and the universal desire to maintain the existing equilibrium have not favoured the rise to conspicuous power and eminence of any individual.

But the somewhat monotonous and generally unsensational course of public events has not been due merely to the fear of change constricting the ambitions of statesmen and peoples; a moderating influence has also been exercised by the constantly increasing power of financial interests. We shall never know exactly when and how financial considerations have curbed the exuberance of petty States or the ambitions of Great Powers. The interests of financiers are as a rule on the side of peace and tranquillity; their power is constantly waxing; their means of persuasion are multifarious and convincing, and can be employed against governments as well as against individuals; an unfavourable policy can even be checked by an artificial stringency of credit which is felt by small and great. Where, as in the United States, a large proportion of the population takes a hand in speculation, thousands of voters are affected by market considerations in the exercise of their franchise. No Power, no person, is too great, no man too humble, to be reached by the pervasive and unseen pressure of financial interests, and financial authority. This force, non-moral as it is, sordid as it may seem, is a growing factor in European politics, and, as a rule, it is exercised for the preservation of peace. It is not only ubiquitous and massive; it is highly organised, highly centralised, and in large measure directed by skilled minds, who understand not only the movements of the Exchange but the secret springs of popular feeling. The obscure sense in the popular mind of the weight and momentum of this unseen force goes far to account for the anti-Semitic movement, which is so widespread in many continental countries.

The age has been prosaic and unromantic; the enthusiasm for the mechanical and scientific triumphs of the early Victorian period has somewhat faded; the belief in constitutional government and universal education as a remedy for all political and social evils has been shaken; the blots on our economic and moral order have been relentlessly drawn to light; self-complacency is no longer fashionable; it is more popular to decry than to praise the world in which we live. The consolations of religion have for the moment lost their efficacy in large sections of the European population. The zeal of the young and ardent is thrown into schemes of social regeneration. Such schemes are everywhere, whether they take the form of personal work among the poor and the sick, or trades-union politics, or visions of progressive legislation moving step by step towards an improved society, or propaganda leading up to the social revolution and common ownership of all land, machinery, and productive organisation; or the blind schemes of murder and destruction nursed in garrets and basements by the half-mad apostles of militant Anarchism. All these schemes alike are materialistic in their aims; their kingdom is of this world; they seek for no spiritual compensations, they admit no spiritual rapture; their professors represent all grades between the extreme of self-devotion and the culmination of hate, envy, and greed. But the belief in the possibility of social reform by conscious effort is the most dominant current in the modern European mind; it has superseded the old belief in Liberty as the one panacea; even Bismarck paid homage to it; and no modern statesman can afford to ignore it. Its substantial achievements, and perhaps its disappointments, are in the future; but its currency in the present is as significant and as pregnant as the belief in the Rights of Man about the time of the French Revolution. The coming age will be occupied by the attempt to translate its ideals into the phrases of practical politics.

CHAPTER II.

FOREIGN RELATIONS OF THE UNITED STATES DURING THE CIVIL WAR.

THE Civil War was so tremendous a struggle that while it lasted the United States could concern themselves with no foreign relations but such as could be held to have some bearing upon it. Within that sphere questions were raised which in the end were happily settled, but which during twelve years so seriously threatened the peace between the United States and Great Britain that they rank in historical importance with the more exciting narratives of wars and conquests.

The secession of the Southern States was a challenge to arms, which Lincoln accepted in his inaugural address by declaring that to the best of his ability he would execute the laws of the Union. It was at once evident that the sea would bear a large part in the contest. On April 17, 1861, Jefferson Davis invited applications for letters of marque and reprisal. On the 19th Lincoln proclaimed his intention to blockade the Confederate ports " in pursuance of the laws of the United States and of the law of nations." On the 24th Seward, the Secretary of State, in order to defeat the adversary's first move, issued the first of a series of despatches instructing the ministers of the United States in Europe to offer their adhesion to the Declaration of Paris, which they had previously refused from a desire to maintain privateering so long as enemy property remained capturable as such at sea. But it was impossible that the Government at Washington should bind that at Richmond; and Great Britain and France agreed to receive the adhesion only with the reservation that it could not affect the existing war. This Seward did not accept, and the proposal dropped. The Congress of the Confederate States, on steps being taken by Great Britain and France to ascertain their policy on the subject, passed a resolution to the same effect as the Declaration of Paris except as to privateering, and the two contending Powers were thus at one on the point of maritime law. In fact, however, the United States issued no letters of marque, and the Confederate States but few; and all the vessels prominent on the side of the latter were either commissioned ships of their navy or tenders of such.

The precedents which had been set during the wars of independence of the United States, the Spanish American colonies, and Greece, had established a general understanding as to the rights and duties of third parties in such cases. Two stages have to be distinguished, to the second of which, the recognition of the separating body as a new member of the family of nations, no third party advanced during the American Civil War. It is therefore unnecessary to discuss the conditions necessary for such a recognition. The first stage is the recognition of the belligerency of the contending parties, which, when the struggle is carried on with the methods and dimensions of a war, is necessary for ascertaining the legal position of those who are brought into contact with it. If, for instance, a Government desires to prevent foreign intercourse with a coast of which it has lost the possession, and where therefore its laws are no longer binding on foreigners, its authority to exclude them depends on the right of blockade, which it can enjoy only as a belligerent. Again, it is only as a belligerent that either party can capture and condemn contraband of war, or search vessels for it at sea. And on the recognition of belligerency follows the duty of an impartial neutrality. Whether the recognition of belligerency is not merely the right of third parties but their duty when a war exists in fact, is still matter of controversy; but the Confederate States, if it had been denied them, might have pointed out that the United States, during their own war of independence, claimed it from Denmark as a duty.

Declarations of neutrality, which are the usual mode of recognising the belligerency of the parties to a conflict, were issued by Great Britain on May 13, 1861, and by France, Spain, and the Netherlands during June. That they were not issued a day too soon for giving notice of their legal position to the individuals concerned, appears from the fact that the British schooner *Tropic Wind* was captured for breach of the blockade on May 21. But the declarations elicited from the United States a repudiation of all known doctrine on the subject. Seward, in his despatches to London and Paris, laid down that there could be no war because the United States were "still solely and exclusively sovereign within the territories" disputed, none therefore until "the revolution should have run its successful course." This was to exclude altogether from international law the recognition of belligerency as distinct from the recognition of achieved independence. When the extravagance of such a plea was too apparent to allow of its repetition, Seward took his stand on the declarations having been unnecessary and therefore premature, because there was no Confederate navy till the *Sumter* put to sea from the Mississippi on June 30. It thus became both the popular and the official view that the declarations of neutrality were not the recognition but the "grant" or "concession" of belligerent rights; that the British declaration —which in truth made nothing lawful in England to the Confederacy or its agents and friends which was not otherwise lawful to them—was the cause of the war by opening to them the resources of England and by encouraging them to rely on British goodwill; and that the same could not be said of the French and other declarations because the resources of those countries were not similarly used by blockade-runners and others—a fact due to the superiority of the British market, though it was asserted that British sympathies were the motive.   It was forgotten that arms were more largely purchased in England by the Government of the United States than by that of the Confederates; and that such purchases and blockade-running, subject to the chance of either being intercepted at sea, are allowed by the law of nations. Such views implied that nothing less than the whole cost of the war could be the measure of the claim which might be made against Great Britain.

The blockade, during the first year of its existence, was far from satisfying that condition of being effective which exists for blockades as well under the Declaration of Paris as under older law.   This was natural, considering the great extent of coast to which it was to be applied, and the fact that the navy which was to apply it had to be created.   It became effective later, but at first the European Powers might lawfully have refused to submit to it.   That they did not take that course may be attributed in great measure to the reluctance to enter on forcible measures which has always placed neutrals at a disadvantage compared with belligerents, who, being already engaged in such measures, hesitate less to extend their area.   But, when all deductions are made, the toleration of the first year's blockade must be allowed to show that goodwill to the Confederate cause, though certainly prevalent in the upper classes of society, was not in Great Britain a force capable of determining government action.   That toleration caused bitter resentment among the Confederate population, who had relied on their dream that "cotton is king"; and so England became the object of aversion on both sides.   The chief source of the feeling in the North probably lay in the disappointed hope that the anti-slavery sentiment, in which England had led the world, would induce her to grant to the Northern cause a benevolent and not an impartial neutrality.

The next incident in order of time was that of the *Trent*.   She was a steamer belonging to a British company, carrying mails under a contract with the British post-office between the Spanish port of Havana in Cuba and the Danish West-Indian island St Thomas.   She was stopped on November 8, 1861, by the United States ship of war *San Jacinto*, Captain Wilkes, and allowed to proceed after four persons, who had run the blockade and come on board at Havana, had been taken from her by forcible but not uncourteous compulsion.   These were Mason and Slidell, charged by the Confederate Government with the duty of trying to open negotiations with the Governments of Great Britain and France respectively, and their respective secretaries, Macfarland and Eustis.   They were on their way to Europe for the performance of their mission, with credentials and instructions which Captain Wilkes failed to discover.   The points of law were all against the captors. First, the *Trent* held no belligerent charter, nor had she taken the four persons on board by special contract with the Confederate Government; and she was therefore not in belligerent service, real or constructive. Secondly, persons in the enemy's military or naval service are the only persons whom it was ever lawful to seize on board a neutral vessel not in belligerent service. The right of a neutral Government to receive, if it pleases, envoys or papers addressed to it, prevents their capture except in enemy territory or belligerent ships. Thirdly, contraband, even could the four persons be treated as such, cannot be captured on a neutral ship unless it has an enemy destination, either immediate or ulterior under the doctrine of continuous voyage. But the *Trent* was bound to a neutral port; and the ulterior destinations of the persons were neutral. The capture, which aroused a tempest of wrath in England, was received with jubilation in the United States. The Secretary of the Navy assured Captain Wilkes that his conduct had the emphatic approval of that department; and the House of Representatives voted him the thanks of Congress. Seward reserved his decision until Earl Russell had in very temperate language claimed the liberation of the four persons with a suitable apology, and Thouvenel, the French Minister of Foreign Affairs, had supported that claim in a reasoned despatch, in which he reminded the United States of the part they had taken in establishing the laws which had been violated. Seward then conceded the British claim, while maintaining the propriety of the capture if only the *Trent* had been brought in for adjudication. Captain Wilkes' reason for not bringing her in when he could have done so without danger, namely to avoid inconvenience and loss to the innocent passengers, he held to be insufficient. Thus the incident ended; but Austria, Prussia, Russia, and Italy expressed to the United States strong disapproval of the capture as being incompatible with the neutral rights always defended by them.

The year 1862 introduces a change of scene. During the remainder of the war the errors consisted in failures to perform neutral duties; and here Great Britain was at fault. The theory of neutral duties had been gradually advanced and rendered more precise; but the British Government and British opinion had lagged behind in the appreciation of the progress. At the point at which they halted, the conception of a neutral's duty extended but little beyond conceding or refusing to one belligerent what he conceded or refused to the other. The prohibition to use neutral territory as a belligerent base was scarcely felt to prohibit more than the departure from such territory of expeditions in the popular sense. The starting from it of a ship in belligerent service was not distinguished from the export of a ship as contraband of war. The neutral's duty to bring his laws and methods of action up to the standard necessary for the adequate performance of his international obligations was imperfectly realised. The sufficiency of British legal provision and

executive action was now to be tested by the activity of Confederate
agents and sympathisers on British soil, under the eyes of the United
States, who had perfected their own Neutrality Laws in 1818. The
result was that two ships, which became famous for the ravage which, as
Confederate cruisers, they wrought on United States commerce, began
their career in circumstances which the arbitrators at Geneva held to
involve Great Britain in liability. Those circumstances need not here
be detailed. It is enough to say that the judgment has met with
general approval, in the writer's opinion well merited; but that the good
intentions of the British Government were above all serious question.
The two ships were the *Alabama,* the name of which has attached itself
to the whole controversy in which she figured, and the *Oreto,* afterwards
called the *Florida.* Both were built at Liverpool and left that port in
Confederate service, but unarmed. The *Alabama* began her fighting
career with a crew which was gathered in England but not engaged in
British waters for Confederate service, and received outside British
waters an armament sent to her from England. The *Oreto* received her
armament at the British island of Green Cay, one of the Bahamas; but
the crew which she took with her on her final departure from British
waters was only just sufficient to carry her into the Confederate port of
Mobile. The United States sought to make Great Britain liable for
other cruisers which had been built or purchased in Great Britain;
but the only one for which the arbitrators found such liability to
exist was the *Shenandoah,* and for her they found it only after she
had succeeded in obtaining at Melbourne an increase of her crew.

But it was not only in the defence of its own territory from belligerent
encroachment that the British Government incurred liability for default
in the performance of neutral duties. The cruisers which had violated
British neutrality gave, by entering British ports, the opportunity of
vindicating it and putting a stop to their ravages. Instead, however, of
being arrested they were allowed to depart after receiving hospitality, as
though, by becoming commissioned ships of the Confederate navy, they
had purged their previous offence. This might have been a justifiable
course if the Confederacy had been a recognised State whose flag
Great Britain was bound to respect, and from which she might have
demanded redress. But to take that course in the case of a belligerent
party from which redress could not be demanded, because it was not
recognised as a State and Great Britain had no diplomatic relations
with it, was to confound the distinction between the recognition of
insurgents as belligerents and their recognition as having established their
independence. For an analogous reason no difference in British liability
arose from the fact that the *Florida,* before she made any captures, had
entered the Confederate port of Mobile and there received her commission. A belligerent body from which redress could not be sought could
not interpose its flag as a defence.

The blockade, now strictly enforced, caused a cotton famine in Lancashire which plunged the operatives into severe distress; but they bore it nobly to the end of the War, for what they perceived to be the cause of freedom. Neither by them nor by any influential member of either House of Parliament was countenance ever given to any proposal for recognising the Confederate States or interfering in their behalf. In November, 1862, when the Emperor of the French was invading Mexico with the avowed purpose of overthrowing her actual Republican government, he proposed that France, Russia, and Great Britain should join in recommending to the United and Confederate States an armistice for six months, during which the terms of a lasting pacification might be discussed. Great Britain refused, and the proposal was abortive. But the maritime commerce of the United States was seriously damaged by the exploits of the Confederate cruisers, all the more because the blockade prevented them from bringing in their captures for adjudication and they consequently burnt them at sea, which multiplied the captures they were able to make and gave them a more odious appearance. This again maintained at the highest point the popular opinion in the United States as to the claims justly to be made against Great Britain.

In favour of Seward it must be recorded, first, that from the beginning he looked to arbitration as a means of settlement. Adams, the United States minister in London, wrote to Earl Russell on October 23, 1863: "I am directed to say that there is no fair and equitable form of conventional arbitrament or reference to which they [the United States] will not be willing to submit." Earl Russell rejected the idea, but by 1866 British opinion on the point had changed. Secondly, notwithstanding some vague references in the correspondence to redress for national as well as private injuries, the convention which, under Seward's direction, Reverdy Johnson, Adams' successor as minister, signed with Lord Clarendon on January 14, 1869, did not provide for national injuries, but for a joint commission before which the private sufferers from the *Alabama* and her consorts might have claimed against Great Britain. The Senate of the United States rejected the Johnson-Clarendon Convention by a majority of 44 to 1 after a very inflammatory speech by Sumner, in which the claim for damages for national injuries was insisted on. As Chairman of the Senate Committee on Foreign Relations Sumner was consulted by Fish in the course of the further negotiations to be mentioned, and replied with a demand for Canada and the West Indies. "The withdrawal," he wrote, "of the British flag cannot be abandoned as a condition or preliminary of such a settlement as is now proposed. To make the settlement complete the withdrawal should be from this hemisphere, including provinces and islands."

Fish, who became Secretary of State on the entrance into office of President Grant in 1869, was thus faced by a task of no common difficulty. If the treaty which was to secure peace between the two

great nations was to be accepted by the United States, it was certain
that it must not distinctly exclude from arbitration the national, or as
they were also called the indirect, claims. If it was to be accepted by
Great Britain, it must not distinctly include them among the subjects
submitted for decision. Add to this that Fish was so far from
believing in the indirect claims which he had in some measure to support,
that he wished them to be adjudicated upon in order that the adverse
decision of the arbitrators might protect the United States against
claims of that nature in the future. Commissioners on both sides met at
Washington and concluded the treaty of May 8, 1871, which dealt with
other questions also, but expressed "the regret felt by Her Majesty's
Government for the escape, under whatever circumstances, of the *Alabama*
and other vessels from British ports, and for the depredations committed
by those vessels." It went on to refer "the *Alabama* claims" to five
arbitrators who should meet at Geneva, in language which the respective
sets of commissioners believed on the one side to exclude and on the
other to include the indirect claims. The proceedings under the reference were commenced; and, when it was found that the printed case
submitted by the United States included those claims, the hidden
difference broke out. The arbitrators declared that, without expressing
an opinion on the interpretation of the treaty, they were of opinion
that the indirect claims were not a good foundation for an award of
damages between nations. The proceedings were then resumed on the
direct claims only, and ended, on September 14, 1872, in an award of
$15,500,000 against Great Britain.

The Geneva arbitration was rendered possible by the insertion in
the Treaty of Washington of three rules by which Great Britain
agreed that it should be governed, while declaring that she could not
assent to them as having been principles of international law in force at
the time when the claims arose; and it was further provided that the
contracting parties should observe those rules as between themselves in
future. This was widely regarded in Great Britain as a serious concession; but it is believed that there is now no important authority in any
country who regards the three rules as having been substantially novel,
or as making any excessive demand on neutrals.

To complete this view of the principal foreign relations of the
United States during the Civil War, it is only necessary to say that,
while that war continued, their Government maintained an attitude of
reserve with regard to the French intervention in Mexico, but that in
1865 it addressed France in terms which have been correctly summarised by Frederic Bancroft as "withdraw or fight." Dates for the
return of the French army to Europe were arranged between the two
Governments; and the French finally withdrew in 1867.

CHAPTER III.

GREAT BRITAIN.

THE elections of 1868 on the extended franchise gave the Liberal party the substantial majority of 112. Disraeli resigned on December 2 and Gladstone accepted the invitation to form a Ministry. The most noteworthy members of his Cabinet were Edward Cardwell, who was Secretary for War, a clear-headed and capable administrator; Lord Clarendon, the Foreign Secretary, a Whig aristocrat, well suited by his genial character and charming manner for diplomatic intercourse, by his industry, skill, and experience for the conduct of foreign affairs, and described by Gladstone as the only living British statesman whose name carried any influence in the councils of Europe; Robert Lowe, the Chancellor of the Exchequer, whose ability was marred by defect of sympathy, narrowness of view, an unfortunate acidity of speech, and excess of cleverness; and Lord Granville, Colonial Secretary, whose dexterity and tact in the management of his equals stood him in good stead as leader in the House of Lords. The Ministry also comprised two orators of mark, John Bright, and the Duke of Argyll; and men of such varied and conspicuous talents and qualities as Lord Hartington, Lord Dufferin, and Goschen. William Edward Forster, as Vice-President of the Council, had the chief responsibility for educational policy without a seat in the Cabinet.

Though he had reached his sixtieth year, the leader was in the prime of life and vigour. Earnest and sincere beyond question, he had enormous industry and driving force. The revolts which his imperious methods occasioned he was generally able to quell by virtue of his dominant personality. But, absorbed as he was at all times in the details of the political conflict, sensitive to the movements of feeling among his own supporters, subtle and elusive in thought and language, his career and policy bear an opportunist stamp, which is singular in one so sincere. His actions and efforts seem always governed by the immediate need rather than by far-sighted purpose; in foreign complications, by the desire to avoid the necessity of intervention, a policy which often failed to achieve its end; in home policy, by the wish to maintain or restore his majority, to carry through the measure of the moment, now leaning upon one section of the community, and now upon another. Those manifestations may have been due in part to the exigencies of parliamentary government; at any rate, no simple formula can be framed to explain the details of his conduct; but, in this, the first Parliament which he led, some unity is supplied by the trend of public events, and the task which was set to him. The forces of emancipatory Liberalism had gathered once more. Restrictions on individual liberty still remained which could without danger be removed; needless privileges were in existence which could be abolished; expenditure could be reduced, and the burden of taxation readjusted. At the same time the Liberal watchword of Liberty did not satisfy all the needs of the situation; the necessity for constructive social legislation, especially in education, was beginning to be felt; and the insistent problem of Irish discontent called for solution.

Gladstone on his accession to power attributed to himself the task of pacifying Ireland. He cannot, at that time, have understood the difficulties of this enterprise; but he pursued it to the end with unwavering devotion. It is characteristic of him that he should have seen in the position of the Irish Church the vital point of grievance; it is natural that the principles which he represented should have carried him to assault this stronghold of illogical privilege. All his own resources, those of his party, and those of the Crown, were devoted to this end, and the Bill was successfully pressed through. More will be said of this measure and its consequences in a later chapter.

No sooner had this question been settled than the more fundamental question of Irish land tenure came in sight. Bright's heroic remedy of land purchase and the creation of an Irish peasant proprietary, though it was afterwards adopted by a Conservative Government, was no doubt politically impracticable at that time. Gladstone himself was in principle averse from interference with freedom of contract; some of his colleagues were even more strictly wedded to the principles of free competition; and the resulting Irish Land Act (1870), fought through by Gladstone with little help from his chief subordinates, while recognising in effect the part-ownership of the Irish tenant, only touched the fringe of the subject, and left the main problems unsolved. Ireland was not pacified, and two Coercion Acts (1870 and 1871) were necessary.

The two greatest administrative measures of Gladstone's first Ministry owed little to its chief. The need of better provision for elementary education was universally acknowledged; and the task of supplying this need was entrusted to Forster. It was reckoned that at the time there were 4,300,000 children who ought to have been at school. Of these, about 1,300,000 were receiving education in schools established by voluntary effort, inspected by Government, and receiving government grants to supplement the school fees and private subscriptions. The main body of these schools were Church of England schools. About another million of children were attending private schools which received no grant and underwent no inspection.

Gladstone himself believed, on the one hand, in the "integrity of religious education"; he held that the religious instruction imparted in the schools should be the exposition of a definite and coherent system of beliefs, not the attenuated common residue that might remain after conflicting creeds had been pruned of their divergent elements; on the other hand, he stood for liberty of conscience, which in his opinion could be reconciled with the rights of the majority by allowing elective bodies to prescribe the form of religious instruction, and permitting individuals to withdraw their children from any religious instruction which offended their principles. Yet the measure that was adopted divided the kingdom of England and Wales, almost at haphazard, into two categories of districts, the schools into two classes of schools. In the one set of schools integrity of religious instruction was maintained, but popular control of religious instruction was excluded, and each school was open to the integral religious instruction of one denomination only. In the other set of schools popular control was fettered and the integrity of religious instruction rendered impossible by the "Cowper-Temple clause," providing that no religious catechism or religious formulary distinctive of any particular denomination should be taught. It was left at the option of the School Boards to teach no religion; they were not permitted to teach any in its integrity. Gladstone denounced one of the most striking features of his own Act when he spoke (1870) of the "popular imposture of undenominational instruction"; and, in fact, the Act for which he was responsible maintained only one of his principles, that embodied in the provision that any parent should be at liberty to withdraw his child from the religious instruction provided. The system established by the Act of 1870 will receive further attention elsewhere; it will be sufficient here to note that the Act satisfied nobody, least of all the Birmingham League, which had advocated universal gratuitous, compulsory, and secular education, and the Nonconformists, who resented the favourable treatment conceded to the "Voluntary" Church of England schools. The Education Act for Scotland passed in 1872 created there a universal system of School Boards and left the question of religious instruction to the Boards. In Scotland this solution presented little difficulty, as the Shorter Catechism was common ground for the great majority of the people.

The other great measure of Gladstone's first Ministry—the reform of the Army—was due to the energy and administrative ability of Cardwell. The first step was to subordinate the office of Commander-in-chief to the Secretary of State for War. This reform was successfully carried out, though the relics of the old dual authority persisted until the abolition of the office and the establishment of the Army Council in 1904. The next step was to establish an effective reserve. The British army had

CH. III.

hitherto been a long-service army, with practically no reserve except the militia. Cardwell (1870) introduced short service, normally six years with the colours and six in the reserve, though the period with the colours could be prolonged or shortened at the discretion of the authorities. He also introduced the system of linked battalions, the battalions of the infantry being grouped in pairs, one stationed at home to be used for recruiting and training, the other to serve abroad, drawing its drafts from the home battalion. This system was fairly well adapted to provide the necessary garrisons for India and the empire in time of peace, and to supply expeditionary forces on a moderate scale; it made, however, insufficient provision for home defence, and was inadequate for the possible and even for the actual needs of foreign service. Soon afterwards (1872) the army was reorganised on a territorial basis, the militia and volunteers being grouped with the regular forces and brought under the same control. The change, however, which excited most public notice was the abolition of the system by which officers on retirement or resignation received payment from those who benefited by the resulting promotion. The Bill framed for this purpose was hung up by the Lords in 1871, and the measure was then carried out by a Royal Warrant, abolishing the system of purchase. The Lords were thus forced to pass the Bill, in order to secure compensation for those who suffered by the reform.

One of the most important measures of this Ministry, and, incidentally, one of the most effective blows at privilege, was an administrative measure carried out by royal prerogative. The Order in Council of June 4, 1870, established the principle of open competitive examination for filling ordinary posts in the Civil Service. Posts in the Indian Civil Service had for about seventeen years been filled in this way; but the Home Service had since 1855 been recruited by limited competitions among nominated candidates, conducted by the Civil Service Commission, established in that year. The new Order was speedily adopted by almost all the chief Departments—the Foreign Office remaining a notable exception. In spite of theoretical and practical objections which can be raised, the system of open competition has worked well, and has freed the public service from all suspicion of jobbery in connexion with such appointments. Many places, especially among those for which technical or professional training is required, are still filled by limited competition among selected candidates, and a very large number of minor posts by the nomination of Heads of Departments, subject to a qualifying examination as to age, health, character, and educational qualifications; but the ordinary clerical and administrative staff, higher and lower, male and female, is now almost exclusively recruited by various types of open competition; and the Order in Council of 1870 has stood the test of time.

Other measures directed towards the removal of restrictions and privileges were the Ballot Act of 1872, which opened the way for the exercise of political pressure by the peasants of Ireland, the abolition of religious tests for degrees, fellowships, and offices in the Universities of Oxford and Cambridge (1871), the repeal of the Ecclesiastical Titles Act of 1851, which prohibited the assumption of territorial titles by prelates of the Roman Catholic Church invested with spiritual authority in England, and the Trades Unions Act (1871), which, while giving to those bodies protection against the embezzlement of their funds, strengthened the laws against " picketing." The establishment of the Local Government Board to control the administration of the Poor Law and other municipal functions (1871), and the Judicature Act of 1873 —which was intended to fuse the Chancery, the three Common Law Courts, and the Admiralty, Probate, and Divorce Courts, together with the intermediate Courts of Appeal, into one Supreme Court of Judicature consisting of a High Court of Justice and a Court of Appeal—were important administrative and constructive reforms which deserve to be set to the credit of this remarkable Ministry. Lord Selborne, the Lord Chancellor, was anxious, in the interests of simplicity, to abolish the further appeal from the Court of Appeal to the House of Lords, and the Bill passed in this form ; but in 1876, when the whole question of appeals had to be taken up not only for England but also for Scotland and Ireland, professional opinion proved too strong for Lord Cairns, and the House of Lords was reconstituted as a second and final Court of Appeal. It may further be noted that a Licensing Bill for public-houses was introduced in 1871, which would within ten years have brought the whole value of the licenses to the credit of the community, and have reduced the number of licensed houses in conformity with the needs and desires of the locality. But, on the one hand, the temperance party were not satisfied and, on the other, the interests attacked were too strong; and the Bill was in consequence withdrawn.

Gladstone did not become Chancellor of the Exchequer until 1873 ; but his influence was powerfully exercised in the interests of economy. Although large sums had to be supplied as compensation for the abolished system of purchase in the army, for the increased cost of education, and for the *Alabama* claims, the expenditure was kept within narrow bounds; and the prosperity of the country was such that in every year of the Administration there was a substantial surplus—amounting in the year 1869–70 to six and a half millions, and in 1873–4 to nearly six— although considerable remissions of taxation were made from time to time, and in particular the last impost of a shilling a quarter on imported wheat was removed. Measured by later standards, the votes for the army and navy were chary ; but they were fortunately not proved insufficient for the actual needs of the country.

The principal foreign questions in which the country was concerned during this Administration were the Franco-German War and the *Alabama* controversy with the United States. The origin and course of

CH. III.

the Franco-German War have been fully set forth in a previous volume. Just before its outbreak Lord Clarendon had died, and Lord Granville had succeeded him at the Foreign Office. It is doubtful whether the utmost resolution, vigour, and despatch could have done anything to prevent the collision for which both countries had been preparing, and which Bismarck was determined to hasten; Lord Granville was not disposed to take a strong line, and, in the result, Great Britain's neutrality, though scrupulously maintained, was regarded by both Powers as unfriendly. The one decisive action taken by Great Britain was to recognise her individual responsibility for the maintenance of the integrity and neutrality of Belgian territory. This guarantee, though it proved to be inexpensive and effective, was not free from apparent risk, and deserves to be reckoned to the credit of an Administration which was not often willing to take such risks.

As an outcome of this War, the Russian Government denounced (October 31, 1870) the clauses of the Treaty of Paris (1856) which forbade Russia to build or maintain ships of war in the Black Sea. The point was probably not worth fighting about, and in any case Great Britain did not intend to fight; but by judicious hints of possible war Lord Odo Russell persuaded Bismarck to propose a Conference of the Powers in London, which solemnly proclaimed the sanctity of treaties, and erased the obnoxious clauses of the Treaty in question. Great Britain obtained, however, an advantage in the new provision which permitted the Sultan to allow the war-vessels of friendly Powers to enter the Black Sea in time of peace in order to maintain the Treaty of 1856.

The *Alabama* question is dealt with in a preceding chapter of this volume, and also, from another point of view, in a later chapter. The depredations of the *Alabama* and other vessels had formed the cardinal point of an undefined series of grievances which had been cherished by the United States against this country ever since the end of the great Civil War. The concessions of Gladstone's Government in this matter were on the liberal side; but there is now little difference of opinion as to the blameworthy neglect of the British authorities, and the price (£3,200,000) paid for reconciliation was moderate compared with the danger of prolonged friction and ill-will. The Foreign Enlistment Act (1870) had already made provision to prevent another *Alabama* from being built and sent forth under similar circumstances. Shortly afterwards, the arbitration of the German Emperor, arranged for by the Treaty of Washington, May, 1871, awarded the island of San Juan off Vancouver to the United States.

The foreign policy of Gladstone's Government, although it was probably judicious, did not add to its popularity with the nation. The feverish energy of legislation harassed vested interests and fatigued the people. The subtlety of Gladstone's mind had involved him in several tortuous transactions, innocent in themselves, but open to hostile comment. The abolition of purchase by Royal Warrant, the formal appointment of Sir Robert Collier, Attorney-General, to a Judgeship in order to confer upon him the qualification required by law for elevation to one of the paid posts on the Judicial Committee of the Privy Council, the nomination of a Cambridge man to fill a living in the gift of the Crown which was reserved for members of the Oxford House of Convocation, in which he was incorporated for the purpose—these were all ingenious moves, harmless in intention, but unacceptable to the British mind. In 1873, it became apparent that Gladstone's ascendancy was waning. A Bill was prepared for establishing a University in Ireland, to include Trinity College, Dublin, the unsectarian Colleges of Belfast and Cork, and the Roman Catholic University, without university chairs of theology, philosophy, or history, and with "gagging" clauses to prevent university teachers from offending the prejudices of any section of their classes. So bad a Bill seems to indicate some temporary failure in the attention or the judgment of the overworked Prime Minister, who was directly responsible. It was thrown out on the second reading by a majority of three (March, 1873). Gladstone handed in his resignation ; but Disraeli refused to take office. He preferred to wait upon the flowing tide of public opinion, and Gladstone consented to remain in power. Another unfortunate transaction came to Disraeli's aid. In July, it became known that Post Office funds to the amount of £800,000 had been diverted from the Consolidated Fund, to which they belonged, to the expenses of telegraphic construction. Of the three responsible officials, the Postmaster-General, Monsell, was retired with a peerage, Lowe was transferred from the Exchequer to the Home Office, and Ayrton was removed from the Office of Works to become Judge-Advocate-General. Though there was no suspicion of malversation, the irregularity was flagrant, and the Liberal Government lost heavily in prestige.

Gladstone himself assumed the office of Chancellor of the Exchequer vacated by Lowe (August, 1873). The question was afterwards raised whether he had not thereby exposed himself to the inconvenient necessity of seeking reelection. It was a nice constitutional point, and, so far as in him lay, Gladstone decided it in his own favour. But his decision was not final or conclusive, and it may be that the prospect of further trouble contributed to hasten his resolution to dissolve. There were, however, other and weightier reasons. In the discussion of the estimates which normally takes place towards the end of the civil year, Gladstone, as Chancellor, pressed substantial reductions upon Cardwell for the army and Goschen for the navy. These Ministers offered resistance, and Gladstone determined to appeal to the country on a policy of reduced expenditure and the abolition of the Income Tax. This resolution, once adopted, was speedily carried into effect and announced on January 24, 1874, to the nation. Hopes were also held out of some relief of local taxation, and of the grant of the franchise to agricultural labourers.

CH. III.

At the General Election which followed Disraeli obtained a majority of 50 over Irish Home Rulers and Liberals combined, and quickly formed his Ministry (February, 1874). The most noteworthy of his colleagues were Lord Derby at the Foreign Office, whose cautious temperament ill accorded with the spirit of his friend and chief; Lord Carnarvon, Colonial Secretary, who also failed to follow his leader when it came to vigorous action; Lord Salisbury at the India Office, at one time a relentless critic, later the faithful ally, of Disraeli; Lord Cairns, his Lord Chancellor, and a great lawyer; Sir Stafford Northcote, a capable administrator trained in Gladstone's school, who was made Chancellor of the Exchequer; and Richard Assheton Cross, Home Secretary, who was responsible for some excellent legislation.

The new Prime Minister was a singular contrast to his predecessor, and all the better suited to the existing temper of the nation. Gladstone was earnest and devoid of humour; Disraeli was ironical and imaginative. Gladstone looked on government mainly from the Treasury point of view; Disraeli had a vivid sense of the romantic aspects of the British imperial position. Gladstone was a High Churchman and the leader of Nonconformists; Disraeli was a Jew, and the champion of moderate evangelical churchmen. Gladstone began life as a Tory, and was driven by his irrepressible energy into the reforming party; Disraeli began life with vague visions of extensive social reform and made his first mark in politics by supporting the Chartist petition (1839); he became a Conservative because the things he most cared for were valued by the Conservative party. Gladstone made more impression in his generation; Disraeli had a shorter lease of power, but bequeathed a tradition and a policy. Gladstone found a strong party and ruined it for twenty years from 1886; Disraeli found a weak party and nursed it into strength.

The parties of which Gladstone and Disraeli were the chiefs were linked by continuous historical succession with the two great sections or factions of the aristocracy, or hereditary oligarchy, which ruled Great Britain in the eighteenth century. But each had been transformed by national changes since the Reform Bill. The Whigs had become Liberals, the Tories had become Conservatives. The Liberal party had absorbed part of the principles of the French Revolution. They stood now for individual liberty, laying especial stress on freedom of trade, freedom of contract, and freedom of competition. They had set themselves to break down the rule of the landowner and the Church, to shake off the fetters of Protection, and to establish equality before the law. Their acceptance of egalitarian principles led them to adopt democratic ideals, to advocate extension of the suffrage, and the emancipation of the working classes. Such principles, though not revolutionary, are to some extent disruptive in their tendency; and their adoption by the Liberals had forced the Tory party to range themselves in defence of the existing order of things.

They professed to stand for the Crown, the Church, and the Constitution. They were compelled by the irresistible trend of events to accept democratic principles and to carry out democratic reforms. They preferred, in fact, to carry out such reforms themselves, in order that the safeguards which they considered necessary might be respected. Democratic principles having been adopted, both parties made it their object to redress grievances ; but the Conservatives showed a natural predisposition to redress those grievances which arose from excessive freedom of competition, the Liberals were more anxious to redress those which were the result of hereditary or customary privilege. The harmony of the State consists in the equilibrium between the two opposing forces of liberty and order. The Liberals laid more stress upon liberty, the Conservatives attached more importance to order and established authority.

Another, but obscurer, element in party psychology is the influence of nationality on political feeling. Wales and Cornwall have throughout the period shown a large preponderance in favour of the Liberal cause. Scotland is by fundamental preference Liberal, though, in 1900, the influence of the Boer War, coupled with aversion from Irish Home Rule, brought about the election of a small Unionist majority. In Wales and Cornwall this result is partly due to Nonconformity ; and in Scotland difference of religion has its political bearing. But, so far as the Celtic portions of Great Britain are concerned, their persistent Liberalism may also indicate some obscure racial bias. In Ireland, where racial hostility is conscious and undisguised, it has led, not to Liberalism, but to a loose and intermittent alliance with the Liberal party.

In foreign affairs the Liberals were led by instinct to avoid all avoidable complications. Palmerston and Russell, indeed, as representing the old Whig tradition, were active in supporting the cause of foreign nations seeking emancipation, and Gladstone himself, when not in office, was easily carried away by such enthusiasms. But a vigorous foreign policy imposes sacrifices on the individual, and thus tends to the diminution of liberty ; hence Gladstone and Granville, when in power, instinctively shrank from measures which might enhance the burden of taxation, and require the increase of armaments. The Conservatives, on the other hand, who stood for the solidarity of the State, took pleasure in actions which manifested forth its splendour and greatness ; moved by the subtle and unconscious influence of the principles which they held, they appealed rather to the pride than to the pocket of the democracy. Both parties have to some extent modified their principles since the time of Gladstone and Disraeli, and both will no doubt modify them further ; but developments up to the present have followed similar lines, for protective duties tend to increase the solidarity of the State and to diminish individual liberty, while property under existing conditions is in the main a form of hereditary privilege which Liberal legislation may consistently aim at curtailing,

CH. III.

as by Irish Land Acts, differential death-duties, differential income-tax, and Licensing Bills.

During the Gladstonian Ministry the chief spectacular interest of politics had been the prolonged duel between the protagonists of the two parties. It was the more regretted that in the new Parliament Gladstone, from the first, took little active part and eventually, in 1875, formally resigned the leadership of the Opposition. Lord Hartington was selected to lead the Liberals in the House of Commons—a duty which he performed with conspicuous self-sacrifice under great difficulties, for although Gladstone declined to lead he did not abstain from interference, and when he interfered he carried a large fraction of his party with him. In spite of all efforts to persuade Gladstone either to lead or to refrain from embarrassing his colleagues, this state of affairs continued to the end of this Parliament and in great measure paralysed the Opposition. On national questions Lord Hartington and Gladstone were seldom in complete accord. Outside the House Gladstone was an unequalled force, and inside the House his action, untrammelled as it was by any official responsibility, found many sympathetic supporters. The position of the official Leader was almost intolerable.

Effective criticism was thus in large measure suspended, and Disraeli was left the more free to pursue his enterprising policy abroad. His first bold and imaginative stroke was the purchase, in November, 1875, of the Khedive's shares in the Suez Canal for four millions sterling. This transaction was prompted by the desire to acquire a substantial, almost a controlling, interest in the British highway to the East; but it has since been also justified by financial success. In 1876, after the impressive visit of the Prince of Wales to India and as a part of the same policy, a Bill was passed enabling the Queen to assume the title of Empress of India, under which style she was solemnly proclaimed in the chief cities of India on the first day of the following year. But these were only minor manifestations of the new spirit inspiring British action. In 1875 the Eastern Question became acute through a rising in Bosnia and the Herzegovina; in 1876 Servia took up arms; and Great Britain, while declining to support Turkey in any enormity she might commit, declined also to associate herself with the other Great Powers in armed intervention to force a cessation of the conflict. Massacres in Bulgaria followed, and Gladstone, making himself the champion of the oppressed nationalities, aroused a somewhat deceptive enthusiasm by his pamphlets and speeches. Russia, perhaps encouraged by Gladstone's agitation and its reception, certainly not deterred by Derby's attitude of reserve, or by Disraeli's clear intimation of warlike possibilities (November 9, 1876), declared war on Turkey (April 24, 1877). The War proceeded with various fortune until the fall of Plevna (December 10, 1877), while Great Britain maintained a watchful attitude, and Gladstone pressed the anti-Turkish agitation. But, on the news that the Russians were advancing on Constantinople, popular sentiment against the "unspeakable Turk" was overwhelmed by the conviction (whether due to reason or passion) that Constantinople at least must be saved, and Disraeli (since August, 1876, Earl of Beaconsfield) found in the popular will the support he needed for energetic action. The British fleet was sent to Constantinople (February, 1878). It is believed that Beaconsfield favoured even more decisive measures, but was outvoted in his Cabinet. It is certain that, when he called out the Reserves to support his demand that the whole Treaty of San Stefano should be unreservedly submitted to a European Congress, Lord Derby finally resigned, Lord Carnarvon having left the Ministry at an earlier stage. But the country was now behind the Prime Minister, and experienced a pleasurable thrill when he reminded his fellow-citizens of their imperial resources by transporting 7000 Indian troops to Malta. In the consciousness of popular support, he pressed the Russian Government hard, and came to an agreement (May 30) by which the principal questions at issue were decided in accordance with British wishes.

The Congress at Berlin which followed was not without importance, although substantial agreement had been reached. There was still a chance of reversing the diplomatic victory. But Beaconsfield, ably supported by Lord Salisbury, maintained the advantage he had gained, and returned to England fairly justified in his proud boast of " Peace with Honour." A convention with Turkey had already been made public which bound Great Britain to defend the Sultan's Asiatic possessions by force of arms, and pledged the Sultan to introduce suitable reforms. In return, the island of Cyprus was handed over on a perpetual lease to British administration. This was the greatest moment of Beaconsfield's life, and it is probable that, if he had dissolved Parliament at this time, he would have been returned with a substantial majority.

But a doubt may still arise whether the results achieved were worth the risks. On the one hand, it may be said that an access of territory was conceded to Bulgaria in 1885, and British interests have not in consequence suffered ; that Batum has not in fact remained a free, unfortified port; that Great Britain has never been called upon to defend the Sultan's Asiatic dominions, and that it is not clear how she could defend them if called upon ; that Cyprus is of little value or importance to us ; that the late Sultan paid no attention to repeated exhortations addressed to him by British Ministers ; and, finally, that, although we could rely upon Austrian support so far as European questions were concerned, had we been forced to take up arms in defence of Turkey's Asiatic frontier, we should have stood alone and in a perilous position. Great Britain was not, in fact, ready for war, and a few thousand Indian troops, more or less, would not have enabled us to face the victorious Russian army, however exhausted. Yet we wrung from the Russians a good deal more than we could have forced them to concede. Our military weakness, if accepted as a ground for inaction, would have prevented us from raising an effective protest against the occupation of Constantinople. And it is impossible to say that, if a bold front had not been shown, the Russians would have stopped short of Constantinople, and, holding Stamboul, that they would have contented themselves with a "big Bulgaria." Constantinople was not only saved for the moment, but has been, until quite recently, more secure than it was before the Russo-Turkish War. Some may be inclined to deny that Great Britain has any vital interest in preserving the rule of the Turks in Constantinople. But, if this be granted, the intervention was necessary, and the subsequent procedure was skilfully carried out.

The greatest drawback to the course of action pursued was that it earned for Great Britain the persistent enmity of Russia during nearly thirty years. She has felt it in Egypt, in Afghanistan, in Tibet, in Persia, in China, and in every dispute with a third party for a complete generation. It has been an inconvenience, and Beaconsfield himself probably paid the heaviest part of the price, for the Afghan War was partly due to Russian hostility and had as much to do with his fall as any other single incident. It has been an inconvenience, and might have been a serious danger. But these perils have now passed, and it may be that Beaconsfield correctly estimated all the risks and decided rather to face them than to accept the alternative.

The remainder of his career was less fortunate. Lord Northbrook had resigned the Governor-Generalship of India in 1876, and Lord Lytton, a highly accomplished diplomatist, was appointed to succeed him. He was soon called upon to face an arduous problem. There had been difficulties since 1873 with the Amir of Afghanistan, and, shortly after Lord Lytton's accession to office, the proposal was made and refused that the Amir should accept a British representative to reside at Herat, or elsewhere, according to convenience. In July, 1878, however, shortly after the Congress of Berlin had concluded its sessions, a Russian envoy was received at Kabul, and the Government decided to force upon the Amir the reception of a British envoy. Major Cavagnari was sent, but was stopped in the Khaibar by Afghan troops. Lord Lytton prevailed on the home Government to persevere, and war began in the winter 1878–9. The course of this War is described in a later chapter; in the result Abdurrahman Khan was set up as Amir; but the conclusion of the settlement was left to another Government and another Viceroy; for on the accession of Gladstone to power in 1880 Lord Lytton resigned.

The original proposal to press upon the Amir a British resident was probably a mistake; if it had not been made, it is doubtful whether Russian overtures would have been entertained. But, after a Russian envoy had been received, the other consequences were apparently inevitable. The War was on the whole advantageous to Great Britain, for

Abdurrahman proved a strong ruler and maintained up to his death a perfectly correct attitude. But it was not popular; the Cavagnari disaster filled Englishmen with dismay; and the prestige of the Beaconsfield Administration was shaken.

The annexation of the Transvaal in 1877 was made by Sir Theophilus Shepstone, probably in the erroneous belief that annexation was desired. The Transvaal Republic was in fact impotent and penniless and in grave danger from the Zulus; and it was not unnatural to suppose that they would welcome the powerful protection of Great Britain. But in 1879 the British Government decided to crush the Zulus. After Ulundi (July, 1879) the Boers were left free from danger and enabled to challenge their would-be protector with success in 1880. But, meanwhile, the massacre of a British force by Zulus at Isandhlwana (January 22, 1879) had dealt another blow to Beaconsfield's Government, which was responsible for the blunders of Shepstone and Chelmsford and for the policy of Bartle Frere. These misfortunes shook the prestige of an Administration and a leader who relied so much upon successful conduct of Imperial affairs; and Gladstone's electoral campaign in Midlothian, initiated in the autumn of 1879, impressed upon the country in the most effective manner every charge which could be brought against the discredited Ministry.

Their output of domestic legislation had, however, on the whole been creditable. They had had to reckon with a period of bad trade, succeeding the excessive inflation of 1873. Nevertheless, the financial administration of Sir Stafford Northcote had been sound, and the establishment of the new Sinking Fund in 1875 was a wise and ingenious measure. The principle was laid down that the charge for the public debt should be fixed at £28,000,000 a year, and that the balance of this sum after payment of interest should go to reduction of debt which would thus, if the principle was maintained, be diminished by a continually increasing proportion. In the session of 1874, a Public Health Act, an Artisans' Dwellings Act, an Act for the protection of the improvements of agricultural tenants, and an Act defining picketing and conspiracy in a manner more favourable to the Trade Unions, were passed. In the following year, the Plimsoll Act for the protection of merchant seamen became law. In 1876, the Education Act was amended and the principle of compulsory elementary education was recognised. In 1877, the prisons of the United Kingdom were by a salutary measure transferred from the administration of local authorities to that of the central Government. In addition, Acts for the prevention of pollution of rivers and to regulate the vivisection of animals were placed on the statute book. The Conservative party seemed to be in possession of the doctrine that their legitimate legislative function is to initiate and carry out useful, if not heroic, measures of social reform. Disraeli put forward the motto: *Sanitas sanitatum, omnia sanitas.* But in that year and subsequent years the record of legislation fell off, mainly owing to the adoption of a policy of deliberate obstruction by Parnell and some of the Irish Home Rule members. The Public Worship Act of 1874, introduced to check ritualistic practices of doubtful legality in the Established Church, was ineffective for the purpose which it was intended to serve, and led to invidious prosecutions which did not further the interests of the Church or of the Government. The Act establishing Commissions for the reform of the Universities of Oxford and Cambridge (1877) eventually bore fruit in a series of moderate and for the most part useful reforms. Finally, in 1879, a disastrous harvest revealed the fact that improved communications and Free Trade legislation had exposed British wheat-growers to effective foreign competition which they were unable to meet; and a prolonged period of acute agricultural depression set in. The industrial and commercial depression that had begun about 1875 reached its lowest point. The formation of the Irish Land League in the autumn of 1879 confronted the Government with another danger the magnitude of which was not perhaps at once apparent.

Under the cloud of disasters abroad, depression at home, and impotence in Parliament, Beaconsfield's Administration met the constituencies in April, 1880, with little prospect of success. The election was fought principally on the question of foreign policy, and Gladstone's denunciations in Midlothian and elsewhere had a striking effect. The Liberals were returned to power with a majority of forty-one as against Conservatives and Home Rulers combined. Beaconsfield in his manifesto to the people had drawn attention to the dangers of the Home Rule agitation and called upon all men " of light and leading " to aid him in resisting it. Little heed was paid to his warning at the time; but a solid phalanx of sixty-one Home Rulers now foreshadowed the difficulties that were to come.

On Beaconsfield's resignation the Queen sent for Lord Hartington, who advised her to the effect that Gladstone was the only possible Prime Minister. The veteran was summoned and accepted the task. Lord Granville became Minister of Foreign Affairs, Lord Hartington accepted the India Office, Sir William Harcourt was Home Secretary, Forster Chief Secretary for Ireland, and, under Radical pressure exercised by Sir Charles Dilke, Mr Joseph Chamberlain was admitted to the Cabinet as President of the Board of Trade. One of the ablest of Liberal statesmen, Goschen, was precluded from accepting office by his aversion from the declared policy of extending the county franchise. Lord Lytton resigned and Lord Ripon was sent to take his place as Viceroy of India. Sir Bartle Frere was, however, retained in office, in spite of Radical attacks, in order that he might, if possible, carry out his scheme for South African federation. When it became clear that federation had no prospect of success, he was recalled (July).

Indian affairs soon claimed the attention of the new Government. Abdurrahman had been recognised as Amir by Lord Lytton; but Ayub

Khan, his rival, a son of the late Amir, was still in the field, and, on July 27, he inflicted a signal defeat on the British at Maiwand. Sir Frederick Roberts, marching from Kabul, relieved Kandahar at the beginning of September, and ended the war. The Cabinet decided to hand over Kandahar to Abdurrahman, and the Afghan question was settled for the time. This decision was made public early in 1881.

During his Midlothian campaign, a report had reached Gladstone that the Emperor of Austria had expressed the hope that Beaconsfield might prove successful in the general election. Angered by the supposed impropriety, he launched into a vigorous attack on Austrian influence and policy. On succeeding to office, he found it necessary to withdraw language used at a time when he had no intention or expectation of returning to power. He offered an apology which produced the desired effect; but the apology as well as the hasty utterance afforded scope for hostile criticism. Good relations with the Government of Vienna were the more necessary, since British endeavour was at once directed to the Balkan peninsula, where certain points connected with the Treaty of Berlin remained to be settled. Layard was recalled from Constantinople, and Goschen was sent on a special mission to adjust the frontier of Greece, to satisfy Montenegro, and to secure, if possible, better conditions for Armenia. Dulcigno was obtained for Montenegro by the mere proposal to occupy Smyrna; the frontier of Greece was after negotiations rectified by the union of Thessaly and part of Epirus; but for Armenia no substantial safeguards were procured.

In Parliament a difficulty at once arose which Gladstone's authority was not sufficient to meet. Charles Bradlaugh, member for Northampton, a declared atheist and Republican, claimed to decline the customary form of oath and to substitute a solemn affirmation as a preliminary to taking his seat. This claim having been rejected, he then demanded to be allowed to take the oath. On June 22, the House declared that he should neither affirm nor swear. At the following sitting he presented himself to take the oath, and was heard at the bar of the House. His request was rejected, and, refusing to withdraw, he was committed to the Clock Tower. In these proceedings the Prime Minister declined to exercise his functions as Leader of the House, and allowed Parliament to take its own course. But on July 1, he proposed a resolution, which was carried, that any Member should be allowed to make an affirmation, subject to the provisions of the existing law which were of doubtful interpretation. Bradlaugh then took his seat; but in the following year the Court of Appeal declared that affirmation was illegal and the seat was in consequence vacated. He was then reelected, and excluded by the House; twice again reelected and twice excluded in the same Parliament. In 1883, Gladstone brought forward an Affirmation Bill which he defended with more than his usual eloquence and conviction; but the Government was defeated by a majority of

CH. III.

three. It was left for the Parliament of 1885 to admit Bradlaugh to take the oath without question, and for another Parliament in 1888 to pass an Affirmation Bill moved by Bradlaugh himself. Bradlaugh lived to win the respect of the assembly which had repulsed him with scorn and hatred, and few will now deny that the course advocated by Gladstone was not less just than generous and statesmanlike. But he was unwilling to imperil his Government by taking a firm stand on the principles which he avowed. He thus weakened his authority, and exposed Parliament to a succession of unseemly brawls. Moreover, when defeated in 1883 on the government proposal dealing with the subject, he did not resign, which seems to show that at a still earlier stage he might without anxiety have taken the risk of defeat.

Except for the difficulties with Bradlaugh the session of 1880 was uneventful. Gladstone repealed the Malt Tax, an old grievance of the British farmer, and substituted a tax on beer. A new Education Act imposed on local authorities the duty of making school attendance universally compulsory. A small advance was made in the direction of enforcing employers' liability for accidents to workmen in their service. Agricultural tenants were permitted by the Ground Game Act to kill and take hares and rabbits on land in their occupation. The Burials Act removed a long-standing grievance of Nonconformists with regard to interments in the churchyards. But a Bill designed to relieve the tension in Ireland by allowing compensation for disturbance to tenants evicted through no fault of their own was thrown out by the Lords, and further time was thus allowed for discontent and disorder to spread.

The existence of grave agricultural distress in Ireland was undoubted. The number of evictions was increasing in an alarming fashion. The circumstances favoured the growing power of the Land League. Political organisation gave point, edge, and direction to the passions inflamed by land-hunger and want. Unorganised, those passions gave rise to crimes such as the murder of Lord Mountmorres (September 25, 1880). Organised, they found a more effective means of coercion in the exclusion from all social and industrial intercourse, first enforced against a land-agent in County Mayo, Captain Boycott. Parliament was called together in January, 1881, to deal with the danger that Disraeli had foreseen. So soon as the protracted debate on the Address was concluded, Forster brought in his Bill for the Protection of Person and Property in Ireland, which permitted the Lord Lieutenant to imprison any person on suspicion and to detain him so long as the Act remained in force. The failure of the prosecution for conspiracy of fourteen Land League leaders in Dublin gave force to the contention of the Government that exceptional powers were needed. But the resources of obstruction were as yet unlimited, and after more than a week the House was still discussing whether leave should be given to introduce the Bill. The Speaker (Henry Brand) then closed the debate by his own authority, and the first inroad was made on the untrammelled freedom of debate hitherto enjoyed by the British Parliament. A few days later, it became necessary to suspend thirty-seven Irish members from the service of the House. By these and similar means the Protection Bill became law on March 2. An Arms Bill shortly followed, and, on April 7, Gladstone was able to bring forward his Land Bill, which was subjected to the fullest possible discussion. Revolutionary as its principles were thought and have proved to be, the necessity of some such measure was admitted, and the House of Lords declined to take the responsibility of rejecting it. Before the end of August the Bill became an Act. The Duke of Argyll resigned. Lord Lansdowne had previously retired from the Government on the introduction of the Compensation for Disturbance Bill.

This session of Parliament was almost wholly taken up with Irish affairs, and neither the Coercion Acts nor the Land Act produced for a time any improvement in the condition of Ireland. The Budget relieved the Income Tax by an additional tax on spirits; and flogging in the army and navy was abolished. Hardly any other legislation could be even considered. But the Government had other and grave anxieties. The Afghan War had hardly been concluded, before discontent in South Africa, encouraged by the belief that the Liberal Government was favourable to Transvaal independence, reached a head. War broke out on December 16, 1880. Sir George Colley, High Commissioner for South-East Africa, and Governor of Natal, suffered a repulse at Laing's Nek, and was finally defeated and killed at Majuba Hill on February 26, 1881. Before this action an offer had been made to the Boer President, and the acceptance was received on March 7. The Government decided to proceed with negotiations as if nothing had happened; and, on March 22, peace was arranged. Sir Frederick Roberts, who had been sent out to take command in South Africa, was recalled immediately after his arrival. The Pretoria Convention was signed in August, 1881, securing a limited independence to the Transvaal Republic under the suzerainty of the Queen.

The action and the inaction of the Government were alike difficult to defend. Concessions which may be reasonable in themselves assume a different aspect when they follow a defeat. Had the Government conceded independence to the Transvaal on their accession to power, had they opened negotiations with a view to a grant of self-government after the failure of federation, or had they determined to prove their military superiority after Majuba and before considering terms, three years of war and many years of sullen hostility might have been averted. The course actually adopted may be described as magnanimous or cowardly according to the prepossessions of the critic; it was certainly apt to secure the maximum of discredit with the minimum of gratitude. But, for the time being, preoccupation with Ireland prevented South African affairs from receiving their due share of attention.

CH. III.

The condition of Ireland had proceeded from bad to worse. Nine hundred suspects were in gaol untried, including Parnell himself; nevertheless, agrarian crime was still rife. On the other hand the attempt to boycott the Land Act had failed, and the new Land Courts were crowded with applications for revisions of rent. Gladstone, influenced by Mr Chamberlain, accepted overtures from Parnell (April, 1882) which resulted in his release and the preparation of a Bill dealing with arrears of rent in Ireland. In consequence, Forster resigned (May, 1882), Lord Spencer having previously succeeded Lord Cowper as Lord Lieutenant. Lord Frederick Cavendish now became Chief Secretary. A few days later, he was murdered in the Phoenix Park (May 6). The hopes of amicable agreement were shattered. Mr George Trevelyan succeeded Lord Frederick Cavendish. A drastic Crimes Act was passed, Irish members being freely suspended during the discussions. An Arrears Act was then pressed through and accepted by the Lords.

Irish affairs were all-absorbing in 1882. Yet Parliament found time for passing Acts dealing with electric lighting, entailed estates, and the property of married women. Meanwhile, a military revolution had taken place in Egypt, bringing the Khedive under the domination of Arabi; Gambetta had fallen from power in France; the Dual Control was tottering, and was brought to an end by the isolated action of Great Britain in bombarding the forts at Alexandria (July 11, 1882). John Bright resigned; but the Government were forced to proceed on the path they had entered. The French Chamber refused the funds for which Freycinet (Gambetta's successor) had asked. Sir Garnet Wolseley landed at Alexandria on August 15, and defeated Arabi on September 13 at Tel-el-Kebir. The military occupation of the country was quickly completed. The British advisers to the Khedive became the effective rulers of Egypt, supported at first by 12,000 British troops. Lord Granville proclaimed to Europe (January 3, 1883) the disinterested intentions of Great Britain, and the Cabinet sincerely believed that evacuation would be possible in the near future. The new members of the Cabinet, Lord Derby and Sir Charles Dilke, approved this policy and shared this belief. Ingenuous Albion, in full sincerity of self-deception, had added to her possessions an important strategic position, a fertile country, and a docile population, and assumed responsibilities which even Disraeli had declined to undertake. The evolution of British administration in Egypt is reserved for treatment in a later chapter. But it must be noted here that difficulties for the British Government began at once in the Sudan, and reached their culmination with the death of Gordon at Khartum on January 26, 1885. Any credit which the Government may have obtained through the excellent conduct of the original expedition against Arabi was destroyed by the disastrous mismanagement of affairs in the Sudan. Action was postponed till success was impossible; the measures taken were as a rule inadequate; the decision to "smash the Mahdi" at

Khartum was announced and then speedily revoked; finally the Sudan was left to a tyrannous anarchy for thirteen years—a result which might have been achieved without moving forward a man, or spending a penny.

The autumn session of 1882 was devoted to the discussion of new rules of procedure in Parliament, which gave power for the closure of debate and for the control of irrelevant discussion and of dilatory motions, and established standing Committees of the House for the discussion of Bills referred to them. By these rules obstructive tactics were impeded.

In 1883, parliamentary business was less exciting and more useful. Childers had become Chancellor of the Exchequer, and was able to reduce the Income Tax. The Agricultural Holdings Act secured to farmers compensation for unexhausted improvements. A Corrupt Practices Act endeavoured to control indirect bribery at elections by imposing a limit on authorised election expenditure. The Coercion Act was vigorously if ineffectively applied in Ireland. Some criminals were discovered and punished, but crime did not diminish. It took a new form in dynamite outrage, which led to the rapid passing of an Explosives Act. The Irish Land League, dissolved by law, had reappeared as the Irish National League (October, 1882). An attempt made to influence the Curia of Rome through George Errington, an Irish Catholic unconnected with the Government, was intended to check crime in Ireland; but the only result was papal intervention against a collection of money for Parnell, which did not check the subscriptions. Parnell, when assailed in the British Parliament by Forster, declined to admit the jurisdiction of the authority before which he was arraigned, or to defend himself there against the charge of connivance in crime.

In 1884, Childers' scheme for the conversion of the National Debt failed, leaving the question to be settled by an abler financier. A Royal Commission on the Housing of the Poor was set up, which collected much valuable information leading to legislation at a later period. Fawcett, the blind Postmaster-General, died after initiating such useful measures as sixpenny telegrams, the Parcel Post, and licensed telephony. The Pretoria Convention of 1881 was modified by Lord Derby on the representations of the Boers; and the word "suzerainty," afterwards a subject of controversy, was omitted from the new Convention, whatever may have been the significance of this omission. Colonial quarrels arose with Germany over the annexation of part of New Guinea, the Cameroons, and Angra Pequeña, and the occupation by German troops of Samoan territory. But the chief business of the session was a Bill for the extension of the county franchise. A motion to exclude Ireland from the operation of this Bill was defeated, and, in consequence, the influence of the Nationalist movement in British politics was enormously increased. The Conservative party insisted on a complete scheme of redistribution to accompany the Franchise Act, and by the help of the Lords they achieved their purpose. In November, the two parties came to an agree-

CH. III.

ment as to the principles of redistribution, and the Franchise Bill passed before Christmas, allowing the franchise to the counties on the same basis as in the boroughs and adding two million voters to the Register. The settlement of redistribution by agreement between parties was an admirable precedent excluding all possibility of " gerrymandering "; but the increase of representation (twelve seats) accorded to Scotland should in strict justice have been accompanied by a diminution of the number of Irish members. In the amicable conclusion of this controversy the Queen played an important part. The Redistribution Bill was introduced in 1885, and it seemed certain that a General Election would take place in the autumn. Mr Chamberlain began to . formulate what eventually became his " unauthorised programme," advocating reform of local government, the encouragement of small holdings and allotments, disestablishment of the Church, free education, the abolition of plural voting, payment of members, and manhood suffrage, and adumbrating schemes for the differential taxation of the rich. Both parties were manœuvring for the Irish vote. The Liberal Government were divided on the question of renewing the Crimes Act, which expired in 1885. They were considering a Land Purchase Act and instalments of Home Rule. Having narrowly escaped defeat for their failure to relieve Khartum, they were confronted by grave dangers arising from the collision between Russians and Afghans at Penjdeh (May, 1885). They weathered this storm, but were beaten on the proposal to put additional taxes on spirits and beer (June 8, 1885) and resigned. After protracted negotiations, Lord Salisbury consented to take office, though in a minority, in order to carry on the business of the country until Parliament could be dissolved   But it was not sufficient to carry on business. A policy was needed for Ireland, and the Conservatives were not in a position to formulate and maintain a settled policy. The result gave an impression of indecision. The Crimes Act was not renewed, and Lord Carnarvon, the new Lord Lieutenant, had an interview with Parnell, in which he was alleged by Parnell to have held out hopes of the creation of an Irish Parliament with power to tax imports from England. In any case, the Conservatives were commonly thought to be more favourable to Home Rule than the Liberals, and Parnell was thereby encouraged to formulate demands which Mr Chamberlain felt obliged to repudiate. Gladstone did not declare himself, but appealed to the country to give him a majority sufficient to enable him to deal with the Irish question without relying upon the help of the Irish members. This declaration decided the Nationalists to throw their whole weight into the scale against him (November).

The Conservatives, having settled the Afghan difficulty in substantial conformity with Gladstone's policy, passed an Act for the Housing of the Poor, another for the protection of young women and children from criminal acts, and established a Secretaryship for Scotland,

dissolved Parliament (November 18).   The elections took place shortly
after and in Great Britain turned principally on Mr Chamberlain's
unauthorised programme and, especially in the counties, on Mr Jesse
Collings' watchword of "three acres and a cow" which attracted the
rural labourer.   In Ireland the sole issue was Home Rule.   In the
result, the Liberals reckoned about 335 votes, the Conservatives about
249, the Nationalists about 86.   Gladstone's independent majority
was not in sight.   His first inclination was to allow the Conservatives to
remain in power and to give them his support in an attempt to settle
the Irish question.   But, meanwhile, it had become known that he himself
was prepared to deal with the problem, and the Conservatives declined
to negotiate.   Lord Carnarvon's resignation seemed to imply a Conservative decision against Home Rule, and the Queen's Speech (January,
1886) was phrased so as to exclude that solution.   The Government had
no sooner announced their intention to introduce a Coercion Bill for
Ireland than they were turned out on an amendment to the Address
relating to allotments for rural labourers.   Gladstone was left with the task
of framing a Government pledged to examine in a favourable spirit the
possibility of granting some form of Home Rule acceptable to the Irish
party, on which his majority depended.   Lord Hartington, Lord Derby,
Bright, Goschen, Sir Henry James, and other men of mark declined
to join him.   Sir Charles Dilke was not available.   Mr Chamberlain and
Sir George Trevelyan joined, while reserving their independence of judgment.   Lord Spencer, President of the Council, whose final conversion to
Home Rule carried great weight, Sir William Harcourt, Chancellor
of the Exchequer, Lord Rosebery, Secretary for Foreign Affairs, and
Mr John Morley, Chief Secretary to the Lord Lieutenant, gave more
unreserved support to the Prime Minister; and a strong Ministry
was eventually formed, though it contained from the first disruptive
elements.

The new Ministry had difficulties to face from the start.   Lord Salisbury had accepted the union of Eastern Rumelia with Bulgaria which
had been safely completed in 1885, but the extension of Bulgaria had
aroused the jealousy of Greece, which demanded compensation from Turkey.
Lord Rosebery continued the policy of Lord Salisbury, and supported
the European Concert in applying pressure to the Hellenes.   War was
thus averted.   Upper Burma, annexed by Lord Salisbury after a short
campaign, was disturbed by rebels and dacoits for many months before
its pacification was completed.   The depression of trade, already acute
in 1885, became accentuated; and, in February, 1886, after listening to
speeches in Trafalgar Square, a riotous mob plundered shops in Piccadilly
and neighbouring streets before their progress was arrested by the police.
The Chief Commissioner of Police was blamed, and his resignation was
accepted.   But all other interests paled before the issue of Home Rule.
Gladstone's proposals aroused dissension in the Cabinet, and on March 26

CH. III.

Sir George Trevelyan and Mr Chamberlain resigned. Nevertheless, Gladstone proceeded, and on April 8 he introduced his Bill. It provided for the establishment of a statutory Legislature consisting of two Orders, one of 28 representative peers, with 75 other members elected by and from the propertied classes, and the other of elected members to the number of 204. The two Orders were to sit together, but either could demand separate voting, in which case the concurrence of both Orders was required to pass a measure. The customs duties and corresponding excise duties were reserved for the Imperial Parliament, but the Irish legislature could impose other taxes. The Irish liability for imperial expenditure was fixed at one-fifteenth of the whole; after this sum had been defrayed, any balance from customs and excise was to be handed over to the Irish Exchequer. Army and navy, foreign affairs, post office, coinage, weights and measures, trade, navigation, and copyright, were assigned to the province of the Imperial Parliament. The Irish legislature was to be precluded from endowing any religious body. There was to be an Irish Executive responsible to the Irish Legislature, which would appoint the judges and magistrates; but the Royal Irish Constabulary were to remain under imperial control for an indefinite period. An extensive measure of Land Purchase was to accompany the grant of Home Rule. But the crux of the whole problem was the exclusion, contemplated by the Bill, of the Irish members from the British Parliament. There were objections almost equally grave to the exclusion or retention of the Irish representatives, and it was on this point more than any other that the Bill of 1886, which excluded them, and that of 1893 which retained them, were attacked.

Lord Hartington and Mr Chamberlain led the attack; Gladstone and Mr Morley were earnest and eloquent in defence; but the Liberal party was broken up, and the Bill was defeated on the second reading by a majority of thirty (June 8). Gladstone decided to dissolve Parliament, and appeal to the people; the answer was decisive; Liberal and Radical Unionists fought side by side with Tories against Home Rule; no other issue was even considered; 315 Conservatives, and 78 Liberal Unionists were returned against 191 Gladstonian Liberals and 86 Irish Home Rulers. Thus the Liberal secession very nearly balanced in Parliament the weight of the Irish Home Rule vote, and this was to be the case for many years to come, until the alliance between Tories and Liberal Unionists seemed to have become part of the established order. The Conservative party was influenced by its Liberal wing; the statesmen who acted with it were in their turn influenced by Tory opinion; and a great change in the party system was thus, by imperceptible degrees, introduced. The most remarkable transformation was that of Mr Chamberlain from the protagonist of Radical Nonconformity into the champion of imperial solidarity; the most noteworthy phenomenon was the fidelity with which Birmingham in particular and the

Midlands in general followed their chosen leader in his gradual change of attitude.

Gladstone resigned on July 30; Lord Salisbury proposed that Lord Hartington should form a coalition Government; this offer was declined, though the Liberal Unionists promised their support to Lord Salisbury. His Ministry comprised Lord Iddesleigh as Secretary for Foreign Affairs, Sir Michael Hicks-Beach as Chief Secretary to the Lord Lieutenant, and Lord Randolph Churchill as Chancellor of the Exchequer and leader of the House of Commons. This meteoric politician was then at the height of his reputation and popularity. In the Parliament of 1880 he had been conspicuous among a small band known as the "fourth party," who, dissatisfied with the policy of the Opposition Front Bench, had made it their business to harry the Government and urge their leaders to greater activity. In Lord Salisbury's Government of 1885 he had been Secretary for India. The principles he avowed were those of Tory democracy; his methods were to popularise the doctrines of the Conservative party by skilful appeals to the impulses of the masses, to win attention by audacious humour and memorable phrases, and to reorganise the Conservative party so as to ensure due recognition for the wishes of the average voter. He alone of the Conservative leaders had a personal hold on the electorate comparable to that possessed by Gladstone and Mr Chamberlain. He had made a determined effort to capture the Tory organisation, and in this attempt had come into collision with Lord Salisbury. In spite of his failure to achieve this end, his influence was such that he was able to secure for Mr Henry Matthews, a leading barrister but untried as a politician, the post of Home Secretary. Of his former allies in the fourth party, Sir Henry Drummond Wolff was employed on special missions to Constantinople and Egypt (1885–7) and afterwards (1887) became British Minister at Teheran. Sir John Gorst had to content himself with the post of Under-Secretary for India. Mr Arthur Balfour, who had worked with the fourth party but had separated from Lord Randolph when Lord Salisbury was attacked, became Secretary for Scotland and shortly after received a seat in the Cabinet.

Lord Salisbury was pledged to initiate a policy of resolute government in Ireland; but, before he could declare the lines on which he intended to proceed, he had to deal with a Cabinet crisis. Lord Randolph had announced a programme of advanced social legislation; but, above all, he was bent on framing a popular budget, and the financial measures which he proposed required the reduction of military and naval expenditure. When his colleagues declined to effect the economies demanded, he gave in his resignation, no doubt in the belief that he was indispensable to his party. Lord Salisbury, after appealing to Lord Hartington, bethought himself of Goschen, a Unionist whose Liberalism was of a very moderate stamp, and an accomplished financier. His accession to the Government proved a great addition to their strength.

CH. III.

William Henry Smith, a good man of business, universally respected, though not brilliant, became leader of the House of Commons. Lord Iddesleigh, who had had great trouble with Lord Randolph, offered his resignation, and Lord Salisbury reluctantly accepted it. The Leader himself returned to the Foreign Office. But, before the arrangements could be completed, Lord Iddesleigh succumbed to heart weakness (January 12, 1887). Mr Arthur Balfour replaced Sir Michael Hicks-Beach, temporarily invalided, as Secretary to the Lord Lieutenant (March, 1887). Lord Randolph Churchill, though he continued to intervene fitfully and sometimes effectively in debate, never recovered his position as a statesman; later, his health broke down, and he died in 1895.

One last effort was made to restore Liberal unity, when Sir William Harcourt, Mr Morley, Lord Herschell, Mr Chamberlain, and Sir George Trevelyan, met at the "Round Table Conference" to discuss a compromise on Irish policy (January, 1887). But the more Mr Chamberlain examined Home Rule, the less he liked it. The Conference broke up without coming to any agreement, though Sir George Trevelyan shortly afterwards returned to his Liberal allegiance.

In order to carry the legislation (described elsewhere) which was considered necessary for Ireland, the rules of the House of Commons were once more reformed, and it became possible for any member to move the closure of a debate which could then, with the consent of the Speaker, be put to the House and carried if at least two hundred members voted in the majority; and, this measure proving insufficient, a time-limit was assigned by resolution of the House, after which the remaining clauses of the Crimes Bill should be put to the vote without amendment or debate. This was the first introduction of the so-called guillotine. Goschen eased his first Budget by taking two millions from the sinking fund. The Merchandise Marks Act, though intended to prevent the passing off of inferior foreign goods as English-made, is generally regarded as having operated mainly as an advertisement of the foreign products affected. An Allotments Act was passed which proved to be of little value in practice.

In 1887, the fiftieth anniversary of the accession of Queen Victoria was celebrated in London by a procession to Westminster Abbey. Between 1861 and 1872, the prestige and popularity of the Crown had waned, owing to the seclusion of the Queen and her unwillingness to take part in public functions. In 1872, the celebration of the recovery of the Prince of Wales from a dangerous illness set the current of feeling moving in the opposite direction. The Prince, afterwards King Edward VII, was constantly willing to take the place of his royal mother on public occasions: Disraeli persuaded the Queen to open Parliament in person (1876 and 1877); her real devotion to public interests became gradually known, and her character won the reverence which it deserved. But the Jubilee

of 1887 first made the nation and the Empire conscious of the inestimable treasure which it possessed in the person of its Sovereign; from
that day onwards the nation and the Crown were in perfect sympathy,
and Victoria became the object of constantly increasing loyalty and love.
On the occasion of this Jubilee, the first Colonial Conference was held,
and contributions of the colonies to imperial defence were inaugurated
by Australia. The Imperial Institute, founded to commemorate this
anniversary, failed to accomplish the expectations of its founders.
In the same year the suppression of a mass meeting in Trafalgar Square,
which necessitated the intervention of the military, attracted a good
deal of attention; and the declaration of Conservative Associations in
favour of Protection and of the exclusion of indigent foreigners, though
contemptuously brushed aside by Lord Salisbury, foreshadowed an important change in public opinion which at a later date profoundly
modified party policy. The mission of Mr Chamberlain to negotiate a
treaty with the United States regulating the right of American citizens
to fish in the waters of Canada and Newfoundland proved ineffectual,
owing to the influence of the American Irish in the Senate.

Lord Salisbury, without contracting any binding alliance, showed
himself friendly towards the Triple Alliance of Germany, Austria, and
Italy. Thanks to the amicable relations thus established, he was able
by successive compacts to clear up all outstanding questions in Africa
(1887–90) and to delimit the "spheres of influence" of the several
European Powers in that Continent. During this period the policy of
incorporating Chartered Companies to administer concessions was revived
by the British Government, and applied in British Nigeria (1886),
British East Africa (1888), Mashonaland and Matabeleland (1889).
This last measure nearly led to a collision with Portugal, who deemed
her rights to be thereby infringed; but the weaker Power had to give
way. By these charters the effective area of British dominion was
considerably increased, with a corresponding extension of British
responsibility. In 1890, Heligoland was ceded to Germany in return
for the recognition of a British protectorate in Zanzibar. Other
agreements assigned to France the "light soil" of the Sahara, and the
protectorate of Madagascar. Lord Salisbury might claim to have had
a voice in the distribution of larger portions of the earth's surface than
any other statesman.

In 1888, William Henry Smith introduced fresh rules for the conduct
of House of Commons business. Goschen successfully converted the
National Debt from a 3 per cent. security to one bearing interest at
$2\frac{3}{4}$ per cent. forthwith, and after fifteen years at $2\frac{1}{2}$ per cent., thus
effecting an immediate saving of nearly two millions, and an ultimate
saving of nearly four millions a year. He also introduced a system of
large subventions from licenses and probate duty to local expenditure;
the additional relief of the rates amounting to about three millions. A

CH. III.

Local Government Bill was introduced establishing elective Councils
to administer the counties in place of the Benches of nominated magistrates which had hitherto managed county business. About the same
time a County Council for the whole of London was set up, which
superseded the Metropolitan Board of Works, but was vested with more
extensive powers. These reforms have had a wide-reaching social effect,
and testify to the irresistible trend towards democratic institutions in
this country.

Meanwhile, the campaign against the National League, agrarian
crime, and boycotting, had been going on in Ireland. The Pope intervened in 1888 to condemn with little result the "Plan of Campaign"
and the practice of boycotting. In 1888–9 the Commission (described
elsewhere) sat, in effect, to try the Irish Home Rule Party. The case
for the prosecution broke down, so far as the letters were concerned;
but, had it succeeded, the blow to the Irish cause could hardly have been
more severe than that resulting from the divorce case (1890) in which
Parnell was implicated. Parnell was ruined in the eyes of English
Liberals; dissensions arose in the Home Rule ranks; and the rest of
his life was spent in an infatuated campaign against the majority
of his own colleagues. In these circumstances, the task of Mr Balfour
was made comparatively easy, and by his useful measures and personal
magnetism he won, towards the end of his time in office, more
popularity in Ireland than has often fallen to the lot of an English
statesman. In 1891, Mr Balfour resigned the post of Chief Secretary to
take the lead in the House of Commons on the death of William Henry
Smith.

In 1889, for the first time the Government took seriously to heart
the necessity of strengthening the navy. Lord Salisbury laid down the
standard of equality with the two strongest foreign Powers. A Bill was
passed prescribing the expenditure of twenty-one millions in seven years
on new construction, and the navy was thus for the time being placed
on an adequate footing. In spite of this extra charge the prosperity
of the country made it possible to meet the financial burdens with ease,
until, in 1890, the embarrassments of the great firm of Barings initiated
a new period of commercial and industrial depression. Nevertheless, in
1891, the Chancellor was able to devote the sum of two millions to
relieving parents of children attending public elementary schools from
the payment of fees. This measure was one of those advocated by
Mr Chamberlain; but its passing was almost a necessary consequence of
the universal enforcement of school attendance. Acts for the establishment of a Board of Agriculture (1889), for the prevention of cruelty to
children (1889), for the abolition of the dues on coal imported into
London (1889), for technical instruction (1889 and 1890), for the better
regulation of factories and workshops (1891), and a Small Holdings Act
(1892), showed a creditable though not excessive zeal for social reform.

In 1891 it was enacted that tithe should be in future collected from the landlord and not from the tenant.

In 1891, in view of the coming elections, the National Liberal Federation formulated what was known as the Newcastle programme. It included the disestablishment of the Churches in Wales and Scotland, local veto by three-fourths of the ratepayers on the liquor traffic in any district, improvement of registration of voters, the abolition of plural voting, proposals for extending employers' liability for accidents to workmen, and for limiting the hours of labour. As an electioneering programme this programme was not calculated to inspire enthusiasm, but rather to unite powerful interests in defence of the Church and the trade in liquor. Coupled with Home Rule, and Gladstone's proposals for the evacuation of Egypt, it formed an unfortunate prelude for the electoral combat of 1892. This resulted in a majority of forty in favour of the policy of Home Rule, which was once more, though to a less extent than in 1886, the dominant issue. In August, 1892, Gladstone resumed office. Lord Rosebery was his Foreign Secretary, Mr Asquith his Home Secretary, Sir William Harcourt Chancellor of the Exchequer, and Mr John Morley Chief Secretary to the Lord Lieutenant.

Gladstone was not able to carry out his policy of evacuating Egypt. On the contrary he was forced in 1893 to take measures further consolidating our position there. Steps were also taken which led, in 1894, to the establishment of a British Protectorate in Uganda. In 1893 a serious controversy arose with France in consequence of boundary disputes between that country and Siam. The Menam was blockaded, and war, for a short time, seemed probable; but the Siamese were persuaded to give way, and the matter was finally settled by prolonged and peaceful negotiations (1896). In the same year (1893) Natal received the grant of responsible government, and war broke out between the British South Africa Company and Lobengula, King of the Matabele. Matabeleland was conquered and added to the territory administered by the Company. This extraordinary Company, directed by Cecil Rhodes, profited by the speculative confidence of the public to raise many millions which were expended on the development of their territory. Much has been accomplished, but the extreme expectations of profit have not hitherto been justified.

In legislation Home Rule held the first place. Gladstone's new Bill, introduced in 1893, adopted the alternative of retaining eighty representatives of Ireland in the Imperial Parliament. It was at first intended that the Irish members should vote only on matters in which Ireland was concerned; but this expedient, destructive of party government, was abandoned; and the Bill, as passed in the Commons on September 1 by thirty-four votes, gave Ireland exclusive control of her own affairs, as well as a share in the control of English and Scottish legislation and finance. The House of Lords rejected the Bill by 419 votes to 41 (September 8), and events proved two years later that they had correctly gauged the balance of popular feeling in the larger island. Home Rule, to which Gladstone had given eight years of his life and for which he had sacrificed the present and the future of his party, still remains written on the Liberal programme; but, since 1893, no responsible statesman has attempted to carry it into effect. This victory of the House of Lords over the representative assembly gave a considerable access of confidence to the Upper House.

A minor issue of this session was a proposal to restore the bimetallic standard in this country. The demonetisation of silver in Germany in 1872 had forced France to suspend her bimetallic system. Had Great Britain then joined with France to support the bimetallic standard by allowing the free coinage of both silver and gold, and by making both metals unlimited legal tender at a fixed ratio, we should probably now have more silver and less gold in circulation and at the banks; but the ratio might have been maintained, and, instead of the progressive appreciation of the standard of value which took place from 1872 and did not cease till about 1900, a similar depreciation would have resulted, with a corresponding stimulus to industry and commerce. The general social effects would have been very complicated; but it is probable that the extended adoption of a single gold standard was premature and pre-judicial to enterprise. Even now that the production of gold has been quadrupled, there is not too much gold for the needs of the civilised world, and its abundance has hardly yet produced any marked effect on the general level of prices. But in 1893 it was already too late. It was then impossible to revert to the original ratio of $15\frac{1}{2}$ to 1 or 16 to 1; and it passed the wit of man to fix any other ratio which would satisfy the chief interests concerned. In these circumstances, Gladstone rightly dismissed the proposal of Mr Chaplin in favour of bimetallism; and, although the question was again raised in the United States at the Presidential election of 1896, it is now universally agreed that bimetallism is no longer practically possible.

In November, 1893, Parliament met again. A Parish Councils Bill was needed to complete the democratic system of local government initiated by the Tories. Some such parish institution was necessary, and at the existing stage of our development the democratic principle provides the only possible basis. The Bill became law in 1894; and, although like other democratic institutions it has probably led to a certain amount of unprofitable expenditure, it has worked as well as most measures work in this imperfect world. An Employers' Liability Bill, introduced in the same winter session, broke down because the Lords insisted on a clause allowing a majority of workmen to agree with their employers on a scheme of mutual insurance approved by the Board of Trade.

Gladstone was now failing, and his retirement was probably hastened by his unwillingness to accede to the demand for increased naval expenditure, accentuated by the loss of the *Victoria*, a first-class battleship (1893). On March 1, 1894, he delivered his last speech in the House of Commons, taking the opportunity to declare that the question of preponderance between Lords and Commons must go forward to an issue, and that his Government adopted as their principle the supremacy of the Lower House. He was succeeded as Premier by Lord Rosebery, who took an early opportunity of declaring that the conversion of England as " the predominant partner" must precede the concession of Home Rule. Sir William Harcourt, the new Leader of the House, was, not unnaturally, incensed to find his claims to the Premiership ignored, and the Cabinet was weakened by the ill-concealed dissension between the Prime Minister and his chief colleague. But Harcourt's budget was the chief event of the parliamentary session of 1894. A small additional tax was imposed on spirits and on beer, and the Income Tax was raised; but the main feature was increased taxation on legacies and inheritance, imposed in proportion to the size of the total estate devised. This new system of taxation, which in 1905–6 brought into the exchequer about thirteen million pounds as against seven and a half millions in 1893–4, has produced great social effects. It is not probable that it has on the whole gravely diminished the net accumulations of capital. It does not seem that it has been to any very large extent evaded by donations during lifetime. But, being levied on the total value of real as well as of personal estates, it has hastened the movement already in progress owing to agricultural depression. Since 1879, the landowners and especially the small squires had been hard hit by the fall in rentals. Many old families had been forced to sell or let their residences and domains. Now, the incidence of the death-duties came as a final and crushing blow to many. Even spread over eight years, the new burden was heavy. And, if an estate changed hands several times at short intervals, the charge was more than many estates would bear. The decay of old families was hastened, old ties of landlord and tenant, of squire and peasantry, were dissolved, and in many cases the place of the old landlords was taken by those who inherited no traditional obligations to the land or its occupants. If the object of the tax had been to depress the ancient squirearchy, and to bring old estates upon the market, the means adopted would have been appropriate; but it does not appear that this was the intention of its framers. The new tax was, in the main, a financial expedient, and as a financial expedient it was a considerable success. This measure and the consequent increase in the navy were the only achievements which this Government could place to its credit. Harcourt's unpopular Local Veto Bill had to be dropped. The campaign against the House of Lords had no hold upon the country. The Irish were dissatisfied and gave no certain support. A Bill for the disestablishment of the Church in Wales was introduced, but aroused no enthusiasm.

The end came by surprise. Following out one of the recommendations made by a Royal Commission, set up in 1888 and presided over by Lord Hartington, Campbell-Bannerman, the War Minister, had persuaded the Duke of Cambridge to resign his office of Commander-in-chief. After he had communicated this intelligence to the House, a hostile amendment of the estimates was introduced on the ground of insufficient stores of cordite, and carried by a majority of seven in a small House. The Government resigned (June, 1895); Lord Salisbury accepted office and after winding up the necessary business dissolved Parliament.

The new Ministry was a Coalition Ministry. The Duke of Devonshire, formerly Lord Hartington, Mr Chamberlain, Lord Lansdowne, and Sir Henry James, with other Liberal Unionists, accepted offices. Sir Michael Hicks-Beach became Chancellor of the Exchequer. Mr Balfour was leader in the House of Commons, Goschen was First Lord of the Admiralty, and Lord Lansdowne Secretary of State for War. The result of the elections was favourable to the new Government, which had a majority of 152 over Home Rulers and Liberals taken together. Mr Chamberlain had probably contributed to this result by holding out hopes of an Employers' Liability Act, and old-age pensions. In the new Government he took the post of Colonial Secretary, with a far-sighted conception of its possibilities, and by his imaginative and sympathetic policy he made himself the most conspicuous figure of the Cabinet, and the most popular Englishman throughout our colonial possessions.

Before the Liberal Government resigned, the war between China and Japan had been brought to an end by the defeat of China and a treaty ceding to Japan Formosa and the Liao-Tung peninsula. France, Russia, and Germany stepped in, and insisted that this important peninsula should be restored to China. Great Britain declined to take part in this action, and stood completely aside, thereby shaking for a time British prestige in the East, but leaving the road open for the subsequent alliance with Japan. Subsequent developments led to the seizure of Kiaochow by Germany in 1897, and the occupation of Port Arthur by Russia shortly afterwards. The British Government vainly endeavoured to save its credit by obtaining the lease of Wei-Hai-Wei (July, 1898). The predominance of Great Britain in the Far East seemed to be at an end.

Meanwhile, an agreement with Russia had been reached with regard to frontiers in the Pamirs (March, 1895) and, after a war in Chitral, that district was annexed by Great Britain in August, 1895. Disputes had long existed with the Venezuelan Government concerning boundaries, and Lord Salisbury declined to proceed to arbitration in respect to part of the territory in question. Thereupon, the American President claimed for the United States the right to decide the points at issue, and to impose upon Great Britain their decision. Lord Salisbury showed great self-possession, and, eventually, an Arbitration tribunal was set up in

1897, and in 1899 decided unanimously in favour of the chief part of the British claims.

Relations with the Transvaal Republic had long been strained, in consequence of the refusal of the Republic to grant the franchise to residents of alien origin. But the whole world was surprised when it became known on New Year's day of 1896 that Dr Jameson, the Administrator of Rhodesia, had invaded the Transvaal with 600 horse. The raid was a complete failure; and an effort was made to prove that it was known beforehand to Mr Chamberlain, or at least to some of the officials at the Colonial Office. The House of Commons set up a committee to investigate the matter, which was unable to find any evidence to substantiate these charges. Dr Jameson was put on his trial and condemned, but released on grounds of health before his term of imprisonment was completed. Rhodes resigned his offices of Prime Minister of the Cape Colony and Managing Director of the South African Company, but suffered no further molestation. The failure of the raid confirmed the Boers in their belief that if they fought they could win, and they at once began to accumulate arms and stores for the struggle which they were not loth to face.

But we are now approaching the present day. We have to deal with questions still burning, and to trench upon issues of current party strife. It will be well to summarise as briefly as possible the course of events since 1895, to avoid so far as possible the criticism of persons and parties, and to concentrate our attention on the main questions that arose during the ten years of Conservative rule. The present Parliament and the present Government can hardly with propriety be discussed.

Lord Salisbury's third Government lasted from June, 1895, to 1900. In 1897, the sixtieth anniversary of the Queen's accession was celebrated in London, and was made the occasion of an unparalleled display of the resources and loyalty of the British Empire. In October, 1899, the Boer War broke out, and the General Election of 1900 was fought on the issue of a fight to a finish. The country by a large majority declared itself in favour of the existing Government and its policy, and for the first time there was a small Unionist majority in Scotland. Lord Salisbury formed a fresh Government pledged to subdue the Boer Republics. The Premier resigned the office of Foreign Secretary, and was succeeded by Lord Lansdowne, whose place at the War Office was taken by Mr Brodrick, now Lord Midleton. On January 22, 1901, Queen Victoria died, and was succeeded by King Edward VII, whose coronation was fixed for June 26, 1902. Two days before the appointed date the country was shaken by the news that the King was suffering from appendicitis, and an immediate operation was necessary. The operation was successfully performed, and the King, happily restored to health, was crowned on August 9, 1902. In March, 1902, the principal countries concerned, excluding Russia, concluded a convention for the abolition of bounties, direct or

CH. III.

indirect, on the production of sugar and agreed to impose countervailing duties on bounty-fed sugar or to prohibit its importation. On May 31, 1902, the Boer War was brought to an end, and the Boer Republics were annexed. The completion of the War allowed Lord Salisbury to retire on July 11, 1902, and he died in August, 1903. He was succeeded as Premier by Mr Arthur Balfour.

When the time came to consider the remission of the war-duty of one shilling a quarter on wheat, Mr Chamberlain advocated its remission as regards colonial produce, but its retention as against foreign produce. During his absence in South Africa this point was decided against him by the pressure of Ritchie, the Chancellor of the Exchequer, who threatened to resign, if Mr Chamberlain's plan were adopted. However, in May, 1903, Mr Chamberlain decided to raise the general issue of Tariff Reform and Colonial Preference, and in September of the same year he resigned, in order to prosecute his campaign more freely. His resignation was accompanied by that of Ritchie and followed by that of the Duke of Devonshire, also a convinced Free-Trader. Mr Balfour, who had shown leanings towards a modification of the principles of unconditional Free Trade, acquiesced in the retirement of the extreme partisans on either side, and endeavoured to carry on the Government without committing himself to any policy which would break up the Unionist alliance. He succeeded in achieving his main object, though for the time his own authority and the prestige of his party were seriously shaken. But in 1905 it became necessary to resign; Sir Henry Campbell-Bannerman succeeded him, and dissolved Parliament in December, 1905.

The general election of January, 1906, was fought on various issues. The preponderating influence with the electors was no doubt dissatisfaction with the Unionist Government, its dissensions, its uncertain fiscal policy, and its long duration. The heavy financial burdens, principally due to the war, swelled the volume of discontent; and the undefined official policy with regard to Tariff Reform was incapable on the one hand of arousing enthusiasm among the voters, and on the other hand gave rise to suspicions that it was proposed to increase the living expenses of the working-class. The employment of indentured Chinese labour in the South African mines was also very unpopular. The Education Bill of 1902 had aroused all the force of militant Nonconformity, and by the increased cost of more efficient education had displeased the ratepayer. Vague social yearnings in favour of improved conditions for the labouring masses operated also in favour of a change, and the out-and-out Socialists either gave their support to candidates directly claiming to represent the interests of Labour, or cast their votes and used their influence in favour of those Liberal candidates who showed themselves not unfavourable to some of their aspirations. The grievances of the Post Office employees, endorsed by the Bradford

Committee, whose report was not accepted by Lord Stanley, the Unionist Postmaster-General, were not without electoral importance. The decision of the Law Courts, which had declared the Trade Unions liable to damages for wrongs committed by their officials, inclined the forces of organised labour to adopt the side of the Liberals, most of whom were pledged to redress this grievance. Home Rule was not made an issue of the election. The total result was an unprecedented majority in favour of Sir Henry Campbell-Bannerman's Government. Less than 160 Conservatives and Unionists were returned, as against about 390 Liberals and Radicals, 80 Irish Nationalists, and 40 Labour members. The Liberals had a majority of about 120 over all other sections combined; but, as they early showed their willingness to act in concert so far as possible with the Labour party and the Nationalists, their gross majority, a majority of very heterogeneous composition, amounted to about 360. Thus ended the twenty years of Unionist ascendancy following on the Home Rule split.

The acts and the fortunes of the Unionist Governments which ruled from 1895 to 1905 may be briefly surveyed under the heads of foreign and colonial policy, education, army, navy, finance, social legislation.

In foreign policy the result of the ten years was the abandonment of the policy of " splendid isolation," and the entrance of Great Britain into understandings with several Powers and one binding alliance. With France our relations reached an extreme degree of tension after the Sudan campaigns and the discovery of the Marchand expedition (1898). This tension was increased by the Dreyfus affair (1897–9) in which the British public took an interest which seemed to our neighbours excessive and indiscreet. But in 1904, owing to the conciliatory efforts of the British Government, the pressure of a shifting Balance of Power, and the personal charm of King Edward, this state of things was happily brought to an end by an understanding mainly concerned with Egypt, Morocco, and Newfoundland, though embracing, so far as possible, all matters of dispute.

Relations with Germany, on the other hand, did not improve. The telegram of the German Emperor to President Kruger in 1896 was resented here. The Boer War was thought to be unjust by the great majority of Germans, as of almost all the chief European peoples, and inflamed the popular animosity against this country. The British understanding with France did not mend matters, and, in 1905, at the Conference of Algeciras Great Britain stood by France while Austria gave her support to Germany, and the serious rift in European harmony has not yet disappeared. Official relations have always been correct; but a strong jealousy between Germany and Great Britain has grown up, accompanied by mutual suspicions, which were not diminished by the later understandings with Russia and lesser Powers. The alliance with Japan was resented in Germany as blocking German designs in the Far East and as a breach

CH. III.

of loyalty to the European community. Proposals for a diminution of armaments made in connexion with the Hague Conference of 1907 were not well received by Germany, and such proposals are not likely to be well received so long as Great Britain maintains her claim to the overwhelming maritime supremacy which is necessary to her safety.

With the United States our relations were at their worst in 1896, at the time of President Cleveland's Venezuelan message The Cuban War gave us the opportunity of showing our goodwill towards the United States in an effective manner, and the two greatest English-speaking nations have since been on much more friendly terms.

With Russia our enduring feud outlasted the Unionist Government. Supposed Russian designs upon India were a constant cause of suspicion. The expedition to Tibet (1904) was partly the result of this mistrust. The alliance with Japan was in the main an expedient adopted to meet the danger of a coalition to destroy British influence in the Far East, and to close the great Chinese market to British goods. But it was also particularly directed against Russian aggression in Manchuria, and the predominance of Russian influence at Pekin. In the War of 1904–5, which was rendered possible by this Treaty, Great Britain in accordance with the terms of the Treaty kept the ring. No other Power could intervene in view of the maritime strength of this country. Thus, without any departure from neutrality, Great Britain's alliance was of material assistance to Japan. But the effects of the War and of the subsequent social disturbances in Russia removed a menace from our frontiers, and rendered the Russian Government more amenable to friendly overtures. The understanding with Russia concerning Persia, Afghanistan, and Tibet (1907) is due in the first place to these causes, and in the second place to improved relations between England and France. It has manifest dangers of its own, but it may be the beginning of a policy of mutual forbearance in the Far East, and of a different grouping of the Powers in Europe.

In the Near East, the amiable sentiments of the British public have constantly urged upon the Government forms of intervention which they knew to be impracticable or harmful. Armenian massacres, the aspirations of Greece, the sufferings of Cretan insurgents, the rights and wrongs of Macedonian Committees, have, each in turn, been made the subject of clamorous demonstrations which, if effective, could only have led to war. British diplomacy has worked long and late and unselfishly in defence of oppressed races; but the preservation of the *status quo*, however unsatisfactory, has been the only guarantee for European peace, and the rivalry of Austria and Russia, with the impotence of the Ottoman Power, have assisted British statesmen to attain their end. And, whatever Government is in power, this policy must be pursued, until the Balance of Power is changed, or one of the rivals is determined to risk a contest. Then, Great Britain will have to decide what her interests in the Balkan peninsula may be, and what sacrifices she is prepared to make in order to protect them.

British colonial policy down to 1903 was dominated by one commanding personality, Mr Joseph Chamberlain. Towards our subordinate colonies he initiated a policy of improvement and development by state funds, a policy of reproductive investment. Towards our autonomous colonies he succeeded in adopting an attitude of sympathy and comprehension which worked miracles. The first outcome was Customs preference for British imports, first granted gratuitously by Canada and afterwards by other colonies. The second outcome was a spontaneous wave of enthusiastic loyalty and imperial pride, which received material illustration during the Boer War. Had the colonies not felt confidence in Mr Chamberlain, doubts might have arisen in their minds whether the quarrel was just and necessary. Australian federation is a visible and permanent fruit of his policy. Another result was the movement for Tariff Reform on the basis of mutual preference between the colonies and the mother country, the result of which is yet to be seen. Something more may be said on this subject under the head of finance, and the details of colonial history are reserved for a later chapter.

The Conservative Government of 1895 made one or two half-hearted or incomplete attempts to deal with the questions of primary education; but it was reserved for the Government of Mr Balfour to tackle the main problem. The problem was forced upon the attention of the Government by the needs of the voluntary schools which provided elementary education for more than half of the children of England and Wales. The government grants, though several times increased, together with the subscriptions of supporters, did not suffice to keep these schools up to the average standard of efficiency maintained by the board-schools. On the other hand, to purchase or rent these schools from the communities that had built and assisted to support them would impose an excessive burden on the public finances. And the friends of denominational religious education, Church of England, Roman Catholic, Jewish, or other, were unwilling to resign the schools which they had hitherto controlled, and to place them under the conditions imposed by the Cowper-Temple clause of the 1870 Act. The defects of that Act demanded a remedy; and every thoroughgoing remedy was barred either by conflicting religious feeling, financial considerations, or other practical difficulties. The Act of 1902 abolished the school boards, and placed the local control of all schools alike in the hands of the county councils, or those of town and borough councils. The existing board-schools were maintained as undenominational schools, and the existing voluntary schools as denominational schools; but, for the first time, the expense of maintaining the latter was placed upon the rates, in so far as the government grant did not suffice. The public authority assumed the direct control of secular education in all schools; but the religious bodies continued to regulate the religious instruction in the schools whose buildings they provided, and were charged with the obligation of maintaining and, if necessary, improving those buildings. By these provisions the existing division of schools into denominational and undenominational was perpetuated, and Nonconformist ratepayers were burdened in many areas with part of the expense of maintaining schools in which religious systems obnoxious to them were subjects of daily instruction, while the similar grievance, which had long been endured under the board-school system by those who were not content with Cowper-Temple teaching, was not removed. From the point of view of efficiency the reform justified the additional cost; but conditions of acute religious strife were induced which have not yet passed away.

Since 1870, elementary education has been made universal and compulsory; the education provided has been improved and a more rational system of inspection has replaced the old plan of payment by the results of examination. But, in the opinion of many, our scheme of elementary education is still unpractical and unsuited to the needs of the great majority of the population, for whose industrial and manual training insufficient provision is made. The concentration (since 1899) of the powers of the old Education Department, those of the Science and Art Department, and the control of educational endowments formerly exercised by the Charity Commission, in the hands of a new Board of Education, was an administrative improvement which has already produced some good results. The age-limit for compulsory education has been progressively raised. Since 1890, when a grant was first made for technical instruction out of money originally intended for other purposes, considerable efforts have been made to provide technical and scientific training in accordance with the needs of the various localities; but the almost complete decay of the old system of apprenticeship has left a gap which these facilities do not go far to fill. By the Act of 1902, the Board of Education and the local education Authorities have considerable powers for the control and encouragement of secondary education; but the coordination of education between the public elementary school and the University is still very imperfect. Mainly through private benefactions and local effort, Universities and University Colleges have been established in many of the leading provincial towns; but private benefaction for this purpose lags in this country far behind the American standard, while public expenditure is not comparable with that of the most enlightened countries of the European Continent. State expenditure on elementary education has risen from about £1,500,000 in 1872 to £16,000,000 in 1908–9; and other expenditure on education has probably increased in a like proportion. But it can hardly be maintained that individual culture and social efficiency have proportionately improved during that period. We have yet to envisage clearly the ends which public education should subserve, and to come to some agreement as to the objects which can with advantage be pursued. For definite and practical objects a much larger expenditure might be profitable; but for the results hitherto obtained the existing expenditure is extravagant. Meanwhile, the religious controversy blocks the path, but does not diminish the cost.

The deficiencies in our military system brought to public notice by the Boer War of 1899 led to a period of active and inconsequent attempts at reform. Mr St John Brodrick, now Lord Midleton, Secretary of State for War from 1900 to 1903, attacked the problem with great energy, acting on the advice of Lord Roberts. The main object of his endeavour was to create an adequate reserve of trained troops, and for this purpose he initiated a plan by which recruits should be invited to enlist for three years only, with the option of extending their service when this term was reached. This plan would have provided in due course of time a large and perhaps adequate reserve of private soldiers, though the *cadres* in which they were to be embodied would have been deficient. But the scheme broke down, owing to the unwillingness of the soldiers to extend their service, and to the consequent difficulties in supplying the drafts for India and the colonies. Arnold-Forster adopted a plan by which the War Office should alternatively enlist men for three years, or for nine years. The nine years' men would supply the drafts for distant service, the three years' men the reserve, and the War Office could control the supply by calling for men of one class or the other or for both according to need. It was his further intention to abolish the linked battalion system, to train recruits in centralised depots, to reduce the term of short service in order to increase still further the reserve; and he had a plan for forming and training a reserve of officers. These ulterior suggestions did not obtain the assent of the Cabinet, and they were finally abandoned owing to the change of Government. Behind all these plans and those subsequently adopted there has been a strong movement for the adoption of compulsory military service; but compulsory military service would not supply the troops for our garrisons in India and the colonies, and is in other respects difficult to accommodate to our needs and our finances. Above all, both parties seem to believe that compulsion would be unpopular with the electorate.

In 1903 Mr Balfour appointed a small committee, consisting of Lord Esher (Chairman), Admiral Sir John Fisher, and Lieutenant-Colonel Sir George Clarke, to consider the reconstitution of the War Office, on the lines indicated by Lord Esher in his note appended to the Report of the Elgin Commission. In pursuance of their recommendations the office of Commander-in-chief was abolished; and the general control of the army was entrusted to an Army Council, consisting of the soldiers and civilians holding the chief administrative posts in the War Office, and presided over by the Secretary of State for War. Mr Balfour

CH. III.

had previously created a Committee of Imperial Defence in which leading political, naval, and military opinion was to be concentrated, and this Committee now received wider functions with a permanent organisation and staff. It was hoped that this Committee would also aid in the task of organising and coordinating defence throughout the Empire. A general staff was also projected and afterwards set up to consider problems of general strategy, and train a body of special officers for staff duties in war and peace. Training of troops was severed from administration, which was largely decentralised, and an Army Accounts Branch was established, which it was hoped might for the future prevent such waste and disorder as had been apparent in the South African War. But the general policy of the Army Council still chiefly depends on the Secretary of State for War and upon Parliament, where his influence is paramount. Responsibility still rests with the Minister of the Crown; but organisation has been improved and the status of the chief military authority has been raised in public estimation. History is not yet, however, in a position to judge of the results of the new system, which has been further developed by Mr Haldane, on the lines laid down by Mr Balfour.

The cost of the army increased from seventeen millions in 1891–2 to nearly twenty-nine millions in 1905–6, a considerable part of this cost being due to an improvement in the pay and other conditions of service. But the beneficial effects of these improved conditions were considerably diminished by the difficulty found in securing civil employment for discharged soldiers—a problem which still occupies the attention of our military authorities.

The Unionist Governments devoted much attention to the navy, which steadily increased in magnitude and effective strength. The growing competition of foreign Powers imposed a progressive burden on the taxpayer; the total expenditure on the navy rising from fifteen and a half millions in 1891–2 to thirty-seven millions in 1904–5, which fell in 1905–6 to thirty-three and a half millions, in consequence of administrative economies. The abandonment of naval stations abroad, the concentration of the main fleet in European waters, the demolition of obsolete vessels, and the use of nucleus crews, resulted in a considerable saving without, as it was believed, loss of efficiency. But the competitive increase in the tonnage and armament of battleships and first-class cruisers bids fair to absorb all possible economies. The Cawdor programme of 1905 foreshadowed an annual expenditure of £8,000,000 on capital ships alone, without reckoning the cost of other classes of ships, harbours, or docks, and, after a short period of relaxed effort, it seems probable that this expenditure may be exceeded in the near future. Our immediate rivals in this field are no longer France and Russia, as in the past, but Germany and the United States, the two most vigorous nations of the world. In 1902, it was decided to modify the system of training for naval officers. Thenceforward, the engineer officers, the marine officers, and the executive officers were to receive the same training during youth, and specialisation was to be deferred until after they had received their commissions.

Irish affairs receive treatment in another chapter. The efforts of the Unionists to combine generous legislation with resolute suppression of crime have up to the present had results which must be described as disappointing. The task of pacifying and reconciling Ireland, which Gladstone took up in 1868, is not yet accomplished, and Mr Wyndham's comprehensive scheme of Land Purchase has been impeded and almost wrecked by the liberality of its own terms, and the rise in the current rate of interest for loans.

The chief measures of social legislation initiated by the Unionist Governments were the Employers' Liability Acts of 1897 and 1900, which secured compensation for injuries received in the course of their employment to various classes of workers, estimated to amount in all to seven million persons, and the Licensing Bill of 1904, which resulted during 1905 and 1906 in the extinction of more than a thousand licenses with compensation paid by levy on the trade, while securing license-holders against dispossession without compensation, and has led and will in natural course lead to further like results. The London Government Act (1899) created in the metropolis a number of Borough Councils to control many of those local services which in other cities are directed by a single authority. It was thought that without such sub-division the responsibility of the London Council might exceed its capacity for executive work, and that its authority in the capital of the Empire might prove to be excessive. Reasons partly similar led to the establishment of a separate and independent authority, to take over the undertakings of all the London water companies (1902). The Unemployed Workmen Act of 1905 was only a tentative and experimental reconnaissance in a difficult and embarrassing country. Minor Acts of collective importance were the Agricultural Rates Act (1896), the Conciliation Act (1896), the University of London Act (1899), the Housing of the Working Classes Act (1903), the Employment of Children Act (1903), and the Aliens Act (1905). But the legislation of Parliament has been supplemented by the activity of many municipal bodies; and a school of reformers has arisen which sees a fruitful prospect in the steady extension of municipal supply of many services to the community, and direct employment of labour by the municipalities. At the municipal elections of 1906 there was a general reaction against the cost of municipal socialism, but it remains to be seen whether this reaction will last.

Great Britain, like most of the chief European nations, has found the problem of national finance increasingly difficult. The policy, inherited from Peel and Gladstone, of reducing expenditure and lightening taxation

CH. III.

has been abandoned, and state expenditure increased from 90 millions in 1891–2 to 140 millions in 1905–6, besides six millions in the latter year charged to capital. After a short struggle to reduce expenditure lasting from 1906 to 1909, public expenditure for 1909–10 is again estimated to show a substantial and progressive increase. The increase is mainly due to expenditure on the army, navy, and education; but all services have become more costly, owing partly to the extension of the field of government activity, and partly to improved remuneration demanded by and conceded to many classes of public servants. In these circumstances, it has become clear that the system of finance hitherto adopted by both parties is not adequate to meet the national needs. Hence arises, on the one hand, the Tariff Reform movement, intended to supplement or replace existing sources of revenue by import duties on manufactured goods, and possibly on some articles of food, with pre-ferential rebates to British colonies, and, on the other hand, the Liberal Budget of 1909, which is a far-reaching attempt to supply present and future needs without abandoning the principles of Free Trade. The supporters of these two schools are now locked in their first serious encounter, the issue of which cannot be foreseen. Both parties now admit the necessity of increased expenditure; they differ as to the merits of rival methods of taxation.

Both parties have been affected by the spread of tendencies, properly called socialistic: the Liberals more than the Conservatives, for it involved a greater sacrifice of principle on the part of the Liberals to abandon the doctrines of free competition in favour of those of government regulation and government beneficence. The Liberal party, in the past supremely individualistic, has found cause to shed a large part of its individualistic prepossessions. The Conservative party was always less individualistic. The prosperity of the State and of the individuals that make up the State depends upon a due balance of individualism and socialism; but the movements of the past century have given so much latitude to individualism that the efforts of this century must by necessity be concerned with correcting the effects of too much liberty. Mr Lloyd George's Budget of 1909 shows this tendency in one shape, Tariff Reform in another; and there are a score of different forms of socialism, consti-tutional, revolutionary, centralised, decentralised, academic, philosophic, aristocratic, democratic, autocratic, predatory, philanthropic, idealist, materialist, Christian, anti-Christian, which can hardly be grouped in a single party. It may be anticipated that both parties will be more or less socialistic for some time to come, and their respective success will depend upon the kind of socialism which their leaders administer. Meanwhile, there is apparent the formation of a new party or section, including men of very varying shades of thought, but agreed in the desire to effect a re-distribution of the national income by one means or another, and adopting the name of "Socialists." The influence, direct or indirect, of this extreme left wing upon politics has already been great; and there is no reason to suppose that it will diminish.

Reviewing the results of the whole period here surveyed, we see a vast increase in material prosperity, a great increase in territory and in imperial solidarity, an increase in national strength though our absolute preponderance has not been maintained. Our export trade, after remaining nearly stationary from 1871 to 1898, increased rapidly from 1899 to 1906. On the other hand, imports showed a fairly steady increase over the whole period, indicating a progressive addition to the total profits arising from our dealings with the rest of the globe. The population of the United Kingdom has steadily increased from thirty-one millions in 1871 to forty-one millions in 1901, though the fall in the population of Ireland has continued. The death-rate has diminished by about thirty per cent.; the birth-rate has also diminished, though in a less proportion. The proportion of pauperism has greatly diminished since 1868, though it has been nearly stationary since 1891. The cost of pauperism has, meanwhile, very greatly increased, owing mainly to better conditions in workhouses and asylums. Social organisation has improved, chiefly through reforms in municipal administration, and the greater efficiency of government supervision. The defects in that organisation are more closely scrutinised, and many evils have been brought to light, few of which are new. Special attention has been directed to fluctuations in industrial employment, to the existence of a large class of persons incapable of continuous employment, to industries carried on under conditions which do not admit of decent existence, to physical deterioration, to the evils of drink, to excessive infant mortality. For these and other social evils remedies are demanded, which will require the application of entirely new principles. The old specific of letting things alone is out of fashion; the manifold responsibilities of the State are recognised. In spite of all expedients to curtail debate and save parliamentary time, the efficiency of Parliament has not increased in proportion to the greatly extended functions now assigned to the legislative authority.

The old rural aristocracy has been to a large extent displaced by newcomers. The rural labouring population has diminished; the urban population has increased beyond all proportion. Emigration has proceeded steadily, with periodical fluctuations, though it has not increased in proportion to the increase of population. The proportion of emigrants proceeding from these islands to the United States has diminished, that destined to British North America and British South Africa has greatly increased; emigration to Australasia has not, until recently, been progressive. The general standard of living has improved, among the wealthier classes to the point of extravagance, among the middle classes and the more prosperous manual labourers to a high degree of comfort; and even in the lowest classes it has probably not deteriorated. The general level of wages for manual labour has risen, and irregularity of

CH. III.

employment is probably not greater than it was forty years ago. Crime has diminished, taking the whole period under review, but of late years it has shown a slight tendency to increase. The consumption of alcohol has diminished in all classes, especially of late years. Gambling on horses and on stocks and shares has become even more prevalent.

In literature few great writers have arisen to take the place of those who have passed away during the period. Ephemeral publications of every description absorb a great deal of energy and talent, and more durable works run the risk of being pushed aside and forgotten. But a public exists which welcomes works on natural science, history, biography, and travels. The interest in social and economic subjects is unfailing. There are many accomplished writers, but few great names stand out from the throng. In drama the taste of the public has demanded light entertainment rather than tragedies and works of poetic imagination, though the plays of Shakespeare still hold the stage. The general scheme of domestic decoration has greatly improved since the aesthetic movement of the seventies; but decorators have relied much on the designers of the eighteenth century, and originality has leant towards affectation. In painting, the conventions of the Victorian school still hold the public taste; the Preraphaelite school has spent its vigour; and the efforts of younger men to find new modes of expression have found little encouragement. The craze for the antique and the rare has diverted funds from the support of contemporary art; but the lack of sincere and spontaneous impulse to artistic production in harmony with our modern life is the main cause of sterility. Museums and picture galleries enshrine the memorials of a creative instinct which no longer exists. In architecture the Gothic revival has passed away, and important buildings are now designed in the grandiose Palladian style; but the public cares little which style is adopted, and the desire for advertisement has produced most of the striking edifices which have been erected in our streets. Domestic architecture in the cottage style, to suit the taste of cultivated people of moderate means, has produced some fantastic and many delightful country residences which, with their gardens and interiors, are the expression of a genuine love of beauty in a narrow class. Of all the minor arts, gardening has been pursued with the greatest sincerity and enthusiasm.

This has been an age of immense material progress, but not an age of conspicuous moral improvement, and with increased prosperity has come a sense of unrest and discontent, and discontent finds sympathetic support from the widespread compassion of the fortunate for the unfortunate. Translated into common sense, this discontent should lead to social reform; but it remains to be seen whether the pervading sentiment of compassion will be used to carry measures framed in the true interests of the whole community, or wasted on palliatives which diminish self-reliance and energy.

CHAPTER IV.

IRELAND AND THE HOME RULE MOVEMENT.

The consequences of the Fenian conspiracy were out of all proportion to the conspiracy itself. It is well known that the execution (1867) of the "Manchester martyrs"—Allen, Larkin, and O'Brien—for their share in the constructive murder of police-sergeant Brett proved the turning-point in the life of Charles Stewart Parnell, and there is not a little truth in O'Leary's remark that Gladstone's conversion to Home Rule dates from the attack on Clerkenwell gaol in the same year. The fact is that, though unimportant in themselves, these events, occurring as they did in England, brought forcibly home to Englishmen the intense hatred with which the English rule in Ireland was regarded by the bulk of Irishmen. Added to this, it was the first time that American-Irish influence had made itself felt in domestic affairs. These incidents furnished food for serious reflexion to a generation which had just succeeded in securing for itself a fuller participation in the government of the country by the acquisition of the household franchise. For good or for evil, the balance of political power had passed into the hands of the democracy, and there was something repellent to it in a system of governing Ireland in opposition to the will of the majority of its inhabitants. The conscience of the nation was touched, and a strong desire was manifested to break with the bad traditions of the past and to do justice to Ireland. There was perhaps more of sentiment than of knowledge in this view of the question. For it can hardly be said that Englishmen generally knew anything of the real causes that lay at the bottom of the Fenian conspiracy. But they were willing to learn, and in Gladstone they found a sympathetic exponent of their desire to act justly towards Ireland.

Himself keenly sensitive to the trend of public opinion, he had already accorded to Ireland a principal place in his political programme. From the question of the disestablishment of the Irish Church, on which, with the majority of Englishmen, he had made up his mind in 1865, he passed on to other objects. The anomalous position occupied by the Established Church in Ireland was only one aspect of the Irish problem. The root of the evil, as it seemed to him, was to be found in the fact that English statesmen had all along tried to govern Ireland in accordance with English ideas and in the interest of a small Protestant minority. But, if Ireland was ever to be pacified and Irish discontent removed, the process must be reversed and an attempt made to legislate for Ireland in accordance with Irish ideas, and for the benefit of the entire nation. He announced his intention, if the opportunity was afforded him, of disestablishing the Irish Church, of settling the Irish land question, and of providing for the educational needs of the Irish people. The opportunity he asked for was given him. His theory appealed to Englishmen educated in the political school of Jeremy Bentham and John Stuart Mill, and at the general election in 1868 he was returned to power with a majority of 118 votes in a House consisting of 658 members. He at once addressed himself to the task he had taken in hand. On March 1, 1869, he introduced a Bill for the disestablishment and disendowment of the Church in Ireland. The Bill, with some modifications made in the House of Lords, received the royal assent on July 26.

Unlike Catholic Emancipation, which was preceded by a long and stormy agitation, dating back to the middle of the eighteenth century, the disestablishment of the Irish Church came suddenly, without any particular demand for it, and was apparently attributable rather to the anomalous position of the Irish Church as a highly privileged and richly endowed corporation in a country the majority of whose inhabitants professed another religion, than to its constituting, at least since the settlement of the tithe question, any oppressive grievance. The Irish Church was an offshoot of the Church of England. It was the Church not of the natives, or of the gentry of Anglo-Norman descent, but of the English planters of the sixteenth and seventeenth centuries. Like them, it had grown rich on the spoils of conquest and confiscation. It was, like the plantation itself, of exotic origin. Notwithstanding its privileged position as the Church of the State, it had from the first had a hard fight to hold its own against Roman Catholicism on the one hand and Presbyterianism on the other. It never was and never could be a missionary Church. This was ground and cause enough in the opinion of philosophic radicalism to destroy it. "It had failed in its mission," said Englishmen, anxious to render justice to Ireland, but a little uncertain where to begin. "Cut it down: why cumbereth it the ground?"

But the Act of Disestablishment was not a simple measure of destruction. Though cut adrift from the State, with its revenues and its privileges curtailed, the Irish Church was left standing as a self-governing body. It was confirmed in the possession of its religious edifices; liberal provision was made for its sustentation; clergymen who wished to retire were enabled to compound for their services; and a fund was set aside to satisfy all vested interests. In itself it suffered nothing by the change. On the contrary, it gained by being freed from political influences, its activity increased, it lost its aggressive-ness, it became more than ever it had been the home of piety and learning, and in the devotion of its members it found ample compen-sation for its loss of material wealth. A proposal made while the Bill was in progress to save it by the concurrent endowment of the Roman Catholic and Presbyterian Churches was rejected; but, to satisfy the sense of justice, provision was made for the discontinuance of the Maynooth Grant and the *Regium Donum*. Henceforth, all three Churches were to stand on the same level. For good or for evil, however, the Act of Disestablishment marks a distinctly new step in the relations between Great Britain and Ireland. It was the first expression of the new political ideal of governing Ireland in accordance with Irish ideas. Those who argued in favour of Disestablishment did so on the ground that the Irish Church had failed in its mission. The same argument would apply to the whole system of the English rule in Ireland. In denouncing Disestablishment as an infringement of the Act of Union, its opponents instinctively felt that more important interests than even the fate of the Irish Church were at stake. In particular, the clause in the Act enforcing the compulsory sale of church property and enabling the tenants of the Church to become, with the assistance of the State, the owners of their holdings, was of serious significance for the future. In passing, it may be noticed that of the 8432 tenants of the Church the great majority took advantage of this clause to become the owners of their farms at an average price of $22\frac{2}{3}$ years' purchase.

Having settled the question of the Church, Gladstone proceeded to attack the land problem. The "Great Famine" (1845–7) is the cardinal fact of Irish history in the nineteenth century. In importance it holds a place beside the Rebellion of 1641–52 and the War of the Revolution. Attention has been drawn in former chapters to the effect of those events on the economic history of Ireland. It has been pointed out how, in consequence of the depopulation created by the wars of the seventeenth century, the English settlers, in their capacity of Irish landlords, tried to extract an immediate profit from their estates by turning their lands into grazing pastures and sheep-runs, and that, while they succeeded in creating a flourishing provision trade and an equally flourishing woollen industry, the natives were driven off to the bogs and sterile parts of the island to make room for cattle. English legislation destroyed the woollen industry; but during the first half of the eighteenth century Ireland was a corn-importing country. This condition of things lasted till England entered on her career of a great manufacturing country. The commercial concessions made to Ireland in 1780, and the encouragement offered to agriculture by Foster's Corn Laws, enabled her to take advantage of the favourable juncture. Ireland became a corn-growing and corn-exporting country. The outbreak of the war with France made agriculture a profitable business, and the Napoleonic period saw Ireland at the height of her prosperity. With the peace there came a decline; but the impetus given to population continued, and in 1841 Ireland numbered 8,175,124 inhabitants. The Great Famine was awful in its consequences; but it was less the Famine than the adoption of Free Trade principles by England that put a sudden end to the artificial prosperity of the country. With the adoption of Free Trade agriculture ceased to be a profitable business, and, step by step, year by year, Ireland has reverted to her primitive condition of a grazing country.

So far as the land question was concerned the immediate result of the Famine was twofold. In the first place, many landlords were irretrievably ruined by their inability to collect their rents, while others, not so hardly pressed, seized the opportunity to eject their non-rent-paying tenants, and to turn their lands into grazing pastures. Secondly, and in consequence of the inability or reluctance of the landlords to forgo their rents for a time, the peasantry, being most of them tenants-at-will, were forced to quit their holdings and constrained to take refuge within the inhospitable walls of the workhouse, or in circumstances of indescribable suffering to seek out new homes for themselves beyond the Atlantic, or to eke out a miserable existence by harvest work in England and Scotland. Parliament met the situation by two Acts—the one, the Encumbered Estates Act, to enable bankrupt landlords to get rid of their lands by removing the restrictions placed by the law on the sale of entailed estates: the other for the relief of evicted tenants, by rendering it obligatory on evicting landlords to give to the Poor Law guardians forty-eight hours' notice of intention to evict, so as to enable them to make provision for the shelter of the persons evicted. The real author of the Encumbered Estates Act was Sir Robert Peel. In pondering over the Irish problem, Peel had reverted to the ideals of English statesmen in the sixteenth and seventeenth centuries. Like Bacon, he argued that Ireland could only be pacified by planting her thickly with English colonists. The devastation created by the Famine had, in his opinion, created a favourable opportunity to put the experiment in execution. As he had foreseen, the market was, in consequence of the Act, flooded with estates. Landlords who, with a little help, might have tided over the crisis were forced to part with their ancestral properties at greatly depreciated prices. But the British capitalist, on whom such store had been set, held aloof. Of the 7216 purchasers for the 3197 estates sold during the next twenty-eight years only 314 were Englishmen. Most of the new proprietors were small Irish capitalists of a not very desirable type. Anxious to make the most of their bargains and bound by none of those scruples that had influenced the conduct of their predecessors, they evicted their defaulting tenants with remorseless energy.

The discontent aroused by the proceedings of the " Exterminators " led to the foundation in 1850 of a Tenant-Right League. The object of the League was to obtain for the tenant what was afterwards known as the "three F's"—a fair rent, fixity of tenure, and free sale—or, in other words, to secure for him a legal recognition of his claim to dual ownership, with the landlord, of the land cultivated by him. The movement spread rapidly. For once laying aside their religious prejudices, Protestant farmers of the north agreed to unite with their Catholic brethren of the south in a demand for legislation on the basis of the proposals of the League. The time seemed propitious. Early in 1852, the Ministry of Lord John Russell was succeeded by that of Lord Derby; but, in consequence of his inability to command a majority, Parliament was dissolved in the summer of that year. At the general election Ireland returned some fifty members pledged to make Tenant Right a cabinet question. Votes were at a premium in the new Parliament, and the Ministry showed a desire to conciliate the Irish contingent. Facilities were afforded the Leaguers to give expression to their policy; and at the same time the Attorney-General for Ireland, Mr (afterwards Sir) Joseph Napier, submitted four Bills for the regulation of the land question, admitting the principle, insisted on by the Leaguers, of retrospective compensation for tenants' improvements. But the House of Lords refused to listen to the proposal; and the Prime Minister, anticipating defeat if he insisted, beat a retreat. His action was resented by the Leaguers, and, transferring their votes to the Opposition, they succeeded in bringing about the fall of the Ministry.

A thrill of joy passed through the country. The fate of Ireland was seen to rest in the hands of its own elected representatives. Without their consent no ministry, it was thought, could be formed, and the price of their consent was Tenant Right. But even then signs of disruption in the ranks of the Leaguers had become visible. The question of the Ecclesiastical Titles, the activity of the Catholic priests, and the violent language of the editor of the *Tablet*, Frederick Lucas, had awakened a feeling of distrust among the Ulster Presbyterians. The hostility of the Catholic Primate, Archbishop Cullen, and the treachery of individual members of the League, completed the mischief. Reduced by desertion to insignificance, the League ceased to be a political factor with which English parties had to reckon. The attempt to create an independent Irish party had failed and its failure discredited parliamentary tactics for more than a generation. Meanwhile, the process of depletion continued. Year by year thousands of Irish men and women quitted the country. Their sufferings were intense; but the prospect for those who remained grew brighter and the idea gained ground with English politicians that "the abstraction of the Celtic race at the rate of a quarter of a million a year was a surer remedy for the inveterate Irish disease than any human wit could have imagined." The Fenian conspiracy destroyed the fond delusion, and revealed a new danger.

CH. IV.

Instead of simplifying the Irish problem, emigration had added to its complexity by introducing a new factor—the American Irish. To the Irishman in America, boiling over with hatred against England, the question of the land had become absorbed in the greater question of national independence. The time had not yet come to put into practice Lalor's advice to link repeal to the land question, like a railway carriage to the engine; but it was coming rapidly.

Meanwhile, on February 15, 1870, Gladstone submitted his Bill for a "final" settlement of the Irish land question to the House of Commons. The Bill contained no recognition of the principle of the "three F's," which its author expressly stated to be incompatible with the rights of property. But it did admit the claim of the tenant to compensation for improvements effected by him, and it gave the force of law to that form of tenant-right which prevailed in Ulster. At the same time it left a loophole of escape for the landlord, by allowing the tenant to contract himself out of the law, with the avowed purpose of assimilating the tenure of land in Ireland to that in England on the basis of pure contract, regardless of the fact that there was all the difference in the world between an independent English farmer, able to make terms for himself, and an Irish peasant, shackled, so to speak, to the soil. Briefly stated, the Bill proposed to recognise Ulster tenant-right wherever it existed; to encourage the creation of leases for thirty-one years; to afford a beneficial right of occupation to the tenant so long as he paid a reasonable, *i.e.* a government valuation, rent, by enabling him to claim compensation for "disturbance," *i.e.* eviction, varying inversely with the value of his holding; and, by the "Bright Clauses," to facilitate the creation of a peasant proprietary, by enabling the Board of Works to advance two-thirds of the purchase money, to be repaid at the rate of 5 per cent. per annum spread over thirty-five years. There is no denying that this was an honest attempt to solve the question; but it must be admitted that the intention of assimilating the law in Ireland to that in England was inconsistent with Gladstone's undertaking to legislate in accordance with Irish ideas. The measure, however, met with little opposition, and after some alterations, further complicating it, in the House of Lords, it became law on August 1.

Having settled the church and land questions to his satisfaction, Gladstone turned to consider the question of higher education. To understand the problem that confronted him, we must go back to the middle of the sixteenth century. At that time, primary education in Ireland rested on two Acts of Parliament, viz. 28 Henry VIII, c. 15, providing for the establishment of parish schools, and 12 Eliz. c. 1, establishing a free school in every diocese. But the education thus provided was, even where the Acts could be enforced, of a very elementary sort, and, in the absence of any means of higher education at home, the Irish gentry of the Pale began to send their sons to be educated in

Spain, France, Italy, and the Spanish Netherlands. But the danger of exposing the more intelligent class of the community to Catholic influences was speedily recognised, and led to the foundation in 1591 of Trinity College. Unfortunately, the remedy came too late. Religion had ceased to be a matter of indifference to the natives, and the Irish gentry would have nothing to do with an institution which was avowedly based on proselytising principles. As it had repelled the Catholics so it failed to attract the Presbyterians, who looked to Glasgow University for their intellectual and theological training. Thus, like the Irish Church, of which it was indeed a branch, Trinity College remained, as it had begun, an institution confined to the English planters, and like her, too, was enriched by the spoils of conquest and confiscation. The Commonwealth left its mark on education in the charitable foundations of Erasmus Smith, as did the Revolution in the Charter schools, and the Union in the Kildare Place schools. A notable effort made by the Irish Parliament in 1787 to deal with the whole question of elementary, intermediate, and higher education, unfortunately led to no result. But the Catholic Relief Act of 1793 was followed by the establishment of a training college for the Irish Roman Catholic priesthood at Maynooth. Nothing, however, was done to meet the educational needs of the country till 1831, when the Irish Secretary of the day, Lord Stanley, carried a measure to combine a scheme of united secular education with separate religious instruction in state-aided schools. The success attending the National School system encouraged Peel to attack the question of higher education in the same spirit, by the establishment in 1845 of three secular colleges at Cork, Galway, and Belfast, called the Queen's Colleges, and combined as a University. But it soon became apparent that a system of secular training, acceptable so long as it concerned itself with the rudiments of learning, was utterly distasteful to a people which, whether Catholic or Protestant, was intensely religious, when it came to teaching such subjects as history, philosophy, and science. Except in Belfast, where a more rationalist spirit prevailed, the "Godless Colleges" were left rigidly alone by extreme Churchmen on both sides. The Church of Ireland had Trinity College, to which parents, if they had sufficient means, could send their sons. The needs of the Presbyterians were fairly met by the new Queen's College at Belfast and Magee College at Derry. The Catholics alone were entirely unprovided for. To supply the deficiency, private benevolence was enlisted, and a Catholic University, of which Cardinal Newman was the first rector, was founded at Dublin in 1854. But, though a university in name, it had no power to grant degrees, and being disregarded by the State, it had from the first a hard struggle for existence.

On the whole, then, there was no question that the subject of higher education in Ireland required serious attention when Gladstone took up the matter in 1872. Unfortunately, Gladstone had no personal

CH. IV.

experience of Ireland, and his attitude towards the problem was rather that of a benevolent sciolist than that of a well-informed statesman. Though theoretically distinct from each other, Trinity College and Dublin University were practically one and the same thing. In his Bill Gladstone proposed to revert to the theory, and, regarding the University as an entity in itself, to associate Trinity College, the Queen's Colleges of Cork and Belfast, together with the Catholic University and Magee College, as colleges affiliated to it. An elaborate scheme was prepared for its administration under the control of the State. But the University was to be a teaching as well as an examining body. The education afforded by it was to be purely secular, and, as the National School system had solved the question of teaching national history by entirely omitting it, so the University was to achieve its end by excluding from its curriculum theology, philosophy, and modern history. None of these topics were to be admitted as compulsory subjects in examination for its degrees. The scheme was greeted with derision and indignation. Catholics and Protestants were unanimous in their condemnation of it. Never, indeed, had an English statesman so thoroughly mistaken public opinion as did Gladstone on this occasion. What Irishmen of all classes and creeds wanted was not secular education, but education based on religion—Anglican education for the Anglican Protestant, Catholic education for the Catholic, and Presbyterian education for the Presbyterian. The Bill was rejected on its second reading, and early in 1874 Gladstone surrendered the seals of office to Disraeli.

Gladstone's failure to solve the Irish problem justified and at the same time gave considerable impetus to a movement which began to make itself felt in Ireland at this time. Home Rule is not simply Repeal in a new dress. It is an idea of European rather than of native origin. It has its roots in that stronger feeling of nationality, which sprang into being about the middle of the century and has led to such diverse results as the consolidation of Italy, the foundation of the German Empire, the separation of Norway from Sweden; to Pan-germanism and Panslavism in Europe, and Monroism in America. The author of the Home Rule movement in Ireland was Isaac Butt. He was a man of singular ability, by birth an Ulsterman, by tradition a Conservative, and by profession a barrister. His progress in his profession had been rapid. At thirty-one he was made a Q.C., and he had already filled the chair of Political Economy in Trinity College, Dublin; but it was his defence of the principles of the Union, on the occasion of the Corporation Repeal Debate, inaugurated by O'Connell in 1843, that first attracted public attention to him. Years went by. He was still a Unionist and a Protectionist when he entered Parliament in May, 1852, as M.P. for Harwich. At the general election in that year he was returned for Youghal, which he represented till 1865. He was defeated at the general election in that year; but was returned to Parliament for

Limerick city in 1871.   In the interval he had acquired a reputation as
the defender of the Fenian conspirators.   More than this, he had from
his intimate connexion with them become convinced that the Fenians
"were not a mere band of assassins actuated by base motives, but real
earnest patriots."   He was led to ponder on "the depth, the breadth,
the sincerity of that love of fatherland that misgovernment had tortured
into disaffection, and misgovernment, driving men to despair, had exaggerated into revolt."   When the Amnesty Association was started in
1868, he accepted the position of President.   The day, predicted for him
by O'Connell, when he would change his political faith, had come.

   It need hardly be said that Disestablishment had created a feeling of
bitter resentment against England among Irish Protestants.   Fenianism,
though scotched, was still alive.   The feeling of dissatisfaction with
England drew Churchmen and Fenians together, and led, in May, 1870,
to the foundation of the "Home Government Association."   The object
of the Association was to secure for Ireland, "under a federal arrangement" by which matters of imperial concern were to be left to the
Imperial Parliament, the management of her own domestic affairs by a
national legislature.   The name of the association was altered to that of
the "Home Rule League," and, in 1873, a branch of it, called the "Home
Rule Confederation of Great Britain" was established at Manchester.
At the general election in 1874 some sixty members were returned to
Parliament pledged, more or less strictly, to the principles of the League.
Unlike O'Connell, however, whom he in many respects resembled, Butt was
neither a parliamentary tactician nor a born leader of men.   His position
was a difficult one.   The party, of which he was the nominal chief, was
composed of the most heterogeneous elements—Orangemen, O'Connellites,
Young Irelanders, Tenant-Righters, and Fenians.   His authority, always
more acknowledged than obeyed, suffered greatly from the fact that he
was overwhelmed with debt and consequently unable to devote his entire
attention to his parliamentary duties.   Moreover, his policy was not
calculated to inspire enthusiasm.   His object, as stated by himself, was
to make an assault along the whole line of English misgovernment, to
bring forward every Irish grievance, in the hope and confidence that, if
liberal-minded Englishmen were made acquainted with the real needs
and wishes of Ireland, "they would come in the end to the conclusion
that they had but one way of giving good government, and that was by
allowing us to govern ourselves."   In the pursuit of this impossible
ideal, he submitted session after session a motion in favour of Home
Rule.   Session after session he brought forward Bills to amend the
tenure of land, to develop the industrial resources of the country, and
to improve the system of municipal and county government.   He was
thoroughly conversant with his subject and spoke with great ability and
marked moderation ; but he spoke to deaf ears.   His Bills were one and
all rejected, and his Home Rule proposal was laughed out of court.   The

CH. IV.

situation recalled the days of the " dignified policy " of Catholic agitation before O'Connell took the matter up.

Most of Butt's followers were quite satisfied with the result; but there were one or two of the party, whom the annual farce of begging for justice provoked to indignation. Joseph Biggar was not the father of parliamentary obstruction; but he was the first to reduce it to a system. The idea of speaking against time had come to him quite accidentally; but, as the importance of the Rule of the House, forbidding contentious measures to be taken after midnight, dawned on him, he recognised what a formidable instrument of obstruction an unscrupulous use of it might prove. If Englishmen would not legislate for Ireland, neither should they legislate for themselves. His opinion was shared by the junior member for county Meath, Charles Stewart Parnell, a Protestant, owning land in county Wicklow. But it was some time before the future leader of the Irish party took an active share in the debates of the House. It was an almost involuntary exclamation that first attracted public attention to him. The Irish Secretary, Sir Michael Hicks-Beach, had, in the course of one of those academic debates on Home Rule, instituted by Butt, alluded to the " Manchester murderers." " No! No! " exclaimed Parnell, adding, when called upon to withdraw, " I do not believe, and never shall believe, that any murder was committed at Manchester." The exclamation and explanation were characteristic of the man.

It is a common reproach against Englishmen that they know nothing of Irish history; but there were probably few members of the House of Commons who did not know at least as much of it as Parnell. His ignorance of everything that preceded his personal experience was astounding, and the fact is of considerable importance in trying to fairly estimate the man and his policy. He had been born and brought up in an atmosphere of intense hatred towards England. This hatred of England kept him steady and gave consistency and force to his policy. In intellectual versatility and in his knowledge of the Irish problem he was greatly inferior to Butt. But he saw, what Butt would never recognise, that, if Home Rule was to be obtained, it was not by trying to persuade liberal-minded Englishmen of its justice, but by making the government of Ireland by the Imperial Parliament an impossibility. England, in short, was to be worried into the concession. Biggar had discovered the way. Parnell began by supporting him; but under his direction obstruction assumed a more definite and intenser form. Other members of the party gave in their adhesion. The session of 1877 saw the system in full swing. A Prisons Bill, introduced by Government, was obstinately contested clause by clause. Seventeen divisions were taken on the usually undisputed Mutiny Bill. But it was during the debate on the South Africa Bill that the policy of obstruction was pushed to its extreme limits. The House was indignant at the open contempt with which it was treated, and pressure was brought to bear on Butt to control his unruly followers. Butt did as he was desired. He was rewarded with the cheers of the House; but his words caused strange searchings of conscience among Irishmen.

The session came to a close on August 13. A few days later, Parnell, addressing a Home Rule meeting in Dublin, declared his utter indifference as to the opinion of Parliament. His words made a great impression on the extreme wing of the party, and at the annual meeting of the Home Rule Confederation at Liverpool Butt was deposed and Parnell elected President in his place. But parliamentary obstruction was only one side of Parnell's policy of forcing Home Rule. Agitation outside the House was as necessary as obstruction inside it. "I think," he said, addressing his constituents at this time, "that that opposition to English rule is best which is most felt....O'Connell gained Catholic Emancipation outside the House of Commons....No amount of eloquence could achieve what the Clerkenwell explosion and the shot into the police van had achieved." His words caused the Fenians to prick up their ears. Fenianism, as we have remarked, was still an active principle in Irish politics. At home it was represented by the Irish Republican Brotherhood, with its headquarters at Paris; in America by the Clan-na-Gael. The object of both associations was the forcible separation of Ireland from England. Neither believed in the possibility of achieving it by constitutional agitation; but, while the former based its hopes on a successful insurrection, for which money and arms were being collected, the latter looked to forcing a conflict between England and the United States as the only practical method of realising its object. But war was a remote chance, and in the meantime some of the Clan-na-Gael, tired of their enforced inactivity, began to wonder if something might not be made of Parnell's agitation. They had no faith in Butt's method; but Parnell's openly expressed contempt for English opinion and his defence of the "Manchester martyrs" obtained their sympathy and paved the way for a closer understanding.

Meanwhile, things were working favourably for Parnell in another direction. The question of higher education, left unsolved by Gladstone, was taken up by Lord Beaconsfield. The old Queen's University was dissolved, and a new Royal University, with power to confer degrees on students educated in any of the Irish colleges, was founded. The creation of a mere examining board did not satisfactorily solve the university question; but it was a considerable step forward, and, early in 1878, a Bill dealing with intermediate education was introduced into Parliament by Sir Michael Hicks-Beach. The Bill made no attempt to go to the root of the matter; but it was favourably received by the Irish party, and it enabled Parnell to point the moral that obstruction, far from having, as Butt asserted, alienated English sympathy, had achieved a notable success.

CH. IV.

The rest of the session passed quietly away, and it seemed as if obstruction was dying down. But appearances were deceptive. For seven years Ireland had enjoyed a succession of good harvests with high prices and a corresponding increase of rents. The general prosperity had served to conceal the defects of the land legislation of 1870. But the harvests of 1877–8 had been greatly below the average, and that of 1879 threatened to prove a complete failure, while prices showed a tendency to fall. Agricultural distress and inability to pay rents led as a natural consequence to evictions on an extended scale. When Parliament met in 1879, the attention of the Chief Secretary, James Lowther, was called to the seriousness of the situation and the pressing necessity of amending the Land Act of 1870. But Lowther turned a deaf ear to the suggestion, and obstruction broke out afresh. To one man, however, the situation seemed to call for immediate action. Michael Davitt, the son of a Mayo peasant, knew by personal experience what eviction meant for his countrymen. A man of small education but of lofty ideals and an ardent social reformer, he had, when little more than a boy, thrown in his lot with the Fenians, and for nearly eight years had paid the penalty as a prisoner in Dartmoor gaol. But his punishment only served to strengthen his views on the land question, and, on being liberated on a ticket-of-leave in December, 1877, he returned to Ireland a confirmed Fenian. Among those who welcomed him was Parnell. An interchange of views followed, and in August, 1878, Davitt sailed for America. Parnell had made a great impression upon him, and in America he exerted his influence with the leaders of the Clan-na-Gael to induce them to support Parnell's policy. Opinion in Fenian circles was divided as to the merits of what was called the "New Departure"; but it was agreed to send a message to Parnell promising support, on condition that he would go for Home Rule pure and simple, and make the land question (with the view to establishing a peasant proprietary) a main plank in his platform. To this overture Parnell made no reply.

Early in 1879 Davitt returned to Ireland. The pinch of famine had begun to make itself felt and evictions were on the increase. To guard against them, Tenants' Defence Associations were formed, and an agitation commenced to secure a reduction of rents. Parnell was induced to attend a meeting arranged by Davitt at Westport in June. It is significant that he was still in doubt as to what attitude to take up in regard to the agrarian question; but he advised his hearers to keep at all costs a firm grip on their homesteads. This was enough for Davitt. The time had come for putting into practice Lalor's advice, to graft a constitutional movement on an agrarian agitation. On October 21, there was a conference of Nationalists and land reformers at Dublin, when the Irish National Land League was established for the purpose of bringing about a reduction of rack-rents and facilitating the creation of a peasant proprietary. Parnell was elected President of the

League, and a resolution was passed requesting him to visit America "for the purpose of obtaining assistance from our exiled fellow countrymen."

On December 21 Parnell sailed for America. But his object in going was not merely, or even chiefly, to solicit relief for evicted tenants. "A true revolutionary movement in Ireland," he said at this time, "should, in my opinion, partake both of a constitutional and an illegal character. It should be both an open and a secret organisation, using the constitution for its own purposes, but also taking advantage of its secret combination." The precise meaning of his words may be disputed; but it is clear that what really took him to America was the necessity he felt of coming to an understanding with the Clan-na-Gael, and of capturing, if possible, their organisation. At heart he was as much a Fenian as any of them, and he would have grasped at any weapon which promised to secure Irish independence; but he was convinced that the constitutionalism they despised was, in the circumstances, the only method that promised success. In this respect his mission was only partially successful. As a body, the Clan-na-Gael would have nothing to do with the "new departure." But there were thousands of Irishmen who were not Fenians, and on them Parnell's arguments made a deep impression. Personally and financially, his tour in the States and Canada was an unqualified success. It was brought to a sudden close by the news that Government was about to dissolve Parliament. Hastening home, Parnell threw himself energetically into the election campaign. Fenian opposition, stronger even in Ireland than in America, dogged his steps and crippled his action. A resolution was passed by the Land League forbidding the application of any part of its funds to promoting the interest of any parliamentary candidate. At Enniscorthy, his meeting was broken up, and he was himself pelted with rotten eggs. But he refused to be discouraged, and, being returned for three constituencies, he elected to sit for Cork city. The general election of 1880 placed the Liberal party, with Gladstone at its head, in power. Out of the 103 members returned by Ireland 65 were professedly Home Rulers. Of these only a minority were unequivocally in favour of a "forward policy"; but they were strong enough to secure Parnell's election as chairman of the party in opposition to Butt's successor, "Sensible" Shaw.

When Parliament met at the end of April, 1880, the attention of Government was at once drawn to the state of Ireland. After some hesitation the necessity of putting a stop to the increasing number of evictions, especially in the west, was admitted by the Chief Secretary, William Edward Forster. A measure of temporary relief was introduced. and a Royal Commission was promised to investigate the working of the Land Act of 1870. The Compensation for Disturbance Bill, as it was called, was, in the opinion of Government, a mere corollary to the Act of 1870, rendered necessary by the exceptional circumstances of the

CH. IV.

situation; but it was vehemently opposed by the Conservatives and rejected by the House of Lords. In Ireland its rejection caused great indignation. Addressing a meeting of tenant farmers in county Kildare, on August 16, Mr John Dillon advised his hearers "to pay no more rent until justice was done them." The Chief Secretary denounced his words as "wicked and cowardly"; but this criticism was fiercely resented by Parnell, and obstruction broke out with redoubled violence. Government was in an awkward position, all the more serious owing to the absence, through illness, of the Prime Minister. From the first, Forster had been extremely anxious to govern Ireland without asking for exceptional powers. His sympathies were entirely on the side of the tenants, struggling against starvation and menaced by eviction. He was convinced that the Compensation for Disturbance Bill would have killed the agitation by acting as a deterrent influence on the small class of unscrupulous landlords, who were seizing the occasion to evict their tenants and consolidate their farms for grazing purposes. But the Bill had been rejected, and, unless he resigned, he had no option but to maintain law and order at all costs. To comply with the demand for a short Act to suspend evictions during the recess was beyond his power. On the other hand, his soul revolted against the barbarous outrages daily recorded in the newspapers, and, as the session drew to a close, his words of warning were mingled with threats of coercion.

Parliament was prorogued on September 7. The situation, in Parnell's opinion, called for immediate action. Notwithstanding the prospect of a good harvest, 15,000 persons, it was calculated, were threatened with eviction. Parliament had refused to protect them; they must be taught to protect themselves. It was perilous ground on which he was standing. Ireland was seething with discontent. During the summer there had been a great development in the operations of the League. Money was flowing in from America, and not money only. Thousands of copies of the *Irish World*, edited by Patrick Ford, openly advocating assassination, were in circulation. But Parnell showed no hesitation. The time for action had come. Speaking at Ennis on September 19, he advised his hearers to resort to boycotting, as the practice came to be called from the name of its first important victim, Captain Boycott, in order to bring obnoxious landlords and land-grabbing peasants to reason. "Depend upon it," he said, "the measure of the Land Bill next session will be the measure of your activity and courage this winter." The *mot d'ordre* had been given. Within a month Ireland was in the throes of an agrarian war. Some landlords, bolder than their fellows, defied the League and continued to evict; but, in general, evictions stopped. On the other hand, agrarian outrages, accompanied in a few cases by murder, increased at an appalling rate. Government watched the rising storm with anxious attention. The reluctance felt to resort to coercion was rapidly yielding to a conviction that the ordinary law was unable to cope with the situation. As the Lord Lieutenant (Earl Cowper) said, it was not so much the outrages themselves that caused anxiety as the universal sympathy shown with the perpetrators of them. On November 2, information was filed against Parnell and the principal officials of the League for conspiracy to prevent the payment of rent, to resist the process of ejectment, to prevent the taking of farms from which tenants had been evicted, and to create ill-will among her Majesty's subjects. The trial lasted twenty days and ended in the acquittal of the accused.

The verdict removed the last feeling of hesitation on the part of the Cabinet. Parliament met on January 6, 1881. The Queen's Speech foreshadowed exceptional legislation for the vindication of law and order, and a new Land Bill. On January 24, the Chief Secretary moved for leave to bring in a Bill for the protection of person and property in Ireland. The motion was fiercely resisted by the Parnellites. Government was entreated to give precedence to its measure of remedial legislation. But Gladstone was inexorable. This time it should not be said of him that he had yielded to intimidation. The patience of the House was sorely tried by the obstructive tactics of the Irish party, and at last, after an unbroken sitting of 41 hours, the Speaker put an end to the debate on his own authority. His action was challenged as a breach of privilege, and, when the Prime Minister rose to propose certain new rules of procedure, he was met with such a storm of abuse as led to the suspension and forcible ejection of the entire Parnellite party. The new rules were passed, and on March 2 the Protection of Person and Property Bill became law. It was followed three weeks later by a Peace Preservation Act. The additional powers acquired by Government no doubt enabled it to confront the Land League with greater confidence; but the recurrence to coercion was a severe strain on Liberal principles, and it was with a genuine sigh of relief that Gladstone, on April 7, rose to move for leave to introduce his new Land Bill. The Bill was a practical concession of the demand for a fair rent, fixity of tenure, and free sale. The "three F's," which in 1870 he had denounced as an encroachment on the just rights of private property, Gladstone now, with some circumlocution, admitted to be not only just but necessary. In a word the Bill expressly recognised a dual ownership in the land, and provided for the creation of a Court to mediate between landlord and tenant as to what constituted a "fair" rent. This Gladstone emphasised as its cardinal feature. No tenant was to be prevented from appealing to the Court; but on the other hand an appeal was not obligatory, and, if they preferred it, landlord and tenant could arrange matters between themselves on the basis of simple contract. When, however, the appeal had once been made, the verdict of the Court was to be binding for fifteen years. At the same time, the principle of the "Bright Clauses" of the Act of 1870, enabling the tenant to purchase his holding, was maintained, and certain defects in that Act as to compensation for disturbance were remedied.

The Bill fairly astonished the Irish members by its completeness. But it was no part of their policy to recognise its merits. On the contrary, they concentrated their attention on its defects. In the first place, the Bill was not a measure for the establishment of peasant proprietorship, and therefore could not command the approval of the extreme wing of the Land League, whose object was the compulsory expropriation of the landlords. But, in the opinion of those who, like Parnell, were willing to accept it as an instalment, its chief defect was that it was not retrospective—that it practically (though not expressly) excluded from its benefits all those peasants, who, for one reason or another, were in arrear with their rent. The Bill received the royal assent on August 22, and a day or two later Parliament was prorogued. On September 14–16 there was a great convention of the Land League at Dublin. The question was what attitude the League ought to adopt in regard to the Act. Parnell's quasi-acceptance of it had greatly annoyed his Fenian allies, and he was in danger of finding himself, as the Marquis of Hartington had shrewdly predicted, in the awkward position of either having to defy them, or of running counter to the wishes of his followers and probably to his own convictions. He struck a middle course. The Act was to be neither accepted, nor rejected; it was to be tested. Select cases were to be submitted to the Court, and judgment suspended till it was seen what interpretation was placed by it on the "fair rent" clause. The fact that Gladstone had himself admitted that the Land Court was the cardinal feature of the Act furnished Parnell with a plausible ground for his proposal. But the attitude he took up and the extraordinary ovation accorded him at this moment by the Dublin populace were regarded by Government as a direct challenge. Speaking at Leeds on October 7, Gladstone roundly asserted that his real object was "to arrest the operation of the Land Act"; but he warned him that "the resources of civilisation against its enemies were not exhausted." Parnell retorted that the charge was "unscrupulous and dishonest." This afforded Government the opportunity it wanted, and a day or two later Parnell found himself lodged in Kilmainham gaol as a "suspect."

His imprisonment (followed by that of several of his colleagues) proved an egregious blunder. The League at once issued a manifesto, calling on the tenants to pay no rent until their leaders were released. Government retaliated by suppressing the League. But this step only added to the popularity of the "uncrowned king," as it became the fashion to call Parnell, while it greatly strengthened his hold over the Fenians. The situation was emphasised by a resolution of the Dublin Corporation, on January 3, 1882, to confer the freedom of the city on him and his fellow-prisoner John Dillon. During the winter, outrages, instead of diminishing, grew in numbers and ferocity;

the gaols were crowded with "suspects"; while the congested state of the Land Court, in consequence of the large reductions of rent granted by it, testified to a nervous desire on the part of Government to bid for popularity.   But, as time went on, it became clear that the Government had suffered a serious defeat.   The question of "a new departure" was broached in the English Press.   Coercion, it was argued, had proved no remedy.   The country, instead of improving, was becoming more hopelessly disorganised; while the discovery, by the police, of the existence of a secret society, known as "Invincibles," whose object was "to remove all tyrants from the country," added to the general feeeling of uncertainty.   Meanwhile, the number of "suspects" had grown to 872, and the responsibility of detaining them in prison weighed heavily on the conscience of the Cabinet.   Yielding to the strain on his nerves, Lord Cowper had tendered his resignation, and, at Forster's suggestion, a Minister of cabinet rank had been appointed Lord Lieutenant in the person of Earl Spencer.

Such briefly was the situation when an overture reached Government from, or on behalf of, Parnell, offering, in the event of his release, to assist in pacifying the country, on condition that the question of arrears of rent was settled.   The offer was scouted by Forster.   Nothing, he declared, would induce him to consent to Parnell's release, except the certainty that he was powerless to cause further mischief.   But, despite his opposition, the negotiations for a compromise went forward.   There was no question of a compact, and still less of a "treaty"; but, through the mediation of Mr Chamberlain, an understanding was reached as to Parnell's desires and intentions.   On the basis of this understanding, the Cabinet, on May 2, came to the unanimous resolution to release him at once, and to review the list of "suspects," "with a view to the release of all persons not believed to be associated with crime."   Forster immediately handed in his resignation.   His successor was Lord Frederick Cavendish.

On Saturday, May 6, the new Chief Secretary, bearing the olive branch of peace, arrived in Dublin.   The same evening, as he and the permanent Under-Secretary, Thomas Henry Burke, were crossing the Phoenix Park, which was full of people, they were set upon by a band of assassins and done to death.   The blow filled the Irish with consternation, and, foreseeing the mischief that was likely to follow, Parnell wrote to Gladstone, offering to retire for a time from parliamentary life.   His offer was not accepted by the Prime Minister, who feared, as he explained to Lord Granville, to lose his "restraining influence."   But a strongly worded manifesto, signed by Parnell, Dillon, and Davitt, denouncing "the cowardly and unprovoked assassination," was deemed necessary in order to exculpate the national party from complicity in the plot.   The murders, of course, put an end to the "new departure" policy.   Five days afterwards, a Crimes Bill, limited to three years but of unprecedented severity, suspending trial by jury and giving the police unlimited power of search and arrest on suspicion, was introduced by the Home Secretary. Every species of obstruction that ingenuity could suggest was resorted to by the Irish members in order to delay its progress. Night after night, for twenty nights, the debate continued, till it was dramatically cut short, on July 1, by the suspension of the entire party. On July 12 the Bill became law. But, severely as he had felt the blow, Gladstone was not to be diverted from his purpose of rendering justice to Ireland; and, simultaneously with the Crimes Bill, a Bill dealing with arrears of rent, on the lines laid down by Parnell, was pushed through Parliament and received the royal assent on August 12. Coercion firmly applied produced its inevitable result. Discontent was driven underground, and, though several horrid murders occurred in the autumn, the country gradually resumed an air of tranquillity. On October 17 a great National Conference was held at Dublin, when the suppressed Land League was revived under the name of the Irish National League. But Government kept a close eye on its proceedings, and the practical suppression of free speech during the remainder of Lord Spencer's viceroyalty frustrated its attempts at agitation.

Notwithstanding his open disavowal of the Phoenix Park murders, public opinion in England and on the Continent refused to believe that the leader of the Irish party was entirely blameless. When Parliament reassembled after the Christmas recess, Forster openly charged him with conniving at crime. But, beyond retorting that the charge was false, and asserting that he had no sympathy with Patrick Ford's dynamite propaganda, Parnell declined to defend himself. The attack, however, was warmly resented by his colleagues, and, as a sign of the country's undiminished confidence in him a public testimonial was set on foot. By the middle of May, 1884, £10,000 had been collected, when the Pope interfered with a strong disapproval of the project. But Ireland had not changed since the days when O'Connell, in the heat of his Catholic Emancipation struggle, had laid down the doctrine that Irishmen were willing to take their theology, but not their politics, from Rome. The attack stimulated subscription, and, when the testimonial was presented to Parnell at a public banquet on December 11, it amounted to about £38,000. Meanwhile, a solemn silence brooded over the land. The inclusion of Ireland in the new Franchise Act excited some curiosity as to its probable effect, and in England it was confidently predicted that it would tend to diminish Parnell's influence. In April, 1885, the Prince and Princess of Wales visited the country; but the black flags that everywhere met their gaze were sufficiently significant of the situation. The time for the expiration of the Crimes Act was drawing on, and the question of its renewal greatly exercised the public mind both in England and Ireland. The Cabinet was believed to be divided on the subject; and, when in May Gladstone announced his intention to renew its chief provisions, the situation created was too tempting to be

resisted by an astute Opposition.   On June 8 Government was defeated
on a budget question by a combination of Irish, Tories, and disaffected
Liberals.   Gladstone at once resigned, and, after some hesitation, the
Marquis of Salisbury consented to form a Ministry.

No compact had been made with the Irish; but it was generally
understood that coercion was to be dropped, and, as a token of goodwill,
Lord Carnarvon, who was believed to favour the concession of a large
measure of local government to Ireland, was appointed Lord Lieutenant,
and general director of Irish politics.   He met with a gratifying reception from the populace on the occasion of his state entry into Dublin on
July 7, and shortly afterwards he had, at his own request, an interview
with Parnell.   What, he asked, did Parnell think of the establishment of a central legislative body for Ireland on the basis of a system
of county boards?   Parnell, astonished and delighted at the question,
recognised his opportunity, and thought that such a proposal would not
satisfy Ireland: in fact, he thought, the central legislative body would
have to be a Parliament, in name and fact.   Carnarvon seemed to assent,
and Parnell withdrew, believing that a national legislature was within
measurable distance.   Meanwhile Government, in pursuance of its policy
of conciliation, had introduced a measure, known as the Ashbourne Act,
to enable tenants on estates, where the owners were willing to sell, to
become the proprietors of their holdings.   In introducing the Bill, Lord
Ashbourne admitted that it was an extension of the principle contained
in the purchasing clauses of the Acts of 1870 and 1881.   Unfortunately,
the "Bright Clauses" in the former Act, advancing two-thirds of the
purchase money, had, in eleven years, only led to the creation of 870
peasant proprietors; while the Act of 1881, advancing three-fourths, had,
since it came into operation, created 733.   The object of the present
measure was to establish a fund of £5,000,000 for the purpose of advancing
the whole of the purchase money at the rate of 4 per cent., repayable in
forty-nine years.   It was, unquestionably, a distinct step forwards in the
direction of creating a peasant proprietary and one fruitful in consequences
for the near future.   The Bill having become law, Parliament was prorogued on August 14.

To Parnell the prospect seemed encouraging.   Speaking a few days
later at Dublin, he declared his conviction that the next Parliament
would see the restoration of the legislative independence of Ireland—the
establishment of an Irish Parliament (consisting of a single Chamber)
and an Irish executive in Dublin, managing Irish affairs, developing
Irish industries, and regulating the life of the nation.   His speech, taken
in connexion with one at Arklow, claiming for an Irish Parliament the
right to impose protective duties, naturally attracted much attention
in England.   Speaking at Waterfoot on August 29, the Marquis of
Hartington expressed his belief that the leader of a party of twenty-six
was slightly overestimating his power both in Ireland and in Parliament.

Mr Chamberlain, who earlier in the year had announced that he was in favour of a scheme conceding to Ireland "the right to govern itself in the matter of its purely domestic business," now declared that, if those were Parnell's terms, he could have nothing to say to them. On the other hand, the Marquis of Salisbury, speaking at Newport, on October 7, intimated, or at any rate led people to believe, that, while determined to maintain the Union, he was prepared to consider any practical plan of Home Rule with an open mind. In November, during the course of his Midlothian campaign, Gladstone, after devoting serious thought to the subject, declared himself in favour of a generous measure of local government; but insisted on the necessity of securing a large Liberal majority independent of the Home Rulers, in order to enable him to deal with the question satisfactorily. Parnell, who was watching eagerly, seized the occasion to invite Gladstone to formulate a plan of Home Rule on his own lines. This Gladstone refused to do. Thereupon Parnell, on November 21, issued a manifesto calling on the Irish of Great Britain to vote solid for the Tories.

The result of the general election of 1885 was satisfactory to no one but Parnell. Eighty-six pledged Parnellites held the balance between 335 Liberals and 249 Tories. It was clear that the latter had gained very little by coquetting with Home Rule, and evidence was soon forthcoming of a desire on the part of the rank and file to return to the traditional policy of the party. Up to this time the state of Ireland, though not free from outrage, had been regarded as fairly satisfactory. It was suddenly found that without "exceptional" powers law and order could not be maintained. In January, 1886, Lord Carnarvon retired from the government of Ireland. His retirement indicated a policy of retreat, which was rendered easier by the appearance, on December 17, of an unauthorised scheme of Home Rule professing to issue from Gladstone. Parliament met on January 21, and a few days later the Irish Secretary, William Henry Smith, asked for leave to introduce a Bill to enable him to deal with the National League. This was Parnell's opportunity. Government was defeated on a side issue and at once resigned. Being called upon to form a Ministry, Gladstone accepted the task, and, in indicating the principles on which his administration was to be based, he announced his determination to try to give effect to the constitutionally expressed desire of the Irish people "for the establishment by statute of a legislative body to sit in Dublin and to deal with Irish as distinguished from Imperial affairs." A consideration of his Bill belongs rather to English than to Irish history; it was defeated on its second reading on June 7, by 343 to 313. A fortnight later Parliament was dissolved.

So far as Great Britain was concerned the general election of 1886 resulted in a victory for the Unionists: in Ireland the Nationalists maintained their position. Lord Salisbury returned to power, and for a time at any rate the question of Home Rule was shelved.   But Ireland, with her needs and aspirations, remained.   The prospect was not encouraging. Owing to a general fall in the price of agricultural produce, it had become doubtful whether the judicial rents, falling due in November, could be paid.   When Parliament met in the autumn, Parnell declared that the situation was more serious than it had been even in 1880.   On September 10 he introduced a Tenants' Relief Bill, for the revision of judicial rents; but the measure was rejected on its second reading by 297 to 202, with the result he had predicted.   During his illness and without his knowledge, Mr William O'Brien and Mr John Dillon, in October, launched the " Plan of Campaign " and another agrarian war broke out. The Plan of Campaign was in no sense a " No Rent " manifesto.   To put it briefly, it amounted to an agreement among the tenants on a given estate as to what abatement they thought to be just on the November rent.   Having agreed on this point, they were then to go in a body to the landlord or his agent and tender the reduced rent as a settlement in full.   In case of refusal, the money was to be handed over to a managing committee and lodged with some trustworthy person, to be used for the purposes of the struggle.   As the law in regard to trades combination stood, the Plan was undoubtedly illegal; but it received the sanction of Archbishops Walsh and Croke.   It was put into operation on about forty estates, when, though resisted by some landlords, it was acquiesced in by the majority, and the winter passed away in comparative tranquillity.   An attempt was made to prosecute the leaders of the movement, but had to be abandoned; and, when Parliament assembled in January, 1887, the Queen's Speech alluded to the necessity for " reforms in legal procedure," " to secure the prompt and efficient administration of the criminal law."

Shortly before the Easter recess Mr Balfour, who had succeeded as Irish Secretary, introduced a new Crimes Bill, possessing the novel feature of permanency.   The Bill, though strongly opposed by the Irish and Gladstonian Liberals, became law on July 18, simultaneously with a Land Bill, conceding the principle of Parnell's Tenants' Relief Bill.   Armed with these two measures Mr Balfour proceeded to the restoration of "law and order" in Ireland.   His task was not an easy one.   Landlords were indignant at the new Land Act, while the Nationalists were infuriated at the renewal of coercion.   It was made more difficult by the close alliance between the latter and some leading members of the Gladstonian party.   Unfortunately, too, at the very beginning of the new Administration a serious collision with the police occurred at a public meeting at Mitchelstown.   One man was killed; and " Remember Mitchelstown " became for long a watchword at Gladstonian meetings.   But the new Secretary held doggedly to his course, administering justice all round and refusing to allow himself to be imposed upon either by the sneers of his opponents in Parliament,

CH. IV.

or by the frantic clamour of Gladstonian Liberals investigating coercion on the spot. Little by little the prospect grew brighter. Mr Balfour's appearance of cynical indifference to anything but accomplishing the task he had undertaken yielded to a deeper and more sympathetic interest in the fortunes of the people he governed. Twice during his administration, in 1888 and in 1890, he introduced Bills to increase the facilities for purchasing land, supplemented in the case of the latter by a measure for the creation of a Congested Districts Board, which was followed by admirable results. But it was probably his Light Railways Bill which, by opening up the country, has done most to entitle him to the gratitude of the Irish peasant.

Meanwhile, the *Times* had been making a vigorous effort on its own account to kill Home Rule by a series of articles, entitled "Parnellism and Crime," in which the charge preferred by Forster against the leaders of the party of conniving at crime was repeated and emphasised. The series culminated in the publication, on the eve of the second reading of the Crimes Bill, of a facsimile letter, purporting to have been written by Parnell shortly after the Phoenix Park murders, excusing his condemnation of them on the score of expediency. The letter produced a tremendous effect. Naturally, it was supposed that a paper of the standing of the *Times* had absolute proof of its authenticity, and Parnell's repudiation of it was regarded as merely another in the long series of deceptions that had marked his parliamentary career. The Tories were jubilant; the Gladstonians correspondingly dejected. The current of public opinion threatened to sweep Parnell into political obscurity. A demand by him for a special committee of the House of Commons to enquire into the fact was refused by Government. He was told that the Courts of law were open to him and he might bring a libel action against the *Times*. This he refused to do, on the ground of the impossibility of obtaining justice from a London jury; but he accepted the offer of a special commission, consisting of three Judges, to enquire into the entire working of the movement. The appointment of the commission was condemned by the Liberals, and severely criticised by Lord Herschell, as establishing "a precedent most novel and fraught with the utmost danger." But, as Parnell said, the Government was determined to have the investigation, whether he liked it or not. The Court sat from September 17, 1888, to November 22, 1889. Public interest in its proceedings, which had grown languid when it was found that no "revelations" were to be expected, suddenly revived when it was elicited that some, at all events, of the letters, which had been the real cause of the trial, were forgeries. The case was settled out of court, the *Times* agreeing to pay Parnell £5000 damages. The Report of the Judges, if on the whole hostile to the movement, rehabilitated Parnell personally in public opinion. But the victory he had gained was almost immediately neutralised by his appearance as co-respondent in the Divorce Court. It is unnecessary to enter into the details of the case of O'Shea *v.* O'Shea and Parnell. The full force of the blow was not immediately felt, and his colleagues, believing the storm would pass over, unanimously reelected him chairman of the party. But an intimation reached Parnell from Mr Gladstone that the continuance of his leadership would imperil the cause of Home Rule. Parnell replied by expressing his determination to " stick to his guns." But Gladstone's attitude and the openly expressed disapproval of Parnell's conduct by the Irish Catholic Bishops produced a strong effect on his followers and ended in their repudiation of his leadership by 45 to 26. After struggling for several months, with the madness of despair, to recover his authority, Parnell succumbed to his exertions, and died of inflammation of the lungs on October 6, 1891.

Parnell's death, however, did not heal the breach between the two sections of the Nationalist party, and the divisions and recriminations between them considerably abated the interest in Home Rule. Gladstone was not unconscious of the fact; but Home Rule had grown to be a principle with him, and, recalled to power at the age of eighty-three, he, on February 13, 1893, again submitted a Home Rule Bill to Parliament, this time unencumbered by any land legislation and with a provision for the retention of the Irish members, on a reduced scale, at Westminster. The Bill was rejected by the House of Lords. Had Gladstone had his way, he would have dissolved and once more have appealed to the country; but his colleagues were averse from the proposal, and early next year he handed over the reins of government to Lord Rosebery. Meanwhile, Mr Morley, as Irish Secretary, had been trying, not unsuccessfully, to give practical expression in his administration of the country to the spirit of Home Rule. His task was rendered easier by the split in the National party, the feeling of exhaustion produced by the long struggle, and the growing desire on the part of Irishmen generally to drop the subject. It was useless, Archbishop Croke candidly admitted, for any reasonable man to hope for a national legislature within measurable time. Speaking at Portadown early in 1894, Lord Londonderry declared that the real policy of the Unionists was the settlement of the land question on the lines of the Ashbourne Act. Outside Ulster, Ireland's prosperity, he insisted, depended on the development of her agriculture, and in his opinion the most pressing need of the nation was the establishment of an Agricultural Department. His words did not pass unheeded.

On the accession once more of Lord Salisbury to office in 1895, a determined effort was made, as the new Irish Secretary, Mr Gerald Balfour, put it, "to kill Home Rule by kindness." In pursuance of this policy a new Land Bill, based on a measure prepared by Mr Morley, was submitted to Parliament in April, 1896. The Bill provided for the gradual and voluntary expropriation of Irish landlords and the

CH. IV,

automatic adjustment of "fair" rents. The acceptance of it by the
House of Lords proved a severe strain on its traditional loyalty to the
Conservatives ; but, after nearly leading to a revolt, it became law on the
last day of the session. Two years later (1898) a Local Government
Act was passed conferring on Ireland the same degree of local autonomy
as was possessed by Great Britain. More important perhaps, however,
was the support extended to an invitation held out by Mr (now Sir)
Horace Plunkett, member for South County, Dublin, to all sections of
politicians to meet together, "to consider the means, outside politics, by
which the material prosperity of Ireland might be stimulated." Notwithstanding some discouragement, a fairly representative committee was
got together and led to the foundation of an Irish Agricultural Society.
By uniting men of different shades of opinion in a common object, the
society had the effect of diminishing the acrimony of party politics.
The work of reconciliation was greatly promoted by the Report issued
in 1896 of a Commission appointed under Lord Rosebery's Administration to consider the working of the Act of Union in so far as it regarded
the financial relations between Great Britain and Ireland. According to
this Report, the Act of Union had imposed a far too heavy burden on
Ireland, inasmuch as the taxable capacity of the country, as compared
with Great Britain, instead of being one-eleventh, had for years been
actually not more than one-twentieth.

The feeling that the Act of Union had not been an unqualified
blessing, as they had hitherto supposed, gained ground in Unionist
circles, and found vent in a great meeting at Cork on December 12,
when Unionists and Home Rulers spoke from the same platform. Still,
there could be no question that, despite the continual emigration, which
was draining off the life-blood of the nation, the country was showing
signs of advancing prosperity. The deposits in the Savings Banks,
which in 1886 had amounted to £4,710,000, nearly doubled that amount
in 1896. The cooperative dairy farming system was beginning to prove
a success; so, too, was the cottage industries movement. Both were
helped forward by the establishment of a number of small credit banks,
based on the Raiffeisen system, which did much to relieve the peasant
from the village lender or "gombeen man." Government watched the
movement sympathetically; and an Agricultural and Industries Bill,
which passed Parliament in 1899, led to the formation of a permanent
Department. No doubt, there was another side to the picture.
Emigration continued at a frightful pace ; between 1886 and 1906 the
population diminished by more than half a million ; large tracts of land
continued to pass out of cultivation ; and in 1898 there was a recurrence
of famine in the west, leading as usual to fresh evictions. Landlords,
who were tired of the everlasting struggle to get their rents, discovered
that sheep and cattle were easier to manage than recalcitrant tenants.
Individuals, mostly well-to-do shopkeepers, were found willing to take

grazing lands on an eleven months' lease, whereby no tenant-right was created. In this way vast tracts of land were cleared of human beings and turned into cattle ranches.

To meet this new danger Mr William O'Brien, the author of the Plan of Campaign, started a United Irish League in county Mayo, the centre of the disturbed district (1899). It took firm root and incidentally furnished the basis for a reconciliation between the two sections of the Nationalist party, under the leadership of Mr John Redmond. It declared war, not indeed to the knife, but what was almost as much feared, to the extent of social ostracism by the familiar process of boycotting, against evicting landlords and "grabbing" graziers. From Mayo the League spread by degrees over the adjacent counties. Even strong Unionists, such as Mr Thomas Wallace Russell, if they did not actually join it, expressed sympathy with its demand for the compulsory sale of landed property (1900). Government itself unintentionally gave an impetus to the movement. Shortly after the foundation of the League, the Congested Districts Board purchased Lord Dillon's estate for something over £250,000. There were about 4000 tenants on the estate paying an average rent of £3 a year. The Board at once reduced rents all round by 10 per cent. Further, it remitted £20,000 arrears and purchased 2000 acres of adjacent grazing land to enlarge the tenants' holdings. The result was that tenants on the neighbouring estates, particularly those of Lord de Freyne, struck for what they called the "Dillon rent." They received the support of the League, and a fresh agrarian war broke out, to which Government, at the instigation of the Irish Unionist Alliance, replied (1902) by putting into force several of the provisions of the Crimes Act of 1887. But coercion was recognised to be only a temporary expedient. It was suggested that a conference should be arranged between the friends of the tenants and those of the landlords. The idea was scouted as ridiculous. All the same, the conference actually met in December; and, having elected Lord Dunraven chairman, it passed resolutions in favour of the total abolition of dual ownership of land on the basis of voluntary sale. The resolutions were confirmed by an Irish Landowners' Convention on January 7, 1903, and on March 25 a Bill was submitted to Parliament, proposing the creation of a new $2\frac{3}{4}$ per cent. stock, redeemable in thirty years, for the purpose of advancing £100,000,000 for the purchase of saleable estates in Ireland, at the rate of £5,000,000 annually. The Bill became law in August.

The unexpected success that had attended the land conference strengthened the desire on the part of men of all parties to join hands in the regeneration of their common country. In August, 1904, the Land Conference Committee resolved itself into an Irish Reform Association. At a subsequent meeting a scheme of Devolution, prepared by Lord Dunraven, was adopted, of which the object was to secure the transference from the Treasury to an Irish Financial Council, whose decisions were only to be reversible by a not less than one-fourth majority vote of the House of Commons, of an annual sum of about £6,000,000, to be employed by the Council for purely domestic purposes. The proposal was greeted by a storm of protest. The fact was that the course of recent legislation was little to the taste of the extreme wing of the Unionist party. They had long been of opinion that the method of "killing" Home Rule by kindness pursued by Government was tending, almost as much as Home Rule itself would have done, to weaken the connexion between the two countries. An attempt made by them in 1900 to capture Sir Horace Plunkett's seat in the interest of one of their own number had only ended in handing it over to the Nationalists. They were more successful in their opposition to the Devolution scheme, and, though unable to secure the removal of the permanent Under-Secretary, Sir Antony (now Lord) Macdonnell, they managed by their protests to force the resignation of the Chief Secretary, Mr Wyndham, and to wring a disavowal from Government.

The strike of the extreme Unionists had its counterpart in the ranks of the Nationalists. Ever since the Liberals had taken up the cause of Home Rule, there had been a tendency to coalition with them on the part of the Irish parliamentary party. But the abandonment of the old policy of neutrality was strongly disapproved by a large section of the Nationalists, especially by those in whom the old leaven of Fenianism was still active. Parliamentarism, it was urged, had proved a failure. The ideal of Home Rule in 1905 was further off than ever. The true policy was one of abstention from Parliament, and of passive resistance to the Administration. Ireland was and would continue to be an independent nation, whether England liked it or not. Until the wrong done to Ireland was made good, there could be no friendship with England. Meanwhile, Irishmen were to adopt an attitude of indifference both to England and the Irish parliamentary party. They were to learn to rely on themselves. There was plenty of work for them to do. The Irish language must be revived and made the language of the nation, emigration, that weakened the national strength, prevented, young Irishmen dissuaded from enlisting in the army, the use of articles of English manufacture discouraged, and so forth. The movement culminated in the *Sinn Fein* policy. Such was the general situation of affairs at the close of 1905, when Mr Balfour's Government resigned.

CHAPTER V.

THE THIRD FRENCH REPUBLIC.

SELDOM has any nation had to face more problems, problems of more vital importance, of more manifest urgency, with fewer apparent resources to aid in their solution, than was the case with France in the summer of the year 1871. Almost half her territory was in the occupation of German armies, under a commander exercising an authority more peremptory and better obeyed than Thiers, who throughout May was, with the help of the Assembly at Versailles, struggling against the Commune in Paris. At the beginning of May, 1871, peace with Germany was not yet concluded. Negotiations were still proceeding on the basis of the preliminaries of February 26, which stipulated for the cession of Alsace and part of Lorraine and the payment of a heavy indemnity, and left further details to a conference on neutral territory, at Brussels. Here the diplomats charged with the duty of concluding the peace seemed to have doubts as to their prospects of success, and to be awaiting a renewal of hostilities.

Though, under the pressure of military occupation, the bulk of the nation, with its representatives in the Assembly and Thiers, desired peace, even at the cost of heavy sacrifices, another party in France, particularly the advanced Republicans in the great cities and above all in Paris, protested against the peace and the sacrifices which were its price, and demanded for France, mutilated in her territory and menaced in her unity, revenge, either immediate or, at least, in the near future. At any time, the choice between that acquiescence and these persistent hopes would have involved risks and doubts. It was specially difficult for a nation which at the moment had no Government; for after the defeat of Sedan the Empire had definitively collapsed. On the other hand, the men who had taken upon themselves the task of organising national defence, Republican deputies and deputies of Paris, had regarded their task as completed upon the cessation of hostilities. The only legal authority still existing in France was a National Assembly which met on February 13, 1871, at Bordeaux, with the immediate duty of deciding between peace and war, and was subsequently charged at Versailles, on the invitation of Thiers and under his direction, with the task of reorganising the forces and resources of the nation, though it had received no mandate to determine the form of government to be eventually established. It is true that this Assembly had chosen as its President Jules Grévy, a Republican, and had, on February 16, nominated Thiers as "chief of the executive power of the French Republic." But the Government thus set up was still provisional; and, while accepting the agreement between itself and Thiers, known as the Pact of Bordeaux, the Assembly clung persistently to its hopes of a restoration of the monarchy. All the parties which for the past hundred years had in greater or less degree swayed the fortunes of France—Legitimists who supported the Comte de Chambord, adherents of the Orleans family grouped round the Comte de Paris, Republicans who believed themselves authorised to link up the threads which had been broken by the *coup d'État*, Bonapartists who, in the face of the decree of deposition of February 28, persisted in their hope of some reactionary movement in favour of the Prince Imperial—all these parties believed themselves to have rights or strove to create them during a period of uncertainty so favourable to the development of their designs and intrigues. No condition of things could have appeared more hopeless for a nation whose soil was in hostile occupation, whose fortunes were wrecked, on the morrow of a civil war which had brought bereavement and ruin and left a legacy of bitter animosities.

Moreover, everything at that time in France seemed to have been cast once more into chaos, principles as well as political systems and material interests. In the history of the Catholic Church, which is so inextricably interwoven with the destinies of the French nation, the events of 1870 counted for as much as the Franco-Prussian War in the realm of politics. The decrees of the Council of the Vatican were the decisive effort of Roman supremacy and of ultramontane doctrines against the liberty of modern societies, against the assertions of reason and of science, and the claims and traditions of national Churches. These decrees indicated so great an increase in pontifical authority that in Catholic countries men might expect the extremest demands on the part of a clergy and of a faithful laity who were themselves incapable thenceforward of offering any resistance to the will of Rome. In France, especially, the religious Orders which had long been proscribed, even under the monarchy, had returned in great numbers to seize, thanks to the Law of Falloux (1850), the direction of popular education, and to conduct the education of the middle classes on Catholic lines, in direct opposition to the University. Moreover many public officials, deputies, and officers of the army and the navy, were inclined from conscientious or interested motives to aid this ultramontane campaign. France seemed, therefore, destined to become the field of this contest between Church and State. Since, moreover, the Council's decrees had almost synchronised with the entry of the Italians into Rome and the end of the temporal power of the Popes, the Church Militant was enabled to excite the zeal of its partisans by compassion for the Church Oppressed and for the fate of the aged Pope, a victim of force and a prisoner in the Vatican. If France, the eldest daughter of the Church, in order to manifest her fidelity, freshly tempered by the Cult of the Sacred Heart, had been willing to become the avenging champion of the Holy See, such a crusade, undertaken immediately after cruel reverses, would have been a convincing proof of the absolute devotion of the nation to the interests and will of Rome.

This, however, was far from being either the desire or intention of many of the French—those who had always nourished a distrust of "priestly government," or those others, among whom were conspicuous the younger members of the Republican party, who were attracted by the doctrines and writings of Comte, Littré, Renan, Berthelot, Taine, and Saint-Simon. A movement of free thought which recalled the efforts of the philosophers of the eighteenth century against the Church, but possessed a more scientifically rigorous method, a wider and more enlightened curiosity; a genuine renaissance of study in the schools, which had been entrusted by Napoleon III to Victor Duruy, a resolute adversary of the Congregations; finally, the formation of numerous societies for popular instruction, more or less inspired by freemasonry, which was becoming more intimately permeated from day to day with the principles of positivism—all these influences had raised up in France against Ultramontanism adversaries who were resolute, well-instructed, and fully accredited. The political struggles aroused by the invasion and the fall of the Empire were to be complicated by acrimonious religious disputes to which the nation had been long a stranger.

If, on the other hand, the middle classes and Thiers, victorious over the Commune, had imagined that the defeat of the labour and socialist party would settle the social question to their advantage, and that the claims of the people and of Paris would be silenced for a considerable time, the event was destined to show them their error. In a country where universal suffrage was still the basis of public life, it was impossible that, even under the pressure of a state of siege which strangled the Press and all socialistic activities, the masses should resign themselves to the total and definitive abandonment of their interests and of their hopes. Moreover, ever since the Republican party had adopted its doctrine and its programme, they had always represented themselves to the people, and especially to the artisan classes with whose aid they were unable to dispense, as seeking political reforms for the sake of the social improvement which they would render possible. The blood-stained days of the Commune had dug a gulf between the people and the politicians. But, as it was essential that the democratic party

CH. V.

should pull itself together, these social reforms quickly forced themselves upon its attention, while the artisan classes, ever since the month of July, 1871, formed the chief support of the political programme and aims of the Republican party. A like anxiety to develop popular education, an equal fervour for all attempts to form professional associations, trade unions, societies for mutual benefit, and cooperative companies, had already determined, on the side of labour, men like Barberet, Chabert, and Tolain, and on the Republican side, men like Vacquerie and Louis Blanc, editors of the *Rappel,* with thinkers like Renouvier and Charles Bigot, to waive their differences in order to cement afresh the alliance between the middle and the lower classes. And, if we wish to appreciate how much strength and hope were left to the labour party, it is enough to observe the extraordinary efforts not only of the Republicans, but of all the middle class parties to attach to themselves the masses—Jules Amigues with money and instructions received from the fallen Emperor, Napoleon III; Mun and La Tour du Pin in the Catholic workmen's clubs placed under the direction of the Bishops; the disciples of Le Play in the Social Peace Societies which had come into being in the year 1871; and last of all the Bishops, as the central bureau of the Catholic Workmen's Associations. "Let us make no error," said a Conservative of the time; "socialism is taking a benign character, but in appearance only and for this sole reason, that, thinking themselves capable of becoming masters of the political world by virtue of their numerical majority, many of the socialists are convinced that they have everything to hope from the regular exercise of universal suffrage." In point of fact, it was still a question, and it was a question of capital importance for France at that time, to decide whether the social peace, which had been re-established and could hardly be maintained by mere force, would be secured by a regular system of legislative measures such as the artisan class would be willing to await and the middle classes willing to grant them without too long delay.

Nor must we forget that, in Europe and the rest of the world, the misfortunes of France had naturally not arrested in any way the course of history, that a critical period had arrived in the progress of the European nations, and that the future of France was involved as much as that of other nations in these world-changes. At this moment new continents, such as Africa, were being opened up by the enterprise or conquest of European peoples, and in other undeveloped continents were being established nations and empires, children indeed of Europe, but children mature and independent, such as the United States of America, Australia, the Canadian and the Africander peoples. Ancient races of the Far East, long time forgotten, like the Chinese and, above all, the Japanese, were taking a fresh lease of life by admitting the commerce, influences, and education of European nations, while Russia and England were extending to the furthest bounds of Asia the limits of their colonial empires, already approaching and rivals in Turkestan. The year 1869 was an important date in the history of humanity, for it was then that General Grant, President of the United States, hammered the last bolt on the line of the Pacific railway from New York to San Francisco. The earth was now girdled by its greatest highway of commerce. Was France to claim her proper share in this universal life, she who had prepared herself for it by her efforts in Algeria, Senegal, and Egypt, and, more recently still, by her enterprise in Indo-Chinese territory? Amid her sorrows, her ruin, and her doubts as to the coming day, would she have the leisure, the resources, or even the desire to take her part?

Thus, at one and the same time, France had before her the task of recreating her material life, her political system, her intellectual and moral existence, her civic unity which had been broken up by the disputes between capital and labour, and, finally, to make an effort, whose extent and tendency could not be for the moment fully gauged, to associate herself with the expansion of Europe in distant and new lands. From this time onward, her simultaneous and successful struggle with all and each of these tasks, with the aid of those wise and patriotic guides who have never been wanting to her, constitutes the history of the latest French democracy.

Her first care was to complete the peace, in order to free herself from foreign occupation. She had no hesitation, between May 4 and May 18, 1871, in submitting to all the conditions which Bismarck, emboldened by the insurrection of Paris and supported by the demands of the Prussian military party, inserted in the Peace of Frankfort. The National Assembly on May 18 ratified the articles signed at Frankfort by Pouyer-Quertier and Jules Favre in the name of Thiers; the obligation to pay a milliard and a half in specie in order to obtain the recall of the invading troops; the right of the army of occupation to be supported generously by France; the right of Germany to be treated by France as the most favoured nation; and, finally, the exchange imposed upon France of the district of Belfort for a whole district of Lorraine lying around Thionville, a region rich in metallurgical industries, and, most important of all, advantageous for the occupation of Luxemburg by the Germans. If France approved these sacrifices, it is because she was ready to pay for them out of her savings. When, on June 20, Thiers carried a vote for a loan of two milliards and a half at 5 per cent., the subscribers upon whom he called replied by offering the Government this sum twice-told, that is to say, the whole sum necessary for the total indemnity for the War. At the end of September, 1871, one milliard and a half was paid to Germany, and two-thirds of the conquered French territory was forthwith evacuated. France showed herself ready to anticipate the payments in order to be quit the sooner if Bismarck had been willing. But she was forced to await a new agreement which was signed on October 12, 1871, and which reduced the army of occupation to 70,000 from 650,000. A third agreement, signed on June 29, 1872, gave the hope of a speedy and final liberation, which the loan of three milliards, voted on July 15, and subscribed seven times over in France alone, and as many times in the rest of Europe, made it possible to realise without delay.

The question at stake for France was not merely that of the payment of a debt, but of the means for assuring her future, her frontiers, and the restoration of the country's well-being. Moreover, in the hearts of many of the French, lacerated as they were by the cruel parting with the people of Alsace, there endured the pertinacious hope of revenge, kept alive by the final efforts of the determined opponents of the peace. Beyond the fifteen milliards which represented the loss by the War, the country resigned itself with great self-denial to the increase in taxation necessitated by the establishment of a national army, which was worked out by the Assembly between April, 1871, and July, 1872. By laying down the principle of compulsory service, of five years' personal service with the colours in the active army, or one year for certain classes of citizens, with fifteen years' obligation to temporary recall to the reserve and territorial forces, France showed that she had grasped of her own initiative, without a master, without a reigning house, almost without a Government, the necessity of this triple burden—military, pecuniary, and social. She voted for the military forces an annual sum of 500 millions, proceeded to the fresh equipment of the foot and artillery forces, and everywhere set up at great expense barracks and camps. And shortly after the formation of a Committee of Defence on July 29, 1872, she had no hesitation in organising the country as a vast entrenched camp, whose fortresses, established as "defensive screens" on the north-east frontier, at Paris, and at Lyons, were to secure for her the means to live and work in peace.

Naturally, there was no lack of deputies and public men to point out the excessive weight of this burden and its unequal division between the children of the people and those of the middle classes, who were partially exempt by virtue of their educational studies. Down to the year 1882, for ten whole years, the nation, the Government, and the Assemblies fought against any essential modification of this military organisation, which seemed to be necessary for the national life. It was only after 1882 that the Ministers of War, Billot, Lewal, and, above all, General Boulanger, on May 25, 1885, decided to propose the reduction of military service to three years, together with the abolition of the dispensations extended to the liberal and religious professions in order to increase the effective total of the army, which was becoming more and more the nation under arms. And it was only after seven years' discussion, on July 15, 1889, that the new law was passed, as by degrees France became aware of her strength and the place she still held in the world. As a sequel to this law and a result of the same reasoning, or owing to the fear engendered in a free nation by permanent armies and a professional army, a further reduction of the time of service to two years, coupled with complete suppression of all the then existing exemptions, passed into law in 1905. There was, moreover, an inclination to reduce the period of liability to recall to the reserve and territorial forces. It is evident that the sacrifices, once eagerly undertaken by the nation for its safety, appear less urgent and more burdensome to the more recent generations which have not experienced the danger, and are not actuated to the same degree by the bitterness of defeat and the desire of revenge.

During these forty years, in which the progress of French military power has never interfered with the expenditure devoted to the navy, though the total cost of national defence amounted to one milliard annually, the French nation has also looked for and found, outside and beyond itself, the conditions and elements of safety. From the month of May, 1872, one of the principal Paris papers, the *Temps*, foretold as inevitable an alliance between Russia and France. When, in the month of September, 1872, the Tsar Alexander II went to Berlin to meet the two Teutonic Emperors, the victor and the vanquished of Sadowa, who seemed to be meditating a union against France, he went not, as was believed in Paris at the time, in order to strengthen this threatening alliance, but to secure France against it, and to permit her to reestablish in peace her finances and her armies. "We need a powerful France," said the Chancellor Gorchakoff to the British ambassador at Berlin, Odo Russell. England agreed with the Tsar. In 1873 the Prince of Wales gave his friendly help to adjust the difficulties with Germany caused by the provocative language of the French Bishops, and in July, 1874, he warned Decazes and the French Ministry to beware for the future of similar incidents. When the Assembly in Paris was invited by Marshal MacMahon to proceed with the organisation of the army by adding a fourth battalion to each regiment, the military party in Germany drove Bismarck to measures of intimidation, which almost amounted to an ultimatum, placing France in a dilemma between loss of honour or a premature rupture. Although they were not allies of France, England and Russia interfered in May, 1875—Queen Victoria by an emphatic letter, Alexander II by a visit to Berlin—and demanded from the German Emperor a disavowal of the provocative conduct of his Ministers. And immediately after this intervention the Tsar said to Le Flo, who had suggested it : " Our relations will become more and more cordial. We have common interests : we should hold together."

The formation by France of such ties, which both resulted from and supported her moderation in external affairs and her strength at home, was hindered by the skill displayed by Bismarck in the Eastern Question; he managed to divert the Tsar's attention, and to embroil him with

France at the Berlin Congress. He contrived, moreover, to foment the colonial rivalry existing between England and France in Egypt and Tunisia. And, so long as the French remained isolated, they lived in perpetual, though perhaps excessive, fear of some accidental rupture, until 1891, when the French fleet, on its entry into the port of Cronstadt, received a welcome such as the representatives of France had nowhere received since 1871. The new era was marked in 1893 by the visit of the Russian fleet to Toulon, and the enthusiastic hospitality offered by the Parisians to Admiral Avellain's crews. It seemed as if an alliance, prepared by Carnot and Alexander III before their deaths in June and November, 1894, had been already sealed, promising to the French all possible security and even all possible hope against Germany. It was, however, only a defensive understanding, which was completed in 1896 by more far-reaching and precise military agreements concluded between President Félix Faure and the Tsar, Nicholas II, who had come to France to review the fleets and the "allied and friendly army." In this form it has existed ever since, unshakable in spite of the external crises, political and social, in Russia, which have put it to a severe test, and it has afforded France security and confidence in herself, proportionate to the place to which she has been restored in the concert of Europe. Hence has followed her reconciliation with Italy, whose King and Ministers had counted since 1873 among the most troublesome and discontented of her neighbours—first by a treaty of commerce in 1898, and then by a formal act of friendship concluded in 1900. Finally, as if mindful of the aid which he had given to France immediately after the War, in 1873 and 1875, the Prince of Wales, now King Edward VII, once more brought to the policy of peace upheld by his nephew Nicholas II the support of England, whose interest it was to check any pretensions on the part of Germany to hegemony in Europe.

To sum up, in 1910, the situation of affairs is strangely altered, since the time when the last armies of France were capitulating at Metz, Paris, and Belfort, flying in disorder towards Switzerland or Britanny, unable from lack of transport, arms, and provisions, if not of courage, to make head against the invaders; while on the other hand Bismarck and the sovereigns of Germany grouped round the King of Prussia debarred unprotesting Europe from holding any communication with France, whose isolation had been made complete by the Revolution of March, 1871. Though the danger resulting from the undue propinquity of the frontier and the capital has made itself felt from time to time, as in October, 1905, and December, 1908, at any rate France has seen the benefit of her burdensome but effective military organisation, and the effect of the alliances grouped about her. At Algeciras, she was able to calculate the value of the sacrifices undergone, and the pledges given to Europe by her moderation. She has fulfilled the programme which Vacherot, one of her most enlightened thinkers, drew up in 1881. "The Balance of European Power is the end towards which our national policy should tend, now that France is able to look beyond herself. This policy does not bring a nation glory, but it enables it to live with honour and security. That balance can only be maintained by means of alliances. France can find opportunity to ally herself now with England, now with Russia, now with Italy, and now again with those three Powers simultaneously, if a common and compelling interest urges such a coalition in the interest of European equilibrium, threatened by the predominance of Germany, strengthened by Austrian support."

It is manifest that the whole of this work of recuperation, which has restored to the French nation consciousness of its own strength, security, and external influence, was based upon the resources of industry and thrift belonging to a people valiant in toil and possessing a country of great natural wealth. It was furthered, in addition, by the care bestowed after 1871 in the management and development of these resources. The robust rural economy which France owes to her climate and her soil, and which manifests itself in the unequalled number of her landed proprietors, inspired a policy of special favour for agriculture and the peasant population. A system of tariff protection in favour of agricultural produce, especially of wheat, was foreshadowed in 1875 by Teisserenc de Bort; it was realised by the laws of March 25, 1885, and March 29, 1887, which laid upon foreign wheat a duty of five francs a quintal, and completed by the customs tariff of January 12, 1892, which the Minister, Méline, prevailed upon the country to accept. In pursuit of a similar policy, Acts passed in July, 1884, 1891 and 1897, favoured the French refineries of sugar and the development of beetroot growing. When French vineyards had been ravaged by the phylloxera, considerable grants were voted by the Laws of 1878 and 1879 in aid of the vine-growers, while bounties to the extent of two millions were voted to foster the culture of flax and hemp, four millions for silkworm culture, an equal sum for silk spinning, and more than twice that amount for the breeding of horses, thoroughbred or half-bred, from French stock.

If the State, in order to provide for the prosperity of agriculture, had merely increased the burden of the taxpayers and the consumers, the benefits of its enterprise would have been open to question, and, probably, in 1881 the establishment of a Ministry of Agriculture, which was to receive in 1905 a grant of 44 millions as against three millions in 1869, would have justified some misgivings. In reality, the State relied less upon Protection than upon the stimulation of energy and progress, particularly after the Law of 1884 had given to small peasant proprietors the right to form themselves into cooperative societies for the improvement of their equipment and of the standard of cultivation. Ten years later, a Law passed on November 5, 1894, placed at the disposition of these bodies the resources of an Agricultural Mutual Loan Society, which in 1905 were increased by loans granted, without interest, up to 40 millions by the Bank of France. In 1905 this society numbered 1113 local branches, and 60 district branches, with nearly 50,000 persons on its books. And, in this connexion, mention must be made of the Agricultural Mutual Assurance Societies, which from 1894 to 1905 have increased almost fivefold, and insure their members against the risks of hail and fire to the amount of over 300,000 millions.

One of the chief needs of an agricultural people is a complete system of schools, professors, and lectures on agriculture. After 1871, by the scientific researches at the National Institute of Agronomy, which was added to the School of Woods and Forests and the Veterinary Colleges of the eighteenth century, by the diffusion of knowledge which was entrusted to the professors of the National Schools, especially the forty Technical Schools of viticulture, horticulture, dairy and cheese farming, and the two hundred professors established by the Departments, it has been proved to French farmers that the secret of their prosperity lies in the substitution of scientific cultivation, based upon methodical experiment, for the simple customs of the past, often mistaken and unproductive. Not since the middle of the eighteenth century had a like effort and a like progress been experienced in French agriculture. Everywhere, great improvement in methods has been manifest; the soil has been enriched by a more judicious and orderly employment of fertilising materials; the adaptation of cultivation to different soils is better understood, and by specialisation the land has become more productive; agricultural machinery has been transformed in these forty years. In short, the agricultural output, which between 1800 and 1860 only rose from four to six milliards, has now reached a total of 11 milliards; the values of land and rents in country districts naturally show a like increase.

This care for the enhancement of the value of the national land has not hindered the industrial development of the nation, which had begun to make itself felt in the time of the Second Empire, as a result of the establishment of railways. One obstacle, it is true, has always stood in the way of this development, the dearth in France of coal, "the bread of modern enterprise." This dearth is sufficiently indicated by noting the 58 millions of tons of coal exported by England in 1907 as against the 10 million tons which France was obliged to import. She has been able to reduce this inferiority by the better development of her mines. A notable success has been achieved in the Pas de Calais, where the output from 1876 to 1903 has been more than doubled, rising from 15 to 35 million tons. To grasp the progress achieved, thanks to this effort, by French industries, we have only to look at the development of machinery. The number of machines in use has gone up from 30,000 to 92,000 in the last 40 years, and has multiplied itself tenfold in power, from 870,000 horse-power to 8,600,000. So early as 1878, when the

Universal Exhibition afforded an opportunity of comparing French industrial effort with that of foreign nations, France was conscious that she could support the comparison, thanks to the impulse of the previous six years of restorative work. The ebullition of joy which Paris manifested in the month of June, 1878, was at one and the same time a proof of achievement and an augury for the future. In the more important manufactures the chief progress has been made in the iron works and chemical works of the east, from Nancy to the Belgian frontier, and in the textile industries of the north and round Rouen. The output of the blast furnaces has been multiplied sixfold between 1870 and 1904. The industrial establishments have been in continual process of augmentation, especially the great factories where labour, capital, and production tend to become concentrated. And, though the chief market for these industries is at home, there is none the less an increase of 22 per cent. to show between 1869 and 1905 on exported goods. Perhaps it is to be desired that the nation should, for its industrial and technical education, make sacrifices equal to those which it has undertaken for the benefit of its agriculture. Initiative has doubtless been shown by the towns, the universities, and private individuals; but, out of 600,000 young men employed in manufacture and commerce, only 20,000 have started with a real professional training.

In the matter of manufactures and commerce, the resources of the State were especially, and at this period lavishly, employed in creating for the nation a material equipment, which had been left in a singularly inadequate condition by the Second Empire, occupied as it had been with other matters. Credit is due to France that, immediately after her disasters, she did not shrink from this increase of burdens, but reasoned that by this means alone she could be enabled to liquidate the claims of her onerous debt. From this period dates the creation of roads and highways with such ramifications into country districts that the strivings of the new life from that time onward touched the tiniest villages and hamlets. The extent of the new roadways has been estimated at 200,000 kilometres, and at 1200 millions the grants given since 1876 for this network; 120 millions are required for its annual upkeep. It has completed the great national and departmental highways, temporarily sacrificed to the need of railroads, and since restored to high honour.

When, in 1878, Freycinet was appointed to the Ministry of Public Works, this engineer, who under Gambetta had organised the outfit for national defence, claimed the equipment necessary for France in time of peace, even five milliards, if required, for the completion of the railway system, the utilisation and development of canals, and the improvement of seaports. The Minister Dufaure decided to issue, as the works required, a loan at 3 per cent. redeemable in 75 years, for this great enterprise (March and June, 1878). The work began simultaneously in all parts of the territory; 2000 kilometres of canals were added in 25 years to the existing 3000, a total which went back to the time of Louis XIV. These canals were freed from all public dues by the Law of February, 1880, and from all private tolls in 1889. Ninety thousand kilometres of new railroad were laid between 1873 and 1906 at a cost of two and a half milliards; the harbour-basins were deepened at Dunkirk, Dieppe, Rouen, Nantes, Bordeaux, and Bayonne, and new basins made at Le Havre, Cette, La Palice, St Nazaire, without counting the improvements carried out at nearly 200 smaller and secondary ports. The total expenditure for twenty years has amounted to 700 millions, to which we must add a new grant of nearly 100 millions voted by the Law of December, 1903, for the benefit of seaports, with the approval of the Chambers of Commerce.

In 1900 the Chief Council of Industry and Commerce declared, rightly, that the country would reap greater benefits from this mighty effort if it were better coordinated and less subordinated to the influences of local politics. The canals and railways should be organised as in Germany, not with a view to mutual competition, but to cooperate towards the diminution of prices and the facilitation of traffic; the seaports should be aided by the economic development of the districts which they serve; maritime commerce, whose prosperity is but mediocre, should be assisted by the development of inland navigation: such were the methods, too long neglected in France, needed to reap the full benefits of the sacrifices undertaken since 1872, by an increase of debt in twenty-five years from 19 to 40 milliards. It is too often forgotten that this debt, which imposes so heavy a burden of interest, more than a milliard added to the annual budget, has nevertheless been a source of wealth, since capital, invested in French securities, has tripled itself in the thirty years from 1870 to 1900, 60 milliards in place of 20, while the increase of foreign securities, nearly 20 milliards in the sixteen years from 1884 to 1900, has proceeded in quite due proportion. The one striking phenomenon of recent years, in which the will of the nation is seen to act contrary to its own interests and its economic development, is the growing diminution in the birth-rate; there are ten births per 1000 inhabitants less since the beginning of the century, and four per 1000 less during the last forty years; while in the neighbouring countries of Europe increase in the population, though also diminishing, is still considerable and continuous.

In this far-sighted policy of development, all has been the calculated and persevering work of a nation which has sought primarily in the instinctive qualities of the race, industry, thrift and good sense, as well as in the munificence of its land and its climate, restoration after defeat, provision for the morrow, security for the future. This nation, which since the French Revolution had tried and overthrown so many

Governments, proved, even at the moment when it was devoid of any
government at all, and ever since, that it was capable of governing itself.
The history of its adhesion by steady stages of progress to the Republican
ideal is peculiarly fitted to throw light upon the way in which the
French since 1871 have made, or rather remade, their destinies. The
National Assembly, elected in the day of adversity to decide the
question between war and peace, for the most part monarchical in
sympathy and yet powerless to give form to the monarchy, could hardly
serve as guide to the nation. Almost at once the nation assumed the
task of giving direction and guidance. In the month of July, 1871,
when the Assembly, by a powerful majority, had decided upon the repeal
of the laws of exile passed against the Bourbons and the family of
Orleans—against the will of Thiers, who would have preferred by postponing this decree to discourage the hopes of the monarchical party—at
the complementary elections held on July 2, out of 111 seats the nation
filled 100 with Republicans of all shades, Republicans by conviction or
tradition, Conservative or Radical, from Duvergier de Hauranne to
Gambetta, Naquet, and Pascal Duprat. In vain did the entire forces
of reaction, royalist and religious, unite together: from the month of
April, 1871, the followers of the Princes of Orleans had been negotiating
with the adherents of the Comte de Chambord for the purpose of
effecting an agreement between the two branches of the family.
Dupanloup was the soul of this coalition, to which Thiers refused to
lend his support, and which was finally frustrated by the Comte de
Chambord, who had come to Paris to be reconciled with the head of the
younger branch, the Comte de Paris (June 30 to July 5). The Prince
showed himself less adaptable than the priest: he preferred exile to
the sacrifice—useless as it probably would have been—of principles of
divine right and royal absolutism, symbolised by the "white flag of
Joan of Arc, Francis I, and Henry IV." Immediately after this
disappointment, the Catholic party in the Assembly and the Bishops
sought for compensation in a French intervention in favour of the Pope
at Rome (July 22), an action which resulted in the retirement of Jules
Favre from office. All these intrigues and plots underwent their first
check in the month of August after the Republican elections. As
adroit at exploiting the unpopularity of the parties of the Right as at
establishing his own reputation for practical and unswerving Liberalism
in the eyes of the Republican party, the French nation, and the nations
abroad, Thiers succeeded, by the *Loi Rivet* drawn up by a group of his
friends, in obtaining from the Assembly, despite its monarchical sympathies, the legal establishment of his authority as head of the Republic.

Certainly, these powers were still limited to the time of the duration
of the Assembly. The Assembly retained the right, formally recognised
in the preamble to Rivet's Law, of framing some day a permanent constitution. But the bestowal upon Thiers of the title "President of the

CH. V.

Republic" was a fact of moment for the future. The provisional and undefined rule which had existed since the month of February, 1871, was beginning to yield place to an embryonic constitution, which took, by popular consent, a Republican form.

Meanwhile, other organisations were called into being by the Law of August 10, 1871—the Councils-General, to which the Assembly, acting upon the ideas of decentralisation which had gained ground in Royalist circles during the previous ten years, had entrusted wider and more active functions. When the Assembly rose for its vacation on September 18, Thiers, in order to watch over the elections to these new bodies, asked the deputies to "take counsel with the country in order to bring their ideas into line with those of the nation." On October 8, 1871, the departmental elections gave fresh testimony in favour of Republicanism of all shades; Republicans formed two-thirds of the members then elected, and already held a majority in thirty departments out of eighty-six. Then, when the Orleanists, the most numerous opponents of the Republic in the Assembly, becoming alarmed at its progress, invited their Princes to take their seats in their midst, Thiers on December 16, 1871, gave a further impulse to the establishment of the new order, to which for the first time he professed unreservedly his own adherence. "I am of the number of those," he said, "whose continual care is the Republic; I have nothing in common with those charlatans who would try this form of government with the desire to bring it to ruin." More and more, henceforth, we shall see the country declaring itself "for the Government of Thiers." The elections of January 7, 1872, gave success to eleven Republican candidates in sixteen electoral areas. In six months the nation had reinforced by more than a hundred members in the Monarchical Parliament the party hostile to attempts at a Royalist restoration.

In this fashion and out of these elements was formed that Left Centre party in the Assembly which played the decisive part from 1872 to 1875. In proportion as the days of misfortune receded into the distance, the days when the country, to put an end to foreign occupation, had chosen that pacific and reactionary Assembly, the gulf widened between this Chamber and the great body of citizens, who were also weary of provisional government, but absolutely opposed to the Assembly in opinions and sentiments with regard to a permanent rule. The majority of the representatives were anticipating and preparing in secret the return of the royal House of France and of a Government devoted to the interests of the Church. And although, refusing the power for himself personally and to the cadet branch the right to claim the power in his stead, the Comte de Chambord, by the Declaration of Antwerp (January 25, 1872), had made known his intention of preventing the birth of "a Revolution Monarchy," the deputies of the Right would never abandon their desire to impose the monarchy upon France. On

the other hand, the people, especially the dwellers in the towns, desired
the triumph of the Republic—"word of magic power over the minds of
the workers." The reason was that the Republic, with universal suffrage
as its base, stood for democratic principles, tendencies, and institutions,
for social progress without violence, by the spontaneous effort of the
popular will of the people, and by the harmony of interests; and, last of
all, it stood for determined opposition to the Clerical party. In spite of
all the efforts of its leaders, and of Gambetta, the "tireless bagman of
democracy," who devoted his entire efforts to reassuring the country
districts and the middle classes, lest they should be led to the side of
Empire by their fear of socialism, the adhesion of France to the democratic idea was rather calculated to estrange the National Assembly from
a Republican form of government than to convert it to that form.
Gambetta felt this so clearly, that, from the end of 1871, he never ceased
to demand in the name of his party the dissolution of this Assembly and
an appeal to a real Constituent Assembly.

What would have happened if the Assembly, in its determination to
work for the restitution of the monarchy, had given the power and a
provisional presidency to the Duc d'Aumale, who expected it in 1872?
Or what would have resulted if the Assembly, when called upon to
dissolve, had refused to do so? Civil war beyond doubt, or, as Thiers
said one day, the time-honoured oscillation from anarchy to despotism,
and from despotism to anarchy. Between the irreconcilable extremes,
the Left Centre was a half-way house, an intermediary, which, for
the part it played in this crisis by the side of Thiers, has earned a
place in the history of France. With its President, General Chanzy,
"republican by virtue of having been the heroic leader of the national
defence," the Left Centre party consisted to a large extent of old
Orleanists who, converted by Thiers, had abandoned their monarchical
leanings, men such as Casimir Périer, Rémusat, Dufaure, and Rivet.
The system of government to which this party in their turn desired to
convert the country and the Assembly was Republican in form, so
as to please popular opinion, and Conservative in policy, so as not to
displease the deputies. With Thiers at their head secretly encouraging
and directing their efforts, this party in spite of everything found the
means to reassure the middle classes and the Assembly as to the possible
dangers to property and religion involved in progress towards Republicanism. By their loyal adherence to Republican institutions, they
afforded to the country at large a sense of security against the intrigues
of the unconverted Monarchists.

By the vicissitudes of this slow groping towards a definite *régime*,
we can judge the importance of this transitional party. Towards
the month of June, 1872, when the elections of Republicans were
becoming more and more significant, especially that of Paul Bert for
Yonne, the Assembly, stirred by indignation against Thiers, began to

CH. V.

become restive. The Orleanists made fruitless advances to the members of the party of the Left Centre; then, on June 20, by the hands of Changarnier and the Duc de Broglie, they sent an ultimatum to the President. They imagined that they would realise their dream more easily under another leader of the executive. Thus opened a campaign against Thiers which lasted for a year and was destined to prove at one and the same time the stubbornness of the Monarchist party and its impotence.

It began by the President's challenge to the majority. On November 13, 1872, he read to the Assembly a message which invited it to give, like the President, their adhesion not only in fact, but in principle, to the Republic. It was understood, of course, that he meant to the "Conservative Republic" which his friends of the Left Centre desired. On November 18 the Assembly took up the challenge, and, at the request of the Legitimist, Audren de Kerdrel, nominated a Commission to censure the conduct of affairs; then, the same day, Changarnier and the Duc de Broglie summoned Thiers to give an explanation of the conduct and language of Gambetta, whom in his adherence to the Republic he had accepted as an ally. To this attack Thiers, seconded by Dufaure, replied by a formal demand for a Constitution, and for the immediate selection of thirty members of the Assembly who should be charged to draw up a scheme. Up to this point, offensive measures seemed to bring him success. His demand, which was also that of his Ministers, was welcomed by a majority of 37, and in Paris by a serried crowd shouting "*Vive la République.*" And, in fact, this "Commission of Thirty," after many changes, was to have the honour of establishing the Republic. The eleven members of the Left Centre, though a minority on that Committee, proved therein the force of their perseverance and their influence.

It would seem that, at this point, the fear of pushing the quarrel still further and of losing his power, which by his own confession he valued for its promise of glory, determined Thiers to retreat, or at any rate to accept a truce. He believed that he saw a warning in the success of an interpellation directed on November 30, 1872, against Lefranc, his Minister of the Interior, by the Bonapartists Rouher and Prax-Paris. He filled the place of the Republican, Lefranc, by Goulard, a member of the Right Centre, and appealed to Fourtou, another member of the same party, rather than to one of his own friends of the Left Centre. Finally, on December 14, he permitted his Minister Dufaure to issue what almost amounted to a declaration of war against the party of the Left, Gambetta and Louis Blanc; while the Government invited the Assembly to restore to the family of Orleans its property, confiscated since 1852, to the amount of forty millions (January 9, 1873).

The steps taken in the months of January and February, 1873, by Dupanloup and his Legitimist and Orleanist friends, to soften the

Comte de Chambord and reconcile him with the Comte de Paris—a third attempt once more defeated by a letter from the Prince, February 13, 1873—and the efforts of the Bishops and the Clericals to involve France in the affairs of Rome, proved very soon to Thiers that between him and the Monarchists there could be no truce, still less an agreement. Accordingly, he made haste to complete his task, the liberation of the whole of French territory; and, assuredly, his chances of coming to an agreement with Berlin upon this question were greater than those of effecting a reconciliation between the party of the Right in the Assembly and his Government. When, on March 17, 1873, Rémusat in Thiers' name read to the deputies the agreement with Bismarck, signed on March 15, for the complete recall of German troops before the prescribed term of two years, the Monarchists affected reluctance in associating themselves with the manifestations of gratitude which the President received from the whole country. They had already brought upon themselves the reproaches of one of their own side, Gontaut Biron, who negotiated this advantageous treaty at Berlin, for their intrigues, which deprived Thiers and his agents of part of the authority necessary for treating with their conqueror. They cared little, provided that their rancour or their ambitions were satisfied at the President's expense. They found another means to show him that they desired his services no longer: they forced the Republican President of the Assembly, Jules Grévy, to resign (April 2, 1873) and replaced him by a fighting President, Buffet. As, moreover, the Left party had been displeased by the advances that Thiers had been making for five months to the Monarchists, and as they showed their displeasure unmistakably by the election in Paris of Barodet, a teacher, in opposition to Rémusat, the most intimate friend and associate of the President, the Government was wholly unprotected against the intrigues and assaults of the Right. So early as the beginning of May the Monarchists had agreed upon a successor to Thiers; failing the Duc d'Aumale, whom the Legitimists finally rejected, or Changarnier, who was too old, this was to be Marshal MacMahon, a Legitimist by birth and family, and a Bonapartist by circumstances.

At this moment, decisive as it was for his authority and his task, the President felt the mistake he had made in estranging the deputies of the Left Centre. As they had been the first to propose to the Assembly, on March 17, 1873, the glorification of the "liberator of French territory," so they were his last resource in this struggle for Republican institutions. Supported by Casimir Périer, Waddington, and Berenger, who had been called to the aid of Dufaure, Rémusat, and Léon Say, Thiers on May 23, 1873, called upon the Assembly to take his side and to decide upon a form of government. Since it was impossible to establish a monarchy favourable alike to the Houses of Bonaparte and of Orleans and agreeable also to the Comte de Chambord, the majority, forming a coalition directed by Broglie and Rouher, resolved simply to demand a President

CH. V.

and Ministers hostile to the Republic, on the pretext that the Republic stood for "Radicalism, anarchy, and moral chaos." By the defection of the members of the Right Centre, of the Target group, upon whom Thiers had believed he could count, they obtained the satisfaction of their desires on May 24, 1873, when, by a majority of 360 to 344, they brought about the downfall of the President and his friends.

From that time the new chief of the executive power, Marshal Mac-Mahon, and the Ministers whom the majority, with its views of the social danger, imposed upon him, the Duc de Broglie, Beulé, Ernoul, Batbie, Magne, Admiral Dompierre d'Hornoy, General du Barail, together with the deputies, that is to say, executive and legislative alike, prepared first to delay, and afterwards to prevent entirely, the establishment of a democratic rule. This struggle only served to exhibit in the full light of day the impotence of the Monarchist parties and the resolution of the nation, which grew daily more marked, to support all shades of Republicanism. If the deputies of the Right had imagined that, after the removal of Thiers and his associates, they could work at their will upon the electors and influence their choice, they were quickly undeceived. Neither the official orders as to candidature transmitted to the Prefects by Broglie, nor the practical censorship imposed upon the Press in virtue of the state of siege, nor the influence exercised upon the mayors of all the communes, whose nomination the Government arrogated to itself by the Law of 1874, were sufficient to prevent the Councils-General and their presidents in the month of August from making an emphatic pronouncement against a monarchy. Moreover, in the country generally, opinion remained sceptical, and was under no illusion as to the chance of a monarchical restoration, which the party of the Right was incapable of uniting to carry through.

From the first moment when they perceived that the coalition was turning in favour of the Bourbons—a change noticeable in June and still more in October, 1873—the Bonapartists Rouher and Raoul Duval separated themselves from it. They had only entered into it in order to bolster up the Republic until the Prince Imperial should attain his majority (January, 1874), in fact, to gain a year's time; thus they were accomplices, not dupes. The Comte de Paris on his side, at the request of his adherents, on August 5, 1873, paid a visit to his cousin, the Comte de Chambord, at Frohsdorf, and was favourably received by him as heir presumptive, on the condition, however, that he should accept and maintain a Legitimist monarchy until he should himself in his turn ascend the throne, when he would be free to adopt such principles as he might prefer. After his return from Austria, the Comte de Paris felt the difficulty of enforcing upon the Orleanists an acceptance of Legitimism and the white flag, which implied the total condemnation of their theories and their history. All that he gained from them was a series of conferences and meetings which resulted, on

October 4, 1873, in the appointment of a committee of nine members and the despatch of a new deputation to the Comte de Chambord. Chesnelong, who was charged with this mission, believed that he could convert the grandson of Charles X to the necessary concessions, and establish him " at the foot of the throne." All these intrigues had no other result than an emphatic letter, a manifesto of uncompromising Legitimism, addressed to France on October 17 from Frohsdorf by the Comte de Chambord. In it he asserted the clearest intention of renouncing the throne rather than surrender his principles and the white flag. The leader of the Legitimists dismissed the Orleanists from his service. By this action he rendered a monarchy impossible, although, on November 27, he conceived the project of going in secret to Versailles to demand of Marshal MacMahon, his faithful subject, his restoration by the help of the army. The powerlessness of the Monarchists then became evident in the action of the Bonapartists, who were emboldened to the point of demanding an appeal to the nation, and in particular in the proposals which Changarnier brought before the Assembly on their behalf—to prolong so far as possible the powers of Marshal MacMahon. They desired, in default of anything better, a military dictatorship of legal and provisory character, half-way between exacting democracy and reviving Caesarism.

Thus the hour was approaching when the members of the Left Centre, though a minority, were to direct the future, because they alone, Conservative Republicans, were the bond between a Conservative Assembly and a Republican nation. It was one of their number, Laboulaye, who was charged to defend Changarnier's proposal and wrest it from the Bonapartists. Together with the prolongation of the Marshal's power, which was, in spite of everything, the prolongation of a provisional Republic, he almost persuaded the Assembly to take into consideration a republican Constitution. But under the influence of Broglie, who, irritated by his persistent failures in the last six months, was bitter against all Republicans, even the moderates, the deputies of the Right refused their support to the project. They came round later, when the Duc de Broglie, in order to maintain himself in power with the Duc de Decazes, was, after the beginning of 1874, forced to go hat in hand, so to speak, in face of the steady progress of the Republic, to implore the help and alliance of Bonapartism. This time, the majority, through fear of Caesarism, was broken up, for the Legitimists had not refused concessions to the Orleanists in order to grant them to the Bonapartists. The Liberal Monarchists shrank from a reconciliation with men like Rouher and Ollivier, whom they had fought for ten years without intermission. The individual members of the shattered Right broke away by degrees and drifted to the Left Centre, in whose hands the whole party of the Left, and its leaders, Gambetta, Ferry, and Brisson, cleverly left the conduct and direction of affairs.

CH. V.

The first decisive sign was the election to the Vice-Presidency of the Assembly, under Buffet, whose authority was diminishing, of a friend of Thiers, Martel (May 13). The second event, which was still more significant, was the defeat of the Ministry of the Duc de Broglie, which was overthrown on May 18, 1874, by the defection of the Legitimists in a body. And, finally, what could be more important to contemporary France than the sight of Casimir Périer announcing at the tribunal of the Assembly the desire of his party, the Left Centre, for a speedy enactment of the laws which were destined to organise the Republic, with its President and two Chambers? Casimir Périer defeated the Monarchists by a majority of four on June 15, 1874. The next day Wallon brought forward a Bill to define the powers of the President of the Republic, and to lay down the method of revising the Constitution.

Every day in that period saw some advance in the schemes, the ideas, the actions, and even the number of the members of the Left Centre, which was strengthened by the adhesion of Montalivet and Léonce de Lavergne. And, on July 29, 1874, when Broglie, a better orator than Casimir Périer, believed that he could force him to beat a retreat with his republican programme, Wallon, the modest spokesman of the Left Centre, who had gained over the Monarchists of the Right Centre and Émile de Girardin, the greatest journalist of his day, was quietly preparing the approaching victory. On January 28, 1875, Laboulaye helped it forward by a speech inspired by an ardent patriotism, which did not, however, finally decide the Assembly to pass the republican declaration, which he demanded. But, shortly afterwards, it accepted Wallon's amendment (January 30), which was passed by a majority of one—an important majority, when we reflect that a Monarchical Assembly, in deciding upon the regular and unlimited succession to the Presidency, had in effect established the Republic.

One month afterwards, again not without difficulty, on February 24, the Assembly established a Senate, to hold office for nine years, appointed by an electoral body composed of all persons elected by the country, from the deputies to the representatives of the municipal bodies, with seventy-five permanent Senators, to be chosen by the National Assembly and afterwards by the Senate itself. On the following day, the Law creating public authorities finally established a Chamber of Deputies, the only one of these authorities which rested on universal suffrage. When in the course of the year the Law of July 16 on the relations of these public authorities, the organic Law of August 2 on the election of Senators, and that of November 30, 1875, on the election of the deputies, had been framed, the Republican Constitution was completed. This Constitution differed widely from those which France had set up in the past, because, for the first time, it was not the work of a Constituent Assembly, and its establishment was regarded by one party as a *pis-aller*, by another as a bargain, by all as a compromise. Only, it was a compromise destined to endure, because it was stamped by the nation's approval, and because the democracy has adopted it and has been able to find in it the expression of its needs and of its aspirations.

Since 1875, the Republican Constitution has been but very slightly modified in the letter. The principal modification was that of August 18, 1883, "The Republican form of government cannot be made the subject of a proposal for revision"—a clause which for the first time placed the political principles and the political life of the nation above party discussions, regrets, and hopes. The suppression in December, 1884, of the permanent Senators, whose places were taken by members elected like the rest, "in such a way as to bring that body into harmony with the democratic character of society," was also an important change. Yet, in spite of all, it amounted to very little. Experience and use have done much more to alter in accordance with democratic tastes the work of the Republicans of the Left Centre, which has proved at the same time sufficiently elastic and very durable. Such monarchical character as inhered in the right conferred upon the President of dismissing Ministers or dissolving the Assembly has become attenuated by lack of exercise to the point of extinction. The aristocratic character of the Senate, which, together with the right of initiating laws, possessed the right to veto all the proposals of the Chamber, has not been able to resist the daily increasing authority of the Lower House over the Ministry, the budget, and the administration in general.

To a certain extent, this current, this evolution, of democracy was the result of the futile attempts made against republican institutions. After Marshal MacMahon had appointed a Ministry of the Left Centre, charged under Dufaure, and later under Jules Simon, with the task of governing together with the two newly-elected Chambers (March and November, 1876), the Conservatives, infuriated by their defeat, persuaded him, first, to dissolve the Chamber (June, 1877), then, with the help of a fighting Ministry (Broglie and Fourtou), to manipulate the elections to their taste; finally, after the failure of this pressure upon the electors, they commenced the employment of force. Although, to complete this effort, the Marshal refused to take the plunge and attempt a *coup d'état*, the newly-born Republic was in grave danger throughout the year 1877. The necessity of defending their work forced the Republicans of the Left Centre to ally themselves closely with the whole of the Left, even the most advanced. Against the menace of a military dictatorship, their chief safeguard lay in the force of the nation's attachment to its liberty.

When the crisis had passed, it was seen that a new Republic, different from that planned by Thiers (who had died on September 8, 1877), a system inspired rather by Gambetta, had been set up in accordance with the republican ideas set forth for fifty years by the partisans of a material and moral development of the entire nation in conformity with the principles of universal suffrage. In consequence of their unwillingness or inability to comprehend this revolution, from 1879 onwards the Left Centre—Dufaure, Jules Simon, and Léon Say—found themselves bereft of their power. Under the presidency of Grévy, who, in January, 1879, succeeded MacMahon, on his resignation before the end of his seven years, authority was in the hands of the democratic Republicans. They decreed, in 1881, the complete liberty of the Press and public meetings, an amnesty in favour of those proscribed after the Commune, and more important still, in 1884, the right of workmen to form societies analogous to the English trade unions. Forgetfulness of class quarrels and interests was the price that the Republicans thought due to the labouring classes whose votes had brought about their triumph. The only dispute was as to the extent of the concessions to be made : the Opportunists, led by Gambetta, who was Minister but a short time (November, 1881, to January, 1882) and died prematurely in December, 1882, and by Jules Ferry, whose spell of power was the longest, from 1880 to 1885, refusing to their Radical colleagues, such as Clemenceau and Floquet, reforms which were too hasty or too sweeping. This division of forces, however, was to become a danger, as was seen on the return to the Chamber at the elections of 1885 of many deputies of the Right; then, in 1886, by the intrigues of the Comte de Paris which resulted in the expulsion of the Princes ; and, finally, by the plot formed at this date round an ambitious and rebellious soldier, General Boulanger, who appealed to patriotic passions irritated by the provocations of Germany in connexion with the arrest of Schnaebele (April, 1887).

Once again parliamentary liberty seemed to be in grave danger, especially as President Grévy, compromised by family scandals, had been obliged to send in his resignation at the beginning of his second Presidency (December 2, 1887). The two Republican parties, Radical and Opportunist, could not agree to elect as his successor the man best fitted for the post, Jules Ferry. The first two years of Carnot's Presidency (1887–94) were difficult. But, once again, the country, warned of the dangers of a military dictatorship by the successes of General Boulanger in secret alliance with the Monarchists (1889), forced union upon all the Republicans. Thus the Constans Ministry found strength to crush this popular idol before the High Court, and drove him into exile, to an inglorious death, and into oblivion.

In one last crisis this democratic evolution was finally completed, at the beginning of the twentieth century. When, after President Carnot, who was assassinated by an anarchist at Lyons (June, 1894), after his successor Casimir Périer, who resigned shortly after his appointment (January, 1895), and after Félix Faure, who only served four years of his time, Loubet (February, 1899) received the Presidential power, which had been shaken by this series of events, the Monarchists, in conspiracy with certain dissatisfied generals of the army, were seeking, in the *affaire Dreyfus*, a roundabout way for overthrowing the liberties of the people. The nation followed the leader of the Opportunist party, Waldeck-Rousseau, when in the month of June, 1899, he did not hesitate to invoke the aid of a Socialist Minister, Millerand: his accession to power carried with it the valuable and decisive support of the masses.

Down to 1905, the Ministers Waldeck-Rousseau and Combes, styling themselves " Ministers of republican defence," relied upon the whole body of the democracy, to whom they offered the Laws upon the right of combination, 1901, upon labour councils, and upon public health, and finally the separation of Church and State. And though, for a brief space, from 1905 to 1907, the attention of the nation was perforce directed towards foreign affairs, yet, at the beginning of 1906, the grouping together in one and the same Ministry appointed by the new President of the Republic, Fallières (February, 1906), of Poincaré, a Moderate, as Minister of Finance, Sarrien, a Radical, as Minister of Justice, Clemenceau, a Socialist-Radical, as Minister of the Interior, Briand, a Socialist, as Minister of Education, indicated the same desire to base the administration of the Republic on the claims of the working classes and the people at large. The last manifestation of this desire was the creation in Clemenceau's Administration, which held office from October, 1906, till 1909, of a Ministry of Labour, and the appointment to it of a Socialist —a measure which earlier, in 1848, had by its object and tendencies produced irremediable division between the moderate Republicans and the democratic party.

There is no room for doubt that the duration of the Third Republic in France, the most long-lived system since 1789, is the result not only of the individual weakness of all the non-Republican parties, but also of the strength which the Republicans have gathered daily, in their progress towards democracy, from the interested devotion of this democracy to their doctrines and their ideals.

The sole force which the French Republic has encountered since 1871 capable of uniting in resistance to it all the parties of the past with certain Republican and democratic elements, was the great party of militant Catholics, the Bishops and the Ultramontane Orders with the fiery deputies of the Right, the forces which Gambetta styled Clericalism when he declared that " Clericalism was the enemy."

The period of the National Assembly seemed the moment favourable to the triumph of this party. Devotional fervour, which had been cleverly implanted among the people by the religious bodies which were freely developing—Jesuits, Eudists, Assumptionists, societies dedicated to St Joseph, St Benedict, St Anthony of Padua, to the Virgin, the Immaculate Conception, and to the Sacred Heart of Jesus (to which the whole of France was soon consecrated), societies of laymen, charitable or intellectual, working men's societies, and leagues of St Vincent de Paul—

had been preparing the opinion of the people in favour of service and obedience to the See of Rome from 1872 onwards. The clergy, thanks to the Law of Falloux, which they upheld against all Jules Simon's attempts at reform, set their hand upon the primary schools, multiplied, in opposition to the *lycées*, the free colleges which were widely opened to the middle classes, and finally, under the pretext of liberty for superior studies, demanded the right to grant university degrees on an equal footing with the State (1873). Throughout the country there was a violent campaign directed by the Bishops, as if they were already masters, against Italy in defence of the Temporal Power, and against Germany and Bismarck to damage the credit of the authors of the *Kulturkampf.* And, summoned by them for like ends, innumerable pilgrimages reached Paray-le-Monial and Lourdes, to the chant of " Save Rome and France." France seemed wholly won over to the Holy See, as the champion of Christ and Rome dreamed of by ardent Catholics.

In reality, the country was taking alarm at the way in which it was being compromised abroad. At the end of 1873, when the German Chancellor, irritated by this campaign against his religious politics, called upon Fourtou and Broglie to punish the intemperate Bishops and later, when he threatened to bring an action himself against them before French tribunals, great emotion was felt in political circles. Decazes was forced to make an apology to Germany (January, 1874) which warned the nation of the danger of these clerical intrigues.

The favour which the Republicans began to experience at elections, in spite of the unhappy recollections of the Commune, proceeded in great part from the dislike and uneasiness inspired in the majority by Ultramontane enterprise. Their programme of resistance, in conformity with the wish of a people who looked to their schools for the resources necessary for their reestablishment, was above all the organisation of studies and of intellectual life in all its branches. The " League of Education," with its million petitioners, demanded schools which should be secular, free, and compulsory. Gambetta, Paul Bert, Jules Ferry, and Jules Simon, led this propaganda. Jules Simon instituted in the *lycées* a system of reform destined to bring secondary studies into harmony with modern needs and modern culture. And the whole scheme of university reform, for which Renan and Taine had been working since 1865, seemed on the point of being realised, to the great advantage of science in France; for science, inspired by the example of Germany, was demanding its status and its right to regenerate the nation. Those private reformers, who did not even wait to see what action the State might take before creating the " Free School of the Political Sciences "—Boutmy, Vinet, and Taine—showed the measure of their faith in the destinies of France when illumined by science.

While the religious Orders were leading Catholics to the assault, believing, in 1873, after the resignation of Thiers, when the hopes of a monarchy were higher, that they would be able to seize the power and use it to the advantage of Rome, the association of Freemasons was turning all the while towards democracy in order to call in the aid of science to strengthen their resistance. The Grand Master waived the obligation upon his initiates to believe in the " Great Architect " and called upon them to maintain all the educational institutions in which the Republicans reposed their hopes of national, intellectual, and political emancipation. The battle, almost always victorious, waged by the democratic party in the electoral divisions under the leadership of Gambetta, whose speeches from 1872 onwards were so many manifestos, was a threefold struggle for liberty of thought, tolerance, and education.

At times, under the Ministry and Presidency of Buffet and MacMahon, the two chief magistrates of a Catholic Republic, in view of the influence of "orthodox" officials, the pressure exercised upon families and interests, the increase of pilgrimages to Lourdes and Rome, and the cult of relics, it might have seemed that the times of the Restoration had returned. " Between the Church and the Revolution," said the Comte de Mun, one of the eloquent leaders of the all-powerful faction, " there exists absolute incompatibility. The Church cannot perish and therefore it will kill the Revolution." It was a military officer serving with the colours who spoke thus. His colleagues, recruited more and more from the religious colleges, pupils of the monks, though they had not his talent, worked with him to gain the help of the army to aid the success of this Ultramontane doctrine—*Gesta Dei per Francos.* But, by refusing its suffrages to Buffet and many others like him, the country showed that it had no inclination to ratify this programme.

Marshal MacMahon, and even the first Republican Cabinets imposed upon him, those of Dufaure and Jules Simon, seemed not to have understood this decision of the electors against the attempts of the Ultramontane party. At any rate, they refrained from carrying it into effect, either because the Marshal, in obedience to the secret counsels of Dupanloup and those of his own wife, awaited a reactionary movement on the part of his Catholic officers on behalf of the Church; or because Dufaure and many others of his party who had remained Catholic in sympathy were afraid of the attacks made by the freethinkers upon their opinions and their faith. It was above all the religious question that began to widen the gulf between the Republicans of the Left Centre and the mass of electors headed by the democratic politicians. The last-mentioned had never pardoned Jules Simon, once a freethinker and Radical, for having, at the time when this question was raised between them and the Ministers of the Legitimist MacMahon, chosen the party opposed to theirs, and for having accepted the Presidency of the Council. The militant Catholics, on the other hand, showed no gratitude towards him for having compromised himself

CH. V.

8—2

on their behalf with his own party. The more regard he showed for the Church, the more exacting they appeared, and the more imprudent abroad. This was the time when the General Assembly of Catholics, under the direction of Chesnelong, and with the encouragement of the whole body of Bishops, demanded from the Marshal-President decisive action in Italy, to support the independence of the Holy See against the national monarchy. They succeeded so far that, irritated and uneasy, Victor Emmanuel and his people were moving towards the Triple Alliance with the Emperors of Germany and Austria, whose object was to watch France and perhaps to stifle her (1882). When, on May 16, 1877, MacMahon appointed Broglie to the fighting Ministry, and dissolved the Republican Chamber, it was with the hope of obtaining from the elections, by means of official pressure, an Assembly that would continuously favour the claims of the Ultramontane party, "the government of parish priests," what was called at the time "moral order."

But the result was a crushing defeat, not only for the Clerical party, but also for the Monarchists who had entered the lists for the last time. France had paid too dear, in 1870, for the error of uniting her interests with those of the Papacy and the cause of the Temporal Power not to understand the danger to which she exposed herself in taking sides against the Republicans with the uncompromising Ultramontane party. The senatorial elections of January 5, 1879, finally gave the majority in the two French Chambers to those Republicans who were most resolute in refusing to tolerate the exacting demands of the Clerical party. Warning was then given of the intentions of this majority, who, in the interests of the Republic, demanded, first of Dufaure (January 20) and then of MacMahon (January 28, 1879), that the offices of the State should be filled by Republicans. Both resigned, in order not to have to execute the necessary weeding out of officials.

This task was entrusted from 1879 onwards, under Grévy's Presidency, to Jules Ferry. An unshakable Republican and an avowed freethinker, this Minister had formerly proclaimed himself an opponent of the alliance of the secular State with the Roman Church, and of the Concordat which was definitely condemned together with Gallicanism in 1870, and a supporter of that separation of civil and religious power which had long been a fundamental article of the democratic programme. At the moment when he was summoned to the direction of Public Education in its relations with the Church, it seemed to him that prudence demanded compromises and half-measures. The important thing was to attack the militant Clericals without irritating the mass of the Catholic party, to respect beliefs while ruining political and Ultramontane plans. He hoped to sow discord between the monks, the forces of Rome organised for contest, and the parish priests, who were more intimately associated with the national life and cared more for the sacraments and for education

than for politics. It was in this spirit that, on March 15, 1879, he
brought forward his Bills for the suppression of the right claimed by the
Congregations of appointing teachers without degrees to the public
schools, for the exclusion of the clergy from university councils, and the
abolition of their right to confer degrees. Article 7 of this Law was the
decisive one; it took from every Congregation that should not have
obtained the recognition and authorisation of the State, and from the
Jesuits in particular, the right of imparting instruction.

It was principally by getting possession of the education of the
young that all the Congregations since 1850 had imposed themselves
upon the French nation: it was the teaching Orders that Jules Ferry
first attacked, limiting his scope in order to be assured of gaining his
end. We shall see that, for more than twenty years, this continued to be
the method of all Republican politicians in pursuance of their policy of
regaining the ground acquired by the Clerical party since 1850; they
have proceeded step by step, in order not to estrange the Liberals and
the Catholics. To appreciate their hesitation, we must remember the
storms of anger aroused by Article 7 of the Law of 1879 among the
Bishops and their faithful flocks. Greatly moved, Waddington, the
chief of the Ministry, resigned; his successor, Freycinet, who was secretly
in sympathy with the members of the Left Centre, supported Article 7
in the Senate, but with so little vigour that the majority of this less
advanced Assembly threw it out. The Chamber, however, forced him
to issue the two decrees of March 29, 1880—one ordering the expulsion
of the Jesuits within three months, the other compelling the Congregations to seek from the State authorisation for their continued
existence in French territory. When these decrees had been issued,
Freycinet began to negotiate with the Papacy, through the mediation of
Cardinal Lavigerie, for a truce in return for a vague promise of non-
hostility towards the Republic. Warned by Gambetta, the Republicans
overthrew Freycinet in September, 1880, and entrusted the carrying into
effect of the decrees to Jules Ferry, who, on his appointment to the
Presidency of the Council, carried a vote for the closing of the Houses
of the religious Orders, though not for the dissolution of the Orders
themselves. The result of all his efforts was rather to increase the
hostility of these Orders to the Republic than to reduce them to obedience
to the democracy.

On the other hand, it was more easy to organise the schools of the
Republic. The Law of June 16, 1881, established the right of the people
to free primary education and thus justified the Government the next
year (March 28, 1882) in making it compulsory. Under certain conditions as to the degrees and character of teachers, this last-enacted Law
proclaimed the freedom of the primary schools; but, on the other hand, it
prescribed the secularity and neutrality of all the state schools. In order
to provide teachers for the work of public education, the Republic under-

CH. V.

took the responsibility for their salaries and their training as regards the Normal Primary Schools of each department. Moreover, the Republic established at Saint-Cloud and Fontenay near Paris Normal Schools of Higher Grade, where the teachers of these Normal Schools, recruited from among the children of the people, received instruction whose influence should penetrate the minds of dwellers in the most remote hamlets—a great concerted effort on behalf of education with which the name of Jules Ferry is still associated. This was the period, moreover, when the Republicans established a scheme for the education of women of the middle classes, a scheme sketched by Duruy and obstinately opposed by the Church, by passing on December 21, 1880, and July 26, 1881, the Laws dealing with schools and colleges for girls, and with the Normal School at Sèvres, whose object was to train mistresses for these schools. Jules Ferry also summoned to the Ministry, to take the direction of Higher Education, the eminent archaeologist, Albert Dumont, whose persistent efforts and moderate views restored life to the French Universities, and multiplied laboratories, professorial chairs, and the numbers of students. Never had any Government or even any Minister showed greater devotion to the interests of science, to the intellectual development of any country or nation.

Doubtless it was the efficacy of the weapon which the democracy had forged for itself by the passing of these laws on education, that disposed the Ministers of the Republic to listen to the offers of reconciliation which came to them at this moment from Rome. Leo XIII, who on February 20, 1878, had succeeded to the uncompromising and passionate Pius IX, while he abandoned none of the deep-seated and guiding principles of Roman policy, desired to bring about their triumph by different means, by gentleness and urbanity rather than by peremptory demands, by adroit concessions rather than by stubborn resistance to modern ideas, by understandings cleverly planned rather than by ruptures with societies, nations, and Governments. Such an understanding appeared to him most urgent in France, where disquieting tendencies were manifested in laws on divorce, on the secularisation of funeral ceremonies, and the suppression of honours paid to Bishops, and of public prayers ; and on November 19, 1885, an Encyclical, *Immortale Dei*, appeared from Rome which called upon Catholics, so far as the interests of the Church and of religious truth permitted, to recognise French political institutions and to take part in the rule of democracy in France. The clergy and faithful in France certainly did not immediately fall into line with this advice. But three years after, in the midst of the Boulanger episode, when the reactionary parties together with the Clericals were hastening to make their attack upon the Republic, Leo XIII published his Bull *Libertas* in the same spirit of gracious submission and gentleness as that of 1885. So well did he succeed that, at length, the Curia, which had so long disturbed, now began to reassure, almost to tempt the Republicans in power—President Carnot, his Ministers and his friends, Tirard, Constans, and Ribot.

In 1889, these members of the Government, deeply attached as they were to the democracy and to secularism, found themselves confronted by the Socialist party, which had been reconstituted since the amnesty under German influence; and, like the Left Centre after May 16, they were then obliged to form alliances with a party whose doctrines and excesses they feared. If the Pope had been more energetic, or had been better able to ensure obedience from the Bishops in France who were obstinately hostile to the Republic, President Carnot's Ministers, above all Freycinet, would perhaps have become reconciled with Leo XIII in order to ensure religious and social peace. But it was not until 1892 that he made known his wishes in the Encyclical, *Inter innumeras*: they were at any rate original and important. French Catholics for the first time received the order from Rome to abandon all attempts at political domination, and to rally to the democracy, "for the civil power, upon every theory, comes from God." To this invitation, Loubet, the chief of the Ministry in France, whose qualities had not yet become known, replied by a promise of liberal and prudent toleration. The Pope, in his turn, replied by a letter to the French Cardinals on May 3, 1892, which brought Mun and the militant Catholics to obey the command and to rally to the Republic. The result was that, at the elections of 1893, the separation of the Church and the State, with the other anti-clerical measures, had almost disappeared from the programmes of the Republicans, even of the Radicals.

In the history of the strained relations between Church and State in France since 1871, the period of Carnot's Presidency (1887–94), especially the years 1893 and 1894, was a sort of breathing-space, a relaxation. With men like Casimir Périer, and still more with Spuller and Méline, chosen deliberately among the most moderate Republicans to arrest the progress of the Socialists who, led by Guesde and Jaurès, at that time numbered fifty deputies in Parliament, the "new spirit" began to inspire ministerial counsels. The anarchist attempts at the end of 1893 and 1894 accentuated and hastened the reconciliation. It even seemed that, apart from political exigencies, a certain way to agreement was being made ready in the minds of men by the moral and neo-Christian movement, first inspired by Renan's school, and supported by a certain distaste for materialistic science and a general aspiration for enlightened altruism, preached by Vogüé, Brunetière, and Paul Desjardins. But these conditions were not destined to endure.

Under the shadow of the understanding which had grown up between the politicians and the faith, the religious Congregations raised their head, protected as they were against the ordinary menaces of anti-clericalism. While men were talking of social and religious peace, journals of violent Ultramontane sympathies, financed from the coffers of the middle class pupils of the Jesuits and Assumptionists, papers such as the *Libre Parole* and the *Croix*, declared war to the death on French citizens of the Jewish and the Protestant faith. Drumont gave the signal in *La France Juive*, which created Antisemitism in France. The journal issued by the same writer spread tenfold the propaganda of the book, excited the priests, and through them the faithful, against the Free-masons and the Jews. Brunetière, in the *Revue des Deux Mondes*, declared war for his part against science and the critical spirit. In 1895 he began a campaign against the democracy, demanding blind submission to the discipline of the Church of Rome.

The Republicans, surprised by this awakening of hatreds and religious factions, yielded so far as to let themselves be forced by the threats of Ultramontane journals to accept the sentence of degradation and exile to Guiana, passed upon Captain Dreyfus, who was accused without proof of having betrayed his country to Germany (December, 1894). This conviction was the proof of the progress made by Antisemitic feeling, and above all of the enormous influence which the Church had obtained, in the four years past, in all classes of society and especially in the army. Thenceforth the Minister for War was in their power through his complicity in a crime against justice. The Chief of the Staff, Boisdeffre, and all the Commanders of Army Corps, formed a sort of military parliament, encouraged by a false patriotism, which began to be called "Nationalism," to aim at the exclusion of the Jews, the Protestants, and even all Liberals, from French citizenship. Though, doubtless, many Catholics did not lend themselves to these proceedings, the Clerical party at least rejoiced in the progress made by these doctrines, and above all in the complaisance of Méline's Ministry, which from 1896 to 1898 pushed the fear of socialism to such a point that they saw and knew nothing of this movement towards a military and monastic tyranny.

The silence, so propitious to intrigue, was rudely broken by the unexpected announcement of Captain Dreyfus' innocence, which was made by Scheurer-Kestner from July, 1897, onwards, and confirmed, to the great displeasure of the Nationalists, civil and military, by Colonel Picquart at the end of the year. In vain did Méline's Ministry at first offer opposition to the solicitations of the family of Captain Dreyfus and of his friends, whose numbers increased daily and included men like Reinach, Jaurès, Zola, Clemenceau, Gabriel Monod, Havet, and Laborie, on the plea that it was impossible to go behind a "judgment given." In vain did the General Staff, attempting to involve the "honour of the army" in the crimes of the Antisemitic party, refuse to recognise in Esterhazy the real author of the *bordereau*, the document upon which the charge of treason against Dreyfus had been based. By slow but sure degrees, the country, the deputies, and the judges, became aware of the machinations of the Clerical party in league with the generals of the army. The elections of 1898 brought about the downfall of Méline's

Ministry. The accession to power of a Radical President of Council, Henri Brisson, who had had no traffic with the Ultramontane party, soon converted his party who up to this time, with the Socialists, had been opposed to a revision of the sentence. The Minister of War, Cavaignac, Nationalist though he was, was forced to make known the forgeries committed at the General Staff by Colonel Henry and his accomplices, with a view to completing finally the ruin of Colonel Picquart and Dreyfus. On the discovery of his crime, Henry passed sentence on himself by taking his own life in prison; and the Government finally ordered a fresh trial (August, 1898).

Another year elapsed before the trial began at Rennes—a year full of efforts made, even in Dupuy's Ministry, from October 30, 1898, onwards, in order to prevent the Court of Cassation from pronouncing its decision. Success was only attained after the sudden death of Félix Faure, who had connived at these hindrances and delays (February 16, 1899), after the election of President Loubet, and the failure of a Nationalist plot organised by Déroulède and Roget; and it was due to the establishment of Waldeck-Rousseau's Ministry, which resolved to bring about the triumph of justice by the help of the Socialists, who did not play them false. It was through fear of socialism that moderate Republicans had let themselves slide into this policy first of indifference to, and subsequently of complicity with, the intrigues which were in danger of bringing about a dictatorship, as in 1851. Similarly, it was the reconciliation with the Socialists, and the inclusion of one of their party, Millerand, in the Ministry for the "Defence of the Republic," which enabled Waldeck-Rousseau, himself a Moderate, and a friend and pupil of Gambetta, to avenge Dreyfus and his partisans. By the Council of War at Rennes Dreyfus was once more condemned; but President Loubet granted a pardon, in anticipation of the decision issued a year later by the Court of Cassation, declaring the innocence of this man whose sole crime was his birth.

The three years' struggle had been severe for Republican Ministers, who could not but see in the "Dreyfus affair" a concerted attempt at establishing, as at the beginning of the Republic in 1876, an Ultramontane rule in France by the aid of the chiefs of the army. Moreover, there can be no doubt but that the Congregations, the "confederate monks," as Waldeck-Rousseau called them, were, this time also, the principal actors. After 1900, Waldeck-Rousseau adopted the tactics and aims of Jules Ferry, and, without threatening the Church or liberty, began the attack upon the religious associations, by enacting for the first time freedom of combination (Law of 1902). His shattered health, which was becoming more enfeebled as his end drew near, forced him to retire (1902). His successor, Combes, proceeded to the legal, and, this time, complete dissolution of those religious associations (other than charitable) which had refused to report to the State their statutes and endowments (1903–4). Faithful to the tactics of all Republican Ministers, he had declared publicly when he entered office, that he would spare the priests while attacking the monks. He relied in this policy upon the Concordat.

Contrary to his calculation, events were hastened forward, either owing to the intrigues of the expelled Congregations, who exercised pressure upon the Curia and the secular clergy to bring about a rupture with France, in the hope of a religious war of revenge, or as a result of the alliance, which was daily becoming closer, between the Socialists in power and the Radical Republicans. When, after the death of Leo XIII, the new Pope, Pius X, whose very name stood as the symbol of an era of non-compromising policy, protested against President Loubet's visit to the King of Italy (April 24–29, 1904), the French Government at first was inclined to meet the insult with silence. With provocative intent, the Pope then made it public. On May 17, 1904, the parliamentary leader of the Socialist party, Jaurès, demanded reprisals. The Government, accordingly, recalled their ambassador, Nisard, from the Vatican.

Thenceforward, the separation between Church and State showed itself to be inevitable, in consequence of the policy of Rome, which had resolved to avenge the dissolution and expulsion of the Congregations, and of that of the French democratic party also, who were no longer restrained by the fear of breaking the Concordat. In a commission established in 1903 to enquire into this grave matter, a Socialist, Briand, had come into prominence by his character, which showed itself alike tactful and firm, resourceful and alert. In the month of January, 1905, after the retirement of Combes' Ministry, his successor as Minister of Public Worship, Bienvenu Martin, came to an agreement with Briand for the purpose of bringing forward a definitive project of Separation which Briand carried in the Chambers at the end of the year (December 9). This Law Briand, Minister of Public Worship in his turn, administered in Clemenceau's Cabinet without yielding, but also without heat, and without arousing the least emotion in the country (1906–7).

Before this Law, as to which the Pope had not been consulted, though in his opinion the nature of the Concordat made it incumbent upon France to consult him, Pius X naturally refused to bow : he would not even take cognisance of its provisions. He enjoined upon the Catholics in France to consider it as null and void. He preferred to sacrifice the property of the French Church rather than permit the faithful to establish the associations for public worship ordained by the legislature to take charge of and administer its goods. Thus it came about that, by the deliberate will of the Holy See, this Law, which its authors had desired to be full of tolerance, equity, and regard for consciences and for vested rights, was transformed in practice into a series of measures of spoliation and persecution.

However, the general indifference of the nation in this crisis, which in other times would have brought about a civil war, has permitted absolute tolerance and freedom in the practice of religion. The Catholic Church has completely lost to-day in France the financial and moral assistance of the State, the right to form any associations except for purposes of charity, the privileges of exemption from military service and from taxation which had hitherto been accorded to the clergy—all of these weapons which had been used against the democracy under the pretext of defending and propagating Catholic beliefs. But it does not appear that the respect due to these beliefs as to all others or religious peace has hitherto suffered any serious hurt.

When we come to follow in detail the sequence of phases through which the union between the Church and State passed after 1871, before it finally ended in the divorce of 1905, we cannot but be struck by the way in which these phases correspond to the evolution of the Socialist party. The Separation was carried out by Jaurès and Briand, that is to say, at the moment when the Socialists began to make their weight felt in Parliament and in the administration. Never, on the other hand, was the domination of the Clerical party over the Assemblies, over education, and over public opinion, so strong as immediately after the Commune, during the period which was, for the labouring classes, a "nine years' terror," during which they seemed to be of no account in the nation.

It is of importance, therefore, to consider the relations between the Church and the State in conjunction with those existing between the Socialist party and the Republic. After the defeat of the leaders and troops of the Commune, there was no Socialist party until November, 1877, when Jules Guesde, with the assistance of Lafargue, the son-in-law of Karl Marx, founded a paper, *L'Égalité*, for a collectivist propaganda, for which *Das Capital* was already put forward at Brussels and Bern as a sort of international Bible, in spite of the resistance of the Anarchists. The amnesty accorded in 1879 to those proscribed in 1871 gave back their leaders to the working classes, and to the champions of the doctrines of Marx their most convinced disciples. The amnesty had been won by the violent demands of a working men's congress held at Marseilles, at which Collectivist orators, such as Lombard, Fournière, and Ernest Roche, gained enthusiastic support for the doctrine of war between classes, in every field, intellectual, economic, and political. In 1880 the party of "Socialist Workers" in France was formed with organisation in six districts; its leaders, almost its apostles, were Benoit, Malon, and Guesde, inspired by the revolutionary doctrine of Marx and Engels, its programme; and its organs were *Le Prolétaire*, *L'Égalité*, and *La Révolution*. "Never before," said a Conservative spectator, "did any doctrine make as great progress in so short a time."

This progress of socialism was soon, however, checked by Republican politicians, who saw, not unreasonably, in the renewal of revolutionary threats, a danger which menaced the development and success of their own ideas among the middle classes and the peasants who were deeply attached to order, social tranquillity, and the rights of the individual. Clemenceau, the most ardent of the Radical leaders, absolutely refused to accept the doctrines of Marx "with his convents and his barracks." This resistance, supported by the chief talent and authority in the country, caused certain of the Socialists to reflect—among them Malon in particular, and Brousse, and subsequently Allemane, Joffrin, and Clovis Hugue, who began to question whether partial reforms obtained by slow degrees would not serve the proletariate better than a total recasting of society, an aim remote and perhaps wholly unattainable. They themselves wanted whatever was possible; and these "Possibilists" were strong enough at the Labour Congress at Reims in 1881 to carry their system in spite of the opposition of Jules Guesde, the overbearing and uncompromising leader, and to break with him at the Congress of Saint-Étienne on September 25, 1882. The Collectivist party thus broke up on a tactical question almost before it was organised—the question whether the war between classes should be conducted by patient sap or by hasty and violent assault.

In 1884, the Republican Government pressed forward a Law, which, in the view of its authors, was likely to alienate the labouring classes from the revolutionary groups by satisfying the interests of their class. By the Law of March 21, 1884, permitting artisans and peasants to form trade unions, in a country where the right of combination did not exist, the Republic conferred a great boon upon the working classes, all the greater in that the right was conferred upon these trade unions to form themselves into groups and even into a universal federation. From 1884 to 1889, every effort was used to develop and encourage cooperative societies of consumers and producers in the spirit of practical socialism inaugurated by the school of Nîmes, by Boyve and Gide. One of the most important enactments was that of 1888, which allowed these societies to compete for state contracts on favourable terms. Under the beneficent eye of a Government that had established a journal in its offices to follow the movement, the first general congress of Mutual Aid Societies was held at Lyons in 1883 and made further claims for liberty. In Parliament the party of social reform daily gained fresh sympathisers; Jaurès, whose conversion from the Left Centre to the Extreme Left began in 1887; Millerand, who went over entirely to the party of extreme Radicalism; and many other Moderates, such as Poincaré, Hanotaux, and Jamais, were in agreement with them in demanding from the Chamber special attention—two sittings a week—for social questions.

At the moment when the Republicans at the Exhibition of 1889 were demonstrating the success of their efforts to give back to a free and industrious France her rank among the nations, they contracted with the Socialist party what may be called a *mariage de raison.*

The meetings of the Collectivist party, Possibilists and Guesdites, held at Paris in 1889 to demand international legislation upon the labour question, made French politicians perceive, by the strength of their organisation and the threats of a general strike, which was attempted on May 1, the necessity of a Concordat with this new religion. This was to be based upon the following conditions: the intervention and assistance of the State, which the political and economic creed of the Liberals had consistently condemned, was to be extended to the furtherance of the moral and material well-being of the proletariate, and the Collectivists on their side were to abandon the hopes of a violent revolution, which they had hitherto put forward in opposition to the needs of the public peace and the demands of the law.

As in all schemes of compromise, there has been ever since this time an alternation of concessions and demands, regulated by circumstances or the claims of one party or the other. In 1890 an important Law (July 8) gave to miners the right of appointing delegates to watch over their safety; an enquiry was set on foot by the Chamber in its Labour Committee upon the possibility of limiting the legal working day in factories. Finally, another Law (December 27) laid down the principle of compensation in favour of a working man whose working contract was broken without cause. This movement for legislation in the interests of labour became more marked in 1891 by the creation of a Supreme Council of Labour, recruited equally from employers of labour and those employed by them; by the promise made by Constans on the question of working men's pensions; and by the institution, on July 20, of a Labour Section in the Ministry of Commerce, and of Labour Exchanges in the provincial towns. A proportionate advance was shown by trade unions and cooperative societies. Something like a reaction set in at the end of 1891, when a strike in the north, at Fourmies, provoked a bloody conflict between the military force and the miners, and still more as a result of the Anarchist attempts of Ravachol in Paris. But the positions occupied by all the Socialist sections—by Brousse and Allemane in Paris, by Guesde, Lafargue, and Camelinat in the north—were already so strong that the progress of socialism suffered no check from these events. On the eve of the municipal elections of 1892, valuable assistance was afforded to them by the democratic middle-class party, followers of Millerand, who set forth in his journal, the *Petite République Française*, the terms of the Concordat arranged between the labouring classes and Republicans, a necessary and fruitful alliance. "We must be either with the people or against them. To accomplish social reforms, we demand the help of all branches of Socialists, no matter how bold their theories, provided that they do not desire to triumph by means other than pacific and constitutional." With the aid of these reforming or radical Socialists, Jules Guesde and his followers conquered Roubaix, a fortress, and the

CH. V.

followers of Brousse gained Paris, a platform; at the elections to the Chamber of 1893, fifty Collectivist deputies entered Parliament, with the idea of winning for men of their way of thinking all the public offices, and using them for the transformation of capitalist and individualist society in accordance with their ideal of the socialisation of the instruments of labour and of production.

The middle classes, however, became uneasy when faced with the theories set forth in 1894 by Jules Guesde in the Chamber, especially after the assassination of President Carnot at Lyons. The election as President of a great capitalist, one of the Casimir Périers of Anzin, and the laws brought forward by Dupuy's Cabinet, which were called the *lois scélérates*, seemed to the working classes indications of reaction and rupture. However, on November 20, 1894, Parliament passed the law to provide "cheap and sanitary dwellings" for working men, and reenacted with greater precision the earlier laws regarding the labour of women and children. "We need social laws," said one of the most moderate deputies, Paul Deschanel, in 1896. Was this declaration very different from the programme of pacific development which Millerand laid down for the Collectivists at St Mandé on May 30, 1896: "Our sole appeal is to universal suffrage. To be invincible we only need to be united." It seemed that a continued accord between Republicans of every shade of thought, except the partisans of physical force, was not only desirable but expedient. The accession to power of Méline's Ministry, which was formed on April 30, 1896, following upon a vote of the Senate against a proposal for income-tax which had been passed by the Chamber of Deputies, brought to a head the resistance of the middle classes to the wishes of the Socialist party.

The Dreyfus affair emphasised this opposition in 1897. Not that in the debate upon this celebrated affair the Collectivists had taken the side of the innocent man. On the contrary, Jaurès, who quickly declared himself against military justice and its errors, was thrown over by his constituents, his friends, and the people of Paris. But, when it became evident in political and professional circles that this Socialist leader was making common cause with Zola, a revolutionary even in literature, and with Clemenceau, the indefatigable opponent of Conservative Ministries, in order to compel the military leaders to recognise their error, the fear took shape and became widely spread, that an anarchist attempt was afoot, planned with the Jews and foreign Powers, to overthrow the army. It is in this fear that we must look for the explanation of the resistance offered by the Ministries of Méline and Dupuy to the revision of the sentence, as much as in the intrigues of the Nationalists, who were as clever as in 1850 at awakening the terror of the "Red peril." On the other hand, these moderate Republicans underestimated the service which, by concealing the faults of certain officers, they were rendering to the Socialists, who had been called upon by the democratic party to defend Republican institutions against any future possible revival of Caesarism. Towards the end of this crisis, the necessary Concordat between the Republic and collectivism, which had been on the point of breaking down, was more firmly cemented. Millerand, who had been at the head of his party ever since 1893, and had in 1896 formulated at St Mandé the demands of the Socialist party, became a member of Waldeck-Rousseau's Ministry, in order to direct, as Minister of Commerce and Industry, what was, in effect, a Department of Labour (June, 1899). It is only necessary to recall the days of June, 1848, and of the Commune in 1870, in order to appreciate the importance of this event in the history of French socialism.

Moreover, this participation of a Socialist in a Republican Government was so much of a compromise that those Collectivists—Guesde, with his followers and friends—who were firmly attached to the doctrine of war between classes and to revolutionary principles, were incensed at the concessions arranged beforehand by Millerand and Jaurès in their agreement with Waldeck-Rousseau. They denounced them at the great party Congress on December 3, 1899, which did not venture to pronounce absolutely whether they were in the right or in the wrong. The party of labour and revolution became daily more hostile to the independent Socialist or reforming party, and broke with the partisans of Millerand, Jaurès, Viviani, and Briand at the Congress of Lyons in May, 1901.

These divisions and disputes did not interfere with the influence that a Socialist Minister was able to exert upon the legislation and political feeling during his tenure of power. In his department, Millerand organised a " Board of Labour " and a " Board of Thrift and Aid," based upon Councils in part elective. One of his first acts was to limit the working day to a uniform eleven hours. This working day was limited in 1902 to nine hours and a half. In 1904 it was fixed at ten hours. The decree of January 2, 1901, established " Labour Councils " for the pacific adjustment of disputes between employers and employed. Another Law, passed on December 29, 1900, settled the hygienic conditions under which work was to be carried on, while a general Law for the protection of Public Health (February 15, 1902) brought under systematic control the dwellings of the working classes, and secured state aid for other improvements. During the three years in which Millerand held office, the attention of the Cabinet, in which for the first time his party had gained a footing, was not distracted for one moment from the task of finding progressive solutions of social problems. When, in 1902, he resigned the Ministry of Commerce, he had decided upon a scheme of reform more fundamental and general still, which he has never ceased since that time to demand from the State, namely, the establishment and organisation of old age pensions for labouring men.

Though this reform, so often demanded, has not yet been realised,

CH. V.

yet the impetus given to the Socialist party by its union with the Republicans has not slackened. Briand, a Socialist, was appointed to the Ministry to apply the law of the separation of Church and State, which was the chief work of their party from 1902 to 1907. In 1907 a Ministry of Labour was created in Clemenceau's Cabinet for the benefit of Viviani, one of Briand's friends. Moreover, with great skill, from 1902 onwards, without the least friction with his friends in office, Jaurès has managed to soothe the anger of the extremists, and has subscribed to the conditions of unification of the Socialist party, in accordance with the example of Collectivism in Germany and under its influence. Thus, for some years, the Socialists have drawn advantage from their revolutionary demands as well as from their participation in the government.

If this party, whose strength in the Republic has waxed in proportion as that of the Church waned, has risks to run, they will come from the excesses of the extremist parties formed on its flanks and among its own members, the Anarchists, the Antimilitarists, who desire to destroy the army which protects the laws they deny, and the "Syndicalists," hostile to Marxism, and still more hostile to parliamentary methods, bent on conferring upon trade unions, grouped more or less closely in a General Confederation of Labour, the powers which now belong to the Republican and middle-class State. The success of the Syndicalists, or the progress already made by them as a result of the fact that public officials are inclined to form common cause with them, appears calculated to break the alliance which has existed for ten years between the Republic and the labouring classes. The problem of the hour is the relations of the Republic with the Socialist party, since such relations are essential and necessary to the life and development of a democracy.

While Millerand was thus engaged in organising labour and arranging for state assistance for the labouring classes, as Minister of Commerce he never forgot that the maintenance and progress of national wealth were the indispensable conditions of the benefits promised by the Republic to the working and poorer classes. In point of fact, nothing has contributed more to the continuance of the economic prosperity of France than the trade with French colonies, which has steadily increased since 1870 from 350 millions to nearly two milliards.

The work of colonising has been for France, ever since her defeat, the constant and almost instinctive care on the part of her Government and her people. She has increased tenfold the population under her sway, as well as the new territories opened to her civilisation and her commerce. The line followed by France in her work of colonisation is naturally the result and development of the system pursued by earlier Governments and prescribed by circumstances: first of all in North Africa. Revolts on the part of the inhabitants of Algeria have become rarer and less important—that of Mokrani in Kabylia in 1881, the most violent, the briefer rising of the Aurès in 1879, and those of 1881 of Bou Amema and Si Tlemcen in the south of Oran, have all tended to establish the permanence of French rule. Round this solid kernel progress gradually proceeded by successive advances. From the province of Constantine, the valley of the Medjerda inevitably led the French towards Tunis, where the acts of brigandage of the Kroumirs on March 31, 1881, gave a legitimate ground for interference. The Treaty of Bardo, concluded with the Bey on May 12, 1881, placed the country under the protectorate of the Republic. This Treaty raised hardly any opposition in Europe, except at first in Italy, and subsequently proved most favourable for the development of the dependency. Commerce has increased in it in twenty years from 27 to 200 millions. A similar phenomenon of expansion is seen in the south, in the oases of the Sahara, where French influence has been established. The attacks of the Touaregs upon French outposts in the Aurès have by degrees compelled the occupation of the districts in the south of Algeria, explored since 1860 by intrepid French travellers. Down to 1880, the boundaries of French territory were Ain-Sefra in Oran, Laghouat in Algeria, and Ouargla at the limit of Constantine. From 1895 onwards, the railroad was extended into the desert towards Igli and El Goleah to facilitate the police work of the French troops. In 1900, the Government decided upon the simultaneous occupation of Insalah, Tidikelt, Touat, and Gourara on the frontiers of Morocco, the most advantageous positions and from a strategical point of view the most important in the Sahara. Moreover, by gentle pressure, France opened for herself the trade routes of Morocco, and the way to the Sudan, which little by little she has succeeded in colonising.

This result was mainly due to the efforts of Faidherbe to open up the *hinterland* of Senegal, of which he had been appointed Governor under the Empire. With method and wisdom this general had subdued the Moorish tribes, who barred the river, and established outposts at Bakel in the interior. More than that, from 1854 to 1865 he had founded a tradition and set an example to a whole generation of officers, enterprising like himself and desirous of spreading French authority as far as the table-lands which separate Senegal from Nigeria. For ten years this was the patient labour of Brière de l'Ille, Gallieni, and Bayol, who in 1881 reached Nigeria by way of the table-lands, and of Archinard and Bonnier, who, in 1894, occupied Timbuktu. The explorations of Binger (1887–9) in the bend of the Niger, of Marchand in the district of Kong, of Monteil about Lake Chad (1891), the conquest of Dahomey by Dodds and Audéoud in 1892, linked by the efforts of Ballot and Destenave with the Niger, and the annexation of the Ivory Coast which was arranged with England in 1892, have in the last years of the nineteenth century established a French empire in the Sudan—an empire consisting of two million square kilometres, whose population, protected as they now are against wars and famine, and for the most part industrious and healthy, will soon outgrow their present numbers and furnish the elements necessary for the development and cultivation of this district, rich as it is in natural resources.

The whole of this development in North Africa was the result of an agreement made between France and England on August 5, 1890, for the union of French Upper Senegal with Guinea, and for the delimitation of the respective spheres of the two nations in the region of Lake Chad along the line from Say to Barua. Another treaty (June 14, 1898) defined more clearly this first agreement, and arranged the union of Senegal with the middle Niger and Dahomey.

France received an important share, although some criticisms were passed on the amount of desert land accorded to her, in this occupation of new territory in the " Dark Continent." The energy of her explorations had well deserved this reward. When the first settlement of African territory took place at the Congress of Berlin in 1885, and the neutrality of the Congo Free State was recognised, Europe, nevertheless, permitted the creation of a French Congo from the Ogowé to the Ubanghi. It was only just to permit France to reap the reward of her energies, and the discoveries of Savorgnan de Brazza. Moreover, encouraged by this international decision, France extended her colonies to the north and north-east of the Congo, thanks to the discoveries and struggles of Crampel, Dybowski, and Mizon, both towards Lake Chad and towards Benue (1888–92). After penetrating the valley of the upper Ubanghi, the French pressed on, in 1896–8, with Marchand as far as the valley of the Bahr-el-Gazal, where their meeting with the army of the English Sirdar, Kitchener, all but provoked a formidable crisis. The Franco-German Convention of the Cameroons (March 15, 1894) had confirmed to France her approach to the territory of Lake Chad by the Sangha which had been explored by Clozel. The Franco-British Convention of March 21, 1899, in return for the French evacuation of the Nile valley, granted to the French Congo exclusive powers of extension in the kingdoms of Chad, Baghirmi, Wadai, and Kanem, territories whose subjection to France was finally accomplished by Liotard and Gentil after the defeat and death of Rabah (1901).

To complete the picture of French colonisation in Africa, we must not omit her establishment in Madagascar in 1895. So far back as the days of Napoleon III, the Hovas, the warlike and dominant tribe in Madagascar, had accepted a French protectorate. They had recognised it once more in 1885. But it needed General Duchesne's expedition, from January 14 to September 30, 1895, and the presence of the French troops at Antananarivo to force upon the Queen and her reluctant aristocracy respect for the terms of the agreements. Meanwhile, by the Treaty of August 5, 1890, England and France had agreed upon the formal annexation of the protectorate of Zanzibar by the one, and that of the great island opposite by the other. From that time no European Power disputed the right of France to Madagascar, not even when she was forced in September, 1896, to substitute a direct rule for a protectorate and to deport the Queen and her Minister Rainalaiarivony to Algeria.

Thus, since 1870, France has become one of the chief Powers in Africa, and, like Russia in Turkestan, whose methods of penetration she imitated, a Mohammadan Power in Maghreb. It was at the same moment that France began to realise, with the conviction of her restored strength, her colonial destinies in Asia.

There, even more than in Africa, it was a sort of reawakening of the past—either of the efforts which the French had made at the end of the eighteenth century to indemnify themselves in Indo-China for the loss of Hindustan, or of the more recent colonial enterprises recommended to Napoleon III by Duruy and Chasseloup-Laubat in 1865 and 1867 at the time of the occupation of Saigon and the neighbouring provinces. The exploration of the Mekong by two intrepid naval officers, Francis Garnier and Doudart de Lagrée, who laboured for three years (1866–9) at the investigation of this great peninsula, demonstrated the importance of finding a path of penetration towards Chinese territory other than the river-course, impeded as it is by rapids. After Garnier's death (1873) France contented herself with a vague treaty with the Emperor of Annam which gave her the protectorate (March 15, 1875). But, after the death of Commandant Rivière, who had been sent to Hanoi to defend French traders, and who was killed in an ambuscade (May 19, 1883), Ferry's Ministry, bent upon colonial enterprise, commissioned Admiral Courbet, first, to force the Emperor of Annam to acknowledge the French protectorate (August 25, 1883), and afterwards to wrest from the Black Flags, who were secretly aided by the Chinese, the delta of Tonkin (Treaty of Tientsin, May 11, 1884).

The Chinese Government then took the offensive, in virtue of secular rights, long since passed into oblivion, and unwilling to have France as a neighbour. Colonel Duchesne, who had been ordered to occupy Langson in virtue of the treaties, was suddenly attacked by the Chinese soldiery in the Bac-le pass. Once more Admiral Courbet received orders to carry out French vengeance. His fleet, by a bold stroke, destroyed on August 23, 1884, in the river Min, the arsenal of Foo-chow. Then, it took possession of Formosa, of the port of Kelung, and of the Pescadores islands, blockading all the southern ports of China in order to hinder the trade in rice. The Chinese had struggled, so long as they believed themselves strong enough by land, to expel the French from Tonkin. Already, they were retiring towards their frontiers, when a momentary panic put to flight General Négrier's brigade before an enemy who believed themselves beaten, just below Langson. The French Chamber, misled by incorrect information, believed that an irreparable disaster had taken place, censured Jules Ferry, and overthrew his Ministry on April 2, 1885.

Immediately afterwards, the news reached Paris that the victories and blockade of Admiral Courbet had finally decided China to accept peace, which was definitely signed on June 9, 1885, at Tientsin. The reward of these efforts was the definitive establishment of a French protectorate in Tonkin and Annam, and its recognition by China, who promised to throw open to French traders and French influence her southern provinces, particularly Yunnan. This was the most extensive attempt made at establishing a European maritime empire in Asia since the events of the preceding century. As a result and by reason of the treaties with Siam (October 3, 1893) and with England (the declaration of 1896 and the treaty of October 7, 1892), the French empire in Indo-China also strengthened and established the position of Cambodia, the other old-established Indo-Chinese kingdom under French protection.

Nevertheless, France does not appear to have thought of imitating Russia, England, and Germany, when these Powers profited by the disturbances in China to occupy Port Arthur, Kiaochow, and Wei-Hai-Wei. At that time the French Government was pursuing other ends in Africa which it judged more important, those which Delcassé endeavoured to realise in Algeria and Morocco. Without any intention of attempting the subjection or even the establishment of a protectorate in this region, which was now almost entirely surrounded by her empires of Maghreb and the Sudan, France was nevertheless uneasy at the anarchy which was threatening the kingdom of Abd-el-Aziz, and formed the scheme of offering him her help, in order to establish special claims on his gratitude. On July 19, 1903, Delcassé published his programme of pacific penetration, which he had drawn up with a view to procuring for France " the privilege and advantage of transforming Morocco into a modern State " in accordance with the treaty agreed upon with Abd-el-Aziz in July, 1901.

By a protocol signed with Italy in 1900, and renewed in 1902, by a promise of help made from St Petersburg in 1901, which was still open, and finally by the Treaty concluded on August 8, 1904, in London, arranging to leave the English absolute liberty of action in Egypt, in return for a similar liberty in Morocco, the French Cabinet seemed to have gained the consent of Europe. Germany alone had been silent when France had intimated her intention of treating Fez differently from Tunis. All at once, either to satisfy the desires of the German colonial party who were anxious to possess a Moroccan port on the Atlantic, or because he was annoyed at the promises made secretly to Spain by Delcassé of a part of Morocco (Treaty of October 3, 1904), the Emperor William II landed at Tangier in March, 1905 ; the dismissal of Delcassé was demanded, and subsequently obtained by a sort of ultimatum addressed to France and Spain in the month of June, 1905.

Relying, however, on the alliance and friendship with England, France did not intend to give up the rights on the borders of the Sherifian empire resulting from her long-established position in Algeria. She agreed to the International Conference at Algeciras in September, 1905, in order to prove that she had no desire for the conquest or economic annexation of Morocco. But she upheld her legitimate claims to a privileged position in Morocco, and asserted them with the consent of Spain, in a new agreement of May 16, 1907. Nothing prevented her, not even the overthrow of the Sultan Abd-el-Aziz by his brother Moulai-Hafid, from exacting vengeance for the massacre of her countrymen by the fanatics of Casa Blanca. She occupied the port and neighbouring district of Shawia, pressing forward with her troops into the valley of the Moulaya and the oases of the south. In February, 1909, Germany recognised the political preponderance of France in this region, which France had undertaken to leave open to the enterprise of German traders.

Thanks to these efforts, the colonial policy of the Republic has led to the establishment of an empire whose extent has been raised from 804,000 square kilometres to nearly 12 millions, with a population of 50 millions and still increasing. In reviewing this policy, we are struck by the small number of wars that it has entailed: none with any European Power, in spite of the dangers of Fashoda and Tangier. In point of fact, it would seem that the French, who found some difficulty in adapting themselves to the conditions and consequences of these enterprises, did not grasp the consequent liability to European disputes.

On the other hand, France has shown great anxiety to associate herself with all the plans concerted between the Powers at the two Peace Conferences of the Hague, and with all efforts to prevent wars by arbitration treaties, while diminishing by international legislation their risks and deadly consequences. The restoration and development of her resources, commercial, agricultural and colonial, a foreign defensive policy directed towards the maintenance of her safety and the Balance of Power —these, and these alone, have been her general aims, her instinctive and national policy.

CH.

CHAPTER VI.

THE GERMAN EMPIRE.

(1)

THE FIRST SEVEN YEARS OF THE EMPIRE.
(1871–7.)

AFTER centuries of dismemberment and impotence the German people had between the years 1866 and 1871 reestablished their claim to rank as a nation. Bismarck's statesmanship and the political and military resources of Prussia had combined to bring about at last the realisation of that new German Empire of which so many generations of patriots had dreamed. Though the time-honoured titles of Emperor and Empire might at first recall the past glories of the Holy Roman Empire, their meaning had undergone a fundamental change; for the future they were to imply no universal claims, no ancient ecclesiastical sanctity, no huge agglomeration of semi-independent institutions of earlier ages; the old names were to stand for a new order of things—the German national State.

War, ever the most potent factor in the founding of States, had brought unity to the German people. Their new State, outcome of this unity, was as yet in the earliest stage of its construction, for only the general outline had been laid down in the Treaty of Versailles of November, 1870, between the North German Confederation and South German States. It was astonishing that a people, while engaged in a life and death struggle with a neighbouring Power, should determine the political setting for its future existence. The next step must be to ensure a corporate political life for the new State, of which the outward form alone had been fixed. In those fateful years from 1867 to 1870 the foundations had been laid of common institutions which had now to be built up and extended over the whole empire. Every obstacle to unity must be removed, so that the new State might be the home of a people united politically as in every other respect. At the same time, it was of importance that what had been acquired should be held against all endeavours from without; the young Power which had sprung up so rapidly must be brought into the circle of the older Great Powers and the lines of its foreign policy must be defined. Thus a great mass of political problems confronted the German people on the conclusion of the War.

Problems connected with foreign policy naturally arose out of the very genesis of the empire in the three Wars of 1864, 1866 and 1870–1. The new empire bore a peaceful character from the outset; Emperor and Chancellor constantly insisted on the fact that Germany, as newly constituted, had her fill of power and entertained no further military ambitions. Nevertheless, there was something convulsive about the impression created by the astoundingly rapid rise of the empire; the smaller neighbouring Powers felt themselves menaced and dreaded a revival of the traditions of the old Empire. The Great Powers, too, were ill-pleased to see the centre of Europe occupied thenceforth by a compact Power of great military strength—a state of affairs which entirely altered the former European constellation. The Germans were soon to learn that a nation of poets and philosophers, the Germany of Goethe and Hegel, with ideals other than political, had been more to the world's liking than the Germany of Bismarck now coming forth into the arena with political claims of its own.

In the first place, the after-effects of the late Wars were not to be so quickly obliterated. Had not Austria-Hungary so recently as the summer of 1870 been on the verge of making common cause with Napoleon III? Such an alliance would have been the natural result of the war of 1866. But the effects of the French war in creating enmities, opposition, and suspicion, were to be of much longer duration. By the terms of the Treaty of Frankfort the French had not only to pay the huge sum of five thousand million francs, but they had also to cede two provinces, Alsace and part of Lorraine. Both provinces, it is true, had formerly belonged to the Empire and a large proportion of their population still spoke the German language. Even without these annexations the breach between France and Germany naturally resulting from the war would not have closed within the next generation, but now it was certain to remain long open.

The motive for the annexations is often misrepresented. Everyone knows the famous words spoken by Leopold von Ranke, the historian, to Thiers in the autumn of 1870, after the fall of Napoleon III. "It is against Louis XIV that we have now to wage war"; that is to say, we have now to fight against the country which has for centuries looked upon the defenceless condition of the Germans as the strongest bulwark of her own hegemony on the Continent. Bismarck's motive for the annexation lay in no faded memories of past imperial history upon which national enthusiasts dwelt, but in the real and pressing necessity for permanent military defence of German unity against all attacks from the west—a unity which had been threatened, so lately as 1866, by the preposterous demand of Napoleon III for the cession of Mainz and a portion of the left bank of the Rhine. This necessity alone impelled him to shift the frontier across the Rhine into the Vosges mountains, for southern Germany had been long enough at the mercy of French artillery. For this reason too, and for this alone, he decided, almost under compulsion from the generals, to acquire the fortress of Metz, situated in the French-speaking area, in addition to Alsace, which with the large German element in its population might be expected to become gradually assimilated to the empire. The annexation, far from being a deed done on the spur of the moment by the caprice of an individual, was the inevitable outcome for both nations of several centuries of their history, and more than one generation of French and Germans alike will have to abide by it.

Any danger to be apprehended solely from the French desire for *revanche* was certainly less than before and would further diminish with the lapse of time. In 1861, shortly before Bismarck took the helm in Prussian affairs, the population of France amounted to 37,400,000 and that of Prussia to 19,100,000; five years later the French population numbered 38,100,000, and that of the North German Confederation 30 millions. After the War and the annexations, the population of France had fallen to 36,100,000, while the German empire had 41,100,000 inhabitants. The rapid increase of the German population and the comparative sterility of the French increased the disproportion; so that by 1905 the population of France only numbered upwards of 39,500,000, whereas that of the German empire amounted to upwards of 60,300,000. As time went on, superior numbers were bound to have a more and more important effect both on the military capacity of the nations and on their economic position.

Nevertheless, from the very outset the new structure of the German empire was burdened as it were by a French mortgage, since every foreign foe could henceforth reckon unconditionally on French support. As in the past Frederick the Great had had to vindicate his conquest of Silesia in a seven years' war against a European combination, so Bismarck in his turn was painfully aware that the incubus of a coalition hourly weighed upon his new creation. The great aim of his policy, from the first, was to prevent the formation of any such coalition.

The internal policy of the empire was fraught with no less difficult problems. The new national State did not include all the German elements, nor was it composed of exclusively German elements. Since 1866 there had been nearly eight million Germans in Austria who had no political connexion with their old country and thenceforward went their own way. It was one of the axioms of Bismarck's policy to regard this severance as irrevocable. On the other hand, the new empire contained many who had no natural place in its system and were included in it against their will: for example, the Prussian Poles and the population of Alsace-Lorraine. Though the regions annexed by Prussia in 1866 had been, to some extent, assimilated to the Prussian nation, yet in Hanover the Guelfic nobility was becoming the centre of a separatist party intensely hostile to Prussia. Furthermore, in the most recent struggle for political hegemony in Germany, religious discord between Protestants and Catholics had been reawakened. In considering the internal obstacles to unity account must also be taken of the far-reaching social changes which had come to pass within the last decades. The middle class had long since been pushing its way to the front, and the development of capitalism received a powerful impetus by the payment of the enormous war indemnity. Not only so, but the working classes were attaining to political consciousness, and social problems of a new order were looming ahead. Such were the internal questions demanding solution at the hands of the new empire, which was now entering upon the task of elaborating its new Constitution.

The two men who together had called the empire into being were destined to direct its affairs for nearly twenty years. First, in virtue of his rank, stands the Emperor William I, an old man of seventy-four at the close of the war, for whom no one foresaw seventeen further years of life and rule. He became in an increasing measure a venerable figure among the crowned heads of Europe, and a personality which strengthened the monarchic principle in the world. His was a fine character: he was imbued with a strong sense of duty and an honest desire for peace, inclining more and more towards Conservatism after his experience of violent European convulsions. His gratitude towards the one man whom he felt to be increasingly indispensable found voice in the famous " Never ! " with which he answered Bismarck's request for dismissal. It was Bismarck, however, the uncrowned founder of the empire, who really wielded the power of the State; yet, during the two decades in which he was omnipotent as a Minister, he held sway for no mere puppet master as Richelieu had done. William never relinquished his royal prerogative, or ignored his own responsibility for all that was done in his name. Yet, though the Emperor sometimes declined to adopt the policy of his Minister and often moderated it, in all important matters Bismarck had his way in the end.

CH. VI.

He united in his person an almost regal combination of functions. As imperial Chancellor he was the sole responsible officer of the empire, director alike of its foreign and its home affairs; at the same time, in the Prussian Government he was President of the Council, Foreign Minister, and for a period (1870–90) also Minister of Commerce. In the exercise of these offices he had, of course, to cooperate with a considerable number of separate authorities established under the Constitution: with the *Bundesrat*, in which the separate Governments were represented so as to vindicate the federal principle in the empire; with the *Reichstag*, elected on the basis of an absolutely democratic equal and universal suffrage, in concert with which the internal consolidation of Germany had to be effected; and, lastly, with both Chambers of the Prussian *Landtag*. Altogether, the machinery of government was extremely complicated and required the hand of a master in political tactics. We do not know what were Bismarck's ultimate objects at every stage, for even his memoirs describe, not so much how things actually happened, as how he, the statesman who was called upon to act, desired his deeds to be regarded by his fellow-citizens and by posterity. For twenty years he held his own in Germany and in the world, keeping the threads of home and foreign policy in his own hand and manipulating them adroitly, ever ready with suggestive ideas and astute lines of action, subduing with irresistible force of will every opponent whether at home or abroad, ever more keenly aroused by any obstacle which lay athwart his path, hardened at last by the sense of power, standing in lonely eminence while friends and colleagues remained far behind. Throughout his whole life he despised pomp and outward honours, desiring nothing but the reality of power; and even this he did not desire for himself, but for that German empire which was his creation and in whose service every force of his being was with passionate devotion exerted and expended.

Germany occupied a central position in Europe among three Great Powers, against two of which she had been very recently at war. On this account it was of vital importance, for her more than any other Power, to prevent coalitions of her opponents by her own strength and adroit foreign policy. During the War of 1870, Bismarck had determined on a permanent political alliance with Russia and Austria, which should minimise the risks of an anti-German coalition and make a war of revenge on the part of France utterly impossible. A Russo-German alliance was a tradition with both countries and both royal Houses; for the dynastic relations dating from the beginning of the nineteenth century were warmly maintained in the friendship existing between the Emperor William I and his nephew, Tsar Alexander II. The Russian Chancellor Gorchakóff had, in the sixties, looked upon Bismarck almost as his pupil in diplomacy, and during the Wars of 1866 and 1870–1 he had observed a friendly neutrality towards Prussia. There were no conflicting interests between the two countries; indeed, the Polish question established a community of interests which Bismarck sought to strengthen further by appealing to the strength of monarchical and conservative opinions in Europe at large, as against the new tendencies which both governments feared.

It was a far more difficult task for the victors of 1866 to arrive at an understanding with Austria-Hungary; but the considerate terms of the Treaty of Prague had paved the way for this; and the fact that the new empire had declined to exert its political force of attraction over the German-Austrian population was calculated to allay Habsburg suspicions. Thus Bismarck managed to bring about a meeting at Berlin, in September, 1872, between the Emperors Alexander and Francis Joseph, both accompanied by their chief Ministers, and the Emperor William. Ostensibly, this meeting was a solemn and brilliant recognition of the German imperial dignity on the part of the two European sovereigns bearing the same title; and the visit of the two potentates implied an impressive guarantee of the position of Germany and a pledge of European peace. Bismarck might well say with pride: "I have thrown a bridge across to Vienna, without breaking down that older one to St Petersburg."

Many were reminded of the league among the three Eastern Powers in the days of the Holy Alliance; but it was impossible to deny that now the centre of gravity of the new combination was Berlin, not, as formerly, Vienna or St Petersburg. This reminiscence of past history affords, however, no exact parallel to the actual facts. No "*Dreikaiserbündniss*," no League of three Emperors, was concluded in September, 1872, as the history books used to relate; there were no written agreements, and Alexander II made a point of reassuring the French ambassador. It should rather be called a "*Dreikaiserverhältniss*," an understanding among three Emperors; or, to use a convenient French expression, an *entente* between three Powers which by a friendly interchange of opinion arrived at a friendly agreement on questions at issue. In the following year (1873) a treaty was actually concluded with Russia, which was signed only by the two monarchs and their respective Field-Marshals Moltke and Baryatinski. Italy, too, seemed already to be inclining towards the new constellation of Powers, for King Victor Emmanuel visited Berlin in 1873. Although Great Britain remained more aloof, Lord Odo Russell, her ambassador, was nevertheless able to report in February, 1874, that "our relations with Germany were never better, more cordial, or more satisfactory than at present."

Bismarck was thus entirely free to watch the shaping of relations

with France. In a treaty of March 15, 1873, France agreed to pay
the rest of the war indemnity by September 5, 1873, although it was
not due until March 1, 1875, while Germany conceded the evacuation
of French territory by July 5, 1873. To all appearances, then, normal
relations were reestablished between the two countries. What they
would be in the future depended partly upon the form of government
which should be adopted in France after the fall of Thiers. Count
Harry Arnim, German ambassador in Paris, an ambitious politician
of legitimist leanings, endeavoured to assist the efforts then initiated
in France for the restoration of the monarchy. Bismarck, on the other
hand, who looked at questions of foreign policy with the eye of a
practical statesman, never with that of a doctrinaire, preferred the
republican form of government for France, although everywhere else in
the world in general he was a firm advocate of monarchic institutions.
A republic, he thought, would not be able to consolidate the latent
forces of the nation and would be less capable of forming alliances with
other Powers in Europe (in which conjecture, for the time at any rate,
he was right); above all, from its very nature, a republic would pursue
a more peaceful policy than a monarchy, which could only regain its
sway over the affections of the French by warlike success, that is to
say, by a war of retaliation against Germany.

So early as December 20, 1872, Bismarck wrote: "It is certainly
no task of ours to render France powerful by the consolidation of her
internal relations and the restoration of a settled monarchy, and thus
to make her capable of entering into alliances with those Powers
that have hitherto been our friends. The hostility of France compels
us to desire that she may remain weak." During the ensuing years,
therefore, he did all in his power to uphold the republican form of
government in France. By this line of action he came into conflict
with Arnim, who appealed to the legitimist opinions of Berlin court
circles and even of the Emperor himself, exceeded his instructions, and
finally embarked on intrigues with Bismarck's enemies at home. The
Chancellor succeeded, however, in obtaining Arnim's recall and, at a
later date, even in bringing about his subsequent criminal prosecution
for the refusal to surrender official papers. It was a struggle in which
Bismarck fought, as his custom was, with implacable energy to the
bitter end, a struggle in which personal animosities were also involved
and the final question of actual supremacy was at issue, but which also
had far-reaching effects upon the system of the foreign policy of the
empire.

Although Bismarck fostered no unfriendly sentiments towards the
young French republic, relations between the two Powers became so
strained in 1875 that war seemed imminent. The ostensible reason
for this tension lay in the French Law of March 13, 1875, by which

the army was to be considerably strengthened, France thus manifesting her fixed intention to build up armaments equivalent to those of Germany. Certain measures adopted by France also appeared in the eyes of the Prussian staff to involve immediate danger to Germany. The subsequent course of events has been frequently described. Certain German diplomats and officers hinted in the course of conversation at the dangerous character of these French preparations; one or two of them used language that might be described as threatening; the officious German press began to publish inflammatory articles, and a leader in the Berlin *Post* in April, 1875, spoke of "war within sight," and took no pains to conceal the source from which it was inspired. The French Government determined to invite the diplomatic intervention of Russia, and, when public opinion in Europe had been thoroughly aroused by an article in the *Times*, Tsar Alexander II appeared with Gorchakóff in Berlin on May 10, 1875, to announce there that peace was assured. Queen Victoria and Lord Derby had taken similar, if less obtrusive, steps. To the French it seemed as if Bismarck had meant to overwhelm them by another war, and that he had only been prevented from so doing by Russian intervention; and certainly Russia, and England too, had made it clear that they would not look on calmly at any fresh humiliation of France. What was the significance of all this from the standpoint of German policy? There is no reasonable doubt that Germany had not the faintest serious purpose of making war; it did not so much as occur to the Emperor to break the peace; and, though a few officers may have shown a bellicose spirit, Bismarck was in no case in favour of a preventive war—a fact now recognised on almost all hands, just as he resisted the leanings of the General Staff in that direction in 1867 and again towards the end of the eighties.

Bismarck's actual intentions can only be judged from his general policy. Presumably his only motive was to make the French think that in certain contingencies he might desire war; probably he meant to warn the newly constituted republic against a policy of armaments and retaliation, and to induce peacefully disposed Frenchmen to set their faces against such tendencies; perhaps, too, the rattling of sabres served the purpose of nipping in the bud any efforts to promote a coalition which might have been facilitated at that time by the *Kulturkampf*, the famous struggle between Church and State then proceeding in Germany. Bismarck's terrorist policy towards France was calculated solely to contribute to the maintenance of peace; but a clever move by the French and one flattering to Gorchakóff's vanity converted a piece of tactical bluff into an apparently serious crisis.

Though official relations between Germany and Russia continued undisturbed, the personal relations of the two Chancellors became

CH. VI.

somewhat strained from that time forward. The Eastern question
soon afterwards cropped up again, reviving the old conflict of interests
between Russia and Austria, and thus disturbing the *entente* of the
three Emperors. At first, only Russia and Austria were involved, but
the third party was thereby confronted with a difficult choice. So early
as the summer of 1876, Tsar Alexander enquired officially in Berlin
whether Germany would remain neutral, if Russia went to war with
Austria over the Eastern question. Bismarck employed all the diplomatic
skill at his command in evading a direct answer to this brutally frank
question; he expressed a friendly feeling for both Powers, and the
distress which a breach between them would cause to him. While
proclaiming in principle the maintenance of neutrality, he made it
perfectly clear at the same time that there was a limit which Russia
would not be allowed to pass in her dealings with Austria without
German intervention—precisely as in the previous year Russia had taken
her stand before Europe for the maintenance of France in her existing
territorial limits. Bismarck's answer was the prelude to the Alliance
of 1879. The consequence was that Russia decided to lead up to her
campaign against Turkey by a different diplomatic road.

During the Russo-Turkish War the Emperor William took a deep
personal interest in the defeats sustained by the Russian army. The
imperial Chancellor, however, absented himself from Berlin during
almost the whole period of the War (April, 1877, to February, 1878),
and obviously wished to avoid any premature pronouncement; he was
determined to observe the strictest neutrality and reserve, and to this
determination he adhered when, after the Treaty of San Stefano, Russia
incurred the risk of war with Great Britain and Austria-Hungary.
Not until Count Shuvaloff had come to terms with Lord Beaconsfield
in London in principle as to the mutual concessions which were necessary
to form the basis of a European Congress did Bismarck express his
willingness that this Congress should be held in Berlin under the
presidency of Germany. But, from the very outset, his one object was
to avoid throwing the weight of German influence at this Congress into
one scale or the other. In his speech in the *Reichstag* of February 19,
1878, he expressed himself to the following effect: "In the mediation
of peace, I do not see why we should arbitrate between divergent
opinions and say: 'It must be thus or thus, and the German empire
supports this side or that'; I rather propose to assume a humbler
rôle, more like that of an honest broker who really means to put the
business through."

And this was the line of action he pursued. The Congress of Berlin
(June 13—July 13, 1878) disclosed a policy of self-denying renunciation
so far as German interests were concerned. While most of the Powers
extended their possessions in the East or had a view to some such

territorial expansion in the future, Germany did not make use of her leading part to secure a share of the spoils for herself, but adhered to her attitude of "satiation" assumed since 1871, and confined herself to the task of mediation without ulterior motive. At this Congress (the details of which do not belong to German history), the trend of Bismarck's policy was to pave the way in European opinion for the relinquishment by Russia of some of her conquests, but to oppose any excessive demands on the part of her enemies. Outwardly, the Congress of Berlin, which brought statesmen from every European country to the capital of the new empire, constituted a magnificent acknowledgment of the position of Germany and one of the greatest achievements of Bismarck's policy. How great a contrast it afforded to the Congress of Paris in 1856, to which the representatives of Prussia were grudgingly admitted at the eleventh hour! Nevertheless, the thankless task of mediation was not without its drawbacks for Bismarck, for it led up to a readjustment of the relations between the Powers which he had till then been able to prevent.

Bitter feeling was aroused in Russia at being thus deprived by Europe of part of the spoils of victory, and this soon gave place to a sense of disappointment, resulting in animosity directed, strangely enough, against Germany. The Panslavonic Press, in particular, fostered the notion that Germany, whose rear had been covered in 1866 and 1870–1, had not shown gratitude for these services in the hour of need, that she could have done more for Russia if she had wanted, and that the humiliation of Russia was therefore to be laid at her door. Perhaps this temper was the psychological outcome of the realisation by Russia that, painful as it might be to her pride, she must henceforth cede her leading position on the Continent to Germany. Russian mortification found expression the following year when, during the discussions as to the execution of the provisions of the Treaty of Berlin, the German representatives on the international commission did not advocate in every detail what Russia desired but voted in accordance with the correct interpretation of the terms of peace. The Tsar in an autograph letter to the Emperor William I, under cover of an accusation against the Minister who was said to have failed to keep his promise, conveyed thinly veiled threats of war against Germany, if she adhered to her present policy.

In face of this attempt to reduce Germany to the condition of an unquestioning supporter of Russia's Eastern policy, Bismarck at once determined to ensure the independence of Germany's attitude and at the same time to protect her against any possible attack; this he did with all the more speed, since he was informed that Russia was at the time making advances to France. While the Emperor William, contrary to Bismarck's advice, tried to settle the differences by a personal meeting with the Tsar, his Chancellor went to Gastein and discussed a treaty of alliance with Count Andrássy, who was then at the head of Austro-Hungarian foreign affairs. The conclusion of the Treaty was postponed for weeks, as the Chancellor encountered serious opposition from the Emperor on the subject. William I was now eighty-two years old, and at his age desired no innovations in policy, but held firmly to the Russophil traditions of his House, desiring no agreement with Austria outside the *entente* of the three Emperors. It was only by threatening to resign office that Bismarck wrung from him a tardy consent to this change of attitude.

The Alliance between Germany and Austria was concluded on October 7, 1879, on the following terms. The two Powers undertook to assist each other with their entire forces in the event of an attack by Russia on either of them; if either of the high contracting parties were attacked by another Power, it was stipulated that the other must give no assistance to the assailant and must at least observe a friendly neutrality towards the ally so attacked; but, if the assailant should be supported by Russia " whether in the way of active cooperation or by military measures threatening the assailed Power," then the obligation of assistance at once operated in full force. This Treaty, which was kept secret until 1887, was solely defensive in character, as its terms clearly indicate. In particular, it implied no breach with Russia: the Emperor William at once communicated the terms of the treaty to the Tsar; and Bismarck thenceforth made every effort to renew friendly relations with St Petersburg. Bismarck had not succeeded in securing any stipulation with Austria for assistance in case of a French attack on Germany; but, as he felt strong enough to resist any such attack single-handed, he was satisfied to have made an Austro-French combination an impossibility and to have ensured the help of Austria against any concerted action by Russia and France; moreover, he was already contemplating the possibility of drawing Italy into the alliance.

It was not without some misgivings that Bismarck carried out his change of front in 1879; to the last, he would have preferred the greater security of an alliance between the three empires. Why, it may be asked, when confronted with the choice between the two Powers, did he not prefer Russia, which was materially the stronger, and equally willing to enter into an alliance? Because he knew that, in a Russo-German alliance, Russia would have had the best of the bargain and would have made use of the German army to cover her rear in a policy of military expansion; and he feared that, in these circumstances, Germany would have to bear the brunt of a coalition between Austria and the Western Powers. The stronger of the two possible allies would have hampered the free play of German policy to a far greater extent, and any counter-move on the part of France or Austria ior bringing about a hostile combination would have found Germany in a position of dangerous dependence on Russia.

In this Alliance a firm basis was created for the foreign relations of the German empire, and the main lines of Bismarck's policy have not been abandoned from that day to this. The Alliance met with unanimous approval from all parties in Germany, Conservatives, Liberals, and Clericals alike, different as might be the special reasons in each case; it also found acceptance with dynasties like Bavaria and Saxony, which had long been associated by traditional friendship with the House of Habsburg. The whole nation shared the conviction that at length the breach was healed which the War of 1866 had created between the States then joined in the German confederation. Bismarck had seen that, considering the large German element in the population of the Austro-Hungarian monarchy, an alliance with Russia against Austria would have been a moral impossibility for the young German empire. Though a link which had once been embodied in the Constitution of the empire had only been reforged in international form, yet the alliance of 1879, which closes the second period of the empire's foreign policy, was none the less the essential complement to Bismarck's solution of the German problem in 1866. Not only did it correspond to the necessity of the two mid-European monarchies, which had been thrown back on each other for support by the current of events, but at the same time it satisfied the national leanings of the two peoples (at any rate of Germans and German-Austrians), for whom this alliance bore an entirely different character from all other alliances.

The home policy of the empire during its first period (1871–7) was in the main determined by the configuration of parties within the *Reichstag*. There were at that time no great historic parties; these only grew up in course of time out of the separate States within the federal union, and the earliest political conflicts were largely the result of the preliminary struggles for constituting the empire; conflicting economic interests operated to a less extent in the first instance. Among the 382 deputies (397 with the addition in 1874 of those from Alsace-Lorraine), the Conservatives, Bismarck's former partisans, were but poorly represented (54 seats in 1871, 21 in 1874, 40 in 1877); they had little sympathy with the new turn of affairs and the abolition of many of their favourite institutions; in fact, they were Prussians rather than Germans. They were at that time without leaders of any eminence and were at first heartily opposed to the parliamentary system. The Free Conservatives or German Imperialists (with 38 seats in 1871, 33 in 1874, 38 in 1877) took a greater interest in the empire and were more adaptable; they tended more and more to support the Ministry and were personally devoted to Bismarck.

The Liberals, on the other hand, though their tactics might differ, were one and all determined on principle that the parliamentary system, which had as yet only received its external form and outline, should attain thorough and complete realisation.   Here also there was a cleavage into two groups.   The National Liberals were the stronger; on them had fallen the succession and traditions of the *Erbkaiserpartei* (Hereditary Emperor party) of 1848–9 and of the *Nationalverein* (National Union) of 1859; they were imbued with a deep sense of national unity, and were at the same time Liberals who had learnt practical wisdom in the school of experience, who wanted, as it were, to graft the old political ideals of the Prussian monarchy on to the new parliamentarian doctrine.   Towards Bismarck they adopted a policy of opportunism.   They were the dominant party in the first three periods of the *Reichstag* (with 120 seats in 1871, 145 in 1874, 128 in 1877), representing almost all parts of Germany equally and also a large proportion of the German intellectuals.   The most important of their leaders were: Rudolf von Bennigsen, President of the *Nationalverein*, 1859–66; Johannes Miquel, Prussian Minister of Finance, 1890–1901, both Hanoverians; two Prussians, Max von Forckenbeck, Chief Burgomaster of Berlin, and Eduard Lasker, a clear-headed Jewish lawyer whose cogent reasoning often carried the day in debates, and a Bavarian, Franz von Stauffenberg; the two national historians, Heinrich von Sybel, and Heinrich von Treitschke, also belonged to this party. The left wing of the Liberals, the *Fortschrittspartei* (party of Progress), with 45 seats in 1871, 49 in 1874, 34 in 1877, remained for the most part in theoretical opposition to the Government and long perpetuated opinions which had taken form in the days of the inner Prussian conflict.   It still included Liberal veterans like Schulze-Delitzsch, founder of the German Societies for mutual assistance (*Genossenschaften mit Selbsthilfe*); and, on the death of Freiherr von Hoverbeck, an East Prussian, the leadership passed to Eugen Richter, a party organiser and debater of an exceptional order, but possessed of less talent for practical politics.

The most peculiar party was the Centre, which, though its name committed it to no definite attitude or policy, was in reality the political organisation of the extreme Catholics and Ultramontanes.   It embodied the *Grossdeutschen* (the party of Greater Germany), who had suffered defeat in 1866, and to whom the exclusion of Austria and the elevation of the Protestant Hohenzollern to the imperial throne were alike distasteful.   They felt themselves now reduced to a minority—according to the census of 1905 the population of the German empire is 62·08 per cent. Protestant and 36·44 per cent. Catholic; but they were determined to organise this minority solidly and make it the basis of a party, the Prussian elements of which (the Rhinelands, Westphalia, and Silesia) were considerably strengthened by the accession of the South Germans, in particular of the Bavarians.

The Centre was federalist, to some extent even particularist in its tenets, in utter contrast to the National Liberals with their Unionist aims and objects. Combining as it did conservative with democratic elements, it hovered between two extremes of policy, at one time presenting itself as the surest bulwark of the throne, at another combining with the *Fortschrittspartei* to champion the parliamentary rights of the people. It possessed solid support in the organisation of the Catholic hierarchy and the whole body of Catholic societies. Of its leaders, Ludwig Windthorst, formerly Hanoverian Minister of Justice, gradually became the most influential personality, dominating the brothers Reichensperger and Heinrich von Mallinckrodt, all three Rhinelanders, and Freiherr von Schorlemer, a Westphalian; Windthorst was unquestionably the most skilful tactician of the Parliament. The Centre increased from 58 seats in the election of 1871 to nearly 100 in 1874, which number has been regularly maintained since. Its hostile attitude towards the Government was intensified by the fact that the uncompromising Guelfs of Hanover, despite their Protestant persuasions, received support from the Centre through the mediation of Windthorst; moreover, the Polish deputies and some of those from Alsace-Lorraine sought to establish sympathetic relations with this party. With these further groups, which were in part openly hostile to the empire, the Centre soon commanded some 130 votes in the *Reichstag*, fully one-third, that is to say, of the total number, and, like the Irish Nationalists in the English Parliament, it could throw this weight now into one scale, now into the other, and make terms for its support.

Of the remaining groups, the Social-democrats alone deserve mention; they held only two seats in 1871 and twelve in 1877.

During the first seven years of the empire, its home policy (also that of Prussia) was determined by Bismarck's attempt to break up the Centre, whose continuance he considered fatal to the future welfare of the empire; in this struggle he was obliged to rely in the first instance on the support of the National Liberals, both in the empire and in Prussia. The characteristic note of this period is to be found in the "*Kulturkampf*" and Liberal legislation.

The *Kulturkampf* had its root in the deep-seated unrest then permeating the Catholic Church. The Declaration of Infallibility, made at the Council of the Vatican, aroused the gravest scruples in many German Catholics. The German Bishops, though at heart opposed to the new dogma, had ended by submitting to it outwardly; but a large number of Catholic professors and priests protested on religious grounds, among them Ignaz von Döllinger of Munich, the greatest scholar among the adherents of German Catholicism.   Their protest led to the formation of Old Catholic communions which repudiated the Vatican; and, when at the first congress in Munich on September 22, 1871, 300 Old Catholic communions were represented, it seemed as though the new movement had a great future in Germany. What line was the State to take, if Old Catholic professors and clergy came into conflict with the Roman Church and appealed for help, or if Ultramontane pretensions provoked a fresh struggle between Church and State?

The leading German Ultramontanes doubtless contrived the formation of the Centre party in order to tide themselves over their internal confusion by means of this external organisation, and so that they might constantly impress upon their adherents the necessity of being on their guard as a confessional minority against aggressive action by the State and the Protestants; nothing would more effectively restore order in their ranks than a fresh outbreak of hostility between Church and State.   Bismarck, on the contrary, looked upon the Centre, which was, in its political essence, a force of Opposition, as a religious party up in arms against the State; its alliance with the Guelfs, and still more that with the Poles, decided him to take the offensive.   The political conflict, which was inevitable from the very nature of the case, was waged not so much in the empire as in the individual States to whose jurisdiction ecclesiastical affairs belonged.   On the motion of the Bavarian Government, the so-called *Kanzelparagraph* (pulpit paragraph) was adopted in the *Reichstag*, penalising the discussion of public matters in sermons in a manner dangerous to the peace.   The final pretext for the struggle was afforded by the Pope's refusal to receive Cardinal Gustav Hohenlohe (brother of the subsequent Chancellor) whom Bismarck had intended to accredit as German ambassador to the papal Curia.   It was on this occasion, May 14, 1872, that he uttered the famous words, "To Canossa we shall not go, either in the flesh or in the spirit."   An Act was passed immediately afterwards excluding the Jesuits and all kindred Orders from the empire.

In Prussia it was chiefly after the appointment of Adalbert Falk as *Kultusminister* (Minister of ecclesiastical affairs and public instruction) that the struggle began over the line of demarcation between State and Church.   Between the years 1873 and 1875, a series of laws was passed which were intended to increase the influence of the State and the German nation upon the life of the Catholic Church and to put an end to all encroachments on the political and social sphere by the Church.   The first "May Laws" (*Maigesetze*) of 1873 forbade public excommunication, instituted a public Court of laymen to decide appeals from ecclesiastical decisions, required that theological students should take a three years' university course and pass a state examination in general knowledge, ordered state inspection of seminaries for priests, and established compulsory notification of church appointments and state veto of the same. In order to cope with the passive resistance of the Catholic clergy aroused by these drastic measures, the May Laws of 1874 made it a punishable offence to omit notification and provided for the administration of vacant bishoprics.

By the Bull *Quod nunquam* Pope Pius IX pronounced this legislation by the State in affairs of the Church to be null and void, whereupon the struggle reached its height in the May Laws of 1875. An Act regulating the suspension of temporalities (" *Sperrgesetz* ") empowered the State to stop payments to the Catholic Church and her ministers, and a convent law suppressed the establishments of all religious Orders except those which undertook the care of the sick.

The more fiercely the *Kulturkampf* raged, the keener was the attack made by the Centre under Windthorst's leadership upon Bismarck's foreign policy, in particular on the friendly relations of the empire towards Italy. In the Arnim affair the Catholics showed decided sympathies in favour of the restoration of the monarchy in France, condemned Bismarck's action, and took sides with his opponent. In the course of the *Kulturkampf*, moreover, the State was obliged to resort to action by the police and in the Courts of law, and the Chancellor was gradually impelled to take steps which put him in the wrong morally in the eyes of large Catholic circles. The Bishops who had been imprisoned for violation of the May Laws were regarded by the faithful as martyrs, victims of another Diocletian, persecutor of the Christians. The number of obedient " State Catholics " (*Staatskatholiken*) remained small, and the Centre united its adherents into an ever firmer phalanx. The Prussian Conservatives, who chiefly represented the orthodox Lutherans, looked askance at the *Kulturkampf*; their distaste increasing as time went on; and the Court, including even the Empress Augusta, condemned it openly. Bismarck's breach with the Conservative party led to his temporary relinquishment in 1872 of the Presidency of the Prussian Council, which he made over to his old comrade von Roon, Minister of War. After the excessively malicious and calumniatory attacks of the *Kreuzzeitung* upon the Chancellor in 1876, the connexion between Bismarck and the party from whose ranks he had risen seemed completely severed.

In these circumstances, the Government in the empire and in Prussia was driven to rely, during the first seven years of the new imperial administration, mainly upon the parliamentary support of the National Liberals, and in this period the consolidation of the empire was achieved on moderate Liberal lines. Bismarck (who still held aloof from economic questions) had as his principal colleague Delbrück, President of the office of the imperial Chancellor, who, like his friend Camphausen, Prussian Minister of Finance, firmly adhered to the principles of Liberal economic policy at home and abroad. The first problem was to build up the economic unity of the empire. The metric system of weights and measures had been already introduced by the Customs Parliament (*Zollparlament*), and in 1873 a uniform monetary system was adopted for the whole empire, namely that of the *mark* as the unit of a currency based on the gold standard : also, in 1876, the *Reichsbank* (Imperial Bank) took the place of the Prussian Bank as the central institution of Germany for exchange, finance, and the issue of notes. Free Trade was made the principle of foreign economic relations, the last protective duties being removed on December 31, 1876.

At the same time the administration of law and justice was unified throughout the empire. Hitherto, the most confusing diversity had prevailed, particularly in civil law ; in the old Prussian provinces the Prussian code (*Preussisches Landrecht*) held good, in other large areas of Germany the common (that is, Roman) law, on the left bank of the Rhine the *Code Napoléon*, and in Baden and Saxony special codes. In 1870 a general penal code had been drawn up, and in 1873, despite the opposition of the particular States, whose judicial supremacy was at stake, the *Reichstag* determined to extend the jurisdiction of the empire to the whole range of civil law, to legal procedure in civil and criminal cases, and to the organisation of justice. The Acts passed in 1876 concerning civil and penal proceedings and the organisation of justice took effect on October 1, 1879 ; the supreme Court of appeal, the *Reichsgericht* (Imperial Court), was shifted to Leipzig, with a view to its absolute independence of the political power at Berlin, despite Bismarck's opposition—this is one of the few instances in which Prussia was outvoted in the Federal Council (*Bundesrat*). A much longer time had to elapse before the *Reichstag*, after most careful preparation, was able to issue, in 1896, the civil code (*Bürgerliches Gesetzbuch*), which came into force on January 1, 1900, and created legal uniformity within the nation such as had never heretofore obtained.

Several of these laws, it is true, were only passed by means of a compromise between the views of the Government and the wishes of the Liberals ; but the question of legislating in regard to the military equipment of the empire led to the very verge of conflict in 1874. The King and the army authorities would have preferred to see the discussion of military expenditure in Parliament restricted, and aimed at getting supplies voted once for all, by a perpetual law (*Aeternat*) ; while the Liberals, in accordance with constitutional doctrine and practice, wished these grants to be submitted with the rest for annual settlement in the budget. A middle course was at that time adopted, the *Reichstag* regulating the effective force of the army and voting supplies for seven years (*Septennat*). This compromise was, in the main, adhered to in the subsequent renewals of the vote, in 1880 and 1887.

The most difficult problem awaiting solution was that of establishing the financial independence of the empire, which hitherto had levied no separate revenue, but had received from the separate States contributions proportionate to their population (*Matrikularbeiträge*). The most delicate and important political points were involved in the settlement of imperial finance : the respective jurisdictions of the empire and of the individual States had to be defined, and institutions developed either on a more centralised or on a more federalistic basis; in this connexion arose the question of transforming the imperial Chancellor's office into a Cabinet of Ministers by the creation of imperial Ministries, which would be an initial step in the direction of reconstituting the empire as a parliamentary State. Finally, the necessity for a separate system of imperial taxation and revenue raised the question whether the existing Free Trade system should be retained and a few taxes for revenue purposes deemed to meet the case, or whether the protective system long demanded from various quarters should be adopted. Bismarck made an attempt to decide these questions with the help of those who had hitherto been his parliamentary allies, and during 1877 treated on several occasions with Bennigsen, leader of the National Liberals, as to his joining the Ministry. When the negotiations between Bismarck and Bennigsen failed, in December, 1877, the Liberal era was doomed, and a new epoch in imperial policy began to dawn.

(2)

THE TRIPLE ALLIANCE AND THE CULMINATING PERIOD OF BISMARCK'S ASCENDANCY.

The apparently sudden change manifested in the course of 1877 was in reality the outcome of long reflexion on Bismarck's part. He had begun to doubt the economic advantages of Free Trade ; the retirement of Delbrück in 1876 was the first indication that the Chancellor's convictions were altering ; the critical condition of the iron industry showed him that in this direction Free Trade was benefiting the foreigner, and he was still more troubled by the fact that agriculture, especially the corn production of the large estates in the eastern provinces, was paying worse and worse in consequence of the importation of Russian corn. His position was very little removed from that of the German-Conservative party, as newly constituted on the basis of the agricultural interest. He was, therefore, the less inclined to see the authority of the Crown and his own great power limited by the parliamentary claims of the Liberals, who to a large extent adhered to Free Trade. Moreover, whatever might be Bismarck's leanings, the old Emperor, a stauncher Conservative than ever at the age of eighty, would not hear of anything approaching a parliamentary *régime,* but demanded a stronger resistance to the rising tide of radicalism.

Thus, after the failure of his negotiations at Varzin, Bismarck began slowly to put about the helm of the ship of State. On the death of Pope Pius IX a few weeks later (February, 1878), he at once recognised the possibility of making peace with the new Pope, Leo XIII, cutting short the *Kulturkampf,* and carrying his new policy with the help of a readjustment of parties. The crisis was hastened in the summer of 1878 by the culpable excesses of Radicalism, and Bismarck determined to open the attack on Social-democracy.

The Social-democratic party had then existed in Germany for just a decade and a half. It had its roots on the one hand in the socialistic theories of western Europe and on the other in the democratic republicanism of 1848, which, though almost extinct in the middle classes, had gained fresh ground among the working people. The leading thinker of this party was Karl Marx, a Rhinelander, who, with his friend Friedrich Engels had published in 1848 the "Communist Manifesto" (*Kommunistisches Manifest*), setting forth the special features of his materialistic view of history and of his socialistic programme, and who during his ten years' exile in London became the head of the "International." In 1867, he had written the first volume of *Das Capital,* a

masterpiece in dialectics, which was thenceforward the book of the law for his adherents. Independently of this, Ferdinand Lassalle, a demagogue of brilliant talents, had in 1863–4 made the first attempt at a political organisation of the working classes by the foundation of the Universal German Working Men's Association (*Deutscher allgemeiner Arbeiterverein*). Between Lassalle's followers and the Marxists, whose leaders in the *Reichstag* were Bebel and Liebknecht, there had at first been the deadliest enmity; but, in 1875, at a congress in Gotha, they combined into a single party, which in the *Reichstag* elections of 1877 secured nearly half a million votes and won twelve seats.

Such were the beginnings of a movement in which the rapidly growing working classes took up arms for their own legitimate social interests against capital, and soon attained to consciousness of their political power. This class movement, however, was permeated with the violent revolutionary spirit of its leaders, and excited the masses to a pitch of exasperation which Bismarck regarded as a grave danger for the empire, then in process of internal consolidation. Though not a direct outcome of the Social-democratic agitation, it was an indirect consequence of the demoralisation caused by it in unscrupulous minds, that, in May and June, 1878, the Emperor's life was twice attempted by men of criminal type who had come in contact with the agitation. On the second occasion—at the time when the Berlin Congress was assembling—the old Emperor was dangerously wounded by a quantity of small shot.

These murderous attempts, which aroused tremendous excitement in the German nation, afforded Bismarck an unexpected opportunity, not only of dealing a severe blow at social-democracy itself, but at the same time of settling accounts with the Liberals.

After the first crime, Bismarck introduced the draft of a Bill for an exceptional law directed against social-democracy, but the *Reichstag* rejected it by a large majority; after the second crime, he dissolved it with the undisguised object of wrecking the National Liberal party hitherto in the ascendant, or else bringing it to heel, in the election which was to take place amid the immense excitement then prevailing. The new *Reichstag* could not do otherwise than assent, in October, 1878, to a Socialists Act (*Socialistengesetz*) prohibiting and heavily penalising the organisation, societies, meetings, and Press of Social-democracy. The Law was passed to cover a period of two and a half years and was reenacted in 1880 and twice subsequently.

During the first years of its enforcement, Social-democracy was materially weakened by the almost wholesale destruction of its external organisation, though the Act could not lastingly impair its internal vitality. An immense feeling of resentment gathered among the masses

CH. VI.

thus deprived of their rights, while the authorised deportation of dangerous persons simply contributed to the geographical expansion of the party. On the expiration of the Act on September 30, 1890, in the year of Bismarck's resignation, it became evident that the growth of the party had not been prevented by these measures, but merely retarded for the time being. Though Bismarck resorted to violent repression of the purely political aims of the Social-democrats, or rather of their revolutionary nucleus, he resolved at the same time to deal with what lay at the root of their legitimate social demands by undertaking extensive legislation for the state protection of the economically weak; the programme of this was announced in the Emperor's message at the opening of the *Reichstag* in 1881.

It was in these stormy times that the various parties in the *Reichstag* in 1879 approached the long premeditated financial and economic legislation with which Bismarck now introduced the second great era of his imperial policy at home. With the tariff of 1879, the German empire left the ranks of the Free Trade States and joined those of the protectionists. Under the new tariff, agriculture, on the one hand, was protected by an import duty on foreign corn, which, though low at first, was afterwards materially increased; while, on the other, manufactures were protected by import duties on foreign goods; at the same time, the duties constituted an important source of revenue for the empire.

Henceforth, it became the guiding principle of Bismarck and his successors in their economic policy to further the interests of agriculture and manufacture, the two most extensive branches of production in Germany, by means of state protection and provision. Naturally, economic considerations began to be involved to a greater extent in the general policy of the empire and to affect the character of parties, which had hitherto been based on constitutional divergences. The initial move towards a new constellation of parties was made when the customs tariff was adopted in the *Reichstag* by an unusual majority, composed of Conservative and Centre, with whom only a few National Liberals were associated. The first result was a split in the National Liberal party in the following year, on account of economic differences; the right wing, which retained the name, became a moderate party, while the left wing, the seceders, drew ever closer to the Opposition till in 1884 they united with the *Fortschrittspartei* (party of Progress) under the name of *Deutschfreisinnige Partei* (party of German supporters of freedom). The ultimate consequence was that Liberalism, torn by internal disunion, was unable to retain or regain its earlier dominance.

The Centre, on the other hand, which had for the first time taken an active part in legislation in connexion with this tariff question, began to move into the position vacated by the Liberals. They became the most powerful single party in the *Reichstag*, and used their power to secure their individual ends. Bismarck was only able to win their cooperation by the repeal, between 1880 and 1886, of most of the Prussian Church Laws passed during the *Kulturkampf*. Although he had tried during the seventies to wreck the ecclesiastical party organisation of the Centre and to increase the power of the State over the Church, he was now obliged to sound a retreat from most of the positions then taken up. The journey to Canossa was made easy and undramatic; but it nevertheless took place. A considerable effect was also produced on constitutional development by this shifting of the balance of power. Within the empire Liberal tendencies towards centralisation under parliamentary supremacy were abandoned; the further development of imperial institutions proceeded rather on the federalistic lines specially advocated by the Centre.

The new era in Bismarck's home policy was to be marked, during the eighties, by a fresh series of great constructive measures.

The message from the Throne of November 17, 1881, declared that the cure for social evils was not to be sought solely in repression, but equally in the promotion of the workers' wellbeing, and announced the insurance of workmen against accident, the establishment of sick-funds, and insurance against old age and incapacity to earn a livelihood. These initial steps in social legislation showed a complete break with the view as to the action of the State held by the Manchester School and with the maxim of *laisser-aller*; at the same time, they implied a return to the political conceptions of the kingdom of Prussia in the eighteenth century and to the ideas of Kant and Hegel as to the moral obligation of the State.

For some years, German economists like Wagner, Schäffle, and Schmoller had been moulding these ideas and preparing public opinion, heedless of the sobriquet *Kathedersozialisten* ("socialists of the professorial chair") applied to them. Similar tendencies were making themselves felt among the parties of the Right, in the Centre, and among the Conservative "Christian Socialists" under the demagogic leadership of the Court-preacher Stöcker, who became also a leader of the Antisemitic party; the scientific theorists were also joined by practical men in the Prussian civil service, like Bötticher, Bosse, and Lohmann. But, in order to carry through the whole of this new legislation, in the face of opposition based on principle and opposition prompted by pocket interest, there was needed the dominating personality of Bismarck, who in 1880 had taken over the Ministry of Commerce also; without him, the reforms might have stopped short after a few futile attempts, or might only have been accomplished after decades of effort. In 1883, the Law with respect to insurance against illness was passed, in 1884 that with respect to insurance against accident, and in 1889, by a narrow majority, the Law concerning insurance against old age and incapacity, which came into force on January 1, 1891.

This legislation has in its social operation produced inestimable benefits. The protective legislation of Bismarck, while preserving the agricultural industry from destruction, had hastened the industrial development of Germany. The more rapid the transformation of Germany into an industrial State, the more urgent it became to remedy the abuses consequent upon the transition. A few figures will show what has been achieved in this direction. In 1907, the number of those insured against illness in the German empire amounted to thirteen millions, those insured against accident to twenty millions, those insured against incapacity to fifteen millions. The amount of compensation paid in all three branches of insurance was, in 1907, 626 million marks (£31,300,000), the total sum for the years 1885–1907 being 6310 million marks (£315,500,000). In recent years the empire has contributed to insurance against incapacity, on an average, fifty million marks (£2,500,000), the state contributions for the years 1891–1905 amounting altogether to 485 million marks (£24,250,000); the capital of the state insurance agencies was, in 1907, 1500 million marks (£75,000,000).

The first task of the immediate future will probably be a simplification of the bureaucratic machinery; next will come the extension of insurance to widows and orphans, perhaps even to cases of unmerited unemployment. Though at first many were keenly adverse to these dangerous experiments in state socialism, all opposition has since died down; indeed, the German system is being adopted more and more as a model by most other Powers. These measures did not, however, produce the political effect which Bismarck had at the same time contemplated, for he had hoped by such means to cut the ground from under the feet of the Social-democratic agitators. It is probable, however, that they mitigated the keenness of social discontent, and facilitated the maintenance and extension of the protective policy.

The economic policy of the eighties had also a predominantly positive side. In the first place, complete tariff uniformity was achieved, the Hanse Towns having hitherto held aloof. It was only after violent opposition that the cities of Hamburg and Bremen agreed to their inclusion in the customs area, which took effect on October 1, 1888; though a separate free port district, for the storage in bond of foreign imports, was excepted in each town. The shipping trade, especially that of Hamburg, began to increase enormously from this time, and the scruples at first entertained by the Hanseatic merchants were thus allayed.

But the most important result of state intervention in private

undertakings was that achieved in railway policy. Bismarck's original idea had been to establish a system of imperial railways through the purchase by the empire of all private lines and the transfer to it of the railways belonging to the separate States; by this means he intended to secure on the one hand a certain and increasing source of imperial income, on the other the centralised control of the whole railway service, as in the case of the postal and telegraphic service. This scheme having been wrecked by the separatist tendencies of the individual States and by Delbrück's opposition, he limited his original programme to the acquisition by the Prussian State of the private railways of Prussia, which was accomplished by the skill of Maybach, Prussian Minister of Public Works. The same tendency in economic policy, the deliberate fostering of profitable industrial enterprise by public initiative, showed itself further in the subventions granted by the State to transmarine steamship lines, and finally in the initiation of a German colonial policy, which will be referred to in connexion with foreign policy. Bismarck also planned the introduction of a state monopoly on tobacco, which was to furnish a permanent internal source of revenue for the empire; but this he did not succeed in carrying through the *Reichstag*.

On the whole, then, the eighties saw an unmistakable strengthening of conservative elements and the forces of authority in political life; the moneyed classes, whose interests had been powerfully advanced both in agriculture and industry by the new protective duties, became the bulwarks of the policy of that era. In the eyes of many, Bismarck appeared to have reverted to the ideals of his earlier days. One section of the Liberals, the National Liberals, chiefly influenced by Miquel, changed more or less with Bismarck, whose masterful personality, with its ever growing authority, seemed to exercise an irresistible attraction. But the Chancellor's new policy was all the more keenly opposed by the Liberal left wing, which in 1884 united the members of the old *Fortschrittspartei* and of the Secession under the designation of the *Deutschfreisinnige Partei*. The new party calculated too openly upon the approaching change of monarch, and under Eugen Richter's leadership rushed wildly into a passionate and personal hostility towards Bismarck, and an opposition devoid of all constructive ideas. In the elections of 1887, however, Bismarck succeeded in uniting both groups of Conservatives and the National Liberals by means of an election agreement ("*Kartell*"), thereby securing a majority of implicitly loyal followers in the *Reichstag*. It was just such a balance of parties which had been his great aim and object from the very outset.

During the last decade of his government Bismarck's personality had increasingly dominated the home policy of the empire; meanwhile, that epoch in his foreign policy was dawning in which his influence on European destinies reached its zenith. Those were the years which even a foreign observer like M. Seignobos, a Frenchman, has characterised as the period of the German hegemony ; this statement must, at the same time, not be taken to imply that the power wielded was extended and used to the utmost as in the case of Napoleon I, but simply that Germany found herself the centre of the ruling constellation of the Great Powers, without, however, utilising her position otherwise than for the maintenance of peace and the development of her resources and alliances.

In the first instance, in May, 1882, the Chancellor supplemented the alliance with Austria-Hungary, which had formed the bedrock of his policy since 1879, by the long premeditated alliance with the kingdom of Italy. Italy had returned empty-handed from the Congress of Berlin, saw herself outflanked by France in Tunis, and felt the need of abandoning her complete isolation. By means of this alliance a solid block of Powers was set up in central Europe, which presented an insuperable barrier to the bare possibility of a union of forces between Russia and France. The two Powers which, so late as the summer of 1870, had been on the point of attacking Prussia as allies of Napoleon III were now united with the German empire in an alliance directed—solely on the defensive—against France.

The Triple Alliance was at first concluded for five years, but was destined to become one of the most durable agreements of modern history; in 1887, it was renewed for another five years, and in 1891, and again in 1902, it was extended for a term of twelve years. The character and stability of the Triple Alliance have unquestionably suffered certain modifications within the present generation, and some of its terms have been altered; beyond doubt, also, the centre of gravity within the Alliance in Bismarck's time lay more decidedly in Berlin than was the case later; nevertheless, it cannot be denied that the newly formed combination had from the first an eminently peaceable character, which it shared with the foreign policy of the empire since 1871, and that it thus made strongly for continuity in European politics.

In any appreciation of the Triple Alliance and its significance for German policy during this first decade, two facts should be borne in mind. In the first place, Bismarck was firmly resolved from the outset, in spite of the agreement with Austria-Hungary and Italy, to maintain the friendly relations with Russia. He did not intend, as he expressed it, to have the wire to St Petersburg cut ("*den Draht nach Petersburg abreissen zu lassen*"). Success crowned his efforts when, at a meeting of the three Emperors at Skiernewicze in September, 1884, he was able to obtain a renewal of the old understanding and also an agreement with Russia for mutual friendly neutrality in the event of either Power being attacked by a third. In the second place, the inclusion of Italy in the Triple Alliance was a step regarded with anything but disfavour by England as a Mediterranean Power, since England had just then fallen out seriously with France about the Egyptian question. Considering these interrelations, it may perhaps be said that Bismarck had by this unforeseen combination caused most European Powers to fix the orientation of their policy by reference to Berlin. And it is one of the strongest proofs of the peaceable character of his policy as a whole that the position thus secured, which amounted almost to a hegemony and precluded all possibility of French reprisals, was not utilised by him to exert any undue pressure on France in her isolation, or to check in any way her assertion of her power in the world. On the contrary, he endeavoured during these years to prove that if France would only give up "staring as if hypnotised into the gap in the Vosges" and live at peace with her neighbour on the lines of the Treaty of Frankfort, she could reckon on the loyal friendship of the German empire in the outside world. Hence, Bismarck everywhere backed the colonial policy which the French Minister Jules Ferry inaugurated on a large scale in Africa and Asia between 1883 and 1885; and, for a moment at any rate, it looked as if the breach created by the events of 1870–1 would be healed in this way.

After Bismarck had secured the strongest possible guarantees for the maintenance of the position of Germany in Europe, the first moves outside the Continent were made, and the empire embarked on its colonial policy. One consequence of the former political disintegration of Germany was that, despite considerable emigration in the seventeenth and eighteenth centuries, the Germans had remained a purely continental people; like Schiller's poet, they had come on the scene too late when the world was already parcelled out, and even in 1871 there were but few to whom it occurred to demand the cession by France of her possessions in Further India. When, however, the empire had been founded, it was natural that a strong nation conscious of itself should resolve on an attempt to retrieve the omissions of the past, so far as might be, at the eleventh hour. From the close of the seventies there was a movement in Germany—at first purely academic— in favour of acquiring colonies, mainly in order to open up to the stream of emigrants some territory where they would not, as in the past, be entirely lost to the German nation—in the twenty years from 1866 to 1885 the United States alone had admitted over two million Germans. But there was a further incentive to the formation in 1882 of the German Colonial Association (*Deutscher Kolonialverein*). The universal enthusiasm for colonial exploration and conquest on African soil which possessed men at this time, especially since Stanley's discoveries and the colonisation schemes of King Leopold of Belgium, necessarily reacted on the Germans. The partition of Mohammadan North Africa had been proceeding since the Congress of Berlin, and the time seemed also ripe for a division of the entire Dark Continent among the European nations. In view of the newly awakened antagonisms among the other Powers, in connexion with their colonial policy, Bismarck thought the moment not unpropitious for Germany, if she were to resolve to make a bid for a share in the process of partition.

Thus the colonial policy of the empire was the outcome of no conscious, formulated plan, but sprang rather from the chance of the moment and the favourable position of affairs; the object of Bismarck was not so much to provide colonies for emigration as to open up new regions to German trade. There had been a prelude to this policy at the close of the seventies in the abortive effort to interest the empire in Samoa, and likewise in the contemporaneous Treaties of commerce and amity in the South Seas, which renounced all projects of acquiring land for colonisation and confined themselves to the object of founding naval stations. Then, in 1881, the idea of the subvention of steamship lines was first mooted, which gave rise in April, 1884, to a Bill for the state assistance of steamer communication with Eastern Asia and Australia. The discussion of this Bill, which did not pass till 1885, marks the beginning of the official colonial policy of the German empire.

The decisive step was taken on April 24, 1884, when the empire extended its protection to the settlement made by Lüderitz, a Bremen trader, on the coast of Angra Pequeña in South-west Africa; Bismarck promised the protection asked for, and gained his point in face of the objection raised by England. The occupation of Togo and the Cameroons followed immediately on the direct initiative of the German empire, men-of-war being despatched thither and an imperial commissioner, Dr Nachtigal, the African traveller. The acquisition of German East Africa was due, in the first place, to the private enterprise of certain bold discoverers like Peters, Count Pfeil, and Jühlke; not till the venture had been crowned by success was any recognition forthcoming from Bismarck, who had maintained an attitude of extreme reserve towards its beginnings. A part of New Guinea and of the adjacent groups of islands was next acquired by means of a joint undertaking of private capital and state subvention. It had been Bismarck's original idea on securing colonies to adopt the English system rather than the French: it was his intention that the trader should go first; the flag should follow in his wake; military and official machinery being dispensed with as far as possible. But it was soon found that individual companies which had received privileges under the protection of the empire were unable to hold their own unaided against native risings, and direct intervention by the State proved necessary, especially in Togo and the Cameroons.

The colonies which Germany had acquired all occupied areas to which no other Power had an indisputable prior claim according to international law. Nevertheless, it was inevitable that public opinion in England should be violently opposed to the course pursued by Germany. The opposition emanated more from the English colonies of Africa and Australia than from the Gladstone Ministry itself; Cape Colony resented the seizure of Angra Pequeña, the Australians the occupation of New Guinea and the Pacific Islands; these Britons beyond the seas would have preferred to oust the troublesome rival from regions which they had long been wont to regard confidently as spheres of future expansion, though they possessed no legitimate title to them. Even the English at home did not at first take Germany's colonial intentions seriously, with the inevitable consequence that, before long, a grave condition of tension was produced between the two countries, upon the details of which Earl Granville's memoirs threw some light a few years ago. That Bismarck nevertheless substantially achieved his end is the more astonishing, if it be remembered that Germany then possessed no fleet to speak of and, in case of need, could have brought no effective force to bear in Africa or Australasia.

It was the international relations of the moment which favoured the policy of Germany, and Bismarck made use of these with consummate skill for attaining his object. England, on her new footing in Egypt, had fallen out with France and was forced to rely on the goodwill of the Triple Alliance; in addition to which she was seriously embroiled with Russia in Afghanistan, so that her hands were full. Moreover, Bismarck had shortly before summoned the Congo Conference in collaboration with France and thereby silenced Germany's sole opponent on non-European questions. Only when, on Ferry's fall, the conciliatory policy towards France proved futile, did Bismarck strike a milder note in the colonial difference with England, and by his son Herbert's mission paved the way for a better understanding and a final settlement. Though at heart no friend of Germany, Gladstone on this occasion seized the proffered hand and called down blessings on Germany's efforts at colonisation; he expressed himself to the effect that England would regard Germany as her friend and ally in the interests of the human race, and would give her every encouragement in her labours for the spread of civilisation.

Thus the transition of Germany to a colonial policy became an accomplished fact. A certain cooperation with England, designated during the ensuing years as the "colonial marriage," was taken for granted. Any profit from German colonies was as yet of course far to seek, and the Germans, like other nations, had to pay heavy premiums on this new departure. Neither did Bismarck allow the colonies to dominate his general policy, which continued to bear chiefly on European affairs.   What, however, the great empire-builder had done was to seize the opportunity of opening up at the last moment a future over seas for his people.

The favourable political situation was destined soon to be disturbed. Since the Bulgarian question had come up in September, 1885, antagonism between Russia and Austria in the East had been reawakened, and, although Bismarck continued to maintain in the matter an attitude friendly to Russia rather than neutral, it sensibly affected the relations between Russia and Germany.   The growth of Panslavic and anti-German movements in Russia, to which Tsar Alexander III allowed freer play than his predecessor, led France, thirsting for revenge on Germany, and instigated by the military adventurer Boulanger, to hold out eager hands for an alliance against the common foe.   Even this danger Bismarck's statesmanship was able to avert.   He soothed the Tsar's grievances and put the finishing touch to his own policy by concluding a fresh agreement with Russia, the " *Rückversicherungsvertrag* " ("Reinsurance Compact")—kept secret even from the members of the Triple Alliance—by which the Skiernewicze settlement was renewed between two at any rate of the imperial Powers.

The inauguration of his Polish policy, involving the expenditure of large sums on the purchase of Polish estates and the settlement of German peasants in the Polish districts of the province of Posen, was intimately bound up with the Russophil policy of Bismarck's last years.

On the other hand, after the elections of February, 1887, which were intensely influenced by the Boulanger episode, he effected a great increase in the army : internally and externally, he was asserting his power.   And thus, although he had to call into play more and more forcible methods of action, the imperial Chancellor maintained to the end his policy of counterpoises, playing off foe against foe and utilising all occasions of mutual animosity among his enemies, and carried the empire, in a position of diplomatic ascendancy, over the double change of sovereign which took place in 1888.

The Hohenzollern dynasty and Bismarck had become indissolubly linked together in the course of a quarter of a century.   It would be difficult to find another instance of such a relation existing between a sovereign with the monarchic consciousness of Emperor William I and a Minister with the dominating force of Bismarck.   The Chancellor was no Richelieu, who quite openly cast his royal master in the shade ; rather, he genuinely felt like a Brandenburg vassal towards his margrave, and it was an honest impulse which prompted him to have himself described on his tombstone as a faithful servant of his master.   The

Emperor was far from being blindly amenable to his Chancellor's policy, and, even in 1879, he withstood long and vehemently the change to an Austrian alliance for which the latter was working. During the eighties, it is true, the feeling took root within the sovereign which found expression in that " Never !" once written by him on a letter of resignation from Bismarck, and he acquiesced in all decisions arrived at by the Chancellor. During this long period a friendship had grown up between the two men, which reveals itself in the deep personal note of their correspondence to the last.

But, the closer the tie had become between William and Bismarck, the further the Crown Prince had drifted from the Chancellor during the last ten years. Frederick William still adhered to the Liberalism of the sixties, which his clever consort Victoria, the English Princess Royal, had fostered in him ; he regarded the revolution in home policy effected since 1879 as a disastrous change, and refused to abandon his personal connexion with Bismarck's Liberal opponents. After the heir apparent had won his early laurels in war, all that awaited him was the difficult task of marking time, as it were, till his fifty-eighth year in unsatisfying leisure, remote from affairs and the exercise of any power. And, when at last his turn came, a still harder lot befell him, for he ascended the throne mortally ill.

He was taken with a disease of the throat, which was diagnosed in April, 1887, as probably incipient cancer, and might then have been arrested by the operation already in contemplation. The optimistic view of the English physician Sir Morell Mackenzie, led, however, to the postponement of the operation, and the malignant character of the disease increased until it was too late. In November, 1887, the Crown Prince could only be saved from suffocation by opening the larynx, and all hope of recovery was gone. It looked almost as if the aged father would survive the son. Then, in March, 1888, Emperor William I fell ill and died a few weeks before his ninety-first birthday. All Europe mourned the death of the man who headed the new line of German Emperors, and who had vindicated the monarchic principle worthily before the world.

The Emperor Frederick III, a doomed man, hastened from San Remo through snow and ice to take up the reins of government. He confirmed Bismarck in his offices, at the same time endeavouring to give expression to his divergent views in a proclamation. Some differences of opinion could not fail to arise : Bismarck succeeded in preventing the marriage of Princess Victoria to the former Prince Alexander of Bulgaria, which would have aroused considerable suspicion in Russia ; but he was obliged to give way when the Emperor, in his last days, insisted on the dismissal of the Conservative Minister von Puttkamer for illegal influence exercised in the elections. But the hundred days of Frederick III—he died on June 15, 1888—were a mere episode, though an intensely tragic one. It was significant for the evolution of Germany that this generation and its ideas—the tendencies of National Liberalism, which Frederick III embodied and represented— found no expression in the conduct of state affairs; this tone of feeling and political aspiration, which is, as it were, a complementary colour between the spirit of the generation of the old Emperor and that of his grandson's, left no mark on history, save an example of heroic devotion to duty in the midst of suffering.

(3)

BISMARCK'S FALL, AND AFTER.

(1888–1910.)

The succeeding Emperor, William II, was only twenty-nine years of age and but newly acquainted with affairs of government when he so unexpectedly ascended the throne. All that was known of him was that he had military tastes, and was happy in his marriage with Augusta Victoria of Schleswig-Holstein-Augustenburg; it soon became evident that a man of almost tempestuous energy had taken his stand at the head of the empire. The circumstances which had so suddenly placed him there account for his honest determination to adhere to Bismarck's policy and principles: "the course remains the same." Nevertheless, the characters of the two men account for the fact that in little more than a year William was familiarising himself with the idea of parting with his grandfather's coadjutor.

The grounds of the rupture and of Bismarck's resignation (March 18, 1890) lay of course, when all has been said, in the individuality of the man who attained in virtue of his birth to the supreme power of sovereign, and in that of the man who for nearly a generation had virtually exercised that power. The one was urged forward by the impulsiveness of youth and perhaps, too, by a feeling that the dominant figure of a Minister had too long overshadowed the wearer of the crown; the other, in the ripe experience of his age, felt that he commanded the situation and was indispensable, and the enjoyment of authority had gradually become with him a passion.

Various tangible differences contributed to complete the breach. Bismarck rightly blamed the impetuosity of the young Emperor in foreign affairs, which was disturbing the tranquil continuity of the *status quo.* In home affairs, the Emperor was bent on arousing high hopes by a social policy on a large scale and by convening an international congress, all of which seemed mere Utopian schemes in the practical eyes of Bismarck. When the elections of January, 1890, had destroyed the majority in the *Reichstag* of Bismarck's *Kartell* (group of allied parties), the Chancellor meditated plans for the overthrow of the Opposition, at the risk of a struggle, perhaps of a *coup d'État,* and for the modification of the Constitution, if that were necessary; the young Emperor very naturally shrank from beginning his reign with measures of this sort. The fall of Bismarck was a disaster to the German nation—not so much as regards home policy, in which, as he grew old, he had delayed many necessary

CH. VI.

reforms, and his successors achieved lasting results; but in the sphere of foreign policy his loss was absolutely irreparable. For eight years the vast wealth of his experience, with which that of no living European statesman could compare, lay idle and unserviceable. The catastrophe was above all painful to the nation, for it regarded as a national calamity the disagreement between the sovereign and Bismarck, whose criticisms of the new policy daily became more embittered.

After March, 1890, political decisions no longer hinged upon the will of a leading Minister, but were subject to the " personal rule " of the Emperor—a personal rule which was of course exercised within the limits imposed by the Constitutions of the empire and of Prussia. Also, as time went on, the power of the Crown varied in character and scope. It was greatest during the Chancellorship of Count Caprivi (1890–4), who conceived of his office as demanding the obedience of a Prussian general to the monarch, and, burdened with the heavy task of remodelling the work of Bismarck, followed in whatever new direction the Emperor led. Caprivi's successor, Prince Chlodwig Hohenlohe-Schillingsfürst, who was Chancellor from 1894 to 1900, was able to take a rather more independent stand. He had a long and successful career behind him, as President of the Bavarian Council (1867–70), ambassador in Paris (1874–85), and Governor of Alsace-Lorraine (1885–94); moreover, he was related to the Emperor and therefore had a different personal status, at any rate until old age gradually sapped his energy. The fourth imperial Chancellor, Prince Bernhard von Bülow (1900–9), by his skill in dealing diplomatically with men, was able gradually to regain a large measure of independence in the exercise of his office. On his resignation, he was succeeded by Dr von Bethmann-Hollweg.

Caprivi's tenure of office, which had to bear the mark of contrast to that of Bismarck, was not without its good results, at any rate in home affairs. The introduction of the two years' term of service (for infantry and foot artillery), the accomplishment of the reform of Prussian finance by Miquel, the gifted Minister of Finance, and other acts of the legislature, showed progress. An attempt at legislation for Prussian primary education on conservative and ecclesiastical lines was ultimately checked by the Emperor himself, who yielded to the unanimous opposition of public opinion. Caprivi's economic policy culminated in the conclusion of commercial treaties with Austria-Hungary, Russia, Roumania, and Italy, by which the protective duties on corn were lowered in return for favoured treatment of German exports. These concessions were in part only carried in the teeth of opposition from the Conservative Agrarians, who founded on this occasion, and thenceforward maintained, in the *Bund der Landwirte*

(League of Agriculturists), an organ of growing power for dominating the rural populace and exercising pressure on political parties. Privately countenanced by the ex-Chancellor, who was living at Friedrichsruhe in high displeasure, the Conservative Agrarians became the most violent opponents of his successor.

The new bearing in the foreign policy of the empire was fraught with more important consequences than the deviation from Bismarck's course in home policy. To begin with, relations with Russia became cooler, while a *rapprochement* with England was effected. On July 1, 1890, the imperial Government made a treaty with Great Britain by which the island of Heligoland was ceded to Germany, in return for certain considerable advantages in respect of boundary lines in East Africa. Stanley, the African explorer, observed that England had got a new suit in exchange for a trouser-button; but, though this was clearly going too far, yet German colonial politicians did complain bitterly of their disappointed hopes when all claim to Uganda, Witu, and Zanzibar was forfeited. The island of Heligoland, lying before the mouths of the Elbe and Weser, in the event of war might attain great strategic importance for the defence or attack of the German coast; but its practical value was not at all apparent at first, and the general public therefore supposed that the Treaty—which was first announced on the eve of the seventy-fifth anniversary of Waterloo—signified an absolute change of front in foreign policy.

This impression was of necessity confirmed in Russia, when the German Emperor and his advisers at the same time determined not to fall in with Russia's proposal for a renewal of the secret "reinsurance compact," which expired in 1890. The action of Germany was prompted presumably by political loyalty to Austria, whose relations with Russia were believed to be sorely strained. In addition to this, the Prussian Government abandoned the anti-Polish policy adopted in 1886—there was a time when the Polish members of the *Reichstag*, under the leadership of Koscielski, actually belonged to the Government majority. All these symptoms of a change of attitude aroused the suspicions of the Russian Government, with the result that advances were made to France in the summer of 1891, and finally an alliance was concluded with the republic. The ascendancy of the Triple Alliance was materially restricted by the formation of this Dual Alliance, and France was liberated from that isolation which Bismarck had to the last so rigidly maintained. The German nation inevitably listened with ever closer attention to the keen criticisms of the veteran ex-Chancellor, and popular confidence in the new directors of affairs was shaken.

After Hohenlohe had become Chancellor (October 27, 1894), so far as relations with European Powers were concerned, the policy of

Germany began to revert gradually to the course pursued by Bismarck ; but at the same time greater activity was displayed in pressing German interests outside Europe, and the era of "satiation" was brought to a close in that direction. The somewhat pretentious term "world-policy" (*Weltpolitik*) has been applied to this new development, and its use indicates that Germany has by degrees ceased to regard exclusively the Continent of Europe in framing her foreign policy. These new tendencies are no chance outcome of the personality of a monarch possessed by exuberant schemes of world-conquest, or of the excessive energy of ambitious statesmen, or even of the wild imaginings of small groups of Pangerman enthusiasts without political influence ; rather, they form part of that strong tide of evolution which irresistibly bore the German State out beyond the bounds of its earlier policy. William II's historical significance lies in the fact that he recognised the inevitable betimes, and put forth the whole energy of his temperament and will to impel the empire along the new course.

The explanation of this turn in German policy must be sought, first of all, in the fundamental fact of the yearly increase of German population and the question of food-supply. In the forty years from 1871 to 1910, the population of the German empire has risen from forty-one to sixty-five millions ; in recent years, the surplus of births has been eight to nine hundred thousand annually, and will soon be not far short of a million. Considering that emigration to North America has greatly fallen off since the middle of the eighties, and that the German colonies—some of them tropical and as yet undeveloped—are for the most part unsuitable for the habitation of white men, and can therefore be quite left out of consideration for the present, the problem at issue is to secure an economic subsistence in the home country for the vast bulk of the annual addition to the population. In a country but moderately fertile on an average, agriculture of course could and can only afford employment to a relatively small proportion : in the main, it is to manufactures that the population must look for employment and maintenance ; that is to say, the sale of manufactured goods must increase *pari passu* with the population, and, as the home market is inadequate for this, the export trade comes to be more and more important.

This fact has been confirmed by the actual process of Germany's development within the last generation. In 1870, she was still a corn-exporting country, and her manufactures for export were moderate in amount ; since then, she has been transformed into a country importing corn and exporting manufactured goods on a constantly and rapidly increasing scale. In 1882, the census of occupations reckoned the number of wage-earners (including members of their families) employed in agriculture as 19·23 millions, in manufactures as 16·06 millions, in trade and commerce as 4·53 millions; in 1895, there were 18·5 millions employed in agriculture, 20·25 millions in manufactures, 5·97 millions in trade; in 1907, 17·68 millions in agriculture, 26·39 millions in manufactures, and 8·28 millions in trade.

In view of these figures it would be an exaggeration to speak of the transformation of an agrarian into an industrial State, for it is the characteristic feature of German development that, in consequence of protective duties, agriculture has retained its economic strength and profitableness, and that its prosperity has not been permanently impaired, as it has been in England, by the growth of manufactures. There can be no denying, however, that the economic structure of the German empire has changed fundamentally within the last generation and is continuing to change. In 1871, 63·9 per cent. of the population lived in communities of under two thousand inhabitants, in 1905, only 42·6 per cent.; on the other hand, in 1871, 1·96 per cent. of the population lived in towns of over one hundred thousand inhabitants, by 1905 the number had already risen to 19 per cent. Thus Germany, while developing into an industrial State, has at the same time become a land of large towns.

A few figures will further illustrate the industrial growth which has taken place. In 1870, there was a demand for 26 million tons of coal; in 1906, for 137 million tons. The production of pig-iron amounted, in 1870, to 1·35 million tons; in 1906, to 12·29 million tons, more than one-fifth of the total output of the world, the United States contributing 25·73 and Great Britain 10·31 million tons. The shipping trade in German ports increased in volume by 53·5 per cent. from 1890 to 1908; the German merchant-fleet, in the years 1900–9, increased 62·6 per cent. in net volume, or 1·08 million tons; the capital of the shipping companies rose from 273 million marks (£13,650,000) in 1899 to 631 million marks (£31,550,000) in 1908. In 1880, German imports amounted in milliards of marks to 2·86 (£143,000,000), German exports to 2·95 (£147,500,000); in 1899, to 4·37 (£218,500,000) and 5·78 (£289,000,000) respectively; in 1907, to 8·75 (£437,500,000) and 6·85 (£342,500,000) respectively. The value of the total foreign trade of Germany has thus risen to 15·6 milliard marks (£780,000,000); it exceeds that of France with 8 milliard marks (£400,000,000) and even that of the United States with 12·5 milliard marks (£625,000,000), and distantly approaches the figure which Great Britain has to show with her 21 milliard marks (£1,050,000,000). Every student will agree that Great Britain, the United States, and the German empire, constitute the group of nations whose industrial and financial development and productive power have made the greatest progress—progress on a scale far surpassing that of all other States.

CH. VI.

Though the population and industrial activity of Germany, her export trade and capital, have thus greatly increased, yet, unlike other Great Powers, she possesses no large oversea dominions which are in a position to receive her surplus men, goods, and capital; for the Germans were so late in entering upon the field of colonial policy that the value of their colonies to meet the economic needs of the home country is for the present almost negligible. Unquestionably, in the great struggle for existence the Germans have entered the lists under less favourable conditions than those nations which have long pursued an imperialistic policy. If, in the world competition diligence and order, technical skill and scientific discovery, in themselves give a favourable chance to German effort, yet the political and economic difficulties to be surmounted are all the greater. Be that as it may, two incentives may be recognised with certainty as determining the policy of Germany in the outside world. The more Germany, for the reasons stated, was obliged to depend on exporting her industrial products, the more zealously she had to strive either to maintain the open door in as many countries as possible beyond the seas, or else, by securing colonies, leases, spheres of influence, or coaling stations, to augment her share in the economic advantages to result from opening up remoter regions, if she was to hold her own among the other far more powerful countries of the world. The second object in view was to afford protection for these vastly increased transmarine interests by the enlargement of the German fleet, which in Bismarck's time had remained of modest size, and was now no longer adequate to the altered situation.

It was this last consideration which prompted the new bent of William II's general policy. The need of expansion, of an eminently economic nature, had manifestly no connexion with a military craving for conquest, which enemies of Germany thought must be inferred from scattered remarks of the Emperor. His statements were sometimes formulated in a vigorous and imaginative form, in order to bring home to his own people the vital questions affecting their existence, and were not always happily calculated to convey to other nations a true impression of the aims of German policy. This, however, does not alter the fact that the Emperor had fully and correctly appreciated the pressing needs of the nation, and has vindicated them before the world. Generations of men still living are too closely concerned in the several aims of this policy for the historian to venture upon any exposition of it in greater detail from authentic sources. Among particular moves in this policy may be cited, for example, the leading part played by Germany in the construction of the Anatolian railway and in the scheme for the Bagdad railway, and, generally speaking, in the economic development of Turkey in Asia; further, the lease of Kiaochow and the acquisition of a sphere of influence in Shantung, in 1897, and the purchase of the Caroline Islands after the Spanish-American War. The same object was also in view in the attempt made to preserve the open door in Morocco after the Anglo-French *entente* of 1904.

It was the Emperor who in every instance gave the initial impulse; at the same time, he bent his energies, first and foremost, on the task of converting the German fleet from its helpless condition into an effective instrument for the protection of maritime interests and transmarine trade as well as for the defence of the home coast. With the completion of the Kaiser Wilhelm Canal in 1895, the connexion between the Baltic and the North Sea had been provided which was the essential preliminary to the pursuance of any maritime policy by Germany; and the *Reichstag* passed the first Navy Act (*Flottengesetz*) in 1898 and the second in 1900, which decreed a gradual and systematic construction of a fleet during a fixed number of years. Every class in the German nation, enlightened by the labours of the *Deutscher Flottenverein* (German Navy League), had realised the necessity of taking up this new burden. The interests of the nation had hitherto been chiefly confined to internal matters; but it now began to drink in the free invigorating breeze of that colonial and naval activity which has made the English so great and powerful a people.

These new tendencies in foreign policy could not but react upon the relations of the empire with other Powers, and in the end they have completely altered the international position of Germany. Although, at the beginning of his reign, the Emperor had drawn closer to England and thereby helped to precipitate Russia into the arms of France, it soon became necessary to assert the independence of Germany's policy as against the wishes of England, chiefly in order to avoid strong pressure from the Russo-French Alliance. It was presumably for this reason that, after the War between China and Japan, Germany took her stand beside the Dual Alliance; the Emperor's demonstration of friendship to the Boers after the Jameson Raid in 1896, though quite intelligible from the general point of view of human sentiment, already betrays a further cooling off towards England, and its final explanation may well be sought in considerations of world-policy alone.

Prince Bülow had since 1897 held the office of Foreign Secretary (*Staatssekretariat des Auswärtigen*) under the aged Chancellor, Prince Chlodwig Hohenlohe; on October 17, 1900, he succeeded to the Chancellorship and supreme responsibility for the entire policy of the empire, taking over the helm with steady, expert hand. At every turn, he found himself confronted with the necessity of choosing between

England and the Dual Alliance, just as, in the seventies, Bismarck had been obliged to make choice between Russia and Austria. It seems that, in 1901, he deliberately rejected the advances of British statesmen, in order that Germany might not become "the sword of England upon the Continent" and have to bear the brunt of any Russo-French onslaught. The determination to pursue an independent course in the end created ill-feeling across the Channel. Some mistakes there were; during the Boer War the sympathies of the Germans as of other nations lay with the weaker side; but at this crisis the Emperor staked his whole influence, nay, some measure of his popularity, against the popular feeling, tempered the bitterness aroused, and withstood every temptation from any other quarter. In the long run, however, apprehensions as to the commercial competition and naval preparations of Germany gained the day in England; indeed, impelled by Chauvinistic sentiment on both sides, the English nation began to accustom itself to the idea of a German peril, and finally to join the ranks of those opposed to Germany. After the Anglo-French *entente* of 1904 and the Algeciras Conference, a change in the old alliances began which introduced a new era in international politics; for the moment it looked as if Germany was to be exposed to the danger of isolation and to a policy of hemming in ("*Einkreisungspolitik*") on the part of her enemies, led, as was thought, by King Edward VII.

The new situation taught a double lesson. The course of the Morocco affair showed that the German empire had been hampered in the free use of opportunities for pursuing its *Weltpolitik* by the union of its opponents old and new. The events of the conflict about Bosnia and the Herzegovina proved that these opponents were not at the time strong enough on the Continent to sever the close connexion between Germany and Austria and to treat the central Power of Europe as a negligible quantity. After these great trials of strength the differences and vexations, to be sure, lost much of their acrimony, and the mists of suspicion were dispelled by frank and friendly discussion, especially in the case of Germany and England.

Even so, the new position of Germany is not without its difficulties. At every step forward, she is confronted by the political and economic opposition of alliances and *ententes*, and fully realises that, despite the Triple Alliance, it is upon her own strength that she must rely first of all in any emergency. This state of things requires that she should strain every nerve. There is no other great nation in the world which would or could have taken upon itself simultaneously the three great charges of a strong army, a considerable fleet, and a far-reaching social policy; and the burden has been increased by the oversea policy adopted, the participation in the Chinese campaign, and the quelling of the South-west African revolt (1904–7). Greatly as the national wealth has grown within the past generation, the growth of the national debt has not been without its effect upon the ordering of imperial finance. A good deal of self-confidence and healthy optimism has been needed to keep to the road once chosen, despite all difficulties. Even if Germany confines herself to maintaining for her part peace in Europe, which since the rise of her empire she has not disturbed, and to securing a sunny place for herself in the world at large, as Prince Bülow expressed it, she will yet learn the truth of that moral law of the existence of nations, that life means struggle.

In view of her geographical and military position, set in the centre of the international constellation of Powers, and impelled by the inward necessity for further development, this country is subjected to a stronger tension of conflicting forces than any other Power, and therefore needs to put forth her strength the more effectively if she is to hold her own. It is only the fullest exercise of her strength which has sufficed since the days of the Saxon and Hohenstauffen Emperors to vindicate the existence of the Germans as a nation. Long centuries of weakness and dismemberment have taught them that, without this determined display of force, the heart of Europe will become an object of attack and spoliation for their neighbours. In the new empire, Emperor, princes, and people, all parties and all ranks, are agreed that these lessons of the centuries, taught by the heights and depths of the nation's history, shall not have been given in vain.

CHAPTER VII.

AUSTRIA-HUNGARY.

The history of Austria-Hungary, during the last fifty years, has presented real unity, despite an outward appearance of great variety. This unity is due to the continuous development of constitutional institutions. That development has not been regular nor free from interruptions; from time to time it has been checked by delays and retrogressions. It originated in periodical oscillation between two constitutional systems, of which the first, rooted in traditional sentiment, was moderate, conservative, aristocratic, and favoured provincial decentralisation, while the second was progressive, radical in its methods and liberal in its formulae, middle class, bureaucratic, Viennese, and favoured centralisation. It was only later, after 1867 and 1871, that the progress became more regular. But, from 1859 to 1909, the purpose remained the same—to adapt the modern system of constitutional and, finally, of parliamentary government, to the Austrian monarchy despite its incongruities of tradition and of race.

The problem was one of extreme complexity. On the ruins of the ancient dynastic and feudal empire, which had fallen in 1848, a modern, popular, and Liberal monarchy had to be constructed. That monarchy needed to consolidate and strengthen itself, on the one hand by concentrating its efforts and resources, on the other by disarming, through wise concessions, the traditional and national antagonism between peoples and sectional divisions; the ancient policy of the Habsburgs, which had been imperial in the extended and medieval sense of the word, had to be replaced by an Austrian or Austro-Hungarian policy, modern, territorial, and popular. On this fundamental problem others were dependent, forming part of it and presenting successive or simultaneous aspects of the whole, such as the adjustment of the relations between the two parts of the monarchy, the Cisleithanian and Transleithanian, by the happy reconciliation of their requisite unity and their historical diversity; the solution, or at least the clear definition and the continuous reduction to simpler terms, of the question of nationalities; the formulation of a foreign policy which would satisfy all the different peoples of the monarchy; the gradual introduction into the organisation of the empire-kingdom and

its subordinate parts of the modern forms of participation by the citizens
in the government and in the administration of their interests and affairs.
This task, accomplished in the infinite and unique complexity of the
Austro-Hungarian environment, despite the intellectual, moral, social,
and economic diversity of the peoples of the monarchy, despite the force
of tradition, weighing heavily on peoples and dynasty alike, gives its
historical value to the reign of Francis Joseph I.

This period of fifty years from 1859 forms only a part of a single reign,
and the figure of Francis Joseph I dominates the whole. The monarch who,
between 1849 and 1859, had given his authority to a process of rigorous
absolutist centralisation, in 1867 confirmed the compromise which established dualism ; he who at twenty years of age revoked the first Constitution which had come into existence in Austria, nearly sixty years later
not only accepts and supports but actually forces upon the privileged
classes and upon his timid Ministers an electoral reform which has established universal suffrage in Austria and renders its introduction in Hungary
probable. The whole of his public and private life is full of similar contrasts. Although a German prince, imbued with German sentiments,
he presides over a transformation of the monarchy which does not favour
the German preponderance ; although a zealous Catholic, he appends his
signature to laws establishing extensive religious freedom in his States ;
although an aristocrat by birth and sentiment, he throws open to democracy
the gates of public life. He humiliates Prussia and Italy, and is afterwards
vanquished by both these countries, with whom he finally enters into an
alliance. After thirty years of defeats and territorial losses, he adds Bosnia
and the Herzegovina to the monarchy, and thus, like the ancient Emperors,
he also becomes *Mehrer des Reichs.* His only son, the hope of his
dynasty, perishes in a mysterious tragedy. His wife, after a troubled
and unhappy existence, is stabbed by an assassin in a foreign land. In
all his misfortunes he has been supported by the consciousness of his
mission and of his duty. Always prudent and reserved, at times over-
cautious, in later life he has laid aside the fire and impetuosity of youth,
to become still more prudent, still more cautious, but in reality, more
courageous. He has grown old, surrounded by the affection of his
subjects and the respect of foreigners ; these he won, in the first place
by his misfortunes, and in the second, by his real goodness and wisdom.
He is now the last survivor of his generation, and the patriarch of the
sovereigns and nations of Europe. Assuredly, the existence of the
monarchy does not depend on him alone ; but, by his good qualities and
his misfortunes he has undoubtedly strengthened the dynastic loyalty
which is traditional in Austria. This man, not in virtue of any conspicuous intellectual gifts, but by his diligence, benevolence, and devotion
to duty, will give his name to the epoch of which his reign, from 1859
onwards, constitutes the unity.

At the first glance, these fifty years divide themselves into five

CH. VII.

periods. From 1859 to 1867 we have the preparation for, and the
establishment of, dualism. From 1867 to 1878 dualism preserves the
spirit of its organisers. From 1878 to 1895 it lives on, warped and
deformed in use, and on the brink of ruin. From 1895 to 1906,
Cisleithania, the dual monarchy, and Hungary are agitated in turn by
constitutional crises. Finally, from 1906 onwards, we begin to perceive
the bold outline of a new policy, of which the first-fruits are the renewal
of the Compromise in 1907, electoral reform in Austria and Hungary,
and the annexation of Bosnia and the Herzegovina.

Ever since the Crimean War, public opinion in the monarchy had
looked for a defeat which should overthrow absolutism. This came at
Solferino. The general discontent in Hungary, of which the slackness of
the Hungarian soldiers in this war gave proof, necessitated the abandonment of the policy of centralisation and Germanisation, and the want of
money led to the abolition of absolutism. Only the upper middle classes,
who had profited by the economic development resulting from the
enfranchisement of the peasants, could furnish the necessary loans; and
they favoured Liberal principles. The aristocracy, which had opposed
Bach, was striving to recover its influence at Court; the foreign policy
adopted by the Emperor—revenge on Italy and extension of his influence
in Germany—was not compatible with the constant threatenings of
internal trouble. Such were the reasons which, in the summer of 1859,
led Austria to take the first steps towards constitutionalism.

And very timid steps they were. Hungary had the chief attention of
the Government; but of Hungarian needs and desires it understood little.
The moderate schemes for reorganisation, which Count Emil Dessewffy,
the zealous and self-accredited spokesman of his country, submitted to
Rechberg, caused great astonishment and were regarded as the work of
a dreamer. For Dessewffy, like all Hungarians, spoke of laws and
rights, whereas for years the imperial Government had recognised only
decrees and imperial grants. Count Leo Thun let loose once more
Magyar national opposition in Hungary by the promulgation of a patent
for the Protestants, which, though relatively liberal, erred in being a
patent, an arbitrary act, a concession. Financial distress led to the first
decisive action. Bruck, the Minister of Finance, in despair, discredited
in public opinion by the disclosure of the expedients to which he had
been obliged to have recourse, unjustly suspected of complicity in the
malversations of the military administration, had committed suicide.
His successor, Ignatius von Plener, an experienced official of Liberal
tendencies, pledged himself unreservedly to a measure of constitutional
reform. On March 5, 1860, an imperial decree convoked the first
legislative assembly of the monarchy as a whole, the "reinforced"
(*verstärkter*) *Reichsrath*.

It was little more than a consultative imperial council. In addition
to the members of the permanent *Reichsrath*, a sort of Council of State

composed of officials, there were to be extraordinary life members, and
38 delegates, to be chosen by the Emperor hereafter on the recommendation of provincial Diets which were to be called into being, but, for
this first occasion, directly nominated by him.   Three-fourths of the
new members were chosen from among the higher aristocracy, the clergy,
and the official classes, only ten from the middle classes.   The Assembly
was convoked for the month of May, so that it might examine the
budget for 1861.   By force of circumstances it exceeded the narrow
sphere which had been assigned to it, and was the first assembly to
discuss in parliamentary fashion the affairs of the entire monarchy.
This was mainly due to the Hungarian members.   They were all
legitimist Conservatives, and they hoped to see the ancient Hungarian
Constitution restored, with such modifications as the social changes of
1848 required, and the relations between Hungary and the monarchy
established on the basis of moderate dualism.   They wished to secure
historical and legitimate rights, respect for tradition and for law.
They found allies amongst the Conservative party of the Austrian
nobility, and especially amongst the nobility of Bohemia.   Ignoring the
historical and constitutional barriers, which, since 1620, have separated
Bohemia from Hungary, Count Clam-Martinič, the chief representative
of this nobility, came to an understanding with Count Anton Szécsen,
the ordinary spokesman of the Hungarian party, on a platform claiming
the due recognition of " historical and political individualities."

This Conservative and autonomist programme was opposed by that of
the more or less Liberal advocates of centralisation, who were officials
and representatives of the German middle classes.   But they were
undecided and timid, above all, fearful of displeasing the Emperor, and
they dared not express, or even avow to themselves, the meaning of their
own aspirations.   They flatly repudiated their colleague Maager, a Saxon
from Transylvania, when he alone dared to state that the real need
of the empire was a modern representative constitution.   In the course
of this session the *Reichsrath* had received from the Emperor the right to
confirm any imposition or increase of taxes, and the raising of any loan.
But the Conservatives were unwilling that the *Reichsrath* should depart
from its consultative *rôle*.   The only result of these discussions was two
addresses to the Emperor, that of the majority, and that of the minority,
both equally obscure and timid—nevertheless, that of the former revealed
autonomist and provincial tendencies, and that of the latter gave
evidence of aspirations towards a centralised and Germanised system.

The Emperor adopted the motion of the majority.   On October 20,
1860, in an imperial Diploma (the October Charter), he declared that,
for the future, he intended to share the legislative power and the right
of imposing taxes and raising loans, for the different sections of the
monarchy with their several Diets, and for the whole empire with a
Reichsrath, consisting of delegates from the Diets.   The reasons for this

great change were set forth to the peoples in a manifesto and in several
rescripts, which prescribed the measures needful for putting it into effect.
Taken as a whole, these constitutional acts produce a confused and contradictory impression. The Diploma is a mixture of centralism, dualism,
and federalism ; moreover, on the one hand, it respects the continuity of
traditional rights, on the other, it upholds the principle of imperial
grants. The only clear statement contained therein is that of the
monarch's intention to break with absolutist centralisation, and to
inaugurate a new and essentially constitutional policy, which was to be
based on a compromise between the unitary and the autonomist principles.

Some months later the October Diploma was, in official language,
completed, but actually superseded, by the February Patent (February 26,
1861), setting up a centralised Constitution. There were several reasons
for this sudden change. In Hungary the Diploma had given rise to a
real revolutionary movement. In order to give the nation a pledge of
the constitutional sincerity of the new system, the Government had
restored the system of administration by *comitats*. The assemblies of
the *comitats* or counties were the traditional home of Hungarian self-
government and of resistance to Austrian interference, and their restoration was the greatest incentive to Hungarian self-assertion. Throughout
the *comitats* the partisans of Deák and those of Kossuth rejected the new
Constitution, demanded the restoration of the Laws of 1848, and acted
as though these had already been reestablished; the sources which
furnished supplies for the army and the exchequer of the monarchy were
thus in danger of being blocked. In Austria the first enthusiasm, aroused
by the proclamation of the new constitutional charter, had been short-
lived. The provincial statutes which Count Goluchowski, Minister of
the Interior, drew almost unaltered from the drafts bequeathed to him
by Bach, presented a reactionary and feudal aspect, particularly galling
to the German middle classes. It was dangerous to irritate these classes,
because they alone could be relied on to support the credit of the State,
at that time lower than ever, and because the new external policy also
required their willing concurrence. The rapid progress of Italian unity
deprived Austria of all hope of regaining supremacy in the peninsula :
she therefore concentrated her efforts on Germany. There she had a
rival in Prussia, who was passing through her brief period of Liberalism ;
in order to meet and overcome her rivalry Austria must have the support
of German opinion, and how could Germans be expected to support
a country which was neither Liberal nor German ? Moved by these
motives and swayed by Schmerling, who had taken the place of
Goluchowski, dismissed after experience of his incapacity, the Emperor
signed the Patent, which, under constitutional forms, brought the
monarchy back to the leading ideas of Bach's system.

The Patent instituted a *Reichsrath*, composed of two Chambers. In
the first, the Chamber of Lords, were represented, by right of succession

or nomination, those who, by birth, position, or merit, belonged to the aristocracy. In the second, the Chamber of Deputies, sat 343 representatives, who were elected by the provincial Diets on the system of the representation of interests. Like the members of the Diet itself, they were divided into four *Curiae,* namely, the great landowners, the Chambers of Commerce, the cities, and the rural districts. In each *Curia* a certain payment in taxes was the qualification for the franchise. The value of the vote varied considerably in the several *Curiae* and provinces: some deputies were elected by two or three votes only, others by between ten and twelve thousand. In every case, the German provinces or districts were favoured and the Slavs treated unfairly. Under the cloak of principle, all principle was ignored; for the sole object was to set up a *Reichsrath* which would not hamper the Government. Moreover, both in the Diets and in the Chamber of Deputies, everything was calculated to ensure a permanent majority of the great landowners, on whose unflinching devotion the Government reckoned in all circumstances. The power of the *Reichsrath* was ill defined and still worse protected; there was no right of calling Ministers to account by interpellation, no ministerial responsibility; moreover, by Article 13, a famous article of the Constitution, the Cabinet might take the place of the Parliament during vacation, with no other obligation than that of accounting for its actions during the following session. On the surface, the system of the Patent is more Liberal than that of the Diploma: in reality, it is certain that, if the Diploma had remained in force, Cisleithanian Austria would have enjoyed greater freedom, and a more regular, less discordant, constitutional development.

In Hungary, the Patent meant a declaration of war. In fact, it treated Hungary as an Austrian province; an autonomous province, it is true, seeing that its internal affairs lay within the jurisdiction of the Hungarian Diet (while those which affected only the Cisleithanian provinces were dependent on the smaller *Reichsrath,* composed of the non-Hungarian deputies), but none the less a province; since all its most important affairs, such as military and financial questions, were removed from the jurisdiction of the Diet, and entrusted to the full *Reichsrath,* where the deputies from Austria and Hungary sat together. In the Diet of 1861, Hungary protested against this violation of the promises made in October, and this return to the ideas of Bach. Through the lips and pen of Deák, "the nation's sage," in an address to the sovereign, the nation asserted the contractual character of the Pragmatic Sanction, and demanded the restoration of her Constitution, "which is not a gift, but was founded on mutual agreement, and sprang from the very life of the Nation." "Law and justice and the sanctity of treaties are on our side, material force is against us." Hungary has a right to "autonomy and legal independence as a State"; her connexion with Austria is a personal union. In the Cabinet there were heated discussions on the reply to be sent to this address; finally, the centralist party triumphed, and the Hungarian Ministers resigned. To the imperial rescript, which rejected every single idea and claim contained in the address, Deák replied by a second address, which ended with the declaration that Hungary adhered strictly to the laws of 1848, that she refused, and always would refuse to send deputies to the *Reichsrath*, that she declared void and invalid all the resolutions which the latter might make concerning Hungarian affairs, and which clearly stated the points at issue. "The rescript does not take its stand on the basis of the Hungarian Constitution, but it considers the imperial Diploma and Patent as fundamental laws; these are acts of absolute power, opposed to the essence of our Constitution. As for us, our duty to our country, our position as representatives, and our convictions, bind us to the Hungarian Constitution, and it is only on the basis of this Constitution that we can deliberate. Between these two different, nay, opposing principles, it is not possible to arrive at a compromise, desirable though it be." Arbitrary power on the one hand, continuity of rights on the other, such were, in fact, the two opposing propositions. A conflict so serious and critical could only result in the dissolution of the Diet. A few months later, the whole of the national administration, which had been reestablished less than a year before, was once more suspended; military government and councils of war resumed their sway in Hungary, and the administration of Schmerling revealed its true colours, appearing openly as the renewal of the system of Bach.

From that moment, its ultimate fate could be foreseen. In the Diet prophetic warnings had been heard. Hungary resumed the passive tactics which had served her in good stead under Bach, and, in addition, she refused to pay the taxes. Deák was the national oracle: the Hungarian Slavs, who had learnt from their experience under Bach, did not hesitate to side with the Magyars and based their expectations on the Hungarian Parliament and Deák's sense of justice. Of the Magyars, the Liberals followed him blindly, and the Radicals and Conservatives drew closer to him daily. Croatia rejected the advances of Vienna, but did not accept those of Pest. Only Transylvania with her Saxons, who were naturally attracted by the system of centralisation and Germanisation, and her Roumans, who, inspired by long-standing hatred of the Magyars, joined the camp of their adversaries, could be said to welcome the system; of the Transleithanian provinces Transylvania alone sent deputies to the *Reichsrath*. But this success was insignificant. In reality, Hungary remained impregnable, waiting until the mistakes of her enemies and the labours of her friends should prepare the way for the triumph of her rights.

Schmerling was assuredly under no delusions on the subject of his chances in Hungary. Victory could only come from without, from the success of the system in Austria, and from the success of Austria in

Germany; such success would have paralysed the Magyar opposition. But this twofold success was not for Schmerling. In Austria the Čechs, after giving the *Reichsrath* a trial, withdrew from it when they found themselves oppressed, ill-treated, and deprived of all hope of obtaining the revision of the constitutional laws which by artificial provisions made them a minority even in Bohemia. The other Slavs shared their passion and their rancour. The Germans, who at first had enjoyed playing at Parliament, soon wearied of the game on discovering that they were really powerless. They were specially interested in financial reforms, and brought to bear upon this subject their *bourgeois* love of order and economy; the Cabinet, spurred on by the Court, which continued to pursue its empty dreams of traditional foreign policy, exasperated the Germans by continually asking them for money, and grew impatient when they refused to grant it. A real constitutional system, or again, a scheme of Liberal political and religious legislation, superseding the Concordat, might have persuaded the majority to make financial sacrifices; but the Cabinet was neither able nor willing to consent thereto. In Parliament ministerial responsibility, with liberty of combination and of public meeting, were demanded, but in vain; the liberty of the Press, which had been partially established by law, was, by the practice of the Courts, turned into absolute persecution, and the Concordat remained intact. Moreover, the annual deficit, on an average fifty million florins, was doubly galling to the parliamentary majority; its orators declared that the nation had come to a financial Solferino, and for what purpose? Failure in Hungary; in Germany, failure which had been acknowledged since the fiasco of the Congress of Princes in 1863; failure even in Austria—what was the good of a Constitution which, at any moment, might be altered or suspended by means of one of its own clauses, namely, the famous Article 13? From 1864 onwards, there was a definite breach between the Cabinet and the majority. The last session, from November, 1864, to July, 1865, was a long death-struggle.

The Emperor had not long continued his early trust in Schmerling. It is possible that he had never placed complete confidence in him: it seems as though Schmerling had never had quite a free hand against Hungary. Was Francis Joseph influenced by his wife, who was devoted to the chivalrous and romantic people of that country? or was he swayed by Count Maurice Esterházy, a Minister without portfolio, an Austrian diplomatist, but a Hungarian legitimist and a zealous Catholic, who in Schmerling's Cabinet represented the internal and external traditions of the policy of Metternich? In any case, the interval of time which elapsed without bringing to Schmerling any part of the promised and hoped-for success, was a gain to the Hungarians. Not far from the sovereign, a group of Conservatives was awaiting the favourable moment when Deák, at their signal, might offer, in the name of the nation, to come to an agreement. So long as Vienna remained intractable, Deák was to remain irreconcilable. In his celebrated *Contribution to Hungarian Constitutional Law*, he asserts the principle of personal union in connexion with an autonomous Hungary. In 1861, the *Reichsrath*, moved by Schmerling, had declared for the Emperor and the Cabinet against Hungary. But from 1863 onwards, the majority of the German deputies had held and had openly stated that, in order to secure the existence of constitutionalism in Austria, it was necessary to come to an understanding with Hungary; however, they insisted that this understanding should be based on the Patent. A year later, having learnt wisdom by experience, they had resigned themselves to making very important concessions to Hungary. Instead of insisting on the presence of the Hungarians in the *Reichsrath*, they were willing that the Diets of Hungary and Croatia should revise the Laws of 1848, so as to bring them into accord so far as possible with the Patent. Then Deák, who had been informed that Schmerling's position, both in Parliament and at Court, was now far from secure, took a step forward. In his well-known declarations of Easter and May, 1865, he formulated the programme, which was afterwards almost wholly carried out by the Compromise. He said, "We are always prepared to take any legal measures to modify our laws so as to secure the safety and solidarity of the monarchy." The Emperor welcomed this programme with joy. He gave proof of his satisfaction in April, 1865, when he spent a few hours in Hungary, and again in June, when he stayed there for several days. On June 26, without telling Schmerling, he called to the Hungarian Chancery George Mailáth, a Conservative. This meant wholesale disavowal of the system; and nothing remained for Schmerling but to tender his resignation, which had been expected and accepted in advance.

The period of the monarchical reorganisation which then ensued lasted for two years; it was only in December, 1867, that the work of reconstitution was completed by the passing of the new Cisleithanian constitutional laws. The forces which brought about this conclusion were the Emperor, the Hungarians, and Prussia; for the Austrian crisis took place at the same time as the German crisis, and the two are connected. The final solution was delayed until the autumn of 1866, on account of the uncertainty of the issue of events in Germany; on the other hand, once the result of these was known, affairs in Austria progressed rapidly; Beust, an antagonist of Bismarck, who had passed from the service of Saxony to that of Austria-Hungary, advised the sovereign to yield to the demands of Hungary, in order to restore to the monarchy its freedom of action in German affairs. In fact, modern dualism owes its origin to Sadowa.

In September, 1865, the February Patent was suspended. The Austrian Germans protested strongly, but in vain; the Čechs, the Slavs, and the Poles, who were delighted, hastened to present their federal and autonomist programmes, all of which opposed centralism and dualism, drawing their inspiration from the ideas set forth in the Diploma.   Count Belcredi, the Minister of State, appeared favourable to their programmes, and had their confidence.   But in Hungary there arose a new force behind Deák, in the person of Count Julius Andrássy, a politician and diplomatist, who had been cured of his revolutionary illusions of 1848 by exile and diligent study ; a man equally capable of negotiating with the Court and of solving the problems of European politics.   The form and legal tenour of the Compromise were due to Deák, its political tone to Andrássy.   From the very beginning of the crisis, Andrássy had laid down the principle of a Liberal government on the basis of an agreement between the two sections of the monarchy, the Germans to have the upper hand in Cisleithania and the Magyars in Transleithania. This continued to be the leading idea of his policy, whilst, under the direction of Deák, a commission of the Diet was drawing up a comprehensive scheme for the organisation of the government for affairs common to both sections of the monarchy.   This scheme had just been completed when, in June, 1866, the Diet was prorogued in consequence of the opening of hostilities.   Thus, it constituted the programme of Hungary— the maximum programme if Austria should be victorious in the war, the minimum should she be defeated.   When, therefore, after the defeat, the Emperor secretly summoned Deák to Vienna, and asked him, " What does Hungary demand ? " the sage of the nation was able to make the justly celebrated reply, " Only what she demanded before Sadowa." But, after Sadowa, she was in a position to accept nothing less.

Andrássy, whom Deák had designated as future Prime Minister, opened negotiations in the name of his country.   On the part of the Austrian Ministers, who desired to make Austria more Slav and more federalistic, he encountered a lively opposition to his policy, until Beust assumed control over the Cabinet.   The struggle between Beust and Belcredi was concentrated on one definite point : the constitutional modifications which the agreement with Hungary had rendered necessary in Cisleithania had to be ratified by the representatives of the countries concerned, but whence were these representatives to be drawn ?   From the old *Reichsrath*, according to the desire of Beust ? or, in accordance with the wishes of Belcredi, from an extraordinary *Reichsrath*, to be freely elected by the Diets without distinction of *Curiae*, a *Reichsrath* which would sympathise with the Slavs ?   The whole question of the Compromise was contained in this alternative ; for it was known, on the one hand, that Belcredi was opposed to dualism, and that the extraordinary *Reichsrath* was certain to amend the Hungarian scheme, and, on the other, that Beust was in favour of dualism and that the smaller *Reichsrath* was prepared to accept the Hungarian scheme as it stood in consideration of the reintroduction into Cisleithania of the centralist Constitution.

The Emperor, under the influence of Andrássy, decided in favour of Beust, and Belcredi withdrew.

Henceforward, matters progressed speedily. On February 17, the Hungarian Constitution was in effect restored by the appointment of a responsible Cabinet, over which Andrássy presided. In May, the smaller *Reichsrath* reassembled; by means of dissolutions and by dint of pressure, Beust had managed to put the machinery of Schmerling into good working order and to make sure of a German dualistic majority. In June, Francis Joseph had himself crowned King of Hungary; thus, after eighteen years of an illegal and absolutist interregnum, he reknit the broken threads of the Hungarian Pragmatic Sanction of 1722–3. In October the Government brought before the *Reichsrath* the laws dealing with the Compromise, of which the economic part had been settled in August and September between the deputations of the two Parliaments. Of its own accord, the *Reichsrath* added some laws which amended the Patent in a Liberal sense, and decided that all these laws, the Compromise, and the revised Constitution of Cisleithania, should come into force at the same time as one whole. Thus it overcame the Emperor's opposition to a part of the revision laws. At the close of the year 1867 the new constitutional fabric was complete in Hungary, Austria, and the monarchy: on the basis of the Compromise, the edifice of dualism had been completed.

Its main idea is as follows. The Austro-Hungarian monarchy is a Power consisting of two States, the empire of Austria (officially entitled "the kingdoms and countries represented in the *Reichsrath*") and the kingdom of Hungary. Each of them is independent and supreme: they are therefore absolutely equal, in a word, they are *peers*. But, since they are in subjection to the same dynasty, they can only be represented and act abroad as a whole; and since, by the Pragmatic Sanction, they have mutually pledged themselves to maintain the rights and integrity of the possessions of the dynasty, they are bound to act together for defence. The organisation suitable for this purpose was set up by the Compromise. It maintained a common diplomatic service, and a unified army so far as command and purely military control are concerned, but the vote of its several contingents was still to remain at the discretion of each Parliament. The sovereign was to be the executive head of these common services, assisted by Ministers acting for both countries, the Ministers of Foreign Affairs, War, and Finance. The last named is merely an administrator of the Common Treasury, which receives the funds contributed by both States for common purposes—the monarchy, which has no private resources, being dependent on their subsidies. To ensure respect for constitutional principles in the government of the empire-kingdom, these Ministers were to be checked by the Delegations. These Delegations do not constitute a Parliament. They consist of two committees, named, in 1867, "international committees"; each is composed of 60 members, each

Parliament electing its own committee, in the proportion of 20 delegates from the Upper, and 40 from the Lower, Chamber. The two committees sit apart, meeting simultaneously once a year, not to legislate—which they have not the power to do—but to vote the common budget, and to scrutinise the administration of the common Ministers. Beyond the sphere of common action, of which we have just traced the limits, there are no affairs in common. Nevertheless, between two States thus politically united, which, for more than three centuries, had been still more closely linked, there must necessarily be affairs of common interest; for instance, the economic, commercial, and financial relations of both countries. As a preliminary, such questions were to be discussed either between the two Cabinets or between "Deputations," elected for each occasion by the Parliaments; they were to be finally settled by the vote of two several laws, Austrian and Hungarian, which were to be in the main identical. Similarly, identical laws were to regulate questions which, although not common, could only be decided by cooperation, such as military organisation, or the ratification of an international treaty. Ten years was the ordinary term for economic conventions between the two States. As a matter of fact, since 1867, as since 1850, Austria and Hungary have formed a single territory for commerce and customs tariff, and their respective contributions towards the common expenditure, originally fixed at 70 per cent. for Austria and 30 per cent. for Hungary, maintained nearly the same proportions for about thirty years, subject to an allowance made for the military districts restored to Hungary in 1873. The Compromise guaranteed constitutional laws to both States of the monarchy. In Hungary, the traditional Constitution, which had been transformed by the Laws of 1848 (these same laws having, in 1867, been adapted to the new system of common affairs), provided for a parliamentary Government. In Austria the Constitution of December, 1867, slightly modified the Patent in a Liberal sense. But it left untouched the essential part, namely, the artificial electoral laws, and Article 13, thenceforward known as Article 14. The internal crises in Austria were due to these laws and that article. The Compromise, taken as a whole, although far from being wholly just or perfectly wise, has at least secured for the monarchy, for the last forty years, a comparatively regular and homogeneous development, which forms a happy contrast with the uncertainty of its progress between 1848 and 1867.

The *Reichsrath*, which, by the revision of 1867, had been reduced to 203 members, still elected by the Diets, found itself confronted by a Cabinet known as the "Commoners' Cabinet," although its President was Prince Carlos Auersperg, "the first nobleman in the empire." Giskra, Minister of the Interior, Herbst, the Minister of Justice, Hasner, Minister of Education, and Brestel, Minister of Finance, gave the tone to the Cabinet. They had before them a heavy task, which they bravely attacked. The following is a list of their chief claims to the honour of posterity : they reformed administration and justice by separating the one from the other ; they organised primary education, which was made compulsory by the celebrated Law of 1869 ; they set in order the finances by the unification of the Debt, by the imposition of a tax on coupons (which meant partial repudiation of the Debt), and by the diminution of the deficit, which was reduced from 39 million florins in 1868 to 3 millions in 1869 : they passed political and ecclesiastical laws which considerably limited the scope of the Concordat. But against all this must be set their serious blunders ; they absolutely failed to understand the modern social movement (Giskra declared that, within the Austrian frontier, the social question was non-existent), and, what was more serious, they blindly opposed the irresistible force of the national movement.

The question of nationalities disturbed and troubled their Ministry, and was the direct cause of their fall. In 1865, when the Patent was suspended, Francis Ladislas Rieger, the leader of the Čechs, a zealous, enthusiastic politician, and an idealist of persuasive eloquence, had endeavoured to come to an understanding with the Liberal section of the Germans, in order that Austria might have, what the Kremsier Diet had almost secured for her in 1849, a Constitution accepted by all her peoples. The uncertainty of the political situation and the distrustful attitude of the Germans caused this scheme to fail ; soon afterwards the tactless intervention of Beust revived and inflamed all the hatred of the Čechs. It was in vain that the celebrated Article 19 of the constitutional Laws of 1867 proclaimed the right of all nationalities to equality and state protection. Since 1848 all the Austrian Constitutions had contained similar clauses, and experience had shown that they were worthless. The Čechs, deceived and deluded by the example of Hungary, adopted passive tactics. They refused to appear in the *Reichsrath* ; they deserted the Diet of Bohemia ; and, in their celebrated Declaration, of August, 1868, they formulated their claim to the recognition of Bohemia as a State on the following lines. Bohemia has the same traditional rights as Hungary ; hence, her relations towards the monarchy can only be adjusted by means of an agreement between her Diet and her sovereign ; a real Bohemian Diet can only exist on the basis of a just and equal electoral law. The Government proclaimed a state of siege in Bohemia. But the Slovenes, in Carniola, made common cause with the Čechs ; the Poles in Galicia, not contented with the extensive provincial autonomy granted to them by Beust in exchange for their vote in favour of the Compromise, demanded new concessions in their Resolution. The Emperor, always ready for conciliation, when this is possible, authorised Beust to open negotiations with the Čechs.

These negotiations failed ; but Auersperg forthwith resigned, and thus inaugurated a long ministerial crisis. Auersperg was replaced by Count Taaffe, who had been a friend of the Emperor from his youth,

and who, like him, was in favour of conciliation.   The majority of the
Cabinet remained persistent Centralists ; Taaffe, unable to convince them,
retired in January, 1870, with his colleagues, Count Potocki, a Pole, and
Berger, a German Liberal, who was more clear-sighted than the rest of
his party.   Hasner then became President of the Council.   But the
opponents of Centralism, conscious of the insecurity of their enemies,
joined forces for a final attack : the clerical party, the Slovenes, the
Roumans, the Italians, and, lastly, the Poles, left the *Reichsrath*.   The
Ministry, having thus lost all prestige and authority, retired.   Potocki
accepted the office of President of the Council, on the understanding that
he was to reconcile the peoples of Austria with each other and with the State.

He failed completely, for he was too centralistic for the Slavs and
too federalistic for the Germans.   Moreover, the importance of the
events which were taking place in Europe threw all questions of internal
policy into the background.   The Franco-German War had set before
the monarchy the problem of an alliance with France against Prussia.   In
spite of Beust and the generals, the influence of Hungary, which was
henceforward decisive, imposed a policy of non-intervention in Germany,
in accordance with the logic of the Compromise.   But the completion of
German unity created other anxieties at the Court of Vienna.   Would
not the new Germany prove expansive and acquisitive ?   Would she not
find support among the Austrian Germans, among whom a national
Radical party was being formed ?   How could Austria defend herself
from this danger except by the help of the Slavs, and more especially of
the Čechs ?   On the frontier of Bohemia the threatening Germans must
find themselves opposed by a contented Slavonic people.   And, moreover,
since the battle of Sedan had put a definite end to the policy of promoting Austrian influence in Germany, since there only remained to the
monarchy the East—the Slavonic East—was it not necessary to make
sure that, here also, Austria would be supported by the Slavs ?   Potocki
was not capable of effecting so great a change ; in February, 1871, he
gave place to Count Hohenwart.

Hohenwart was a high official who, up to that time, had diligently
served the Liberal scheme of administration.   The programme of his
new Ministry had been drawn up by Schäffle, the Minister of Commerce,
a German by origin, and a professor of political economy in Vienna.
Schäffle, under the influence of the economic and social doctrines which
he had adopted, was hostile to the middle class capitalists.   Hence, he
wished to replace the Liberal system of the 1861 Patent by a Conservative system, resting on the higher nobility and the lower middle classes.
He therefore appealed to all the enemies of German Liberalism, to its
political enemies, the clerical and the feudal party, and to its national
enemies, the Slavs.   His policy found expression in schemes for electoral
reform lowering the franchise, for the extension of the power of the
Diets and provincial autonomy, for the legal establishment of equal rights

CH. VII.

for nationalities. It failed; yet its failure was not due to the energetic opposition of the Germans, as they claimed, but to the blindness of the Čechs and to foreign intervention. For Bohemia, the Ministry, in agreement with the Čechs, proposed a law dealing with nationalities, which would have provided for the Germans and Čechs real equality without oppression on either side, and Fundamental Articles. These articles were to be the Bohemian Compromise: they assigned to the Diet of Prague almost all the functions of the *Reichsrath*, without trenching on the province of the Austrian Delegation; thus they established federalism in Cisleithania. Did the national interests of the Čechs urgently call for such a revolution in the Constitution? It was afterwards apparent that far slighter modifications of the Constitution of 1867 would have sufficed to provide for extensive national development. But they sacrificed themselves to their allies, the Conservative nobility, whom they had joined in 1861. Clam-Martinič, led astray by feudal romanticism, proud and unforgiving, wished to obtain for Bohemia exactly what Hungary had obtained, to humiliate the German Liberals, and perhaps even to make his will felt by the Emperor. Beust protested against the Fundamental Articles in the interests of external policy (for Austria was already on the way to a reconciliation with Germany), and Andrássy on behalf of the rights of Hungary. In order to avert a very serious crisis, the Emperor requested the Čechs to make some concessions, which concessions Clam-Martinič forbade them to grant. On October 27, 1871, Hohenwart fell from power, and a month later Prince Adolf Auersperg, younger brother of Carlos, assumed the direction of affairs, together with the second German Liberal Ministry.

In the hands of Hohenwart, Schmerling's system had produced Diets favourable to federalism. In the hands of Lasser, the new Minister of the Interior, backed up by enormous governmental pressure, and by a corruption which was at that time without precedent, it produced a German majority. The first care of this majority, which had learnt wisdom by experience, was to strengthen its own position. Lasser succeeded where the Ministry of the Commoners had failed—in establishing direct election to the *Reichsrath* (Law of April 2, 1873). Henceforward, the *Reichsrath* was independent of the Diets; it was no longer possible for a whole province to remain without representatives in Parliament to the detriment of its prestige and authority. In this way, the Law of 1873 gave the death-blow to the old passive tactics; it destroyed the chances of federalism. On the other hand, it added to the injustice of Schmerling's electoral legislation instead of reforming it. The privileges of the German middle classes were increased now that the complement of the Chamber was raised from 203 to 353 members, the number of deputies from the towns and the Chambers of Commerce being doubled, while those from the country districts were only increased by two-thirds: in Moravia, the German population had five times as much electoral power as the Čech.   Hence, the *Reichsrath* remained powerless against the Emperor.

The majority, thus consolidated, took up the political and religious legislation, which had become inevitable since the denunciation of the Concordat in consequence of the proclamation of the dogma of infallibility (1870).   The Laws of 1874, in a spirit of moderate Liberalism, determined the civil status of the Catholic Church, and the application of the principle of religious liberty.   The Emperor refused to sanction a law dealing with the religious Orders.   This legislation, together with a judiciary reform, which provided for a timid and precarious introduction of the jury system, constitutes the sole success of the Auersperg Ministry.   It had many failures to counterbalance this.   The financial crash in Vienna (1873), following a period of frantic speculation, which practically dated from the Compromise, not only shook the economic equilibrium of Austria, but revealed corruption in the very highest circles of the Government—even in the Cabinet, for one of its members was forced to resign in consequence; it affected the moral authority of the middle class Liberals.   The Conservative party, with its Catholic, Christian-Socialist, and, later, Antisemitic tendencies, profited by the crash, which also strengthened the anti-Centralist coalition.

All the Slavs were involved in it, except the Ruthenes, who sought from the Germans protection against the oppression which they still suffered in Galicia at the hands of the Poles.   The latter enjoyed, at the same time, the advantages of power and the benefits of opposition; they were represented in the Cabinet by a Minister for Galicia, but they professed to draw a careful distinction between the Emperor, towards whom they professed infinite devotion and implicit obedience, and the centralised Ministry and the Parliament, which they found it profitable to oppose, seeing that, at regular intervals, their opposition had to be disarmed by concessions.   The southern Slavs had formed an alliance with the German Catholics, under the able direction of Hohenwart.   The Čechs persisted in holding apart, but the democratic movement of the " Young Čechs," who bitterly opposed the influence of the nobility, and declared themselves in favour of an active policy, gained rapidly in strength. Adolf Auersperg, like his brother before him and Schmerling before both of them, tried to solve the Bohemian question by violence and a state of siege.   The parliamentary majority was even more extreme than h the blindness of national prejudice prevented it from seeing that disputes made Austria powerless as towards Hungary, and th deprived the Parliament of the strength to struggle against th attacks of absolutism.

In Hungary, the Compromise had inaugurated a and regular development.   Andrássy and his Minister of Justice, Joseph Eötvös, the Religion, and Lónyay, the Minister of reconstruction of the territorial integrity of the kingdom. The Principality of Transylvania had been simply reincorporated into Hungary, in accordance with the Law of 1848. With Croatia, Hungary had concluded the Compromise of 1868, which conceded to the Croats for their internal affairs a fairly wide autonomy and the exclusive use of their own language. In addition to this, Croatia was allowed forty representatives in the Lower Hungarian Chamber and three in the Upper. This Compromise was in some respects obscure, and, throughout, it has given rise to disputes which were occasionally serious. The military frontier districts, originally organised as a defence against the Turks, were now divided between Croatia and Hungary. The political administration was reformed in a modern sense; the liberty of the *comitats* was not suppressed, but subjected to a ministerial control which was sufficiently powerful to prevent it from degenerating into its former condition of licence and actual rebellion; justice was transformed by the institution of a professional magistracy nominated by the Government. The law of nationalities of 1868 reconciled, by truly liberal provisions, the rights of the Magyar tongue as the state language, and those of the other tongues spoken in Hungary. This law bore the stamp of Deák's sense of justice and of Eötvös' political intelligence; but Magyar arrogance soon enforced an interpretation which was contrary to the spirit of its authors and to its own letter. In external politics, Andrássy established the influence of Hungary. He had invented the idea of the Delegations, and he knew how to make this instrument serve his purposes, which were wholly inspired by the interests of his country. He also knew how to use the great influence which he had acquired over the Emperor and Empress.

But, before long, there was reaction. The work of the restoration and organisation of the Hungarian State had exhausted Deák's party, which was losing all its best men. Deák, a worn-out old man, was living in partial retirement; Eötvös had died in 1870; Andrássy had been made Minister of Foreign Affairs in 1871; and Lónyay was discredited on account of corruption. The support of the Magyar country districts was bringing to the front Koloman Tisza, who, since 1861, had been at the head of the party which opposed Deák. He was a very typical representative of the national nobility of middle rank, which had never been affected by the atmosphere of Vienna. During 1873 and the following years a terrible financial crisis devastated the country: in some years, the deficit rose to 62 million florins—one-fourth of the receipts; the national credit was ruined. To extricate the country from this dangerous situation a new strong party was needed, vigorous with the our of youth. It came in the shape of the Liberal party, formed under patronage of Deák, and consisting of his own followers combined with of Tisza. A few months later (January 29, 1876), Deák died, ed by the tears of the nation and the dynasty, the respect of his ts and of Austria. An epoch of Hungarian history came to an

end with him.   He bequeathed to his country an undisputed legacy—
the modern State of Hungary, restored on the lines of dualism.   Tisza
was soon to breathe a new spirit into the form which Deák had created.

While his young and brilliant colleague, Koloman Széll, was reforming
the finances, Tisza took in hand the renewal of the economic Compromise,
that is to say, the decennial commercial and financial arrangements with
Austria.   His own past tradition, and the economic embarrassment of
the country, necessitated his obtaining in the new agreements advantages
for Hungarian trade and commerce, together with supplies for the
Hungarian budget.   But Austria, who, by the arrangement of 1867, was
bound to bear two-thirds of the common expenditure, and almost the
whole of the old debt, was very conscious of her economic superiority,
and, not without reason, looked to the economic Compromise to compensate her for the equality which had been imposed upon her by the
political Compromise.   Finally, Hungary triumphed all along the line.
The Austrian Bank became the Austro-Hungarian Bank, although
Austria retained a predominant control therein; the new fiscal tariff
established the increase in duties which the Hungarian budget needed;
and Hungary's proportionate contribution towards the common expenditure was not raised.

The Austrians, who since 1867 had been watching the rapid development of Hungarian influence, attributed their own misfortunes to the
defective organisation of dualism.   From time to time the Radical section
of the German majority demanded the suppression of the Delegations.
The Law of 1873 had retained in force the election of the Delegates of
the Chamber of Deputies by provinces; on the other hand, the Delegates
of the Hungarian Parliament were elected by the whole Chamber—
that is, by the majority.   Thus, the one Delegation was heterogeneous,
the other homogeneous; and, on more than one occasion, when the two
were at variance, the Delegates of the Chamber of Peers, and those of
the minority of the Austrian Chamber of Deputies had won the victory
for the Hungarians against the majority of the Austrian Deputies.   As
a matter of fact, the weakness of Austria was due to the impotence of a
Parliament which had sprung from a false and deceptive electoral law,
and which did not possess the support of the country.   The centralist
Germans shut their eyes to this truth.   Their wilful blindness was the
swift cause of their ruin.   And, as usual, it was external policy which
led to a complete change of system in Austria.

From 1867 to 1870, Beust had prepared the way for revenge on
Prussia.   But Andrássy watched him closely; he pointed out to Beust,
and, occasionally, to the foreign diplomatists, that henceforward, the
monarchy must consult the wishes of Hungary with regard to her foreign
policy.   Sedan changed the situation.   Austria's former jealous hostility
towards Berlin was succeeded by friendship.   Beust was not the man to
carry out this policy for long. · His fall was hastened by the ill-will of

CH. VII.

the Emperor-King, who could not forgive him for having originated the policy of Potocki and Hohenwart, though he had perceived the danger of it at the eleventh hour. A week after Hohenwart's dismissal, he was asked to send in his resignation, and was succeeded by Andrássy. Under this statesman, the policy of the monarchy became a truly Hungarian policy; as a matter of fact, after 1866 and 1870, it could never have been anything else. Despite the opposition of both Delegations and both Parliaments, Andrássy had long been preparing the monarchy to claim Bosnia and the Herzegovina as her share of the inheritance of Turkey. By the Congress of Berlin she acquired them. Thus, the occupation of these provinces constituted the triumph of the personal policy of the Emperor-King and his Minister. Hungary, whose opposition had been due to her hostility towards the Slavs and to her ancient sympathy for Turkey, which had been revived in 1849, did not maintain a futile attitude of sulkiness, when the occupation had become an accomplished fact. On the other hand, the Germans were steadfast in their opposition ; the Eastern policy was expensive, and it increased the Slav population of the monarchy; they refused to accept the logic of facts. The Catholic Right and the Slavs took advantage of this blunder, and identified themselves with the new Eastern policy. Thus they were ready to support the Emperor in a change of system, henceforward inevitable.

Auersperg, between the demands of his majority on the one hand, and the resistance of the Court on the other, had, like Schmerling, soon come to the end of his resources; after 1876 the Ministry dragged on a maimed existence. In July, 1878, he handed in his resignation : but matters were somehow patched up and Lasser was the only one to retire. He had been deputy in 1848, head of a Department under Bach, a Minister under Schmerling ; he was the very soul of the Cabinet, the incarnation of that Germanising and absolutist bureaucracy, whose narrow Liberalism exhausted itself in sullen anti-clericalism and respect for constitutional forms. The Emperor was not in favour of a sudden change. But it was forced upon him by the obstinacy, the blindness, and the wounded pride, of the chief members of the majority. They were simple enough to believe that no other system could last for more than six months, not realising that they themselves had owed all to the grace of the sovereign. Taaffe, together with a provisional Ministry, " made " the elections. Schmerling's machine worked as well in his hands as in those of Lasser ; in accordance with the desire of Taaffe and the Emperor, the vote of the great Bohemian landowners threw the Liberal party into a minority in the *Reichsrath*. There was a complete change, as was inevitable, in consequence of the transformation of external policy and the whole social and intellectual evolution in Austria.

The Austro-German alliance was signed in 1879 by Haymerle, Andrássy's successor, but it was really the work of Andrássy. It bears the Hungarian stamp ; the Slavs rejected the very idea of an alliance ;

the Austrian Germans would have had it more close—not international, but, for Cisleithania at any rate, constitutional.   But neither Hungary nor the dynasty wished it to be so close as to imperil independence, or more lax, for they looked to it to protect them, in their Eastern policy, from the hostility of Russia.   Eastern policy, as appealing to the Slav peoples, demands that at least some part of the Slavs in the monarchy should not have to complain of oppression ; on the other hand, the dynasty, always concerned about the national aspirations of its German subjects, and possible intrigues of Prussia, has never, since 1860, dared to favour the Slavs, except when it felt sure of the disinterestedness of Germany.   Moreover, in 1878, the Slavs were not what they had been in 1848, or even in 1859 and 1860.   Under the protection of the constitutional system and the influence of the Germans, a national middle class had grown up amongst the Čechs, a product of the development of trade and industry and of the spread of education. The Universities, which were still German, produced scholars, lawyers, and officials, who remained Čech at heart ; these men inspired and organised the lower middle classes, the artisans, the peasants, whom an increase of wealth and a better system of education had rendered more conscious of their nationality and more exacting in their demands. The Conservative aristocracy sided with them.   Thus the German party, which was falling to pieces, found itself confronted by a solid phalanx.   The financial crash of 1873, which led to a general economic crisis, had shaken the Liberal ascendancy.   The lower middle classes, who had hitherto been Liberal-Radical, began to return to clerical Conservatism.   This party had been clever enough to perceive the weak point of their opponents ; the Jews, who play an important part in the commercial and financial life of Austria, constituted one of the forces of German Liberalism, and it was easy to point to them as the cause of all the evil.   This the clergy did not fail to do ; thus began the period of Antisemitism.   The great Conservative, clerical, and feudal nobility realised how many weapons it possessed against the detested Liberalism of the narrow and prejudiced middle class.   The first Congress of the Austrian Catholics (May, 1877) revealed to close observers the imminent formation of new political parties.   Thus, the German Liberals were weakened and attacked on all sides ; they were too self-satisfied to perceive their own mistakes, too much puffed up with nationalist pride to seek safety in an agreement, at which they might quite well have arrived, with the Liberal Čechs of the middle class.   Should the dynasty desert them, they must perforce succumb.

After the elections of 1879, Count Taaffe became President of the Council, which office he retained for fourteen years (August, 1879, to October, 1893).   He changed his colleagues and his programme several times : at first his Cabinet was Liberal-Conservative ; from 1880 to 1890 it was Conservative-Nationalist ; and from 1891 to 1893 it reverted to its former colours. Nevertheless, throughout these fourteen years, the leading idea of the Prime Minister remained the same, namely, to strengthen the power and authority of the Emperor, his former playmate, whom he served all his life with unshaken fidelity, and to be the "Minister of the Crown" as opposed to the parliamentary Ministers. Although he did not meddle with the forms of the Constitution, Taaffe intended that the Emperor should be in reality supreme in high policy, in diplomatic and military affairs, and that the bureaucratic administration should govern internal affairs in his name, subject to the control, but not to the compulsion of Parliament. This system necessarily involved the depression of Parliament. To the parties who supported him, Taaffe systematically declined to make any concession of principle concerning the Constitution or the administrative organisation; but he did grant them some practical concessions in questions affecting the rights of individuals, and, more especially, those of nationalities. Naturally, these concessions were not obtained without bargaining, and the Minister did not suffer in the bargain. His enemies, the German Liberals, constantly reproached him for weakening the State. It is scarcely paradoxical to maintain that he did exactly the contrary. The defeat of the Fundamental Articles and the long duration of the Auersperg Ministry had led the opponents of the Constitution to despair of a sudden and complete constitutional change. Taaffe inured them to the application of the Constitution, which they detested; he proved that it might even be of service to them; thus he strengthened it, and he strengthened the State, for his reading of unsatisfactory clauses rendered them tolerable even to those against whom they had been directed. National struggles had existed before his time; he was not responsible for them. On the contrary, by making Parliament the field of combat for national struggles, he undoubtedly lessened the danger which they represented to the State, and he contributed towards preparing the way for the condition of equilibrium and national agreement towards which Austria was slowly progressing.

The gradual breaking up of the parties favoured his policy. The German Liberals, who had been placed in a minority by the elections of 1879, were still more weakened by the elections of 1885, for the electoral reform of 1883 had given the Čechs an assured majority among the great landowners of Bohemia, and, by lowering the franchise, it had placed in the hands of the lower middle classes a great number of constituencies in the towns and country districts. Moreover, the Liberals were divided, and the Nationalist Radicals were making headway against them. The three groups which supported the Ministry—the Čechs, the Poles, and the Catholic Centre—were almost equal in numbers, but widely different in aspirations and interests; they were only united in their hatred of Liberal Germanism, and their fear lest, by a sudden change of policy, the Emperor might begin once more to favour it. They were thus at the mercy of the Ministry, whose real strength lay in the gradual disintegration and separation of the political groups. Its success and long life must be attributed to the skill and facility with which it contrived to take advantage of this process.

After the struggle with the finances had continued for ten years, Dunajewski, a Slav Minister, succeeded in getting them into order. From 1877 onwards the State began to resume the railways, which it had sold for a very low price at a time of great pressure. A system of state insurance for the working classes was set up, and, on the other hand, the system of incorporated crafts was revived. However, this vaunted panacea was of no avail to the industrial lower middle class, the artisans. Finally, the organisation of the Austrian *Landwehr* was strengthened by military laws in accordance with the wishes and demands of the Emperor. Although the Triple Alliance was anything but popular with the majority, it was never seriously attacked.

The various parties of the majority gained distinct advantages, albeit considerably fewer than they had hoped for. In 1878, the Čechs had been obliged to abandon the hope of obtaining decisive concessions in exchange for their return to the *Reichsrath* after ten years' absence : they had to content themselves with promises and one portfolio. Afterwards, in the Bohemian Diet and in the Bohemian deputation to the *Reichsrath* they obtained the majority and secured a national University—founded in 1882 by dividing between the Čechs and the Germans the old University of Prague—together with a number of secondary schools. By the decrees of 1880 and 1886, their language was placed on an almost equal footing with German in Bohemia and Moravia for public or official life. A number of Čechs were admitted to the ranks of the Austrian administration without being obliged to conform to German standards. In moments of irritation or depression, Rieger himself was wont to deplore this "policy of crumbs." Nevertheless, the results obtained by it were really valuable, as was shown several years later. It was under Taaffe that the progress which the Čech nation had been making since 1848 assumed such solid proportions as prevented any aggressive or durable return to the policy of Germanisation.

The Poles established their sway in Galicia, as Taaffe had handed over to them the second nationality of the country, the Ruthenes, who, since 1848 and 1861, sought the protection of the German Liberals. Under pretext of developing autonomy in the country, the Polish nobles made it their private preserve, allowing no voice to Vienna, to the Government, or to the *Reichsrath*, save for grants of favours to themselves, such as the construction of railways more or less strategical, or the remission of taxes. The Catholic Centre had, for its share, the schools and the general Conservative spirit of the administration ; in 1883 the principle of denominationalism was restored by a side-wind ; in 1888, Prince Liechtenstein wished to have it proclaimed openly. But there was such lively resistance, not only on the part of the German Liberals, but also on that of the Young Čechs, that the Emperor himself intervened to have the proposal withdrawn. The Ministry, undermined by this shock, began to decline from that date onwards.

The parliamentary bargaining, which was the daily routine of Taaffe's system, was only possible in the political conditions established by the Constitution of 1861, with deputies elected, not by a really popular vote, but by a limited and distorted franchise—deputies who represented, not the people, but cliques. Now the Government had exhausted its store of concessions, and, at the same time, the evolution of intellectual, economic, and political life was creating new, spontaneous, and popular forces, which attacked the system. Bohemia was the cause of its ruin. From 1861 onwards, and more especially from 1867, the Austrian question had centred in Bohemia. For the question of nationalities in Cisleithania is essentially the question of Čechs and Germans. The party of the Old Čechs had forfeited their influence by following blindly the lead of the nobility; their policy was denounced as reactionary and anti-national by the Young Čechs, who were Liberals and Radicals, and who invoked the tradition of Hus; finally, their uncertain attitude towards Liechtenstein's proposal completed the reversion of feeling. The elections of 1889 gave the Diet of Bohemia to the Young Čechs. The Government, to defeat them, attempted to reconcile the Old Čechs and the Germans; and the Emperor intervened in person. But the force of public opinion brought about the failure of the scheme, and, in 1891, the Young Čechs obtained all the Čech seats of Bohemia in the *Reichsrath*. Taaffe, after making a vain attempt to come to an understanding with the German Left, proposed an electoral reform on the basis of what was almost universal suffrage, which would have revolutionised the condition of Austrian politics. The combination of his Liberal enemies on the Left and his clerical friends on the Right, forced him to withdraw. In his last project he had risen above himself, and given to Austrian politics a new and fruitful impulse which was almost revolutionary.

From 1893 to 1896, there was but one question in Austria, that of electoral reform. The original narrowness and injustice of Schmerling's system had increased tenfold during the last thirty years. The middle classes, to whom it had confined the electoral franchise, had, under the influence of economic and social changes, melted away; in the interval between the elections of 1885 and those of 1891, the proportion of electors to the population had fallen from 70 to 61 per mille in the towns, and from 77 to 75 per mille in the country districts. The working classes, although daily increasing in numbers and social importance, had no place in the Constitution. The agitation in favour of universal suffrage, which had begun several years before, was supported, in the first place, by the Socialists, who, since 1888, had united to form a single party; secondly, by the Christian-Socialists, whose programme, highly tinged with Antisemitism, received the growing support of the lower middle classes; thirdly, by the German Nationalists, from hatred of the Moderate Liberal middle class; and lastly, by the Young Čechs, because of their opposition to their Conservative nobility and the Old Čechs. This coalition of all the political and national opponents of the German middle classes, this remarkable combination of extreme national sections and new international or supernational parties, Socialist and Antisemitic, was profoundly significant. Only by electoral reform could the Austrian Parliament be charged with new life and vigour; only by the removal of the barriers to the franchise was it possible to merge the narrow self-interested cliques, which were enthralled by the Nationalist spirit in its most vulgar form. For these could only be swept away by the popular flood of men who, in order to live, must needs work, and who, without in any way sacrificing their own nationality, would refuse to subordinate their existence and their interests as men to the self-interested subtleties of Nationalist politicians. Taaffe had identified himself with this just point of view. He had committed the Government to electoral reform, and thus made it inevitable. The coalition Government which succeeded him, and in which the German Liberals and the clerical and Polish Conservatives had, for want of a programme, pooled their selfish interests and their terror of innovations, strove during the two years of its barren existence to find a formula by which it might decently bury the question of reform. This reform was finally voted under the next Ministry, a coalition Cabinet of officials, with Count Badeni, a former Governor of Galicia, as President. The electoral reform, which was promulgated in June, 1896, merely completed the work of Schmerling. To the four *Curiae* already in existence it added a fifth, the *Curia* of universal suffrage, in which all Austrian citizens above 24 years of age, whether privileged electors or not, were enrolled. There were 72 representatives of this *Curia*, which comprised $5\frac{1}{2}$ million voters; the four privileged *Curiae* retaining 353 seats for 1,700,000 electors. It was a caricature of Taaffe's scheme, and it involved the inevitable failure of his great idea; it meant, not the substitution of economic struggles for national disputes, but the addition of one to the other. But, for this very reason, it also meant the certainty of a new reform within a brief period. The reform of 1896 marks the close of an epoch in Austrian history; it prepares the way for a ten years' crisis, during which the internal conditions of Austria and the relations between the two States of the monarchy were alike transformed.

In Hungary Tisza remained in power for exactly as many years as Taaffe in Austria. He also changed his colleagues more than once, but never changed his policy. His system was essentially national—a system of Magyarisation; while in Austria the efforts of Germanisation were relaxed, in Hungary the forces of assimilation were being stretched to their utmost limit. At the slightest manifestation of national spirit, not even political, but purely literary or religious, the Slovaks, and still more the Roumans, were accused of Panslavist or seditious sentiments, and severely punished. From these persecutions, and the injustice of the electoral laws, which sanctioned every kind of pressure and corruption, they took refuge in passive tactics. In 1873, the Saxons of Transylvania lost a great part of their former privileges. The Croats opposed more lively resistance. Their autonomy was irksome to the national zeal and domineering instincts of Tisza; both were still further stimulated after that the occupation of Bosnia and the Herzegovina had aroused in Croatia the desire and the hope of forming a great southern Slav State, which, together with Austria, and Hungary confined to the limits of the Drave, would constitute the third section of a triple monarchy. The Hungarian and Croatian Compromise was renewed in 1879, and again in 1889, but not without difficulty. There were riotous scenes at Agram in 1883. Order was restored, but Tisza had to give way; and the recollection of these conflicts gave to Hungarian and Croatian relations, in spite of their superficial correctness, a sense of hostility and insecurity.

The finances, which had once more been drained by the cost of the occupation of Bosnia, were set in order by Wekerle, one of Tisza's ablest colleagues. The formation of a state system which included all the important railways, with the exception of one, secured for Hungary the control of the commercial land routes to the East. Baross, a Minister of genius, introduced into this system the well-known "Zone tariff"; and the consequent reduction in prices led to an enormous increase in the number of travellers, and the rapid development of trade and commerce. The reform of the Chamber of Magnates secured for this assembly greater authority and dignity, and at the same time, by the institution of a qualification of 3000 florins paid in land-tax, it diminished the number of hereditary members, which had hitherto been excessive; it also introduced an aristocracy of merit, by the creation of fifty life magnates, nominated by the King. But all these reforms, though useful in themselves, did not constitute sufficient justification for so protracted a Ministry. Tisza, like Taaffe, but in a different way, had demoralised Parliament: he was the head of a clique rather than a party; he looked upon power as an end in itself, and, although himself incorruptible, he strengthened his position by obtaining material advantages for his followers, such as salaried posts or seats on the boards of industrial or financial companies. He fell from office in 1890, owing to the hatred of his enemies and the lassitude of his own party.

There ensued several years of political and ecclesiastical conflict. The majority of the Magyars are Catholics; but the Protestants are numerous and influential. Mixed marriages are of frequent occurrence; by the Law of 1868, the children of such marriages were to be brought up in the religion of the parent whose sex they have inherited. But the civil registration was in the hands of the ecclesiastics, and the Catholic priests, encouraged by Rome, began, in defiance of the law, to baptise all the children of mixed marriages and to inscribe their names in the parish registers. Thus it became necessary to transfer the civil registration to the secular administration; and public opinion, reform having been begun, insisted that it should be complete, demanding civil marriage. Tisza's successor, Count Szápáry, being opposed to civil marriage, withdrew. Under Wekerle, who succeeded him, Szilágyi, Minister of Justice, proposed the reform; it was accepted by the deputies, but rejected by the magnates, under the influence, so it was said, of the Court. The Ministry resigned, but it was found impossible to replace it. Then Wekerle and Szilágyi, recalled to power, and fortified with the King's consent, passed the law concerning civil marriage; then they again withdrew, for the King could not forgive them for their resistance to his will. Count Khuen-Héderváry, the *Banus* of Croatia, was called upon to form a Cabinet for the second time within a few months. He was high in the King's favour, and it was thought that he was destined to become the Hungarian Taaffe; again he was unable to find colleagues amongst the majority. (He has been more successful in 1901.) Then Baron Bánffy, President of the Chamber, formed a Liberal Ministry, which passed the latest political and religious laws. In sum, these laws instituted lay civil registration for all, together with religious freedom; they placed the Jewish faith on a footing of equality with the various Christian religions. They had, moreover, a national bearing, for they transferred to state agents the important functions of civil registration hitherto exercised by the priests, who, among the orthodox Slavs and Roumans, were agents of Nationalist and anti-Magyar propaganda, or were looked upon as such. Hence, Hungary gained a twofold victory, which doubly strengthened her position.

The fusion of Hungarian parties and the change of system established in Austria in 1879 exercised a very perceptible influence on the working of dualism. The preponderance of Hungary in the monarchy, which was the inevitable consequence of the system established in 1867, became more and more marked. Tisza controlled a solid and loyal majority, but it was at the same time strong and exacting. On the other hand, Taaffe's Parliament was weak and disunited. In consequence, the Court did not treat the two Delegations in the same way; it made concessions to the Hungarians, but exercised authority over the Austrians. In external policy, besides Count Kálnoky, who had succeeded Haymerle in 1881, Tisza was the only person of importance. The Austrian Parliament, Conservative and Slav, was averse from the Triple Alliance, which, however, accorded with the ideas and sentiments of the Magyars. The government of Bosnia and the Herzegovina, the occupied provinces, had been attached to the common Ministry of Finance. Kállay, a Hungarian, received this portfolio in 1882. He understood the problem, pacified and reorganised the two provinces, assured their material prosperity.

He had been a diplomat before he became a Minister; his traditions were Conservative; his administration and politics were directed by the general interests of the monarchy.   But Hungary, whose Kings had formerly reigned over Bosnia, looked upon the country as belonging to her, and the Austrians were incensed that they should have to pay two-thirds of the expenses of its occupation, and at the same time, enjoy no more authority over it than the Hungarians, perhaps even less.   On all sides, they saw the advance of Hungarian influence and Hungarian claims, and the decay of the former unity of the monarchy.   In 1889, the army exchanged its old unitary title of Imperial Army for the dualist title of Imperial and Royal Army; many Austrians thought that even the dynasty was abandoning its time-honoured ideal of unity.   Then, why should Austria saddle herself with the burden of dualism for the sake of a precarious and delusive union?   In 1887, the economic Compromise had again been renewed without much difficulty; but, in 1897, the task promised to be both difficult and dangerous.

It was to fulfil this task that Count Badeni had been called to power in Austria.   His success in Galicia had won for him the reputation of a capable administrator.   But he knew nothing about the rest of Austria or the *Reichsrath*.   His methods were those of cunning and violence rather than those of an accomplished statesman.   His fall was rapid and complete.   He had only one success, his electoral reform, and that was, to a great extent, due to his predecessors.   The Chamber which resulted from it, and which was elected in 1897, was quite unlike those which had preceded the reform.   Even more clearly than the reform itself, it bore the stamp of the social transformations of the last twenty years, and of the political changes heralded by the method of Count Taaffe.   The united German Left, the old middle class party, had lost its unity, and one-half of its numbers; on the Right, it was being abandoned by the group of great landowners, who were inevitably attached to the Government; on the Left, it was losing the deputies from the towns and country districts, " the Progressives," who, henceforward, were scarcely to be distinguished from the Populist party, the ancient German Nationalist party, which had grown to be the largest of the German parties.   The Clericals, whether Conservative or dema-gogic (Christian-Socialists or Antisemites), had won a great number of seats.   Bohemia and Moravia had elected a majority of the Young Čechs. Among the representatives of universal suffrage, there figured for the first time fourteen Socialists (Germans, Čechs, and Poles).   The 425 deputies were divided into 24 groups.   The Slavs, together with the German Catholics, made up a majority, but they did not possess the majority of two-thirds which was required to bring about any change in the Constitution.   In view of this minute subdivision of parties, Count Badeni wished to reintroduce the system of Count Taaffe; but the time for it had passed by, and the pupil lacked the master's cunning.   The

renewal of the economic Compromise constituted his chief difficulty.   In
order to obtain a majority inclined to ratify the concessions which
he was making to Hungary, Count Badeni granted to the Čechs the
"linguistic" decrees of April 6, 1897, which are described below.   But
thereby he aroused opposition on the part of the Germans, and produced a
parliamentary crisis which, after more than ten years, is not yet concluded.

The question of Bohemia is, as we have said, the central point of
the constitutional question in Austria.   It is in order to maintain their
relations with the Germans of Bohemia that the Germans of the Alpine
provinces of Austria are in favour of centralisation, and it is in order to
secure for themselves a compact and formidable base of Germanic support
against the attacks of the Slavs that the Germans of Bohemia adhere to
this policy..   As Herbst once said, they gravitate towards Vienna; for them
Bohemia is merely "a geographical expression."   At present they are
asking for it to be divided in accordance with the linguistic boundaries;
the German parts, the "closed German territory," to have a national
administration, which would be independent of Prague, and subject to
the direct authority of Vienna.   The Čechs are federalists.   For them,
Austria is not a State, but rather a collection of States, namely, Bohemia,
Moravia, and Silesia, countries subject to the Crown of Bohemia; Galicia,
Tyrol, Archduchy of Austria, and others.   They hold that all these
States have as much right to exist and to preserve their integrity as
Austria herself, which they unite to form.   They therefore refuse to
accept the division of Bohemia according to the preponderance of
German or Čech nationality.   The decrees of 1897, which practically
required from every government official employed in Bohemia and
Moravia an equal knowledge of Čech and of German were doubly galling
to the Germans.   In the first place, these decrees imposed a special rule,
the same for both countries, which virtually created for them a special
body of government officials, thereby seemingly consecrating the idea of
federalisation and preparing the way for its fulfilment.   In the second,
the decrees required of all government officials an equal proficiency in the
two languages, thereby favouring the Čechs, who, through tradition, and
for purposes of education, had always learnt German, while the Germans
of Bohemia had, from pride, long refused to learn Čech, which they
looked upon as an inferior language.   These decrees were no revolutionary
innovation, for those of 1880 and 1886 had formed precedents, indeed,
the 1880 decrees worked perhaps an even greater change, taking into
consideration the time at which they appeared.   But the whole of the
political, the social, and consequently, the national, atmosphere of
Austria had changed.   In 1880, the Germans had confined themselves to
verbal protest; in 1897, their hostility assumed the positive and effectual
form of popular manifestations and parliamentary obstruction.   For the
time being, they were victorious; but it was their turn to be surprised
when the Čechs met the withdrawal of the decrees—which constituted

CH. VII.

the triumph of the Germans—with obstruction that proved likewise invincible. For neither Germans nor Čechs were any longer inclined to accept without demur the dictates of bureaucracy. Although not yet capable of establishing for themselves a new national order of things, by coming to an agreement with each other, they had, nevertheless, arrived at a stage of sufficient strength and maturity to enable them to withstand any change in the existing national order of things made without their collaboration, and opposed to their interests. They had arrived at what has been correctly termed " negative national autonomy."

Neither by gentleness nor by force could Count Badeni overcome the German opposition: his attempt to use violence led to a parliamentary revolution, disturbances in Vienna, and, in December, 1897, to his own resignation. A provisional Ministry, under Baron Gautsch, adjourned Parliament, in order that the Ministry might exercise its power of promulgating the budget by decree, together with a provisional Compromise with Hungary. It was the first time that the famous Article 14 had been applied in this way, and it involved a practical suspension of the Constitution; but otherwise the life of the State would have been obstructed. The semi-parliamentary Ministry of Count Francis Thun-Hohenstein, formed in March, 1898, was similarly driven by opposition to the use of the same expedient. When the opposition threatened to prevent the election of the Austrian Delegation, thus impeding the action of dualism, the Court became agitated and, in October, 1899, Count Clary, assisted by a Cabinet of officials, took office. He announced that the language question would be settled by legislation. Within two months, the opposition of the Čechs forced him to withdraw. After an interval, the Emperor entrusted to Körber the task of coming to an agreement with the Germans and the Čechs. In many ways, the new Prime Minister recalled the statesmen of the period of enlightened despotism. He was an official of wide experience and great ambition, with an exceptional capacity for hard work (at certain times, he directed as many as three departments at once); with ideas, which were in many cases very Liberal, he combined methods which were occasionally peremptory and almost despotic. He had no real sympathy with Parliament, he did not believe in the value of its help, nor was he sincerely convinced of the need to put it in working order. He invented the system of non-political politics; that is to say, he set aside the national and political questions and endeavoured to concentrate the attention of the people on economic and material subjects, which bring them together. Nevertheless, the essential problem of Austria, that is, the problem of nationalities, is always certain to reappear in the foreground, and imperiously to demand a solution.

Körber began by bringing in Bills on the language question; these bills, which were regarded unfavourably by Čechs and Germans alike, did not succeed in disarming obstruction. He then tried a dissolution. But the elections of January, 1901, brought still more strength to the National-Radical parties; the number of declared Pangermanists was trebled, and they announced in public that it was their desire to see Austria absorbed into Germany. On this Chamber the Ministry tested the value of its formula. It placed before the Chamber a programme of important works, such as the improvement of navigable ways, the proposed connexion of the basins of the Danube, Elbe, Oder, Vistula, and Dniester, to be accomplished by a network of canals; the construction of a new railway system which was to cross the Alps, bringing Bohemia and Upper Austria into communication with Trieste. This gold mine, for it required a loan of about a thousand million *Kronen,* was joyfully welcomed by all the parties; but, no sooner had the credit been voted, than they returned to the burning question of the languages. The Čechs led in obstruction, but all parties were annoyed by the stagnation of Parliament and the helplessness of the Government. Körber, attacked by both Court and Parliament, was obliged to resign in December, 1904. In consequence of the development of the Hungarian crisis, Baron Gautsch, his successor, suddenly found himself confronted by the question of universal suffrage. This Prime Minister, who had at first very decidedly opposed Reform, ended by yielding to the manifestations of popular feeling; in February, 1906, he brought in the scheme for the introduction of universal suffrage into Austria. In the following April, parliamentary difficulties compelled him to retire, but his successors, Prince Conrad Hohenlohe, and, a month later, Baron Beck, declared themselves still more openly in favour of Reform.

The decline of constitutionalism in Austria had necessarily increased still further the power which Hungary had possessed in the monarchy since 1867. The Compromise enforces, as one of the preliminary conditions of the union of the two States, the exercise of a constitutional system in Austria. Hungary was, therefore, in a position to make her own terms for accepting the application of Article 14 to the renewal of the economic agreements. She was in control of the situation, and Baron Bánffy had no difficulty in obtaining from Count Thun, not only concessions of form, which were highly flattering to her self-respect, but also very material advantages, namely, a considerable extension of Hungarian influence over the Austro-Hungarian Bank, and a more advantageous distribution of the common customs receipts. On his side, he agreed that the new arrangements should remain in force, not for a given period of time, *i.e.* ten years, but merely until they should be revoked. As revocation could only be accomplished by means of a law, and therefore with the consent of the monarch, he was left in control of the situation, and the decennial crisis of dualism was effectually prevented. These arrangements aroused the opposition of the Extreme Left or Kossuthian party, whose programme consisted in the substitution of personal union for dualism. In order to overcome this opposition, Baron Bánffy, and Tisza, his patron, attempted a parliamentary *coup d'État*; but it failed, owing to the secession of the most distinguished members of the majority, and Baron Bánffy fell from power. Under Koloman Széll, the new Prime Minister, the spirit of Deák seemed to recover its advantage in the Liberal party over the system of Tisza. By a new coalition the Liberals won the support of the National party, which had hitherto centred itself round Count Albert Apponyi. They gained thereby in numbers, moral authority, parliamentary value, and influence throughout the country, and, what was more important, henceforward they were able to avail themselves of the eloquence, patriotism, integrity, and popularity of Count Apponyi. The economic questions were settled by the "formula of Széll": this made temporary provisions which were to be valid until 1907. That year was the date not only for the expiration of the new economic arrangements—which, for the first time, assumed in Hungary the form of autonomous laws, not treaties with Austria—but also for the termination of the commercial treaties with foreign countries. Thus, in 1907, Hungary was to control the economic future of the monarchy. A new fiscal tariff was drawn up with the consent of Austria to take effect in 1907.

The Ministry had won the sympathy of the Opposition by its attempts to purify and protect parliamentary representation, as evidenced in the law prohibiting members from taking part in the direction of companies having dealings with the State, and that which transferred to the Supreme Court the right of invalidating elections. But hostility was again aroused by a projected military law. The party of independence and of 1848, that is to say, the Nationalist Kossuthian Opposition, is, on principle, antagonistic to the common institutions and especially to the common army, for it claims the right to a national Hungarian army. To the Court, the essence of dualism consists in military unity. The conflict thus did not admit of compromise. Széll, overcome by the Opposition, resigned. Finally Count Khuen-Héderváry was made President of the Council; but, suspected by the Opposition and almost equally by the majority, and weakened by the remembrance of his former failures, he was obliged to retire at the end of a few months. He was succeeded by Count Stephen Tisza, son of Koloman Tisza, a well-informed and gifted man, hard-working and energetic, but obstinate and inflexible, superior to his father in ability, but more unfortunate. In order to make matters easier for him, the sovereign granted some military concessions. These were as follows: the existing flags and banners of the common army were to be exchanged in the Hungarian regiments for new ones which were to bear insignia denoting the sovereignty of Hungary; the Hungarian regiments were to be commanded by Hungarian officers only; though German was to remain the common language for military purposes, the use of Magyar was to be extended. But Tisza had too many enemies; as a strict and zealous Protestant, he was exposed to the hostility of the Catholics; as his father's son, he incurred the hatred of

the Kossuthian party. He also met with personal hostility; Count
Apponyi abandoned the Liberal party as soon as Tisza was made head
of it, and Count Julius Andrássy, son of the first President of the
Hungarian Council, who had inherited his father's ability, assumed an
attitude of reserve and suspicion.

Tisza wished to effect a radical parliamentary cure. In order to curb
obstruction it was necessary to introduce closure into the Hungarian
Parliament; he therefore proposed to reform the rules of the Chamber.
A President, who was devoted to him, attempted to pass this measure by
violent means; whereupon a group of dissidents, led by Andrássy and
Széll, left the Liberal party; turbulent scenes ensued in the Chamber,
and Parliament was dissolved. By the elections of January, 1905, the
Independent party, which was opposed to the Compromise, and still
more to the way in which it had been administered since 1867, became
the largest party in the Chamber; together with its allies, the Dissidents
and the Catholics (the latter formed a "popular" party which had
originated with the political and ecclesiastical campaign of 1894), it was
in the majority. Five months were spent in the attempt to form a
Ministry, chosen from among the coalition, the latter demanding important military concessions which the King refused to grant. Then, in
June, 1905, General Fejérváry, who for fifteen years had been Minister of
National Defence in the Liberal Cabinets, and who possessed the entire
confidence of the sovereign, sacrificed himself to form a Government
which would protect the King and attempt to reconcile the Crown and
the parliamentary majority. The latter proved unmanageable. In order
to reduce this majority, the Government under the guidance of Kristoffy
threw out the idea of an electoral reform, which was to introduce universal
suffrage into Hungary.

The aim of the Reform was the same in Hungary as in Austria.
First, to extend the suffrage with a view to opening the door of politics
to the working classes, who bear the heaviest share of the public burdens,
and who care little to discuss the details of the language question or the
subtleties of public law; not to eliminate from public life the question
of nationalities, for this would have been impossible, but to put it in
competition with economic and social questions, and hence to secure
the active, normal existence of the State. The electoral system of
Hungary is even worse than that of Schmerling; its extreme complexity
—there are thirty-six electoral qualifications—gives clear evidence of the
intention to confine the electoral franchise almost exclusively to the
Magyars, and, amongst these, to a few privileged classes. The electoral
arrangements give to the Magyars a representation which may be twelve
times as great in proportion to their numbers as that of the Roumans,
for instance. The procedure for deciding upon electoral qualifications
allows the Minister presiding over the offices in which the lists of voters
are drawn up to exclude practically all the electors whom he disapproves

CH. VII.

from the exercise of their rights. The proportion of electors to the population, which has been steadily decreasing for some time, has now sunk to 52·5 per mille. One-fourth of the electors are officials or employees of the State. Under these conditions, and in consequence of historic tradition, the political and parliamentary staff is chosen almost exclusively from one caste, that of the lesser nobility, whose education is purely formal, juridical, and verbal, and who adhere to the old "gravaminal" policy of seeking out and denouncing any real or fancied attack on the constitutional rights of Hungary. Under the projected Reform, which trebles the number of electors, this petty and turbulent element ought to yield to the force of the workers, to the productive element; for the labouring classes, which had hitherto been excluded from the electoral body, would constitute one-third of it. Without impairing the Magyar hegemony, the Reform ought to secure for the non-Magyar nationalities a representation which, if not proportionate to their numbers, would nevertheless be considerable. It should thus compel the Magyar parties to unite, for how could they continue their vain discussions about trifling points, when they found themselves confronted by the serious question of nationalities in a Parliament thus transformed? Moreover, among the deputies of the minor nationalities (the Roumans, Slovaks, Serbs, and Germans) the Court hoped to find allies who would join with the Magyar moderate element in securing the uninterrupted working of the dualist forms of government for affairs common to both countries.

It was not without hesitation that the sovereign had identified himself with Reform. Count Goluchowski, Minister of Foreign Affairs, and Baron Gautsch, represented to him that universal suffrage would prove infectious; if it were granted to Hungary, how could it be withheld from Austria? Would it be possible to preserve the continuity of the external policy of the monarchy, and, more especially, to maintain the alliance with Germany, which forms the mainstay of this policy, in the face of Delegations elected (though indirectly) by universal suffrage, Delegations that would prove more exacting and less manageable than before? It was the obstinacy of the Hungarian coalition, which rejected all his attempts at conciliation, that finally decided the Emperor-King. Even when thus threatened, the coalition remained obdurate; in vain Count Andrássy opened direct negotiations with the King in its name. Then the Fejérváry Ministry announced the dissolution of the Chamber; the Parliament buildings were occupied by soldiers, and a colonel read the decree of dissolution from the platform. At the same time, the commercial treaty, which had recently been concluded between Germany and the monarchy, was put in operation by a royal decree, in defiance of the Constitution. There was no really serious movement on the part of the people in response to this twofold attack on constitutional law. Then the coalition yielded. Wekerle, the Prime Minister, identified with political and ecclesiastical reforms, formed a coalition Cabinet, in which Francis Kossuth, son of the great Louis Kossuth, together with Count Apponyi, stood for the Independent party, and Count Andrássy for the dissidents, who had become the Constitutional party. The "compact" made with the Crown secured, in the first place, indemnity for the members of the Cabinets of Tisza and Fejérváry, and for the officials who had served them; in the second, parliamentary ratification of the commercial treaty with Germany; in the third, the normal working of the government and the administration in Hungary, and the satisfactory conduct of affairs common to both countries; in the fourth, the postponement of any change in the army until the electoral Reform should be put into effect. This was to be done so soon as current affairs and arrears had been cleared up. The Reform was to be at least as extensive as that designed by the Fejérváry Ministry, and based on the principle of universal suffrage (April, 1906). The old Liberal party decided to dissolve itself, and in the May elections the Kossuth party obtained an absolute majority in the Chamber.

A period of transformation and rejuvenescence in the history of Austria and Hungary began with the almost simultaneous accession to power of the respective Ministries of Beck and Wekerle. The forms of government which, in 1867, had been instituted in Austria, Hungary, and in the dual system, expressed very nearly the equilibrium of political, economic, social, and national forces at that date. Since that time these forms of government had remained practically unchanged whilst, on the other hand, the equilibrium was being shifted. This had given rise to parliamentary difficulties, to crises of obstruction, and to that surprising and ridiculous phenomenon, a monarchy which, in external affairs, tries to play the part of a Great Power and occasionally succeeds, whilst, so far as home affairs are concerned, it is unable to obtain for itself a peaceful existence and an assured future. Since 1906, electoral Reform has been accomplished in Austria and promised to Hungary beyond recall; the economic Compromise has at length been renewed, and, for the first time, to the equal satisfaction of both States; external policy has been revived and reinvigorated by a bold offensive in the East, which is not without errors or defects, but which, by forming new ties of mutual interest between the two States and by exposing them to common dangers, has strengthened the feeling of solidarity and brought them together. All this affords a new guarantee for the duration of the Austro-Hungarian monarchy, which has sometimes appeared to be on the point of vanishing, and which has so often been declared essential to the well-being of Europe.

In Austria, Baron Beck formed a mixed Cabinet of officials and members of Parliament (May, 1906). He withdrew all the schemes for the economic Compromise which his predecessors had put forward, thus asserting the complete freedom of Austria in the requisite negotiations.

He then gave his undivided attention to the electoral Reform, which had matured under the Governments of Gautsch and Hohenlohe and was now ready to be put into execution. It only required a few modifications. The Chamber of Peers deemed it revolutionary, and, in order to obtain their support, the Government was obliged to fix, by law, a maximum and minimum for the number of Life Peers, that is to say, to furnish a guarantee against the wholesale creation of Peers. The new electoral Law of January 26, 1907, granted the right to vote to all Austrians above 24 years of age, who had not forfeited their rights, and who had resided in a commune within the constituency for a year. It suppressed the *Curiae*. Henceforward, each parliamentary district was to have its own deputy. These constituencies, which were divided into two classes (urban and rural respectively) and which were, so far as possible, of homogeneous nationality, differed considerably in extent and population; their boundaries were determined by law, once for all. By means of this inequality, and of the unchangeable nature of the law, it was found possible to safeguard, within the requisite proportions, the privileges of certain nationalities, whose hostility might have imperilled Reform. Hence, it did not establish absolute equality and perfect justice. The Germans, who formed 35·8 per cent. of the population, were allowed to retain 45 per cent. of the seats; whereas the Čechs, for a population of 23·2 per cent., had only 20·6 per cent., and the Ruthenes 6·2 per cent. for a population of 13·2 per cent. The aggrieved nationalities protested; not one, despite the justice of its complaints, wished to impede the success of a Reform which was, in the main, beneficial to all of them, but they reserved for themselves the right of removing this remaining injustice in the future.

The Reform was justified by the elections of 1907, which completely upset the proportions of the different parties. The Parliament elected by universal suffrage was quite unlike the old Parliament of *Curiae*. In the new Chamber, which has 516 members, the two strongest parties were no longer the nationalist but the economic parties, namely, the Christian Socialists, who had 96 seats, and the Social Democrats, who had 87; on the other hand, the Pangermans had fallen from 15 to 3. Among the different German parties, the votes were distributed as follows: 720,000 Christian Socialists; 514,000 Socialists; 146,000 Agrarians (this is a mixed party, economic and nationalist, but less irreconcilable than the old nationalist parties); 146,000 Populists (the nationalist party of the lower middle classes); 116,000 Liberals (upper middle class and intellectuals); 71,000 National Radicals; 20,000 Pangermans. Similarly, among the Čechs, mixed parties, such as Catholics and Agrarians, had gained considerably at the expense of the purely nationalist parties, and the Social Democrats had obtained two-fifths of the whole votes. It was, in fact, the dawn of a new Austria—an Austria which was stronger than the old one, and quite determined to live.

The history of the Parliament in 1907 and 1908 furnishes additional proof of the efficacy of this reform.   There are still fierce national struggles, possibly more violent than heretofore, but they are no longer able to impede the action of Parliament.   Obstruction has become the weapon of the weakest sections, and in their hands it has lost its force. In decisive moments, the great parties, more especially the economic parties (*i.e.* the Socialists, Christian Socialists, and Agrarians), have shown clearly and vigorously that they do not intend to allow the people's Parliament to be paralysed.   Thus the sovereign has been justified in his faith in universal suffrage; he has been rewarded for his energetic and unfaltering support of it.   But all the difficulties are not yet surmounted ; far from it.   The national struggle is raging in Bohemia today with unparalleled violence; it has led to the fall of Baron Beck, and it has placed Baron Bienerth, his successor (1907), in a position which presents difficulties seemingly inextricable.   But the electoral reform has indicated the path which leads to solutions ; an understanding between the peoples, becoming more and more conscious of their own strength and of that of their opponents.   Advance in democracy has naturally involved advance in national autonomy which, by entrusting to each nationality a national administration and the care of its own exclusively national interests, will eliminate the chief causes of strife and promote agreement concerning the important political and economic interests common to all.   In the rescript which summoned Baron Bienerth to the Ministry, the Emperor proclaimed his faith in parliamentary government, thus showing that he comprehends the needs and interests of his subjects more clearly than many of those subjects themselves, and that he is determined to continue in the way opened out by the electoral Reform.

In Hungary, constitutional procedure, which had been interrupted by the Fejérváry Ministry, was reestablished under the *régime* of the coalition. The officials who had served under his unconstitutional system, and who had been less protected, or at any rate, less openly protected by the King, than their superiors, were dismissed from office.   The Magyar national feeling was appeased by a new educational law, the work of Count Apponyi, calculated to ensure the rapid development of the Magyar tongue, and by a more pronounced encouragement of trade than heretofore, which, in accordance with the programme of its promoter, Francis Kossuth, would seem to prepare the way for the fiscal separation of the two States, and the economic independence of Hungary.   But Hungary has been perturbed by the secession of the Croats, whose cooperation had materially contributed to the Pyrrhic victory of the coalition in the recent struggle with the King.   The Croats declared that, in spite of the promises which had been made to them, they had not been adequately rewarded, and that they were no better treated than before.   There was rioting at Agram and the Constitution was suspended by the *Banus*. The Hungarian Government, despite its air of indifference, perceives the danger of this situation and desires to come to an agreement; but the difficulty is enhanced by the unreasonable attitude of the extreme parties on both sides. Electoral Reform has been the cause of no less embarrassment. Count Andrássy, whose task it was to establish universal suffrage without weakening the national Magyar character of the Hungarian State—which he did not wish to do, even had the majority permitted it—gradually worked out a scheme of compromise, by which plural voting and the skilled delimitation of constituencies were to keep the nationalities in check under a system of universal suffrage. With a view to the changes in the political situation which Reform will necessitate, the present coalition is tending towards a real amalgamation. The Constitutional party and the Kossuth Independents have drawn together during the last three years, the latter having made most of the advances. The King will certainly not give up universal suffrage. It remains to be seen whether the Magyar parties will unite on a common-sense programme for practical moderate action, such as the economic and social development of the country, reconciliation with Croatia and the nationalities without loss of the requisite unity of the Hungarian State, some form of union with Austria, whereby, under a system which would more clearly define the independence and sovereignty of both States, their political and economic solidarity would be more firmly secured.

The economic Compromise concluded under the administration of Beck and Wekerle already bears the stamp of a new adjustment of political bearings. Since 1867, the formula of the Compromises had always been the same, namely, Hungary, in return for the "national" sacrifice imposed on her by the community of diplomacy, and more especially, of the army, demanded economic concessions which the Austrian Ministers, under pressure on the part of the Court, invariably ended by granting. Baron Beck reversed the formula, for he sold political advantages to the Hungarians, in return for economic advantages for Austria. For the first time in these negotiations, the Austrian Cabinet allowed itself to be swayed, not by the dynastic interests connected with the common diplomatic and military organisation, but by interests purely Austrian, namely, the requirements of the finances, of trade, and of the Austrian people. In fact, the task of the Beck Cabinet was facilitated by the general economic situation and the reaction on Hungary of the European financial crisis; it was not a suitable moment for Hungary to quarrel with Austria, her best customer and chief creditor. The agreement, after a keen conflict of interests, settled the bulk of the economic questions still pending between the two States, with the exception of that of the Bank, which, by mutual consent, was reserved for subsequent negotiations. Hungary was gratified by the form of an international treaty, instead of that of a union, and by a guarantee that, in future commercial agreements with foreign countries her independence and sovereignty should be more clearly emphasised, and, lastly, that the Austrian market should be opened without restriction to her loans. Austria gained the declaration and confirmation of the principle of commercial freedom between the two countries, and of equality of their respective subjects before the fiscal laws; the institution of arbitration to settle any difficulties which might arise in connexion with the economic Compromise (this last she had demanded in vain for forty years); the recovery of her liberty in the matter of railway tariffs which, for the last ten years, had been curtailed to the advantage of Hungary; finally, a favourable settlement of the proportional contribution towards the common expenditure, which, henceforward, was to be at the rate of 36·4 for Hungary and 63·6 for Austria. Hence, on this occasion, neither country profited at the expense of the other, the Compromise being in conformity with the interests of both countries, as conceived by them. This Compromise did not, like those which had preceded it, give rise to bitterness and malice. It was adopted in both States before the end of 1907. On January 1, 1908, the constitutional interregnum that had lasted ten years came to an end.

The pessimists called this Compromise "the Compromise of Separation," and foretold that, on its expiration in 1917, the last traces of the economic union between the two States would disappear. But it rather seems as though the new Compromise had strengthened the ties between them, in that it subordinated form to matter, promoted free and equal discussion between the two contracting parties, and proved to the Hungarians that dualism is not detrimental to Hungarian sovereignty, and to the Austrians that it does not necessarily involve sacrifice and humiliation on their part.

Since 1866, the monarchy has become an Eastern Power and is now that alone; its external policy being wholly concentrated on the Balkans. The occupation of Bosnia and the Herzegovina in 1878 had been the first step in this direction. Since then, the necessity of consolidating this conquest, and the shock resulting from internal trouble, had impeded the Austro-Hungarian advance. The external policy of the monarchy, which was characterised by caution under Count Kálnoky, and by timidity under Count Goluchowski, faithfully followed the lead of Germany. In the autumn of 1906, Count Goluchowski was sacrificed to the ill-feeling of the Hungarians, who blamed him for having postponed the conclusion of the constitutional struggle. He was succeeded by Baron Aehrenthal, formerly ambassador in St Petersburg, who was expected to be the promoter of an Austro-Russian agreement of a still more intimate nature than that contained in the programme of Mürzsteg. But he prided himself on his modern, practical, and economic policy; in order to assist the development of Austro-Hungarian trade in Macedonia, he started the scheme of the Novibazar railway, which was to connect the Bosnian system with the Turkish line towards Salonica. Russia, to salve her wounded feelings, made overtures to England, but, at that moment, the Young Turks took a hand, and the whole of the Balkan card-table was overthrown. Austria-Hungary had good cause to fear that the regenerate Turks would take it into their heads to demand that her occupation of Bosnia-Herzegovina should come to an end, and, naturally, she would never have consented to this. In October, 1908, in order to settle the matter, the Emperor-King proclaimed that the law of succession established by the Pragmatic Sanction of 1722–3 was to be extended to those two provinces, in other words, that they were annexed by the monarchy. The complications which ensued have not yet been completely solved. Nevertheless, the annexation is irrevocable. Austria and Hungary are at one in their desire to maintain it.

On December 2, 1908, Francis Joseph I celebrated the sixtieth anniversary of his accession to the throne. On the occasion of his Jubilee (December, 1898), Europe had viewed with fear and distrust the future of the monarchy, which seemed inevitably doomed to dissolution at the death of Francis Joseph. But ten years have elapsed since then, and the prognostications are wholly different. The acute crisis has been dispelled solely by the internal forces of the monarchy. The external dangers, that is to say, Pangermanism and Panslavism, appear much less serious today than at that time. Pangermanism has been swept aside by universal suffrage, and the Panslavonic feeling is growing weaker; moreover, it suffers from the reaction due to the enfeeblement of Russia and the Balkan evolution. There is still a violent struggle between the nationalities, but the inevitable solution is in sight. The union between Austria and Hungary has, in reality, been strengthened by the new Compromise and the new Eastern policy. It seems as though all the Austrian, Hungarian, and Austro-Hungarian questions could be settled from within. It is in this that the progress consists; herein lies the great security for the future.

It would be equally unjust to attribute to Francis Joseph alone all the honours of this far-reaching and peaceful transformation, and to deny that he had any part in it. His wisdom, self-control, moderation, tact, and freedom from prejudice, have done much to help it on its way. Much will depend upon his successor. But fifty years of national and constitutional life have endowed the peoples of the monarchy with the strength to enforce their wishes side by side with those of their sovereign, and, if necessary, in opposition to him. They are of age, and can control their own destinies if they wish to do so, provided only that they agree amongst themselves. They have come to realise the common interest which keeps them united in the monarchy and in time they will become conscious of the strength by means of which they can govern it in accordance with their own interests. The monarchy no longer rests on the power of the dynastic tie alone, but also on their conscious desire for union. Herein lies its great internal change; herein lies its mighty new strength; this is the great, the enormous result of the reign of Francis Joseph.

CHAPTER VIII.

UNITED ITALY.

WHEN the last French soldier had sailed from Civita Vecchia and the papal mercenaries laid down their arms at the breach of Porta Pia, the task of national union, to which three and a half centuries earlier Machiavelli had urged the princes of Italy, was at length accomplished. Therewith a new epoch opens in the history of the peninsula; the stirring days are past and the problems that absorb Italian statesmen will be henceforth predominantly domestic. During the six years subsequent to the opening of the first Italian Parliament at Rome (November 27, 1871) the great historic party of the Right, whose enlightened conservatism had presided over the fortunes of the young monarchy, was in rapid disintegration. A great cause had evoked great leaders, but, the goal once reached, the tension slackened. No statesman of first-rate ability was brought to the front, and men of second rank were confronted with racial, political, ecclesiastical, and social problems which would have taxed the genius of a Cavour in the plenitude of his powers. The Right attempted to deal, and not unsuccessfully, with the perilous situation caused by the intrusion of the secular power into the ecclesiastical capital; they wrestled with the financial chaos and reduced it to some degree of order; they maintained a cautious foreign policy; they laid the basis of a new military organisation and set about the creation of a navy. But they had grown timid; they were absorbed in political and financial expedients, while fiscal oppression and widespread poverty were engendering discontent and a new and passionate ideal of social regeneration was permeating the democracy of Italy. Internal dissension parted the Lanza-Sella and the Minghetti sections, and was only kept in check by fears of a Radical administration under Rattazzi. Eagerly watching to grip and throw the leaders of the Right stood the men of the Left, compact, united, big with promises, impatient of a sterile Republicanism. Their leaders had supported Sella in restraining Victor Emmanuel from his chivalrous but mad impulse to involve the nation in the *débâcle* at Sedan, and had spurred the recalcitrant and hesitating

Right to the final consummation of Italian hopes at Rome.   Rattazzi's death in the summer of 1873 paved the way for a Minghetti Cabinet, and the general elections of the autumn of 1874 gave the new premier a substantial majority.   But the Left, despite unscrupulous official pressure and corruption, had strengthened their position; and among their deputies sat Saffi, leader of the popular party, who with Signor Fortis and other Romagnuol democrats had been arbitrarily arrested at Villa Ruffi during the elections.

Among the most odious of the taxes imposed (1869) to fill the maw of the ravenous exchequer was the grist tax, known all over Italy as the " tax on hunger"; and the extension of the tobacco monopoly to Sicily in 1874 had aroused fierce opposition.   In 1876 a big scheme of railway redemption and state management, introduced at a time when a thousand million *lire* of forced currency were in circulation and Italian paper stood at 10 per cent. discount, gave the Left their chance.   There were ominous signs, too, of insubordination among the Tuscan deputies of the Right, who were disappointed at their exclusion from office and irritated by Minghetti's unsympathetic attitude towards the desperate financial situation at Florence, caused by the sacrifices she had made when, a sleepy provincial town, she was summoned to become the capital of Italy. Minghetti, unconscious of the gathering storm, having triumphantly announced, on the opening of the spring session, that the finances had found their long-desired equilibrium, and having traced the lines of his railway policy, was met by a hostile vote.   A motion was carried (March 18, 1876) condemning the oppressive incidence of the grist tax. The long reign of the Right was at an end, and on March 28 the first Ministry of the Left sat in the Parliament at Rome.   The new premier, Depretis, had been one of the earliest disciples of Mazzini, but long since had made his peace with the monarchy and had served as pro-dictator of Sicily.   In addition to the Presidency of the Council he took the Department of Finance; Baron Nicotera, the famous Calabrian patriot, who had organised the party victory, held the portfolio of the Interior, and Zanardelli, a clever Radical jurist, that of Public Works.   An early opportunity was taken to dissolve the Chamber and " work the elections " in accordance with approved Italian practice.   Nicotera drove the electoral machine at tremendous pressure; the prefects were lashed by disciplinary measures, threats, and promises, to feverish activity on behalf of the government candidates; and, aided by the widespread desire for change and disgust at the long dominion of the *Consorterie*, a crushing defeat was inflicted on the Right, who returned to the new Chamber (November, 1876) a disorganised rump.

The Depretis Ministry assumed power with a heavy load of promises. The forced currency was to be redeemed, the hated grist tax abolished, and a more equitable distribution of public burdens was to relieve the poorer taxpayer.   The resources of the country would be developed, trade fostered by an extensive scheme of railway construction, existing treaties of commerce revised in a free trade direction. They promised to introduce a comprehensive measure of electoral reform, to maintain the right of public meeting and the freedom of the Press, to organise free and compulsory secular education, to observe rigidly the Law of Guarantees, and to meet any encroachment of the ecclesiastical power by an unflinching assertion of the paramount authority of the civil Government. Victor Emmanuel, despite the scared countenances of his late advisers and their croakings of imminent revolution and chaos, accepted the new situation with absolute sincerity; and, bluff, honest soldier as he was, inserted with his own hand a clause in the Speech from the Throne expressing his full and frank confidence in the Ministers he had called to office. Signor Crispi, the most outstanding figure of the Left, was elected President of the Chamber, and all fair auguries seemed to attend the birth of the new Ministry.

But it is one thing for advanced politicians to combine in opposition: another to work harmoniously in a wide programme of progressive legislation. The new Ministers were tried administrators, but three only had experience of office; they had no Foreign Minister equal to Visconti-Venosta, no financier of Sella's capacity: some, of forceful individuality, were moved by personal ambition. There was little cohesion and less willingness to sacrifice private aims to the common weal. Moreover, they lacked originality: their opponents' Railway Bill was adopted with the addition of a clause empowering the State to lease the railways to private companies. The tardy abolition of the grist tax (1884) made no sensible diminution in the price of bread; and an increase of the duties on corn from 2s. 6d. to 5s. 3d. a quarter in April, 1887, followed by a further increase in February, 1888, to 8s. 9d., made the abolition a mere mockery of the poor. Reform was sacrificed to clamorous interests, and the petty crafts of parliamentary legerdemain became paramount. With all their faults, the Right had been a political party: the Left initiated the system of government by factions and sectional interests. For a whole decade, with two short interruptions, the premiership was held by Depretis, a man in whom Cavour, thirty years before, had discerned, beneath an austere and resolute exterior, a petty mind and infirm will. Personally clean-handed and averse from ostentation, the new premier had a profound insight into the darker places of the human soul and was skilled in playing on the baser motives that sway the actions of men. Cynical, cold, devoid of enthusiasm, he relied for his ascendancy on his consummate tactics, his adroitness in parliamentary fence. In his hands, Italian politics degenerated into a welter of corruption unparalleled in the history of the monarchy. Ill-assorted *connubii* of hostile party leaders had already been known in Italian politics: to Depretis belongs the inglorious distinction of having elaborated the shameless promiscuity of alliances known as *trasformismo*, which has ever since fouled the streams of parliamentary life in Italy. With Minghetti's aid and under the pretence of uniting moderate men from all parties against the " insolence of the piazza" and the extra-legal agitation of the Extreme Left, Ministers were chosen from those heads of factions and interests who commanded most votes in the Chamber; it was a system negative of all political rectitude and destructive of healthy party distinctions.

An act was passed (July 15, 1877) making elementary education compulsory for children between the ages of six and nine, but no adequate machinery for enforcing attendance was provided, and the burden of expenditure was laid on the communes ; a Bill, introduced during the domination of the Right to regulate the employment of women and children, was carried in 1886 so far as regarded child labour alone ; a considerable, though somewhat timid and complicated, Electoral Reform Bill was carried in 1881, which extended the franchise from 621,896 voters (1879) to 2,017,829 (1882) ; some energy was shown in suppressing brigandage in the south.   But the closing years of the Depretis Ministry were years of inertia, of a petty hand-to-mouth policy, of grave financial miscalculation, and of a light-hearted embarcation on a disastrous career of African adventure. The annual effective expenditure (excluding railways) which during the last six years of the Right (1871–6) had averaged £43,460,850 rose under the first six years of the Left to £48,284,580.

On January 9, 1878, the whole Italian nation was plunged into profound grief by the death of its first King, whose imperturbable courage and faith, sterling honesty, and burly good sense, had been essential factors in its emancipation. Many have been the pompous titles added by fear or flattery to the names of princes; to Victor Emmanuel belongs the unique distinction of having been known to his people as the King who was an honest man (*Il re galantuomo*). Twenty-nine days later the last Pope-King passed away. One of the latest acts of Pius IX had been to send Monsignor Marinelli, his own father confessor, to the dying Victor Emmanuel with his blessing and with the Blessed Sacrament which was administered by the royal almoner, Canon Anzino. The new King, Humbert I, took the oath to the Constitution on January 29, 1878, and was acclaimed with confidence and loyalty : on February 20 one of the shortest conclaves in the history of the Papacy and one of the least distracted by external pressure, elevated to St Peter's chair, Cardinal Pecci, known as Leo XIII.

On June 2, 1882, a heavier sorrow even than that evoked by the death of Victor Emmanuel fell upon the people of Italy: Garibaldi, their darling hero, last survivor and best loved of the four great creators of Italian Unity, closed the glorious drama of his life at Caprera where, his patriotic warfare done, the scarred warrior had laid aside his sword and turned to his plough. Victor Emmanuel's death had left him inconsolable: the disclosure of the incompetence and folly that led to the betrayal of

Italian hopes at Tunis had touched the old soldier to the quick. He suffered himself to be drawn into a popular demonstration of protest at Palermo and never recovered from the fatigue and excitement of the journey.

The advent to power in August, 1887, of Crispi, the old revolutionist and member of the Expedition of the Thousand, was viewed with small favour by the Court. Although the new premier had given the watchword that rallied the bulk of the Republicans to the monarchy; although he had sacrificed his dearest principles and friendships to the common good of the Unitary movement—the House of Savoy never forgot or forgave his opposition to the Napoleonic alliance, which he consistently distrusted, and believed (not without justification as the sequel proved) to be pregnant with humiliation to Italy. The country at large, however, was won by his undoubted force of character and by his imperturbable faith in the future of his country. After the last six slumbrous years of Depretis' rule, a premier who could govern with vigour and act with promptitude made a powerful appeal to the party of order. Everyone in the government departments, from highest official to humblest doorkeeper, felt the grip of a strong hand on the reins when Crispi was in the saddle; and, had but sagacity and insight informed his will, he might have worn down opposition. But he was proud, impatient of criticism, self-centred, difficult of access. Nursed in conspiracies, his hot southern imagination saw plots and dangers everywhere; his impulsive temperament led him into the strangest inconsistencies. Now, he threatened to occupy the Vatican with Italian troops: now he opened negotiations for an understanding with the Papacy. He would free the workman from the slavery of capital: then he would pursue Radicals and Socialists with implacable hostility and appeal to all parties of order to unite against the menace of subversive propaganda. In addition to the Presidency of the Council, Crispi bore the burden of the Foreign Office and of the Interior, and, in spite of his enormous capacity for work, these responsibilities induced an irritability of temper that gave his enemies easy prize. But it was not until 1891 when, confident in his quasi-dictatorship, he dared to lay a reforming hand on the bureaucracy and grew restive under the tutelage of the Right, that he fell into the trap prepared for him by a combination of party groups (January 31). A coalition of the Right and Left Centres under the Sicilian patriot, Marchese di Rudinì, and Baron Nicotera, succeeded in forming a Cabinet among whom were tried and incorruptible administrators such as Luzzatti, Luigi Ferraris, and Professor Villari. The new Ministry met the Chamber with an admirable programme of retrenchment, but it lacked cohesion and vigour and was unskilled in, or contemptuous of, the art of lobbying. Its indecision in face of riots at Rome irritated the extremes of Right and Left alike; and a proposal to reduce the number of Army Corps roused the opposition of the Court and

CH. VIII.

military party; in May, 1892, the Left under Signor Giolitti returned
to power.

The new premier, who had climbed at a comparatively early age
from a modest position in a government office to political eminence, was
a man of amazing intellectual suppleness and versatility; of indefatigable
industry; a precise and lucid rather than an eloquent speaker; an
adroit organiser and accomplished master of the art of electoral corruption.   Giolitti was the first to attempt the creation of a Liberal and
monarchical party that should include 'all progressive politicians who
were willing to break definitely from the anti-dynastic Extreme Left;
but he was indifferent as to means and careless of principles, if only he
could maintain his footing on the slippery heights of power.   Ill-hap
pursued his first Ministry, some of whose members were conspicuous
neither for capacity nor integrity.   A crushing exposure of grave irregularities in the relations between eminent politicians and Tanlongo,
Director of the Banca Romana, was met by Giolitti with denials of
complicity   But the shameful indictment was too well authenticated,
public disgust too profound; and, though Tanlongo and his accomplices
were acquitted by juries, it was only as a protest against the immunity
of more highly placed culprits.   Meanwhile, the Ministry, besmirched
and discredited, were too demoralised to grapple with the growing
unrest in the peninsula and the more serious agrarian insurrections in
Sicily.   A wave of national revulsion swept them from power; and an
almost universal cry for Crispi, as the one strong man able to deal with
the situation, again lifted the veteran leader of the Left into the saddle
(December 14, 1893).   Crispi's iron hand was soon felt.   Martial law
was proclaimed; the Labourers' Unions in Sicily were dissolved; 271
popular associations were suppressed—55 in Milan alone.   The premier,
whose perfervid imagination, worked upon by police spies, saw a vast
conspiracy aiming at a Federal Republic and plots to sell Sicily to
France or Austria, had recourse to a brutal policy of repression that
recalled Bourbon and Austrian days.   Savage and indiscriminating
sentences by military commissions, arbitrary arrests of men suspected of
holding advanced opinions, revolted the popular conscience and prepared
a soil wherein the seeds of socialism rapidly germinated.   On December 4,
1894, an impotent report of the Parliamentary Commission on the
bank scandals deplored the "indelicate relations" between responsible
politicians and the banks of issue; and, a week later, Giolitti, flourishing
a bundle of papers, declared in the Chamber that he held in his hand
Crispi's moral ruin.   A committee of five appointed to examine the papers
reported next day that the premier and other prominent politicians had
received considerable sums from the Banca Romana for the purpose of
electoral and press corruption.   Crispi, by a daring stroke, prorogued the
Chamber and quashed all discussion (December 12, 1894).   Giolitti, it
was found, had used a private correspondence between husband and wife

to help to drag the premier down ; and, although party warfare in Italy is not over-chivalrous in its methods, this action was felt to be a blow beneath the belt. Shamed by the general disgust, he left the country for a time. Crispi, having ridden the storm and won the acquiescence of the monarchy, now headed for a thinly disguised dictatorship. During the process of revising the electoral register in accordance with a law passed July 11, 1894, voters suspected of hostility to the Ministry were struck off the rolls and in all a purge of 813,320 electors was made out of nearly 3,000,000. Crispi then dissolved the Chamber and, by a vigorous application of the government screw, obtained an overwhelming and more subservient majority. The elections were a mere parody of representative government; and it has been estimated that the 336 official candidates were returned by about 600,000 electors out of a population of 31,000,000. Even this could not prevent a small but resolute band of Socialist deputies and some of Crispi's bitterest enemies from appearing on the benches of the Extreme Left ; and, led by the fiery Cavallotti, the campaign against the premier was resumed with unabated rancour. Crispi's position however was too secure to be shaken : he was even spoken of as Minister for life. But Africa, the grave of reputations, ruined him. Lured by grandiose visions of a vast Italian empire in Erythrea, his forward colonial policy met its Sedan at Adowah ; and, in March, 1896, he was hurled from power amid the execrations of the people. King and army demanded an avenging campaign to wipe out the shame of defeat; but lack of money no less than the temper of the nation forbade, and a peace Ministry was formed. A period of rapid ministerial changes ensued and between March 10, 1896, and June 26, 1898, four Cabinets were made and unmade.

The opening months of 1898 were marked by ominous indications of a social upheaval. The people were losing faith in their rulers and, amid the widespread disorder, the teachings of the extreme democrats fell on willing ears. At the celebration of Cavallotti's funeral (March, 1898) the authorities with alarm beheld the bannered hosts of socialist and revolutionary clubs march through the streets of Milan and Rome—a veritable review of the forces of democracy. Those alone who have had personal experience of Italy in the nineties can appreciate the utter misery and dejection of her people in those distressful times. Wheaten bread, owing to bad harvests and the high tariff (in December, 1894, the import duty on corn had been raised to 13s. the quarter), was a luxury of which the more fortunate *contadini* on feast days bought precious morsels weighed out with niggard hand. Gaunt, half-starved labourers, mattock in hand, gathered on the piazzas and shouted for " bread and work." Early in 1898, in the Mantovano, in the Marches, and in the Napoletano, the smouldering discontent blazed out into open riots ; the Puglie were in revolt; and, while King and Senators were uttering pleasant platitudes in celebration of the fiftieth anniversary of the Constitution,

Sardinian peasants were dying of hunger. The half-suppressed troubles in the centre and south were soon answered by grave disorders in Tuscany and the north; for a whole day Florence was in the hands of a mob, and the troops, after standing idly by, were tardily and without necessity ordered to fire on the people. Similar scenes were witnessed in Pavia, where the popular young Muzio Mussi of Milan was killed while attempting to prevent bloodshed. The indignation at Milan was profound, and some workmen who struck work in protest on the morning of May 7 were harried by the police; troops were called out and bleeding victims mutely called for vengeance. Sporadic risings occurred in various quarters of the city, and a rabble of hooligans, factory girls, and excited workmen paraded the streets, breaking shop windows and perpetrating some acts of petty larceny. As yet no serious development had taken place, and prompt, vigorous, and concerted action would have restored order. But, owing to the imbecility of the authorities, sufficient force was displayed to provoke, not to overawe, and they allowed the riot to make head. Discontented and unemployed labourers from the suburbs poured in; parts of the city lay for a time at the mercy of the disaffected of all classes, and three barricades of tramcars were erected. Meanwhile, martial law had been proclaimed and General Bava-Beccaris appointed dictator; reinforcements were hurried up, and soon the Piazza del Duomo was a mass of soldiers and artillery. Old men rubbed their eyes—the days of Radetzky and the Austrians seemed to have come back again. A remorseless and indiscriminate repression followed, which rapidly degenerated to a vicious man-hunt in the streets. No attempt at a stand was made, for the rioters were unarmed and unorganised. Some labourers going to work were shot down; even women and boys met a like fate. The figures may tell their own tale. The number of civilians killed—men, women, and children—was officially returned (and certainly below the mark) at 82; the wounded were counted by hundreds: one soldier only was killed, by a tile thrown from a roof; 23 were wounded, mostly by stones.

After the rifles and cannon had finished, there came the turn of the prisons. A raid was made on everyone suspected of advanced opinions: deputies, editors of Socialist, Radical, and Catholic papers, were dragged from their homes and ostentatiously led handcuffed through the streets; sentences of imprisonment varying from 3 to 12 years were inflicted. The procedure at the military Courts was a mere travesty of justice. No evidence of organised sedition or insurrection was forthcoming; any article expressive of advanced opinion, any phrase of "subtle irony," was held to be a constructive incitement to violence. Rich and cultured Milan, the moral and intellectual capital of Italy, beheld the jack-boot and sabre enthroned in her midst, and an indelible impression was left in her memory of a savage, military tyranny.

When the grave news of the three days at Milan reached Rome, losing none of its sinister aspect by filtering through the minds of scared officials, the more timid saw looming before society the dread spectre of the red republic.   Thirty provinces were placed under military rule; Courts-martial with feverish zeal inflicted centuries of imprisonment on a multitude of suspects; a general suppression of popular organisations —Socialist, Republican, Catholic—followed; even village banks and cooperative societies were raided and dissolved.   After a ministerial crisis, General Pelloux succeeded in forming a coalition Cabinet from the monarchical parties, and in his opening speech to the Chamber dwelt on his past record as a Liberal and promised substantial reforms.   But no less than four service members (two generals and two admirals) held portfolios, and soon the habits of the quarter-deck and of the parade ground led his Ministry to a series of harsh and coercive measures which alienated the Left.   By July, however, the situation had become so far normal that the military tribunals were abolished; and the corn duties (which had been reduced to 8s. 9d. per quarter on January 25 and wholly abolished on May 6) were on July 1 reimposed at 13s., reduced to 8s. 9d. on the 4th, and on August 16 again raised to 13s.   The popular parties regained activity and a petition signed by 360,000 persons demanded a general amnesty from the monstrous sentences inflicted by the military Courts.   In the local elections of the north and centre the popular candidates swept the board, and the year closed with a partial amnesty which restored to liberty, but not to full civil rights, 2700 political prisoners.

The year 1899 dawned under fairer auspices.   A period had been put to the disastrous tariff war with France and a new treaty of commerce atoned for many of the Government's mistakes.   But the calm was a delusive one; on June 1 a Bill was pushed forward by the Government incorporating certain political ordinances (*provvedimenti politici*), which empowered the Prefects or the police to proclaim public meetings and conferred arbitrary powers on the Government for the suppression of any association regarded as subversive of social order or of the Constitution.   The Extreme Left, led by Signor Pantano, declared that the Bill involved a breach of the *Statuto*, and decided to obstruct its further progress.   After a fortnight's heated debate and a futile attempt by the Conservative leader, Baron Sonnino, to pass guillotine resolutions, the measure had made no progress; and on June 22, having obtained a provisional vote for six months' supplies, Pelloux prorogued the Chamber until the 28th.   On the 23rd he promulgated the ordinances by royal decree (*decreto legge*).   When the sittings were resumed, the majority gave the premier a Bill of indemnity, and on the 30th, after a scene of unparalleled violence in which the voting urns were overthrown, the session was abruptly closed.   In December, a general amnesty was granted, but with reservations which largely neutralised its effects as an act of grace.

CH. VIII.

On February 22, 1900, an unexpected check heaped confusion on the Government. The Court of Cassation at Rome, with admirable independence, declared that the *decreto legge* of June 23 had no legal validity, and once again the undignified conflict was resumed on Pelloux' attempt to legalise its provisions. To checkmate obstruction, revised standing orders were prepared, which, it was intended, should be provisionally enforced without debate. This flagrant overriding of parliamentary privileges only intensified obstruction and embittered the conflict. Pantano spoke through a whole sitting, and on April 3 he and Zanardelli, together with their followers of the Constitutional and Extreme Lefts, walked out of the House in protest, and the revised orders were adopted by the remaining deputies. Pelloux prorogued the Chamber, and on April 5 withdrew the *decreto legge*.

The disorderly scenes were renewed with even greater acridity on the resumption of the sittings on May 15. The Extreme Left met all attempts to apply the new orders with indomitable obstruction; the sitting closed in violence and confusion, amid the defiant strains of Garibaldi's hymn. Pelloux, with his enormous and subservient majority reduced to impotence, dissolved the Chamber, and, confident of victory, appealed to the country to decide between himself and the obstructionists. The elections fixed for June 3 found the popular parties prepared, and an alliance of Radicals, Republicans, and Socialists, fought with unity and enthusiasm. The Government obtained its majority by the usual electoral methods; but, while the official candidates were returned by narrow margins, those of the Union of popular parties were elected by triumphant majorities. In the progressive north the Opposition polled a majority of 70,000 votes, while the ministerialists carried the corrupt and reactionary south by 90,000. The Extreme Left increased its members from 60 to 98, and, exultant in its moral victory, confronted the discredited majority. At the first trial of strength, Pelloux surrendered (June 18); and the Crown, anxious for an issue from a perilous situation, appealed to the patriotism of the venerable President of the Senate, Saracco, who, by his exalted position and honourable record, stood above all parties. A ministry of conciliation was formed; the vote of April 3 was rescinded, and a Committee of Procedure, including three deputies of the Extreme Left, drew up modified standing orders, which were passed almost unanimously. Thus the crisis ended to the profound relief of all parties (July 2), and the attempt of reactionary politicians to set back the clock in Italy ignominiously failed. The obstructionists had played a perilous game, and nothing but a consciousness of the tremendous issue at stake and the conviction that the better sense of the nation was behind them could have justified their action.

Never had the monarchy driven so close to the breakers. Pelloux acted, if not with its approval at least with its acquiescence, and the disservice wrought to the House of Savoy was serious. On July 29 Humbert I was to inaugurate a gymnastic festival at Monza. The municipality of Milan had refused to attend the King at the railway station; and, by an amazing lack of forethought on the part of the police authorities, no precautionary measures were taken for his safety. With the indifference to danger characteristic of his House, Humbert mingled freely with the crowd, whose coldness and indeed hostility were manifest. The ceremony ended, the ill-fated King was about to depart, when Bresci, an Italian anarchist from America, mounted the royal carriage, and deliberately aimed, with fatal effect, four shots at his breast.

Humbert I inherited his father's courage, but not his genial personality and force of character. He was well-meaning and loyal to his coronation oath, but his political outlook was a narrow one; and towards the end of his reign, as we have seen, he suffered a small clique of military and reactionary politicians to blind him to the signs of the times. The Prince of Naples, who ascended the throne as Victor Emmanuel III, while steadfastly opposing any reduction in armaments, has frankly accepted the more liberal and enlightened policy that the country demanded. Holding a high ideal of the kingly office, his enlightened and cultured mind and simplicity of life have brought a much-needed standard of clear thinking and clean living to the Italian Court. And, while it would be a grave error to assume that the monarchy is deeply rooted in popular affection or that the House of Savoy evokes any passionate enthusiasm in the country, it has undoubtedly gained in esteem during the present reign and is loyally accepted by all save the revolutionary extremists.

The vacillation of the Saracco Ministry in face of some labour troubles at Genoa brought about its fall in February, 1901; and the young King, resisting pressure from the Right, boldly charged Zanardelli with the formation of a Cabinet from the two Lefts. The Radicals, however, refused office owing to fundamental differences with regard to military expenditure, and the Cabinet was chiefly composed of members of the Constitutional Left (February 14).

The Zanardelli-Giolitti Ministry marks a new departure in Italian politics. For the first time since 1870 the working classes felt that in disputes between capital and labour the sword of state would not be flung into the capitalist scale; and old-fashioned parliamentarians were shocked to hear a responsible Minister of the Crown speak of the legitimate aspirations of the workers to a better place at the banquet of life. Giolitti, after a long eclipse, resumed his policy of demonstrating to the democracy that political liberty and social reform were compatible with loyalty to the House of Savoy. It was understood that freedom of speech and of public meeting, though not legally formulated, would be unquestioned, that combinations among workmen would be unchallenged and a neutral attitude observed towards strikes so long as they were conducted within the limits of the law. Labour was not slow in taking advantage of the novel situation. The number of industrial strikes, which in 1900 amounted to 383, increased in 1901 to 1042; the strikers from 80,858 to 196,540. In agriculture, the increase was even more startling—from 27 strikes in 1900 to 629 in 1901. From the Alps to Sicily considerable increases of pay were gained, especially by agricultural labourers. The new policy of non-intervention was, however, early in 1902, severely strained by a gas strike at Turin and by a threatened general strike of railwaymen. A corps of engineers was sent to take the place of the strikers at Turin, and the railwaymen were forbidden, as public servants, to leave their work. When the prohibition was met by defiance, those of the men who were subject to military service were called under arms; and absence from duty thus became equivalent to desertion. Meanwhile, the Government promised to use its influence with the companies to obtain an amelioration of the men's condition; and, partly at the expense of the Government, partly at the charge of the companies, a contribution of nearly a million sterling was made to their provident funds.

The compact group of the popular parties exercised its controlling pressure with unsuspected moderation, and its influence on legislation showed itself in the important social measures that were added to the Statute Book. The Employers' Liability Act and the (contributory) Government Old Age Pension Scheme of 1898 were amplified and amended; the Factory Acts of 1886 regulating child labour were strengthened and extended to women, who, together with children under thirteen, were excluded from labour underground and from night work; an important measure was foreshadowed, creating a national (contributory) Maternity Fund to provide for the maintenance of women operatives during the month of abstinence from work after child-birth required by the Act. The octroi duties on bread and flour products were abolished; permissive legislation for the municipalisation of public services was passed; facilities for the creation of local agrarian credit institutions in the south were given to the Banks of Naples and Sicily. The efficacy of social legislation in Italy is, however, intimately involved in the attitude of the Government towards armaments and administrative probity. The crushing burden of taxation—in no other European country is the proportion to income so high—renders any increase of civil expenditure impolitic, and for lack of funds to provide an adequate staff of inspectors the laws are largely evaded. The Law of July 18, 1904, creating a superior Council of Public Charities and conferring on its Commissioners wide powers of coordination, reorganisation, and control, appointed only four inspectors to deal with the 40,000 charitable foundations of the kingdom.

The firmness shown by the Government in the face of a general strike

at Rome in April, 1903, and in suppressing disorder in the south, won
approval even from Conservatives, and they were applauded for asserting
their independence of Socialist pressure.   The Extreme Left, however,
grew restive, and soon dealt the Ministry a heavy blow.   An interpellation from a Socialist deputy (June 5) on the proposed return visit
of the Tsar to Italy, and hot protestations against arbitrary arrests on
Italian soil, said to have been dictated by the Russian secret police,
added to charges published in the *Avanti* of maladministration and
corruption in the Navy Department, led to the fall of the Ministry
(June 17); but the Cabinet was reconstructed, without Giolitti, on
June 25, and Zanardelli, by an adroit speech, won a vote of confidence.
The advanced Socialist wing at once organised a vigorous agitation
against the proposed Imperial visit; and in October the King handed
to Zanardelli an autograph letter from the Tsar, intimating a renunciation of the journey.   The veteran statesman, profoundly affected by the
humiliation of Italy, laid down his charge, and on December 26 passed
away from earthly strife.

On August 4, 1903, the Chair of St Peter, rendered vacant by the
death of the venerable and politic Leo XIII, was filled by the elevation
to the papacy of the devout Cardinal Sarto, Patriarch of Venice, under
the title of Pius X: his election was largely due to the ill-feeling
engendered among some of the Cardinals at the exercise of the Austrian
veto against Cardinal Rampolla, the French candidate.

Giolitti was generally indicated as Zanardelli's successor; after the
refusal of portfolios by the Radical and Socialist leaders, Sacchi and
Turati, a Cabinet was formed (November 30), mainly of Conservatives
which included Luzzatti, the most eminent of Italian financiers. Luzzatti's
promise of a big surplus of two and three-quarter millions sterling for
the year 1903–4, and the reduction of the petroleum duty by 50 per
cent. were happy auguries for the new Ministry; but the inevitable defects
of a *trasformismo* Cabinet were soon manifest.   Their tolerance of
violence among strikers was regarded by the Right as the price paid for
the support of the Extreme Left; and the Government, yielding to
pressure, swung round to a more resolute policy which led to angry
meetings of protest at Milan.   On September 16, 1904, a Committee of
Resistance was formed, which declared a general strike in order to force
the resignation of the Government.   The threat was not taken seriously;
and great was the consternation when, on the 17th, the citizens of Milan,
Genoa, Venice, and Turin, beheld civic life paralysed and an attempt
being made to terrorise society and overthrow the State by starvation
and darkness.   Many hardships were suffered, especially by the sick and
helpless.   Shopkeepers who refused to close saw their windows smashed;
the railway lines converging on Milan and Genoa were torn up to block
the advance of troops.   At Rome, Florence, and Naples, the strike was
less general, but characterised by the same anarchic violence.   The

Mayor of Milan was forced to haul down the flags that had been hoisted on public buildings, in celebration of the birth of an heir to the throne; and they were trampled under foot amid cries of " Down with the House of Savoy."

But Giolitti refused to fan a riot into a revolution: the authorities were instructed to resort to force only in the event of definite criminal acts. The troops behaved with admirable self-control in face of great provocation, and the movement soon came to an end. Three dastardly assassinations disgraced the strikers in the northern cities, and about a hundred soldiers and police were more or less injured. The revulsion was profound. Even extreme politicians felt that the fundamental laws of social life had been brutally violated; and an appeal to the country was made amid a reaction of anger and disgust. Abandoning their usual apathy at elections, the middle classes made a determined effort to inflict a crushing defeat on the popular parties, and the desire of the Catholic electors to bear their part in the struggle between the powers of order and anarchy was so intense that the hand of the Vatican was forced. The declaration of the Cardinal Penitentiary on the occasion of the general elections of 1874 that it was inexpedient for Catholics to vote at political elections, known as the *non expedit*, and subsequently interpreted by the Holy Office to imply absolute prohibition, was partially withdrawn; and the Bishops were instructed to permit the Catholic laity to vote in order to combat the subversive parties and uphold the principles of social order and respect for religion. The boycott of Italian political life by the Catholics that had begun in 1861 with Don Margotti's manifesto *Nè eletti, nè elettori*, was at length removed. For the first time in the history of United Italy political meetings of Catholics were held at Milan, and the haughty isolation of the Catholic nobility of Rome was changed to active participation in the turmoil of political elections. The rout of the popular parties at the first ballots was significant. At Milan an avowed Catholic was elected, while, of the Extreme Left, Turati alone, who had opposed the general strike, was returned: at Mantua, Livorno, Parma, Naples, even at Reggio-Emilia, the cradle of socialism, a flood of reaction overwhelmed their candidates. The triple alliance of Socialists, Republicans, and Radicals, which had dissolved in mutual recrimination, was renewed in face of the common disaster; some seats were retrieved at the second ballots, others were won from the Conservative Opposition by the help of Government pressure; but the verdict of the country was unmistakable. The interest evoked by the contest in the cities was unique; 85 per cent. of the electorate are said to have gone to the polls at Florence, and the official average of the whole kingdom was returned as 67 per cent., a higher percentage than that of any other general election since 1861. The Communal electors subsequently confirmed and emphasised the verdict of the political electorate.

In the new Chamber, Giolitti had an overwhelming majority, even against the section of the Conservative opposition led by Baron Sonnino and the Extreme Left combined. But the latter, although purged of its more subversive elements and reduced in numbers by about a score, was, by the energy of its members, still potent for mischief; its favour was deemed worth buying, and the Government supported the Radical Leader, Marcora, in his candidature for the Presidency of the Chamber (December 1). The winter session of 1904 closed with an optimistic financial statement by Luzzatti, who indicated a surplus of over a million and a quarter sterling, and announced that the *agio* on gold had at length disappeared.

The railway conventions were now approaching their term, and a strong movement declared itself in favour of state administration. Giolitti was opposed to state management; but the universal irritation caused by the obstructionist tactics of the railway employees and their threats to strike in the early months of 1905 forced the hands of the Government. On Giolitti's resignation through illness (March 4) Fortis succeeded in forming a Cabinet pledged to railway purchase (March 28). Clauses negative of the right to strike were included in the Bill presented early in April, and were carried by an enormous majority. A threatened strike collapsed, and the men were solaced by promises of increased wages and an augmented pension fund. On June 30, 1905, the transference of management took place, and within a few days the purchase money was raised at home at 3·65 per cent. The haste and levity with which this enormous responsibility was assumed were remarkable even in Italian legislation, and the action was aptly compared by a leading politician to that of a man who would set forth in evening dress to climb Mont Blanc. A long period of disastrous railway chaos ensued, partly no doubt due to the accumulated defects of twenty years' private management. The whole carrying trade and passenger traffic of the country were dislocated, and goods consigned to Italy were landed at foreign ports, owing to lack of trucks at Genoa and Venice.

Fortis' power gradually crumbled, and the Ministry resigned on February 1, 1906. Baron Sonnino, who for personal integrity, breadth, and precision of view, and profound knowledge of the economic condition of the country, stood head and shoulders above his colleagues, but whose support of the reactionary Government of 1899 had been remembered against him, was now called to office; the prolonged political chaos— there had been five crises in little more than a year—seemed destined to give place to order and good government. The Conservative leader appears to have aimed at the formation of a Ministry of all the talents. So wide was the range of his choice that all previous examples of *trasformismo* paled into insignificance. Never had such an array of probity and ability been seen since the days of Cavour and Ricasoli:— Luzzatti and Carmine from the Right Centre; Boselli and Salandra from the Centre; Guicciardini and Bacelli from the Left Centre; the Republican Pantano and the Radical Sacchi from the Extreme Left. On March 8, 1906, Sonnino unfolded an admirable programme of economic and social legislation, including a comprehensive scheme for the regeneration of the south, whereby he proposed to reduce the land tax by 30 per cent. on assessments below £240 pending the completion of the new cadastral survey; to grant subsidies to agrarian credit banks; to exempt the lowest assessments from the family tax and the tax on cattle; and to compel landlords to make certain advances to cultivators for seed and other purposes. Increased subsidies to the communes for elementary education, the opening up of remote districts by additional roads, tramways, and light railways, the repeal of the press laws, were also included in the scheme. On the 16th, Luzzatti promised a magnificent surplus of nearly two and a half millions sterling. But the new premier was lacking in qualities that make the successful leader of men. Autocratic in temperament, devoid of personal magnetism, a good speaker but no orator, he had small experience of, and cherished the utmost contempt for, the petty arts of parliamentary *finesse* that play so large a part in the science of government in Italy. The Extreme Right was irritated at the inclusion in the Cabinet of an avowed Republican, and of a notorious Anti-clerical as Minister of Public Worship; threatened interests were active, and, while the Ministry were occupied with measures, Giolitti had returned and was busy with men: with consummate skill he brought the disaffected forces into line, and the confederation of integrity and capacity succumbed to the first assault of menaced interests and disappointed ambitions (May 17). Giolitti came into power: by restoring the secret service fund (which Sonnino had discontinued) he was able to tune the Press, and, appropriating much of his predecessor's programme, he succeeded in carrying several measures during the brief summer session. Luzzatti's long-prepared scheme for the conversion of the debt was triumphantly realised; Sonnino's measures for the economic regeneration of the southern provinces, previously attacked in opposition, were now adopted with some modification in the interests of the landlords, and the drastic report of the Royal Commission on Navy Administration was decently interred.

The winter session of 1906 closed with the announcement of an estimated surplus for the financial year 1905–6 of over two and a half millions sterling, despite the extraordinary expenditure of nearly a million and a half in aid of the sufferers from earthquake in Calabria and from the eruption of Vesuvius. The railway chaos was yielding to the energy of the new Director; and by the authorised expenditure of over thirty-six millions sterling for the purchase of rolling stock and the improvement of the permanent way, and of twenty-four millions for the construction of new lines, it was hoped to place the service on a satisfactory footing.

The status of the Pope and the relations between the Civil Power and the Papacy are defined by the Law of Guarantees (May 13, 1871). The Pope's claim to sovereign honours and prerogatives is recognised, and, his person being declared sacred and inviolable, all attacks, or incitements to attack, are subject to the same penalties as those directed against the King; he is guaranteed the use of the Vatican and Lateran Apostolic palaces and of Villa Gandolfo, with their artistic and literary treasures, and a perpetual net annual endowment of £129,000. The absolute spiritual authority of the Pope and his control of all papal seminaries, academies, and colleges are also recognised, and the fullest liberty to hold conclaves or councils is granted. The Government surrendered the privilege of nominating to benefices and offices in the Church, provided that Italian subjects only were appointed; Bishops were exempted from the oath of allegiance to the King; the *exequatur* and the *placitum regium* were abolished, except so far as regards temporalities. These and other clauses of the law were so many conditions imposed on the Papacy by superior force; they were never recognised by it and the proffered annual endowment has, owing to French pressure, never been accepted. The law, like so much modern Italian legislation, was too hastily drafted, and an ill-defined borderland of overlapping interests and jurisdictions has been a source of much friction. But, on the whole, it has worked well, despite papal assertions of the impossibility of compromise; though there have been intrigues with the enemies of Italy and much angry hostility on the surface, the personal relations between Pontiff and King have been generally conciliatory. Pius IX resigned himself with dignity and good humour to the new situation; he resolutely declined to listen to any proposal to leave Rome and always remained on excellent terms with Victor Emmanuel II. Leo XIII, while equally inflexible in upholding papal claims to temporal sovereignty, maintained the same friendly personal relations with the monarchy, and mutual concessions for the solution of practical difficulties were the rule during his long pontificate. During the reign of Victor Emmanuel III, and especially since the diplomatic rupture between the Papacy and France, relations have been even more cordial, and the protectorate of the Catholic missions in the East has been transferred to Italy. Official hostility has been relaxed on either side, and, but for the violence of extremists in both camps and financial considerations at the Vatican, together with the fear that an avowed reconciliation with the monarchy would loosen the ties between the Papacy and the Catholic world and accelerate the tendency towards the creation of national churches, the kiss of peace would already have been exchanged. A significant declaration by an illustrious Italian Bishop was published in November, 1904, rejoicing that the *non expedit* was ended, and the Temporal Power dead and buried. In July, 1905, the venerable Bishop of Cremona published the details of a remarkable interview he had at Florence in 1879 with Cardinal Manning, who, drawing up his tall ascetic figure, solemnly warned him that it was madness for the Papacy to think of regaining the Temporal Power; that no European State would lift a finger to restore it, and that, by asking the monarchy to give up Rome, they were asking it to commit political suicide.

The encyclical *Il Fermo Proposito* (June 11, 1905), practically shelving the *non expedit* and expressly calling on Catholics to prepare to take part in parliamentary life, is a tacit surrender to an accomplished fact and the end of futile claims to temporal dominion. But the occasion and manner of the changed policy at the Vatican have sorely tried the feelings of the Catholic democracy. They complain that what was refused during a whole generation to national sentiment has been conceded to fears of Socialism in the moneyed classes, and that the Church has allied herself with a party in the State, her avowed enemy for half a century. The triumph of the Spanish Cardinals in the Curia and the suppression of Don Murri's organ, the *Cultura Sociale*, with its "American" policy of interesting the clergy in moral and social reform, have been followed by the encyclical *Pieni l' Animo* (July 28, 1906), which requires the absolute submission of the priests to episcopal authority in all their social and political activities and prohibits any connexion with the *Lega Democratica Nazionale*, any utterance of words that tend to provoke hostile feelings against the upper classes, or any breath of concession to the exigencies of modern life. In the fields of philosophy, theology, and science, the triumph of medievalism has been complete. The syllabus *Lamentabili*, July 3, 1907, and the encyclical, *Pascendi Dominici Gregis* (September 8, 1907), are a reversion to the attitude of the syllabus of 1864. The Church, with maternal vituperation, denounces her modernist children as factors of heresy, destroyers of all religion, and lures to atheism; the Bishops are urged to eradicate modernism from the seminaries by means of press censors and vigilance committees acting in secrecy, and to block every aperture by which a ray of advanced thought may penetrate. Despite penalties of major excommunication, the modernist leaders have decided to persist in their effort to raise the scientific and philosophical equipment of the priesthood and remove it from its present position towards all that concerns the problems of the modern world.

The end of the nineteenth century, and the opening of the twentieth, have been remarkable for the advent of two new forces into Italian politics which give some promise of a healthier tone in public life. The more recent of the two—that of the organised Catholic laity—points to the active cooperation of an orderly Conservatism, which has too long passed by on the other side; the earlier and more important movement, that of organised socialism, has given the democracy a new hope and a constructive faith, which have largely weaned it from the solvent forces of anarchism. Its rise has been rapid. In 1879 the young Andrea Costa, breaking away from the International, began to preach the Marxite faith in Italy. He taught that the days of barricades were past; the old doctrine of violent revolutions to be achieved by a few men of ideas, acting upon and leading the unconscious masses, must give place to the patient work of propaganda among the proletariate; the workers must be educated to act as a self-conscious force in a class struggle for economic emancipation, culminating in their inevitable victory and in the collective possession and administration of the wealth of the community.

Socialism, however, made little way till early in the nineties, when Filippo Turati and other enthusiastic young Marxites founded the *Critica Sociale,* and began an active and fervent propaganda. The new social gospel made an irresistible appeal to the ardent young intellectuals of cultured and industrial Milan and the north generally, and by the adhesion of thinkers such as Lombroso, Ferrero, Antonio Labriola, and Anna Kuliscioff, of poets and authors as Graf, de Amicis, and Ojetti, of professional men as Ferri, the eminent criminologist, and Bissolati, of economists as Loria, the movement sprung at a bound into robust maturity. In 1893, the party divided into opposing camps: the *Riformisti,* under Ferri, who were willing to accept the monarchy so long' as it was not ranged against them, and to work temporarily with Radicals and Republicans for definite measures of reform that had socialistic tendencies; the *Intransigenti,* under Turati, rigid and exclusive Marxites who would have no compromise with any form of capitalistic society. In 1896, by a curious evolution, the leaders changed positions · Turati became chief of the *Riformisti,* and Ferri of the opposing group. At the congress held at Rome in 1900 the two groups were alike confronted by a new section, the *Sindacalisti,* led by the fiery Neapolitan, Arturo Labriola, who, more uncompromising even than Ferri, insisted on the fundamental revolutionary character of socialism and looked for victory from the direct action of the organised workers—*operai sindacati* —fighting for their own hand.

In 1903 the party organ, the *Avanti,* was captured from the *Riformisti,* and Turati's colleague Bissolati gave place to the more aggressive Ferri as editor. At the socialistic congress of 1904 at Bologna the clash of principles, embittered by personal antagonism, led to angry scenes in which Ferri, passionately pleading for the unity and integrity of the party, intervened as peacemaker between Turati and Labriola and carried the Right and Left Centres with him in a resolution which declared that, while asserting the necessity of combating capitalistic society by revolutionary propaganda, unity must be sought in the varied activities of all socialists. The resolution was a compromise, and its supporters were known as *Integralisti.* Such was the growing

CH. VIII.

importance of the Socialist party that the meeting of the congress at Rome in 1906 evoked scarcely less attention than that of the Chamber itself. The veteran Andrea Costa presided, and debates, hot and passionate, proved how wide and deep was the schism. Ferri again dominated the assembly, and with the aid of the *Riformisti* carried by a large majority—26,947 against 5278 of the votes represented—a resolution affirming that the party, while agreeing to make use even of general strikes as a means, would avoid an excessive or too frequent use of that weapon. Fundamental questions, such as that of passive resistance to military service, were not faced, and although broadly it may be said that the advocates of the catastrophic, as opposed to the evolutionary and parliamentary principle, had lost in numbers and influence, the gulf that separated the groups was not bridged. Ferri remained director of the *Avanti* and, by his aggressive energy and powerful eloquence, the acknowledged leader of the socialists in the Chamber. Although their deputies were reduced in the 1904 election from thirty-three to twenty-seven, the Socialists then polled 316,790 votes, and the party, monopolising as it does the labour movement in Italy, wields an influence out of all proportion to its numerical strength. The Socialists are naturally strongest in the industrial north; they have a large following in Parma, in the villages of the Romagna, of Reggio-Emilia, and among the labourers of the Po valley; some headway has also been made in Naples and the south. The election statistics of 1904 give 177,439 Socialist votes to the north; 108,231 to the centre; and 31,120 to the south, including the islands of Sardinia and Sicily. So far as the immediate demands of the parliamentary group are concerned, they amount to little more than a compendium of urgent social and political reforms of which many have been accepted by enlightened Conservatives, such as Professor Villari and Baron Sonnino. The old Republican party has waned in numbers and importance as social questions have more and more imperiously demanded solution; but the Constitutional Radicals who, while refusing to utter the socialist shibboleth, yet differ from the socialist programme only in minor details, are a force to be reckoned with, and number in their ranks men of the highest capacity and integrity.

The story of Italian finance, since 1870, is that of a grievous and increasing burden of expenditure patiently borne by a country poor in natural resources and young in the practice of industry. The system of national book-keeping is a complicated one, and the mass of printed matter dealing with public finance is portentous.

The effective expenditure which, in 1871, amounted to £40,531,000, rose in 1881 to £49,183,000; in 1890–1 to £64,601,000; in 1900–1 to £66,094,000; and in 1906–7 to £74,252,500. The lean years of recurrent deficits, 1885–6 to 1896–7, have since given place to handsome and gradually increasing surpluses, amounting to £378,440 in 1897–8, and to nearly four millions sterling in 1902–3. In 1906–7 the surplus of effective revenue over expenditure was £3,929,900. These sums, however, owing to varying deficits in the categories of railway construction and financial operations, finally worked out in 1897–8 to a deficit of £44,220, and to a reduced surplus in 1902–3 of £2,788,520; the final surplus in 1906–7 however amounted to £4,073,900. The National Debt is oppressive in its magnitude. From £323,618,000 in 1871, it steadily increased to £505,343,000 in 1897. Ranging between 512 and 521 millions during the next decade, it fell to 508 millions in 1905, rose again to 521 millions in 1906, and in 1907 reached £524,797,000, of which however £14,059,000 were railway bonds raised in June, 1905, at 3·65 per cent., and £4,280,000 raised in December, 1906, at 3·50.

The increase in local indebtedness is also a matter of grave concern. The provincial and communal debts, which in 1877 stood at £34,235,000, had in 1899 increased to £56,671,000, to which should be added a depreciation of communal property by sales of woods amounting to ten millions sterling. The annual local expenditure has increased from sixteen millions in 1871 to over twenty-six millions sterling in 1899. In local, as in national taxation, the incidence falls with crushing effect on the poorer classes, who contribute a disproportionate amount of their income owing to the large revenue drawn from indirect taxation (food and drink). Some relief has been afforded by the abolition of the octroi duties on bread and flour products; but the condition of the labourer is a serious problem, for to millions of Italians wheaten bread and even salt are still luxuries. In local as in national expenditure reform is a moral as well as a political question. Enlightened and upright statesmen of all shades of opinion concur in demanding a purification of the public services, and bewail the lack of honest and efficient administrators. Italy still awaits the courageous and resolute reformer, who shall grapple with the shameless corruption which is so exhausting a drain on the national resources.

In the race for armaments, Italy has not yet decided whether to run with the great Powers or with the small. Her army, organised on German lines in 1875 by General Ricotti, is nominally composed of a permanent force of about 250,000 men and a first reserve of about 500,000: a second reserve, the *milizia mobile*, numbers 310,000, and a third, the *milizia territoriale*, about 2,225,000. The total strength in 1901—since when confidential returns have been issued to the military authorities alone—was officially returned as 3,366,920 officers and men, excluding the African forces. But the paper strength is subject to important reservations. The legal period of training is, for financial reasons, considerably curtailed in practice; the *milizia mobile* is rarely called out, and a competent Italian military authority has recently declared that in the event of mobilisation nine-tenths of the second reserve would join the colours deficient in training: in point of efficiency the third reserve is probably in even worse case. The proportion of conscripts who fail to pass the medical examination and are either rejected as physically unfit or referred back for a year, is a high one, and for the past thirty years has averaged about 48·6 per cent.

Army expenditure has increased from six millions sterling in 1871 to nearly twelve millions and a quarter in 1906–7; naval expenditure from over a million in 1871 to over six millions in 1906–7. The number of officers and men on the navy rolls has risen from 15,215 in 1873 to 59,587 in 1906. The proportion of army and navy expenditure, about 21 per cent. of the whole, is considerably lower than that of the Great European Powers; in proportion to private incomes it is, however, much higher.

In 1906, the extraordinary and continued improvement in the national finances and the serener political atmosphere made it possible to carry out the great scheme of debt conversion contemplated since 1899 and already elaborated in 1903 by Luzzatti. In 1871 the minimum quotation for the *rendita* on the Paris Bourse was 50·50: in 1905 it never fell below 103·55, despite the reduction of the net interest in 1894 from £4. 6s. 9d. to £4 per cent. Meanwhile the average rate of exchange for gold in London fell in 1905 to 25·14. Of the gross amount of Italian consols, 400 millions sterling, no less than £327,640,000 was subjected to conversion. The Bill, laid on the table at three o'clock of the afternoon of June 29, 1906, became law at eight o'clock amid a scene of unparalleled enthusiasm. Rising as one man, the whole Chamber turned to where Luzzatti sat, a simple deputy, and united in a magnificent ovation to the father of the financial *risorgimento* of Italy. The heroes of the conversion were, however, as Luzzatti modestly said, the patient Italian taxpayer and the thrifty and patriotic Italian emigrant. By the conversion, the net 4 per cent. *rendita* was to be reduced to 3·75 per cent. from July 1, 1907, to January 1, 1912: it it was then to be reduced to 3·50 per cent., and guaranteed from further conversion up to January 1, 1921. So successful was the operation that holdings to the amount only of £187,000 were refunded and not a breath disturbed the money markets of Europe. On the eve of the conversion the *rendita* was quoted in Paris at 105·10: on the morrow at 104·80: during the first six months of 1907 it averaged 102·50. The annual economy to the exchequer was estimated at £800,000 for the first, and £1,600,000 for the second period. The position of the Finance Minister after the conversion recalls that of the winner at dice in the opening *terzine* of the sixth Canto of *Purgatory*— clamorous interests plucking at his sleeve asking for relief. Luzzatti's original purpose was to exonerate the poorer taxpayer by reducing the duties on the first necessities of life; but the prospective saving is already engulfed, as former surpluses have been, by the increased demands of railway construction, military and naval expenditure, state employees and protected interests. The economic expansion which rendered this conversion possible has been no less remarkable. Exports and imports (excluding the precious metals) amounted in 1872 to £93,790,890. Some slight increase in imports took place in the later seventies; between 1880 and 1887 the rise in imports was more marked, while the exports remained stationary. Under the increased protectionist duties and the disastrous tariff war with France, the volume of foreign trade, which in 1887 reached £104,283,360, contracted in 1888 to £82,661,440, the exports to France having fallen from £16,192,240 to £6,814,320. Some slight recovery ensued, and foreign trade remained at an average of about eighty-seven millions until 1897, when a rapid and sustained revival took place. In 1898 it rose to £104,676,180, and by progressive increases reached in 1907 the handsome total of £193,181,500.

Many causes have contributed to this happy result—the termination of the tariff war with France; commercial treaties with Germany and Austria; the increasing utilisation of hydro-electric power; the growth of cooperation; the sobriety, industry, and alert intelligence of the Italian workman; the new ideas and heightened standard of comfort introduced by returning emigrants. The growth of cooperative banking has been striking. From 64 in 1871 the number of *Banche Popolari* has increased to 832 in 1906; the two pioneer banks of Milan and Bologna, founded in 1866, have increased their turnover, the former from four and a half millions sterling in 1870 to one hundred and six millions and a half in 1906; the latter from £437,452 to £7,624,187. The savings entrusted to the 750 banks which made returns to the Cremona Congress in 1907, amounted to twenty-eight and three quarter millions sterling. The amount of deposits in credit, ordinary, and Post Office Savings Banks has increased from £26,046,000 in 1876 to £152,724,000 in 1906. During the period 1881–1905, £16,604,584 have been given or bequeathed to charitable institutions, which in 1900 possessed property worth £88,198,228. Excluding credit associations, the number of legally constituted cooperative societies has increased from 1203 in 1897 to 4042 in 1906, among which the 50 Agricultural *cooperative* have increased to 622, and the Builders and Decorators *cooperative* from 349 to 818. A remarkable development has recently taken place at Reggio-Emilia under the auspices of the socialists, who by means of the Labour Bureau (*Camera del Lavoro*), have federated no less than 425 workmen's associations, of which 175 are cooperative, 38 provident societies, and 212 trades unions. Under the new law (July 7, 1907) which facilitates the concurrence of cooperative societies in contracts for State Railway construction, 39 of the Reggio-Emilian *cooperative* have combined and contracted to construct and work the Reggio-Ciano line of about 20 miles.

The increase in exports of manufactured goods since 1892 has been

CH. VIII.

more than threefold, in imports of raw material more than twofold. The exports of raw and manufactured silk have risen from £13,248,500 in 1897 to £27,347,000 in 1906, and the home production of raw silk from a million and a quarter tons in 1876 to over six millions in 1906. The struggle for supremacy between Lyons and Milan has, since 1892, ended in a victory for the Lombard capital; in 1905 the total quantity of silk conditioned at Milan was 9439 tons as against 7010 at Lyons. In 1903, 191,654 operatives were employed in the Italian silk industry.

The cotton trade, from small beginnings, has attained large proportions: the home market has been captured and the value of cotton exports increased from £827,968 in 1888 to £4,952,915 in 1906. In 1903 the industry gave employment to 138,880 operatives, despite a large increase in the use of steam and hydro-electric power. The woollen industry, although highly protected, is a sickly one, and is of relatively small importance. Some progress has been made in iron, steel, and chemical manufacture. The production of steel, largely due to high tariffs and a virtual monopoly of government orders, especially for armour plates, has increased from 4212 tons annually during 1881–5 to 135,856 tons during 1900–4. There can be no doubt that, as the latent potentialities of hydro-electric power are increasingly harnessed for the service of Italian industry and vexatious fiscal impediments removed, a great impetus will be given to home manufactures. The amount of water power available has been variously estimated at from two and a quarter to ten million horse-power, of which, in 1904, 490,000 horse-power only had been tapped.

But with little iron, no coal, and exiguous mineral resources generally, Italy is, and probably will long remain, chiefly an agricultural country. Her exports in 1905 amounted to twenty-four millions sterling—less than those of Belgium, whose population numbers less than seven millions, little more than one-fifth of the Italian total; and, according to the census of 1901, no less than 16,836,551 persons in Italy were dependent on agriculture. In her agriculture, however, a *risorgimento* is still to seek. Italy is not naturally a fertile land. With one-tenth of barren rock and one-third mountain, she has, except in Lombardy and Venetia, but few plains of rich alluvial soil, and south of the Tiber, no great rivers. The mysterious *pellagra* and malarial fever are permanent scourges; untamed watercourses ravage the soil; earthquakes and volcanic eruptions periodically leave ruin and desolation in their train. The dweller in the bleak and sullen north, his ears ringing with Mignon's *Kennst du das Land*, conjures up visions of Italy as a land of fatness, laughing with corn and wine and oil; a land of golden-hued orange trees glowing in the sunlight, and lemon groves laden with cooling fruit. But over vast tracts of the south, how grievous is the reality! The traveller in the Basilicata, in Calabria, in Lecce, beholds fever-stricken deserts;

hopeless, helpless misery; the piteous aspect of villages each, with sadly appropriate nomenclature, possessing its *Via Addolorata.*

Much agricultural progress has, however, taken place in the north, owing to cooperation, rural credit banks, and improved methods of culture. *Casse Rurali*, the first of which was established by Dr Wollemborg in 1883, have profoundly influenced the development of peasant farming in north Italy and have starved out the usurer. In 1892 the system was vigorously taken up by the clericals, and a rapid growth ensued; in ten years the *Casse* increased from 93 to 1099. In 1906, 1467 were in operation, or, including the analogous *Casse Agrari*, 1663, only a few score of which were unsectarian.

The political emancipation of the south was achieved in a few months; forty years have passed, and its economic emancipation is still to seek. The fiscal and economic burdens of unification have fallen with terrible incidence on the south; it is estimated by Professor Nitti that the old kingdom of the Two Sicilies pays in direct taxation £1,200,000 annually more than it ought. The problem is that of a bigger Ireland, of an *Italia Irredenta* far more urgent than that of the provinces still Austrian—a riddle which yet awaits its Oedipus.

The evil in its urban aspect is centred at Naples: in its rural aspect in the Basilicata. Nitti has proved that in Naples alone of the great cities of Italy the consumption of food per head has been decreasing, and that there alone the diseases due to innutritive, unwholesome, and insufficient food have steadily increased instead of diminishing. A confidential report by Dr Franzoni, prepared at the request of the Zanardelli Government, gives an appalling picture of the exhaustion and misery in the once fertile but now miserable and derelict Basilicata —squalid fields; deserted farms, unsaleable, unlettable; fiscal extortion of incredible ferocity; a population inhabiting filthy hovels in abject misery and troglodyte promiscuity. The causes specified by Dr Franzoni are manifold—lack of capital, ravages of floods, deafforestation, the advent of railways and consequent competition of external produce, the grievous burden of taxation, lack of roads, prehistoric methods of cultivation, *latifondi*, absenteeism, suppression of the religious Orders, monstrous usury, corrupt and inefficient administration.

The statistics of illiteracy tell their own tale: in the Basilicata, in 1901, after a quarter of a century of nominally compulsory education, 75·4 per cent. of the population were illiterates as compared with 17·7 in Piedmont. The increasing exodus of the able-bodied male inhabitants from this land of despair has assumed alarming proportions. Since 1899 emigration has doubled, and in 1906, out of a total population of about half a million, over 18,000 expatriated themselves, of whom 98 per cent. crossed the ocean to the lands of promise in the west. The Basilicata is the only province of Italy where the population per square mile has shown a decrease instead of an increase. The result of emigration has

CH. VIII.

been twofold : while on the one hand, wages, during the past five years, have doubled, and relatively considerable sums of money have been sent from America to the families left behind by the emigrant, on the other, owing to the grievous financial position of many of the landowners, crushed between the heavy taxation and increased wages, fewer hands have been employed and more land has gone out of cultivation. The Apulian aqueduct voted in 1902, a vote of two and three-quarter millions sterling in 1904 for public works in the Basilicata, and a law to encourage the growth of industries at Naples, were so many partial attempts to deal with the problem. But it was not till 1906, when Sonnino introduced his measures for relief, that any statesmanlike effort to grapple with the problem as a whole was made. The Naples law (July 8, 1904) contains great potentialities. A large zone of territory free from duty on raw materials has been set apart for the encouragement of manufactures. Already factories are springing up and a Genoese company, founded under the auspices of the chief iron and steel works in Italy, has acquired about 270 acres of land on which it is proposed to erect blast furnaces and rolling-mills capable of an annual turn-over of a million tons of raw material and steel products. The works for the construction of the great Apulian aqueduct begun in 1904 are estimated to involve an expenditure by the State of four millions sterling, and, by the Communes of Foggia, Bari, and Lecce, of another million. Grave technical defects have, however, been indicated by eminent engineers and geologists; and local medical officers in the province of Lecce, and especially at Gallipoli, unanimously attribute the increased mortality, which it was one of the objects of the aqueduct to check, not to bad water but to the insufficient quantity and bad quality of the food of the inhabitants.

The problem of southern unrest is, in Sicily, complicated by racial characteristics and historical traditions. The islanders, with their intense local patriotism and strains of Saracen and Norman blood, have ever been distinguished by their passionate love of independence, and it was always easy to raise a separatist movement there, whether under Spanish or Bourbon rule. The economic misery of the southern mainland finds its parallel in the island. Illiteracy and emigration are as prevalent as across the straits—127,603 emigrants left Sicily in 1906—whole populations are largely maintained by money sent by relatives from America, and a new form of usury has been created to supply passage money and landing capital to emigrants. Sicily, more than any other agricultural region of Italy, has been hit by American competition, and the *mosca olearia* pest, as on the mainland, has wrought havoc with the olive crops. Two-thirds of the *agrumi* (lemon, orange, etc.) plantations are in Sicily, and the fall in prices in these products has been disastrous. Sulphur too, another Sicilian staple, has severely depreciated in value. Here, as on the peninsula, huge estates, short leases, lack of

capital, monstrous usury, and a corrupt administration, are evils imperatively demanding broad and statesmanlike remedies. Crispi, in 1894,
confronted by the agrarian insurrections, made a bold attempt to deal
with the problem, but his schemes were wrecked by the powerful landed
interests represented in the Chamber.

In the Napoletano and in Sicily a further complication arises from
the corroding of social life by the *Camorra*, and the *Mafia*. Among
populations accustomed for centuries to regard the official machinery of
the law as something hostile, venal, superimposed by a foreign despotism,
secret societies find a congenial soil. In their better aspect, they constitute a sort of rough popular justice and a degenerate chivalry; they
keep the ring clear for the play of those fierce passions, which from time
immemorial have made personal revenge of injury a sacred law: in their
coarser aspect they are but gangs of criminals, blackguards, and ratteners,
whose only bond is a community of antipathy to all established order or
government. The apotheosis of criminals, such as Palizzolo and of the
disgraced Minister Nasi in Sicily; the immunity of the former and the
tardy and derisory sentence passed on the latter; the deplorable revelations at their trials of perversity, jobbery, and lack of principle in high
places, leave an impression of widespread corruption on the mind. It
is one of the ironies of the Nasi scandal that the incriminated Minister
held the portfolio of Public Instruction in more than one Government
and authorised the use of Mazzini's *Duties of Man* as a reading book in
Italian schools.

The prevailing tendency of Italian diplomacy since 1870 has been
towards alliance with Germany. Even down to October 13, 1874, a
French frigate remained at Civita Vecchia at the Pope's disposal;
and, until Gambetta routed the forces of clerical and monarchical
reactionaries in 1877, there was a very real danger of seeing the French
bayonets at Rome again. Moreover the determination of the Italian
Government to create a powerful modern navy was held to be a menace
to French interests in the Mediterranean. In 1878 Italy had returned
empty-handed from the Berlin Congress, though cherishing hopes of an
Italian protectorate in Tunis, to which she had been urged by Austria
and Russia, but from which she had abstained from fear of wounding
French susceptibilities: in 1881 she beheld her statesmen outwitted and
herself forestalled by the French occupation. To her utter stupefac-
tion, no protest was raised by Great Britain or Germany, for it was
not then known that France had been paid for her acquiescence in
the secret acquisition of Cyprus by an invitation to compensate herself
in North Africa. The Treaty of Bardo (May 12) was a response to
Lord Salisbury's *Prenez Tunis*, addressed at Bismarck's suggestion to
Waddington at Berlin, and it fanned Italian hostility to France to
fiercest flames. In October, Bismarck, who had always desired formally

CH. VIII.

to include Italy in the German-Austrian alliance, contrived, in spite
of irritation caused by the Irredentist agitation, a meeting between
Humbert I and Francis Joseph at Vienna. To the amazement and
disgust of Italian patriots, their King returned an Austrian colonel, and
(May 20, 1882) an alliance was concluded with the arch-enemy of
Italian independence.

The popular sympathy with Arabi Pasha, to help whom Menotti
Garibaldi was raising an Italian legion, made it impossible to accede to
a formal invitation to join Great Britain in the occupation of Egypt,
and since 1882 some coolness had arisen between the two nations. But
in 1884 it was indirectly intimated to the Depretis Ministry that, in
view of French activity, the occupation by a friendly Power of certain
positions on the Red Sea littoral would not be regarded unfavourably at
Downing Street. Secured by the *Triplice* from attack by land, and by
agreement with Great Britain from attack by sea, the Government
decided on a forward policy in Africa. Early in 1885 Beilul and
Massowah were occupied by an Italian expedition, H.M.S. *Condor*
having preceded it with orders to observe and report. The new policy,
which had been acquiesced in rather than approved by Depretis, was
inaugurated with no clear grasp of the magnitude of the issues involved
and, indeed, against the personal advice of Lord Cromer to the Italian
Consul-General at Cairo. The abandonment of the Sudan by Great
Britain was an unforeseen blow, but the occupation was made good and
subsequent operations on the mainland evoked protests from King John
of Abyssinia. Early in January, 1887, rumours reached Rome of hostile
forces gathering under Ras Alula; but the Minister of War, Count
Robilant, airily declined to attach importance to the movements of a
"handful of raiders" (*quattro predoni*). On January 26 Depretis rose
in the Chamber, ashen pale, and with faltering voice read a telegram
announcing that a whole battalion of 500 men had been cut to pieces
at Dogali. A force of 20,000 men was sent to retrieve the disaster, but,
after a period of inaction on either side and many losses from dysentery
and fever, the expedition was recalled. In the anarchy that followed
the death of King John in 1889, Menelik of Shoa was promised Italian
support against his rival of Tigri; and the ambiguous Treaty of Accialli
with the Shoan Chief, negotiated by Count Antonelli, nephew of the
famous Cardinal, was interpreted by Crispi to involve the suzerainty of
Italy over Abyssinia; money was coined with the impress of King
Humbert, wearing the Ethiopian crown, and the African possessions
were constituted (January, 1890) a *Colonia Eritrea*. Brilliant victories
over the dervishes at Agordat (December 21, 1893) and Cassala
(July 19, 1894) were hailed with transports of joy in Italy; and Crispi,
who had returned to power in 1893, sailing on the full tide of success,
aimed at a vast African empire. On January 14, 1895, General
Baratieri, Governor of the colony, defeated Ras Mangascia at Senafé,

and the premier proposed to occupy the province of Tigri. But at the end of the year large Abyssinian armies were threatening the Italian outposts; a force of 2350 men was routed and a garrison at Makalé compelled to surrender. Hastily formed and ill-disciplined reinforcements were despatched from Italy, and Crispi angrily telegraphed to Baratieri demanding an "authentic victory." The Governor, concentrating his forces, advanced, and on February 7, 1896, sighted the enemy under Menelik. The Abyssinian army retired to Adowah: Baratieri remained inactive, and hinted at withdrawal. On February 22 General Baldissera was appointed to supreme command; and on the 25th Crispi despatched a furious telegram to Baratieri, characterising the operations as "military phthisis," and declaring that the country was prepared for any sacrifice to save the honour of the army and the prestige of the monarchy. Goaded, perhaps, to a desperate effort to retrieve his position before the arrival of his superior, Baratieri advanced with 20,000 men to meet the enemy 80,000 strong at Adowah. He was a dashing Garibaldian soldier of the old school, but over-weighted by the command of an expedition that demanded high powers of organisation. His army service was inadequate, and he was a long distance from his base. The columns lost touch; a whole brigade went astray; and on March 1 the Italian army was routed, losing all its artillery. The long retreat through mountain defiles, harassed by a savage and hostile population, was more agonising even than the defeat. The disaster was complete and overwhelming; 254 officers, including two generals, and nearly 4500 men were killed; 45 officers and 1500 men captured. The attempt to hunt with the lions in colonial aggrandisement had ended in humiliation; the suzerainty over Abyssinia was abandoned, and the colony, finally delimited by the Treaty of Peace signed September, 1900, was reduced to a territory of about 80,000 square miles; in December, 1906, an agreement on Ethiopian affairs was signed by Italy, France, and Great Britain. Up to 1906 African adventures had cost the State £17,591,567. The balance sheet of the colony of Erythrea is a melancholy one. Out of a population of about 300,000, only 2800 are Europeans, and the annual charge on the Italian exchequer is about £320,000. The total imports in 1905 were valued at £516,367, of which Italy contributed £138,852; the total exports £270,897, of which only £31,303 were home consignments. A small caravan trade, totalling £209,965 in 1906, was done with Ethiopia. In 1905 the Italian Government assumed direct administration of the Somaliland Protectorate, after the unhappy results of exploitation by two private companies.

Since the end of the tariff war with France in 1898, and the subsequent acquiescence of the Republic in Italy's claims on Tripoli, the sister Latin nations have drawn closer. Popular Italian sentiment has always favoured an alliance with democratic France rather than with Germany; an agreement on Mediterranean affairs was effected

in December, 1901, and, early in 1902, the French ambassador, in
a speech to the French colony at Rome, declared that a conflict
between the two Latin nations was no longer possible. The visit of
President Loubet to Rome in the spring of 1904 sealed the bond of
amity, and support was given to France at the Algeciras conference
even at the cost of some friction with Germany. The Triple Alliance,
nevertheless, has been maintained: it was renewed in June, 1902, in
conformity with the new situation and still remains one of the bases
of Italian foreign policy, tacitly accepted but not loved. The *Italia
Irredenta* agitation for the redemption of the Trentino and the other
Italian-speaking provinces from Austrian rule has, since 1897, been
overlaid by the more absorbing question raised by the Balkan policy
of the Dual Monarchy. The menace of an Austrian Albania, with
an Austrian Biserta at Valona commanding the Straits of Otranto
is intolerable to Italian diplomacy, which appears to overestimate the
capacity of the Gulf of Valona as a possible naval base: equally insufferable to Austria is the prospect of an Italian occupation of Albania.
Officially, both Powers are bound to maintain the *status quo*, and repeated
statements have been made by successive Foreign Ministers in the Italian
Chamber that Italy and Austria are in full accord with regard to
Albania. But, while officially the attitude of both Powers is correct, each
is pursuing among the Catholic population of northern Albania a policy
of "pacific economic penetration" by means of the religious Orders
and schools, and, generally, by shipping subsidies, and strenuous efforts
at commercial supremacy. Increased armaments on both sides; anti-
Austrian agitations in Italy; the exploitation of her dynastic relations
with Montenegro; the pressure of the Pangermanic movement in
Austria, and rival railway policies—these are disturbing elements in
the situation that demand the utmost delicacy and sagacity on either
side. The strategic railway projected by Austria through the Sandjak
of Novibazar between Uvatz and Mitrowitz would place her in direct
communication with Salonica and the Aegean, and cut across all lines of
penetration from the Albanian ports to the east; and, if the additional
railway, which is already being studied at Vienna, descended the coast of
Albania from Cattaro, the province would be enclosed in a girdle of
steel and necessarily fall under Austrian control. To counter this,
Italian diplomatic support and the promise of a subsidy of £1,600,000
have been given to the rival Servian scheme of a Danube-Adriatic line.
Italy, in her present economic position, perhaps stands to lose more by
a European convulsion than any other nation, and in the face of the
ever-gathering, ever-shifting stormclouds in the Balkans she will need
all possible wisdom and fortitude in her statesmen.

CHAPTER IX.

THE LOW COUNTRIES.

HOLLAND.

THE political history of the kingdom of the Netherlands during the greater part of the period (1870–1905) of which this chapter treats is of no great general interest. The death of Thorbecke left the Liberal majority in the States General weak and divided, and, as there was also a dearth of statesmen of mark and intellectual distinction, there is little of moment to record beyond the succession of Ministries. The task of forming a Cabinet was confided by the King in 1872 to Gerrit de Vries, who held office until 1874. His Ministry saw the beginning of the war with the Sultan of Achin in north Sumatra, which was for so many years to drain the resources of Holland. An expedition of 3600 men under General Köhler sent against the rebel Sultan (April, 1873) had to retreat with heavy loss, many dying from disease, including the commander. A second larger expedition under General van Swieten was successful; the Sultan was deposed and his territory occupied. This war, however, involved the home country in heavy expenses, and was very unpopular in Holland. The provision of the necessary funds increased the difficulties of a Ministry which could not rely upon the support of a united party. In June, 1874, they resigned, and were succeeded by another Liberal Ministry under Jan Heemskerk, which held office for three years. Heemskerk, who had been Prime Minister from 1866 to 1868, was a capable man; but during his second Ministry he can scarcely be said to have been in power. He administered affairs not because he had the loyal support of his party, but rather because it was felt that "the King's government must be carried on." He had to contend against the opposition of the Progressives under Joannes Kappeyne and of the Anti-revolutionary party, which, after the death of Gulielmus Groen van Pfinsterer (May, 1876), found a new leader, Abraham Kuyper, who effected a considerable change in its aristocratic character by infusing into it the principles of democratic Calvinism, which he himself professed. This Ministry passed a useful measure of reform in the judiciary, and attempted to deal in a temporising spirit with the thorny question of primary education. Their proposals, however, gave satisfaction neither to the advanced Liberals, nor to the Anti-revolutionaries, nor to the Catholics. Heemskerk resigned and was succeeded by the leader of the Progressives, Joannes Kappeyne, who found himself after the election of 1877 supported by a majority of 16 in a House of 80 members. His Ministry was marked by the creation of an eighth department of State, that of Commerce and Waterways. His treatment of the primary education question, which refused to grant the subsidies to the "private" schools, was carried in the teeth of the bitter opposition of the Anti-revolutionary (Calvinist) and Catholic parties, who were united in desiring full state support for religious instruction. But the Cabinet were confronted with the difficulty of providing "ways and means" in conse-quence of the cost of the protracted Achin war; and, although a succession duty and other unpopular taxes were forced through the Chamber by a narrow majority, the Finance Minister, Johan George Gleichman, found himself unable to meet the deficit, which confronted him, without having recourse to a loan of 44 million florins. In these circumstances the proposals of the Minister of Waterways, Tak van Poortvliet, to make a number of new canals were not favourably received, and were rejected (May 20, 1879) by 40 votes to 39. This led to the resignation of the Ministry. Kappeyne asked for the support of the Crown to revise the Fundamental Law, but this the King refused.

William now asked a member of the Anti-revolutionary party, Constantius Theodorus Count van Lynden van Sandenburg, to form a "Ministry of affairs" composed of moderate men of all parties. He succeeded in doing so, and, which is more wonderful, though he had not the hearty goodwill of any section of the Chamber, he remained in office for the greater part of four years (1879–83). The divisions in the ranks of the Liberal majority and the steady support of the King enabled van Lynden by his tact and resourcefulness to carry on the government during a period of much disquietude and uncertainty. A series of disasters fell at this time in rapid succession upon the Royal House, which seemed to threaten the extinction of the line of Orange-Nassau. In 1877 Queen Sophia died; in 1879 Prince Henry, the King's brother, for some years Stadholder of Luxemburg; a few months later (June 11) the Prince of Orange, aged 39 years; in 1881 Prince Frederick, the King's uncle; and in 1884 Prince Alexander, his younger and sole surviving son. It cannot honestly be said that the national regret at the tragically premature deaths of the two young princes was called forth by regard for their personal qualities. William ended his days at Paris, and at the time of his decease had estranged himself from his countrymen by his continued residence in a foreign capital, whose distractions he preferred to the more homely life in Holland. He was, however, a man of parts; but Alexander was sickly in body and enfeebled in mind, and his death was an important event only because he was the last heir-male of the famous family of Orange-Nassau with whose fortunes those of Holland had been for three centuries so closely bound up. The King had in January, 1879, taken in second wedlock the youthful Princess Emma of Waldeck-Pyrmont, and the birth of a daughter, Princess Wilhelmina (August 31, 1880), caused general rejoicing throughout the country.

During van Lynden's Ministry the public interest in Holland was much stirred by the events, which followed the uprising of the Boers of the Transvaal against English rule and led to the formation of the South African Republic. It was also still much occupied by the continuance of the Achin difficulty. The Administration fell through an adverse vote (66 against 12) on a proposed modification of the electoral franchise, February 26, 1883.

The Liberals having now a very narrow majority and being split into hostile fractions, the task of conducting the administration was again, for the third time, confided to Jan Heemskerk at the head of a coalition Ministry of neutral character. By the death of Prince Alexander (June 21, 1884), the question of providing for the succession of a female sovereign and a Regency became urgent. A modification of the Fundamental Law was necessary, and provision was made for Queen Emma to become Regent during her daughter's minority with full powers. The parliamentary deadlock made, however, that larger revision of the Fundamental Law, which had been so long deferred, a matter of vital necessity to the country. The unsatisfactory financial position, due to the pressure of the Achin campaigns, the call for an alteration in the conditions of military service and provision for the national defence, and for extension of the suffrage in a democratic direction in order to combat more effectively the active Socialist agitation under the leadership of Domela Nieuwenhuis, compelled the Government to take this revision seriously in hand. The opposition of the King was withdrawn, and in 1887 the revision became an accomplished fact. The First Chamber was to consist of 50 members, chosen as before by the Provincial Estates. The Second Chamber of 100 members to be elected every fourth year by an electorate which included all males of 23 years and upwards, being householders or lodgers at a certain minimum rent or possessing " signs of fitness and social well-being "—a formula reserved for definition in a future law. By this reform the number of electors was raised from (about) 100,000 to 350,000.

The first elections under the new system resulted in the victory of the Anti-revolutionary (27) and Catholic (25) coalition over the Liberal groups (46). One independent Conservative and one Socialist (Domela Nieuwenhuis) were also returned. In April, 1888, a new Ministry came into office under Baron Aeneas Mackay, a man of moderate and conciliatory views. One of the first efforts of the Coalition was to secure that subsidising of the " private " schools by the State, which had been denied them (1889). The private schools thus supported must number at least 25 scholars, must conform to the official regulations, and must be organised by a society or body recognised by the law. The death of King William, who had been for some time incapacitated by ill-health, took place on November 23, 1890. During his long reign the people knew that their King, whatever his prejudices or mistakes, had been heart and soul devoted to the welfare of the nation, and, though he had never made any effort to win popularity, the traditional loyalty of the Dutch to the House of Orange-Nassau rendered the person of the last male representative of the race an object of deep-rooted affection, and his death was generally mourned. An attempt of the Coalition Ministry to introduce a system of universal personal military service alienated the Catholic wing of their supporters, and at the elections of 1891 the Liberals obtained a majority.

The new Ministry under the leadership of Cornelis van Tienhoven, a man of moderate views, was generally of a Progressive type, and contained a number of able men, notably Nicolas Gerard Pierson, Minister of Finance, and Tak van Poortvliet, Minister of the Interior. Failure had always attended hitherto the attempts of finance Ministers to meet the constantly recurring deficits and to make the budget balance by means of an income tax. Pierson succeeded. He imposed a tax on all incomes of 650 florins and upwards derived from commerce, industry, or salaries, but not on the interest of capital, on rents, or agricultural profits; he placed, however, a tax upon capital above 13,000 florins. He was able, at the same time, to remit the tax on patents, and to lower the land tax and various duties. Under his skilful management funds were found for the much-needed reorganisation of the national defences as well as for social reforms. The Liberal party was, however, once more to be divided and the Ministry shattered, by differences of opinion on the question of the extension of the franchise and the interpretation of the qualification under the Act of 1887—"signs of fitness and social well-being." Tak van Poortvliet brought forward in 1893 a proposal for practically universal suffrage. He understood by "fitness" being able to write, by "social well-being" not having received assistance from public charity. His proposal, if carried, would have raised the number of electors from 350,000 to 800,000, but it was strenuously opposed. The moderate Liberals under Samuel van Houten's leadership conducted a campaign against it in the Chamber, in the Press, and on the platform, and they had as allies the Conservative section of the Anti-revolutionary party headed by Alexander Frederick de Savornin-Lohman, and the bulk of the Catholics. On the other hand the radical Progressives supported Tak, as did also the democratic Calvinists (Anti-revolutionary party) under Kuyper, and a small group of Catholics who followed Schaepman. The parties were broken to pieces, and, the States General being dissolved in March,

1894, an appeal was made to the people. The election was fought not on the ordinary party lines, but as a contest to the death between "Takkians" and "anti-Takkians" or "van Houtians." The results of the polling showed that the van Houtians were in a majority, and the Takkians could only muster 46 votes against 54 opponents. The Ministry therefore resigned, and was replaced by a Cabinet formed by Jonkheer Johan Roëll with van Houten occupying the post of Minister of the Interior in succession to Tak van Poortvliet. It was on van Houten, therefore, that the duty fell of preparing an alternative project of electoral Reform. His proposals were finally accepted in 1896, and contained the following provisions. The members of the Second Chamber are to be returned by 100 single member districts; all males, being Netherlanders, and 25 years of age, are electors, provided they come under one of the following categories: (1) persons who pay in direct taxation at least one *gulden*, (2) householders or lodgers paying a certain minimum rent and with certain conditions as to length of residence, (3) proprietors or hirers of vessels of at least 24 tons, (4) earners of salaries or wages varying according to the place of habitation from 275 florins to 550 florins per annum, (5) holders of investments of 100 florins in the public funds or of 50 florins in the Savings Banks, (6) persons who have passed certain examinations. This scheme raised the number of electors to about 700,000.

The elections of 1897 after a severe struggle resulted in the return of an increased number of Progressives, and the Roëll-van Houten Ministry resigned, giving place to a Liberal concentration Ministry drawn from the various sections of the Liberal party under Pierson, who resumed his place as Minister of Finance, and Hendrik Goeman Borgesius, Minister of the Interior. This Ministry passed a number of useful measures of social, educational, and administrative reform : among these a law which made it obligatory on parents to send their children to school until the age of 13, and at the same time raised the salaries of teachers and the subsidies of the State. At last, in 1898, after a quarter of a century of wrangling and discussion personal military service was established, students and ecclesiastics excepted. In this year (August 31, 1898) Queen Wilhelmina attained her majority, an event which was celebrated with much enthusiasm, and many expressions of grateful recognition were offered to the Queen Mother for the admirable way in which she had for the past eight years discharged the duties of Regent.

The following year was rendered memorable for Holland by the gathering on the initiative of the Tsar Nicholas II of the first International Peace Congress at the Hague. The sessions, at which delegates from all independent States were present, were held from May 18 to June 29 at the royal residence known as The House in the Wood. A few months later (October 10) the Boer War broke out, which aroused among the Dutch an intense feeling of sympathy for their kinsmen in South Africa. The fugitive President Paul Kruger took refuge in Holland. He received a most friendly welcome from the Queen in person, and in this she reflected the feeling of the country, which was for a time very bitter against England. The Ministry, however, did its utmost to preserve a correct attitude, and to maintain friendly relations with a Power which it was hopeless to oppose. This attitude, together with a certain measure of unpopularity attaching to the laws establishing personal military service and obligatory school attendance, led to the overthrow of the Liberals at the elections of 1901. The orthodox Calvinists (Anti-revolutionaries) and the Catholics of all groups united on the basis of a defence of Christian belief against a party whose profession of religious neutrality they denounced as "paganism." Kuyper, to whose talents and energy the victory at the polls was largely due, became the head of a Coalition Ministry.

Earlier in this same year (February 7, 1901) Queen Wilhelmina was married to Prince Henry of Mecklenburg-Schwerin. It was a match of affection, which commended itself to the Dutch people, whose deep-rooted attachment to their Queen and dynasty was most touchingly shown in the spring of the following year (April, 1902) when her very serious illness threatened to expose the Netherlands to the danger of a disputed succession to the throne. Socialism had for years been a growing force, having its chief centres in the large towns, especially in Amsterdam and in Friesland, under the leadership of the eloquent young advocate, van Troestra. In 1903 the Socialist propaganda bore fruit in the threat of a general strike unless the Government were prepared to concede the demands of the Democratic Labour Party. The Ministry met the threats with firmness. The military were called out, and an "Anti-strike" Bill introduced and carried. The determined attitude of the authorities met with the success it deserved, and the strike was a complete failure. The rebellion in Achin again assumed serious dimensions in 1902, involving a costly campaign, which resulted in 1903 in the submission of the Sultan. In 1904, however, hostilities once more broke out, and there was sanguinary fighting, in the course of which a number of women and children met their deaths at the hands of the Dutch troops. The news aroused much indignation, and the conduct of the war was severely arraigned in the Second Chamber. When the general election of 1905 drew near, the sections of the Liberal party which had been so long divided sank their differences in a united assault upon the Ministerialists, whose popularity had been gradually diminishing. After a close struggle 45 Liberals with 7 Socialists were returned against 48 followers of Kuyper. There was thus a narrow majority against the Government dependent on the Socialist vote. Kuyper therefore resigned and was succeeded as Prime Minister by a moderate Liberal, Goeman Borgesius.

During the period with which this chapter deals the Kingdom of the Netherlands had been progressing steadily in material wealth and general well-being. The population had more than doubled since 1845, and amounted to more than 5,000,000. The poldering of the estuary of the Y (1873–7) had converted yet another district of many thousands of acres, once covered with water, into fertile pasture land, with the North Sea Canal passing through its midst. This fine canal, fifteen miles long and capable of conveying the largest ships, has given to Amsterdam a new outlet to the ocean, and has done much to restore its commercial and maritime prosperity; while the port of Rotterdam has, since the opening of its new waterway, made even more rapid strides. Rotterdam is a great emporium of German trade, and the tonnage of the ships visiting it is now twenty-five times greater than half a century ago. Agricultural depression during the last decades of the century was severely felt, the trade in butter and cheese especially suffering from Danish competition; but with the advent of the twentieth century there were signs of revival. The fisheries remain, as they have been for centuries, a profitable source of occupation to many thousands of the seafaring population.

In the general diffusion of culture, and in intellectual and scientific distinction, Holland can compare favourably with any other country. While the reader must be referred on this head to the brief sketch of literature in the Netherlands which was given in the previous volume; two fields of study may be indicated in which deserved preeminence has been attained—critical theology and national history. The representative names are Abraham Kuenen and Robert Fruin. The former has gained a world-wide reputation. But the work of Fruin has been scarcely less remarkable, for by his influence and example he created a school of historical workers whose researches in the national archives, conducted on sound and scientific principles, have been most fruitful.

This account of the period 1870–1905 would not be complete without mention being made of the great revival of Dutch painting which it has witnessed. There are some critics who have so high an opinion of the merits of the modern School, that they venture to think it not unworthy to take rank with that which in the seventeenth century made Dutch art famous. This may be confidently stated—that not since the age of Rembrandt has there arisen in any other country such a group of con-summate artists, distinguished for the originality and variety of their genius, for their technical skill and richness of colouring, as in the Holland of our own times. The names of Josef Israels and Hendrik Willem Mesdag, of the three brothers Maris, of Anton Mavre, Vincent van Gogh, and Albert Bilders, are familiar to all lovers of art, and besides these may be mentioned others of great merit—Rochussen, Bles, Roelofs, Bosboom, and of younger men, Neuhuys, Blommers, van Bor-selen, van de Sande Bakhuysen, de Haas, Duchâtel, and Haverman.

CH. IX.

The qualities of this school show that the Dutch race of today have inherited from their forefathers an artistic temperament singularly sensitive to the poetry of form and colour, and the power to give it outward expression.

BELGIUM.

The outbreak of war between France and Germany was a cause of great anxiety and no small danger to Belgium. Fortunately, in no small measure owing to the exertions of the King, steps had been taken to maintain an efficient army of 100,000 men with an adequate reserve, and to fortify the valley of the Meuse. Hostilities had no sooner begun than the Belgian Government gave orders for the mobilisation of the troops for the defence of the frontiers. This prompt action, and the declaration of Great Britain that she would resist any violation of Belgian territory, secured the neutrality of the country. After Sedan, a body of French soldiers fled for refuge across the frontier; but they were at once disarmed and interned.

It has already been told how in this year (1870) a Catholic Ministry under Baron d'Anethan took office. Aided by a split in the Liberal ranks the Catholics had at the elections of August obtained a majority in both Chambers. The restriction of the franchise to the moneyed middle class, the great mass of the people being without votes, had given the Liberals a long lease of power. They had used it in trying to banish religion from the schools, and so far as possible from civil life, and at the same time in not unsuccessful efforts more and more to centralise the administration and to make it increasingly bureaucratic. They also consistently refused to regulate by legislation the hours or the conditions of labour or to reform the law on military service. In their case, the name of Liberal signified rather that the party consisted of free-thinkers and Anti-Clericals than of men devoted to the cause of progress and reform. The Catholics on the other hand must not be regarded as in any sense a purely Clerical party. The distinction between them, apart from their attitude towards religious questions, might perhaps be thus expressed; the Catholic party was in its principles democratic and essentially national; the Liberal party oligarchic and cosmopolitan, with French leanings.

In 1871 Malou succeeded Baron d'Anethan as head of a Cabinet composed of moderate men. This was largely owing to the determination of the King that the Ultramontanes should not be allowed to commit the Belgian Government to take any active part in the agitation for the restoration of the Pope's Temporal Power. Nothing very note-worthy occurred during the seven years of their tenure of office. The voting qualification for electors to provincial and communal Councils was lowered to 20 *francs* and 10 *francs* (direct taxation) respectively, and a law was passed making personal service in the army obligatory. Faced however by the opposition of a section of reactionaries in their own ranks as well as by the whole Liberal party, which had gained strength in adversity, the Administration did not retain its hold on the electorate. In 1878 the Liberals were once more in a majority, and Walthère Frère-Orban became Prime Minister. His tenure of office was signalised by a resolute attempt to secularise education.

A Bill was introduced and carried after fierce opposition, by which the system of primary education, which had subsisted since 1842, was completely subverted. All communal schools were placed under the strict supervision of the State, and the teaching of religion was strictly forbidden, although an attempt was made to conciliate the Catholics, by the introduction of a clause permitting the clergy of all cults to give instruction in the school buildings out of school hours to the children of such parents as desired it. The private schools were allowed to exist, for the privilege of freedom of education was conceded by the Constitution; but in the choice of schoolmasters, and indeed of all persons employed in the public service or under the local administrations in the magistracy or the notariate, on railways or in charitable institutions, an exclusive preference was given to the pupils of the state schools. The Catholics met the attack with an organised resistance. The Bishops appealed to the faithful for funds, and so liberal was the response that soon private Catholic schools were built in almost every commune in the kingdom. This appeal was accompanied by drastic action. The clergy, carrying out the instructions of the episcopate, refused absolution to all teachers in the "Godless" schools and to the parents whose children frequented them. The Government replied by the refusal of public assistance or employment. But the influence of the clergy prevailed. Many of the state schools were almost deserted. In Flanders over 80 per cent. of the children went to the Catholic schools. The intervention of the Pope was requested; but the Holy See declined to take any action, and such was the resentment felt that the Belgian envoy at the Vatican was recalled. To maintain the struggle the Liberal party needed all their strength; but a split took place between the two sections, known as the Doctrinaires and the Progressists, on the question of the extension of the franchise. This was fatal. The elections of 1884 resulted in the return of a large Catholic majority; indeed so permanent has been the revulsion of feeling against the Liberals, that the party has remained excluded from office for a quarter of a century. The new Ministry, at first under the presidency of Malou, and afterwards of Auguste Beernaert, set to work without delay to undo the educational legislation of their predecessors. The Liberals had established a special department of education. This was abolished. Authority over the schools was restored to the communal Councils, which had the power either to maintain a public (state) school, or to "adopt" and give a grant to a private school, provided that it conformed to the regulations and submitted itself to the inspection of the State. At the demand of 25 heads of families, the commune was required to provide a Catholic or a neutral school, as the case might be; but the teaching of religion was made compulsory, whenever the parents desired it. Under this law, in a large number of communes the unsectarian schools ceased to exist, and the religious education passed into the hands of the Catholic clergy. Some members of the Cabinet would have proceeded still further in a reactionary direction; but the King, seeing that the aims and views of this ultramontane section were arousing strong hostility in many municipalities and communes, insisted on their removal from the Ministry. Their place was taken by moderate men. The Schools Law of 1884 has worked well, and the settlement of the religious question embodied in it has not been since disturbed.

During the next few years, the Catholic majority devoted themselves to the furtherance of a policy of social legislation, and several useful Acts were passed. The Liberal Doctrinaires and Progressists were still divided on the subject of electoral Reform, and did not prove formidable adversaries; but a new party arose—*le parti ouvrier belge*—whose opposition, as the years went on, had to be seriously reckoned with. Socialism, based upon the principles of Karl Marx, had been making great headway among the Flemish industrial classes, especially at Ghent and Brussels, while among the Walloon population, who worked in the coal mines and factories of the south and east, a revolutionary socialism of the French type had taken root, with headquarters at Liége and Namur. Serious strikes, in 1886, had to be suppressed by military force. A Government Commission was nominated to enquire into the grievances of the strikers, and, in 1887, councils of arbitration were appointed to settle disputed questions between employers and employed. Fresh strikes and disturbances took place, however, in 1888, with the result that the Socialist party determined to set on foot a vigorous agitation to secure representation in Parliament, whose watch-cries were to be universal suffrage and reduction of the military service. In making these demands they found the Liberal Progressists willing to act with them up to a certain point; but the violence of the Socialist leaders alienated gradually all moderate men, who were not prepared to accept the doctrines of collectivism pure and simple. The principle of revision of the Constitution was at length agreed to, and the Chambers were dissolved in 1892. The result of the election was an increase in the Catholic majority, which numbered 92 to 60 Liberals. But the Catholics did not even now possess the two-thirds majority required by the Constitution. Much discussion ensued; but no definite decision was for some time arrived at. Meanwhile, the *parti ouvrier* continued its agitation; and a general strike was threatened unless universal suffrage was conceded. The Chamber, however, rejected the proposal to establish universal

suffrage (April, 1893). Nevertheless, it was felt by all sections of the Catholic party that a wide extension of the franchise was called for, and the compromise of universal suffrage safeguarded by the plural vote, as proposed by a Catholic deputy—Albert Nyssens—was ultimately adopted (September 3, 1893).

This system gave a vote to every male citizen of 25 years of age and upwards; but it granted a supplementary vote to all fathers of families, to the owner of real property valued at 2000 *francs*, or of investments bringing in an income of 100 *francs*, and two supplementary votes to everyone possessing diplomas of higher education and to certain functionaries, with the proviso that no one should have more than three votes in all. The first election under the new system, which increased the possible total of votes tenfold, was held, October 14, 1894. The result gave an overwhelming majority to the Catholic party, who numbered 105. The Liberals only succeeded in holding 18 seats; but the Socialists made a great stride forward and had 29 representatives in the new Chamber. They now began with renewed vigour, under the leadership of Emile Vandervelde, to conduct an active agitation in the country, while they found in Parliament an opportunity, if not of thwarting the will of the majority, at least of expounding their aims and views with insistence and ability. The first care of the Ministry of de Burlet, who had succeeded Beernaert in April, 1894, was to carry out a reform of the provincial and communal electorate on the same lines as the parliamentary. An attempt was again made to terrorise the Government by means of a general strike and by riots, but the authorities were firm, the military was called out, and the strike collapsed. The passing of these electoral reforms strengthened the hold of the Catholic party upon the administration of the country. In 1895 an education Bill was introduced, which completed the work of 1884. Religious instruction in public schools was made compulsory, and the communes were forbidden to give free education to the children of parents able to pay a fee. At the same time, social reform in many directions occupied a foremost place in the programme of the Catholic party, and Acts were passed dealing with old age pensions, workmen's dwellings, and employers' liability; much was also done for the encouragement of thrift by subsidies to the Savings Banks, and to mutual societies.

The partial elections of 1896 resulted in raising the number of Catholic deputies to 111, while the Liberals numbered 12, and the Socialists 29. The next elections in 1898 left the relative strength of the parties practically unaltered. In 1896 Count de Smet de Naeyer became head of the Ministry in place of de Burlet. One of the first acts of his Ministry was a law making Flemish, as well as French, the official language of the country. The Flemish movement thus, in 1897, attained the realisation of its aim. All laws were henceforth to be published in the two languages. The results of the last elections, which had left the Liberal party in a hopeless minority, and had actually destroyed the more moderate wing of that party, the Doctrinaires, had led to a demand for proportional representation. The great Catholic majority, as is so often the case, having an overwhelming superiority over all opponents, began to split up into groups, and they found themselves in face of a resolute Socialist minority, which was bold and enterprising, and did not scruple to make full use of all the arts of parliamentary obstruction. The split in the ranks of the majority caused, in the early part of 1899, a change of Ministry, Count de Smet de Naeyer giving place to van den Peereboom. The new Prime Minister however found himself confronted by organised obstruction from the Socialists, and after a brief tenure of office he resigned, and Smet de Naeyer returned to his former post.

A Bill for the adoption of a system of proportional representation was now pressed forward and carried. By this measure, in every *arrondissement* each party receives a number of seats proportional to the votes recorded in its favour, provided these exceed a certain fixed minimum. The first elections under the new system were held in May, 1900, and, as had been anticipated, resuscitated the almost defunct Liberal party. The Catholics were still in a decided majority, the actual distribution of seats being, 85 Catholics, 31 Liberals, 32 Socialists, 3 Radicals, 1 Christian Democrat (dissentient Catholic). The burning question at this time was that of military service. The Belgian army had been raised by conscription mitigated by a somewhat indulgent system of substitution. The measures now proposed modified the compulsory system by encouraging voluntary enlistment while at the same time reducing the time of active service and the numbers with the colours. The real aim of the Catholic party was, in opposition to the wishes of the King and of his military advisers, to adopt for Belgium the Swiss rather than the German model of army organisation. At the same time, the subject of social reform was always in the foreground of the settled policy of the Catholic party, and laws were passed regulating contracts of labour, protecting workers from insanitary conditions, and guaranteeing to married women the free control of their savings. But the activity of the Catholics in their social legislation only stirred the Socialist leaders, whose growing influence with the industrial masses it was intended to undermine, to more bitter and determined opposition. The demand was made for universal suffrage pure and simple; and, in April, 1902, attempts were made to force the hand of the Government by strikes and riots. But the authorities were firm, the strikes failed, and public opinion refused to be terrorised. There were many loud words, but the general strike— threatened for April 18—proved a fiasco, in face of the determination of the employers, and the promptness with which the authorities quelled all riotous disturbances by calling out the troops and civic guards to the assistance of the police.

A month later (end of May, 1902) the returns of the parliamentary election confirmed the Catholic party in their long tenure of the reins of power—by giving them a majority of 26 over the combined forces of the Liberals and Socialists. Under the capable leadership of Count de Smet de Naeyer, the policy of the Catholic party continued to follow frankly democratic lines. Smet de Naeyer was a skilled financier. With a rate of taxation per head of the population about one-half of that paid in England and much less than one-half of that paid in France, the budgets could boast of annual surpluses, despite the large amounts expended in providing old age pensions, in subsidies to mutual societies, on the promotion of technical education, and other measures for the encouragement of thrift in the working classes. Probably more is done in Belgium than in any other country, through the agency of a network of savings banks, mutual societies, and building societies, to encourage the investment of savings and to provide loans secured by life insurance policies for the purposes of agriculture or for the purchase of dwelling houses. The old age pension system established by the Laws of 1902 and 1903 entitles every workman who deposits one *franc* to an old age pension fund in a savings bank to receive an addition of 60 *centimes* from the State until a sufficient amount stands to his credit to provide an annuity of 360 *francs* per annum. Shortly after the passing of the amended Act of 1903 the government grant to more than two hundred thousand pensioners amounted to 15,000,000 *francs.* The partial elections of 1904, though the strength of the Liberal party was increased, left the Catholics with a majority of 20 votes.

The whole of the period which we have been considering was one of uninterrupted industrial progress and commercial prosperity. It was also marked by the first steps for the acquisition by Belgium of colonial possessions. These steps were solely due to the initiative of King Leopold II. The remarkable personality of the King had a large share in shaping the destinies of the country. During the whole of his reign his strength of character, his trained experience, his diplomatic skill, and his varied culture, exercised a constant and growing influence. The wisdom of Leopold I built up the Belgian State; his son with equal abilities was cast in a very different mould. Leopold II was not content to play the *rôle* of the constitutional ruler of a petty neutral kingdom. He wished that his people should have a place in the world movement of colonial expansion. By his patient diplomacy, capacity for organisation, and undaunted resolution in the face of difficulties that seemed insuperable, he succeeded in creating the Congo Free State under his own sovereignty. The Geographical Congress (1876), summoned by King Leopold to meet at Brussels under his presidency, led to the formation of the International Association for the suppression of the slave trade and the opening out of Central Africa. Of this International Association King Leopold was the moving spirit.

CH. IX.

He enlisted the services of Stanley, and a Belgian expedition under his leadership in 1879 made its way to the Upper Congo. There however it found rivals in a French expedition under Brazza; and the Portuguese also advanced claims to the possession of the Lower Congo. Only by the exercise of much tact and adroitness did King Leopold succeed in preserving a way of access from the coast to the navigable reaches of the river above the Cataracts. At the Congress of Berlin, November, 1884, a vast domain in Central Africa was recognised as the sphere of influence of the International Association, and was erected into an independent State under the sovereignty of the King of the Belgians, with the proviso that freedom of commerce and freedom of religion should be guaranteed, and that slavery should be suppressed and no trade monopolies granted.

It was more difficult for King Leopold to win the assent of the Belgian people to his assumption of the sovereignty. The large majority of the Belgians felt no eagerness to throw away the advantages which Belgium enjoyed as a neutral State under the protection of the Powers by running any risk of being drawn into the vortex of international politics. The King, however, addressed himself to the two Chambers, and their approval of his acceptance of the sovereignty was given, April 28 and 30, 1885. King Leopold needed also the financial help of the Belgian people; and, to make it clear that his African enterprise had not been undertaken for personal aggrandisement but for the ultimate benefit of Belgium, he devised to the Belgian State by a will dated August 2, 1889, his possessions in the Congo; and a treaty was concluded between the Free State and Belgium, by which the latter advanced 25,000,000 *francs* for the purposes of railway construction and the opening of the Upper Congo territory to commerce. It was not without strong opposition that the Chambers thus officially associated themselves with the King's projects, and after the extension of the franchise in 1894 this opposition became more and more accentuated. A fresh loan of 5,600,000 *francs* was granted indeed in 1896, but only by 61 votes to 57, and there were 20 abstentions. Nevertheless, by the energy of the King, all difficulties were gradually surmounted. The railway to Stanley Pool above the Cataracts was at last completed and opened for traffic in 1898. The commerce of the Congo State has progressed by giant strides. The exports, which reached a total of 1,980,441 *francs* in 1887, amounted to 15,146,976 *francs* in 1897, and had risen in 1903 to 54,597,836 *francs*. Since 1898 other lines of railway have been rapidly pushed into the interior. Now that the Congo Free State has been transformed into a Belgian Colony (1909), it may be hoped that the pressure of public opinion will correct any irregularities and abuses.

King Leopold II died on December 17, 1909, and was succeeded by his nephew, the Count of Flanders, as King Albert I.

CHAPTER X.

THE IBERIAN PENINSULA.

SPAIN.

BETWEEN the year 1871 and the present time, Spain has progressed, through internal disorder and colonial disaster, to a condition of comparative material prosperity, and towards a state of political stability. The most vigorous of living Spanish novelists, Don Vicente Blasco Ibañez, speaking through the mouth of a character in his story *La Catedral,* observes that Spain has been dragged on by the general advance of Europe, but has herself contributed nothing, and has made no spontaneous movement. Don Vicente speaks with the licence of a domestic critic. A foreigner will prefer to say that Spain has at last begun to awake from delusions, and to learn to look at facts. Her course during these years has been divided into six stages: the reign of Amadeo of Savoy (January, 1871, to February, 1873); the Republic (February, 1873, to December, 1874); the restoration of the Bourbon dynasty by the *pronunciamiento* of Murviedro (December 28, 1874); the reign of Alfonso XII (December, 1874, to November 25, 1885); the Regency of Doña Maria Cristina (November, 1885, to May, 1902); and the period since the present King, Don Alfonso XIII, attained his majority. These six stages may be grouped into three divisions. From the arrival of Don Amadeo until the proclamation of Alfonso XII, Spain was contending with anarchy; from the close of 1874 to the end of 1898 she was struggling to retain the remnants of her colonial empire; since she had to pay the penalty of centuries of error by the disasters of that year, she has begun, for the first time, to endeavour to make full use of the neglected resources of her own soil. The realities of her history will be best grasped by adhering to these divisions, rather than by giving undue attention to such distracting, and frequently meaningless incidents, as changes of Ministry.

The reign of Don Amadeo was in itself but a part of a period. It represented nothing more than the hopeless attempt of a body of military and civil conspirators to set up an imitation of the government of William III in Great Britain, without the aid of any one of the conditions which rendered the Revolution settlement of 1689 possible. No party supported his throne. Three real parties existed in the country —the Republicans, who had been represented by 63 votes in the Constituent Cortes, the Carlists, and the Alfonsists. The last of the three was as yet weak. It was hampered by the youth of its candidate, Don Alfonso, the son of Isabel II, and by the discredit which the personal weaknesses of the Queen had brought on the Bourbon family. The Carlists were formidable. They were, however, divided among themselves. The official head of their branch of the Bourbon family, Don Juan de Bourbon, was disposed to coquet with constitutional principles. He was even prepared to be content with the position of Regent for his cousin Don Alfonso. Their party manager in Spain, Don Cándido Nocedal, was averse from the use of force. He agreed with Don Antonio Cánovas del Castillo, who became the official leader of the Alfonsists in 1872, in thinking that the monarchical parties should wait until the revolution settlement broke down by its own inherent weakness, when the country would turn to them for salvation. The policy of both, which Cánovas was in time to make effective in the interest of his own party, was accurately defined by the Jacobite cant phrase, "box it about and it will come to my uncle." But Don Juan de Bourbon was repudiated by the bulk of his followers, and by his own sons, Don Carlos and the younger brother Don Alfonso. There were a few Carlists, of whom the most famous was Ramón Cabrera, in favour of concessions to Liberalism; but they had little influence and in the end drifted into the ranks of the Alfonsists. The real strength of the Carlists lay in the clergy, and the influence they exercised over the country people in all parts of Spain, and more especially in the Basque Provinces, Navarre, Upper Aragon, Catalonia, and Valencia. The clergy were deeply offended by the choice of a King from the House of Savoy, which had just occupied Rome, and had made the Pope "the prisoner of the Vatican." They were even more sensibly affected by the irregular payment of their stipends, and by the fear that the religious budget would be suppressed, and that they would be thrown on the voluntary contributions of the faithful who, in spite of the ardent Roman Catholicism of the Spaniards, have always been very niggardly to the parish clergy. Therefore, the priests were well disposed to do all they could to promote a Carlist rising.

The revolution settlement had in fact no support except the army. This would indeed have been sufficient if the army had been united and well-handled. Amid the indifference, local patriotism, and factions of Spain, the army is the only great national secular institution. So long as it is united it can control "the machine," the centralised administration which interferes in all Spanish life, through its local unofficial instruments, the *caciques*, when it does not act by direct order. Therefore it can command the services of place-hunting politicians, and it can secure the election of Cortes with an obedient majority by administrative pressure or corruption. During the revolutionary period a third means of coercion was much employed—the notorious *partido de la porra*, "party of the cudgel." They were hired gangs of ruffians who terrorised the voters. But in 1871 the army had been deprived by the assassination of Prim of the only leader who was popular with the ranks, commanded a personal following among the officers, could hold the stick and strike with it. Moreover, the army was subject to the action of a strong dissolvent. When in 1867, Prim made his abortive attempt to persuade the garrison of Valencia to revolt, he had promised the abolition of compulsory service. This promise was repeated by the Republicans, and by some of the politicians who served the Government of Don Amadeo. It deeply offended the officers, who knew that voluntary service would mean the destruction of the army; but it was very popular with the soldiers, who desired nothing better than to be free to return home. In the meantime, and apart from the Carlist intrigues of the clergy, the country was menaced by growing disorder. A great recrudescence of the endemic brigandage of Andalusia had followed the revolution of 1868. The "Kidnappers," Palma *alias* Bando, Pulli, Pitoño, and others, blackmailed the orderly population. Many of them were enrolled in the *partido de la porra*, and had their official protectors in Madrid. Anarchism and socialism began to increase in the towns, and agrarian socialism, the natural fruit of large estates owned by absentee landlords and worked by gangs under exacting middlemen, became rampant in the south.

From January, 1871, to September, 1873, all these elements of disorder grew, till they threatened the very existence of the national unity and the State. Don Amadeo's share in this access of fever was that of a transient and embarrassed phantom. He and his beautiful wife were insulted, and his life was threatened. His Ministers pursued factious quarrels, and their feuds were promoted by Republicans and Carlists in the Cortes, who combined to make government impossible by joining with any section of malcontents on any question. Six ministerial crises and three general elections in twenty-four months served only to manifest the instability of the artificial monarchy of Don Amadeo. He was at last told by the army chiefs that he must agree to the suspension of constitutional guarantees, and rule by the sword. The King was resolved to reign as a constitutional ruler, and refused his consent. His fall became a mere question of time, and he availed himself of a military question to escape from a desperate position. The officers of the artillery refused to obey General Hidalgo, formerly a member of their own corps, who had been responsible for the murder of several of his colleagues at the San Gil barracks in 1866. The Prime Minister of the day, Ruiz Zorrilla, insisted on dismissing them. The King attached his name to the decree, resigned his crown, and left Spain on February 12, 1873.

During this sterile agitation in Madrid the Carlists had gained ground. They were at first represented in the field only by such men as the Cura de Santa Cruz—a brutal fanatic who enforced his demands for blackmail by shooting men, and by stripping, tarring and feathering, or flogging women. Santa Cruz operated in Navarre and Biscay; but he had imitators elsewhere. In 1872 the Carlist Princes were encouraged to take the field themselves. Don Juan de Bourbon had resigned in favour of his eldest son; and, on May 1, Don Carlos crossed the frontier of Navarre from France, relying not only on his own partisans and on deserters from the army but on republican cooperation. His following was easily scattered at Oroquieta on May 4 by General Moriones, and he fled back to France. Serrano, then Prime Minister, came to the north, and entered into a convention with the Carlist leaders at Amoravieta. He promised an amnesty to all, even to deserters from the army. The convention exasperated the Liberals in all parts of Spain, but especially those of the towns of Navarre and Biscay, who considered that they were left at the mercy of their hereditary enemies, the country people and their clerical leaders. After the abdication of Don Amadeo, the Cortes, which had just been elected by Ruiz Zorrilla and the *partido de la porra* to support his monarchy, proceeded to proclaim the Republic. The deputies endeavoured to retain control of affairs by means of a committee till new Cortes were elected. It was set aside forcibly by the real Republicans; and Señor Figueras was named interim president.

The simmering disorder of the country now boiled up with frightful rapidity. First came the paralysis of the army. General Gaminde, who held the command in Catalonia, concentrated his troops at Barcelona, and endeavoured to induce them to proclaim Don Alfonso. The soldiers, misled into the belief that the Republic would abolish compulsory service, refused to follow him. He fled to France, and most of the officers went into hiding. The soldiers disbanded themselves, and the open country was left to the Carlists. The example set at Barcelona was widely followed. The army was not wholly disbanded, but it was much weakened, and discipline was all but destroyed. In Catalonia one column murdered their general, Cabrinetti, and then surrendered to the Carlists. The forces of Don Carlos increased rapidly. He reentered Spain on July 17, 1873, and before the end of the year he had forty-five thousand men in arms. In Navarre and the Basque Provinces, where he occupied a compact body of territory, with the exception of a few fortified towns, his troops were regularly organised. In other parts of Spain the Carlist forces were never more than *guerrilleros*—numerous in Catalonia and Valencia, but confined to a few wandering bands in La Mancha and Estremadura. By the end of 1875 they had risen to 75,000 men with 143 guns, with the same differences in the various parts of the country. In Navarre and the Basque country a regular army was based on a territory with a civil administration, a revenue, a capital at Durango, cannon foundries, Courts of law, and even a university at Oñate. Supplies were received across the French frontier by the connivance of Marshal MacMahon's Government.   Elsewhere the Carlists continued to be composed of *guerrilleros* and bandits.

Great as the peril from the Carlists was, it was thrown into the background for a time by an even more pressing danger.   The proclamation of the Republic was followed all over the south by an outbreak of the deeply-rooted and ancient particularism, local or even tribal, of Spain.   In Andalusia and Murcia big towns and little threw off the control of the central Government and assumed practical independence under the name of " cantons."   At Carthagena, the cantonalists seized nearly the whole fleet, and the navy was even more completely disorganised than the army.   The few troops left in the south were concentrated at Córdoba.   The cantonalists quarrelled among themselves; but they agreed in refusing to pay octroi duties (*consumos*) or to remit taxes to Madrid.

The Republican leaders, Figueras, Pi y Margall, and Salmeron, proved incapable of dealing with the crisis they had provoked.   All were professors, journalists, and talkers, who had received the worthless superficial education given in modern Spain.   They had acquired what knowledge they possessed from easily read French sources, and were moreover divided in opinion.   Emilio Castelar, a man of the same stamp, but of more fluent and redundant eloquence, and of better natural capacity, did not at first obtain a position of leadership.   Figueras was terrified by the Republic when he saw it.   He fled the country in May rather than face the first Cortes, which were elected in the midst of prevailing turmoil, but only by about a third of the electors.   The deputies chose as his successor Pi y Margall, a Federalist Republican, who endeavoured to deal with anarchy by leaving freedom to provide a remedy.   The country was brought to the verge of disintegration.   Under the influence of fear the deputies set him aside and put Salmeron, a Unitarian Republican, at the head of affairs.   Salmeron made an effort to restore order.   A small force, composed in part of trustworthy troops, but very largely of officers left without employment by the disappearance of their regiments, was sent to Andalusia under the command of Manuel Pavia.   He brought the troops at Córdoba to order, and crushed the cantonalists of Seville after a fierce fight.   His success showed that the army could still save Spain, and that no other force could.   But, if the army was to do the work, it would inevitably resume its predominance.   Salmeron's fear of militarism overpowered his fear of anarchy, and he stopped Pavia in full career of victory.   With the deputies, fear of anarchy continued to be more acute than dread of the soldiers.   Salmeron was set aside on September 7, 1873; Emilio Castelar was put in his place, to save society; and the Cortes were prorogued till January.

Nobody doubted that Castelar was commissioned to rescue the country by the use of force.   He was as much responsible for all the mischief that had happened as any man; but the fact that he did his work with an avowed disregard for his reputation for consistency and a single eye to the good of Spain put him in a category apart from other Republican leaders. The artillery officers were brought back on their own terms, and a conscription of 120,000 men was raised. The docility of the mass of Spaniards to a vigorous central Government made it possible to carry out the measure, but it killed the Republic. Freedom from the "blood tax" was in the eyes of the overwhelming majority of the population the one good they could obtain from the Republic. When the promises made to them were falsified, they returned to the old attitude of submission to the central authority and the local *caciques*. Cantonalism was broken down, though the cantonalists held Carthagena for some months, and the army resumed the position to which it is entitled by the fact that it alone can act as a national secular institution. In the absence of an accepted monarchy by divine right, and in view of the utter incapacity of the Spaniards to combine for a definite political purpose, the *exercitus* is the *populus*.

The deputies, who had made Castelar dictator in September in order that he might save the country by means of the army, were frightened at the consequences of what they had done. When the Cortes met again in January, 1874, it was notorious that they would condemn his policy as being too military, and it was no less notorious that the army would not tolerate a return to the anarchy of the spring. When the Cortes were about to pass a vote hostile to Castelar on January 3, they were expelled by Pavia, who had recently been appointed Captain-General of New Castile. Pavia's summary measure surprised nobody and offended very few. The restoration of the son of Isabel II was now seen to be the one possible solution. It was delayed, because Don Antonio Cánovas, who had organised the Alfonsist party thoroughly, preferred to gain time for preparing public opinion. It was also his wish that the army should first suppress the Carlists, and then summon free Cortes. No Cortes elected in such circumstances could have been free in any other sense than that in which an English Chapter is free to elect the Bishop presented to it by the Crown. But Don Antonio's course would have preserved a decent appearance of leaving the decision to the civil power. An interim military Government, with Serrano at its head, was set up. It kept the Carlists at bay, and even succeeded in forcing them to raise the siege of Bilbao. In December, 1874, Don Alfonso, who was now over sixteen, and therefore of age, issued a proclamation drafted for him by Cánovas promising an amnesty and constitutional government. In that month the army acted on the facts of the situation. Two battalions stationed at Murviedro were induced by General Martinez de Campos to proclaim Don Alfonso, and the armies in all parts of Spain followed their example. He was formally received at Madrid on January 14, 1875.

With the establishment of Don Alfonso XII, Spain reached a tenable position half-way between the absolute monarchy of Don Carlos, with its following of priests, Basques, and *guerrilleros*, on the one hand, and Republican anarchy on the other. Carlists of constitutional leanings rallied to Don Alfonso, and so did many who had been Republicans so long as the Republic was the only alternative to Don Carlos. The professional politicians naturally adhered to the power which disposed of offices. The Pope recognised the young King, and, though the Church did not receive all it had been promised, it was conciliated by the payment of its budget, and by an article in the Constitution of 1876 which forbade the public manifestation of any other form of worship. This article has not in practice prevented the opening of dissenting chapels, native and foreign, nor has it seriously limited the activity of foreign Protestant teaching missions to which large numbers of workmen send their children because they give a better education than native schools. We cannot dwell on successive Ministerial changes, which were not in any case the result of conflicts on questions of principle, but were mere alternations in office of the place-hunting coalitions, respectively led by Antonio Cánovas, and Práxedes Mateo Sagasta. The centre of interest has shifted in Spain since 1874. Irreconcilable Carlists and Republicans have continued to intrigue, and from time to time down to 1886 there were local outbreaks of military disorder. But the mass of Spaniards have ceased to believe that they would gain by any change in the form of government. The establishment of a money qualification for voters in 1876 was submitted to with indifference. The restoration of universal suffrage in 1889 produced no effect on the character of the elections to the Cortes. The country was tired of agitation, and asked only to be allowed to live in peace, and to have an opportunity for attaining some measure of material prosperity. It has, in the main, been granted what it asked for. The level of Spanish public life has continued to be low. The administration has not been less corrupt than of old, nor less unintelligent and dilatory. But politicians have abstained from the excesses of Narváez and González Bravo. The administration has not prevented the country from profiting by the great stimulus given to its wine trade by the ravages of the phylloxera in France, or by the great development of the mining industry of Biscay due to foreign—mostly English—skill and capital. Roads, railways, and irrigation works have combined to raise Spain to a level of industrial activity which would render a return of the disorders of 1868–74 intolerable. At the two great crises of its recent history the politicians and the people of Spain have shown themselves capable of averting internal armed strife. The politicians, military and civil, had been taught by the events of 1868–74 that excess of unscrupulous intrigue would recoil upon themselves.

The first crisis came on the death of Alfonso XII in November, 1885. The young King's reign had, on the whole, been prosperous. The Carlists had been swept out of Valencia and Catalonia in the course of 1875. By the end of January, 1876, they were crushed in Biscay, and

CH. X.

the *fueros* were abolished. A settlement with the Church, the Constitution of 1876, a modified version of the Constitution of 1844, and a composition with the national creditors, permitted the country to return to quiet at home, and to honourable relations with its neighbours. The King's marriage with his cousin Mercedes, daughter of the Duke of Montpensier, in January, 1878, healed a family quarrel. After her death in June, he married Maria Cristina, daughter of the Archduke Charles Ferdinand of Austria, in 1879. This marriage gave Spain a profitable connexion with a great Power. The King's foreign policy was not fortunate. A desire to obtain a place for Spain among the Powers of Europe led him into making advances to Germany, and caused deep offence to the French, who, as the chief owners of the Spanish railways and the chief purchasers of Spanish wine and wool, have a strong financial hold on the country. He was insulted in the streets of Paris in 1883, and in 1885 a dispute about the Caroline Islands rendered the German connexion extremely unpopular. It was settled by the tact of Prince Bismarck, who referred the question to the arbitration of the Pope. Don Alfonso showed courage and humanity in visitations of flood and epidemics. Yet he lost the respect of his subjects. He had been surrounded from his youth by members of his mother's Court, who helped if they did not instigate him to indulge in excesses which ruined his health, and filled the palace with scandals as in the reign of Isabel. On his death various members of his family, headed by his mother, entered into intrigues against his widow. Alfonso had left two daughters, and his queen was with child. The aim of the family intrigue was to oust her from the regency. The danger of a return of Bourbon stock-jobbing, corruption, and clericalism, was met by a determined rally of politicians, civil and military. The ex-Queen Isabel was forced to withdraw, and a male member of the family, who permitted himself to indulge in insolence, was sternly punished. Maria Cristina was established as Regent, with Sagasta as Prime Minister, and the support of all parties, even of those Republicans who followed Castelar. The birth of her son Alfonso XIII, on May 17, 1886, strengthened her position, and it was confirmed by her tact, her devotion to her son, the dignified order of her life, and her political judgment.

The second crisis was far more serious. It came in 1898, when Spain lost the remains of her colonial empire. On October 10, 1868, one month after the revolution in Spain, a Cuban rising began at Yara. It smouldered on, till Martinez de Campos brought it to a termination—or rather to a pause—by the convention of El Zanjón in 1878. He succeeded more by making promises of concessions than by force. His promises were repudiated by the home Government; a second rising in the eastern end of the island—the so-called "Little War"—was brutally crushed. Then Cuba simmered in discontent till the final revolt of 1895. It is superfluous to insist on the vices of Spanish colonial administration.

The Spaniards have never been able to take any other view of a colony than that it should be treated as a milch cow to be milked for the exclusive benefit of Spanish traders and officials. On that point all parties were agreed, and they were ready to combine to meet every colonial request for self-government with insulting denial. The Spanish immigrants engaged in trade, and settled in the towns, were the most noisy opponents of all concessions. They were organised into regiments which never fought the insurgents in the bush, but were always at hand to coerce their rulers when they might suspect them of an inclination to yield to Cuban demands. From the day when they displaced General Dulce in 1869 down to that on which their clamours forced General Primo de Rivera to send Admiral Cervera's squadron to destruction, these men were the prime cause of the evil done in the island. Their chiefs were capitalists who profited enormously by disorder, for they acted as contractors to the army and made vast illegitimate profits. Unhappily, they had the support of politicians at home and notably of Cánovas. Cuba provided so many opportunities of rewarding political services that no party chief would willingly consent to administrative reform. The services of Cánovas to his native land, which were considerable, were largely counterbalanced by his arrogant obstinacy, and wilful blindness towards the colonies. He assured his countrymen that, if they had been unable to control their vast possessions on the mainland, they could always in the end quell a limited territory like Cuba, because they could shed more blood. He would not face the probability that the United States would intervene. When hard pressed from Washington he would, indeed, make a pretence of drawing up schemes for the self-government of the island. His schemes, and those of other politicians, were transparently and childishly fraudulent. Cánovas would advise other politicians to yield, and would himself yield on particular points, as when he counselled Castelar to apologise, and pay an indemnity for the seizure of the *Virginius*, in 1873, or when he himself settled some rather dubious claims patronised by the United States Government. But he would not hear of any serious concessions to the Cubans.

The renewal of the rebellion in 1895 found Spain in an even worse position than she had held in 1869. The total abolition of slavery in 1886, without indemnity to the owners, had displeased them and had not conciliated the blacks. The fall in the price of sugar had made it less possible for Spain to find resources for the support of the War in the island. The amount of American capital invested in Cuba had doubled since 1878, and the American people had stronger reasons for intervening than ever. Spain might have conquered, if adequate military measures had been taken; but the conduct of the War was inept. Martinez de Campos was sent out in the fatuous hope that he would be able to conciliate the insurgents. He failed, and reported that not only the creoles, but many even of the immigrants from Spain, were irreconcilably

CH. X.

hostile to the government of the mother country. He added that the authority of Spain could be restored only by barbarous methods which he was not willing to apply. The General was recalled in 1896, and replaced by General Weyler, who was willing and even eager to apply the methods of barbarism. His policy was to destroy the crops and houses, and concentrate the population in the towns, in order to starve the rebels in the bush. This policy began to shock the Spaniards themselves, and the burden of the War grew insufferable. The murder of Cánovas at Santa Agueda on August 8, 1897, saved him from seeing the results of his own policy. The United States, which had shown much patience, intervened at last, and Cuba was lost in 1898.

At the same time Spain's possessions in the Philippines were torn from her. She had never occupied the islands fully, and the population was oppressed by religious Orders which performed the functions of a parish clergy. A revolt had broken out, about the time of the final rising in Cuba; but the Philippines were lost because the United States took them as a prize.

Yet this year of disaster and of punishment saw the beginning of a new and better era for Spain. As in 1885, politicians and people rallied to avert internal disorder. The monarchy passed through a crisis which in the opinion of hasty observers threatened it with destruction. The burden of the Cuban debt was honestly assumed. The foreign debt was left untaxed, and foreign holders were paid in gold. The credit of Spain improved. Freed from the strain of colonial wars, and the temptation to waste their scanty capital on colonial enterprises, the Spaniards have begun to develop the resources of their own country. Having been at heart tired of Cuba, they soon reconciled themselves to their loss, and learned to consider it a gain. The proof they gave of probity and self-control raised them in the estimate of other Powers. To Spain, together with France, has been entrusted the duty of policing the coast of Morocco. The majority of the young King, which was attained in 1902, was welcomed as the beginning of a new era. His marriage in 1906 to a grand-daughter of Queen Victoria was welcomed by the great majority of his subjects as a proof that he would frankly take his place among constitutional sovereigns. The courage shown by the young couple when a savage attempt was made to murder them on their wedding day, and their boldness in coming unguarded among their people on the morrow, touched popular sympathies. The total disintegration of the Liberal parties has thrown political power into the hands of the moderate and constitutional Conservatives, who on the whole best represent the wishes and opinions of the average Spaniard. There is a very fair prospect that Spain, chastened by her sufferings between 1868 and 1874 into a horror of domestic war, and cured by the disasters of 1898 of all inclination towards foreign adventures which are far beyond her resources, is settling down to a period of recuperation. The establishment of cordial relations between France and England is a great element in her favour, for it has suspended their rivalries at Madrid, and secures her the friendly offices of her chief customers and creditors.

Though the period of violent political unrest has apparently passed, other causes of disorder exist, and the country is still far from the possession of a good Government. The material progress of the nation has produced its inevitable effect. The poor, whether in town or country, have experienced some improvement in their condition, and for that very reason are awakening to desires which were unknown to their fathers Having gained something, they are eager to win more. The agrariai discontent of the south has never been removed. So far back as 1862 it was manifested by the revolt headed by the horse-doctor, Pedro Alanio, at Loja. The rising was suppressed with ferocity, and the Government made it an excuse for forbidding trade unions and socialist propaganda. The revolution of 1868 paralysed the hand of the State for a time. Agrarian and urban socialistic longings were found to have spread widely under the surface. During 1873 Alcoy, in Murcia, was the scene of some dreadful outrages perpetrated by workmen on their employers. The brigandage of Andalusia has its root in the misery of the agricultural population, who are collected in gangs on the *cortijos*, or granges, of absentee landlords, and are exploited by middlemen bound to them only by the cash nexus. The brigand is the popular hero who is supposed to avenge the poor on the rich. The restoration of order brought no sufficient improvement in the state of the agricultural labourers. In 1883 strong measures had to be taken to break up the secret society known as the *Mano Negra* (the Black Hand) which terrorised the landowners and their agents. In other parts of Spain, small holdings and *métayer* tenancies are common. The unrest of the labouring class has not been shown so violently as in the south. Yet it exists and is justified by the wrongs of a class on which the weight of taxation falls heavily. The excessive emigration of the agricultural class to the River Plate, to Cuba since the island became independent, and to the west of the United States, is stimulated by misery. Some of the emigrants return when they have made a little money, and most of them remit part of their earnings home to their families. But the returned emigrants, known in Spain as *Indios*, and the remittances, alike serve to spread the conviction that men can prosper better anywhere than at home. There is a growing though still unenlightened understanding of the fact that the poverty of the lower orders is due to a bad fiscal system, and to protection carried to a point at which it all but strangles the movement of trade: a sense of wrong, a wish to escape, and a tendency to revolt, are spreading.

If this is the case with the ill-organised country population, it is still more so in the towns and the mining districts where combination is easy. Strikes, provoked less by long hours of work and bad wages than

CH. X.

by a scandalous truck system, have been frequent in Biscay. They would have been still more violent if the Government, in its eagerness to maintain peace, had not occasionally compelled the employers to make concessions. In Barcelona, which has always been turbulent, the workmen have fallen under the influence of militant socialists. The result has been a long series of revolts and of bomb outrages in theatres and on religious processions. These excesses have been suppressed, but in ways which have intensified the evil. There is no doubt that torture was used to extort confessions from large numbers of people arrested at random. It was not applied as by the Inquisition and the old criminal procedure, on a regulated system and under the supervision of magistrates, but at the discretion of the lowest class of police agents. These cruelties were quoted by Michael Angiolillo, as his justification for murdering Cánovas. The memory of the torturings in Monjuich has done much to excite the social hatred of the poor against the rich—a sentiment once hardly known in Spain, but now too common.

This hatred and distrust of the employers has had one consequence of a peculiarly unfortunate character. The merchants and manufacturers of the maritime provinces, which contain the larger part of the population, and much the larger part of the wealth of Spain, have many reasons to resent the corruption, the perpetual interference, and the delays of the central administration. The burden is most acutely felt in the most industrial province of Spain, the principality of Catalonia. It led to a revival of " regionalism," that is to say, a demand for Catalan self-government. The demand was often advanced in terms offensive to other parts of the country. Yet it had much in it to invite sympathy and cooperation. There was at least a possibility of the formation of a national party grouped round the united Catalans (the *Solidarios*) to insist on administrative reform. The hostility of the workmen has postponed, if it has not destroyed, the hope of the formation of such a party. They are convinced that the employers, and their agents the lawyers, have no other aim than to acquire entire command of the local administration in order to be able to exploit the working classes without fear of check. These divisions of course tend to confirm the power of the overstaffed, meddlesome, and dilatory central administration.

The literary movement in Spain during the last forty years has had two features of undoubted novelty and real interest. The two most popular writers of books of entertainment in this period have both been didactic and vigorous assailants of all that the conservative Spaniard praises as *castizo*, *i.e.* truly national and Spanish. The *Episodios Nacionales* of Benito Pérez Galdós, though obviously modelled on the tales of Erckmann-Chatrian, have a genuine originality. Their literary merit is not great, but Galdós has the Spanish capacity for telling a story and giving reality to his characters. His *Episodios* are significant because they give a succession of pictures of the history of Spain from the administration of Godoy down to the present day, from the Liberal point of view. The returns of circulating libraries show that they are far more popular than the works of any contemporary writer. Blasco Ibañez, who sat in the Cortes as Socialist deputy for Valencia, is a far more emphatic enemy of the old order of Spanish life. In *La Catedral, La Horda, Sangre y Arena,* and other books, he assails the Church, and boldly argues that the purely Spanish things and ideas beloved of the Conservatives have been the causes of the material ruin and intellectual stagnation of the nation. Then, it is certainly not without significance that the dominant figure of Spanish literature has been neither poet nor novelist, but the very copious and learned historian and critic, Marcelino Menéndez y Pelayo—author of *Los Heterodoxos Españoles, Las Ideas Estéticas en España,* and of innumerable monographs. Menéndez, who wrote his *Heterodoxos Españoles* in a spirit of militant Roman Catholic orthodoxy, has never recanted his opinions. Yet the reader who compares that work with the later writings of the author will note a marked alteration in tone, and will be materially helped to appreciate the change of spirit which has come over the country. Señor Menéndez has been surrounded by a school of writers, some of them his own pupils, who have devoted themselves to the study of particular passages in the literary and political history of Spain.

PORTUGAL.

The history of Portugal since the year 1871 has continued to present the same kind of contrast with the contemporary course of affairs in Spain as that observable during the preceding generation. Portugal has escaped great internal convulsions and serious disaster abroad. The continuance of peace has allowed of a certain development of industry. Trade and revenue have increased. But this being granted, nothing can be adduced which tends to show forth the intellectual or moral improvement of the nation, nor are there more than extremely faint indications of future advance. During this period of nearly forty years the bulk of the population has remained suffering and discontented but impassive, while the weight of a most unfair taxation has grown till it has become crushing, while a constantly increasing expenditure has more than kept pace with a growing revenue, and the national treasury has passed through a bankruptcy. This has happened because the country has been governed by contending factions of professional politicians who have had no other aim than their own immediate personal advantage. There have been bread riots made by starving people. There has been one Republican rising, the work of a handful of briefless barristers, journalists, and students, which was instantly crushed. There has been one professed attempt to bring about a reformation from above, which was discredited by the manifest self-seeking of the pretended reformers, and defeated by a great political crime. When the temporary interruption in the course of parliamentary faction had been brought to an end by murder, the political world of Portugal returned to its familiar contentions, unchecked —unless indeed a tardy murmur of expostulation from the trading class of Lisbon is destined to have some effect.

The most visible part of Portuguese contemporary history, its parliamentary kaleidoscope, has gone constantly round and round. Ministerial crises, or reconstructions due to personal quarrels, have occurred at the rate of nearly one a year, without producing any other result than a rearrangement of the items composing the Regenerator and the Progressive parties. Reform Bills have been passed, and the constitutional machine has been modified in a democratic sense. The main result has been that the Upper Chamber has been changed from an hereditary to an elective senatorship—whereby the number of places of dignity and emolument open to professional politicians has been increased.

The outer world has affected Portugal in two ways. In 1875 Marshal MacMahon, then President in France, who had been asked to arbitrate on the respective claims of Great Britain and Portugal to Delagoa Bay, decided in favour of the smaller country. This decision gave a stimulus to the reviving colonial activity of the Portuguese. They began to extend in South Eastern Africa and to advance great territorial claims which soon brought them into sharp collision with Great Britain. The details of these conflicts belong to the history of the partition of Africa, which was one of the great historic movements of the nineteenth century. Their reaction on Portugal has been on the whole most unfortunate. Between 1880 and 1890 Portugal suffered several disappointments, and in the latter year was forced to submit to an ultimatum presented to it by Lord Salisbury. That part of the people of Portugal who take any interest in public affairs held the monarchy responsible for the humiliation inflicted on the national pride. It was to some extent soothed by a few manifestations of resentment, such as the return of the Order of the Garter by the King Dom Luiz, and the refusal of tradesmen in Lisbon to open their shops during a visit paid to the port by a British squadron. But the Liberal monarchy, already far from strong, was distinctly weakened by the discovery that it could not save Portugal from the consequences of being a small State, or enable her to indulge ambitions out of all proportion to her resources.

The disappearance of the Empire in Brazil in 1889, and the establishment of a Republic, had a very similar effect on Portugal. The Portuguese emigrate largely to their former colony and prosper there. Many return with the fortunes they have made, and some of them bring back a belief that there is a healing virtue in the name and form of a Republic. In 1891 a Republican rising was organised at Oporto with money contributed by returned emigrants. It was headed by Alves Veiga,

a lawyer and journalist, and it found its only effective support in some
600 soldiers whose services were bought. The population of Oporto
remained indifferent and the rising was easily put down. Yet a militant
Republican party was established in Portugal, and refugees who crossed
the Spanish frontier entered into relations with the party in that
country. Their influence was confined to a portion of the inhabitants
of the towns, and was trifling. Nevertheless, they introduced one more
element of weakness and possible disorder.

On the death of Dom Luiz on October 9, 1899, he was succeeded by
his son Dom Carlos, a gentleman of sporting tastes and profuse habits.
He was married to Marie Amélie de Bourbon, daughter of the Count of
Paris, who brought him a large fortune, but he habitually anticipated
his civil list, and became heavily indebted. Successive Ministers met
his demands by advances of money from the Treasury, and the monarchy
became a partner with place-hunting politicians in robbing the revenue.
The French Queen was followed by French religious Orders and Jesuits,
who had no legal right to be present in the country. This invasion
aroused the hostility of the University of Coimbra and of the politicians.
An anti-clerical agitation arose; but the unstable governing factions
could not carry out any definite policy of repression. It is impossible
to say with confidence how far clerical intrigue combined with the
financial embarrassments of the King to produce the strange crisis of
1907–8. Clerical influence was certainly not employed to avert it.

The employment of dictatorial powers to tide over some pressing
crisis had not been unusual in Portugal. But, before 1907, this peremptory device had only been used by some political faction which was itself
in haste to restore the normal working of the Constitution—that is to
say, the habitual alternations in office, and divisions of the spoils among
the professional politicians. In this year, however, Dom Carlos entered
on a course which had undeniable novelty. He found in João Franco,
a wealthy man of apparently resolute character, a Minister who was
prepared to govern without the Cortez. Parliamentary government was
suppressed, and Portugal was promised an honest administration. There
is no reason to suppose that, if this venture had been made with a
serious purpose, it would have met with any national resistance. The
Portuguese knew that João Franco told the truth when he said that the
politicians, Regenerators and Progressives alike, were greedy unscrupulous
adventurers, who pilfered the revenue. If they had found any substantial relief in the King's *coup d'État* they would have dispensed with
constitutional forms. But it soon became obvious that the change in
persons was not to bring with it any lightening of the burden on the
taxpayer. Franco exposed the roguery of the politicians, and made a
show of retrenchment. But he was forced to increase the pay of the
army on which he had to rely, and the King was aided by a collusive
arrangement which freed him from his debt to the Treasury and

received an increase of his civil list. It became obvious that what was taken off with one hand was to be imposed by the other—and the people remained indifferent. The politicians were exasperated by the loss of their profits, and by measures of repression. The King, who entertained a confidence which had the appearance rather of infatuation than of courage, exposed himself in the streets of his capital. On February 1, 1908, while driving through the streets of Lisbon with his wife and his two sons, he was assailed by a gang of assassins. He and his eldest son were murdered. His second son, Manuel, the present King, was wounded. The Queen had an extraordinary escape in the midst of a fusillade of carbines and revolvers.

The crime stands alone among the many regicides of the present age in that it was absolutely successful. The royal family was terrorised. Franco fled the country. Constitutional government was restored, and the professional politicians resumed all their power. The quiescence of the nation was absolute. The Republicans made no movement. The political life of Portugal appears to be concentrated in factions of office-seekers, who have only been stimulated by their victory in 1908 to a more reckless pursuit of personal feuds. The remedy must be found outside the professional political world. It can only be provided by honest and patriotic Portuguese prepared to unite for the creation of a healthy public opinion, and to act together for the real good of the docile and long-suffering majority of the people of Portugal, whose somewhat too passive good qualities are recognised by foreign observers, but have been cruelly abused by their masters.

CHAPTER XI.

SCANDINAVIA.

SWEDEN.

CHARLES XV died in September, 1872, without male issue, and was succeeded by his younger brother, Oscar, on the thrones of Sweden and Norway. The new King was a man in the prime of life—he was born in January, 1829—and had had many years, as heir presumptive, in which to prepare for his high calling and to gain experience and information. King Oscar II was undoubtedly a personage of far more significance than his brother. Endowed with a clear judgment, a quick mental grasp and an unusually retentive memory, he was, moreover, possessed of exceptional culture and of varied knowledge, attained by means of profound study as well as extended travel in Scandinavia and abroad. As a writer on military history he had won distinction, and the University of Lund had presented him with the degree of Doctor of Philosophy, in genuine recognition of his scholarship. The artistic endowments which had also distinguished his elder brothers were prominent in King Oscar, and found their chief scope in the domain of music and poetry. He was an eminent orator, and his literary productions revealed a sensitive, poetic soul. To these advantages of talent and culture were added a noble character, a stern sense of duty and rectitude, with a benign and captivating, yet withal kingly manner. King Oscar was a humane man in the full sense of the word, filled with the sincerest endeavour to benefit the two nations whose sceptre had been entrusted to him. The impulses of his nature occasionally found expression in a certain vehemence and impatience in the presence of opposition, or revealed themselves in outbursts of enthusiasm and sanguine hopes; but his subjective preferences and sentiments were in the end ever subordinated to his mature experience of the world and his judicious rule of life. His imposing and noble presence, which grew more majestic and august with the passing of the years, commanded the respect of all who came in contact with him. Despite his personal merits, the new King had in the beginning to encounter some disfavour on the part of the general public.

His predecessor, with less sterling qualities, had won the hearts of both his peoples, by his faults as well as by his merits, and his successor suffered by comparison. Public opinion was slow to veer round and do justice to King Oscar's personality; but in time he gained a popularity more deep-rooted and widespread than had fallen to the lot of Charles XV.

This was increased no doubt by his marked inclination for constitutional rule. During the reign of Charles the more personal monarchy, characteristic of the first two kings of the Bernadotte dynasty, yielded to the constitutional demand that the responsible Ministers should effectively control the government. But this change had been accepted with great reluctance by Charles, who only under compulsion consented to suppress his personal views, and did not desist from lending his ear to private counsellors and friends to the detriment of his official advisers. A measure of uncertainty had prevailed in constitutional affairs, and a veiled strife was waged between the traditional personal monarchy and the ever-growing constitutional tendency. On the accession of Oscar II this uncertainty and this opposition ceased. The new King respected the position and the demands of his counsellors, and, although his own judgment always carried weight by reason of his experience, intelligence, and seriousness of purpose, he did not press his views longer than was consistent with the responsibility of his counsellors and the claims of the parliamentary situation. The establishment of the annual two-Chamber Diet in 1866 secured the political power of the Diet, and the reform which in 1876 introduced a responsible Prime Minister has further contributed to diminish the personal influence of the King. But in Sweden, owing to the equipoise between the two Chambers and to King Oscar's personal tact and authority, the Constitution did not develop into a true parliamentary government, though the tendency was in that direction. In Norway, on the other hand, where the royal authority lacked the secure position which it occupied in Sweden, the parliamentary principles implicit in the Constitution of 1814 came into full effect during his reign and reduced the monarchy to a mere figurehead.

The external outlook of the united kingdoms was overclouded at the time of Oscar's accession. The abandonment of Charles XIV's Russophil policy, which followed on the alliance with England and France of 1855, had made the relations with Russia very strained. The vague hopes of a reunion between Scandinavia and Finland, cherished in a number of eager Scandinavian circles, and favoured not least by Charles XV himself, together with the hatred of Russia displayed by the Swedish public and their enthusiasm for Poland during the Polish rebellion, had inspired the Russian Government with a certain distrust of Swedish policy, while on the other hand the value of the guarantees given by the Treaty of Alliance had practically disappeared on the breaking up of the Anglo-French friendship and the heavy defeat of

France in 1870. The Scandinavian plans, which the two preceding Bernadottes had favoured, had proved an absolute fiasco, and a feeling of resentment was left in defeated and mutilated Denmark, who had had to fight her battle alone, in spite of all promises. In Germany Prussia, under the guidance of Bismarck, had carried all before her, and had created a new German Empire, which appeared as the first Power in Europe; her aggrandisement had taken place partly at the expense of Scandinavia; moreover Sweden's sympathies had all the time been with the adversaries of Prussia, and especially during the Franco-Prussian War, when enthusiasm for France, grief for her misfortunes, and hatred toward Germany were deeply felt among the Swedish people, and not least by the romantic King. The new monarch had to allay the suspicions of Swedish designs against the peace, conceived, not without cause, by her powerful neighbours, and to maintain in foreign policy a firm, neutral, and peaceful attitude; his efforts clearly showed that the Government looked to actual realities. King Oscar himself entertained sympathy for Germany and German culture, and his display of firmness and impartiality soon convinced every neighbour of his sincere desire for peace. During the conflicts, which disturbed the rest of Europe, Sweden and Norway faithfully maintained the part of a neutral and impartial spectator. It was not until towards the end of Oscar's long reign, that the feeling of secure external peace was to be again disturbed by Russia's forcible incorporation of Finland, which awakened sorrow and sympathy in the Swedish people, and brought the two northern realms into more direct contact with their Russian neighbour, and still more by the dissolution of the union of the two Scandinavian kingdoms, at a time when mutual relations throughout the European world were becoming strained.

The domestic policy of Sweden under King Oscar II was marked by no dramatic events, striking revolutions, or imposing personages, but it displays the pertinacious endeavour of its statesmen to keep pace with the rapid economic and intellectual development of the country. This task devolved in the first place on the new two-Chamber Diet, which first assembled in 1867, and thereafter met annually. It was soon clear that the great expectations of finding in this Parliament an organ of reform more prompt and pliable than the old Diet of Four Estates had been extravagant. At the outset, the First Chamber comprised the representatives of the Estates of the Nobility and Clergy, drawn from the higher and still mostly noble bureaucracy, and from the educated and wealthy classes, especially the class of landed proprietors. This Chamber was, of course, characterised by a certain conservatism, but also by varied experience of the requirements of the State. It was a true House of Peers in the best sense of the word. In the Second Chamber, corresponding to the former Estates of the Burghers and Peasantry, the peasants soon showed that they possessed a decided preponderance, and skilful leaders among them were not long in forming a strongly-organised party, the "Agricultural party" (*landtmannapartiet*), which during the next few decades entirely ruled this Chamber and thus constituted the most powerful section of the Diet. By its side there was a section known as the "Intellectual party" (*intelligenspartiet*), chiefly consisting of urban representatives; at first, it often went hand in hand with the majority in the First Chamber; but, like that majority, it lacked firm organisation.

Opposition between the two Chambers has been a marked feature throughout all succeeding developments. The First Chamber, however, has always managed, in sharp conflicts, to vindicate its full equality, perhaps mainly because the question of supply is decided by a common vote, when the First Chamber, together with a minority from the Second, often determines the issue. The result has been a complete dualism within the Diet, which for decades hindered the progress of all important political reforms, and caused fruitless party strife. Another result has been that the Government has been able to lean at will either upon the majority of the First Chamber or upon that of the Second, or, again, to take up a position independent of both as a mediator. It is true that the opposition between the two Chambers diminished considerably in the process of time, the First Chamber being more and more exclusively dominated by the large landowners, whose common interest with the peasants during the customs conflicts of the eighties declared itself; but, at the same time, Radical ideas forced their way in, especially among the representatives of the big towns, and a Liberal party of modern character was formed, which has been of growing importance. The opposition between this party, which from 1905 onwards has obtained a slight preponderance in the Second Chamber, and the Conservative party, supported by the landowners of both Chambers, has gradually become the chief factor in politics in Sweden, as in other civilised countries of today. During the last decade the Socialists have succeeded in gaining a footing in the Diet.

On no question have the two parties carried on a more protracted struggle than on that of the national defences, which during the first few decades of the new phase of representation were the chief domestic topic discussed. The army and navy of Sweden were thoroughly antiquated when the great European crises of the fifties and sixties roused the nation from its sleep, and a national sentiment of defence found its vent in the so-called volunteer movement (*skarpskytterörelsen*). From the beginning, however, the reform was blocked by the peasant party, who made any increase in the grant for defences conditional on a complete and absolute remission of the old burdens of military tenure establishment (*indelnings-verk*) and of land-taxes (*grundskatter*) on "unprivileged" land. The question was fought for a score of years. In vain did the Government bring forth one scheme after another to reform the defences—schemes constructed on every possible plan ; the opposition between the two Chambers wrecked every one of them. In vain did Baron de Geer, the creator of the new form of representation, work at this reform during his second Ministry, 1875–80, and after him the Agricultural party's own Government under Count Arvid Posse (till 1883). It was reserved for Themptander, in 1885, to carry through a first trifling extension of the training-period of those liable to military service, in return for which concession a reduction of 30 per cent. on the old land burdens was granted.

Before this reform had advanced any further, a fierce dispute about the customs had arisen and crowded out all other questions. During the general depression which prevailed in the eighties there was great distress in agriculture, produced by the fall in prices that followed the flooding of the market by American corn. The cry for protective duties for agriculture and industry became general, although it meant a reversal of the whole customs policy of Sweden as developed in the middle of the century and established by the commercial treaties of the sixties. The struggle between Free Trade and Protection agitated the Swedish people more than any other question since the days of parliamentary reform. After the protectionists had succeeded in gaining a majority in the Second Chamber, the Free Trade Ministry of Themptander resigned in 1888, and heavy duties on corn were introduced. In 1892 the new system was completed by the protection of industry. In the First Chamber the protectionists gradually won a stronghold. As representative of the new agricultural majority Erik Gustaf Boström, a landed proprietor, became Premier in 1891 and remained in power, with a short interruption between 1900 and 1902, until the spring of 1905. Boström was a skilful tactician, and an energetic and clear-sighted statesman, with a sharp eye for reality and essential points of policy. In the course of his career, he detached himself more and more from his party and took up a mediatorial attitude towards the contending factions, though always with a strongly pronounced Conservative leaning.

Supported by the great economic improvement which came in the nineties, and by a new tide of national sentiment, Boström succeeded, in 1892, in carrying through another step of the defence reform ; the training-period of the conscripts was more than doubled ; in return, the remaining 70 per cent. of the old land burdens was annulled. But the reformers could not be content to accept this as final. With the growing spirit of nationality, fanned by the conflict with Norway and the events in Finland, the goal so long aimed at was at length reached—a trained army, based upon universal compulsory service (1901). Strong fortresses were begun with the new century at Boden in the extreme north and outside Göteborg, and the Swedish fleet was practically created anew ; so that at the end of Oscar II's reign Sweden was, in proportion to her population, one of the best armed States in Europe.

CH. XI.

With the final realisation of the great defence reform, the question of the extension of the franchise forced its way to the front. This question was embraced especially by the Liberals, who found it the most popular plank in their platform. Already in 1896, schemes began to be proposed by the Government to deal with this knotty question. After the elections of 1905 the first Liberal Ministry was formed under Staaff, a lawyer; but its Franchise Bill, based upon election to the Second Chamber by universal suffrage in single-member constituencies, was defeated the very next spring, owing to the opposition of the First Chamber; and the Ministry was replaced by a Conservative Government under Lindman. He succeeded in passing a Franchise Bill based on proportional representation in elections to both Chambers; but, in order to win over the Second Chamber, the Government had to make considerable concessions to Radical ideas—universal suffrage, a lowered rating for eligibility to the First Chamber, payment for members of that Chamber, as well as for those of the Second, and a reform of the municipal franchise, which will considerably democratise the municipal authorities, and not least the provincial assemblies, which elect the First Chamber. It is probable that, as a result of this reform, which was finally ratified by the Diet in 1909, the peasants will gain the predominance in the Upper House, while organised labour will hold sway in the Lower. Thus the dualism of Swedish representation will not cease, though the principles of opposition will be changed. This issue of the franchise struggle was both unexpected and unpopular; but a rescinding of the resolution of 1907 was, from the first, practically out of the question.

By the side of the great political questions, which determined the grouping of the parties and led to changes of Ministry, the domestic policy of the country has chiefly aimed at the continuous remodelling of the community on modern lines, and supporting, regulating, and protecting the inner life of the nation. This development in prosperity and culture naturally forms the essence of the history of the Swedish people during the last decades. Its economic life during this period has been exposed to very great variations, the great prosperity in the early seventies being followed by an economic depression, which yielded in the nineties to a still more brilliant expansion, till, a few years after the new century had opened, a reaction set in, which culminated in the serious financial crisis of 1907–8. The industrial life of the country has presented the same vicissitudes as the general economic life of Europe; but, on the whole, economic development in Sweden has progressed with a rapidity unparalleled in the history of that country. Agriculture—of old the country's primary source of prosperity and still supplying a livelihood to over half the population—has made considerable progress by bringing new land under cultivation, by improved methods, and more intensive development. The farmer, during the last few decades, has devoted himself more and more to stock-raising;

so that Sweden, which before 1880 was a corn-exporting country, now imports corn, but in its place exports dairy produce. Forestry, which supplies Sweden's chief article of export, has multiplied its yearly output during the same period. So, too, with the mining industry: through the active working of the large Norrland ore fields at Kiruna and Gellivare, which began in this century, Sweden should become more and more prominent as an iron ore exporting country. A special railway-line, the most northerly in the world, from Luleå on the Gulf of Bothnia, past the great ore fields, across the frontier to the icefree harbour of Narvik in the West Fiord, has been built to deal with this valuable export. Yet, perhaps, the advances in industry are the most remarkable. During the reign of Oscar II, the number of workmen has been increased more than fivefold and the value of output more than sevenfold, and the section of the population that lives by manufactures has risen from one-sixth to one-third. A great industrial era began in Sweden towards the end of the nineteenth century. The use of electric power in the service of industry promises to make Sweden, with its numerous waterfalls that are easy of access, a great industrial power. The system of railways, begun in the fifties, has grown to such an extent that Sweden stands first in the world in the proportion of railway mileage to population. The history of the telephone and telegraph tells of similar success. The statistics of trade for the country correspond, of course, to the economic development in general; and maritime commerce, which was for a long time depressed, has taken a new lease of life and is opening up direct communication with the most distant seaports. One sign of the growing riches of the country is the increase in the state budget, from about 60 million *kronor* (£3,330,000) in 1872 to over 200 million in 1907. The population rose from four millions in 1863 to over five and a half millions in the same period, exclusive of the million Swedes who left their native shores for America during the second half of the nineteenth century.

The great material development has brought with it in Sweden, as elsewhere, a number of new problems and dangers. Above all, the rise of a large class of artisans has accentuated several problems difficult of solution. Legislation has not been able to keep up with the fresh demands on it, and the socialist movement has gained much ground among the working classes since the end of the eighties. In Sweden this movement has presented itself as an unusually denationalised class movement, and in its wake anarchist tendencies have forced their way in and aggravated incessant strikes and lock-outs. This constitutes a danger to the whole industrial future. In 1908 and 1909 conflicts between employers and employed became especially violent; and, in the latter year, a general strike broke out, which for a while threatened the foundations of the whole social structure of the country. The labour question has become more and more the pivot of domestic policy in Sweden.

CH. XI.

The intellectual advance of the nation has also been rapid during the last four decades. Swedish scholarship found worthy representatives in every branch of knowledge; especially in the domain of natural science, in which Torell, Retzius, and Arrhenius have achieved world-wide fame. In geographical discovery, Swedes, notably Nordenskjöld and Sven Hedin, have been pioneers. In literature Viktor Rydberg and August Strindberg, and more recently Fröding and Selma Lagerlöf, have been distinguished figures; while Swedish art, above all in painting and music, has had excellent and original representatives. The Press has grown into a power that meets the demands of the modern community, and the education of the people is not surpassed in any other country. The creation of two new Universities, in Stockholm and Göteborg, and the establishment of a number of technical schools, have materially increased the facilities for obtaining higher education.

Thus the reign of Oscar II has been, in an exceptional degree, a flowering time of peaceful culture. Its end was, however, disturbed by the acute conflicts between Sweden and Norway, which finally led to the dissolution of the Union. This event, the most important in the political fortunes of the Scandinavians during this reign, is discussed in the following section.

NORWAY AND THE DISSOLUTION OF THE UNION.

Under the long rule of Oscar II, Norway also made considerable progress in many branches of industry. The natural resources of the country are, however, small; arable land forms but a very small percentage of its extensive territory, while even wooded ground is relatively insignificant; minerals are by no means so abundant and good in quality as the Swedish. Fishery and the timber trade supply the chief articles of export. Quite recently, the manufacturing industries have made good headway, and in her numerous waterfalls Norway, like Sweden, has a valuable source of power, though lack of capital, of raw material, and of convenient markets, constitute a serious drawback. Norway's chief branch of industry is still, as of old, her maritime commerce, and her mercantile marine has long been one of the largest in the world. During the second half of the nineteenth century it increased tenfold. As this increase depends mainly on trade between foreign ports, the continued development of the maritime commerce is itself dependent, to a large extent, on the economic policy and advance of other countries. The influx of tourists has become of growing importance to the finances of the country. But the economic depression of the early years of this century fell very heavily on Norway.

The second half of the nineteenth century was also a period of great intellectual activity in Norway. Her literature aroused admiration through the great dramatist Henrik Ibsen, the lyric poet and novelist, Björnstjerne Björnson, and the novelist Jonas Lie. Norwegian art, especially music, represented by Grieg, flourished, while learning has been represented by notable men, such as the gifted philologist Bugge. In polar exploration Fridtjof Nansen gained European renown. A curious linguistic movement, in favour of an artificially constructed language, *Landsmaal*, threatening to displace the present standard language, essentially based on Danish, must be regarded, in the main, as a manifestation of deep-rooted nationalism. It may entail a serious danger to the intellectual development of Norway.

Political life has been largely controlled by the country's relations to Sweden. The question of the Union has influenced the fortunes of parties and cabinets in Norway much more than in Sweden, where it only began to be of importance in domestic policy from the middle of the last decade of the nineteenth century. All the great questions in the political life of Norway during this epoch were connected, in some way, with the predominant question of the Union.

From the beginning, the Union suffered greatly from lack of clear definition. According to the Swedish conception, Norway was ceded to Sweden by Denmark in the Treaty of Kiel, although the King of Sweden, after a short war with his new and rebellious subjects, came to an agreement with them which guaranteed to Norway in domestic matters an independent position and a distinct entity. The Norwegians, for their part, maintained that they were an independent nation, and that the Union was legally based on their own free decision and the election by the Storthing of Charles XIII as King of Norway. On one point, however, both were originally agreed, namely, that the Fundamental Law of November 4, 1814, was the original Act of Union, which was supplemented by the *Riksakt* of 1815. It followed, that any change in the Norwegian Fundamental Law required Swedish consent; and, when that conclusion became obvious, the Norwegians soon came to assert the new interpretation that the *Riksakt* was the sole compact. Thus the general historico-political as well as the juridical principles of the Union were subjected to different interpretations. Not less unsatisfactory were the actual terms of the Union, since the compact lacked provisions for the administration of foreign affairs. The King conducted them on the lines of the Swedish Constitution and with the counsellors prescribed by it. In a word, the administration of foreign affairs under the Union was Swedish. This was disputed by nobody, and was implied by the convention of Union. The Consular Service, on the other hand, was from the beginning a matter of joint arrangement. Also, in external emblems and other details, the subordination of Norway was manifest.

CH. XI.

Charles XIV appointed Norwegians to the legations and the Foreign Office in Stockholm, and in 1835, on his own authority, gave a Norwegian Cabinet Minister a seat in the Swedish Diplomatic Council. On his accession to the throne Oscar I granted perfect equality as regards minor and emblematic details.   But, on the Norwegian and on the Swedish side alike, there had grown up a feeling of dissatisfaction with the legal organisation of the Union; and a committee, appointed in 1839, was deputed to draw up a scheme for a new Act of Union, based on a complete equality of rights and obligations.   That was the beginning of the futile attempts to revise the Union.   These failed, owing to the fact that on the Swedish side there was a desire to develop and strengthen the Union, preferably by setting up a common Parliament, while Norway with her newly awakened, sensitive national sentiment feared the Swedish amalgamation plans and rejected every attempt to strengthen the connexion.   But, without closer union, a satisfactory scheme of common administration in foreign affairs was scarcely possible.   Another circumstance that rendered more difficult a rearrangement and in the end made it impossible to maintain the Union was the essentially different position of the monarchy in the two countries.   In Sweden there was a strong constitutional monarchy, in Norway a kingship possessing only a suspensive veto and lacking *inter alia* a free control of the military forces of the country and the right to dissolve the Storthing and demand a new election. Both the first large union committee, whose proposal was presented in 1844, and a later one of 1865, whose proposal was formally rejected by the Storthing in 1871, failed in their attempts to revise the Union.

The first serious conflict which threatened the existence of the Union turned on the abolition of the post of *statholder* (King's lieutenant in Norway).   In 1859–60 the Storthing resolved that the King's right to appoint a statholder in Norway should cease.   On the Swedish side the proposal was not disputed; but it was claimed that the King's consent to this change in the Norwegian Fundamental Law should be given in the combined Council of State, since that law had come into existence through negotiations with Sweden.   The Storthing angrily disputed this demand, and declared that the *Riksakt* was the sole compact.   As no unanimity could be arrived at, Charles XV had to refuse his sanction to the decision of the Storthing.   Not till after Charles' death did the Storthing renew their decision about the statholdership, and King Oscar II was face to face with his first great difficulty on the subject of the Union.   His Swedish counsellors yielded this time, not on the principle, but because the question was of so little intrinsic importance, and the office of statholder was abolished in 1873.   This was a considerable success for Norway, because it implied that Norway by herself had the right to revise her Fundamental Law, and that Sweden had lost the right to consider alterations in the original document of the Union, however significant they might be for its existence.

By far the most important occurrence in the political life of Norway under the government of Oscar II before the dissolution of the Union, and the actual turning-point in its history, is the assertion of parliamentarism in Norway. As a matter of fact the King's power, according to the Constitution, was so poorly equipped as against the Storthing, that the supremacy of the latter would have been established long before, had not the King been at the same time King of Sweden. Charles XV had still maintained his right to chose his Norwegian Ministry at his own discretion and to refuse his sanction to resolutions of the Storthing that seemed to him to threaten the Union. The introduction of yearly Storthings, from 1871 onwards, increased the power of the Storthing, however, and at the same time the great Liberal party arose through the uniting of the peasants and the Radicals under the able and unscrupulous leadership of Johan Sverdrup, a lawyer. In order to obtain greater influence in the Government, the Storthing resolved in 1872 to alter the Fundamental Law so as to give the members of the Council the right to take part in the deliberations of the Storthing. The King gave his consent only on certain conditions, including the concession to him of the right to dissolve the Storthing and appeal to the electorate, which conditions were rejected by the Storthing. The conflict was now engaged. The most significant fact was that the Liberal party now advanced the preposterous theory that the King, even for changes in the Fundamental Law, only possessed a suspensive veto, and resolved to push forward the reform in this way. Thus the position of the monarchy as an independent power in Norway was at stake; if the voice of the Storthing were to prevail, it could then, by means of fresh reforms, deprive the King of any other of his rights.

Besides the fact that the Fundamental Law clearly prescribed methods of procedure for alterations in itself which differed widely from those laid down for other legislation, the Storthing had repeatedly acknowledged the King's veto in connexion with the Fundamental Law, and the jurists of Norway itself always maintained the same opinion. Amid increasing tension the Storthing, in 1874, 1877, and 1880, passed the change in the Fundamental Law already mentioned; each time the King refused his sanction. The third time the Storthing declared the resolution had become a Fundamental Law without the King's sanction, and requested the Government to publish it accordingly; the Government refused. The Storthing had recourse to the Court of Impeachment (*Riksret*), composed, according to the Norwegian Constitution, of the Supreme Court of Judicature and the Lagthing, one section of the Storthing. But, as the Liberals were not sure of the issue, proceedings were postponed until after the new elections of 1882. By means of violent agitation the Liberals won a brilliant victory at the polls, and in 1883 the Selmer Ministry was impeached. It was now possible to pack the Lagthing with staunch Liberals; and, by diminishing the number of members of

CH. XI.

the Supreme Court and irregularly disregarding every protest raised against the parliamentary members of the Court of Impeachment, a strong party tribunal was created, which in February, 1884, sentenced Selmer and seven other Cabinet Ministers to be deprived of their offices, and three others to be fined. The procedure showed a shameless disregard of legal forms and principles; so that Oscar II could justly declare, on the report of the Council of State, " that the management of legal proceedings and the composition of the Tribunal have been interfered with, in violation of the principles of an impartial administration of justice." He continued to assert his right, but accepted the resignation of the Selmer Ministry with an expression of gratitude. After abortive attempts to form a new stable Conservative Ministry, King Oscar was obliged to take the bitter and humiliating step of entrusting the formation of the Government to the leader of the Liberal party, Sverdrup. Although the Storthing had to content itself with adopting a fresh resolution about the participation of the Ministry in its deliberations, which now received the royal assent—a conclusion which formally left unsettled the question of the King's veto in constitutional matters—in reality, the assembly had gained a notable victory. No constitutional device could obscure the fact that the Storthing had carried its point, overthrown the Ministry that had opposed it, and entrusted its own leaders with the government of the country. The day of parliamentarism had arrived, and the power of the Norwegian King was broken. Amid acute party struggles between Conservatives, Moderates, and Liberals, and rapidly changing Ministries, the development of the Norwegian State has from that point gone hastily forward towards a consistent evolution of the usual Radical programme, universal suffrage, trial by jury, and so forth; and, like all uncontrolled party rule, Norwegian parliamentary government has been marked by the oppression of those who are opponents, recompenses to partisans, and doctrinaire legislation. At the same time, it has undoubtedly set free many sources of popular energy which were formerly fettered.

The fall of the royal power in Norway in reality also determined the fate of the Union. It may therefore seem strange that Sweden looked on at the constitutional struggle in Norway without attempting any other intervention than an ineffective utterance from the Government, to the effect that the King's veto on any change in the Fundamental Law of Norway was one of the essential principles of the Union. But the issue of the statholder question had deprived Sweden of the formal right to intervene, and a large section of the Swedish people were indifferent to the crisis in Norway or ignorant of it, or they applauded the brilliant victories of parliamentary ideas. This, together with Oscar II's peace-loving nature, explains why he did not use every effort to vindicate by force his clear right and the original compact with his dynasty. But by this inaction the Union was doomed.

Perhaps nothing contributed more to open the eyes of the Swedes in this matter than the Norwegian Military Service Act of 1885. By means of a mere change of name it transformed a large part, and that the most efficient, of Norway's regular military forces into a local defensive body, thereby withdrawing them from the common army of the Union, which was the real guarantee of its existence.

Proposals were now made from the Swedish side to alter the Fundamental Law so as to amend what was most deficient in the Union, the arrangement of the Foreign Office. The Swedish Cabinet proposed (1886) an addition to the *Riksakt*, by means of which the Diplomatic Council should formally be turned into an institution of the Union, consisting of three Swedish and three Norwegian Ministers. The Norwegian Government rejected the proposal because it was stipulated that the Minister for Foreign Affairs should be a Swede, and they declined to confirm this stipulation by law. Some years later, the proposal was again taken up. The Sverdrup Ministry had now rapidly become disintegrated; and, in 1889, a Conservative Ministry was formed by Emil Stang. This Government, which was friendly to the Union, in January, 1891, agreed with the Swedish Government upon a similar proposal, in which the stipulation as to the nationality of the Minister for Foreign Affairs was omitted. The Liberals grudged the Conservatives this success; they already had a new programme of their own; and the Storthing threw out the Bill. A Radical Government under Steen came into power.

The vital struggle as to the continuance of the Union now began. The new Radical programme contemplated the appointment of a separate Norwegian Minister for Foreign Affairs, a point that was stubbornly maintained subsequently. Sweden could not accept this, since it annulled the external unity of the two realms, which alone gave value to the Union, and would also, by reason of the far stronger position of the Storthing as against the King in comparison with that of the Riksdag, impose a serious disadvantage upon Sweden. On the other hand, the idea of a common Foreign Minister, Swede or Norwegian, was approved in principle; and this was officially stated by the Swedish Minister for Foreign Affairs in 1893. In order to pave the way for its own reform programme, which could evidently not be carried into effect at once, the Radical party in Norway took up the question of a separate Norwegian Consular Service. This was alleged to be necessary for the commerce and maritime trade of Norway, although the leading Norwegian shipping companies declared that they were not desirous of any change in the joint Consular Service, which had always worked advantageously. In 1892, the Storthing passed the momentous resolution for the establishment of a Norwegian Consular Service and requested the King's sanction to it as a purely domestic matter. The King refused his sanction, as he was bound, however powerless, to do, since it was a direct attack upon the Union; a joint

CH. XI.

institution of this kind, which had existed since the beginning of the Union, could not be abolished without negotiation with Sweden; and, according to the unequivocal words of the *Riksakt*, the King's decision could only be given in a combined Council of State. But the King of Norway might be coerced, and the Steen Ministry sent in their resignation, thinking the King would not succeed in forming or supporting another Government opposed to the will of the Storthing. However, the Conservatives did not leave the King in the lurch; and in 1893 Emil Stang again accepted office in open hostility to the majority in the Storthing. In vain did the angry Storthing withdraw the grant to the joint Consular Service; the Government succeeded in covering the deficit from the surplus of other revenues. In vain did it refuse the grant to the Diplomatic budget; the Swedish Treasury advanced Norway's share in this item. In its animosity the Storthing even reduced the Civil List of the King and Crown Prince. A new Radical victory at the polls, though with only a slight majority, finally induced the Stang Ministry, after a two years' struggle with the Storthing, to send in their resignation; but the King refused to form a new Government on Radical conditions, and the Stang Ministry had to remain in office. Things looked threatening, and in the spring of 1895 King Oscar called a secret committee of the Riksdag to confer upon the aspect of affairs. In Sweden the indignation against the challenges of the Norwegian Radicals was growing. Norwegian nationalism had aroused the Swedish national spirit. The Riksdag thoroughly approved the King's attitude, and urged a general revision of the articles of Union. A sign of the feeling against Norway was the denunciation of the existing Suedo-Norwegian mutual tariff law, which was held to favour Norway economically. Additional supplies were voted in view of a possible war, and at the head of the Foreign Office there was a staunch supporter of the Swedish national movement. Among Conservative circles in Sweden there was a strong current of sentiment in favour of a firm attitude on the question of revision, to be backed if necessary by an appeal to arms. The Radical party in Norway could evidently get no further with mere resolutions that could not be upheld by force, and the Storthing had to beat an ignominious retreat. The decision about the Norwegian consuls was revoked, the grants to the Consular Service and the Diplomatic budget were renewed, and the money advances from Sweden were made good. A coalition Ministry under Hagerup took the reins of government, and in a large union committee were buried for a time the burning controversies of the preceding years.

This union committee, the third in order, came to no unanimous decision. Its proceedings, in which the Norwegian Radicals had certainly not taken part with any intention of coming to a genuine agreement, served in the main only to demonstrate the honest endeavour of Sweden, as well as of the Norwegian Conservative party, to secure, on

perfectly equal terms and by means of a common Minister for Foreign
Affairs and a common Consular Service, an equitable adjustment of the
Union ; at the same time it demonstrated the equally determined aim of
the Norwegian Radicals to prevent it.   This brought about a few years'
respite in the bickerings about the Union.   But during this pause the
Norwegian Radicals got ready to take their revenge for 1895.   Further
strengthened by the new elections, in 1898, they again assumed the government.   Against the King's veto, the symbol of the Union in the canton of
the Norwegian flag was struck out, regardless of the fact that this was
arbitrarily altering an agreement made with Sweden.   Already in 1895 the
development of the Norwegian armaments had begun ; in 1901 a row
of fortifications along the eastern frontier was commenced, obviously
intended to serve one purpose only, the disruption of the Union.   These
warlike measures, the object of which could not be misunderstood, led
to similar defensive preparations in Sweden, further accentuated by
Russia's high-handed proceedings in Finland, which seemed to point to
the necessity of the Scandinavian peoples making common cause.   Under
this conviction the Swedish Government once more opened negotiations
with Norway.

Hitherto it had been maintained in Swedish circles that the question
of the Consular Service could not be solved unless in connexion with a
reform of the Foreign Office, and the union committee had worked on
that presumption.   The Norwegian Radicals asserted the opposite, and
were ready to resume their old programme of the early nineties.   The
Swedish offer now accepted the principle of a separate settlement for
the Consular Service.   In the autumn of 1902 preliminary negotiations
between delegates from the two countries were set on foot, and resulted,
after a few months' work, in a summary notification to the general
public of a preliminary agreement.   This was the famous *communiqué*
of March 24, 1903, declaring that an understanding had been come
to for the establishment of a separate consular system for each of the
two countries on the condition that the relations of the respective
consuls to the Foreign Minister and the legations should be regulated
by similar, unalterable laws, subject only to revision with the consent of
both contracting parties, and guaranteeing that " the consuls should not
overstep the proper limits of their activity and that the necessary
collaboration between the Foreign Office and the consular system of
the two countries should be thus secured."   Though this document
achieved little, it held out some hope of success.   Therefore the Radical
Ministry gave place once more to the Hagerup Ministry, and the King
commissioned the Councils of the two countries to draw up a final scheme
for the consular question on the basis of the *communiqué*.   Everything
now depended on whether an agreement could be come to about the
"similar ordinances " ; and here insuperable difficulties soon presented
themselves.   On the part of the Swedes, the claim had to be insisted

upon that the Norwegian consuls should be placed to some extent under the control of the Foreign Office. The Norwegians declared that they could not accept this, but they had no other expedient to propose than to rely upon the tact and goodwill of the future Norwegian Consular Board for harmonious cooperation with the Foreign Office. With no further guarantee it was impossible for the Swedish statesmen to disorganise the Foreign Office of their country and of the Union. Every suggestion from the Swedish side, however moderate and considerate it might be, was rejected, and finally, in February, 1905, the Norwegian Government broke off the negotiations.

The failure of the negotiations roused great excitement in Norway. The Radical party again came into office, under Michelsen, a ship-owner. Its programme this time was, in effect, the rupture of the Union. The animosity toward Sweden was stirred up to the highest pitch. The grossest invectives were hurled by the Radical Press of Norway against the Government and the people of Sweden, and in the foreign Press distorted accounts of Sweden's design to assert her supremacy and her breach of faith were circulated—all in order to cover the attack upon the Union which had been planned long before. The path the Norwegian Radicals were now determined to follow led to the dissolution of the Union, not by open action, undertaken with a full sense of responsibility, but by a misuse of the forms of law. In vain did the Crown Prince of Sweden, in the capacity of Regent, with the concurrence of every member of the Cabinet and both Chambers of the Riksdag, propose (April, 1905) a new offer for negotiations on the basis of a common Foreign Minister and a separate Consular Service. With this offer, made in a strictly official form that allowed of no misinterpretation, the Swedes had gone as far as they possibly could. Every consideration for Sweden's historic right, her numerically superior population and greater contribution to the collective forces, and the divergent Constitutions of the two realms, was sacrificed in order to preserve the Union, the safeguard of the external security of the two peoples. The offer was rejected. Instead, the Storthing resolved to establish a Norwegian Consular Service within an appointed time. When the King, as could have been foreseen, refused his consent to this, the whole Ministry tendered their resignation. Although the King refused to accept it, as he was unable "at the moment" to form a new Ministry, every member of the Norwegian Government simply resigned his official position. After this had been announced in the Storthing (June 7), the Storthing declared that, since the King had announced his inability to form a new Government, he ceased *ipso facto* to reign, and consequently the Union with Sweden was dissolved. The retiring Ministry were commissioned to officiate provisionally.

This was revolution. Norway had violated her Fundamental Law and the *Riksakt*. But the people of Sweden also had a voice in the

matter.   Exasperation at the manner in which the rupture of the Union
had taken place, the manifest perversion of justice, and the unwarranted
accusations against the old King and against Sweden itself, flared up and
found expression in the warm protestations of loyalty which poured in
from every part of Sweden to King Oscar.   The Riksdag, summoned to
an extraordinary meeting, was agreed that only after formal negotiations
between the two realms and upon certain conditions, contained in an
Address to the King of July 28, 1905, could they recognise the dissolution of the Union, and public opinion was unanimous in supporting this
clearly formulated course.   On the Norwegian side there was haste to
comply.   After a general election had declared for the dissolution of
the Union, the Storthing addressed to the Swedish Government a formal
request for a discussion; whereupon four members of each Government
met in Karlstad at a conference which, on September 23, resulted in a
number of agreements, all of which were in substantial conformity with
the conditions laid down by the Riksdag.   The first condition was the
establishment of a neutral zone, consisting of a narrow strip on both
sides of the frontier from the Skaw up to 61° lat., within which no
fortifications were hereafter to exist, nor troops to be stationed.   Thus
Norway was bound to demolish the continuous line of fortifications along
the frontier of Sweden, which had been put in working order or had
been built up in the last few years, from Fredriksten to Kongsvinger.
The last-named old fort, which lay within the neutral zone, but not so
close to the Swedish frontier as to constitute a direct menace to Sweden,
was, however, to remain in its then condition, with a limited garrison.
This concession was the only one which the Norwegian negotiators
succeeded in obtaining.   Furthermore, the old privilege of the nomadic
Laplanders as to reindeer pasturage on both sides of the frontier was
secured, as well as the right to export Swedish ore from the iron ore
fields of Norrland by the port of Narvik.   Among the other articles
was an engagement that for the future certain classes of dispute should
be referred to the permanent Arbitration Court at the Hague.   These
agreements, which were approved by the Riksdag and the Storthing,
received King Oscar's sanction on October 26, 1905.

Thereby the Union was formally and legally dissolved, and each
kingdom went its own way after all mutual claims had been peaceably
adjusted.   Still, the tension had been high before the final settlement
had been come to, and at one moment during the Karlstad conference
a war, for which both sides were prepared, nearly broke out.   Such a
war would have answered no useful purpose, since a forcible reestablishment of the Union could not have been considered desirable and would
only have led to interference on the part of the European Powers.   As
the result of a general election, the Norwegians declared for the preservation of a monarchical form of government; and the Storthing elected
Prince Charles, younger son of the Crown Prince Frederick of Denmark

and his wife, the Swedish princess Louisa, to be King of Norway. The new King, who was married to the youngest daughter of the King of England, assumed the name Haakon VII. The venerable old King Oscar II, the evening of whose life had been clouded by these events, did not survive them long. He passed away on December 8, 1907, and was succeeded by his son, King Gustavus V.

The rupture of the Union has undoubtedly diminished the external security of the two Scandinavian States. By herself Norway is a small, weak Power, owing to her poverty and her scanty population; her independence may easily be seriously threatened in certain circumstances. She has sought protection by entering into a Treaty (1907) with England, Russia, Germany, and France, by which these countries have guaranteed to Norway her territorial integrity. For Sweden, too, the divorce from Norway made the international position more difficult and dangerous; but, at the same time, the dissolution of the Union was felt as a relief from the continual conflicts with Norway, and national feeling in Sweden had grown during the conflict to a fuller and clearer consciousness than it had possessed for centuries. In her national homogeneity and territorial compactness, which do not invite conflicts with other Powers, and in a highly developed and numerous army of defence, she possesses the guarantee of continued peace and security from without. Sweden has tried to strengthen these guarantees in her own way, by acceding to the Baltic and North Sea Conventions, concluded in the spring of 1908, which guarantee the possessions of the different contracting parties along the coasts of these seas. To the Baltic Convention, Sweden, Denmark, Germany, and Russia were parties; to the North Sea Convention, Sweden, Denmark, Germany, Holland, and Great Britain.

DENMARK.

After the loss of Schleswig and Holstein (1864) Denmark became one of the smallest Powers in Europe, and the question of her existence as an independent State might well cause anxiety to her statesmen. The recent losses had brought one advantage with them, in that the German element of population was now entirely divided off from the Danish State. Unfortunately, the purely Danish population in north Schleswig, some 200,000 souls, had also come under the German dominion. The Peace of Prague, 1866, it is true, held out a prospect of the return of north Schleswig through the well-known clause about a future vote of the people in that district, but the defeat of France in 1870 and the agreement of 1878 between Prussia and Austria to annul the Prague clause frustrated the hopes the Danish people had cherished to the very last for the reunion of Danish Schleswig. In the population of that district, however, the Danish national spirit has continued with undiminished vigour, and the Danes have felt it obligatory to maintain and strengthen the national and cultural bond.

The unhappy issue of the conflict with Germany naturally awakened a strong national feeling against that Power, which Prussia's attempt to Germanise north Schleswig by force helped to keep up. Danish policy has, for its part, always observed an unswerving neutrality, dictated by the country's situation; but it could scarcely conceal the fact that the Danish people now looked for support rather to the Powers which were possible opponents of Germany—in the first place to England and Russia, with which countries Denmark was closely allied dynastically, since the heirs apparent of both these countries (afterwards King Edward VII and Tsar Alexander III) had wedded Danish princesses. The disaster of 1864 also produced a certain animosity against Sweden and Norway, who had left Denmark alone in her struggle; but the cultural ties with the Scandinavian Powers were kept up as keenly as before and strengthened by means of currency and postal conventions, by a conscious striving for greater conformity in legislation, by scientific gatherings of Scandinavians, and so forth. The dissolution of the Union of Sweden and Norway and Denmark's attitude towards it again produced a feeling of coolness, this time on the part of Sweden, but this too is likely to pass away before long. The tension between Denmark and Germany has noticeably decreased of late. The economic and intellectual relations between the two countries have proved to be so close that an amicable feeling even in political matters could not be permanently excluded. Both Denmark and Germany were parties to the Baltic and North Sea Conventions of 1908.

With wonderful energy the people of Denmark, after the War of 1864, set themselves to the task of developing Denmark's internal resources and civilisation. Zealously they turned to the chief natural source of plenty in Denmark, the soil. The *Hedeselskabet* (society for the cultivation of the heaths), formed in 1866, has gradually changed half of the barren Jutland moorlands into productive fields, meadows, or woods. Danish agriculture is among the most highly developed in the world. From a corn-producing country Denmark has become more and more a stock-farming country. The surplus of such products, especially butter, bacon, and eggs, constitutes Denmark's chief export. By the side of agriculture Danish manufactures have made great strides—they support one-third of the population. Foreign trade, after a period of depression towards the middle of the nineteenth century, has also been exceedingly prosperous. The United Steamship Company of Denmark has played a great part in the development of the maritime commerce. Esbjerg was founded in 1868 as a seaport for the growing export trade to England. The free port of Copenhagen (since 1895) has contributed materially to the prosperity of the Danish transit trade. The development of the Danish railway system belongs mainly to this period. Whether the prosperity of Denmark can reach a yet higher level, is doubtful. The little nation has braced up her energies to the fullest extent that the country's resources render possible ; and the result attained to by the work of the last few decades is, in its way, extraordinary.

Denmark's intellectual culture must also be ranked very high. Danish art and *belles lettres* have been long renowned ; characterised less by lofty invention and striking originality than by a high average standard, they bear witness to an old, refined culture which is maintained by a large section of the population. In the ethical and religious life of Denmark sharp contrasts exist between the critically negative, radical, and cosmopolitan spirit, represented by the author and historian Georg Brandes and his numerous followers, and conservative national principles, upheld by positive religious currents, either of an orthodox tendency (inland missions), or evangelical (Grundtvigianism, etc.). These variances have been fought out mainly among the middle class and peasant population, which latter has risen more and more to a social equality with the former. During the last twenty years serious social conflicts have taken place between this middle class and the working classes, imbued with socialistic ideas. The enlightenment of the masses in Denmark has proceeded rapidly, especially through the high schools for the people, which are a distinctly Danish institution and have spread from Denmark over Scandinavia and Finland. In all branches of scientific knowledge Denmark has had illustrious representatives, especially perhaps in history, philology (Vilhelm Thomsen) and medicine (Finsen).

This fertile internal development under the long reign of Christian IX has proceeded in spite of unusually violent political divisions. The King himself was at first, as a German and the founder of a new dynasty, received with a certain coolness by the Danish people ; but his thoroughly honourable, lovable, and unpretentious nature won him an ever-growing popularity. He was not a man of commanding intellect or even of any learning ; but he had a naturally sound judgment and was thoroughly trustworthy, faithful, and loyal to the Constitution. After the latter had received its final form (1866) and the sharp disputes were at an end, there began a complete remodelling of the Danish political parties ; several scattered liberal or radical fractions joined a great Liberal party which soon had a majority in the Folkething. This united party, whose most conspicuous leader during the seventies and eighties was Kristen Berg, aimed at controlling the Folkething and reforming the State according to its ideas. In opposition to it the Conservatives and National Liberals made common cause ; they had their main support in the Landsthing, and accordingly maintained that this institution had an equal constitutional position with the Folkething. The royal House of

Denmark naturally sided with this Conservative party, which defended constitutional ideas against the parliamentarism of the Folkething. After several changes of Ministry, Jakob Estrup became leader of the Government in 1875. For nearly two decades, with rare courage, tenacity, and power he maintained the political independence of the monarchy and the Landsthing against the Folkething. When the Liberal majority in the Folkething tried to coerce the Government by stoppage of supplies and the systematic rejection of every Bill, Estrup made use of the power which the Constitution gave the King of issuing provisional Acts, among them also finance Acts (in 1877 for the first time), and, backed by the Landsthing, defied the increasingly furious attacks of the Folkething. The climax of the struggle was reached during the years 1885–94, when the Government ruled for nine years without a legal grant of supplies. Year after year, the Estrup Ministry ruled by means of a provisional budget and carried out the fortification of Copenhagen—one of the chief demands of the Conservatives. But the whole political life of Denmark suffered from these constitutional struggles. At last a split occurred in the Liberal party, and a moderate fraction approached the Conservatives, who for their part were longing to come to some agreement. In 1894 Estrup made way for a moderate Conservative Ministry, a legal Bill of supply was again established, and the defensive works that had been undertaken were approved of. But the party disputes were not at an end. The development threw the centre of gravity of power more and more into the Folkething and, as the general elections of 1901 were strongly in favour of the Liberals, King Christian was forced to accept a Liberal Government. This change of policy was welcomed with great joy. Yet it has hardly been accompanied by the success expected, even if a policy of reform has been accelerated.

The leading personality on the Liberal benches during the rise of the party was Jens Christian Christensen, formerly an elementary school teacher, whose parliamentary talents raised him to the leadership of the Folkething in the nineties, and then to the Government, first as Minister of Church and Education and then (1905–8) as President of the Council. The old King, Christian IX, died in January, 1906, and was succeeded by his son, Frederick VIII.

CHAPTER XII.

REACTION AND REVOLUTION IN RUSSIA.

THE Crimean War had so thoroughly discredited the reactionary system of Nicholas I that for a time even the officials seemed to be Liberal. The first and greatest of the reforms of Alexander II—the Emancipation of the serfs (March 3, 1861)—was a political and social measure of the first magnitude, challenging countless vested interests, and carried through, after many revisions and hesitations, entirely from above and by a great effort of public spirit on the part of the sovereign. The outlines of the settlement were broad and liberal; but the labour bestowed on it had been immense, and the sympathies of the official world were for the time exhausted. Alexander II was not a strong man, his Court, at which the German landowners from the Baltic provinces possessed a disproportionate influence, reflected the mood of the country gentry, whose interests had suffered most from the Emancipation; officialism was scared by the rapid growth of public opinion, which had received the strongest nourishment from the great peasant question, and had imperatively demanded a share in its solution.

The Emperor, naturally, sank back into his old surroundings. A notable turning-point in opinion came with the Polish rising of 1863. The Poles had the support of Bakúnin, Hertzen, and other enemies of the bureaucracy; they were so foolish as to claim the Lithuanian and White Russian provinces where the population was mainly Russian; General Mieroslawski even sought to sow confusion in Russia by disseminating Radical ideas there, while recommending the death penalty for a similar propaganda in Poland. A national reaction followed, especially on the vain threat of French intervention.

Public interest in reform was not, however, extinguished; and the Emancipation Act evidently needed supplementing by changes in local government, the legal system, and the relations of the peasants towards their superiors. But, owing to the increasing conservatism of the ruling caste, these reforms were conceived in a less liberal spirit. The reform of the Universities in 1863 was comparatively successful. At the beginning of the reign the limitation of the number of students had been withdrawn, and a multitude of young men of humble origin had been admitted. The students organised themselves for certain corporate objects, such as the formation of secular Sunday Schools. A few revolutionary proclamations appeared; and in September and October, 1861, a riotous demonstration took place in St Petersburg. The rules of June 12 abolished the right to form corporate organisations; they were followed by speeches, demonstrations, and arrests. The Emperor then issued the Statute of 1863, which conceded to the University authorities a considerable measure of independence from police control.

The Law of January 13, 1864, second in importance only to the Emancipation of the serfs, instituted Zemstva or County Councils, elected indiscriminately from all classes, in the central provinces of the Empire. Each district elected a Zemstvo; the district Zemstva elected to the Zemstvo of the province. Their competence embraced " affairs of local well-being." But this Law was early subjected to considerable limitations. The institution of a practically new system of law Courts and the introduction of trial by jury followed (December 2, 1864). The old system stood condemned on all sides, and in principle the change was most beneficent; but two grave defects were allowed to pass into the actual Law—political cases were to be tried by a special Court without a jury, and officials could only be tried with the consent of their superiors. Moreover, the Law was only put into operation with extreme timidity and delay. The drafting of the Press Law of 1865 was seriously modified under the influence of Valúyeff, the Minister of the Interior; the preliminary censorship was abolished for the newspapers of the capital, but the punitive censorship which replaced it was vested, not in the law Courts, but in the Minister himself; so that this measure, introduced as a reform amid the enthusiasm of the educated classes, was hardly a reform at all. This Act ends the reforming period, though self-government in a more restricted form was extended to the towns (1870), and the reorganisation of the army on the basis of conscription (1874) was conceived by Dmitry Milyútin in an exceptionally broad and liberal spirit. The obligation of service was extended to the privileged classes; only sons were exempted; the period was reduced from 25 years to 5, to be followed by 8 to 10 years in the war reserve. Between 1861 and 1881, the army was put upon a territorial basis, the training of officers was much improved, and the military law Courts were reformed.

After Karakózoff's attempt on the Emperor's life (April 15, 1866) many Liberals became more conservative; the Liberal Minister of Public Instruction, Golovnín, gave place to Count Dmitry Tolstóy; and the police of St Petersburg was entrusted to General Trépoff. The two leading Radical monthlies, the *Contemporary* and the *Russian Word*, were suppressed; and an appeal was issued inviting the aid of the people to combat pernicious ideas subversive of religion, order, and property.

CH. XII.

As for these "pernicious ideas," the Russian Government, since the French Revolution of 1792, had been waging an intermittent war with an almost imaginary enemy. The Decembrists of 1825 were undoubtedly dangerous because of their high position and their high intelligence; they were vaguely tinged with socialism, but they were few in number, and their attempted revolution was hopeless. The dreamy socialist thinkers of 1849, called the Petrashevtsy, who included the writer Dostoyevsky, were hardly more numerous and of no political importance. But these two abortive movements were of no account as against the repressive system which, throughout the reign of Nicholas I, lay like a dead weight on the whole population. Byelinsky, the first great Russian literary critic, did much towards creating a reading public with a high standard of intelligence. Meanwhile, Fourier and the French socialists obtained increasing influence; in the Russia of the autocracy it was the tradition of individualism that was deficient. In spite of the rigorous censorship, Russian thought, though emancipated, was not at this time revolutionary. The Liberal wave of the forties was strongly felt in Russia; but men so different as Katkóff and Bakúnin were at first intimates and fellow-thinkers. Of the two chief schools of thought, the Westernisers and the Slavophils, the former were not revolutionary, nor the latter reactionary: the censorship, curiously enough, was most severe towards the conservative and patriotic Slavophils. Then came the preeminence of Hertzen, who led the campaign against the abuses of the representative system. He was as much a Liberal as a socialist; before all things he was a great moral force; and his paper, the *Bell*, published in London, penetrated even to the Emperor's cabinet.

Early in the reign of Alexander II a deep division becomes observable among Russian political thinkers, corresponding to that which was in progress in official circles—between those who wished to go forward and those who wished to go back. In each case it was the enemies of compromise who showed most will and conviction; thus, while the Government became more reactionary, the educated classes became increasingly revolutionary. Hertzen at this time represents the Liberalism of the "conscience-stricken gentleman," swamped by the so-called "men of mixed class" who were streaming into the Universities. Retaining their sympathy with the peasant world from which they had sprung, these men entered an atmosphere of intelligence entirely foreign to that world, without gaining foothold within the charmed circle of authority. Chernyshevsky, who has been called the father of Russian socialism, set the tone to this new class in the *Contemporary*. His mind was acute and powerful, and shrank from no conclusions. In his view, the welfare of a nation depended not on its corporate wealth but on the comparative distribution of well-being; and he made this principle his point of departure. Like the Slavophils, he wished to preserve the primitive socialism of the village commune; but he looked

forward to a Russia which, by a chance of history, should escape the
capitalist stage of modern Europe and achieve its development in
accordance with the theories of modern socialism.

Chernyshevsky welcomed enthusiastically and even extravagantly the
Emperor's earlier pronouncements on peasant reform ; but for the allotment of land to the peasant he set up a revolutionary standard, and,
as concessions at first suggested were gradually whittled away, he passed
into a permanent mood of bitter hostility. It seems certain that he
inspired the university protests of 1861 ; the *Contemporary* was stopped
for eight months, and, for alleged complicity in a violently revolutionary
manifesto, he was sentenced to seven years of penal servitude. His
work was continued by the brilliant young critic Dobrolyúboff, who
poured contempt on the impotence and characterlessness of Russian
life and on the timid Liberals who preached patience and moderation.
Dobrolyúboff died before his friend's catastrophe ; but the bitterness
of both became much more extreme in Písareff, another young man fresh
from the student's bench, who developed the protest of Dobrolyúboff
into a complete egoism, isolating the sacred personality of the egoist
from all that was dominating in environment, from all that was
authoritative in the present or in the past. He despised politics and
he could not have been of any party ; at the most he admitted groups of
kindred spirits : his *Russian Word* was continually in controversy with
the *Contemporary*. But his influence over a certain section of opinion
was great, since he met its instincts as the apostle of negation ; for four
years (1862–6) he wrote from a prison cell. The "nihilist" type had been
presented in literature in the *Fathers and Children* of Turgénieff : but,
while the critics of the *Contemporary* regarded the brilliant character-
isation of Bazároff as a pitiful caricature, Písareff avowed it and extolled
it. With his gospel of annihilation he led his generation into a blind
alley, the end of all civilisation. When Písareff was drowned at the age
of 27 (1868), his ideas were in a state of transition ; certainly, he had
not said his last word ; but his strange teaching was exaggerated still
further by his followers ; and it is thus that we reach the so-called
"short formulae" of the nihilists, such as :—"man is an animal," "the
belly is the centre of the world," "love is simply a sexual attraction,"
"photography is higher than art."

The word "nihilism" has been far too loosely applied. At this time
the movement was chiefly literary ; there were as yet no terrorist organisations and only isolated terrorist acts ; and, before these became
common, there had been a strong reaction from the ideas of Písareff
amongst the Russian revolutionaries. The Government, however, did
not perceive this ; and, unfortunately, there existed no strong body of
central and moderating opinion to mediate between reactionary and
revolutionary thought. Nine-tenths of the population consisted of an
ignorant and recently emancipated peasantry. Among the educated

classes were only scattered groups of individuals, each possessing its own shade of view, and free expression was discouraged. Hertzen, living abroad, had misjudged Russia. The *Bell* had alienated patriots by its Polish sympathies and estranged revolutionaries by its censure of Karakózoff. At home the silence of Liberal opinion was seldom broken after 1864. Several attempts had been made by the gentry to persuade the Emperor to "crown his edifice" by summoning representatives of the people, and, in 1865, the Moscow gentry repeated the request: "truth," they pleaded, "will reach your throne without hindrance." Alexander, in replying, claimed "the exclusive right to initiative in the chief sections of this gradual work of completion," and hoped to meet with "no more embarrassments of this kind from the gentry of Russia."

In 1870, the Government took advantage of the downfall of Napoleon to declare itself free from the restrictions imposed on it in the Black Sea by the Treaty of Paris; and even Slavophils believed that this relief to the national pride might be followed by concessions to the Russian people. Under the direction of Ivan Aksákoff, Samárin, and Prince Cherkassky, the City Council of Moscow drew up a loyal and convincing appeal to the sovereign, pleading especially for "freedom of opinion and the printed word, without which there is no room for sincerity." The address was returned as "couched in an unfitting and unbecoming form." Samárin himself had had to print abroad his patriotic work on the *Frontiers of Russia*, in which he stood for the old culture and social system of Russia against the feudalism of Baltic Germans and Poles. The Slavophil organ of Aksákoff, *Moscow*, was suppressed in 1869; and until 1880 the party of national traditions had no other means of public expression of its views than occasional speeches in the Slavonic societies of the capitals. Even Katkóff, the editor of the *Moscow Gazette* and the ally of Count Dmitry Tolstóy, came into open conflict with Valúyeff over the limitations placed on the powers of the Zemstva and on the Press. Valúyeff resigned (1868), but only to be replaced by the reactionary Timásheff, formerly Chief of Gendarmes; and in the licensed Press only the most pliable could survive. However, the admirable monthly, the *Messenger of Europe*, was successfully conducted on Liberal lines by Stasyulévich and Asényeff.

Thus isolated from the public the Government went on towards the great catastrophe. The real leader of the reaction was Count Dmitry Tolstóy. His tendencies were unmistakable; he had conducted an official persecution of the Catholics, and his criticism of the project of Emancipation was so reactionary that the Emperor wrote on it "This is not a criticism but a lampoon." He had served in the Ministry of Public Instruction, and had been Chief Procurator of the Holy Synod. During his long tenure of office (1866–80) the chief sphere of Count Tolstóy's repressive activity was the Universities and the schools. His object being to drive out the new generation of men of mixed rank, it was necessary to begin from the bottom. Scholars of the "Real Schools" were subjected to a revised syllabus, and refused access to the Universities; the Gymnasia, retained as nurseries for the Universities, were remodelled on strictly classical lines (1871). It must be remembered that in Russia educated men are comparatively few, and in great request as officials or professional men; and, as the school certificate and university diploma are required for any higher public appointment, they have a high market value. This explains the effectiveness of exclusion from studies as a punishment, the indignation which it has always excited among the students when applied to their leaders, and the chivalry which has so often induced whole masses of them to challenge the same fate. Tolstóy frankly aimed at a diminution in the number of students and a monopoly for those whose means enabled them to prepare for the school entrance examinations in the dead languages. Transition from one grade of school to another was also made as difficult as possible—and all this at a time when the results of the Emancipation were carrying Young Russia irresistibly forward in pursuit of instruction. Tolstóy became and remained the most unpopular man in Russia. The ordinance of 1871, which established his system, was enforced with certain modifications till recent times. The Universities lost most of the rights conferred on them by Golovnín's statute, and passed practically under police supervision. In 1869 the primary schools were removed from the control of the Zemstva, and put under the supervision of government inspectors, whose duties were largely of a police character. The books supplied to the pupils and the political opinions of the teachers were henceforth closely watched; and in Poland and the western provinces the schools were turned into an engine for Russifying the population.

The Zemstva had begun their work with great enthusiasm; their members received a training in public business conducted on the principles of publicity and responsibility, and their officers were in close contact with the people. They were therefore distrusted by the Government, and their powers and representative functions were constantly diminished. They retained the constructive work of school organisation; but they lost the right of control. Valúyeff, who was almost as hostile to the Zemstva as to the Press, aimed at making the local Governors as absolute as himself; in 1866 he obtained from the Emperor an order which forbade the appointment of officers by the Zemstva without the Governor's consent; and this act of administration, like many others, has remained in force much longer than the law which it so arbitrarily amended. The Zemstvo executives had their own elected Presidents; the Marshals of the Gentry presided over the full assemblies, and in 1867 they received ample powers for closing debates; the printing of resolutions or debates was made subject to the consent of the Governor. In consequence of this policy many of the most active members lost all interest in their work.

CH. XII.

The new law Courts also found many devoted workers, qualified to set up a high standard of dignity and independence. But a single sentence of acquittal in a press case led to the removal of all such cases to a Court without a jury. Provincial judges were put into relations with the Governors similar to those of other officials. Count Pahlen (1868) lost no time in attacking the new system: the examining magistrates were made removable, and in 1874 he obtained the right to exercise a veto even over the list of private lawyers. Other laws, which removed political cases from the cognisance of juries, must be judged differently, since they were called forth by exceptional circumstances of an alarming kind.

Between 1865 and 1870 forty-four press warnings were issued by the censorship, and seven periodicals, including those of Aksákoff and Katkóff, were stopped for terms ranging from two to six months. In 1868, Timásheff, in defiance of the law, obtained permission from the Committee of Ministers to forbid the sale of any newspaper on the streets. This measure, declared at the time to be temporary, was never abrogated; and the precedent for evading a regular decision of the Council of State was followed in a number of other regulations. From 1869 to 1871 there were twenty-three warnings; six periodicals were stopped, and nine deprived of their sale on the streets. In the next five years the figures rose to 72, 16, and 45, and those for 1878–9 were still higher. In 1873 editors were made liable to expulsion from their posts if they refused to divulge the names of contributors. In 1879 the Government assumed the power of forbidding a paper to print advertisements; the penalty of suspension or suppression was extended to provincial papers, which were already subjected to preliminary censorship. These measures were applied to practically all the chief Russian periodicals, except the revolutionary publications, which were printed abroad and distributed in secret. Works of Mill, Spencer, Lecky, and Finlay were excluded from circulation in Russia.

Thus there was open war between the Government and the Russian "Intelligence"; let us turn now to the vast background of peasants. After the Emancipation, the peasants were for a time forgotten, but the reform went forward of itself. In 1863 the emancipating law was applied to the serfs of the sovereign and of the imperial appanages, and in 1866 to those of the State. All these received a more liberal allotment of land than the former serfs of the gentry; and the peasants of the appanages were from the first put into a position much closer to that of personal proprietors. Meanwhile, the impoverished landlords were glad to allow the redemption of the land on the terms prescribed, and in ten years two-thirds of their serfs had acquitted themselves of their old obligations. But the accident of bad crops in northern Russia in 1867–8 made it clear that the peasant had the greatest difficulty in discharging his new dues to the State. It was proved that the governmental burdens of the peasant often exceeded the whole income from his holding, and could only be met from other sources. Thus the purely agricultural districts, where there were no earnings from factories or cottage industries, were being exhausted; a peasant who had bread all the year round was becoming a rarity. Prince Vassilchikoff showed that, whereas the ordinary landowner was paying $3\frac{3}{4}d$. an acre, the peasant was paying $2s$.—besides an almost equal sum levied for special purposes. Three bad crops in succession led in 1873 to a famine in the grain-growing provinces; the peasants sold their cattle to buy bread, and were therefore unable to manure their land. The Government advanced some £260,000; it remitted taxation, and the arrears of two years; much help was also obtained from private charity; but repressive measures were at the same time adopted. In 1874, Committees, consisting partly of local officials, replaced the "arbiters of the peace" who had satisfactorily carried out the first application of the Emancipation Law. The police colonels received disciplinary powers over the peasants elected to responsible posts in the governance of their class.

The Emancipation found Russian industry in a very primitive stage, and it inflicted great loss on the old serf-worked factories. A fury of speculation set in after the Crimean War, followed by a financial crisis in 1858–9; and the fever of railway development at the end of the sixties again led to a crisis in 1873–4. Speculation reached greater dimensions than ever from 1878 to 1880, to be followed by seven years of depression. These figures show that the periods of commercial vigour corresponded with those of great public interest in reform, and also that Russia already reflected in a marked degree the commercial fluctuations of western Europe. The second of these phenomena implies that, for good or for evil, Russia had passed into the stage of capitalism. Many of the former serfs, unable to pay the redemption dues on their holdings, streamed into the towns; and, as Russian peasants, after migration, still maintain a permanent connexion with their native village, the peasant turned artisan was still a peasant; he bore his share of the village taxes, and in old age returned to his native place; thus was developed an army of " go-aways," who brought the peasantry into contact with modern conditions of life and thought. In the factories, the introduction of machinery made the employer more independent of the worker; and, though wages were higher, prices rose faster still. The Government scarcely attempted to face these new questions. The employers of the St Petersburg district favoured reform; but the Moscow manufacturers were hostile to new methods of working, and nothing was done. One effect of this advent of industrialism was to divert many able minds from the pursuit of the public welfare; and there was an alarming increase of corruption and bribery, especially in the official world.

Naturally, this negative record does not cover the whole life of a nation full of tension after the promise and inception of far-reaching reforms. Russian thought was rapidly being revolutionised, and becoming absolutely independent of the received order of things. The Russian mind is acute, and it had become embittered : the Intelligence, though small in numbers, was compact, and ready to follow any powerful thinker who could express its instincts. It was completely severed from the Government ; and it is, therefore, all the more remarkable that this period of reaction should be marked by a revulsion from the negation of Písareff. His literary nihilism was discarded ; it gave place to a generous devotion to the needs of the people, and to the arduous and almost impossible task of educating the masses. Under existing conditions, enthusiasm was not likely to respect lawfully constituted authority ; and, in accordance with Russian instincts, the movement was in character socialistic.

The first to recall Russian thought from the blind alley of Písareff was Professor Lavróff. From his exile in the province of Vyatka, he sent to the *Week* in 1868 his notable *Historical Letters,* and after his escape from Russia he established the revolutionary periodical *Forwards* in London (1873). Lavróff aimed at the creation of a moral system for the Russian revolutionary Intelligence ; returning to the school of Hertzen, he placed supreme emphasis on the sacred value of character, and he urged on Young Russia the duty of devoting itself to the people from which it had sprung. The young student was able to study because the peasant tilled and the artisan worked ; and he owed such light as he could give in return to the struggling and ignorant masses. The teaching of Lavróff was infinitely deepened by a much more profound thinker, Mikhailovsky. This eminent writer, who contributed to *Notes of the Fatherland* from 1868 to 1883, was the exponent of a whole system of philosophy, described as " sociological individualism." He acknowledged two standards—the development of individual character, and the welfare of the people, defined as those who labour—and he maintained that these two ideals, if rightly understood, are complementary to each other. To the struggle for existence he opposes the struggle for individual completeness, which, he says, involves the fullest sense of the world around us. Like Chernyshevsky, he believed that Russia could escape the period of capitalism, and he wished therefore to strengthen the village commune, while aiming at the formation of character in its individual members. Mikhailovsky's teaching was intensely moral, but it was quite unrestrained by consideration for established civil or religious systems ; and his influence largely helped to develop the strong rationalism of present-day Russian society. At the same time, he greatly deepened the sense of the debt of the Intelligence to the labouring classes.

Under its own self-chosen masters Russian thought had thus become contemptuously regardless of the negative direction imposed by the

Government. The chief care of the thinkers was how best to smuggle contraband ideas past the censorship. Meanwhile, the conservative Slavophils were punished precisely because they spoke and wrote quite plainly. In a few very limited circles, however, protests of a more practical character were preparing—conspiracies for organised propagandism or for revenge on certain typical representatives of the administration. There were three main tendencies, each with a small number of adepts and a much larger number of active or passive sympathisers. The Socialists of Lavróff were for propaganda and the preparation of a new world; the Anarchists of Bakúnin were for rousing the peasants to immediate insurrection; the Jacobins, such as Necháyeff and Tkachéff, attached less importance to the cooperation of the people and conspired to seize on power by a violent *coup d'État*. At first only the two former tendencies commanded any popularity. The proclamations of 1861, " To the young generation," " To the landlords' peasants," etc. were aggressive and sometimes insolent; but they were the work of individuals or very small groups; the bloodthirsty proclamation, " Young Russia " (1862), had even less authority. The far more moderate manifestos of the secret societies, " The Great Russian " (1861), and " Land and Liberty " (1863), were more serious; several officers took part in the first; the second was an attempt to unite all the revolutionary groups; it met with little success until 1876. Karakózoff, who fired at the Emperor in 1866, was indeed a member of a very small revolutionary group; but he was a neurotic, and his design had been discountenanced by his fellow-members. The repression which followed was a turning-point in the movement. Many of the chief revolutionaries were now beyond the frontier; there they created a literature of periodicals and pamphlets which was smuggled in large quantities into Russia. The *People's Business* of Bakúnin appeared in Geneva in 1868, and his pamphlet *Statecraft and Anarchy* followed in 1873, the same year as the *Forwards* of Lavróff. The disturbances in the Russian Universities had continued, and the University of Zurich was for a time the chief meeting ground of revolutionary students. The first organised conspiracy was the work of the Jacobin Necháyeff, and it was neither general nor popular. There were riots at St Petersburg University in 1869, and Necháyeff tried to make the students bring forward political claims. He acted as secretary of an imaginary committee, and planned a vague system of wholesale murder; he ordered and carried through the murder of a rebellious associate; but he could not collect more than £30 in Moscow, and the whole scheme was discovered. The Government gave the case full publicity, and eighty-seven persons were brought to trial in 1871. Necháyeff had escaped, but was handed over by the Swiss Government and sent to penal servitude.

Despite this disillusionment, Bakúnin went on preaching from Geneva a general rising of the peasants. Lavróff advocated a propaganda of a slower and more reasoned kind. In St Petersburg, Nicholas Chaikovsky had gathered round him a knot of young revolutionary idealists, who held classes for working men and distributed books and pamphlets. Similar groups were formed in Kieff and Odessa. It became the fashion to learn a trade and live the life of a workman. Arrests continued, and most of the followers of Chaikovsky passed under lock and key. It was now (1872–5) that whole masses of students decided to turn their backs on the towns and live among the peasantry. Great sacrifices were often made; high office, aristocratic homes, were abandoned for a workman's bench in a factory, or a bed on the cold ground; but only a few of the rarer spirits ever got into real touch with the peasants. Many turned back at the first contact with the rough peasant life; most lived on aimlessly in villages, meeting each other with pass-words and surreptitious greetings and never extending their circle. Two or three talks with peasants earned a fictitious reputation for success, and inspirited the whole fraternity. In the end, confounded by the police system, by the distrust and hostility of the peasants, and by the sense of their own ignorance and failure, they drifted back to the towns. Here they lived without passports—that is, in a permanent state of conspiracy. Countless arrests were made by the Government, and each trace of a propagandist visitor was taken to imply the existence of a powerful local organisation. Many persons, such as the future regicide, Kibálchich, were arrested for trivial offences, were kept in prison for years without trial, and became confirmed revolutionaries. Huge and long delayed trials, such as that of 193 persons in January, 1878, gave the bolder spirits the best chance of airing their views. There was a premium on violence, whether of the police or of their opponents; the passportless wanderers, desperate and nerve-shaken, rapidly passed into the mood of terrorism, and the professional class and even some of the Zemstvo workers were more or less in sympathy with this new mood.

It was at this point that Russia drifted into the War with Turkey, which is treated in another chapter. The War was preceded by a strong and genuine movement amongst minds with Slavophil tendencies; but there was too evident a contrast between a liberating policy abroad and suffocation both of Poles and Russians at home. Panslavism required as its basis a true Slavophilism at home, without which the whole strength of the idea was gone; and in Russia, as we know, the Slavophils were forbidden to speak freely. Hence the comparative failure of the officially patronised Congress of Slavs at Moscow in 1867. Ignatyeff took up the cause of the Bulgarians as against the Greeks (1872) and Slavophil men and money went to Bulgaria in 1875. Slavophils helped to prolong the struggle between Turkey and Servia; and it is notable that some Russian Liberals and even some revolutionaries volunteered with the Servians. It was undoubtedly a national movement which carried Alexander II into war. But almost everything in this war seemed calculated to mortify the Russian people. Turkey flattered western Europe and derided Russia with a semblance of constitutional rule; the two main armies, nominally led by Grand Dukes, were blocked by apparently insignificant fortresses; in glaring contrast with the devoted bravery of the soldiers stood forth the disgraceful peculation of military officials and contractors; the tide that carried Russia to the gates of Constantinople brought her face to face with a war with half Europe; the Treaty of Berlin was a humiliation; the one Russian gain, Bessarabia, embroiled her with her only ally, Roumania; for the Russian protectorate of the liberated States was substituted a European guarantee of them against Russian aggression; the victories of Russia gave a constitution to Bulgaria, whilst she herself remained under police rule. To the outburst of mortified patriotism from the Slavophils the Government's only answer was to suppress the Slavophil committees.

The mood of those malcontents who had decided to live without passports was now fully ripe for terrorism. The most prominent actors were not the leaders of revolutionary thought, but very young men and women. Beginning with prison escapes and rescues, they passed without plan and almost unconsciously to armed resistance against arrest, and to murders of traitors, spies, and lower police officials. From this it was an easy step to the murder of a Governor, or even to plots against the life of the Emperor. As this process evolved itself, a gap opened between the simple propagandists and the more violent revolutionaries; these last, becoming more compact and businesslike, adjourned the realisation of their vague social theories, resolved to dispense with any active popular support, and organised themselves on a basis of conspiracy pure and simple.

The first act that marked this evolution was peculiarly characteristic of the issues involved. The student Bogolyúboff, imprisoned for his share in a notable demonstration before the Kazán Cathedral, refused to uncover before General Trépoff, who, as head of the police, was visiting the prison. In defiance of law, Trépoff ordered him to be flogged. A young girl, Vera Zasúlich, who did not know Bogolyúboff, sought an interview with Trépoff, fired at him, threw her revolver on the ground, and surrendered herself (February 5, 1878). The Minister of Justice recommended a trial with a jury; the defence disclosed other arbitrary proceedings of the police, and the jury acquitted the prisoner. The police attempted to rearrest her, but she was rescued by the crowd outside the Court, and passed over the frontier. The censorship allowed full discussion of the trial, and after it even some men of moderate opinions altered their view of terrorism. The terrorists gained confidence, and the effective work of the revived society "Land and Liberty," which aimed specially at "disorganising" the Government, dates from this time. Spies were the easiest prey, and murders were committed in Rostóff, Odessa, Moscow, and Kieff. One hundred and fifty students were expelled from Kieff University, and their passage through Moscow provoked a students' demonstration and violent police measures.

The revolutionaries had now succeeded in printing their papers in Russia, and this facilitated the stricter organisation of their authority, which was chiefly the work of Alexander Mikhailoff. In Kieff the chief mover was the high-strung and moody Osinsky, styled "the empirical creator of terrorism"; but he found more than his match in the versatile police officer Sudéikin. In August the head of the Third Section of the police, General Mézentseff, was killed in broad daylight in one of the central squares of St Petersburg, and the murderer, Kravchinsky (Stepniak), not only escaped but was able to circulate his printed justification of the deed. All political cases had by this time been removed from the cognisance of juries: they were now handed over to Courts-martial. Most of the ten members of "Land and Liberty" in St Petersburg were arrested; but Mikhailoff soon restored the organisation.

The Courts-martial were accompanied by an appeal from the Emperor to his people. It was not long unanswered. The Zemstva, as the only official elective institutions in Russia, could claim a special authority. Since 1870 there had been occasional meetings of Zemstvo Liberals. In 1878 they held a conference at Kieff, to which they invited several prominent revolutionaries. These they urged to desist from terrorism; meanwhile, the Zemstva would ask the Emperor to restore local government, the law Courts, and the Press, to the same condition as before the reaction, and also to summon representatives from every Zemstvo to St Petersburg. No promise was given; but terrorism did in fact cease, and some revolutionaries joined the Liberals in a "League of Oppositional Elements." Some ten Zemstva sent answers to the Emperor's appeal. The most notable address was that submitted to the Zemstvo of Chernígoff. It threw a searching light on the evils that were sapping Russian loyalty. "The struggle with destructive ideas," it said, "would be possible only if the public possessed its own weapons—freedom of speech and of the Press, of opinion and of instruction." Its author, Petrunkévich, was exiled to Kostromá (1879), and afterwards was allowed to buy an estate in Tver, where he became one of the central figures of a later Liberal movement. A similar address was drawn up at Tver. Liberal demonstrations in St Petersburg called forth a strong expression of displeasure from the Emperor. The wholesale arrests continued: there were strikes and street conflicts in St Petersburg. In February, 1879, Prince Kropotkin, Governor of Kharkoff, was shot down by the hysterical Goldenberg, who afterwards betrayed his colleagues. In March Mirsky fired at General Drenteln, the successor of Mézentseff. In April Solovyéff fired five shots at the Emperor, without effect. To meet the emergency, the Government divided Russia into six districts, each under a Governor-General with full powers. Gurko in St Petersburg, Totleben in Odessa, and Chertkoff in Kieff, arrested and exiled wholesale; passports were rigorously examined, and the whole population of the capital was subjected to the espionage of the concierges. The Government had been very slow to apply the death penalty, but armed resistance was now punished with death; Osinsky was hanged for this in Kieff.

The revolutionary movement was now avowedly controlled by "Land and Liberty"; the central Society had provincial branches both in town and country, notably on the lower Volga. It was joined by the artisan Khaltúrin, who had been vainly trying to organise a "Northern Union of Workmen"; and the peasantry were represented by a youth of singular daring and feverish activity, the ex-student Zhelyáboff. This was a typical "man of mixed class," who combined peasant vigour and devotion with the abnormal half-educated intelligence of the new generation. For such men the pace was too slow; but many of his comrades were doctrinaire socialists who reprobated terrorism. In June, 1879, Zhelyáboff and fourteen of his associates resolved to form an inner circle called "The Will of the People" to carry through the revolution by terrorism, retaining if possible the wider organisation, as representing those vague socialistic principles which were common to all the revolutionaries. The sense of the general meeting was against terrorism, but henceforth " Land and Liberty " disappeared as a whole.

The "Will of the People" remained as a small self-appointed committee; and from the peaceful majority was formed a new body called "the party of the Black Partition" (*i.e.* partition of property), which eschewed both politics and terrorism, and aimed at achieving a distant social revolution by propaganda alone. The separation was friendly, and the organ of the Black Partition was at one time printed at the secret press of the " Will of the People." The split followed the lines of division previously noticed. The " Black Partition " were the Lavróff propagandists of the past and the Social Democrats of the future. The "Will of the People" now consisted of the Bakúnin insurrectionists organised on Jacobin lines, who later became the Socialist Revolutionaries. Plekhánoff, Stefanóvich, and other experienced revolutionaries headed the " Black Partition "; the younger and more vigorous leaders joined the " Will of the People." They were men of action as opposed to the thinkers, and they received the larger share of the passive sympathy accorded by the public.

The "Will of the People," as Sophia Perovsky and many of its members knew, broke the sequence of the Russian revolution. Not only did it commit the revolutionaries to a hopeless struggle of force against the Government, but even in case of victory it was certain that no national assembly would adopt their ill-conceived ideas. But this only made their activity more desperate and feverish. They were acting " for the good of the people"; but the people looked on, and only individuals gave passing help. The few conspirators were proscripts, harried by constant fears from one lodging to another. The life was an impossible one; in so small a number every arrest made a sensible gap, and even Zhelyáboff could see that terrorism was using itself up.

The conspirators at once organised a hunt after the life of the Emperor. They had their own mining experts; Kibálchich possessed an unusual knowledge of explosives. In the summer of 1879 fifty persons worked at the construction of three mines at Odessa, Alexandrovsk, and Moscow. The Emperor's train was to be destroyed on the road from Livadia; but the mine at Alexandrovsk failed to explode, and that at Moscow destroyed the wrong train. In January the Society's press was tracked down, but those in charge defended it long enough to enable them to destroy all compromising papers. Khaltúrin next obtained work as an enameller at the Winter Palace, mapped out the rooms, and with remarkable patience and boldness worked daily at a mine two stories below the Emperor's dining room. A plan of the Palace was found on an accomplice, and stricter guard was kept within its walls; but the dynamite hidden under Khaltúrin's pillow was not discovered. On February 17, 1880, he fired his mine: ten soldiers were killed and fifty-three wounded; but, owing to a fortunate delay, the Emperor was not in the dining room. Khaltúrin escaped, to suffer for another crime under another name in 1882.

Under the existing system, the destinies of Russia depended on the mood produced in a few leading individuals, and especially in one. The ruthless crime at the Winter Palace had different results from its predecessors. The Liberal movement was still strong in the Zemstva; and in January the opportunist Valúyeff suggested that the public should be allowed to take a larger share in business of State. Meanwhile, a Supreme Disposing Commission was established to deal with revolution, whose head, General Loris-Melikoff, was invested with dictatorial powers over other Ministers and all the resources of the State. Melikoff had commanded a Russian army in the late war, and had been disgusted by the disorganisation and peculation which he had witnessed. As Governor-General of Kharkoff, he had applied his extraordinary powers with wisdom and clemency. He had much moral courage and a strong sense of order, and his views were those of a liberal-minded official. He was hostile to any kind of national assembly, and to any concession that might be attributed to fear or even to public criticism; but he desired that local self-government should be developed, and that the law-abiding population should not suffer from measures directed against the revolutionaries. He appealed for its support as "the chief force that could help the Government to restore the regular course of public life." These words met with a grateful hearing, and Melikoff's rule is known as "the dictatorship of the heart."

Four programmes were before the public. The Slavophil scheme, as elaborated by Koshéleff, was as follows.   Autocracy must remain unimpaired; but, as the autocrat cannot know everything, he must be kept in touch with his people by a permanent consultative assembly, elected by the Zemstva and dealing with all new legislation, including the budget.   The Liberal " League of Oppositional Elements," founded in the south, had become the Zemstvo Union; its programme, published so late as 1882, claimed freedom of person, conscience, speech, and association, local elective law Courts, the right to prosecute officials, and a new system of local government, freed from the class basis and the limitations imposed on the subject nationalities; it suggested an Imperial Duma, with direct control of the administration, and also a Federal Duma, elected by the assemblies of the enlarged areas into which it proposed to divide the empire; this scheme, which was the germ of the future " Cadet" programme, would have established parliamentary government and decentralisation.   Thirdly, radicals and revolutionaries demanded a Constituent Assembly.   A fourth suggestion, originating with a small group of officials, was limited to the introduction of delegates from the Zemstva and town councils into the existing Council of State.

Moderate representations were received by Melikoff from various cities and Zemstva (1880).   No utopian theories were put forward, and the terms chosen showed remarkable restraint.   Terrorism was described as " the madness of a few individuals," and gratitude was expressed for the first measures of the dictatorship.

Loris-Melikoff, though he had almost at once to stand fire from the revolutionary Mlodetsky, carried out his ideas without perturbation. He freed the Zemstva from some vexatious restrictions and sent four Senators to report on the working of the existing Zemstvo law.   After consulting with editors and leaders of thought, he allowed to the Press a measure of liberty; and a Commission was appointed to revise the Press Law.   An immediate outburst of journalistic activity ensued. Aksákoff could now express his strong Slavophilism in the *Rus*; and the *Voice*, the *Zemstvo*, the *Country*, and *Order* gave utterance to more Liberal opinion.   The Courts-martial and Governors-General were retained; but repression became more discriminating, and many prisoners who had never been brought to trial were set free.   The irresponsible " Third Section" (political police) was made a branch of the Police Department of the Ministry of the Interior, under the direction of Plehve.   Besides all this, there were important changes in the *personnel* of the Ministry.   Count Dmitry Tolstóy was dismissed amidst general rejoicings; Pahlen had already been replaced by Nabókoff as Minister of Justice; Greg, the discredited Finance Minister, gave way to a Liberal, Abaza; and a more pronounced Liberal, Sabúroff, became Minister of Public Instruction.   After six months of work, the Supreme Disposing Commission was dissolved, and the dictator became Minister of the Interior, with something like the powers of a Prime Minister.

CH. XII.

The almost universal demand for some kind of Constitution had still to be met. Melikoff licensed joint-meetings between various Zemstva; he referred for their decision the revision of laws on the peasants; and on February 9, 1881, he laid before the Emperor a report embodying his views. He had previously taken pains to repudiate the ideas of both Slavophils and Liberals: he now urged that the reforms of the reign should be completed, and that for this purpose the opinions of local men should be heard. The ancient *Zemsky Sobór* of the Románoffs, recommended by the Slavophils, he rejected as out of date, and the imperial Duma of the Liberals as exotic; but further means were to be devised for consulting the people. The projected reforms were to be prepared by the Government from materials collected by it and submitted to drafting Commissions in the autumn. Their conclusions should then be debated by a General Commission, consisting of members and a president nominated by the Emperor, with elected delegates from the Zemstva and chief towns. The powers of this Commission were to be strictly consultative; and its conclusions, with the comments of the Minister concerned, would come before the Council of State for further discussion.

Melikoff's proposals did not err on the side of boldness; and the Emperor, after some hesitation, on March 13, before starting for the Michael Riding School, returned Melikoff's draft with his approval, and desired that it should be read to the Council of Ministers on March 26. At the Riding School he said to his wife, "I have just signed a paper which will, I hope, make a good impression and show Russia that I grant her everything that is possible."

It was all that was possible for himself—more perhaps than could have been expected; for in Russia the greatest social reforms come easier to the sovereign than very small political concessions. The peasants would have received it with indifference, the gentry with tempered gratitude, the revolutionaries with derision. The "Will of the People" now possessed twelve local branches, with special sub-committees for propaganda amongst officers, students, and workmen, for Press work, and for the manufacture of explosives. The actual members were about five hundred; and the more determined were divided into fighting bands of some ten persons each. In February, Zhelyáboff picked his volunteers; Kibálchich gave lessons in the handling and throwing of bombs, Bogdanóvich undermined the Little Sadóvaya, and Zhelyáboff the Stone Bridge. On March 13, 1881, six bomb-throwers were at their posts, awaiting the signal from Sophia Perovsky. The Emperor, after visiting the Michael Riding School, was driving down the deserted Catharine Canal, when a boy of nineteen, Rysakóff, threw a bomb which killed many of his escort. Alexander dismounted to attend to the wounded, and walked fearlessly down the street towards the assassin. "What, that one?" he asked, "why, he's nice-looking." He had hardly turned back when another conspirator, Grinevetsky, threw a second bomb, which tore all the lower part of his body to pieces; he was able to whisper, "Home quick...take me to the palace, to die there"; he reached the palace unconscious, and died the same afternoon.

Zhelyáboff, already arrested and in a neighbouring prison, openly showed his joy at the sound of the explosions; but the monstrous act was the deathblow to his party. The chief danger—the very general passive sympathy with the revolutionaries—was removed. Propagandist work among the peasants became almost impossible, and the leaders of the "Black Partition" soon crossed the frontier. The police could now deal with the terrorists; and Plehve soon succeeded in capturing nearly all the conspirators. The terrorist organ boasted of the execution of the death sentence, and a letter was even sent to Alexander III proposing terms of peace. Threats of further vengeance were printed during the trial of the ringleaders; but five, including Zhelyáboff, Perovsky, and Kibálchich, were condemned and hanged. The ranks of the terrorist organisation were thinned past refilling (March, 1881, to February, 1883). Fresh plots were concerted, the most notable being that of Vera Figner, for the occasion of the new Emperor's coronation in May, 1883; they led to the formation of a patriotic league to protect the sovereign's life, and the ceremony passed without accident. The last notable murder was that of Sudéikin, Chief of the Detective Department, in December, 1883. He had entered into relations with the terrorist Degáyeff which enabled him to lay hands on Vera Figner. Degáyeff escaped to Geneva, but was compelled by his associates to return to Russia and kill Sudéikin. A final attempt to revive the terrorist organisation was made by the bold and resourceful conspirator Lopatin, who was arrested in St Petersburg in 1884.

Though the project of the General Commission had not been published it had become known, and many references to it were introduced into the addresses from the Zemstva to the new Emperor. They all strongly condemned sedition; but all agreed that the real remedy lay in the personal contact of the sovereign with his people. The Liberal Press spoke in a similar sense; but Slavophils, such as Aksákoff, while still bent on their own combination of autocracy with a national assembly, used all their influence on the side of authority, and the semi-official Katkóff went still further. Memoranda were sent in by persons who had ties with the official world, and Melikoff at this time received three—from Gradovsky, from the Pole Vielopolski, and from Chichérin—each paying its due to the panic of the time. Gradovsky recommended a national assembly, "to identify the causes of disorder." Vielopolski's note condemned constitutional aspirations as a disease, but also condemned centralisation, and advised the extension of the Zemstvo system to his own fellow-countrymen. Chichérin, while denouncing even the constitutionalists as a band of rebels, urged the execution of Melikoff's scheme, or the submission of all legislative projects to selected experts.

CH. XII.

Alexander III, with whom the decision rested, was a personality in the very strongest contrast with the nervous spirit of the time. He had immense physical strength, was slow and easygoing, and had a great reserve of will-power. His mental limits were narrow; he was no thinker, but he knew his own mind. Not at first destined for the throne, he went much his own way in the matter of education. His tastes remained those of a military Grand Duke, and his manners and habits were those of a simple country gentleman. He was extraordinarily obstinate and had violent outbursts of temper; but, after a somewhat wild and profitless youth, he became a model husband and father; he was absolutely honest and had the highest sense of duty; in spite of all his strength, the Crown was for him an immense burden. His extreme shyness imparted to the Court a narrower and duller atmosphere during his reign; but the intrigues which were natural to such conditions were well controlled, and there was always a master who could keep everyone in his place.

It is believed that he at first intended to issue Loris-Melikoff's project as the last testament of his father; anyhow, the Minister made an announcement to this effect on March 17. Three days later, the Emperor called together a special conference; nine Ministers were for publishing the project, and five members, specially invited, were against it. While the Ministers were still discussing, an imperial manifesto had already been drafted by Alexander's former tutor, Pobyedonóstseff. It appeared on March 23. "The Voice of God," it said, "orders us to stand firm at the helm of government...with faith in the strength and truth of the autocratic power, which we are called to strengthen and preserve, for the good of the people, from every kind of encroachment."

Full reaction did not set in at once. Melikoff resigned, and Abaza, Milyútin, and Sabúroff followed him; though Nabókoff stayed on to be superseded later, Melikoff may be said to have replied to his adversaries with the first declaration of Cabinet solidarity. The new Ministry was also more or less homogeneous: it represented the Slavophil formula of autocracy, coupled with local self-government and Chichérin's principle of consultation with experts. In this there was nothing inconsistent with autocracy, since the experts were not representative and were chosen by the Government. Count Ignatyeff became Minister of the Interior, and issued a circular which censured the bureaucracy and declared that the reforms of Alexander II would be developed with the aid of local men. But distrust of the representative principle implied distrust of public opinion and of the Press. The *Russian Courier* was stopped for four months and the Liberal *Voice* for six, and an attempt to replace the latter by the *New Gazette* was at once crushed. In a word, the time of free expression of opinion was ended.

A majority of the Zemstva declared themselves against the expert principle in legislation. Ignatyeff applied it in the important Commission of Kakhánoff, which was appointed to revise the system of local government, and in an enquiry into the reduction of the peasants' redemption dues. But it was clearly shown that the summoning of a few picked experts was no substitute for the proposals of Melikoff; and, though adverse resolutions were repressed by the Governors, twelve Zemstva petitioned for the right of electing the men who should represent the public. The general opinion was unmistakable. The Slavophils continued to urge their old scheme of a revival of the ancient *Zemsky Sobór*. Their plan, as elaborated by Golokhvástoff, excluded all constitutionalism, imitation of the West, or restriction of the autocracy. An assembly, chosen by each class separately, would meet the autocrat, to be harangued on the sanctity of property, on loans to peasants and redemption dues, and on the diminution of drunkenness; later, a Congress might discuss local government. Ignatyeff, supported by General Skobeleff, favoured some such scheme; he was strongly opposed by Katkóff, Tolstóy, and Pobyedonóstseff. But the Emperor was tired of the whole question of reform, and by May, 1882, the struggle was over. Tolstóy succeeded Ignatyeff as Minister of the Interior, and reaction triumphed for twenty-two years.

Tolstóy remained Minister till his death in 1889, and his traditions were continued by his successor, I. Durnovó, a routine official, to 1895. On Prince Gorchakóff's death in 1882, Giers obtained the Foreign Ministry in preference to Ignatyeff, and held the post till 1892. Pobyedonóstseff continued to be Procurator of the Holy Synod till 1905.

The Government was now quite cut off from the people. It was taken for granted that each office-holder was the executor of commands from above; that each was chosen, not so much for any opinion which he might represent, as for his supposed ability to do a certain definite piece of work to order; that the monopoly of criticism was vested in his superiors, and, finally, in the sovereign. In principle, there was complete centralisation; but it was quite impossible for the Emperor to read a tithe of the reports for which he had the ultimate responsibility. The empire was vast, and it was growing; but private initiative was suspect as such, and official action was governed by telegraph from a far corner of Russia. The repression of all criticism made official arrogance inevitable; a more serious danger was the general lack of training in common sense, presence of mind, and personal responsibility. The public silence also inevitably entailed an atmosphere of intrigue. The worst effects of the system were not to be felt till the death of Alexander III.

It was Pobyedonóstseff who supplied this system of government with a formulated creed. He was a man of fine intelligence and a first-class jurist; he won the confidence of three Emperors; he had conviction, and he was plain-spoken. A thorough despiser of human nature, he turned reaction into a system of philosophy. According to him, modern

Europe was a solemn warning to unspoilt Russia. Parliaments were nothing but nests of the most selfish and sordid ambitions; the Press existed chiefly to disseminate falsehood; instruction was dangerous in itself; trial by jury was simply a field for the "arts of casuistry." Law was no substitute for absolute power: it was "a vain fancy." Practically, the most important of real forces was "inertia." Pobyedonóstseff's gospel was autocracy and an official Church; but, though he was an almost inspired talker, the positive side of his creed remained extremely vague, and in the end he must be classed as the doctrinaire nihilist of officialism. His long administration of the Church brought it into direct conflict with all ideals of enlightenment, and turned the theocratic power into the weapon of a political clique. The monastic caste, though markedly inferior in intelligence to the parish clergy, became more predominant over it. Timeserving was at a premium, and the clergy were more and more cut off from their parishioners.

The strictly political side of the same doctrine was developed by Pázhukin (1885). He saw salvation in the system of close compartments for each separate class: the patriarchal landlord directing the peasant's life and thought, the peasant carefully isolated from all outside influences; while all the reforms of Alexander II, except the Emancipation, were condemned as sinning against these canons. "A Zemstvo elected without a class basis means all, and all means no one." The new law Courts were "filled with persons who had no ties with the locality." Katkóff gave his last energies to anticipating or explaining the wishes of the new rulers (to 1887), and his successor, Gringmuth, continued till 1907 to hound the public against Zemstva, students, Jews, and Englishmen. Suvórin's *Novoë Vremya*, conducted with consummate tact, continued to be an admirable register of the breezes of court favour.

Melikoff's Press Commission had lapsed on his downfall; and journalists remained till the end of the century under the harrow of Tolstóy's special ordinance of 1882. Papers which had received a third warning could only be continued under the preliminary censorship. A council of four Ministers could stop any periodical without warning and forbid the editor to engage again in any similar enterprise. From 1882 to 1889 fourteen papers were stopped, and upwards of sixty were warned, deprived of their street sale, or forbidden to print advertisements. Before Tolstóy's death very few papers remained, and these were thoroughly cowed; nevertheless, the warnings, stoppages, and prohibitions under his successors continued. A new growth of public interest produced a number of periodicals—the *Russian Review* (1890), *God's World* (1892), and the *New Word* (1894)—and revived others, such as the *Wealth of Russia* and the *Russian Gazette*. All the papers were lowering their prices and increasing their circulation. But fresh barriers were erected; and from 1896 newspapers were only licensed temporarily, so that they could be crushed without explanation. Sipyágin's hand was less heavy

(1899–1902); but Plehve (1902–4) was prodigal of measures of repression. Prince Úkhtomsky, a strong Conservative and personal friend of the Emperor, suffered for publishing the fact—attested by the Zemstvo President, Count Bóbrinsky—that the Governor of Tula was concealing the existence of a famine in his province. Such was the practical application of the paradoxes of Pobyedonóstseff. This system was continued till Plehve's death in 1904.

The Press being thus muzzled, the inevitable protest came from the students of the Universities, who were being taught the lesson that learning can only be free in a free State. Their grievances were not primarily political; and, indeed, the revolutionary organisations were themselves for a long time quiescent or ineffective. The students claimed independence for the Universities as learned institutions, the abolition of the system which shut up the different faculties in close compartments, and the right of association for the support of their poorer comrades and for the maintenance of the code of student honour. In 1882 there were disturbances and protests from the students of Kazán and St Petersburg; and two years later Delyánoff introduced the new University Statute, which destroyed the reforms of Golovnín. After further protests from the five chief Universities (1887), the powers of the official inspectors were enlarged, and new class limitations restricted the admission of students. One new University was founded; but the Government showed a predilection for modern High Schools, of which many were established under Alexander III and Nicholas II. It hoped to put a premium upon "useful knowledge"; but the men turned out by these institutions were as radical as the rest. In 1899, a very general strike of students led to the closing of the Universities. Bogolyépoff, who had succeeded Delyánoff, introduced new "temporary rules" restricting students' associations; and many of the protesting students were sent to serve as privates in the army. Bogolyépoff was killed by the student Karpóvich. Enquiries were instituted, with no result. In 1904 the repression was worse than ever, and the protests were more frequent. Professors, like Paul Vinográdoff, who in these years sought at once to restrain the students and to draw attention to abuses, suffered for any display of independence. The more vigorous students threw themselves into the socialist propaganda among the working men. The higher teaching of women was greatly developed during this period. Attempts were also made to organise home reading and university extension lectures; but here again the Government took fright; manuscripts had to be sent in, and any deviation might bring punishment; Milyukóff, one of the ablest lecturers, was banished to Ryazán; the movement was extinguished in 1902. Police discipline and Tolstóy's block system still reigned in the secondary schools, but a few exceptional peasants were able to surmount its barriers. In the Zemstvo schools the power of the inspectors was absolute whenever asserted, and many a schoolmaster was driven from his post. A number of church schools were founded; but the average priest was so ill-qualified for educational work that Pobyedonóstseff's attempt to place primary education under clerical control was abandoned. The Government, however, was not altogether regardless of education; it established several well staffed primary schools, training colleges for teachers, and special schools under the Ministries of Finance and Communications.

The law Courts had lost all the guarantees of independence before 1882. The Minister of Justice, Manasséin, was hostile to the spirit of the new institutions. In 1887, though supported only by a minority in the Council of State, he obtained power to close the Courts to the public at his own discretion. The lists of jurymen were further revised, persons of small property being excluded; in 1889 class representatives nominated by the Government replaced the juries in whole categories of cases. The next blow was aimed at the very foundation of the new system. The elected Justices of the Peace, who presided in the local Courts, had done their work well; but they were in touch with the Zemstva, and Pázhukin desired to replace them by a new class of nominated officials, called Land Captains, who should combine with their judicial duties the supervision of the peasants as a class. Pázhukin was put at the head of the chancellery of the Ministry of the Interior and brought forward his scheme, which, in spite of the opposition of Manasséin and of the majority in the Council of State, was adopted by Alexander III.

The Land Captains were nominated, not by the Minister of Justice, but by the Minister of the Interior; they had no legal training; the ideal set before them was not law but common sense; and their duties were so extensive as to include interference in quarrels between man and wife. As belonging to the administrative system, they had a discretionary power of imprisonment without form of law. Even in the towns judges of lower official standing, removable at pleasure, replaced the Justices of the Peace. The independence of the judges grew less and less, and, from the Senate and higher Courts down to the Land Captains, the administration of the law was varying, contradictory, and extremely dilatory. The exemption of all officials from trial without permission of their superiors remained as an established principle; and conditions of life were often in fact determined by the Code of exceptional ordinances, drafted by Plehve in 1881, which regulated the application of a state of siege. Thus the life of the great reforms was crushed under a heap of circulars, ordinances, and regulations, nominally temporary but far more permanent than the laws which they modified; and their governing assumption was that the commonplaces of civilised Europe were false when applied to Russia.

The war against the Intelligence naturally lasted longest in these three fields—the Press, the Universities, and the law Courts. The period of idealism and aspiration came to an abrupt end with the murder of Alexander II. Educated Russian society was prostrated. There was a strong revulsion of educated opinion, not only against the revolutionaries, but also against every importation of Western innovations. "It is time to go home," said the Slavophils. But when Ignatyeff fell and the Slavophils themselves were suspect, the moral reaction gave place to sheer apathy and the pursuit of purely selfish interests. Meanwhile Leo Tolstóy cuts himself off from the world to live the life of self-perfection. Others preach that man exists for art. Chékhoff, who has been styled "the poet of the twilight," finds his whole epoch monstrous and ridiculous: "men only eat, drink, sleep, and die." Yet it is the same man who writes: "Our Russia is rich with every variety of life; I am sure that we are on the eve of something great." His time is indeed a turning-point. The theorists of both political extremes had ignored one possibility, namely, that Russia, like other countries, might pass through the stage of capitalism. This development was already upon them; it raised economic questions of the first magnitude which could only be solved by common sense; and the days of both the extreme doctrines were already numbered.

Even the peasants, the pet playthings of both parties, so far from being born socialists or born reactionaries, had in them the makings of a petty *bourgeoisie*; to the manipulation of all their superiors they opposed a shrewd attitude of "non-committal." They were the vast background of the population; and it was gradually recognised that their economic future was a question which challenged the very existence of the State.

Loris-Melikoff, in one of his first reports, had roundly condemned "the immobility in peasant reform." The financial aspects of the question were ably handled by the Finance Minister Bunge (1881–7). He found that the Government had gained by the terms on which it had paid off the landlords at the Emancipation; and he diminished by 12,000,000 *roubles* the redemption dues in Great and Little Russia, inviting the Zemstva to allot the relief. Still larger reductions were granted in 1885; and, though the arrears were more than 12,000,000 *roubles*, the Government still gained. In 1885–6 the poll-tax was removed; but at the price of new burdens on the Crown peasants. Meanwhile the payments of the "landless peasants" were lightened. Bunge also tried to improve the collection of the revenue, and in 1881 he joined the Ministers Ignatyeff and Ostrovsky in their attempts to aid the peasants to acquire more land. For this purpose was founded the Peasants' Bank, at first designed to help the more needy to get level with their neighbours and therefore offering help only on condition of special distress, but afterwards applied to the creation of private holdings in general. The Bank had an income of only some £500,000 a year, and for some years it did considerably less in transferring land to the peasants than the peasants had done for themselves. In 1885, under the influence of other ideas, there was founded a Land Bank for the gentry, who were rapidly selling off their estates in consequence of the depression of agriculture in general. With this Bank was incorporated in 1890 the Mutual Land Loan Society, founded in 1866. Peasants' Bank and Gentry Bank worked side by side, with separate staffs, but in the same buildings; they represented two different sides of one and the same operation; and, certainly, in the transference of land the gentry received the greater consideration.

The third question with which Bunge dealt was the spontaneous and irregular migration of peasants. It had gone on for over fifty years; and, though legally permission was necessary, 40,000 persons dispensed with it each year between 1876 and 1881; as was to be expected, many of them failed to find new homes. A new system of licensing these migrants was established and worked successfully (1881). Starting from the principle that migration was normal and necessary, a Commission proposed to put it partially under the control of the Zemstva; but their work was cut short by Count Tolstóy's accession to power. Tolstóy's Law of July, 1889, contained an empty threat of bringing back those who had migrated without license; but it freed those who were licensed from military service and from Crown taxes for a term of years. It also helped them to acquire land in Siberia, and even in Europe; but the communal system and the antiquated mutual guarantee of the local taxes were retained in the new settlements. With or without this Law, some 400,000 persons migrated to Siberia between 1887 and 1894, mostly from south Russia.

Loris-Melikoff, in one of his first reports, had planned a reform of peasant administration. After more than two years of work, a complete scheme was presented by the important Commission of Kakhánoff. The existing commune was to be superseded as an administrative unit by a kind of parish council of all classes; the canton was to become a simple territorial unit without distinction of class, with a chief appointed by the District Zemstvo; a Court for all classes was to be set up under the Justice of the Peace. For many years public opinion in Russia had been practically unanimous in favour of these changes; but, on the accession of Tolstóy to power, the Commission was first diluted with new nominated members and then dissolved (1886), and Pázhukin was instructed to draw up a new plan. Pázhukin's Land Captains, bad as judges, were even worse as administrative officials. They could revise the programme of any communal or cantonal meeting and refuse to confirm any election. They could punish without appeal any elected officer of commune or canton. They had control over the reserves of corn, and even the divisions of family property were under their supervision. They were, from the first, quite unfit for the dictatorial powers which they wielded, and they steadily deteriorated. They were not local patriarchs but officials of the central machine; and for the peasants they represented the beginning of that policy of suspicion which had been already practised with such ruinous effect on the educated classes. No officials were in greater odium; and later the word Land Captain summed up the popular hatred for the reactionary system of government. By a Law of 1886 a labourer's breach of contract became a criminal, instead of a civil, offence. By the Law of December 26, 1893, a later development of the system of Tolstóy and Pázhukin, the sale of communal land was placed under official control; the non-communal land acquired by individual peasants could only be sold to members of the same commune, and thus an unnatural check was placed on the acquisition of private property. This measure was popular with some enemies of the Government, because it bolstered up the commune and favoured socialism; but it was perhaps the greatest legislative mistake of the period. In 1893, the periodical redivisions of holdings by the commune were placed under the Land Captains.

A similar reactionary spirit inspired the important Zemstvo Law, which was issued, despite opposition within the Government, in 1890. Control by the Governors was drawn closer, especially in respect of the local budgets; class distinctions were emphasised; the franchise of the gentry was raised; the number of peasant members was reduced, and they were to be chosen by the Governor from a list of successful candidates. The Land Captains were made members *ex officio*, and the so-called " third element "—that is, doctors, schoolmasters, etc., in the service of the Zemstva—was excluded altogether. Even thus emasculated, the Zemstva remained the strongest champions of reform. In 1900, Zemstva were forbidden to raise their budgets by more than 3 per cent. every year—a purely mechanical arrangement which often delayed the satisfaction of local needs.

Railway and factory development had been the chief task of Reutern, Finance Minister under Alexander II. Bunge was called upon to deal with the depression of trade which succeeded the speculative activity of the mid-seventies (1880–7). Wages fell, or if nominally maintained were diminished by arbitrary and extravagant fines. This led to great strikes, such as that of 2000 men in Moscow. In St Petersburg many factories dismissed half their hands; in Chernígoff and Kostromá, two-thirds. In Vladímir nearly two-thirds of the silk factories stopped work. Thousands of discharged workmen were returning to their native villages. Cottage industries were dying out; and Russia could not revert to purely agricultural conditions. The crisis drew attention to the needs of the new race of factory workers. The Moscow employers, enjoying a superfluity of labour and still working under semi-patriarchal conditions, feared factory reform and had so far succeeded in shelving it; but those of St Petersburg, who were largely foreigners, had to create their own labour supply and favoured a system of efficient labour and higher pay, with shorter hours, and no stoppage of work. Moscow stood out for what it called "the freedom of the people's labour"; but Bunge obtained sanction (1882) for a Law forbidding child labour and the night-work of persons under 21. Factory inspectors were appointed to carry out the Law; they met with constant opposition in the Moscow district; their reports revealed that the hours sometimes amounted to 18, and children of three were found working with their mothers; the system of fines was quite arbitrary and monstrously exorbitant; most workers slept in the working rooms; the employers made large sums out of the workmen by the factory shops. In June, 1884, the schooling of factory lads was safeguarded. On June 15, 1886, was issued a new Factory Act which owed much to the initiative of Count Dmitry Tolstóy. The Law enumerated the legitimate causes for dismissal and for leaving work; strikes were made criminal; and leadership in a strike became a specially grave offence. The factory inspectors received far more power; they were to revise all rules of factories, the engagement of workmen, the tariffs of factory shops, and the imposition of fines. They were to mediate in all disputes and prosecute for any infringement of the law. They were backed by Factory Committees under the local Governor, which could issue any special regulations as to housing and medical attendance.

It was a sincere attempt of the bureaucracy to secure material advantages for the workman; in insurance, for instance, it was so favourable to him as to be unfair to the employer; but both were denied the right of looking after their own interests, and the new law was resented by both. The protests of Moscow drove Bunge from office, and his successor, Vishnegradsky (1887–92), had to relax the law in favour of the employer (1890). The inspectors discovered all sorts of artifices for evading the payment of workmen; and in some places disorders ensued which caused the interference of troops.

The principles of paternal government were now to be tested by a phenomenal growth of Russian industry. Commercial activity rose in 1887; from 1895 it developed with prodigious rapidity. When the Catharine Railway united the south Russian coal to iron, factories began to spring up like mushrooms; by 1899 there were seventeen huge factories in the Donets district, only two of which worked on Russian capital. Enormous dividends were sent abroad; the price of land where there was coal increased threefold; the railways and ports were unable to deal with the traffic. In two years (1895–7) the face of south Russia was entirely changed. Between 1886 and 1899 the national output of iron was more than quadrupled, till it exceeded that of France. The number of workmen and the value of all goods increased rapidly from 1887 to 1893; and between 1893 and 1897 the former was nearly doubled and the latter tripled. Other trades developed only less rapidly. The workers in threads increased from 400,000 in 1887 to 643,000 in 1897.

Knoop developed an extraordinarily successful business which might almost be called a dictatorship of the cotton trade ; clients secured from him factories ready made and ready staffed, often without being allowed any voice in the plans ; England was Knoop's chief supplier. It was only later that large Russian capitalists began to learn from the object lesson going on before their eyes ; and even then a comfortable share in the new development remained with the foreigner. All this movement was in close connexion with European trade ; for it was the presence of large sums in Western Banks that brought capital into Russia. In the nineties the St Petersburg Exchange was still a desert ; from 1893 it was crowded with carriages, and later reactions did not stop the growth of activity. Companies were started almost entirely on credit, which, as we shall see, was greatly facilitated by the Government ; but the inevitable crash of 1899 and the subsequent war and troubles at home, if they were fatal to individual houses, left the general trade still progressing. The factory operatives increased in ten years (1887–97) from $1\frac{1}{4}$ millions to 2 millions and now exceed 3 millions ; minor trades are not reckoned in these figures. Russia found by experience that she had new and lucrative markets to develop at home ; the immense resources of the country—particularly of the Caucasus (naphtha), Central Asia (cotton), and Siberia (corn, farm products, and minerals)—are well known. In his last book (*For the Knowledge of Russia*, 1907), the Conservative patriot Mendeléyeff gives abundant proof that Russia has passed for good or evil into the capitalist period, and that any theoretical bolstering up of agriculture against industry will be fatal even to agriculture itself. The patriarchal isolators of the peasants have had their day, whether they be reactionaries or revolutionaries ; the development of civilisation in Russia is destined to resemble that of Western Europe.

Russia was always like a big family ; there was a deep solidarity between the artisan and peasant population ; and it was ominous that these years of exceptional industrial prosperity should have been a time of severe agricultural distress. It is common for some part of the country to be "under famine" ; but the famines of 1891–3 were nothing less than a national calamity. Twenty provinces suffered in the first two years, including the chief grain-producing districts ; there were no adequate reserves of corn, and the peasants were threatened with extinction. The population had been growing fast ; the divided and subdivided holdings were too poor to support cattle or horses ; and the fields were only half tilled and manured. Some had to find unnatural substitutes for bread ; some ate the straw roofs of their empty barns ; scurvy and typhus became rampant : the feeblest workers would lie for days on their stomachs to save the scanty store for the others. The dilatory and suspicious Government was compelled to alter its policy, and permit professional men and even students to engage, like its own officials, in the work of relief. This was just the tonic which the Russian

Intelligence required; it revived in a much more practical form the missionary ardour of the seventies; and young men streamed into the country to serve as schoolmasters and doctors. The work was an education, and the service of the Zemstva offered a wide field for self-devotion.

With these new factors, began a new and fateful reign (November, 1894). The life of Alexander III had been consistent and complete; he had blocked all outside initiative; he had himself faced the enormous burden of autocracy, and worked—in some cases with effective common sense—at the ordinary business of government. Steps had been taken to safeguard the great wealth represented by the state forests; the army had been put into a much more rational uniform; the navy had been increased. He died doing his duty as he conceived it; but Russia was now rising from a long sleep; and much more was required of his successor. Nicholas II was a man of amiable disposition, weak will, and only moderate ability. As Crown Prince he had travelled in the Far East, had been President of the Trans-Siberian Railway, and had therefore gained acquaintance with the question of emigration; these interests set the tone to the earlier policy of his reign. Since 1891 constitutionalism had again been in the air. Under the direction of Nathanson a group called the "Right of the People" had put forward a general programme of reform, such as might reconcile moderates and radicals. The Zemstva, in their addresses to the Emperor on his accession, were much more modest. Nine Zemstva asked that their representatives should be summoned to share in the drafting of laws. The most notable address was that of Tver. "We trust," it said, "that our happiness will grow and strengthen under an exact observance of the law, not only by the people, but by the officials; for law, which represents in Russia the expression of the will of the Monarch, should stand higher than the chance views of individual officials. We ardently believe that the rights of individuals and of public institutions will be kept unshaken." It suggested that the sovereign would find "a new source of strength in relations with representatives of all classes of the Russian people, which are alike devoted to the throne and to the country." The chief author of this address was the brilliant barrister Rodicheff. The Emperor's reply to the deputations (July 29, 1895) upheld the principles of autocracy and characterised as "senseless dreams" the claim to participate in affairs of internal administration. Rodicheff was excluded from the audience and forbidden to live in St Petersburg, as a special mark of displeasure. Three of the Zemstva withdrew their addresses after this, but Chernígoff stood firm. It declared its loyalty but made its requests still more precise, and enumerated in the clearest terms the chief hindrances to practical reform. There continued to be informal communications between Zemstvo Liberals and occasional private conferences under the guidance of Petrunkévich.

Few changes were made in the Ministry, and behind the scenes there remained the powerful influence of Pobyedonóstseff. But the close of the last reign had been marked by a change of far-reaching importance in the appointment of Witte as Minister of Finance in place of Vishnegradsky. The retiring Minister had sought to foster industry by a protective tariff, and his policy was developed by his successor with great boldness. Witte had raised himself by sheer ability, first to the management of the South-Western Railway, and thence to the Ministry of Ways of Communication. He was little troubled by moral scruples and far too clever to be blind to the gross defects of the bureaucracy; he had made many enemies on his road. But he saw into the future, and during his administration (1892–1903) he set his mark on every part of the financial, industrial, and railway administration, and committed Russia irrevocably to the capitalist system.

Witte's financial policy was definite and drastic, and it was carried through in the face of widespread opposition. A fixed value for Russian money was the first necessity for financial credit; since 1856, both the silver and the paper *rouble* had lost all stability as a medium of exchange; the exchange value varied from 19*d.* to 31*d.* in two years (1888–90). Witte at once proceeded to stop speculation in paper *roubles* on the Berlin exchange by threatening private banks in Russia with the loss of credit from the Imperial Bank (1893); in 1894 he was able to secure a constant standard for the credit *rouble* which was fixed at two-thirds of the old metallic *rouble*; and in 1897 a gold *rouble* equivalent to it in value was adopted as a standard, and permanent restrictions were placed upon the issue of paper *roubles*. It was objected, especially by the party of agriculture, that the increased security of the new system was obtained at too heavy a sacrifice for a country naturally poor; but the change was not only salutary but imperative. Less convincing was the vast increase of the "free balance." By economy combined with heavy taxation, Vishnegradsky had increased the money reserve of the State from 56,000,000 *roubles* in 1886 to 236,000,000 in 1893. In 1901 the gold reserve in the Bank was 648,000,000 *roubles* against a note issue of 630,000,000, and in 1899 the balance had been considerably better; it was urged that excessive power was thus placed in the hands of the Minister of Finance; yet it was Witte who secured for Russia the means and the credit which were to carry her through the Japanese War. Meanwhile, between 1887 and 1901 foreign loans had increased the State indebtedness by a sum computed at 1,853,271,633 *roubles* nominal value, or 942,093,750 *roubles* capitalised at 4 per cent. after numerous conversions. A temporary panic (1887) among German investors was balanced by the readiness of France to lend money to Russia; this eagerness was as much political as financial. German credit has again been utilised, though to a lesser extent, and it is notorious that the finances of Russia have for some time mainly depended on foreign loans.

A vast extension of the system of state monopolies was a prominent feature of Witte's policy. Down to 1889, less than one-fourth of the small railway systems was under direct state control; but Witte as Finance Minister at once set about making the railway service a monopoly of the State. He bought up private lines and made new state railways at a very rapid rate: and in 1900 the State owned more than 60 per cent. of a greatly increased railway system. The profits of these transactions were exaggerated by various manipulations of figures. Down to 1903, it was only in three years (1896, 1898, and 1899) that the State could claim any actual profit from the working of railways, and the deficit of 1900 has been calculated at sixty-one million *roubles*. Since 1900 the Government has had to meet larger and larger deficits, notably in consequence of the expenses of the Siberian Railway and the unsatisfactory management of the Eastern Chinese Railway; in 1903, Witte had to protest against the spending of large sums on lines of purely strategical importance. His protests were justified, but his whole system of railway finance was hazardous; the highest praise that can be awarded to his policy is that by affording facilities of transport it hastened the industrial development of Russia.

The appropriation by the Government of the important spirit monopoly was also carried out by Witte. From 1819 to 1827 there had been such a monopoly; the sale of spirits decreased under it, and the right of sale was then farmed out until 1863, the consumption again increasing. From 1863 to 1894 the sale was thrown open, the State levying an excise; the consumption fluctuated, but the profits of the State increased considerably. In 1885 the number of places of sale was limited, and Alexander III gave instructions for drawing up a plan of state monopoly. His wish was to limit drunkenness: Witte realised his idea in 1894, when the sale of spirits was resumed by the State without any adequate compensation, except in the Baltic provinces, and in Poland.

The measure was, no doubt, in part an attempt to cope with the prevailing vice of drunkenness, but the moral advantages of the change are very doubtful. A great number of illicit dramshops have sprung up, the lower police winking at their existence. Drunkenness centres principally in those places which possess legal dramshops, though the number of these has been greatly diminished. Tearooms have been provided by local semi-official committees, but even their promoters do not pretend that they have been very successful. The sale of spirits, apart from illicit sales, which do not appear in the returns, has undoubtedly increased; even years of bad harvests have been marked by an increased consumption; the consumption of alcohol in Russia is much less per head than in any other country in Europe; but it is irregular, and drunkenness is frequent.

Government credit and the loans negotiated through foreign bankers were unsparingly used by Witte in his efforts to foster Russian industrial activity. The building of factories was encouraged by extensive orders from the Government, which often accepted shares in the companies which carried them on. Banks were assisted in a similar way; cheap rates of transport were conceded to commercial products. The commercial crisis of 1899 was largely due to this systematic policy of inflation; but the industrial development which it produced is not likely to disappear. Witte has claimed that not a single tax was left unaltered by him; practically the whole fiscal burden was thrown on the indirect taxes, and this is one reason why passive resistance by non-payment of taxes became almost impossible. His policy was strictly protectionist, and left room for all sorts of manipulation with regard to various countries and articles of export. The tariffs of 1850, 1857, and 1867, which tended towards free trade, had benefited the landowners and the St Petersburg factories. Moscow was less enterprising, depended less on improvements from abroad, and had a greater fear of competition. Moscow influences prevailed in the tariff of 1891, and very large duties were imposed on coal, cast iron, and other necessary imports. Witte continued this process, and cast iron came to cost three times as much in Russia as in England. Naturally other interests, especially the agricultural, considered themselves to be sacrificed to the iron trade. In 1892, Germany excepted Russia from the reduced duties on grain accorded to other countries. In 1893, Russia slightly reduced the duties on French imports and greatly increased those on German goods. On February 10, 1894, both Germany and Russia reduced these aggressive duties by a Treaty binding for ten years. A tariff war with Germany was hardly compatible with the fact that Germany buys about half of the Russian export of rye. In spite of the tariff, German imports continued to increase, chiefly because of the businesslike methods of German traders. English imports, however, underwent a continuous decrease, in spite of a commonly expressed preference for English goods; branches of trade which had been almost English monopolies began to pass out of English hands into German, although it was against Germany that the new tariffs had been chiefly directed. Witte has boasted that during his administration the Russian exports had come to exceed the imports. But this is no advantage when the chief export is grain, when the consumption of bread per head has fallen off 70 lbs. in the year, and when the necessary agricultural implements are prevented from entering the country. The Russian peasant, it is calculated, pays, as compared with the German, two and a half times as much for cotton and sugar, four and a half times as much for iron, six times as much for coal. The apparent wealth accruing to the State from these various sources was unscrupulously exaggerated, and systematic efforts were made to produce a deceptive appearance of prosperity.

The greatest achievement of this period was the opening of the

CH. XII.

Siberian Railway, which drew more attention to the emigration question. In 1892 Durnovó had ordered the Governors to discourage migration, but Nicholas II knew that it was normal and necessary. He replaced I. Durnovó (1895) by Goremýkin, whose reports on the peasant question had won his confidence; large sums were spent on emigration and allotments, and the privileges of the settlers were increased. At the same time enquiries were made into the causes which were driving the peasants from their homes; migration was found to be largely due to the burden of taxation.

From 1899 to 1903 there were repeated dissensions in the Ministry. Ostrovsky advocated drastic reform. Pobyedonóstseff resisted change, and even enquiry, in the interests of public tranquillity. When, in 1899, Goremýkin wished to extend Zemstvo representation to outlying provinces, Witte represented him as a dangerous innovator, and succeeded in ousting him from his post. Sipyágin was preferred to Plehve for the post of Minister of the Interior, and appointed a Commission to " complete " the Emancipation Act. This Commission reported in 1903, after Sipyágin had been assassinated, and Plehve had succeeded him (1902). The report laid down as immutable principles the class distinctiveness of the peasants, the inalienability of peasant land, and the inviolability of the traditional system of land tenure—principles opposed, in fact, to those of the Emancipation Act, and formulated in the spirit of the subsequent reaction. This report Plehve endorsed, and it received some support from a manifesto issued by the Tsar in the same year, proclaiming as against the renewed activity of socialism the sanctity of property.

Meanwhile, Witte had been making his own enquiries into the " exhaustion of the centre of the empire." A decline was shown (1901) in the crops ranging up to 27 per cent.; the grain sown was less by 35 per cent. than thirty years before. Oats were giving place to potatoes, and horses were disappearing; the arrears of taxes were enormous. Strengthened by these returns, Witte succeeded in setting up a rival Commission to deal with " the needs of agricultural industry " (1902), which appointed local committees of a semi-representative kind. Thus an appeal was at last made for the cooperation of the Zemstva, and Witte's agricultural committees mark a turning-point in Russian history. But, hitherto, the peasant question had been a weapon in the battle between conflicting Ministers; and Witte's sudden change of front in favour of the Zemstva proved to be only another move in the game.

The Zemstva and larger town councils had a full share in the new activity which followed the famine of 1891. The more energetic members gravitated to the Provincial Board, which was nearly everywhere more Liberal than the District Boards. Politics were forbidden, but economic questions could be discussed and dealt with. This work was inspired by

the highest public spirit.   The initiative fell to the Provincial Zemstvo
Board of Moscow under its President, Dmitry Shipóff (from 1893), a
country gentleman of rare wisdom and integrity; and associated with
him were other men of ability, such as Golovnín, Múromtseff, Kokóshkin,
and Chelnokóff, all destined to win distinction in a wider field.   Their
work was based throughout on careful statistical investigation, and each
new enterprise was tested in one district before it was generally applied.
The grants of the Provincial Zemstvo were always largest to those
District Zemstva which were themselves ready to spend money on
improvements.   Shipóff and his colleagues brought the school within
two miles of every inhabitant of the province of Moscow and the hospital
within five.   Particularly admirable were the equipping of small medical
outposts and the beginnings of adequate provision for the insane.
Clover was supplied to the peasants, and there was a notable improvement in the cattle.   Veterinary doctors were established, and imported
cattle were inspected.   Factories were compelled to drain their premises.
The Zemstvo engaged to find water for villages.   One thousand miles of
road were constructed.   Great pains were taken to create village libraries.
In all these departments, each of which was committed to one man, the
Zemstvo worked without pay and was always ready to raise the rating
rather than defer improvements.   The work was interrupted by the
constant interference and prohibitions of the Government; twice, Laws
on the medical administration, which had been signed by the Emperor,
were denied execution by the officials; for all that, the Moscow Zemstvo
changed the face of the province.   The same statistical basis was taken
elsewhere, and the same main lines were followed.   The Zemstvo of
Samara established one of the first bacteriological institutes, and by
a war of many years' duration succeeded in almost banishing cattle-
disease from the province; excellent work was also done in Tver,
Vorónezh, Tambóff, Chernígoff, and notably in Vyatka, where nearly all
the inhabitants were peasant farmers and there was practically a peasant
Zemstvo.   The smaller town councils were less progressive; but that
of Moscow, when once composed of Liberals, could achieve even more
than the Zemstva.   Wholesale improvements were carried out, such as
a new water supply, the drainage of half of the city, a pension scheme
for employees, and a very remarkable development of the schools and
hospitals.   There was hardly a prominent member of the first Duma who
had not learnt his experience either as a member or as an employee of
the Councils of Local Government.

In 1894 several Zemstvo presidents were summoned to a semi-official
congress on agriculture, under Prince Shcherbátoff.   Shipóff proposed
that these should act as a distinct section of the Congress, and, as the
Ministry consented, half the Congress joined this section.   Shipóff,
as chairman, then for the first time broached the idea of parish councils
to be elected from all classes.   Informal meetings were afterwards held

at his house, and a small permanent committee was formed. A Conference held at Nizhny Novgorod in 1896 excited the fears of the Governor, but was openly supported by Witte. At this, the reactionaries raised the scare of a *Zemsky Sobór*; Goremýkin, always fully informed by Shipóff, had so far been neutral; he now forbade the next meeting in St Petersburg. From 1896 to 1902 there was a series of semi-official Congresses on the decay of cottage industries, the prevalence of fires, and the needs of agriculture; Shipóff made use of these and other occasions to renew the informal conferences of Zemstvo presidents, but the attendance sank lower and lower. The Congress on cottage industries, early in 1902, showed that hopes were again rising. After discussion with Petrunkévich, Shipóff called a congress for June 2, 1902. Some sixty came, and political questions were raised for the first time. The Congress suggested a common programme for the promised agricultural committees; it called attention to the inequalities of civil rights, the hindrances to public instruction, the limitations imposed upon the Zemstva, the defects of the financial policy, and the need of a free Press. On May 7–8, 1903, during the semi-official Congress on insurance there was another Conference; the Zemstvo men agreed that all laws on local questions ought first to be submitted for discussion to the Zemstva and that elected representatives from the Zemstva should assist in drafting such laws.

Witte's agricultural committees met under these conditions (1902–3). Most of the original members were officials; members of the Zemstvo Boards were included, and, in a few districts, all the members of the Zemstva. The consultation of peasants was severely restricted; but Count Heyden, formerly a high official and now a devoted worker on the Free Economic Society, managed to organise an excellent peasant representation in his district. In one district none but officials were allowed to vote; and in one province the Governor declared that no committee was required. There was discord in the Ministry itself; Plehve, like Pobyedonóstseff, was dead against the committees, and Witte was only using them as a pawn in his struggle with Plehve. Accordingly, Plehve sent precise instructions to the presidents to burke the discussion of all important questions. There was hardly an article of Witte's original programme but was excluded in one or more districts; and free discussion was hampered in every way. Reports of the proceedings were hushed up by Marshals and by Governors; and several were omitted from the official record. Yet the results were considerable: 118 committees contented themselves with marking time; 181 declared for enlightened Conservatism; and 418 were pronouncedly hostile to the existing system. Many committees asked for freedom of the Press, a national representation, and inviolability of person—that is, freedom from imprisonment without law, and from search or arrest without warrant. Weighty protests against the existing *régime* were made in Kostromá, Tambóff, Kharkoff, and Sudzha; the report of Vorónezh was even more daring.

The only result of the committees was a very great increase of public interest. Witte, in a memorandum, tried to turn their reports into a condemnation of the Ministry of the Interior; he paid the penalty of his manœuvres and was deprived of power, being appointed to the honorary post of President of the Committee of Ministers. In January, 1904, the conclusions of Sipyágin's rival Commission were submitted to new provincial committees much more carefully selected. In March, 1902, was abolished the system, already almost extinct in practice, by which each village society was made corporately responsible for its taxes. In the autumn of 1903 Shipóff had great difficulty in restraining the Zemstvo men; the more advanced minority summoned a separate Congress, but the solidarity of all Zemstva on non-party grounds was too valuable an instrument to be sacrificed, and the Congress came to nothing. Plehve cancelled the reelection of Shipóff as Zemstvo president in Moscow; in his place was chosen a much more pronounced Liberal, Golovnín; but Plehve continued his policy of undiluted repression till the summer of 1904. This brought him into conflict with all classes and especially with the students. The Press was silenced, and numberless persons were exiled by administrative order.

The Zemstvo men, as representatives, had not said too much; the movement of thought had long since passed far beyond their modest requests for political liberties. If economic questions engaged attention, it was partly because political reform seemed at present unattainable, but partly also because these questions suggested a radical reconstruction of society. In 1882, "V. V.," a dogmatising writer of the anti-Western school, had issued a book on *The Future of Capitalism in Russia*, adopting the old theory that it had no future at all. But in 1883, Plekhánoff and other members of the "Black Partition" founded a society called the "Liberation of Labour," which, acting entirely from abroad, recognised capitalism as inevitable and gave its main attention not to the peasantry but to the growing nucleus of factory workers. The work of the society was inconsiderable until 1893, when a wave of the socialistic ideas of Karl Marx passed into Russia. As against the vague creed of the earlier revolutionaries, here was an imposing system of thought, complete in itself and gloriously disregarding all that did not enter into its scheme. Marx was ill understood, but his works were read everywhere, and the usual tendencies of Russian thought were freely read into them. This movement of gradual propaganda, confident of the future, was a step forward from the confused thought and action of the last generation; but it arbitrarily anticipated a happy victory for Social Democracy in Russia before the *bourgeoisie* had rooted itself there; it preached the theory that "the worse things are now, the more complete will be the crash";

and, generally, it depended far too much on the inevitable and on a majority of voices to encourage any remarkable initiative in its adherents. The Marxists, such as Plekhánoff and Struve, at least gave the deathblow to the doctrine that Russia was exempt from all ordinary laws of development. For the best of them, including Struve himself, Social Democracy was but a phase of development; but it certainly reached the masses. Marxist periodicals began to appear in the legitimate Press—*The New Word* (from 1897), and *Life* (1899–1901). Much wider was the influence of Maxim Gorky (from 1891), whose cynical attitude towards the educated classes and glorification of the proletariate prove him a natural product of this movement. The appearance of an exclusive class creed for the masses greatly increased their interest in public questions.

The striking spread of education, mainly due to the work of the Zemstva, began to show itself in the statistics of the yearly recruits; very many of the Zemstvo employees were socialists, and many Zemstvo schools and book-stores took a strong socialist tinge. The "go-aways" carried back socialism from the towns into the country. Deported workmen had a very different influence from the old missionary students. But the centre of activity was in the great factories, and in the constant migrations of workmen from one to another. In 1896, at the fair of Nizhny Novgorod, the employers set the example of "demands" addressed to the Government. The earlier workmen's organisations, directed by theorising and quarrelling propagandists, were easily crushed by exile and imprisonment (1895–6). But Lénin and others took a successful initiative in the summer of 1896, and the strike of nineteen cotton factories in St Petersburg for a twelve hours' day and other purely industrial demands thoroughly alarmed the Government. Witte, with his leanings to state socialism, was not unready to secure an ally in the proletariate. The Factory Law of June 15, 1897, limited the hours to 11½, or to 10 of nightwork. In March, 1898, on the initiative of some of the socialist groups, was held a Congress which formed a "Workmen's Social Democratic party." Divisions and jealousies were manifest from the outset, and the drafting of a programme was deferred. Central and local Committees were alike at once arrested, and the organ of the party was destroyed. In the confusion which followed, there was no central initiative except that of individual periodicals. Serious questions divided the groups. The "Liberation of Labour" was discredited as acting from abroad. Old propagandists, realising that the party as yet existed only on paper, considered a democratic basis impossible, and, so long as conspirative methods were inevitable, wished to keep a dictatorship. Most of the workmen, who were hardly Social Democrats at all, only wanted a practical campaign for winning practical concessions from the employers. This so-called "economic" tendency prevailed for a time even amongst the propagandists; and even labour newspapers preached indifference to politics. The workmen organised permanent funds, less for the propaganda of the party than for supporting local strikes; and there was an increasing strike movement all over Russia. In the autumn of 1898 began a commercial crisis, aggravated by a serious famine; the Government spent huge sums on the starving, but closed other relief agencies. A well-organised strike of fourteen days was carried through in the Caucasus; the movement spread along the Siberian Railway to Krasnoyársk.

The Government had recourse to very unusual methods. After the first series of strikes, even the temporising *Novoë Vremya* had exhorted it to take up the workmen's question; the reply was an order to newspapers to print no article on the subject without authorisation by the police. But in April, 1898, the Chief Police-Master of Moscow, Dmitry Trépoff, in a lengthy secret report, proposed to combat the propaganda of revolutionaries by counter-propaganda of the police and support of the workmen against their employers. This was confessedly a move by the police of the Minister of the Interior as against the factory inspectors of the Minister of Finance ; and as such it was supported by Pobyedonóstseff, the Grand Duke Sergius, and, it would appear, Plehve ; in 1899 and 1900, circulars were issued in this sense. Zubátoff, a former revolutionary who had become Chief of Detectives in Moscow, in a series of talks with imprisoned workmen claimed to be working for their class. He supplied money for a labour newspaper and subsidised labour propagandists—amongst others the priest Gapón. In Minsk he organised a labour club and even an " Independent Labour party." In Moscow he arranged public lectures on the labour question by well-known economists; the free discussion after these lectures helped him to discover and remove Social Democrats. Similar societies under the patronage of Governors and Bishops were instituted elsewhere ; the Minister of Finance addressed a strongly worded remonstrance to the Emperor. In Moscow the workmen distrusted Zubátoff; but in Odessa, one of his agents, Shayévich, protected from the City Prefect by the Central Department of Police, organised a strike which at last got out of hand and had to be stopped by the troops.

The exposure of the manœuvres of Zubátoff quite discredited the non-political tendency amongst the Social Democrats. The more resolute wing of the party now assumed the lead in a new paper, the *Spark* (*Iskra*). It wished to create a real party by formulating the socialist doctrine as a class creed and superimposing it on the discontent of the workmen. The organisation was to be not democratic but conspirative; terrorism was condemned as impotent and disintegrating; propagandism was the task of the present, though Lénin and his friends did not shrink from the idea of an ultimate insurrection. They were so rigorously logical as to separate the interests of the peasants entirely from those of the workmen; for the peasants they desired such impoverishment as would make the small farmer a hired labourer and drive him into the proletariate. The uncompromising vigour of the *Spark* secured for it many friends and many enemies. At the second congress of the whole Social Democratic party (1903) the original split was greatly widened ; and the programme of Lénin became the creed of the extreme wing known under the name of the "majority men." The "minority men" continued moderate ; they were willing to keep up relations with other parties and to make use of parliamentary institutions even under a monarchy. The ultimate aim of both wings was a democratic republic. Their relative strength varied in different localities; and at the meetings of the whole party they prevailed in turn.

The students' movement of 1899 culminated in a demonstration on the Kazán Square in St Petersburg, which was dispersed with bloodshed (March 17, 1901); several leading writers issued a united protest. Meanwhile, strikes became more political. In November, 1902, the local committee of the Social Democrats conducted in Rostóff-on-the-Don a great strike of factory and railway men. Still more imposing was the strike of July, 1903, at the petroleum wells of the Caucasus. The employers refused all concessions and summoned the troops ; the answer of the workmen was to fire the wells. In October, 1904, the union of workmen in Baku began to talk of an armed rising. The strike of December 26 aimed at political concessions : freedom of organisation, Press, speech, and person, with a Constituent Assembly. It also demanded an eight hours' day. The employers, this time, conferred with the men ; but Cossacks fired into an unarmed crowd, killing six and wounding twenty. In the two next days the workmen again fired the wells : " these," they said, " are the candles for our dead." But this is already the beginning of a later period.

Marxism soon lost its hold over the best minds. Its dead monotony of principle and action called forth a natural protest of individuality, national or personal. One symptom of this protest was the growth of the new Socialist Revolutionary party, formed by veterans of the " Will of the People" almost at the same time as the Social Democratic. It gave all its attention to the peasants. To these the extreme logic of the " S. D.'s " offered no hope ; but the " S. R.'s " were less *doctrinaire* and in much closer touch with practical life ; the " S. R." propagandist really lived amongst the peasants ; he had to learn that their grievances were simple and economic, and that they had no republican ideals for the empire. Here the conditions of missionary work demanded initiative and resource ; and the " S. R.'s " were far more enterprising than the " S. D.'s." Their audience was ignorant and apathetic ; and, believing in the influence of isolated protests, the party contained a special militant section, which renewed the practice of terrorism. The most notable assassinations of the new period were the work of commissioned or uncommissioned " S. R.'s." Terrorism was a method of political warfare licensed by the party for those who believed in it. Most " S. R.'s " were simply resolute champions of protest in a time of gross misgovernment; they had no fixed theory and might easily become ordinary radicals. Their propaganda had at first very little success. But in May, 1902, crude and elemental disorders broke out amongst the peasants of Poltáva and Kharkoff. The attacks on property were punished with flogging and heavy fines, and the mood which followed was favourable to the "S. R.'s."

A far more important sequel of the Marxist phase was the growth of a new and robust idealism, based upon the rights and the duties of the individual, whether personal or corporate. To Russians a Liberalism of tradition was denied by history; this was the Liberalism of conviction. Many of its elements already existed in the instincts of the Liberal gentry and of Zemstvo work; but the creed itself was only now formulated and chiefly by reasoned converts—Berdáyeff, Struve, Bulgákoff, and Novgorodtseff. This view was expressed later in the reviews, *A New Road* (1904) and *Questions of Life* (1905). The new movement had far-reaching results. Even those who remained Marxists felt compelled to meet it half-way. When the new school split up into two sections, its influence was only increased; Berdáyeff and Bulgákoff helped to strengthen the budding romanticism of Russia, which had notable representatives in the poet Balmont and the writers Merezhkovsky and Rózanoff; and Struve and Novgorodtseff became prominent workers in the formation of a Russian Liberal party. There had existed, since 1899, in Moscow an informal club of progressives called the *Besyeda*. To this belonged enlightened Conservatives such as Count Bóbrinsky; but the predominance gradually passed to ardent Liberals, the twin Princes Dolgorúkoff and the exceptionally able and devoted organiser, Prince Shakhovskóy. These last united with old Zemstvo Liberals, like Petrunkévich and Rodicheff, professional men like Vinográdoff and Milyukóff, and radical writers like Korolyénko, to form a political group known as the "Liberators." Amongst the Liberators were Nabókoff, born for eminence in parliamentary life, and Kokóshkin, a constitutional expert and a speaker of rare lucidity. The Liberators were formally united only by their contributions to the paper *Liberation*, the first really important organ of Russian Liberalism, which, on the refusal of the Government to license it, was published in Stuttgart (from July 14, 1902). The editor was Struve; he printed also pamphlets and documents of the first importance. In December, 1902, Struve declared for the organisation of a broad Liberal party; this party, he explained, must be both constitutional and democratic (February, 1903). The other Liberators remained in Russia, and formed small local branches. They held a small conference near Lake Constance (August 2–3, 1903). On November 21 was formed out of their elements a special group, called the Zemstvo Constitutionalists, which aimed at making the general movement of the Zemstva as progressive as possible. On January

16–18, 1904, was formally founded the "Union of Liberators"; its council was allowed to coopt new members. The Zemstvo Constitutionalists met again on March 7, and declared for a representative assembly. The Union prepared a draft constitution; but the general mood at the opening of the Japanese War (1904) did not favour the Liberators. Their chance came in the autumn.

To complete the picture of the empire, we must follow the policy of the reaction westwards and eastwards. It had two kindred principles: aliens within the empire were to be forcibly Russianised, and a moral barrier was to separate Russia from Western Europe; meanwhile, Russia, as the missionary of the one true faith, was to annex and Christianise the East. The root idea depended for its vitality on religious considerations. But, under the rule of Pobyedonóstseff, the Russian Church had at this time lost much of its moral significance. Imperial expansion might console many for the growing demoralisation at home; but the officials, who were the chief agents in the expansion, were more demoralised than the rest. Meanwhile, each increase of territory or addition to the system of regulations enhanced the power of the local agents of the Government, and diminished the control of the nominally autocratic sovereign.

Finland especially challenged the attention of the reactionaries by reason of its nearness to St Petersburg and its acknowledged constitutional liberties, confirmed before its annexation to Russia in 1809. It possessed a Diet, elected from the four classes of the population, and a national executive council, called the Senate (from 1816). The Emperor was sovereign, but as Grand Duke of Finland; he was represented by a viceroy or Governor-General. Senate and Diet had access to the Emperor through a Secretary of State living in St Petersburg, who was distinct from the Russian Ministers. Bills were submitted to the Diet after the preliminary consent of the Emperor. The population consists of Finns, with an admixture of Swedes; the Russian element is inconsiderable. Nicholas I did not summon the Diet, and issued some enactments on his own sole authority. Alexander II granted a separate coinage in 1860, and in 1863 summoned the Diet and expressly recognised "the principles of constitutional monarchy"; he named a committee to codify the statutes of the Constitution. The Diet was to be summoned every five years. The army was restricted to service within the grand-duchy, and the burden of military service was made much lighter than in Russia (1878). Alexander III signed the constitutional guarantees; but the Penal Code of 1888 was referred to a commission at the Russian Ministry of Justice. The economic progress of the country was rapid; and the Finns, despite Swedish opposition, had succeeded in legalising their language and creating a very creditable mass of literature. Language rights were now demanded for Russian;

and this question led to the resignation of the Secretary of State, and a censorship of Finnish newspapers (1891). A knowledge of Russian was made obligatory for public servants.

Nicholas II confirmed the liberties of Finland; but in 1898 he appointed Bóbrikoff as Governor-General, and in January, 1899, the Diet was called upon to sanction a complete reorganisation of the military regulations: Finland was to become a military district of Russia, the officers were to be Russians, and the old Finnish staffs were abolished; the oath was to be to the Emperor as such. In May, other proposals put the period of service and the number of recruits on the same basis as in Russia; the Finnish army was not to be increased, and the supernumerary recruits were to be drafted elsewhere; a knowledge of Russian would secure a curtailment of the period of service. The Diet agreed that Finland should contribute more soldiers and that they should defend the empire in general, but it rejected the Russian proposal; nevertheless, this was enforced. On February 15, 1899, the Emperor, under the influence of Pobyedonóstseff, issued a manifesto declaring that Finnish Bills must be drafted by Russian Ministers in conjunction with the Secretary of State for Finland, and need only be submitted to the Diet if they concerned Finland alone. In August, Plehve was appointed Secretary of State for Finland. There was a national protest, not accompanied by any disorders. Bóbrikoff made the censorship more severe; and the Finnish postal system was now merged in that of Russia. The Senate pointed out that, according to the statements of successive Emperors, the fundamental laws could only be changed by a unanimous Diet. A thoroughly representative deputation proceeded to St Petersburg, where it was refused an audience; a petition of 500,000 persons, signed in ten days, received no reply. A Russian police was introduced into Finland. From 1901 to 1905 was conducted an orderly and almost unanimous movement of passive resistance. All officials except those belonging to the party of Old Finns had resigned; recruits refused to serve; pastors would not read out the conscription lists. In spite of spies, *gendarmes*, and suspensions of newspapers, Bóbrikoff could not prevail. In 1904 he was assassinated by Eugene Schaumann. These troubled years gave a great impetus to the spread of Social Democracy in Finland.

The Baltic Provinces (Esthonia, Livonia, and Courland) are peopled by Esths and Letts, with a German nobility and trading class; the religion is the Lutheran. The Esths and Letts were emancipated in 1816–9: many of them were small farmers, but the hired labourers resented the feudal custom of forced labour; many feudal rights remained, and the subject races were excluded from the provincial Diets. Here, as elsewhere, the labour question had become acute, especially since the rise of factories around Riga. The Germans had been perfectly loyal since their annexation in 1721, and they had always taken a large share in the administration of the empire. The German culture and German bye-laws of these provinces had remained intact. After 1870, the unification and growing power of Germany roused Russian jealousy. Antigerman sentiments were encouraged by Russian agents among the Esths and Letts, and they were incited to claim rights for their languages as against the German. Forests were fired and estates wrecked, and as a remedy the revising Senator, Manasséin, recommended closer union with Russia. From 1885, Russian was introduced as the official tongue. Lutheran churches were not to be built without leave of the Procurator of the Synod (1885). Conversion to Orthodoxy was pushed with all the resources of power; and pastors were imprisoned for receiving back their repentant parishioners. In 1886 the schools of the local Lutheran consistories were placed under the Russian Minister of Public Instruction. From 1887, Russian was introduced into Dorpat University; and from 1889, no lectures might be given in any other language. Even in private schools, German was forbidden. The local law Courts were suppressed, the town councils reduced to insignificance, the mayors nominated, the Press was put under the Russian censorship, and the local bye-laws were abolished. German place names were changed for Russian. As the German nobles possessed immense influence at Court, Nicholas II relaxed the tension, and they recovered or retained much of their local power; but Germans were not popular in the empire, and the Esths and Letts did not forget the encouragement given to them when the disorders of 1905 put the German landlords at their mercy. The Lithuanians (provinces of Vilna, Kovno, Grodno, and Suwalki), like their kinsmen the Letts, developed a language movement, which was repressed during this period.

Poland, after the insurrection of 1863, was reorganised by a Constituent Committee (1864–6) under Nicholas Milyútin and Prince Cherkassky, who believed that the Polish peasants might be finally estranged from the gentry, and become a support of Russian autocracy. The country was redivided into ten provinces; the peasants received their holdings in perpetuity, with indefinite rights of access to the forests and pasture of the gentry; escheated property could only be bought by Russians. Most of the monasteries of the national religion (Roman Catholic) were confiscated. But the Milyútin idea was quite impracticable, for there was no Russian element in Poland except the officials; and the Russification in Poland became very early a policy of sheer repression, exasperated from time to time by the evident signs of its failure. Russian was made obligatory for official correspondence and university lectures (1869–70). General Gurko and the Curator of Education, Apukhtin, worked for the day "when Polish mothers would lull their children to sleep with Russian songs"; every inquisitorial method was brought into play. The secondary schools were entirely Russianised. Poles were excluded from government posts in Poland. Polish literature and even the Polish language were taught to Poles in

Russian. Russian was also made obligatory in primary schools. Priests
were constantly transferred, fined, or arrested. Russian law Courts were
introduced in 1876. Poles were not allowed to sell their land to foreigners
(1885). Prussia replied by expelling Russian Poles, and the Law of 1885
was repealed in 1897. Shuváloff (1894) and Prince Imeretinsky (1896)
recognised the failure of the policy of repression; the former relaxed
the severity of the administration; the latter recommended considerable concessions; but the main grievances remained, and were
aggravated by the arbitrariness of officials. Under Imeretinsky, Russian
was introduced even in private trading concerns.

Young Poles, excluded from public service, streamed into commerce.
Thus was formed a native middle class. Poles took a leading part in
the industrial and commercial development of the Russian empire.
Between 1876 and 1896, the number of working men increased sixfold
in some trades; huge factories replaced small ones; Warsaw grew
rapidly, and Lodz became a great town.

The Polish rising was followed by a return to sober common sense.
In Galicia the Conservative Stańczyki began a wary policy of detail,
which, between 1859 and 1872, won the confidence of the Austrian
Emperor and the grant—through circulars rather than through statutes—
of practically complete autonomy. On the other hand, the Prussian
Government repressed the language and schools of its Poles, and later
took measures to drive them from their land; its policy, except during
a short period, was to turn the Poles into a mere proletariate. The
example of Austria was not lost on Russian Poland. Here a very
pronounced development of positivism led to a general enthusiasm for
"organic work" or "work at the foundations," of which the chief
exponent was the brilliant publicist Swiętochowski. The narrow traditions of the old Poland of the gentry gave way to ideals far more
broadly national. This general tendency later divided itself into three
main channels. Polish socialism may be dated from Limanowski (1868);
it did not take root till 1876, when an ambitious but futile plan of
conspiracy was designed by Szimanski. In 1878 was pompously announced the creation of a socialist party; there were many arrests; a more
compact group, the "Proletariate," had more success, until crushed with
the greatest severity in 1885. Later arose a "Workmen's Union," which in
1893 joined with the remnants of the "Proletariate" to form the new and
formidable "Polish Socialist party." So far, most of the propagandists
had aimed at a cosmopolitan programme; but the party, as soon as it
really took root, showed itself to be profoundly national. From 1895 to
1899, it was able to carry out 186 strikes, of which 127 were successful.
It aimed at separation from Russia and a democratic republic. Radically
opposed to this party was the small group of "Conciliators" consisting
mainly of the richer gentry, and stronger in Lithuania and White Russia
than in Poland; their organ, the *Country* of Pilc, was in St Petersburg.

They copied the Polish Conservatives of Galicia, and hoped for concessions from the Russian Government to a loyal Poland; but Russian administrators regarded them as wolves in sheep's clothing. They had a fleeting success, when Nicholas II visited Warsaw and they organised a remarkable demonstration of loyalty; but the disillusionment which followed the visit made them extremely unpopular.

Much more conspicuous ability characterised the Middle party. Out of the new moral and intellectual Poland inspired by Świętochowski, arose the Society for Public Instruction and, in 1886, the "Polish League" with its national fund, closely associated with the newspaper, the *Voice*. Reorganised in 1895 as the "National League," it became the dominant moral force in Russian Poland. Count Potocki and the able publicist Poplawski were later joined by Roman Dmowski, expelled from Warsaw University for celebrating the centenary of the Constitution of 1791. Living in Galicia, Dmowski made the League the basis of a political party, the National Democrats. His breadth of conception and his practical resource were unusual, and he soon became the accepted dictator of both League and party. In his *Thoughts of a present-day Pole* (1902), he defined their principles. Poland, however sorely tried, was never to wander from sound sense; socialism would produce a horde only fit for partisan warfare; the Russian Government sought to rob Poland of her individuality, and must therefore by Poles be regarded as, in the deepest sense, revolutionary. Poland was to save herself by the development and concentration of all the moral forces within her. Russia "regarded the whole Polish nation as a plot," and was therefore to be met at every turn with a stubborn resistance, by the joint self-assertion of thousands of workers, and, eventually, by the effective boycott of everything Russian. The political virtues and the political organisation which were required would be created in the long and patient struggle. The educated classes would thus be brought into the closest contact with the peasants, who required of them no new basis of morality but only political education. The peasants, who had become enterprising small farmers, offered an admirable soil for this propaganda. Peasant energies were directed to practicable objects, the foundation of private schools using the Polish language, the banishing of Russian from the business of the parish meetings. Thus the country was covered with numberless groups of workers, who, later, would follow the lead of the National Democrats.

The party from 1897 to 1901 aimed at independence; but from 1901 it gave up the idea of an armed rising. Rather, it would seek reunion by playing off against each other the three partitioning empires. Though Poland was partitioned, the Polish people must remain indivisible. Austria was too weak to offer any salvation; but Russia, after quite failing to annihilate Poland, would find her own self-evident interest in granting local government, which would turn this discontented people into a bulwark, and would make every Austrian or German Pole wish to be reunited with his compatriots in the Russian empire. Dmowski's policy was directed against Germany to the profit of Russia; but he refused to sink the individuality of Poland even in a Russian Liberal party; a parliamentary Russia might be more exacting than an autocratic one. When the *Voice* was suppressed in 1894, these views were much more openly preached in the *All-Polish Review* of Dmowski and Poplawski, which from 1895 appeared in Cracow and had subscribers in all the three "Partitionments"; for the peasants, there was the *Pole* with 5000 subscribers. The party, definitely organised in 1897, issued its revised programme in October, 1903; its watchword was autonomy within the Russian empire. It now represented most of the gentry and middle class, all the peasantry, and a considerable section of the working men. The priests were welcomed as valued and honoured helpers. Meanwhile it had bridged the gap between gentry and peasants.

In White Russia (the provinces of Vítebsk, Minsk, and Mohiléff), most of the gentry are Polish, the middle class is Jewish, and the peasants are Russians. Here Poles were disqualified from acquiring land. The Roman Catholic priests were under a constant persecution; they could not leave their parishes without permission. The Uniat Church had been crushed in 1839; and in 1873 the remnants of this Church were pursued into the Polish diocese of Kholm. Forcible conversions to the Orthodox Church excited a stubborn resistance from the Uniats, and this led to the use of troops. Yet in 1897 there were still 80,000 Uniats holding out, whose marriages and children the Russian Government refused to recognise.

In Little Russia (the south-western provinces of the empire) vague traditions of republicanism lingered on from the time of the free Cossacks. The Little Russians are far more independent and enterprising than the Great Russians; their land-tenure is in effect proprietary and not communal; they have taken a very prominent part in the recent development of industry. A literary movement for preserving the Little Russian dialect has met with support within the educated class; it is semi-political, and extends into Galicia; it has been strongly opposed by the Russian Government; but the latter has encouraged the Little Russian peasants as against their Polish landlords. On this side, Bessarabia, with a population of Moldavians, Jews, and Russian settlers, was added to the empire in 1878.

There are some $5\frac{1}{2}$ millions of Jews in Russia. The vast majority of them live in the western and south-western provinces; here some of their monuments go back to the beginning of the Christian era, and the Russian Jew can almost claim to have a second fatherland. It was the partition of Poland (1772) that brought the Jews into the Russian empire; they were welcomed with the promise of equal rights with Russians. Limitations began in 1804; but Nicholas I attempted to merge the Jews in the rest of the population (1840–5); and in 1835 they received access to the ordinary schools, and in 1859 to the first Guild of Merchants. Educated Jews (1861), craftsmen (1865), and veterans of the army (1867), were admitted into the interior of the empire. A Commission reported in favour of a further equalisation in rights (1879), but was dissolved. Among the few terrorists there had been several Jews; and Alexander III showed the bitterest animosity against the race as a whole. Within their area, the Jews have a complete economic supremacy and use it to the full. In 1880 a series of armed attacks was made upon them, never properly investigated, but apparently due to the idea that here were victims handed over by the officials for spoliation. The "temporary rules" of May, 1882, which evaded the ordinary process of legislation but have been retained ever since, confined the Jews to towns and "townships" of the fifteen provinces described as the Jewish Pale. A Commission for the drafting of permanent laws declared for the opposite policy, and was dissolved. New ordinances excluded Jews from all direct share in local government, even in towns where they constituted nearly half the population and paid three-quarters of the taxes. Only a small percentage of Jews (10 per cent. of all the scholars) were admitted to schools almost entirely supported by Jewish taxes; the arbitrary selection from the applicants led to grave abuses. Special taxes on Jewish meat and candles, levied from 1835 onwards, were supposed to provide special schools for Jews; but the money was administered by the Government and often spent on general purposes, such as roads or police. Lacking school diplomas, the Jews found many careers closed; they could not be civil servants or officers in the army; but the number of recruits taken from them was disproportionately large. They might not acquire or lease property outside the towns, even in the Pale; they were debarred from agricultural pursuits, and from work in factories outside the towns. Jews were forbidden to live within a given distance of the frontier.

By these regulations, mostly instituted between 1882 and 1892, the Pale was impoverished, and the Russian population was encouraged to contempt and violence. But the effect on the police was more serious. They were charged with the interpretation of these complicated rules; they could settle what Jews might live in the interior provinces as "craftsmen," and which members of a Jew's family might live with him; the occasions for bribery were unlimited. Great numbers of Jews emigrated; some returned with a foreign education; some became an economic menace to other lands. The towns of the Pale were filled with paupers, and epidemics became frequent. The *pogróms* or mob-attacks on Jews were renewed in 1903 at Kishinéff; they were chiefly due to police incitements. Many Jews became revolutionaries; apart from the small terrorist-anarchist groups which formed at Byelostók, Odessa, and elsewhere, there was created a powerful organisation allied

to the Social Democrats, the *Bund* ; and later local militias were formed
for self-defence.   But the Jewish middle class was Liberal and peaceful.
A scientific association investigated the Jewish monuments in Russia ;
a society was formed in the south for providing legal defence to Jews ;
and this, joining hands with the Jewish group in St Petersburg, helped
to create a strong Jewish section of the Cadet party, which gave to the
first Duma one of its ablest politicians in Vináver.

Russia was isolated from western Europe by the Treaty of Berlin
and the Triple Alliance.   Alexander III, in difficulties with his people,
wisely eschewed all but peaceful relations with his neighbours.   Visits and
compliments were exchanged ; and, though in 1884 a combination aimed
against France was rejected, Russia and Germany by a secret treaty
engaged themselves to benevolent neutrality if either were attacked.
Russia was unable to prevent the union of Eastern Rumelia with
Bulgaria, and the enforced abdication of Prince Alexander of Bulgaria
did not restore Russian influence in that principality.

German diplomacy brought about the one real success of Alexander's
reign.   The Triple Alliance of Germany, Austria, and Italy had been
renewed in 1887, and, as it enjoyed the goodwill of England, the
Emperor's thoughts naturally turned towards France.   When Berlin
refused to lend (January, 1888), a whole series of Russian loans was taken
up eagerly in France (1889–91).   The breach with Germany had been
widened by the attempts to Russify the Baltic provinces and by the tariff
war.   When the Empress Victoria of Germany accepted Prince Alexander
of Battenberg as a future son-in-law (1888), the Emperor hurried troops
to his frontier ; and, though the match was broken off, the irritation
on both sides remained.   The steps by which the Alliance between
France and Russia was reached are elsewhere recorded.

The Russian people, at first, seemed to be almost as enthusiastic as
the French.   Doubtless, very different motives contributed to this
common result ; but the Alliance became an important factor in European
politics, and the Russian Government derived solid advantages from the
loans raised in France.   On August 24, 1898, Count Muravyéff, the
Russian Foreign Minister, issued a circular proposing a Peace Congress
of the chief Powers of the world—a sign that the isolation of Russia was
at an end.   If the outcome of the Congress, which sat from May 18 to
July 29, was not equal to the conception, there were nevertheless tangible
results.   Meanwhile Germany, aided by Austria, was extending her
political and economic influence over the small Slav States of the
Balkans, and heading off the Russians from Constantinople by securing
a firm hold there.   The Pangerman idea was thus in direct conflict
with the Panslavist, and it assisted the German pursuit of material
advantages.   In 1898, King Charles of Roumania, himself a Hohenzollern, conceded a direct way of communication between the German

and Turkish capitals. In 1899 a German company obtained leave to build a railway from Konieh to the head of the Persian Gulf. However, Montenegro remained firm in friendship for Russia; and Servia could not afford to forgo Russian support. Bulgaria was reconciled to Russia by the brutal murder of the patriot Stambuloff (1895), and by the baptism of Prince Boris into the Greek Church. Ferdinand was recognised as Prince, and received at St Petersburg. The Greeks are no friends of the Balkan Slavs; but Nicholas II helped to mitigate the penalties of the Graeco-Turkish War (1897); while Germany had throughout the conflict been friendly to Turkey, whose army had been trained by German officers. In England the public mind was still confused by distrust of Russian schemes of aggression and dislike of autocratic government; but Russia was no longer thought to be so dangerous to the peace of the world. Turkish misrule in Macedonia caused prolonged disorders and European intervention. The joint action of Austria and Russia effected very little; Bulgaria seemed on the verge of war with Turkey; and Russia appeared about to resume her policy of liberator in the Near East. Such a policy would have aroused wide sympathy in Russia. But at this moment Japan claimed the settlement of very different issues, and the resources of the disorganised empire were expended in an unpopular war, conducted at the greatest possible disadvantage.

The foreign policy of Russia—negative on its Western side, except in respect of the French alliance—had been one of rapid expansion in the East. This was of a piece with the anti-Western bias displayed at home, of which the natural complement was a political and religious crusade Eastwards.

The cession of Batum and Kars by the Treaty of Berlin riveted Russia's hold on the Caucasus. This very populous district is a strange medley of races, languages, and religions. The Georgians, who are Christian, are a military race, with a nobility of their own. The Armenians, also Christian, form the middle class; the Tartars, who are Mussulmans, the working population. The task of Russia was to keep order among the three races. The Armenians gave most trouble. Scattered also over the eight neighbouring provinces of Turkey, they hoped for an autonomous State of their own, and influenced English public opinion in this sense. Forty thousand Armenian emigrants carried this propaganda from Turkey into Russia. Those who remained were exposed to the Kurdish massacres of 1894. In 1895, Russia joined in the ineffective demands of the Powers for reforms in Turkish Armenia. In 1903, Plehve appropriated the funds of the Armenian Church for administration by the Russian Government. A rapid development of the petroleum wells of Baku, chiefly by foreign capital, added to the other elements of unrest. Labour questions became acute, and the great strikes of 1903–4, organised by the Union of Baku workmen, threw these important provinces into complete chaos.　Meanwhile, the monk Uspensky dreamed of a Russian religious hegemony extending southward through Syria and Palestine as far as Abyssinia, Egypt, Ethiopia, and the Sudan.　In 1889 a Cossack adventurer, Ashinoff, seized the ruined fort of Sagallo in the French colony of Obok ; he was dislodged, and was disavowed by the Russian Government. Russians and Abyssinians exchanged visits ; and Leontieff became Governor of the equatorial possessions of the Emperor Menelik (1900). But Hanotaux' plan of linking up the French Congo with Abyssinia in concert with Russia, and thus heading off England from the Sudan, failed in 1898 with Marchand.

The Tartars of east and south-east Russia are by language, religion, and culture in close touch with the Mussulmans of Central Asia.　They are peaceable and loyal, but have a strong corporate feeling.　Their pious foundations were taken out of their hands ; they could only build mosques by leave of the local bishop ; they were hindered in the founding of schools.　The nomad Kirghiz resented the ill-regulated intrusion of Cossack settlements.　The absorption of the Caucasus, and the conquest of the major part of the Khanates of Central Asia between 1864 and 1879, brought Russia close to the frontiers of Persia, Afghanistan, and India.　As Gorchakóff pointed out to the English alarmists in 1864, Russia was in these regions a civilising force, compelled to advance till she had neighbours who could secure order on her frontier. Incidentally, her advance enabled her to respond effectively to the hostile action of England, by precipitating the collision between British India and Afghanistan (1878–81).　The process of expansion proceeded ; and the tribes of the Atrek and Kopet Dagh, and the Tekkes and Sariks of the Merv oasis, came under Russian rule (1881–4).　The Shah accepted the rearrangement of frontiers, and an Anglo-Russian boundary commission was appointed to delimit the Afghan frontier.　In 1885 the Penjdeh incident nearly led to war.　A railway, primarily strategic, was constructed, in spite of extraordinary difficulties, by General Annenkoff between the Caspian and Samarkand (1885–8); the Trans-Caspian railway was later extended from Merv to the Afghan frontier, and from Samarkand in the direction of Kashgar ; a separate line links Orenburg with Tashkent ; only 438 miles separate the Russian railway system from the British-Indian.　In 1895 a boundary commission of Russians, Englishmen, and Afghans, delimited the Pamirs.　There was a forward school in Russia as in England; but it had few adherents, and was practically limited to the reactionaries.　The more general view was that India, if conquered, could not be held, or its enormous coast line defended : Russia could neither find the necessary funds, nor an efficient body of administrators.

Very different was the question of Persia, which, through the outlet of the main Russian waterway, the Volga, has long been in close relations with Russia. In 1892, the Imperial Bank of Persia, directed from London, advanced a loan to the Persian Government; in 1898 the Shah turned to Russia; and in 1903 was founded the Bank of Persian loans, which was strictly a Russo-Persian enterprise; the northern custom-houses of Persia passed under Russian control. The Russian trade with Persia is greater than the British; and, as the country divides geographically into northern and southern zones, the question was settled for a time by the Convention of 1907.

The first Governor of Trans-Caspia, General Kuropatkin, was an able administrator; the form of rule was military, but the Mohammadan laws and customs were not entirely disregarded, and the conquest represents a real advance in civilisation. As settled government prevailed, industry made rapid progress, especially in Tashkent; in spite of bad railway administration, cotton is exported, and other natural resources await development. But there were now eighteen millions of Mussulmans within the empire, and the great revival in the literary and political culture of Islam made itself felt in Russia. The Mussulmans, organised by Topchibásheff, formed a party in the first Duma.

The wastes of Siberia had long been regarded chiefly as a place of banishment. The progress of the political struggle added yearly to the tale of exiles; and, when the attention of western Europe was attracted, something was done to reform the prison system. It was largely to the exiles that north-east Russia and western Siberia owed a remarkable development of initiative and enterprise; but the material was supplied by the rapidly increasing emigration of peasants. These were the real pioneers of empire; there sprang up a hardy and independent race bound by every tie to Russia, but feeling acutely the defects of the bureaucratic system and the need of local self-government. Eastern Siberia, however, long remained as a road to something beyond; and, as the swarming population of China was approached, the balance of vital force and of migration told against Russia. The Pacific had been reached at the close of the seventeenth century; the Amur region had been secured by Count Muravyéff (1858–60), and Vladivostók was founded. Alaska was sold to the United States in 1867; but Saghalín became completely Russian in 1875. The Trans-Siberian Railway was suggested by Muravyéff. It was begun in 1891, and opened in 1901. The enterprise was imperial in character, and the Crown Prince cut the first sod on the far side. The railway was strategic—the stations are far from the towns—and its course was changed by political events. Instead of passing along the Amur, it went southward to Harbin and Vladivostók; and from Harbin a line was carried through Mukden to Port Arthur. Its length was to be 5542 miles, and the cost £100,000,000. The difficulties were enormous. All the great rivers that run northwards had to be bridged; Lake Baikal in summer was crossed with ferries; the track is in constant danger from sudden thaws and floods. The distance and the vastness of the undertaking gave ample room for peculation, and the service has been hampered by numberless thefts. The resulting advantages are very great. The journey to the Pacific was greatly shortened for passengers and mails; the government orders for rails helped to develop the Russian iron trade; the Siberian coal-fields were opened up; Siberian corn and farm produce and Chinese tea were brought through at cheap freights to the markets of Europe; most important of all was the immense impulse given to emigration.

In turning their backs on Europe, the Russian reactionaries sought to find a substitute for reform in imperial expansion. The theory, as expounded by Prince Úkhtomsky, was that Russia, as really an Asiatic Power, had a mission to apply autocratically to Asia the benefits of modern inventions. The Orthodox Church rejoiced in the task of expanding Christendom. But the practical application of such theories was in the hands of distant and self-seeking officials; and there arose in the Far East a party of adventure, wielding extensive powers, and powerfully backed at St Petersburg. It was thus that the Russian Government, averted from the West, came into contact with an Eastern nation which sought to assimilate Western culture. On the worst chosen ground, the Russian Government joined issue with a modern army full of the initiative and patriotism of freedom; and the wave started by Japan was to roll back to the confines of Austria and Germany.

The Russian Government was not prepared for the rapid triumph of Japan over China (1894–5); but, with the aid of France and Germany, it upset the Treaty of Shimonoseki, and Japan lost many of the fruits of victory. Russia lent a large sum to China in 1895; and, by the Conventions of 1896–8, the Eastern Chinese Railway was enabled to complete the Russian system through Manchuria to the sea. Port Arthur, occupied by Russian warships in 1897, was leased from China in 1898. The Boxer revolt and the European intervention which followed it were made the pretext for the occupation of the whole of Manchuria. Evacuation was promised (1902) but delayed; and fresh demands were submitted to the Chinese Government (1903). Still more hazardous was the intervention of the Russian Government in the affairs of Korea. Here was the natural outlet for overcrowded Japan. There followed a conflict of diplomacy, which the Japanese cut short by beginning war.

CHAPTER XIII.

THE REFORM MOVEMENT IN RUSSIA.

THE initial reverses in the Japanese War produced deep mortification in Russia. Public opinion was not at all bitter against Japan. But troops went to the front with an excellent spirit; it was a point of honour to win; there were many volunteers for the medical service. Public bodies sent ambulances; individuals contributed to the Red Cross Society. Yet the Russian conduct of the War was more humiliating than the Japanese victories. The enormous difficulties of transport were vigorously handled by Prince Khilkóff; the mischief was in the fighting line. The systematic misrepresentations of the official telegrams only exaggerated the effect of private news; the Viceroy Alexéyeff was deeply mistrusted, and the few exceptions only proved the incapacity of officers of all ranks. Peculation was rampant; goods sent to the Red Cross were sold in Moscow; and one of the donors, the merchant Morozoff, was severely rebuked for protesting. The Zemstva joined in a wide organisation of war relief; even this innocent cooperation excited the wrath of Plehve. He still relied on the system of suspicion; of the troops forwarded an excessive proportion consisted of Jews, Poles, and over-aged reservists. On July 28, 1904, he was blown to pieces near the Warsaw Station at St Petersburg by the revolutionary Sazónoff. The sinking of the *Petropávlovsk* outside Port Arthur (April 13, 1904) had preceded his death, and the disastrous battle of Liaoyang followed close upon it.

For more than a month Plehve's place remained unfilled. The birth of a Crown Prince was celebrated by an edict finally abolishing corporal punishment. On September 8 Prince Svyatopolk-Mirsky was appointed. He was amiable, distinguished, and enlightened, and his governor-generalship in Vilna had been marked by wisdom and clemency; he received a number of journalists, and frankly asked for the confidence of the public. This unexpected appeal was welcomed by addresses from Zemstva, town councils, and other public bodies. There was an epoch of enthusiasm and trust. The Liberal weekly, *Right*, and even the *Novoë Vremya*, boldly asked for Press freedom and the civil liberties (November 2). The censorship practically stopped working. Many of Plehve's exiles were brought back. In October, some of the Liberators conferred in Paris with Poles and with Socialist Revolutionaries, to establish, if possible, a common platform.

The Liberators prepared for action. A great opportunity now offered. After some discussion between Shipóff and Prince Mirsky, it was agreed that a political conference open to all Zemstvo members should meet without official recognition. This conference was held in St Petersburg on November 19–22; and Shipóff privately reported its proceedings to Prince Mirsky, who informed the Emperor.

Ten "points" were submitted; an eleventh was added later. Eminent reformers from all the Zemstva were present, and the speeches were marked by unanimity and moderation. The conference conceived that its task was to avert a revolution by inducing the Government to grant reforms. The "eleven points" included inviolability of person and dwelling; freedom of conscience, of speech, of the Press, of meeting, and of association; equal civil rights for all Russian citizens (notably for the peasants); the abolition of the class basis in local government, a wider Zemstvo franchise, and smaller territorial units. The last point led to some disagreement; all wished to petition for some kind of elected national assembly; sixty, led by the Liberators, voted that it should have legislative functions, and thirty-eight, led by Shipóff, that it should only be consultative; but almost all agreed that it should fix the budget and control the actions of administrative officials. Other requests were for the abolition of exceptional laws, an amnesty for political prisoners, and freedom of public instruction. Prince Mirsky would not receive any deputation; and the resolutions were delivered to him by Shipóff in the form of a letter.

The eleven points were supported with enthusiasm by the educated opinion of the country. Many Zemstva and some town councils hastened to declare themselves. In some places discussion was prevented, but telegrams and addresses continued to come in, all advocating reform.

About the time of the Zemstvo conference appeared two pronouncedly radical newspapers, *Our Life* (November 14) and the *Son of the Fatherland* (November 30), both directed by Liberators. Their unmeasured criticism revived the activity of the censorship, which not only stopped the *Son of the Fatherland* for three months, but gave two warnings to the *Pravo*. Circulars forbade any articles on the Zemstvo conference or the question of a national assembly, and unlicensed news of addresses from public bodies (November 14–December 12). Nothing was to be printed on suggested changes in the system of government (December 14). The newspapers continued to speak out, and more punishments followed.

The public replied with a series of banquets and meetings, mostly organised by the Liberators for the fortieth anniversary of the law Courts of Alexander II. The law only recognised the right of public meeting for members of a given profession, and that only under close

CH. XIII.

restrictions. On December 3, at a banquet of the Union of Writers
in St Petersburg, 600 persons signed a claim for a constitution. In
Moscow, on December 4, a banquet of lawyers, professors, and journalists
accepted the Zemstvo programme with some additions. The same day,
400 St Petersburg lawyers marched down the streets and passed a resolution of protest in the Town Hall. From December 2 to 18 similar
meetings and banquets in the provinces demanded free law Courts, as
promised forty years before. Other professions followed the example
of the lawyers. The engineers met in St Petersburg (December 18)
and signed a programme, ostensibly of reforms required for the material
development of the country, but really of far more general scope. If
each profession met separately to adopt a political programme common
to all, the unanimity of the public would be strikingly displayed; it was
the acute mind of Milyukóff which saw most clearly the strength of this
weapon. On a programme drafted by Vernadsky was organised the
Academic Union of professors. On December 31 was held a banquet of
doctors. The Government, fearing to dissolve the banquets by force,
punished the keepers of the respective restaurants. This only drove the
demonstrations into the streets. In St Petersburg (December 11) and
in Moscow (December 19) students and schoolboys were attacked by the
police; Moscow University was closed.

The reverses in the War continued. General Kuropatkin, after announcing an advance, had to retreat in disorder. The fleet was crippled.
Reinforcements from the Baltic fired in panic on the Hull and Grimsby
fishermen (October 22), and there was an anxious delay before compensation was paid. In Russia the raising of recruits and the sending off
of reservists sometimes led to serious disorders. Before the surrender of
Port Arthur (January 15, 1905), the Emperor did something to come
to terms with public opinion. He summoned his chief advisers; the
Grand Dukes and Pobyedonóstseff opposed concessions; Witte hesitated,
and his hesitation was reflected in the sovereign's pronouncements of
December 25–7. The edict of December 25 foreshadowed several reforms.
The peasant legislation was to be harmonised with the other laws;
official arbitrariness was to be punished; the law Courts were to be
more independent; and the exceptional ordinances were to be revised.
The Zemstva and town councils were to have a wider franchise, and less
restricted functions; a smaller territorial unit was to be introduced into
the system. Religious toleration and the rights of aliens were to be
extended; the Press laws were to be regularised; and some factory
legislation was promised. Each Minister concerned was to draft the
suggested reforms, but there was no talk of a national assembly.

The edict was vague in wording and confused in order; it was
followed, two days later, by an official communication condemning the
reformers as instigators of riots, and declaring the claims of the public
meetings to be inadmissible in view of the unchangeable principles

sanctioned by the fundamental laws of the empire.   Meetings would be
forbidden, and officials who took part in them would be subjected to
special punishment.   The Zemstva were not to touch questions outside
their competence ; the Press was ordered to restore calm.   Here, as in each
later pronouncement, the sovereign claimed to be taking an initiative
his own, without any reference to public opinion.   More newspapers
suffered from the censorship.   Liberal Zemstvo men were roughly
handled in the streets of Tambóff.   On January 19, at a religious
ceremony in St Petersburg, a shot from a saluting battery threatened
danger to the life of the Emperor, who left the capital, not to return for
more than a year.

   At this point, the workmen entered into the movement.   Under the
influence of Zubátoff, there had sprung up in St Petersburg an Association of factory workers, privileged by the police and directed by the
priest Gapón.   It was allowed to work for a reform of the factory laws
and to collect funds.   In the course of 1904 Gapón had created eleven
district branches, whose electors and delegates all rendered him implicit
obedience.   At the great Putíloff factory the dismissal of two workmen
produced a strike of 13,200 persons.   A deputation, headed by Gapón,
demanded an eight hours' day, higher pay, better sanitary conditions,
and the right of election to arbitration committees.   These demands
were refused by the employers as ruinous ; and, without any disorder,
Gapón's whole organisation was brought into play.   Other large factories
struck work ; a strike committee was elected ; and relief committees
were established at each branch.

   As all further negotiations with the employers failed, it was decided
that Gapón, followed by all the strikers with their wives and children,
should present a petition to the Emperor.   This petition included not
only the economic demands of the workmen but the political demands
of the professional classes.   Gapón's followers simply meant to make an
appeal to their sovereign.   Gapón himself insisted that no arms should
be carried, but there is some reason to think that he contemplated
"rescuing the Tsar" from his counsellors.   Troops barred each approach
from the factories to the city; the bands of workmen, some of which
marched with ikons and church music, were mostly stopped in the
suburbs, where in several cases the troops fired on them.   Gapón fell
unwounded under a corpse at the Narva gate, but many passed the
cordons in small groups and walked up the Nevsky Prospekt ; they were
driven back by dragoons from the Winter Palace; there was firing on
the Nevsky; and in the Alexander Garden a volley from the troops
brought down some of the urchins who had climbed the trees ; later, the
crowd was again fired upon near the Moika canal.   The demonstrators
offered practically no resistance, except for the erection of some barricades in the Basil Island (January 22).   Gapón, after shaving his beard,
attended a meeting of protest in the evening, and then escaped over the

frontier; he joined hands with the revolutionaries, and gambled, nominally for the success of the cause, at Monte Carlo. Later, he returned to enter into relations with Count Witte's Government, and was killed by the revolutionaries as a traitor in 1906.

The Government went its own way. Prince Mirsky, who had lost all influence, gave way to Bulýgin, appointed to draft the promised reforms. General Trépoff became Governor-General of St Petersburg, with extraordinary powers, and later Assistant Minister of the Interior, with an independent control of the police of the empire. Trépoff was honest and fearless; he had sympathies with the workmen and with the Zemstva; but he was at home only in the routine of repression. He arranged a "deputation" of carefully selected workmen to ask the Emperor's pardon for the great procession. With Kokóvtseff, he issued an appeal to the working class to stand by the Government. Four hundred employers, when consulted by Kokóvtseff, would not make personal concessions to save the Government, and asked for general reforms (February 4–7, 1905). Two hundred Moscow manufacturers claimed that industrial questions could not be settled without civil rights for all Russian subjects, including the workmen.

Trépoff expelled many workmen from the capital, and these took home to the provinces exaggerated accounts of the events of January 22. The Social Democrats, who had done no more than join in the procession, now claimed the initiative in a huge social movement. Big factories and printing presses struck work in Moscow. Strikes followed in Kovno, Riga, Sarátoff, Vilna, Revel, and Mohiléff. Thirteen of the chief railway lines in European Russia stopped work; the Government put nearly all railways under martial law, and allowed the railway officials to arrest refractory employees. One after another, the Universities closed their own doors. The Minister of Public Instruction was for coercion; but the Ministers as a body decided to consult the Councils of the Universities. Most of these declared against a renewal of studies, and the Ministers decided not to reopen the Universities till September 14. Meanwhile, there began a series of innumerable murders of police officers, especially in the Jewish Pale. Isolated policemen were shot down in the dark, and the criminals nearly always escaped. On February 17 all else was thrown into the shade by the murder of the Grand Duke Sergius in the Kremlin at Moscow. The criminal, Kaláyeff, was a thorough enthusiast, but the crime was organised by the Socialist Revolutionaries, under the inspiration of the police agent Ázeff. The people in general showed no regret for one who as Governor-General of Moscow had persecuted all classes alike. Meanwhile, in January and February, in St Petersburg, Moscow, and other large towns, students or schoolboys were attacked by hooligans in the streets; priests sometimes showed their sympathy for these attacks, and there were already signs of instigation by the police. In the Caucasus, where murders of policemen were especially frequent, something like open war broke out between Mussulmans and Armenians, and the authorities looked on. Things were nearly as bad in the Jewish provinces. In Poland, the National Democrats, while seeking their advantage in the general confusion, had counselled calmness and organisation, but the socialists came into conflict with the police. Strikes spread on so vast a scale that they quickly alienated the business classes. The National Democrats issued a direct condemnation of all action that might lead to an armed rising. Their own policy was much more effective; they persuaded the peasants to refuse to do their business at the parish offices in the Russian language; in two-thirds of these offices the Russian tongue *de facto* disappeared. In Poland, as in the Caucasus, the Government replied by introducing martial law. But the general disorder was too serious to admit of delay, and Yermóloff, Minister of Agriculture, a persistent friend of reform from above, persuaded the Emperor to give shape to the promises of December, and to summon a national assembly.

On March 3 an imperial manifesto maintained the ancient principles of government, and appealed to all Russian men to remember their debt of service (a phrase which was later twisted into a text by the reactionary Union of the Russian People). But a rescript of the same date to Bulýgin declared the sovereign's intention of "henceforth, with God's help, summoning the worthiest persons elected by the population to share in the drafting and discussing of legislative proposals." The Emperor did not blind himself to the difficulty of combining this transformation with the necessary preservation of the "immutable fundamental laws," and, following an old precedent, in a separate edict he commanded the Ministers to discuss all suggestions sent in by public bodies or even by private persons. The Government hastened to publish the first results of its own work. Ordinary legislation was more precisely distinguished from imperial ordinances (June 19). To leave the Orthodox Church ceased to be a criminal offence, and religious teaching was to be given according to the confession and in the language of the given locality (April 30). In the western provinces aliens were allowed to acquire land; the gentry received the right of electing assemblies; and Polish and Lithuanian were licensed in private schools (May 14). Some limitations were set to the most vexatious of the ordinances affecting the Jews (June 29). The Ministry of Agriculture and Imperial Domains was replaced by a more competent organ of administration (May 19), and several sums due from the peasants to the Treasury were remitted (April 30). The right of four Ministers acting conjointly to stop newspapers was abolished, but the Minister of the Interior could take this action, subject to its confirmation later by the Senate (June 5). Trials of state criminals were put on a more regular basis (June 29). At the same time the Grand Duke Nicholas was put at the head of a newly formed Committee of Imperial Defence, with

more than the full rights of a Minister (June 21). The best of these
measures were no more than palliatives, and all of them came too late.
Much more direct was the effect of the invitation to the public to send
in memorials. It was practically an invitation for parties to form and
draw up their programmes.

The initiative lay at present with the Zemstvo men, and more
particularly with those of them who were also Liberators. This section
met separately in March and declared formally for universal, equal, direct,
and secret suffrage. The Liberals, as we may henceforth call them,
decided to ask for elective representation on the Commission which was
to shape the national assembly. They pronounced for two Chambers.
They also adopted almost unanimously the principle of compulsory
expropriation, with compensation, and the increasing of the peasant
holdings. This they did, because they feared the popularity of the
socialist parties, and because they did not feel strong enough to carry
the ramparts of the bureaucracy without the support of great masses of
the population. It was a policy of aggression; it alienated Shipóff
and the Moderates; it split the unity of the national movement; and it
complicated the simple political issue with vast social questions.

In April the Liberals held a larger Congress, to which some Zemstva
declined to send delegates. It pronounced for a legislative, not a consultative, parliament, and ratified all the decisions of the Congress of
February; it also refused to take part in the local committees of the
Government for the suppression of agrarian riots. Political discussion
was going on all over the country. The organising committee of the
Zemstvo Liberals invited town councillors to its next congress; Shipóff
and the Moderates arranged a meeting of their own (June 4).

The Zemstvo Liberals were being driven forward by the professional
class, which was profoundly radical, and had very few capable politicians.
This class rapidly developed the idea suggested by the banquets of 1904.
From each profession was organised a union, and each union had a
similar programme, of a content almost purely political. The union of
Engineers was the most energetic and one of the most radical. The
Academic union was more moderate. Clerks, primary school teachers,
doctors, lawyers, Jews, chemists, writers, women, teachers in secondary
schools, and railway employees, all formed unions in April or in May;
and the same months witnessed a series of meetings in which the several
unions took as their watchword a Constituent Assembly, with equal
rights for all religions and nationalities and for both sexes. Milyukóff
desired to make the unions a school from which could be developed
a more compact Liberal party, as opposed to the revolutionaries; while
he held back the unions, he used them to press on the Zemstvo Liberals,
with whom he had from the first been in the closest touch. In his new
party the Zemstvo men would supply the leaders and the unions the
weight of numbers. He brought to this task singular versatility

and tactical resource, and gradually established a strong personal authority.

In May all the unions were gathered together in a Union of Unions, an immense body which on general questions could claim to express the opinions of a large section of the Russian people. Fourteen unions sent delegates to the first Congress, which met in Moscow on May 21; it arranged for bi-monthly meetings, and appointed a committee to promote joint action. The sum contributed by each union was trifling (£2. 10s.); but the scheme at least realised on a huge scale the forbidden right of association, and there was no doubt as to the democratic character of its programme. Milyukóff became its President.

The Congress of Professors in April adopted Milyukóff's definition— "constitutional democratic principles"—and claimed self-government for the Universities. The Academy of Sciences, the highest learned body in the country, declared for immediate freedom of the Press. On April 7 a meeting of printers demanded an eight hours' day. The warnings of the censorship ceased almost entirely. The Railway union marked the junction of the professional class and the working class, for it included both. Two thousand five hundred Moscow workmen petitioned Kokóvt-seff for the rights of association and striking, and for industrial Courts with equal representation of employers and employed. The Minister's answers were not hostile. The Social Democrats made many converts; strikes took place all over Russia, and processions with red flags some-times ended in conflicts with the police. In Poland there was during two months an epidemic of strikes, extending to the railways; the Polish socialists, whilst abandoning the demand for independence, claimed a special Constituent Assembly for Poland; meanwhile, the schoolboys under the direction of the National Democrats refused to remain in schools where they were taught in Russian. The Law of June 19 allowed teaching in Polish in private schools; but such scholars were still denied access to public posts. For all that, these schools were organised on a vast scale, and a national Society (the "Mother of Schools"), whose collecting-boxes stood everywhere, practically took the education of the country into its own hands. In the Caucasus there was still chaos, and the tolerant Count Vorontzóff-Dashkoff was appointed Viceroy.

Still more threatening were the growing disorders among the Russian peasantry. They began in the impoverished provinces of Orél and Kursk (February 23) and became more organised when they spread to Chernígoff. The solidarity of the commune, artificially preserved by the reactionaries, could in a time of excitement be turned to the profit of revolution. A village would move as one man; it would call in other villages, and the whole mass would present itself at midnight before the manor-house, cut down the timber, wreck the gardens, pillage the barns, and carry off the plunder in carts brought for the purpose. Sometimes the cattle were taken; less often the house itself was wrecked; but violence to persons was very exceptional. The example of the south-centre was followed in Vítebsk, Lublin, and Bessarabia, and still more extensively in the Caucasus. Disorder spread to the provinces of Podolia, Vorónezh, and Nizhny Novgorod. Petitions streamed in from the peasants asking for seven acres per head, relief of taxation, the remission of the remaining redemption dues, freedom to rent land or to leave the commune, the liberation of agrarian rioters, the grant of state lands to those who tilled them, partial expropriation of landowners with compensation by the State, a legal limit to the extent of estates, freedom from special class laws, freedom of instruction, and especially the abolition of the Land Captains. Most of these claims reflected the influence of the Socialist Revolutionaries, and were adopted, despite the Land Captains, at the ordinary communal meetings. The peasant's idea was that the projected National Assembly was summoned chiefly in order to give him land; and curious compromises, on the basis of joint occupation, were made between landlords and peasants for the interim period.

Meanwhile the great battle of Mukden had ended in a confused retreat (March 23); and now the Baltic fleet was destroyed in the battle of Tsushima (May 27–8). This was a crowning catastrophe; and the censorship, completely disorganised, could not prevent its importance from being immediately realised. The official world was as if bewildered; the local authorities lost their heads; the word bureaucrat became the current term of abuse.

On the news of Tsushima, the Moderates and Liberals of the Zemstva reunited in a coalition congress held in Moscow (June 6). Marshals of the gentry and members of the town councils also attended. The congress adopted a direct address to the sovereign; it spoke of the criminal negligence and abuses of his counsellors, and urged the speedy summons of representatives of the whole empire. "Do not delay, Sire"; it ended, "in the terrible hour of the nation's trial, great is your responsibility before God and Russia." The Emperor received the deputation on June 19; the spokesman was Prince Sergius Trubetskóy, who, like Shipóff, had won the respect of all parties and classes. In simple language, he exposed the dangers which threatened society in general; few of the Emperor's counsellors could enlighten him as to the real state of things; it was all-important that the sovereign should be put in full touch with his people. The Emperor listened attentively, and returned the most gracious answer. "Dismiss your doubts," he said; "the will of the Tsar to summon national representatives is unchangeable"; he asked his hearers to invite the cooperation of all in the task of reform. His words were published, and their effect was immense; old men shed tears that they had lived to see this day. But the *Rus* was stopped for a month for its bold comments, and two other papers suffered.

Meanwhile, the reported details of the scheme for a National Assembly quite failed to satisfy progressive opinion. The Union of Unions, meeting in congress (June 6–8), demanded a Constituent Assembly, to finish the war and change the system of government. On the initiative of the engineers, several of whom had been arrested, a form was drawn up by which members of each implicated union declared their membership and invited arrest. The arrested were set free without trial. The Union of Unions held a third Congress in St Petersburg and in Finland on June 14–16. The advanced radicals carried a resolution condemning the scheme of a Duma before it was published, and urging that the elections should be boycotted. Milyukóff was now losing control: he turned for cooperation to the Zemstvo Liberals (July 24); the chief obstacle was a resolution of the Union of Unions covertly sanctioning terrorism. Not long afterwards, he and certain of his colleagues were arrested. He was soon set free; but his connexion with the Union of Unions was practically at an end; on the other hand, his task of forming a Liberal party in Russia was nearly accomplished.

A Peasants' union had joined the Union of Unions. It became an imposing reality when some of the more clear-headed of the Socialist Revolutionaries, dropping out of their propaganda all questions as to the form of government, circulated the enticing formula: "all the land for those that labour." Villages began to adopt this programme wholesale. Revolutionary propagandists had long been active in the navy; when the Black Sea fleet visited Odessa for its summer manœuvres, a petition for better food was preferred on the *Prince Potemkin*; the ringleader, Matyúshenko, was at once shot down, and the sailors in revenge killed most of their officers and took control of the ship. Admiral Krüger did not dare to engage the mutineers, and sailed away with the other ships. The *Potemkin* terrorised Odessa, where the sailors gave Matyúshenko a public funeral; but, in the absence of any further plan, they interned the ship in Roumania and later returned on a promise of pardon.

On June 15, members of various town councils had decided to create an organising committee similar to that of the Zemstvo Liberals. On the 28th, a Congress of 86 town councils met which unanimously condemned the published outlines of the government scheme for a Duma, and approved a draft of the Zemstvo Liberals, which included women's suffrage. Zemstvo men and town councillors now planned a great joint Congress for July 19 in Moscow. Trépoff ordered the organising committee to dissolve, and threatened to use force if the Congress met. The committee informed the Government that it had repeated its invitations, and 235 persons attended the Congress. The police entered the place of meeting and bade the assembly disperse; the President, Count Heyden, and the Chairman of the committee, Golovnín, refused, referring to the Emperor's appeal for cooperation; and the police withdrew. The Congress gave its preliminary approval to a draft of a constitution made by Múromtseff, Kokóshkin, and Shchepkin. A sort of Grand Remonstrance was also drawn up, enumerating the failures of Ministers to realise declared intentions of the sovereign, and a shorter address to the people was adopted and signed by the majority. It was couched in loyal terms, and discountenanced all violence; but it invited the people to meet as the Congress had done, without regarding police prohibitions. Golovnín presented the resolutions in person to General Trépoff; but the Government took no action, except to punish Moderate and Liberal papers for their reports of the proceedings.

A month later, on August 19, at last appeared the Act establishing an imperial Duma. The Duma was expressly declared to be consultative, and all alterations in the Duma Law were to be the exclusive business of the sovereign. For all electors there were two stages of election, and for most three or even four. Each village assembly sent men to the canton; the canton chose delegates; the delegates chose electors. The lesser gentry chose delegates, and these in conjunction with the greater gentry chose electors. The holding in land which entitled to a direct vote for the electors ranged in different provinces, according to value, from 250 acres to 2000; there was a similar franchise for other property and for commercial undertakings. Persons without property in country districts (doctors, schoolmasters, etc.) were excluded altogether. In the towns there was a high lodger franchise (a monthly rent equivalent to £10–11); the factory workmen as a class were entirely left out. Twenty-seven towns had their own members. The rest of the country elected by provinces: first, a peasant was chosen from each province, and then all the electors united to choose members for all the remaining seats. Thus a majority of one in a province could carry all the seats but one for that province: this was, in fact, a premium on quick changes in public opinion, and a temptation to manipulation by the local officials. Each class could only choose delegates from its own members; hence the large number of peasants in the Duma. No man could be elected except for his own district, and thus many capable men were debarred from election. The control of the lower peasant elections was put in the hands of the Land Captains; but there was a right of appeal. Local electoral committees controlled the higher elections, and the Senate was the supreme arbiter.

The Duma thus elected was in general to sit in at least four sections; later events led to the dropping of this regulation. It was to choose its own presidents, a concession given late in the day at the instance of General Trépoff. Its members were inviolable, unless charged at law with criminal offences; they received £1 per day, and took a solemn vow to the Emperor and Autocrat. The Duma appointed its own clerks and ushers, but not its police. It could discuss the public part of the budget, alienation of state property, and the railway administration; it could interpellate the Ministers on the conduct of the officials; it could discuss any Bills drawn up by the Ministers. It could itself initiate laws; but here the procedure was cumbrous in the extreme. No action could be taken for a month, after which the Minister returned the Duma's Bill with his criticisms. In case of disagreement with him, the Duma required a two-thirds majority to press the Bill further. The Bill then passed to the already existing Council of State, a nominated and purely bureaucratic body. If the Duma disagreed with the Council of State, a joint committee of both sat under the presidency of the latter. The last step was the assent of the sovereign. In case of delays on the part of the Duma, its consent could be dispensed with altogether. The Press was admitted, except to sittings specially closed by the President or a Minister. The Peace of Portsmouth followed on August 29.

The public was eagerly discussing whether to take part in the Duma. The Union of Unions was sharply divided; some argued for a general political strike. But the Liberators were all against boycott, and Múromtseff set to work to draw up an order of procedure inside the Duma on the basis of the new Law. Even the more moderate of the Zemstva and town councils asked for the immediate grant of the civil freedoms as necessary for the conduct of the elections. Another Zemstvo Congress, including Poles, Cossacks, Caucasians, and Siberians, met without hindrance on September 25. It decided to elect to the Duma, in order to make it legislative and secure universal suffrage. The Congress voted almost unanimously for compulsory expropriation of land, with compensation to private landholders. This was the last great Congress. With the Zemstvo Liberals, the influence of Milyukóff had become more and more paramount. They had broken with the moderate minority and had turned the Zemstvo into a party weapon. It remained to constitute the new Constitutional Democratic party; and this was fixed for October 25.

By the Edict of September 9, the university professors were to choose their own Rectors and Deans of Faculties, and to be responsible for the internal order of their respective institutions; the inspectors of discipline were now subordinated to the elected Rectors. The students set about organising university meetings for the general public. Their leaders were revolutionaries, and their guests were of the most motley character; sometimes they numbered several thousands; violent speeches were in a few cases followed by damage to the arms and portrait of the Emperor; a severe rebuke from the elected Rector of Moscow, Prince Sergius Trubetskóy, passed unheeded; and soon afterwards he died suddenly, while pleading at the Ministry of Public Instruction for a more general reform. University Councils pressed the Government to license public meetings outside. On October 25 a decree accorded this right with many reservations; notice had to be given some days in advance; the programme and names of speakers had to be submitted;

CH. XIII.

and in case of any deviation, the meeting could be closed with heavy punishments. On October 28 the police, after a very clear warning, temporarily seized certain university buildings. While the Commission of Kobekó sat revising the press laws, the censorship was unusually severe.

In the centre, in the south, and especially in the Baltic provinces, peasants burnt down manor-houses, escorted the landlords to the railway, and appropriated land. The more moderate confined themselves to very orderly meetings; their language was plain, and their demands were radical; but it was clear that they were breaking loose from the propagandists and finding their own natural leaders. With very few exceptions, all were profoundly loyal to the monarchical principle; they quite understood that the Duma meant access to the sovereign, past the Land Captains. On August 16 the Peasants' union held its first Congress in Moscow; delegates came from twenty-three provinces; it joined the Union of Unions, but exercised a sobering and restraining influence, notably on its own propagandist organisers; however, the Radical land programme was adopted in its sharpest definition and was for a long time to complicate the transition to constitutional government; the peasantry of whole provinces held Congresses reminiscent of the Federations of the French Revolution.

Much closer was the bond between the professional class and the workmen. The mass meetings in the Universities were under the direction of socialists, who in Kieff and Odessa boldly demanded a democratic republic. In October the strike movement rapidly spread. On October 20 it was wrongly reported that the Congress of the Railway union had been arrested in Moscow; at once the railway men in Moscow struck work for the civil freedoms and a full amnesty; the example was followed by nearly every railway in the empire. Factories were immobilised and the Government was paralysed. Prince Khilkóff and Count Witte were informed that the strikers would only stop for an immediate grant of the civil freedoms, a Constituent Assembly, and universal suffrage. On the 27th, Trépoff ordered the troops not to spare their cartridges; the same day, all the unions joined the strike; they sent men to stop all work in banks, business offices, law Courts, schools, and even in the Senate. Chemists, doctors, and magistrates refused to work; the newspapers did not appear; the electric light was cut off and there were fears for the water supply; silence reigned in the streets and the inhabitants prepared themselves to stand siege against famine. The workmen now put forward purely political demands, and began to organise on a permanent basis. A Council of Workmen Delegates from the different factories met on October 27 and secured the obedience not only of its own class but of the professions; it ordered employers to close their works under threat of wrecking (October 30); it bade the workmen cease all payments for food or lodging while the strike lasted, and threatened any purveyors who might protest. In the midst of this turmoil, the new Liberal party, the Constitutional Democrats (a name soon shortened to "Cadets"), was holding its first meeting in Moscow. Thoroughly frightened, the Government gave way.

The Emperor was ready to dismiss his trusted but unpopular Ministers, Pobyedonóstseff, Trépoff, and others. He was not ready to accept as their successors men who were unknown to him and represented the demands of the people. He had, therefore, no alternative but to turn to the opposition inside the bureaucracy, that is, to Count Witte, whose nominal post of President of the Ministers was now made that of a Premier with a Cabinet. Witte framed the Manifesto of October 30 and the accompanying government communication. The Manifesto upheld the integrity of the empire and the principle of cooperation between sovereign and people; in the clearest terms it promised freedom of conscience, speech, meeting, and association, and the widest possible extension of the franchise. The Duma was made frankly legislative; that is, no law was to be made without its consent; its control over the acts of officials was to be made effective. The communication frankly traced the existing confusion to the contrast between the system of government and the aspirations of the thinking public; while rejecting the hysterical demands of extreme groups, it assumed that the majority of Russian subjects were not unreasonable; all the civil freedoms were essential and should be conceded in practice at once; the Council of State should be recruited with elected members; repression should not be applied to acts which clearly did not threaten society or the State.

Officials and police felt themselves abandoned by the new edict. The murders of policemen were past reckoning. In the summer, the reactionaries had begun to unite to defend their vested interests under the name of "Genuine Russians." They were urged forward by the *Moscow Gazette* and formed provincial branches, weak in numbers but strong in the support of the police, who had close contact with the casual criminal class. In very many cities and towns the educated radicals were attacked by mobs under the eyes of the police. In Kieff and Odessa, where revolutionary Jews had been prominent, it was still worse. Here, on the destruction of the Emperor's insignia, the responsibility for which has never been fixed, crowds dispersed the demonstrators, fell upon the Jews, and plundered their shops wholesale for three days; brutal murders were committed; official complicity in these outrages was hardly disguised; plunderers and soldiers, even before the *pogróms* began, alleged the permission of the Emperor and assigned a limit of three days, which was practically always adhered to; in every case troops and police were able to stop the *pogróms* without fighting as soon as they chose. All these facts were established by the Government through investigations on the spot; telegrams from General Trépoff suggested his connivance.

CH. XIII.

In St Petersburg, the workmen almost seemed to be masters of the situation. The Council of Workmen Delegates now represented 74 factories and four trade unions; it controlled the Union of Unions, whose saner members had followed Milyukóff into the Cadet party. The Council stopped the general strike at midday on November 1, "to arm for the final struggle for a Constituent Assembly and a democratic republic." It was punctually obeyed all over Russia.

The Cadets feared revolution; while claiming a Constituent Assembly, they were sobered by the Manifesto. Shipóff's Moderates received it with genuine gratitude, and united under the name of Octobrists. Before the issue of the Manifesto, Witte had asked Shipóff to help in forming a Cabinet, reserving only the more specialist posts. Shipóff was ready; but he saw that a Reform Minister must carry the public as a whole; and he insisted that the Cadets should be represented. Count Witte was prepared to invite not only Count Heyden but Múromtseff and Petrunkévich. He invited the Cadets to name three to confer with him; but they did not send their best men, and their spokesman demanded a Constituent Assembly. Witte could not imperil the Emperor's autocracy; and these negotiations came to nothing. Witte now limited himself to the Moderates; but he had meanwhile secured as Minister of the Interior the staunch reactionary P. Durnovó. Shipóff therefore withdrew from the combination, and separate negotiations with his friends, Prince Eugene Trubetskóy and Guchkóff, also broke down by reason of the general distrust of Witte. Of the reformers only Prince Urúsoff accepted office, and the rest of the Cabinet was chiefly formed of officials.

In Finland, four years of passive resistance had culminated in an almost unanimous strike, lasting for eight days. A kind of national militia, the Red Guard, was organised; and the strike was conducted with perfect order. A manifesto was issued which promised the restoration of the old Finnish liberties and a reform of the Diet on the basis of universal suffrage (November 17), and the strike ceased at once. A Diet was elected, the first since 1899, and met in December; it sat for three months, and passed a Bill reforming its own constitution and another conceding universal franchise for men and women and the principle of proportional representation. These Bills were confirmed by the sovereign. In Poland, on November 5, a procession of 200,000 persons, with national flags and national songs, marched through the streets of Warsaw; and at a great meeting on the next day the National Democrats put forward the demand for autonomy. An orderly congress of peasants from 1200 communes repeated their claims. To a deputation of Poles Witte returned a contemptuous answer, and on November 10 all Poland was placed under martial law. The Polish socialists still kept up their agitation; and strikes and murders continued. On November 8, the sailors at Cronstadt mutinied. This was the result of revolutionary propaganda; but the mutineers had no plan at all; they wrecked some houses, but were quickly brought to order, and the ringleaders were handed over to a Court-martial.

Disregarding some overtures from Count Witte, the workmen went on with their organisations. The Council of Workmen Delegates had a capable leader in Khrustalyéff, a lawyer of peasant origin. On November 11 the Council decreed that no one should work more than eight hours a day. Many employers closed their factories, and the attempt failed. The Council now declared a second general strike as a protest against the punishment of the mutinous sailors and against martial law in Poland. This strike had little support from the public; and on November 20 the Council stopped it, "to save the strength of the workmen for a decided engagement." The Council came to be nicknamed the "working men's Government"; and people asked whether Witte would arrest Khrustalyéff or Khrustalyéff arrest Witte. The Union of Unions was by this time the satellite of the Council; it had lost all authority and common sense, and, by drowning the public in floods of words, it helped to bring on the inevitable reaction.

On October 31, Witte summoned the chief editors, asked for their cooperation, and promised them a press law. The censorship opened all subjects to public discussion and remitted many punishments. At this time anything could be printed. Social Democrat newspapers appeared openly, forbidden books were published, and political caricature was free. The result was a deluge of literature, violent attacks on the *bourgeoisie*, and an atmosphere of hysteria and unbridled licence; picture postcards plainly recommended political assassination. The Government hurried on the new Law, which was issued on December 7. The programme of any newspaper, if not criminal or immoral, was to be sanctioned; deviations from it could be prosecuted at law and heavily punished; incitement to strikes or mutinies and the circulation of false or disastrous news were declared criminal offences; books remained under the former *régime*.

Witte also secured material relief for the peasants. By the Manifesto and decrees of November 16 the redemption dues, the heaviest burden of the peasantry, were reduced by one-half for 1906 and then remitted altogether; and loans for the purchase of land were issued on better terms. But there was famine in the grain-producing provinces, and the agrarian riots spread everywhere; in some districts no estate remained untouched. Revolutionaries announced that the Duma was to give all the land to the peasants. The movement soon passed beyond their control. Huge crowds gathered openly, and the police were powerless; there was brutal maiming of cattle; violence to person remained rare. The Peasants' union tended to diminish the excesses. In Krolévetz, Sumy, and Pokzóvskoe, officials were expelled and self-government attempted. In the Baltic provinces, the Lettish workmen and labourers gathered in thousands, besieged and stormed the castles of the German

CH. XIII.

landlords, engaged the local troops, overthrew the local authorities, held all the open country, and declared a republic.

Even the troops began to waver in their allegiance. Some seized the Siberian railway and hurried homewards. The disorders of Cronstadt were repeated at Vladivostók. At Sevastopol revolutionary sailors seized a ship and gave battle under Lieutenant Schmidt. Soldiers mutinied at Kieff, Vorónezh, Bobrúisk, Ekaterinodár, Novorossiisk and Moscow. Their usual demands were for better pay, food, and general treatment; but strangely mingled with these claims were undigested formulae of the propagandists.

On November 19, the last Zemstvo Congress met in Moscow. The majority were already Cadets; but the agrarian disorders had had their effect on the gentry and the Moderates were uniting in a new party, the Octobrists, to develop loyally the principles of the Emperor's Manifesto. The Cadets, on the other hand, still leant towards the Left, which they hoped to assimilate and control. The Congress nearly split up on the question of a Constituent Assembly; in the end it recommended universal suffrage and constituent functions for the Duma. It asked for a full amnesty and the abolition of the death penalty; and it promised moral support to Witte, so long as he really developed the Constitution. It approved of autonomy for Poland.

The distrust of the country put Count Witte at the mercy of the reactionaries. The chief force in the Cabinet was now Durnovó. He was master of the police, and he was frankly for repression. General Trépoff, who had become commandant of the imperial Palace, could press such a policy at the Court. The workmen were talking of another general strike when the Government took action. The committee of the Peasants' union was arrested (November 29); on December 5 the Government laid hands on Khrustalyéff. Martial law was proclaimed at St Petersburg (December 12). Severe punishment was imposed for strikes, especially of the railwaymen. Meetings were forbidden. The extremists replied with a revolutionary manifesto inviting the withdrawal of deposits from the Savings Banks, the non-payment of taxes, and an open conflict with the Government; this manifesto they tried to print in all the papers (December 13); those which consented were confiscated; forty printing presses were closed in St Petersburg alone. The Council of Workmen Delegates was largely responsible for a general strike of the postal and telegraph men (December 14) which for two months disorganised the whole service. On December 16 almost the whole Council (190 persons) was arrested. On December 18, the Government issued a weighty impeachment of the revolutionary parties. These proclaimed a third general strike in St Petersburg. This strike was insignificant; but the news travelled to Moscow where workmen came on to the streets and fought with the police. The Moscow revolutionaries were unready and disunited; but there was a sporadic series of street skirmishes in the north-western part of the city (December 22–January 1). A committee tried to coordinate the scattered bands; barricades were hastily erected and telegraph wires were stretched across the streets. The insurgents were a few hundreds; the peaceful inhabitants were between two fires; shots fired from the windows of their houses brought down the vengeance of the troops. The result of this futile revolt was to disgust and frighten all sober people; and the Moscow rising was the turning-point in the story of these troubled years. Throughout, the events in the capitals had been hastily reproduced in other towns; and to this period belong attempts to dispense with established authorities in Sarátoff, Rostóff, Novorossiisk, Ekaterinoslav, Sochi, Sukhúm, and Pyatigórsk.

Count Witte made his greatest concession under the influence of the Moscow rising. A decree extending the franchise was suddenly launched on December 24. Taken together with the Manifesto of October 30, it completely altered the character of the Duma. It conceded votes, and with votes also eligibility, to almost all those excluded by the Law of August 19. The franchise was given to all taxpayers; the extension of the lodgers' franchise introduced the whole professional class; the whole class of workmen was now enfranchised on a similar basis to that of the peasants; there were excluded only factories with less than 50 workmen, the poorer craftsmen, the lower employees in offices, and servants. The Law allowed preliminary electoral meetings without the police; the elections were to be controlled by more popular bodies, and the verification of them was entrusted to the Duma itself. Though there were still the same stages of election, universal suffrage had been virtually granted. But the enormous importance of these concessions was overlooked in the universal disorder and the drastic repression that followed it.

The measures of Durnovó soon passed the bounds within which they might have secured moral support. Punitive columns had been sent down to the more disaffected districts. The riotous peasants had returned home, and offered no resistance. Villages were cannonaded, and innocent and guilty perished alike. In reprisal, General Sákharoff was killed in Sarátoff, and the brutal Luzhenovsky in Tambóff; the account of the treatment of Luzhenovsky's assassin, Spiridónova, after her arrest, raised a storm of indignation and led to the murder of two police officers. In the Baltic provinces, the stewards pointed out their chief enemies, who were summarily dealt with. Livonia and Courland long remained in a state of ferment; and there were numerous tales, not without foundation, of men buried alive by the soldiers or tortured in prison. In Georgia, General Alikhánoff burnt villages and reigned by terror.

In the central Police Department at St Petersburg, a gendarme, Kommissároff, printed at the government expense violent appeals to riot, which were circulated by the "Union of the Russian People" all over the country. The Assistant Minister of the Interior, Prince Urúsoff, who had done all that he could to prevent *pogróms*, brought the matter

CH. XIII.

before Witte ; but the Premier, who knew how powerful were the friends
of the Union at the Court, dared not do more than dismiss Kommissároff.
Urúsoff resigned his office and became a candidate for the Duma.

Everybody was now preparing for the first Russian parliament. The
Government was recovering from its panic, and set itself to increase its
powers again. The Manifesto of March 5 excluded from parliamentary
discussion the fundamental laws of the empire and the constitutions of
the legislative bodies. The Ministers received power to issue temporary
laws when the Duma was not sitting. The old Council of State was
reconstituted. For legislative purposes it was to consist, half of
nominees of the sovereign, and half of members elected from the clergy,
Universities, Zemstva, gentry, and commercial committees ; the President
was chosen by the sovereign. The Council received equal legislative
rights with the Duma. The two Houses could not deal with estimates
founded on existing laws, ordinances, or imperial commands, or with
credits for war or the imperial household ; ordinary military and naval
estimates were to be discussed if the Ministry could not cover them from
money in hand. If the Houses did not pass the budget, the Government
could substitute the estimates of the preceding year. When they disagreed, the Government could take the estimate nearest to that of the
preceding year (March 23). Details of loans and currency were reserved
to the Minister of Finance (April 10), and other important financial
functions to the nominated members of the Council of State. All these
ordinances were made fundamental and unchangeable. Army, navy, and
foreign policy were declared prerogatives of the Emperor; the liberties of
the Manifesto of October were again enumerated, but the room left for
limitations and exceptions robbed them of all real meaning (May 6).

A mass of ordinary legislation was hurried through before the
Duma met. The severest penalties were imposed for the possession
of explosives (February 22) ; arrangements were made for the use of the
troops for police purposes (February 20), and wreckers of property were
made materially responsible for the losses they caused (May 9) ; strikes
of country labourers were to be rigorously punished (April 28) ; " false
reports " on the action of officials or on public calamities entailed
imprisonment or fines (April 5); "false rumours" on the financial position
of the Government involved from one to two years of prison (May 5) ;
the press law was tightened (March 31), but the preliminary censorship was abolished for books (May 9). The right of meeting was
practically nullified by a decree of March 17, which required a license
in each case from the administrative authorities, forbade assemblies in
restaurants, hotels, or inns, and limited the use of professional establishments to meetings for professional objects. The right of association
was still more severely limited by a decree of the same date ; all societies,
including even political parties, had to obtain legalisation from the
Government ; the programmes had to be submitted in detail ; any

deviation entailed prohibition; membership of officials, association of workmen, and the union of two societies were specially restricted; the penalties under both these Laws were imprisonment and fines. A decree of March 17 made a bid for the settlement of the all-important land question without the Duma; local agricultural committees were to be constituted, consisting mainly of officials; they were to consider measures for the relief of the peasants and the extension of their holdings.

Meanwhile, the elections were proceeding. The spokesmen chosen by the peasants to speak direct to the Tsar were not so much party men as persons possessing the general confidence. Their main thought was, of course, land; and most of them on reaching St Petersburg massed instinctively under the title of "non-party" and diligently attended meetings of various parties to discover who would do most for their class. Not more than seven reactionaries, mostly peasants, were elected to the first Duma. Workmen began by boycotting the elections: but joined in when they saw that the Opposition would win; the "majority men" of the Social Democrats remained self-excluded, and of the more moderate "minority men," at first only ten were elected. The issue lay between the Cadets and the Octobrists. The Octobrist plea for sobriety had been seriously prejudiced by the measures of Durnovó; Shipóff was beaten in Moscow, and sixteen Octobrists under Count Heyden and Stakhóvich formed a nucleus round which rallied some forty other members. The Cadets alone conducted an organised electoral campaign; they understood the Government's electoral law better than it did itself; and over 150 of their carefully chosen candidates were elected. Milyukóff had been excluded on formal grounds; but he was always in the lobbies, and every decision of the House was referred to him. There was always a line of possible cleavage between the strong Right wing of the Cadets, which included nearly all the ablest men, and the Radicals of the professional class: but the strong hand of Milyukóff held together not only the party, but the Duma itself. A third party, the Labour group, was only formed at Sarátoff during the elections; it originated in the Peasants' union, which since the diminution of repression had again rapidly grown in numbers; its platform was: "all the land for those who labour"; in St Petersburg it received the adhesion of many peasant member͟ ͟d it soon numbered 90. The various alien races grouped themselve͟ ͟ ͟r and claimed self-government; the Poles (26) were all Nationa͟l The claim for Polish autonomy was favoured both by the ͟ the Labour group.

There was a new Ministry to face the Duma. C͟ he had successfully negotiated a foreign loan for i͟ was dismissed. Durnovó also left office. ͟he ne͟ possessed the personal confidence of the Emper͟ and from the start he did not believe that t͟ with the Duma. Most of his colleagues͟

CH. XIII.

notable was the Minister of the Interior, Peter Stolýpin, a country gentleman who had served with credit in high provincial posts and, as Governor of the turbulent province of Sarátoff, had kept his head amidst the general panic of the authorities.

On May 10 the Emperor visited St Petersburg, received the Duma at the Winter Palace, and delivered with great spirit a simple appeal to its patriotism. In the Tauris Palace the distinguished jurist Múromtseff was elected President, almost unanimously. The Cadets, fresh from the polls, hoped to carry the ramparts of the bureaucracy by moral force; in order to secure the unanimity of the Duma, careful account was taken of every element in it. As the Emperor's speech contained no programme, the Duma assumed the initiative in its Address to the Throne, worded with restraint, but presupposing a decisive authority in the people. It spoke of "strictly constitutional principles," of "perfecting the principles of a national representation"; it demanded control over the executive, responsibility of Ministers and their dependence on the majority of the Duma, a reform of the newly constituted Upper House, and for the Lower full competence in legislation, a monopoly of financial control, and the right of receiving petitions. The programme included the removal of all civil disabilities of class or nationality, the final abolition of the death penalty, expropriation of land for the benefit of the peasants, freedom of association for working men, free education, readjustment of the taxes, and local government for all races resting on universal suffrage; the Duma took on itself the care of the soldiers and sailors; the Address concluded with an imperative appeal for an immediate amnesty for "all acts which have resulted from religious or political convictions." On the demand for a complete amnesty, the Octobrist Stakhóvich invited a solemn condemnation of the countless and incessant murders of officials; leaning towards the Labour group, the Cadets refused his amendment; and its few supporters left the House. The rest unanimously adopted the whole draft.

Goremýkin replied on May 26. He separated the matters which the Duma might discuss from those which it might not. He declared the proposal of expropriation to be "inadmissible"; the civil liberties oug... rtainly to be secured, but the exceptional ordinances must be r... deal with murderers and robbers; his own programme dealt ...with the land question, and promised Bills for the abolition ...or the revision of some indirect taxes, and for punishing ...of officials. His speech was followed by a storm of ...he whole condition of the empire; the Ministers, ...y questioning, kept their seats for a time and then ...nsure was, hereupon, carried amidst the greatest ...ven dissentients.

...lete deadlock; the Ministry did not resign, ...ssolved. All interest was centred in the

sovereign, and it was seen that his principal advisers were not in the Cabinet. Múromtseff's order of procedure was discussed and adopted. The Ministry submitted many important projects of reform, including the extension of peasant land-tenure, the reorganisation of local law Courts, the compensation of those who had suffered from wrongful action of the officials, and the punishment of criminal conduct in the government service. The Duma brought in Bills as to its right of initiative in legislation, on administrative imprisonment, on civil equality, on freedom of conscience, as to the abolition of the death penalty, the revision of the press laws, the freedom of meeting and association, and the right to strike. Time was found to pass one government Bill through all the stages of legislation; it was a vote of £1,500,000 for famine relief. The issue before the country, however, was not any individual measure, but the question who was master.

Depending entirely on the support of the people, the Duma frequently turned itself into a public tribune for exposing the abuses of the administrative system; interpellation of Ministers was used effectively by the Cadets and extravagantly by the Labour group. The most notable interpellation was on the fresh *pogróm* at Byelostók. Here, after many murders of policemen, the Union of the Russian People hounded on a mob against the Jews, and murders and robberies continued for the usual three days; the commanding officers and the civil authorities looked on. The Duma sent down its own commissioners to Byelostók and printed its report. Prince Urúsoff unfolded the whole story of Kommissároff, and pleaded for direct communication between sovereign and people (July 4). Stolýpin, alone among the Ministers, gained in reputation from these debates.

Yet these few weeks of tension were doing much for the political education of the members. Under the able discipline of the Cadets, the initial flood of words began to abate. The agrarian disorders continued, and in Odessa gangs of desperate robbers invaded the restaurants; but the total of terrorist acts showed a marked decrease. All eyes were on the Duma; letters from whole village communes promised support, if it were touched. Meanwhile, country gentlemen protested against this whirl of change; and the official world, though timid and correct, showed its deep resentment; at poorly attended gatherings the reactionaries sent telegrams to the *Government Messenger* begging the sovereign to dissolve the "seditious" Duma.

The Labour group brought in a Bill to expropriate all land and allow only small holdings on the basis of personal labour. The Cadets, instead of frankly opposing this wild scheme, based their Bill on no[t] dissimilar principles. An enormous Land Committee was constituted and the Duma proposed to organise its own local committees to collect materials. The Court was inclined to end the crisis by accepting a Ministry from outside the bureaucracy. Communications were opened

CH. XIII.

with Shipóff; he was summoned to the Emperor and invited to take steps to form a Cabinet. This was the turning-point; for Shipóff, as was known, would not take office without a frankly national Ministry. He aimed at a patriotic coalition of all the central forces for the establishment of constitutional rule, and, with this object, he offered the majority in the Cabinet to his rivals—the Cadets. But Milyukóff and his party refused to join in the coalition. The choice now lay between a Cadet Ministry and the bureaucracy. The Court was half disposed to yield; direct negotiations were opened with Milyukóff by General Trépoff.

The conflict had already become more acute. On July 3 the existing Ministry had published everywhere a government communication, as an antidote to the popularity of the Duma's Land Committee. It recounted the causes of impoverishment, and promised to the peasants ten specific measures of relief, including facilities for sale, the conversion of communal into personal property, and perhaps even the sale of land to peasants by the Government under cost price; it openly and at length combated the propositions introduced in the Duma; and it ended with an injunction to trust to the constant solicitude of the Emperor. On July 16 the Duma again called on the Ministry to resign. On July 17 it adopted the draft of an address to the people in reply to the government communication, which in spite of Milyukóff's influence was passed on July 19. The Labour group now left the House, because it did not consider the address strong enough; and the Octobrists abstained from voting because they did not want any address at all. For a moment at least, the unanimity of the Duma had disappeared, and a debate on a vital issue had ended in a fiasco.

Stolýpin was strongly against a Cadet Ministry; Trépoff urged that 30,000 workmen might march on Peterhof; the veteran Goremýkin replied that 60,000 would be better; this sturdy interjection ruled the decision, and Stolýpin was appointed Premier with orders to dissolve and with authority to summon a new Duma on the same electoral law. Early on Sunday, July 21, without any notice to the President, the decree of dissolution was posted in the streets: a second Duma was summoned for March 5, 1907; next day followed a Manifesto, which upbraided the members, and summoned "all well-intentioned Russians to unite for the support of the legal power." Troops were moved into St Petersburg, and soldiers guarded the doors of the Tauris Palace. Some 200 ex-members, including President, Vice-Presidents, and the Cadet and Labour leaders, gathered on Sunday night at Viborg in Finland; the Octobrist and Polish leaders also came, but withdrew; the rest issued an appeal to the nation not to pay taxes, not to grant recruits, and not to consider itself bound by foreign loans until the Duma was restored. But the Cadets possessed no organisation for conspiracy, and the initiative was left to any town or village which

might think fit to renew the movement of the preceding October. Thus the appeal was nothing more than a last summons to the Ministry to surrender on moral grounds which it did not admit. Stolýpin was not frightened; he allowed the members to return to St Petersburg, and there they scattered of themselves. The revolutionary parties and some of the Labour members issued two separate appeals proposing an incoherent plan for a rising. Armed risings did indeed break out among the Russian troops at Sveaborg in Finland, among the sailors at Cronstadt, and on a cruiser off Revel; but these feeble attempts were easily suppressed. The vast majority of Russians strongly disapproved of the dissolution; but the country was confused and in part alienated by the tactics of the Cadets; and, above all, it had been exhausted by the disorders of the preceding winter.

In the void thus created Stolýpin was master of the situation. He defined his policy as presenting two fronts. He would fight revolution, that is, all attempts to impose changes on the Government by violence; but he would separate the revolutionaries from the peaceable population, secure for the latter all the guarantees of civil liberty, and, assuming the initiative which the Government had so far left to the Duma, use the interval before the next session to introduce reforms in detail. He began with a circular ordering the exact observance of laws by the officials, but he refused to give up the exceptional ordinances.

Terrorism, revived by an offshoot of the S.R.'s, under the name of Maximalists, was met by the institution of field Courts-martial with closed doors (September 1); one day was allowed for preparing an accusation, two for the trial, and one for the execution of the sentence. The Socialist Revolutionaries were reduced to the insignificance of a "cottage industry"; the death penalty was made applicable to ordinary robberies and even to insults to officials. Over 600 persons were executed under this ordinance; but ordinary crime only increased. A decree of August 18 dealt severely with propaganda in the army.

Stolýpin had invited Shipóff, Heyden, and other Moderates to join him; they required effective guarantees of the civil liberties which Stolýpin could not obtain, and he was left to fight his battle for reform almost alone. A brutal attempt on his life did not change his course, but he was hampered on every side. Much of the money voted by the Duma for famine relief had been misappropriated; and the reactionary Assistant Minister Gurko was found guilty of criminal negligence. The Ministers adopted a large part of the Liberal programme by placing on the market appanage lands (August 25), communal lands (September 9), and cabinet lands (October 2). A very valuable measure abolished many class restrictions on the peasants; they were granted full rights of admission to the government service, could leave or join village communes, and could partition family property and elect their Zemstvo members without interference (October 18). The

Law of November 22 went much further; any head of a family could claim his communal holding as personal property; the claimant could also demand that his holding, instead of being as usual in several strips, should be united in one place; but the final decision of doubtful points was left to the Land Captains; and there was room for much injustice to the remaining members of the commune. This Law was nothing less than a revolution against state socialism; it favoured the development of personal initiative and a better standard of cultivation. The Government applied it at once without waiting for the new Duma; but it was long before the peasants availed themselves of it.

Stolýpin declared himself a constitutionalist, but not a parliamentarist. He stood on the Fundamental Laws; he would not be dependent on a parliamentary majority, yet he required a Duma with which he could work. But his supporters were few at the Court, and still fewer in the country. There sprang up a concealed and chaotic class warfare. Instead of the open agrarian riots of the preceding winter, there was an unending series of individual attempts, made at night, to burn this or that barn on the squire's estate. The Government replied with wholesale sentences of banishment without trial, which in this year reached the enormous figure of 35,000. The prisons were crowded to bursting point, and epidemics broke out. The Zemstvo franchise had not been widened, and now the threat of expropriation lost one Zemstvo after another to the Liberals. The new Zemstvo executives got rid of their radical employees. For the Cadets, political propaganda was made impossible. The Cadet party was refused legal recognition; officials were dismissed for belonging to it; the Cadet clubs were closed; those who had signed the Viborg appeal were struck off the roll of electors. The Octobrists were still only a potential party. They had no Press and no organisation; their meetings were like private gatherings. The temporary paralysis of the mass of middle opinion favoured the reactionaries. Courtiers and officials who resented any change from the old system now united to work on the mind of the sovereign. They had complete freedom of speech; they had the good will and often the active support of the local Governors; they were backed by many of the wealthier landowners now organised as the "United Gentry"; they had their own theorists, such as the doctrinaire Samárins of Moscow, who now reprinted their suggestion that the Duma should be replaced by drafting commissions attached to the several Ministries and elected partly by lot (November). But their chief spokesmen were men of a lower type, semi-official adventurers who saw their chance in the nominal establishment of representative institutions; such were the chief organisers of the Union of the Russian People. These inveighed against Stolýpin as a radical; they obtained almost entire control of the machinery of the Church; they sometimes terrorised local officials; in some provinces they enrolled prominent landowners in their

Union, but in general they depended on the small traders; travelling agents made promises of material gains, indiscriminately enrolled their hearers, and then departed; except in the south-west they had no support of numbers; but to the Emperor they represented themselves as the national party of loyalty.

In the Cabinet itself no principle of solidarity was maintained, and many of the changes made were to the disadvantage of Stolýpin. The local Governors were practically emancipated from his control by the exceptional ordinances. The electoral Law could not be modified without consent of the Duma, but it left considerable latitude of interpretation to the Senate and to the Minister of the Interior. These powers were freely used to disfranchise various classes of voters; notably, all the peasant migrants to the towns, who were the most intelligent of their class. Unsatisfactory candidates were struck off the rolls or exiled; Jews were told that if they voted they would be expelled. Lists of candidates were officially circulated for the Reactionaries and the Octobrists. Other parties were punished for naming their candidates. In towns voting papers were withheld by the police from a quarter or even a third of the voters; polling places were reduced in number; the days for polling were not announced or even deliberately announced wrongly; peasant farmers were called away to their communes, under threat of fines, on the days fixed for the polling of small landowners. A circular from the Synod instructed the priests to "take an active part and guide their flocks," threatening the refractory "with the wrath of God"; priests were to become candidates, wherever possible. In some towns the Reactionaries took away voting papers or even arrested their opponents.

The disorders were all on one side. The Cadets, sobered by their misfortunes, abandoned their "storming tactics" for a regular siege of the bureaucracy. The peasants showed a remarkable instinct of discipline. To secure unanimity, they privately chose their candidates in advance, regarding them as "consecrated to chastisement." They mustered in full, the younger voters taking the leading part. In spite of all devices for influencing the elections, the choice of peasant electors was a complete triumph for the Opposition, and especially for the Labour group. The list included doctors, schoolmasters, statists, engineers, students, writers, and editors. It was only the peasants who deliberately reelected men disqualified by the Government; they even chose men who had been exiled administratively; and one such was set free to sit in the Duma. The small landowners showed less initiative. Yet here the peasant farmers carried the day, and even many of the successful priests were their choice. The large landowners chose mostly members of the Right or Octobrists. Eighty-four per cent. of the town electorate polled; where Cadets joined forces with the Left they invariably prevailed; and, where they opposed each other, they in a few cases let through members of the Right or Octobrists. All efforts to manipulate the list of chosen electors were in vain. The final elections yielded :—12 Reactionaries, who desired to displace Stolýpin and abolish the Duma; 34 Independent Tories; 17 Moderate Right or Conservatives, under Count Bóbrinsky, who detested revolution but welcomed the institution of a Duma; 32 Octobrists; 24 Non-Party; 37 Independent Liberals; 123 Cadets, robbed of their chiefs and again led by Milyukóff from outside; 101 members loosely united in the Labour group; 14 of the non-conspirative People's Socialists; 35 Socialist Revolutionaries; and 54 Social Democrats. Most of the new members were young professional men with secondary education; where eminent Zemstvo men were cancelled, obscure revolutionaries sometimes passed; more than a quarter of the whole House had at some time undergone administrative punishment.

On the Left there was not a single able politician; but the Social Democrats, mostly "minority men," commanded attention by their apartness, frankness, and discipline. The Cadets had to depend for a majority on agreements with other parties; but by their ability they assumed and kept the leadership of the Duma; their moderating influence on the Left was very marked. Both Cadets and Labour group, giving up all idea of aggression, set themselves to keep the Duma from dissolution as long as possible, and thus failed to use many opportunities for a weighty protest. The 36 Mussulmans usually voted with the Cadets. In Poland, only a minority of the Socialists still believed in violence; and the Moderate parties, led by Dmowski, carried all the seats. He gathered in the Poles elected from other provinces, enforced the strictest discipline, and, seated between Cadets and Labour group, decided several issues.

The second Duma met on March 5, 1907. Throughout, the atmosphere of tension was almost intolerable. Approach to the House was hedged about in every way; spies were attached to several of the members, and, outside, their gathering places were nearly all semi-conspirative. Stolýpin entered the Duma as its master, and his able speeches were listened to with respect. His attitude was conciliatory, but he was unwilling and unable to make any real concessions. He required an understanding with a constant and intelligent majority and good constructive work in the Committees. For this the mutilated Assembly had neither the ability, nor the time to acquire it. It was with difficulty that the Cadets prevented the Left from refusing the yearly recruits, from seizing on the sovereign's right of amnesty, and from declaring for expropriation of land without compensation. Almost every sitting was interrupted by provocations from the reactionaries. Their plan was always to demand a public condemnation of revolutionary terrorism. On May 30, the House found itself listening to a formula on terrorism from each of the nine parties. Much the best, that of the Poles, simply stated that terrorism was incompatible with parliamentary institutions; and this would have passed but for the party jealousy of the Cadets. The House was left without any formula. Meanwhile, Pikhnó

urged at Court a *coup d'État* on the part of the sovereign; Gringmuth
proposed a military dictatorship, and Professor Martens prepared foreign
opinion. Suddenly, the discovery of a plot to kill the Emperor was
announced, and the Duma was invited to congratulate him on his escape.
A group of conspirators, whose services had been refused by the Socialist
Revolutionaries, had consulted with a Cossack, Ratmíroff; on the advice
of his officer, he had promised to send telegrams as to the movements of
the Grand Duke Nicholas and Stolýpin. The telegrams were sent, but
the conspirators went no further. Declaring the plot to be instigated or
imaginary, the Left block decided to boycott the demonstration as aimed
at themselves. The vote of congratulation was adopted unanimously by
the rest in a half empty House. Thus the Duma was again discredited.
More was to follow. On the vaguest evidence, an Act of accusation was
framed against all the Social Democrat members of the Duma; the Act
was loosely drawn up; generally omitting dates, it strung together pronouncements of the party since 1905; beyond the published programme
of the party it brought evidence against not more than one-third of
the persons accused. Here was a weapon ready for use. Meanwhile,
the fate of the Duma was warmly debated by the Ministers and at the
Court. Stolýpin's hand was forced by the reactionaries; and by June 14
the question was practically decided. The Premier suddenly demanded
a secret session. He spoke for a few minutes, asking the speedy consent
of the Duma to the exclusion of all the Social Democrats; and the Act
of accusation, which had not previously been communicated even to the
persons accused, was then read out. The Duma referred the matter
without delay to a committee for investigation of the evidence. Without
waiting for its decision, on the morning of June 16, while the members
were in their beds, a Manifesto was published dissolving the Duma.
The members, it stated, had not been real representatives of the needs
and wishes of the population; and the manner of election would therefore be changed by the authority which had granted the Duma, the
Emperor responsible to the throne of God.

The new electoral Law, prepared in advance, followed without delay.
Five provinces which had always sent Opposition members lost fourteen
seats. Siberia lost six out of twenty-one. Central Asia, full of Mussulmans, was disfranchised altogether. The Caucasus out of twenty-nine
seats lost nineteen. In Transcaucasia, as in Vilna and Kovno, special
seats were created for the small Russian population. Out of thirty-six seats
Poland retained only fourteen; and of these two were allotted to the
Russian residents. Of the towns of the empire only seven retained seats
of their own; the rest were merged with their respective provinces. In
each of these seven, the representation was equally divided between two
categories of voters; for the first category was established an exceedingly
high rating. Many classes were formally disfranchised. The preponderance of the country members of Russia proper having thus been

CH. XIII.

assured, measures were taken to put their election entirely into the hands of the larger landowners. They were able to determine the choice even of the peasant members of the Duma. In 34 out of 53 provinces, the number of "electors" was so distributed as to give the landowners an absolute majority over all other classes, including town-voters and workmen; in most other cases they were practically supreme. The Minister of the Interior, and under him the local Governors, received extensive powers for the further interpretation of this most complicated law; it was they who defined without appeal the categories of the voters and could separate nationalities or unite two separate districts. The whole law may be regarded as a partial triumph of the supporters of the class-basis and the reactionary scheme, but also as a partial victory for Stolýpin. At least there was a Duma, with undiminished powers of legislation.

From June 16, 1907, onwards, the Government attempted a wholesale liquidation of its grievances, a process which seemed to have no end. Of the Social Democrats, who were tried with closed doors, thirty-one were sent to Siberia. Most of the other ex-members were carefully isolated from their constituents; many were expelled from their posts; some were imprisoned; some went into hiding. In the winter (December 25–31) those who had signed the Viborg appeal were condemned to three months imprisonment and permanently deprived of the franchise. Trials for offences committed in 1905 went on until 1909, when thirty-two death sentences were pronounced in Ekaterinoslav. New "obligatory ordinances" of the police imposed fines up to £300 or imprisonment up to three months on those who published or circulated any articles "arousing a hostile attitude to the Government." The discretion was left with the police themselves; thus, many provincial papers were crushed, and the rest found it best to submit each number to the police in advance; there was no unity of system, and articles which passed in the capitals were fined when reprinted elsewhere. The right of meeting within the Universities was restricted (1907), and female students were excluded from their new university rights (1908). From the law Courts high legal officials were dismissed for their independence; many persons condemned for *pogróms* were publicly pardoned by the sovereign (1908). Local Governors exceeded in arbitrariness all that was done by the central authorities. Wholesale expulsions of peasants culminated in the formation of bands of brigands. In some villages the malcontent majority burned down the houses of any who had property. The field Courts had been discontinued, but death sentences by ordinary Courts-martial showed a constant increase; in 1906 and 1907, 4131 officials were killed or wounded and there were 1503 executions. In 1908, the attacks on officials sank to 1009, but the executions rose to 825; after the revolutionary organisations had been stamped out, the crimes were symptomatic of sheer social disorder; many criminals escaped, but whole batches were condemned without discrimination.

The second dissolution was followed first by complete prostration, next by indifference to public interests and a feverish search for other excitements. But then began a healthy rally of public opinion. Struve drew attention to the economic development of the country, as a school of detail and as the decisive factor in politics. Such was also the tendency of important merchants of Moscow, and even of many of the peasants; cooperative societies multiplied. The Cadets set themselves the sane ideal of a constitutional Opposition. After all, there remained a national assembly, free discussion of the budget, and more freedom of the Press than under Plehve. There were many able business minds which had not yet accepted political organisation; and out of these Guchkóff, whose moment had now come, sought to make an effective party of Octobrists or Conservative Reformers. He could expect support from merchants, small traders, and enlightened but sober country gentlemen. Even the gentry of the Right were rather Tories than reactionaries, and had no great affection for unreformed officialdom. A sharp natural line separated all these elements from the few reactionaries. These were nearly all dependent on the old *régime,* and for them the real issue was between vested political interests and financial publicity. Their only method was still to flog the corpse of the dead revolution; and Purishkévich announced that he and his friends were going to the third Duma in order to destroy it.

The new elections were held in October, 1907. This time, the Law worked of itself. The elections immensely strengthened the hands of Stolýpin; they finally proved that there was no national basis for the reactionaries. The third Duma met on November 14, 1907. It was in complexion a House of the upper class, with a predominance of country gentlemen who had served in the army, in the upper branches of local administration, or in the bureaucracy. There was a sprinkling of merchants. The few prominent reactionaries were young men unknown except for the extremeness of their views. The Moderate Right (70), with some six men of distinction and parliamentary ability, followed Stolýpin and drew more and more away from the Extreme Right. The Octobrists (153) included a large number of able men with court rank, administrative experience, and established reputations. Their leader, Guchkóff, was the real master of the Duma. Milyukóff carried St Petersburg with a vote of 22,000, and the Cadets numbered 54. The new President, the Octobrist Khomyakóff, exhibited composure and shrewd good sense, and exercised on the House a sobering influence which promised stability.

The Duma had still to create the middle term between the Government and the country; its failure would involve the failure of Stolýpin. After a while, in the Committees hard work began for all the leading men irrespective of party; a whole mass of government information had to be mastered; frequent and informal discussion with heads of

Departments of the Government proved educative for all concerned. Stolýpin was in close touch both with the Moderate Right and with the Octobrists. Guchkóff and the Octobrists supported Stolýpin against the more reactionary Ministers; theirs were the Departments which the Duma chose to criticise. For the first time, the budget was discussed in detail. The chief ground chosen for patriotic criticism was the mismanagement of the army and navy. The Duma refused to pass a credit for new warships without a thorough naval reform. Guchkóff, in a telling speech, exposed the unpunished favourite, Admiral Alexéyeff, and made the whole question a test of the sincerity of the constitutional Manifesto (June 6, 1908). Three days later the army estimates were brought forward. Guchkóff pleaded for a system where character and talent should replace nepotism, and ended by naming Grand Duke after Grand Duke and inviting them to resign their military posts. On the estimates for Public Instruction, von Anrep offered a strongly critical analysis of the whole policy of this Ministry from the days of Count Dmitry Tolstóy. The session ended without dissolution. The Government secured the money for the battleships from the Council of State; but the Emperor dissolved the Committee of Imperial Defence under the Grand Duke Nicholas (August 21).

In the vacation, the reactionaries tried hard to oust Stolýpin. Count Witte had renounced his constitutionalism of 1905; and a first-rate financier with foreign ties was very necessary, if the Duma was to be abolished. Duma and Stolýpin were attacked as undermining the prerogatives of the Emperor by encroachments in the domains of foreign policy, the army, and the navy. The enormous number of death sentences in January, 1909, increased the moral tension. An extraordinary revelation further excited public opinion. The police spy Ázeff had for years been a member of the Central Committee of the Socialist Revolutionaries; he had known of, but not averted, the murders of Sipyágin, Plehve, and the Grand Duke Sergius. Ázeff was allowed to disappear, and Lopukhín, formerly Chief of the Department of Police, was sent to penal servitude for acquainting the Revolutionaries with Ázeff's real position (May). Meanwhile, Stolýpin had sometimes succeeded and sometimes failed in his attempts to bridle reactionary officials; and the temporising *Novoë Vremya* printed articles for and against him side by side. New appointments to Ministries reflected the continual hesitations of the sovereign. The Premier was, however, able to send revising Senators to investigate the administrative abuses in Moscow and Turkestan (September–December, 1908). Senator Gárin discovered in Moscow a whole system of blackmailing practised by the secret police. The City Prefect, Rheinbot, was put on trial, and the Governor-General, Hörschelmann, was displaced. Mishchénko was removed from Turkestan, Pyeshkóff from Kharkóff, and Prince Gorchakóff from Vyatka. Meanwhile, from February, 1909, onwards, there was a steady and rapid fall in the number of executions; and at Easter a telegram from the Minister of War required that only murders of exceptional brutality should be punished with death. Stolýpin began to replace martial law by milder measures. These were very material triumphs; and, in March, while Stolýpin was in the Crimea, recovering from a serious illness, the reactionaries made a desperate attack upon him at Court, for submitting to the Duma, in accordance with the fundamental laws, the estimates for the new naval staff. The Premier hastened back from the Crimea. After a sharp crisis, he was retained in power, but received orders to redraft the Fundamental Law in question. Before the end of the session, the Duma confirmed the temporary land Law of November 22, 1906, with the important modification that existing holdings could be claimed as property without reference to the village commune. The incidental difficulties of the Law were simplified; and the Act was an instance of successful cooperation on a vital question between Duma and Government (May 20).

The struggle as to the system of government in Russia had meanwhile assumed a much wider scope. In Finland, after the Manifesto of November 17, 1905, the Red Guard passed into the hands of socialist workmen; it became so troublesome that the middle class organised in opposition a White Guard; there were conflicts, in which members of the White Guard were killed. The Red Guard tried to prevent the passage of loyal Russian troops at the time of the mutiny at Sveaborg; it was disowned even by the socialists, and was disbanded by the Finnish Senate. In 1907 it was partially replaced by the *Voima* (Force), originally a gymnastic association on a national rather than a party basis; imported stores of fire-arms were discovered. The first Diet elected on the new franchise met in the spring of 1907. Early in 1908, the Socialists carried a wild resolution for the active defence of the rights of Finland, and the Diet was dissolved. At the Russian Court, former supporters of Bóbrikoff were again prominent. They appealed for a patriotic policy; Stolýpin agreed, but invited the cooperation of the Duma. In an able speech he outlined the case of the Russian Government; Russian revolutionaries had hatched plots with impunity in Finland, and in such a matter unity of control was imperative. Milyukóff replied with a masterly review of the case for Finland. Stolýpin, without further consultation, put his policy into execution. By the Ordinance of June 2, the Cabinet was to discuss any matters which concerned the whole empire; it was to see all state papers of Finland; the Secretary of State for Finland could not report separately to the sovereign. This amounted to an abrogation of the constitutional independence of the country; and the Government entered upon a serious conflict with the Finnish Diet, which is not yet concluded.

In Poland, hardly any concessions had been made and martial law was continued. But, as Russian Liberalism became practical and constructive, the Polish question attracted its intelligent interest. An article by Struve on "A great Russia" (January, 1908) outlined a whole series of ideas. The new *régime* called for the development of a strong and Liberal patriotism. Russia's *rôle* in Europe was the defence of Slavonic interests; but western Slavs could not trust Russia whilst there was administrative anarchy in Poland; a contented Poland would not be a danger to Russia, but the advanced guard of the Slavonic world. The present system served the interests not of Russia but of Germany, which, being unable to assimilate its own section of Poland, depended on the continuance of even worse repression beyond the frontier. The forward policy of Germany and Austria south-eastwards could only be successful at the expense of the minor Slav States; English influence no longer opposed Russia in Turkey; it was Germany that sought there an outlet in the direction of Persia. For every reason, moral and material, the friendship with England should be strengthened and developed. The antecedents for this view went far back. It now drew together under the name of New Slavophils leading men of the Moderate Right, the Octobrists, the Peaceful Reform, and the Cadets. In the summer of 1908, Dr Kramarz and other eminent Slavs of Austria were received by all parties and everywhere insisted that a Liberal policy in Poland was the condition of their confidence in Russia. In July a Congress of the various Slavonic peoples was held at Prague; before their brother Slavs, the Russian delegates, Bóbrinsky, Maklakóff, and others, declared for an understanding with Poland. The expropriation law of the Prussian Government had led to an extensive boycott of German goods in Russian Poland.

The enthusiasm of the Congress had not subsided, when, after a previous meeting between the two sovereigns, Prince Ferdinand declared the independence of Bulgaria, and Austria the annexation of Bosnia and the Herzegovina. The annexations roused the greatest indignation in Russia; the independence of Bulgaria was welcomed with satisfaction, but the Bulgarian Government was regarded as treating with a German Power to the disadvantage of another Slavonic people. When Count Pourtales, the German ambassador in St Petersburg, suddenly demanded and secured from the Russian Government a full retreat from even the moral championship of Servia, the humiliation made manifest the need of union between Government and people. So enlightening was the action of Germany that reactionaries like Bashmakóff and Liberals like Milyukóff found themselves discussing at a common Slavonic Congress what was to be done for the people of Poland.

Revolution in Persia and in Turkey surrounded Russia with constitutional movements; and two reactionary sovereigns were deposed. A greater interest attached to the possibility of an economic and political conflict between Germany and England, and, consequently, to the relations of Russia with both countries. Up to 1904, only the official

Press in Russia could speak freely; the legitimate annoyance of the Russian Government at the anti-Russian policy of England had become stereotyped and traditional; the friendship between the reigning Houses of Russia and Prussia was, likewise, traditional, since the time of the Partition of Poland; yet Englishmen and Germans who had lived long in Russia almost invariably maintained that it was the German who was disliked. There were reasons why this should be so. Russians at large were more nearly touched by their own system of government than by questions of foreign policy, and here the Germans were constantly presented to them as the agents of power. Baltic Germans were strong at the Court; they held many of the highest administrative posts and were in every chancellery; they had, for instance, a disproportionate share in the work of the Courts-martial. German stewards with scrupulous exactness collected the revenues of their absent masters. German firms captured the strategic posts of trade, and German managers ruled Russian workmen. Owing to a strong contrast of character between the two races, their use of their power was often contemptuous and rarely sympathetic.

Meanwhile, English capital was only lent to the Government distrustfully and in driblets; and English merchants had not enough knowledge to enter the far more profitable path of private enterprise in Russia. The alliance of England with Japan, and the supply of contraband of war by some English firms, gave new fuel to Russian indignation. Yet, in the general public, this irritation was only superficial. During the war, Germany relieved Russia of all solicitude for her western frontier; but with the rising movement for reform came open ill-will against Russian Germans, and against the official world of Germany which was believed to be on the side of reaction. It was to the German Emperor that Schwanebach addressed his impeachment of Witte and of the October Manifesto. Meanwhile, freedom of the Press proved that the subsidised organs were alone in their antipathy to England. The political ideals both of Cadets and of Octobrists were learnt chiefly from England, the study of whose constitutional history had aroused in Russia an enthusiasm hardly intelligible to a present day Englishman. The difference was that the Cadets sought to apply English principles and the Octobrists felt a kinship with English instincts. All three Dumas, representing different aspects of Russian opinion, were remarkably friendly to England, and England supplied the staple of the precedents and parallels for quotation. The attitude of the British Government in the time of transition was tactful and sympathetic; the beginnings of constitutionalism coincided with the agreement as to Persia; and at Revel the King of England toasted both sovereign and people. During the Balkan crisis, friendly support was given to Russia. This goodwill, coming not after but during the transition, was of material service to it. With the beginning of steady constructive work, the ties were naturally

CH. XIII.

drawn closer. Struve put forward as one of his ideals "the economic penetration of Russia by England"; industrial England might put its movable capital in contact with the unworked resources of rural Russia. Visits of sixty Polish merchants and of the future Minister of Commerce, Timiryázeff, to England (September, 1908), and the establishment of an Anglo-Russian Chamber of Commerce in St Petersburg, coincided with a new interest in Russia amongst English commercial men. But here, too, everything was not to be settled in a day. Effective publicity in financial affairs, a reign of law, and the liberation of enterprise, would, as they were realised, set free the influx of English capital. In other words, apart from all political formulae, closer ties with England depended on progress in Russia.

Under these conditions a lively interest was taken in a visit to England of the President of the Duma with the leaders of all the Moderate parties (June and July, 1909). The invitation was signed by seventy of the most representative Englishmen. The visitors were received by the King, and entertained in the House of Commons, by municipalities, by Universities, and by Chambers of Commerce. The heartiness of their reception was everywhere more than conventional. The solidarity between Russian parties was increased by the journey; and it was in the Mansion House that Milyukóff formally renounced the tactics which had placed the Cadets in direct opposition to the Tsar. The two sovereigns, meeting at Cowes, exchanged cordial references to the national reception of the Duma. For England, the discovery of the friendliness of the Russian people introduced a profoundly important factor into the balance of foreign relations.

CHAPTER XIV.

THE OTTOMAN EMPIRE AND THE BALKAN PENINSULA.

The year 1870, so important in the history of western Europe, marked the beginning of a new era in the Near East. Before that time, outside the borders of the kingdom of Greece and the principalities of Roumania, Servia, and Montenegro, the Christian population of the Balkan peninsula was classified not by race but by religion. All the Christian subjects of the Sultan in south-eastern Europe, whatever their nationality, came under the spiritual jurisdiction of the Ecumenical Patriarch; they were therefore regarded as Greeks. But when, on March 10, 1870, Abd-ul-Aziz signed the firman creating the Bulgarian Exarchate, he laid the foundations of a new Power. Christian and Greek were thenceforth no longer synonymous in European Turkey; another nationality, long forgotten by Western statesmen who knew nothing of the medieval glories of the Bulgarian Tsars, arose as a competitor of the Hellenes, hitherto regarded as the "sick man's" only heirs. The Greeks saw at once the full import of a step which Fuad Pasha in his political testament had recommended in the interest of Turkey, and which Ignatyeff had supported in that of Russia. The Ecumenical Patriarch only managed to postpone for two years the appointment of the first Exarch, and then excommunicated him and his adherents as schismatics. The Bulgarian Exarchate, indeed, came to bring not peace but a sword. Henceforth the rivalry of the Christian races of the Balkan peninsula was as serious an obstacle to the settlement of the Eastern question as were the jealousies of the Great Powers, and the situation became much what it had been before the Turkish conquest. Then, the mutual animosity of Slavs and Greeks had aided the Ottomans to extend their dominions in Europe; now the conflicting ambitions of Hellenes, Serbs, Bulgarians, Albanians, and Roumanians facilitate the retention of Thrace, Macedonia, Albania, and Epiros by the Sultan, whose policy it has been to play off one Christian nationality against the other, always favouring that which for the moment was weakest.

CH. XIV.

The Franco-German War, which enabled the Italians to enter Rome, provided Russia with an opportunity for tearing up the Treaty of Paris. On October 31, 1870, the Russian Chancellor announced, in a circular to the Powers, that his Imperial master no longer considered himself bound by the restrictions imposed upon his sovereignty in the Black Sea; and the Convention of London (March 13, 1871), which resulted, abandoned the neutrality of the Euxine. A further Turco-Russian Convention permitted both States to build Black Sea fleets. Sevastopol could be restored; the Russian navy might once more become a menace to Constantinople. But the next Russo-Turkish War came too soon for Russia to avail herself of this advantage.

The Eastern question remained dormant during the three years which followed the appointment of the first Bulgarian Exarch. But, in 1875, the outbreak of an insurrection in the Herzegovina led to the most important developments which south-eastern Europe had witnessed since the creation of the modern kingdom of Greece. Bosnia and the Herzegovina more nearly resembled Crete than any other part of the Turkish empire. Their inhabitants, though divided into Christians and Mussulmans, were all of the same Slav race, with this difference only, that most of the Christians were Orthodox Serbs, while a minority consisted of Catholic Croats. Of Turks, as in Crete, there were practically none, except the functionaries sent from Constantinople. Thus, the Mussulman oppressors in these two Slavonic provinces belonged to the same stock as their Christian victims, who were nominally their equals before the law, but were virtually debarred from giving evidence in the higher Courts, and could only obtain justice against members of the dominant creed by enormous bribes. Some years before the outbreak, the British Consul had uttered the significant warning that "without some powerful intervention, Bosnia and the Herzegovina might soon witness scenes similar to those which have lately terrified Europe in Syria." No Christians were employed in the administration; the police purchased their places and reimbursed themselves by extorting money from those whom it was their duty to defend; and, worst of all, the exactions of the tax-farmers were such that the peasant seldom kept for himself more than one-third of his crop. It was this last iniquity which occasioned the ultimate outbreak in 1875.

The harvest of 1874 had been a very bad one, yet the tax-farmers did not on that account diminish their demands. The unhappy peasants of Nevesinye, a place a little to the east of Mostar, were unable to pay and rose in revolt. The insurrection, at first regarded by the Turks as a merely local disturbance, soon spread. The Catholic clergy, who had long looked to Austria for aid, were excited by the recent visit of the Emperor to Dalmatia; the Orthodox Serbs turned their eyes to Montenegro, whence help had so often come, and where the fugitives from Turkish tyranny were only awaiting the moment to strike. A manifesto was issued, demanding vengeance for the battle of Kossovo (1389), the Waterloo of the medieval Servian empire, and for the five centuries of servitude which it had caused. The agitation extended to Bosnia; volunteers came down from the crags of the Black Mountain; and the movement, which had at first been directed not against the Sultan but against the local authorities and the Mussulman landowners, developed into a revolt against Turkish rule. All attempts at conciliation failed. The Powers sent their Consuls to confer with the rebels, but in vain; the Porte made its usual promises, but its Christian subjects had heard them before. Count Andrássy, the Austro-Hungarian Foreign Minister, addressed a note to the Turkish Government, urging the real equality of Christians and Mussulmans before the law, the abolition of the system of farming the taxes, and the formation of a local assembly representative of both religions to control the administration. This famous document, intended to secure peace, was as barren of results as were the negotiations of the Austrian Baron Rodich with the insurgents. Unsubdued in the field, and encouraged from both Servia and Montenegro, they now increased their demands, and insisted that one-third of the land should be handed over to the Christians. A final effort of the three Emperors to make the Sultan carry out reforms met with no support from the British Government, then pledged to Disraeli's Turcophil policy. Servia and Montenegro armed; and on July 1, 1876, Servia, and on July 2 Montenegro, declared war against Turkey on behalf of their brother Serbs. The moment had at last come, so the Prince of Montenegro told his subjects, to restore the Servian empire, which had fallen with Murad I and should revive with Murad V, the new Sultan.

The situation of the Turkish empire in the summer of 1876 might, indeed, justify the sanguine rhetoric of Prince Nicholas. The insurrection in the Herzegovina had not only aroused the sympathies of the two neighbouring Serb States but quickened the national feeling of the Bulgarian peasants. Economically, the condition of the Bulgarians during the later years of Ottoman rule contrasted favourably with that of some independent Christian races. Midhat Pasha, the most Liberal of Turkish statesmen, had been for four years Governor of the Vilayet of the Danube, as Bulgaria was then officially styled, and his residence at the provincial capital of Rustchuk had conferred great material benefits upon the thrifty, laborious population. In fact, the Russian officers, who visited Bulgaria during the war of 1877, found that the "little brothers," whom they had come to free, were better off under the Turkish yoke than many of their own *mujiks* under the benevolent despotism of the Tsar. In the words of an impartial eye-witness, to exchange places with the Bulgarian *râyah* "would have been no bad bargain for the Russian peasants." But a revolutionary committee, composed of educated men, had existed for several years at Bucharest, and had extended its branches across the Danube. Despite the heroism

CH. XIV.

of Vasil Levski, an ex-deacon, who was the chief of these itinerant "Apostles" and died on the gallows at Sofia, where a monument still preserves his memory, the efforts of these intellectual leaders had exercised little influence on their stolid and unimaginative countrymen, till the Serbs of the Herzegovina gave them the example of another Slavonic nationality struggling to be free. A new revolutionary organisation was founded in Roumania; wooden cannon were hollowed out of cherry-trees, and on May 2, 1876, the insurrection broke out at Tatar-Bazardjik. In itself it was of little importance, but the cruelty with which it was suppressed aroused the indignation of the whole civilised world. The credit of having first disclosed to the public the horrible massacre of Batak was due to the enterprise of an English newspaper correspondent, whose story, so far from being exaggerated, was amply confirmed by the British and American Commissioners. The village of Batak, on the northern spurs of Rhodope, was preparing to join the national movement, when a force of Bashi-Bazuks under the command of Achmet Aga of Dospad and his colleague, Mohammad Aga of Dorkovo, arrived there. After some attempt at defence, the villagers surrendered on the distinct promise that their lives should be spared. Then began what Baring, the British Commissioner, stigmatised in his official report, drawn up after a visit to the spot, " as perhaps the most heinous crime that has stained the history of the present century." Achmet Aga and his men spared neither age nor sex. Some of the victims were butchered in cold blood; others were burned to death in the school; others again perished amid the flames of blazing petroleum in the church. For more than two months the stench of the unburied corpses kept every living soul away; and when the British Commissioner arrived he found no one but a solitary old woman in this once flourishing village. Only after his arrival did the survivors begin to return from the woods where they had found shelter. It was estimated that 5000 out of a population of 7000 had perished at Batak alone, while the Christians slaughtered throughout Bulgaria in that fatal month of May made up a total of 12,000.

The "Bulgarian Atrocities" aroused the indignation of the whole Christian world. In England Gladstone's famous pamphlet ran through many editions, while the most powerful orator of the day levelled all his moral force, all his rhetorical skill, against the system of government which could not only allow, but reward, such crimes. Lord Derby, the Conservative Foreign Secretary, telegraphed to Constantinople that "any renewal of the outrages would be more fatal to the Porte than the loss of a battle"; and an Ottoman official, perceiving when it was too late the full political import of the Batak massacre, asked one of its authors how much Russia had paid him for a deed which would furnish her with a fresh excuse for intervention on behalf of the persecuted Slavs of the Balkan peninsula. Since that day there have been atrocities in the

Turkish empire on a far larger scale; but the Armenian massacres had much less effect upon politics than the butchery of Batak.

Meanwhile, a revolution had broken out in the heart of the Turkish capital. The national party, discontented with the lack of firmness shown by Mahmûd Neddim, the Russophil Grand Vizier, raised the cry of "Turkey for the Turks"; at Constantinople several thousand *softas*, or theological students, forced the Sultan to dismiss his Minister; at Salonica the French and German Consuls were murdered. Matters reached a climax when, on May 29, Mehemed Ruchdi, the new Grand Vizier, and his confederates, having obtained a *fetvah* from the Sheikh-ul-Islâm authorising the deposition of Abd-ul-Aziz on the ground of his incapacity and extravagance, declared the throne vacant and on the following day proclaimed his nephew Sultan under the title of Murad V. Four days later, the death of Abd-ul-Aziz prevented all danger of a restoration. The cause of his death has been much contested; five years afterwards, Midhat Pasha and others were tried and convicted of the Sultan's assassination; but the trial, held under the shadow of Yildiz, was an absurd travesty of justice, and it was the opinion of a British doctor[1], who saw the dead man's body, that Abd-ul-Aziz committed suicide by cutting his arteries with a pair of scissors. The removal of his uncle did not, however, confirm Murad on the throne for long. The tragedy of his sudden elevation to power affected a mind naturally feeble; the national party soon recognised that he was not the man to direct the fortunes of the empire in a time of dire distress. On August 31 he was deposed in his turn, and his brother Abd-ul-Hamid II took his place. Murad vanished in the palace of Cheragan on the Bosporos, which had witnessed his uncle's tragic death, and his fate remains one of the mysteries of Constantinople.

Seldom has a Sultan begun his reign under greater difficulties than the astute diplomatist who now ascended the throne. He found Bosnia and the Herzegovina in revolt against his authority, Servia and Montenegro fighting on their behalf. The two Servian States, although they had begun the war nearly at the same time, were of very different calibre and had very different leaders. Prince Milan of Servia, who had now come of age, was a man of considerable natural shrewdness, but he was no soldier, while his character had been spoiled, as is that of most Orientals, by a Parisian education, and further marred by the bad example of his Regents. He was suspicious and jealous of Prince Nicholas of Montenegro, a man of much diplomatic ability and far greater force of will, whose poetic nature never lost touch with realities, who had already taken part in one war against his hereditary enemy, and whose people, in the words of Tennyson, were a nation of "warriors beating back the swarm of Turkish Islâm for five hundred years."

---

[1] The late Dr Dickson of Constantinople, who communicated this to the author.

Between these two rulers there could be no unity of purpose, for neither was willing to cede to the other the headship of that great Servian empire, which it was the ambition of each to revive. Milan, accordingly, entered into the struggle against his will, and in deference to public opinion, which would have severely punished an Obrenovich who should have abstained from championing the cause, in which his rival, the pretender Peter Karageorgevich, was fighting as a volunteer among the hills of "lofty Bosnia."

The Servian army, increased by a body of volunteers, was under the command of an experienced Russian officer, General Chernaïeff, whose plan of campaign was to invade the Turkish territory on the south and east by the valleys of the Morava and the Timok, while at the same time despatching detachments to the frontiers of Bosnia and of the Sandjak of Novibazar. But the Russian commander's strategy was frustrated by the inferior material of which the Servian forces were composed. Unlike the Montenegrins, the Serbs had been at peace for two generations with their former masters, for whom they were no match in the field, while the Bulgarians, cowed by the massacres, did not rise as was expected. Chernaïeff, indeed, crossed the Turkish frontier to the south, and carried the Turkish camp by a sudden attack. But, while one Ottoman general checked the Servian advance to the east at Zajechar and laid the important strategic post of Knajajevats in ashes, another descended the valley of the Morava, and completely defeated the retreating army of the south at Aleksinats. Prince Milan, from his headquarters at Parachin, had already invited the Powers to intervene. An armistice was granted, but the negotiations for a settlement were hindered by the ill-timed proclamation of Milan as King of Servia at Deligrad on September 16, at Chernaïeff's suggestion, and the fighting was resumed. The Serbs made a desperate stand at Djunis, but in vain; Aleksinats was lost; all southern Servia was in the power of the Turks, and the road was open to Belgrade. Then the Tsar intervened to save Servia from annihilation. General Ignatyeff handed a Russian ultimatum to the Porte, demanding the conclusion of an armistice within 48 hours with both Servia and Montenegro. The Turkish Government yielded; on November 1 an armistice of two months was signed, which was subsequently extended till March 1, 1877, when a definite peace was concluded between Prince Milan and the Sultan. Servia neither lost nor gained by the War of 1876; her territory was left undiminished; her finances were unencumbered by a war indemnity.

Meanwhile, the Montenegrins had fought with far more success than their Servian allies. The forces of the Black Mountain were divided into two armies, that of the north, under the command of the Prince, which invaded the Herzegovina, and that of the south, under Bojo Petrovich, his cousin and subsequent Prime Minister, whose instructions were to watch the Albanian frontier. The northern army defeated the

Turks with great loss at the village of Vuchidol, and the advance guard
reached the old castle of Duke Stephen only a few miles from Mostar.
But bad news from the south compelled the Prince to hasten back to
the defence of his country, only to find that his cousin had twice routed
the enemy at Medun near Podgoritsa. Another Montenegrin victory at
Danilograd in the Zeta valley and the capitulation of Medun concluded
the campaign of 1876. Montenegro signed an armistice with the Porte
on the basis of *uti possidetis*; Bojo Petrovich was sent to Constantinople
to negotiate peace, with instructions to ask for an increase of territory,
including the cession of the then Turkish fortress of Spizza, which commands the bay of Antivari. The Porte was willing to cede Spizza, but
declined to give up Nikshich, whereupon the Prince recalled his envoy
and prepared for a second campaign.

European diplomacy did not remain idle while Servia and Montenegro were keeping their truce with Turkey. The British Government
had sent the fleet to Besika Bay near the mouth of the Dardanelles,
when the Bulgarian troubles began, and the language of the Prime
Minister was warlike; but, on the proposal of Lord Derby, a Conference
of the Powers for the settlement of the Eastern question assembled at
Constantinople. On the day of its opening (December 23), Midhat
Pasha, who had just returned to power, obtained from Abd-ul-Hamid II
the publication of a decree, creating a Turkish Parliament composed of
two Chambers, and proclaiming the equality of all Ottoman subjects
before the law and the integrity of the Ottoman empire. This last
doctrine provided a pretext for the rejection of the proposals submitted
by the Conference, of which the principal were the rectification of the
Montenegrin frontier, and the autonomy of Bulgaria, Bosnia, and the
Herzegovina, under Governors-General to be named by the Porte with
the consent of the Powers. These propositions were examined by a
national Council, convoked for the purpose; and, on its refusal to accept
them, the Conference broke up in January, 1877, and Prince Gorchakóff,
the Russian Chancellor, addressed a circular note to the other Powers,
asking what measures they proposed to take for enforcing the decisions
of Europe. The British Government made one further attempt to preserve peace. A fresh Conference was held in London; and, on March 31,
the representatives of the Powers signed a protocol, taking cognisance of
the conclusion of peace between Turkey and Servia and of the promised
reforms, and calling upon the Porte to make those reforms effective
and to place the Turkish army on a peace footing. Meanwhile, Midhat
Pasha had fallen, and with him all hope of serious reform had disappeared; the Parliament which he had created was without experience
of public life, while dependent on the Government; and it supported the
Government in rejecting the London protocol. War was now inevitable;
Russia signed a military convention with the Prince of Roumania for
the passage of her troops across his territory, and on April 24 the

Russian troops crossed both the European and the Asiatic frontiers of Turkey. Five days later Montenegro reopened hostilities.

Turks and Russians alike realised that Roumania was the key of the situation. Powerless in the Black Sea, where the Turkish fleet was then superior, the invaders could only attack Turkey by land, and in Europe every facility for doing so was placed at their disposal by the principality, which lay between the Danube and the Russian frontier. The Porte, which still took the strictly legal view of Roumania as a vassal State, not only protested against the convention as a violation of the Treaty of Paris, but also ordered the bombardment of the Roumanian town of Calafat on the Danube—an act which provoked a declaration of war by Roumania, and the proclamation of Roumanian independence on May 21. A month later, the Russian troops crossed the Danube almost without opposition at two points, one facing the Dobrudja, the other opposite Sistova, and Bulgaria became the theatre of the War. The Tsar, confident of the success which seemed to await him in this Slavonic province, attended a solemn thanksgiving in the church of Sistova; and General Gurko surprised Trnovo, the medieval Bulgarian capital, traversed the Balkans by the low pass of Hainköi, entered the valley of the Tundja, and took the Shipka pass in the rear. It seemed as if this daring officer would reach Adrianople, or even appear at the head of his cavalry before the walls of Stamboul. A panic broke out at the Turkish capital; Abd-ul-Kerim, the Ottoman commander in Europe, was deposed; Mehemed Ali, a German renegade of French extraction, took his place, while Suleiman was recalled from Montenegro to Thrace. Then the fortune of war turned; Gurko, despite the desperate bravery of his Bulgarian allies, was defeated at Stara Zagora and driven back to the Balkans; Osman Pasha, hitherto stationed in compulsory idleness at the " virgin fortress" of Vidin, occupied Plevna, whose defence was to be the most heroic episode of the campaign. That small town, easily captured in the first Russo-Turkish War of the century, proved to be the chief barrier to Russian success in the fourth and last.

The siege of Plevna began on July 20 with a Russian repulse, which was followed ten days later by a second and far more crushing defeat. The Roumanians, who had hitherto taken little active part in the War, now crossed the Danube, and Prince Charles was appointed Commander-in-Chief of the allied forces before the beleaguered town. On September 11 they attacked the strongest of all the defences of Plevna, the " indomitable Grivitsa redoubt," and after three attempts placed the Roumanian colours on its summit. But the assault upon a second redoubt failed. Unable to take Plevna by storm, the allies shut in the garrison so closely on every side that at last Osman's supplies ran out; he was compelled to resort to a general sortie, and, after performing prodigies of valour, surrendered on December 10 with all that was left of his gallant army. Meanwhile, the Turks had in vain endeavoured to

dislodge the Russians from the Shipka pass, and in Asia had lost, for
the third time in history, the strong citadel of Kars, captured by an
Armenian general, Loris-Melikoff. On the west of the Balkan peninsula,
the Montenegrins, after craftily luring their enemies into the Zeta valley,
had surprised and driven them back with great loss, and Prince Nicholas
achieved the military feat of which he is still most proud—the capture
of Nikshich after a four months' siege. Everywhere—in Montenegro, in
Bulgaria, in Asia Minor—the Turks were worsted. Now a fresh enemy
appeared in the field. Two days after the fall of Plevna, Servia again
declared war against Turkey. It seemed as if, unaided, the Turkish
empire must collapse before this combination of Christian nationalities.

But the Russian advance had alarmed those powerful interests, which
had so long prevented the disappearance of Turkish rule from Europe.
Austria-Hungary, since she had been driven out of Italy in 1866, had
looked upon the western half of the Balkan peninsula as the peculiar
sphere of her diplomacy; the Emperor Francis Joseph had, indeed,
promised his neutrality during the War in the meeting which he had had
with the Tsar at Reichstadt on July 8, 1876, on condition that the
occupation of Bosnia and the Herzegovina should be his share of the
spoil; but the Austrian Government was anxious lest this condition
should not be observed by the victorious Russians, who would by
such a concession have been convicted of betraying that Panslavonic
cause, of which Russia had constituted herself the champion. In
Great Britain, the Prime Minister was an avowed friend of Turkey—
an attitude attributed by his friends to political insight and dread of
Russia, by his foes to his Jewish blood and his Asiatic imagination—while public opinion, although deeply moved by the Bulgarian
atrocities, was still under the influence of the country's traditional
policy towards her old ally of the Crimean War, and was not prepared
to see the Russians installed at Constantinople. The occupation of
the new Rome had, indeed, been expressly discountenanced by the
Tsar; but he had now returned from the seat of war to Russia, and
his generals, careless (after the fashion of military men) of diplomatic
conventions, might seek to win eternal fame for themselves by planting
the cross once more over Santa Sophia. While the Porte appealed to
the Powers for their mediation, the Russian, Servian, and Montenegrin
armies continued to advance. Gurko recrossed the Balkans, took Sofia
and routed Suleiman near Philippopolis; Skobeleff and Radetzky
surrounded the Turkish army, which had fought so valiantly in the
Shipka pass, at the neighbouring wood of Shéjnovo on January 9, 1878;
eleven days later the Russians, as in 1829, entered Adrianople. The
terrified Mussulmans fled before them to the fastnesses of Rhodope, and
the brutality of the Cossacks towards these refugees almost equalled that
of the Turkish irregulars to the Bulgarians. The Serbs, more fortunate
than in the previous campaign, defeated the Turks at Pirot, while

Prince Milan, amidst general enthusiasm, entered the ancient Servian town of Nish in triumph—an achievement which has ever since endeared the ill-fated Obrenovich dynasty to the citizens. A third Servian victory at Vranya completed the successes of this brief war. At the same time, the older branch of the Servian stock realised the great ambition of Prince Nicholas to reach down to the Adriatic ; the coveted fortress of Spizza on the bay of Antivari, the town of Antivari itself, and the old pirate stronghold of Dulcigno fell before the victorious Montenegrins, whose poetic ruler addressed an ode to the sea, to which he had at last cut his way. He was on the point of beginning the siege of Skutari-in-Albania when the news of the armistice reached him, while the same intelligence cut short the Roumanian siege of Vidin. On January 31, the document suspending hostilities had been signed at Adrianople. Events in England had, more than aught else, contributed to the conclusion of the armistice. The Conservative Cabinet was divided, but its most powerful member was ready to risk a war, for which he had said that Great Britain was better prepared than any other Power ; and there was a war-party out of doors, excited by music-hall ditties and bellicose leading articles, which asked for nothing better than another victory over the rival whom British troops had beaten little more than twenty years earlier. Not yet entrenched in Egypt, even though she had half the Suez Canal shares in her pocket, Great Britain still regarded the occupation of Constantinople by a Great Power as a menace to her Indian empire, while the intemperate language of men like Edward Freeman only damaged the cause which they had at heart. Accordingly, the British fleet was ordered to Constantinople—a destination at once altered for Besika Bay after the resignation of Lord Carnarvon, the Colonial Secretary—and Parliament was asked to vote £6,000,000 for armaments. As the Russian lines were now moved close to Constantinople, a part of the British fleet was ordered to enter the Sea of Marmora for the protection of British life and property at the capital. The forces of the two Great Powers were within a few miles of each other; war seemed to be inevitable. The Grand Duke Nicholas established his headquarters at the village of San Stefano, the British Admiral was stationed off the island of Prinkipo.

At this moment another nationality intervened to complete the confusion of the situation. The Greeks had hitherto taken no part in the struggle. The insurrection of the Slavs in Bosnia and the Herzegovina, the first Servian and Montenegrin campaigns, had found the Hellenes merely interested spectators ; the Bulgarian rising naturally could not have been expected to command their sympathy. But when Russia, the great Orthodox Power, which had been one of the three benefactresses of the young Greek kingdom, entered the field, the position changed. There were some who wished to avail themselves of this Russo-Turkish War, as they had desired in that of 1854, to excite insurrections in the Greek provinces of Turkey; while the national pride rejected the idea of a fresh, and perhaps final, settlement of the Eastern question, in which Greece, the oldest factor in the problem, should be ignored. It was felt at Athens that party dissensions must cease in the face of this crisis in which the future of Hellenism, the realisation of "the Grand Idea," might be at stake. A coalition Cabinet, an "Ecumenical Government," as it was called, was formed in June, 1877, under the presidency of old Admiral Kanáres, who more than fifty years before had fired the Capitan-Pasha's ship at Scio, and who had as colleagues no less than four ex-Premiers. Such a "Ministry of all the talents" has never been constructed in Greece before or since; but, in similar circumstances, it has lately been imitated in Servia, by the coalition Ministry of all parties in February, 1909. Following the advice of the British Government and the national disinclination of the Hellenes to identify their cause with that of the Slavonic elements in the Balkan peninsula, the majority of the Cabinet declined the invitation of the Russian Minister during the siege of Plevna to join in the conflict and share in the spoils. But, when the news of the Russian advance on Adrianople arrived, the excitement of the populace became intense. The "Ecumenical Government," whose chief was already dead, resigned; and one of its members, the most experienced of Greek statesmen, Koumoundoûros, who formed the new Cabinet, had to satisfy public opinion by supporting insurrectionary movements in Epiros, Thessaly, and Crete, and by preparing to join in the war. The Greek forces had reached Domokós, when the conclusion of the Russo-Turkish armistice convinced the Greeks that, if they attacked Turkey now, they would fight alone. Great Britain promised that the Greek claims should be considered at the coming Congress; the Greek troops were recalled, but the insurrections went on. The movement in Epiros was soon suppressed; but that in Thessaly was more serious. The picturesque villages which gleam on the slopes and nestle in the folds of Pelion rose in rebellion; a provisional Government was formed, which proclaimed union with Greece; and the fall of Makrinitsa, the headquarters of the insurgents, is still associated with the death of the Englishman Ogle, whose name is borne by a street at Volo. At last, British intervention in May ended the insurrection in Thessaly, while in Crete, which demanded complete autonomy, desultory fighting continued.

The Treaty of San Stefano, which had meanwhile been signed by the Russian and Turkish delegates on March 3, 1878, was not calculated to satisfy Hellenic aspirations. That abortive instrument, still regretted in Bulgaria, would have restored the Bulgarian empire of the Middle Ages, and, while hopelessly dismembering Turkey, would have put a final end to Greek ambitions in Macedonia. It provided for the creation of a vassal principality of Bulgaria, with a frontage on both the Euxine and the Aegean, and with an inland frontier which marched with the Danube

CH. XIV.

on the north and comprised the Macedonian lakes of Prespa and Ochrida, once the home of the Bulgarian Tsars, and the seat of the Bulgarian Church.   To Servia, as the reward of her two campaigns, was assigned a considerable slice of territory, which included Nish, while her south-western frontier was drawn in so favourable a manner as almost to touch the enlarged eastern boundary of Montenegro.   The two Servian States would thus have practically joined each other, and an all-Servian railway might have united Belgrade with the Adriatic.   To these territorial advantages were added the recognition of Servian independence and the cessation of the tribute, which since 1867 had been the last vestige of Turkish suzerainty.   Montenegro was more than trebled in size, and doubled in population; she was to retain her recent conquests of Nikshich, Spizza, Antivari, and Dulcigno; Bilek and Gacko in the Herzegovina, Podgoritsa and the medieval Montenegrin capital of Jablyak on the side of Albania, Priepolye in the Sandjak of Novibazar, were included in the enlarged principality, while diplomacy calmly assigned to Prince Nicholas the unruly Arnauts of Plava and Gusinje.   Montenegrin independence, which had really existed for five centuries, was at last formally recognised by the Sultan.   Roumania, which had rendered such splendid service to Russia during the siege of Plevna, was treated far less generously than the Bulgarians, whose country had, indeed, been the theatre of operations, but who had played a much less important part in the actual fighting.   While the independence of Roumania was admitted by the Porte, Russia acted with base ingratitude towards her Latin ally.   She was resolved to acquire at all costs, preferably at that of her Roumanian neighbours, the southern part of Bessarabia, which she had been compelled to surrender after the Crimean War, and which had been joined to Moldavia by the Treaty of Paris.   She, therefore, obtained from Turkey in lieu of part of the war indemnity the barren district of the Dobrudja, which lies between the Danube and the Black Sea, with the object of exchanging it compulsorily for the far more desirable strip of Bessarabia.   For herself Russia stipulated also for Ardahan, Kars, Bayazid, and Batum with a strip of coast in Asia, so that Trebizond and Erzerum would become the first important towns within the new Turkish frontier.   In order still further to cripple her adversary, she insisted on the demolition of all the Danube fortresses, and a war indemnity, which, after the above-mentioned deductions, still remained large.   On behalf of the Christian populations still left under Turkish rule, she demanded autonomy for Bosnia and what remained of the Herzegovina under a Christian Governor-General, subject to modifications thereafter to be made by Turkey, Austria-Hungary, and herself; in Crete the Porte promised " to apply scrupulously the Organic Law of 1868," and to introduce " analogous arrangements adapted to local requirements into Epiros, Thessaly, and the other parts of Turkey in Europe"; finally, by Article 16 it engaged " to carry into effect, without further delay, the improvements and reforms demanded by local requirements in the provinces inhabited by Armenians, and to guarantee their security from Kurds and Circassians." The subsequent Armenian massacres form a striking commentary on this article.

The Treaty of San Stefano was a wholly Slavonic settlement of a question which concerned other races as well. It would have given the final blow to the Turkish empire in Europe by cutting the remaining Ottoman territory in two separate parts, and by imposing a Bulgarian barrier between the two chief cities of European Turkey. More than that, it would have aggrandised the Bulgarian at the expense of the Greek nationality in Macedonia and Thrace, and would have sacrificed the Albanians to the greater glories of Montenegro and Bulgaria. From every part of the ceded districts came protests against this flagrant violation of justice and ethnology. The Greeks addressed an erudite disquisition to the British Government on this complete disregard of their historic claims; the Mussulmans appealed to Queen Victoria as the Empress of a hundred million Moslem subjects; the Lazes begged for British protection to prevent the cession of Batum and the consequent ruin of Trebizond; the Serbs protested against the inclusion of Servian regions in Bulgaria; the Albanians formed a league to "resist until death" any attempt upon the inviolability of their land; the Roumanians were justly indignant at the loss of Bessarabia. But what chiefly moved the British Government to oppose the treaty was the conviction that the "big Bulgaria" of San Stefano would be merely a Russian province, a constant menace to Constantinople, and a basis for a future Russian attack upon it. The idea of the late Sir William White had not then gained acceptance in England, that our true policy in the East is the formation of strong and independent Balkan States, which would serve as a barrier between Russia and her goal and might even become the allies and the outposts of a reformed Turkey against Muscovite aggression. Yet close observers of the attitude of the Bulgarians during the War might have noticed that the "little brothers," whom the Russians had come to free, were very glad of freedom, but had no desire to exchange one despotism for another, even though the latter were Orthodox and Slavonic. At that moment, however, all the appearances justified the British suspicions. The past policy of Russia towards the Eastern Christians had not been disinterested; her past relations with Greece proved that what she did not want was the erection of a really strong Christian State on the ruins of Turkey. All the circumstances attending the birth of the new Bulgaria pointed in the same direction—the Prince to be "freely elected by the population," and the future administrative organisation to be drawn up by an assembly of notables, "under the supervision of a Russian Commissioner," who would watch for two years over its application. Nor was Great Britain the only Power opposed to the Treaty. Austria-Hungary had greater interests in the Balkan

CH. XIV.

peninsula; she had been promised at Reichstadt the occupation of Bosnia and the Herzegovina; she contemplated that *Drang nach Osten*, which would be as effectually barred as the Greek advance towards Constantinople by a "big Bulgaria," which would have cut her off from Salonica. In France, the new Foreign Minister, Waddington, who had been educated in England, had strongly British sympathies, whenever French interests did not conflict with them.

Even before the Treaty of San Stefano, Austria-Hungary had proposed the summons of a Conference to Vienna, which subsequently became the Congress of Berlin—the capital of the Power least interested in the Eastern question, and the abode of the great statesman who had both the frankness to offer himself as "an honest broker" and the authority to secure the acceptance of his friendly offices. Russia was willing to entertain the proposal, provided that she might select what clauses of the treaty she pleased for discussion at the Congress. The British Government, on the other hand, demanded the examination of the treaty as a whole, and followed up its demands by action. Lord Derby, indeed, declined to be responsible any longer for a warlike policy with which he had long been out of sympathy, and resigned the Foreign Office to Lord Salisbury, the late British delegate at the Constantinople Conference, who lived to make the sorrowful confession that in her pro-Turkish policy Great Britain had "backed the wrong horse." Lord Beaconsfield then called out the reserves and ordered a force of native Indian troops to Malta, while his new Foreign Secretary in a circular addressed to the other Powers summed up the British Government's objections to the Treaty of San Stefano. The mobilisation of the Austrian army, the indignation of Roumania at Russian ingratitude, the discontent at home—all contributed to induce the Tsar to listen to the British arguments. Through the mediation of Count Shuvaloff, the Russian ambassador in London, a secret agreement, which speedily found its way into print, was made between the two Governments for the modification of the "big Bulgaria," and the way was paved for the meeting of the European Areopagus at Berlin.

The Congress of Berlin, which opened on June 13 and closed on the same day of the following month, was the most important gathering of statesmen that has ever met since the last great liquidation of the Eastern question at Paris in 1856. All the Great Powers were represented by their best men—Great Britain by the Prime Minister and the Foreign Secretary; Russia by Prince Gorchakóff and the Russian ambassador in London; France by Waddington; Austria-Hungary by Count Andrássy and Baron Haymerle; Italy by Count Corti, her Minister for Foreign Affairs; Germany by the "Iron Chancellor," who was elected president of the Congress. Each Power was also assisted by the counsels of its ambassador in Berlin, while Turkey, the object of these deliberations, sent Karatheodori and Mehemed Ali, the one

a Greek, the other a German, to plead Moslem interests at the Congress.
The admission of Greece was championed by Lord Salisbury, in pursuance of the British pledge to see that Greek claims should not suffer
from Greek neutrality in the war.   He pointed out that the creation
of the Bulgarian Exarchate had made the Greeks and Bulgarians rivals,
and that, while Bulgaria enjoyed the protection of Russia, Greece
was unrepresented at the Council which was about to decide on the
future of the East.   The Congress decided, however, that the Greek
delegates, Theodore Delyánnes and Alexander Ragkavês, should merely
be admitted, like those of Roumania, to state their views without the
right of voting.   Thus, none of the small States immediately concerned
in the settlement were allowed direct representation at the council-
board.

The Congress of Berlin, in spite of the threatened departure of the
British delegates at a critical stage of the negotiations, accomplished
its work, and drew up on July 13 what has been ever since, at least on
paper, the charter of the Balkan peninsula.   The Treaty of San Stefano
was almost entirely nullified by the Treaty of Berlin.   Instead of a "big
Bulgaria" stretching from the Danube to the Aegean and from the
Black Sea beyond the Macedonian lakes, it created a small "autonomous
and tributary principality under the suzerainty of the Sultan," which
was bounded by the Danube, the Balkans, the Black Sea, and the Servian
and Macedonian frontiers, and had a harbour at Varna.   South of the
Balkans, there was artificially formed an autonomous province, known
by the diplomatic name of "Eastern Rumelia," and placed "under the
direct political and military authority of the Sultan," but administered
by a Christian Governor-General "named by the Porte, with the
assent of the Powers, for a term of five years."   The recent history
of Moldavia and Wallachia might have suggested the reflexion that
national feeling will sooner or later join together what diplomacy has
severed.   But for the moment the separation of Bulgaria into two
sections was regarded as a triumph of British statesmanship and a
diminution of Russian influence.   Such is the shortsightedness of the
ablest diplomatists that, when the union of the two Bulgarias came only
seven years later, it was the British Government that supported and
the Russian that condemned it.   It was further provided that the Prince
of Bulgaria should be "freely elected by the population and confirmed
by the Porte, with the consent of the Powers," and that no member of
any reigning dynasty should be eligible.   Until a Bulgarian Assembly
of Notables should have drawn up an organic law for the principality,
a Russian Commissioner was to direct the administration, but the
duration of this provisional arrangement was limited to nine months.
The organisation of Eastern Rumelia, on the other hand, was entrusted
to an European Commission, which was allotted three months for its
labours.

CH. XIV.

While the articles affecting Bulgaria were intended to minimise Russian influence in the eastern Balkans, the clauses regarding the Serb population were favourable to the growth of Austria in the west. In pursuance of the Reichstadt agreement, and on the proposal of Lord Salisbury, Bosnia and the Herzegovina were to be " occupied and administered by Austria-Hungary," which thus became what she had been for two decades of the eighteenth century—a Balkan State. Arguments, alike practical and historical, could be advanced for this arrangement. The two provinces contained few Turks, and were distant from the Turkish capital, while the coexistence of two Slav races and of three religions, Orthodox, Roman Catholic, and Mussulman, suggested the administration of a strong foreign Power as the best means of securing order and good government, which should be the aim of practical statesmen in the Near East rather than exclusive attention to the doctrine of nationalities. Austria-Hungary had already a number of Croatian and Servian subjects ; and, though the Magyars had sympathised with the Turks during the war, so lately as 1869, Count Andrássy had alluded to the ancient historical claims of the Hungarian Crown to Bosnia, the north of which had been annexed by Austria in 1718. Moreover, the British Foreign Secretary saw in an Austrian occupation the best means of preventing a chain of Slav States from stretching across the Balkan peninsula. But this was not the only blow dealt by the Berlin Treaty to the hopes of Servian and Montenegrin patriots. Article 25 further gave to the Dual Monarchy "the right of keeping garrisons and having military and commercial roads" in the Sandjak of Novibazar, which remained as a Turkish wedge between the two Servian States, a funnel through which Austrian influence could penetrate into northern Albania and Macedonia. A further Convention, dated April 21, 1879, between Austria-Hungary and Turkey, while confirming this treaty right, stated that Austrian troops would only be placed at the three points of Priboy, Priepolye, and Bielopolye, which last place was almost immediately changed for Plevlye. In accordance with the views of Austria, the territorial additions made to modern Servia at Berlin were not in Stara Serbia, the ancient land of the Servian Tsars, which still remained Turkish, but at Nish and Vranya, and in the Bulgarian-speaking district of Pirot—a total increase of one-fourth of the former principality. Servia now obtained the formal recognition of her independence ; but, like the other two Slav States, she was to pay her share of the Ottoman debt for these new possessions. Montenegro, now also recognised at last as a sovereign State, had to be content with twice, instead of thrice, her original territory. She received the important places of Podgoritsa, Spuj, and Jablyak, and the Albanian towns of Gusinje and Plava with the villages depending on them. She obtained an outlet on the sea at the bay of Antivari, but was forced to restore Dulcigno to Turkey and to cede Spizza to Austria. The former of these grievances was redressed in 1880; the latter has never been forgotten, for the twin forts of what has since 1878 been the southernmost village of Dalmatia command the bay and dominate the Prince's palace on the shore. Yet further, to prevent Antivari becoming a possible landing-place for Russian forces and ammunition, it was provided by Article 29 that all Montenegrin waters should "remain closed to the ships of war of all nations," that the principality should have neither fleet nor naval flag, and that the maritime and sanitary police of the small strip of Montenegrin coast should be in the hands of Austria-Hungary. These inexorable conditions were a bitter disappointment to Prince Nicholas. He saw the Herzegovina, the cradle of his race, the stony land where he had fought so valiantly against his hereditary enemy, occupied by his arch-foe—that *Erzfeind* who is now so much more feared at Cetinje than the *Erbfeind* of other times. He saw, too, Spizza—the poor man's "ewe lamb," as his ardent admirer Freeman called it—taken from him, its captor, by a Power to which it had never belonged.

A still greater injustice was perpetrated by the articles dealing with Roumania. Roumanian independence was made conditional on the retrocession of south Bessarabia to Russia in exchange for the Dobrudja with an additional strip of territory to the south, extending as far westward as the walls of the famous fortress of Silistria. Against this cruel condition Prince Charles and his high-spirited people protested in vain. Russia insisted on thus rewarding the splendid services of her Latin allies, to whose assistance her victory had been largely due, while the additional piece of land given as a consolation to Roumania was benevolently taken from Bulgaria. The empire of the Tsar was thus once more bounded by the "accursed stream," which, after twenty-two years of union, again separated the free Roumanians from their brothers in Bessarabia, a region historically and ethnographically a Roumanian land, while the Dobrudja contained large Bulgarian and Turkish elements, and was still as desolate as at the time when Ovid had lamented that it was his place of exile. Moreover, the consignment of a Bulgarian population to Roumanian rule tended, and was perhaps designed, to sow discord between the two adjacent States. The energy of Roumania has, indeed, made the best of this compulsory exchange; a splendid bridge now spans the Danube, uniting the trans-Danubian province to the rest of the country, and making the barren Dobrudja a highway, by the now flourishing port of Constantsa, from Berlin to the Bosporos. But the ingratitude of Russia still rankles in the mind of the Roumanians, and has had the effect of driving the "Belgians of the East" into the orbit of the Triple Alliance. The other and much more plausible condition of her independence—the abolition of Jewish disabilities—Roumania has sometimes evaded and sometimes ignored. It is argued by Roumanian statesmen that in their country, and especially in Moldavia, the Jewish question is not religious but social and economic, and that the admission

CH. XIV.

of the Semitic foreigners to full rights would swamp the native population. In order, however, to obtain the recognition of the Powers the
Roumanian Government had to revise Article 7 of the Constitution,
which permitted the naturalisation of Christian aliens only; but, even
then, the naturalisation of the Jews was limited by various legal restrictions, with which a preoccupied Europe did not trouble to interfere.
Other less contentious clauses of the Treaty excluded men-of-war from
the Danube below the Iron Gates, and entrusted to Austria-Hungary
the removal of that natural obstacle, which was accomplished in 1896.

Greece received by the Treaty of 1878 no increase of territory.
Delyánnes had told the Congress that, in view of the general desire
of a pacific settlement, his Government would be content for the time
being with the annexation of Crete and of the Turkish provinces
bordering on the Greek kingdom—an arrangement which, as he justly
argued, would be a guarantee of peace. Accordingly, the Congress, on
the proposal of Waddington, invited the Porte, in its 13th protocol, so
to rectify the Greek frontier as to make the northern boundary of Hellas
march with the Peneios on the east, and with the Kalamâs, which flows
into the sea opposite the southern half of Corfù, on the west. An
article of the Treaty reserved to the Powers the right of offering their
mediation to facilitate this settlement. Crete, on the other hand, was
to remain Turkish, the Porte promising to apply the Organic Law
of 1868, while the rest of the Turkish empire, for which no special
administration was provided, had to be content with the prospect of
a similar organisation, the details of which were to be worked out by
special commissions, representing the native population. This Article,
which was destined to cover Macedonia, Thrace, Albania, and the larger
part of Epiros, remained a dead letter.

Such were the main provisions of this new Charter of the Near East,
so far as it affected Europe. In Asia, the Black Sea frontier, as fixed at
San Stefano, was preserved at Berlin; the Porte ceded Ardahan, Kars,
and Batum to Russia, but retained Bayazid; while the Tsar promised
that Batum should be made "a free port, essentially commercial." Eight
years later, his successor, despite the protests of the British Government,
repudiated this solemn promise. Finally—most futile of all these pledges
—by Article 61 the Porte undertook "to carry out, without further delay,
the ameliorations and reforms demanded in the provinces inhabited by
the Armenians, and to guarantee their security against the Circassians
and Kurds." Periodical statements of these reforms were to be made to
the Powers, who would "superintend their application." A special
responsibility for the protection of the Armenians devolved upon Great
Britain in virtue of the Cyprus Convention, which had been signed on
June 4, and the publication of which during the Congress came as a
thunder-clap upon the diplomatic world. By this Convention, Great
Britain engaged to join the Sultan in the defence of his Asiatic

dominions against any further Russian attack, and the Sultan promised, in return, "to introduce necessary reforms" there, in consultation with his ally. In order to enable the latter to fulfil her engagement, he assigned to her the island of Cyprus as "a place of arms" in the Levant, on payment of an annual tribute, and on the understanding that a Russian evacuation of the recent Asiatic conquests should be followed by a British evacuation of Cyprus. Thus Lord Beaconsfield "consolidated" the Turkish empire by assigning the administration of Bosnia and the Herzegovina to Austria-Hungary, and that of Cyprus to Great Britain, with which its sole historical connexion had been the conquest by Cœur-de-Lion nearly seven centuries earlier. His own opinion of these diplomatic achievements was summed up in the memorable phrase, in which he told the British people on his return from Berlin, that he had brought them "peace with honour."

The experience of the thirty years that have elapsed since the signature of the Berlin Treaty forces us, however, to add the following notes upon its provisions and the observance they have received. It has not proved in any sense a permanent settlement of an eternal question; it has not secured the peace of the Balkan peninsula; it has not ensured the just treatment of the Christian races which it left under Turkish rule. Almost every signatory Power, and more than one small State, has violated some provision of this solemn international instrument. Turkey has broken Articles 23 and 61 by doing nothing to reform the lot of the Macedonian and Armenian populations, while no Power has taken effective steps on behalf of the latter; Russia has torn up Article 59 by closing and fortifying Batum; Austria-Hungary has arbitrarily extended the provisions of Article 25 by annexing Bosnia and the Herzegovina; Roumania has defied Article 44 by her persecution of the Jews; Greece has received only a portion of the territory indicated as hers in the 13th protocol; Bulgaria has contemptuously and successfully ignored two whole series of clauses by the union of Eastern Rumelia and the recent declaration of Bulgarian independence; the Montenegrin frontier has been modified by an armed demonstration; while Crete has protested against her situation to such purpose, that four of the signatory Powers have placed her under the government of a Greek Commissioner. Two short but desperate wars, one of them fratricidal, have demonstrated the futility of supposing that any parchment bonds will heal the racial jealousies or restrain the racial ambitions of centuries in a part of Europe —if Europe it can be called—where the claims derived from medieval, and even ancient, history are constantly invoked as if a thousand years had been as yesterday. Yet, if the Treaty of Berlin presents a sadly lacerated appearance today, it has nevertheless marked an advance towards the ultimate solution of the Eastern question. Whatever theorists may say, the thirty years of Austrian occupation in Bosnia and the Herzegovina, with which we may compare the British occupation of Egypt and the

CH. XIV.

French protectorate of Tunisia, have converted two wild Turkish provinces into a pattern Balkan State ; free Bulgaria has, on the whole, proved to be a success ; while the exemption of the Macedonian Greeks from Bulgarian rule has, at least, led later Greek politicians to bless the name of Lord Salisbury for his services in helping to destroy the Treaty of San Stefano.

The three years immediately following the Berlin Congress were occupied with the delimitation of the new frontiers and the establishment of the new order of things, which, in the case of Bosnia, Montenegro, and Greece, proved to be more difficult than had been expected. Sixteen days after the signature of the treaty, the Austrian troops under Baron von Philippovich crossed the Save in four columns, the chief column following the historic route along the Bosna valley which Prince Eugene had taken on the occasion of his famous dash on Sarajevo in 1697. But the Austrians had reckoned without the fanaticism of the Bosnian Mussulmans. On August 3 the Moslems of Maglaj treacherously cut to pieces a squadron of hussars, and a series of skirmishes followed, until the second column, having captured the ancient city of Yaytse (Jajce), where the last Bosnian King had met his death, effected a junction with the main body and pressed on to Sarajevo. When the Austrians approached, an insurrection broke out in the capital; the Turkish governor was deposed; and a fanatic, named Hajji Loja, preached a holy war against the Christians. On the 19th the Austrians opened fire upon the city, which, after a desperate resistance, fell into their hands; a large part of the town perished in the flames, and the grave of many an Austrian soldier still bears silent testimony to the fury of the defenders. Meanwhile, a guerrilla warfare had broken out in the rear, under the command of Muktija Effendi, an Albanian from Novibazar, who was joined by some Turkish regulars. The Bosna valley was once more the scene of constant conflicts ; and the Herzegovina, which had at first submitted to Baron Jovanovich almost without a blow, became restive. It was necessary to send four more army corps to the relief of the army of occupation. The valley of the Bosna was then cleared; the Herzegovina was subdued by the end of September; and on October 20 the last stronghold of the Bosnian insurgents surrendered. In 1882, however, another insurrection broke out in the Herzegovina, and it was not till the appointment of the late Baron von Kállay to direct the destinies of the "Occupied Territory," that the constructive work, which has gone on ever since, began. At last, after thirty years of Austro-Hungarian occupation, the two former Turkish provinces were annexed to the Dual Monarchy on October 7, 1908.

The military occupation of the three points in the Sandjak of Novibazar began with the entrance of the Austro-Hungarian troops into Plevlye on September 10, 1879. The Austrians sent only one civil official there, and the Turkish administrative, judicial, and financial authorities continued to exist, while Turkish troops were stationed in the same towns as the Austrian garrisons. The friendly relations which were maintained during the period of this mixed occupation between the Austrians and the Turkish authorities were largely due to the tact of Ferik Suleiman, the perpetual Pasha of Plevlye, who was appointed soon after this strange and hybrid arrangement began. The exclusion of Turkish irregulars from the Sandjak by the Austro-Turkish Convention also had an excellent effect, while Ottoman pride was characteristically salved by the diplomatic device of forming the three towns and the four small intervening watch-posts occupied by the Austrians into a new and smaller Sandjak of Plevlye. But with the natives of this district, mostly Serbs—for here was Rascia, the nucleus of the old Servian empire—the "Europeans" were never popular. These "enslaved" Slavs were never allowed by their free Servian and Montenegrin neighbours to forget the Treaty of San Stefano; and they regarded the Austro-Turkish wedge which prevented the union of the two States on either side of them as an obstacle to that dream of a revived Servian realm, which, five centuries since the death of Stephen Dushan (1355), is still ever present to the imaginative minds of the scattered Serbs. Hence, when, in part compensation for the annexation of Bosnia and the Herzegovina, Austria-Hungary withdrew her troops from the Sandjak on October 28, 1908, they were regretted only by those who had made their living by ministering to the wants of the soldiers. Europe was told that this act of renunciation signified the definite abandonment of the Austrian advance to Salonica, of which Plevlye had been sometimes regarded as the first stage. The initials of the Emperor Francis Joseph on the hill-side at Plevlye mark the furthest point which the Austrian double-eagle has reached since it threatened, for a moment in 1689, the walls of Uskub.

While Austria was thus taking up her new position as the "sentinel of the Balkans," her neighbour, the Prince of Montenegro, was unable to obtain the two Albanian districts of Gusinje and Plava, which had been assigned to him at Berlin. The inhabitants were first-class fighting-men, who cared for neither the Congress nor the Sultan, and objected to have their homes and themselves transferred without their consent to another State, which, being admittedly better governed than their own, might interfere with their time-honoured privileges of lawlessness. The Sultan's first envoy, Mehemed Ali, they murdered as he fled from his burning house; the second they refused to obey. Accordingly, in 1879, hostilities broke out between them and the Montenegrins; and the "Albanian League," which had been formed to combat the Treaty of San Stefano, was revived, probably at the suggestion, certainly to the satisfaction, of the Porte. Turkey was thus able to make the national sentiment of a race, which had had no separate existence since the days of Skanderbeg, and no great local leader since Ali of Janina, an excuse for not carrying out its inconvenient engagements. A compromise, suggested by Count Corti, the Italian ambassador at Constantinople, according to which Montenegro should receive instead of the towns of Gusinje and Plava a portion only of the former district and a larger strip of territory between Podgoritsa and the lake of Skutari, was accepted on April 12, 1880, but proved to be impracticable, owing to the determined opposition of the Albanians. Those who inhabited this region were Roman Catholics, and, if the Mussulman Albanians had objected to Prince Nicholas as a Christian, the Catholics repudiated him as what was worse—an Orthodox one. Prenk Bib Doda, the Mirdite Prince, whose territory to the south of the Drin was not menaced by the proposed aggrandisement of Montenegro, marched at the head of his tribe to the aid of his brothers in faith, and ere long 10,000 men were on the frontier.

Meanwhile, Gladstone had returned to power in England, and his well-known Montenegrin sympathies facilitated a solution of the question. The plenipotentiaries of the Powers met in conference at Berlin in June to consider the best means of securing the performance by Turkey of the unfulfilled engagements made there two years before, and proposed, in lieu of Count Corti's scheme, that Montenegro should receive the town of Dulcigno and a strip of seaboard as far as the river Bojana. This proposal the Porte refused to accept, on the ground that Dulcigno contained a Moslem population, and secretly urged the Albanians to resist its cession. Thereupon, at the suggestion of the British Government, a naval demonstration of the Powers was held in September before the old Venetian colony, while Montenegrin troops approached it by land. As the Porte still held out, and the admirals were anxious not to bombard the town, this existence of *Dulcigno far niente*, as Count Beust wittily called it, might have continued indefinitely, had not the British Government suggested the seizure of the rich custom-house at Smyrna. The mere suggestion had the desired effect; the Turkish commander drove out the Albanians, and at last, on November 26, the Montenegrins peaceably occupied Dulcigno. Prince Nicholas publicly expressed his gratitude to Great Britain. Dulcigno is not the natural frontage of the Black Mountain; indeed, it is a mere open roadstead, and the neighbouring bay of Val di Noce has never been exploited. But, at any rate, Montenegro, if she still lacks a good harbour, if her coast was, till this year, bound by Austrian fetters, has a seaboard of 30 miles, and she owes its extension, as she owed her brief occupation of Cattaro in 1813, to the aid of a British fleet. Doda was exiled, and has only lately returned. Oroshi, his capital, was laid in ashes.

The rectification of the Greek frontier, suggested at the Berlin Congress, gave even more trouble than that of Montenegro. Lord Beaconsfield had told Greece that she had a future, and that she could accordingly afford to wait. She had to wait three years before she obtained one portion of the new territory indicated as her due; she is waiting still for the remainder. The Porte pursued its usual dilatory policy, and the "Albanian League" made its appearance in Epiros, as well as in northern Albania. When the Greek delegates at last met the Turkish Commissioners at Preveza early in 1879, their deliberations proved futile, and the venue was removed to Constantinople, where the negotiations could be supervised by the Powers, but with the same negative result. The accession of Gladstone to power in England in 1880 was hailed in Greece as in Montenegro, for the new Prime Minister was gratefully remembered as the author of the last extension of Hellas sixteen years earlier. At the Conference held in Berlin for the settlement of the Greek and the Montenegrin questions, the frontier adopted was in Epiros the river Kalamâs, in Thessaly the crest of Olympos, and this line was so liberally drawn that both Janina and Metzovo would have been ceded to Greece. Athens went wild with excitement at the news; Trikoúpes, then Prime Minister, at once accepted the proposal of the Conference, and, when the Porte rejected it, mobilised the Greek army. A change of Ministry in France, however, seriously injured the Greek cause. Hitherto, the British and French Governments had been the best friends of Greece; but Barthélemy Saint-Hilaire, the new French Minister for Foreign Affairs, whom the Greeks had ingenuously regarded as a Philhellene because he had translated Aristotle, adopted arguments which his British colleague qualified as those of the Turks. The result was that the Porte, finding the Powers disunited, made a firmer resistance; and a Conference of their representatives at Constantinople finally, on May 24, 1881, limited the new territories of Greece to Thessaly and that portion of Epiros which formed the district of Arta, whose famous bridge became, and still remains, the boundary. The British delegate, Goschen, admitted that Greece deserved a larger share of Epiros, and a journey from Arta or Preveza to Janina will convince the traveller of the predominantly Hellenic character of that unredeemed district. But the arrangement was the best that could be made under the circumstances. In Thessaly the Greek kingdom gained a valuable province, which had been Turkish for wellnigh five centuries, while at Arta it recovered the historic capital of that medieval despotat of Epiros, which, when the Crusaders partitioned the rest of Greece, became the chief refuge of Hellenism.

The most important creation of the Berlin Treaty—the principality of Bulgaria—was entrusted to Russian hands during the interregnum which lasted until a Prince could be elected. The Russian Commissioner, Prince Dondukoff-Korsakoff, was a rich man who kept open house and was personally popular; but he treated the country as a Russian province. All the chief posts were filled by the Russian "liberators," in disregard of the fact that the Bulgarian peasants are extremely suspicious of foreigners. At first, while the memories of Turkish rule were fresh in men's minds, recognition of Russia's services reconciled the natives to this alien domination; but political gratitude, even in the Balkans, is usually short-lived; and ere long the Bulgarians began to show that they had not ceased to be Turkish *râyah* in order to become Russian subjects.

Yet further to strengthen the hold of Russia, the Commissioner framed a Constitution, at once ultra-democratic and ultra-conservative, which was so devised that the Prince could be checkmated by the people and the people by the Prince, while the real power would remain with the Tsar; unfortunately, paper constitutions never produce in practice the results which they are intended to achieve. It never occurred to the astute framer of the Bulgarian charter, that he had not provided against one contingency which actually occurred—the union of Prince and people against their "liberators." Meanwhile, Bulgaria, a land of peasants without the smallest experience of parliamentary institutions, was suddenly endowed with a single Chamber, or ordinary *Sobranye*, elected by manhood suffrage, with free, compulsory, elementary education, equal electoral districts, payment of members, and a free Press. As against these democratic provisions, the Ministers were made independent of the Chamber, and the creatures of the Prince, who was given the further power of dissolving the *Sobranye* whenever he chose. No second Chamber was instituted, nor would it have been easy to devise one in a land without an aristocracy, without great fortunes, and without either a leisured or a highly cultured class. But for great changes, such as the election of a Prince, the nomination of Regents, the extension, cession or exchange of territory, or the revision of the Constitution, an extraordinary assembly, or Grand *Sobranye*, was declared necessary. This body was formed of twice the number of members composing the ordinary Chamber. The Constitution was passed by an Assembly of Notables, held not at Sofia, the newly chosen capital, but at the ancient imperial city of Trnovo, on April 28, 1879. Next day, Prince Alexander of Battenberg, son of Prince Alexander of Hesse and nephew of the Tsar, Alexander II, was elected first Prince of Bulgaria. Two months later, the new ruler set foot in his principality and took the oath to the Constitution at Trnovo.

Prince Alexander at the time of his election was only 22 years of age. But he had already seen service in the land of his adoption. He had taken part in the Russo-Turkish War, had crossed the Danube at Sistova and the Balkans with Gurko; he had fought at Nova Zagora and had stood in the trenches at Plevna; at the time of his election he was serving as a Prussian lieutenant at Potsdam. But, if his military experience and his tall, martial bearing fitted him for one part of his duties, his complete lack of both political education and statesmanlike capacity were serious drawbacks to the performance of the other. He was obstinate, talkative, and apt to quarrel with his advisers, and he had the great disadvantage of having to trust for some time to interpreters in his intercourse with them. A stranger to the tortuous politics of a newly emancipated oriental land, in which personal questions naturally played a prominent part, he was certain to make mistakes in the closet, though he redeemed them on the field of battle.

For the first two years of his reign, the Prince, who had ascended the throne as the nominee of Russia, naturally inclined towards the Russophil, or Conservative party, although the Nationalists, or Liberals, were in a majority. Finding himself unable to work with his Parliament, in 1881 he suddenly issued a proclamation announcing his resignation, unless irresponsible authority were conferred upon him for seven years, and appointed the Russian General Ernroth president of the provisional Administration. A packed Assembly, held at Sistova under threat of the Prince's instant departure on the steamer which lay ready in the Danube, conceded his demands; the *coup d'État* had succeeded, and he was, to all appearance, master of the country. But Russia was the power behind the brand-new Bulgarian throne; two more Russian Generals, Soboleff and Alexander Kaulbars, arrived from Petersburg to assume the posts of Premier and Minister of War, and representative institutions were reduced to a small Chamber which had no function beyond that of voting the budget. Both the Prince and his people, however, soon resented the tactless conduct and imperious ways of the Russian generals, who treated the free Bulgarians as Asiatics, and detested their ruler as a German. Accordingly, in 1883, he restored the Constitution of Trnovo, and his two Russian Ministers retired to their own country.

Meanwhile, the International Commission had drawn up the organic statute for Eastern Rumelia; and in 1879 Alexander Vogorides, son of a Rumeliote who had been first Prince of Samos, and himself a Turkish official, was appointed the first Governor-General. Aleko Pasha, as he was called in the Turkish service, thus represented in his own person the three nationalities of the province—Bulgarians, Greeks, and Turks —whose languages were all declared to be official. The Rumelian Constitution was more conservative than that of the neighbouring principality. The local assembly consisted of 56 members, of whom 36 were elected on a property or educational franchise, while the others were either nominated or *ex officio* members. Politics were excluded from its discussions, which were occupied with financial and administrative questions; the "spoils system," which is the curse of all Balkan States, was avoided by a permanent civil service, and the chief posts were filled by well-to-do Rumeliotes of good family. Six Directors conducted the administration, the chief of whom, the Secretary-General, was, like the Governor, a Rumeliote with Samian experience, Gavril Krstyovich. Under these circumstances, Eastern Rumelia was materially better off than the principality; the Thracian plain is naturally the richest part of the two Bulgarias; and the absence of political agitation is the greatest of blessings that any Balkan land can enjoy. Only in the Rhodope

CH. XIV.

mountains, where a half-English, half-Polish adventurer, named St Clair, had been hailed as a "saviour" by the Mussulman insurgents at the close of the war, twenty-two communities of 19,000 Bulgarian Moslems formed the so-called "Pomak Republic," independent alike of Turkey and of Eastern Rumelia, to which the Berlin Treaty had assigned them.   One of the authors of the massacres of 1876 maintained himself as the chief of this band of fanatical robbers, until, in 1883, the Porte, heedless of the Berlin Treaty, annexed the "Republic" by the cheap device of decorating and giving official uniforms to the leading "Republicans."

Nationalist feeling was maintained, despite the prosperity of Eastern Rumelia, by the Bulgarians of Sliven ; and, when the first Governor-General's five years of office expired, there was an Unionist party, which advocated the nomination of Prince Alexander as his successor.   For the moment, the Unionists were defeated, and Krstyovich was appointed under the name of Gavril Pasha.   But the tactless exercise of the Porte's right of veto on Rumeliote legislation, and the wish for a Bulgarian customs union, increased the desire for political unity.   On the morning of September 18, 1885, Major Nikolaieff and other officers surrounded the Pasha's *Konak* at Philippopolis, while the Unionist leader, Stoianoff, entered his room and told him that he was a prisoner.   The aged Governor-General yielded to superior force ; he was drawn round the town in mock triumph with a Bulgarian schoolmistress holding an unsheathed sabre by his side, and then sent away to Sofia and thence to Constantinople. Not a single drop of blood stained the revolution ; the Union of the two Bulgarias under Prince Alexander was proclaimed, and a provisional Government formed to await his decision.

The Prince had been forewarned of the conspirators' plans, but he hesitated at first to defy Turkey and the Powers by accepting the offer which they now made him.   Stambuloff, then Speaker of the Chamber, plainly told him that, if he did not advance to Philippopolis, he would have no option but to retire to Darmstadt.   Bulgarian opinion wanted the Union, and would abandon a Prince who had not the moral courage to achieve the national desire.   Alexander, accordingly, ordered the mobilisation of the army, and on September 21 entered Philippopolis. The *Sobranye* at once approved the Union, and voted an extraordinary credit for its defence.

To the general surprise, the Sultan contented himself with protests and merely defensive preparations, while Great Britain, where Lord Salisbury was then in power, strongly supported the Union, in direct opposition to the policy adopted after San Stefano.   The Tsar, Alexander III, was indignant at his cousin's audacity ; he struck his name out of the army list, and recalled all Russian officers from Bulgaria.   Still more violent was the opposition of Bulgaria's two rivals in the Balkans, Greece and Servia.   Both countries demanded territorial compensation for the aggrandisement of the principality, and the Cretans proclaimed once more their union with Greece.

The only serious danger was on the side of Servia. On March 6, 1882, Prince Milan, to show the superiority of his position, had been proclaimed King, Servia being raised to the dignity of a kingdom. But the glamour of this title did not make King Milan popular; his life was attempted in the Belgrade Cathedral; his peasant subjects rose in rebellion against the arbitrary measures of his " iron Minister," Kristich; while the Karageorgevich pretender was more threatening because he had married a daughter of Prince Nicholas of Montenegro. Dynastic reasons, therefore, suggested a spirited foreign policy as the best means of raising the prestige and increasing the popularity of the Obrenovich family. Nor were there lacking other motives for a conflict. The Bulgarians coveted Pirot, the Serbs desired Vidin; and the river Timok, by changing its course, had created a delicate question of frontier between the mutually jealous neighbours. A tariff war yet further embittered their relations, so that the news of the Philippopolis revolution found both King and people predisposed for war. The result was a complete surprise. When, on November 14, Servia began hostilities, the general belief was that the " King of Servia and Macedonia," as the Belgrade populace styled Milan, would have a triumphal march to Sofia. Appearances pointed to such a conclusion, for the Bulgarian army was denuded of its Russian instructors, whose places had been hastily taken by young officers, while the Servians had had the experience of two campaigns. But the Bulgarians were fired with zeal for the national cause; even the Moslems of the principality rallied to the side of a leader who had shown them toleration; recruits from Macedonia crossed the frontier, and the main body of the Servian army, when on November 16 it approached the picturesque village of Slivnitsa, which lies on the direct route to Sofia, found Prince Alexander facing it at the head of his hastily collected forces. The battle of Slivnitsa, which lasted for the next three days, was the Bulgarian principality's baptism of fire. The night before the battle, the raw Bulgarian levies were still doubtful; but, when the fighting began, the splendid example of the Prince inspired them with firmness. The critical moment was reached on the third day, when a rumoured march of the Serbs on the capital from the south caused a panic at Sofia and the Prince had to reassure the terrified citizens by his presence. The alarm proved to be false, the Serbs were defeated at Slivnitsa; their siege of Vidin was quite fruitless; King Milan asked in vain for an armistice; and the Bulgarians, after a two days' battle at Pirot, occupied that coveted town. The road to Belgrade lay open to the invaders, but next day Austria intervened to save her *protégé*, and informed Prince Alexander that, if he advanced further, he would find an Austrian army before him. Thus, on November 28, ended this fourteen days' fratricidal war; an armistice was signed in Pirot, and on March 3, 1886, the Treaty of Bucharest restored the *status quo*. Bulgaria gained from Servia neither territory nor money by her victory; but she had established in the eyes of Europe that right which comes of might to the possession of Eastern Rumelia. A diplomatic compromise was made at Constantinople, by which the Sultan appointed the Prince of Bulgaria his new Governor-General of Eastern Rumelia, thus preserving the letter of the Berlin Treaty, and relinquished his right to keep a Turkish garrison there in return for the purely Turkish district of Kyrdjali and the adjacent home of the Pomaks in the Rhodope. Thus, in the eyes of Turkish theorists, Eastern Rumelia remained a separate province, united by a limited personal union with the principality; while the practical Bulgarians regarded it as southern Bulgaria, whose administration was merged in that of Sofia, and whose 91 representatives sat with their northern brothers in the same National Assembly.

The Bulgarian triumph at Slivnitsa had yet further increased the excitement in Greece. Delyánnes, then in his first premiership, made preparations for war against Turkey, and reintroduced the forced paper currency, which has existed ever since. Warlike demonstrations took place at Athens and in several Greek country towns; a large force of men was mobilised; and the situation became so critical, that the Powers intervened, and finally, on May 8, 1886, ordered their fleets to blockade the Greek coast from Cape Malea to the frontier of Thessaly. The French Government alone took no part in this blockade, which was organised by the Gladstone Ministry and carried out by the Duke of Edinburgh, who, as Prince Alfred, had been offered the Greek crown twenty-three years before—circumstances which made Great Britain and the great Philhellene temporarily unpopular. Delyánnes then resigned; and, though fighting took place on the Thessalian frontier, Trikoúpes was able to prevent further hostilities. Greece disarmed, and the blockade ended. But the feeling against Bulgaria continued.

Prince Alexander did not long enjoy his triumph. An enemy more insidious than Servia was scheming for his overthrow. Russia had not forgotten his audacity in achieving for himself what she had failed to accomplish for her own ends at San Stefano. There were discontented officers in the army, whose services had not been adequately rewarded and who were ready to play the Russian game, certain to be disavowed in case of failure, sure to be recognised in case of success. Of these officers the chief were Bendereff, the acting Minister of War, and Gruieff, the head of the Military Academy. The conspirators, some 80 in number, selected the moment when Sofia was stripped of troops in consequence of a rumoured Servian invasion, and at two o'clock in the morning of August 21, 1886, entered the palace, and forced Alexander, by pointing their loaded revolvers at his head, to sign a paper abdicating the throne. Three hours later he was driven to the monastery of Etropol and next day to the Danube, where he was conveyed on board his yacht, and on the morning of August 23 landed on Russian soil. Thus, the Prince of Bulgaria, like Prince Couza of Roumania twenty years before, was kidnapped and deposed before Europe could say a word. Obviously, the romance of the Middle Ages was still to be found in the prosaic capital of modern Bulgaria.

Sofia remained for three days in the hands of the conspirators. As not infrequently happens in Balkan States, a churchman, in the person of the Metropolitan Clement, was found to pronounce his blessing upon the band of traitors, and to assume the presidency of a provisional Ministry, which assured the people of the Tsar's protection. But, as the Balkan proverb says, " the clouds are high, and the Tsar is far off"; Stambuloff, at that time Speaker of the *Sobranye*, and Lieutenant-Colonel Mutkuroff, who was in command at Philippopolis, appealed to their fellow-countrymen against the conspirators, and dissolved the provisional Government. The next step was to discover the kidnapped sovereign's whereabouts and to bid him by telegraph return to his faithful people. Alexander accepted the invitation, and a fortnight after his abdication reentered his capital. But the "hero of Slivnitsa" had lost his nerve under the trials of the last twelve months. A poor diplomatist, he was induced by the Russian Consul, who met him on his landing at Rustchuk, to despatch an obsequious telegram to the Tsar, which concluded with the expression of his readiness to resign his crown to the sovereign whose father had given it. Alexander III disliked his cousin, and had grown distrustful of Bulgaria; he telegraphed back that he could not approve the Prince's return. This fatal mistake cost the latter his throne. Despite the pressing arguments of Stambuloff, he publicly announced his abdication on September 7; and, after appointing that energetic statesman, with Mutkuroff and Karaveloff, as Regents, next day left Bulgaria for ever. Under the name of Count Hartenau, the first Prince of " the peasant State" lived for seven years the happier life of an Austrian officer, an example of the rule that assassination or abdication is the fate of most Balkan rulers.

Russia, having got rid of Prince Alexander, made a bold but mistaken attempt to recover her lost influence. As her agent for this purpose she selected Major-General Nicholas Kaulbars, brother of the former Minister of War, ostensibly to "assist" the Bulgarians at this crisis. But the methods of this strange diplomatist alienated more than anything else the sympathies of the stubborn peasants from their Russian patrons. While the Regents wisely desired the interregnum to be as short as possible, Kaulbars was resolved to postpone the elections to the Grand *Sobranye*, which was to choose the new Prince. With this object he stumped the country as an imperial anti-election agent, only to find that his interference had increased the national spirit of the people. The Grand *Sobranye* met, and on November 10 unanimously elected Prince Waldemar of Denmark, brother of Queen Alexandra and brother-in-law of the Tsar. Prince Waldemar, not meeting with the autocrat's approval, declined the offer; and for the next six months the Bulgarian

Crown went a-begging, while Russian plots, despite the departure of the ineffable Kaulbars, continued to undermine the principality. Various candidates were put forward—the Princes of Mingrelia, Oldenburg, and Leuchtenberg, and the King of Roumania, were all mentioned. At last, three delegates, sent to find a Prince, discovered at Vienna the man whom they sought in the person of Ferdinand, youngest son of Prince Augustus of Saxe-Coburg and descended through his mother from King Louis-Philippe. Except in point of age—he was at this time 26 years old—the second Prince of Bulgaria bore no resemblance to the first; by training and temperament he was the exact opposite of his future subjects. A poor horseman and an officer only in name, he was fonder of botany than of sport; he was a Roman Catholic, while they were preponderantly Orthodox; he was a stickler for etiquette, while they were convinced democrats. But he was well-connected, wealthy, and willing; and, accordingly, on July 7, 1887, he was at Trnovo elected Prince of Bulgaria. Russia, however, protested against his election, and long refused her consent; this refusal involved his social boycott by the Powers but had no other serious consequences. In fact, the absence of a Russian agent was a positive advantage. The Prince, who is one of the ablest of Balkan diplomatists, bided his time; and for nearly seven years his great Minister, Stepan Stambuloff, defied Russia and won the admiration of Great Britain as "the Bulgarian Bismarck."

Alike in his methods and in his fall, the son of the Trnovo innkeeper resembled the German Chancellor. During his long tenure of the premiership, he was absolute master of Bulgaria; for the Prince was at first much in the position of our George I, ignorant of the language and the customs of his subjects, and Stambuloff was for some years indispensable to him. The Minister had no constitutional scruples; he held that his end—the maintenance of Bulgarian freedom—justified his means, which included the manipulation of elections and the persecution of political opponents. He saw clearly that it was the interest of Bulgaria to establish friendly relations with Turkey; he was thus able to secure Turkish support against Russian schemes and to establish Bulgarian schools and bishoprics as the nucleus of a Bulgarian propaganda against the Greeks and Serbs in Macedonia. Russophil conspiracies he suppressed with the utmost severity, and Major Panitsa, who had trusted that Russia would save him from the penalty of his treachery to his Prince, was tried by Court-martial, and shot as a traitor. Assassination then became the weapon of the discontented; one of Stambuloff's colleagues was shot by his side at Sofia; his agent was stabbed in the street at Constantinople. These acts of violence rendered it imperative to provide for the future of the throne; the Prince, in 1893, married a Bourbon Princess, Marie-Louise of Parma; and the birth of an heir, who received the name of the ancient Bulgarian Tsar Boris, gave Bulgaria the promise of a national dynasty. The marriage proved, however, to be the cause of Stambuloff's fall. United to a Bourbon, the Prince naturally desired society for his wife and due social recognition for himself, while at the same time he felt strong enough to dispense with his too powerful and most uncourtierlike Minister. The relations between them became so strained that at last Stambuloff resigned, and Prince Alexander's former secretary, Stoiloff, became Premier. Like his German prototype, the fallen statesman vented his spleen in newspaper interviews, which called down upon him signal retribution. The end came on July 15, 1895, when the one great man of modern Bulgaria was brutally assaulted at Sofia by three assassins; three days later he died of his wounds; and the tardy trial of his murderers cast suspicion upon the Government and discredit upon the country.

Freed from all control, the Prince now made his peace with Russia. The sacrifice of Stambuloff was followed, in 1896, by the conversion of Boris to the Orthodox faith, after a more than usually unseemly theological controversy. Russia thereupon recognised Prince Ferdinand, whose policy thenceforth became steadily Russophil. The officers implicated in the kidnapping of his predecessor were reinstated; Russian training was encouraged in the army; Russian Grand Dukes came to celebrate the anniversaries of Shipka and Plevna. At the same time, the Prince was careful to cultivate the good graces of his suzerain. His neutrality in the Graeco-Turkish War of 1897 was rewarded with further concessions in Macedonia, which embittered his relations with Greece, while internally the principality made steady material progress, of which the Balkan exhibition in 1907 gave Englishmen a proof. A serious agrarian revolt, and the beginnings of a socialist movement were the shadows which fell upon "the peasant State."

Servia, after her unsuccessful war with Bulgaria, was mainly occupied with the domestic squabbles of the royal family. King Milan, though an able man, had the vices of the Europeanised oriental, while his beautiful wife, Queen Natalie, possessed a strong will of her own. International politics widened the breach between the royal pair, for the King was an Austrophil, while the Queen, as befitted the daughter of a colonel in the Russian army, was an adherent of the Tsar. At last, Milan obtained a divorce from his wife, and followed this domestic victory by granting a Constitution far more Liberal than that of 1869.

Scarcely, however, had this new charter come into force, when he abdicated in favour of his son, Alexander, on March 6, 1889. As the young King was only thirteen years of age, three Regents were appointed to govern the country, the chief of them being Jovan Ristich, the ablest Servian statesman, who twenty-one years before had been one of Milan's own guardians. The bickerings of the divorced couple and the Queen's assertion of her right to reside in her son's capital, however, kept Servia in a constant ferment, till at last they not only both consented to live abroad for their country's good, but made up their private differences, in

CH. XIV.

order to save the throne from the Karageorgevich pretender. Meanwhile, Alexander, who had been hitherto apparently immersed in the study of constitutional history, suddenly amazed his Regents by ordering their arrest at his dinner-table on April 13, 1893, proclaiming himself of age, and dissolving the *Skupshtina*. The success of this *coup d'État* directed against the Regents encouraged him to make another against the Radicals. Accordingly, on May 21 of the following year, he abolished the Constitution of 1889 and restored that of twenty years before. This drastic act was followed, five years later, by a wholesale proscription of the Radical and Russophil party, which the Court sought to implicate in the attempted assassination of Milan, Commander-in-Chief since 1898, by a certain Knezevich, said to be an agent of the pretender (July, 1899). In August, 1900, Alexander, who had hitherto been successful, committed the serious political mistake of marrying a lady-in-waiting of his mother, Madame Draga Mashin, widow of a Bohemian engineer and herself of "Bohemian" tendencies, which Belgrade gossip speedily exaggerated. This union proved his ruin. The Tsar, indeed, hastened to congratulate the King, and in the following year the death of Milan, who had retired in disgust, removed one of the constant irritants of Servian public life. But the lack of an heir, the suspicion that Queen Draga was scheming to secure the succession for one of her brothers, and the petty jealousies of Belgrade society, rendered the King's position insecure. In vain he granted an amnesty to the proscribed Radicals ; in vain, in 1901, he celebrated the anniversary of the Turkish evacuation of Belgrade by the issue of a Constitution more Liberal than that of 1869, but less Radical than that of 1889, giving the country the safeguards of a second Chamber and a Council of State. Discontent grew apace in a soil so congenial to political intrigue as is that of the Servian capital. The first sign of the coming tragedy was the proclamation of King Peter Karageorgevich by an adventurer at Shabats in 1902. To secure himself against similar conspiracies, the King appointed a military Cabinet, and on April 7, 1903, perpetrated a third *coup d'État*, by which he suspended the new Constitution until he had rid himself of the Radical elements which it had produced, and then revived it with a Senate and a Council devoid of a single Radical. The final blow to Radical hopes was the abolition of the ballot. Thus deprived of their constitutional remedies, the Radicals were driven to seek refuge in the usual Balkan device for desperate emergencies—a palace revolution.

The Serbs are fond of historical anniversaries, and the conspirators appropriately selected that of Michael's murder in 1868 for the assassination of the King, to whom they, as officers, had all taken the oath of allegiance. Their motives were as sordid as those of any hired band of bravoes. Colónel Mashin, their leader, was brother of the Queen's first husband and her personal enemy ; others, it was said, were well paid for their murderous work, while behind the actual assassins stood the smug, black-coated politicians, ready to profit by what was cynically proclaimed to be a "glorious revolution." On the night of June 10, 1903, the conspirators met at the "Servian Crown" to arrange their plans; the 6th regiment occupied the approaches to the palace; the door was exploded with dynamite; and in the ensuing darkness the murderers groped about, till at last they found the royal couple hiding in a cupboard. The wretches, who wore the King's uniform, showed no mercy to their sovereign. The last Obrenovich fell, clasping his wife in his arms, while the ruffians who profaned the name of officer stabbed and outraged the body of the Queen. Throwing the two mangled corpses out of the window, the assassins continued their work in the city. The Queen's two brothers, and also the Prime Minister and the Minister for War, were shot in cold blood; the occasion was seized for gratifying private revenge; and Belgrade proved to the world that she was still, after a century of practical freedom, inhabited by thinly polished barbarians. Nor was this impression diminished when, in the morning, the capital was decorated with flags, the church bells rang, and dance music enlivened the squares. When night fell, two carts conveyed the bodies of the King and Queen to their last resting-place in the church of St Mark, where the second and least conspicuous Obrenovich Prince had been buried.

The country experienced but a short interregnum. Prince Peter Karageorgevich may not have been privy to the murders; but it was he who profited by them, for on June 15 the National Assembly unanimously elected him King. The new sovereign, who nine days later mounted the blood-stained Servian throne, had spent 45 of his 57 years in exile— now in Hungary, now at the Court of his Montenegrin father-in-law, now at Geneva—and was therefore practically a stranger to the land, over which his father Alexander had ruled for sixteen years. He was the puppet and the prisoner of the regicides, to whom he owed his crown; yet by retaining them about his person he offended the moral sense of those nations, like Great Britain, which regard political expediency as no excuse for murder. Of the Great Powers, Austria and Russia, traditional rivals for influence in Servia, alone recognised him, till in 1906 the retirement of the chief conspirators induced the British Government to send a Minister to Belgrade. Meanwhile, the palace became once more a hotbed of scandals, owing to the freaks of the Crown Prince; the garrison of Nish conspired for a restoration of the Obrenovich dynasty, still represented by a natural son of Milan and by a cousin of Alexander. married to Prince Mirko of Montenegro, whence covetous eyes were ever directed towards the Servian throne; and a tariff war with Austria-Hungary injured the material interests of the peasants. Such has so far been the result of this Karageorgevich restoration.

The history of Montenegro since the completion of her territory in 1880 has been very different from that of the other two Slav States.

CH. XIV.

Prince Nicholas has had to solve the problem of converting an Homeric society of fighters into a modern commercial and agricultural community. With the exception of an occasional brush upon the Albanian frontier, his warriors have kept the peace. From Turkey he has had nothing more to fear; indeed his relations with the Sultan have become excellent; while Austria-Hungary he has wisely so far abstained from attacking. None the less, he has instituted for defence a standing army based on compulsory service. Admirable roads now traverse and connect the old with the new and more fertile Montenegro, which was the result of the Berlin Treaty and the subsequent arrangements. A railway has been opened from Antivari to Virbazar, and steamers furrow the blue waters of the Lake of Skutari. A new code was introduced in 1888, and in 1905 the Prince, on the advice of his eldest son, came to the conclusion that it was time to grant parliamentary institutions. The first Montenegrin Assembly met on December 19 of that year, and, already, the Black Mountain has had its full share of cabinet crises and political conspiracies. So long, however, as Prince Nicholas lives, he will always be the real ruler of Montenegro. Socially and politically alike, he has gained importance by the splendid marriages of his daughters, notably by that of Princess Elena in 1896 with the Prince of Naples, now King Victor Emmanuel III. This Italian connexion, though not popular in Italy, has made Montenegro much better known in Europe and has stimulated Italian commercial enterprise on the eastern shore of the Adriatic. A series of picturesque anniversaries—the 400th of the foundation of the first Slavonic printing-press, the bicentenary of the Petrovich dynasty, and the Jubilee of the battle of Grahovo—have all drawn attention to the stirring annals of "the smallest among peoples," while in August, 1910, the Prince celebrated his fifty years of rule. Nor has Prince Nicholas, while active as a diplomatist and statesman, ceased to enrich Servian literature. One of his two dramas, the "Empress of the Balkans," possesses special interest, since, under the thin disguise of an historical play, it contains his opinions on Balkan politics.

Even more prosperous has been the course of the one Latin nation of the Near East. Roumania, which became a kingdom in 1881, has been chiefly occupied with social questions. Antisemitism, due to economic rather than to religious causes, has been one characteristic of contemporary Roumanian history; agrarian riots—twice, in 1888 and 1907, assuming the proportions of an insurrection—have been another. Riches and poverty are brought into sharper contrast at Bucharest than at other Balkan capitals, with the inevitable result. The ability and long experience of her German King have been of immense value to "the Belgium of south-eastern Europe," while the literary fame of "Carmen Sylva," his accomplished Queen, has conferred distinction on her adopted land. Armed and fortified more strongly than in 1878, Roumania has proved a serviceable outpost of the Triple Alliance, though she has never drawn the sword since then. In Balkan politics she has coquetted, now with Greece, and now with Bulgaria, in the interval suspending her diplomatic relations with the former, and once talking of war with the latter. The Kutzo-Vlach movement in Macedonia has chiefly determined the attitude of Roumania to both these States.

The settlement of 1878 embraced, as we saw, besides the Balkan States, the island of Cyprus and the Armenian provinces still left to the Sultan, the island of Crete and the rest of the Turkish dominions in Europe. The British Government, according to the terms of the convention, occupied Cyprus in July of that year. A High Commissioner was appointed, as had been the case in the Ionian Islands, and in 1882 a more Liberal Constitution was announced. At present Cyprus, dependent on the Colonial Office, possesses a legislature of 18 *ex officio* and 12 elected members, representative of the Greek majority and the Moslem minority. While, however, material progress has been achieved, the payment of the Turkish tribute, fixed at £92,800 a year, has proved a handicap to the island, which Bosnia was spared. The present occupation of Cyprus may be regarded from three national standpoints. The Turkish Government has gained by the punctual payment of a settled sum; the British have found that neither as "a place of arms" to command an eventual Euphrates railway, nor as a commercial speculation, has the island realised the hopes of Beaconsfield; the Greeks, though economically better off and politically better governed, demand union with Greece, and quote as a precedent the cession of the Ionian Islands. British statesmen have replied that, if Great Britain were to withdraw, she would be bound to restore Cyprus to Turkey, to which three of the Seven Islands had never, and only one had for any length of time, belonged, while they refer to the disinclination of the Moslem minority to be united with the Greek kingdom. But the maps used in the Greek schools already represent Cyprus as part of "unredeemed Greece," although it has not been governed by Greeks since the close of the twelfth century; and, whenever Crete obtains union, Cyprus will be further encouraged to demand it. Finally, regarded as a guarantee of Armenian reforms, the Anglo-Turkish Convention of 1878 has been a complete failure.

The Armenian, Cretan, and Macedonian questions have been the most serious problems which Europe has had to face in the Near East since the Treaty of Berlin. The Armenians are in a position different from that of all the other Christian races of Turkey. While the Greeks, Bulgarians, Serbs, and Kutzo-Vlachs can look for support to Athens, Sofia, Belgrade, and Bucharest, the Armenians have no Armenian State to which they can turn for protection. In that respect, they resemble the Albanians, but with this important difference, that the Albanians are first-rate fighting men who can defend themselves, while the

CH. XIV.

Armenians, with the exception of a few in the Russian service, are not. Unfortunately, this unwarlike race has as its neighbours the savage Kurds, the Albanians of Asia Minor, who treat it much as the Arnauts treat the Serbs of Old Servia. Divided between Russia and Turkey, deprived for more than five centuries of the last remnant of national independence, the Armenians, in a secret petition presented to the Congress of Berlin, had disclaimed political ambition and had begged for an arrangement modelled on that of the Lebanon, under a Christian governor. Instead of this, the collective wisdom of Europe was content with a vague promise of security and reforms. Great Britain did indeed send consuls to report on the condition of Asia Minor; but even Gladstone, when he came into power in 1880, dropped the Armenian question at a hint from Bismarck.

Down to 1889 the question attracted no further attention. But in that year the first news of outrages in the Armenian provinces of Turkey reached England. Abd-ul-Hamid II had, meanwhile, established a system of highly centralised personal government; Midhat's short-lived Parliament had long been dissolved, and its author had died in exile; the Palace had superseded the Porte, and the Sultan's favourites had more influence in the affairs of the empire than his Ministers. At the same time the Armenians had become the objects of suspicion to the Sultan and the Tsar alike, and both Russians and Turks professed to discern an "Armenian peril" in the material progress of these clever and industrious, but unpopular, men of business. When the cry of oppression was raised, the Turkish authorities merely prosecuted a Kurdish chief, who was acquitted, but ultimately exiled. The Armenians, on their part, were already agitating; their societies, of which the chief bore the significant name of *Hindchak* ("the Bell"), sounded the alarm in the ears of somnolent diplomacy. The Kurds, reinforced by the fanatical Mussulmans whom the events of 1878 had driven "bag and baggage" into Asia, redoubled their exactions; conflicts arose, and the Armenian massacres began.

For three weeks in the late summer of 1894 the district of Sasun in the province of Bitlis became the scene of horrors which recalled those of Batak. The Kurds, aided by Turkish troops, under the command of Zekki Pasha, destroyed 24 villages and butchered, with the most revolting cruelty, every Armenian whom they could find. Zekki was decorated for his "services"; but Great Britain demanded the appointment of a Commission of enquiry, which British, French, and Russian delegates should accompany. The Commission, officially designated as intended "to enquire into the criminal conduct of Armenian brigands," conducted its proceedings with the partiality which might have been expected from this statement of its object, and proved as dilatory as most Turkish official bodies. In vain, the three Powers presented a scheme of Armenian reform; in vain, great meetings were held in London and Paris on behalf of the Armenians. An Armenian demonstration at Constantinople on September 30, 1895, only resulted in a massacre of many in the capital and of many more at Trebizond. But this was nothing compared with what was to come. While the ambassadors were presenting a new scheme of reforms to the Sultan, which he promised to see carried out faithfully, a gigantic massacre was taking place in Asia Minor. During part of October and the whole of November the Armenians were murdered wholesale, the murders being organised by the Sultan's officials, headed by Shakir Pasha. The British ambassador wrote home that "over an extent of territory considerably larger than Great Britain" all the large towns save three and almost all the villages had suffered, and that a moderate estimate put the loss of life in those six weeks at 30,000. Still, however, the massacres continued; Van, hitherto spared, was selected for the next great holocaust; while the Powers, fearful of reopening the Eastern question by active intervention, which would have aroused mutual suspicions, left the Armenians to their fate and contented themselves with demanding the presence at Constantinople of a second *stationnaire* for the protection of their own subjects. But Europe was soon to learn that, under the very shadow of the embassies, the unhappy Armenians could be butchered with impunity. A body of the latter, more desperate than the rest, indignant at the supineness of the Powers and infuriated at the forced resignation of the Armenian Patriarch and the irregular appointment of his successor, seized the premises of the Ottoman Bank and only left them under promise of a safe conduct and the protection of the ambassadors. Scarcely had they been shipped on board a French steamer, when the infuriated Sultan took a terrible vengeance upon their innocent compatriots. For the next two days, August 27 and 28, 1896, the streets of Constantinople were the theatre of an organised massacre. The Armenian quarter was attacked by gangs of men, armed with clubs, who bludgeoned every Armenian whom they met, and forced their way into the houses of Armenians, or foreigners who had Armenian servants, in pursuit of their victims. Police officers and soldiers aided, and even directed, this Turkish St Bartholomew; and it was not till the representatives of the Powers, who had seen with their own eyes what had occurred, sent a strongly worded note to the Palace, that the order was issued to stop the slaughter. Some 6000 persons perished in this horrible carnage, and, in the words of a British diplomatist, it seems to have been "the intention of the Turkish authorities to exterminate the Armenians." The perfect organisation of the shambles was proved by the fact that scarcely anyone who did not belong to that race perished, and that these few exceptions were due to such accidents as will happen even in the best regulated massacres.

The "disturbances at Constantinople," as they were euphemistically called by diplomatists, convinced even the most incredulous that the

previous massacres in remote parts of the empire had not been mere
inventions.　Gladstone, for the last time, sallying forth from his retirement, as he had done at the moment of the Bulgarian atrocities, twenty
years before, branded Abd-ul-Hamid II as "the Great Assassin";
French writers pilloried him as "the Red Sultan." But no steps were
taken to punish the author of the Armenian atrocities.　Germany,
anxious to obtain concessions in Asia Minor, avowedly supported the
Sultan, and reaped the reward of her selfish policy.　Austria-Hungary
was too deeply interested in the Balkan peninsula to risk a policy, of
which it was difficult to foresee the results.　Russia had cynically
declared through the mouth of Prince Lobanoff, that she did not desire
the creation of another Bulgaria in Asia Minor.　Lord Salisbury, again
Prime Minister and Foreign Secretary, solemnly and publicly warned
the Sultan of the consequences of his misgovernment, and suggested
the eventual necessity of employing force.　The French ambassador at
Constantinople advocated the despatch of a fleet as the only means of
intimidating Abd-ul-Hamid ; and among British residents at the Turkish
capital the opinion was expressed that Great Britain should, and could,
have acted with more vigour.　The British ambassador sorrowfully
confessed to a leading Englishman that his mission had been a failure ;
the most that can be said is that Great Britain, having greater responsibilities towards the Armenians, did a little more than any other Power
for their support.　Further, but smaller, massacres took place at Tokat.
Then a new phase of the Eastern question attracted public attention ;
all eyes were fixed on Crete, and the sufferings of the Armenians were
forgotten by a preoccupied Europe.

Crete, as we saw, had received a promise at Berlin that the Organic
Law of 1868 should be applied with any modifications that might seem
equitable.　Accordingly, on October 25, 1878, the island received a
supplementary constitution, called the Pact of Halepa, from the consular
suburb of Canea, where it was signed.　This additional charter, which
merely modified the Organic Law, provided that the Governor-General
should hold office for five years, and should be assisted by an adviser of
the opposite religion ; that there should be a General Assembly sitting
publicly for 40, or at most, 60 days in the year, and composed of 49
Christians and 31 Mussulmans ; that Greek should be the language of
both the Assembly and the law Courts ; that natives should have the
preference for official posts ; and that, after the cost of local administration had been deducted from the insular revenues, the surplus should
be divided in equal shares between the imperial treasury and the schools,
hospitals, harbours, and roads of the island, upon which practically
nothing had been spent since the days of the Venetians.　Paper money
was prohibited, newspapers were allowed, and an amnesty and the
remission of arrears of taxation completed the benefits to be conferred

upon the islanders. In theory, at any rate, the Pact of Halepa was the high-water mark of Ottoman concessions to Crete.

For the next eleven years the island almost realised that rare form of happiness which consists in having no history. For the larger portion of that period Crete was governed by Photiádes Pasha, a Greek of conciliatory disposition and administrative capacity. His successor, a Greek from Epiros, was unpopular, and in the year of his appointment the union of the two Bulgarias caused the Cretans to demand union with Greece. It was not, however, till 1889 that a fresh insurrection took place, which, originating in the mutual disputes of the Christians, developed into a movement against the common enemy. The reply of the Sultan was to issue a firman, on November 24 of that year, which virtually repealed the Pact of Halepa, and placed the Assembly, now reduced to 57 members, under the influence of the Governor-General, a Mussulman, and therefore inclined to favour the dominant Mussulman minority. Desultory disturbances went on in the usual fashion of that turbulent island, which no Government has found easy to govern, until the Sultan, in 1895, at last yielded to the violent importunities of the Cretans, and appointed Alexander Karatheodori Pasha, a Christian, as *Vâli* (Provincial Governor). The increase of the numbers of the Assembly to 65—40 Christians and 25 Mussulmans—seemed to have dissipated the dangers of further disputes.

But the Cretan Moslems, like most minorities accustomed to the exercise of power, were resolved to demonstrate the futility of attempting to govern Crete through the medium of a Christian. Murders of Christians began; a Christian Committee of Reform was founded and embittered the situation, while Karatheodori, who had made himself personally popular to the Mussulmans, was deprived by his Government of the means of paying his *gendarmerie*. The appointment of a Turk as his successor, instead of satisfying the Moslem party, disgusted both sides, for the Mussulmans wanted a military Governor, while the Christians desired another Christian. Such was the state of tension, when the insurrection, which was to end in the practical destruction of Turkish rule over Crete, began on May 24, 1896, with a sanguinary conflict in the streets of Canea. Too late, the Sultan accepted the advice of the Powers, revived the Pact of Halepa, promised to summon the General Assembly, and to grant an amnesty, and appointed a Christian Governor in the person of Georgi Berovich, who had been Prince of Samos. One Commission, comprising European officers, was to organise the *gendarmerie*; another to reform the tribunals. This arrangement, accepted by the Christians, was regarded by the Mussulmans, who derived their inspiration from the Palace, as one of the usual paper reforms, which they were expected to resist; and the arrival of the Turkish officer, who had been connected with the Armenian massacres at Van, encouraged their resistance. The customary delay in beginning the work of organising the police made the Christians also suspicious; and a Mussulman outbreak at Canea on February 4, 1897, followed by the burning of a large part of the Christian quarter, renewed the civil war. The Christians occupied Akrotiri, the "peninsula" between Canea and Suda bay, and proclaimed union with Greece.

Meanwhile, the news of a massacre at Canea had caused immense excitement at Athens. Trikoúpes, who had counselled quiet at the time of the last insurrection, was now dead, and Delyánnes, the bellicose Minister of 1885, was once more in power. But even the strongest of Greek statesmen could no longer have resisted public opinion. Greece had incurred enormous expenses for the maintenance of the Cretan refugees at Athens, while there were numbers of Cretans established in Greece, whose influence was naturally in favour of intervention. Prince George, the King's second son, left the Piraeus amidst enthusiastic demonstrations with a flotilla of torpedo boats to prevent the landing of Turkish reinforcements; and on February 15 a Greek force under Colonel Vássos, with instructions to occupy Crete in the name of King George, to restore order and to drive the Turks from the forts[1], landed a little to the west of Canea. The same day the Admirals of the Five European Powers, whose ships were then in Cretan waters, occupied the town, whence the last Turkish Governor of the island had fled for ever. The insurgents on Akrotiri now attacked the Turkish troops, until the Admirals forced them to desist by a bombardment, which caused intense indignation at Athens and some disgust in London among those who remembered Navarino. A note of the Powers promising autonomy on condition of the withdrawal of the Greek ships and troops met with an unfavourable reply; and, though the Admirals issued a proclamation of autonomy, they followed it up by a blockade of the island, and by another bombardment of the insurgents at Malaxa above Suda bay.

The conflict between Hellenism and its hereditary foe could no longer be confined to "the great Greek island." In Greece a body, called the "National Society," forced the hand of the Government; an address from 100 British members of Parliament encouraged the masses, ignorant of the true conditions of British politics, to count upon the help of Great Britain; the King, in a speech to the people, talked of putting himself at the head of an army of 100,000 Hellenes. The secret history of the weeks immediately preceding the War is still only a matter of surmise; but the opinion is now held in Greece, that King George expected the Powers to prevent hostilities at the last moment; he could then have yielded to their pressure without risking his position with his subjects. Neither he nor the Sultan wanted a war, from which the latter knew that, if successful, he would gain nothing, and at the outbreak of hostilities he was less unpopular at Athens than the German

---

[1] Parliamentary Papers: "Turkey, No. 11 (1897)," p. 59.

Emperor, whose officers accompanied the Turkish army.   The Emperor's
policy throughout had been bitterly hostile to the country of which his
sister would one day be Queen, and he is still held largely responsible for
the war.   Among the Greeks, who had not been at war with Turkey
since the struggle for Independence, there was intense enthusiasm,
unfortunately unaccompanied by organisation.   Greece is a profoundly
democratic land, where the soldier does not recognise a social superior in
his officer, where the critical faculty is highly developed, and the natural
tactics of the country are aptly described by the phrase "klephtic war"
(κλεφτοπόλεμος), while the fine military qualities of the Turks had been
schooled by German instructors.   Thus, the contest was unequal, even
though a band of red-shirted "Garibaldians" of various nations under a
son of the great captain came to the aid of the Greeks, and money
poured into the war fund from abroad.

On April 9, armed bands of the "National Society" crossed into
Macedonia; further conflicts occurred on the Thessalian frontier; and
on April 17 Turkey declared war.   True to his traditional policy of
dividing the Christian races of the Near East against each other, the
Sultan secured the neutrality of Bulgaria and Servia by an opportune
grant of bishoprics, commercial agents, and schools in Macedonia.   An
Austro-Russian note to the Balkan Courts warned them not to interfere
in the struggle.   Thus any hopes of common action by the Christians
were dissipated, and the ring was confined to the two combatants.

The "Thirty Days' War" was an almost unbroken series of Greek
disasters.   The Greek navy, which was superior to that of the Turks,
and upon which great hopes had been placed, effected nothing except
the futile bombardment of Preveza, the capture of a cargo of vegetables
at Santi Quaranta, and that of a Turcophil British member of Parliament.
This inaction is one of the mysteries of the War.   No doubt, a bombardment of Smyrna or Salonica would have mainly damaged the Greek
populations of those cities; but Turkish islands could easily have been
taken, and better terms thereby obtained at the peace.   Probably the
paralysis of the fleet was due to considerations of diplomacy.   On land,
the campaign naturally fell into two divisions—one in Thessaly, the
other in Epiros.   In Thessaly Edhem Pasha, the Turkish commander,
after severe fighting in the Melouna pass, and an obstinate battle at
Reveni, occupied Larissa, whence the Crown Prince's troops had fled in
disorder; in Epiros the battle of Pente Pegadia ("Five Wells") between
Arta and Janina saved the latter town.   The Turkish advance across
the Thessalian plain aroused a reaction at Athens.   The indignant
crowd marched on the unprotected palace, and the King owed his
throne to the prompt intervention of Rhálles, the most influential
leader of the Opposition, and the idol of the Athenians, who was
forthwith appointed Prime Minister.   Colonel Smolenski, "the hero of
Reveni," the one officer who had distinguished himself, repulsed the

Turks in a first attack on Velestino, the scene of the legend of Alcestis, but had to yield in a second battle; the classic field of Pharsalos was the scene of one Greek defeat, and the unknown village of Gribovo in Epiros that of another; and the climax was reached when, on May 17, the battle of Domokós opened to the Turks the Phoûrka pass which leads down to Lamia. A panic seized the Athenians at the news; the royal family durst not show itself in the streets; the royal liveries were changed; pictures of Smolenski took the place of royal portraits in the shops. Then the Powers intervened; an armistice was signed on May 19 and 20 in Epiros and Thessaly, and Colonel Vássos, who had already left Crete, was followed by the rest of his men. A treaty of peace was concluded at Constantinople on December 4, which provided for the evacuation of Thessaly by the Turkish troops, and the cession for the second time of that province to Greece, except one village and certain strategic positions, which bring the Turkish frontier very near Larissa. Greece was ordered to pay a war indemnity of £T.4,000,000, and accepted an European control of her finances. In 1898 the Turks left Thessaly and with them almost all the remaining Moslem *begs* (landowners). A series of quiet years followed the war, broken only by the "Gospel Riots," a disturbance arising out of the translation of the New Testament into the vernacular. Theotókes, a lieutenant of Trikoúpes, became the leading force in Greek politics, and, after the assassination of Delyánnes in 1905 for his attempt to suppress the Athenian gambling-hells, and the subsequent split in the Delyannist party, was able to form a long administration. Greece has recovered from the wounds of 1897; her finances are more flourishing; her paper currency has approached par; and her internal politics have been, till last year, steadier than in the days of "grandfather" Delyánnes—a patriot, but more of a demagogue than a statesman. But in the summer of 1909 the renovated Turkish Government assumed a menacing attitude; Greece had to abandon for the time the cherished union with Crete, and a body of officers, in the name of army reform, demanded the removal of the Royal Princes from their commands, and took up a threatening position outside Athens. Three cabinet crises followed in rapid succession, and for a moment the abdication of the King and his withdrawal with his whole family from the country were rumoured. The "Military League" under Colonel Zorbâs has forced its policy upon the terrorised Chamber; but the revolt of a naval officer, named Typaldos, was easily suppressed in the classic waters of Salamis. It has now been decided to convene a National Assembly to revise the Constitution; and on March 29, 1910, the Military League, after an existence of seven months, was accordingly dissolved.

The settlement of the Cretan question long vexed the diplomatists of Europe. Eighteen months were spent in the search for a Governor. A Swiss Federal Councillor, a Luxemburg Colonel, a Montenegrin

Minister, were in turn proposed, until at last, owing to the influence of
the Tsar, Prince George of Greece was appointed High Commissioner
of the Powers.   Meanwhile, Germany, followed by Austria, had retired
from the European Concert on the Cretan question, and the forces of
the four other Powers, supported by their fleets under the command of
the Italian Admiral Canevaro, had occupied the coast towns, the British
holding Candia, the Russians Rethymno, the French Sitia and the islet
of Spinalonga, the Italians Hierapetra, and all four Canea.   In these
places, especially within the cordon of Candia, the Mussulmans were
herded, while the Christians held the whole of the open country, and
a migratory assembly, presided over by Dr Sphakianákes, issued decrees
under the seal of Minos.   An attack upon the British in the harbour
of Candia and the murder of their Vice-Consul on September 6, 1898,
hastened the settlement of the Cretan question.   Admiral Noel's energy
achieved what diplomacy had long striven to obtain; the ringleaders
were hanged; and, two months after the affray at Candia, the last
detachment of Turkish troops left the island; the fort on the islet
in Suda bay was thenceforth alone occupied by Ottoman soldiers.   Such
was the state of affairs when, on December 21, 1898, Prince George set
foot in the island.

The Prince's appointment, originally made for three years, lasted for
nearly eight, and for the first five Crete remained tranquil.   Naturally
popular with the Christians, he endeavoured to reassure the Mussulmans,
whose numbers had dwindled by emigration to such an extent that the
census of 1900 showed them to be only one-ninth of the population.
A *gendarmerie* of Cretans officered by Italian carabineers took the
place of the Montenegrins; and each of the four Powers advanced
£40,000 for the initial expenses of the new administration.   An
assembly met to adopt a new Constitution, which provided the Prince
with five Councillors, one of them a Mussulman, and created a Chamber
of deputies, ten of whom were nominees and the rest elected every two
years.   A Cretan flag, Cretan postage-stamps and small coins, were
further proofs of autonomy.   But, early in 1904, discontent became rife
in the island.   The Prince, influenced by his Greek secretary, descended
into the arena of party politics against Venizélos, the ablest of the
Cretan politicians, who was accused of advocating the erection of Crete
into an independent principality, on the lines of Samos—a proposal
strongly denounced at Athens.   The Italian Foreign Office warned the
Prince to act constitutionally, and a crisis was reached when, in March,
1905, the Opposition took to the mountains and established its headquarters at Therisso, a strong position already famous in the annals of
Cretan warfare.   The insurgents there declared themselves a provisional
National Assembly, proclaimed union with Greece, and held out till winter
forced them to surrender to the Consuls of the Powers.   The following
summer Prince George, weary of Cretan politics, resigned, despite a

petition of many deputies in his favour. Thereupon, the Four Powers, whose representatives in Rome had since the time of Admiral Canevaro formed a Cretan Areopagus under the presidency of the Italian Foreign Minister, entrusted to King George the selection of a new High Commissioner. His choice in September, 1906, fell upon Zaïmes, the most Conservative and most silent of Greek statesmen, and the choice has been fully justified by results. Little more was heard of Crete, till, in October, 1908, the news of the annexation of Bosnia and Bulgarian independence caused the proclamation of union with Greece which has hitherto been without effect.

Armenia and Crete had scarcely ceased to occupy the attention of Europe when a third question, more complex than either of them, became acute. Macedonia is the land of conflicting races and overlapping claims. During a large part of its history it has been entirely Greek; in the Middle Ages it was alternately under the hegemony of Bulgarian, Servian, and Byzantine Emperors, until the conquering Turk put all these Christian races under his dominion. But the memory of their respective sovereignties lives on, while of late years a fourth propaganda, that of the "lame" or Kutzo-Vlachs, the work of a certain Apostolos Margarites, has been encouraged by Roumania. Religious differences revived these racial hatreds. The firman creating the Bulgarian Exarchate in 1870 provided that, outside of what is now Bulgaria, a petition by two-thirds of the inhabitants could secure the transfer of a district from the Patriarch to the Exarch; and "Patriarchists" and "Exarchists" thenceforth represented respectively the Greek and the Bulgarian cause in Macedonia, while Servia and Roumania, seeing the political advantages of an ecclesiastical propaganda, began to agitate for the restoration of the Servian Patriarchate of Ipek and the erection of a separate Roumanian Church. The Treaties of 1878 naturally made the Balkan States regard Macedonia as their promised land. Servia, cut off from expansion in Bosnia and the Herzegovina by the Austrian occupation, and bound by a secret treaty not to agitate there, looked to the north of Macedonia and to Uskub, where her great Tsar Dushan had once been crowned; Bulgaria remembered the frontiers which were awarded her at San Stefano; Roumania, recognising in the Kutzo-Vlachs long-lost kinsmen, hitherto considered as Greeks, saw that, by first fostering and then sacrificing them, she might claim compensation nearer home; while Greece regarded these newer nationalities as upstarts who had no rights in the home of Alexander the Great, the land redeemed from the barbarians for the Byzantine Empire by Basil "the Bulgar-slayer." Austria-Hungary, for her own purposes, was glad to divert the attention of Servia from the Bosnian Serbs, and that of Roumania from the Roumans of Transylvania; while, at the same time, established in the Sandjak of Novibazar, she might contemplate a descent upon the valley of the Vardar and upon Salonica. For reasons of its own, the Turkish

Government, too, was glad to increase the confusion of races. The Turks in Macedonia are a mere handful; and Turkey maintained her empire by dividing her subject nationalities, favouring now the Bulgarian, now the Serb, now the Greek, and in 1905 the Kutzo-Vlach, according to the weakness or importunity of each. Needless to add, the usual Turkish misgovernment continued; of the reforms stipulated in Article 23 of the Berlin Treaty not one had been carried out by the Porte.

The Austro-Russian agreement of 1897, which aimed at preserving the *status quo* in the Balkans, and pledged the two ancient rivals to abstain from exercising a separate influence there, had the effect of stifling the question, but only for a time.

The first impulse to the Macedonian agitation came from Bulgaria. The principality was full of Macedonians, who occupied posts in the army, in the schools, and on the Press. A Macedonian Committee, which had its seat at Sofia, addressed a memorial to the Powers in 1899, advocating an autonomous Macedonia under a Bulgarian Governor-General. But the president, Boris Sarafoff, was aware that Europe thinks of the Balkan races only when they are cutting each other's throats. Bulgarian bands crossed the Macedonian frontier, a Bulgarian emissary shot a Roumanian professor opposed to the propaganda of the Committee, and the whole world became aware of the existence of a Macedonian question, when Miss Stone, an American missionary, was captured by a gang of political brigands. Meanwhile, Old Servia was the scene of Albanian feuds, which culminated in the murder of Mollah Zekko, a donkey-boy who had risen to be the leader of a movement for an autonomous Albania, and whom even the Sultan feared and conciliated. So serious was the state of things, that Moslems as well as Christians were agreed[1] "that the provinces of Turkey in Europe cannot be allowed to remain in their present deplorable condition." Austria and Russia, the two Powers most directly interested, were of the same opinion; their Foreign Ministers met at Vienna and drew up in February, 1903, a modest scheme of reforms for the three *vilayets* of Salonica, Monastir, and Kossovo, which the other Powers supported. They recommended the Sultan to appoint an Inspector-General for a fixed number of years; to reorganise the *gendarmerie* with the aid of foreign officers, and to compose it of Christians and Moslems in proportion to their numbers; and to establish a separate budget for each of the three *vilayets*, upon the revenues of which the cost of local administration was to be a first charge. The Sultan accepted the Austro-Russian reform scheme, but its only result was to increase the disorder. The Albanians of Kossovo, suspecting interference with their liberties, rose in rebellion, shot the Russian consul at Mitrowitz, and

---

[1] Sir A. Biliotti in Parliamentary Papers: "Turkey, No. 1 (1903)," p. 274.

held up the Sultan's envoys at Ipek. The Bulgarian bands, despite the dissolution of the Macedonian Committees by the Bulgarian Government, blew up railway bridges, and mined the Ottoman Bank at Salonica. The Greeks were terrorised by the Bulgarian Committeemen and plundered by the Turkish irregulars. This state of things induced Austria and Russia in October, 1903, to issue a second edition of their reform scheme, called, from the place of signature, the Mürzsteg programme. This programme, which was also accepted by the Sultan, attached Austrian and Russian Civil Agents to Hilmi Pasha, the Inspector-General who had been appointed a year earlier ; entrusted the reorganisation of the *gendarmerie* to a foreign general, aided by military officers of the Powers, who were to divide Macedonia among them ; and demanded the reform of the administrative and judicial institutions of the country with the participation of the Christian population. General de Giorgis, an Italian officer, was appointed to command the *gendarmerie,* and his successor is another Italian, Count di Robilant. All the Powers, except Germany, sent a small contingent of officers, subsequently slightly increased, and Macedonia was, for police purposes, divided up into five *secteurs,* the British taking Drama, a rich district almost wholly peopled by Pomaks, the French Seres, the Italians Monastir, the Austrians Uskub, and the Russians Salonica. Most of the *vilayet* of Kossovo, the worst of all, and part of that of Monastir, were excluded from this arrangement. An agreement between Bulgaria and Turkey for the prevention of armed bands helped to improve the condition of Macedonia in 1904.

But, in the autumn of that year, a new disturbing element arose. Unable to obtain protection for their fellow-countrymen against the Bulgarians, the Greeks organised bands in their turn ; and Paul Melâs, one of their leaders, who fell in Macedonia, became a national hero at Athens. The rival parties, which took their titles from the Greek Patriarch and the Bulgarian Exarch, and were secretly encouraged by consuls and ecclesiastics, murdered one another in the name of religion, which in Macedonia is a pretext for racial animosity ; while the Sultan widened the breach between Greece and Roumania by recognising the Kutzo-Vlachs as a separate nationality, with the right of using their language in their churches and schools. These national quarrels spread beyond Macedonia ; the Bulgarians destroyed the Greek quarters of Anchialos and Philippopolis ; the Roumanians demonstrated against the Greeks resident in their country ; a common danger caused Greeks and Serbs to fraternise. Meanwhile, the British Government, disgusted with the slow progress made by the Mürzsteg programme, proposed in 1905 its extension to the *vilayet* of Adrianople, and the appointment of a Commission of delegates, nominated by the Powers, under the presidency of the Inspector-General, for the purpose of framing financial reforms. The Sultan at first refused to allow foreign interference in his finances ; but the occupation of Mitylene by an international fleet forced him to recognise the four financial experts whom the other Powers had already sent to Salonica as colleagues of the Austrian and Russian Civil Agents. In 1908, all the arrangements made for the pacification of Macedonia—the appointments of Inspector-General, civil and financial agents, and *gendarmerie* officers—originally made for two years, were prolonged for six. The civil and financial agents were, however, suppressed in the following year. But still the bands increased, while the British proposal to increase the *gendarmerie* met with no support from the other Powers, mainly occupied with the rival railway schemes of Austria and Servia. In short, European intervention in Macedonia has been so far unsuccessful. If the taxes have been better collected and administered, if the Turkish troops have committed fewer outrages, the strife among Greeks, Bulgarians, and Kutzo-Vlachs has been bitterer than ever.

The Eastern question suddenly entered on a new and acute phase in the summer of 1908. The " Young Turks," or party of reform, whom diplomatists had hitherto been wont to regard as dreamers, had long carried on a secret propaganda, which had made great progress in the army. A bloodless revolution took place in Constantinople on July 24, the Sultan restored the Constitution of 1876, all the nationalities of the empire temporarily fraternised, a general election was held, and a Turkish Parliament met. This grant of constitutional liberties to the subjects of Turkey proved a serious embarrassment to a Christian Power like Austria, whose wards in Bosnia and the Herzegovina did not enjoy similar privileges. At the same time, the internal difficulties of the new Turkish Government suggested to Austrian and Bulgarian statesmen that this was the moment for realising their long-deferred hopes. There seems to have been an understanding between the Austrian Emperor and Prince Ferdinand that each would help the other against Servia, which was thus taken between two fires. Accordingly, on October 5, 1908, Bulgaria declared her independence and the Prince was proclaimed at Trnovo "Tsar of Bulgaria," a title since altered to "Tsar of the Bulgarians." Two days later, Austria-Hungary annexed the two provinces which she had occupied for thirty years. The Italian Minister for Foreign Affairs treated the matter as merely the destruction of a diplomatic fiction; but Great Britain protested against the unauthorised departure from treaty provisions. Servia armed, and demanded a strip of Bosnia which would unite her with Montenegro; while the Prince of Montenegro announced that, if the Austrian annexation were allowed, he would be no longer bound by the restrictions imposed at Berlin upon the bay of Antivari. The proclamation of the union of Crete with Greece increased the difficulties of the situation, and the evacuation of the Sandjak of Novibazar by the Austrian troops was not regarded as adequate compensation. Turkey has, however, accepted £T.2,500,000 for all the domain lands in Bosnia and the

CH. XIV.

Herzegovina. Thus, the Treaty of Berlin has suffered three more breaches, but so far, as in 1885, Europe, like Turkey, has accepted accomplished facts, and Servia has been forced to forgo all territorial concessions. All the Powers have recognised the independence of Bulgaria, and the annexation of Bosnia and the Herzegovina; Austria, while retaining Spizza, has suppressed or modified other limitations on the freedom of the bay of Antivari. Crete is not yet united with Greece, but the troops of the four Powers were, in July, 1909, replaced by *stationnaires*. At present the Cretan question is dormant.

Meanwhile, a counter-revolution had broken out in Constantinople. The "Young Turks," however, held their own; the army of Salonica, the cradle of the Liberal movement, marched upon the capital; on April 27, 1909, Abd-ul-Hamid II was deposed, and his next brother proclaimed Sultan under the title of Mohammad V. The dethroned ruler was conveyed to Salonica—a striking instance of that poetic justice which has ever illuminated the tragic annals of Byzantium.

To sum up the results of the last three decades, Turkey has lost Bosnia and the Herzegovina, Bulgaria, Thessaly and part of Epiros, a portion of Albania, and—in all but the name—the island of Crete. Roumania and Servia have thrown off the last shreds of vassalage, and both they and Montenegro have been enlarged at her expense. Thrace, Macedonia, Albania, and part of Epiros alone remain of the once vast Turkish empire in Europe; Cyprus and Egypt are practically British; Tunisia, over which the Sultan claimed a vague suzerainty, is a French protectorate. Tripoli, coveted by Italy, is the only fragment left to the Turks in Africa; even in Asia, their original home, their frontier has receded. It remains to be seen whether reforms aided by European and Balkan jealousies can prevent the end of European Turkey.

CHAPTER XV.

EGYPT AND THE EGYPTIAN SUDAN.
(1841–1907.)

SATISFIED with the hereditary governorship of Egypt, which was affirmed by the Five Powers of Europe in 1841, Mehemet Ali, already over seventy years of age, abandoned all idea of further aggrandisement and devoted himself for the next seven years to the social and material improvement of his country, with an aggregate of results which caused him to be ranked by his admirers in Europe with Saladin, Peter the Great, Napoleon, and Cromwell. His boundless ambition had led him to sacrifice almost everything to the dream of becoming the head of a powerful empire, independent of the Porte. With this end in view, he introduced various European sciences, arts, and manufactures into Egypt, and the works issued from the printing press which he had imported in 1821 were solely intended for the instruction of his military, naval, and civil officers. Hardly able to read and write, and ignorant of the language of his adopted country, he nevertheless created a new era for Egypt and raised a State sunk in misery into one of comparative prosperity. He left behind him canals and roads, factories and arsenals, schools and hospitals, and introduced into the Delta the cotton plant, which was destined to add so greatly to the wealth of Egypt. He was an oppressor of barbarous habits, but he had the merit of protecting his people from all oppression but his own, and, though severe, he was not wantonly cruel. In 1847, he laid the first stone of the Barrage, fourteen miles below Cairo; but in the following year the "Lion of the Levant" was attacked by senile dementia and resigned in favour of his son, Ibrahim, the hero of Konieh and Nezib, who was already in his sixtieth year and only reigned four months.

In 1849 Abbas, a grandson of Mehemet Ali, came to the throne shortly before his grandfather's death, and in a short reign of five years, by reason of his hatred of Europeans, did much to stem the progress of civilisation. His troops were driven from Nejd, while the Wahabi State regained its independence; but, on the outbreak of the Crimean War, he placed his army and his fleet at the disposal of the Sultan. The power of the Pasha of Egypt within his own dominions was almost supreme, and he could cause any one of his subjects to be put to death, without the formality of a trial, and without assigning any cause; a simple horizontal motion of his hand was enough to decree the sentence of decapitation, with which thefts were often punished. Other offenders were exiled to the army in Upper Egypt or were made to work on the canal *corvée*. Cruel, avaricious, and sensual, Abbas I was murdered by his own slaves on July 13, 1854.

He was succeeded by his uncle Said, an amiable and liberal-minded prince, who retrieved much of the mischief done by his predecessor and raised the army to 50,000 men, though he lacked the vigorous intelligence and force of character of the founder of the dynasty. The initiation of the idea of railway construction must be credited to Mehemet Ali; but it was not until 1855 that the first railway was made between Alexandria and Cairo. British influence with the Pasha surpassed for the moment that of France. Robert Stephenson was appointed the engineer, and for some years, until Egyptians had been trained, the drivers and stokers were mostly Englishmen. Egypt thus preceded Turkey and most European countries in railway construction.

For centuries the most enlightened rulers of Egypt had paid special attention to the possibility of restoring communication between the Mediterranean and the Red Sea. In 1845, after some twenty years of indomitable perseverance, Waghorn succeeded in conveying the mail from Bombay to London in thirty days by the overland route which traversed Egypt from Suez to Alexandria, whence the letters were despatched to Trieste and, later, by French influence, to Marseilles. But it was not until November 30, 1854, that Ferdinand de Lesseps obtained from Said Pasha a preliminary concession for accomplishing the great work which Napoleon had abandoned, and Robert Stephenson (in 1846) had pronounced impracticable. After accepting the modifications recommended by an international commission, comprising representatives of seven Powers, the final concession was signed by the Pasha on January 5, 1856. Meanwhile the British Government, under the influence of Lord Palmerston, the Foreign Secretary, endeavoured, for a variety of political reasons, to throw obstacles in the way of the enterprise, and so far succeeded as to prevent the Sultan from granting his sanction to the concession. Palmerston, mindful of Napoleon's invasion of Egypt and of Louis-Philippe's intrigues to establish a French protectorate in the days before the bombardment of Acre, strongly objected to the establishment of a powerful French company on Egyptian soil, and foresaw that, if the Canal were successfully made, Great Britain would be the country most interested in it, and would therefore be irresistibly drawn into a more direct interference in Egyptian affairs, which he deemed it was desirable to avoid, because she had already enough upon her hands and because any unnecessary intervention on her part might lead to a rupture with France. This remarkable forecast was justified; for, in spite of the commercial advantages of the Suez Canal, there can be no doubt that it has often rendered acute the political differences between the two Powers which strove for so many years for supremacy in Egypt. It was also argued that the Canal might cause England to lose her trade with the East, just as Venice had suffered by the discovery of the Cape route.

English opposition rather stimulated than discouraged the enthusiasm of Lesseps, while it also stirred up the national feeling of France, and thus enabled him, in 1858, to launch on nearly every Bourse in Europe a company with a capital of £8,000,000. Rather more than half of this amount was subscribed for, chiefly in France; and eventually, in 1860, Said Pasha was induced to take up the remaining unallotted shares. Disregarding British objections and the indifference of the rest of the world, and not waiting for the consent of the Porte which was withheld till 1866, Lesseps, accompanied by a dozen Europeans and 100 native workmen, began the stupendous work on April 25, 1859, by cutting a small trench in the narrow belt of sand on the shore between Lake Menzala and the sea, and named the desolate spot Port Said in honour of the Viceroy. The very site, however, of the future town had to be formed, and this was done by spreading over the sand the mud dredged from the adjoining lake, which the summer heat soon hardened into a sufficiently firm foundation for the workshops that rapidly sprang up along the line of the new harbour. The pioneers were dependent for fresh water on Damietta, 30 miles away, whence Arab sailing boats reached them at very irregular intervals. On this unpropitious site arose, within ten years, a French town of nearly 10,000 inhabitants, well laid out in streets and squares, with docks, quays, churches, mosques, hotels, and a freshwater canal.

It is to Said Pasha's credit that he encouraged, under French influence, the discovery and preservation of the old monuments of his country, and founded the Bulak Museum in Cairo. But his contact with Europeans led him into extravagant expenditure, which caused him, in 1862, to take the first step towards Egypt's bankruptcy, by contracting for the Government a loan of £3,292,800 at an annual charge of 8 per cent. without any adequate arrangement for repaying the sum borrowed.

At his death on January 18, 1863, Ismail, the son of Ibrahim and grandson of Mehemet Ali, succeeded to the throne and to this national debt, in his thirty-third year. By the end of 1876, this reckless spend-thrift had raised the debt, nominally, to 91 millions, though in reality it considerably exceeded this figure. A country of some six million inhabitants, mostly peasants with less than one acre of cultivated land apiece, had thus added to its financial burdens at the rate of seven millions a year. Yet, when, at Ismail's professed desire, Stephen Cave investigated and reported upon the details of Egyptian finance in 1876, he stated that for the enormous debt there was " absolutely nothing to show but the Suez Canal, the whole proceeds of the loans and floating debt having been absorbed in payment of interest and sinking funds, with the exception of the sum debited to that great work." The total amount sunk by the Egyptian Government in the Suez Canal exceeded sixteen millions; yet Egypt had no longer any share whatever in the vast profits of that undertaking. Each loan cost the State more than 12 per cent. per annum, while the railways loan of 1866, contracted nominally for three millions at seven per cent., actually cost 26·9 per cent., including the sinking fund. The terms of borrowing became increasingly disadvantageous, so that of the great £32,000,000 loan of 1873, which pledged every available security of real value, only £20,700,000 reached the Egyptian treasury. Foreign adventurers swarmed around Ismail and battened on the unscrupulous despot, who was his own Finance Minister and kept no accounts, and whose inveterate love of speculation and trickery made him an easy prey. Even when he could afford to spend some of the borrowed money upon himself or upon the country, he always contrived to obtain the least possible value for his expenditure, and, while funds were being raised in enormous quantities, his people were subjected to the most cruel exactions. Not only was the taxation of land increased by fifty per cent., but no faith was kept with those from whom the money was extorted. The discontent caused by the perpetual plundering of Ismail's agents made foreign intervention inevitable.

Though the settlement of 1840–1 had made Egypt virtually independent, the relation of its ruler to the Porte was still that of a Governor-General, ranking little higher than that of the Governor of Bagdad. Ismail, soon after his accession, began negotiations with Constantinople which resulted in two imperial firmans (1866 and 1872). By these he received the title and rank of Khedive, insured the succession to the throne directly from father to son, instead of its passing to the eldest male of the family of Mehemet Ali, as had been fixed by the treaty of 1840, and rid himself of limitations of his prerogative with regard to the strength of his army, the right of contracting foreign loans, and that of concluding commercial treaties. These firmans were approved by the Five Powers, and all that the Khedive nominally gave in exchange for independence was the doubling of his yearly tribute to the Sultan. But it is an open secret that the *bakshish* extorted from the Egyptian treasury by Abd-ul-Aziz, his Ministers, and every official through whose hands the prolonged negotiations passed, amounted to more than a million pounds. Ismail's policy was to buy from the Porte the freedom which Mehemet Ali had failed to gain by force of arms.

Early in 1864, the Suez Canal works came almost to a standstill; for, by Lord Palmerston's instructions, the British ambassador in Constantinople protested to the Porte against the employment of forced labour on Turkish territory for the benefit of a foreign company. Lesseps saved the situation by persuading the Khedive to submit the question to the Emperor Napoleon as arbitrator, who decided that the withdrawal of Egyptian labourers, thousands of whom had already died from exposure and insufficient rations, was a breach of Said Pasha's original contract, and he accordingly awarded the Company a payment of about £3,000,000 from the Egyptian treasury. The Company lost no time in substituting machinery for manual labour; and on November 17, 1869, the Canal, of a total length of 100 miles, was opened for the traffic of 48 ships, the first vessel to pay the dues flying an English flag. It may be calculated that Egypt contributed nearly one-half of the capital by which the Canal was built, and yet received no pecuniary benefit of any kind. The inauguration of the Canal was made the occasion of a series of magnificent *fêtes,* attended by the Empress Eugénie of France, the Emperor of Austria, the Crown Prince of Prussia, the Grand Duke Michael of Russia, Prince Henry of the Netherlands, and hundreds of distinguished guests, whose expenses were lavishly defrayed by the Khedive from and to Europe and during their stay in Egypt. Some six weeks before the opening ceremony, as it had been represented to the Khedive that the Empress would wish to visit the Pyramids of Giza, he ordered a road seven miles in length to be constructed, connecting them with Cairo. Ten thousand peasants, driven by the lash, carried out the work in the appointed time, in spite of intense heat. Ismail, then at the height of his grandeur, turned a deaf ear to the creditors who were becoming alarmed at his extravagance, dreamed of founding a new empire in Africa, and never reckoned on the possibility of the downfall at Sedan, which helped to bring about his own collapse.

The importance of the Suez Canal to the commerce of the world depended upon the economy of time and distance effected by it as compared with the route round the Cape—for instance, the saving from London and Marseilles to Bombay was respectively 4840 and 5940 miles—but it was not until 1872 that the receipts of the Company exceeded the expenses. The gross receipts gradually rose from £264,000 in 1870 to £4,804,000 in 1907, while the number of ships paying canal dues increased from 491 to 4267 in the same years. The ships in 1907 belonged to 20 different nations, 2651 being British, while Germany came next on the list with 580 vessels. For many years the British ships numbered more than three-fourths of those passing through the Canal; and when, in 1875, Disraeli became aware that Ismail was negotiating in Paris for the mortgage of his only remaining unpledged asset —the Canal shares originally allotted to Said Pasha—he at once borrowed £4,000,000 on his own authority, bought the shares from the Khedive, and had his prompt action ratified by Parliament, thus causing his country for the first time to become a partner in the Canal enterprise. Three English Directors were appointed to the Board of the Company, a number afterwards increased to one-third of the body.

The success of Said Pasha's original loan proved to be the ruin of Ismail; for, at the accession of the latter, Egypt's credit as a borrower stood high in Europe, while the price of Egyptian cotton rose enormously in consequence of the Civil War in America. With the downfall of the Confederate Government came the collapse of the cotton boom; but fresh loans enabled him for a time to extend the railways, schools, and public works of the country, to provide some 10,000 dependents with daily food at his chief Cairo palace, to send military expeditions to the Sudan, to waste money in every possible way, and, by fair and unfair means, to raise his own personal holding of land from 30,000 to 916,000 acres, mostly cultivated by forced labour.

When Ismail could no longer borrow at ruinous rates of interest he, on April 8, 1876, suspended payment of his treasury bills, following the example of the Ottoman Government some six months earlier.

On May 2 the Commission of the Public Debt was instituted by Khedivial decree, France, Austria, and Italy each selecting a commissioner, though Lord Derby, the Foreign Secretary, declined to appoint one from England. The British Government refused any interference in the internal affairs of Egypt, and paid small attention to Cave's report and to the financial arrangements negotiated by Goschen and Joubert, which resulted in the appointment of two Controllers-General of Egyptian finance, one French and one English—the Dual Control; but eventually, in 1877, Major Baring (now Lord Cromer) was nominated British Commissioner to the Public Debt by Goschen, to whom the Khedive had privately applied for a suitable official.

Ever since the treaty of 1841 England had been regarded as the special champion of Turkish suzerainty, while France had adopted the *rôle* of protector of the Viceroys; but, in April, 1878, Great Britain, on the eve of the Berlin Congress, brusquely departed from her former attitude and joined the French Government in demanding a full enquiry into the financial condition of Egypt, to which the Khedive was obliged to consent. In order to check his arbitrary power, he was induced to recognise the principle of Ministerial responsibility; the Dual Control was suspended; Nubar Pasha, an able Armenian, Sir Rivers Wilson, and Blignières, were appointed Ministers and remained in power for five months, while most of the Khedivial property was ceded to the State, on the security of which the Domains Loan of £8,500,000 was at once raised.

Early in 1879, Ismail, by encouraging a mutiny in his army and by intriguing against his own Ministers, showed his unwillingness to resign his autocracy and demanded the retirement of Nubar, whom he accused of undermining his authority. Nubar was succeeded as Prime

Minister for four weeks by Prince Tewfik, the heir apparent, and then
by Sherif Pasha, while the European Ministers were dismissed and many
leading officials resigned, including the Commissioners who had been
enquiring into the finances of Egypt. Ismail's resumption of power
caused some embarrassment in Europe; for Great Britain was still
honestly striving to avoid the burden of increased responsibility;
France hesitated between a natural desire to exclude England's supremacy
and the fear that a joint occupation with her neighbour would prove a
certain cause of disagreement between herself and England; Italy
secretly befriended the Khedive, while vaguely hoping that she might gain
some advantage from his imminent downfall; Russia held aloof; and
Turkey waited anxiously to see if her suzerain rights were endangered,
fully aware that not one of the Powers would consent to a Turkish
occupation. Ismail's hope that he had defied Europe with impunity
received a severe shock from an unexpected quarter. Germany had
never displayed much interest in Egyptian affairs, and the world was
therefore astounded to learn that Bismarck threatened active intervention in Egypt in order to protect the interests of certain German
creditors of the State. Matters were thus brought to a crisis. England
and France joined Germany in demanding the deposition of the Khedive
by the Sultan; and, on June 26, 1879, a telegram reached Cairo from
Constantinople, addressed to "Ismail Pasha, late Khedive of Egypt,"
informing him of his deposition and of the nomination of his son Tewfik
in his stead.

When the blow fell, nothing became Ismail better than the dignity
with which he accepted the inevitable; he salaamed to the new Khedive
and retired to Naples with his personal attendants and some 300 ladies
of his harem. In 1887 he was invited by the Sultan to Constantinople,
where he passed the last eight years of his life, a state prisoner, hoping
against hope that some lucky chance would assist his return to power in
Egypt.

Tewfik Pasha succeeded to a bankrupt State, an undisciplined army,
and a discontented people, and could bring nothing to cope with these
but youth and inexperience, for, unlike his brothers, who were of better
maternal parentage, he had not been educated in Europe. An attempt
was at once made by Turkey to tighten her hold upon Egypt by a new
firman, the clauses of which both England and France contested in the
interest of the new Khedive, whose right to contract loans was, however,
withdrawn, while his standing army was limited to 18,000 men. The
Anglo-French Dual Control was revived; confidence was restored with
a new Egyptian Ministry; half the annual revenue was set aside for the
creditors of the Egyptian Government; and matters seemed at last to be
on a more satisfactory basis until February, 1881, when the Khedive
dismissed his War Minister on the demand of some mutinous regiments.
Before the end of the year, the whole Ministry was dismissed in order to

appease other disaffected officers, headed by Arabi, a colonel of peasant origin, who, on February 5, 1882, became War Minister. While the Khedive chafed under the power of his rebellious army and of the national anti-Turk party, which the officers professed to represent, Turkey saw another chance of interfering and sent two Commissioners to Egypt, who were only withdrawn by the Sultan when England and France each sent a man-of-war to Alexandria. The two Powers thus took the strong line of deciding that Turkish intervention was inadvisable and acted loyally together; for Barthélemy Saint-Hilaire said that his Egyptian policy "was summed up in the absolute necessity, as in the past so in the future, of perfect frankness between the two Governments and joint action on every occasion." Early in 1882, Lord Granville reluctantly yielded to pressure from Gambetta; and a Joint Note was addressed to the Khedive with the view of strengthening his authority, which rendered European military intervention an absolute necessity. This attempt to free the Khedive from military domination failed. Great Britain and France despatched fleets to Alexandria, while all the Powers decided that Egypt was a matter of general European interest, and that the Sultan should be invited to attempt to restore order by sending to Cairo a Special Commissioner. In the meantime, the Khedive was threatened with death if he obeyed the Anglo-French advice to dismiss Arabi from the Ministry; and the rebels seriously talked of deposing the Viceroy and exiling all his relations.

Turkey, faithful to her diplomatic traditions, sent two Commissioners with diametrically opposite instructions, each to report independently to the Sultan; but, within a few days of their arrival, the hand of European diplomacy was disagreeably forced by an anti-Christian massacre in Alexandria on June 11, 1882. Arabi became more than ever master of the situation. The work of the Government was at a standstill, panic spread, and by June 17, 14,000 Christians had left Egypt, while thousands more were anxiously awaiting steamers to carry them away. On June 23, the Six Powers met in conference at Constantinople, to decide upon what terms the Porte should be invited to lend troops to restore order in Egypt; but, before the Sultan had made up his mind to be represented at this Conference, British patience, after eighteen months of useless negotiation, was exhausted, and Arabi's folly in raising batteries to defy the British fleet necessitated the bombardment of Alexandria, on July 11. At this time there were no less than 26 warships in the harbour, representing ten foreign navies. On July 3, the British Admiral had been instructed to prevent work on the fortifications and, if it were continued, to destroy the earthworks and silence the batteries.

The French fleet sailed away; for the French Government, on being invited to cooperate, had already informed the British ambassador in Paris that the proposed bombardment would be an act of war against

Egypt and that such an act, without the express consent of the Chamber, would violate the French Constitution.

On July 12, when the batteries were all silenced, the Egyptian troops set fire to the town and left it to be pillaged by the mob, which took the opportunity of outraging some Turkish ladies and of murdering several Europeans. Gladstone's Cabinet, which lost Bright at this juncture, refused for several hours to allow troops to be landed to counteract the work of the incendiaries, because it involved "the assumption of authority upon the Egyptian question." But England, now determined to substitute order for anarchy, obtained the partial cooperation of France, until mistrust of Germany brought about the fall of the Freycinet Ministry and finally ended the question of French military intervention in Egypt. An appeal to Italy was answered by friendly assurances, coupled with the evident desire to abstain from active alliance, inspired by a natural reluctance to separate from the European Concert and by fear of an ultimate collision with France.

The Sultan expressed himself willing to issue a proclamation denouncing Arabi as a rebel and also to enter into a military convention with Great Britain, indicating the manner in which 5000 Turkish troops were to be employed; but the diplomacy of the Porte was more than usually tortuous, with the consequence that the convention was still unsigned on September 13, the date on which Lord Wolseley defeated the Egyptian army at Tel-el-Kebir.

For two months after the bombardment of Alexandria there were two rival Governments in Egypt—that of the Khedive, practically a prisoner in his palace near Alexandria (although he was supported indirectly by Great Britain), and that of Arabi, backed by the Egyptian army; yet both of these professed equal hostility to the British invasion of Egypt. On July 20, the British Government announced its intention of sending British troops to Egypt in default of foreign cooperation, in order to restore the Khedive's authority; the House of Commons voted the necessary money by a large majority; the troops reached Alexandria; and on August 18, the British fleet sailed thence with the military transports. The rebel army was drawn up to oppose the advertised landing at Aboukir; but the fleet, contrary to expectation, steamed straight for Ismailia, from which point the advance to Cairo had been secretly planned. In spite of the complaints of Lesseps, the troops were gradually poured across the desert from the Canal, the enemy retiring before them. After an unsuccessful attack on the British camp at Kassassin, Arabi entrenched himself in a strong position at Tel-el-Kebir. In the early morning of September 13, about 13,000 British soldiers drove twice the number of Egyptians from their entrenchments and captured all their 70 guns; Arabi Pasha was one of the first to fly, while officers and men vied with each other in the rapidity with which they cast away rifles and uniforms and assumed the garb and habits of

CH. XV.

peaceful peasants engaged in tilling the fields. The 11,000 troops in and near Cairo surrendered unconditionally, by Arabi's orders, as soon as a handful of Englishmen had pushed on to the capital, and within a week all the outlying garrisons had laid down their arms. On September 19, a laconic Decree, signed by the Khedive, appeared in the *Journal Officiel,* "The Egyptian Army is disbanded." So ended an undisciplined force which, in Lord Cromer's words, could mutiny but could not, or would not, fight. In spite of the unconcealed satisfaction of the Egyptians at the arrival of English troops and a petition signed by 2600 European residents in Alexandria in favour of a permanent British occupation, Lord Granville announced that he " contemplated shortly commencing the withdrawal of the British troops from Egypt." Lord Dufferin was despatched from Constantinople to Cairo on a special mission " to advise the Government of the Khedive in the arrangements which would have to be made for reestablishing his Highness' authority." His first step was to obtain the release of all prisoners under the rank of major who were confined on charges connected with the mutiny. The British Government handed the ringleaders over to the Khedive, with the stipulation that no sentence of death should be carried out without the approval of the British authorities. Arabi was defended by two English barristers, and, after a protracted and unedifying trial, Lord Dufferin arranged that Arabi and four other Pashas should plead guilty to the charge of rebellion, and be sentenced to death; and that the Khedive should commute the sentence to one of banishment. Ceylon was chosen as the place of exile; and there most of the Pashas lived in comfort for over 18 years, when the survivors were allowed to return to Egypt. Riaz Pasha, the Prime Minister, objected so strongly to the injustice and impolicy of this leniency that he resigned office.

Shortly after the military occupation of Egypt, the British Cabinet intimated to France its intention to withdraw from the Dual Control, and on February 4, 1883, Sir Auckland Colvin was appointed as the first Financial Adviser to the Egyptian Government. Great Britain declined to listen to French protests on this point; the French Government "resumed its liberty of action in Egypt," and, until the signature of the Anglo-French agreement in 1904, remained more or less persistently hostile to England.

Lord Dufferin, on February 6, 1883, submitted to the Foreign Office his proposals for the reorganisation of Egypt in an eloquent despatch which concealed both from the British and the Egyptians the extreme difficulties which he was clear-sighted enough to foresee; and, though he recommended the formation of a Legislative Council and Assembly, he hinted that the masterly hand of a Resident would have to bend everything to his will. Before returning to Constantinople he caused the Khedive to prohibit the bastinado, which until then had been invariably used to extort confessions, and he arranged for the reconstruction, under

British chiefs, of the departments of Irrigation, Army, Justice, and Police. He had hardly left Egypt when that unfortunate country was paralysed by outbreaks of rinderpest and cholera, the latter introduced by pilgrims returning from Mecca. The British Government sent medical officers from England and India, who were powerless to do more than make recommendations which the Egyptian officials were both unwilling and unable to carry out. Gladstone's Cabinet refused to entertain the idea of a protectorate and was still bent on withdrawing from the country as soon as possible. Sir Evelyn Baring (afterwards Lord Cromer) was appointed as Agent and Consul-General and took up his new duties in Cairo on September 11, 1883.

In spite of the unwillingness of the Cabinet, the British occupation, dreaded by Mehemet Ali and foreseen by Kinglake in *Eothen,* had already lasted twelve months—a logical sequence of the labours of Waghorn and Lesseps, and of the magnificent follies of Ismail.

Egyptian sovereignty in the Sudan (or the country of the blacks) dates from 1819, when Mehemet Ali sent troops thither and ultimately established his authority over Sennar and Kordofan. The Victoria Nyanza Lake was discovered by Speke in 1858 and the Albert Nyanza by Sir Samuel Baker in 1864, while in 1866 Suakin and Massowah were assigned to Egypt by the Sultan. In 1871 Baker conquered and annexed the Equatorial Provinces, having been engaged by the Khedive for four years to subdue the countries south of Gondokoro, to suppress the slave trade, and to open to navigation the great lakes of the Equator. He tried to change the name of Gondokoro to Ismailia in honour of his master, and, by establishing military posts and making maps, laid the foundation of future government. He was succeeded in 1874 by General Charles Gordon, who had been fired by the Khedive and Nubar Pasha with their dream of a Central African empire, and who only stipulated that his salary should be £2000 a year instead of £10,000 as proposed by Ismail. In the following year Darfur and Harrar were annexed to Egypt, and steamers were taken up the Nile to ply on Lake Albert Nyanza. In February, 1877, Gordon, already Governor-General of the Equatorial Provinces, was promoted to be Governor-General of the Sudan, and astonished the Arabs by the rapidity of his camel marches and his feverish love of inspecting outlying districts. The Egyptian Sudan then consisted of an area some 1300 miles long by 1300 miles in breadth at its widest part. Gordon found that no trade worthy of the name was carried on excepting in slaves and ivory; and he resolutely set himself to harass the slave dealers in every possible way. After a series of engagements against rebel slave hunters in 1879, Gessi, one of Gordon's officers, shot Suleiman, the son of Zobeir Pasha, the most influential black in the Sudan and the recognised chieftain of some 11,000 troops. Gordon's crusade against the slave traders, who were usually in collusion with government officials, followed by his prompt resignation so soon as he heard of Ismail's downfall, greatly contributed to spread discontent throughout the Sudan, while the disastrous War in Abyssinia in 1875, where Prince Hassan had been taken prisoner, and 900 Egyptians, armed with rifles, had fallen before King John's swords and spears, had by no means discouraged Sudanese rebellion.

Gordon's departure for England coincided with the return of the slave dealers. The Egyptian Government became universally hated; the Treasury was empty; and the army was worthless, without pay, discipline, or loyalty. Everything was ripe for the Mahdi, who, in August, 1881, proclaimed his mission to conquer Egypt, overthrow the Turks, and convert the whole world. He declared war equally against orthodox Mohammadans, Christians, and pagans, and thousands of fanatics who had eagerly assimilated his mysticism flocked to his standard. In consequence of Colonel Stewart's valuable reports on the growing movement, several British officers were appointed in the spring of 1883 to the staff of the Egyptian army in the Sudan, under the command of General Hicks, who found his recommendations paralysed by Cairo intrigues, until he was appointed Commander-in-Chief in July. Lord Granville took the extraordinary and undignified line of disclaiming all responsibility in Sudanese affairs; the Egyptian Ministers failed to realise the military and geographical situation; and Hicks, with a worthless rabble, was allowed to start from Duem on September 8, 1883, to attempt the reconquest of Kordofan from the Mahdi. His army was led astray by false guides into the desert, where those who did not succumb to thirst fell an easy prey to the Mahdi's hordes, about 30 miles south of El Obeid. Hicks and his staff died like men, fighting, within a mile of a large pool of water of which they were in complete ignorance. So soon as rumours of Hicks' defeat reached Cairo, Sir Evelyn Baring impressed upon the British Cabinet the uselessness of separating Egyptian from Sudanese affairs; and Lord Granville informed him that in no case would British, Indian, or Turkish troops be sent to reconquer the Sudan, and that, as Egypt had neither soldiers nor money, it was necessary to abandon the Sudan to its fate. This decision was very unpopular in Egypt and resulted in a change of Ministry in January, 1884, while votes of censure on Gladstone's policy were moved in both Houses of Parliament. Public opinion in England and Egypt was strongly in favour of an attempt being made to relieve the loyal garrisons in the Eastern Sudan, then beleaguered by Osman Digna, a former slave dealer, who had been appointed as the Mahdi's Emir, and whose prestige had been greatly increased by unsuccessful Egyptian expeditions against him in the neighbourhood of Suakin. The new Egyptian army, commanded by Sir Evelyn Wood, which was hardly a year old, was considered too raw to be despatched, and General Valentine Baker was hurriedly sent to the Red Sea with his newly formed *gendarmerie*, some of whom had been recruited from Arabi Pasha's army defeated at Tel-el-Kebir. On February 5, 1884, Baker's force of 3500 men, marching to relieve the Tokar garrison, was attacked by less than 1000 of the enemy. His men threw down their arms, fled, and allowed themselves to be killed without making the least resistance. It was thus conclusively proved that the Egyptian peasant of that day was incapable of fighting. Baker's defeat caused a panic at Suakin. Admiral Hewett was obliged to land a small force for its protection, and he was placed in civil and military command of the town. Sir Gerald Graham was sent from Cairo with 4000 British troops and fought two successful engagements in March at El Teb and Tamai, near Suakin, though Tokar had in the meantime capitulated; but his victories were rendered almost useless by the refusal of the British Government to advance troops from Suakin to Berber.

Early in 1884 the proffered services of General Gordon had twice been refused by Sir Evelyn Baring and the Egyptian Ministers; but when it was found that the most suitable Egyptian Pasha (Abd-el-Kader, who had lately been Governor-General of the Sudan) declined to go thither, Gordon's appointment to Khartum, to carry out the best policy of withdrawing Egyptian troops and civilians from the interior of the Sudan, was rapidly approved in London and Cairo. Lord Granville took the General's ticket; Lord Wolseley carried the hand-bag which contained all his outfit; and the Duke of Cambridge held open the door of the railway carriage. Gordon reached Cairo on January 24, and there met Colonel Stewart.

Public feeling in England was strongly in favour of Gordon's mission; the Cabinet placed great faith in his powers of personal magnetism and quite failed to realise that his past popularity in the Sudan had been with liberated slaves and victims of oppression, and not with the ruling classes whose place had now been taken by the followers of the Mahdi. Gordon himself disbelieved in the wide spread of the religious movement and at first talked confidently of being able to execute his mission in three or four months, though his sagacious companion, Colonel Stewart, was no sharer of his optimistic views. Gordon, at his own request, was again appointed Governor-General of the Sudan, and arrived at Khartum on February 18. During his brief stay in Cairo a dramatic meeting took place at the British Agency between Gordon and Zobeir Pasha. This Pasha, who claims descent from the Abbaside dynasty of Khalifs, must have strange views on the steadfastness of British policy. When Gessi had caused Zobeir's son to be shot, in 1879, a letter was found from the father inciting the son to revolt, and consequently Zobeir was tried in Cairo for rebellion against the Khedive and was condemned to death. This sentence was, however, commuted into residence in Cairo with a pension of £1200 a year from the Khedive. On January 22, 1884, while on his way to Egypt, Gordon suggested that Zobeir should be watched and deported to Cyprus; yet three days later, upon accidentally meeting Zobeir in Cairo, he experienced a "mystic feeling" that he could trust him, and recommended that Zobeir should accompany him to Khartum in order to settle the affairs of the Sudan after evacuation by Egypt. No official in Cairo at that time supported Gordon's demand for the ex-slave hunter. But the mystic feeling in favour of the cooperation of Zobeir grew into a settled conviction, as Gordon came to closer quarters with the appalling difficulties of his task. His arguments in favour of trying to form a buffer State under Zobeir's command, between the Mahdi's forces and Egypt, gradually won over Colonel Stewart, Nubar Pasha, the astute Prime Minister of Egypt, and Sir Evelyn Baring. Gordon's repeated requests for Zobeir, cogently backed in Cairo, were, however, negatived in March, 1884, by the British Cabinet, which feared the Anti-Slavery Society and parliamentary opposition. During the advance upon Khartum Zobeir was deported as a prisoner to Gibraltar, but was allowed to return to the Sudan in 1900, where he is now a peaceful farmer.

By May, 1884, Berber and the Bahr-el-Gazal province had fallen into the hands of the Mahdi, and all communication between Khartum and Egypt was cut off, while, on September 18, Colonel Stewart was murdered on his journey north with despatches from Gordon.

In April, 1884, Gladstone's Government was urged by Lord Wolseley, Sir Evelyn Baring, and others to prepare for a military expedition to rescue Gordon; but four valuable months were lost in indecision, and it was not till October that Lord Wolseley was able to begin the Nile campaign, which then became a race against time rather than a fight against man. Disregarding local military advice, Lord Wolseley persuaded the Cabinet against the desert route from Suakin to Berber (280 miles) and the Nile march from Berber to Khartum (200 miles), for, mindful of the success of his Red River Expedition, he preferred the long river route of 1650 miles from Cairo to Khartum. He was also considerably influenced by the important fact that Berber was already in the hands of the enemy. The army was thus struggling upstream, against cataracts, with 800 special "whalers" built in England to convey the troops, Canadian "voyageurs" to navigate the rapids, and even West African Kroomen to carry the stores around the cataracts. Every detail was well thought out by the military staff—time alone was lacking. By Christmas day the main part of the expeditionary force was concentrated at Korti. Gordon, standing heroically alone, without any trustworthy subordinates, with 34,000 useless mouths to feed, forced to reduce the rations of the garrison to crushed palm fibre and gum, was so closely hemmed in by the dervishes that his life was obviously in imminent danger from treachery within and storming parties without. Lord Wolseley therefore resolved to divide his force into two columns, the smaller, under Sir Herbert Stewart, to march across the desert to the Nile at Metemma, while the larger, under General Earle, continued its advance up the river in order to capture Berber, as advised by Gordon. This desert march of 160 miles was no part of the original programme. Camels, though proffered and refused months before, could not be procured in sufficient numbers, and much delay was caused by having to establish forts at the desert wells and by compelling the transport to double and treble its journey.

On January 17, 1885, the desert column was attacked by the dervishes in force, armed with rifles captured from General Hicks, and after several sharp engagements, during one of which Sir Herbert Stewart was mortally wounded, the troops reached the Nile and found four steamers which had been sent by Gordon to meet the expedition. On the 24th Sir Charles Wilson steamed on towards Khartum, under heavy fire from the banks, only to learn on the 27th that the Mahdi had entered the capital and that its heroic defender had been killed. Various gallant incidents occurred during this forced march which added lustre to the prowess of the British army. The river column also met with the enemy and lost its General at Kirbekan.

Encouraged by Gordon's arrival, the inhabitants of Khartum had decided not to fly, because they chose to believe that he was only the precursor of an English expedition which should capture the Sudan for England. This belief arose, in spite of the deathblow which Gordon had himself dealt to his mission when he announced, both at Berber and at Metemma, on his way to Khartum, that Egypt had abandoned the Sudan.

The failure of the "too late" expedition to relieve Gordon, "the hero of heroes," raised intense excitement in England ; and, as the lowness of the Nile and the limited force available precluded any immediate action, the British Government announced its intention of renewing the campaign in the autumn for the purpose of overthrowing the power of the Mahdi and of constructing a railroad from Suakin to Berber. But in May, partly because Russian relations with Afghanistan had made a European war possible, enthusiasm died away, evacuation was ordered, and the whole of the Sudan, with the exception of the Red Sea ports, was surrendered to the rule of the Mahdi and Osman Digna, which lasted for thirteen years, during which time the country was devastated and almost depopulated.

An armed truce prevailed until 1889, when the Khalifa, who had succeeded the Mahdi on his death, five months after the fall of Khartum, impelled to action by famine among his followers, caused one of his chiefs to attack the Egyptian army at Toski on August 3. The dervishes were utterly defeated, and their project of invading Egypt, which had been maturing for years, entirely collapsed. The defeat of Osman Digna near Tokar in February, 1891, permitted Egypt to reoccupy and tranquillise part of the Eastern Sudan, and to remain content for about five years behind a settled frontier.

CH. XV.

Among the garrisons abandoned by Egypt in 1883 none were in more imminent danger than the soldiers quartered on the Abyssinian frontier, who found themselves between the triumphant hordes of the Mahdi and the savage Abyssinians.   Admiral Sir William Hewett was therefore sent on a diplomatic mission to King John, who agreed, in consideration of annexing the fortresses and their munitions, to allow the Egyptian garrisons to retreat peacefully through his dominions while the Italians, fired with colonial ambition, occupied Massowah on the Red Sea coast.   Fighting soon occurred between the Italians and the Abyssinians, who pursued their invariable custom of slaughtering the wounded and mutilating the prisoners and the slain.   A second mission was consequently despatched in October, 1887, under Gerald Portal, with letters from Queen Victoria to King John, to bring about peace between him and the Italians.

Early in 1889 King John determined to attempt the capture of Galabat, with the idea of marching thence to Khartum.   His troops stormed the town successfully, but he himself was killed by a stray bullet, and the Abyssinians were eventually routed by the Mahdi's troops.   After this, both parties seemed tired of hostilities, and some trading between them ensued.

While the eyes of Europe were eagerly turned on Gordon at Khartum, a small band of Englishmen in Egypt was trying to evolve order out of chaos, prosperity out of discontent.   The country was dangerously near to bankruptcy; French hostility was active; and the other European Powers, excepting Italy, openly sympathised with France, while Turkey fomented discord by proposing at intervals that Halim Pasha should replace Tewfik as Khedive.   Gladstone and Lord Granville were bent on withdrawing the troops from Egypt, and could hardly be made to understand that a country in which all Europe has interests cannot be treated as Afghanistan or Ashanti.   To gain time, they despatched at different times two officials, whose missions were complete failures.   Clifford Lloyd reached Cairo in the autumn of 1883 to inspect reforms and naturally found that none as yet existed.   He became Under-Secretary of State for the Interior, initiated many useful improvements, offended several Oriental susceptibilities, and was compelled to resign office in May, 1884.   Lord Northbrook's mission (1884) resulted in nothing but increased depression among the English officials in Egypt.

British Ministers in 1884 found that the Egyptian question was a subject more complicated and fraught with more dangers than any item of foreign policy in which England had been concerned for more than half a century.   They were obliged, for instance, to hold three cabinet meetings on three successive days in April of that year before they arrived at the momentous decision of forcing Egypt to abandon the Sudan.

Lord Salisbury, in 1885, sent Sir Henry Drummond Wolff to Egypt as a Joint Commissioner with the Sultan's nominee, to settle, if possible, the most thorny points of the Egyptian question; but, after eighteen months of discussion, the Sultan, under the influence of France and Russia, refused to ratify the Convention, and no result was achieved except that Egypt became saddled with the presence of a permanent Turkish Commissioner.

Egypt, by a single impression of the Khedive's seal, had decided that the Egyptian peasant must not be flogged, and had then determined on the further reform that he should not be forced to give his labour gratuitously. For centuries it had been the custom every year, with the aid of whips made of hippopotamus hide, to force the people to clean out the canals, in which they often had no personal interest. In theory the annual canal clearing required the services of one-eighth of the population during three months; but, as the rich found no difficulty in evading the duty, a severe burden fell upon the poorest peasants for at least half the year. France put every difficulty in the way of allowing Egypt to abolish the *corvée* and to pay the labourers a small wage; but the British Government temporarily agreed to provide the funds by postponing the payment of the money due to England on account of the interest on her Suez Canal shares. It was not until after eight years of diplomatic squabbling that money was permanently found to pay for the free labour which had taken the place of the *corvée*.

The first six years of the British occupation were an unceasing struggle against bankruptcy, for it was not until 1888 that the annual deficit was replaced by financial equilibrium. This happy result was in some measure due to Sir Evelyn Baring's courage and success in facing the Powers in 1885 with a demand for permission to raise a new loan of nine millions sterling to pay off the Alexandria war indemnities, to wipe out the deficits of four preceding years, and to provide a million pounds for new works of irrigation. This extra million, skilfully spent, saved the irrigation system, the agricultural crops, the government taxes, and the finances of Egypt. Since those struggling days, when the Finance Ministry had difficulty in providing the monthly pay of government officials, an annual surplus has been gained, taxation relieved by £2,000,000 a year, revenue increased from £9,000,000 (in 1883) to more than £16,000,000 (in 1907), and Egyptian credit raised to a level little below that of the richest European Powers. During the same years the annual expenditure has risen with the growing revenue, but has been so well controlled that the increase has amounted to little more than half the extra revenue, thus allowing for the formation of a Reserve Fund. This is the more remarkable, because much of the extraordinary expenditure on railways, canals, and public buildings has been provided out of annual revenue. The only increase in taxation has been in the tobacco duty. A sound fiscal policy, honest administra-

CH. XV.

tion and encouragement to native proprietors of small holdings of land, aided by the efforts of the industrious peasants, have succeeded in producing a transformation in a quarter of a century which appears to be unique in history.

Our limits forbid an enumeration of the various benefits which have accrued to Egypt during British rule, but a few of them may be briefly set down. Next to finance, the success of which is due to Lord Cromer himself, the two departments in which British officials have achieved great renown are those of irrigation and the army, for in both the necessary control has been entrusted to experts, and there has been no international interference. The British engineers, when summoned from India, found themselves obliged to grapple with chaos resulting from half a century's want of technical skill and administrative morality. Canals were cleared and extended, drainage of the land introduced, and the great Barrage below Cairo utilised. This dam, though built by forced labour, had cost the Government nearly two millions sterling, and, owing to faulty foundations, had remained practically useless until Sir Colin Scott-Moncrieff rendered it capable of doing excellent service. When the British engineers had been at work for ten years, the cotton crop and sugar crop were both trebled, and the country, which had been entirely roadless, was being gradually covered with a series of light railways and agricultural roads. Many minor reforms in agricultural irrigation bear testimony to the value of the English occupation; but they are eclipsed by the success of the magnificent dam at Assuan, which was begun in 1898. More good has already accrued to Egypt by the expenditure there of three and a half millions than by the hundred millions of Ismail Pasha's debt. Work is now in progress to add to its usefulness by heightening the existing dam, which will more than double the storage capacity of the reservoir; by this addition water will be provided during the summer to irrigate a million acres of land now lying waste in the northern tracts of the Delta. Exploration and surveying are being carried out with the view of creating future reservoirs in the Sudan and of controlling the waters from the Great Lakes to the sea. To the Egyptian Irrigation Department must be accorded the praise of having most benefited the people and of having made the fewest errors of judgment.

The agricultural population has invariably appreciated the labours of the Anglo-Indian Irrigation Inspectors, and in 1888, when some thousands of acres in Upper Egypt were threatened with absolute failure of the inundation in consequence of a low Nile flood, and were only saved by the personal exertions of Mr Willcocks, the grateful inhabitants put their religious fanaticism on one side and insisted on the Christian attending a thanksgiving service in the mosque of the chief town, side by side with the Egyptian Minister of Public Works, who came specially from Cairo to attend the ceremony.

Before the British occupation the army conscripts were torn from their homes, chained together like convicts, and, escorted by their shrieking women, despatched to distant garrisons whence they seldom returned. When Sir Evelyn Wood became the first English Sirdar of the Egyptian army it had been well proved that the troops, officered only by Egyptians, were quite useless; and the new military advisers were reminded of Ibrahim Pasha's dictum after his successes in Syria, that no Egyptian should ever advance beyond the rank of sergeant. Six thousand peasants were taken straight from the land, and, to their astonishment, found themselves well fed, well clothed, unbeaten, paid punctually, and even allowed furlough to visit their families. As the power of the Mahdi grew, it became obvious that Egypt must possess a larger army and several regiments of black volunteers from distant parts of the Sudan were enrolled.

In 1887 the composite force of Egyptians and Sudanese had lived down its doubtful reputation and was entrusted with the defence of the southern frontier at Wadi Halfa; but it was not until 1896 that a forward advance was made to reconquer the Sudan. On March 1 the Italian troops were totally defeated by the Abyssinians at Adowah, and rumours were afloat that the dervishes contemplated an attack on Cassala. Lord Salisbury, when invited to create a diversion in Italian interests, at once gave orders to reoccupy the once fertile province of Dongola. It was decided to employ only Egyptian troops under the command of the Sirdar, Sir Herbert Kitchener; but a British battalion was sent from Cairo to Wadi Halfa for moral assistance, and Suakin was garrisoned for six months by a contingent from the Indian army. Dongola was occupied on September 23 after two fights, in spite of an outbreak of cholera and unprecedented storms, which washed away the desert railway on which the army was dependent for food and stores. While the army was fighting, the financiers were wrangling as to who should pay for the expedition. The British Cabinet decided that Egypt should provide funds to reconquer her lost territory. Egypt had the money in her treasury and was willing to pay, but could not do so without the consent of the six Commissioners of the Debt. Four of them authorised payment; but two dissentients, representing France and Russia, appealed to the law Courts and compelled the Egyptian Government to refund the money. The matter was eventually settled by the British Government lending £800,000 to Egypt at $2\frac{3}{4}$ per cent. interest. News from the Sudan, brought by Slatin Pasha and other escaped prisoners, had confirmed rumours that the Khalifa's rule was crumbling to decay; and the Chancellor of the Exchequer announced in the House of Commons on February 5, 1897, that Egypt could never be considered permanently secure so long as a hostile Power was in occupation at Khartum, and that it was England's duty to give the final blow to the Khalifa. Before the close of that year, the Egyptian troops had

CH. XV.

constructed a desert railway from Wadi Halfa towards Berber, Abu Hamed and Berber were both wrested from the dervishes, and Cassala was taken over from the Italians, who were glad to get rid of an expensive possession.

Early in 1898, in consequence of the threatening attitude of the dervishes, four British battalions were sent from Cairo to strengthen the Egyptian force between Berber and the Atbara river; and, on April 8, the Sirdar destroyed the entrenched camp of 12,000 dervishes, nearly all of whom were killed or taken prisoner. The desert railway steadily and rapidly advanced, plans, long and secretly thought out, were deliberately matured, and by the end of August the Sirdar had with him a force of 22,000, including two British brigades, massed about 40 miles north of Khartum.

On September 2 Sir Herbert Kitchener's victorious army captured Omdurman, the stronghold of Mahdiism; and two days later a religious service, under the British and Egyptian flags, was held at Khartum in memory of General Gordon, near the spot where he fell thirteen years before. The Khalifa fled from Omdurman into the wilds of Kordofan, wandered about for a year, and was then killed with all his principal chiefs by a force under Sir Reginald Wingate, the present Sirdar of the Egyptian army. The economy practised in the Sudan campaign of 1896–8 was noteworthy, for, after deducting £1,200,000 spent on railways and telegraphs, the actual costs of the military expedition only just exceeded one million pounds.

Hardly were the two flags floating over the capital, when news reached Khartum that six white men were encamped at Fashoda, a village on the White Nile, some 300 miles to the south. Lord Kitchener despatched all newspaper correspondents to Cairo and hurried by steamer to Fashoda, which he reached on September 18, to find that Major Marchand had arrived there with 100 native troops from Senegal, and had already hoisted the French flag. The Egyptian flag was also hoisted, a salute was fired in honour of that event, and some delicate negotiations took place on the subject between Paris and London. The British Government adopted a very firm attitude, and eventually Major Marchand received orders to haul down the tricolour and return to Europe. That the incident may not be needlessly recalled to mind, the name Fashoda has been removed from the maps of the Sudan, and the village is now called Kodok.

In January, 1899, an agreement between the British and Egyptian Governments regulated the political status of the Sudan, giving a valid title to the exercise of sovereign rights in the Sudan by the King of England in conjunction with the Khedive, based on the right of conquest. The southern frontier was left undefined. It was also provided that the supreme civil and military command of the Egyptian Sudan should be vested in the Governor-General, who must be appointed by Khedivial decree on British recommendation, and that no foreign consuls should be allowed to reside there without the previous consent of Great Britain. No serious opposition to this agreement was encountered in Europe, partly because it was provided that in all matters concerning trade with or residence in the Sudan "no special privileges would be accorded to the subjects of any one or more Powers."

In the ensuing ten years, the Sudan has slowly advanced towards fiscal and material prosperity. The financial deficit is gradually lessening and, with growing resources, it is confidently expected that the burden on the Egyptian budget will be lightened year by year. The retirement of Belgian troops from the south-western districts of the Bahr-el-Gazal, the settlement of the frontiers of Abyssinia and Uganda, and a more definite understanding as regards the Darfur frontier, have diminished the external difficulties of the Sudan Government. Excluding the Egyptian and maritime boundaries, there are some 4000 miles of frontier to watch, while the neighbouring tribes are savage and under merely nominal control, so that peace has frequently been disturbed and raids have taken place. The gradual extension of the telegraph system to more remote districts has aided the band of English administrators who, under the Sirdar as Governor-General, have done much to provide security and protection for the inhabitants. The population, greatly reduced under Mahdiism, is increasing rapidly and now exceeds two millions; in spite of locusts, cotton and cereals are gradually covering the irrigated land; imports and exports are yearly increasing; while at Port Sudan, on the Red Sea coast, an arid desert has been transformed into a well-equipped harbour, which will greatly add to the economic development of the resources of the country.

The future prosperity of the Sudan depends upon its agricultural development for which two essentials are needed, labour and water. Unlike the Egyptian, the Sudanese prefers fighting to tilling the soil, while long years of tribal warfare and inherent laziness have caused him to relegate agricultural work to his women folk, though the present generation is being gradually trained to cultivate the land. When the English had reconquered the Sudan they found the region of the great swamps blocked by weed barriers, called *sudd*. Some of these were three-quarters of a mile in width and being perfectly firm were overgrown with long reeds and high grasses. The White Nile wandered for nearly 400 miles through these marshes, entered them as a fine river but emerged a somewhat insignificant stream, having lost by evaporation and by the absorption of the water plants more than half the supply brought down from the Lakes. The marshes varied in width from five to twenty miles, and, after some months of experiment in 1900, it was found that the *sudd* could be removed. The entire channel has been free to navigation since 1902; but the question of keeping the Upper Nile permanently free from *sudd* and of preventing a waste of water in the marshes still remains an important problem under consideration. Years spent on surveying and levelling have resulted in the Nile being mapped, while a series of permanent gauges on both the Blue and White Niles have been erected throughout the limits of the Egyptian Sudan. The water levels are now daily recorded, and a register of the highest importance is thus kept.

Until the close of Ismail's reign, Europeans in Egypt were, in respect of all criminal and civil questions, under the sole jurisdiction of their own consuls. This was in virtue of the Capitulations, or concessions contemptuously conferred on foreign traders by the Ottomans when they were the terror of Europe. Some of the consuls were accustomed to use their influence to urge upon Egypt the payment of most preposterous demands, and in 1876 there were £40,000,000 of foreign claims outstanding against the Government. In that year, Nubar Pasha, after eight years of weary negotiation, succeeded in obtaining the consent of all the Powers to the creation of the Mixed Tribunals, which were made competent to try all suits in which the plaintiff and defendant were of different nationalities. The judges of the Mixed Tribunals are nominated by the Great Powers, with the approval of the Egyptian Government, by whom their salaries are paid, and it was agreed that their jurisdiction should be based on the *Code Napoléon*. The new Tribunals had the right of curtailing the Khedive's power of contracting debts in the name of Egypt and thus indirectly brought about Ismail's deposition.

The Native Tribunals, instituted in 1883 under Lord Dufferin's auspices and based on a French model, were new creations dealing with all civil cases in which both parties are Egyptian subjects, and with all criminal cases in which an Egyptian is the accused party. The Department of Justice was practically left in Egyptian hands, until it was discovered in 1889 that the Brigandage Commissions, which had temporarily superseded the Native Tribunals, had allowed witnesses to be tortured and innocent persons to be imprisoned, if not hanged. In 1891 the Egyptian Government consented to appoint Sir John Scott as Judicial Adviser. His tact and knowledge of the country enabled him at once to inaugurate a sound judicial system; and those who were firmly persuaded that no Egyptian could withstand the temptation of a bribe or condemn a Pasha to prison must allow that the standard of efficiency among Egyptian Judges is at the present day not only high but steadily rising. Out of a total staff of 1600 in the Department of Justice, only 36 are now Europeans.

Soon after the British occupation of Egypt, attempts were made to improve the public security of the country by appointing European police officers to counteract the evil influence of the Mudirs of the provinces; but every Egyptian Minister proved more or less hostile to the new system, until, in 1894, a compromise was effected by the appointment of Mr (now Sir Eldon) Gorst as adviser of the Ministry of the Interior, with a small body of English inspectors who successfully prevent some of the abuses of the past.

The old order of Mudirs has passed away in a cloud of corruption and nepotism, and the modern occupants of that post are carefully chosen from amongst those who have learnt to rule the villagers without resorting to the whip or unjust imprisonment. Before the British occupation, and even for a year or two after it, the prisons were crowded to excess, not only with convicted criminals, but also with accused persons who had to wait months or years without trial, while many innocent witnesses were imprisoned with them, because it was considered more convenient to detain them until they were wanted. The inmates, half starved, covered with vermin, lacking exercise and occupation, were kept, with no change of clothing, in insanitary dormitories, which were annually visited by typhus and relapsing fevers. Gradually, the old prisons have been ventilated and made sanitary; many new gaols have been built for both sexes; reformatories for children have been instituted; trades are taught; proper diets and clothing are provided and "gaol fever" has been abolished; while the work of the police has been made more easy by the successful establishment of the system of finger prints.

The sturdy Egyptian, living for the most part an outdoor life in a good, sunny climate, knew nothing of Public Health questions until Mehemet Ali, under quarantine pressure from Europe, established a military sanitary service, followed by a Board of Health and hospitals for treating sick civilians. Clot Bey, an able Frenchman, was placed at the head of the medical department and found himself obliged, in 1827, to open a medical school in order to furnish surgeons and apothecaries for the army, which then consisted of 200,000 men. This was actually the earliest government school in Egypt, and by steady perseverance all prejudices were overcome and human dissection was permitted for the first time since the reign of the Ptolemies. In spite of dire visitations of plague and cholera, the population of Egypt gradually increased, partly in consequence of the introduction of vaccination, for it is said that, before Clot Bey's time, 60,000 children usually died of smallpox every year.

The sanitary department and medical school were, after 1858, left entirely in Egyptian hands, and proved to be quite useless during the cholera epidemic of 1883. In the following year Englishmen were appointed as heads of the Public Health Department of the Interior and of the International Quarantine Service, which had been formed at the request of Europe to prevent exotic disease, human and veterinary, from entering Egypt. There were then in existence twenty-three government hospitals, insanitary, ill-furnished, and served by old soldiers who had been discharged from the army. The inmates consisted entirely of government employees, prisoners, foundlings, idiots, and prostitutes, all sent and detained by order of the Mudir or Governor. The public firmly believed that the sick were beaten and robbed by the orderlies, and were then put to death by the doctors. Refractory patients were fettered in chains, anklets, and handcuffs, while sick men transferred from the prisons, wore, until they died, heavy chains six feet long round their ankles. The one state lunatic asylum, near Cairo, was in an even more pitiable state. Three hundred lunatics—for it was only the most dangerous to society who were incarcerated by the police—eked out a miserable existence in filth, hunger, chains, and nudity. The most maniacal were confined in dark dungeons, where they were chained to the walls and floor. There was no resident doctor and the chief treatment employed was venesection. The British Government and its representatives in Egypt were, in the early years of the occupation, so deeply engaged in the race against bankruptcy and in protective measures against the dervishes, that little could be done except by the removal of flagrant horrors, but money was gradually forthcoming to build new hospitals, renovate and equip old ones, provide accommodation for infectious diseases, and create Hygiene, Vaccine, and Anti-rabies Institutes, all now doing excellent work under Europeans. The chief hospital in Cairo has had the advantage of English nurses since 1888; and many generations of Egyptian students, trained since that time in the Medical School attached to it, have carried away into distant parts of Egypt and the Sudan the practical knowledge of what a hospital should be. The lunatic asylum, now under resident British doctors, matron, and steward, has been so enlarged and reformed that it is difficult to discover the buildings where the horrors were enacted a quarter of a century ago. To the asylum and to the general hospitals in country towns thousands now willingly travel for medical advice, which their parents not unnaturally shunned.

When the Public Health Department was reorganised in 1884, it was found that no sanitary house, hotel, or hospital existed in all Egypt. Three-fourths of the primitive town drains ended directly in the Nile or in canals which supplied drinking water to the villages on their banks, while the remainder found their way into large, stagnant ponds surrounded by houses, in which cattle were watered and children paddled. The principal towns have now been supplied with pure drinking water and drainage schemes are being gradually introduced.

Twice since 1883 cholera has been imported by pilgrims returning from Mecca and has successfully been grappled with. The fear of this disease, with its attendant quarantine restrictions and dislocation of traffic and commerce, has proved to be the best ally to the Public Health officials. Khedivial and Ministerial decrees have been signed, money voted, experts engaged, and material provided for fighting other enemies such as human plague and cattle plague. Quarantine officers see that pilgrims returning from the Hadj are examined and washed, while their property is disinfected; the supervision of steamers ensures their travelling in comparative comfort on the sea, though they are still plundered by Beduin and poisoned by sewage-infected water in the Hedjaz.

Plague was absent from Egypt from the middle of the nineteenth century till 1899, and though the recent outbreaks have in some districts obstinately recurred, the disease has been well controlled and has never blazed out as it did in former periods of Egyptian history. "Egyptian ophthalmia" is more rife in the Nile valley than in any other part of the world, but it is slowly yielding to education and the crusade against dirt. Aided by a munificent gift from Sir Ernest Cassel, eye hospitals and dispensaries are springing up to which the more enlightened Egyptians willingly subscribe. Many chronic diseases, which sap the vitality of the agricultural labourers, have been discovered of recent years; and a highly trained European staff is endeavouring to restore to the Egyptian student in the English tongue the modern fruits of that knowledge which was for so many years almost a monopoly of his forefathers in the famous cities of Memphis, Heliopolis, and Alexandria.

It is greatly to the credit of Mehemet Ali that, uneducated as he was (for he did not learn to read till he was 47 years old), he placed a high value on the education of children. He established elementary schools in the towns and forced boys to attend them. This measure was so unpopular that mothers actually blinded their sons or cut off their right forefingers to prevent their being able to write, rather than have them clothed, taught, fed, and paid at government expense. The succeeding generation slowly woke up to the fact that, unless their children were sent to school, they would be unable to enter the service of the Government, though they still expected all instruction to be given to them gratuitously; but the parents of today are perfectly willing to pay moderate school fees.

During the worst financial years before Ismail's downfall, the government expenditure on education reached only £29,000 a year; and, though this sum was more than doubled under the Dual Control, it was not until 1890 that the Ministry of Finance felt rich enough to increase the grant to £81,000. Since then, the education budget has gradually risen until 1908, when provision was made for the expenditure of £450,450, besides special credits for the construction and maintenance of school buildings. The census of 1897 showed that 88 per cent. of males and 99·5 per cent. of females in Egypt were unable to read and write. The village school, which had hitherto contented itself with teaching a few children how to spell and how to learn by rote whole chapters of the Koran, in consideration of grants-in-aid came under government supervision. The primary and secondary schools, directly under the Ministry of Education, increased in number as finances permitted and in efficiency when English teachers were introduced. Every effort has been made to encourage training schools for teachers of both sexes, and the success of a few secondary schools for girls shows that the idea is gaining ground that education need no longer be a male monopoly. Ismail established in Cairo the first school for girls ever known in the Ottoman empire.

Though much of the correspondence in government offices was conducted in the Turkish language, France held for three-quarters of a century the intellectual domination of Egypt. The upper classes knew, as a rule, no European language but French, and it was but natural in the early years of the British occupation that a very large majority of pupils elected to continue their school studies in French in preference to English. But the tide slowly turned, and, since 1899, after the reconquest of the Sudan, and especially after Great Britain's attitude at the time of the Fashoda incident, the increase in scholars on the English side became more marked, so that in 1905 they outnumbered the French class by 1962 to 370. The technical colleges comprise a school of agriculture, a polytechnic school of engineering, a medical school, and two schools of law, besides training colleges and industrial schools. There is every difference between the orderly, clean, well-appointed government school of today and the insanitary establishments of the past, in which the students were never trained to use their brain or eyes except by committing to memory whole chapters of an Arabic work, often incorrectly translated from a European edition already out of date. A similar change may be noted in the physical and moral aspect of the scholar.

But Great Britain, which has with some success been helping a handful of young Egyptians to awaken intellectually, has now to face the problem of how far the pendulum must swing towards granting self-government. No European acquainted with Oriental races can doubt the absurdity of suddenly bestowing autonomy on a country saddled, as Lord Cromer has said, with "one of the most complicated political and administrative machines which the world has ever known." Even if a far greater number of Egyptians had acquired the necessary character and ability, they would be unable to cope with the executive impotence too often caused by administrative internationalism and the all-powerful Capitulations, which grant equal rights to sixteen different kinds of foreigners. The ever increasing number of European residents, about half of whom are Greeks and Italians, constitutes one of the difficulties of government; it was calculated in 1852 that there were not more than 6000 foreigners in Egypt, but in 1882 the number had risen to 100,000, and today there must be at least 150,000.

The present Nationalist party came gradually into existence during the few years of unrest which followed the death of the Khedive Tewfik on January 7, 1892—an event accelerated, if not caused, by the incompetence of his native doctors. During those years relations were, unfortunately, strained between the young Khedive, Abbas II, and the British Agency. Mustapha Kamel, a bold young man with great gifts of eloquence, placed himself at the head of the self-styled "Nationalists,' and conducted from Paris a press campaign against British rule. Since his death in March, 1908, no leader of eminence has yet been found to succeed him, but the multiplication and unbridled licence of Egyptian newspapers has forced the question of Nationalism on the attention of the world. Though many of the unthinking youths of the day proclaim themselves members of the party, they have no right to pretend that they are in any measure representative of the feeling of the country. The movement is distinctly Mohammadan and takes no account of the Copts and other Christians.

The bulk of the people is still crassly ignorant and quite indifferent to local politics; for even in Cairo and Alexandria, where the agitation is hottest, only one per cent. of the voters can be induced to come to the poll to elect members for the Provincial Council or General Assembly. Few of the elections are contested and the great majority of the population is entirely apathetic. The extreme Nationalists demand the immediate withdrawal of the army of occupation and the substitution of Egyptians for Europeans throughout the whole administration, so that all authority should be in native hands. British zeal for education and for encouraging the spirit of independence, together with liberty of speech and writing, have brought about a condition which is opposed to the ruling authority. But the Young Turk party in Constantinople has fully recognised that the Egyptian Nationalists have no grievances except those of sentiment, and that Egypt should rest content at present with the municipalities and local commissions which have been established during the last twenty years.

For a score of years after the British landed in Egypt, reproaches were levelled against them, chiefly by France, for not having fulfilled their promise of evacuating the country; and the reply invariably given by British Ministers was that the necessary work of reform to put the Government of Egypt on a firm basis was not yet completed. It is significant that dwellers in Egypt never raised that question, though French newspapers, published in Cairo, used to print in large letters on their front sheet the unfulfilled rash promises of British statesmen. During these twenty years the views of the public both in England and in France changed considerably. The English gradually came to be proud of the reforms initiated by a handful of their countrymen and fully recognised that it would be shameful to abandon an unfinished task. The French people found that their investments in Egypt became more valuable every year that the helm was in British hands, and it was slowly conceded that the great national sentiment of France for Egypt, which had existed ever since Napoleon's "Battle of the Pyramids," did not justify her in provoking England to war. Both nations were looking for a convenient occasion honourably to bury international susceptibilities. The opportunity presented itself in the summer of 1903, when it had become evident that continued misgovernment in Morocco, culminating in revolution, called loudly for the intervention of Europe. As a result of diplomatic negotiations, on April 8, 1904, an Anglo-French agreement was signed by Lord Lansdowne and M. Paul Cambon, the French ambassador at the Court of St James. Besides dealing with various debatable questions in Newfoundland, Nigeria, Siam, Madagascar, and the New Hebrides, the French Government diplomatically recognised for the first time the predominant position of Great Britain in Egypt. "The Government of the French Republic, for their part, declare that they will not obstruct the action of Great Britain in that country by asking that a limit of time be fixed for the British occupation or in any other manner." Germany, Austria, and Italy subsequently adhered to this agreement; although difficulties afterwards arose between France and Germany resulting in the Algeciras Conference, Egypt gained financial liberty by means of several important clauses; the English position in Egypt, by official sanction, ceased to be in any way irregular, while France was compensated elsewhere for any apparent diminution of her political status in the Valley of the Nile. As further concessions to France, the British Government recognised the Suez Canal convention (signed in 1888, but not made operative) which had for its object the neutralisation of the Canal at all times and to all Powers, and the final conversion of the Egyptian Debt was postponed till 1912, in consideration of the sacrifices of the bond-holders in the past.

On May 6, 1907, Lord Cromer relinquished his great work in Egypt and was succeeded by his former subordinate, Sir Eldon Gorst. The country, found by Lord Cromer in 1883 in the midst of military and financial ruin, has become, not only freed, but prosperous; the land, once wrested from its owners and forfeited to creditors, is being redeemed; contentment has taken the place of misery; and even the regenerated Anglo-Egyptian Sudan bids fair to become self-supporting. Lord Cromer's position was unique, and as a benevolent despot he compelled the lasting respect of the Oriental by his common-sense justice. During his early years as British Agent and Consul-General he did not enjoy the complete confidence of the Cabinet; but, little by little, he won the trust of successive British Ministries, and thus obtained a secure hold over his office—an advantage which has often been denied to great Englishmen in situations highly momentous for the welfare of the empire.

CHAPTER XVI.

THE BRITISH EMPIRE IN INDIA.

THE Mutiny was the last great danger from human agency that has seriously threatened the existence of British power in India. Sir John Lawrence, who had lived through the heroic age, inaugurated as Governor-General a more prosaic but happier era. The conquest of India proper within its natural frontiers was over. By a self-denying ordinance Britain had deliberately set limits to her own dominion; and the feudatory States of the interior, with frontiers defined, dynasties established, and continued existence guaranteed, were left encircled in the peaceful ocean of the *Pax Britannica*. Sir John Lawrence' viceroyalty gave India a needed space for recuperation after the prolonged horrors of the Mutiny, and served as a trial period for testing the new imperial Constitution. The exhaustion of the land was too recent for more than a few tentative essays in the new work of conciliation, concentration, and reform, which may properly be said to date from 1869—the point of departure for this chapter.

The period to be dealt with is likely to suffer in interest when compared with those that have preceded it. The annals of sound administration are dull. There are few striking episodes except that of the Afghan War. Within India itself, the foes that Englishmen are called upon to meet are those intangible enemies plague and famine, folly and ignorance. Even after the conquests that extend the frontier, the real struggle, with few exceptions, only begins when the sword is sheathed. The victories and defeats of the administrator and the political officer provide a less stirring narrative than those of warring armies, though the attempt of a Western nation to solve the problems of Eastern dominion by the standards of its own civilisation should be of the profoundest interest. There is henceforward far greater continuity in Indian history. The division into viceroyalties becomes less satisfactory as a principle of classification. We often find that the solution of any important question, though finally effected by one Governor-General, has been mooted, prepared, and developed by his several predecessors. The time is too recent for official secrets to be divulged, and it is not easy to apportion to each man his due meed of credit. Especially is this true of the more permanent officials, the pillars of the Supreme Government, who serve Viceroy after Viceroy, bear the heat and burden of the day, and leave the guerdon and the praise to others. Such men are sometimes called upon to administer a policy which in its earlier stages they have conscientiously opposed, and their lips are sealed in the face of criticism and obloquy. Finally, the treatment of the period must be subject to considerable reserve; for many of its problems are yet unsolved, and it deals largely with the work of living men. An atmosphere charged with the heat and dust of controversy still hangs over much of the field to be surveyed.

In 1868, the Earl of Mayo, who had thrice held the office of Chief Secretary for Ireland under Conservative Administrations, was appointed by Disraeli to succeed Sir John Lawrence. His name was received with a popular clamour of dissent, for which there was little justification; and, when Disraeli fell from office before the Governor-Generalship was technically vacant, Gladstone, the new Prime Minister, was loudly but vainly urged to cancel the appointment. On his arrival in India, the Viceroy found the most pressing question of foreign policy to be that of the north-west frontier. The annexation of the Punjab in 1849 had carried British dominion up to the base of the mountains of Afghanistan; but it would be a mistake to assume that the frontiers of the two countries met in a clear-cut and indisputable boundary line. From Baluchistan northwards to Chitral there was, and still is, a debatable zone of tribal territory lying along the spurs of the hills, and pierced by the passes that debouch into the plains of the Punjab. Till 1893, the fierce and warlike tribes which occupy this region nominally owned the suzerainty of the Amir of Afghanistan, though they were completely beyond his effective control. The western and northern frontiers of Afghanistan were equally indefinite; and many years were to pass before the loose and chaotic territories that form the Amir's dominions received, owing to the jealousy of two great European Powers, a well-defined but artificial boundary line.

It is a standing problem for Indian strategy to decide the best line of defence to be held in northern India in view of the rapid advance of Russia southwards from central Asia. A retirement to the Indus, the subjugation of the tribal zone, the partition of Afghanistan or its conquest as far as Herat and the Oxus—all these policies have had their advocates. But the course adopted, with some wavering in detail, has been to stop at the base of the mountains, leaving to the tribes a nominal independence limited by the presence of isolated British garrisons at strategical points, and to guarantee the inviolability of the buffer State of Afghanistan. The Afghan question, as Lord Mayo found it, was, to some extent, a legacy from his predecessor, and a few words must be said on Sir John Lawrence' treatment of it. Dost Mohammad, whom the issue of the lamentable First Afghan War had left upon the throne of Kabul, died in 1863. His death was followed by an inter-necine conflict between his sons. Sher Ali, the heir designate, held the throne for two years on a very precarious tenure, and was then driven from Kabul and Kandahar by his elder brother Afzal. Afzal died in 1867, and, as his eldest son Abdurrahman waived his claim to the succession, he was succeeded by another brother Azim. In 1868 Sher Ali, from his base at Herat, almost the only one of his ancestral territories left to him, began a victorious campaign which ended by placing him in possession of all the dominions of Dost Mohammad. These dominions he ruled with more or less success during the next decade. The interregnum had rendered the policy of the Indian Government exceedingly difficult. Lawrence was only anxious that Afghanistan should be strong and independent, and he was intensely opposed to interference in its internal affairs. Dost Mohammad had expressed a desire, in 1857, that after his death his sons might be left, in the time-honoured Afghan fashion, to fight out the question of sovereignty for themselves; and, as he had loyally refused to take advantage of British difficulties in the Mutiny, Lawrence felt bound to respect his wishes as far as possible. His policy was therefore to recognise the *de facto* ruler. For two years, however, it was by no means easy to decide which of the two claimants to the throne would make good his position, and British policy was driven into a rather unedifying and tortuous course. It was prepared to recognise one or all of the candidates for sovereignty, in so far as they were strong enough to establish themselves. In 1867, Lawrence actually held official relations with one claimant as Amir of Kabul, and with another as ruler of Herat. The Afghans contended, with some force, that this policy was a direct incentive to successful revolt. No Amir could be expected to set a high value on British support, which was likely to be transferred to his most formidable rival at the very time that he most required it.

The factor that complicated the question in later years—the approach of Russia to the frontiers of Afghanistan—only began towards the end of Sir John Lawrence' viceroyalty. After the occupation of Samarkand (1868), he pressed on the Home Government the desirability of agreeing with Russia upon a line of demarcation between the spheres of influence of the two countries, the crossing of which line should involve war with Great Britain in all parts of the world. Lawrence believed that, if such an understanding were arrived at, the Government of India would be freed from apprehension, and might welcome the civilising influence of Russia on the turbulent races of central Asia. The British Government had indeed no right to set a limit to Russian expansion other than the frontier of Afghanistan, for that expansion bore the closest possible resemblance to the advance of the English from the sea coast to the Himalayas; and, in fact, no overt objection to the Russian absorption of Khokand, Bokhara, and Khiva was ever made by England, though envoys from the doomed States appealed to her for assistance. Lawrence has been rather unfairly charged with neglect of the frontier problem. His inactivity was due to a reasoned conviction, and not to carelessness; and he succeeded on the whole in marking out the course which British policy was to follow under the guidance of his successors, till its reversal at the hands of Lord Lytton. So soon as Sher Ali had consolidated his power, Lawrence granted him a present of arms and money. Further than that he was not prepared to go. When he was asked to comment upon the famous Minute of Sir Henry Rawlinson in 1868, which suggested the occupation of Quetta, the formation of a close alliance with the Amir, and the grant of a subsidy, he clearly showed his dissent from what was soon to be known as the "Forward" policy. He declared, with the acquiescence of Henry Maine, Sir Richard Temple, and John Strachey—an authoritative consensus of opinion—that it would be impolitic to decrease any of the difficulties that Russia would naturally encounter in an invasion of India, by meeting her half-way in a difficult country and in the midst of a hostile and exasperated population. The true defences of British India against any possible invasion from without, or rebellion from within, lay in a rigid abstinence from entanglements in Afghanistan, a compact and efficient army holding the inner lines of communication, a careful husbandry of finance, and the acquiescence of the Indian peoples in the justice and advantages of British rule.

Sher Ali met Lord Mayo in conference at Amballa in March, 1869, and laid before him very definite proposals for a closer alliance. He asked for a new treaty, a fixed annual subsidy, assistance in arms and men whenever he required it, a full recognition and guarantee of the claims of himself and his dynasty to the throne of Kabul, and the acknowledgment as his heir of his favourite younger son Abdulla Jan. Such terms went far beyond the Lawrence policy, and neither the Home nor the Indian Government was prepared to accept them. The Viceroy was charged with the difficult task of refusing all the Amir's proposals without alienating his friendship. He accomplished what might almost seem an impossible feat, by his diplomatic handling of the Conference, fine courtesy, and great personal charm. Sher Ali, coming from his own barren and semi-barbarous country to the magnificent pageantry and military pomp of the Durbar, representing in its most effective form the power and resources of British India, showed an almost pathetic eagerness to win the approval and countenance of the Viceroy. Instead of his eagerly desired treaty, he took back with him only the written promise of Lord Mayo that the British Government would assist him with arms, ammunition, and money, at its own discretion, and would give him its strong moral support, whatever that somewhat intangible commodity might be worth. Yet he was apparently contented, and on his return to

Afghanistan made some earnest though occasionally misguided efforts to
carry out the reforms in his administration that Lord Mayo had pressed
upon him.

The proper complement of the Lawrence policy of non-interference
in Afghanistan was a clear and friendly understanding with Russia. The
result of negotiations between the two Governments in Europe and the
mission of Douglas Forsyth to St Petersburg in 1869 was a general
agreement that the Oxus should be the boundary of Sher Ali's dominions
to the northward, and that Russia should respect the integrity of his
country, so long as he renounced all intention of interfering in Bokhara.
In 1871, the Russians objected to Badakshan being included within the
Afghan frontier; but after two years they waived their claim and
accepted the British line. In detailed delimitation of the boundary
much remained to be done in subsequent years; but the understanding
with Russia on the main question was an important landmark in the
history of the central Asian problem. It might, however, with advantage
have been more definite. The constant and ever increasing correspondence of General Kaufmann, Governor of Russian Turkestan, with the
Amir was certainly not in accordance with Russia's pledge that Afghanistan should be considered to lie outside the sphere of her influence.
The despatches from Kaufmann were not welcomed by Sher Ali, who
disclosed his uneasiness to Lord Mayo. The Viceroy informed him that
they were merely complimentary, and deprecated his objections. Subsequent events were to prove that the Indian Government would have
been well advised if they had requested the Russian authorities to
communicate with the Amir only through British representatives.

The geniality and tact of Lord Mayo, which had been so happily
displayed in his negotiations with Sher Ali, performed an important
service in the dealings of the Indian Government with the feudatory
Princes. Since the Mutiny the relations of the Supreme Government
with the Native States had entered upon a new phase. The fact that
the thrones of Indian dynasties now rested ultimately on the faith of
treaties and the sanctity of a solemn pledge increased the moral
responsibility of Great Britain for any case of misgovernment, while
it tended also to limit her power of intervention and control. It was
unthinkable that the Indian Government, in its capacity of suzerain,
should keep silence in the face of gross tyranny or maladministration;
too punctilious a respect for a Prince's right might mean toleration of
his people's wrong; yet, now that the policy of lapse and annexation
was barred, the means by which these evils were to be encountered were
not too clearly indicated. The practical solution was only gradually
worked out in the course of the next thirty years, though Lord Mayo
outlined the attitude of his successors. Henceforward, it was the part of
the Viceroy to press personally upon the chiefs the need of righteous
government and the responsibilities of their high office, while carefully

avoiding any appearance of official dictation or of injudicious meddling in their internal affairs. In the event of grave abuses continuing after the resources of remonstrance and moral persuasion had been exhausted, it was recognised that the action of the paramount Power must be limited to the establishment of regency councils, temporary administration through a British Resident, or, in extreme cases, as in that of the Gaekwar of Baroda, in 1875, the deposition of a sovereign though not of his dynasty. Lord Mayo frankly, yet diplomatically, pointed out to the chiefs that, if England were not disinterested, she would be only too glad to see their peoples weak, poor, and disorderly; she deliberately preferred to take the honourable risk of fostering their growth into rich, strong, and well-ordered communities.

Internally the period of Lord Mayo's rule was notable for the advance made in all departments of social, economic, and administrative reform. The path of progress was resumed, which had been inaugurated by Lord Dalhousie but interrupted by the cataclysm of the Mutiny. The Department of Public Works, which was spending money lavishly and injudiciously, was drastically reformed. An attempt was made to set on foot a system of elementary education, and a determined advance was made with that policy of developing the material resources of the country by the construction of railways and canals which has been sedulously carried on down to the present time. But the most important reform was in the Department of Finance, where Lord Mayo was called upon to meet a very serious crisis. The last three years of his predecessor's rule had shown a deficit of nearly six millions sterling, and the prospects of his own first year of office were gloomy in the extreme. Much of the credit for the actual expedients adopted belongs to the Viceroy's able advisers, Sir Richard Temple, and the Strachey brothers (John and Richard); but Lord Mayo shared in their labours, gave them his ungrudging support, and strengthened their hands by his expressed determination, at whatever cost, to avoid another deficit. The temporary crisis was first averted by prompt and uncompromising measures. Reductions amounting to over a million were forced upon the great spending departments; the salt duties were increased in provinces where they had before been low; and the Viceroy risked his popularity by a sharp rise in the income tax. By these heroic expedients the estimated deficit for the first year of his Governor-Generalship was converted into a small surplus. It remained to provide for the future by means that strained the administrative machinery less severely. The Financial Department of the Government of India was reorganised and overhauled in the interests of economy, and the whole system of its control of the finances of the Provincial Governments was altered. Hitherto grants to the Provincial treasuries were made annually by the Governor-General in Council, and every penny was allocated to a special purpose. In the event of any money being saved, it was not to be retained by the local authorities, but returned to the Imperial treasury. It was therefore to the advantage of each Provincial Government (its legitimate needs being unlimited) to ask for as much as possible, and spend as much as it could get. By the new system a fixed yearly grant, subject to revision every five years, was made to each province, to be allocated and distributed within certain limits to its various needs without interference from the Viceroy and Council. The deficits of five and three-quarter millions for the years 1866–9 were converted into surpluses amounting to nearly six millions for the four following years; and the most satisfactory feature was that the change was brought about, for the most part, by economy, retrenchment, and reorganisation. The revenue to be raised was actually reduced from £51,600,000 in 1868–9 to £50,100,000 in 1871–2. There are few instances on record of a great financial crisis more successfully dealt with.

In 1872 Lord Mayo was assassinated by a Pathan fanatic when visiting the convict settlement in the Andaman Islands. His period of office had hardly lasted long enough for a final verdict to be pronounced; but in achievement and still more in promise it had signally falsified the ungenerous criticisms passed on his appointment, and had afforded another proof of Disraeli's well-known insight into character and his faculty of choosing men. Lord Napier of Merchistoun was hastily summoned from Madras as acting Governor-General till a successor could be sent out from England. The premier's choice fell upon Lord Northbrook, the head of the Baring family, a sound and cautious administrator of the Whig school, at that time holding office as Under-Secretary for War. His viceroyalty was on the whole singularly uneventful. Except for the year of famine, 1873–4, India enjoyed a period of financial prosperity. Her foreign trade was now beginning to feel the beneficial effects of the Suez Canal, which had been opened in 1869. Lord Northbrook was able to abolish the income tax in 1873, and to take an important step towards the adoption of Free Trade principles in India. From the year 1860 the rate of duty on all imports had been 10 per cent. *ad valorem* and 3 per cent. on most exports. The import rate had been reduced to $7\frac{1}{2}$ per cent. in 1864 and in 1875 it was lowered by Lord Northbrook to 5 per cent., while all export dues were swept away, except those on oil, rice, indigo, and lac. Orthodox economic opinion in England had as yet no doubts about the universal advantage of *laisser faire* in fiscal policy, and the Home Government pressed upon the Viceroy a much further advance in the Free Trade direction. But, though Lord Northbrook personally required no conversion on this point, he appears to have doubted whether he could afford to give up the revenue which these duties yielded to the exchequer. He was supported by official opinion in India, which is never wont to be swayed overmuch by *a priori* reasoning. The only other important feature of his internal policy was the attempt to deal with a famine by means which have since become part of the

CH. XVI.

routine machinery of Indian administration. A serious scarcity was threatened in Bengal and Behar in 1873–4. The Viceroy and Sir George Campbell, the Lieutenant-Governor of Bengal, determined that not a soul should perish of starvation, if they could help it. Immense purchases of rice were made in Burma; transport and distributive agencies were rapidly extemporised; and relief works were widely established. No considerations of economy were allowed to conflict with the Viceroy's purpose. As a result, the loss of life was practically *nil*; valuable lessons, both in what to aim at and what to avoid, were learnt for future occasions; and over six millions sterling were spent from the Indian exchequer.

Lord Northbrook's relations with the Amir of Afghanistan were less happy than those of his predecessor. Sher Ali's acquiescence in the policy pressed upon him by Lord Mayo was largely due to personal reasons, and the Viceroy's tragic death snapped the closest tie that bound him to the British Government. He had already been greatly dissatisfied with an award given by British commissioners in a dispute as to the province of Seistan between himself and the Shah of Persia. He showed a growing uneasiness at the rapid advance of the Russian line of conquest. One after another, the central Asian States were absorbed and incorporated in that vast empire. The Russian outposts were pushed ever nearer to the northern frontiers of his kingdom. The advance was probably far less deliberate than it appeared at the time either to Sher Ali or to observers in England. As Prince Gorchakóff pointed out in his able Minute of 1864, Russia, in approaching Afghanistan, was influenced by the same imperious law that had led the armies of Great Britain across the plains of Hindustan and the Punjab till they reached the mountains. She was urged irresistibly onward in spite of her oft-repeated protests, genuine enough at the time when they were uttered, that her chief desire was to know where to stop. But Sher Ali could hardly be expected to realise what only the coolest heads in England were capable of understanding. Nor, if he had done so, would it have added to his peace of mind to discover that the two greatest European Powers were being drawn by a magnetic attraction to a region of contact of which his own kingdom formed the centre. A conference held at Simla in 1873 between Lord Northbrook and an Afghan envoy did not, unfortunately, do much to mend matters. The Amir, whose alarm had been intensified by the Russian conquest of Khiva in June, pressed, as he had done before, for a closer alliance. But Lord Northbrook was not allowed by the Liberal Government, fearful of complications in Afghanistan, to do more than reiterate the vague assurances of support given by Lord Mayo. Sher Ali earnestly implored the Viceroy to give him a written promise that Russia would be considered as an enemy if she committed aggression on his frontier. It was only with the greatest difficulty that he could be made to understand that European diplomats could not categorically admit the possibility of "enmity" on the part of a friendly State. Though there were many weighty objections to any hard and fast alliance with a semi-barbarous Power whose political future was so doubtful as that of Afghanistan, it is probably to be regretted, in view of after events, that the opportunity was not seized of making the connexion with Sher Ali more binding. Then, if ever, was the time to do so at the spontaneous request of the Amir, who, seeing that he must enter into closer relations with one or other of his European neighbours, had deliberately given the preference to Great Britain. It was certain now, as it had not been in Sir John Lawrence' time, that Sher Ali was a strong and capable ruler. A treaty carefully drawn up and free from any burdensome conditions on either side might well have been regarded as a logical outcome of the Lawrence policy rather than as its reversal. But the moment was allowed to pass. In 1873 it was the Liberal Government that held back, rather against the weight of Indian opinion, just as two years later it was the Conservative Administration that put strong pressure in the other direction upon Lord Northbrook and his Council.

Sher Ali was bitterly disappointed. He soon afterwards proclaimed his younger son Abdulla Jan as his heir, and treacherously arrested and imprisoned the latter's eldest brother, Yakub Khan. He angrily resented the dignified rebuke administered by Lord Northbrook; but, though he seems henceforward to have listened with greater tolerance to the insidious promptings of Russian agents, he still showed no tendency to welcome the presence of Russian troops near his frontier. By care and diplomacy he might probably have been won back to his old friendly attitude; but, at this juncture, a change of Government in England prejudiced and precipitated the whole question. In 1874 Disraeli became Prime Minister, with Lord Salisbury as Secretary of State for India. They approached the Afghan problem from quite an opposite standpoint to that of their predecessors. They had conceived a lively dread of the power of Russia in Asia, and they suspected Sher Ali of equivocal dealings with her. That the existing state of things was not altogether satisfactory has been already indicated. As Lord Salisbury afterwards forcibly pointed out, the ill-defined dominions of the Amir were being "brought within a steadily narrowing circle, between the conflicting pressures of two great military empires, one of which expostulates and remains passive, while the other apologises and continues to move forward." The new Cabinet had been greatly impressed by a Minute from the able pen of Sir Bartle Frere, suggesting that, in view of the critical situation in Asia, it could no longer be regarded as satisfactory that the only representative of the British Government in Afghanistan should be a native Mohammadan agent. They therefore desired the Viceroy to press upon Sher Ali the admission of a British Resident into his country, to be stationed in the first instance at Herat and afterwards

at Kabul. Against this change of front on the part of the Imperial
Government, the Viceroy, supported by his whole Council, lodged a
weighty protest. He pointed out that the sudden reversal of policy
must necessarily bewilder and alarm the Amir. On two occasions, in
1869 and 1873, Sher Ali had himself earnestly prayed for a closer
alliance with Great Britain, and expressed lively apprehension of Russia's
designs. He had been assured again and again that his fears were
groundless. He was now suddenly to discover that the British Government, for no apparent reason that did not already exist in 1873, had
contracted a severe attack of Russophobia, and were thrusting upon him
the alliance they had hitherto refused to concede, saddled with the
one condition that he had consistently declined even to discuss. These
arguments made no impression on Lord Salisbury, who continued to
exert pressure upon the Viceroy. He suggested, in a much criticised
despatch, that the mission might avowedly be directed to objects of
lesser political interest which "might easily be found or if need be
created." Lord Northbrook was not the sort of man to carry out a
policy of *finesse* of this nature, and resigned his office, ostensibly for
personal reasons (1876).

Lord Northbrook was succeeded by the second Lord Lytton, the son
of an eminent man of letters and himself a man of literary distinction,
striking talents, and impulsive temperament, under whose guidance
India within three years drifted into the Second Afghan War. The
responsibility for this result, which at the time was popularly attributed
almost wholly to the Viceroy, must be shared by Disraeli, and was due to
his grandiose conception of foreign policy. The Viceroy, however, was
given a very free hand, and the actual shaping of the policy in detail
was left to him almost entirely. He was empowered to concede most of
the demands that Sher Ali had put forward in 1873, which, if granted
at the time, might have made the Amir the firm friend of the British
Government. Unfortunately, everything was made to depend on the
fatal condition that a British representative should be stationed at
Herat. A plausible pretext for a mission was found in the assumption
by the Queen of the title "Empress of India," which had been proclaimed
by Lord Lytton at a great Durbar on the Ridge of Delhi on January 1,
1877. To Lord Lytton's request that he would receive an envoy to lay
before him the full import of this ceremony, the Amir sent a polite
refusal on the ground that it was unnecessary. He further allowed it to
be known that, among other reasons, he feared his own inability to
protect an envoy from the fanaticism of his subjects, and that, if he
received a British ambassador he could not refuse to grant the same
privilege to the Russians. Lord Lytton considered this an act of grave
discourtesy, and warned Sher Ali that he was isolating himself from
British alliance and support. He failed however, on this point, to carry
with him three members of his Council. Sir William Muir, Sir Henry

Norman, and Sir Arthur Hobhouse, held that it was not dealing fairly with the Amir to lay stress on the temporary and complimentary character of a mission, the real intention of which was the establishment of a permanent embassy in Afghanistan; and they declared that, however advantageous it might be to Great Britain to have an agency in the country, the Amir was perfectly justified by the Treaties of 1855 and 1857 in declining to receive it. There is little doubt that the dissenting Councillors were in the right; but the Viceroy was impulsive and impatient. He was convinced that Sher Ali was actively intriguing with Russia, though the evidence on which he depended was far from conclusive. Ultimately, no doubt, Sher Ali did enter into relations with the emissaries of the Tsar; but for a long time his only idea was to maintain his territory unviolated by either of his European neighbours, and, down to a very late date (May, 1877), all letters from Russian officials were opened in the presence of the British native-born representative and communicated to the Viceroy. Sher Ali was, indeed, in Lord Lytton's picturesque phrase, an earthen pipkin between two iron pots. None realised that fact more clearly than he did himself, and his chief desire was by every means in his power, by every desperate expedient, to keep his European suitors with their embarrassing attentions at arm's length.

At the end of 1876, the British occupation of Quetta, by arrangement with the Khan of Kalat, naturally appeared to the Amir as the first step in a general British advance upon his frontier. Early in 1877, Lord Lytton once more pressed his demands in a prolonged conference at Peshawar between the Amir's envoy and Sir Lewis Pelly. The conference could have but one issue. Syad Nur Mohammad, the Afghan ambassador, was not to be dislodged from the position that to admit a British Resident into Afghanistan was impossible. Neither the Viceroy nor the Home Government seems to have grasped the sound reasons for this objection. For an Amir to lie open to even the shadow of a taunt of being the puppet of a foreign nation is fatal to his prestige. The Afghans are, and always have been, intensely jealous of outside domination in any form. The First Afghan War was a striking example of this trait in the national character; and, in after years, Abdurrahman, in spite of his real admiration and friendship for the British, would never admit for a moment the proposal of a resident envoy at his Court. Nor did the Viceroy in his impatience place himself in the position of Sher Ali, consider the limitations of his knowledge, or understand how difficult it was for him to be sure of the good faith of the British Government. It was a common report in the Indian bazaars at this time that the marriage of the Duke of Edinburgh with a Russian Princess implied a conspiracy between England and Russia for the partition of Afghanistan. An oriental ruler, standing in a position of such isolation as Sher Ali, and ignorant of the dynastic inter-

relations of European Courts, had no trustworthy means for testing such
a rumour. He only knew that he was face to face with a people who
might be as merciless as they were undoubtedly powerful, and whose
policy in the last resort, as he shrewdly suspected, would be determined
by their own interests.

The Viceroy's brilliant special pleading made no impression upon
Syad Nur Mohammad. In his attempt to prove that the Amir had given
an "anticipatory consent" to the admission of a Resident, and that
British obligations were limited to the Treaty of 1855 (the Treaty of
1857 being for a temporary purpose only and Lord Mayo's letter containing no binding pledge), Lord Lytton played a rather disingenuous
part, which caused the Amir to doubt the good faith of Great Britain
altogether. It is more than likely that from this point he definitely
turned to the Russian alliance. He had no love for either of the
great European Powers; but by Lord Lytton's precipitancy he was
driven to the conviction that, if he must enter into close relations with
one or other, it had better not be with the nation which had in the past
interfered by armed force in the affairs of his country.

In March, Syad Nur Mohammad, whose health throughout the conference had been in a precarious condition, died, maintaining his position
to the end with a certain quiet and pathetic dignity, and saddened by
the fatalistic conviction that his efforts were destined to be in vain.
Lord Lytton seized the occasion to declare the conference at an end,
though a successor to the dead envoy was already on his way from
Kabul, charged, so rumour ran, with instructions to concede the
British demands. All communications were now broken off with the
Afghan Court. In May, Lord Lytton justified his conduct of the
negotiations in a long and able despatch, which has been adversely
criticised as lacking the impartiality desirable in a great state paper.

Within a few months the Afghan problem, through the outbreak of
international complications in Europe, entered on a new and startling
phase. In 1876 the misgovernment of the Turk in Europe caused armed
insurrections in Servia and Montenegro. In the following year Russia
declared war upon Turkey, and in January, 1878, her armies crossed
the Balkans. Lord Beaconsfield, who believed that England could not
afford to permit the disintegration of Turkey, stood aloof from all
proposals to coerce the Porte, ordered the British fleet to pass the
Dardanelles, and brought some regiments of Indian troops to Malta.
The Russian Government, finding a quarrel forced upon them in Europe
by Great Britain, endeavoured as a diversion to stir up trouble on the
Indian frontier. The two countries were now on the brink of war;
but, partly through the mediation of Germany, a settlement was agreed
to at a conference of the Great Powers, and ratified by the Treaty
of Berlin. Unfortunately the pacification came too late to avert the
Afghan War. The electrical disturbance which had hovered over the

Western world round the storm centres of London and St Petersburg passed away eastwards, and exerted its destructive energy against an oriental ruler who could know little of the real causes of dispute. On June 13th, the day on which the Congress of Berlin held its first sitting, a Russian mission under General Stoletoff started from Tashkent for Kabul; and it had been for some weeks in the Afghan capital before the news of the Peace was known in Asia. Sher Ali had vainly endeavoured to stay Stoletoff's progress, using the same arguments that he had already employed against the British; but a hint was thrown out to him that, if he proved obdurate, the Russians could put forward a dangerous rival to his throne in the person of Abdurrahman, his nephew, who had long been their pensioner. The unfortunate Amir bowed to necessity, and there is some evidence to show that he now definitely signed a treaty with the Russian Government.

When the news of Stoletoff's reception by Sher Ali reached Lord Lytton, his worst fears of Russian aggression seemed to be realised. He promptly despatched a letter to the Amir, demanding that a like privilege should be accorded to Great Britain; and, without waiting for a reply, he announced his intention of sending Sir Neville Chamberlain as his representative. The death at this point of Abdulla Jan, the Amir's youngest son, which was reported to have almost unhinged his reason, delayed the setting out of the embassy. Meanwhile, ten days after Lord Lytton's letter, Stoletoff had left Kabul on the news being brought to him that the British intended to send a mission. No reply was received from Sher Ali to the Viceroy's despatch, and on September 21 an advance party of Sir Neville Chamberlain's mission under Major Cavagnari was challenged at Ali Masjid, a lonely frontier post, and prevented from entering the Khaibar pass. Though the Afghan officer showed great courtesy to the British commander, he made it quite clear that his instructions would oblige him to oppose the further progress of the mission by force. The situation was now very critical; but a more conciliatory statesman than Lord Lytton might not have considered the resources of diplomacy to be exhausted. It was clear that Russia was far more to blame than Afghanistan for the sending of the mission, and it was she, as Lord Lawrence contended, who ought to have been called to account. In view of the settlement at Berlin, Stoletoff's entry into Kabul might fairly be regarded as an unfriendly act, and pressure should have been exerted at St Petersburg for his recall. There is little doubt, in view of what subsequently happened, that the demand would have been complied with. Neither the Home Government nor Lord Lytton seems to have understood that Russia's action at this time was far less an attack on India than a counterstroke directed at British policy in Europe, which, whatever its justification, was certainly unfriendly to Russia. The mission having been withdrawn, it was obviously the right policy for the British Government, even if it had any doubts upon the

CH. XVI.

point, to assume in its dealings with the Amir that the departure of Stoletoff was welcomed by him, and to endeavour by all possible means to reestablish friendly relations with Afghanistan. Granted that there was no other way of preventing the installation of a Russian envoy in Afghanistan, the ethical question still remains whether the Indian Government had a right to force a representative of its own upon Sher Ali, who was nominally an independent Prince.

Lord Lytton eagerly seized upon the incident at Ali Masjid as affording him a plausible pretext for a war which he had long believed to be inevitable. He described the arrest of the mission with undoubted exaggeration as a forcible repulse, and clamoured for permission from the Home Government to launch across the frontiers the troops that were already massed at the entrance of the passes. But the Cabinet imposed upon him a few weeks' delay, and an ultimatum was despatched to the Amir requiring a definite acceptance of the British terms within a specified time. The belated reply that reached the Viceroy was considered unsatisfactory, and meantime war was declared on November 21, 1878. The mountain boundary of Afghanistan was pierced simultaneously by the advance of three columns. Sir Samuel Browne marched through the Khaibar to Jalalabad. Major-General Roberts entered by the Kuram valley, and drove the enemy from the heights that command the Peiwar pass. General Stewart marched from Quetta upon Kandahar. There was little organised opposition, and the military occupation of the country between Kabul and Kandahar was speedily carried out. In December, Sher Ali fled northwards to Afghan Turkestan, leaving his son Yakub Khan to make what terms he could with the invaders. Russian support proved a broken reed in the hour of trial. General Kaufmann cynically bade the Amir make peace with the British if they gave him the chance, and plainly told him that Russia would neither send troops nor further his expressed intention of going to St Petersburg to appeal to the Tsar in person. All that Russia appears to have done is to have extracted a pledge from the British Government in London that the integrity of Afghanistan should be respected. Sher Ali, worn out with anxiety and disease, died at Mazar-i-Sharif in February. The earthen pipkin was crushed at last. It is impossible to withhold a certain measure of sympathy from the deluded Amir, or to resist the conviction that the tragic sequel might have been avoided by more considerate and less precipitate statesmanship on the part of the Viceroy.

The Cabinet now determined to recognise Yakub Khan, Sher Ali's eldest son, though the Viceroy's personal opinion was in favour of proceeding to the disintegration of Afghanistan. The new ruler was compelled by the Treaty of Gandamak, in May, 1879, to surrender all the points in defence of which his father had forfeited his crown. He agreed to conduct his relations with foreign States according to the advice of the British Government, to permit a British officer to reside at Kabul, and to surrender to British control the districts of Kuram, Pishin, and Sibi with the guardianship of the Khaibar and Michni passes. In return for these concessions the Amir was to be supported with arms, money, and troops against any foreign aggression, and to receive an annual subsidy of six lakhs of rupees.

The Treaty of Gandamak was the high-water mark of the Disraeli-Lytton policy, and all the objects for which the War had been entered upon seemed secured. But the fair prospect was only too soon to be overclouded. Once more, England had to learn by bitter experience that it was impossible to govern the turbulent Afghan nation through an Amir supported by foreign bayonets. In July, 1879, Sir Louis Cavagnari took up his residence at Kabul. On September 6, only a few days after the envoy's last laconic message, "All well," had been telegraphed to the Viceroy, the terrible news came over the wires that he and all his suite had been massacred three days before by the disorderly Afghan army, which had risen in revolt. Yakub Khan's precise degree of innocence or guilt was never ascertained; but he seems at any rate to have made no serious attempt to protect the embassy. The murder of Cavagnari was a staggering blow to Lord Lytton, for it shattered his hopes at the moment of their realisation; but he set himself doggedly to recover lost ground. Retribution was not long in falling upon Afghanistan. Stewart reoccupied Kandahar; Roberts once more traversed the Kuram valley and moved on Kabul. He defeated the rebels at Charasia and entered the city. A stern vengeance was meted out to all those whose complicity in the murder could be proved. Yakub Khan surrendered himself as a suppliant, abdicated the throne, and, after an inconclusive enquiry into his conduct had been held, was deported as a state prisoner to India.

The difficulties of the army of occupation were, however, but beginning. In the winter there were many serious risings round Kabul, and it was only by hard fighting that Sir Frederick Roberts kept his communications with India open. In the spring of 1880 Sir Donald Stewart, by his victory at Ahmad Khel, cleared the road between Kandahar and Kabul, and joined Roberts at the latter place. In the meantime, the Indian Government was anxiously seeking for a way out of the *impasse* in which it found itself. It was in effective occupation of only a small part of Afghanistan. To subdue and hold down the whole country with the forces at its disposal was utterly beyond its power. To withdraw, without establishing some form of government, was to abandon Afghanistan to anarchy. The solution came from an unexpected and not altogether friendly quarter. Abdurrahman Khan, the nephew of Sher Ali, had been living since 1868 in exile beyond the Oxus under Russian protection. He now appeared in northern Afghanistan, with the connivance of his patrons, who probably believed that his presence there would be an embarrassment to the British. The

Indian Government, having reviewed and reluctantly rejected the claims of all other candidates, determined to offer the throne to Abdurrahman. The decision was a singularly bold one; but Lord Lytton seems to have correctly gauged the character of the future Amir, and his famous leap in the dark was thoroughly justified by success. But, before his decision could be formally ratified, he had ceased to be Viceroy. In April, 1880, Gladstone succeeded Lord Beaconsfield as Prime Minister, with the Marquis of Hartington as Secretary of State for India. They had been returned to power largely on an outspoken and sweeping condemnation of the foreign policy of the Conservative Government. Of that policy the Afghan War formed an important part, receiving a special measure of unfavourable criticism. It would have been impossible for Lord Lytton to serve under men who had opposed his policy for the last four years; and when he heard of the fall of Lord Beaconsfield's Government he tendered his resignation.

Internally, his viceroyalty had been marked by the occurrence of a famine which in extent and severity was hitherto unparalleled. It lasted for two years (1876–8), affected the whole of southern, with part of western and central India, and left behind it a deadly sequel of fever and cholera. Such a calamity could not be averted, as Lord Northbrook had averted the Behar scarcity in 1874. The desire to save life had to be tempered with a stern resolution to practise the severest economy. Sir John Strachey and Sir Richard Temple rigorously administered the finances on these principles. About eight millions sterling were spent by the Indian Government; but even so, over five million persons perished from starvation or disease, while the economic loss to the country from remissions of land revenue and land going out of cultivation cannot be exactly estimated. Two all-important results were the establishment of a special famine insurance fund, for the maintenance of which new revenue amounting to a million and a half was thenceforth to be raised, and the appointment of a Commission, under the presidency of General Richard Strachey, which carefully collected and compared the experience of the past, and laid down regulations, afterwards embodied in the Famine Code of 1883.

One of the most widely criticised acts of Lord Lytton's viceroyalty was the passing of the Vernacular Press Acts (1878), which placed the censorship of the native Press in the hands of the Executive. Opponents of the policy, including three dissenting members of Council, contended that repressive legislation was not required, and that it was invidious to make a distinction between English and vernacular newspapers. In view of the fact that the Acts were safely repealed by his successor, these criticisms may be considered justified; but the problem was a difficult one. *A priori* maxims as to the danger of driving the evil of sedition underground, or the peril of sitting on the safety valve, hardly apply without qualification in an oriental State, where the ordinary criteria of sound judgment are not valid. The real charge against Lord Lytton is, not that he inaugurated a deliberate attack upon the freedom of the Press, but that he committed an error of judgment as to the time at which the State should step in and exercise its controlling power.

In the sphere of finance, Lord Lytton gave a loyal support to the great reforms of Sir John Strachey, whom he persuaded to leave his Lieutenant-Governorship of the North-West Provinces for the thankless post of Financial Minister (1876). Chief amongst these were the equalisation of the salt tax throughout India and the consequent abolition of the famous customs line formed of cactus hedge, wall, and ditch, which stretched across the peninsula for 2500 miles and was guarded by an army of revenue officials. Another great stride was made in the direction of establishing Free Trade in India. The Lancashire cotton manufacturers were loudly clamouring for the abolition of the import duties levied at Indian ports on the produce of their looms. The House of Commons, by a resolution passed unanimously, called upon the Indian Government to sweep away the imposts as soon as the finances could bear the strain, and Lord Salisbury pressed the reform upon the Viceroy. The pressure was unnecessary, for Lord Lytton was at one with his Finance Minister in eagerly desiring the change—not, as he was careful to state, to secure the political support of the powerful Lancashire interest, but because he was convinced that Free Trade would ultimately prove the best policy for India itself. In spite of the fact that the Afghan War and the famine subjected his financial policy to a severe test, Lord Lytton abolished duties on twenty-nine articles in the tariff in 1878, and in the following year did away with those levied on the coarser kinds of cotton cloth. In carrying this reform, he showed that he had the courage of his convictions and was not afraid to risk the imputation of unworthy motives. Throughout, he supported Sir John Strachey against the majority of his constitutional advisers, this being the only instance in recent times of a Governor-General exercising his legal right to override the expressed opinion of the majority on his Council. Lord Lytton's avowed desire was to make India a great free port open to the commerce of the whole world. The pressure of special circumstances prevented him from fully realising his ideal, but he definitely committed the Indian Government to the course which was ultimately completed by his immediate successor. In 1880, Sir John Strachey, who had occupied almost every important post from that of Acting Viceroy downwards, left India and afterwards served a long period on the Council of the Secretary of State (1885–95). Through the faulty system on which the accounts of the Military Department were kept, a serious error had been made in estimating the cost of the Afghan War. This was the only blot upon his extraordinarily successful administration; and it is noteworthy that that part of the war charges (fifteen millions) which fell upon the Indian Exchequer was paid for out of revenue—a striking proof of his financial skill.

CH. XVI.

Few Viceroys have been submitted to fiercer criticism than Lord Lytton. This was partly due to the fact that his Afghan policy—the domain in which he was least successful—almost monopolised public attention because of the space it occupied in the party conflicts of the day. Even here, though the verdict of history has on the whole gone against him, time has greatly modified the severity of contemporary judgments. He took long views, but pressed them too impetuously on his subordinates. He was apt to be impatient of opinions that clashed with his own, and there was a precipitancy about many of his actions which conflicted with true statesmanship. Of an unconventional cast of mind, he was not always punctilious enough in regard to those trifles which are no longer trifles for a man in his high position; and the literary faculty, which he found it so hard to curb, of employing the most striking and picturesque phrase to express his meaning, was sometimes misunderstood by men accustomed to the studiously neutral style of Indian official papers. His internal policy had many merits, and in some respects he was in advance of his age. He was in favour of introducing a gold standard into the coinage of India, and, if the change had come when the value of the rupee stood at about one and ninepence, the saving to the revenues would have been very great. He advocated that formation of a North-West Frontier Province distinct from the Punjab, which was only carried out thirty years later; and he put forward a bold and striking, though possibly premature, scheme for the creation of a native Indian Peerage and the summoning of a great Indian Privy Council of feudatory chiefs. Sharing the imaginative political conceptions of his friend and leader Disraeli, he did not underrate, as the men of his generation were apt to do, the effect of pageantry, sentiment, and symbolism on Eastern minds. The Royal Titles Act, which conferred the designation of Empress of India upon the Queen, excited open disapprobation and even ridicule in England. The criticism was founded in part on high constitutional grounds. The leaders of the Liberal party disliked the distinction between England and India implied in the new designation for the Crown, which seemed to them to indicate that, while sovereignty at home was based upon the supremacy of law, in India it depended upon the power of the sword. In their view the Act was dangerously like an admission that Great Britain was faltering in her expressed intention of gradually extending to India the benefits of free institutions. Criticism in India was far less vocal; but the attitude of the Civil Service, honourably distinguished by its care for realities and disregard for show, was hardly sympathetic. At the great Durbar on the Ridge of Delhi the majority of its members who were present stood by acquiescent but not enthusiastic. Many were converted when they noted the effect of the gorgeous ceremonial on the assembled feudatory chiefs, some of whom gained on that day for the first time a clear conception of the majesty of the empire in which they occupied a high and honourable place.

In 1880, Lord Ripon, who had in former years been Secretary of State for India, was appointed Viceroy to succeed Lord Lytton. He went out with instructions to effect a peaceable settlement with Afghanistan. The Liberal Cabinet was firmly resolved to return as far as possible to the state of things which existed before 1876. Lord Hartington pointed out with some force that the only result of two successful campaigns and lavish expenditure had been the disintegration of the State which the British Government desired to see strong, friendly, and independent, the incurring of new and unwelcome liabilities in regard to one of its provinces, and a condition of anarchy throughout the rest of the country. In July, Abdurrahman was formally acknowledged as Amir, with the understanding that he was to have no foreign relations with any Power except Great Britain. He was to be defended from outside aggression so long as he observed this condition, but he was not required to admit a British Resident into his country. It was not however originally intended that he should succeed to all the dominions of Sher Ali. Kandahar was to be separated from Kabul and to be ruled by an independent Prince, while Herat remained for the time in the power of Ayub Khan, a son of the late Amir. The British forces were preparing to evacuate the country, when the news came that Ayub Khan had marched upon Kandahar and almost annihilated a British brigade at Maiwand. Roberts, who was at once despatched from Kabul by Stewart with a force of 10,000 men, accomplished his famous march of 313 miles in twenty days, and defeated Ayub Khan at the battle of Kandahar. The episode was not allowed to interfere with the evacuation of the country, and the British forces were withdrawn through the Bolan and the Khaibar passes. The independent ruler that had been set up in Kandahar proved a failure, and his opportune resignation was accepted. Kandahar was evacuated in 1881 and handed back to Abdurrahman, in spite of the protests of a party in England which wished this important strategic post to be retained permanently in British hands. The sacrifice proved well worth making. Nothing bound the Amir so closely to the British alliance as the cession of a place he had always ardently coveted. For a time, however, it looked as though Kandahar were destined to fall into other hands. Ayub Khan, marching from Herat, seized and held the city for a few months; but he was finally defeated by Abdurrahman, who thus regained both Kandahar and Herat. In 1883, his subsidy was increased to twelve lakhs. The dominions of Dost Mohammad were now consolidated under a very capable and independent Amir with a firm conviction of his own divine right to rule. There was very little altruism in his attitude to the English, and he was not disinclined on occasion to cause them trouble on the frontier; but he clearly understood that, while it was Russia's interest to dismember his country, it was Great Britain's to keep it intact. Thus, though he was determined to debar all Europeans from

CH. XVI.

entering his territories, he was content to put himself under the protection of the British Government, accept its aid in money and arms, and fulfil his part as an outpost in defence of the northern frontier of India.

The Afghan question thus happily settled, no other serious foreign problem occurred during the viceroyalty of Lord Ripon. The country enjoyed a time of peace and prosperity. The financial reforms of Sir John Strachey bore their full fruit in years of rising revenue and surplus budgets. Under these favourable circumstances the Free Trade policy inaugurated by Lord Northbrook and Lord Lytton was carried to its natural completion. In 1882, the remaining duties on cotton goods and the general five per cent. tariff on imports were abolished—reforms which resulted in remissions to the Indian taxpayer amounting to two and a half millions sterling. In this prosperous interval between the Afghan War and the era of difficulties due to famine, plague, a falling exchange, and increased military expenditure, a great impetus was given to political and social reform. Lord Ripon, a life-long Liberal, had a robust faith in the efficacy of Western political ideals and theories as applied to orientals. Down to the time of his rule immense material benefits had been procured for the Indian races by a disinterested bureaucracy, which preferred to work for the people rather than through the people. In the minds of those natives who responded most promptly to the influences of British rule there was gradually growing up a natural and healthy desire for an active share in the work of government, and even for a part in the social life of men who had taught them to believe that, in theory at any rate, there was no such thing as inequality of race. To these aspirations Lord Ripon showed himself peculiarly sympathetic, and he probably believed that some sacrifice of efficiency was worth incurring in order to train the subject races in the rudiments of self-government and self-control. Every reform affecting the moral or intellectual well-being of the people received his hearty support. An elaborate enquiry was held into the state of education throughout India, and measures were taken for the improvement of primary and secondary instruction, which had hitherto received a very small share of state support in comparison with that lavished upon the colleges. Lord Lytton's Vernacular Press Acts were repealed, and all restrictions were thus removed from the free expression of opinion on political and social topics. Increased powers of self-government were made over to local boards and municipalities, and the elective principle received considerable extension. Subsequent experience was to show that the instinct for the working of such institutions is of very slow growth; but, though as yet bodies of this nature have to be carefully supervised and controlled by British officers, the experiment has proved well worth making. To Lord Ripon fell the duty, in 1881, of handing over to the Hindu dynasty of Mysore the government of its dominions, which for the past fifty years had been administered by the British.

The native approval of Lord Ripon flared up into widespread enthusiasm when his championship of their cause seriously embroiled him with the European population. In 1883 there was stirred up one of those delicate and dangerous questions underlying the surface of Anglo-Indian society which it is much more convenient to ignore than to face. Many natives of ability and education had risen to high positions on the judicial bench, and it was proposed, in a Bill framed by Mr (now Sir) Courtenay Peregrine Ilbert, to confer upon them criminal jurisdiction over European British subjects. Hitherto it had been a recognised rule, that, save in the Presidency towns, no European could be tried except by a European magistrate or judge. A fierce agitation was at once set up against the measure by the European residents in India. Feeling on both sides became lamentably embittered, and the Bill was only passed in 1884 by a compromise which permitted Europeans to be cited before magistrates of native birth who had attained the standing of district magistrate or sessions judge, with the proviso that the accused might claim to be tried before a jury half of whom were to be of European or American birth. On the resignation of the Viceroy in 1884, remarkable manifestations of regret were evoked from all classes of the native population, and the route of his journey from Calcutta to Bombay was attended by enthusiastic crowds.

Lord Ripon was succeeded by the Earl of Dufferin, a statesman and diplomatist whose full and varied career afforded the finest possible training for his new post. As a former Under-Secretary of State for India and British Commissioner in Egypt he had an expert knowledge of Eastern questions, and as ambassador at St Petersburg and Constantinople he had studied at first hand the foreign policies of England's most formidable rival in Asia and of the great European Mohammadan Power. His diplomatic skill and personal charm were destined to allay the embittered feelings of the European population, which had been aroused by his predecessor's eagerness for reform.

The field of Lord Dufferin's activity in foreign politics lay mainly in the north-west and south-east. The occupation of Merv by Russian troops in 1884 once more raised the question of the demarcation of a boundary between Afghanistan and Russian territory in Asia. The first meeting of British and Russian Commissioners charged with this task took place at Sarakhs in October, a month before Lord Dufferin's arrival in India, the portion of the frontier line to be demarcated being that between the Hari Rud and the Oxus. The Russians unscrupulously occupied much of the territory in dispute, and the Afghans, with the natural wish to forestall them, kept pushing their outposts forward. The British Commissioners were thus left in an embarrassing position, being hampered by the fact that the Home Government had not accurately defined the extent of the claims which they regarded as essential. Another source of difficulty was that, the Commissioners being subordinate to the British and Russian Foreign Offices, the Indian Government had no direct control over the proceedings. The Russians had warned off the troops of the Amir from Penjdeh, which they definitely claimed for themselves. The Afghans, however, occupied the place; and, in March, 1885, they were attacked and driven out by Russian troops. This high-handed action made the situation extremely critical. The popular voice in England clamoured for war, which was only with great difficulty averted by the statesmanlike forethought and restraint of Abdurrahman and the skilful diplomacy of Lord Dufferin. Fortunately, when the incident occurred, the Amir was actually on a visit to the Viceroy at Rawal Pindi. Abdurrahman was never anxious to extend his dominion in the turbulent region of the north-west; he was honourably desirous of conferring a service on his protectors, and quite determined to avoid at all costs, what he knew would be an unmitigated calamity for Afghanistan, the outbreak of war between his powerful European neighbours. He professed his readiness to abandon all claims to Penjdeh if he were allowed to hold Zulfikar. To this peaceful solution of the difficulty Lord Dufferin bent all his energies, declaring that a war between England and Russia would be a combat between a whale and an elephant. He realised, with broad-minded tolerance, that the advance of Russia to the borders of Afghanistan had, in great measure, been imposed upon her by an irresistible law, and he believed that, if the present position were accepted, and her future progress limited with her own consent, the general interests of humanity and civilisation would be benefited. This happy consummation was reached by the labours of the Afghan Boundary Commission in 1885–6, supplemented by an agreement signed at St Petersburg in 1887. The demarcation of the frontier from the Hari Rud to the Oxus fixed the main line barring the advance of Russia in the direction of British India, and thus settled an important question in the world policy of Asia. The war panic, however, did not pass without leaving a permanent mark on India. The hurried preparations burdened the Exchequer with a sum of two millions, and one of the results was an increase in the permanent strength of the army, both native and European. From the spontaneous offers of assistance made by the feudatory chiefs in 1885, sprang the institution of the Imperial Service troops maintained by native States for the defence of the whole empire. The conference of Abdurrahman with the Viceroy at Rawal Pindi was in all respects satisfactory. Lord Dufferin won the confidence of the Amir as completely as Lord Mayo had gained the goodwill of his predecessor. He understood, what Lord Lytton with all his ability had failed to perceive, that by the necessities of his position the Amir of Afghanistan could not make certain concessions which seemed altogether advantageous to the Indian Government. Strong and able as Abdurrahman's administration was, it was also to Western eyes barbarous and cruel. The Amir himself cherished no illusions as to the very limited advance in the direction of civilisation made by his subjects, and he was determined at all hazards to exclude from his country the interference of the British official with his coldly observant eyes. Lord Dufferin tentatively proposed to send British officers to organise the defences of Herat; but, when he saw that the Amir instantly took alarm, he wisely refrained from pressing the point upon him.

On the eastern frontier of India Lord Dufferin completed the conquest of Burma. The First and Second Burmese Wars had shorn that country of its maritime provinces, Arakan, Pegu, and Tenasserim. The Third was to reduce the whole of it to subjection. Relations with the independent Burmese Government had for some time been very difficult to maintain upon a friendly footing; but they grew rapidly worse after the accession in 1878 of King Thibaw, an oriental despot of the most savage type. In 1879 the British Agent had been withdrawn from Mandalay. In 1885 the Indian Government ascertained that the King was preparing to enter into relations with the French administrators of Indo-China, while at the same time he threatened to impose a heavy fine upon a great British commercial company. An ultimatum was promptly despatched to the Court at Ava, demanding the reception of an envoy at Mandalay, a permanent Resident at Court, and an immediate answer to both demands. As the reply was unsatisfactory, General Prendergast invaded the country by a flotilla of boats up the broad stream of the Irrawaddy. So rapidly was the blow directed that Thibaw was taken completely by surprise, and surrendered unconditionally when the British expedition approached his capital. Within a fortnight from the beginning of the advance, the country was nominally subdued. Thibaw was deported to India, and the country was annexed by proclamation on January 1, 1886. The difficulties of the occupation were, however, as great as the conquest had been easy. The disbanded soldiers of the Burmese army took cover in the jungles, and for two years maintained a desperate guerrilla warfare by murder, rapine, and dacoity. Further reinforcements were drafted into the country; and in spite of climatic and local difficulties of every kind British sovereignty was made effective.

The Burmese henceforward enjoyed the benefits of humane and civilised government; but it must be admitted that Lord Dufferin's action was sufficiently high-handed. It would be hypocritical to pretend that mere misrule on Thibaw's part would have brought upon him so crushing a doom. As in the case of Sher Ali, the near approach of another European Power proved his undoing. The real reason for the war was the desire to forestall the designs of the French, who had theoretically a better right than the British to extend their influence over Burma, for they came by the express invitation of the King. England, however, for good or ill, considered that she could not afford to see the country absorbed by any Power except herself.

In the domain of social reform, Lord Dufferin carried through, in

1885, the great agrarian measure known as the Bengal Tenancy Act, which his predecessor had initiated. It aimed at ameliorating the lot of the peasantry, who through their ignorance and poverty were often at the mercy of the landlords. The Government stepped in to check the free play of economic competition, where it pressed too hardly upon a submerged proletariate. The Bill gave the ryots a certain fixity of tenure, defined the limits under which rights of occupancy could be acquired, checked and limited the practice of indiscriminate eviction, and generally provided for the interests of the cultivators of the soil. Later Acts followed on the same lines relating to Oudh and the Punjab. An important reorganisation of the Civil Service followed upon the recommendations of a Commission presided over by Sir Charles Aitchison, which sat in 1886–7 to enquire into the possibility of giving natives a larger share in the administration of the country, and so carrying out the promise made in the Charter Act of 1833 that no man should be disqualified by reason of his religion, place of birth, descent, or colour from holding office under the Company—a promise that had been definitely reaffirmed in 1858 on the part of the Crown. From 1855, vacancies in the Covenanted Civil Service were filled by open competition after examination held in London. The necessity of crossing the sea practically guaranteed that only a small proportion of successful candidates would be natives of India. In 1870, an Act of Parliament empowered the Governor-General in Council with the approval of the Secretary of State to draw up special rules for the admission into the Covenanted Civil Service of men of native race, without the need of their passing the examination held in London. Anglo-Indian opinion was strongly against the reform, and by the mere dead weight of inertia effective action was postponed till Lord Lytton's time. In 1879, however, rules were at last framed and the Statutory Civil Service was founded, members of which were to be natives of India appointed by the local Governments. One-sixth of the posts ordinarily filled by Indian civilians selected in England were ultimately to be set apart for them. The Statutory Civil Service proved a failure, and it was discontinued on the recommendation of Lord Dufferin's Commission. Henceforward, the Civil Service was divided into three branches, the Imperial Indian Civil Service, recruited in England, but open to Indians who cared to make the journey and were successful in the competition, the Provincial, and the Subordinate Civil Services, both of which were recruited in India and filled almost entirely by men of native origin. To the Provincial Civil Service were now assigned many of the administrative and judicial posts hitherto held by members of the Covenanted Civil Service.

Though he did not actually carry them out, Lord Dufferin prepared the way for important reforms in the constitution and procedure of the Legislative Council of the Governor-General, as established by the Indian

Councils Act of 1861. He recognised that the more moderate demands of the Indian National Congress, which first met in 1886, were based upon political aspirations that were to some extent natural and proper. His policy was to grant speedily and with a good grace whatever could be safely conceded, to declare plainly that such a settlement must be regarded as final for a number of years, and to repress any incendiary agitation, in the direction of which native political activity normally tends to run. He declared that he would personally feel it both a relief and an assistance if he could rely more upon the experience of Indian advisers in the consideration of questions that came before the Council. He proposed, therefore, to increase the number of additional members, who, added to the Executive Council, transform it into a legislative body. The new members were, so far as possible, to represent various native classes and interests. His proposals, though modified to some extent by the Home Government, were embodied in Lord Cross' Indian Councils Act of 1892, which became operative in the viceroyalty of Lord Lansdowne. The additional members were to be at least ten, and at most sixteen, in number, and not more than six of them were to hold official positions; five were to be appointed on the recommendation of the non-official members of four Provincial legislatures and the Calcutta Chamber of Commerce. The Provincial legislatures were themselves enlarged by additional members, who were to be nominated by various municipalities, University Boards, and commercial associations. The representative, though not the elective, principle was in fact tentatively introduced. The Legislative Council had hitherto been allowed no opportunity of criticising the financial policy of the Government, except when it was found necessary to impose new taxation. The budget was now to be laid annually before the Council, every member of which, speaking in turn, had the right to express his views upon it. Subject to much the same safeguards as have been found necessary in the House of Commons, the right of interpellation was also granted, both as a concession to native demands and as affording the executive an opportunity of defending its measures. These concessions did not satisfy the extreme party of Indian reform; but they were of no mean significance. Men of native birth, seated side by side with the highest executive officers, were henceforward able to make their opinions known at the Viceroy's council-table. They were listened to with deference, and, though their opinions might not prevail, it was at least incumbent upon the Governor-General and his Ministers to reply to their criticisms and endeavour to win their approval. The Government thus openly acknowledged that it not only desired, as it had always done, the moral and material welfare of the millions committed to its charge, but also held it of the greatest importance to work towards the realisation of that high aim, so far as possible, with the approval, and even through the agency, of the ruled.

In December, 1888, Lord Dufferin handed over his office to the

Marquis of Lansdowne. New problems and new dangers were arising in India. The era of comparative prosperity which dated from Lord Mayo's time, and had proved buoyant enough to withstand the strain of war and famine under Lord Lytton, was now definitely approaching its end. A cloud of troubles, due to falling exchange, bad harvests, and frontier wars, was looming up to burst over the country in the next decade.

Abdurrahman had remained consistently faithful to Great Britain. His loyalty was never really in doubt; but his cordiality towards different Viceroys varied with their personal characters and the policies they were called upon to follow. Lord Lansdowne could hardly be expected to win the intimate place which his predecessor had held in the Amir's regard; but the main reason for a certain estrangement that now sprang up between Abdurrahman and the Indian Government was to be attributed to a gradual change in British frontier policy. The belt of tribal territory left between the British boundary line and Afghanistan was necessarily a constant source of trouble. The Indian Government was held account-able for any depredations the tribesmen might commit against the Amir's country, but was alike unable to foresee and to prevent them. On the other hand, it was easy for Abdurrahman, remaining himself in the background, to foment disturbances among the tribes, if he wished, for any reason, to put pressure upon his ally. A school of Indian adminis-trators arose which advocated the substitution of a real for a nominal control over these semi-independent clans, the rectification of the Afghan-British frontier, the extension of strategic railways, and the gradual reduction of all the turbulent districts to order. The chief arguments against this policy were the great cost, the wide extent of country to be controlled, and, above all, the risk of offending the Amir, whose continued loyalty claimed from Great Britain every concession that was compatible with her own security. For ten years after 1885, the Indian Government made some cautious steps in the direction of what is known as the Forward policy. The movement stopped far short of the schemes of Lord Lytton and never contemplated a rupture with Afghanistan; but it was sufficiently marked, especially when Sir Frederick Roberts was Commander-in-Chief (1885–93), to cause uneasiness to Abdurrahman, who viewed the gradual approach to his frontiers with great jealousy, and strongly preferred that the tribes owning his religious headship should be left independent. In 1888 a mission under Mr (now Sir) Mortimer Durand was on the point of starting for Afghanistan to explain and justify British policy, but was postponed in consequence of the rebellion of Ishak Khan, who rose against the Amir in Afghan Turkestan. Things drifted from bad to worse. Abdurrahman had causes of complaint against the Russians for acts of aggression in the Pamirs, the only region where the Afghan-Russian frontier had not been demarcated, and he looked with increasing suspicion and dislike upon the British railway lines creeping nearer and nearer to Kandahar. In 1890 the tension was extreme and Lord Lansdowne declared that, up to the eve of his departure, all the conditions of the frontier problem were calculated to lead to a rupture with Afghanistan. In 1892 it was proposed to send a mission under Lord Roberts to confer with the Amir. Considering that Lord Roberts was a devoted adherent of the Forward policy, and had played the principal part in the Second Afghan War, the choice of an envoy was not particularly tactful. But the Amir proved equal to the occasion, and managed to delay the mission on plausible pretexts till Lord Roberts had left India. Sir Mortimer Durand took his place, and met the Amir at Kabul in 1893. The results were thoroughly satisfactory. It was decided that the Afghan boundary line both on the Indian frontier and in the Pamirs should be settled as soon as possible. The Amir's annual subsidy was raised from eighty thousand to a hundred and twenty thousand pounds, and further supplies of arms and ammunition were promised him. From that date till his death in 1901, the cordiality of his relations with the British Government remained unimpaired.

During Lord Lansdowne's period of office a serious monetary problem which had long been impending came to a head. The decline in the value of silver throughout the world was a disturbing economic feature of the latter part of the century which no human foresight could have met or warded off. It was due partly to increased production through the opening of new mines, partly to the demonetisation of silver by Germany and the renunciation of bimetallism by the States of the Latin Union. The silver coins throughout the greater part of Europe thus became token money only, but the effects on India were far more momentous. Before 1873 the value of the rupee had approximated closely to two shillings. From that date it began to fall. The decline became accelerated after 1885 and in 1890 the rupee was worth only one shilling and fourpence. In 1890–1 there was a temporary rise due to special legislation in America; but after 1892 the value of the rupee was again on the downward grade. India was affected in most of her dealings with the outside world, and especially with England. Since the two countries had not the same standard of value, the loss fell altogether upon India, the silver-using country; for her liabilities in London, including the interest on her public debt, payments for public works, pensions, and the upkeep of the India Office, had to be discharged in gold. Year by year, as the fall continued, she was called upon to pay a greater number of rupees for each pound sterling. Further, with the annexation of new territory and the increased expenditure on railways and public works, the amount to be remitted home constantly tended to increase. Larger and larger quantities of gold had to be purchased with depreciated and rapidly depreciating silver. In 1892, when the value of the rupee had by no means touched bottom, it was estimated that nearly six million pounds more revenue had to be raised by taxation from the Indian peoples than would have been necessary if the rupee had retained the value it bore in 1873.

Other economic evils naturally followed. It was impossible for the Finance Minister to make accurate estimates for even a few months ahead. A further temporary rise or fall of a halfpenny in the value of the rupee confounded the most painstaking and careful forecasts. The violent fluctuations checked and discouraged mercantile enterprise, and hampered the flow of capital from Europe. The artificial stimulus given to the export trade was a poor compensation for other evils, and, by an inexorable economic law, could not ultimately have anything but an impoverishing effect upon the general welfare. To meet the increasing charge, further taxation, some of it retrograde and economically vicious, was found to be necessary. The salt dues were enhanced and an income tax reimposed—two methods of raising revenue to which Indian statesmen are rightly loth to have recourse. It is not surprising that, at the end of the decade 1880–90, the Indian Government warned the authorities at home that, unless a remedy could speedily be found, the country was drifting rapidly to financial bankruptcy and political ruin. In 1892, they approached the India Office with the suggestion that a fixed ratio between gold and silver should be established by international agreement; failing that, they were prepared to let economic orthodoxy go by the board and close the Indian mints to the free coinage of silver, with the aim ultimately of introducing a gold standard. In accordance with this policy, Indian representatives were despatched to the International Monetary Conference at Brussels, but without result. Bimetallism being for practical reasons impossible, and the alternative of additional taxation not one to be faced, the Home Government reluctantly fell back upon Lord Lansdowne's second proposal, and, fortified by the report of Lord Herschell's Commission of 1893, agreed to the closing of the Indian mints to the unrestricted coinage of silver—a measure which was carried out in the concluding year of Lord Lansdowne's period of office. The immediate effect was slight. Lord Elgin, who became Viceroy in 1894, was confronted with the prospect of a serious deficit, to meet which the five per cent. import duties abolished in 1882 were reimposed on all goods except cotton cloths. Within the year even that exception was removed, though, to prevent the duties from being in any way protective, a countervailing excise duty was levied on the products of Indian cotton-mills. The rupee continued to decline in value till 1895, when it reached the lowest point at thirteen pence. From that date the effect of the closing of the mints and the restrictions on the import of silver began to be felt, and the rupee gradually rose till it touched one shilling and fourpence, the amount at which the Government proposed to introduce a gold standard at the rate of fifteen rupees to one pound.

In Lord Elgin's time an important military reform was finally carried out which had been advocated by many Viceroys. The old system of three separate Presidential armies under three Commanders-in-Chief was abolished. A Commander-in-Chief for the whole of India was appointed, with four Lieutenant-Generals as his subordinates. The reform was typical of the change that had passed over British dominion in the East. The original arrangement dated from the time when each of the three Presidencies was surrounded by a zone of hostile territory. From three centres the irresistible onset of British power had spread, like the waters of three converging rivers, till it had covered the whole peninsula. For many years Madras and Bombay had possessed no frontier. The pressure from foreign Powers was felt only on the far north beyond the barrier of the Himalayas, or, further still, beyond the protected or subsidised States of Baluchistan, Afghanistan, Kashmir, Nepal, Bhutan, and the independent Burmese tribes, where the limits of British influence marched with the frontiers of Persia, China, Tibet, and the French possessions east of the Mekong. That great exterior line was rounded off in 1895 at the one point where the demarcation, as it affected Russia and Afghanistan, had been left incomplete, by the Commission which adjudicated debatable territory in the Pamirs.

A controversial question was settled in 1895 for some years by the report of a Commission on opium. The cultivation and preparation of this drug in British districts is a state monopoly from which a considerable revenue is obtained. The Government regulates the extent of poppy culture, and manufactures the finished product at the state factories of Ghazipur and Patna—one of those exceptional functions which vividly recall the fact that the Indian empire sprang from a trading company. A body of reformers in England had long called upon the State to relinquish the traffic for moral reasons, even at the cost of severe financial loss. They averred that the effects of opium, except when used medicinally under strict supervision, were pernicious and degrading; and they held that the Chinese, with whom the chief export trade is done, were unrighteously coerced into permitting the importation of the drug by the Opium War of 1842. The apologists of the Government, however, maintained that the real reason for the destruction by the Chinese of the opium chests in 1842 was not the effects of the drug upon the population, but the drain of bullion from the country to pay for the excess of imports over exports. Whether, even so, England was justified in going to war, to teach an oriental nation a sounder view of the phenomena of international trade, is perhaps open to question; but there seems good reason to hold that the Chinese Government in the Treaty of Tientsin (1858) admitted opium of their own accord as a legal article of import. The Commission found that the evil effects of the drug in India had been greatly exaggerated; they drew a parallel between its temperate use and that of alcohol in England, and intimated that prohibition was not more necessary in the one case than in the other. They threw upon the Chinese Government the burden of taking action if it wished the importation of opium forbidden, and claimed that the state monopoly really amounted to a restriction of cultivation, since it was confined to definite areas. The Indian product was at least opium in its best and purest form. Deprived of it, the Chinese would only have recourse to the home-grown supply, which was in every way inferior. Finally—a reason that probably outweighed all others in the opinion of politicians—the Commissioners considered that the Indian revenues could not at present afford the financial loss that would be entailed by prohibition. The report has by no means put an end to the anti-opium agitation, the promoters of which are prepared to challenge many of the statements of fact put forward by the Commission; but the question has, since 1908, entered on a new phase through the agreement with China for a gradual decrease of the export trade.

Few Viceroys have had a sterner struggle with adversity than Lord Elgin. The evils of unstable exchange brought about a series of financial deficits. The country was visited by famine and plague; and to these evils was added a serious frontier war. The famine of 1896-7, which, radiating from central India, reached as far as Rajputana and Upper Burma, first put to a severe test the Code of 1883. The mortality in British territory was estimated at 750,000 deaths; and the cost of relief, exclusive of remissions of revenue and charitable funds, amounted to over five millions sterling. Yet so terrible was the problem to be faced, and so much was done under adverse circumstances, that these results were considered relatively successful and economical, and only a few changes in detail were recommended to be made in the Code. Before these could be carried out, at an interval of only two years, Lord Elgin's successor, Lord Curzon of Kedleston, was called upon to deal with an even more terrible famine, that of 1899–1900. Coming, as it did, before the country had fully recovered from the ravages of the previous one, and attended by an outbreak of cholera and malarial fever, it taxed the resources of the Government to the extreme point. The cost of relief amounted to over six millions, and more than a million persons are said to have perished in British districts alone.

The bubonic plague broke out in India in 1896. Identical with the epidemic described by Thucydides, which visited Athens in B.C. 431, with the Black Death of the Middle Ages, and the Great Plague of London in 1665, this scourge of nations has had a strange and interesting history. It came originally from the East, probably from the most populous centres of the Chinese empire, and moved slowly westwards till it reached the shores of the Atlantic. After periodical and destructive outbreaks lasting through several centuries, it gradually receded by well-defined steps to its original home in the East. It lingered longest in the south-east of Europe, where the boundaries of the two continents meet under the suzerainty of the Turk. Even in Asia it appeared, for more than a hundred years, to lose its virulent and destructive force, tending to become merely endemic in certain localities.

At the end of the nineteenth century the plague seemed to be endued with a new and baneful activity. In the autumn of 1896 it appeared in Bombay, causing an exodus of the population, and dealing a serious blow at the commercial prosperity of the city. In 1897 it spread through western and central India, and in 1898 the first cases were reported in Calcutta. The Administration was confronted with a new problem requiring the most delicate handling. To frame counsels of perfection was easy; the difficulty was to apply them. It was often found impossible in practice to employ the preventive measures recommended by science, owing to the panic of the native population and their unconquerable opposition to isolation hospitals, house to house visitation, segregation camps, and inoculation. In the early stages of the campaign against the disease, serious riots broke out in Bombay, and, owing to incendiary writings in the vernacular Press, the law in regard to seditious publications was made more stringent—a measure which, however necessary, naturally intensified the popular discontent. After 1898, milder methods of prevention and cure were employed, which proved actually more successful in action, as they conflicted less with the prejudices of the people. In spite of the most devoted efforts, little real progress has been made towards stamping out the plague in India. To keep it fairly under control seems now the utmost that can be hoped for, and it remains a most serious and ever present problem for Indian statesmen.

By the Durand agreement of 1893, the hill State of Chitral, abutting on the mountain range of the Hindu Kush, had been embraced within the British sphere of influence. An agency was established at Gilgit and British political officers occasionally visited the capital. In 1895, the native Government was overthrown by one of those violent revolutions which occur periodically in the history of all oriental States. The ruling chief was assassinated, and all the forces of disorder united for a brief moment in an attempt to drive out the British representative, who was closely besieged in Chitral itself. He was only released, and the Chitralis defeated, after an invasion of the country by 16,000 troops. Though the Viceroy advised the retention of Chitral, Lord Rosebery's Government decided upon an evacuation of the country. But the Liberal party lost office before the troops could be withdrawn, and the Conservative Ministry of Lord Salisbury reversed their decision.

But the Chitral rising proved only the harbinger of further troubles, and soon the whole extent of the tribal country was aflame with rebellion. To this effect many causes contributed, each of which was in turn hailed as the main reason for the war by partisans in England. The tribesmen were intensely jealous of their independence, and they looked with growing distrust upon the Forward policy of the past ten years, the construction of roads and railways up to the limits of their territory, and the nearer and nearer approach of the outposts of British power.

CH. XVI.

They were taught by the fanatical priests of their religion that the boundary line lately drawn between their territory and Afghanistan was intended, on its southern side, to be also the northern frontier of British India, and, untrue as the insidious suggestion was, their suspicions and fears were natural enough. But other great events at this time were sending a thrill through the whole Mohammadan community. The crushing victory over the Greeks obtained by Turkish arms aroused the warlike fervour which is never wholly extinct in the breast of the true believer. The abuse of the Sultan, which was common on popular platforms in England at this time, is credibly alleged to have aroused strong anti-Christian feeling ; and the Amir of Afghanistan himself had lately published an academic treatise on the *jehad* or holy war against infidels as enjoined in the Koran.

The War subjected British arms to the severest strain imposed upon them since the Mutiny. In June, 1897, a rising took place in the Tochi valley. In the following month, fierce attacks were made by the Swatis on the fortified posts at Chakdarra and the Malakand, which had been occupied by British troops since the Chitral expedition. In August, the Mohmands raided within twenty miles of Peshawar, and the Afridis besieged the fortified stations on the Samana Ridge, where a Sikh garrison made a gallant resistance, dying to a man at their posts. The Afridis next captured all the British positions in the Khaibar, defended though they were by tribal levies of their own countrymen. The challenge thus given was speedily accepted. Retribution fell first upon the Mohmands. The Malakand field force, under Sir Bindon Blood, invaded their territory in September, 1898. Operations were concluded in the following January after fierce fighting and considerable loss of life. The campaign in the Tirah valley did not begin till October, when Sir William Lockhart took command with an army of 40,000 men. The heights of Dargai were brilliantly stormed at a cost of two hundred casualties. The country was traversed and the villages were destroyed; but the march was everywhere harassed by desperate rearguard actions, and some of the hardest fighting in the campaign was experienced when the enemy's territory was being evacuated by two separate routes at the end of the year. On the return from the Tirah valley the Khaibar posts were again occupied by British troops. Under threat of another invasion in the spring, the Afridis agreed to pay the fines imposed upon them and to surrender their arms. British losses in the war amounted to three hundred killed and nine hundred wounded.

In January, 1899, Lord Elgin was succeeded by Lord Curzon of Kedleston, who had served in Lord Salisbury's Government as Under-Secretary for India and for Foreign Affairs, and left what promised to be a brilliant career in the House of Commons at an unusually early age to take up his new office.

The first problem that demanded solution at his hands was the settlement of the north-west frontier. The Tirah campaign was barely concluded when he took the oath of office. More than ten thousand troops were still quartered over the border in Chitral, the passes, Lundi Kotal, and the Tochi valley. A shrewd statesmanship was required to guide and shape the policy of the future. The advocates of the Forward policy held that the expenditure of lives and money, the despatch of punitive expeditions, and the construction of strategic railways, were unavoidable steps in the demarcation of a scientific frontier. The extreme adherents of this view looked forward to the time when the tribal territory should be finally subdued and the frontiers of India and Afghanistan should coincide. To men of the opposite school the approach to the mountain walls seemed a needless, costly, and hazardous course of aggression, though they were not clear as to where the line should be drawn, now that the barrier of the Indus had once been passed. Before he left England, Lord Curzon was looked upon as a champion of the Forward policy ; but he proved no supporter of it in office, if it meant extending British dominion till it touched the Afghan frontier. He was, on the other hand, no devotee of the Lawrence school, if that required the evacuation of Chitral, Quetta, and the points already reached. Indeed, though the basis of his policy lay in a fresh and independent study of the problem, it proved in operation something of a compromise between the two warring sections. British troops were gradually withdrawn from the Khaibar, the Malakand, Dargai, and the Kuram valley, and their places were taken by tribal levies trained and commanded by British officers. All interference with the religion or independence of the tribes was eschewed ; but they were firmly made to understand that order must be kept on the borderland. Within the British lines there was a certain concentration of force and a numerical increase in the garrisons. The traffic in arms and ammunition was, so far as possible, suppressed, and strategic railways were pushed forward to Chaman, Dargai, and Jamrud. The widespread conflagration of 1897–8 has been succeeded by twelve years of peace on the north-west frontier—an eloquent testimony to the success of a policy that happily combined the advantages of economy, military efficiency, and respect for the independence of the tribesmen.

Lord Curzon's border policy was rounded off and completed by an administrative reform of the first importance—the separation of the north-west frontier districts from the Lieutenant-Governorship of the Punjab. The Punjab had itself in the past been the typical frontier province of British India, and had produced a famous school of administrators, who ruled their districts almost untrammelled by Government interference with a personal and benevolent autocracy. But, as the boundary line of British India shifted further and further away towards Afghanistan, the status of the Punjab approximated to that of the more constitutional and settled Provinces. Lord Lytton, it will be remembered, had proposed the creation of a separate frontier charge under specially appointed officers subject only to the Supreme Government; but the projected reform remained in abeyance, till it was carried into effect by Lord Curzon in 1901. Even then, the change was stoutly resisted by many of the Punjab officials, who were loth to see their extraordinary powers curtailed. The new province was made up of the trans-Indus districts of the Punjab, together with the political charges of the Malakand, Khaibar, Kuram, Tochi, and Wana.

The peace observed along the north-western frontier of India had as one of its happiest results the continuance of satisfactory relations with Afghanistan. Abdurrahman, who had met Lord Curzon in earlier years, and had formed a high opinion of his character and abilities, died in 1901. The greatest testimony to the unique position he had obtained was the peaceful succession of his son Habibulla, which was directly contrary to the Afghan precedent of an internecine conflict between the sons of a dead Amir. Down to the present time, the new ruler has succeeded fairly well in maintaining his power and in holding back his unruly subjects from serious depredation on the frontier; but he does not appear to possess his father's abilities, and there are not wanting signs that the Afghan question will again become a very difficult and dangerous one for Indian statesmen.

The other Asiatic Power with which Lord Curzon had important dealings was Tibet. Though the suzerainty of the Emperor of China was nominally recognised, the government of the country was really in the hands of the Dalai Lama or Buddhist High Priest of Lhassa, or of those who controlled that sacred pontiff. British relations with Tibet dated back to the time of Warren Hastings, who on two occasions sent missions to the country in the hope of establishing trade. In 1887, the Tibetans invaded the protected State of Sikkim, but were repulsed with loss. In 1890, a convention was agreed upon between the Indian Government and China, whose sovereign rights over Tibet the British found it convenient to recognise, for the opening of commercial intercourse between the two countries. The Tibetans, however, did their best to render the concession valueless. They refused to cooperate in a demarcation of their frontier line or to meet the Chinese and British representatives in a conference. In 1904 a mission under Colonel Younghusband was sent to penetrate into the country and negotiate a settlement. Resistance was offered to the progress of the mission by the troops of the Dalai Lama, a mere rabble, which were repulsed with some loss of life on their side. Lhassa was entered for the first time by a European army. The Dalai Lama abdicated, and a treaty was negotiated with his successor, which was afterwards modified in some important particulars by the Secretary of State. Lord Curzon's action in Tibet seemed hardly consonant with his former unaggressive policy upon the frontier, and earned the adverse criticism of a section of the Liberal party in England. It was said in defence that the Dalai Lama was known to desire an alliance with the Russian Government; but there were many who doubted the moral right of the Indian Government to force trade relations upon an independent country, or to deny it the privilege of negotiating with other European Powers.

In 1903, Lord Curzon visited the Persian Gulf, which lies beyond the range of a Viceroy's ordinary autumn tour. The destiny of Persia is one of the most uncertain of Asiatic problems. Russia presses upon her from the north, Great Britain from the south, though the influence of the two Powers is very different. Great Britain holds in her hands the bulk of the foreign trade of southern Persia, and claims a general control of the whole Asiatic coast line from Aden eastwards to Baluchistan, whether the shore itself be under the sovereignty of independent Arabian tribes, the Ottoman Government, the sultanate of Oman, or the Shah himself. Since 1853, the waters of the Gulf—an early theatre of British effort and enterprise in the seventeenth century—have been cleared of pirates and opened to vessels sailing under every flag. Great Britain has never coveted territorial possessions on either shore. It is her avowed policy to preserve the integrity of Persia, to further the commercial and political development of the country, and to prevent it from falling under the sway of a rival European Power, and so forming the base for an assault upon India.

While England approaches Persia from the sea, the pressure exerted by Russia upon the northern frontier is far more direct. Her conquest of the Turcomans and absorption of Khiva and Bokhara have made the boundaries of the two empires conterminous for about a thousand miles. The development of navigation on the Volga and the construction of the Transcaspian railway have given to Russia the bulk of the trade with northern Persia. But the commercial weapons of Russia are monopoly and prohibition. She has laid an interdict upon the making of railroads in Persian territory, and has often opposed measures that might regenerate the country. And further, Russia is said to aim at more than a preponderating influence. Persia naturally looks north, and the capital itself is within a hundred miles of the Caspian, now to all intents and purposes a Russian lake. A body of Persian Cossacks, trained and commanded by Russian officers, is by far the most efficient part of the Persian army. Were Russia left a clear field, all indications point to the gradual but complete absorption of Persia into the huge framework of the Muscovite empire; but the commercial and political rivalry of Great Britain bars the way. Persia stands on a different level from that of the central Asian khanates, though she is hardly more able than they to resist by material force the relentless advance of Russia. She possesses an ancient though decaying civilisation; and the glamour of her past still faintly illumines her present degeneracy.

Down to 1887, the influence of England in Persia, at one time great, had steadily tended to decline, but the appointment of Sir Henry Drummond Wolff to Teheran in that year did much to restore her waning prestige. Lord Curzon had consistently advocated, for many years before his viceroyalty, the extension of British interests in southern Persia by the establishment of consulates in the ports of the Gulf and the trading cities inland, the extension of telegraphs and the development of the Nushki-Seistan trade route. As Viceroy he did much to realise all these projects. It was hopeless now, even if it were desirable, to supplant Russia in her predominant position in the north—the natural and fitting outcome of her great military and political strength in that region. But Russia was credited with the desire of proceeding ultimately to the annexation of the northern provinces of Persia, especially of Khorasan, and penetrating by way of Seistan along the Afghan frontier to a port on the Persian Gulf. On all such aspirations, if really entertained, a check was put by the British Foreign Secretary's pronouncement in May, 1903, that Great Britain would regard the establishment of a naval base or of a fortified port in the Persian Gulf by any other Power as a grave menace to British interests, to be resisted by all possible means. Lord Curzon's visit to the Gulf was the complement of this notable declaration; but the final development of the policy was not reached till after he had laid down his office. On September 1, 1907, a convention was signed with Russia at St Petersburg relating to Persia, Afghanistan, and Tibet. In Afghanistan there was practically a mere recognition of the *status quo.* The suzerainty of China over Tibet was acknowledged; and the country was closed alike to Russia and Great Britain except so far as it was opened to the latter by the Treaty of Lhassa in 1904 and the Anglo-Chinese convention of 1906. In regard to Persia the agreement was far more important. It sums up and ratifies a solution to which the work of diplomatists and boundary commissions have been directed for many years. The two Powers promise to respect the integrity and political independence of Persia. Great Britain binds herself to set no barriers in the way of Russian influence in northern Persia exercised through political and commercial concessions granted by the Shah, while Russia engages to respect in like manner the position of Great Britain in the south-eastern provinces. Both Powers were impelled to a definite agreement by the knowledge that the Persian problem, already difficult enough, was soon to be complicated by a new factor. Persia has proved receptive to the new spirit stirring among the peoples of the East, and has endeavoured to establish a form of parliamentary government. But constitutionalism is not easily brought to the birth in oriental countries, and in the period of transition there will be many tempting opportunities for either England or Russia to intervene, unless they are bound by clear and valid terms.

At the end of the century, the finances of India emerged from the long depression in which they had been plunged during the period of unstable exchange.   After 1899, the Finance Minister found himself each year in the possession of a handsome surplus.   Accordingly, an Act was passed, on the recommendation of Sir Henry Fowler's Commission, to make the British sovereign legal tender in India at the value of fifteen rupees. The desired result was obtained, and a steady flow of gold to India set in. The profits of the silver coinage were paid into a gold reserve fund, which, when Lord Curzon left India, amounted to nearly nine millions sterling.   The expedient adopted has worked well in practice and has signally falsified the prognostications of those who opposed the closing of the mints.   Theoretically, however, the monetary position of India is very anomalous.   Gold is the standard of value, but as yet the Indian mints have not begun to coin it.   The silver coinage is really a token currency with an exchange value above its intrinsic worth, so that the Government makes a considerable profit on it ; but it is still legal tender to any amount.   The improvement in the finances enabled Lord Curzon to grant valuable remissions of taxation after the terrible famine of 1899–1900.   In 1902 over a million and a quarter of the land tax was given back to the most distressed provinces, and in the two following years the incidence of the salt tax was made lighter than it had been since the days of the Mutiny.

In internal affairs Lord Curzon's period of office formed an important landmark.   Every department and branch of the administration was subjected to a searching and impartial test.   The method employed was in nearly every case the same—preliminary investigation by a strong commission, followed by an independent consideration of their report and prompt legislative action.   Procedure by commission, so often a plausible way of shelving inconvenient questions, was abundantly justified by the extraordinary complexity of the field to be surveyed, and became in Lord Curzon's hands a preparation for drastic action.   The numerous reforms can be only briefly specified here.   On the military side, the native regiments were rearmed, the artillery was strengthened, and the transport service was reorganised.   Contingents of the Indian army played a prominent part in the task of defending the British empire in many lands.   They fought against the Boxer insurgents in China, and against the Mullah in Somaliland.   In 1905 a thoroughgoing reform of the police service, which in its lower branches was notoriously corrupt and oppressive, was inaugurated.   An important agrarian measure was passed, designed to free the cultivators of the soil in the Punjab from oppression at the hands of the money-lenders.   A new Department of Commerce and Industry was established, with a sixth member of the Viceroy's Council as its President.   The procedure of government Departments was simplified and improved.   A determined assault was made upon the abuse of the system of report writing, described by the Viceroy as the most perfect and pernicious in the world.   It had grown within recent years to such a pitch that it threatened to clog the whole administrative machinery. The education problem was thoroughly sifted by a conference at Simla and the labours of a University Commission. A large annual grant was set aside for the extension of primary schools. On the position of higher education the Commission produced a cautiously worded but rather discouraging report. The old theory, put forward in 1854, that a college education opened to the higher classes would "filter" down to the masses of the people, had proved a vain hope. A university degree was looked upon by the clever Bengali as a mere passport to a post in the provincial or subordinate Civil Service. The Universities themselves, mere examining boards, fostered a system of "cramming" which, deleterious enough even for Europeans, produced the most deplorable results, from an educational point of view, when applied to the imitative intelligence and facile memory of oriental races. In 1904 the Senates of the Universities were reorganised in the hope that the new governing bodies, mainly composed of the teaching staff, would frame regulations more with regard to sound educational principles and less with the aim of turning out as large a number as possible of qualified or partially qualified graduates.

The educational policy of his Government, more than anything else except the partition of Bengal, brought Lord Curzon into conflict with the so-called National party in India. That party is the outcome of the higher education given in the colleges. It is nourished on a careful study of English classics, especially the political philosophy of the Whig and Liberal schools of thought. Its avowed aim is the establishment in India of a democratic and constitutional government—a transplanting of the full-grown tree of the Western State to Eastern soil. It had first risen to prominence in 1885 from the organised demonstrations in honour of the retiring Viceroy, Lord Ripon; and, from that year onward, an annual meeting was held in one of the big cities of India under the title of the Indian National Congress. The Congress remains as yet officially unrecognised, but its existence, embarrassing as it is to the Indian Government, is the natural outcome of some of the best and most liberal aspects of British rule. It has done excellent work in calling attention to legitimate grievances, and, were it more under the control of the moderate constitutional party, its beneficial activity would be greater than it is. Many of its members have been men of ability and public spirit; but its aims as formulated in recent years are considered by most Indian statesmen to be considerably in advance of what is at present practicable. It endeavours, not always with success, to combine democratic ideals with national aspirations which are at bottom intensely aristocratic. The attempt to disguise this fundamental cleavage, and to bridge over the diversities of race feeling, weakens the Congress as an effective Opposition to the Indian Government. It is thoroughly representative only of the comparatively small section of native Indians who know English. Its claim, so loudly made, to speak for the great mass of the cultivators of the soil, has little justification, and it is, as a rule, looked upon with distrust by the feudatory chiefs and the bulk of the Mohammadan community.

The Congress, inclined at first to welcome Lord Curzon, became alienated from him when, with characteristic outspokenness, he declined to advance along the path it had pointed out, and forced it to perceive that his interest lay in social and administrative reform rather than in constitutional experiment. Yet Lord Curzon was always eager to extend the sphere of action open to men of native birth, and no Viceroy was ever more inflexible in meting out stern chastisement to any European who had insulted or ill-treated a member of the subject races. He freely risked his popularity with the army and the European inhabitants in his firm determination to punish such lapses severely.

On January 1, 1903, Lord Curzon proclaimed King Edward VII, who had himself visited India in 1875 when Prince of Wales, as Emperor of India at the coronation Durbar at Delhi—a pageant which surpassed even that of 1877. In 1904 the Viceroy came to England for a few months, but was reappointed for a further term of office. He carried through on his return an administrative reform of the first importance—the partition of Bengal, which had often been suggested in the past. The original Presidency of Fort William had been already lightened in 1836 by the formation of the North-West Provinces (combined with Oudh in 1877 and renamed the United Provinces of Agra and Oudh in 1901), and by the creation of Assam in 1874 as a separate Commissionership. The time was now ripe for a further subdivision. The Lieutenant-Governor of Bengal was expected to administer the affairs of a population nearly twice as great as that of the United Kingdom. No one denied that the task had grown to be beyond the capacity of a single man, and that it was destined to grow still heavier year by year. The Indian Government accordingly decided to divide the province. Many alternative schemes were considered, and, to a certain extent, the plan adopted was modified in accordance with outside criticism. Finally, a new province was created, by amalgamating fifteen districts of the old province of Bengal with Assam, under the title of Eastern Bengal and Assam.

Before the reform was completed, a fierce popular agitation broke out against the change. Though partly genuine, and, in so far as that was the case, largely based upon a misapprehension of the facts, it was mainly directed by the literary class, and deftly manipulated to suit the aspirations of the Indian National Congress party. What the Viceroy described as a mere adjustment of administrative boundaries was represented as the partition of a homogeneous nation and as a deliberate attack upon the social, historical, and linguistic ties of the Bengalis. The extreme presentment of the opposition case tended to assume, as Indian political movements so often do, an element of the grotesque; but the saner members of the National party, supported by

CH. XVI.

a small English section, argued that the particular method selected by the Indian Government, whatever its abstract merits, should have been abandoned on the ground that no political change can be really beneficial which is strongly opposed by national sentiment. They could not deny the necessity for some change; but they proposed that the ruler of Bengal should henceforth be a Governor instead of a Lieutenant-Governor, and that he should be assisted, as in Madras and Bombay, by an Executive Council. Lord Curzon replied that the establishment of an Executive Council in Bengal would divide and weaken the responsibility of the Governor or Lieutenant-Governor; for that province, with its variety of races and civilisations and its many complex problems, still above all others required a strong personal control. Here was revealed the wide gulf that separated the official and non-official views. Looking mainly to the efficiency of the administration, the Viceroy and his advisers desired to decentralise as little as possible; while the National party only saw in the proposed change a favourable opportunity for advancing in the direction of constitutional and representative government, and to impose definite limits upon the autocratic power of the head of the executive.

Lord Curzon declined to be moved from his purpose by popular clamour, and the reform was duly carried out in 1905. It was the last important act of his viceroyalty. In 1904 the Commander-in-Chief, Lord Kitchener of Khartum, with a view to the simplification and concentration of business, had proposed certain changes in the elaborate military department in India which, in Lord Curzon's opinion, would tend to make the head of the army dangerously independent of the civil power. In the face of this conflict of opinion, the Home Government found itself in a difficult position. Misunderstandings and recriminations ensued; and Lord Curzon, considering that he had not received the support to which he was entitled, resigned office and returned to England in 1905. He was succeeded by the Earl of Minto, great-grandson of the first Earl, who had been Governor-General from 1807 to 1813.

Lord Minto's task has proved no easy one. The agitation against the partition of Bengal has developed into a demand for Indian Home Rule. The advent to power of a Liberal Government at the end of 1905, with Mr John Morley (soon created Viscount Morley of Blackburn) as Secretary for India, aroused many extravagant hopes; and, when it was found that, though he lent a sympathetic ear to all Indian reformers, he declined to reverse Lord Curzon's action in Bengal, or make rash constitutional experiments, a considerable amount of open discontent was manifested. India is now passing through a period of unrest. Even in the National Congress there has been an open breach between the moderate and the extreme party. A disconcerting feature has been the outbreak of an anarchist propaganda and the occurrence of murderous attacks upon Europeans. It has been found necessary to curb the licence of the Press by drastic measures against seditious journalists, to pass an Explosives Act, and to extend the summary jurisdiction of the Courts in cases of violence.   But, while the methods of repression have been prompt and stern, neither the Viceroy nor the Secretary of State has faltered in following the policy of reform to which they were already committed.   Lord Morley has appointed a native Indian to the Executive Council of the Viceroy, and two others to the Council which advises him at the India Office.   By the Indian Councils Act of 1909 and by Regulations authorised under the Act, the number of members serving on the Viceregal and Provincial Legislative Councils has been nearly trebled.   An official majority is still retained on the Viceroy's Council but has been dispensed with on the Provincial Councils.   The Executive Councils of Madras and Bombay are to be enlarged, and new Councils may be created in Provinces ruled by Lieutenant-Governors.   In the Constitution of the Legislative Councils the principle of election is to be introduced side by side with that of nomination.   Special electorates of Mohammadans, landowners, and trading communities have been formed to secure the representation of classes and interests rather than of territorial areas.   Much greater latitude than before has been given to the Councils in regard to interpellation, criticism, and the initiation of business; and it seems likely that the changes will effectively associate the people of India with the Government, not only in the work of legislation, but also in that of actual administration.

The main characteristics of British Indian history since the Mutiny are not difficult to discern.   Internally, there have been sweeping political, social, and economic changes.   Though India is still mainly an agricultural country, the mill, the factory, and the workshop have sprung up in many districts with all the influence, partly progressive, partly degrading, which they are wont to exercise over the life of a people.   The foreign sea-borne trade has been multiplied five times in value since 1857, and the immense improvement in communications has not only brought great economic benefits, but has done something to break down the ancient barriers of race, caste, and faith.   If these developments have not produced a more marked increase in the prosperity of the bulk of the population, that is because, by an inexorable law, good government in India produces its own problems and difficulties. It stays the ravages of famine, interdicts civil war, and forbids infanticide, only to find itself called upon to support a population pressing ever nearer and nearer to the verge of subsistence, now that the former checks on its increase have been removed.

External ly, the only important acquisition of territory has been the annexation of Burma.   But, though elsewhere the land frontier, having reached the mountains, has on the whole remained stationary, it has been rectified and settled.   British supremacy has radiated outwards, beyond the administrative boundary proper, over protected or subsidised States and political spheres of influence, till it comes into touch with other great Asiatic Powers, Western or Eastern—Persia, Russia, China, Siam, and French Indo-China. The process which continually demarcates and defines political boundaries in Asia, though it removes some dangers to the world's peace, creates others. The storm centre shifts from the frontiers of European Powers to the protected States occupying the margin of territory between their great Asiatic empires. Any European Power that finds its frontier endangered by some outburst of anarchy in a semi-civilised country may be driven to armed intervention, but it will not easily persuade its jealous rivals that it has no ulterior aims. Therein lurks the peril of the situation. The maintenance of peace, for example, between England and Russia, may depend, quite apart from all other causes, upon the power of the Amir of Afghanistan to impose upon his turbulent subjects an order and a discipline which are alien to their nature.

The history of the rise of British dominion in India has in the course of this work been carried down from the first meeting of a small body of Elizabethan traders in the hall of a City Company to a sketch of the vast empire of today. So rapid has been its growth and expansion that the whole tale is rounded off within the compass of a *History* whose title is "Modern." When all qualifications and deductions have been made, it may be justly claimed that Great Britain has built up a model system for the administration of an oversea empire under sub-tropical skies. It is interesting to observe how abiding were the lines of policy and how permanent were the instruments which from the beginning she brought to the solution of the problem. The Factory, with its President and Council, is the direct parent of the Viceroy and his Executive Council. Just as each member today holds a separate portfolio for which he is responsible, so each of the subordinate officials of the old Presidencies was head of a branch factory or special department. English rule in India has ever been, as Burke pointed out, a government of writing and a government of record. The administration has always been carried on with a formidable machinery of despatches, minutes, and reports. In the earliest days of the Factory period, as now under the imperial Government of the Crown, those members of Council who dissented from the opinion of the majority were expected to enter a written and signed protest, to be forwarded for the information of the authorities at home. The old corrupt Covenanted Civil Service of the Company was purified by Cornwallis; and its later history made it a worthy forerunner of the imperial Civil Service with its lofty traditions and honourable record of devoted work. The salutary tendency which impels British thinkers to criticise their best institutions has not spared this Service; but no responsible voice breathes a word against the ability or cleanhandedness of its members. They have their own rewards and are led onward by the allurement of an honourable ambition; yet few have ever risen high without dedicating far more of their abilities and powers to the service of India than a narrow conception of their duty required of them.

If England, for the past hundred years, has held the fate of India in the hollow of her hand, India, in turn, has exercised a potent influence over the destinies of her suzerain. She has afforded a unique training ground for soldiers and statesmen. She has attracted and engrossed the genius of some of England's most gifted sons. She has taken heavy toll of English talent and English lives. The resources of her commerce and the prestige which her possession confers have set Great Britain in the foremost place among the nations of the world. The defence of India and the maintenance of free communications with her shores is a problem which increasingly dominates British policy and British diplomacy. The pathway over the seas is dotted throughout its length by coaling stations and fortified posts. British possessions in the Mediterranean— the milestones and relics of the great continental wars of the eighteenth century—acquired a new and unexpected value when the Cape route was abandoned for that of the Suez Canal and the Red Sea. Gradually and imperceptibly, Great Britain tends to extend her control over the shores and waterways along the line of intercommunication. The occupation of Egypt and Cyprus, the control of the Persian Gulf, the policing of the Arabian Sea, are all ultimately due to the desire to keep open the approaches to India. No effort, no sacrifice has been considered too great to retain the splendid prize; but that determination has gone hand in hand with a consistent and sustained attempt to ameliorate the condition of the Indian peoples, to confer upon them the benefits of Western knowledge and Western ideals of government, and so to justify on high political and ethical grounds the existence of an empire which, in the peculiar circumstances of its acquisition and development, has assuredly no parallel in the history of the world.

CHAPTER XVII.

THE FAR EAST.

CHINA.

THE Tientsin Treaty of 1858 and the subsequent Conventions opened to the Chinese a new view of their relations and duties towards the Treaty Powers. Down to that date the old idea of supremacy which had hitherto dominated their political conduct had prevailed, and they were now for the first time brought face to face with the policy of the equality of States. By the terms of the Treaty of Tientsin foreigners—missionaries and others—were to have, for the first time, the right of travelling and of residence in the interior of the empire, and the privilege of being represented by diplomatic agents at the Court of Peking. Though the Chinese agreed on paper to yield these privileges, they were in spirit as much opposed to them as ever; and their subsequent conduct was in strict keeping with the traditional policy of yielding only as much as they had not the power to withhold.

In 1856, the Mussulmans of Yunnan rebelled against the Chinese Government and established themselves at Talifu. Trade between Burma and Yunnan and thus with the rest of China was in consequence interrupted. Nevertheless, in 1868, Major Sladen penetrated from Mandalay to Bhamo and visited Talifu. In 1873, the Mussulman rebellion was suppressed; and, in 1874, the British Government, being desirous of establishing a trade route between north-eastern Burma and south-western China, sought from the Tsungli Yamên passports for another expedition commanded by Colonel Horace Browne. This expedition assembled at Bhamo and there awaited the arrival of Augustus Margary, of the British Consular Service, who travelled from Shanghai *via* Hankow to act as interpreter to Colonel Browne. In due course, he arrived at Bhamo (January 17, 1875), and brought so glowing an account of the treatment he had received *en route* that no antagonism was anticipated. Before, however, the expedition was ready to start, rumours reached the camp that opposition was meditated. Margary offered to go ahead of the expedition and to test the disposition of the Kakhyens and Chinese who occupied the intervening territory. He reached the Chinese frontier without hindrance; but at Manwein, a city near the boundary, he was murdered, and at the same time Colonel Browne's escort was attacked. So large was the opposing force that Colonel Browne deemed it advisable to retire; which he did, reaching Bhamo in safety.

Sir Thomas Wade at once demanded reparation for the crime, insisting that an enquiry should be held on the spot. This was agreed to by the Chinese, who, however, carried out their part of the bargain in so dilatory a manner as to nullify the effect intended; whereupon Wade hauled down his flag and left Peking. In response, however, to an appeal from the Tsungli Yamên he agreed to meet Li Hungchang in negotiation at Chifu. Here they came to terms, a condition of which was that an envoy should be sent to London to apologise for the crime. Fortunately, a Mandarin named Kwo Sungtao was chosen for this office; and so effectively did he execute his commission that he was left in charge of the newly established legation at the Court of St James.

Meanwhile the Emperor T'ung-Chih had arrived at man's estate, that is to say, he had reached the age of sixteen, and was thus bound to assume the imperial sceptre and to take to himself an Empress. Hitherto the affairs of the empire had been administered by the Empresses— Tz'ŭ An, the widow of the late Emperor Hsien Fêng and the titular Empress Tz'ŭ Hsi, the mother of the Emperor T'ung-Chih. These two ladies now handed over the reins of power to the young Emperor and sought among the daughters of the Manchu magnates a lady to share his throne. Their choice fell upon Aluté, the daughter of Ch'ung Chi, a Manchu official. On October 16, 1872, this imperial marriage took place, with the usual pomp.

It had long been felt that the non-reception of the foreign representatives at Peking placed them in an anomalous position, and the fact that T'ung-Chih had come of age invalidated the excuse that his youth precluded him from granting official audiences. In answer to the applications of the foreign representatives, he granted them an audience on June 29, 1873. The good effect of this step was somewhat marred by the fact that the ceremony was held in a hall used for the reception of subordinate Mongolian Princes. Doubtless a similar slight would have been prevented in the future if T'ung-Chih's reign had been prolonged. But an attack of small-pox proved fatal to him, and on January 12, 1875, his Imperial Majesty became a " guest on high." Sinister rumours were current as to the nature of the disease. It was certain that he had rebelled against the Dowager Empresses; but, however that may be, his death placed the regency once more in the hands of the Dowagers, whose first duty was to nominate a successor to the throne. Their choice fell on the son of Prince Ch'un, the seventh son of Tao Kwang (1820–50), aged four years.

CH. XVII.

This selection met with opposition, since it violated the custom that the heir to the throne should be of a later generation than the last occupant. The Dowager Empresses were, however, sufficiently powerful to ignore this usage; and the infant sovereign ascended the throne without further opposition, under the title of Kwang Hsü, or "Succession of Glory." But the Dowagers had to overcome another objection to their hasty election. At the time of the death of T'ung-Chih his widow Aluté was *enceinte*; and, according to usage, the Regents should have waited until it was proved whether the infant were a son or a daughter. Fortunately for them, the death of Aluté solved the difficulty, and Kwang Hsü was left the unopposed occupant of the throne. Considerable ill-feeling had lately arisen against the Japanese in consequence of their having demanded reparation for the murder of shipwrecked Japanese sailors by the natives of the east coast of Formosa (1874). The Japanese failing to obtain satisfaction landed troops in Formosa, and war was only averted by the intervention of Sir Thomas Wade, who undertook to induce the Chinese to comply with the demands of the Japanese (1874).

At the same time, a strong anti-foreign current of opinion prevailed throughout the empire. Missionaries were attacked, and in some instances murdered. It is always difficult to reach the cause of these outbreaks. Commonly some local circumstance or the presence of an inimical official sets the spark to the train; and when once the fuse is lighted a Chinese mob quickly passes beyond control. A French missionary was murdered in Szech'uan, and mission premises were destroyed in several parts of the country.

European demands could not, however, be permanently ignored; and, in the second year of Kwang Hsü's reign, the Chinese Government agreed to open four new ports to foreign trade—Pakhoi, Wênchow, Ich'ang and Wuhu (1876). Unfortunately, this further opening of the country to foreigners was followed by a disastrous famine (1878). Nine millions are said to have perished, and many more would have suffered the same fate had it not been for the missionaries, who organised relief works for the benefit of the sufferers. This evidence of goodwill was not without its effect on the Chinese Government, from which a circular letter of thanks was received by the foreign representatives at Peking.

A period of comparative tranquillity followed throughout the empire, and the Tsungli Yamên had time to devote to the affairs on the northern frontier. They had been too much occupied in suppressing the T'aip'ing rebellion and the Mohammadan revolution in Yunnan to pay attention to such outlying districts as Kashgaria and Kuldja. But, now that their hands were free, they set about reviving the old order of things. The agitations, which had led to the overthrow of Chinese power in central Asia ending in the triumphs of Yakub Khan in the districts of Kashgaria and Yarkand (1864–9), had so disturbed the Russian frontier that, with the consent of the Chinese, the Russians had occupied the province of Kuldja (July, 1871) on the understanding that, so soon as the Chinese were able to reoccupy the territory effectively, it should be restored to them. This time had now come. Yakub Khan had died suddenly (1877), and the Chinese were supreme within their own frontiers. They, therefore, renewed negotiations with the Russians, whom they found ready to treat.

With strange ineptitude, they appointed (August, 1878) Chunghow as their ambassador, whose only qualification was that he had carried a message of apology for the Tientsin massacre to the French Government. He now concluded an agreement (October, 1879) which left the best part of the province to the Russians. This arrangement was condemned at Peking, and the ambassador's crime was aggravated by his returning to China before he had the imperial sanction to leave his post. For these misdemeanours he was promptly condemned to death—a sentence which would probably have been carried out, had it not been for the intervention of Queen Victoria, who, shocked at a sentence so disproportionate to the crime, pleaded for his life.

Meanwhile, Kwo Sungtao had been recalled from London, and the Marquis Tsêng had been appointed in his place. Fortunately for China, Tsêng was ordered to take up the negotiations which Chunghow had mismanaged. He recovered nearly all the land ceded, in consideration of a sum of money, which the Chinese Government was ready to pay. In April, 1881, the senior Dowager Empress, the widow of Hsien Fêng, died, or, as the Emperor expressed it at the time, "drove the fairy chariot and went a long journey"; and this put an end to the disputes that used to occur when there were two pilots at the helm. But the danger of entrusting the affairs of the empire to one head, however able, soon became apparent. For some time the relations between France and China with regard to Tonkin had been signally unsatisfactory—not so desperate, however, that a conciliatory attitude might not have averted the threatened evil. But Tz'ŭ Hsi showed a determined front to all overtures for peace, and thus, as is shown in another section, brought about a war which dragged its slow length along from 1882 to 1885.

One fruitful cause of diplomatic disputes during 1885 and previous years was the chronic question of the *likin* tax, an impost levied on the passage of goods into the interior, and falling with unjust incidence on foreign commodities. This tax was, like our income tax, in its origin, a war tax, and, also like our income tax, has long survived the cause of its imposition. The *likin* fell with special weight upon opium. When once this article of commerce crossed the boundaries of the foreign settlements, it became a prey to the tax-gatherer and contributed a considerable part of the incomes of the local officials. The evils attending the collection of *likin* were so patent that Lord

Salisbury (in 1885) proposed to the Marquis Tsêng, when Chinese Minister at the Court of St James, the drawing up of a convention which should impart regularity to its collection. It was finally agreed that a toll of eighty *taels* per chest, in addition to the thirty *taels* of import duty, should be imposed on all opium imported into the country, and that, in consideration of this additional payment, opium should be free from all further imposts of every sort. This proposal was readily welcomed at Peking, though it met with considerable opposition in the provinces. Under the old system, local Mandarins squeezed as much out of the opium as it would bear, and sent to Peking as small an amount of the tax as the Central Government would accept; whereas, under the new convention, the whole eighty *taels* went into the court exchequer. In spite, however, of this extra tax illegal perquisites continued to be levied from the trade by the provincial Mandarins.

In 1889 the Emperor came of age; and, as in duty bound, the Dowager Empress chose for him a wife, who happened to be the daughter of her brother, General Kwei-hsiang, and therefore a cousin of the Emperor. This young lady, Yeh-ho-na-la by name, was officially described as "a maiden of virtuous conduct, and becoming and dignified demeanour." The age at which the Emperor had arrived, however, entailed more than the taking of a wife. It meant that he had reached the stage in the imperial career when he should take over the reins of power; and with many laudatory expressions he accepted the resignation of the Dowager Empress as Regent and took upon himself the burdens of empire. The two imperial personages kept up for a time an antiphonal chant of praise; but the harmony was not of permanent duration.

At this epoch the diplomatic world at Peking was surprised by the appearance of an imperial edict containing a proposal of the Emperor to receive the foreign ministers in imperial audience on lines "in accordance with the reception of the twelfth year of the reign of T'ung-Chih" (1873), and a command that they should be entertained at a banquet given by the officials of the Tsungli Yamên. This privilege was graciously accorded, but unfortunately the Emperor suggested for holding it no other place than the Tsze-Kwang-Ko, where his late Majesty had granted the solitary audience on record. The only difference in procedure on this occasion was that each Minister was given a separate audience, instead of all being received together. It was generally felt by the diplomatic body to be derogatory to the sovereigns whom they represented that they should be received in this pavilion, and they allowed it to be known that for the future they would prefer to forgo the privilege. The Emperor yielded to the protest of the foreign ministers, and received the newly arrived Austrian and British plenipotentiaries in the Chêng-Kwang Hall of the palace. A still further advance was made in international usage when, in 1898, Prince Henry of Germany

visited Peking. On this occasion the Emperor greeted the Prince with
the cordiality due to royal personages, and returned his visit after the
short interval prescribed by etiquette. But still greater favours were
accorded to the Prince. The Dowager Empress received him in state,
and confided to him her intention of receiving the ladies of the legations
on her approaching birthday.

From 1878 onwards the progressive party, led by Li Hungchang,
had been urging on the Throne the advisability of constructing railways
for commercial and military purposes. Their first design was to construct a line which would serve the purpose of exploiting the coal mines
at K'aip'ing, a place situated half-way between Taku and Shan-hai-Kwan.
The first step was to get the imperial sanction to the undertaking.
This the united influence of Li Hungchang and Tong Kingsing, a
Cantonese merchant, succeeded in doing. But so successful were the
arguments used against it at Peking that the imperial sanction was
withdrawn. Li Hungchang and his confederates, among whom was
Claude William Kinder, a railway engineer, were not, however, to be
thus rebuffed; and, if a railway was impossible, they declared themselves
content to have a tramway, the trucks of which were to be drawn by
mules. At the same time Kinder, with his own hands, constructed
a railway engine out of old iron, and, when this strange motive power
was completed, it was quietly placed on the rails and made to do the
work of the mules. Another edict was sought to sanction the evasion.
This was granted. The construction of this line fired the imagination
of Li Hungchang, who proposed to the Throne that a line should be
constructed connecting Taku on the coast with T'ungchow, twelve
miles from Peking. Li pointed out that the line from K'aip'ing to
the sea coast would be of great commercial advantage, while its
continuation to Shan-hai-Kwan on the one hand and T'ungchow on
the other would add enormously to the military strength of the empire.
But he had determined enemies to deal with in the capital. So
powerful was this party that the Dowager Empress was unable to
thwart them; and, following the usual course in such circumstances,
she ordered the several Viceroys to report to her on the subject.
One or two, notably Liu Ming-chuan, memorialised in favour of the
project, and Chang Chihtung gave a qualified approval. He argued
that the construction of railways near the coast constituted a danger,
since it would enable invading forces to pass rapidly into the interior
of the country, and, further, "that the same prudence which made
England veto the Channel Tunnel should make China veto the Tientsin-
T'ungchow railway." But he held that trunk railways were necessary
to maintain the commercial advantages of China, and he advocated
the making of such a line from Peking to Hankow on the Yang-tsze,
760 miles in length. Much to his own surprise, his proposal was
accepted, and he was ordered to take up the viceroyalty of the two

Hu provinces so that he might be able personally to superintend his mission (1889). Li also gained his point; and the line from Tientsin now enters the Imperial City at the Chien Gate.

Meanwhile, reforms were being initiated in other directions. For many centuries the system of competitive examinations throughout the empire had remained unchanged, the ancient Chinese classics being the subjects which tested the abilities of the candidates. This system had no affinity to modern requirements, and Prince Kung (1866) recommended to the Throne that subjects of modern foreign literature should be admitted to the curriculum. It often happens, however, that projects which are recommended to and approved by the Throne remain entirely inoperative, and such was the case on this occasion. Much the same failure attended the institution of schools and colleges. A school of modern science which was opened at Peking failed to attract pupils, and had to be closed. It required further impetus to impel the Chinese along the path of progress.

The year 1887 saw a move in an important direction. It may be said generally that there is no coin in the currency of China, the only coin being that locally known to Europeans as "cash," twenty of which equal in value about a penny. At this time, in a moment of progressive zeal, the Dowager Empress issued an edict on reforms in the currency and directed that the officials should combine to produce a uniform system throughout the empire. This is a much-needed work; and one or two Viceroys, amongst whom was Chang Chihtung, set up mints which did well for a time, but in times of difficulty were allowed to fall into decay; recently, however, Chinese copper and silver coins have been struck and have come into circulation.

Although peace had been proclaimed between France and China and a Treaty arrived at (1885), the ambitions of the Republic were not satisfied; and a further convention (1887) was signed and sealed, by the terms of which the towns of Lungchow in Kwangsi and Mêng-tzu in Yunnan were to be open to foreign trade. This was so obviously an attempt to draw the trade of southern China through Tonkin that the Hongkong merchants became alarmed and agitated for the opening of the West river, which, taking its rise in Yunnan, runs through Chinese territory to the sea near Canton. The Chinese, for the time being, successfully resisted this proposal, and it was not until lately that the privilege of trading up the river in question so far as Nanningfu, 560 miles from its mouth, has been accorded (1902).

The year 1888 may be said to have seen the beginning of what Lord Salisbury described as "the battle of concessions," and its inception took place in a most unlikely quarter. For three hundred years Portugal had been the only European country which had held a footing on the mainland of China. In the year 1557, the Chinese rented to the Portuguese traders the peninsula of Maçao for 500 *taels* per annum,

Down to the year 1848, the Portuguese continued to pay this sum and held undisturbed possession of the territory. In that year, the Governor, Amaral, declined to continue the payments. The distance of the disputed piece of land from Peking made the Chinese Government regard the transfer with comparative indifference; but, at all events, it left the Portuguese in possession, though at the sacrifice of the life of the Governor, who was assassinated in broad daylight in the main road near the town. By a Treaty signed in 1887 the Chinese guaranteed "the perpetual occupation and government of Macao and its dependencies by Portugal, on the same footing as any other Portuguese possession." Portugal, at the same time, agreed not to alienate Macao and its dependencies without the consent of China.

In an important memorial presented to the Throne in 1889, a note of warning was struck by the Governor of Kiangsu as to the intentions of Russia in the Far East. He pointed out "that Russia overlaps us on the north round the Chinese Province of the New Dominion, Mongolia, and Heilung Kiang; and to the east round Kirin....Her left eye looks covetously at Korea, and her right at Mongolia." The design of constructing a line of railway which was to connect Moscow with Vladivostók would have been enough to have suggested this warning, and a Treaty concluded between Russia and Korea in the preceding year added a special point to the Governor's forecastings. Under its terms Russia was to "be allowed to trade at Kiong-Lyng as well as at the ports of Chemulpo, Gensan, Fusan, and the town of Seoul." This was one of the first steps taken by Russia in the course which led up to the War of 1904, and it would never have been carried through except for the help of Li Hungchang, who at this time was a warm supporter of Russian schemes. Chang Chihtung was powerless in face of Russia backed by Li.

Another man who might have stood as a shield to Korea against Russia was the Marquis Tsêng, whose policy led him to oppose the machinations of the Dowager Empress and Li Hungchang. He was, however, removed from the thorny path he would have had to follow, by death in circumstances which gave rise to suspicions of foul play. He was taken ill after a dinner given him by some of his colleagues, and died a few days later, on April 12, 1890.

Though the Chinese may be from time to time induced to adopt progressive methods, as a rule they revert in course of years to their former ways. An attempt had been made after the War with France to establish a fleet, and Captain Lang of her Majesty's Navy was seconded for service as Admiral. For a time things went well, but indifference supervened; and, finding it impossible to maintain the standard of discipline necessary for the fleet, Admiral Lang resigned his appointment, and after his retirement the fleet greatly deteriorated.

There had lately been uneasiness in the relations with foreigners in

CH. XVII.

the empire, and Admiral Lang's resignation entailed from a Chinese point of view the necessity of making some concession. With little persuasion, therefore, the Tsungli Yamên was induced to sign a convention with Great Britain (1890) opening the important trading centre of Chung K'ing to foreign trade. This city stands at the head of the four hundred miles of rapids which separate it from Ich'ang and is practically unapproachable by steamers. Two or three gun-boats have, after infinite trouble, made the passage, but, unless some method is adopted for clearing a passage down the rapids, native junks must remain the only means of trade communication between the two cities.

In this year (1890) the Duke and Duchess of Connaught visited China; but the Chinese found pretexts for avoiding a royal reception at Peking, and the Duke and Duchess were therefore obliged to confine their visit to the Treaty Ports. At this time and during the following year (1891) central China was in a disturbed state, and a feeling against foreigners was dominant. Besides the reasons for hostility already enumerated, strong opposition had been offered in the United States and Australasia to Chinese immigration. The Chinese complained that, while their countrymen were being thus excluded from white communities, the Powers were demanding that China should be thrown open to foreigners and foreign trade. The passing of the Geary Exclusion Act, May, 1892, by which the landing of Chinese in the United States was prohibited, aroused so much opposition that the Act was never enforced. But the hostility which it provoked produced a strong feeling in China, and probably had much to do with the ill-will which found expression during the early nineties. During this epoch several missionaries lost their lives (1891), and two Swedish missionaries were murdered at Hankow under circumstances of great atrocity.

Though Burma had been annexed to the British Crown, the boundary between that country and the French acquisitions in the neighbourhood of Siam had never been clearly defined; but in 1894 a Convention was signed with the French Government by which it was arranged that a commission should be appointed to mark out the boundaries between the two territories, and, meanwhile, it was agreed that a neutral zone should be established on the joint frontiers. By this agreement it was laid down that the Emperor of China should not cede either the State of Munglem or that of Kianghung to any other nation without previously coming to an agreement with her Britannic Majesty. But in spite of this compact China ceded to France during the following year (1895) a portion of the reserved territory. This breach of faith was strongly resented by the British Government, which insisted that the district of Kokang and part of Wangting should be granted to Great Britain by way of compensation, which was done (February, 1897).

Korea, which for centuries had held the anomalous position of a country tributary to two separate Powers, was destined at this time once more to attract international attention. During the reign of T'aitsung of the T'ang Dynasty (A.D. 627–650), the King of Korea, who had never yielded full obedience to the Emperor of China, taking advantage of the accession of a new line of Chinese sovereigns, began to resist any interference with the internal affairs of his kingdom. Resenting this attitude on the part of his tributary, T'aitsung espoused the cause of a small State, which had revolted against the King of Korea, and placed a large army on the frontier. Dismayed at this display of force, the King yielded the point in dispute; and Korea renewed her payments to China.

A chance incident, in 1875, foreshadowed the Chino-Japanese War of 1894–5. In that year it happened that a Japanese man-of-war was surveying the coast of Korea and was fired on without notice by a fort. Japan replied to this action by preparing a punitive expedition against the offending district. The Koreans, however, came to their senses in time to prevent hostilities; and a treaty was made under which two ports were opened to foreign trade and the right of sending a minister to reside at the Court of Korea was granted to the Japanese. In these negotiations Korea had been treated as an independent kingdom, and the tribute formerly claimed by Japan was allowed to drop. The hostile attitude assumed in 1875 by Korea towards the foreign Powers was due to the machinations of the King's father, T'aiwên Kun, who had presented an unyielding front to all reforms. So unmanageable was he that the Chinese Government despatched an envoy to kidnap him, and T'aiwên Kun was safely brought to Paoting Fu in China. Unfortunately, the Chinese allowed him later to return to his native country. He had no sooner arrived on the Korean shores (1884) than, at his instigation, an attack was made on the Japanese legation. Another expedition was fitted out to avenge this outrage. When events reached this critical stage, the Chinese despatched an army to the "Hermit Kingdom." Meanwhile, suggestions for peace were thrown out; and Count Ito and Li Hungchang met at Tientsin to arrange terms of amity.

In the course of these consultations it became obvious that China was unwilling to give up her suzerainty over Korea, which was capable of being used as a lever to enforce conditions with Japan. The two plenipotentiaries agreed that, if events should necessitate the despatch of either Chinese or Japanese troops to Korea, notice of the intention to send them should be given to the other Power.

Affairs had become so entangled in Korea that European nations took keen interest in the imbroglio. Russia began to cast longing eyes on Korean territory, and so imminent appeared the danger (1885) that the British Government occupied the islands known as Port Hamilton, off the coast of Korea. This roused so much opposition on the banks of the Neva that, after the lapse of two years (February 27, 1887), the British flag was hauled down, and the islands were returned to their previous owners on the understanding that in no case should they be handed over to any other foreign Power.

Korea at this time once more attracted international attention. In 1884, a rebellion had broken out in that misgoverned peninsula, and the leader of the outbreak, Kim-ok Kiun, had sought safety at Tōkiō. For a time his absence secured peace in the Korean capital. But, like most exiles, he continued to conspire; and so disturbing was his influence that it was determined to decoy him on to Chinese soil, where he might be put out of the way with the least inconvenience. Emissaries were sent to entice him to Shanghai, where he was murdered (1894). His body was carried to Korea, accompanied by his murderers, who were accorded a cordial welcome, while the ex-rebel's remains were subjected to every insult. This murder still further inflamed the political passions of the rebels known as the Tong Haks, to whose banners the people flocked. In their difficulty the Koreans appealed to China for help; and that Power, ever ready to pose as a suzerain, despatched two thousand troops to the neighbourhood of the Korean capital, at the same time, as by treaty bound, giving notice to Japan of their action. In response, the Japanese despatched an equal force to the peninsula and collected at Hiroshima a reserve army in case of emergency. These preparations had a moderating effect on the Tong Haks, and China and Japan made ready to withdraw their troops.

In the interests of permanent peace, however, Japan proposed to China that they should conjointly urge on the Korean Government the adoption of reforms in the administration of the kingdom. True to her reactionary policy, China declined to have anything to do with such a project and reminded Japan that, since Korea had claimed independence as an empire, she should be left to carry out her own reforms. Japan next turned to Korea itself; but, meeting with no satisfactory response, the Japanese minister, Otori, presented an ultimatum calling upon Korea to accept the reforms within the next three days (July 20, 1894). On the 22nd an unsatisfactory reply was received, and an attack was at once made on the capital. The city was taken without serious opposition and the King was made a prisoner. Meanwhile, both empires prepared for war. On July 21, several Chinese transports sailed for the Yalu river which forms the northern boundary of Korea, and for Asan on the south-western coast of the peninsula. On the part of Japan three men-of-war were sent to guard the coast; and on July 25 they sighted two Chinese men-of-war. An engagement followed, and within an hour one of the Chinese ships was driven ashore, while the other escaped to Wei-Hai-Wei. At the close of this action a Chinese man-of-war, escorting a transport, the *Kowshing*, appeared on the horizon. The man-of-war yielded herself a ready prey; but the *Kowshing*, a British vessel, refused to haul down her flag or to obey the Japanese order that she should follow the squadron to a Japanese harbour. Thereupon, the Japanese opened fire and sent the transport to the bottom with fifteen hundred men. The fleet protecting Asan having thus been disposed of, the Japanese opened the assault on that stronghold. The Chinese occupying force was commanded by General Yeh, who, so soon as the Japanese ships approached the harbour, vacated the city and marched off to Ping Yang, a position of great strength further north. Thus deprived of its garrison, Asan was straightway occupied by the Japanese, who followed the flying Yeh to Ping Yang. At this point Yeh was joined by two *corps d'armée* under the command of Generals Ma and Tao, who arrived on September 14 before the doomed city. On the next day the Japanese opened fire, and after a fierce assault captured the city, only to find that the garrison had made its escape by the northern gates. The Japanese had, however, before attacking the city, occupied the passes leading from the northern gates. As the fugitives showed themselves, the Japanese opened fire on them, slaughtering fifteen hundred of their number; the remainder, continuing their flight, made their way northward across the Yalu.

Two days after the date of this battle, a naval engagement took place off the mouth of the Yalu river. Both Chinese and Japanese had been busily engaged in landing troops on the coast of Korea and were so engaged when the fleets met off the island of Hai-Yang. So far as numbers were concerned, the two fleets were equal, and there was no hesitation about entering on the conflict. The Chinese adopted the older formation, placing their ships in line, while the Japanese steamed round them, taking every advantage of their formal antagonists. The battle lasted three hours; four Chinese ships were sunk, while another was so severely damaged that she was run aground. The Japanese did not lose a ship, though two were badly injured. After this victory the Japanese presented themselves on the bank of the Yalu. Contrary to Chinese expectations, instead of attempting to cross the river at the point where the southern road strikes its bank, they marched a few miles higher up and found little difficulty in crossing the stream. The Chinese had retreated to Chiulien-ch'êng, a city of considerable strength, but deserted it on the approach of the foe. In the same way they occupied and deserted Antung, Fênghwangch'êng, and Hsiuyen, all places of importance. Having thus driven back the enemy, the Japanese contented themselves with marching on Yingkow, the town of the treaty port of Niuchwang.

Successful so far, they now attacked Port Arthur on the Liao-Tung peninsula. The attacking force under Marshal Oyama landed at Hwayuenk'ow and without difficulty occupied the cities of Kinchow and Talienwan, both of which had been deserted by the Chinese. At Port Arthur the harbour was encircled by a continuous chain of forts, which had been constructed on the newest principles by French engineers. On November 21, the Japanese advanced to the attack. For a short time the Chinese fought well; but towards the end of the day they took to flight and made their escape northward along the line of the coast.

This defeat was of so overwhelming a nature that Li Hungchang memorialised the Emperor, suggesting that overtures of peace should be made. The Emperor consented and appointed an envoy. But no plenipotentiary powers having been conferred on him, he was not recognised at Tōkiō. At this time only one more stronghold remained to the Chinese. This was Wei-Hai-Wei, a fortified place of great strength on the north shores of the Shantung promontory. This position was held by Admiral Ting, who had fought at the battle of the Yalu, and who exerted himself to inspire his men with courage against the persistent attacks of the Japanese under Admiral Itō. This was difficult, and, after losing five ships of war, he surrendered the position. Having at the same time secured the lives of his surviving men, he committed suicide (February, 1895). This brought the War to a close, and the field was left open to the peacemakers. With persistent folly, the Chinese again sent an unauthenticated emissary, who was treated by the Japanese as his predecessor had been; and it was not until Li Hungchang presented himself at Shimonoseki (March 19, 1895) that negotiations were begun. The first meeting was held two days later, and after some successful sittings Li, on returning to his hotel, was shot in the face by a Japanese fanatic. Fortunately, the wound was slight and only for a while delayed the proceedings. On April 17, the Treaty of Shimonoseki was signed. By this treaty China ceded to Japan the Liao-Tung peninsula, the island of Formosa, and the Pescadores group. A war indemnity was fixed at 200,000,000 *taels*, which was to be paid in eight instalments. The cities Shashih, Chung K'ing, Soochow, and Hangchow were to be opened to trade "under the same conditions, and with the same privileges and facilities as exist at the other open cities, towns, and ports of China," while Japanese vessels were allowed to navigate the waters of the Upper Yang-tsze, the Wusung river, and the canals connecting Shanghai with Soochow and Hangchow. Until these conditions were fulfilled, China consented to the occupation by Japan of Wei-Hai-Wei. The ratifications of this treaty were exchanged at Chifu on May 8.

But the end was not yet. While critics were expressing surprise that Li Hungchang should have consented to the cession of the Liao-Tung peninsula, meetings were being held by the ministers of Russia, Germany, and France, which ended in the presentation to Japan of a collective note, in which the Mikado's Government was urged to forgo the cession of the territory, on the ground that any foreign Power possessing Port Arthur would dominate Peking. With great wisdom, Japan assented to this proposition, in return for the payment of an additional indemnity of 30,000,000 *taels*. Then followed a succession of secret conferences between Li Hungchang and Count Cassini, the Russian minister at Peking, which ended in a secret convention, the terms of which have never been officially published; but it is believed that they included guarantees to China for the integrity of the empire, especially in the event of any further attempt on the part of Japan to obtain a footing on the mainland; while China bound herself to afford facilities for the construction of a system of Russian railways through Manchuria, together with certain contingent rights along the coast line of northern China.

In 1896, Li Hungchang was sent to represent China at the coronation of Nicholas II, Tsar of Russia. He went to St Petersburg with the Cassini Convention in his pocket and obtained the ratification of it by Prince Lobanoff, the Russian Minister for Foreign Affairs. To meet her financial engagements arising out of the Shimonoseki Treaty China found to be no easy task, and opened negotiations with England for a loan of £12,000,000 sterling. Against this arrangement Russia entered a violent protest. So strong was the pressure brought to bear on China that the Tsungli Yamên begged the English authorities to allow them to forgo the loan. Having achieved this triumph at Peking, the Russian Government changed the venue of the negotiations to St Petersburg and arranged with the Chinese minister at that Court to furnish China with the necessary supplies. This arrangement was opposed by Great Britain; and, finally, the money was advanced by the Hongkong and Shanghai Banking Corporation, with the assistance of a German Bank.

On November 1, 1897, two German missionaries were murdered in a village near Chining Chow in the province of Shantung. The murder was peculiarly cold-blooded, and, so far as it was possible to discover, it was entirely causeless. The German Admiral, Diedrichs, resolved on immediate action; and, steaming into the harbour of Kiaochow in the incriminated province, took instant possession of the island of Tsingtao within that port. The Germans demanded an indemnity of 200,000 *taels* of silver; the rebuilding of the chapel destroyed during the riot; the repayment of the expenses incurred by Germany in the occupation of Kiaochow; the dismissal from the public service of Li Pinghêng, the Governor of Shantung; and the infliction of the severest penalties on the actual murderers. A ninety-nine years' lease of the captive territory and the cession of mining rights and railways within its boundaries were also demanded and granted. Full use has been made of these privileges; a line of railway has been constructed and opened to Tsinan Fu, the capital of the province, while a typical German town has already come into existence at Tsingtao.

Other cessions followed. Russia opened negotiations at Peking for permission to winter her fleet in Port Arthur (1897). This was readily granted, and led to a further request for the lease of the port on the same terms as those accorded to Germany. This was also granted without demur. The importance of this position may be judged from the fact that Port Arthur lies only one hundred and sixty-three miles from Taku and still nearer to Chifu, constituting the key to the position of northern China. The Convention by which this concession was granted was signed on March 15, 1898. On July 1 of the same year Sir Claude Macdonald signed a Convention by which Wei-Hai-Wei was leased to Great Britain, so long as Russia was in occupation of Port Arthur. Not to be behindhand, the French Government demanded the port of Kwang Chow Wan, and accepted an assurance from the Chinese Government that that portion of the empire should be recognised as being under French influence. At the same time, Great Britain asked for and was granted an accession of territory at Kowloon on the mainland opposite Hongkong, consisting of an area of two hundred square miles, together with an assurance that no other foreign Power would be admitted to any territorial rights in the valley of the Yang-tsze Kiang. While these negotiations were being carried on, Prince Kung died at Peking, after having guided the foreign policy of the empire for nearly fifty years. In the following year (1899) China gained one political victory in a matter of concessions. Encouraged by the success which had attended the efforts of others, the Italian minister at Peking opened negotiations for the lease of the port of Sanmên on the coast of Chekiang. To this unnecessary request the Chinese returned such an answer that nothing more was heard of the matter.

During the year 1898 the questions connected with the spread of Christianity in China came once more prominently to the front. The two parties to the controversy—respecting the rights of missionaries and their converts—were powerful and determined. On the one side were the native converts, few in number, though, as has since been proved, firm in purpose, backed by European missionaries and diplomatic action ; and on the other the great bulk of the non-Christian natives, who enjoyed the full support of the Mandarin class. This official antipathy may be said to have arisen in the seventeenth century, when, in opposition to the Jesuit missionaries, the Dominicans insisted on the question of the religious nature of the worship of ancestors being referred to the Pope. As it had already been declared by the reigning Emperor K'anghsi (1662–1722) that the rites were not religious, this reference to Rome was regarded as an insult to the Chinese Throne. But, apart from the religious difficulty, there has always been a political side to the question, and the Roman Catholic priests have given offence by the adoption of the emblems of official rank. Apart from its obvious impropriety, this assumption confers the right of entry into Courts of justice and entitles the wearers to interfere in legal cases. Missionaries of all societies, Roman Catholic as well as Protestant, have been accused of using influence in favour of converts in the native Courts of justice ; and, doubtless, Roman Catholic missionaries have freely used their influence for political as well as religious aims.

All this makes the action of the Chinese Government in 1899 the more astounding; for on March 15 in that year an imperial edict was issued, officially granting to missionaries of all creeds a political status of an important character. This edict was issued in obedience to pressure brought to bear on the Government by the French legation, and was at once put in force by the Roman Catholic missionaries. To their credit be it said, the privileges proffered were declined by the Protestants; and by a recent edict (1908) they have been withdrawn.

Another matter which created odium against Roman Catholic missionaries was a clause in the French Treaty of 1860, which entitled them to recover religious buildings which may have been snatched from them during the outbreaks of the past. Many of these buildings have for more than a century been converted into temples and dwelling-houses, and the attempt to restore them to the foreign owners must necessarily give occasion for bitter disputes. But probably the most direct cause of the numerous outbreaks against missionaries is the existence of orphanages conducted by Sisters of Mercy. To the practical Chinese it is unthinkable that men and women should leave their native countries to establish these institutions with no other object than that of benevolence. As the Tsungli Yamên said, in all the Chinese provinces native orphanages exist, making the institution of foreign homes superfluous. The orphanage at Tientsin was the direct cause of the massacre in 1870.

On the whole, the Chinese have a case, more especially against the Roman Catholic missionaries. The wisdom which guided Father Ricci and his comrades in the sixteenth century has long since ceased to direct the counsels of the missionaries. One marked feature of Chinese life is the publicity in which the people live. It is not considered a trespass freely to enter a neighbour's house, and, if there should be shown any disposition to resent the intrusion, it is at once held to suggest that the householder has some sinister motive for secrecy. Reared in this belief, the people are at a loss to explain on any other grounds the isolation in which Roman Catholic priests live. This is the most prominent of the causes which have led up to missionary riots, and to some extent it is fostered and promoted by increased knowledge of foreign affairs. In the western province of Szech'uan disturbances have of late (1899), also, been of frequent occurrence, and are to be traced more or less directly to the ill-feeling aroused by the wars with France and Japan. One of the numerous placards, which were issued to stir up the hostility of the natives against foreigners, warned the English, French, and Americans, that, if in the future they wished to preach their doctrine in China, they must drive the Japanese back to their own country.

Until lately Hunan has been regarded as the most anti-foreign province in the empire, and it was from this locality that the most virulent anti-foreign documents were issued. One of these, entitled

"A Death-blow to corrupt Doctrine," had a wide circulation and did infinite mischief; while, later, an illustrated work of the same nature, full of scandalous insinuations and baseless charges, had been issued to the people. The Roman Catholics call their faith " the Religion of the Lord of Heaven." It so happens that the Chinese word for "pig" has the same sound as that signifying "lord," and the author of this blasphemous work throughout its pages translates the " Religion of the Lord of Heaven " by the " Religion of the Heavenly pig." It was discovered that a man named Chow Han, holding the rank of a Taotai, was the author of these works. But so accurately had he given expression to the feelings of the people that no efforts of the British legation could move the Tsungli Yamên to take adequate action against him.

Although religious questions occupy a foremost place in the charges levelled against foreigners, other matters fill up the cup of their misdeeds, and among the chief of these is the opium traffic. There can be no question that very great evil is produced by this drug. But it is easy to overestimate the mischief. It is commonly stated that a man who has smoked long enough to have acquired the *yin*, or "craving," is incompetent to become a father; and it is frequently asserted that 40 or 50 per cent. of the male population are slaves to the *yin*. The teeming population of the country is the best answer to this exaggerated charge; and in great parts of the country, especially in the low-lying river beds, small doses of opium produce the salutary effect which they are known to have in the fens of Lincolnshire. But there can be no doubt that, speaking generally, the evils attending opium smoking are vastly greater than the good it effects; and it is not to be wondered that men like Chang Chihtung, who have the good of their country at heart, should desire to see it abolished. Chang Chihtung writes : " Assuredly it is not foreign intercourse that is ruining China, but this dreadful poison... Opium has spread with frightful rapidity and heart-rending results through the provinces. Millions upon millions have been struck down by the plague...The ruin of the mind is the most woeful of its many deleterious effects. The poison enfeebles the will, saps the strength of the body, renders the consumer incapable of performing his regular duties...It consumes his substance and reduces the miserable wretch to poverty, barrenness, and senility. Unless something is soon done to arrest this awful scourge in its devastating march, the Chinese people will be transformed into satyrs and devils."

Since the appearance of Chang Chihtung's work, however, a gigantic effort has been made to abolish opium smoking altogether in the Middle Kingdom. On September 20, 1906, the following edict was issued by order of the Emperor : " Since the first prohibition of opium, almost the whole of China has been flooded with the poison. Smokers of opium have wasted their time, neglected their employments, ruined their constitutions, and impoverished their households. Thus, for several decades China has presented a spectacle of increasing poverty and weakness...The Court is now determined to make China powerful; and it is our duty to urge our people to reformation in this respect. We decree, therefore, that within the limit of ten years this harmful filth be fully and entirely wiped away. We therefore command the Council of State to consider means for the strict prohibition both of opium smoking and of poppy growing."

Altogether, there is much to be said for the Chinese complaints against foreigners. The Chinese have everything that they want within the empire; and if foreigners force themselves upon China, it is maintained that they should submit to the country's laws.

In the later eighties these grievances found expression in a series of outrages along the valley of the Yang-tsze Kiang. At Chin Kiang an organised attack was made on the foreign settlement, in the course of which the British consulate was burned to the ground. Other localities suffered in the same way. In Kwangsi, in Szech'uan in the west, and in Shantung in the north, similar outrages were perpetrated. And this at a time when foreigners were contributing considerable sums of money for the alleviation of the distress caused by one of the recurrent floods of the Yellow river, and increased by a bad harvest.

The national disgrace entailed by the War of 1894–5 brought home to the Emperor and some of his advisers the imperative necessity of introducing reforms into the administration of the empire. Individual reformers had long been at work; and, in particular, K'ang Yuwei, who had earned for himself the title of the "Modern Sage," had plans cut and dried for revolutionising the body politic. Like most reformers, K'ang exaggerated the efficacy of his remedies; but in an interview granted to him by the Emperor he told so plausible a tale that Kwang Hsü adopted his views with enthusiasm. Everything was to be changed, from the Officers of State to the wearing of the queue, and the Emperor was by the stroke of his pen to create a new heaven and a new earth for China. The reactionary party at Peking appealed to the Dowager Empress to resume the reins of power. Nothing loth, she accepted the invitation, and, facing her imperial nephew, told him he must once more resign all rule into her hands (1898). This he did, and in quick succession edicts appeared reversing his decrees, and ordering the instant punishment of K'ang Yuwei and his associates. Fortunately for the "Modern Sage," he had notice of the coming storm and escaped; but his brother and five others were executed.

This reversal of official policy was reflected in the popular movements throughout the northern provinces of the empire. In Kiangsu, Anhui, Shantung, and Chili, disturbances, directed mainly against Christians, broke out. From the disorder which followed emerged a society known as the *Iho Ch'üan*, or Society of Boxers (literally patriotic harmonious fists). China is honey-combed with secret societies, and this one required

CH. XVII.

but the touch of the official hand to give it life and vigour. Edicts appeared in the *Peking Gazette* which gave imperial support to the agitation. The Powers, the people were told, cast looks of "tiger-like voracity on the empire." Viceroys and Governors were ordered to unite their forces and act together without distinction of jurisdiction. Never, they were told, should the word "Peace" fall from their lips, but each should strive to preserve his ancestral home and graves from the ruthless hands of the invader. This is a specimen of the exhortations issued by the Dowager Empress, who had a complete belief in the magical powers professed by the Boxers. An edict, signed by the Emperor, declared that, "finding there was no probability (or even possibility) of his having a child, he had besought the Dowager Empress to select some suitable person to be adopted as heir to the Emperor T'ung-Chih." P'uchün, a son of Prince Tuan, was upon this chosen to be the heir apparent.

Meanwhile, the political horizon became so overcast that the foreign ministers urged the Tsungli Yamên to suppress the Boxer movement, and in reply received assurances that everything was being done which could possibly conduce to that end ; and they pointed to the arrival of a large army, commanded by General T'ung Fuhsiang, as proof of the sincerity of their assurances. Unfortunately, T'ung's record was a bad one, and from the date of his arrival matters assumed a still more threatening aspect. In October, 1899, three British officers went to Luk'ou to inspect the railway bridge there under construction. This they found occupied by a party of T'ung's soldiers, who, instead of leaving the bridge when asked to do so, pelted the foreigners with stones. From this time matters went from bad to worse. The Boxers drilled openly, and constantly threatened foreigners and their native servants. At this juncture it was announced that Yühsien, the notoriously anti-foreign Governor of Shantung, had been transferred to the Governorship of Shansi. Against this appointment the foreign representatives remonstrated, but in vain. All through the winter of 1899–1900 matters continued extremely grave, and in April, 1900, Favier, the Vicar Apostolic of the Roman Catholic Mission at Peking, reported to the French minister that Christians had been massacred and villages burnt in the neighbourhood of Paoting Fu. In the following month an attack was made upon the railway works at Fêngt'ai near Peking. The Boxers burnt the station and tore up the railway.

Matters had now reached such a pitch that the foreign representatives applied to the Admirals at Taku for additional guards, and in response 340 men from the ships arrived at the various legations in Peking. At this crisis the appointment of Prince Tuan, a professed Boxer, to the chairmanship of the Tsungli Yamên, made the situation clear ; and it was felt that even the legations could no longer be regarded as places of safety. In this whirlpool of disorder, the Boxer army mustered and marched to rapine. So critical was the danger that the Admirals were again telegraphed to for reinforcements; and Admiral Seymour, at the head of a force of about 2000 men, left Tientsin for the capital on June 10. At first they met with little opposition; and an advance party reached Antung, where they found the railway line destroyed, and a large force of Boxers holding the position. On June 17 Admiral Seymour found that the line had been cut behind him at Yangtsun. The trains that attempted to communicate with Antung were unable to get through. Finding that weight of numbers made it impossible for him to advance, he determined to retreat to Tientsin by river. On the 22nd the force arrived abreast of the Siku arsenal, which opened fire on the flotilla. Accepting this challenge, Admiral Seymour attacked the arsenal and took it. In it were found large quantities of rice and ammunition. A small party of marines were sent to cut their way through to Tientsin by night, but were forced to retire. On the morning of June 23 the Chinese made a desperate attempt to recapture the arsenal, but were repulsed after hard fighting. Happily, a messenger succeeded in making his way through the Chinese lines to Tientsin, and a relieving force was sent which returned with the expeditionary troops to Tientsin on June 26.

Meanwhile, the Taku forts had been taken by assault on June 16, an act that was held by the Chinese to constitute a declaration of war. The imperial troops now joined the Boxers and the legations at Peking and the foreign settlements at Tientsin were besieged. The settlements at Tientsin were in a very unprotected state, and, had it not been for the fortunate arrival of a force of 1700 Russians, the probability is that they would have been destroyed and the legations taken. As it was, the foreigners in the settlements were powerless. Their communications with the Taku forts were cut off, and their defensive works were of the crudest. On June 15, the Boxers set fire to parts of the native city, and, having sixty guns at their disposal, were able to play havoc from the city walls on the settlements and their surroundings. At length, on June 24, a relieving force of 2000 strong made its way through from Taku, and, with this increase of numbers, the allied commanders prepared to attack the city. During the whole of July 13, the allies bombarded the city wall, and the next morning they advanced to the attack. Just before sunrise the Japanese sappers made an attempt to blow in the outer city gate. The Chinese met them with a tremendous fire, and a bullet cut the electric wire which was intended to ignite the charge. Second Lieutenant Inouyé then pluckily rushed forward and exploded it with a lighted fuse. This gate only led into an enclosure; one of the soldiers, however, climbed the wall, and opened the gate from the inside. Thereupon, the Chinese fled, and the city was occupied by the allied forces.

Instant preparations were now made for the relief of the legations

CH. XVII.

at Peking; and, on August 4, a relief column composed of 18,800 men taken from the allied armies set out on their march to Peking. At Peitsang, Yangtsun, and Hosiwu, engagements were fought in which the Chinese were easily routed. T'ungchow, twelve miles from Peking, was found to be evacuated; and, in the middle of the night of the 13th, word was brought to the British commander that the Russians had commenced their attack on the city wall of Peking and were asking for reinforcements. These were supplied from the Japanese lines, but the honour of being the first to relieve the legations was reserved for General Gaselee, who, in obedience to a note from Sir Claude Macdonald, entered the city by the Water Gate on the southern wall.

For eight weeks the legations had withstood a strict siege. When it was reported to them that Seymour's relief column was to start on June 10 from Tientsin, Sugiyama, of the Japanese legation, went to the station to welcome it. There he found T'ung Fuhsiang's troops in possession. These bandits set upon the helpless Japanese and beat him to death. This may be said to have marked the beginning of the war in Peking. On June 19 the Chinese Government wrote to the legations, giving the foreigners twenty-four hours in which to leave the capital. The ministers in consultation wrote to the Tsungli Yamên to ask for an interview. No answer to this proposal having been received on the following day, the ministers, with the exception of Baron von Ketteler, the German minister, agreed to await events. Von Ketteler set forth alone to pay the proposed visit and was shot dead within a few hundred yards of his legation. Peace was no longer possible, and the foreigners of all nationalities retreated to their legations. The British legation, being the largest and best appointed, formed the refuge of all those who, as the siege progressed, were driven out of their places of retreat. The Peit'ang, under the direction of Bishop Favier, withstood all the assaults of the enemy.

That such small bodies of men should have succeeded in keeping so large a force at bay would suggest that the besiegers were not anxious to proceed to extremities; and, in fact, as the relieving force approached the capital, attempts at conciliation were made by the members of the Tsungli Yamên. The Chinese Ministers sent civil letters and presents to the different legations. On the arrival of the column, the Chinese made but a faint-hearted defence; and, as it entered the southern gates, the Dowager Empress, with the Emperor and Court, sought safety in flight to Si-an-fu, the capital of the province of Shensi. Thus for the second time this lady was driven from her capital by foreign invading forces (1860 and 1900). Prince Ching and Li Hungchang were appointed plenipotentiaries to arrange terms of amity.

The Chinese proposals were singularly inadequate, and were at once dismissed. In their place, it was demanded that due punishment should be inflicted on the officials implicated in the Boxer movement; that an indemnity should be paid; that the Taku and other forts between Peking and the sea should be dismantled; that the importation of fire-arms should be prohibited; that permanent legation guards should be established; that the Tsungli Yamên should be abolished; that the provincial examinations in those districts where foreigners had been murdered should be suspended for five years; and that a rational system of intercourse with the Emperor should be arranged.

After much discussion these terms were virtually conceded by the Chinese; and Princes Tuan and Tsailan were sentenced to death, three other high officials were condemned to commit suicide, and three other high-placed Mandarins were beheaded. It was further agreed that Prince Ch'un should proceed to Berlin to convey to the German Emperor the expression of the regrets of the Son of Heaven for the assassination of Baron von Ketteler, and that another mission should be despatched to Tōkiō to apologise for the murder of Sugiyama. The indemnity was fixed at the sum of 450,000,000 *taels*. With the signing of this protocol (September 7, 1901) peace was restored, shortly followed by the death of Li Hungchang after a brief illness on November 7, 1901.

The Boxer movement had been eagerly watched by the Russian Government. When the Boxers appeared to be making way, some anxiety was felt in the outlying posts occupied by the Russians in Manchuria—at Blagovestchensk, among other places. The growth of this town had been rapid, and a small force of Russians found themselves opposed to a large Chinese population. The disparity between the two nationalities so alarmed General Chichegoff, the Governor, that he ordered all Chinese to cross to the south side of the river Amur. There was some hesitation about obeying this order, upon which the Governor commanded his soldiers to drive the people across the river. This they did at the point of the bayonet, 4500 people being drowned in the process.

Meanwhile, the relations between Japan and Russia had become threatening. The demand for the retrocession of Port Arthur at the end of the War had aroused the suspicion of the Japanese, and the persistent way in which Russia continued to pour troops into Manchuria provided further food for reflexion. The agreement by which China, in addition, granted permission to Russia to make railroads connecting her Siberian system with Vladivostók and Port Arthur gave further indications of Russian policy. If, however, Russia had stopped there, matters might have been arranged; but she cast longing eyes on the port of Masampo on the south-eastern coast of Korea. This movement elicited a vigorous remonstrance at Seoul, and Russia found it advisable not to proceed with the demand (1899). Thus baffled in Korea, the Russians devoted more detailed attention to Manchuria; and this culminated in an agreement made on November 11, 1900, with the Tartar general at Mukden, by which Admiral Alexéyeff invited the Chinese to resume the government of the country under the protection of Russia, the latter to have the right of navigating the Yalu and cutting timber on its banks. This produced another protest from Japan. The position of affairs was at this time considerably altered by the conclusion of an offensive and defensive alliance between Great Britain and Japan (1902). The effect of this treaty was instantaneous; but still Russia refused to believe that Japan would proceed to extremities against her, and considered that the British nation was satisfied with an agreement (1899) in which it was declared that the portion of the Niuchwang railway line inside the Great Wall was within the British sphere of influence, and that any railway north of the same barrier was within that of the Russians. After some delay in the negotiations, Japan sent an ultimatum to St Petersburg, in which she proposed to recognise Manchuria as Russia's sphere of influence, provided Russia would recognise Japanese influence as paramount in Korea. Not receiving a reply to this message, Japan withdrew her ambassador from St Petersburg on February 6, 1904, and three days later Admiral Uriu sank two Russian cruisers which were lying at Chemulpo in Korea. Later on the same day, Admiral Togo attacked the Russian fleet at Port Arthur and sank two battleships and one armoured cruiser. The causes and results of this War are dealt with in a separate chapter.

The victory of Japan came as a revelation to the Chinese, to whom it naturally occurred that, if the Japanese could do such things, they might do likewise. This idea made the Chinese seek to discover wherein the great strength of the Japanese lay. They found the explanation in Western learning, and they hastened to establish reformed schools and colleges throughout the empire. The learning of Confucius was at a discount; and all public temples except those under special imperial guarantee were converted into schools. Numbers of Japanese professors were imported to instruct the youths, and on the other hand thousands of Chinese young men were sent to study in Japan. At the same time, five commissioners were sent in 1905 to Europe and America to examine the systems of government adopted in those continents. The problem which the commissioners were called upon to solve was a difficult one; and it is questionable whether the time they devoted to the task—three months—was sufficient for their purpose. On their return, they requested the Throne "to issue a decree fixing on five years as the limit within which China would adopt a constitutional form of government." Four of these years have already sped, and the first step towards a constitutional government has only recently been taken by a decree establishing provincial assemblies.

But, though there may be delays, much has been accomplished, and since the war of 1904–5 a general desire for foreign education has been everywhere shown. One remarkable development has been the translation of European works into Chinese. In military matters vast strides in advance have been made, and the recently (January 2, 1909) dismissed

Yuan Shikai had already shown how much may be effected by the zeal and energy of a single man. At recent autumn manœuvres the regiments under his command showed a sense of discipline and order which was most remarkable and suggested the idea that the old order of military things had indeed disappeared. In other directions much progress is to be observed—notably in the construction of railways. The practically minded Chinese have readily learned to value this new mode of transport, and the work is proceeding. Already (1907) 3539 miles of railways have been constructed and are in operation, while 1285 miles are under construction.

The history of the foreign customs affords an example of what a foreigner may accomplish in China. In 1905 Sir Robert Hart was able to return an income from the foreign customs of £5,281,000, a sum which alone out of the various sources of Chinese revenue furnished an acceptable security for foreign loans. A postal system, also established by Sir Robert Hart, is returning an increasing income year by year. In 1904 it yielded 400,000 dollars and in 1905, 600,000.

If a new era is to begin for China, the almost simultaneous deaths of the Emperor Kwang Hsü and of the Dowager Empress Tz'ŭ Hsi, announced in November, 1908, may perhaps be destined to serve as the landmark from which the initiation of the new order will have to be dated. The death of Tz'ŭ Hsi, at any rate, closed an eventful epoch.

ANNAM.

For many centuries Annam, consisting of the provinces of Tonkin on the north, Annam in the centre, and Cochin China on the south, had been in an intermittent state of disorder. At the time of the expansion of England in India the position tempted the ambitions of the French King, who was desirous of founding an Asiatic kingdom as a counterbalance to our Indian empire. At this time King Gialong of Annam had been dethroned, and through the influence of the Bishop Pigneau de Behaine had petitioned for the help of France to recover his Crown. The Bishop promptly escorted the ex-monarch's son to Paris, where he was received with cordiality by Louis XVI, who concluded a treaty with him in 1787. In consequence, however, of the French Revolution the full design was allowed to lapse into oblivion, though Gialong was restored to the throne with French assistance.

In 1824, the French officers remaining in the country were expelled and foreigners were thenceforward excluded. Many French and Spanish missionaries were put to death; a condition of affairs that existed until the Anglo-French campaign in China, which ended in the Treaties of Tientsin (1858), furnished a convenient opportunity for despatching an expedition to the country. The result of this mission was the capture of the important city of Saigon, where the French established themselves in March, 1859. The occupation of this city was the beginning of an Indo-Chinese conquest, resulting in the cession to France of the provinces of Saigon, Mytho, and Bienhoa, with the islands of Pulo-condore (1862), the establishment of a French protectorate over Cambodia (1863), and the occupation of the three provinces lying to the south-west of Saigon (1867). In 1866, an expedition was organised for the exploration of the Mekong river. This stream was found to be no waterway, a fact which compelled the explorers to seek some other route by which they might reach the Chinese province of Yunnan; and, in this search, they struck the Red river, which connects Yunnan Fu with the Gulf of Tonkin.

At this time Yunnan was in the hands of Mohammadan rebels, and the Chinese were anxious to secure a safe route by which they might import arms to their forces in that province. They therefore furthered the French project and gave the explorers letters of recommendation to the authorities at the provincial capital. On the other hand the French, while anxious to do all they could to support the expedition, were unwilling to commit themselves irretrievably. Captain Senez, who commanded the vessel in which it was arranged that Dupuis, the explorer, should take his passage northward, arrived off the coast of Tonkin in November, 1872. Without delay he proceeded up the river to Hanoi, and at once opened communications with the authorities. He found them to be less complacent than he had anticipated, and he had no sooner sailed again for Saigon than direct opposition became apparent. Upon this, he seized some native boats, and, having loaded them with arms, ascended the river. His progress was watched by the natives, who refused him supplies. He had, however, the satisfaction of handing over his cargoes to the Chinese Commandant of Yunnan Fu. On his return to Tonkin, he found that the opposition of the Annamese officials had become intensified. At the same time, a request was made to Saigon that the Governor should send an official to adjudicate on the points in contention. In reply to this appeal Garnier, who had taken an active part in the exploration of the Mekong, was sent to Hanoi (1873). He immediately issued a proclamation informing the people that he had been despatched to promote trade and to further the prosperity of the province. In reply, the Annamese authorities notified the people that they were quite able to take care of themselves and did not want any interference on the part of the French. Thereupon, Garnier issued a further proclamation, announcing that the country was open to foreign trade, and demanding the surrender of the citadel of Hanoi, as well as the issue of instructions to the native Governors to obey the orders of the French, and the granting of permission for Dupuis to enter freely into Yunnan. This document Garnier treated as an ultimatum, and, when acceptance of it was refused by the Annamese, attacked the citadel and captured it without difficulty.

Being now committed to offensive operations, Garnier and his subordinates attacked the fortified places within their sphere of action and made themselves masters of the delta of the Red river. With a courage begotten of contempt, Garnier disregarded the threatening attitude of the Annamese and Chinese troops now in the field against him. A considerable force of these allies advanced to recapture Hanoi. Garnier placed himself at the head of the garrison and sallied out to meet the enemy. When leading on his men, he stumbled and fell, and was immediately stabbed to death. A like fate overtook his second in command.

Though so far successful, the Annamese were anxious for peace, and sent an emissary to Saigon to ask for the appointment of a plenipotentiary. In reply, the Governor of Saigon appointed an emissary to arrange a treaty with the Annamese. This document assumed that the Annamese had the right to make a treaty without reference to their suzerain power, China (1874). Tolerance was promised to missionaries and their converts, and the internal peace of the country was guaranteed. The terms of this Treaty were, however, ignored by the Annamese, who, as time went on, became more active in their oppression of the Christians within their dominions. For some time France endured these outrages ; but in 1882 affairs reached such a point that she felt bound to intervene again, and Captain Rivière was despatched to Hanoi to support French interests. Following in the footsteps of Garnier, Rivière attacked the citadel, and lost his life in so doing.

Meanwhile, China had been silently watching events and had encouraged the "Black Flags" to support the Annamese in their opposition to the French. These irregulars gave backbone to the Annamese forces, as the French were beginning to find out. They saw the futility of protracting this state of warfare and demanded the conclusion of a treaty which would cede to them Tonkin. Already, a similar proposition had been brought forward at Peking by the French minister Bourrée, who suggested that the portion of the province of Tonkin north of the Red river should remain tributary to China, while the portion south of the Red river should be ceded to France. In return, France was to defend Tonkin against all comers. The conclusion of this Treaty (December, 1882) was irregular. By tradition and law Annam was one of the dependencies of China, and the King therefore had no power to conclude a treaty without the concurrence of his suzerain. Its terms were no sooner communicated to the Tsungli Yamên than Prince Kung repudiated them. Meanwhile the French troops again took the field, and, in spite of a warning that an attack on the city of Sontai would be treated by the Chinese as a declaration of war, laid siege to and captured that fortress. About the same time the strongholds of Hanoi and Haiphong also fell into their hands. The loss of these places produced consternation at Peking. The King of Annam formally declared

CH. XVII.

war against France, and the occupation of Hué, the capital city, followed
(1883).   But while fighting was going on negotiations were in progress ;
and the plenipotentiaries of the two Powers at this time came to an
understanding that France was to assume a protectorate over Annam
(1883).

Li Hungchang was the only man who could lead China out of the
entanglements into which she had fallen, and the Dowager Empress
acted wisely when she appointed him Commander-in-Chief in south
China.   Subsequent events proved that he carried with him powers
beyond those attaching to his military command ; for, on arriving at
Shanghai, he proceeded to open negotiations with Tricou, the newly
arrived French minister.   So promising did these *pourparlers* prove
that Li hastily returned to Peking to urge on his imperial mistress the
advisability of making peace with their enemies.

On the question of peace or war the Peking Cabinet was divided ;
and Prince Kung was dismissed from all his offices for venturing to
advocate a pacific policy.   While the issues were still confused, a chance
meeting at Canton between Captain Fournier, commanding a French
man-of-war, and Detring, of the imperial Customs Service, led to
further complications.   By some argument which has never been explained, Detring persuaded Fournier to steam northwards to Tientsin for
the purpose of opening negotiations with Li Hungchang, without any
regard to Tricou at Peking.   Behind the back of the minister, Fournier
was authorised from Paris to play the part of a plenipotentiary, and
with as little delay as possible these two agents concluded the Convention
known by Fournier's name.   This document was signed on May 11, 1884,
and by its terms France undertook to protect the southern frontiers of
China, while China on the other hand agreed to withdraw her garrisons
from Tonkin and to respect the treaties concluded between France and
the kingdom of Annam.   A verbal undertaking was at the same time
given by Li that all Tonkinese garrisons near the boundaries of
Kwangtung and Kwangsi should be evacuated within twenty days from
the date of the Treaty, while the fortresses abutting on Yunnan should
be evacuated within forty days.   In case of non-observance of these
limits of time, France should be free to expel the laggard garrisons.
The Fournier Convention was arrived at under a vow of secrecy, Tricou
being informed that, though negotiations had been going on at Tientsin,
nothing definite had taken shape.

The two agents parted, holding divergent views on the limits of
time at which the main fortified posts in Tonkin were to be evacuated
by the Chinese.   General Millot believed himself to be within his
rights when he ordered Colonel Duchesne to occupy Langson.   On
approaching the walls of this fortress, the French encountered a Chinese
force, the commander of which declined to give way before the invaders,
as he had not received any instructions to that effect ; while, through
a further misunderstanding, an engagement was precipitated, in which

the French were defeated and put to rout. The news of this disaster caused consternation in Paris, and Jules Ferry at once despatched remonstrances to the Tsungli Yamên, where the French minister was met by the round assertion that the French troops were the invaders, and that the Chinese commander was only doing his duty according to the terms of the Treaty. A reference to this document proved that the Chinese were technically in the right. Both sides stood to their guns, and an end was put to the prevailing uncertainty by the presentation of an ultimatum demanding that the terms of the Fournier Convention should be carried out at once, and that the Chinese troops should evacuate Tonkin without delay. Negotiations were reopened at Shanghai, while at the same time a French fleet was blockading the northern coast line of Formosa. Some doubtful successes were obtained by the French arms in this direction, but a more substantial though less honourable advantage was gained by an attack made on the Chinese fleet in the harbour of Foo-chow. As it was there understood that negotiations for peace were in progress, no opposition was offered to the entrance of the French fleet, which opened fire on the Chinese ships, most of which were in a few minutes either sunk or disabled. It was now plainly impossible that the French representative could remain at Peking. He therefore hauled down his flag and took up his residence at Shanghai. The Chinese now poured troops into Tonkin, but success did not attend their banners. Langson was successfully occupied by the French, and other places of less note fell into their hands.

Sir Robert Hart had throughout these proceedings been active in the interests of peace, and had charged his representative at Paris to lose no opportunity of laying the Chinese aspect of the quarrel before the French Ministry. The result of these efforts was that a protocol was signed on April 4, 1885, which was followed by a Treaty, signed on June 9, by the two most important Articles of which (1 and 11) it was laid down that "France engages to reestablish and maintain order in those provinces of Annam which border upon the Chinese empire. For this purpose, she shall take the necessary measures to disperse or expel the bands of pirates or vagabonds who endanger the public safety... nevertheless, the French troops shall not, under any circumstances, cross the frontier which separates Tonkin from China, which frontier France promises both to respect herself and to guarantee against any aggression whatsoever. On her part China undertakes to disperse or expel such bands as may take refuge in her provinces bordering on Tonkin, and to disperse those which may be tempted to form there for the purpose of causing disturbances amongst the populations placed under the protection of France ; and, in consideration of the guarantees which have been given as to the security of the frontier, she likewise engages not to send troops into Tonkin." The signature of this Treaty restored peace to Tonkin, and it has been maintained down to the present time.

CH. XVII.

Bismarck once described the colonial positions of the three great Powers in the epigram, "England has colonies and colonists; Germany has colonists but no colonies; France has colonies but no colonists." This last clause accurately represents the case of France. The French colonies have formed the happy hunting grounds of political partisans who have successfully competed for the administrative posts in the far-off regions. This was eminently the case with Annam down to the year 1896. Prior to that date, swarms of office-holders swelled the annual budgets and added little to the efficiency of the administration. They knew nothing of the languages of the natives, and cared nothing for the maintenance of civil law and order.

In these circumstances, the colony became a heavy burden on the Parisian exchequer, and constant outbreaks disturbed the relations of the colony with the mother country. Fortunately for all concerned, M. Doumer was appointed Governor-General of Indo-China in December, 1896, and he at once, by his administrative ability, changed the aspect of affairs. The principal items of his programme of reforms were the improvement of the financial situation of Indo-China, and the creation of a financial policy suited to the country and its needs; the pacification of Tonkin; the organisation of a Government-General; the completion and the reform of the administration of the protectorate; and the extension of the influence of France and the development of its interests in the Far East, particularly in the countries adjoining the colony—that is, in Siam and China.

M. Doumer's first step towards the attainment of these objects was to constitute a Legislative Council, which was divided into four committees, the first dealing with military and naval affairs, public works, railways, commerce and agriculture; the second with legislation and administrative organisation; the third with the budgets; and the fourth with other financial matters. Under this reformed administration the colony flourished abundantly. The foreign trade of the colony increased from 162,000,000 of francs in 1893 to 400,000,000 in 1902. Of these sums the share of France increased from 30,000,000, or less than one-fifth, to 148,000,000, or more than one-third. Happily for the colony, the reforms introduced by M. Doumer have been maintained, and there is every prospect that the colony will continue its successful career in the future.

THE PHILIPPINE ISLANDS.

The Philippine Islands first appear in history in 1520. In that year Magellan, in pursuance of the Papal Bull which divided the world of discovery between Spain and Portugal, steered his course in the direction of the Spice Islands. In this quest he found himself in touch with a group of islands, which were subsequently named, after Philip II, the Philippines. Here he met his death in 1521. This archipelago consists of upwards of 1600 islands of all sizes. The whole surface is extremely volcanic—23 volcanoes being active at the present time; and between 1880 and 1896 the surface of the land was disturbed by 221 earthquakes. The Philippines contain a population of 7,572,199, which mainly consists of aborigines and Malays, with a liberal sprinkling of Chinese.

Among these inhabitants missionary friars actively pursued their work of conversion, and, although constant quarrels disturbed their relations with the civil authorities, much good work was done. Schools and colleges were established and charitable institutions as well as hospitals were founded.

The wars and rumours of wars that perennially disturbed the relations between the Spaniards and the natives were further complicated by the advent of Chinese expeditions, which commonly ended in frightful massacres. In 1591 an envoy from Japan arrived, demanding the allegiance of the native King to the Emperor of Japan. This visit caused much anxiety; but the Governor-General by his judicious treatment of the ambassador succeeded in inducing him to conclude a treaty of peace with Spain.

In 1762 the alliance entered into by France and Spain against England brought England into the field as a competitor for the ownership of the Philippines. Without much difficulty, the British effected a landing and hoisted their flag on Port Santiago, where it flew until January 30, 1764, when news of the Treaty of Paris reached Manila. During the nineteenth century the disputes between the natives and the Spaniards led to some formidable insurrections. In 1872 a rebellion against the Spanish yoke broke out, led by a distinguished Filipino, Burgos. This outbreak failed, through a misunderstanding of the signal agreed upon; and after some sharp fighting the Spaniards gained a decisive victory.

But, though this particular revolt was thus brought to an end, peace was not secured. In course of time the rule of the friars had become harsh and tyrannical, and simultaneously there had grown up a desire for more extended liberty among the natives, many of whom had visited Europe, while some few had represented the Philippines in the Cortes at Madrid. In consequence of the resulting dissatisfaction a series of outbreaks occurred, which showed the advisability of granting administrative reforms to the archipelago. Commissioners were appointed from time to time to study the political conditions; educational facilities were given to the natives; and changes were brought about in the system of civil administration. These reforms did not, however, satisfy the Filipinos, who demanded the expulsion of the friars; a political administration similar to that granted to Cuba; the return to the owners of the land seized by the friars; the prevention of insults to the Philippine natives; and economy of expenditure. In 1896 a petition was addressed to the Emperor of Japan, inviting him to annex the islands. The Japanese Government forwarded this document to Madrid, thus putting the Spaniards in possession of the revolutionary plan which was on foot. Martial law was proclaimed and numerous arrests were made; but the action of the Spanish authorities was hampered by a serious outbreak in Cuba, which demanded the presence of a large force of men. The Governor-General deemed it wise, in these circumstances, to offer an amnesty to all those who should lay down their arms. Many Filipinos accepted this offer, and the revolutionary movement would probably have died out, had it not been for the appearance, on July 2, 1897, of an edict imposing severe restrictions on the movements of the people in the towns, who were placed under pain of being treated as rebels. The reply to this edict was a document urging all to take up arms, demanding the expulsion of the friars, popular representation, freedom of the Press, and more just laws in general. In face of this uprising, the Spaniards thought it wise to negotiate, and appointed Pedro Paterno, a Filipino, to negotiate with Aguinaldo, who represented the insurgents. A treaty was the result, by the terms of which the Filipinos were to lay down their arms, and Aguinaldo and other leaders were to be deported from the archipelago.

Affairs were still in an unsettled condition, when news of the declaration of war between the United States and Spain reached Manila. The first local incident of this War was the destruction of the Spanish fleet at Cavite on May 1, 1898. Two months later, American troops were landed in Luzon; and on August 13 Manila surrendered to them. General Merritt, who commanded the troops, was nominated Governor; and on the following day he issued a proclamation in which he declared the abolition of Spanish authority and the continuance of municipal laws, extending protection to places devoted to religious worship, art, science, and education. By the Treaty of Paris, December 10, 1898, peace was restored, and the Philippines were ceded to the United States. Meanwhile, General Aguinaldo had returned to Manila on May 19, 1898, on board a United States man-of-war. There seems to have been some confusion about the terms on which this agitator was allowed to return. By the Americans he was given considerable latitude of action, which he stretched according to circumstances. On landing, he immediately began to organise an army and a government under the American flag, and notified his fellow subjects that the American Government was for the future merely to exercise a protectorate over the islands, leaving the natives to govern themselves. These measures led to friction. He, however, continued to promise to the people national independence, and formed a Cabinet for the government of the archipelago. He established a Philippine Republic, with himself as President.

Gradually, the relations of the Americans with the Filipinos became more strained; and on February 4, 1899, the shooting of a native soldier who attempted to cross the American lines in the darkness produced an outbreak of hostilities. Thus war again broke out, and the American troops overran the archipelago without serious difficulty. In August Malalos, the insurgent capital, was taken, and central and northern Luzon were subdued. By November, 1899, all organised opposition had ceased, though guerrilla warfare and brigandage continued. In April, 1901, Aguinaldo was captured, and other prominent insurgent officers were afterwards taken. The insurrection was declared at an end on July 1, 1901, when the President of the United States issued a proclamation handing over the islands to a civil Government, of which Judge Taft was appointed the head. Under this new form of administration three Filipino members were added to the Commission, which it was intended should be ultimately superseded by a Philippine Assembly, to consist of from fifty to a hundred members, composed of representatives from each province; and thus, it was hoped, would be established a distinct separation of State, Church, and military interests. All these functions had, under the Spanish rule, been exercised by the Spanish Governor-General, and no such thing as a representative assembly was known. Under the present American scheme "the governing body itself is composed partly of Filipinos; the majority of the provincial Governors are natives; the Chief Justice and certain other members of the supreme Court are likewise Filipinos; the judges of the Courts of first instance are largely native born; and the municipal officials, with the exception of the health officer in certain places, are always Filipinos."

It is admitted on all hands that the Filipinos are not as yet ripe for self-government. Meanwhile, the Americans are educating them up to the level required for this; and, in the interval, the condition of the archipelago is improving; trade is increasing, as is shown by the fact that the total trade in 1905 amounted to £12,701,064, an increase of £925,618 over that of the preceding year; and education is spreading. "I firmly believe," said President Roosevelt in his message to Congress in December, 1904, "that you can help them (the Filipinos) to rise higher and higher in the scale of civilisation and of capacity for self-government, and I most earnestly hope that in the end they will be able to stand, if not entirely alone, yet in some such relation to the United States as Cuba now stands."

THE MALAY PENINSULA.

A glance at the map is sufficient to show how completely the Malay peninsula with the islands which start from its southern point separates the China Sea from the Indian Ocean, and it is, therefore, not surprising to find that its shores formed the scene of a constant struggle for the mastery between the Dutch and the English during the early days of Eastern exploration ; indeed, it was not until towards the end of the eighteenth century that British supremacy in the peninsula was definitely recognised.

The British flag was hoisted at Penang on August 11, 1786, and Malacca surrendered to the British just nine years later. The Crown colony known as the Straits Settlements, comprising Penang, the province of Wellesley and the Dindings, Malacca and Singapore, was established later. Connected with these settlements are the Federated Malay States, which consist of the sultanates of Perak, Selangor, the Negri Sembilan, and Pahang. The relations between these States and Great Britain were established gradually, and were formed in the haphazard way which has marked the incorporation of so many of our colonial dependencies. Down to the year 1873, when Sir Andrew Clarke was appointed Governor of the Straits Settlements, the government of the Malay States was still in its pristine condition : every necessary as well as every luxury of life was heavily taxed ; in the law Courts the decisions depended solely on the relative wealth or influence of the litigants, and the punishments were barbarous ; a system of debt-slavery existed, under which not only the debtor but his wife and their most remote descendants were condemned to hopeless bondage ; forced labour was exacted for indefinite periods and entirely without remuneration ; and the Rajah had the right to compel all female children to pass through his harem.

Sir Andrew Clarke brought with him to Singapore instructions from the Colonial Office to examine into and report upon the political systems of the several States. Enquiry revealed to him the barbarous systems existing under the rule of the Rajahs, and he at once determined to improve on the instructions given him in Downing Street. Without much difficulty he persuaded the Sultans of Perak, Selangor, the Negri Sembilan, and Pahang to receive British Residents at their Courts and to submit to their advice on political and financial matters, leaving out of account all social customs and religious rites.

The new system appeared to work well and had been in operation about a year when Birch, the Resident at Perak, was murdered with the connivance of the Sultan of that State (1875). This proceeding alarmed the Colonial Secretary of State, who severely censured Sir Andrew Clarke for having exceeded his instructions. The government at Perak by British officers in the name of the Sultan was forbidden ; the duties of the Residents were limited to the " giving of influential and responsible advice"; and the Resident of Perak was warned that " the Residents have been placed in the native States as advisers, not as rulers, and if they take upon themselves to disregard this principle they will most assuredly be held responsible if trouble springs out of their neglect of it." These instructions were plausible, and, if the Malays were capable of tempering the evils of despotism by statesmanship, would have been judicious and wise. But the constitution of Malay society made this impossible.

The Malay people may be divided into two classes. On the one hand are those who can lay claim, however indirectly, to royal lineage, and on the other the main body of the people, who by enforced labour are compelled to supply a quota of the revenue. It is from the first class that the exercise of any reforming power could alone be expected; but their personal interests are bound up in the present system. The people are inherently indolent, and so long as their labour can produce enough to maintain life they are content. In view of this position, the British Government, after mature consideration, determined to revert to the policy of Sir Andrew Clarke, and, through the European advisers on the staffs of the sultanates, to secure step by step the complete control of the administration. The results have proved eminently satisfactory. By the year 1884 slavery had been abolished throughout British Malaya; in 1888 Pahang, the largest State of the Federation, accepted a British Resident; in 1895 the small States forming the Negri Sembilan were placed under one native ruler; and in the following year the four States —Perak, Selangor, the Negri Sembilan, and Pahang—were combined in a Federation for the purpose of mutual assistance, continuity of policy, and uniformity of administrative methods.

The main wealth of the Federated Malay States consists of the tin mines, which supply the greater part of the world's tin. In 1901, out of the total export trade valued at $71,350,000, tin represented $61,689,000, or more than 86 per cent. of the whole. In the same year tin paid as export duty $8,439,000; and the opium, spirit, and gambling licenses brought in $3,726,000. A marked feature in the financial condition of the States is that owing to the indolence of the natives the revenue of the country is nearly all paid by Chinese immigrants. Thus the tin is produced entirely by the industry of the Chinese miners; and the sums derived from the opium, spirit, and gambling licenses are drawn from them.

The Federated Malay States cover an area of 25,000 square miles, and, with the province of Wellesley and Malacca, they include the whole eastern shore of the Straits of Malacca. Excluding Pahang, for which no returns are available, the population of the Federated States amounts to 570,454. Of this total 61 per cent. are foreign immigrants, chiefly Chinese, and only 39 per cent. are Malays. Each of the four Federated States is governed by a State Council consisting of the Sultan, the British Resident, the secretary to the Resident, a number of Malay chiefs, and one or more prominent Chinamen to represent the interests of the Chinese community.

Under British administration the Federated States have flourished abundantly. They have obtained security of life and property; slavery and the exaction of unpaid labour have been abolished; free education and free hospital treatment have been provided for all; more than a

CH. XVII.

thousand miles of metalled roads have been constructed, and 300 miles of railway have been built. The revenue of the States has been raised from $400,000 in 1875 to $22,500,000 in 1902; meanwhile the foreign trade has increased from $1,500,000 to $127,000,000.

SIAM.

Siam was first introduced to the notice of European historians by Portuguese explorers and adventurers. The trading of these pioneers was little better than smuggling and buccaneering, while they sold their military support to the highest bidder, irrespective of the merits of the causes which they espoused or assailed. During the sixteenth century, the Portuguese enjoyed a monopoly of the foreign trade of Siam, and it was not until the beginning of the seventeenth century that the Dutch sought to enter into competition with them. This intrusion was resented by the Portuguese, who spread reports hostile to the political honesty of the new-comers. An embassy which was sent to Java discovered the falsity of these charges, and for some time the Dutch settlers stood high in favour at Ayuthia, the then capital of Siam. But the Dutch influence did not last; and at the present day little is left to mark the residence in the country of the natives of Holland except the ruins of the Dutch factory, still visible in the jungle near Paklat, on the banks of the Menam. During the seventeenth century, the Jesuits were active in the Far East and established a mission in Siam. It so happened that a Greek named Phaulkon at that time stood high in favour at the Court of Siam, and, being a proselyte to the Roman Catholic Church, he gave active support to the Jesuit missionaries. A cleavage was thus developed which produced two hostile parties—the nationalists, who served their own gods, and the missionaries with their converts. In order to strengthen the Jesuit party, it was arranged by Phaulkon that King Louis XIV should send an embassy to King Phra Narai of Siam; and, in 1685, an envoy presented himself at the Court of Ayuthia bringing a letter from the French monarch together with a collection of presents. A return mission was sent in the following year under the direction of Father Tachard, a Jesuit missionary. One or two missions followed; but their effect was partly nullified by the fact becoming known that, much as the French King desired Siamese trade, he cared far more for the spread of his religion. King Phra Narai became alarmed since these designs were supported by the arrival from time to time of small detachments of French soldiers, nominally as guards of honour to the King. The death of Phra Narai in 1688 brought matters to a climax; and the national party at once took action. Under a Minister of State named Opra Pitrachand they at once took the field. They seized the next heirs to the throne and sent Phaulkon to execution. The late King's brothers were murdered, and Opra

Pitrachand usurped the throne. The French soldiers were transported to Pondicherry, and a state of war prevailed.

Meanwhile, relations were opened between the British Government and Siam. Sufficient encouragement was given British merchants to settle in the country, and, as the first arrivals concerned themselves with trade only and left the natives in undisturbed possession of their own religion, they were cordially welcomed. But troublous times were ahead for the nation. Fierce persecutions broke out against the Jesuit missionaries and their converts, which were in the end checked by the presence of a French fleet off the coast. Wars with Burma also frequently occurred; and in 1767 the Burmese captured and destroyed the capital city of Ayuthia. During these years Siam had been blotted out of history, so far as Europe was concerned, and it was not until 1822 that she again appeared on the surface. In that year John Crawfurd was sent to Bangkok as envoy by the Indian Government with instructions to obtain commercial facilities but not to conclude a treaty. Up to this time it had been the practice of the King's Ministers on the arrival of a vessel to ransack her cargo, to purchase at a low cost those articles which suited their taste, and to retail them to the native merchants at their full value. Against these impossible conditions Crawfurd protested strongly, and succeeded in inducing the King to modify them in the direction of free trade. Four years later Captain Burney followed in Crawfurd's footsteps, and concluded a treaty, by the terms of which free trade was established between the merchants of both countries, without the intervention of any third parties. This was a distinct advance; but on the other hand trade was limited to certain centres, and Englishmen were bound to conform to Siamese rules and regulations of life.

The conditions of this treaty were before long violated by oppressive monopolies and its provisions became a dead letter. A few years later (1833), the United States of America sent an envoy, who concluded a treaty with Siam similar to that of Burney. Later, in 1850, Sir James Brooke was despatched by Queen Victoria to negotiate a treaty with the King; but the attitude of the officials and people had become so hostile that Sir James took his leave without even opening negotiations with the Government. This unpromising attitude did not however continue long; and in 1855 Sir John Bowring, her Majesty's Superintendent of Trade in China, was received in Siam with every sign of hospitality, and succeeded in concluding a treaty which was a distinct advance on all previous efforts. By it a British consul was to be established at Bangkok who should try all cases in which British subjects were defendants; the free exercise of the Christian religion was permitted; and liberty to build churches was granted. All imports except opium, which was to be imported free, were to pay a duty of 3 per cent. *ad valorem*; and all exports were to be taxed according to the specifications in the tariff attached to the treaty. Merchants were allowed to buy or sell without let or hindrance, and a most-favoured-nation clause was inserted.

About this time the French idea of a colonial empire in Indo-China began to take shape, and a desire was developed to extend and establish the French boundaries in and about Annam. As matters then stood, the eastern frontier of Siam was the range of mountains running north and south on the left bank of the Mekong, and, on the plea that the territory on the left of the river from the frontier of Yunnan to the sea had formerly belonged to Annam, France laid claim to it as suzerain of that country, and she further demanded that the bordering territory measuring fifteen miles on the right bank of the Mekong should be handed over to her on the same conditions. On October 3, 1893, a treaty was signed at Bangkok giving effect to these conditions. But, meanwhile, the French had found it necessary to send two gunboats to Bangkok and to blockade the Menam in order to enforce their claims. This action was so threatening to the interests of Great Britain that she was almost drawn into war to protect her rights (July, 1893). Fortunately, this catastrophe was averted, and a treaty between the two Powers (England and France) was subsequently entered into (1896) guaranteeing the integrity of Siam proper. By this instrument Great Britain and France consented to refrain from any armed intervention or the acquisition of any special privileges in the Siamese possessions included within the basin of the Menam; and at the same time the preponderating influence of Great Britain in the western, and of France in the eastern portions of the Siamese dominions, were tacitly recognised.

Later still—1907—a treaty was signed between Great Britain and France, the chief feature of which was the cession to France by Siam of the territories of Battambang, Siem-reap, and Sisophon in return for the territories of Dan-saï and Kratt, as well as all the islands situated to the south of Cape Lemling, including Koh-Kut. Moreover, a further agreement has been arrived at by which the Malay States of Kelantan, Trĕnggânu, and Kedah, have been recognised as being under the influence of Great Britain; and in return Siam secures a loan with which to construct a railway system, by which it is hoped that direct railway communication will soon be established between Bangkok and Singapore; and Great Britain relinquishes those exterritorial rights which place foreign subjects of British nationality outside the jurisdiction of the native Courts.

The main object of the policy, which France had pursued on the eastern frontiers of Siam—to promote the French trade in Indo-China—has not been attained; and the construction of the line of railway from Bangkok to Korat shows that the direction of trade is westward rather than eastward. France is so far from gaining a monopoly of the trade with Siam that, as appears by the returns of 1905, 86 per cent. of the export trade and 79 of the import trade of that year fell to the share of the British.

CHAPTER XVIII.

THE REGENERATION OF JAPAN.

In the preceding volume the history of Japan was traced down to the year 1871, closing with the record of the deposition of the territorial barons from their ancient positions as quasi-sovereigns of their fiefs, and the conversion of those fiefs into prefectures, administered by officials of the Government at Tōkiō. The final step was thus taken in the unification of the government of the empire.

Great as had been the changes during the thirteen years in which Japan had been open to foreign intercourse, they were as nothing compared to those which followed during the succeeding years, and which it is the object of this chapter to describe. In order that a proper appreciation may be formed of their character and of the onerous task imposed upon the Ministers who carried them to their final accomplishment, a short description of the social conditions of the people as they were until 1871 seems desirable.

First in rank came the *Kuge* or court nobles, the attendants at the Court of the Emperor at Kiōto, who, invariably tracing their descent from collateral branches of the imperial family and therefore sharing to some extent the prestige of the Emperor's divine origin, were, though poor and landless, recognised without question as the highest in the land next to the imperial family. They performed no military duties; their time was passed in the seclusion of the Court, in the performance of court duties, in studying court etiquette and polite accomplishments. At the time of the Restoration they numbered one hundred and fifty houses; they stood apart, a class by themselves.

The *Daimiō* or territorial nobles were the descendants of great military adventurers of the Middle Ages who enriched themselves by taking permanent possession of lands which they had won by the sword, or had received from the *Shōgun* as rewards for their services. They had no claim to the ancient lineage of the Kuge; but on the other hand they were feudal chiefs of territories that in some cases comprised entire provinces. All were wealthy, though in varying degrees; all were practically sovereign lords of their fiefs, governing them as petty kingdoms, exercising independent administrative and judicial powers within their limits, issuing their own paper currency, framing their own laws, and supporting their own armies. The armies of the Daimiō were composed of *Samurai*, military retainers of the chief, a greater or less number being maintained in each fief in proportion to its wealth and magnitude. Each Samurai wore two swords, and the right of wearing arms and of using them in their lord's service was solely vested in this class. From their lord they derived subsistence for themselves and their families, and in return they rendered him the most unquestioning loyalty and obedience, and were ready at any time to sacrifice their lives for his sake or at his command, either by their own or an enemy's hand. The majority devoted their time exclusively to military training; to fencing, riding, and learning the use of the spear and the bow; but the highest in rank and the more intelligent acted as counsellors to their lord, and as administrators of the public affairs of the fief, fulfilling the same functions that in a kingdom are discharged by Cabinet Ministers and permanent officials. The Daimiō and their retainers constituted the Samurai, the first of the four classes into which the registered population was divided.

The remainder of the population consisted of three classes which, in order of social rank, were *Nō*, farmers, *Kō*, artisans, *Shō*, traders; but just as, at the top of society, the class of Kuge stood by itself, apart from and above the four classes, so in the very lowest strata were found two other unclassed sections of the population, the *Eta* and *Hinin*—the latter word meaning "not human"—the pariahs of the nation, who lived entirely apart from their fellow countrymen, whose avocations were the slaughtering of animals, tanning, burying the bodies of executed criminals, and similar pursuits, regarded with loathing and detestation. The touch, even the presence, of these outcasts was looked upon as contamination by the three lower classes of citizens.

While the latter were immeasurably above the Eta and Hinin, the social conditions in which they lived rendered them little better than serfs in comparison with the haughty military class, the Samurai. Iyeyasu, the founder of the Tokugawa dynasty of the Shōguns, in the legacy or testament which he left for the guidance of his successors, thus defined the relative positions of the Samurai and the other three classes: "The Samurai are the masters of the four classes. Farmers, artisans, and merchants may not behave in a rude manner towards Samurai, and the Samurai is not to be interfered with in cutting down a fellow who has behaved to him in a manner other than is expected." These principles were guiding laws throughout the whole period of 265 years during which the Tokugawa dynasty held sway, and even for the first few years of the present Emperor's reign. In the struggles which preceded the modern Revolution, in all the political movements that followed during the succeeding decade, the lower classes had neither voice nor part. They were never consulted; they never thought of obtruding their voice in discussions or their persons in fighting. The lot of the commoners was to obey, to furnish the means that were required for the maintenance of the Samurai, to be left without any security as to the continued safe possession of what they might acquire for themselves, to remain contented not only in the station of life but in the actual locality in which they were born, each man, no matter what were his tastes and abilities, being bound to follow in the footsteps that had been trodden by his direct forefathers. Rigid sumptuary laws prescribed their dress; none was allowed to ride on horseback. When in the presence of a Samurai, they either prostrated themselves upon the ground in an attitude of craven humility or, if circumstances required them to stand, they did so with bent backs, with eyes fixed on the ground, and spoke with bated breath, using words expressive of the most profound respect for their auditors and utter depreciation of themselves. If struck, no thought of retaliation ever entered their minds; if murdered in pure wantonness, as often happened, no thought of vengeance or legal punishment of the assailant occurred to their families or successors.

It was with these materials that the founders of modern Japan had to begin their great work. No more unpromising task has ever been carried through with greater success to a triumphant issue.

In 1871, the Emperor was served by a body of Ministers who, throughout the civil and military struggles which culminated in the Revolution, had given proof of being possessed not only of moral and physical courage, of strong and persevering determination, but of many attributes of wise and far-seeing statesmanship. They formulated in the Emperor's name their new policy, which was outlined in the oath taken by the young Emperor early in 1868, before an assembly of his own Court and of the territorial nobles. This oath was subsequently known as the "Charter Oath," and consisted of the following five clauses: a deliberative assembly shall be summoned and all measures shall be decided by public opinion; high and low shall be of one mind in the conduct of the administration; matters shall be so arranged that not only the government officials and Samurai, but also the common people, may be able to obtain the objects of their desire and the national mind may be completely satisfied; the vicious and uncivilised customs of antiquity shall be broken through, and the great principles of impartiality and justice coexisting with heaven and earth shall be taken as the basis of action; intellect and learning shall be sought for throughout the world for the purpose of firmly establishing the foundations of the empire.

In carrying out the policy outlined in these clauses, the Government had to face the most deeply rooted conservative prejudice, and the constant terror of assassination, which has, down to recent years, been a recurring incident in Japanese politics; to obtain all the best services of a heterogeneous population; to accomplish great domestic reforms simultaneously with the management of foreign affairs that bristled with present humiliation and future menace.

The downfall of the feudal system entailed the abolition of the old class distinctions. The court and territorial nobility were merged under the title of *Kwazoku* or nobles. The remainder of the Samurai, irrespective of gradations of rank and influence in their particular fiefs, were newly grouped under the title of *Shizoku*, and the rest of the population under that of *Heimin* or commoners, the Eta and Hinin being included in these. Class disabilities of every kind were abolished, and every office in the Government was thrown open to all ranks of the people. The nobles were permitted to go abroad with their wives and families for purposes of pleasure or study: the Samurai to lay aside their treasured swords and betake themselves to trade or agriculture; the commoners to choose their occupations at will. All sumptuary laws were abolished.

Further reforms were inaugurated before or soon after the close of 1871. The foundations of a national army, recruited by universal service, were laid; a beginning was made with the navy; railway, postal, and telegraph services were organised; a scheme of compulsory education was founded which provided facilities for the education of every child in the empire; and a mint was established which turned out an honest uniform coinage in the place of the debased and varied tokens previously current in the fiefs.

The internal difficulties which faced the new Government were sufficiently serious to absorb all the attention of the Ministry, and they were complicated by international questions demanding a degree of diplomatic skill to which the Ministry, either in its individual or in its collective capacity, could lay no claim. The Ministry was further handicapped by its consciousness of the country's military impotence and pressing financial difficulties. The Government had neither army, navy, nor war chest, while claims were either being actually pressed or threatened, which affected the territorial integrity and the prestige of the empire. Finally, the Ministry had also before it the question of the revision of the Treaties which controlled Japan's international relations with Western Powers.

The original Treaties between European Powers and Japan were concluded on the same basis as those already existing between European and other oriental nations. All these Treaties, without exception, reserved to the European contracting Power a complete system of exterritorial jurisdiction over its citizens residing within the limits of the oriental Power. This reservation was as necessary at the time the first Treaty was concluded with Japan as it continues to be in the case of China at the present day. Japan had no known system of law; no organised Courts of justice or competent legal officers; torture was an incident of every criminal trial; the death penalty was daily inflicted for offences against property or person of the most trivial character; and the prisons were *infernos* of human suffering. The assent of the Shōgun's Government was given to these Treaties, not only under threats of force which it had no means to resist, but in ignorance of the ordinary international rights of sovereign States. When the Emperor's Government came into office, it had to assume the obligations of the Treaties, and to face in its foreign relations a condition of affairs which was now known by it to be derogatory to the national prestige of a civilised State. The national laws had no application to foreign residents; none of the latter could be punished for criminal offences or civilly sued except in Consular Courts of their own nationality; and these Courts—even those which were actuated by an honest desire to use their powers with equity and whose judges possessed the knowledge and experience that are essential for the administration of justice— could only administer their own laws. No foreign Power, except Great Britain, had made any legal provision by which sanction could be given without delay to Japanese laws and ordinances, however urgent and necessary they might be for the safety not only of natives but of foreigners. Before any law could be made effective against foreigners of other nationalities, the consent and approval of its terms by their respective Governments had to be severally obtained, and many of these Governments, however well disposed to Japan, had no legal machinery, such as existed in the British Orders in Council, by which they could deal with their citizens in a foreign country in respect of offences unknown to their own laws. Great Britain had done all that lay in her power to render her jurisdiction effective. Her Consular Courts were presided over by men whose qualifications would have fitted them for similar duties in their own country, whose honesty and impartiality were never once questioned, and who were vested with very extensive powers both of civil and criminal jurisdiction. A Court of Appeal, presided over by a judge of the professional status of a member of the High Court of Justice in England, was founded in Shanghai. The majority of the other Powers were represented by merchant consuls without legal or official experience of any kind; and, where consuls *de carrière* were maintained, as in the cases of France, Russia, and the United States (Prussia was content with merchant consuls), their experience and training were entirely political or official, and gave them no qualifications for the efficient exercise of judicial functions. An appeal from their decisions could only be made in civil cases to Courts in Europe or in the United States—a procedure altogether beyond the means or comprehension of a Japanese suitor. None had any power to inflict the death penalty or even a long sentence of imprisonment, and several were vested with no higher functions than those of a committing magistrate. As the higher Criminal Courts were in some cases not less distant than the Civil Appeal Courts, it is not difficult to infer that gross miscarriages of justice were frequent in serious cases. In fact they were the rule, rather than the exception.

In addition to the exterritorial clauses, the Treaties also contained customs tariffs, by which both import and export duties were fixed on an average *ad valorem* basis of five per cent.; and, while the Government was at its wits' end for money, it could not, during the continuance of the treaty tariffs, look for a single penny of increased revenue from its customs. No confidence was placed during the last years of the Shōgun's Government in its ability to protect the large foreign community resident in Yokohama against its subjects in rebellion, whose gathering cry was "expulsion of the foreigners from Japan." Great Britain and France, therefore, maintained garrisons of considerable force in Yokohama—that of Great Britain especially forming in itself a small army complete in every military detail—and continued to do so during the first seven years of the Emperor's rule. The presence of these garrisons was galling in the extreme to the Government, so soon as it had learned that in ordinary international intercourse between civilised nations it would have been regarded as a sign of conquest.

Very early in its existence the Government appealed to the foreign diplomatic representatives in Japan for their help in procuring from their own Governments an amelioration of the Treaties; but, finding little sympathy, it despatched an embassy on a large scale to the United States and Europe with the object of obtaining for Japan complete judicial and tariff autonomy (1871). Iwakura Tomomi, a court noble of high rank, was chosen ambassador, and four of the ablest members of the Government were attached to him with the title of vice-ambassadors.

The embassy was absent for nearly three years; but, as might have been foreseen, it wholly failed in its main object. Not only was it well known to European Governments that social conditions in Japan were such as Europeans could not accept, but a strong bias was created by the rigid inhibition still laid by the Japanese Government upon the profession or practice of Christianity by its subjects, and by the severe penal consequences which any violation of that inhibition entailed. At the close of 1869, a persecution was instituted on a large scale against the inhabitants of certain villages who, it was suddenly discovered, still practised the doctrines of Christianity taught to their forefathers by Jesuit missionaries three hundred years previously, having clung to these doctrines throughout all the long interval, without help or encouragement from Christian Europe, at the risk of social ostracism and legal tortures by their own people; and this persecution still continued when the embassy sailed. If, however, the embassy failed in its main object, its results deserve more than a brief mention. Besides the purely diplomatic staff, officials of every department of the public service

were attached to it.   They investigated and reported, with the minute
painstaking detail that characterises Japanese administration down to
the present day, on the civil, military, and commercial conditions of
every country which they visited, and there was no important country in
the West that they did not visit.   The result was a series of reforms at
home which may be said to constitute the foundations of modern Japan.
Military instructors were engaged in France, and naval instructors in
England, to create a national army and a navy.   Men of high scientific
qualifications were also engaged to develop the system of national education, and to establish colleges of science and medicine; to commence
the preparation of codes of laws, which should take the place of the
semi-barbarous laws derived from China and ultimately justify foreign
Governments in submitting their citizens in Japan to native jurisdiction.
Torture in criminal trials, if not wholly abolished, was shorn of its worst
features.   The punishment of crime was brought more into consonance
with modern Western ideas by the abolition of the death penalty for
offences not of the first order of gravity; the sale of children or of
young girls to brothels was forbidden; acts and customs which violated
the European sense of decency were also prohibited; and, though last,
far from least, the public inhibition of Christianity was withdrawn and
the way paved to universal religious toleration.   Many of the reforms
were at first rather apparent than real; but all became questions of
practical politics and their effective accomplishment was only a matter
of time.

Every recommendation made by the embassy, every step taken on
that recommendation, was influenced by the burning desire to procure
the abolition of exterritoriality.   Social reforms were made in order
to raise the standard of national civilisation to a level with that of
Western nations; military and civil systems and educational institutions
were started, so that the Japanese might be able to back their demands
by force, should these not be granted in response to the arguments of
right and justice.

The story of the diplomatic negotiations which finally culminated
in the realisation of Japan's aspirations is too long to be told with
any approach to fulness in this chapter.   From first to last, eight
Japanese Ministers for Foreign Affairs were engaged in the negotiations.
Proposal after proposal was brought forward as a basis upon which
revision might be proceeded with, each in turn only to be rejected
by the Western Powers to whom they were submitted as asking too
much, or by the Japanese as granting too little.   Two conferences sat
at Tōkiō—the first in 1882, the second in 1886—both presided over
by the Minister for Foreign Affairs and attended by the diplomatic
representatives of all the Treaty Powers.

At the first conference, Great Britain was still represented in Japan
by Sir Harry Parkes, a man of masterful and determined character,

CH. XVIII.

whose knowledge of Japan, acquired during eighteen years' residence, commencing almost contemporaneously with the first political movements against the Government of the Shōgun, was wide and profound. This knowledge, combined with his character and irresistible energy, gave him a commanding influence among his colleagues which was successfully exerted to keep the discussions within practical bounds; and the result of the conference was the establishment of certain broad principles on which, as it seemed at the time, new Treaties might be based. The second conference held its first meeting in May, 1886. Sir Harry Parkes had in the interval been transferred to China. His United States colleague, also a man of long experience and considerable ability, had left Japan, and there was no one of the representatives of the Treaty Powers in Japan whose ability, knowledge or personal character enabled him to take any decided lead in the proceedings. All the representatives were ostensibly of equal rank; all claimed the same rights to a full hearing. The representative of Great Britain, with all her immense commercial and shipping interests, surpassing at that period the aggregate of all other Powers, with the rights and claims of a large resident British population to guard, had only the same vote and voice in the proceedings as the representatives of Austria and Spain, who had neither trade nor citizens to protect, or as those of small Powers such as Belgium and Portugal.

But, although the second conference failed to produce revised Treaties, an agreement was arrived at on so many points that it was comparatively easy to deal with the remainder. Advanced education, and the growing influence of a Press which was never silent on the subject of the recovery of the national rights, had by this time developed considerable political activity among the mass of the people, who had never before meddled in state affairs. Under the growing pressure of public opinion, the Japanese Government pressed steadily forward to the attainment of their great object. Agreements were made with some of the Great Powers, which gave rise to temporary hopes of a solution of the question; but none succeeded in satisfying the Japanese people, who, as time went on, became more and more averse from accepting any settlement short of the entire abrogation of the existing Treaties. When the Constitution came into force, and the first Parliament met, its earliest efforts were devoted to urging on the Government the revision of the Treaties on the basis of absolute equality between the contracting Powers. In two instances the national wishes were gratified. Mexico, whose commercial intercourse with Japan was of the most insignificant nature and who had no subjects to protect from the tender mercies of Japanese administration and justice, concluded a Treaty on equal terms in 1888. Four years later, Portugal withdrew her diplomatic and consular representatives from Japan, as one of several measures of economy necessitated by financial stress at home. Japan, thereupon, denounced the exterritorial clauses of the Treaty and assumed complete jurisdiction over Portuguese subjects in Japan, on the ground that Portugal had failed to discharge her obligations, implied in the Treaty, to provide efficient means for the judicial control of her subjects, whose number was not inconsiderable. The embassy of Iwakura, the two Tōkiō conferences, the Mexican and Portuguese Treaties in their different aspects, were the most prominent incidents from an international point of view in the long series of treaty negotiations.

Taught by the experience of the two conferences that negotiations in Tōkiō were hopeless, the Japanese transferred their activity to Europe and dealt, not with all foreign Powers in conference, but with each separately under the pledge of diplomatic secrecy. Here at last accord was reached. Little by little during the course of the laborious negotiations the difficulties in the way of an understanding were removed; and, on July 18, 1894, the representative of Great Britain signed a Treaty which conceded everything for which the Japanese had worked. Where Great Britain, whose interests in Japan were still paramount, led the way, the other Western Powers had perforce to follow. Some of them did so slowly and reluctantly and with greater regard to the interests of their citizens in Japan than had been shown by the British Foreign Office; but all finally consented; and on June 30, 1899, the Emperor was able to proclaim to his subjects that "his long-cherished aspirations, exhaustive plans, and repeated negotiations had at last been crowned by a satisfactory settlement with the Treaty Powers" and that exterritoriality in his dominions was at an end.

It was a proud day for the nation, celebrated with public rejoicings such as might have been expected at the close of a long and successful war with a powerful enemy. It was the first experience in history of the unreserved submission of Europeans to the jurisdiction of an oriental State; and was regarded at the time with much misgiving by those who were affected. Time has, however, justified the experiment. The step having been taken by their own Governments, foreign residents in Japan had perforce to accept it; and the Japanese, in their triumph, could on their side afford to be generous and use their newly acquired powers with moderation. Individual cases of hardship occurred, where Courts of law violated the spirit of European equity in dealing with cases which were wholly novel to them; a very heavy load of taxation was imposed where none had been leviable before; inquisitorial regulations, foreign to advanced sentiments of personal liberty, had to be endured; but, on the whole, Europeans have succeeded in accommodating themselves to their surroundings, and have been dealt with by the Government and its local administrators on the same terms as Japanese subjects. Only one of the five members of Iwakura's embassy, Prince Itō, survived to witness, twenty-eight years later, the realisation of its object.

Born a simple Samurai of the Chōshiu clan, one of the many

thousands of the same position, Prince Itō, in his early youth, discerned the material advantages of Western civilisation. At that period, Japanese were forbidden under pain of death to leave their native shores; but, in their thirst for knowledge, Itō and four fellow clansmen braved this penalty and, secretly leaving their homes, succeeded in making their way to England. Two of the five, in order to acquire a practical acquaintance with navigation, shipped before the mast in a British sailing vessel, the *Pegasus*, and worked their way in her as common sailors all through the voyage round the Cape to England. These two were Prince Itō and Marquis Inouyé. Throughout all the stages of Japan's development, Marquis Inouyé steadily worked side by side and in complete harmony with Prince Itō, and was only second to him in the great services he has rendered to his country and in the distinction he has merited and won. Both remained long enough in England to acquire a thorough practical knowledge of the language and to see and learn much besides; but both hastily returned to Japan when they heard of the troubles which culminated in the bombardment of Shimonoseki. After these events, both remained in the clan, but both had incurred the odium of their fellow clansmen, the more prejudiced and ignorant of whom regarded them as in some degree responsible for the misfortunes which had fallen upon their lord. Attempts were made to assassinate both. Inouyé escaped with his life, but, to this day, bears the scars of the terrible wounds he received. Itō's escape from death was due to a young girl, scarcely in her teens, who, with a courage of which Japanese history affords several examples among women, succeeded in hiding him from the band of wouldbe murderers who were searching for him, and subsequently became his wife.

On the accomplishment of the revolution, Itō was clearly marked for the service of the imperial Government by the reputation which he had acquired in his own influential clan for exceptional ability, and his knowledge of the English language and of European customs caused him to be chosen for an office in which he would be brought into constant intercourse with foreigners. The port of Kōbé (Hiōgo) had very recently been opened to foreign trade and residence. Arrangements, which demanded unusual tact and business capacity, had to be made for the settlement of foreigners in it, and Itō was chosen to carry them out and for the purpose was appointed Governor. In that office he laid the foundations of what is now the greatest commercial port in the Far East. In less than two years he had completed his task. He was then transferred to Tōkiō as Vice-Minister of the Board of Works, and, after having been another two years in that office, was appointed one of the vice-ambassadors in Iwakura's mission. In every crisis of the empire, whenever a mission of diplomacy which demanded exceptional tact, firm decision, sacrifice and broadmindedness, or elaborate investigation, had to be sent abroad, Itō was chosen as the ambassador. He was the first

Prime Minister when the system of responsible government was introduced and he has held that office no less than four times. To the time of his death (1909) he retained the respect and gratitude of his countrymen, and, whether in or out of office, he was the confidential adviser of the Emperor in every emergency of the State.

Like all young students, he was, from the first, attracted by constitutionalism, and sought to develop in his countrymen a capacity for representative government. His thoughts were shared by other political leaders and students, and their realisation was foreshadowed in the first clause of the Charter Oath, under which clause the first National Council of the empire was convoked in 1869 at Tōkiō. It was composed of representatives of all the feudal clans, one representative being nominated by the authorities of each clan. It was, we should remember, a council of Samurai only. Public opinion was still their prerogative. The rest of the people were unconscious of political rights, and indifferent to their acquisition. The Council was dignified by the name of Parliament but possessed no legislative power, its functions being merely to debate and to advise, without any substantial expectation that its advice would be taken. It remained in session for a few months at Tōkiō, and summaries of its proceedings were published. Proposals were debated for admitting foreigners into commercial partnerships with Japanese, for abolishing some of the privileges of the Samurai, such as the practice of *seppuku* (vulg. *harakiri* or disembowelment) in expiation of offences, and that of wearing two swords; but they were rejected almost unanimously. The general mass of the people, on the very rare occasions on which they were referred to, were mentioned in terms of haughty contempt, and the whole spirit of the assembly was that of conservatism in its most rigid aspects. It was soon dissolved, and no attempt was made to repeat the experiment until 1874.

Throughout the intervening period, the Press had been steadily growing in ability and influence. Many writers in it had been educated in the United States and had there imbibed, in an exaggerated form, the doctrines of constitutional government, without acquiring the capacity of recognising the unfitness of their own countrymen, who had only recently been liberated from the iron fetters of feudalism, to exercise the rights and privileges of a people who had imbibed the spirit of constitutionalism almost with the first breath of life. In the extravagance of their aspirations and in their methods, which included the undisguised advocacy and the practice of assassination, they strongly resembled the Nationalists of British India at the present day. Their cry was for the creation of a deliberative and legislative assembly, elected by and from the people in fulfilment of the terms of the Charter Oath. The influence of public lectures and outspoken memorials to the Government was added to that of the Press, with the result of extending political knowledge and aspirations, not only among the Samurai but among the commons. In 1875, the first important steps were taken towards the fulfilment of the Oath. The chief local authorities of the different prefectures were convened in Tōkiō under an imperial rescript, to form a deliberative council, "in which the measures that might be thought necessary for the welfare of the people should be discussed, and the sentiments of the people made known to the Emperor." This council was not elective, being composed entirely of officials who owed their appointments to the central Government; but it was intended to be the means of the gradual introduction of constitutional forms. In the same year the Genroin, or Senate, was also constituted under an imperial rescript. It consisted of officials selected by the Emperor as a consultative body for deliberating and advising on the measures submitted to it by the several departments of the Government.

Neither of these bodies possessed any legislative powers. The Emperor still remained the sole source of all law. Neither of them could claim to be representative; but their functions gave them somewhat of a parliamentary character. It was the original intention that the council should meet yearly; but, after its first meeting, the pressure of international difficulties in regard to Korea and the domestic crisis of the Satsuma rebellion, followed by the assassination of the ablest member of the Government, provided abundant reason for its not being convoked again until 1879, when it met once more, on this occasion under the presidency of Itō. The meeting was utilised to procure the acceptance of a law for the formation of urban and prefectural Assemblies, to consist of representatives elected by and from the people of each locality, with an effective voice in the administration of local affairs. These were the first representative popular assemblies in Japan; and, while at first they seemed to promise little hope of success, they served as schools of training in popular representation. Meanwhile, political agitation continued throughout the country with unabated vigour, and the pressure that was brought to bear on the Government, combined with the hope engendered by a better spirit that manifested itself in the local assemblies, had at last their due effect. In the year 1880, the Emperor in a further rescript declared that a national Parliament should be established in 1890, "in order that the imperial purpose of gradually establishing a constitutional form of Government might be carried out."

Agitation at once ceased. The imperial promise was given, and the most persistent agitators were satisfied. Itō was the member of the Government chosen by the Emperor for the preparation of the draft of the Constitution, and he spent the next succeeding years in Europe studying the constitutions and laws of various countries, and extracting from each whatever appeared to be most suitable to the peculiar conditions of Japan. In 1884 he returned to Japan with his material, and his arduous task of drafting the Constitution was commenced with the aid of able advisers, both of his own and other nationalities. The preparation of the Constitution was however only one of the burdens laid upon him. Complications which occurred in Korea, described in another part of this chapter, demanded his presence in China early in the following year; and at the close of the same year a step was taken for remodelling the whole form of the Government, amounting almost to a second revolution in its drastic changes, for which he was mainly responsible.

The form of central government eventually adopted on the completion of the Revolution was framed on an ancient Chinese model which had served in Japan prior to the first Shōgunate in the early Middle Ages. A similar system was universal among the feudal principalities. Its main principle was that the chief posts should be filled by men of high rank who exercised only a nominal authority, while the actual administrators of the several departments of the Government, men of ability but without the prestige of high social status or long descent, should hold only subordinate positions. The principal members of this Government were a Chancellor of the Empire, who was directly responsible to the sovereign, and two Ministers known as a Minister of the Left and a Minister of the Right, who had no administrative responsibility and performed no functions beyond that of giving the Chancellor the benefit of their advice and the prestige of their names. Beneath them were the heads of the various departments, who together formed a Council of State and were responsible to the Chancellor as the representative of the Emperor. The Chancellor's authorisation was required to give validity to any act done by a member in his executive capacity, and the Chancellor alone was responsible to the sovereign and the sole medium of communication with him.

The first Chancellor of the Empire was Sanjō Saneyoshi, and the Ministers of the Left and Right were Iwakura Tomomi and Shimadzu Saburō. Beneath them, either at the head of the several departments of the Government or holding important positions in them, were men such as Saigō, Ōkubo, Kido, Itō, Inouyé, Ōkuma, and Itagaki, and many others whose names are now historical—all simple Samurai, possessing no qualifications of rank or descent to differentiate them from thousands of others born in the same class of life. Sanjō and Iwakura were both court nobles (*Kuge*) of high degree. Both had not only lent their names to the promoters of the Revolution, but had taken an active part in it. Both had been closely associated with the Emperor from his youth and possessed his confidence and friendship. Shimadzu was the father of the feudal lord of Satsuma, the latter having succeeded to the chieftainship of the clan by adoption, and therefore, though far below Sanjō and Iwakura in rank and lineage, possessed the social status of the highest orders of the territorial nobility. These three nobles gave the prestige of their names to the Emperor's Government in its early

CH. XVIII.

days when ancient lineage and high rank were still the most important factors in influencing the people in general, both Samurai and commoners. Sanjō and Iwakura were both men of ability, industry, and courage, and, apart from birth, possessed every qualification for their high offices. It was under Shimadzu's guidance and influence that the Satsuma clan cast its lot with the Reformers before the Revolution, and his own and his clan's services were therefore properly recognised by his appointment as Minister of the Right. But he had no sympathy with the subsequent drastic reforms of the new Government. His whole character was that of rigid unbending conservatism, and in a very few years he resigned his office and withdrew to his native province, taking no further share in the imperial administration.

Iwakura died full of honours, loved by his sovereign and reverenced by the people to the last, in July, 1883. Kido died in May, 1877 ; and Ōkubo was assassinated almost to a day a year later, paying with his life for his share in the suppression of the Satsuma rebellion. The fate of Saigō is told below. Itagaki and Ōkuma both seceded from the Government, the former in 1873 and the latter in 1881, in disapproval of its unwillingness to hasten the establishment of constitutionalism, and became the leaders of independent political parties. The five Ministers last mentioned were, in their several spheres, the most prominent active members of the first Government of the Emperor. Their removal left Itō unquestionably the ablest civil administrator still in office.

In 1885 Sanjō was still Chancellor of the Empire, and the Minister on whom the whole nominal responsibility of the Government fell. Age was however telling on him ; the increasing complications of both domestic and foreign affairs were not only intensifying the burden of his office, so much so as to render the efficient performance of its duties beyond the capacity of one man, even if in the prime of vigorous manhood, but at the same time proving the system unsuited for the prompt and efficient transaction of the business of the State. Itō, with his expert knowledge of Western institutions, came to the rescue ; and, at the close of the year 1885, an imperial rescript proclaimed the abolition of the old and the foundation of a new form of administration. Sanjō was relieved of his office at his own request. A Cabinet was created consisting of ten Ministers of State, nine of whom were also chiefs of the principal executive departments. At their head was a Minister-President without a portfolio, and both the Minister-President and every member of the Cabinet were personally in their several capacities responsible to the Emperor, and were appointed and directly controlled by him.

The formation of the Cabinet was an important onward step on the path leading to constitutional government, and the appointment of Itō, the official charged with the preparation of the Constitution, as the first Minister-President under the new system satisfied the hopes of the nation that the question would be treated as one of the most important among the many which the Government undertook to solve. One change which was part of the new system may be mentioned as illustrating the spirit of the times. Hitherto, the Minister for Foreign Affairs was the lowest in rank of departmental chiefs. Henceforward, he ranked in the Cabinet next in order to the President. The President and the Minister for Foreign Affairs were charged with solving the two most important public questions of the day—the establishment of constitutional government as it is understood in the West, and the revision of the Treaties. The work and progress of every other department, whether Finance, Army, Navy, Commerce, Communications, or Law, were ancillary to those two great questions, and whatever success was achieved in these departments was valued mainly as contributing to the realisation of the two main national aspirations.

Four years' laborious preparation followed, and at last, on February 11, 1889, the Emperor with all due solemnity bestowed upon his subjects, amidst universal popular rejoicing, the Constitution framed by the best intellects of his country. In the summer of 1890 the first general election took place, and in the following November the new Parliament met.

The first few years of its existence were not promising, and their record is little more than that of a continuous struggle on the part of the majority of the members of the lower House against the executive Government and of factious opposition to every measure submitted by the Government to the consideration of the House. The more advanced Radical section of the people, who took an active share in domestic politics, had been in some degree disappointed by the Constitution. They had hoped for one modelled on that of England, under which the Government would have been responsible to Parliament and held their offices at its will. What was granted was a Constitution modelled on that of Germany, under which Ministers were responsible to the Emperor and held their offices solely at his will. Many of the members had, during the agitation which preceded the grant of the Constitution, suffered both heavy fines and long imprisonment and still cherished bitter animosity against the Government at whose hands they had suffered. There was, besides, a strong animus among the members against what was called the Sat-Cho combination, which was prominent not only in the Cabinet but among the permanent officials of every department of the State, both military and civil. Satsuma and Chōshiu had been the two most powerful feudal clans prior to the Revolution, and had contributed most, both by moral and physical force, to the overthrow of the Shōgunate. If their services to their Emperor and country were great, the rewards which they assigned to themselves were in proportion. Throughout all the intervening years they had never lost their grip on office, and had never ceased to exercise its privileges in favour of their own fellow clansmen. When the first Parliament met, the Minister-President and eight of the other nine members of the Cabinet hailed from one or other of the two clans: the officers of the navy were said to be exclusively recruited from Satsuma, and those of the army from Chōshiu, while the majority of civil offices throughout all the departments of the Government, from assistant-Ministers of State and judges down to policemen and postmen, were shared amongst the less distinguished cadets of the two clans. The antagonism of the people at large to this combination, constantly and forcibly fulminated in the Press, found expression in the Diet. Government measures, both of legislation and finance, were ruthlessly obstructed by every device that the utmost ingenuity could invent. On the other side, the Government made free use of the weapons which the Constitution placed at its disposal; and suspensions and dissolutions followed each other with a rapidity that almost seemed to nullify the existence of the Diet.

The early struggles between the Government and the Diet had one important result on the foreign policy of the Government. They were to some extent the cause of the War with China. The diplomatic representative of China at Tōkiō urged on his own Government a firm resistance to the Japanese demands in regard to Korea, as he was convinced that political discord in Japan would prevent the Government from venturing to declare war, while the Government, on the other hand, were led to run this risk largely through their despair of reconciling the opposition of the Diet. They judged the patriotism of their countrymen better than the Chinese diplomatist. From the moment at which war was declared, and throughout its continuance, the opposition in the Diet was stilled, and every measure brought forward by the Government was passed without dissent, almost without debate. The same experience occurred ten years later when war broke out with Russia, the people from the highest to the lowest being once more solidly united against a foreign foe. In the intervening period of peace, when the conditions in which Japan found herself imposed on her a national expenditure more than twofold what it had been before the first war, opposition to the Government was still a continuing characteristic of the Diet; but there were occasional sessions in which a more harmonious spirit prevailed and many important measures were passed, notably those which embodied a new Civil Code of Law and Procedure (1896–9)—measures of pressing importance in view of the cessation of exterritoriality which was imminent at the time.

It is impossible in the space that is available in this chapter to describe in detail the struggles between the Government and the lower House which have been the principal characteristic of parliamentary proceedings in Japan, or to give any intelligible account of the numerous parties of which the lower House has been made up, or of their political platforms.   On the one side, there has been a continual effort to subject the Government to the House, to render its continued existence impossible without the support of a majority of the House—in fact, to establish the purely party government which was the darling object of the leaders of the Radical party before the Constitution; on the other, to maintain in all its integrity the principle of the Constitution, that the appointment of the Ministers and their continuance in office rest with the Emperor alone.   The reformers have freely used the chief weapon which the Constitution placed in their hands, that of either rejecting *in toto* or drastically amending the financial bills submitted to the Diet by the Government.   The financial condition of the country subsequent to the Chinese War, the policy of military and commercial progress, with the consequent necessity of providing for an enlarged national expenditure, caused this weapon to be always available and effective.   The Government, on the other side, has met the implacable opposition of the Diet with repeated suspensions and dissolutions. Reformers have, on occasion, shown themselves not unwilling to sacrifice important interests of the State to their own personal advancement or to the suppression of their opponents.   Some of them have not been guiltless of corruption in a more degrading form.   On the other hand, the successive Governments have endeavoured to stifle opposition or even discussion by an uncompromising use of the Emperor's authority and name.   The House of Peers is mainly an elective body, only 53 out of a total of 328 members holding their seats solely from the accident of birth.   It has throughout conserved its dignity both in the proceedings in its own Chamber and in the general policy of acting as a bulwark against untimely or violent reform.   It has had the advantage of including among its members not only chosen representatives of the wealth and intelligence of the nation, but all the survivors of the men who have made modern Japan, all the "elder statesmen" as they are called, men who were already in office in 1871, and the most distinguished representatives of the military and naval services and of science and literature.   A House composed of such elements could never fail to exercise great influence in political life; and the House of Peers has on several occasions used its powers with effect.   Whenever it has done so, it has been with the approval and sympathy of the best elements among the people.

The experiment of constitutional government has not been without some marked success in its short life, or without definite promise for its future.   The rules of the two Houses provide for the speedy transaction of business; and, on all occasions when passions are not stirred by the venom of party antagonism, measures of prime importance are passed with a celerity which might fill British Cabinets with envy.   There are no purely academic debates.   Eloquence is unknown, but so, too, is the stammering, hesitating, diffident speaker.   The Japanese are entirely free from selfconsciousness, and a member of Parliament addresses the House with as much ease, as much confidence in himself, as a rector in England speaking to an audience of respectful villagers in his own parish. Party government has not yet come, but parties have on more than one occasion proved their power, and the realisation of the ambition of their leaders is less visionary than was that of the first agitators for any form of constitutional government.

It is now necessary to return to 1871, the first year in which the central Government started on the course of reform contemplated by its leaders. What they gradually succeeded in accomplishing has already been briefly indicated. Space does not admit of describing the various stages in the progress that industry, perseverance, and patience, under the best teachers that the West could give, enabled Japan to make from this year onwards till 1894, when in the War with China she gave to the world the first real demonstration of what she had done. Some internal opposition was experienced in the early days of wholesale reform, and revolts occurred in a few districts under the leadership of Samurai, formerly supporters of the Revolution, who either thought their services had been insufficiently rewarded, or had taken part in the Revolution in the belief that its success would be the prelude to a crusade against all foreigners, ending in their general expulsion and Japan's reversion to her old customs and policy of exclusiveness. The revolts were easily suppressed, though not without bloodshed; and the reforms of the Government received the active sympathy of the nation at large, an extraordinary desire manifesting itself among all classes for the acquisition of Western knowledge and, as a first aid to that end, of the English language.

In 1872 the first incident occurred which was to bring Japanese diplomacy prominently before the world and to offer the first proof of the courage and determination with which Japan was prepared to deal with international questions and of the ability which she could bring to their solution.

The Peruvian ship *Maria Luz*, on her voyage from Macao to Peru with 322 contract Chinese labourers on board, had been disabled by a gale in the Pacific and had consequently put in to Yokohama in distress. Peru had no treaty with Japan, and her ships and subjects coming to Japan had therefore none of the exterritorial privileges enjoyed by those of the Treaty Powers. The *Maria Luz* consequently became subject to Japanese jurisdiction from the time she had entered the territorial waters. Shortly after her arrival, a Chinaman was found at night alongside the British flag-ship on the China Station, the *Iron Duke*, which happened to be in Yokohama harbour, and was taken out of the water in a condition of great exhaustion. He stated that he had escaped from the *Maria Luz* and had swum the intervening distance of fully two miles; that he and his fellow countrymen had been confined in the ship against their will, after being originally either enticed on board at Macao by fraudulent promises or actually kidnapped.   The coolie trade between Peru and Macao was at that time notorious for the cruelty with which it was carried on, both by Peru which obtained by it a supply of forced labour for her guano diggings, and by Portugal, to whose colony of Macao it brought a large annual revenue.   The British chargé d'affaires, when handing over the fugitive to the Japanese authorities, called their attention to these facts, and very forcibly urged on them their duty not to permit " the Government to be disgraced by affording the smallest possible countenance to the abominable traffic in which the *Maria Luz* was engaged."

The suggestion was promptly adopted.   A public enquiry was held— the first trial ever held in Japan with open doors—where both parties were represented by counsel, members of the English Bar practising in Japan, and where verbatim reports of the proceedings were taken.   The master of the *Maria Luz*, his officers, and the coolies were examined, and precedents furnished by international law were carefully and exhaustively investigated, with the result that all the coolies were released from their servitude, which was declared to be contrary to the law of Japan, and sent back to China.   Throughout the proceedings the Japanese had the full moral support of both the British and United States diplomatic representatives, but met with strong opposition from those of other Powers.   This opposition was fearlessly faced, and no warnings as to the possible penalty which they might ultimately be called upon to pay for their humanity caused the Japanese to waver from what they considered to be their obligations as a nation.

On the release of the coolies, the master of the *Maria Luz* returned to his own country.   Peru despatched a diplomatic mission to Japan, and, as she possessed at that time one of the most powerful ironclads afloat, the *Independencia*, she threatened to back her diplomacy by force if her demand for an apology and an indemnity was refused. But it was intimated to her that the British fleet would await the arrival in Japan of the *Independencia* and her consorts, and the Peruvian vessels were recalled ere half their voyage had been completed. Diplomacy procured the submission of the question to the arbitration of the Tsar of Russia, whose decision, given nearly two years afterwards, was entirely in favour of Japan.

The result of the case was far-reaching.   The Government of China, roused to shame by the publicity of the case, instituted a blockade of Macao, which effectually prevented the ingress from the mainland of junks carrying kidnapped labourers.   Portugal, unable in consequence of this blockade to carry on the traffic on a profitable scale, was at last roused to forbid its continuance in Macao ; and the way was paved for the opening of diplomatic intercourse between Japan and China on a new footing, which was destined to be very speedily used in the solution of the important pending questions of the Riukiu Islands and Korea.

CH. XVIII.

The Riukiu Islands, lying midway between Japan and Formosa, were regarded as an appanage of the daimiate of Satsuma, by which they had been invaded and conquered in the year 1609, the clan claiming that, in their annexation, they were only restoring an authority which had existed centuries previously. The ruler of the islands used, however, the title of king, and till 1395 ruled what was really an independent kingdom. In that year the islands came under the suzerainty of China and commenced the payment of an annual tribute; but they continued to enjoy complete autonomy till 1875, when they were formally annexed by Japan, and constituted a prefecture on precisely the same conditions as prefectures in the main islands.

In the latter part of 1871, a Riukiu junk was wrecked on the south-eastern coast of Formosa, and her crew of sixty persons were murdered by the Bhotans, one of the eastern Formosa savage tribes. The Riukiuans appealed for help to obtain redress not to their suzerain China but to Japan. The matter was at once taken up by Japan; but precedent demanded that, prior to active measures, the views of the Government of China should be ascertained, as to whether that Power held itself responsible for the misdeeds of the inhabitants of Formosa as its subjects and reserved to itself the rights of controlling and punishing them. It was also advisable to ascertain definitely the position which China assumed with regard to Korea.

Since the invasion of Korea by Hideyoshi at the close of the sixteenth century, when the whole country was devastated by the Japanese armies and the inhabitants were treated with ruthless cruelty— the memory of which, even to this day, causes the words " the accursed nation" to be an ordinary Korean vernacular equivalent for Japan— commercial intercourse between the two countries was confined to narrow limits. A Japanese trading settlement was maintained at Fusan; but it was under conditions which, if less humiliating, were not less restrictive than those imposed by the Japanese on the Dutch at their factory at Desima in the harbour of Nagasaki. Subsequently to the unification of the Government under the present Emperor, an intimation of the changes which had occurred in Japan was sent to Korea; but the mission bearing it was received with contemptuous insult by the Korean authorities, and later endeavours to open relations by further missions had no better result. These facts did not become publicly known until 1873, when some Korean despatches were published in which Japan was mentioned in degrading terms and upbraided for having forsaken the ancient civilisation of China in favour of that of the barbarians of the West. It was afterwards proved that these despatches were forgeries, but at the time they were accepted as genuine. Public opinion in Japan (that is, in this period the opinion of the Samurai alone) was at once aflame. An immediate declaration of war against Korea was eagerly demanded, not without the sympathy of some of the most influential members of the Government. But China stood in the way, and her possible interference could not be lightly regarded in the actual condition of Japan.

Soyejima, Minister of Foreign Affairs, who was recognised as one of the most profound Japanese scholars in Chinese classical literature, was ordered to proceed to Peking as ambassador (1873). The choice was a fortunate one. In addition to his Chinese scholarship, the ambassador was gifted with tact, perseverance, and diplomacy, and he succeeded in carrying all his points with the Chinese Government. China disclaimed all authority over the eastern half of the island of Formosa, and acknowledged the rights of Japan to punish the savages inhabiting that part of the island for the murder of the Riukiuans, thereby recognising Riukiu as being under Japan's protection. As regards Korea, China acknowledged that, both in its internal administration and in the conduct of its foreign affairs, that country was independent. Incidentally, Soyejima secured another diplomatic triumph. The audience question was still unsettled when he arrived at Peking. The diplomatic representatives of the Western Powers for several years had been pressing a demand that they should be received in audience by the Emperor with the formalities observed in European Courts. They had not yet succeeded in overcoming Chinese scruples when Soyejima arrived upon the scene as ambassador, a rank which he alone held among the foreign representatives. By his firmness he put an end to the procrastination of the Chinese authorities, and by his expert knowledge of Chinese tradition and customs he was able to secure that no veiled discourtesy should mark the proceedings. The audience took place: as ambassador, Soyejima properly took precedence of his European colleagues, and he was accordingly received by the Emperor of China in person without the degrading prostrations which had been for generations past regarded as indispensable.

The final step in the incorporation of Riukiu with Japan, a culmination which the considerations of race, language, and geography, as well as politics, rendered natural and proper, was taken two years later. Formosa and Korea, on the other hand, continued to be questions of acute contention, and Korea was the principal subject of Japan's foreign policy down, it may be said, to the present time.

Soyejima returned to Tōkiō from Peking, and Iwakura from Europe in the autumn of 1873. National indignation against Korea was at its height; China's non-intervention was apparently secured; and war was eagerly demanded by a large section of the Samurai, supported by influential members of the Government. Others equally influential, with Iwakura at their head, recognised Japan's unfitness, both from her military and economic conditions, to prosecute a foreign war successfully, and were as resolute in favour of peace as their colleagues were for war. Their differences had to be settled by the Emperor, who decided in favour

CH. XVIII.

of peace. Five members of the Government at once resigned their offices. One carried his resentment so far as to raise an armed revolt, and within a few months paid for his audacity with his head. Iwakura narrowly escaped assassination, and more serious consequences followed later.

Another outlet than Korea had to be found for the warlike aspirations of the Samurai. The Formosan expedition was accordingly undertaken. Early in 1874, a force of over 3000 men was conveyed with great difficulty to the island and landed. Insignificant military operations were carried on with little loss either to the invaders or to the savages they had come to punish, and, after the occupation of a small and remote part of the island had lasted for about seven months, the force was withdrawn, having achieved nothing besides provoking the serious irritation of China, who awoke too late to the fact that the integrity of her dominions was being violated.

The only result of her tardy protests was to furnish Japan with reasonable grounds for the demand of an indemnity to cover the expenses of the expedition. This was strenuously resisted by China, and for a time a rupture was imminent between the two Governments. By the intervention of the British Minister at Peking, peace was preserved, and an arrangement was made by which China agreed to recognise that Japan had rightfully undertaken the expedition for the protection of her own subjects, and to pay a sum of 500,000 *taels*, one-fifth as compensation to the families of the murdered Riukiuans, and the remainder to recoup the cost of roads and buildings constructed by the Japanese during their occupation and left by them on their evacuation. By this arrangement both parties were satisfied.

In September, 1875, a Japanese gunboat, which was surveying the mouth of the river Han in Korea, was fired on by a Korean fort. The insult to the flag was promptly avenged. A landing party from the gunboat stormed the fort and slaughtered the garrison and many innocent rustics in the vicinity, and then, having first taken as booty all the military implements, guns, banners, drums, etc., that were found in it, set fire to the fort. Once more, the Korean question came to the front and once more there were loud demands that Korea should be punished by war. Japan was now in a position very different from that of 1873. In the intervening two years substantial progress had been made in the acquisition of Western science and methods. The foundations of a mercantile steam marine and of a navy had been laid; the conscript army, recruited from all classes of the people, though small, was well drilled; and the Government was no longer dependent solely on the Samurai for its fighting material or obliged to defer to their clamour, however loud. Japan was united within itself and had the confidence which springs from experience. It could therefore have undertaken war with every hope of success; but the determination was adopted of endeavouring in the first place to induce Korea to conclude a treaty of friendship and commerce as a preliminary step towards drawing the hermit kingdom out of its seclusion.   An embassy, accompanied by a fleet of war vessels and of transports carrying troops, was accordingly despatched to Korea in January, 1876; and in a little more than a month a treaty was signed, and the members of the embassy had made a peaceful entry into the capital.   The provisions of the Treaty were generally similar to those of the Treaties originally concluded by Japan herself with Western Powers, which, as she afterwards complained, had been unjustly extorted from her by those Powers in her ignorance of international equity and her military helplessness.

This Treaty may be said to make Japan's third triumph in diplomacy. The *Maria Luz* case put an end to the slave trade of Portugal in the Far East.   Soyejima solved the audience question in Peking.   The seclusion of Korea was now ended.   In all three cases, Japan succeeded where Western Powers had failed.

The success of the Government enabled it to employ its enhanced prestige in the promulgation of further domestic reforms.   The national demand for Treaty revision and a parliament continued to find expression both in the Press and on political platforms; but the most unsparing use was made of press and public meeting laws of exceptional severity and a rigorous censorship.   Editors and speakers were consigned to prison for long periods, and newspapers were indefinitely suspended on the fiat of the Home Office whenever their utterances threatened the public peace or their criticism of the Government became too outspoken; and the completion of reforms, which had been tentatively essayed in 1873, was initiated early in 1876.   These reforms concerned the Shizoku or Samurai.

When the fiefs were mediatised and the chiefs deprived of their revenues, the Government, of necessity, undertook to provide for their retainers, who, unfitted as they were by their previous training and experience for bread-winning occupations, must otherwise have starved. Pensions were assigned to them, based on their former hereditary or life allowances, and paid out of the revenues of the fiefs, now collected by the imperial Government in the form of land taxes.   This system continued until 1873, when a scheme of voluntary commutation was promulgated under which hereditary pensions could be commuted, at the will of the holders, for six, and life pensions for four, years' purchase, the purchase money being paid one-half in cash and the other in 8 per cent. bonds, redeemable in three years.   This scheme naturally found no large acceptance on the part of the pensioners; but, though its success was small, such were at the time the financial difficulties of the Government that it was only enabled to meet the obligations under it by a loan of $2,400,000 (then worth about £500,000) from an English bank.   The financial difficulties increased rather than diminished during the succeeding two years, and the continued payments of the Samurai pensions became a serious burden on the resources of the nation.   It was therefore decided that commutation should be made compulsory, on a basis varying from five years' purchase in the case of large pensions to fourteen years in those of the smallest, the payments being made in bonds bearing interest of from 5 to 7 per cent. (1876).

This measure was accepted without protest by the sufferers, though its results were in many instances cruel in the extreme. The number of the Samurai who, either from natural capacity or through training, had a modicum of commercial or industrial aptitude was infinitesimal. In blind ignorance, many at once sold their bonds and, with the capital thus raised, entered into trade. Japan has never been wanting in adventurers who in their unscrupulousness, cunning, and mercilessness to their victims, are worthy compeers of the worst products of the exchanges of Berlin and Paris. To these the Samurai, with their small capital, offered a ready prey. Some opened small shops, willing for a livelihood to accept what they had, only five years previously, regarded as contamination. But, as a native writer said, "however skilful in wielding the halberd or the sabre, they know nothing of the abacus; they bought in the dearest and sold in the cheapest markets," and bankruptcy was soon the result. New institutions and new pursuits afforded, on the other hand, humble occupations to many. The new police force was almost entirely recruited from them—a fine force, marvellously efficient in the performance of its duties and in the prevention and detection of crime, ready to undertake active military service when occasion called for it, incorruptible, and as courteous and ready to help the stranger as the police of London. The rapidly extending railways gave openings to others as guards and signal-men; and in the Press, yearly expanding at that period in quantity and in circulation, and in the public influence which it exercised, they were found not only as reporters and writers, but as compositors, printers, and doorkeepers.

Instances were known of their serving as stokers on small coasting steamers, as domestics in the houses of foreign residents. These were the fortunate among their order. Hopeless poverty and social ruin were the lot of many. An epidemic of burglaries of the worst form according to Japanese law, in which the offenders were armed with swords and ready to use them, broke out at this period in Tōkiō. Many of them were committed by destitute Samurai, who paid for their offence by felons' deaths on the scaffold. The ranks of licensed prostitutes were largely recruited from their daughters, who performed what was regarded as the noblest act of self-abnegation in order that their parents might be provided with the common necessaries of life.

Time has atoned for much of what the Samurai underwent at this period. Those who survived it with honour, no matter how humble the means which enabled them to do so, continued to instil into the minds of their sons and daughters the ethical principles which they had imbibed in their own youth. The zealous and conscientious service which they formerly rendered to their feudal lords was by their sons given to the Emperor. All offices, both military and civil, were thrown open to all classes of the Emperor's subjects. The Samurai were, in feudal days, the brains of the country. That they retained a marked intellectual superiority over their fellow citizens was soon shown. From among them have come, not all, but a great majority of the successful candidates in open competition for appointments in the naval, military, and civil services. The most prominent members of the legal, medical, and engineering professions are Samurai; and, while all the outward and visible marks of their status are gone—their picturesque dress, their swords, their haughty demeanour—they are still a class apart in the general registers of the people and enjoy the social consideration which is given in the most democratic countries of the world to long descent and gentle blood.

While, as has been said, the edict for the commutation of pensions was received uncomplainingly, another, which had preceded it by a few months, proved too severe a test for many of those against whom it was directed. It has been mentioned that, in 1873, the Samurai were permitted to discontinue the wearing of their swords. Some, in the general wave of democratic innovation that was inundating the country, had done so, but they were the exceptions rather than the rule. The majority still clung to the only outward mark that remained to them of their status, to the sword which was "the living soul of the Samurai." The new edict (1876) peremptorily forbade the continuance of the practice. Armed revolts on the part of those who refused to obey broke out in three places. They were promptly suppressed; but they were soon followed by a fourth, which tested the resources of the Government to the utmost.

Among the five Ministers of the Crown who resigned their offices at the crisis of 1873 the most prominent was Saigō Takamori, originally a Samurai of the Satsuma clan. In feudal days Saigō was one of the chief councillors of his lord, and in the military operations which preceded the revolution, he commanded the Satsuma forces in the field. His prestige, his strong character, his commanding personality (he was exceptionally tall and powerful for a Japanese), and his position as chief representative of the most powerful clan of the empire gave him a commanding influence in the first Ministry of the Emperor, and the Emperor's own fiat was required to override his wishes in regard to the policy to be adopted towards Korea. When that fiat was issued, Saigō resigned and withdrew in umbrage to his native province of Satsuma, where he was said to devote his time to farming and field sports. But these pursuits were only a cover for preparations to carry out his own policy in defiance, if necessary, of his former colleagues, the ablest of whom was, like himself, a Satsuma Samurai, who had continued in the service of his sovereign. First and foremost, Saigō was a Samurai and as such clung tenaciously to the Samurai privileges. Every step taken by the Government to diminish those privileges met with his disapproval, above all the creation of a conscript army from all classes of the people. In his own clan his all-powerful influence was used to maintain the Samurai on their old footing and to train them as soldiers who should be as efficient in modern warfare as they had been in the days of swords and spears. He was able to do this with little difficulty. His whole life, his services made him the subject of enthusiastic devotion on the part of his fellow clansmen. Even the loyalty which both he and they owed, under all the teaching and traditions of feudalism, to their feudal lord, gave way when it became a question of choosing between obedience to Saigō or to the lord.

The conditions which continued to characterise the old daimiate of Satsuma, even subsequent to the great change of 1871, lent themselves to the successful promotion of his designs. Satsuma was always the most powerful of the daimiates in feudal days. It was also the most exclusive, the one which most strictly guarded its *imperium in imperio*. Its geographical position in the extreme south of Japan, with a frontier of hills, crossed only by steep and narrow passes, its capital town at the head of a long narrow bay whose approaches from the sea could be easily guarded, facilitated the maintenance of its exclusiveness. In 1871, when all the other clans in the empire, including Chōshiu, Tosa, and Hizen, almost the equals of Satsuma in strength, wealth, and reputation, accepted, without even a murmur, the edict of the Government which destroyed the jurisdiction of their lords and imposed upon them strangers from other parts of the empire as their new Governors, Satsuma contemptuously rejected the officials sent from Tōkiō and, returning them on the same steamers that had conveyed them to Kagoshima, continued to administer its own affairs precisely as it had done before the revolution. The Government of the Emperor had not the means to enforce compliance to its orders. What was possible was done in humouring the lord of the clan with all the honours that could be conferred on and shown to him, in heaping honours on Saigō himself, and in employing other members of the clan in every possible capacity in the government service. But all in vain; the clan continued to maintain its exclusiveness; and communications throughout the whole empire were at that time so limited and so jealously guarded in Satsuma that very little could be learnt at Tōkiō of what was actually taking place within the clan.

The new edict of the Government broke down the last fences which had hitherto bounded Saigō's patience. His Samurai were now well equipped with modern weapons and well drilled in their use, and they retained all their old skill in the use of their terrible swords, their dauntless courage, and their hereditary contempt for all who had not been born in their privileged class. The Government had its conscript army of about 40,000 men, mainly recruited from the peasants and tradesmen, whose compeers in Satsuma still were serfs. While Saigō was living in seclusion at Kagoshima, he had no opportunity of estimating the results of efficient military training and discipline, and he regarded the whole government army with contempt, believing that its units would scatter and fly like frightened hares when called to face the swords of Samurai, as they would have done in feudal times.

The gauntlet was thrown down, and on February 15, 1877, Saigō marched out of Kagoshima at the head of 14,000 men on his way to Tōkiō, for the purpose, in the words of his own curt manifesto, " of addressing some enquiries to the Government." Early in the same month the Emperor had proceeded from the capital to Ōsaka for the formal opening of the newly constructed railway between the great commercial city of Ōsaka and the old court capital of Kiōto, linking the two cities which in former days had stood at the extreme poles of social life—Ōsaka, wealthy, progressive, but despised; Kiōto poor, conservative, but aristocratic, even sacred. In the midst of the festivities the first intimation reached the Government of disquieting occurrences in Kagoshima. One of its members, a Satsuma Samurai, was at once sent to the spot to endeavour to conciliate the malcontents and to preserve peace; but his mission proved fruitless, and the Government was forced to accept the challenge which had been flung at it.

The campaign which followed lasted over seven months and was as bitterly fought on both sides as any in European history. The tactics of the Satsuma clansmen resembled those of Prince Charlie's Highlanders in 1745. They fired a few volleys with their rifles, then, sword in hand, rushed upon their enemies and endeavoured to bring them to close quarters. The Government had at first little confidence in the steadiness of their conscripts, and in the early stages the first fighting line was composed mainly of policemen who were Samurai like the clansmen, equally skilled in the use of the sword, equally fearless, and many, as members of rival clans, animated by traditional hatred of Satsuma. But it was soon found that the soldiers could be trusted, and numbers and discipline produced their inevitable result. The clansmen, at first victorious, were gradually beaten back, and their surviving remnants were finally hopelessly surrounded. Saigō and a few hundred of his most devoted followers broke through the lines and, leaving the remainder to save their lives by surrender, entrenched themselves on a hill near Kagoshima, determined to die rather than surrender. This was the last incident in the struggle. The hill was stormed by the imperial troops, the leaders and the majority of followers were killed, only 200 wounded being made prisoners by the Imperialists (September 24, 1877). More than 40,000 fighting men had from first to last been engaged on Saigō's side, though his available fighting strength never exceeded 20,000 to 22,000 men at one time. The aggregate of the Government troops engaged numbered over 65,000. Saigō's losses in killed and wounded exceeded 18,000, while those of the Government troops were 17,000, in all nearly one-third of the forces engaged on both sides. The cost of the campaign to the country was 42,000,000 *yen* (£8,400,000), and as it had to be defrayed by an increased issue of the existing inconvertible paper currency, this became depreciated, with disastrous results to the general economic condition of the empire.

Heavy as the cost was, both in life and treasure, the results of the struggle were not bought by the nation at too dear a price. Feudalism received its last blow. Satsuma, beaten to its knees, was crushed and placed under the administration of officials from Tōkiō. No murmur of rebellion has ever since been raised, and as, where Satsuma failed, no other clan could hope for success, this was the last, as it was the most formidable, armed opposition that the Government has had to face. Internal peace has since continued unbroken. The campaign conveyed two important lessons—it showed that the Government could rely on the loyalty of its own servants. Four of the Emperor's leading Ministers, some of the most distinguished generals in the army, and a large number of subordinate officials of every grade, both in the central and local government offices, were Satsuma Samurai. Not one man among them forsook the Government during the struggle. Even Saigō's own brother, like himself a distinguished soldier, though he did not take the field, continued to discharge his duties in the War Office; and the navy, officered exclusively by Satsuma men, never wavered. More important still, it proved that the Samurai no longer possessed the monopoly of the fighting spirit of the nation and that the mass of the people could be trained into trustworthy soldiers. The rebellion was the first practical test of the men who have since proved themselves to be among the most formidable soldiers of the world, and of a military organisation which has shown itself to be efficient and complete in every detail.

Since the termination of the Satsuma rebellion Korea has, apart from the question of treaty revision, been the keynote of Japanese foreign politics. That this should be the case is natural from the geographical propinquity of the two countries which rendered Korea of immense strategic importance to Japan, and from the internal conditions of both. In Japan there was always a war party, keen for the unimpaired maintenance of the imperial prestige, anxious for fields in which to display the national military spirit and efficiency, anxious also for the personal glory of military success, and cherishing the memories of the successful invasion of Korea by Hideyoshi in the sixteenth century and of its traditional conquest by the mythological Empress Jingo in prehistoric times. How Korea's repeated affronts to Japan made her, during the first decade of the Emperor's Government, the object of this party's aspirations has to some extent already been told. Korea continued to be their object during the succeeding two decades. Twice war was demanded and only avoided by the firmness of the Government and by energetic diplomacy backed by a display of force strong enough to drive all thought of armed opposition from the minds of the impotent Koreans. When war at last did break out—not with Korea but with China—Korea was its ostensible cause and it was the real cause of the later war with Russia.

The possibility of Korea's absorption by Russia was present as a perpetual nightmare to the most thoughtful and peace-loving members of the Emperor's Government, from the moment at which they were first in a position to devote their minds to foreign politics. They knew of Russia's longing for an open harbour such as the Korean coasts offered in several places, and saw the perpetual menace to Japan which such a harbour would constitute in Russia's hands. They knew of Korea's incapacity to resist foreign aggression, not only from her ignorance of all modern military science, but from her own internal disorganisation, from the wholesale corruption that was rife in every department of her Government, and from the want of national spirit or patriotism among her people, engendered by centuries of misgovernment, cruelty and oppression. Their own history taught them the impossibility of any country maintaining exclusiveness against the rest of the world, and their experience showed them that it was not hopeless for a people to remedy the neglect of centuries and take its place with dignity among the nations.

When Japan, playing the same *rôle* as that played by Commodore Perry in her own case, opened Korea to the world, Japanese statesmen were not solely influenced by their desire to put a stop to the continued recurrence of petty affronts which they had suffered. They hoped that foreign intercourse would, in time, help to end internal disturbance in Korea, to foster a national spirit of independence and patriotism, to secure some degree of honesty and efficiency in the Government, and to lead the nation at large into the paths of European civilisation. In cherishing these hopes, they failed to estimate rightly the different characters of their own and the Korean people. Their own lower classes were not less servile, not less apathetic than those of Korea; on the other hand, while the upper classes of Japan, as represented by the Samurai, were wholly indifferent to self-interest, full of high-spirited patriotism, of lofty ideals of personal honour, and always ready for any sacrifice on behalf of their lords, while feudalism still existed, or, when it ended, of their country, the Korean upper classes were not less entirely devoted to the interests and the enrichment and aggrandisement of themselves or their families. Hence, not only was progress impossible, but peace and order were neglected, and a corrupt system of administration was sedulously maintained in force.

With such a governing class—a class whose chief weapons were duplicity and treachery—it is not surprising that all hopes of reformation were falsified. From the conclusion of the first Treaty down to the

Chinese War, Korea's history was that of continued misgovernment and repeated disturbance, one party endeavouring to oust another from the spoils of office. The country continued to be an unceasing source of anxiety, as always threatening the peace of the East and offering itself as a ready prey at any time that Russia should choose to lay hands on it. Japan, notwithstanding her honest intentions, was not herself wholly irresponsible either for Korea's political anarchy or for the failure of the people to advance. She was, on more than one occasion, most unfortunate in the officials who represented her in Korea and in their ill-judged participation in the sordid struggles of Korean politicians. Men standing high in her military and civil services took part in the horrible murder of the Queen. The Japanese private citizens who took advantage of the new Treaty by taking up their residence at the open ports, included among them, at least in the first decade, the very worst possible types of unscrupulous adventurers, whose methods partook equally of the qualities of the bully and the swindler. Among all the transformations which have taken place in Japan nothing is more marvellous than that of the lower classes. The timid, cowering serfs of feudal times have become fearless soldiers; many of them have also in their daily lives developed into truculent and offensive ruffians. Numerous specimens of this class found their way into Korea, and their behaviour towards the gentle, broken, submissive natives was such as might have been expected. Their misconduct was noted by every impartial European who visited Korea, and it received little, if any, restraint from the Japanese officials whose privileges of exterritoriality should have first been used for the preservation of order among their own citizens and the stern punishment of their offences.

From 1882 to 1904 four distinct crises occurred, spoken of by Japanese writers as the " Korean affairs " of 1882, of 1884, of 1894, and of 1904. The two last were the immediate preludes of the Chinese and Russian Wars. These have been narrated in other chapters of this volume.

The condition of Korea during the early years after her opening presented a strange similarity to that of Japan immediately after the Restoration. There were two parties in the country—the one led by a few clever but ambitious young men, who, seeing to what Japan had attained in economic and military development, were anxious that Korea should pursue the same path with the same end in view and ultimately become a strong and united nation. They therefore desired to cultivate foreign relations to the utmost, and, most of all, to strengthen friendly relations with Japan. There was however a background to these young men's designs. They were still sunk in domestic intrigue, and they hoped to utilise Japan as a lever in their own favour in domestic politics. On the other side, there was the Conservative and anti-foreign party, which hated every element of Western civilisation and intercourse and clung to Chinese suzerainty and to the doctrines of

Chinese philosophy, whose dearest wish was to see Korea resume her ancient exclusiveness. The two parties, which, it is to be remembered, consisted, as in Japan, only of the upper classes, kept the country in a state of continual unrest, and the miseries of the common people, harried by both parties, were increased by continued extortion and oppression.

From 1880, when the building of a legation was completed, the Japanese envoy resided in the capital, but made little advance in cementing friendly relations with the Government, which was mainly composed of members of the Conservative party, or in promoting reform. At the head of this party was the Tai Won Kun (in Chinese, T'aiwên Kun), actual father of the King, who had been the adopted son of his predecessor. In the summer of 1882 a mutiny occurred among the Korean soldiers in the capital, consequent upon their having been defrauded of their pay, and, in the general disorder which ensued, the soldiers, incited by the Tai Won Kun, attacked and burnt the Japanese legation, and killed several members of the staff. The survivors, with the Minister at their head, fought their way out of the legation through the mob which surrounded it, and succeeded in reaching the sea, where they were rescued and conveyed to Nagasaki by a ship of the British navy, the *Flying Fish*, which happened to be engaged in surveying the coast.

As in 1873 and 1875, a cry for war was, once more, raised in Japan; but, once more, prudent counsels prevailed, and after protracted negotiations, backed as usual by a strong display of force, Korea made full reparation by the payment of an indemnity, an apology, and the punishment of those who could be proved to have taken part in the attack. One incident, however, marked the negotiations which was pregnant with grave future results. Korea, frightened by the presence of the Japanese military and naval forces, appealed to her suzerain China for assistance. The appeal was answered with a promptitude unprecedented in modern Chinese history. A strong Chinese military and naval force was despatched to Korea, ostensibly for the protection of the King, and for a time a collision appeared to be imminent between China and Japan. It was avoided by Korea's acceptance of Japan's moderate demands. The Tai Won Kun was decoyed into the Chinese camp, placed under arrest, and conveyed to Tientsin as a prisoner, so that the most disturbing element in Korean politics seemed to be removed; but from that time onwards China maintained in Korea, not very far from the capital, a permanent garrison of well drilled and equipped soldiers, varying in number from two to three thousand. Its alleged purpose was the maintenance of the King upon his throne and his protection against his own rebellious subjects. China assumed this duty as the suzerain to whom the King was entitled to look for aid in time of need. The Japanese, on their side, kept a small force of two companies of infantry as legation guards in Seoul. This was the "affair of 1882."

CH. XVIII.

During the next two years, Treaties were concluded by Korea as an independent Power, free from all control of China in her foreign relations with the principal Western Powers, including Great Britain ; and, by 1884, the diplomatic and consular representatives of these Powers were resident in the capital. A new minister represented Japan. Many Koreans had visited Japan in the course of these years, and what they saw and learnt there taught them that the main hope of their country's national independence and material progress lay in her adoption of Western civilisation. On their return, they naturally allied themselves with the Progressive party, and they succeeded in obtaining to some extent the King's sympathy with their ideas. The Conservative party was, however, still sufficiently strong both in itself and in the support of China, to control the King and to limit the exercise of his principles of Liberalism, and to retain for its members all the chief offices of the State. Hostility increased between the rival parties, and culminated in a conspiracy on the part of the Progressives to overthrow the Government and establish their own members in its place.

On the night of December 4, 1884, a banquet was given to celebrate the opening of a new post-office, at which the principal Korean Ministers and all the foreign representatives except the Japanese were present. Towards the close of the banquet an alarm of fire was raised, and both hosts and guests hurriedly dispersed. As they did so, an attempt was made to murder one of the principal Ministers. The leaders of the Progressive party then made their way to the palace and easily persuaded. the weak, terror-stricken King that his life was in danger and that his only resource was to appeal to the Japanese minister for protection.

The Japanese minister was, as has been stated, not present at the banquet. Two letters from the Court, one of them an autograph letter from the King, reached him in quick succession at his legation, both entreating him in urgent terms to proceed at once to the palace for the purpose of protecting the sovereign's person. The legation guard, consisting of 130 soldiers, under the command of a captain, was at once paraded and marched to the palace, where they took possession of all the gates, and effectually cut off the King from all communication with his responsible Ministers. Whether the Progressive conspirators had hoodwinked the Japanese minister, or whether the latter was a conscious partner in their design of destroying for ever by one *coup d'État* the Chinese and Conservative party of the Korean Government, has never been publicly explained and only the confidential archives of the Tōkiō Foreign Office could solve the doubt. Be that as it may, the conspirators had now the matter in their own hands. The principal Ministers were arrested during the night, hurried to the palace, and ruthlessly butchered along with court officials, eunuchs, and others, who were known to be favourable to them ; and the King, helpless in the hands of the conspirators, at once conferred the vacant posts upon their leaders.

The Chinese soldiers were stationed at some little distance from the capital. The conspirators were able to prevent any information reaching them until the tragedy was over, and it was only on the following day that they received an appeal for help from the surviving Conservatives. The *raison d'être* of the Chinese garrison was to protect the King against his rebellious subjects. Here was a case in which it was clearly the duty of the commanders to act, if they were ever to do so, and they had no hesitation in assuming the responsibility, even at the risk of a serious collision with the Japanese. The troops were marched to the palace; a brisk encounter took place between them and the Japanese guard, in which the latter, though hopelessly outnumbered and fighting, not against a rabble, as in the affair of 1882, but against soldiers as well disciplined as themselves, fought with their usual fearlessness. The inevitable result followed. The Chinese gained possession of the palace and of the King. The Government was once more in the hands of the Conservatives and the conspirators' game was over. Some of them escaped out of the country; those who were found met with the same mercy that they had shown to their political antagonists.

Simultaneously with the attack on the palace, a general anti-Japanese riot broke out throughout the whole capital, and the populace vented its hatred by destroying the residences of the Japanese traders scattered through the capital, and in many cases murdering the inmates. The minister and his overpowered guard made their way back to the legation, fighting their way through the streets, and found themselves, with all the remnants of the Japanese civil population who had taken refuge in the legation, in a state of siege, without provisions or the means of procuring them. The situation was desperate. But the minister showed no lack of courage, promptitude, or determination. The soldiers were formed into a square, with the wounded and fugitives in their centre, and, with the minister and his staff at their head, as in 1882, they once more fought their way through the streets and reached the coast, after a toilsome march, the hardships of which were intensified by a heavy snowfall in the night. The legation was burned by the mob, after its evacuation.

When the news of the events that have been described reached Japan, the usual cry of the war party again broke out and was fully vented in the Press, on this occasion more against China than against Korea. China was accused of having wantonly used her troops in Korea to attack Japan's representative and to imperil the lives of himself, his guard, and his countrymen—the indiscretion, to use the mildest term, of the representative being ignored. The Government was wiser and better informed than the Press and showed the same restraint and prudence that it had exhibited in previous Korean complications—in fact, in every incident of its foreign relations. Its two ablest and most experienced members were commissioned to negotiate. Inouyé, the

CH. XVIII.

Minister for Foreign Affairs, suspended his treaty revision labours in order to proceed to Seoul, and Itō his preparation of the Constitution to proceed to Peking. The missions of both were successful. Japan was not guiltless in the affair, and the reparation demanded from Korea was very moderate. Inouyé obtained it in full. The negotiation with China was more complicated. China was at the time flushed with triumph at her successful resistance to France and little disposed to give way before a Power such as Japan, whose military strength was, she believed, in no way superior to her own. It was only Prince Itō's personality that finally, after repeated and long protracted discussions, induced Li Hungchang to assent to an acceptable agreement. Its principal stipulations were that both Powers should withdraw their troops from Korea; that both should have the right of sending them back, should circumstances in Korea render that course advisable or necessary; but that, whenever either Power proposed to exercise that right, notice should be given in advance to the other; and that Korea should be encouraged to work out her own reformation, especially in the training of an efficient army of her own people.

The Korean affair of 1884 was thus ended; but Chinese influence continued to be paramount in Seoul, and Chinese traders, presenting a vivid contrast in their conduct and methods to the Japanese, to absorb the trade of Korea. Friction repeatedly occurred; but peace was preserved for ten years, when the result of the War of 1894 entailed the complete renunciation of China's suzerainty and ended the active interference of her officials in the domestic administration of Korea. Japan's influence now supplanted that of China, and the former Power enjoyed an unique opportunity to act in Korea's regeneration. She proved that she was honestly desirous of performing this task conscientiously and thoroughly by allotting its discharge to Count Inouyé. But Inouyé made the one great mistake in his brilliant career. He proceeded too rapidly. Legislative, financial, and administrative reforms were imposed on the Koreans with a rapidity that could only be bewildering to a nation that had been stagnating for centuries and that had none of the receptive qualities of the Japanese. While Count Inouyé remained in Korea, all apparently went well; but, so soon as his commanding influence was withdrawn and the supervision of the reforms he had inaugurated was left to a less gifted official, all quickly reverted to chaos.

The Queen of Korea was a woman of as great strength of character and intellectual ability as her husband was the reverse. She was filled with ambition both for herself and her country; but its welfare depended in her eyes on its continued association with China and the conservation of Chinese civilisation. The Tai Won Kun, her father-in-law, who had been released from his detention in China and permitted to return to Korea, shared her predilection for China; but between him and the Queen feelings of bitter antagonism existed. The

Queen used her influence with the King to procure the nomination of her own blood relations to all the highest offices of the State; even Count Inouyé, while in Korea, had found it expedient to yield to her in this respect. The Tai Won Kun desired these offices for his own relations and disciples. That desire could never be satisfied while the Queen lived, and a plot was accordingly formed into which the representative of Japan allowed himself to be drawn. On the morning of October 8, 1895, a sudden attack was made on the palace by the Tai Won Kun, at the head of a crowd which included some Koreans but was mainly composed of Japanese. Among the Japanese were some civilians of the worst type of educated rowdies, a class which had lately appeared and risen into prominence in the political life of Japan, whose arguments were those of the cudgel and the sword-stick; but the majority were soldiers and government employees, including even officials of the legation. An entry was effected into the Queen's apartment, where she and some of her ladies were ruthlessly murdered with every circumstance of cruelty and indignity that unrestrained savagery could dictate. It was subsequently asserted that the actual murderers were Koreans disguised as Japanese; but it was not denied that Japanese officials were present.

When the news of this incident was confirmed in Japan, all the participants in it were promptly recalled. The military officers were tried by Court-martial, but acquitted on the grounds that they had taken part in a *coup d'État* on the instructions, which it was alleged they were bound to obey, of Japan's chief representative in Korea. The latter, a lieutenant-general in the army and a viscount in the peerage, was arraigned before the ordinary criminal Courts; but his trial was not carried beyond the preliminary Courts which, in Japan, fulfil the functions of the police Court and grand jury in England. All proceedings in these Courts are carried on with closed doors, and it can therefore only be presumed there was not sufficient evidence to justify the committal of the accused to public trial for complicity in the crime of murder. His share in the plot was not a crime, and the only penalty that could legally be inflicted upon him for it was the cessation of his employment by the Crown and the condemnation of his countrymen. These were not wanting, and many of his compatriots urged on him the old Samurai atonement of *seppuku* (*harakiri*).

The price which Japan had to pay was a heavy one. No murdered Queen in history has been more heavily avenged. The incident might be called the remote cause of the War with Russia. The King took refuge in the Russian legation in Seoul, and two years elapsed before he again ventured outside its walls. All that Japan had done or tried to do was undone. Russian influence took the place of Japanese, and the country's retrogression into administrative chaos was rapid. It seemed only a question of time, at what date Korea would become a Russian possession in name as it was gradually becoming in fact—when the War with Russia once more enabled Japan to assert her interest and her influence. Korea now stands to Japan in much the same relation as that of Egypt to Great Britain. The task of her reorganisation was undertaken by Prince Itō, who, having nearly reached the allotted age of threescore years and ten, might well have demanded the repose to which his long services had entitled him.

Under the Treaty of Shimonoseki, signed on April 17, 1895, which terminated the War, the island of Formosa, together with the outlying group of islands known as the Pescadores, were permanently ceded to Japan. Some sentiment influenced the demand for its cession, made by the victorious Japanese, as it was claimed that Formosa was occupied by their ancestors in the thirteenth century and that geologically it formed a link in the continuous chain of islands that constitutes the empire. The practical reasons were its strategic importance, commanding the narrow straits, which are the highway for all the shipping entering the China Seas from the south, and the promise of its providing a valuable field of emigration for the increasing population of Japan. Little had been done by the Chinese during their long occupation to develop the resources of the island; but it was believed to offer immense possibilities in agriculture and mining, given good government and intelligent administration. It was known to possess valuable coal-fields, and a considerable quantity of gold had been found in it by primitive methods of surface washing; its tea commanded high prices; its sugar and rice were exported in large quantities to Japan and China; and it was the chief source of the camphor supply of the world.

The physical conditions of the country are peculiar. It lies almost due north and south, its length being 221 miles and its breadth varying from 60 to 90 miles. The western half consists entirely of low plains which are thickly populated by industrious emigrants from southern China; the eastern, of forest-clad mountains which rise abruptly from the plains to a height of 7000–8000 feet and continue eastwards to the sea where they also rise abruptly from the coast in granite cliffs to the height of 5000–6000 feet. The entire eastern coast line, unbroken by a single harbour, when viewed from ships, the largest of which can approach quite close to it, presents one of the most sublime and awe-inspiring views of the world. Only the western half of the island was ever brought under the effective domination of China. The eastern half is sparsely inhabited by untamed savages of the most bloodthirsty type, to whose gloomy mountain fastnesses the Chinese were never able to penetrate.

The cession of the island to Japan was received with such disfavour by the Chinese inhabitants that a large military force was required to effect its occupation. For nearly two years afterwards, a bitter guerrilla resistance was offered to the Japanese troops, and large forces—over 100,000 men, it was stated at the time—were required for its suppression. This was not accomplished without much cruelty on the part of the conquerors, who, in their march through the island, perpetrated all the worst excesses of war. They had, undoubtedly, considerable provocation. They were constantly attacked by ambushed enemies, and their losses from battle and disease far exceeded the entire loss of the whole Japanese army throughout the Manchurian campaign. But their revenge was often taken on innocent villagers. Men, women, and children were ruthlessly slaughtered or became the victims of unrestrained lust and rapine. The result was to drive from their homes thousands of industrious and peaceful peasants, who, long after the main resistance had been completely crushed, continued to wage a vendetta war, and to generate feelings of hatred which the succeeding years of conciliation and good government have not wholly eradicated.

The first steps in the civil occupation of the island were not more promising than the military occupation. Many of the officials were undoubtedly honest, and sincerely desirous of performing their duties as much in the interest of the natives as in that of their own country and countrymen; but among them were also many who united flagrant corruption with tyrannical abuse of their executive powers. All, whether honest or dishonest, were entirely ignorant of the local dialects, and they made the fatal mistake of employing as interpreters and informants the subordinate officials of the former Chinese Yamên. These men, the most dishonest and unscrupulous products of the official system of China, created what was almost a reign of terror. They levied wholesale blackmail on the most wealthy and prosperous of their countrymen, and, when their demands were refused, they procured the execution or ruin of many innocent persons by fabricated evidence which the Japanese were incompetent to test.

Whatever were their early shortcomings, the Japanese have since made ample amends for them, and the results which they have already achieved speak well for their capabilities as colonists. Harbours have been improved; railways, waterworks, and roads constructed; schools and hospitals founded; modern scientific methods introduced into the sugar and camphor industries; and, while native adults are being furnished, for the first time in their lives, with the concrete example of honest executive and judicial administration, their children are being trained in Japanese sentiment and Japanese methods, so that they may grow into patriotic subjects of the empire. For ten years, the island was a heavy burden on the Japanese finances, large annual subventions being required from the Treasury; but, in 1906, it became financially independent for the first time, and its revenue has since increased, owing to the profits derived from camphor, salt, tobacco, and opium monopolies, so that a large surplus can be annually applied to permanent productive works. Attempts are now being made to penetrate the mountains in the east and to subjugate the savage inhabitants; but, in view of the natural difficulties which have to be overcome, this task will require years for its accomplishment. The island is governed as a crown colony, the inhabitants neither possessing the parliamentary franchise nor being liable to military service.

In the island of Saghalín, fishing settlements were established by Japanese during the eighteenth century, and, very early in the nine-teenth, it was explored by a Japanese navigator and proved to be an island. It remained, however, a *terra incognita* to the Shōgun's Government, which took little notice of the Russian encroachments that were gradually made on it. When it did awake to the threatened loss of the island, it was too late, and the best terms in regard to it that could be obtained were that it should be occupied in common by the subjects of both countries, an agreement being concluded to that effect when the first Treaty with Russia was made in 1855. Subsequent endeavours to set up the 50th parallel of latitude as the line of demarcation of the spheres of the two countries failed, and Russian settlements steadily grew in number, until they extended to the extreme south and Russia was in virtual occupation of the whole island. Japan, unable by reason of her military weakness and internal disorganisation to oppose this aggression, yielded to necessity, and by a Treaty signed at St Petersburg in 1875 ceded the whole island to Russia, who, in return, recognised the chain of the Kurile Islands as Japanese territory.

Consolation was found at the time for this very unequal transaction in the thought that the climatic conditions of Saghalín rendered it unsuitable as a colonising field for Japanese, and that the loss was a small price to pay for the removal of a possible cause of serious friction between the two Powers. But, as time went on, it was realised that Japan had parted with an integral portion of her dominions, and in doing so had exchanged an island rich in possibilities for a few barren and inhospitable rocks. By the Treaty of Portsmouth (1905), the island south of 50° was ceded to Japan as one of the conditions of peace, and she has now the opportunity of testing her colonising capacity in a sub-arctic climate as well as in the sub-tropical climate of Formosa, while in Saghalín there is no hostile population to subdue. The original cession of the whole island to Russia proved to be not without advantage to Japan. It left her free to expend her energies and her money, both to a very large extent, on the development of the resources and defences of the island of Yezo, as much a part of Japan as Ireland is of the United Kingdom, while Saghalín is merely an outlying island which could be perfectly well spared at a period when no surplus population required an outlet from the main islands. Even Yezo was threatened by Russia, when Japan, during the struggles of the Revolution, was apparently in hopeless anarchy and military impotence. A very able Russian official was stationed at its principal port under the guise of a consul; a large mission of the Russian Church was maintained under Bishop Nicholai, the noblest and most devoted Christian missionary who has given his life to Japan since the days of Francis Xavier; Russian hospitals were also established, and Russian influence insidiously but steadily spread among the natives. It was, probably, only the knowledge that all she did was carefully watched by the able and determined British minister in Japan, who never shirked responsibility and who always had at his call the whole British fleet in Chinese waters, that prevented Russia from establishing a foothold in Yezo whence Japan might have had considerable difficulty in dislodging her.

The history of Japan's international relations during the Meiji period may be closed with the mention of two further incidents. The first was the Boxer movement in China, which is fully described in an earlier chapter. Japan has not, however, received the credit she deserves for her share in its suppression. When the foreign communities of Peking and Tientsin were surrounded and threatened with annihilation by overwhelming Chinese hordes, when distance rendered it impossible for relieving forces to arrive from Western countries in time to save them, Japan came to the rescue, and quickly landed at Taku an army of 21,000 of her best soldiers, fully equipped in every military detail. Throughout the campaign, this army was distinguished by no less skill on the part of its generals and no less bravery on the part of its soldiers, than were the British and American allies by whose side it fought. The evil record made for themselves by the Japanese soldiers in Formosa, under conditions of great provocation and temptation, was thoroughly erased by their conduct in northern China. It was as strongly marked by discipline, restraint, and humanity as that of some of the European armies was by the reverse of these qualities. What the Japanese saw of the Russian generals and soldiers in this campaign filled them with self-confidence and enabled them to meet the Russian armies in Manchuria without a shred of doubt as to the side to which victory would ultimately fall. Great Britain learned, for her part, that she need not hesitate to accept the Japanese as worthy allies. Having learned that lesson, she had no hesitation in concluding with Japan the defensive alliance, first signed on January 30, 1902, and amplified and strengthened on August 12, 1905. By these Treaties, Great Britain and Japan became the guarantors of peace in the Far East. Great Britain was relieved from the expense of maintaining in Eastern waters a powerful modern fleet—a burden which might have proved insupportable under the new conditions that are manifesting themselves in the present year, 1910. Japan obtained the final acknowledgment of her status as a great and civilised Power. The Charter Oath of the Emperor was thereby fulfilled to its last clause, and the "foundations of the empire were firmly established."

CH. XVIII.

CHAPTER XIX.

THE RUSSO-JAPANESE WAR.

ON April 8, 1902, a Treaty was signed between China and Russia. By its terms Russia undertook to respect the integrity of China and to evacuate Manchuria; China agreeing to be responsible for the safety of Russian subjects and enterprises in that province. Thus the prospect of peace in the Far East was, after many dark and stormy days, once more bright. Russia had, by her lease of the Liao-Tung peninsula, reached her long sought goal, an icefree port on the Pacific, and her communications with that port seemed safe. Japan, having secured a working agreement with Russia as to Korea, felt free to develop her legitimate sphere of influence in that kingdom, now that she was relieved from the menace which an apparently permanent domination of Manchuria had constituted. The evacuation was to be completed in three periods of six months each, and at the end of each period a section of the province, defined in the Treaty, was to be restored to China. In October, 1902, Russia duly met her engagements; but in the following April the second section was still in the hands of Russian troops. The Chinese ambassador at St Petersburg, in reply to enquiries, was informed that any further evacuation must be conditional on his Government agreeing to certain concessions and guarantees as to Manchuria not mentioned in the original Treaty. This China, supported by Great Britain, the United States, and Japan, refused to do. Almost simultaneously with the formulation of these fresh demands a marked increase in the activities of Russian subjects in northern Korea took place. A Russian speculator, Bezobrazoff, who was engaged in exploiting a concession obtained from the Korean Government, carrying with it the right to cut timber on the Yalu and Tumen rivers, had interested influential personages in the Tsar's *entourage* in his schemes. Work was begun on the Yalu in April, 1903, and on this pretext Russian troops were moved towards the river. This was a direct violation of the agreements with regard to Korea which had been concluded by Russia and Japan. The latter had expended much blood and treasure in order to secure a predominating interest in the Korean peninsula. She had recognised that, with Russia established there, not only would her own natural field of development be at once closed but her existence as a nation would be eventually threatened. The rapid growth of Russian power on the Pacific coasts, the enforced cession of Saghalín in 1875, and of the Liao-Tung peninsula with the hard-won Port Arthur twenty years later, had aroused profound distrust of Russian designs in the minds of Japanese statesmen. Japan accordingly made representations at St Petersburg that the proceedings of the agents of Russia in the Far East did not square with her pledges to withdraw from Manchuria, and offered a fresh treaty for acceptance, which, while safeguarding Russian interests in Manchuria, defined in unmistakable terms Japan's position in Korea. After various *pourparlers*, Russia's answer was presented at Tōkiō on October 3, 1903. This proposed to place certain restrictions on Japan with regard to Korea, but left Russia free to develop her interests on the Yalu, and to do as she pleased in Manchuria. Several months of negotiation followed, during which Russia was gradually strengthening her military position in the Far East. At length, on January 13, 1904, Japan agreed to regard Manchuria as outside her sphere of influence, but required in exchange, as an irreducible minimum, that Russia should give a similar undertaking as to Korea. In view of Russian military movements actually in progress, the Japanese ambassador was instructed to press for an early reply to this communication. None having been received by February 4, the Emperor determined to end the negotiations, and, on February 5, diplomatic relations with Russia were severed. On the next day, the first orders for mobilisation were issued in Japan.

It might well fill the world with amazement that an Asiatic people, relatively small and comparatively untried in war, should deliberately challenge one of the great military Powers of Europe to a trial of strength in circumstances which compelled them to become the aggressors, and to flout their mighty enemy in what was *de facto* his own territory. For Japan could not gain her object, which was to stop Russian aggression in Manchuria and Korea, by sitting still within her islands, and defying Russia to come on. But the chances at every step in the negotiations which led to the outbreak of war had been carefully calculated, on one side at least. The Japanese statesmen and soldiers knew that for their purpose the measure of Russia's strength was not the vast array which impressed Europe, but the number of ships and soldiers which she could deliver and maintain in what was to be the theatre of war.

In the beginning of February, 1904, Russia had, east of Lake Baikal, approximately 80,000 field troops, 25,000 fortress troops, required to garrison Port Arthur, Vladivostók, and the minor defences in the maritime province, and some 30,000 railway troops and frontier guards. These forces were scattered over the immense area lying between Lake

Baikal on the west, Vladivostók on the east, Nikolaievsk on the north, and Port Arthur on the south, the two main groups, about Vladivostók and Port Arthur, being 900 miles apart. The rate at which the immense resources of European Russia in men and *matériel* could be made available in the Far East was dependent upon the capacity of the Eastern Siberian Railway. The cost of laying the 5500 miles of line between Moscow and Vladivostók, and the extension of 600 miles from Harbin to Port Arthur, had caused the standard of construction to be the lowest which would meet the requirements of commerce. Neither the permanent way, nor the number and accommodation of stations and sidings, nor the quality and quantity of the rolling stock, was suited to the strain of the heavy traffic which the formation and maintenance of a great army would involve. But the chief difficulty was Lake Baikal. There was, at the beginning of 1904, still a gap of more than 100 miles of mountainous country in the railway which was being constructed round that lake, and, until this line was completed, everything had to be transported across thirty miles of inland sea. By January 27, 1904, the steamers which ordinarily performed this work were frozen in; all troops had to march across the ice, and until the end of February, when a light railway was constructed on the ice, all stores had to be hauled across on sleds. During the latter half of April traffic across the lake was almost at a standstill because of the thaw, and it was not until May 5 that the steamers were able to resume work. Most of the reservists, and much of the transport and *matériel* required to fit the troops already stationed east of Lake Baikal to take the field had to come from Europe. At the same time, the rolling stock and railway *personnel* on the Manchurian railway had to be increased. Fortunately for Russia, the resources of Manchuria and of the neighbouring Chinese provinces made the importation of foodstuffs unnecessary; but even with this advantage no very considerable reinforcements could be delivered in Manchuria before the end of April. Thus Japan could calculate that, even under the most favourable conditions, Russia would not for some months be able to put more than 80,000 troops in the field, and it was highly improbable that even this number could be concentrated on any one battlefield.

The land forces of Japan at the outbreak of hostilities consisted, approximately, of an active army of 180,000 men with a first reserve 200,000 strong, and 470,000 other trained men, or about 850,000 trained men in all. Behind this there was a reserve of population capable of bearing arms of about 4,000,000. From these land forces about 150,000 men, organised in divisions, could be mobilised immediately.

The naval forces in the Far East were more evenly divided. Japan had six first-class and one second-class battleships, six first-class cruisers, besides two purchased in Europe which reached Japan about a week after hostilities began; twelve second-class and thirteen third-class cruisers. Russia had seven battleships, nine first-class, two second-class, and six third-class cruisers. Thus, on paper, Russia's battle fleet was slightly superior; but it was divided. Seven battleships, four first-class and two second-class cruisers were at Port Arthur, four first-class cruisers at Vladivostók, and one at Chemulpo. It was necessary to send out naval reinforcements from Europe in sufficient strength to avoid defeat in detail, and the preparation of a fleet for such a voyage was a matter of many months.

The situation of the two Powers at the moment when diplomatic relations were broken off affords a striking example of the value of a complete understanding between statesman, soldier, and sailor at each step of negotiations which may culminate in war. The Boxer rebellion, her relations with China, her wish to secure an icefree port in the Pacific, had decided for Russia the number and distribution of her troops east of Lake Baikal. The desire to evade obligations which might involve the abandonment of promising undertakings led her to drift into a situation which threatened war, under what were, at the time, very unfavourable conditions. Japan had on the other hand calculated to a nicety how long she could afford to wait for satisfactory guarantees from Russia. Statecraft had secured for Japan the military advantage of the initiative, and left her free to prosecute an offensive campaign, since Russia could not collect sufficient transports in the Pacific for any serious expedition against the Japanese islands.

The necessary prelude to offensive operations on land was the command of the sea, which involved an attack on the enemy's main fleet at Port Arthur. As to the next step, it was clear that neither army, when concentrated in strength, could live for long in Manchuria without the assistance of a railway. This limited the possible lines of operations to two, the Vladivostók-Harbin line, and the Port Arthur-Harbin line. It was of importance to the Japanese to force the Russians to fight before the arrival of reinforcements from Europe. Landings could be made on the coasts of western Korea and of southern Manchuria earlier than on the coast about Vladivostók, which is icebound until the end of April, and this was in favour of the southern line. But the chief factor which determined the choice was undoubtedly Port Arthur itself. The most glorious and popular achievement in the Chinese War had, in the eyes of the Japanese people, been the assault and capture of Port Arthur. By the intervention of Russia, Germany, and France, Japan had been forced in 1895 to yield up this fortress, and her exasperation was not lessened when Russia obtained possession of it two years later. It is not too much to say that the national sentiment of Japan regarded the capture of Port Arthur as the first objective of the War. Apart from national sentiment, Japan went to war, first, to ensure her own predominance in Korea, secondly, to force the Russians to withdraw from Manchuria. The overthrow of the Russian empire on land was out of the question; but, if Japan were to secure these objects for the future, she must gain the command of the sea in permanence, not merely for the duration of the campaign. To obtain possession of the only icefree port in the Pacific which Russia held was the surest, and indeed the only real, guarantee for this.

The Japanese plan of campaign was therefore: to attack at once the Russian ships at Port Arthur and Chemulpo; under cover of this attack to reinforce the Legation guard at Seoul, and to move a division across the Korean Straits in order to force the Korean Government to acquiesce in and prepare the way for an advance of an army through Korea to the Yalu; as the progress of the naval operations permitted, to land other armies on the southern coast of Manchuria with which to prosecute the siege of Port Arthur and to cover the siege operations. For the development of this plan it was of great importance to Japan to anticipate Russia in Korea, in order to secure the ports of that country for her own uses, to prevent them from serving as bases for operations of the Russian fleet, and to force the Korean Government, in which the Russian and Japanese parties were nicely balanced, to adopt an attitude of benevolent neutrality. Russian patrols were known to be on the Yalu, and a cruiser, a gunboat, and a transport with troops on board from Port Arthur, were in Chemulpo harbour. Secrecy and rapidity of action were essential. Accordingly, at 6 a.m. on February 6, four battalions at peace strength, so as to avoid the stir of mobilisation, were embarked at Sasebo and, escorted by seven cruisers and twelve torpedo boats under Admiral Uriu, sailed for Chemulpo, while the main fleet under Admiral Togo made for Port Arthur. On the afternoon of February 8, the Russian gunboat *Korietz* steamed out of Chemulpo harbour and, meeting the scouts of Uriu's squadron, fired the first shot of the war. The gunboat returned, and that evening the Japanese flotilla appeared and began disembarking troops, which on the next day occupied Seoul. During the forenoon of February 9, the Russian ships *Variag* and *Korietz*, on Uriu's summons, gallantly came out to meet the Japanese fleet and were overwhelmed.

Meanwhile, on this same eventful morning of February 9 Togo had been busy at Port Arthur. The entrance to that harbour was difficult of navigation, and, to be ready for emergencies, the Russian fleet had a week before moved into the roadstead. There it was surprised during the early hours of the 9th by the Japanese mosquito flotillas, and two battleships and a first-class cruiser were badly damaged by torpedoes. The arrival of Togo's main fleet brought on a general engagement, in which four more Russian ships were seriously injured. Thus, before any formal declaration of war had taken place, more than half the Russian naval strength in the Yellow Sea had been put out of action, and, at a cost of six men killed and 45 wounded, the command of the sea which was the foundation of the Japanese plans was, for a time at least, assured.

The unexpected completeness of Togo's success allowed the original plan to be modified, and, to avoid the long and difficult march from Fusan to Seoul, the twelfth Division was shipped, as soon as it had mobilised, direct to Chemulpo, where it had disembarked by February 21. On March 10 the advanced guards of this division were in touch with the Russian vedettes on the Chechen river. With a screen of troops established in Korea, and Togo ready to counter every attempt of the Russian ships to break out of Port Arthur, the time had arrived when a concentration in northern Korea could be begun. A First Japanese Army, composed of the Guard and second Divisions, together with the twelfth Division already in Korea, had been organised and placed under the command of General Kuroki. The ice off the harbour of Chinnampo began to break up in the first week of March, and soon afterwards the earliest troops of the Guard and second Divisions began disembarking at that point. Japan had chosen the moment for beginning hostilities with such nicety that she was able to use the harbours of the north-western coast of Korea for her scheme of concentration, the moment they became available. Any earlier rupture of diplomatic relations would have involved long marches through roadless Korea, a later might have found the ports in Russian hands. By March 29 the whole of Kuroki's troops had disembarked; and, by the 20th of the following month, after weary struggles with the Korean roads, which the thaw had converted into rivers of mud, the First Japanese Army had driven back the Russian outposts and was concentrated behind the Yalu.

While the Japanese transports were plying to and fro, Togo was ensuring their safety by ceaseless activity before Port Arthur. Torpedo attacks and attempts to block the mouth of the harbour were frequent. Early in March, the arrival from Europe of Admiral Makaroff, an able and energetic officer, had infused new vigour into the Russian fleet, which began to leave the shelter of the harbour. The Japanese succeeded in laying mines secretly in the channels generally used by the enemy's ships, and, on April 13, the battleship *Petropávlovsk*, in returning to port, was sunk by a mine, with Admiral Makaroff and about 600 men on board, while a second battleship, the *Pobieda*, also struck a mine and was injured.

During the two and a half months which had elapsed since the outbreak of the War, something had been done towards grouping the scattered Russian forces in positions from which they could act in concert. On March 27 General Kuropatkin, who had been appointed Commander-in-Chief in the Far East, arrived at Liaoyang and took up his duties. He was a general with a European reputation, who had earned his chief title to fame as Skobeleff's right-hand man in 1877 and had been for some years at the head of the War Ministry at St Petersburg. He formed a plan of campaign which was suited to the circumstances. The command of the sea gave the Japanese power to land

troops wherever the natural conditions were favourable. The mountainous
character of the greater part of the country limited the possible lines of
advance from the coast which the Japanese armies could use ; and, for
the same reason, these armies must eventually operate up the great Liao
valley along the line of the Manchurian railway. The routes from
Korea and from the southern and western coasts of Manchuria met at
Liaoyang. Kuropatkin accordingly decided, after providing garrisons
for Port Arthur and Vladivostók, to make his first concentration at
Liaoyang and, while watching the coasts and delaying the Japanese
advance with detachments, to refuse a decisive battle until he had
assembled sufficient strength to allow him to assume the offensive with
effect. Some such plan is usually forced upon a Power which is compelled
to fight in or for a distant dependency against an enemy on the spot.
If Government, people, and subordinate leaders are prepared to accept
the sacrifices which it involves, and support the commander of their
armies loyally, the inevitable difficulties may be overcome ; but, at best,
the advantage of the military initiative must, for a time at least, be
yielded to the enemy, and some loss of territory and prestige must be
faced. If, on the other hand, the Government press their general to guard
this place or that, if the people, angry at the apparent immunity with
which the enemy takes what has been theirs, clamour against him, and if
subordinate leaders stubbornly refuse to give way before an enemy they
despise, then only a commander with a genius for war and an iron will—
such a commander as is seldom vouchsafed to a nation—can put this
plan into execution.

Kuropatkin was faced with such difficulties from the outset. Up to
the date of his arrival in the Far East, the supreme command of Russia's
naval and military forces had been exercised by her Viceroy, Admiral
Alexéyeff. He had been chiefly responsible for the conduct of affairs
which led up to the outbreak of hostilities, and his position naturally
carried great weight. For various reasons he was disposed to disagree with Kuropatkin's proposals. In the first place, he was deeply
interested in the various enterprises for the development of Manchuria.
Further, he and many of the military commanders who had hitherto
served under his orders were inclined to look with contempt upon a yellow
race, whose military methods and organisation they had neglected to
study, and to scorn even the appearance of giving way. Last, his
training and education led him to look at the problem from a naval
point of view. He saw that, if Russia was to regain command of the
sea, a fleet must be organised in Europe and sent to the Far East. Port
Arthur, as the only icefree harbour provided with docks which could
receive this fleet, had even greater value than it possessed as the base and
refuge of the fleet already in Eastern waters. Alexéyeff knew that the
declaration of war had found the fortifications and armament of Port
Arthur in an incomplete condition, and was very apprehensive of the

danger of leaving the fortress to look after itself. He was not soldier enough to understand that the place must fall to the ultimate victor, no matter how often it changed hands in the course of the War, nor did he see that for the Russians to engage the enemy before they were strong enough to strike a decisive blow was to make bad worse. Alexéyeff found at the Russian Court many who could not brook to see their interests abandoned to the enemy without a struggle and were therefore prepared to support his views, and Kuropatkin was thwarted by men who did not understand the wisdom of his proposals. That he was not the man of blood and iron needed in order to cope with the situation does not absolve those who made that situation impossible for one who was both a skilful leader and a gallant soldier.

At the end of April, the Russian field troops east of Lake Baikal were distributed in four main groups. There were some 45,000 men along the Manchurian railway, chiefly about Liaoyang under the direct command of Kuropatkin; some of these troops were still on their way to join him, some had been pushed as far south as Niuchwang: Lieutenant-General Stoessel had 19,000 in Port Arthur and the Kwantung peninsula, Lieutenant-General Linevich about 16,000 around Vladivostók: last, 19,000 men were deployed along the southern coast of Manchuria and the Korean frontier under Lieutenant-General Zasulich. These figures represent the approximate numbers of effective fighting troops; the paper strengths were much higher, but every regiment was, from a variety of causes, below its war establishment.

It is with General Zasulich's command, which was already in touch with Kuroki on the Yalu, that we are first concerned. On April 22, when Zasulich himself arrived on the Yalu, his force was watching a front of some 170 miles from Pitzuwo on the coast to a point about 50 miles up the river. This distribution was in agreement with Kuropatkin's reiterated orders that the enemy were to be watched and delayed without committing the troops to a decisive battle. Zasulich appears to have misconceived his *rôle* completely, and to have made up his mind from the outset that, if he were attacked on the Yalu, the strength of his position and the quality of his troops would give him victory. The bulk of the Russian troops were grouped about Antung, and a point a few miles further up the right bank of the Yalu opposite Wiju. Here they had constructed strong but very conspicuous entrenchments on the low hills commanding the four mile width of open sandy plain, which, broken only by the many channels of the Yalu and its tributaries, formed the valley separating the two armies. The Japanese had already crossed the river in face of the Chinese in 1894; and, by means of spies and of every known form of reconnaissance, they had accurate information of their enemy and his position. Kuroki, who could dispose of 40,000 men, inferred that Zasulich, who had troops extended far along the coast of southern Manchuria, and had occupied Antung in strength, was appre-

CH. XIX.

hensive of a landing on his right, and he determined to play on that fear. He, therefore, decided to keep the Russians employed near the mouth of the river, and to make his real crossing at and above Wiju. By April 28, Kuroki's plans were far enough advanced to allow him to fix May 1 for the attack, and, after some preliminary skirmishes and bombardments, the chief bridges were completed by April 30. On the morning of May 1 the valley was shrouded in a dense mist, and when this lifted the Russians found their left threatened by immensely superior numbers. At 7 a.m. Kuroki ordered the general attack. After two hours of sharp fighting the Russian left was driven from its first position, and the Japanese were firmly established on the right bank of the river, while the large proportion of the Russian force about Antung was still expecting the main attack to be delivered against it. By 10 a.m. Zasulich had reached his left flank and, after taking in the situation, he ordered a general retirement. But it was now too late; the Japanese right, swinging round, cut in on the Russian line of retreat, and only desperate and gallant fighting by the rearguard prevented the retirement from becoming a rout. The first battle with equal weapons, under modern conditions, between yellow and white troops, had ended in a decisive victory for the former; the Russians lost 1800 killed and wounded, 600 prisoners, 21 guns, and 8 machine guns; the Japanese 1021 killed and wounded.

The importance of this success to Japan could hardly be overestimated. The prestige of Russian troops stood very high before the War, and the fact that they had been met and decisively beaten in battle was to stand Japan in good stead when she went to the exchanges of Europe for the means to prosecute the campaign. Though Japan owed her victory to the blunder of a subordinate general, the moral effect of the success on her troops was as great as if their prowess alone had won the day. She had chosen for the training of her army the best German instructors available, and these had set themselves to adapt the natural fighting qualities of the people to the conditions of the twentieth century. The soldiers produced by this system were by nature sturdy, cleanly, and abstemious, by religion and tradition eager to sacrifice their lives for Emperor and country, by training equal to the requirements of a modern war. They were led by officers who had received a scientific education of a standard similar to that of the military schools of Europe. But, with all this, there was very naturally a certain anxiety until the system had stood the ordeal of battle with a European foe, and the telegram sent by the Japanese general staff officers to their German instructors from the field of battle gave expression to the exultation of the whole people in the fact that their theories had been put to the test and not found wanting.

The characteristics displayed by the Russian soldiers in this battle marked them throughout the War. The men were dogged and determined fighters, patient under hardships, but slow and quite incapable of thinking for themselves; the junior officers—particularly of the Siberian regiments

—were not abreast of modern progress in their profession; the seniors were too much given to intrigue and to quarrels. In the result, the Russian army in the Far East was a ponderous and clumsy machine, capable of gallant fighting on the defence, but with little power of manœuvre or of initiative, and its want of capacity to seize such chances as the fortune of war presented forced it continually to follow the movements of an adversary, who had the courage to assume and the skill to keep the offensive.

Kuroki's victory had made Japan paramount in Korea, and cleared the way for the next step in the campaign, the isolation of Port Arthur. While the First Japanese Army was assembling along the Yalu, a Second Army, consisting of the first, third, and fourth Divisions under General Baron Oku, had been quietly collected in transports at Chinnampo. On May 3, Togo reported that his efforts to block the mouth of the harbour at Port Arthur had so far succeeded as to prevent the egress of battleships and large cruisers; and by dawn on May 5 the first transports of Oku's army were anchored off Howtushih, a place on the southern coast of Manchuria, some twelve miles southwards of Pitzuwo, where the Japanese had landed in 1894. Though the coast presented great physical obstacles to a disembarkation, which involved the assembling of a fleet of eighty transports, and though the landing of the fighting troops alone required eight days, no attempt at interference was made by the Russians; yet Port Arthur, with its channels still open to navigation by destroyers and torpedo boats, was only sixty miles away, and General Stoessel had men busy fortifying the neck of the Kwantung peninsula at Nanshan, not forty miles off. Zasulich had withdrawn northwards to Fênghwangch'êng after his defeat on the Yalu, and his cavalry, which had been watching the coast, fell back with him. The Japanese had kept the size and composition of the forces which were disembarking in Manchuria almost entirely secret, and in the absence of any troops through which to gain information the Russians had relied upon native rumour. This had wildly exaggerated the number and extent of the Japanese landing. Towards the end of May, Kuropatkin had directed the cavalry to resume touch with the coast; but the Japanese had then established a screen on land which could not be penetrated. On May 14, Oku cut Port Arthur off from direct communication with the outside world. Five days later the main body of the Japanese tenth Division under General Kawamura had completed its landing at Takushan. This small force of less than 10,000 men was destined to act as a connecting link between Kuroki on the right and Oku on the left. But it played a part out of all proportion to its size, for rumour represented it as an army of several divisions, and it was not until long afterwards that its real strength was known. The Russian intelligence department was never able to correct the data upon which its calculations of Japanese strength were based, and this affected Kuropatkin's strategy throughout the War.

CH. XIX.

By May 21, the fifth Division had joined Oku, who left it with a cavalry brigade to protect his rear against any Russian movement from the direction of Yingkow, and marched with the first, third, and fourth Divisions against Port Arthur. Simultaneously, a Japanese squadron demonstrated along the coast toward Yingkow, as if searching for landing-places, and this stopped all idea of a Russian advance southwards along the railway. The position in Port Arthur was curious. General Stoessel was the senior officer on the spot, but, as he had had no experience of the charge of an important fortress, General Smirnoff had been sent specially from Europe to be fortress commandant. Kuropatkin, fore-seeing difficulties, ordered Stoessel to leave shortly before communication with the outside world was cut; but Stoessel suppressed the fact of the receipt of this order, and remained. Thus the situation was from the outset unfavourable to unity of command.

Under the supervision of General Kondratenko, the senior engineer in Port Arthur, the neck of the Kwantung peninsula at Nanshan, where it is only 4000 yards wide, had been strongly fortified. It was this position, washed by the sea on either flank, which Oku now proposed to attack with his three divisions, about 39,000 strong. To hold it, Stoessel had sent the fourth Eastern Siberian Rifle Division under General Fock, who deployed but a small part of his force in the entrenchments, keeping the bulk under his own hand. After some preliminary fighting on May 25, Oku made his attack on the 26th, assisted by four gunboats and four torpedo boats, no larger vessels of Togo's fleet being able to stand in close enough to be of use in the shallow waters of Kinchow bay. Weeks of careful preparation had made Nanshan almost a fortress. Assault after assault, delivered with all the devotion of which the Japanese infantryman is capable, was stubbornly repulsed. The Russian guns ran short of ammunition early in the day; but Fock had his large reserves in hand, and by a bold counter-stroke might have secured the victory, had he been a man to dare. As the sun was setting, the infantry of the fourth Japanese Division, wading breast high through the ebbing tide in Kinchow bay, turned the Russian left and at last secured a foot-hold in the position. Fock had already telegraphed to Stoessel, who remained all the day in Port Arthur, that the situation was extremely critical. He received in reply an order to retire, which was executed in some confusion, 82 guns falling into Japanese hands. Though not less than 15,000 Russians had been in the immediate neighbourhood of the battlefield, barely a fifth of that number had been engaged; yet so well had that small body fought that they left 700 of their comrades to be buried by their foes, of whom 4613 officers and men were killed and wounded. The spoils of victory included Dalny, with all the equipment of a modern commercial harbour, which was occupied on May 29; but its waters had been so thickly sown with mines that it was some weeks before it could be used. Mines had already inflicted a heavy loss on Togo, the battleships *Hatsuse* and *Yashima* having been sunk by this means on May 15; on the same day a second-class cruiser was lost by collision in a fog. With the help of that extraordinary power of reticence which was not the least of the aids to victory employed in this war, the loss of the *Yashima*, unobserved by the Russians, was concealed for many months, though all her crew were saved and were drafted to other ships.

At the beginning of June the Japanese were ready to engage in direct operations against Port Arthur; the eleventh Division had landed and, joining the first Division, had formed a Third Army under General Baron Nogi, who was to conduct the siege. This left Oku with the third, fourth, and fifth Divisions for the advance up the railway towards Yingkow. The first troops of the tenth Division had meanwhile reached Hsiuyen and Kuroki had occupied Fênghwangch'êng with the First Army. This distribution was in great measure due to the mountainous character of southern Manchuria. Three roads only led from the coast into the valley of the Liao—the first, by which Kuroki was advancing, through the Motien pass; the second, followed by the tenth Division, through the Fenshui pass; the third, allotted to Oku, followed the railway. On each the number of men who could be fed was strictly limited; for even the railway was of little assistance, until Talien bay had been cleared for shipping, and rolling stock been landed. Kuropatkin, for whom rein-forcements were now arriving steadily, had on his left Zasulich's force, reinforced to 20,000 men, under Lieutenant-General Count Keller, in touch with Kuroki; in the centre, General Mishchenko with 3000 Cossack cavalry watched the tenth Division; on the right, Lieutenant-General Stackelberg had 35,000 men distributed along the railway at and south of Yingkow, while as a central reserve there were 50,000 men around Liaoyang and in Mukden. The obvious course for the Russian Com-mander-in-Chief was to hold in check two of the Japanese columns and concentrate all his efforts on crushing the third; but, as often happens in war, the obvious course was the most difficult. Kuropatkin had not the transport to enable him to send a large force into the mountains at a distance from the railway, and, were he to develop his strength against Oku, a successful advance by either of the other Japanese columns would cut his line of communications. His information led him to believe that the enemy, particularly the central column, was much stronger than was actually the case, and so far his subordinates had failed conspicuously. Therefore he proposed to make his concentration yet further in rear, at Harbin, and was preparing to evacuate Liaoyang when Alexéyeff inter-vened, and, supported from St Petersburg, demanded an immediate effort to relieve the pressure on Port Arthur. So Stackelberg was sent south-ward with 26,000 men to draw upon himself as large a part as possible of Oku's army, but to avoid a decisive battle. The landing of the eleventh Division left Oku free to bring 37,000 men against Stackelberg, whom he met and defeated at Telissu on June 14 and 15, in a battle in which the Japanese lost 1190 killed and wounded, the Russians more than 4000 killed and wounded, and 16 guns. Bad weather, difficult country, and want of ammunition checked the Japanese pursuit and allowed Stackelberg to withdraw from an expedition during which he was throughout acting on faulty information, for the Russians believed the greater part of Oku's army to be completing the investment of Port Arthur. Immediately after Telissu, Oku was reinforced by the sixth Division from Japan.

The scene of real struggle was now for a time shifted to the rear of the army, whose progress depended on the rate at which panting coolies and Chinese carts could haul stores through the Manchurian roads converted into quagmires by torrential rains. With occasional skirmishes, toilsome marches, and long halts, the Second Japanese Army crawled into K'aip'ing on July 8. The other Japanese columns had, with no less difficulty, made some progress in the mountains. Kuroki had by June 24 collected sufficient supplies to permit his advance from Fênghwangch'êng, and on June 30 had secured the important Motien pass. Vacillation and uncertainty at the Russian headquarters were responsible for this. It was feared that the mysterious centre column would cut off Stackelberg; so troops were withdrawn from the left to oppose it just when Keller needed them most, and returned to him too late to be of use. On July 4, and again on the 17th, Keller tried hard to wrest the pass from Kuroki, but the Japanese, enjoying for once the luxury of defending strong positions, were not to be shaken.

The tenth Division began its forward movement on June 25, and two days later had possession of the Fenshui pass. Then, as the difficulty of supplying the centre column had not proved so great as had been anticipated, it was decided to strengthen it by the tenth Reserve Brigade from Japan, which, with the tenth Division, formed the nucleus of the Fourth Army under General Count Nodzu, who assumed command on July 16. So the three armies were drawing in towards the Liao valley, but their progress was slow, for important events elsewhere had, even more than the obstacles presented by nature, checked the rate of advance.

For some time the four powerful Vladivostók cruisers had been making their existence felt by raids from that harbour, and a Japanese squadron under Admiral Kamimura was keeping them in check. On June 12 the Russian ships left the port, evaded Kamimura, and sank three Japanese transports in the Straits of Korea, the majority of the troops on board perishing. The cruisers regained Vladivostók on the 20th, after scattering a quantity of merchant shipping. On June 23 Admiral Witthoft, who had succeeded Makaroff, sailed out of Port Arthur with six battleships, four cruisers, and their attendant destroyers and torpedo boats. This showed that the Russians had repaired their battleships secretly, that the channels of Port Arthur were navigable by their largest ships, and that, owing to the Japanese losses, the Russian fleet at Port

Arthur was numerically superior to anything Togo could bring against it. For a short time the command of the sea hung in the balance. Had Witthoft attacked and gained even a partial victory, or had he evaded Togo and joined the Vladivostók squadron, the Japanese land operations must inevitably have been seriously compromised. But Witthoft did not perceive his chances, and on sighting one of Togo's divisions steamed back to port without fighting. This revival of Russian naval activity seriously alarmed the Japanese, the despatch of reinforcements and supplies was temporarily stopped, and by this all four armies were more or less affected. Togo at once resumed torpedo boat attacks on the harbour, and the blockade was made more stringent, while on June 26 Nogi began active operations against the land defences by capturing Stoessel's advanced positions.

The convergence of the Japanese armies now made it desirable that the controlling mind should be nearer the scene of action. So Marshal Oyama, who had been appointed to the supreme command, left Japan on July 6 and established his headquarters at K'aip'ing. During its halt at that place Oku's army had been living almost from hand to mouth, and, partly from want of supplies, partly owing to bad weather, he was unable to move forward until July 23. Stackelberg had fallen back on to the fourth Siberian Corps which had assembled under General Zarubeieff at Ta-shih-chiao. Here they were joined by Mishchenko's cavalry, which gave Zarubeieff, the senior general, a force of 36,000 men. Oku, who had 55,000 to bring against him, attacked on the 24th, but during daylight could make no impression on the Russian position, and had begun to try his fortune under cover of darkness, when the Russians were found to be retreating. Zarubeieff had heard that Nodzu's army was advancing, and, in agreement with Kuropatkin's instructions that he was not to risk a decisive defeat, had ordered a withdrawal, which was carried out almost without molestation. The Russians lost about 2000 killed, wounded, and missing, the Japanese 1044 killed and wounded. The chief prize of the victory was the harbour of Yingkow with its connecting lines of railway, which supplied the Japanese with a valuable base, and made the long and difficult line of communication to Talienwan unnecessary.

After Ta-shih-chiao Nodzu was joined by Oku's fifth Division, which henceforward formed part of the Fourth Army, and with this reinforcement he was able to push back the Russians in front of him and to join hands with Oku at Haicheng on August 1. On the right Kuroki anticipated Keller, who, having been reinforced by the tenth Army Corps from Europe, was slowly preparing to attack the Motien pass, when the Japanese assumed the offensive on July 31 and secured the whole of the valley of the Lan-ho. In this fighting Count Keller was mortally wounded. The Russians lost 2000 killed and wounded, the Japanese 989.

The Japanese armies were now in two groups, separated by thirty miles of mountainous country, each group being about sixteen miles from Liao-yang, round which Kuropatkin had collected his whole available force, and where he was receiving daily reinforcement. The Russians were already in superior numbers to the three Japanese armies in front of them, and the time had come for them to strike one of the enemy's groups boldly before it could unite with the other. But Kuropatkin was in no mind to be bold. He credited the Japanese with at least two divisions more than they possessed; they had all the prestige of victory, and he believed they would attack at once; his thoughts were therefore turned rather to warding off than to striking blows. So difficult is it for a commander to wrest from his adversary the initiative which, maybe through no fault of his own, he has been forced to renounce. Thanks to the enemy's inaction, the Japanese were able to tide over an anxious period of delay, for once more lack of supplies brought their armies to a standstill. It was necessary to clear Yingkow harbour of mines and to build up a new line of communication for Oku's army, while Kuroki in the mountains was in continual difficulties, and his men were at times on half rations.

The pause was filled by renewed activity round Port Arthur. By July 23 Nogi had been joined by the ninth Division and a reserve brigade, which gave him 60,000 men. He at once began to press his attack. The Russian field and garrison troops in the fortress numbered 41,600; and these could be increased to 50,000 with the addition of sailors from the fleet and a body of partially trained civilian inhabitants. The deficiencies in the land defences had been to a great extent made good by improvised works ably designed by General Kondratenko, and the armament was supplemented by guns from the fleet. Nogi had complete information of the state of the defences at the beginning of the War, and he did not apparently give sufficient credit for the work that had been done since. He had carried the place by assault before, and seems to have thought he could do so again; for, on the night of July 26, he opened his attack on the outlying works, and, fighting two days and two nights, eventually turned the line of defence, when the Russians fell back. He had lost 4000 men in merely clearing the way for his real work. The attack on the main defences was at once begun; and, after many failures, by August 8 two small outlying forts on the eastern face had been taken at a cost of 2200 killed and wounded. Nogi's energy had an unexpected result. Alarmed for the safety of the fleet, the Tsar authorised Admiral Witthoft to break out and try to reach Vladivostók. So, on the morning of August 10, six battleships and four cruisers steamed out of harbour. But the ships were in poor trim for battle; the repairs had not been completed; indeed, some of the guns that had been landed had not been replaced. Even so, the Russian ships had all but gained a fair start of Togo's main squadron—such are the difficulties of blockade in these days of steam—when a chance shot killed Witthoft and temporarily disabled the flagship which was leading. This gave the Japanese the long-sought opportunity of bringing the enemy to a battle, which ended in the virtual annihilation of the Russian fleet. One battleship, two cruisers, and four destroyers escaped to neutral ports where they were disarmed ; one cruiser, the *Novik*, after a gallant fight, was beached on the island of Saghalín ; five battleships and a cruiser, all more or less severely injured, were driven back into the harbour ; thus the sting of the Port Arthur fleet was finally drawn.

The Japanese siege artillery was now ready for action, and, after two days of cannonade, all too short to damage the works seriously, Nogi began a general assault on August 20. Then was seen the curious and horrible spectacle of chivalrous devotion and *berserker* contempt for death at grips with every engine of destruction which modern science has devised. For two days and nights this wonderful infantry flung itself against powerful works, manned by a stubborn and unyielding foe. Small remnants, left by the waves of assault, clung desperately to such positions as they had won, till they were forced back at last, human endurance being incapable of more, with a gain of two small redoubts and a loss of more than 15,000 killed and wounded. Such a lesson was needed to teach these heroic soldiers that there were limits to the power of their valour. So the siege settled down to the slow business of sap, mine, and counter-mine, while the main armies returned to active attack and defence.

Oyama had stores enough for an advance on August 18 ; but, as the weather then made movement impossible and as Kuropatkin showed no signs of taking the offensive, the Japanese Commander-in-Chief decided to wait and see how Nogi fared. When it became clear that not a man could be spared from Port Arthur, Kuroki began the nine days' struggle known as the battle of Liaoyang. Kuropatkin had for months been fortifying positions six miles south of that town on the left bank of the Taitzu-ho; and for their defence he had the third Siberian Corps and tenth Army Corps with the seventeenth behind them as a reserve, and on his centre and right the second Siberian and first Siberian Army Corps with the fourth Siberian Corps in second line, a total of about 140,000 men. Besides these, the first troops of the fifth Army Corps had already reached Liaoyang, and its main body was at Mukden on the way south. Oyama had under Kuroki on his right 40,000 men in three divisions and a reserve brigade; in the centre, under Nodzu, 35,000 men in two divisions and two reserve brigades; and on the left, under Oku, three divisions of 60,000 men. Thus Kuropatkin was from the first slightly stronger in numbers, and during the battle he received about 10,000 men in reinforcements. On the 24th the Russian forces were well in advance of the main fortified positions, and Oyama's first object was to push them back on to these. Kuroki, having the most difficult country to traverse, was directed to begin. There ensued four days of fierce fighting in the hills and valleys of the Tan-ho. By August 28, General Bilderling, who commanded on the Russian left, had been compelled to draw heavily on his reserves. But Kuroki, still isolated, was by no means secure, till Kuropatkin, persuaded by the advance of the Second and Fourth Japanese Armies that the time had come for him to man his defensive works, ordered a retirement. Oyama had determined, on the previous day, to move to the assistance of his gallant lieutenant, and had set Oku and Nodzu free to attack. On August 29 the three Japanese armies were in touch, and on the 30th Oyama began his main attack on the Russian south front with the Second and Fourth Armies. Kuropatkin's positions had been strengthened with much skill and labour and were sternly defended, so that here the Japanese could make no progress. On the east front Kuroki's hard-fighting Guards had met with greater success, and by the 31st had thrust so far into the Russian position that they were for a time in extreme danger. Fortunately for them, Kuropatkin had sent his reserves to help in warding off the fierce attacks on the south front, and he could not seize the opportunity when it occurred. As the south front could not be penetrated, Kuroki was ordered to cross to the right bank of the Taitzu-ho, and begin a turning movement against the Russian left. To meet this movement, Kuropatkin had to form a new reserve and to move it across ground cumbered with the paraphernalia of a great army. Thus it was not until September 2, when Kuroki was firmly established north of the river, that the Russian Commander-in-Chief was ready for his counter-attack. Then Kuroki's twelfth Division threw the movement into confusion by surprising and almost annihilating one of the leading Russian brigades. With this, Kuropatkin lost heart and ordered a retreat, which was carried out skilfully and in good order on September 3. The victory won was far from decisive, the attacks of the Second and Fourth Japanese Armies had been continually repulsed, and it was by sheer desperate fighting, which left Kuropatkin no breathing space to organise a counter offensive, that the day was won. The Japanese, who had lost 23,615 killed and wounded, were far too exhausted to pursue ; the Russians, who had been almost entirely on the defensive, lost 16,500.

It had become apparent to the Japanese Government that both the carrying capacity of the Siberian railway, which had been steadily improved since the outbreak of hostilities, and the power of resistance of Port Arthur, had been underestimated, and that the further development of the military strength of the country had become a necessity. A law amending the terms of service in the army, so that troops hitherto available only for home defence could be sent abroad, was accordingly promulgated. The War Office at St Petersburg was equally busy in preparing reinforcements for Kuropatkin. After Liaoyang, the Russians had retired on Mukden and taken up a position behind the Sha-ho, whither Oyama had followed them leisurely. During September, Kuropatkin was reinforced by the first Army Corps from Europe, and by a newly formed sixth Siberian Army Corps, which gave him an effective force of about 220,000 men. The Japanese efforts were directed rather to restoring the regiments already at the front to their full strength, and by the end of September Oyama had 160,000 men. These were extended on a front of 90 miles, from the mountains on the east across the Sha-ho, where it bends southwards to join the Taitzu-ho into the Hun-ho valley. The extent of ground occupied by both armies in this campaign was a new feature in war, and had become possible because of the improved means of communication which science has placed at the disposal of generals in the field. Here, for the first time, we see the directing mind far from the shock of battle, controlling by telegraphs and telephones the movements of widely separated armies.

His access of strength convinced Kuropatkin that the time had come for him to attack and on October 2 he issued a flamboyant proclamation to his army announcing his decision. The relative position of the Japanese armies was unchanged. Kuroki occupied the right, Nodzu the centre, and Oku the left. Kuropatkin proposed to hold Nodzu and Oku to their ground and to throw his weight against the Japanese right. For this he formed his army into two wings and a reserve. Bilderling, with two and a half corps, was to advance on either side of the railway against the Second and Fourth Armies, Stackelberg, with four and a half corps, was to move through the mountains against Kuroki, while three and a half corps formed the central reserve. Bilderling started a cautious advance on October 4; but the cumbrous Russian machinery was not suited to a swift offensive in mountainous country, and it was not until the 10th that Stackelberg, after painfully pushing in Kuroki's advanced troops, was able to develop his strength against the Japanese right. Then Oyama, confident that Kuroki's tried fighters would hold their own, like a skilled boxer who has parried with his right, struck back heavily with his left. On the 11th and 12th Bilderling was steadily forced back, and Kuroki, cooperating, defeated the fourth Siberian Corps which formed the connecting link between Stackelberg and the Russian right. This threatened Stackelberg's line of retreat and induced him to look to his own safety rather than to the defeat of Kuroki. The last days of the battle, as the Russians fell back fighting on to the Sha-ho, were remarkable for a dramatic struggle in the centre, where, on the left bank of the river, rose out of the valley a bare hill crowned by a single tree with the village of Sha-ho-pu at its foot. On the 14th this was twice captured, and twice recaptured by the Russians, Kuropatkin himself directing the struggle from the hill-top. On the 15th a skilful surprise gave both village and hill to the Japanese; but on the next day General Putiloff, collecting a force from the *débris* of many failures, led it at dusk once more to the assault. Taking the exhausted enemy unawares, he drove them from the summit and captured 14 guns. The village was once again taken by the Japanese; but the Russians were not to be moved from the hill to which the captor had now proudly given his name. Putiloff Hill thus became an advanced post to the lines behind the Shaho, into which the Russians had withdrawn and on which the Japanese attacks could make no impression. On the 19th weariness put an end to the fighting, which had cost the Russians 32,300 killed, wounded and prisoners, the Japanese 20,300. A long truce of recovery and preparation for the severe Manchurian winter followed this ten days' struggle.

After the failure of the bloody assaults of August on Port Arthur, Nogi had perforce to resort to more deliberate methods. Siege batteries were built, parallels opened, and a heavy bombardment of the Russian works begun. On September 19 a series of attacks was initiated upon advanced works on the northern and north-western fronts, which ended in the capture of Fort Kuropatkin in the north, and in good progress towards a prominent hill which, under the name of 203 Metre Hill, was to play a prominent part in the siege. After a month of sapping and bombardment, a general attack on the main defences of the eastern face was begun on October 26 and lasted for five days. The ditches of many works were entered; but the Russians by fierce hand to hand fighting drove their enemy out again, and, though some of the chief forts were seriously damaged, none at the end remained in Japanese hands. These attacks had cost the Japanese 151 officers and 1970 men killed and wounded.

Meanwhile, the pressure of events elsewhere had made the reduction of Port Arthur a matter of great urgency. By the middle of October the Baltic Fleet, the preparation of which had been for months a topic of newspaper discussion, had actually put to sea under Admiral Rozhdestvensky. On the night of October 21 a division of this fleet, in crossing the Dogger Bank, passed through a group of Hull fishing smacks, and opened fire upon them. One smack was sunk, two of the fishermen were killed and eighteen wounded. The news of this astounding event did not reach England till the evening of the 23rd, by which time Rozhdestvensky had passed down Channel without reporting the incident. Such a wave of indignation swept over Britain as might have forced a weak Government into war. Fortunately, Mr Balfour and Lord Lansdowne never lost control of a critical situation, and on October 28 in a speech at Southampton the Premier was able to announce that the Tsar had expressed his regrets, promised compensation, and agreed to detain the responsible officers. The whole matter was to be referred to arbitration. Accordingly an international Commission of Admirals met in Paris in January, 1905. The Russian defence was that they had been attacked by torpedo boats concealed among the fishing smacks. There is no reason to doubt that the mistake was made in good faith, absurd though the explanation sounded to English ears at the time. The Baltic Fleet had been mobilised with difficulty, the crews were untrained, and many of the hands were landsmen. Rumours as to Japanese designs were

rife and a condition of nervous anxiety pervaded the fleet. In the
darkness the signals for the movements of the steam trawlers were mistaken by credulous, suspicious, and not over-skilful eyes for those of
torpedo boats. The Commission found by a majority that the torpedo
boats were mythical and awarded compensation for the damage done, but
agreed that the situation justified Rozhdestvensky's anxiety.

While Europe had been on the verge of war, the Baltic fleet had
continued its voyage, and had ceased to be an empty menace. So the
seventh Japanese Division was landed at Dalny to reinforce Nogi, and a
steady stream of drafts was poured into the divisions which had lost so
heavily. A third assault was attempted against the eastern forts on
November 26, but with no better success. Without pause, Nogi directed
his efforts to the north-west front, and on the next day began a series of
attacks on 203 Metre Hill. By sapping, desperate assaults, and continuous bombardment, the assailants worked their way forward foot by
foot, until on December 5 the prize was won, but at a terrible cost.
Since November 25 the Japanese had lost 13,000 men, 9000 of these
falling round 203 Metre Hill; in the works there, which had been blown
to pieces by high-explosive shell, 400 Russian corpses were found. The
importance of this capture lay in the view over harbour and town which
the hill, though not in the main line of the defences, commanded. With
modern artillery it is unnecessary that the man who aims the gun should
see the target. If an observer can see where the shells alight, fire can be
directed with complete accuracy. So, with a good observing station in
their hands, the Japanese were able to make certain that the warships
remaining in the harbour should not again put out to sea. Saps were
now begun from 203 Metre Hill towards the western forts, and the
eastern forts were steadily undermined. On December 15 the garrison
suffered a heavy loss in the death of General Kondratenko, who had
shown himself the only high commander in the place with a single purpose
and character strong enough to subordinate all else to its attainment.
On the 18th, one of the eastern forts was taken by assault, after mines had
been exploded beneath it; and another fell ten days later. The generals
in the fortress were now at open disagreement—the one side for surrender, the other for fighting; but, on January 1, Stoessel solved the
problem by sending a flag of truce to Nogi without the knowledge of his
council. On the same evening the capitulation was signed, and the
Japanese had gained the first of the great objects of the War. Though
the situation had become desperate after the fall of the eastern forts, it
was Stoessel's clear duty to keep Togo and Nogi employed to the last
possible moment, and at the time of surrender the means of defence had
not been exhausted. 878 officers, 23,491 men marched out as prisoners
of war, and provisions for three months and $2\frac{1}{2}$ million rounds of small
arm ammunition were found in the place. Had there been loyal cooperation between the higher commanders, and a more skilful use of the

resources of the fortress during the early days of the siege, the defence might well have been prolonged till the arrival of the Baltic fleet, when Togo's work would have been greatly complicated. But, if Stoessel proved unequal to his task, nothing but honour is due to the Russian soldiery, who bore themselves nobly throughout the 148 days of siege, in face of a foe whose courage, skill, and determination have rarely been excelled in war. 28,200 Russians were killed or wounded during the siege. The capture cost the Japanese the huge total of 57,780 killed and wounded, while the losses from sickness were very heavy, as they always are where a large force is kept for long in one place.

As the fall of Port Arthur had set 100,000 men free to join Oyama, it became imperative for Kuropatkin to brave the winter, and to act before Nogi's army could arrive. The numbers of the Russian army were approaching the limit which the single line of railway could maintain during the winter, when hard weather increased the needs of the troops, and made traffic more difficult. The rate at which reinforcements arrived had therefore steadily diminished. Early in January, Kuropatkin could put 250,000 men in the field; these were organised in three armies—the First under General Linevich, the grey-haired veteran who had been throughout the war in command at Vladivostók, the Second Army under General Grippenberg, the Third under General Kaulbars. While this reorganisation was in progress, Alexéyeff was recalled; and the Russian Commander-in-Chief became the supreme representative of the Tsar in the Far East.

During the three months since the battles on the Sha-ho the Japanese War Office had been busy making good Nogi's enormous losses and increasing his strength, so that Oyama had received only the eighth Division and sufficient men to replace the wear and tear of war, which gave him a strength of 185,000 men. Kuropatkin desired to delay Nogi's arrival; so, on January 8, he sent a force of about 6000 Cossack cavalry under General Mishchenko to raid the Japanese communications. For a cavalry dash the force was too large, and was encumbered with too much transport. It moved down the Hun-ho valley, round the Japanese left, and reached the base at Yingkow on the 12th. The alarm had been given everywhere, and the posts were manned by small bodies of infantry sufficient to repulse a cavalry who knew not how to use their rifles. On the 15th Mishchenko returned to the Russian lines in safety, having accomplished little beyond gaining information of Nogi's movement and destroying a few hundred yards of railway which were quickly repaired. On the night of January 24, Grippenberg began another effort. A great part of the Second Army, which formed Kuropatkin's extreme right, was on the right bank of the Hun-ho. Grippenberg crossed that river on the ice, succeeded in surprising the advanced troops on Oku's left, and captured the village of Hokutai, which formed part of the Japanese main position. On the 26th, the fight resolved itself into a struggle for the possession of the adjoining village of Sandepu. The village was taken by the Russians, but they were unable to drive the Japanese from a work on its outskirts, and it was finally evacuated and left in flames. Still, Grippenberg's right continued to make progress and Oku's left was slowly pressed back, until the night of the 27th brought reinforcements which Oyama had collected on learning the extent of the Russian successes. Grippenberg clamoured for support so that he could make good his gains; but Kuropatkin had not the nerve for bold enterprises. Remembering the counterstroke on the Sha-ho, he watched the Japanese centre and right, fearfully clinging to his reserves. Grippenberg, enraged against his chief, was ordered back, and on the 29th both armies were in their old positions. This fruitless fighting had cost the Russians 10,000 killed and wounded, the Japanese 8900. The one result was that Grippenberg broke out openly into recrimination against Kuropatkin, and was deprived of his command.

It was important that Oyama should use the access of strength derived by him from the addition of Nogi's army and from the new formations due to the alterations in the Japanese terms of service, before the thaws of spring turned the plains of Mukden into a morass. The disposition of the reinforcements, which had been used already with such good effect during the war, was again employed to bewilder Kuropatkin. A Fifth Army, composed of a reserve Division and the eleventh Division from Port Arthur under General Kawamura, was moved through the mountains and extended Kuroki's right; the presence of the eleventh Division was allowed to become known, and convinced the Russians that Nogi's army was about to carry out a great turning movement against their left. The First, Fourth and Second Armies retained their relative positions from right to left, and were rearranged and strengthened by reinforcements. Nogi's army, with the exception of the eleventh Division, was moved with great secrecy into a position on the left bank of the Taitzu-ho, where the general disposition of the troops in front shielded it from prying eyes. Last, a general reserve of 20,000 men was formed under the direct control of Japanese Headquarters. Oyama thus had about 300,000 men under his orders. The Russians still held approximately their old positions on the Sha-ho, the First Army under Linevich being in the mountains on the left, the Third Army under Bilderling in the centre, and the Second, now under Alexander Kaulbars, stretching down to and across the Hun-ho. Kuropatkin posted his reserve at Mukden, and had altogether about 310,000 men. Of the rival armies the Japanese was considerably the stronger in infantry, the Russian in cavalry; the artillery was fairly evenly divided, but the Russian guns were far superior.

Kuropatkin, once more, proposed to anticipate the enemy; but, once more, the Japanese struck while the Russians were still preparing to move. On February 23, Kawamura advanced through the mountains and attacked the Russian extreme left. The next day Kuroki assailed the whole front of the Russian First Army. Linevich was, on the whole, able to hold his ground, but Oyama's plan had fulfilled its purpose. Kuropatkin expected attack on his left and, seeing in Kawamura's army his real danger, hurried his reserves to his left flank. On the 27th, when the Russian Commander-in-Chief was committed to this movement, Nogi crossed the Hun-ho quietly, and on the 28th was in line with Oku menacing the Russian right. Then began a slow but irresistible wheel, in which Nogi and Oku gradually bore back Kaulbars, while elsewhere a doubtful battle raged to and fro, in attack and counter-attack, round the Russian earthworks. Kuropatkin hastily assembled a new reserve for a counter-attack against Nogi; but the patchwork organisation of the battlefield could not work smoothly, and the attack was not ready until March 6 when it was repulsed. That evening Kuropatkin began to prepare for retreat on Tieling. During the 7th Nogi, supported by Oyama's reserve, extended his left steadily northwards, and Kuropatkin ordered Linevich, who had held his ground through twelve days' fighting, back into new lines which had been fortified in front of Mukden on the right bank of the Hun-ho. Throughout the 9th and 10th, Linevich continued to repulse all attacks on his front, and, though Bilderling and Kaulbars suffered heavily as they withdrew, they were able by gallant fighting to prevent Nogi from cutting the line of retreat and bringing about a new Sedan. The weary Japanese occupied Mukden but were never able to turn the retreat of the stolid Russian columns into a rout. By March 14 the Russian armies had passed through Tieling, and a week later were astride the railway in new positions some 80 miles north of that town. Oyama occupied Tieling on the 16th and fixed his head-quarters there, pushing outposts to within 12 miles of the Russian advanced troops. Thus the two armies faced each other with little change till the end of the War. The exhaustion of men and stores, which was the consequence of the fourteen days' battle round Mukden, and the thaws of spring, made both commanders disinclined to undertake lightly the difficulties of active operations. The Japanese had lost 71,014 killed and wounded during the battle, the Russians about 60,000 killed and wounded and 25,000 prisoners, and an immense quantity of *matériel*. Immediately after the battle, Kuropatkin, who felt that he had no longer the confidence of the army, tendered his resignation to the Tsar, asking at the same time to be employed in a subordinate capacity. Linevich was appointed as his successor, and Kuropatkin took over the command of the First Army.

The fall of Port Arthur had made the time of the arrival of the Baltic Fleet in the Far East a matter of minor importance. Accordingly Rozhdestvensky had made a long halt at Madagascar, partly in order to train his inexperienced crews, and partly to await an additional squadron, which was composed of the dregs of the Russian naval

establishments. Steaming slowly eastwards, while overcoming all difficulties of coaling and feeding his fleet in a manner which displayed
exceptional powers of organisation, Rozhdestvensky united his various
squadrons in the China Sea on May 9. His fleet consisted of eight
battleships, four of them slow vessels of old type, four armoured and
eight protected cruisers, of which about half were out of date, nine destroyers, and a number of auxiliary ships. The bottoms of all these ships
were foul with their long voyage. Togo had had four months in which
to refit his ships and rest his crews. He had four modern battleships,
one battleship of old type, and three coast defence battleships, eight
armoured and fifteen protected cruisers, with a swarm of gunboats, torpedo
boats and destroyers. The Japanese squadrons were homogeneous, and
almost all the ships of the most modern type. The impossibility of carrying
coal sufficient for fighting a battle and at the same time for making the
wide *détour* round the islands of Japan, compelled Rozhdestvensky to take
the direct route to Vladivostók by the Straits of Tsushima. Togo had
established a complete system of reconnaissance over all waters by which
the Russian ships could approach, and had fixed his base at Masampo,
on the Korean side of the Straits, whence he could bring the enemy to
battle close by, if the latter attempted to force the direct route, and
could anticipate him if he chose the more circuitous way to Vladivostók.
At 5 a.m. on May 27, one of Togo's lookouts reported by wireless telegraphy that the Russian fleet was steaming for the Straits of Tsushima;
and henceforward the faster Japanese cruisers were able to observe
unharmed and report every movement of their enemy. Rozhdestvensky
advanced in three long columns with his unarmed auxiliary ships in the
centre, a formation which served indeed to protect these, but allowed
Togo to concentrate an overwhelming fire against the leading ships.
The battle began, about 2 p.m., to the east of the island of Tsushima,
the Japanese engaging the enemy at 7000 yards, a range at which the
superior training of their gunners enabled them to make the most of
their weapons. By steaming across the Russian fleet, so as to bring
every possible gun to bear, the Japanese developed a crushing fire, while
that of the Russians was comparatively ineffective. In less than three-
quarters of an hour the battleships leading the two main columns were
out of action and Rozhdestvensky was severely wounded. By nightfall
every attempt of the Russian ships to break through to the north had
been frustrated, and all cohesion in the fleet had been destroyed. During
the night the Japanese torpedo boats continued the work which the heavy
cannon had begun, and on May 28 a general chase of the flying enemy
completed the work of destruction. Four battleships, four armoured
and three protected cruisers, five destroyers, and five auxiliary ships were
sunk; four battleships and two hospital ships were captured; three protected cruisers, one destroyer, and two auxiliary ships reached neutral
ports and were disarmed; two protected cruisers and two destroyers

CH. XIX,

alone reached Vladivostók. Thus the question of the command of the
Pacific was definitively settled.

It was fitting that the last great success in the War should have been
gained by the one genius whom the struggle had produced. The success
of Japan was only possible if she held the command of the sea.
Togo's shoulders had borne the greatest weight of responsibility, and
his brain had designed the only absolute and unanswerable victory.
On land there was a deadlock. On the side of Russia the Siberian
railway was, with the advance of spring, again working at its full power;
but it would be many months before the losses of Mukden could be
replaced, and a sufficient superiority accumulated to restore lost confidence and enable an offensive campaign to be attempted again. The
country was torn by internal dissension, in many places open rebellion
was rife. The War was thoroughly unpopular, as a disastrous colonial
enterprise to be got rid of at any reasonable cost, not a vital struggle
to be fought out so long as any power of resistance remained. Japan,
with all her prestige of unbroken triumph, had little behind the
bold front she presented to her enemy and to the world; her resources
both in men and in money were nearly exhausted. The campaign on
land gave little promise of a decisive result. There was no place which
Japan could seize, so as to crush, once and for all, her enemy's power
in the Far East. A siege of Vladivostók, another and more formidable
Port Arthur, was out of the question. She could at most hope for
another Mukden, leading to a similar position of stalemate. Both
armies were tied to the single line of railway, the artery through which
flowed their life's blood. With a theatre of operations limited on the
one flank by inhospitable mountain country, and on the other by the
frontier of a neutral State, brilliant combination and decisive manœuvre
were impossible. Before the battle of Tsushima, friendly Powers, led by the
United States, had begun to make tentative overtures of mediation; but,
until her last venture on the sea had been staked, Russia was unwilling
to listen to advice. When, however, the naval campaign had been finally
decided, the time was ripe for negotiation. So on June 10, at the
suggestion of the President of the United States, the belligerents agreed
to nominate representatives to consider terms. No armistice was declared,
and fighting went on; but on the part of Japan this was rather a
rearrangement of her cards, so as to provide her plenipotentiaries with
the strongest possible hand, than a seeking of decisive results. Two
divisions of reserve troops under General Hasegawa drove the Russians
out of north-eastern Korea, and appeared to threaten an advance on
Vladivostók, while one expeditionary force was landed in Saghalín and
secured possession of that island without difficulty, and another occupied
the mouth of the Amur.

The Japanese representative, Baron Komura, and the Russian, Count
Witte, met at Portsmouth in the United States of America at the

beginning of August, and three weeks of anxious negotiations followed, during which the chief stumbling-block to an agreement was Witte's refusal even to consider the payment of an indemnity by Russia. At last on August 29, when hopes of peace had sunk very low, Baron Komura was able to announce that his Master had, in the interests of humanity, agreed to waive his demand for any payment of money. The Russians offered half Saghalín, and the Japanese, much to the surprise of Witte, accepted the offer from first to last.

The chief articles of the Treaty of Portsmouth were those which recognised the preponderating influence of Japan in Korea, agreed to the evacuation of Manchuria, and ceded to Japan the Liao-Tung peninsula, including Port Arthur and Dalny, together with the southern part of the island of Saghalín. The world in general was astonished at the moderation of the Emperor's Government, and the disappointment of the Japanese populace showed itself in serious rioting. The uniform and apparently decisive success of their armies and fleets had aroused hopes for which there was no justification. The statesmen of Japan had arrived at a correct appreciation of the conditions, for it is now certain that an indemnity could have been wrung from the Tsar only at a price which would have at least equalled its value. The War had cost Japan about £100,000,000 and Russia slightly less; despite her victories, the former had to pay more for her loans than the latter. Each nation had mobilised about 1,000,000 men; of these, 230,000 Japanese and 220,000 Russians had been killed or wounded, or had died of sickness.

The success of Japan cannot be ascribed to the greater valour of her troops. Splendid as was the courage of the Japanese soldiery, the Russians, whom no glimmer of success had come to cheer, fought with a dogged determination which commands equal respect. Nor can it be ascribed altogether to the leadership of her armies, for Kuropatkin had assembled at Liaoyang a greater force than Oyama could bring against him; strategy can rarely expect to do more. It is true that on the sea the genius of one man was supreme. With no margin for failure, Togo had borne, through days of deep anxiety, the responsibility of making possible and of sustaining the war on land. The apparent ease with which he won each decisive success tends to conceal the merit of his achievement, for the blockade of Port Arthur may take rank with the blockade of Brest. But, since her fleet alone could not give Japan the victory, we must look elsewhere for the cause of her triumph. In the island kingdom statesman, diplomat, soldier, and sailor had worked together as a well-trained team to develop the maximum of offensive power; on the other side the national spirit of Russia had never fired her armies or her fleets, nor singleness of purpose inspired her leaders. Japan had been victorious because she had learnt from her German tutors that war is the business, not merely of the soldier or of the sailor, but of the nation as a whole.

CH. XIX.

CHAPTER XX.

THE EUROPEAN COLONIES.

EVER since the discoveries of the fifteenth century revealed to the nations of Europe the existence of new lands beyond the seas, a stream of men bearing a knowledge of Western civilisation has gone forth to their conquest and occupation. The few years under present consideration form a brief period in this long process. Yet they have seen an awakened interest in colonisation and an extension of the field of enterprise which give them a unique significance. The comparative tranquillity of domestic and foreign affairs in most countries of Europe has favoured a great outburst of colonising energy, for which the growth of population and industry has provided the principal motive. The growth of population has swollen the stream of emigration; the expansion of industry has increased the desire to control sources of supply for raw materials and markets for finished products. A rapid improvement in means of communication and transport has facilitated intercourse between distant parts of the world. A vast store of accumulated wealth in old countries has been available for investment in new. Modern ideas have stimulated the imaginations of nations, and a keener spirit of rivalry has stirred their ambitions. Thus there has resulted an immense extension of European influence into undeveloped lands and over primitive peoples. Old commercial interests have been transformed into political connexions. New scenes of action have been found. The tropical interior of Africa, the neglected archipelagos of the Pacific, and parts of Asia, have become the possessions or spheres of influence of the Great Powers. What form colonisation may take in some of these newly occupied territories the future will declare; the outstanding feature of recent activity has been the keen competition for spheres of action, and the rapid partition of almost all available territory amongst the chief nations of Europe, the United States, and Japan.

While the opening of fresh fields of enterprise and the coming forward of new nations to assume the colonising *rôle* form an interesting and important chapter of recent colonial history, the maturing of results in the older centres of colonisation makes up the main part of the story. The transformation of colonies into nations is a development of deep significance, and one which the present generation has witnessed. In considering this development, it is with British colonisation that we are chiefly concerned. In Canada, Australia, New Zealand, and South Africa, the process of settlement and State-building proceeded, during the first half of the nineteenth century, so surely and rapidly as to foreshadow the formation in these countries of new peoples at no distant date. That promise has been slowly fulfilling itself. In recent years, under the influence of "laws of political and economic gravitation," the greater English colonies have been taking shape as nations and States. It is in this development that we find the idea which informs and interprets their recent progress. Politically and socially, they have all been in a process of formation and transition; and, though each has been passing through a different stage of development, they have all been moving towards the same goal in obedience to the same impulse. Political institutions have been fashioned; a social order moulded; standards of life and civilisation set up; national ideals formed; and, behind all this, has been in each case the conscious and unconscious struggle for unity and national being. Nor must it be forgotten that this process of growth has taken place amidst conditions that differ much from the environment of earlier colonial societies. Modern progress has brought these great colonies very near to the life of the Old World which has accelerated and controlled their growth. They have drawn largely on its resources of wealth and population, and their freedom to shape their own course has been qualified by their situation in the midst of the complex play of forces, political and economic, which modern conditions have generated. But, while they have in some respects shared the same influences, and felt the same impulse, they have experienced the greatest variety in those general circumstances which give its particular character to a nation's history. The geographical surroundings, the races concerned, the opportunities of economic progress, the political problems, the degree of pressure from foreign Powers, the domestic difficulties involved in the presence of native peoples, have been different in each case. Amid diverse scenes, and with varied experiences, these new nations have been growing up; each has its own story and its own chequered tale of progress.

The modern development of Canada takes its character from two great events which have been described in the preceding volume of this work—the confederation of the provinces, and the transference of the vast western territories to the new Dominion Government. Through many difficulties the little group of British colonies had been steered at last into the broad path of their permanent interest. The acquisition of the west completed the wide theatre of their history; political union gave them the strength and organisation necessary if they were to take advantage of their great opportunities and aspire to a high national destiny. The indispensable conditions of progress were thus provided; the work of building a nation and developing the vast resources of the country remained to be done. Brief as is the time that has elapsed since confederation, the colonies that then emerged from the gloom of their early troubles and bargained doubtfully for union are far removed from the Dominion of today, with its confidence, ambition, and growing solidarity. Grasping a definite national ideal, and aided by the resources which our modern control over nature has afforded, the Canadians have laboured to overcome the obstacles that historical conditions and the geography of the country opposed to their union and progress. Hard toil and great sacrifices have been required, but today they look back on part of their task well done.

In 1867, when the union was formed, the canal system of the country was inadequate and rudimentary, and railway building was in its beginnings. There were no efficient means of communication between the Canadas and the maritime colonies, or between the east and the west. Each colony tended to be in closer connexion with the neighbouring States of the Union than with its sister colonies. The settlement of the country had always been regarded from a local point of view ; and the competition of the United States had limited its progress as well as drawn off enterprising young Canadians to wider and busier scenes. Save for Lord Selkirk's small but historic colony on the Red river, the fertile plains of the interior lay unoccupied. The mining community of British Columbia was isolated in the valleys and mountains of the Far West. The manufacturing industries of the country were of little importance ; agriculture and trade were suffering from the denunciation of the Reciprocity Treaty with the United States; but in Ontario settlement was being extended along the valleys of the Ottawa and its tributaries, and the population had already grown far beyond that of Quebec. In the maritime colonies political life too often centred round petty issues ; in the united provinces it struggled under the incubus of a race feud. The French had not been drawn into closer sympathy with the English, and treasured as jealously as ever their own life and nationality. To unite the two races in work for the common good, to give a real unity to the far-divided members of the Confederation, to open to colonisation the great western territory, to develop the economic strength of the country, and thus to create in their vast half-continent a strong nation capable of resisting the absorbing influence of the neighbouring Republic, was the task before the Canadian leaders. It will be convenient first to follow out in its broad outline the course of political history, and then to survey and summarise the results that have been achieved.

The new problems that came to the front after confederation dissolved the old political groups. The Radical tradition of Papineau gradually spent its force in Quebec. The Grits of Ontario had realised some of their democratic principles and abandoned others. New issues formed new parties—Liberal and Conservative—which have since, in turn, held the reins of government. The Anglo-French Conservative party, which came into power in 1867 under the leadership of Sir John Macdonald, and carried out the work of confederation, governed from 1867 to 1873, and again from 1878 to 1896. Its long tenure of office during a formative period gave it a controlling influence over the future destiny of Canada. It stood for a strong national government, Protection for the encouragement of industry, energetic railway construction to promote the unity and settlement of the country, the strengthening of the imperial connexion, and close commercial relations with the mother country rather than with the United States. These principles, accepted with some qualifications and some accentuation by the Liberal party when it came into power in 1896, may be regarded as the guiding lines of Canadian policy.

In the first years after confederation, the most important question was the building of railways to unite the provinces. At the elections of 1872 Sir John Macdonald had been returned to power. The Intercolonial Railway was then in course of construction, and a transcontinental line was projected. The financing of so vast an undertaking was a matter of immense difficulty, and, while plans were being discussed, a grave scandal was caused by the discovery that one of the capitalists with whom the Government was negotiating had contributed to the Conservative party chest. Macdonald resigned (Nov. 1873), and Mr Alexander Mackenzie formed a ministry, which, on a dissolution, gained an overwhelming victory at the polls. The four years of Liberal government saw much legislation of a useful character. The North West Territories were separated from Manitoba. Treaties were made with the Indians, and their relations with the Dominion Government placed on the happy basis on which they have since remained. It is well to remember, however, that the relatively small numbers of the Indians and the abundance of land in Canada have combined with the just and sympathetic policy which the Government has pursued to save the country from the ever-present native question which has troubled some colonies. A Supreme Court of Appeal was established, the election laws were amended in a democratic direction, and a local option temperance measure was passed— an experiment in licensing reform which had little lasting result. But in its commercial policy, and its dealings with the problem of a trans-continental railway, the Liberal Government was not fortunate. In 1874, it took powers to construct the railway as a public work, and planned to utilise the vast water stretches on the route. It made surveys, and proposed to proceed gradually as the country seemed able to bear the expenditure. Little was done, and the dissatisfaction of British Columbia increased so much that it threatened to secede from the union. An attempt, also, to negotiate a new reciprocity treaty with the United States broke down completely (1874). Meanwhile, Canada was passing through some lean years. Already suffering from the competition of the fertile

prairies and strong industries of the United States, it felt severely the
depression which followed the financial crisis of 1873 in that country. In
these circumstances, Macdonald launched into Canadian politics the issue
of Protection. Appealing to the national sense that was making itself
felt, he proposed "the adoption of a National Policy which, by a judicious
readjustment of the tariff, will benefit and foster the agricultural, the
mining, the manufacturing, and other interests of the Dominion." In
1878 the Conservatives were returned to office by a large majority, and
they remained in power for eighteen years. The construction of the Pacific
railway was taken up more determinedly. Since the resources of the
country seemed inadequate for the task, Macdonald turned, as he had
turned before, to private contractors, and in 1881 concluded an agreement
with a group of capitalists. The policy of building gradually was
abandoned in favour of the bolder plan of building straight across the
Continent. Generous terms were conceded to the Company, including
large grants of money and land; and, throughout, the Government gave
it a whole-hearted support. The financial and engineering difficulties
were successfully overcome, and in four years the great national enterprise
was completed. Canada gained a new sense of unity, and the way was
open for the settlement of the west. Just before the work was finished,
the country was disturbed by a revolt of the half-breeds settled at
St Lawrence on the Saskatchewan, who had become anxious as to the
security of their lands (1884). Some Indian tribes joined them; but the
rebellion was promptly suppressed, and Riel, who had instigated it, was
executed, in spite of the efforts of Quebec to secure his reprieve. In 1885,
the Conservatives dealt with the franchise for the Federal Parliament.
Their measure aimed at establishing a uniform franchise based on a small
property qualification, to take the place of the provincial registers which
had hitherto been in use. The Act proved unpopular, and when the
Liberals returned to power was speedily repealed (1898).

Neither protective tariffs nor the opening of the west brought
immediate prosperity to Canada. The lean years continued. Industry
made but slow progress, and the eastern farmers were engaged in a hard
struggle. In these circumstances, the Liberal party, which still adhered
to Free Trade, continued to advocate closer commercial relations
with the United States, to be attained either by treaty, or, as some
desired, by a Customs Union. An annexationist element in the party
also made itself heard; but its strength was small and gradually waned.
The Liberal policy was, however, suspect, whether it took the form of
commercial union or unrestricted reciprocity (1891), and could not compete with the protective policy by this time strongly rooted in Canadian
life. Commercial union portended political union, involved heavier
direct taxation, threatened the young Canadian industries, and seemed
inimical to the imperial connexion as well as destructive of the national
idea. From Washington the Liberals received little encouragement,

and gradually they shifted their ground to "a fair and liberal Treaty of Reciprocity" (1893). Meanwhile, various events were undermining the Conservative position. In 1891 Macdonald, whose personal popularity and patriotic instinct had been a great strength to his party, died. Throughout a life wholly devoted to the service of Canada he had played a great part in shaping her policy and fortunes, on which he left the imperishable impress of a great and strong man. Death removed other leaders in quick succession, and some political scandals further affected popular confidence in the Government. The Liberal party had freed itself from the suspicion of disloyalty; accepting the able leadership of Mr (now Sir Wilfred) Laurier, it secured the support of Quebec; and by an active electoral campaign in 1896 it drove its opponents from power.

The accession of the Liberals to office was followed by a decade of immense activity and progress, during which questions of tariffs and commercial treaties, immigration and settlement, and new projects of railway and canal construction occupied the principal attention of the country. The Liberals had fought the election under the banner of Free Trade; but the new Government, nevertheless, made terms with the manufacturers and accepted, substantially, the protective tariffs and bounty system of their predecessors. The much denounced National Policy passed out of party politics into the region of national ideas. The fruitless "pilgrimages to Washington" to secure reciprocity treaties were abandoned. New bounties were given to the iron and steel industry. The protective policy was modified in 1897 by the grant of a preference of $12\frac{1}{2}$ per cent., afterwards increased to $33\frac{1}{3}$ per cent., in favour of Great Britain. In order to encourage trade with the mother country the Conservatives had previously suggested reciprocal preferences; the Liberals gave an unconditional preference—at once a proof of patriotic feeling and an offering to the fallen god of Free Trade. Germany, not admitting the right of the various parts of the British Empire to make special tariff arrangements with each other, seeing that they were fiscally independent, regarded this action as unfriendly to herself, and in 1901 excepted Canada from the most favoured nation treatment which she accorded to the British Empire. Canada retaliated in 1903 by imposing a surtax on German imports. A tariff war thus ensued which checked the expansion of German trade with the Dominion, and which was only brought to an end in March, 1910. The development of markets for her produce over-sea and on the Continent had become of great importance to Canada; and, had it been possible, she would gladly have followed up the grant of preference by negotiating a commercial treaty with the mother country, as, in 1907, she succeeded in doing with France and, in 1910, with her powerful neighbour. In 1905–6, a Commission enquired into the tariff, which was afterwards revised in the interests of the manufacturers.

In other directions, the Liberal Government exhibited great energy

CH. XX.

in the development of the country's resources. Though some political questions of considerable interest arose, which will be mentioned in another connexion, the chief attention of the Government was turned to the problems of the west, where the energies of the country were concentrated on a great work of colonisation. The resources of Canada were widely advertised through Europe. Free grants of land were offered to settlers. Immigrants were procured in great numbers, and for some time without much discrimination. In recent legislation, however, the Canadian Government has asserted its right to reject certain classes of immigrants, to impose a small financial qualification, and to deport undesirables. The country needs most the small farmer with capital and the farm labourer, and has not yet the expanding industrial life which would enable it to offer a wide and varied field of employment. At the same time fresh schemes of railway and canal construction were projected, to open up new stretches of territory and to facilitate the carriage of produce to ocean ports. Transport became the centre of the problem of western settlement. A second transcontinental line, the Grand Trunk Pacific, was commenced in 1903, the Government undertaking to build the eastern section, and the Grand Trunk Company, which was to administer the whole, the western section. Schemes for reaching Hudson's Bay by a railway from Winnipeg, and for connecting Georgian Bay and the river Ottawa by canal, were also formed.

It is now possible to look beneath the shifting surface of politics and survey the substantial results which have been achieved in the upbuilding of the country. In British Columbia, much progress has been made since the first rush of gold-seekers in 1858 transformed the fur-trading stations of the Hudson's Bay Company into a self-governing colony. As in the Pacific States of America, mining was followed by more enduring industries. The great resources which the country has in its forests, fisheries, coal deposits, fertile land, and commanding commercial situation, have been in part developed. Settlement has extended along streams and valleys, by the side of lakes and railways; but difficulties of communication and transport have necessarily limited its progress. After a few years of activity mining declined, until in 1896 fresh discoveries in the Kootenay district led to a revival, and improved methods placed the industry on a stronger basis, though dear labour and insufficient transport facilities still limit its progress. With the Klondyke "rush" of 1899 and the simultaneous revival in British Columbia the gold production of Canada reached its highest point, from which it has since steadily declined. From the time of the gold discoveries British Columbia was confronted by the common problem of the Pacific seaboard—an influx of Chinese, and later of Japanese, coolies. The labouring classes expressed their strong aversion from the Oriental immigrant by determined agitation, and compelled the Dominion Government to take action. Twice a

Commission examined the question, with the result that exclusive legislation of increasing severity has been directed against the Chinese. In the case of Japan a diplomatic agreement for the restraint of immigration was negotiated in 1907. This question, so liable to inflame feeling, has, together with certain troublesome financial relations, caused some friction between the province and the Dominion Government.

The plains of the interior have been the scene of a greater change. Until 1869 they were under the control of the Hudson's Bay Company. That body served the empire well by exploring and holding a vast stretch of territory; but it possessed neither the means nor the inclination to open its hunting grounds to the more fruitful operations of the settler. Yet its presence was not the chief obstacle to colonisation, and no rush of immigrants followed the purchase of its rights. The great problem of communications required first to be solved. In the United States, when once the barrier of the Alleghanies was passed, the configuration of the country favoured an uninterrupted advance of population across the central basin of the Continent. This was impossible in Canada, where, north of Lake Superior, a great desert stopped the westward march of colonisation. Thus, during the middle years and far into the last quarter of the nineteenth century, the immense tide of European emigration flowed into the cities and plains of the United States. It was a question of comparative advantages, and western Canada, inaccessible and little known, could not compete with the Mississippi and Missouri valleys, where railways were opening the way for the colonist. But the course of events and the energies of the Canadians have steadily changed the situation in favour of the Canadian west. Apparently without mineral wealth, its principal advantage has been a capacity to produce the great cereals; hence, it needed markets and facilities for transporting its grain before it could compete with the grain-growing States and attract the enterprising farmer. Railway construction was an essential condition of settlement. When the Canadian Pacific was carried across the Continent the work was begun. This bold speculation in the possibilities of the north-west was abundantly justified by the result. Population and commerce followed, and, when the initial difficulties had been overcome, settlement proceeded rapidly. Much capital has already been invested in railway construction, and new land is thus continually being brought within the reach of the settler. The Canadian Northern, combining smaller lines, has become a great artery of trade in the Saskatchewan basin. The Grand Trunk Pacific, now building, will open a new route from east to west and develop another belt of prairie. General conditions have at the same time become more favourable to Canada. The demand for foodstuffs in European markets has increased, while the United States has shown some tendency to diminish its exports of this kind, thus enlarging the supply sought from Canada. At the same time, the best lands of the United States have already been distributed. Thus, in the balancing of advantages, western

Canada has become one of the most attractive parts of the American Continent. The stream of immigration that flowed into the Missouri valley has been turning north-west, overflowing into the plains of Canada, and moving further north so far as climate, soil, and means of communication will allow.

The energetic policy of the Government has enabled the country to reap the benefit of the changing conditions. After confederation, the provincial immigration agencies were centralised under the single control of the Minister of Agriculture, and the resources of Canada were more widely advertised in Europe and the United States. In recent years this policy has received a strong stimulus; the Government and the great steamship, railway, and land companies concerned have vied with each other in procuring immigrants. By the Land Act of 1872 the land system of the United States was borrowed and applied to the circumstances of western Canada with great success. Provision was made for the survey of land in townships, with reserves for educational purposes, and the practice of making free grants of land under certain conditions, which had been abandoned, was restored. Thus, the acquisition of land was made easy for the comparatively poor man. The improved methods of procuring immigrants and placing them upon the land bore rapid fruit in the advance of settlement. By scientific enquiry on experimental farms the Government has also done much to solve the agricultural problems of western farming. Ignorance of the conditions and of the requisite special methods of tillage, together with inflated hopes, combined to cause many failures at the beginning, and the prospects of the country were clouded. But the necessary knowledge and experience have been acquired and diffused with the best results; and, in addition, an admirable financial system has been created to assist the farmer. Mixed farming has begun to take the place of the single crop. The west has valuable pastures. In Alberta, horse and cattle ranching on a large scale was one of the first industries; it also assumed some importance in Manitoba and Saskatchewan, though the large ranch is now disappearing with the entry of the cultivator.

Already a large result vaguely outlines itself. A great agricultural community is being planted in the west. Many different races are mingling to form it, though the Anglo-Saxon element predominates, and the Anglo-Saxon passion for material progress controls the spirit and fortunes of the country. Farmers from Ontario, Canadians returning from the United States, Americans, who have proved valuable citizens, and a large number of English, are settled side by side with colonists from almost every European country, since Canada in her eagerness for immigrants opened her doors wide. Thus the present time finds her engaged on the task of building up new provinces out of these diverse elements, and welding them into union with the older provinces by ties of common interest, sympathy, and patriotism. The assimilation of the new elements must follow the extension of settlement, if national unity is to be maintained.

The main strength of the Dominion is still concentrated in the eastern provinces. Prince Edward Island, Nova Scotia, New Brunswick, have undergone little change. During thirty years, 1870–1900, their population scarcely increased. Agriculture, fishing, and lumbering remain their chief industries, though coal-mining and the iron and steel industry have become important in Nova Scotia. Newfoundland remains outside of the Dominion. In 1895 it made a proposition for union, but without reaching an agreement. Its economic life still centres in the fisheries; and the development of the interior, though beginning, has not proceeded far. In Quebec the growth of population has pressed upon the resources of a not too productive soil. The French, unwilling to mix with the English in the other provinces, have gradually displaced them along the line of the Ottawa as well as in the eastern townships of their own province, where they form today a larger proportion of the population than in 1850. At one time they dreamed of planting their race in the plains of the west and encircling the English, but the idea vanished and they have had very small share in western settlement. Though not untouched by the influences of modern progress, they still retain, amid the feverish activity of the Continent, the singular simplicity of their old life. Migratory bands of labourers leave Quebec to supply the permanent or periodical needs of expanding industries elsewhere, such as lumbering in Ontario, harvesting in the west, and, more especially, the manufacturing industries of New England. In 1900 there were 374,000 French Canadians in the United States, nearly five times as many as there were at the same time in Canada west of the Ottawa river. An agricultural people, their surplus numbers have drifted under economic pressure into the nearest industrial centres. Ontario has increased in wealth and population; but its agriculture has undergone a change common to the whole east. When, in the seventies and eighties of the last century, the competition of the prairie States and the falling prices of wheat depressed the fortunes of the farmers, mixed farming, dairying, fruit-growing, and stock-raising were substituted for the single crop system. The Government came to their assistance with education and organisation. Scientific knowledge and cooperative effort were applied to the solution of agricultural problems. The hand of progress extended a new opportunity which was eagerly grasped: the improvement of cold storage by a new system of mechanical refrigeration enabled the Canadian farmers to build up an immense export trade in cheese, butter, hams, and fruit, and thus in time to regain a measure of prosperity.

More important has been the industrial progress of the country. In 1870, the manufacturing industries were at an early stage of development. The comparatively free commercial relations with the United States and the mother country, as well as the want of fitting general conditions for the maintenance of the great industries, reduced them to repairing and the preparation of raw materials for export. But a change came over the scene. Political union was followed by an ideal of national being which included the desire of a broader and more independent economic life. The systematic Protection of manufactures was begun. Other conditions became more favourable to industrial progress. Improvements in means of communication, the growth of an agricultural community offering a large market in the west, the demand for wood pulp of which Canada can provide a great supply, the increasing use of water power, and the investment of American capital in Canadian enterprises, have all contributed to alter the situation. Great difficulties were presented by the want of skilled labour, and, for a long time, of capital. The mineral resources of the country have been more developed ; but, though varied, they have not proved to be very great. Large coal-fields exist; but they are situated more conveniently for commerce than for industry. Some solid results have, however, been achieved. While the application of simple manufacturing processes to raw materials has remained the chief feature of Canada's industrial life, to this has been added the manufacture of cottons and woollens, agricultural implements, wood pulp, and paper. In addition, the iron and steel industry has been extended during the last twelve years under the liberal bounty-policy of the Laurier Government. In Ontario many small manufacturing towns have grown up, as the seats, some of one industry, others of several industries, in addition to the larger centres such as Sydney, Quebec, Montreal, Toronto, Kingston, Hamilton, and Winnipeg. Scarcely any of the industries could dispense with the Protection they receive, the burden of which the country bears with little complaint for the sake of the national ideal which it appears to further. No Labour party has been formed. Even Trade Unionism is very much localised and dependent on American organisation. The sense of a common interest still inspires the workers of a country which contains few very rich men and no marked distinction of classes.

The development of means of communication and transport has played a very important part in the recent history of Canada, whether economic progress, political union, or the extension of settlement, be considered. To the railway, and to the river highway supplemented by the canal, the Canadians have looked for the uniting of a country which nature has divided. The work of improving the channel of the St Lawrence has remained uncompleted. In 1870 a Dominion Canal Commission laid down a policy which, with some amplification, has since been carried out. Today, after a century of labour, ocean-going steamships can pass to the western shore of Lake Superior, whence there is a channel of fourteen feet to Montreal, and from Montreal to the sea of over twenty-seven. Railway building has been more important. The first decade of construction in Canada (1850–60) was not happy in its results, and left troubles behind its speculations. Much inferior work was done at a high cost. The lines proved unprofitable and, though Ontario gained, the British investor suffered. The Government, which was already guaranteeing the interest on capital expenditure in certain cases, was compelled to intervene further by assisting the Grand Trunk and managing the Northern. With the progress of the country, the larger lines were lifted out of the morass of debt and difficulty in which they were involved. Confederation gave a new impetus to construction, and bore fruit in the Intercolonial and the Canadian Pacific. The former was constructed, and is still managed, by the Government; but, built for a political end, it has never proved a commercial success. The needs of settlement and commerce and the competition to secure through traffic have been responsible for the immense activity of later years, under which the railway mileage of the country has increased to almost 23,000 (1908), while at the same time the larger systems have been much improved, and many small lines have been consolidated. Though some dissatisfaction with the services of the railways has existed amongst the western farmers, the graver abuses that often follow in the absence of competition have not appeared. Problems of construction have occupied the attention of the Government far more than those of regulation. Railways have mattered so much to the country that the Government soon abandoned the idea of trusting solely to private enterprise to provide them. The misfortunes of the sixties, the political purpose of some of the lines, and the difficulty of raising the necessary capital drew the State in various ways into railway business. It has given moral support and subsidies of land and money, as have also the provinces and municipalities, besides sharing in some cases and assuming in others the whole responsibility of both construction and operation. Nevertheless, the individual has always been allowed great freedom in carrying out public works. In 1907, the national debt was little more than one-third that of Australia. Thus the railway system of Canada stands midway between the state system of other English colonies and the private ownership systems of the mother country and the United States.

These substantial changes show, in a general way, how far the economic development and consolidation of the country has proceeded. It remains to survey the influence of confederation on political life and unity. Through a long period of Canadian history, a want of sympathy and cooperation between French and English proved an obstacle to progress. Religious, social, and economic differences, as well as a great unlikeness of character, combined to separate them, and at one time political conditions aggravated the evil. Canada could not hope to be strong until a sense of common interest and mutual confidence bridged the gulf between the two races; and no more hopeful change has passed over the country during recent years than the growth of these feelings. The French remain as determined as ever to preserve their nationality and institutions. The Catholic Church still exercises her controlling

influence upon their life, and, though steadfastly loyal to the British
connexion, has opposed an intermixture of races which would divert its
sheep from their fold.   But, while the French community remains what
it has always been—an offshoot of eighteenth century France, now attached
to a strenuous Anglo-Saxon colony—its outlook and sympathies have been
widened.   It has acquiesced in, if it has not sympathised with, every step
in the expansion of Canada, and even in uncongenial imperial activities
and ambitions.   The control which the French possess over the government of their own province, the caution which has sought to keep race
issues out of party politics, the increasing prosperity of the country, the
wise and inspiring leadership of a statesman of their own race, and
the recognition by England and France of the possibilities of a lasting
national friendship, have all acted most favourably on their relations
with the English.   Doubtless the rivalry of race and religion is not yet
buried, and there remains an underlying separation of feeling, as between
two different communities ; but, none the less, since confederation, there
has sprung up a sense of common interest, and an effective and enduring
cooperation which has meant much for the progress and unity of Canada.

Self-government, the federal system, and the extension of municipal
institutions in the provinces, seem now to have finally overcome the chief
political difficulties under which the country formerly laboured.   The
Constitution has proved equal to the stress of circumstances for more
than forty years, and seems well adapted to the conditions and the genius
of the people.   There has been little straining of the different parts of
the Dominion against each other.   Except in the case of Quebec, provincial feeling does not arise from deep distinction of character, but from
a long-standing isolation and autonomy, and thus diminishes under
modern influences.   A strong national Government was created, and has
shown some tendency to grow stronger.   Its relations with the provincial
Governments form the chief feature of recent constitutional history.
Macdonald, who preferred a legislative to a federal union, superintended
somewhat closely the course of provincial politics.   In 1879 he recommended the Governor-General to remove from office Letellier de St Just,
the Lieutenant-Governor of Quebec, on account of the manner in which
he had exercised his constitutional power of dismissing Ministers.   In
a prolonged dispute over the boundaries of Ontario, which commenced in
1871 and was only finally settled by decisions of the Privy Council in
1884 and 1888, he maintained with the greatest tenacity the claims of
the Dominion against those of his own province.   He declined, however,
to disallow an Act passed by the Quebec Government in 1888, which
gave compensation to the Jesuit Order for their estates confiscated in
1773 and also referred to the Pope the distribution of the money granted
—on the ground that, since the property had been vested in the provincial
Government, the matter was one of purely provincial concern.   On
another occasion, Manitoba vindicated provincial rights in regard to

railway policy. It had been agreed by the Dominion Government that the Canadian Pacific Railway should not, for twenty years after its construction, be exposed to competition within twenty miles south of the main route. Manitoba resisted this monopoly so determinedly that the railway was compelled to abandon its exclusive rights in return for a loan from the Dominion. In the control of the liquor traffic it proved difficult to fix the boundaries of provincial and national power; and the Scott Temperance Act (1878), passed by the Dominion Parliament to confer local option on cities and counties, was contested before the Privy Council, where its validity was confirmed.

Education was reserved for provincial legislation, but the religious divisions of the country have made it a battlefield of province and Dominion. The Constitution confirmed to religious minorities such educational rights as belonged to them by law at the time of the union; and this confirmation was inserted in the Act by which, in 1870, the province of Manitoba was created. The Government of the new province continued for some years the existing denominational system of education, but, finding it inefficient and expensive, substituted in 1890 a non-sectarian system. French Roman Catholics of the province, believing the change would prove fatal to their schools, carried the question before the Privy Council, which decided, on the one hand, that they had never enjoyed any right to state maintenance of their schools, but only a right to found and carry them on at their own expense, and, on the other, that the Dominion Government had power to intervene if necessary to secure the remedy of their grievances. In 1871, when a similar situation arose in New Brunswick, Macdonald refused to interfere, and the dispute was settled by arrangement between the religious bodies concerned. In 1895, however, the Conservative Government determined to put pressure upon Manitoba, and endeavoured unsuccessfully to carry a remedial law through the Dominion Parliament. The question became an important issue at the elections of 1896. On being returned to power, the Liberal party, which had defended provincial rights and non-sectarian education, rejected their predecessors' policy of coercion, and entered into negotiation with the provincial Government. An amicable settlement of the dispute was thus secured, which removed the real grievances of the Catholics by giving them protection for their language and religious teaching in their schools. In 1905, when the provinces of Alberta and Saskatchewan were formed, the state-aided denominational system which existed in the Territories was secured in the Constitution of the new provinces.

In the three provinces created since confederation, the Dominion Government exercises one set of rights which the older provinces never resigned. Land, forests, and water power remain under its control; but, in return, a larger subsidy has been given to the new Governments. When the whole working of the Federal Government is surveyed, it must be admitted that the controlling influence of the national authorities has generally been exercised with wisdom and tact. No fresh legislation has been required for defining the respective powers of Dominion and province. But the financial relations between them, fixed by special treaties in accordance with the conditions and requirements of each province, have been less satisfactory. The agreement with Nova Scotia caused much discontent in that province, and its subsidy had almost immediately to be increased. In 1887, and again in 1903 and 1906, conferences of provincial premiers were held in order to discuss the whole question, and in 1907 a Bill was submitted to the imperial Parliament to ratify a new arrangement. British Columbia, which claims special treatment owing to the high cost of administration in mountainous country, still remains dissatisfied.

No sketch of any part of Canadian history would be complete which ignored the close relations between Canada and the United States. Their greatest importance lies in the strong influence which the United States has exerted on the economic and political development of Canada, though controversies and negotiations concerning boundaries, fisheries, and trade occupy a larger place in history. Two kindred peoples, having a common frontier, for the most part artificial, of four thousand miles, could not fail to be drawn in many respects into a common life. The social structure of Canada and the methods of her politics are American, though her political principles and institutions are English. She has borrowed much from the experience of the United States and exhibits the same impetuous progressive spirit, though in finance she has pursued a more cautious policy. Over the whole Continent population and capital have flowed where the best opportunities drew them, with little regard to the political boundary. The greater prosperity and the busier urban and industrial life of the United States not only prevented Canada from securing a large share in the stream of emigration from Europe to America, but also drew away from her borders many of her most enterprising citizens. And when, under changing conditions, the resources of Canada began to be more developed, Americans and American capital contributed much to the process. Hence, extensive commercial intercourse has always existed between the two countries. From the time that Canada lost preferential treatment in the British market to the time, fifty years later, when imperial preferences were again discussed, a reciprocity treaty with the United States remained the principal object of her commercial policy. The necessities of Protection, however, limited her bargaining power, and consistent discouragement from the United States turned her attention to the development of oversea trade. A friendly spirit has generally marked the relations of the two countries, and, especially during the last few years, American politicians have shown a disposition to respect the ambition and achievements of Canada.

Some particular controversies deserve notice here. The Treaty of

Washington, in 1871, attempted a settlement of the perennial dispute concerning American encroachments on the inshore fisheries of Canada. Free trade in the products of the sea fisheries was agreed upon, and the Americans were admitted to the inshore fisheries on payment of an indemnity. The Treaty remained in force for twelve years (1873–85). On its abrogation the troubles recommenced. As a result, a commission was appointed by the British and American Governments to consider the question. The proposals which it made were approved by the Dominion Parliament, but rejected in the American Senate. Canada then offered a *modus vivendi*, which has remained in force. Meanwhile, in 1886, another fishery dispute arose. On the ground of their sole sovereignty over that part of the sea which lay west of Alaska, the United States claimed to exclude the Canadians from the Behring Sea seal fisheries. Great Britain, on behalf of Canada, maintained that Behring Sea was an open sea, and her contention was upheld by the arbitrators to whom the matter was referred. The jurisdiction of the United States was restricted to the three-mile limit; regulations were made for the conduct of the fishery; and the Canadian sealers received compensation. The American ownership of Alaska produced another and more vexatious controversy. Its boundary with Canada was regulated by an Anglo-Russian Treaty of 1825, the meaning of which admitted of doubt. The question assumed increased importance when gold was discovered on the river Klondyke, since the main sea approach to the gold-fields by the Lynn Canal passed over territory which the Americans claimed. In 1903, it was agreed to submit the question to a body of arbitrators consisting of three Americans, two Canadians, and the Lord Chief Justice of England, who, on the principal practical question involved, whether the boundary should follow the general contour of the coast, as Great Britain contended, or pass round the heads of the inlets, as the United States contended, gave their decision by a majority vote in favour of the American claim, to the intense chagrin of Canada. Newfoundland has also been involved in a fishery dispute of a most serious character with the United States. Under the Convention of 1818, the Americans enjoy the right to take fish of every kind off the west coast of the island. By legislation in regulation of the fisheries, Newfoundland has recently restricted the privileges which the Americans have enjoyed, to an extent which the Americans claim to be an infringement of their treaty rights. Circumstances compelled the mother country to override the colonial Government and arrange a *modus vivendi* with the United States. The whole question has now by mutual agreement been submitted to the Hague Tribunal.

Thus, the dawn of the twentieth century finds the expansion of Canada still proceeding. The colonisation of the country has been a constant struggle for unity and national being against geographical divisions, race strife, and the assimilative power of the neighbouring republic. Recent years have seen Canada progress a long way towards the realisation of these ambitions. Political conditions and economic prospects have both been transformed, and, as they have improved, national aspirations have grown stronger. Canada has outgrown the old conception of colonial status and takes her place with pride as a member of a great empire. Her past history and present position foreshadow a future of great promise.

Heirs of the same political ideas as the Canadians, and more closely united in race and position, the Australians have been engaged, though perhaps less consciously, on the same task of forming a State and a nation. In the isolation of far away seas they worked out the beginnings of their life, and laid the foundations of a group of separate societies. Forces born of contiguity, kindred character and ideals, and the possession of a common country, steadily drew them together, until modern progress, sweeping them more completely into the world's general life, applied external pressure to hasten their union. The federation of the Australian colonies was thus the consummation of a process of growing together which forms perhaps the principal feature of their recent history. After 1870, pioneers, attracted by the wealth of pastoral plains or the discovery of precious metals, joined up in the interior the expanding frontiers of settlement in the various colonies—save where nature had planted the impenetrable desert to divide them; and even across this barrier the explorer found a path and the line of telegraphic communication was carried. In every colony economic development showed itself, though in different degrees, in the growth of agriculture and commerce, the multiplication of railways, the increase and concentration of population, and the beginnings of the manufacturing industries. A new generation of men, natives of the land, fashioned new ideals of social and political welfare, which bore a general resemblance over the whole Continent. The trend of progress gradually produced and revealed the identity of interest and character between these contiguous societies; so that, at last, political union followed, not easily, but without violent effort or transformation. Thus, in recent years, economic growth, political union and the shaping of distinct ideals, have carried Australia out of the colonial into the national stage of existence. In New Zealand a similar development has taken place. Peopled by the same race, pursuing the same industries, and colonised at much the same time as several of the neighbouring colonies, its life and fortunes, though separate, have resembled theirs.

In Australasia settlement started from a number of points on the coast, and was carried thence into the interior. The explorer, the stock-raiser, and the miner, pioneered the way. Exploration was almost complete and the limits of habitable land fairly well known when the period we are surveying opened. Between 1872 and 1877, Forrest and Giles, by different routes, traversed the central deserts of the Continent, which alone remained unpenetrated, and enabled Western and South Australia to be connected by telegraph in 1877. Meantime, the surer work of the settler linked South Australia to her eastern neighbours. From the coastal regions of the eastern colonies the sheep-farmers were moving further and further west and mingling in the plains of the interior. In New South Wales they wandered towards the barrier range which separated them from South Australia. On Cooper's Creek and the Diamantina, and on the streams that flow into the Gulf of Carpentaria, the squatters of Queensland and South Australia met in the early eighties. At the same time, new discoveries of gold and silver at Silverton and Broken Hill (1883) on the western borders of New South Wales, at Palmer (1873) and Mount Morgan (1883) in Queensland, as well as others of less moment in New South Wales and elsewhere, dispersed population from place to place. Western Australia in 1870 was a mere fringe of settlement on the borders of a great desert; but pastures were found on the northern and western rivers, and new oases of human activity were formed. Then gold was found in the interior at Kimberley and near Yilgarn (1886–7), and, with the discoveries that followed (1890–3) on the Ashburton and Murchison, at Coolgardie, and Kalgoorlie, towns sprang up in the desert whose population soon surpassed that of the older settled parts. In Tasmania, tin was found at Mount Bischoff (1871), silver at Zeehan (1885), and copper at Mount Lyell (1886). The mining industry opened up a large district, and contributed much to improve the prospects of the island. In New Zealand, discoveries of coal and gold led to the formation of many small towns in Middle Island, and forged new links between the provinces.

Pastures and mines were thus the attractive forces whose action resulted in the dispersion of population through the Continent, and sheep-farming and gold-mining formed at one time the principal industries of all the colonies. A more general progress has diminished their relative importance; but, between them, they still supply the greater part of Australasia's immense export trade. From 1870 until 1890, the pastoral industry continually expanded. Then came long years of trouble, falling prices, labour disputes, financial difficulties, and the worse enemies of drought and disease. New South Wales and Queensland suffered the most; New Zealand almost escaped. After 1902, prosperity slowly returned. The westward migration of the stock-farmers transferred most of the great runs to the plains of the interior. The movement has been stimulated by land legislation and agricultural settlement, aided by artesian bores, and rewarded by fine pastures. In Queensland, cattle and not sheep now occupy the coast-lands. Formerly, wool was almost the only product of the industry which found a foreign market. But, with cheaper transport and progress in the art of refrigeration the trade in frozen meat has now become half as valuable as that in wool; in addition, dairy products, hides and skins, horses, cattle and sheep, swell the volume of pastoral exports. After 1870, gold-mining offered for many years a

CH. XX.

diminishing field of employment, though the conditions continually varied
in the different colonies.   Between 1871 and 1897, the total annual output
of Australasia never exceeded ten million pounds, and was often less than
six.   Since 1897, it has increased rapidly owing to the great discoveries
in Western Australia, and also to an increasing production in other
colonies, especially in Queensland.   The " golden age " of Victoria, New
South Wales, and New Zealand belongs to the third quarter of the
century, that of Queensland and Western Australia did not dawn until
the last quarter.   The mining industry, like the pastoral, has expanded
its range in recent years, and includes coal, lead, copper, and tin, as well
as the precious metals ; but the latter form much the largest part of its
product, into which the great industrial mineral, iron, scarcely enters.

The dispersion of settlement has been the work of the sheep-farmer
and miner ; concentration has resulted from the progress of agriculture
and new land laws ; while the rise of urban centres is connected with
the expansion of commerce as well as with industrial and railway policy.
When the gold fever first waned, men turned from the mine to the land,
and the farmer began to establish himself by the side of the stock-master ;
but the rise of agriculture to a position of great importance amongst
Australian industries is a recent development.   The early difficulties
which confronted the farmer—the locking up of land in the runs of the
squatters, the high rate of wages, the want of means of transport and of
markets for produce—have been steadily combated.   In the early sixties,
New South Wales and Victoria endeavoured to make land available for
agricultural settlement by allowing intending purchasers to make free
selection on the squatters' runs.   While this policy secured its end and
many farmers were established on the land, it had also other and
unexpected results.   The genuine and the pretending settler not being
carefully distinguished, far more land passed into private hands than was
ever placed under cultivation.   When one colony took a step forward,
competition compelled the other colonies to follow.   But Queensland
and South Australia, with simpler problems before them, acted more
cautiously, and did not adopt free selection.   Victoria and New South
Wales in time modified their systems.   In Victoria the conditions of selection were made more stringent (1878), in New South Wales the selector
was restricted to the eastern and central divisions of the colony, and the
western was reserved for the stock-master, who received here greater
security of tenure.   But the progress of agricultural settlement continued
to be slow, and the colonial Governments adopted new measures.   The
large estates which blocked the way became a general object of attack.
During the nineties, all the colonies passed laws authorising the purchase
of land from large owners for division into small holdings to be let on
perpetual or long lease.   New Zealand, where the evil was greatest, led
the way.   Some colonies only allowed voluntary purchase; but most gave,
or quickly added, compulsory powers.   Other methods of expropriating

the large owner or of promoting closer settlement, such as special taxation of large estates and the sale of land to village communities or
labour settlements, have been adopted ; for repurchase of the land is an
expensive operation, to which financial considerations fix a limit.   By
these and other means agriculture has been extended in suitable districts,
and a variety of forms of tenure offering easy conditions to *bona fide*
settlers have been created.   In addition, in most of the States, agricultural
colleges have been established ; and in all, except Tasmania, Government
has the power of rendering financial aid to the farmer.   The Governments have done much to make land accessible and improve means of
communication.   They have had to contend against past mistakes and
powerful interests, which have hitherto been too strong for them.   Yet
the farmer's worst enemy is, after all, not the squatter but the climate,
which fixes for his operations limits that Governments cannot much
extend.

These efforts have not been without large results, as the recent agricultural progress of the country shows.   Since 1870, the area under cultivation has been more than quadrupled.   New South Wales and Victoria
have ceased to be dependent on South Australia for food products.
Sugar, fruit, and wheat, the last being still the principal crop, have
become important exports.   Fruit-growing, like dairy-farming, has been
extended, as improved means of refrigeration have opened the English
market.   The vine is cultivated in New South Wales and Queensland,
though chiefly to supply the Australian demand.   On the coast-lands of
Queensland cotton and sugar were first grown in the sixties.   In the face
of American competition cotton soon ceased to be a profitable crop ; but
the cultivation of sugar was much extended in the eighties.   Then falling
prices ruined many of the planters, and a reorganisation of the industry
followed.   Small farms took the place of large, and the Government
came to the rescue (1893) by guaranteeing the interest on loans raised to
establish central mills in which the cane is crushed.   The agricultural
development of tropical Australia has not been carried very far, and was
soon found to involve labour problems of great difficulty, which will be
discussed in another connexion.

The rapid expansion of Australasia's great productive industries, and
the corresponding expansion of her foreign commerce, have been made
possible by the improved means of communication which have given the
interior lands access to markets and cheapened the cost of moving produce.
The general character of Australian trade has not been much changed,
but its basis has been broadened, its volume much enlarged, and its
direction somewhat modified.   During the last twenty years, Great
Britain has supplied a diminishing, and Germany and the United States
an increasing, proportion of the imports ; while the latter two countries,
as well as France and Belgium, have also taken an important place as
buyers or distributors of Australian produce.   Large quantities of capital

have been borrowed from Great Britain to be invested in the development
of the country and, in periods of extravagant borrowing such as 1886 to
1891, have caused imports to exceed exports in value, though the ruling
tendency has been in the opposite direction.   Much of this capital was
devoted to the building of railways.   In 1871 the railway mileage of
Australia was only 1030 miles, by 1907 it had been increased to
15,758.   More than one-fifth of this was laid down during the decade
1871–81, and nearly two-fifths in the following decade, which was a
period of immense activity.   The financial and other troubles of the
nineties made borrowing more difficult, slackened production, and
diminished very much the rate of construction.   Not all the lines were
of great value.   The cost of some was unnecessarily high; there were
duplications and unprofitable extensions into remote districts.   Except
in Western Australia, private enterprise played no part, for without
the aid of the State the work could not have been done.   Democratic
communities insisted on government action in the opening up of the
country; Government alone seemed to have the power and credit to
procure the necessary capital, and, if its work was costly, it was quick
and sure.   The private capitalist would not take the great risks; the
Governments, if not always wise, were ambitious and active.   Even in
Western Australia, state initiative and control assumed the upper hand
in 1892, when there were important lines to be constructed.   The policy
of all the colonies was to connect the lands of the interior with the
nearest or largest seaport of the same colony.   Owing to the political
influence which their large population gives them, the great ports have
exercised a strong influence on railway policy in their respective colonies,
and have prevented the formation of interior distributing centres, as well
as placed some petty hindrances in the natural course of intercolonial
trade.   Each colony directed its action according to the supposed
interests of commerce and settlement within its own borders, and,
whether from lack of foresight or from rivalry, no two contiguous States
adopted the same gauge.   Thus, great as the work of the railways has
been in promoting the settlement, prosperity, and unity of the country,
it has been in some respects hampered by the emulation of cities and
colonies.   The state management of the railways has not been a commercial success, or prevented every abuse of their power; but the
financial loss is small, and the people gain in having a substantial control
over one of the great agents in the production of national wealth and
strength.   In New Zealand, railways were extended most rapidly during
the seventies, and, by bringing the various settlements into closer communication, they contributed to render antiquated the provincial political
organisation.   Thus, Australasia has on the one side of her account her
railways and other public works, and on the other side the immense
public debt which has been accumulated in the course of their construction, amounting in 1907 to over 66 millions for New Zealand and nearly

228 millions for Australia. New Zealand contracted its principal loans in
the seventies; Victoria, New South Wales and Queensland in the eighties;
Western Australia in the nineties.   The financial burden is heavy, but
the greater facilities for economic development provide the means of
bearing it; and, except in Western Australia, the colonies have been
spared the necessity of granting huge blocks of land to private companies—the policy followed by Canada.   It is scarcely possible yet to
compare the efficiency and cost of the means adopted by the two
countries.

The economic expansion which we have hitherto considered was a
normal development along the old lines of progress—a larger production
and export of staple commodities.   But the years under review have also
seen the beginning of manufacturing industries in some of the colonies.
Industrial activity was necessarily very slight in a land of small, and for
the most part dispersed, population, divided into a number of States
which, raising their tariff walls against each other, limited the free
market of the manufacturer.   But with the progress of the country, a
concentration of population in the chief towns took place, and, as the
production of gold began to decline, a desire to broaden the field of
employment made itself felt.   In Sydney, Melbourne, Brisbane, Adelaide,
and in the larger towns of New Zealand, manufacturing industries were
established which have since assumed considerable importance.   The
chief are still those which prepare raw materials for export; but, as
was natural, the woollen and leather industries have also prospered,
though the greater industries which rest on iron, cotton, silk, and
earthenware, have not yet been founded.   Their products are still imported, for the most part from Great Britain, as well as miscellaneous
and cheaper articles from Germany and other countries.   The mother
country had left the colonies free to choose their own tariff policies.
Victoria in 1877 definitely adopted Protection, and most of the other
colonies under the pressure of financial necessities drifted in the same
direction, except New South Wales, which in 1873 abandoned high
tariffs and, save for a brief period in the nineties, maintained free trade
until the end of its separate history.   New Zealand, like Victoria,
though later, accepted Protection on its merits; but definite theories
played a smaller part than circumstances in guiding the policy of the
other protectionist colonies.   The difficulty of collecting direct taxes
in young, sparsely-peopled countries led Governments to rely for their
revenue on tariffs, soon raised by extravagance to a protective level.
The tariff is but one of the factors which influence industrial and general
progress; but it is interesting to observe, in the case of the two great
colonies which followed different policies, that New South Wales has
outstripped Victoria in the growth of population and wealth, while
Victoria has, against greater difficulties, maintained an industrial activity
equal to that of New South Wales.

CH. XX.

The rise of manufacturing industries accentuated a feature of Australian life which has always been apparent—the large proportion of urban to rural population.   As a result, partly of geographical conditions and partly of policy, Victoria, New South Wales, South Australia and Queensland, have all tended to concentrate their industrial and commercial activity.   Australia has but few ports, and, in a great trading country, they have naturally acquired a special importance, which has been increased by the policy of the railways : workers drifted into them from the uncertain employment of the mining fields ; and, when industries were founded, they were founded where the population was already concentrated.   Melbourne and Adelaide today contain nearly 43 and 46 per cent. of the inhabitants of their respective States ; and in other colonies the capital city is only less powerful.   In New Zealand, where different conditions prevail, urban life is more distributed.

In addition to the economic progress which drew the people of the different colonies together and multiplied their mutual interests, must be noted the increasing likeness of their social and political development, and of the ideals of welfare which they formed.   In Australasia there were seven distinct communities.   But rival Governments, although a formidable obstacle to political union, did not shape different societies, and expressed nothing more than the difficulty, in earlier times, of directing the affairs of a dispersed population from a single centre.   The different colonies were peopled by men of the same stock and the same classes. The circumstances of their origin and history varied ; but they shared the same religion, race instincts, and ideas of social order.   During recent years, this homogeneity has been powerfully expressed in their policy, and has perceptibly increased.   The aboriginal population has never much affected the course of Australian development.   In Tasmania it is now extinct ; in Victoria and New South Wales negligible ; and even in Western Australia it has not been large or formidable enough to influence social progress.   In New Zealand the situation has been different ; but the Maoris, though much has been done to preserve their old life, appear now to be a dying race.   Immigration to Australia has been confined almost entirely to English-speaking people, and no serious problem of assimilation has presented itself in any colony.   Nor have the numbers of immigrants ever been large except during the busy years 1881–5. Between 1870 and 1906 the total net gain to population from this source was only 605,578 ; and, so great was the falling off as a result of the recent financial and industrial troubles and droughts, that, in the decade 1896–1905, it was little more than 5000.   The immigrant seeks the new country whose open opportunities and prosperity offer the strongest demand for his services.   The scarcity of suitable farming land available for settlement, the absence of expanding industries, the distance and expense of the journey, have weakened the attractive power of Australia in competition with other countries.   Nor have the Australian colonies maintained that free policy which has admitted multitudes to the cities and prairies of America. The practice of assisting immigrants was abandoned by Victoria in 1873, South Australia in 1886, New South Wales in 1887, and Tasmania in 1891. The Labour parties have not favoured the immigration of artisans, and the freedom of employers to introduce workmen under contract has been limited. The demand for the farmer remains small, so long as much of the best land is locked up for pastoral uses in the possession of individuals and companies. More-over, burdened with new responsibilities towards the weaker members of society and doubtful of the capacity of the country to employ a large influx of people, the Australians have further legislated to exclude, not only the diseased and criminal, but also the poor who might become a public burden. Thus, in days when cheaper means of transport have made possible greater movements of population, the land problem, dull times and a cautious policy have combined to restrict the flow of popu-lation towards Australia. In the last few years strong forces, particularly the desire to increase the defensive power of the country and to develop the tropical parts by white labour, have been operating in the other direction, and greater efforts to secure settlers have contributed to the considerable increase of immigration since 1905.

While, in the case of the European, the Australian colonies have sought to select, in the case of the Asiatic they have developed a policy of practical exclusion. Here they faced a far more difficult problem. Close to the populous districts of southern and eastern Asia, Australia, with its vast unpeopled tropical plains, has become more and more afraid of an extensive Asiatic immigration. Very early in the century, when labour was scarce, the squatters imported Chinese and Hindu coolies as shepherds, and after them natives of the New Hebrides. The sugar planters of Queensland also recruited Kanakas from some of the Pacific islands. Meanwhile, a spontaneous Asiatic immigration began. During the first gold rushes Chinese entered the country in considerable numbers, and from the mines drifted on to the runs and farms of New South Wales and into the furniture trade of Melbourne. Between 1855 and 1861, Victoria, New South Wales, and South Australia passed their first exclusion laws, imposing duties on masters of vessels carrying Chinese. The immigration ceased, and the laws were repealed. The gold dis-coveries in Queensland were followed by an influx of Chinese into that colony. An exclusion law passed by the Queensland Government in 1876 was reserved by the Governor and disapproved by the Secretary of State. New Acts were framed in the two following years, imposing a poll tax on the Chinese immigrant. In 1881, a fresh agitation broke out in the other colonies and was followed by restrictive legislation. Another outbreak of alarm, in 1888, caused the strengthening of these laws. A high poll tax was placed on the Chinese immigrant, who was excluded from mining and naturalisation; and a limitation according to tonnage was placed on the number of Chinese which a vessel might bring. In the same year, a judicial decision of the Privy Council confirmed the right of a colony to regulate the admission of aliens. Subsequent Laws in Western Australia, New South Wales, and New Zealand (1897-9), impose an educational test which proves an effectual means of exclusion. Save for the few capitalists who desired to import coolies, the policy of a "White Australia" expressed in these Laws had the approval of the whole country. From a working-class jealousy of a cheaper form of labour, it has been elevated to the position of a national ideal which aspires to preserve the type by refusing to admit into the community an element so far different in ideas and standard of life as to be incapable of assimilation, and thus possibly a menace to free institutions and social welfare.

In their political development the various colonies proceeded on parallel lines. The Constitutions which they chose for themselves in 1885 differed in some important respects, and have never been completely assimilated. On the whole they have worked well, in spite of some difficulties in acclimatising English institutions under new conditions. A tendency to enlarge the functions of Government, as well as to make democratic changes by extending the franchise, increasing the authority of the Lower House, and limiting the duration of Parliament, has been generally evident. But of constitutional reconstruction there has been very little, save in the case of colonies whose development had lagged behind. Western Australia had received only partially representative government in 1870, and responsible government was not granted until 1890. At intervals, the cry for this concession was raised when some energetic politician stirred the colony. But the imperial Government refused to hand over a vast country to a small community, though offering to separate, and grant self-government to, the south-western district. The Western Australians preferred to retain "Western Australia one and undivided," and waited for political progress until gold discoveries brought them immigrants and wealth. In New Zealand, the provincial Governments, established in 1852, were abolished in 1875. They had become expensive, inconvenient, and unnecessary, as the better organisation of local government diminished their work, and improved means of communication lessened local differences. The composition and powers of the Legislative Council and its relations to the Assembly were in several colonies the cause of prolonged struggles. In Victoria, South Australia, and Tasmania, the Council was an elected body ; in New South Wales its members were nominated. In 1873, Henry (afterwards Sir Henry) Parkes made an attempt to place the Council of New South Wales on an elective basis; but the colony was not dissatisfied with the nominated Council, and the attempt failed. The elective Council of Victoria proved a strong body, and collisions with the Assembly began at once, and were continued in fierce strife throughout the seventies. The tariff, land taxation, and the payment of members, were among the subjects of dispute. The struggle resulted in deadlocks, the stoppage of public business, damage to public credit, and even in an appeal for imperial intervention. In the end, the Assembly failed to establish its supremacy over the Council; but the latter was by an Act of 1881 made more representative of the opinion of the colony. In Tasmania and South Australia the elective Councils also exerted a real influence. But in these colonies the Councils possessed the power of amending money bills, and greater moderation marked their differences with the Assemblies. South Australia, however, in 1881 provided a constitutional means of dealing with a deadlock between the two Houses, by vesting in the Governor the power either to dissolve both Houses simultaneously or to add new members to the Council. Manhood suffrage has been adopted in every colony except Tasmania; and in 1893 New Zealand led the way in extending the franchise to women. South Australia followed in 1894, and even the Conservative Upper House of Victoria gave way to a general movement. Within a decade, women's suffrage was granted throughout Australasia, without producing much immediate apparent influence on the course of politics.

Throughout Australia government has remained centralised; but the extension of a measure of local self-government into settled districts, which have generally been incorporated as boroughs or shires under elective Councils with limited powers, has continued at varying rates in the different colonies. The process was most rapid in Victoria and Queensland, slower in New South Wales, where incorporation remained voluntary (and often undesired) until 1905. More important has been the progress in educational organisation. In all the colonies there has been a movement to extinguish the dual control of education which resulted from the original dual system of denominational and national schools; to withdraw state aid from denominational schools; to establish an Education Department of Government under the direction of a Minister responsible to Parliament; and to render education compulsory, free, and secular, while allowing at the same time facilities for religious instruction by the denominations. Secondary education has been less thoroughly organised; and in this field private schools, generally exempt from all government supervision and control, play a large and increasing part. To the Universities of Sydney and Melbourne have been added those of New Zealand (1870), Adelaide (1874), and Tasmania (1889).

The political life of Australia has a character of its own. The methods and spirit of English politics were less easy to introduce than English constitutions. In societies which had no hereditary aristocracy, no established Church, no large leisured or learned class, no wealthy manufacturers, the material for a Conservative party was wanting. Thus everywhere groups rather than two stable parties were formed, with the consequence that the life of Administrations was usually very short and the political situation continually changing. Payment of members produced a professional class of politicians, and gave the electorate more control over their representatives. Power passed into the hands of the wage-earning and trading classes, who used it to promote new ideals. The large landowners, failing to sympathise with the prevailing tendencies, neither guided nor followed. New leaders were bred and trained in the strenuous atmosphere of the political arena. As the democracies became conscious of their power, the desire to expand the functions of the State grew stronger. More and more, Governments were expected to take an active part in the development of the country, and the spirit of earlier days in Australian history, when the State ruled all things, returned. The State had always been the great landlord; it had been called upon to build and manage railways and waterworks, to control education, and to defend nascent industries; now, it was further required to organise and aid producers by loans, as well as to uplift the masses by regulating their conditions of employment, their hours of labour, and their wages. Of its work in some of these fields we have already spoken; of its efforts to realise Australasia's latest ideals of social welfare some description remains to be given.

In Australasia, the laws regulating industrial and social conditions were, until recently, less advanced than those of older countries, owing to the peculiar labour conditions that prevailed and the comparative absence of manufacturing industries. But the last fifteen years have seen these arrears made up and bold experiments ventured upon which have attracted the interest of the world. While New Zealand has been perhaps the most progressive of the colonies, the competition and close relation that exists between them all has compelled all to act. Undoubtedly, the movement has been accelerated by the formation of Labour parties. Before the great industrial struggles that distressed Australia between 1886 and 1892, the working classes took little organised part in political life. The trade unions, not long established, relied on the more familiar weapon of the strike. During the eighties there was great activity in the federation of unions; the Amalgamated Miners' Association and the Amalgamated Shearers' Union were formed. A feeling of unrest spreading through industrial circles foretold the imminence of the great struggle which broke out in 1890. The Shearers' Union aspired to control all shearers' labour by preventing the employment of non-unionists. They were supported by the Carriers' Union and the Wharf-labourers of Sydney, as well as by the Newcastle Miners and the Marine Officers' Association. Many industries were paralysed, the Broken Hill silver mines were shut down; the intercolonial steamship service was practically suspended; and the whole of the eastern colonies and New Zealand were affected. The general unemployment imposed too severe a financial strain on the unions, and the strike collapsed, only to be renewed again in 1891 with more violence by the shearers of Queensland and New South Wales. The stock-masters, however, succeeded in

importing non-union labour from the southern colonies, and once more
the strikers succumbed.   By the same means a strike at the Broken Hill
mines in 1892, where the employers sought to substitute the contract
system for day work, was defeated.   In this prolonged battle capital
proved stronger than labour.   The strategy of the unionists was not the
wisest; and, though their cause evoked much sympathy, they failed to
convince the country that the power they sought could be exercised for
the general good.   Moreover, the times were unfavourable for the old
methods of industrial warfare.   Twenty years of prosperity, among the
happiest in Australian history, were drawing to an end.   The excited
activity that characterised them had been stimulated by extensive
borrowing, the multiplication of credit institutions, not all prudently
managed, and an unjustifiable speculation which was followed by a
reaction bringing a contraction of employment.   The general depreciation in the value of great staple commodities such as wool, wheat, and
metals, especially affected Australia.   Financial troubles began in 1891
and reached a crisis in 1893, in which year half the banks in Australasia
closed their doors.   Many other difficulties had to be faced; none the less,
the real work remained and recovery soon began, though the immense
activity of the preceding period was not repeated.   In these circumstances
labour leaders began to organise their followers for political activity, that
they might use the State to impose on capital some at least of the terms
which labour unaided had failed to extort.   In every colony a Labour
party was formed, having its strength in the industrial, mining, and
grazing communities rather than among the farmers.   With different
fortunes in different colonies, and with many vicissitudes, the Labour
parties have exerted an increasing influence on political life.   In New
Zealand, where the Conservative classes had controlled the policy of the
country for thirty years, the working men, allying themselves with the
old Liberal party, formed a Progressive party which has remained in
power since 1891.   In South Australia and Victoria, they have generally
worked with the Radicals.   In Queensland and New South Wales they
have maintained their distinctness and followed an opportunist policy.
Practical and not doctrinaire, their leaders have concentrated attention
on social and industrial reforms, inspired by the belief that Government can secure for every worker a higher level of material welfare;
and by their definite ends and determined action they have made the
Labour parties perhaps the most powerful political force in the country.

In 1894 an important Factory Act was passed in New Zealand,
which placed even the smallest workshops under government supervision.
It was the beginning of much legislation, which has since followed in all
the colonies, inspired by the idea of bringing industry under state
regulation.   Factory Acts became general and were followed by Shop
Acts, less drastic, owing to the political strength of the small traders.
Bolder experiments were soon made in New Zealand and Victoria,

CH. XX.

and speedily copied in other colonies. The Factory Act of Victoria, 1896, established wages boards in certain industries, the number of which has since been much increased. The boards were specialised bodies, elected by employers and employees, having power to fix a minimum wage and to regulate the conditions of apprenticeship. In 1894, an Act was passed in New Zealand providing for compulsory arbitration in industrial disputes. A dispute was to be carried, first, before a local Conciliation Board, and, if not settled by that, before a Court of Arbitration. Experience discredited the Conciliation Boards, and New South Wales, in dealing with the problem in 1901, set up simply a Court of Arbitration, while the New Zealand Act was amended to allow a dispute to be carried directly before the Court. The effect of these measures can scarcely yet be estimated. If they have not realised the expectation of the wage-earning classes, they have not quenched their hope of increasing benefit from the state regulation of industry. The Wages Boards have certainly mitigated, though they have not eradicated, the evil of sweating, and they have acquired a broad influence in the regulation of industrial conditions. Much the same can be said of compulsory arbitration. Without altogether preventing strikes, it has greatly diminished them; and the power which the Courts have of giving to particular decisions a general application renders the process of arbitration a powerful means of industrial regulation. But common sense levels down the results of interference, just as the interaction of all sides of industrial life extends its range. State regulation does not yet appear to have injuriously affected the expansion of industry, while it has operated to improve the conditions of the worker, to shorten hours of labour, and diminish the employment of children. The burden is, perhaps, borne by the consumer in higher prices, and felt most by the best workers, fettered by average standards. But the gain may be greater than the loss.

The most important of the more purely social reforms has been the concession of old age pensions. New Zealand, in 1898, established a non-contributory system, under which age, poverty, and good character qualified natives of the islands for a pension. New South Wales and Victoria followed in 1900. The New South Wales scheme closely resembled that of New Zealand; but Victoria followed a more economical policy and worked its pensions into a general plan of provision for the aged poor. All three systems have been successfully worked, though the financial burden and administrative difficulties proved greater than had been anticipated. In the regulation of the liquor traffic no great experiments have been made. The principle of local option has been generally accepted, and various forms, from the reality in Queensland and New Zealand to the shadow in Western Australia and Tasmania, have been established.

To be united at some time in a single State seemed the natural destiny of the Australian colonies, even at the time when, for administrative convenience, they were divided. Their continual expansion overcame to a great extent the obstacles of distance and dispersion and closely interweaved their affairs. The likeness in the political and social development of the several colonies, as well as a rising consciousness of new general interests, slowly prepared the way. The federal idea, in different forms, appeared continually on the horizon; but it was not until 1900 that union was accomplished. From 1863, delegates of the various colonies met in occasional conferences on matters of common interest. But such meetings, though not useless, were hard to summon and possessed no power. Fiscal union was at one period strongly desired, and the imperial Parliament in 1873 passed the Australian Colonies Duties Bill, in order to set the colonies free to make such tariff arrangements with each other as they wished. But differences of commercial policy changed the situation, and in 1881 the idea was abandoned. Evidently, political union could not be pursued along the path of fiscal union. Meanwhile, a vague apprehension of trouble to come spread through the colonies, as new neighbours appeared in their distant waters. The occupation of the Pacific islands had begun; and questions arose in New Caledonia, Fiji, the New Hebrides, New Guinea, and Samoa, which deeply concerned the Australians. Only by union could they make their voice heard in external affairs. Hence, in 1885, a Federal Council was created to deal with certain defined matters, including marine defence, the influx of criminals, and relations with the islands of the Pacific. The new body was permanent; but it had neither executive nor money, and it failed to obtain general support. New South Wales and New Zealand were never represented, and South Australia only once. Inadequate as the Council was to act as the engine of federal action, the nation was disinclined for the great effort required to fashion a new constitution. Economic prosperity absorbed energy and attention, and the rivalries of the colonies were accentuated with their progress. The various Governments were unlikely to overcome the real obstacles in the way of union, and it was necessary that the people should supply the motive force. The increasing gravity of external problems forced the matter into the front again in the later eighties; and Parkes, who had suggested and then disregarded the Federal Council, now gave his support to the larger policy.

A convention of delegates from the colonial Parliaments met at Sydney in 1891 and speedily framed a constitution. The adversities of the following years delayed progress; but the conversion of opinion proceeded, and a popular movement was organised. A new constituent assembly was elected, and, meeting at Adelaide in 1897, reconsidered the work of its predecessor. The proposals adopted were referred to the vote of each colony, and were accepted at once in Victoria, Tasmania, and South Australia, but in New South Wales and Queensland only after certain amendments. Western Australia delayed a little longer in the hope of further concessions. New Zealand decided not to enter the federation. While she desired to cooperate with Australia, she doubted the advantages of a close union. The sentimental impulse of the national idea could not be very strong in her; while the possible commercial and financial gain seemed not to outweigh the loss of legislative independence and the absence of her leading politicians during a great part of the year. Australia was far off, and New Zealand was prosperous in isolation; nor was there the impelling consideration of defence, since this was rather an imperial than an Australasian question. The Federation Act was welcomed by the imperial Parliament, and received the royal assent in July, 1900.

In framing their Constitution the Australian colonies proceeded with deliberation. They chose a federal rather than a unitary system, as required by their geographical conditions and as alone practicable in the circumstances. They rejected the close form of union adopted by Canada in favour of the looser form of the United States; at the same time, they followed the example of the mother country by grafting the Cabinet system on to their institutions. While preserving in full vigour the autonomy of the States within their own spheres, they did not deny to the new Government a range of power adequate to secure its utility and strength. They gave to the democratic principles which had prevailed in the colonies an even fuller exercise in the new Constitution; so that, in a very real sense, the Federal Government is of and by the people, to whose vote its acceptance was referred, by whom constitutional amendments must be approved, who directly elect both Houses of Parliament, as well as decide between them in case of obstinate differences.

In forming the national Government, the machinery of State Constitutions was not disturbed. The States remained separate entities, sovereign within their own spheres, intact in their territories, capable of remodelling their own institutions, and in direct relations with the imperial Government; but they surrendered to the new Government certain specified powers, including the control of commerce, customs duties, the postal services, external affairs, defence, family and commercial law, immigration and naturalisation, the right to construct and acquire railways, as well as to take over and consolidate the state debts. The States retained the control of education, police, and land, together with a coordinate, though inferior, power of legislating on matters over which the Commonwealth exercised authority. A Parliament, an executive Council, and a High Court of Justice, constituted the organs of the new Government. The Parliament consists of a Senate and a House of Representatives. The qualification for members and for electors is the same for both Houses; the members of both are paid, and paid alike. The Senate embodies the federal principle in the Constitution, and in it each original State has six representatives. Senators are chosen for a period of six years, each State forming a single constituency, except in the case of Queensland; one-half of the members retire every third year. The

House of Representatives contains twice as many members as the Senate, divided amongst the States in proportion to population, and is dissolved at least triennially. Thus both Houses are in touch with popular opinion; but the predominance of the Lower House is secured by the dependence of Ministers upon its support, and by the fact that the Senate, while it can reject or advise on money bills, cannot initiate or amend them. The Constitution also makes provision in case of a prolonged dispute for a simultaneous dissolution or joint sitting of the two Houses. The executive power is vested in the Governor-General appointed by the Crown and a Council appointed by the Governor-General, of which Ministers are always members, though all members are not necessarily Ministers. The High Court has original jurisdiction in certain defined matters and a general appellate jurisdiction. From its decisions an appeal can be made to the Privy Council, though, in cases of "constitutional powers," only by certificate of the Court, while, in other cases, the right is subject to limitation by statute—an arrangement which represents a compromise between local and imperial sentiment on this question. By a provision which became known as the "Braddon blot," the Federal Government was bound for ten years to distribute three-quarters of its revenue from customs and excise amongst the States, which could ill afford to lose suddenly their main financial resource.

The formation of the Commonwealth opened a new phase in Australian history. The policy of the country suffered no change, for the new State spoke with the same voice as the old colonies. But the unity which had been attained by years of progress was now recognised in institutions and could be carried forward to completion; while the ideals which had been shaped severally and locally could now receive a national expression. To this work the new Government turned. National action speedily gave a new emphasis and scope to the white Australia policy. The importation of Kanakas was prohibited (1901), and those already on the plantations were required to be deported by 1906. The Commonwealth Government was forbidden to enter into mail contracts with steamship companies employing coloured labour in the carriage of the mails (1901). Educational tests were imposed on immigrants, with the object of excluding Asiatics and other coloured peoples (1901 and 1905). Bounties were offered to sugar planters who used only white labour.

With the formation of the Commonwealth, tariff barriers between the States were removed, and inter-state trade rapidly increased. On the fiscal question opinion was at first naturally divided. The expenses of government necessitated a high scale of duties, and the feeling in some of the States in favour of protecting Australian industries remained strong. A protective policy was, in consequence, definitely adopted, and the question has now ceased to provide a main line of political division. But, while determined to secure so far as possible the home market for its own manufacturers, as successive increases of the tariff have shown, the Australian Government has favoured a policy of imperial preferences. In the interests of the mother country it slightly modified the tariff of 1907, by granting small preferences on certain classes of goods, and in her extensive markets it would welcome a preference for the products of Australia's agricultural and pastoral industries. The Labour party proved to be very strong in the Commonwealth Parliament, and three times (1904, 1908 and 1910) a Labour Ministry has taken office, though only on the last occasion has it obtained real power. The regulation of industry in the interests of workers has in consequence been a prominent question; but the industrial legislation of the Commonwealth has been limited by difficulties in defining the respective spheres of the State and the nation. This situation has combined with other causes to spread the opinion that the relations between the Federal and State Governments must be revised by an increase in the powers of the former. The character of this change has an important bearing on the development of Protection, government regulation of industry, land legislation, and fiscal measures in the interests of labour. It has been the principal issue in the election at which the policy of the Labour party, desirous of strengthening and extending Federal control, has quite recently secured the support of the country (1910). An increase of Federal revenue is required as well as an increase of Federal power. Hitherto the Commonwealth has derived almost the whole of its revenue from Customs, Excise, and the Post Office. The States have had wider resources. In addition to the funds received from the Commonwealth, they raise money from public works, various forms of direct taxation and the sale and rental of Crown lands. A change in the financial relations by a revision of the Braddon Clause and the transference of the state debts to the Commonwealth is now under consideration, and the future will probably also see an extension of Federal taxation. With railway problems, so vital in young countries, the Commonwealth has, as yet, been little concerned. The handing over of the lines by the States, provided for in the Constitution, though it has been contemplated, has not yet been effected. The building of transcontinental lines has not had the importance which it possessed in Canada. But, on strategic and political grounds, an overland connexion with Western Australia is desired, and money has been voted for the survey of a route from Kalgoorlie to Port Augusta. The country traversed is unlikely to be commercially developed, and the assimilation of gauges in the eastern colonies has been a question of more urgent importance. The site of the capital, which the Commonwealth Act fixed in New South Wales, though not within 100 miles oı Sydney, was, after much trouble, settled in 1908 by the choice of the Yass-Canberra area, about 150 miles southwest of Sydney.

New Zealand, which suffered far less than Australia from the calamities of the nineties, has recently made great progress in wealth and popu-

lation. Australia also has recovered since 1902, though the activity of
earlier years has not been repeated. Time seems to be cementing the
union she has formed, and at the same time confirming the New Zea-
landers in their determination to remain apart. Both countries pursue
their separate yet similar history inspired by strong ambitions and a
growing national spirit. They have worked out their destiny, attaining
maturity and a distinct character, within the shelter of the British
empire, to which today they add the strength and energy of two new
nations.

We take up the thread of South African history at a point where it
begins to bear a similar character to that of the great sister colonies.
The exploration of Central Africa and the mineral discoveries of Kimberley and later of the Transvaal, opening a new phase in the economic
development of South Africa, induced Great Britain to attach to that
country a greater value as a field of commerce and colonisation. New
opportunities, together with the competition of other Powers for territorial possessions, stimulated her to extend her sovereignty into the
interior and along the coast, enveloping the independent Boer States.
At the same time, progress and common problems interwove more and
more the life and interest of the English and Dutch communities; so
that the political divisions, produced by a clash of ideal and civilisation
between Briton and Boer in the first half of the century, proved to be
increasingly detrimental to a country which racial and geographical
conditions made a single whole. The idea of restoring unity to a land
unhappily divided thus became a strong motive force in its history.
Much tact and wisdom were required to reconcile and harmonise the two
opposed ideals—the one stubborn and tenacious as the other was strong
and assertive—in whose cooperation and blending the best prospects
for South Africa were to be seen. But, in the difficult circumstances,
mistakes worse than those of the past were repeated, and a melancholy
train of events so far emphasised their antagonism that, at last, the
relations between the two races and the political future of South Africa
were committed to the arbitrament of war. The establishment of British
sovereignty over the Boers followed, and permitted the union of South
Africa in a single State.

Signs were not wanting in the early seventies that British policy in
South Africa was undergoing a change. Griqualand West was annexed
in 1871, and self-government granted to the Cape Colony in 1872. In
the same year, the dispute with the Portuguese about the territory south
of Delagoa Bay was referred to the arbitration of the French President,
Macmahon. His decision, delivered in 1875, was entirely in favour of
Portugal, which, however, in the meantime, had agreed not to part with
the territory to any third Power, and, later, by a convention of 1891,
conceded to England the right of preemption of any of her possessions

CH. XX.

south of the Zambesi.   A movement to secure the confederation of the
South African colonies was also on foot.   The advantages of such a
course were already apparent, and the Orange Free State seemed not
unwilling to agree.   Lord Carnarvon despatched James Anthony Froude,
in an unofficial capacity, to promote the cause in the Cape Colony ; but
his indiscretion in stirring up trouble between the colonists and their
Government had an opposite result.   However, in 1877, a permissive
Federation Act was procured from the imperial Parliament.   At this
point the policies of union and expansion merged in a remarkable event,
pregnant with great results.   The position and conduct of the Transvaal,
especially in its dealings with native peoples, excited the concern of all
South Africa.   Trouble menaced it from several sides ; but its most
serious entanglement was a territorial dispute with the Zulus, who, under
their new King, Cetewayo, had restored their military organisation and
become most formidable opponents.

Sir Theophilus Shepstone, an experienced administrator in native
affairs, was despatched to the Transvaal, with discretionary powers to
annex the country if the majority of the inhabitants so desired.   Finding
the government bankrupt and in apparent collapse, and the people
unprepared to resist the enemy, he proceeded to exercise these powers,
although the Boers were by no means willing to purchase protection at
the price of independence.   At this juncture Sir Bartle Frere arrived in
South Africa as Governor of the Cape and High Commissioner.   A man
of clear and far-reaching aims, he believed that British sovereignty must
sooner or later be extended over the whole of South Africa as far north
as the Portuguese dominions.   He therefore accepted the annexation of the
Transvaal, made war on the troublesome Transkei Kafirs, and, while conceding to the Zulus most of the land in dispute, demanded of Cetewayo
the immediate dissolution of his military polity.   The result was a war
which lasted through the first seven months of 1879.   Commencing with
a disaster to the British arms at Isandhlwana Hill (January 22), which,
but for the heroic defence of Rorke's Drift, might have had serious
consequences, it was crowned at last with complete success in the
decisive victory of Ulundi (July 5).   The Zulu power was broken,
and Zululand, divided among thirteen chiefs, was placed under a
British Resident.   Suspicion of German and Boer intentions induced
Great Britain to annex St Lucia Bay in 1884, and Zululand itself in
1887.   Unlikely as it was that the warlike Zulus could have been induced
without blood to discard their institutions and mode of life, the tragic
incidents of a war which the Home Government had desired to avoid
discredited Frere's action in England, and he was superseded in South-
East Africa, though retained in his post at the Cape in order to forward
the great object of South African union.

Meanwhile, the Transvaal had become a scene of trouble.   The great
majority of the Boers opposed annexation ; but the imperial authorities

disregarded their protests, believing that they would accept the accomplished fact. An unpopular Governor and an unsympathetic and unwise administration failed altogether to conciliate them. The freest of republics was denied even an elementary measure of self-government. In these circumstances, fortune did not aid the attempt to push forward the project of confederation. The Cape Dutch were incensed at the treatment of their kinsmen, and the Cape Parliament, disliking to be hurried by Downing Street, rejected the proposal. In December, 1880, the sullen anger of the Boers blazed into rebellion, and they raised at Paardekraal the standard of revolt. Sir George Colley, Governor and Commander-in-Chief in Natal, advanced with slender forces to disperse them and relieve the invested British garrisons. At Laing's Nek and Ingogo he found determined opponents; pushing on, he met defeat and death on Majuba Hill (Feb. 27, 1881). This slight encounter, magnified by the great results which followed it, became for the Boers a burning memory and a proof of British impotence and irresolution. The British Government refused to continue the War for the barren end of retrieving its military prestige, and concluded with the Transvaal the Pretoria Convention, by which the Boers regained their independence under British suzerainty. Three years later, the agreement was qualified by the London Convention. The express assertion of suzerainty was not repeated, but the Transvaal agreed to make no treaty, save with the Orange Free State, without the consent of Great Britain. For the protection of white residents in the country some further provisions were inserted; but, as subsequent events proved, they were not sufficiently explicit to serve their intended purpose. Such is the chequered story of the first annexation of the Transvaal. The false initial step might, not impossibly, have been maintained, had not fatal errors followed. The final issue, confused and humiliating as it was, was the best escape from a dilemma which knowledge, wisdom, and good faith throughout, might have avoided.

The central interest of South African history shifts at this point to the Cape Colony, where hitherto the course of politics had been smooth. English and Dutch were not hostile. If the Dutch were chiefly farmers and the English chiefly traders, yet they intermarried freely and were conscious of common interests. The development of the interior had given a great stimulus to the progress of the Cape, and in 1874 its Government had adopted a vigorous policy of railway construction which had revolutionised the conditions of commerce and communication. No organised parties sprang into being on the grant of self-government, since there was no material for their formation. With abundance of land, there was no land question among the whites; with no established Church, no ecclesiastical controversies; with no industries or large towns, no marked separation between rural and urban interests; and, though native questions raised difficult problems and the Dutch feeling was opposed to the liberal policy which the Cape had earlier laid down, the

CH. XX.

division of opinion within the colony was not sharp. The struggle
of the Boers for independence, however, awakened the slumbering race
sentiment of the Dutch, and provoked an outburst of feeling which
perpetuated itself in a new organisation of political parties. In 1882
the Africander Bond was formed. Inscribing the sacred doctrine of
colonial self-government on its banner, it took for its motto the union of
South Africa; but it appealed mainly to the Dutch, and had little
sympathy with the British ideal of expansion, progress, and unity under
the British flag. It quickly secured the official use of the Dutch language in Parliament and the law Courts. Subsequent events somewhat
estranged its sympathies from the Transvaal; at the same time, under
the influence of Cecil Rhodes, who understood and worked with the
Dutch, its views were broadened and its latent anti-British sentiment
died down.

Rhodes had come out to South Africa in 1871 and taken part in
the diamond rush to Kimberley, where, later, he consolidated the mines
in one strong monopoly, and built up the immense fortune which he
devoted to his imperial schemes. From 1884, when he entered Cape
politics, he played an important part in all South African affairs, but
particularly in the policy of expansion into the interior, which had
become at that time the dominant issue in South African politics.
Frere had induced the imperial Government to occupy Walfisch Bay
(1878), though it refused to annex the whole coast line as far north
as the Portuguese dominions, with the result that, in 1884, the Germans
established themselves in these parts, and threatened by eastward
penetration to join hands with the Boers moving westwards, and enclose
the British south of the Orange river. Access to the interior, with
its prospects of mineral and agricultural development, was vital to the
economic progress of the Cape. While Germany was transforming her
tentative footholds into sure possession, the strife began. North, south,
and west, the Boer farmers trekked in search of land, unrestrained by the
Conventions of 1881 and 1884, which had fixed the boundaries of the
Transvaal. In Zululand they established the New Republic, in Bechuanaland the twin republics of Stellaland and Land Goshen. The New
Republic was recognised by Great Britain in 1886, and incorporated
with the Transvaal in 1888; but, against the other republics which
barred the route into the interior, an expedition was despatched under
Sir Charles Warren in December, 1884, and they were dissolved. A
British Protectorate was proclaimed as far north as lat. 22°; and in
September, 1885, the southern part of Bechuanaland was constituted
a Crown colony, to be annexed to the Cape in 1895. The far-seeing
missionary John Mackenzie urged upon the imperial Government the
northward extension of its influence. But it was left to Rhodes to carry
out this important work. To close Matabeleland to the Boers and add
this vast and rich domain to the British empire was his ultimate ambition,

and in the foundation of Rhodesia he left the most enduring monument
of his courageous energy. In 1888, a treaty was negotiated with Lobengula which barred Matabeleland to foreign enterprise, and in the following
year Rhodes founded the British South Africa Company for the colonisation and development of the country. No northern limit was fixed to its
sphere of operations, for its ambitious promoter already dreamed of a
British Dominion that should stretch from Capetown across the interior
of Africa to the mouth of the Nile. In 1890, the pioneer expedition set
out, and forts were established at Salisbury, Victoria, and Charters, round
which towns in time sprang up. The expense of the undertaking proved
very great, and serious political and climatic difficulties confronted the
new settlers. The Portuguese disputed their position, until an Anglo-
Portuguese agreement (1891) defined the Company's territory on the east.
The Transvaal in 1890 withdrew all claim to land north of the Limpopo,
which enabled Rhodes to repel by force an attempt of the Boer farmers
in 1891 to trek into Matabeleland. In 1893 war broke out with the
Matabele, who disliked the restraints placed upon their raids into
Mashonaland. But the Company's police proved equal to the task,
and Bulawayo was captured without disaster, though in the pursuit of
Lobengula a small party of English were cut off and destroyed. A
second outbreak in 1896, when Rhodesia was denuded of its police,
proved less serious, and was allayed by a personal visit of Rhodes to the
native chiefs. Meantime, the agricultural and mineral development of
the country proceeded. The railway was carried north from Kimberley
to Bulawayo in 1897; and, in accordance with the agreement made
with Portugal in 1891, another line was constructed from Beira on the
coast of Mozambique to Salisbury. Other extensions have followed.
This early penetration of Rhodesia by railways has much facilitated its
occupation; but the Company has had to maintain a long and unremunerative struggle in developing the promising resources of the country.
Nor has its policy and government been altogether acceptable to the
settlers, many of whom would have preferred direct imperial control.

At the time when the struggle for the interior was just beginning, a
new problem was suddenly introduced into the vexed politics of South
Africa. The conflict over the expansion of the Transvaal was succeeded
by a conflict over its domestic concerns. The existence of gold in the
country had been suspected for some years before the extensive discoveries of 1886 placed the Boers in possession of the richest mines in
the world. A rush of immigrants followed, and a heterogeneous population with a large English element was gathered on the Witwatersrand,
where the town of Johannesburg sprang into being. An alien and progressive community was planted in the midst of a nation of farmers, and
the prospects of assimilation were remote. Jealous of the independence
they had won, and fearful lest their distinct national being should be
lost, the Boers, by raising the qualifications required for the franchise,

effectually excluded the Uitlanders from any share in the government of the country, though in a few years they formed the majority of its inhabitants. Their language had no recognition in legal and political life; they were taxed without representation; and, though life and property were secure, they were in many respects in the position of a subject population. The middle classes chafed because a defective Government denied them the conveniences of civilisation, the capitalists because it hampered the progress of the mining industry. In 1890 the Boers established a Second legislative Chamber; but the concession was illusory, for, though the vote for this Chamber was easily obtainable, the new body had no real power. In 1892 the National Union was organised on the Rand, with the object of securing reform of the administrative and electoral systems, responsible government, the equality of the English and Dutch tongues, the independence of the Courts of Justice, and free trade in South African products.

The prosperity, and then the troubles, of the Transvaal deeply affected the other colonies. As with regard to native affairs, so with regard to railways, immigration, customs, the relations of English and Dutch, each was interested in the policy of the other. When the Transvaal became the centre of a great industry with a growing commerce, Cape Colony and Natal hastened to improve their harbours and extend their railways, in order to share in its activity. When an influx of English carried a race question into its politics, they felt the severing influence in their own. But the Transvaal, under the guidance of President Kruger, failed to recognise the common interests of all the South African States or to enter with them on a broader life. Cape Colony was estranged by a policy which placed high duties upon its produce, excluded its citizens from office in the same way as other immigrants, and opposed the development of its railways. The Transvaal, on its side, was mortified by the attitude of Great Britain towards its desire of expansion. After long negotiations and delay, Swaziland was, in 1894, placed under its control; but, in the following year, Great Britain annexed the territory between Zululand and Mozambique, thus finally taking from the Boers their cherished hope of securing a seaport. Meanwhile, a railway question had been the cause of a sharp struggle. By an arrangement with the Orange Free State the Cape system was extended across that colony and was continued to Johannesburg in 1892. A rival line from Delagoa Bay, commenced in 1887, entered the Transvaal in 1890 and reached Pretoria in 1895. The Cape route was favoured by its earlier completion and superior management; but the other had the great advantage of being shorter. A contest for the traffic of the mines ensued, in the course of which the Transvaal Government, in violation of the London Convention, closed the drifts over the Vaal to imported goods—an action that awakened a storm of indignation in South Africa and called forth an ultimatum from Great Britain to which Kruger yielded.

But, though Rhodes, who had become head of the Bond Government at the Cape in 1890, gained a victory in the matter of the railways, as he had previously foiled on west and north the Boer ambitions of expansion, and though Kruger's unfriendly policy had assisted him to conciliate and capture Dutch sentiment at the Cape, yet the isolation of the Transvaal still stood between him and the realisation of his great ideal of South African union. At this stage in the struggle, circumstances seemed suddenly to offer him the chance of overthrowing his adversary by one doubtful stroke. As the Boers refused the desired concessions to the Uitlanders, and the imperial Government failed to intervene effectually, the National Union began to contemplate an armed uprising. Rhodes offered them the assistance of the mounted police of the Company, whom he concentrated at Pitsani ready to act if necessary, on the condition that the Transvaal should accept the British flag. To this the conspirators were unwilling to agree, and a deadlock ensued, in the midst of which Dr Jameson, who commanded the Company's force, taking the matter into his own hands, invaded the Transvaal (Dec. 29, 1895), only to be intercepted by a strong party of Boers and to surrender at Doornkop (Jan. 2, 1896). The discreditable conspiracy thus collapsed in confusion and defeat, and the precipitate action of Dr Jameson revealed the deeper scheme of Rhodes as a design against the independence of a friendly State. The result was to extinguish all prospects of voluntary reform in the Transvaal, to drive the Orange Free State from its friendship with Great Britain into a close alliance with the sister republic, and to plunge South Africa into a turmoil of race hostility which ended at last in the storm of war. The task of the imperial Government, represented by Mr Chamberlain, was rendered as difficult as it could well be. Instead of standing on its legal rights and demanding the redress of specific grievances, it proceeded to the root of the matter, and pressed on the Transvaal proposals for constitutional change. The atmosphere of suspicion which preceding events had created was fatal to any understanding. A conference at Bloemfontein between President Kruger and Lord Milner, who had been sent out as High Commissioner in May, 1897, produced no result. Both sides were preparing for a struggle, and the weaker, with well-judged policy, struck quickly. In October, 1899, the sister republics issued an ultimatum. Thus the two ideals which represented the main streams of South African life came at last into determined and fatal collision.

The outbreak of war found Great Britain in an unhappy position. Confident in her immense power, incredulous of the Boer intentions, reluctant to precipitate a conflict, she was suddenly involved in a struggle whose seriousness she had failed to realise, and for which she had made no adequate preparation. The sympathy of most civilised nations was with her opponents, though her colonies and the great majority of the English people gave enthusiastic support. Counting on her unreadiness, the Boers proposed to invade Cape Colony and Natal. They expected to defeat the small bodies of troops opposed to them and to secure the support of the Cape Dutch. If they succeeded so far, they anticipated that one or more of the Great Powers would intervene, and that Great Britain would thus be compelled to recognise the complete independence of the Transvaal, and perhaps the union of South Africa under the Dutch flag. In the first few weeks of the War, the British were obliged by their inferiority in numbers to act on the defensive. General White, who commanded in Natal, withdrew his troops from the frontiers of the colony, after repulsing the Boers at Talana Hill (Oct. 20) and Elandslaagte (Oct. 21), and concentrated them at Ladysmith. In the west, defences were hastily improvised at Mafeking and Kimberley. The great railway junctions of Nauwport and Stormberg on the northern frontier of Cape Colony fell into the hands of the Free State burghers, who also threatened De Aar. But, exposed as this part of the country was, the invaders showed no great energy or definiteness of purpose, and waited on events. East and west also, the Boers paused in their advance to invest Ladysmith and Kimberley, whose long resistance gave time for British reinforcements to arrive. When Sir Redvers Buller reached South Africa in November, the War entered on a second stage. The British took the offensive, divided their forces, and endeavoured to relieve the invested towns. Events did not confirm the wisdom of this policy, for the relieving forces were not strong enough to achieve their ends. Lord Methuen, who, with 13,000 men, advanced to the relief of Kimberley, defeated the Boers at Belmont (Nov. 23) and Graspan (Nov. 25), and forced the passage of the Modder river (Nov. 28–9), only to suffer a tragic and costly reverse in an attempt to storm the heights of Magersfontein (Dec. 10). On the same day General Gatacre lost part of his force at Stormberg. The Commander-in-Chief was not more fortunate, being driven back from the passage of the Tugela at Colenso (Dec. 15). This series of disasters roused the imperial Government and the colonies to a sense of the gravity of the situation. Lord Roberts and Lord Kitchener were despatched to take command, and for months immense reinforcements were poured into South Africa. Meanwhile, intervention was discussed by some of the Powers; but their mutual rivalries and the supremacy of the British navy proved insuperable obstacles.

The new offensive movement initiated by Lord Roberts opened a third stage in the War, wherein success was transferred to the British arms. Advancing northwards, he relieved Kimberley, and overtook and penned the investing army of Cronje in the valley of the Modder at Paardeberg, where it surrendered (Feb. 27, 1900), to the intense discouragement of the other Boer forces. Serious resistance in the Free State was at an end, and Bloemfontein fell almost immediately. As the Boers retreated in the west, the task of relieving Ladysmith became more practicable. Attempts to approach the town by way of Spion Kop and Vaal

Kranz had failed; but at the end of February Buller stormed Pieter's Hill and the long siege was raised. In May, Mafeking, obstinately defended by Baden Powell, was relieved by a force from Rhodesia. In the same month, the Orange Free State was annexed. In June, Lord Roberts advanced on Pretoria, and defeated General Botha at Diamond Hill. The annexation of the Transvaal followed in September.

The great actions of the War were now ended; but the Boer peoples were unsubdued, and, tenacious of their independence, waged an obstinate guerrilla warfare for another two years. Their wandering commandos, under daring and skilful leaders, frequently surprised and defeated detached bodies of British troops, and had to be systematically hunted down—an operation which their mobility and the immense area of the country rendered extremely slow and difficult. The devastating and embittering character of this final stage of the War inflicted the severest injury on the distracted country. At last, in May, 1902, worn out by the fruitless struggle, the Boers sacrificed their independence, and accepted the British terms at Vereeniging. Failing to secure decisive success at the beginning, they had no chance of ultimate success. Singlehanded, they could not sustain a prolonged contest against the great resources of the British empire. Yet they had proved a formidable enemy. Their ample preparations, a central position, familiarity with the ground and the climate, and the moral impulse of a struggle for independence, gave them great advantages. Stubborn and skilful, though not invincible, in defence, swift in movement, and capable of individual initiative, but wanting the resolution for effective attack, their military qualities, like their democratic military organisation, fitted them far better for the defence of their native land than for the invasion of an enemy's.

Within a brief interval of each other died the two protagonists of this national struggle in South Africa. Kruger died an exile broken by age and failure (1903). His life had measured the life of the two republics, in whose fortunes he had played no mean part. As a boy he left the Cape in the Great Trek, and he lived to guide the Transvaal through the last troubled years of its history to the fatal issue in which his work and ambition were finally dissolved. In him was incarnate the invincible conservatism of the old Dutch spirit, as in his opponent the progressive energy and broad outlook of the modern world. Rhodes died in South Africa (1902), at the moment when the cause for which his life and fortune were spent had achieved a costly and terrible success. Working for great ends with such means as came to his hand, he made mistakes which time has covered, and achieved results destined to endure. His imagination and unstinted labour contributed in no small measure to shape the progress of South Africa.

The great result of the War was to bring all the South African communities under British sovereignty and so to prepare the way for their union. But before this could be realised, a tremendous task of reconstruction had to be faced. The Boers were restored to their farms, and an attempt was made to plant British settlers in the Orange River Colony and the Transvaal. The overtrading and speculation which the commercial activity of the years of war had stimulated were now followed by a strong reaction in the seaports and large towns, and depression settled upon the whole of South Africa. The mine-owners complained of the difficulty in recruiting native labour, and desired permission to import coolies from China. Anxious to serve the immediate interests of a great industry whose prosperity was vital to the country, the Home Government consented, in spite of the strong dislike of this course which was manifested in all parts of the empire. In the meantime, Legislative Assemblies were set up in the two conquered States. A change of Government in England in 1905 produced a change of policy in South Africa. The importation of Chinese ceased; and full self-government was granted to the Transvaal in 1906, and to the Orange River Colony in 1907.

This bold and generous concession opened the way for South African union. It conciliated and broadened the outlook of the Dutch leaders; it also assimilated the political status of the four great European colonies. Natal had received self-government so far back as 1893. At the time, the concession caused some anxiety in Great Britain, since the colony contained a native population, numbering many times that of the white, and a large Hindu community, employed on its sugar plantations or in retail trade. The progress of Rhodesia had not been rapid enough to justify the same change in its case; but, when the Company's administration was reconsidered after the Jameson " Raid," an imperial Commissioner assisted by a Legislative Council, in which the elected members have been given a majority, was placed over the south-western part. In 1907 the Earl of Selborne, appointed High Commissioner in 1905, reviewed the situation in a memorable document, and showed the impossibility of South Africa enjoying a real control of its own affairs save as a single State. The railway agreements, which had been arranged for distributing among the rival systems the traffic of the mines, and the Customs Convention, which, first made by the Cape Colony and the Orange Free State in 1889, had been extended at last so as to include all the colonies, though useful as temporary measures, offered no effectual and satisfactory means of forming a railway and commercial policy for South Africa as a whole. The dependence of the Cape Colony and Natal on the trade of the Transvaal was a vital consideration.

In other ways, painful experience reinforced the same conviction. The problem presented by the native population had grown more urgent and more complex with the lapse of time, and demanded the consideration of a South African authority. Successive annexations of territory had brought many new peoples under the government of the colonies. With the prohibition of tribal wars, the numbers of the natives increased so rapidly as to press, in places, upon the resources of the country. Scarcity of land caused trouble between black and white, and, by forcing the native into new fields of employment, raised the question of his industrial education. The progress of the mining industry created a rapidly increasing demand for his labour which could not easily be satisfied, and both the agricultural and the mining industries were embarrassed by labour difficulties in spite of the immense black population. In all the colonies there had been a tendency to disintegrate or modify the tribal system, and bring the native under the control of white magistrates and special legislation; but each had followed its own policy—whether as regards land tenure, political rights, special codes of law, education, taxation, or the liquor traffic—with a resulting diversity which, though it reflected to some extent a difference of conditions, was also caused by divergent ideals, and produced many unhappy consequences. Only in the Cape Colony had much been done to assist the native to become a useful citizen, and in the Cape Colony the liberal policy which had never denied the franchise on grounds of colour began to awake apprehensions in the early nineties, and was modified by raising the qualifications of the voter. At the same time, however, Rhodes, in the Glen Grey Act (1894), so called from the district to which it was first applied, endeavoured to lay down a broad policy, which, by giving to the native security in his land and earnings, the opportunity of education and some local self-government, might breed in him habits of industry and self-respect.

One other important development, increasing the complexity of the whole question, was the steady differentiation, under modern conditions, of classes among the natives, from the native in the tribal state, subject to chiefs and holding land under communal tenure, to the educated native or coloured man of Cape Colony, who owned land and exercised the franchise. Basutoland, which was attached to the Cape in 1871, was in 1884 restored to the imperial Government, under whose control it has enjoyed comparative independence and prosperity. In Zululand, on the contrary, which was annexed to Natal in 1897, the colonial Government has experienced severe trouble, culminating in the rebellion of 1906. A numerous and vigorous people, denied the congenial pursuit of war and not yet inured to peaceful occupations, the Zulus have been difficult to handle; but a more sympathetic and personal system of government would probably have prevented or removed many of the grievances of which they complained. In a sharp clash of opinion with the mother country arising out of this incident, Natal vindicated her right, as a self-governing colony, to control her own native policy. The occurrence was but one feature of a situation with which a single authority for the whole country could best deal. Other problems also required united action for their solution—such as those offered by the Asiatic immigrant, against whom Natal and the Transvaal were legislating; by agriculture, in which the necessity of scientific methods

CH. XX.

and common plans was apparent; and by the mining industry, with its labour problems which affected all the colonies in a variety of ways. Evidently, an Africander nation, guiding its own destinies, could only be shaped under common political institutions. The conviction that the time was ripe for action grew among the leading men of the country, and passed from them to the people. Finally, the tariff question forced to the front the vaster problem of which it formed a part. A convention of members of the South African Governments, assembled to discuss tariffs, gave place to a convention summoned to consider union. Sitting in secret from October, 1908, to February, 1909, first at Durban and then at Cape Town, and proceeding with singular unanimity, it framed a Constitution for a united South Africa which was forthwith submitted to the Parliaments of the four colonies. The Transvaal accepted it, Natal and the Orange River Colony offered some objections natural from small communities merging themselves with larger, the Cape offered more vital objections to some of the principles of the scheme. In a final meeting at Bloemfontein the suggested amendments were discussed and in part adopted. The Constitution, thus changed, was accepted by the people of Natal on a referendum, and by the Parliaments of the other colonies. Embodied in a Bill, it passed the imperial Parliament in September, 1909. In the thirty-two years that had elapsed since Lord Carnarvon's Federation Act the drama of South African union had been played through all its tragic scenes.

The aim of the Convention was to unite the two European races in effective and enduring cooperation. It did not seek to solve the great political and economic questions which confronted them, but only to create a Government, based on sure and equal principles, to which the future of the country might be safely entrusted. To achieve that end, many opposed forces and antagonistic interests needed to be harnessed together. Four separate colonial Governments, as well as the imperial Government, exercised political power within the bounds of the intended State. Three railway systems, on whose profits the financial stability of the four colonial Governments largely rested, worked in irreconcilable competition. The two white races had but just emerged from the War into which their conflicting ideals and mutual distrust had plunged them. By their side, and several times more numerous, lived an immense black population, as to whose treatment and future there was no agreement. Rival interests divided town from country, the coast from the inland. In the circumstances, the immense area of the country, the race divisions and the natural clinging of the old colonies to their historic autonomy seemed to demand a federal union. Yet, on the other hand, the geographical unity of South Africa, the intermingling of English and Dutch, the economic interdependence of all the colonies, the difficulty of dividing functions between a federal and state Governments in view of the oneness of

South African problems, and considerations of economy, favoured the opposite course. Thus the Convention, ignoring the example of other and kindred States and regarding only the needs and history of its own country, decided to make a complete end of existing political machinery and to establish in South Africa a unitary State. The old colonies have become provinces, and new provincial Governments have taken the place of their old Constitutions. But the new Governments are subordinate bodies, without rights and powers guaranteed in the Constitution. They are the agents of the Union Government, from which they receive their authority and to whose supervision they are subject. Though the new Constitution is not without a trace of federal ideas there is no attempt at a balancing of powers, either between the parts of the Union and the whole, or between legislative, executive and judicature. The central agent of the Government is a Parliament which is, or is soon to be, a sovereign body. The executive is dependent upon it, for the cabinet system of government is definitely adopted; the law Courts cannot restrict its action, for they do not interpret the Constitution; there is no matter, not even the amendment of the Constitution, which is not ultimately within its determination. Save for a few temporary provisions to make easy the passage, South Africa commits itself unreservedly to the new order. The two races come together on terms of complete equality. Both languages receive the same recognition in political life, and the principle of the equal value of the vote throughout the Union is substantially maintained. No attempt has been made to settle prematurely the great problems raised by the native population. The native appears in the Constitution, in order that his existing rights may be guaranteed and not that his future status may be determined. That work is left to the Union Parliament, in which the point of view of the native is represented by four members added to the Upper House on the ground of their knowledge of the native mind. Special provisions relating to finance and railway management are designed to preserve the railways from political interference and to guard the interests of both inland and coast. The difficulty of the capital was overcome by a compromise. Cape Town had historic claims and climatic advantages, Pretoria is at the heart of South Africa. So the Convention decided to separate, what everywhere else are united, the centre of administration and the seat of Parliament, and fixed the former at Pretoria, the latter at Cape Town. Such are the main principles on which the Union was formed. The actual machinery of Government may now be briefly described.

At the head of the Union is the Governor-General appointed by the Crown. The Parliament consists of two Houses, a Senate and a House of Assembly. The Senate contains forty members, holding office for ten years, of whom eight are nominated by the Governor-General, and thirty-two are elected in equal numbers for the four provinces, for the first time by the old Legislative Assemblies, for the future, unless Parliament

CH. XX.

shall otherwise determine, by the Council of each province together with the members of the House of Assembly who represent the particular province. The members of the House of Assembly are directly elected. Their distribution among the provinces is to be proportionate to population, though the Orange Free State and Natal at first receive a larger proportion than this principle would ensure them. The qualifications for the franchise are those obtaining in the old colonies, until Parliament otherwise provides; but any disqualification on grounds of colour must be approved by a two-thirds majority of both Houses sitting together. In each province the electoral divisions are to contain the same number of voters, though on certain defined grounds the strict numerical principle may be departed from, to the extent of 15 per cent. more or less than the quota. The principle of proportional representation, adopted for the Senate, was abandoned for the Assembly in deference to the views of Cape Colony. Members of both Houses must be British subjects of European descent. The supremacy of the Lower House is secured by provisions forbidding the Senate to originate or amend money bills, and arranging for a joint session in case of dispute at which a decision is to be made by a simple majority vote. The provincial Governments are designed to be administrative bodies free from party politics. They consist of an Administrator appointed by the Governor-General and holding office for five years, an elected Council sitting for three years and not subject to dissolution, and an Executive Committee of four chosen by the Council to act with the Administrator. The Councils control all purely local institutions and works, agriculture, subject to certain conditions, education (excluding higher education) for five years at least, and other matters referred to them by Parliament. Though they may raise money by direct taxation, the Union Government has effective financial control over them, and their ordinances require the consent of the Governor-General. A Board of not more than three Commissioners, appointed by the Governor-General for five years, and under the presidency of a Minister, is to manage the railways, ports, and harbours of the Union. It is to conduct the administration on business principles, for the general economic development of the Union, and not for profit.

Mr Herbert Gladstone (now Viscount Gladstone) was appointed first Governor-General of South Africa, and the meeting of the first Union Parliament was fixed for the autumn of 1910. With its assembly a new chapter will begin in the history of the country. Dutch and English are not separate in South Africa but freely intermingled; in one State many silent influences may lay to rest the clash of ideals, and blend, or teach cooperation to, forces that ill-starred events have in the past driven into hostility.

Some of the conditions which have encouraged the union of groups of English colonies in single States capable of developing a national life have also been acting upon the empire as a whole with a similar, though weaker, influence. Two opposite tendencies have indeed been apparent in its recent constitutional development. On the one hand, the new nations forming within its borders have claimed more and more to control their own affairs, and in every field of government have taken over powers from the mother country; and, on the other hand, both they and the mother country have been developing a sense of mutual interest and a realisation of the need for common action which, not very long since, was almost absent. Both of these tendencies require some consideration.

In the legislative sphere the independence of the colonies has become more complete. The imperial Parliament shows no disposition today to legislate for a self-governing colony save at its request; and since 1899 the imperial power of disallowing colonial Acts has not been exercised except in the case of Acts that clashed with imperial interests. The judicial connexion with the mother country has also been weakened. In 1887, the decision of the Supreme Court of Canada was made final in criminal cases; the Australian Commonwealth Act allows only a limited right of appeal from the Courts of the Commonwealth to the Privy Council; and both the Australian and South African Parliaments have power to restrict the matters on which leave to appeal may be asked. Imperial troops have been entirely withdrawn from the Dominions, which organise their own military defences and have in most cases laid the foundations of local armies. Already, they exhibit an unwillingness to rely exclusively on the imperial navy or to be content with voting annual subsidies towards its cost, seeing that they have no voice in their expenditure. Australia, dissatisfied with the agreements of 1887 and 1903, by which she paid for the maintenance of a small squadron in Australian waters to guard her trade, is now, in cooperation with the mother country, beginning to form a navy which shall be under her own control. New Zealand remains content to offer an annual contribution; but Canada, which has hitherto taken no direct part in imperial defence, proposes to follow the example of Australia. In the exercise of the prerogative of pardon it has become the practice, since 1877 in Canada and 1895 in Australia, for the Governor to act on his own responsibility only when imperial interests appear to be concerned. The attempt of the mother country to maintain some control over the native policy of a self-governing colony has failed in the one or two cases where, owing to peculiar circumstances, it was made. In Western Australia the care of the aboriginal population was at first vested in an independent Department; but in 1897 this was subordinated to the Government of the colony. In 1906 Natal successfully resisted the attempt of the imperial Government to supervise its conduct of native affairs.

While the foreign relations of the empire remain under the exclusive control of the mother country, in the making of treaties a compromise

CH. XX.

arrangement is being slowly worked out which recognises the right of the great colonies to determine and promote their own interests in international affairs, without giving them that unlimited freedom of dealing with other States which would be tantamount to independence. Since 1867, Canada has always been represented in the negotiation of treaties affecting her, and recently has conducted negotiations by her own Ministers with France, the United States, and Japan. In 1877, it became a recognised principle that all colonies might separately adhere to or withdraw from commercial treaties negotiated by the imperial Government; and, in 1900, the principle was further extended to other treaties. The question of immigration into a colony has been responsible for some special difficulties. As the greater colonies developed a national sense, they became determined to control the influx of unassimilable races into their midst, and their action necessarily affected the relations of Great Britain with the foreign countries concerned as well as the relations of the different parts of the empire. As a result of much discussion and some friction, the imperial Government has admitted the claim of the colonies to control or prevent such immigration, while they have yielded to its representations so far as regards the form and method of their legislation. But the unity of the empire is not of such a character that every subject enjoys the right of free movement throughout its borders; the native of India may be excluded from South Africa or British Columbia, and the undesirable Englishman may be turned back from the ports of Canada or Australia.

Thus, in every field of Government, whether in legislation, justice, administration, or foreign policy, the great Dominions have assumed an increasing control of their own affairs. Clearly and fully the mother country has been throwing upon them the burden of their own destiny, which they in turn have taken up with promptness and courage. Yet the logical and at one time not unexpected result of such a policy—the gradual dissolution of the empire—has not followed. The commercial and maritime progress of other countries, the widespread interest in colonial affairs, the awakening of the East, the competitive spirit of the age, have created a new situation, in which the belief that the disunion of the empire is an inevitable result of national growth within its borders and carries no evil consequences has gradually lost its force. While there has been no desire to abandon the policy of freedom for individual development, the feeling has grown that, in the changed circumstances of the age, this policy does not satisfy every imperial need, and that some constructive ideal is required to supplement its influence. For the conception of the empire as a group of many communities, each having its own ends to realise, there has been substituted a conception of the empire as a whole, having common interests for the maintenance of which more adequate means of action need to be devised. The idea of federation, which had been growing in colonial politics, was thus sown in imperial politics, and showed its first form of life in a Conference of colonial premiers held in London in 1887. Too much was not attempted; but it was evident that the colonies were developing a sense of a united empire as distinguished from a controlling mother country which might become a creative political force. In 1894, a second Conference was held at Ottawa. It made a number of recommendations designed to promote the unity of the empire, of which the more important concerned the improvement of means of communication and the adoption of a policy of commercial preferences. As a result, the imperial Parliament removed such legislative restrictions as hampered the freedom of the colonies in this latter respect. A third Conference met in London in 1902, at which it was decided that the Conference should become a fixed institution and be summoned every fourth year. The Conference of 1906 took the name of Imperial Conference and gave to the greater colonies that of Dominion. Though the Conference has no continuous existence and has no executive power, its periodic assembly is a recognition of the fact that a new ideal of imperial unity has been born. The chief problems that it has discussed—imperial defence, trade relations, and means of communication—indicate the main lines along which an attempt has hitherto been made to realise this ideal. Perhaps the greatest advance has been made in the matter of defence. For a long time the feeling has been gaining ground that in this matter all members of the empire must accept a measure of responsibility and give their cooperation. In 1885 New South Wales sent a contingent to the Sudan and other Australian colonies prepared to do the same. During the South African War all the great colonies volunteered prompt and generous assistance. An attempt has been made by the Conferences to frame a general scheme of military defence. Moreover the Dominions have begun to accept a liability as regards the maritime defence of the empire. In 1902 several colonies made promises of annual contributions to the cost of the imperial navy. Australia and Canada have gone further and are organising navies of their own, as stated above. But the most striking manifestation of colonial interest in imperial defence was given by the large offers of assistance which the discussions of naval policy in the House of Commons in March, 1909, called forth from New Zealand and some of the Australian States. Much also has been done to facilitate intercourse between different parts of the empire by a reduction of postal rates, the laying of new cables, and the improvement of steamship services. But, in the matter of trade relations, a serious division of opinion has been apparent. The colonies, while not desiring an imperial Customs Union, wish to see imperial trade encouraged by a policy of mutual preferences; and, following the example of Canada in 1897, the greater colonies have granted preferences of varying amount and value to the mother country. The latter, adhering to Free Trade, has been unable to give any special advantage to colonial commerce; though a movement, initiated by Mr Chamberlain in 1903, to secure a change of her commercial policy which would make this possible, has received strong support. Thus, during recent years, in various ways a centripetal tendency has manifested itself in the development of the empire; but at the same time it has been controlled and limited by the strong instinct of autonomy and self-interest which actuates each member.

The story of progress, though not of change, is interrupted when we turn to the oldest centre of European colonisation—the islands and coasts of the Caribbean Sea. The nineteenth century has been a troubled interval in the history of most West Indian communities. New conditions have forced them to make considerable readjustment of the rigid social structure and limited economic interests which they had developed in different circumstances. As an ever-widening area for the production of tropical crops has been brought under cultivation, their commercial importance has waned, not only relatively but actually. Their history, at the same time, has lost something of the picturesqueness associated with its earlier chapters, though it has undoubtedly gained a profounder interest since the abolition of slavery gave to the negro some control over his own fortunes, and to both black and white the problem of cooperation presented itself under the new conditions of freedom. A great work of social and economic reorganisation thus forms the central thread of that history. On the political side it has much variety. If the great European Powers ceased after 1815 to make the West Indies a cause or arena of strife, yet the internal fortunes of most of the islands have been chequered and changing. Some communities have struggled for independence, some with it. In other cases, the Powers in possession have been labouring to adapt their colonial systems to modern democratic ideas. Everywhere the great problem has arisen of fashioning a government that, both in its local and central agents, should be wise and efficient, as well as just between race and race.

When, in 1834, the emancipation of the negroes was begun in the British West Indies it was intended that a temporary system of apprenticeship should break the step from slavery to freedom; but unforeseen abuses influenced the imperial Parliament to impose on the planters restrictions of such severity that, in 1838, they terminated all apprenticeship, and the great revolution was thus suddenly completed. Once set on foot, this movement inevitably spread through all these closely related islands. Through Haiti it had already passed, when the doctrine of the rights of man first entered the colonial field. In the Danish islands, a riot at Santa Cruz (1847) precipitated the grant of freedom. In Guadeloupe and Martinique, the concession was made in 1848, but a system of long contract service followed. In the Dutch islands, the negroes worked out their freedom between 1863 and 1873. In the Spanish islands, where

the negroes were fewer in proportion to the white population than elsewhere, and the relations between the two were on the whole better,
emancipation was delayed—in Porto Rico until 1873, in Cuba until 1886.

"A race has been freed, but a society has not been formed." In these
words Lord Harris, Governor of Trinidad, briefly expressed the problem
which confronted the West Indian communities.   The future status of
the negro and the maintenance of the plantations were both involved.
Free labour might have suited the planter as well as slave labour, had it
been obtainable.   But, where the negro could squat on fertile land and
maintain himself with little effort, he had no inducement to work on his
former master's estate.   In British Guiana, Jamaica, Grenada, and also
in the French islands, the tendency of the negroes to occupy small
holdings, quickened in places by the harshness of the planters, resulted
in the formation of a strong peasant proprietary, threatening the old
plantation system.   Scarcity of land prevented this development in
Barbados; and in the Dutch, Danish, and French islands labour laws
acted as a check.   While the negro, becoming wage-labourer or peasant
proprietor, was gaining in happiness and often in self-respect, the planter
was suffering, especially in the English islands.   His compensation for
the loss of his slaves had been inadequate, and the labour problem
presented the greatest difficulties.   In 1847, a second blow, scarcely less
heavy than emancipation, fell upon him.   The mother country adopted
a free trade policy, and in a few years his advantage in the English
market was taken away.

The resulting depression was rendered worse by a want of harmonious
cooperation between the imperial and colonial Governments in the
measures required to ease the process of adaptation to the new conditions; and with Jamaica and British Guiana there arose serious
difficulties, which for a time frustrated progress.   The mother country
assisted the colonies with loans of money, and recommended new forms
of taxation, improved methods of production, the importation of East
Indian coolies, and economy of expenditure, as well as legislation
regulating the condition of the freed negroes.   Under a system of
indentured labour, large numbers of coolies were procured, chiefly from
the East Indies, to supply the needs of the plantations—of whom many,
when the time of their service was completed, remained to settle in the
islands.   In British Guiana and Trinidad, whose decline was arrested by
this means, the Asiatic element in the population has become very
considerable, and it is important also in Jamaica, the Leeward and
Windward Islands, and Martinique.   Where the labour difficulty could
be overcome, the sugar industry generally continued, though to a
diminished extent and with declining profits.   Many large estates were
broken up into small holdings, on which, in some parts, the negroes
raised the cane to supply central crushing mills.   In some of the British
islands the white population began to decrease, while the coloured

increased rapidly. The French planters were assisted by preferential tariffs which preserved for them the home market; the Spanish by the great natural resources of Cuba, its proximity to the United States, and easier labour conditions. In the course of time, however, all began to feel the competition of the beet-sugar industry of Europe, encouraged as it was by bounties. In some islands sugar cultivation was abandoned or still further reduced, and an attempt was made to develop other industries. The cultivation of cocoa was introduced into Grenada and St Lucia, and extended in Trinidad. In St Vincent arrowroot became an important product, in Antigua cotton, in Montserrat limes. Jamaica, never exclusively dependent on sugar, now further developed such subsidiary industries as the cultivation of tobacco and coffee, the cutting of dyewoods, and ranching, and after 1870 built up a considerable fruit trade with the United States. British Guiana was assisted in 1889 by discoveries of gold in a branch of the Mazaruni river. Thus, while cane sugar remained the staple crop, flourishing in favourable conditions, struggling and declining in unfavourable, miscellaneous exports began, after 1880, to form an increasing proportion of West Indian trade.

The last decades of the century were, however, a period of severe trial for most of the British islands. From 1880 to 1895, the price of sugar fell continuously. British Guiana, Barbados, and most of the Windward and Leeward Islands, still mainly dependent on this one crop, were especially affected. In 1897, a Royal Commission was appointed to enquire into the causes of the depression and to consider the general prospects of the islands. The Commissioners found that the competition of bounty-fed sugar was chiefly responsible for the serious position to which the cane sugar industry was reduced, and they made many recommendations designed to broaden the basis of economic life in these colonies. As a result, agricultural experiments have been made with a view to the introduction of new crops, particularly cotton; and the fruit trade with the mother country has received a great stimulus by the establishment of a direct line of steamers between Bristol and Jamaica subsidised by the imperial and Jamaican Governments. The export of bananas and limes from Jamaica and Dominica to the United States has become of great value, while the sugar trade with Canada has increased as a result of the preference granted by the Dominion to British-grown sugar. In 1902, also, a Convention of the Powers interested, with the exception of Russia, arranged for the abolition or restriction of the bounty system from 1903 onwards. Unhappily, the natural calamities— hurricane, earthquake, and volcanic eruption—to which the West Indies have always been exposed have recently occurred with great frequency, and added to the strain upon the resources and endurance of the islands.

The course of their political development may now be briefly traced. Save for the troubles of which Cuba has been the centre, the West Indies have since 1815 enjoyed conditions of peace and security unparalleled in their modern history. The transference of some of the Spanish islands to the United States has been the principal territorial change. The United States, ever since their colonial days, have maintained a close commercial connexion with the West Indies; and, in the period of expansion before the Civil War, the annexation of Cuba was one of the ambitions of the southern leaders. During the years of reconstruction, expansion became unpopular, and opportunities of making acquisitions in the West Indies were rejected. American interests in Cuba, however, increased, and the unhappy misgovernment of that island by Spain brought on the War of 1898, which resulted in the disappearance of Spain from the Caribbean Sea and the acquisition of Porto Rico by the United States. Cuba has not been annexed, as such action would have a disquieting effect in South America, and there is a difficulty in receiving Cuba into the Union either as a State or as a Territory. But the United States demand that the Cuban Government should maintain security of life and property, and liberty. The possessions of England remain the same, though she has been involved in some territorial controversies. The prolonged dispute with Venezuela concerning the boundaries of British Guiana, which assumed great importance on the intervention of the United States, was settled by arbitration in 1899, and the larger part of the disputed territory was awarded to British Guiana. Other boundary disputes between French Guiana and Brazil (1900), and British Guiana and Brazil (1904), were settled by the same means.

Wars of independence and a social revolution that has reacted on political life have rendered the internal political history of the islands more perturbed. The once rich and fair island of San Domingo, the pearl of the Antilles, has been the seat of two communities, of which one has seen a prolonged experiment in negro self-government, with European political institutions. San Domingo, the Spanish part of the island, declared its independence of Spain in 1821, only to be merged in the Haitian republic in 1822, and freed itself from Haiti in 1844 to fall again under the dominion of Spain in 1861. The independence which it recovered in 1865 it vainly sought to surrender to the United States in 1871. Since that date it has enjoyed a quieter existence under a liberal constitution. The history of Haiti has been even more chequered. An arbitrary and corrupt Government, republican only in form, and disturbed by periodical revolutions, of which one in 1849 resulted in the establishment of a brief empire, has scarcely commended the great experiment which it represents. The exclusive policy, which has virtually shut out the foreigner, has not only restricted the development of the island, but, by banishing the influence of a stronger race more experienced in the practice of self-government, seems to have prevented the negro from making political and economic progress.

The sentiment of Cuban independence was born in the great colonial revolution at the end of the eighteenth century, though it languished during the golden days of Cuba's prosperity which followed. When the emancipation of the slaves began in the other islands and prosperity declined, the Creole chafed more and more against a corrupt and extravagant Government, as also against a colonial system under which privilege and office were reserved for the Spaniard. In 1868 a civil war broke out and lasted ten years, with the result that Spain so far modified her policy as to grant Porto Rico and Cuba a barren right of representation in the Cortes of the mother country. In 1895 further changes were made, including the formation of a Council of Administrators to advise the Governor; but the civil war was renewed, until the intervention of the United States, in 1898, secured the independence of the island. Guadeloupe and Martinique became departments of France, sending deputies to the French Parliament, and, with the introduction of universal franchise and other democratic measures, political power in the islands passed into the hands of the negroes. The English, as in previous centuries, found it a difficult problem to organise the government of their scattered islands on the most efficient and economical basis. The federation of all the islands has been considered; but they lack that sense of union which would bring about a demand for it, and the possible increase of expense has seemed a serious obstacle. There has thus been a tendency to make small groups. The Leeward Islands have generally formed a single Government, and in 1871 their federal constitution was revived. The Windward Islands form another, of which in 1833 Barbados was made the seat of government, to be separated again in 1885. With them Trinidad and Tobago were also for a time included; but they were detached in 1876, united as a single Government in 1889, and incorporated as one colony in 1899. British Guiana, like Jamaica, has always formed a separate Government. British Honduras was detached from Jamaica in 1884.

Contrary to the general tendency of our colonial policy since Lord Durham's famous Report, there has been a contraction rather than an extension of self-government in the West Indies. Though the negro has in many parts made economic progress, he has not yet exhibited much political capacity; and neither the small white population, nor the untutored black, can be given dominion over the other. This has been the principal cause of retrogression. Declining prosperity and particular occurrences have also played a part. In 1865 the negroes of the south-east of Jamaica rose in rebellion, complaining of oppression and insecurity in the tenure of their lands. The insurrection was suppressed by Governor Eyre with promptitude and vigour, but with an undue and unjust severity which necessitated his recall. After this deplorable event, the historic legislature of the island, whose latter years added little glory to a notable career, surrendered its continuance in favour of a stronger Government. Grenada and St Vincent lost their representative institutions in 1876. The Constitution of Honduras, modified in 1853 by the admission of elective members to the Council, was modified again in 1870 by their exclusion. Thus, at the present time, the Bahamas, Barbados, and the Bermudas, where there has been no change, have representative institutions without responsible government; British Guiana, Jamaica, and the Leeward Islands, a Legislative Council, partly elective and partly nominated; the Windward Islands, British Honduras, Trinidad, and Tobago, Legislative Councils, composed partly of official and partly of nominated members. In British Guiana the Council is known as the Court of Policy, and, in the discussion of finance, is joined by some additional elective members in a sitting known as the Combined Court.

The course of West Indian history seems isolated from that of other colonies during recent years. There is no unity of development discernible in the variety of its details. The West Indies have ceased to be the scene of activity and strife which they formerly were, and which other new lands have become, while they exhibit no large result achieved for civilisation by the efforts of centuries. Their greatness was so much the greatness of a single industry that they seem to have shared for a time in its eclipse. Nature, which limited their chances of progress, circumstances which divided them from each other, human policy which gave them an unfortunate social structure, forbade them to aspire to the greatness and national being which other groups of colonies have attained. A scattered group of islands, in the possession of different Powers, inhabited by different races, each strong in local pride, though their problems have been similar, they have never risen to a sense of common interest nor desired the unity which they could not attain.

From this survey of the development of the older colonies we may now turn to consider the colonies and dependencies which have recently been founded as a result of the revived activity of the Great Powers. The new movement has not involved much migration of Europeans, nor, again, has it consisted in the mere establishment of commercial stations; but, as was the case in India, it has brought about the partition and subjection of vast tropical areas with immense populations. Commerce rather than settlement has been the chief end in view, and dependencies rather than colonies have been formed. Africa and the Pacific have been the spheres of action. Such a process has many aspects of interest. The story of the partition can be told; the attempts to utilise the conquered territory explained; the policies of the various Powers towards the native peoples indicated; but we cannot yet estimate the significance for Africa and Europe of this new and close contact between them.

For centuries, colonisation in Africa was confined to the coast. Though the Portuguese traversed the continent from Angola and Mozambique, their occupation of the interior was never effective, and even on the coast their claims were ill-defined. Africa possessed few attractions. It had been drawn into the life of Europe only because it offered harbours on the route to India, a source of supply for the rough labour needed in tropical colonies, and a scanty trade in such commodities as palm-oil and gold-dust.   During the middle years of the nineteenth century, France was active and ambitious in Africa.   She established her power in Algeria, and, extending her influence also along the Senegal to the source of the Niger, planned the union of these dependencies in a great West African empire.   In South Africa England had strong colonies; but, with a dominion vaster than public sentiment approved, she refused to extend her dominion northwards where Dutch exiles were planting new States. In her West African settlements she took little interest.   Their prosperity had departed with the abolition of the slave trade.   They had become little more than places of repentance, where something might be done to atone for the wrongs of which they had been the scene.   Gambia, Sierra Leone, the Gold Coast, and Lagos, which was acquired in 1861, formed the group; from all of which, save Sierra Leone, England trusted ultimately to withdraw.   But destiny was too strong for her.   First the Danes (1850), and then the Dutch (1871), handed over their forts, and thus left her for the time the only Power established on the historic Guinea coast.   As the trade in tropical commodities increased, the English developed commercial interests on the Niger mouth, in the Cameroons, and in Zanzibar, which interests German merchants came to share.

Meanwhile, a generation of great explorers was opening the way for the rapid occupation of Africa.   When Livingstone died in 1873, the chief problems of African geography were near to their solution.   Stanley, De Brazza, Thomson, and other bold travellers, completed the work.   The courses of the Niger, the Nile, and the Congo were made known, and the commercial value of the interior regions of a neglected continent was revealed.   Signs of a new period dawning followed each other quickly. The English changed their policy in South Africa;. the French increased their activity in West Africa.   In 1879, King Leopold of Belgium formed the Brussels International Association for the exploration of Central Africa.   This body divided itself into national committees, of which the Belgian concentrated itself on the Congo and prepared the way for the Congo State. ˙ In 1882 England commenced that fateful intervention in Egypt which led on to a protectorate, to the conquest of the Egyptian Sudan, and the control of the upper waters of the Nile.   Most significant of all was the entrance of Germany into the colonial field.   In that country the prophets of colonisation had often lifted up their voices, but the disciples had been few and scattered, until the great impulse which brought her political unity concentrated in this field also her divided energies.   In 1878 the German African Society, and in 1882 the German Colonial Society, were formed.   The arguments of merchants with substantial interests in Africa, the commercial needs of a great empire, the course of events in Africa, at last convinced Bismarck that the time had come for action.   In Damaraland and Namaqualand German missionaries had taught, and German merchants traded, for forty years; and, since Great Britain hesitated to undertake the responsibilities of government outside of Walfisch Bay, a German protectorate was in 1884 proclaimed over the remainder of the coast. Togoland and the Cameroons also were immediately afterwards annexed; and Great Britain, thus anticipated in several quarters, now hastened to extend her sovereignty over the mouths of the Niger and the Oil rivers. It was in these circumstances that in 1884 an international Conference assembled at Berlin to consider certain African questions. The main interest was concentrated on the Congo. The State which King Leopold had created received recognition, and the Congo basin was declared open to the trade and navigation of all nations. All the Powers concerned bound themselves to suppress the slave trade. They declared occupation of territory to be valid only when effective, and they defined a "sphere of influence" as an area within which some one Power possessed a priority of claim. This preliminary agreement facilitated very much the peaceful settlement of the subsequent territorial controversies.

Africa is not divided into very clearly marked geographical areas, but the problems of partition have had certain definite centres and are capable of being grouped. West Africa, the western Sudan, and the Niger basin, formed one sphere of operations; the Congo basin another; the upper Nile and the region of the great lakes a third; Africa south of the Congo and the lakes a fourth. Outside of these there remain Morocco, the Mediterranean littoral, Abyssinia, Somaliland, and the surrounding islands. In West Africa, the French, extending along the Senegal to the upper waters of the Niger, broke the power of the independent native States, once part of a great Moslem empire in Central Africa, which barred the way, and in 1881 established a protectorate over the left bank of the upper Niger. They occupied points on the coast between the existing settlements of the English and Portuguese, which they linked up with their acquisitions in the interior. They overthrew the kingdom of Dahomey in 1892–4, and in 1893 entered Timbuktu. Thus, by their earlier and superior energy, they secured the upper Niger and much of the country within its great bend; while closing the door on the expansion of the English and Portuguese settlements, whose natural hinterland this would have been. On the lower Niger the course of events was different. The English merchants established there united in 1879 to form a single Company, which, after a severe struggle, defeated and bought out a rival French institution. By Treaties with the Sultans of Sokoto and Gando (1885), it secured access to the Benue and Lake Chad, which the Germans, operating from the Cameroons, were preparing to close. In 1886 it received a charter of incorporation as the Royal Niger Company, and undertook the task of penetrating and administering an immense country. A triple contest had now begun for the trade of the central Sudan. The French from the west, the English up the Niger and Benue, the Germans from the Cameroons, all pressed towards Lake Chad, where they met, and, by a series of agreements between 1886 and 1906, divided their spheres of influence. England left to Germany the area between the Cameroons and British East Africa, which Germany divided with France, resigning to her the territory east of the Shiré and making her England's neighbour in Darfur and Bahr-el-Gazal. France thus gained the opportunity of extending her North African empire to the Nile and the Congo; but, while she linked up the French Congo with her other possessions, her advance to the Nile was frustrated by the simultaneous approach of the English southwards from Egypt.

Thus has North-western Africa been divided up. In the northern corner lies the untamed empire of Morocco whose trade and seaports have proved a dangerous cause of dispute amongst the Powers. Then Spain holds Tiris, and the English the river Gambia, though its trade is now largely in French hands; while, between Cape Roxo and the river Cajet, Portugal retains a last foothold on the coast which her navigators first explored. Save for these two places, the French hold all the coast from Cape Blanco to the English colony of Sierra Leone, now an important commercial emporium through which much trade with the interior passes. Liberia, a negro republic, adjoins it, while on the historic Ivory Coast the French again are established. The Gold Coast retains its ancient name, though it has added a considerable hinterland. It still yields gold with other more valuable products, but suffers from want of means of communication. In Togoland, as in the Cameroons, the Germans have made considerable progress. To the east lies the territory subjugated by the French in 1892–4, and east of that the colony of Lagos, now included in Nigeria. In 1900, the Royal Niger Company, after conquering the Sultan of Nupé in 1897, surrendered its political privileges to the Crown; and the vast areas which it had governed, together with Lagos and the Oil rivers, were formed into the two protectorates of Northern and Southern Nigeria. Shortlived as it was, it takes a place amongst the great commercial Companies which have extended and upheld imperial as well as trading interests in distant and difficult lands, in the face of severe rivalries and great financial difficulties. Enveloping Nigeria and the Cameroons as well as the older and smaller settlements, and stretching from the Mediterranean in the north and the Atlantic in the west to Darfur and the Congo east and south, sweeps the great dominion of the French, to whom has fallen the interior, immense in area though often of little value. In 1902, it was divided into five administrative territories, with a Governor-General resident at Dakkar.

Between the Portuguese settlement of Mozambique in the south and Somaliland in the north, the Sultan of Zanzibar ruled, having control of the coast and vague claims over the interior. The commerce of his kingdom was largely in the hands of English and Indian merchants, and its administration was in 1878, and again in 1881, offered to the British Government. In the partition of Africa, his territories have been divided between England and Germany. Though England and France had agreed in 1862 to recognise the independence of Zanzibar, German emissaries in 1884, taking advantage of the weakness of the Sultan's position in the interior, negotiated treaties with some of the inland tribes, and, in 1885, a German East Africa Company was formed to develop the territory thus acquired. About the same time a British East Africa Company was formed, and the two associations were soon in competition. An Anglo-German agreement in 1886 made the first delimitation of their respective spheres, and confined the Sultan's territory to a narrow strip of coast, of parts of which both Powers speedily obtained leases. A revolt of the coast population in the German sphere, lasting for two years (1888–9), resulted in the supersession of the Company by the imperial Government and the purchase from the Sultan of the leased territory (1890). The claims which the Germans had acquired on various parts of the coast and in the interior placed them in a position to circumvent the English on the north and west, and to gain access to the upper Nile. By an important agreement in 1890, which settled many difficulties, their sphere was more expressly delimited. They surrendered their claims on the coast between Witu and the river Jub. The northern boundary of their territory was carried from the Victoria Nyanza to the Congo State, excluding them from the upper Nile; and a line was drawn on the south from Lake Nyassa to Lake Tanganyika dividing their possessions from British Central Africa. The British Government declared a protectorate over the islands of Pemba and Zanzibar, and the dominions of the Sultan were thus finally partitioned.

While Germany thus withdrew from the contest for the upper Nile, France and the Congo State remained as rivals of Great Britain. In 1890, the British East Africa Company, which had received a charter in 1888, asserted its authority in Uganda—a country divided at the time by fierce feuds of a mixed religious and political character. The resources of the Company proved unequal to the task, and two years later it withdrew; but its action resulted in the proclamation of a British protectorate in 1894. In the following year, the Company, which had remained in control of the coast, sold its assets to the State, and the British East Africa Protectorate was formed. To this Company the British owe their position in East Africa, for, though it never prospered, it carried British influence into the interior, and, when it failed, stronger hands took up its work. England thus secured her position on the upper Nile, and, by leasing the Lado enclave to King Leopold, enabled him also to attain an end which he had sought since 1884. But the arrangement which had been made by the two Powers in 1894—that King Leopold should have the Bahr-el-Gazal basin and Great Britain a strip of territory between the Albert Nyanza and Tanganyika, linking up her East and Central African possessions—was rescinded, in consequence of the opposition of France and Germany. The attempt of the French to reach the Nile at Fashoda was foiled by the English conquest of the Sudan (1898).

The British East African possessions are now organised in the three protectorates of Uganda, East Africa, and Zanzibar. Experience has shown that East Africa is of more commercial value than Uganda, and, owing to its altitude, capable in part of European settlement. In 1895, the construction of a railway was begun from Mombasa to the Victoria Nyanza, which it reached in 1902. The possession of Uganda is of great political importance, since it both secures the command of the upper Nile and offers to the spread of Islamic movements the barrier of a Christian native State. The Germans have obtained a strong grip of their territory, where considerable economic progress has been made; but its natural advantages have not proved to be very great.

In the Congo basin, an international and half-philanthropic under-taking issued in the formation of an independent State, which, in the process of time, has become a Belgian dependency. The labours of English and American explorers prepared the way for its foundation ; but the State itself was organised by King Leopold, whose position as its sovereign was recognised by the Berlin Conference and the Great Powers. By successful war and more successful diplomacy, he enlarged its territories and raised its status. At the same time, he drew it into such close connexion with the Belgian kingdom, to which in 1889 he bequeathed it, that the expectant heir at last demanded a mismanaged patrimony. Its history would be a fine tale of European energy applied to the development of a tropical country, had not the work been marred by a cruel spirit of exploitation gaining the upper hand. The first ten years of its existence were a period of great activity, during which a marvellous change came over the land. Splendid pioneering work was done. Experienced missionaries and travellers explored the great streams. The drink traffic, the slave trade, and cannibalism, were much diminished. The ancient Arab dominion in Central Africa was over-thrown after a hard and costly struggle (1890–3). Routes of communi-cation were opened, and railway building commenced. A despotic system of government was organised with energy and skill. Under the King were three Administrators-General, of whom the Governor-General resided at Boma. At the same time, by successful negotiations with England, France, and Portugal, the frontiers of the Congo State were advanced to the Nile and rounded off on north and south.

So much enterprise in exploration, expansion, and economic develop-ment soon involved the Government in financial difficulties. The Belgian Parliament was on several occasions invited to make loans to the King, in return for one of which, in 1890, it was agreed that the Congo State might be taken over at any time in the succeeding ten years and six months—a stipulation of which the Belgian Parliament did not think it worth while to take advantage. In the same year the King obtained from the Great Powers a relaxation of the Berlin Act permitting him to levy import duties. Gradually, a new spirit asserted itself. The original ideals were neglected, in view of the opportunities of profit which economic development brought and the necessities which political progress created. Companies were founded to develop commerce, and large areas were placed under their control. The Government claimed monopolies in rubber and ivory—the staple commercial articles—and private trade dwindled away in a region that was nominally open to the enterprise of the world. At the same time, the international character of the State disappeared and Belgian officials displaced those of other nationalities.

But it was by its treatment of the native peoples that the Congo State attained that evil eminence which accumulating proof shows it to have well deserved. The system of administration lent itself to abuses. Large powers were devolved upon men not always adequately paid or capable of bearing their responsibilities. The supervision of their conduct in the interior was impossible from places so distant as Boma and Brussels. The native was wronged by the disregard of his system of landownership and of the tribal rights to hunt and gather produce in certain areas, as well as by a system of compulsory labour in the collection of produce on behalf of the State, enforced by barbarous punishment and responsible for continual and devastating warfare. In the large territories placed under Companies there was no adequate provision to prevent misgovernment, and in these the abuses were worst. The Berlin Conference ventured on a careless and unhappy experiment, when, without guarantee or security, it committed a mighty population to the care of an autocrat. In 1896 the Aborigines Protection Society took up the cause of the Congo native, and in 1904 a Congo Reform Association was founded; but diplomatic pressure produced little change. Finally, the Belgian Parliament taking up the question, the Congo State was in 1908 transferred to Belgium, and its rulers have thus become responsible to the public opinion of a nation.

Africa south of the Congo State and the great lakes has been divided between the Portuguese operating from their historic settlements, the English advancing northwards from Cape Colony, and the Germans. The ambition which the Portuguese cherished to unite Angola and Mozambique in a transcontinental dominion was frustrated by the activity of the English in Central Africa. Since 1878, English missionaries and traders had established interests in the region between Lakes Nyassa, Tanganyika, and Bangweolo. This region the Portuguese endeavoured to secure, and an important expedition was despatched under Major Serpa Pinto to extend their claims in the Zambesi basin (1889). In 1891, an Anglo-Portuguese agreement divided the disputed territory.

Mashonaland was secured to the British South Africa Company, and a British protectorate was formed in Central Africa, a large part of which was in 1894 added to the Company's sphere of operations. The share which Portugal has thus obtained in the partition of Africa, though not commensurate with her historical place in its occupation, has been more than commensurate with her capacity to develop its resources. Since the suppression of the slave trade, her colonies have not flourished, and they are now a burden on her finances. German South-west Africa has been already mentioned. The Anglo-German agreements of 1885 and 1890, and a German-Portuguese agreement in 1886, fixed its boundaries, bringing it at one point to the Zambesi. But the colony has proved expensive and disappointing. Namaqualand is dry and barren, though Damaraland is capable of development and, possibly, of European settlement. In 1904 a serious revolt of the Hottentots and Hereros arrested their progress, and has only recently been suppressed.

In the eastern horn of Africa Italy marked out for herself a sphere of expansion. Occupying first the bay of Assab in 1870, she secured her hold in 1882, and extended her influence along the Red Sea coast to Obok, where the French had established themselves in 1862. The dependency of Eretrea thus created proved expensive; but the Italians intended to use it as a base from which to penetrate Abyssinia. That mountain kingdom lay aloof and independent. In 1868 it had been involved in war with England. When the proud warrior king, Theodore, offended by the action of the British Government, threw the British consul and other European residents into prison, Abyssinia was invaded and Magdala stormed; but no lasting intervention followed. Italy was less happy. Near Adowah, in 1896, her forces suffered a disastrous defeat and her intention was foiled. Meanwhile, on the other side of the horn she established a protectorate over a large part of Somaliland, where she found a rival in Great Britain, with whom the country was divided. The prosperity of British Somaliland was disturbed by a destructive war, which broke out in 1903.

Such, in brief outline, is the process by which Africa has been conquered and partitioned. Africa has been an easy prey because of its divisions, its military weakness, and its low civilisations. Though no one of the incoming Powers has established its position without a struggle, only in Morocco and Abyssinia has the native opposition proved really formidable. More serious difficulties have been encountered in the settlement of rival claims. England and Portugal came to the brink of war over Central Africa in 1891, as did England and France over the Sudan in 1898, and France and Germany over Morocco in 1904. The wide field of enterprise which has given scope to the ambitions of every colonising Power, a spirit of reasonableness, and the definite principles previously agreed upon for the decision of doubtful questions, have made it possible hitherto to reach a peaceful settlement of all disputes. The political divisions have not been formed according to geographical divisions—no one of the great river basins belongs exclusively to a single Power—but exhibit a strange diversity, being, in each sphere, a resultant of the forces which historic position and, later, energy and foresight gave to the competing Powers. England owes much to the happy possession of points of access to the interior from south and north, much also to the energy of private persons acting singly or through Companies, and to the far-reaching conceptions of a few great leaders; as usual, she owes least of any Power to the direct intervention of Government. France, too, has expanded her rule from historic settlements, and owes her great dominion to the imagination which outlined, and the steadfastness which pursued, a vast ambition. The pertinacity with which the Germans discovered weak points in existing claims, the swiftness of their action, their unyielding diplomacy, have enabled them, while starting without advantages, to secure extensive possessions. Belgium owes her share to the activity of her late sovereign, who by benevolent profession rescued a mighty domain from the international scramble to transform it into an estate for private gain. The Portuguese hold, much diminished, the heritage bequeathed them from a distant past.

The necessity of making the tropical regions of the world contribute more largely to its general economic needs has called forth the great colonising movement which has subjected Africa, with its millions of inhabitants in their varying stages of progress, to European Powers. The contact of higher and lower civilisations, not simply in commerce but also in government, and in the economic development of the continent which has resulted, has necessarily raised far-reaching issues. But the work of conquest and political organisation is too recent for us to estimate its effects on the peoples of Africa, and that of economic organisation is but beginning. One general end the Powers have had in view—the suppression of the slave trade at its sources—now practically achieved after a century of effort. Domestic slavery—an ancient African institution—is a different problem, but it has been discouraged in lands under direct British government. Tribal life continues and is deliberately preserved. The transformation of the native economy has not been attempted. Whether desirable or not, it is beyond the strength of any Government yet established in tropical Africa. Economic development in most cases proceeds but slowly. Governments are poor, for their subjects are poor; and the problem of adapting taxation to the organisation of primitive peoples, though varying in difficulty, has nowhere been found easy. The immense task of associating the native in the development of the country on European lines requires so considerable a change in his ideas and life that it may take a long time to carry out, save where it is attempted by methods of compulsion which public opinion more and more decisively condemns. Yet, without the aid of the native, the value of these tropical regions to their European conquerors is much diminished. In Europe, the occupation of Africa has increased wealth and trade, and cheapened some of the comforts of life; what it will mean for Africa cannot yet be judged.

In another part of the world, new ground has been broken. The many archipelagos of the Pacific, discovered by Spanish and Portuguese navigators in the sixteenth century, remained, with the exception of the Philippines, neglected, until they were rediscovered, in the latter part of the eighteenth century, by rival French and English explorers who opened the Pacific once more to European enterprise. But, though Australia and New Zealand were colonised, the annexation of small groups of islands offered no advantage, and the Pacific Islanders continued to live their life in peace or war as was their wont. In time, however, missionaries penetrated into Hawaii, Fiji, the New Hebrides, and elsewhere; and, when Australia began the culture of cotton and sugar, labour traders visited the Loyalties, the New Hebrides, the Solomons, and other groups, to kidnap or hire the natives for work on the plantations. In 1864, France planted a penal settlement in New Caledonia, which she had annexed in 1853. German traders established themselves in Samoa, Fiji, the Caroline and Marshall groups, as well as in some of the larger islands off the coast of New Guinea. Thus, in various ways, the Pacific groups felt the touch of European life, and, becoming the scene of its competing energies, were partitioned and annexed. To this issue England led the way. In 1874, influenced by the abuses connected with the labour traffic, which required regulation and oversight, the commercial interests of Sydney, and the fear lest some other Power might anticipate her, she annexed the Fiji Islands, whose Governor was in 1875 created High Commissioner of the Western Pacific, with jurisdiction over British subjects in those parts.

In the ensuing thirty years, the Pacific was mapped out into spheres of influence and the smallest islands passed under the protection of some foreign Power. In 1878, the United States established a coaling and naval station at Pago Pago in the Samoas. Both English and French were interested in the New Hebrides, islands near both New Caledonia and Queensland; but for a time they were content with a policy of mutual exclusion, which in 1887 gave way to joint control. The French, meanwhile, turned to Polynesia, and annexed the Windward Islands of the Society group, to the intense irritation of New Zealand. Australia was more concerned as to the intentions of Germany in New Guinea; and, determined to forestall her, the Prime Minister of Queensland in 1883 annexed the non-Dutch part of the island to the British empire. The mother country repudiated the action. But Australian instinct had divined the truth; and in 1884 Germany annexed parts of northern New Guinea, Great Britain thereupon annexing the remainder. In 1885 and 1886, the three Powers with the chief interests in the Pacific came to a general agreement as to their respective spheres of influence. Germany mapped out a great area in Micronesia and western Melanesia in proximity to the historic possessions of the Dutch, including the Carolines, Marshalls, part of the Solomon group, and northern New Guinea. The French claimed a sphere of influence in Melanesia, of which New Caledonia was the centre, and another in Polynesia, with the Society Islands as its centre. The English sphere extended from south-east Melanesia and Micronesia over Polynesia, almost enveloping the French. Samoa and Tonga were for the time neutralised. In 1892 England annexed the Gilbert and Ellice Islands, in 1893 the southern Solomons, and in 1898 Santa Cruz and the Swallow group. In this last year Hawaii ended the vicissitudes of its political development and became a dependency of the United States. In 1899 Germany bought the Spanish rights in the Carolines and Pelew, and divided the Samoas, important for their harbours and situation, with the United States. Great Britain relinquished her claims in Samoa, in return for a greater freedom of action elsewhere, and proceeded to further annexations. She established a protectorate over Tonga, the Manahiki and Cook Islands, which latter two groups were in 1902 placed under the government of New Zealand. By a Convention of 1906 her joint control with France in the New Hebrides was continued and strengthened. Both Australia and New Zealand disclaimed responsibility for this arrangement, on the ground that they had been allowed no real opportunity of considering its terms.

For Great Britain expansion in the Pacific was a natural result of the commanding position which she held there; but her action was hastened by the competition of other Powers and the strongly expressed apprehensions of her Australian colonies. Other influences played a part. The protection of native peoples inspired the annexation of several groups, as also did the interests of imperial communications. A path of possessions across the ocean links up Canada and Australia, helping to guard a great commercial and telegraphic highway. Germany has sought to secure her commercial interests by political power, and to find in the Pacific, as in Africa, that open sphere for her colonial ambition which has existed scarcely anywhere else. The penal settlement of New Caledonia, commerce, and the protection of the natives, have induced France to make considerable efforts. In Hawaii and Tutuila America holds securities for her trade, and in the Philippines fruits of the only war which affected this great partition.

The majority of these islands are not, and perhaps will not be, extensively colonised by white men. In very few cases has any effective government been established. Annexation has generally meant the protection of white residents and, perhaps, the maintenance of order. Of the English islands Fiji and Tonga are securely held. Fiji is governed as a Crown colony, having since 1904 a Legislative Council with an official majority, on which two natives represent their race. Economic development has proceeded apace, and the colony has a flourishing trade with Great Britain and Australia. Coffee and cotton cultivation have given place to sugar and copra. In Tonga a native King still reigns, though a British Resident ensures an effective control of the Government. British New Guinea, now administered by the Commonwealth, has also made progress. In the eastern part gold has been discovered; but the west remains wild and unsafe. In the Solomons, two deputy commissioners control the labour traffic and exercise the functions of government along the coast. Of the French islands, New Caledonia remains a penal settlement under the control of a Governor and Privy Council; the Society group is governed from the beautiful island of Tahiti; the Marquesas are under a Commissioner. As in Africa, Germany has devoted great energy to the development of her possessions. Her protectorate of New Guinea includes her share of that island as well as the Bismarck archipelago. On the island a Company had control from 1885 to 1889, when it was bought out by the Government. Hawaii has made considerable progress since its annexation by the United States. In all the Pacific Islands the native population tends to decline in numbers—whether from disease, alcohol, change of habits, or the loss of freedom of spirit consequent on contact with the superior energies and faculties of the white race—though the principle of preserving and not destroying native institutions and tribal life has received general recognition.

In the midst of these new influences, yet not much affected by them, lie those groups of large and small islands which form the Dutch East Indies, always the most famous of Dutch colonies. Of recent years the reform of their colonial system has occupied the chief attention of the Dutch, rather than any great extension of their activity. They have modified their strictly commercial *régime* in sympathy with the changing spirit of the age, and have taken up something of the civilising *rôle* now assumed by colonising Powers. Abandoning the illiberal policy which guarded their islands as a government preserve, they have opened the door to private enterprise. At the same time, they have remodelled a fiscal administration resting on government cultures and forced services and substituted more modern forms of taxation. Before 1870, all the cultures had been abolished except those of coffee and sugar. In the succeeding twenty years, the transition from forced to free labour was made in sugar cultivation; the coffee culture still remains. As the Government withdrew from business, so it was able to enlarge its activities for the general good by developing an educational system and building railways. The changed conditions have encouraged economic progress. Individual enterprise and free labour have given more elasticity and strength to industry, with the result that the trade of Java has increased very much since 1870, though the sugar industry, here as elsewhere, has been depressed by a period of low prices. The Internal Possessions, Java with Madura, remain by far the most important of the group. They alone are securely held and effectively governed. The process of penetrating the larger islands has continued to be very slow. In 1899 the Dutch assumed direct control of western New Guinea, which they had previously ruled through the Sultan of Tidor. In Celebes only two Residencies, or provincial Governments, have been established, and the same number in Borneo, where Dutch rule is for the most part nominal. Some districts of Sumatra are effectively occupied; but the island is very little developed and its products are chiefly forest products. The Government remains highly centralised, and still endeavours to make these colonies what they have always been, save under exceptional circumstances—a source of profit to the mother country. Unhappily, a long war with Achin, which began in 1873 and continued for thirty years, has swallowed up recent surpluses.

The acquisition of a part of Borneo by Great Britain forms a singular story even in the varied annals of her colonial history. When, in 1833, the China trade was opened freely to British merchants, James Brooke secured a grant of land in Sarawak from the Sultan of Brunei, who had maintained his independence of the Dutch. Winning the confidence of the natives, he was offered and accepted in 1841 the Government of Sarawak, to which five years later Great Britain attached the island of Labuan, ceded to her by the Sultan as a naval station. Dignified, conciliatory, and sagacious, he was able to intervene between the two races inhabiting his kingdom, Malays and Dyaks, oppressors and oppressed, and, while guarding the privileges of the one, to secure the rights of the other. The complete success with which he solved the problem of governing these Asiatic peoples was witnessed in their devotion to him and his successors, as well as in the order and prosperity of this part of the island. In the course of time, another British subject acquired rights in the neighbouring territory of North Borneo, east of the river Kimanis (1878); and, in 1881, the British North Borneo Company was chartered. This Company, the first of the great modern chartered Companies, has been rather an administrative than a commercial body; and subsidiary Companies have been formed to carry on trade and agriculture. In 1888, its territory, together with Sarawak and Brunei, were placed under British protection. The Governor is appointed by a Court of Directors and approved by the Secretary of State; like the Rajah of Sarawak, he is advised by a Legislative Council of European officials and native chiefs. The administration of Brunei was, in 1906, surrendered by the Sultan to the Resident.

Such in its brief outline is the story of recent colonisation. The main course of the work accomplished has been directed by young communities controlling their own life. Yet, from any point of view, the whole development must be regarded as a marvellous manifestation of European energy. Europe has supplied the stream of emigrants and capital without which the new lands could not have achieved their rapid progress ; and it has continued, in the words of Adam Smith, to breed and form men capable of laying the foundations of new States.   The explorers, traders, and governors of recent times have paralleled the feats of their predecessors.   It is possible that their efforts will not bear equal fruit in the birth of European societies in other continents, since many of the lands occupied have proved unsuitable in climate to become the homes of white races.   In some new countries, moreover, the period of beginnings and experiment is not yet past, and it remains for the future to declare the form which their colonisation will take.   But, if in certain directions the efforts of the colony-builder have been yielding a diminishing return, the substantial result remains, that almost all the vacant lands and weaker races of the world have passed under the control of Europe and been drawn into its economic and political life.   The transformation in many cases of a commercial connexion into political sovereignty, and the consequent assumption of governing responsibilities over millions of people, constitute a change fraught with so great significance that its influence will only slowly be worked out.

The great power and prestige of Germany, and the exertions which she has put forth to increase her commerce and influence in distant parts of the world, give to her colonial experiments and policy a singular importance.   Her expanding population and industries have compelled her to seek outlets for her trade and people in oversea possessions.   But her struggle for unity delayed so long her entry into the colonial field that she has failed to acquire lands where white communities can be formed ; and her recent acquisitions have been for the most part trading and plantation settlements whence raw materials to feed her industries can be supplied.   Want of experience in dealing with primitive peoples has involved her in frequent and expensive wars; but, with conspicuous energy and system, she has applied herself to master the problems of colonisation and to develop the territories she has occupied.   Her great strength, power of organisation, and willingness to make sacrifices to achieve her purposes, mark her determined entry into the colonial field as one of the most pregnant developments of recent years.

Of less importance, but of great historic interest, has been the virtual withdrawal of one of the oldest colonising Powers.   The enduring work of Spain was done in the earlier centuries of modern colonial history.   After the loss of her great empire her energies slackened, though her name and power lingered on in the West Indies and the Philippine archipelago.   Here also, towards the end of the nineteenth century, she surrendered her place to an Anglo-Saxon Power of unresting activity and bold ideals.   It is possible now to look back upon her work without prejudice.   The first of European peoples to plant colonies in distant lands, she created and maintained her own policy in government and economics.   Her exclusive principles never commended themselves altogether to other Powers, and her system was not copied; but it will be admitted that she knew how to plant her civilisation wherever she held sway, and to secure her authority even when her strength and maritime greatness declined. Her dominion lasted long and died hard; today, in the two continents where it existed, several young nations own her their parent.

The last word may be of the British empire. The experience of the past has not been wasted on the mother country; and, with more fortune and greater wisdom, she has been steering through the difficult waters in which she formerly made shipwreck. Her colonial policy has been inspired by an understanding and a wise recognition of facts. Settlers in new countries form societies; such societies, as their strength grows, desire the control of their own life; common interests draw contiguous societies together, and union creates and fosters the sense of nationality. Perceiving the course of this development, the mother country has continually readjusted the ties that bound her to her colonies, so that they might be appropriate to the stage of growth which each colony had reached. Wherever possible, she has conceded to them the full control of their own affairs; and she has encouraged contiguous colonies to unite, so that in dimensions, resources, population, and economic strength, the indispensable material foundations of a self-governing State could be formed. Thus, an issue which once burst upon her with the suddenness of accident and disaster, rudely breaking the thread of her work and transforming its political significance, has since been sought and is in course of achievement, though in a manner that gives a greater freedom to natural processes of growth and saves the continuity and completeness of the work of the race, at once creating nations and retaining them in the unity of a great State. Slowly the British empire is shaping itself into a league of Anglo-Saxon peoples, holding under its sway vast tropical dependencies as well as many small communities of mixed race. Strong bonds of common loyalty, race, and history, as well as the need of cooperation for defence, unite the white peoples. But the course of progress has carried the empire to an unfamiliar point in political development. Loose and elastic in its structure, it may well take a new shape under the influence of external pressure, political and economic.

CHAPTER XXI.

THE REPUBLICS OF LATIN AMERICA.

(1)

HISTORICAL SKETCH TO 1896.

THE tendency of modern developments in Latin America has been indicated elsewhere; nor is it possible to narrate here the internal history of all these republics. Four of them demand separate treatment as possessing more distinct and significant histories: namely, the United States of Brazil, the United States of Mexico, the Argentine Confederation, and the Republic of Chile. The other countries may be very briefly treated, mainly in two groups: first, the group of five small States lying between Mexico and the Isthmus; secondly, the group of four extensive republics in tropical South America.

The five States of Guatemala, Honduras, Nicaragua, San Salvador, and Costa Rica, assumed upon emancipation the novel and inappropriate name of Central America, in order to suggest some geographical pretext for separation from Mexico. These States, owing to their situation near the shortest transcontinental routes, are prominent in the external relations of Latin America; but it would be useless to trace their relations with one another or their internal history, half tragical, half farcical, but always disorderly, except in Costa Rica, which has preserved a long tranquillity. Occasional and partial efforts towards a federation have hitherto been foiled by separatist tendencies, acting through a long and wearisome series of wars between Governments, besides civil wars and revolutions.

The vast tropical region of South America, intersected by the westward and southward curve of the Andes, is divided among four republics —Venezuela, Colombia, Ecuador, and Peru—which, though not homogeneous in character, may be grouped together in a historical summary. Bolivia, a fifth tropical State, can hardly be included in any historical classification, consisting largely as it does of a loose collection of Indian tribes, with a Government of European origin in the capital; thus, the history of Bolivia need only be touched in regard to its external relations, which have crushed it into remote interior forests and mountains and excluded it from direct access to the sea. The other four tropical republics have not yet emerged from the phase of internal struggles which followed on emancipation—struggles of personal ambition, of contests between centripetal and centrifugal forces, between progress and reaction, between clericalism and liberalism, between the rights of autocratic presidents to rule and the right of their subjects to revolt. The equilibrium, more or less stable, which has perhaps been reached in the temperate regions further south, has here been retarded by the large survival of indigenous Indians, by the large intermixture of negro elements, and by the absence of any considerable European immigration. Bolívar denounced the ignorance of his countrymen in words not quite inapplicable today :—" The majority are *mestizos, mulatos,* Indians, and negroes: an ignorant people is a blunt instrument for its own destruction—to it liberty means licence, patriotism means disloyalty, and justice means vengeance." The desire of every educated or half-educated man to live at the expense of the State is a fruitful source of disorder; for the educated classes lead the ignorant to civil war, ostensibly for the sake of principle, but, in fact, largely for place and profit. The intervals between these revolutionary episodes have usually been periods of autocracy, more or less complete ; and the character of the Government has been in fact the character of the reigning autocrat. The merits of these personal administrations are difficult to estimate ; but there is probably justice in the general opinion that the man who, by success in civil war, brings about a period of peace has served his country well, if only his government is moderately free from tyranny and selfishness. Thus Ramón Castilla, who in 1843, by victory in war, gave to Peru peace under his own government and generally guided affairs down to 1862, may, perhaps, be justly regarded as the best of Peruvian statesmen. Even Guzmán Blanco, who dominated Venezuela for twenty years (1870–89), and seems a perfect type of farcical immorality in politics, gave to his country peace and the opportunity of economic progress.

The written Constitutions of these republics are models of constitutional law, based upon European and North American experience ; and some real constitutional efforts may be traced from about the middle of the nineteenth century. One symptom of these efforts appears in the more definite adoption of a federal form of government by New Granada and Venezuela. New Granada in 1863 assumed the name "United States of Colombia"; but, during the conservative and clerical autocracy of Nuñez (1884–94), federal government was suspended.

One strange effort at reaction deserves mention. García Moreno, who was President of Ecuador from 1864 to 1869, and then, after an interval of disorder, ruled again down to his assassination in 1875, imposed upon the country a system of extreme ultramontane clericalism. He surrendered to the Church all ecclesiastical patronage, declared papal bulls to be valid without the "pass" of the Government, and forbade heretical worship. In fact, he induced the reluctant Pius IX to accept a supremacy over the republic of Ecuador such as the Papacy had scarcely possessed over any European monarchy in the Middle Ages.

The little State of Paraguay, chiefly inhabited by Guaraní Indians speaking their own language, has a terrible history. Its first dictator, Francia (1815–40), set the example of that brutal and capricious tyranny which was afterwards often imitated elsewhere. The third dictator, Francisco Lopez (1857–70), by his insane schemes of empire, ruined his country. In 1865 he invaded both Brazilian and Argentine territory. This drew upon him the combined attack of his three neighbours, Brazil, Argentina, and Uruguay : and the population of Paraguay was almost wiped out in five years of war (1865–70), which only ended with his death.

In Brazil, the Emperor Dom Pedro II was declared to be of age in 1840. The following decade was a period of pacification and slow progress, introducing forty years (1850–89) of internal order and peace, unparalleled in South American history, and accompanied by a great advance in economic prosperity. This peace and progress were largely due to the character of the Emperor himself, a kindly and slightly eccentric philosopher, devoted to the service of his people, careless of royal state, but shrewd enough in maintaining the monarchy, whose ultimate fate he foresaw. He used to call himself the best republican in his dominions, and might fairly have called himself the most republican ruler in South America. After some early and futile attempts to use English parliamentary methods, he exercised a paternal autocracy over subjects to be guided and controlled like children. The people were generally indifferent to forms of government; Ministers, deputies, and officials owed their positions to the Emperor, and representative institutions had no more essential reality than in the neighbouring republics. His foreign policy with regard to the river Plate was prudent and successful : Brazilian intervention led the way to the fall of Rosas in 1852, and definitely reestablished the threatened independence of Uruguay. The Paraguayan War (1865–70) could hardly have been avoided, but the chief burden fell upon Brazil ; whereas Argentina won the chief benefits from the opening of the river and the disappearance of a menacing despotism in the interior. Since that time the States touching the Atlantic have abstained from international wars, though they have not always observed strict neutrality in regard to the internal disputes of their neighbours.

The last twenty years (1870–89) of Dom Pedro's reign comprise two movements—the agitation against slavery, and the growth of republicanism. In 1850 the slave trade was abolished; in 1871 it was decreed that all children thenceforth born should be free ; between 1850 and 1887 the number of slaves fell from 2,500,000 to 750,000. But from 1884, the question of complete abolition agitated the country. Finally, during the Emperor's absence in Europe, the Regent, his daughter Isabel, forced through Parliament in 1887 a Bill for immediate abolition. The Emperor's fall was prepared by this grant of liberty to all his subjects and also by widespread apprehensions concerning the supposed absolutist and clerical tendencies of the heiress apparent, Isabel, and her husband, the Comte d'Eu. Republican doctrines had been gathering strength for a generation; the slaveowners were bitterly hostile to the Court; the people felt no enthusiasm for monarchy; and now Dom Pedro's failing health and deliberate neglect of precaution provided the opportunity for bloodless revolution. In 1889 a military conspiracy deposed the Emperor.

The country accepted with indifference the change from hereditary monarchy to military dictatorship. A federal Constitution was proclaimed for the "United States of Brazil"; but, in fact, General Fonseca, the leader of the recent mutiny, ruled as he chose, until he was induced, by revolt in the south and by the disaffection of the fleet, to resign in favour of the Vice-President, General Peixoto. The rigorous despotism of Peixoto provoked in 1893 the revolt of the *Gauchos* of Rio Grande do Sul and also of the fleet stationed at the capital. Although the insurgents disavowed royalist designs, there was obvious probability of an alliance between royalism and insurrection.

For six months, from September, 1893, the vast harbour of Rio was the scene of civil war. Warships of every maritime nation were present to protect their trade, and, in January, 1894, one of their commanders was at length provoked to take action by an attempt of the insurgents to prevent merchant-ships from approaching the custom-house. The insurgents having fired on three United States merchant-ships, the United States squadron, after ineffective remonstrance, followed by due warning to the insurgent admiral, cleared for action, and moved up to protect their merchant-ships. This menace sufficed to achieve its object. Six weeks later, the insurgent admiral, faced by overwhelming forces, took refuge with his men on board Portuguese warships, whose commander refused to give up the refugees. Peixoto, who had ruled by terrorism during war, was inexorable after victory. Numbers perished by sentence of Court-martial, and greater numbers were simply killed by soldiers, often after torture. Civil war, marked by indescribable atrocities on both sides, still dragged on in Rio Grande and was not finally closed till October, 1895.

Meantime Peixoto, at the close of his term of office in November, 1894, retired into private life and died six months later. It may be argued that he acted throughout with the simplicity of a soldier, and that, apart from his sanguinary methods, his stern maintenance of authority, even in defiance of law, was necessary to the subsequent peace and order of the country. Since his time, Presidents have been elected under official influence and have ruled under republican forms; but personal authority is mitigated by the vast size of the country, and by the semi-independence of the provinces.

A dispute with the Argentine Republic concerning the frontier in Misiones was settled in favour of Brazil in 1895 by the arbitration of the President of the United States. In a country comprising so vast a tropical region, not completely settled or even completely explored, other questions have naturally arisen concerning frontiers and even concerning authority over parts of its recognised territory.

Mexico between 1835 and 1848 lost more than half of her territory to the United States; the conquest of Texas, California, and New Mexico, has been related elsewhere. In 1838–9 occurred the incident known as the "pastry war," when a French squadron occupied Vera Cruz to claim compensation for injured French citizens, among them a baker whose shop had been looted. British mediation was offered, and a strong British squadron watched the proceedings of the French, who eventually accepted a settlement and evacuated the port.

Benito Juárez, a pure-blooded Indian and a man of disinterested character and high capacity, was President from 1858 to his death in 1872, and laboured through a period first of civil war and then of foreign invasion to extricate the country from the vortex of revolutions and *pronunciamentos.* From 1855 he pursued the "war of reform," improving the police and the educational system, abolishing the *fueros* or privileges of clerical and military Courts, depriving the Church of its lands and—with limited exceptions—of the power to hold land, disqualifying the clergy for office, suppressing convents, separating Church from State, and finally, in 1861, expelling the Papal Nuncio and five Bishops.

In 1861, in order to avert a joint French, British, and Spanish expedition against Mexico, Seward proposed that the United States should undertake to pay the interest on the Mexican debt, in return for a mortgage on a large part of the Mexican national property. This proposal aroused apprehension in Europe and was allowed to drop. The three European Powers then invited the United States to joint action in coercing Mexico to fulfil her financial obligations and protect foreign residents. The invitation was declined; and in January, 1862, Vera Cruz was occupied by 8500 Spanish and French troops with 700 British marines. The French and Spaniards advanced into the interior, negotiations meantime proceeding with the Mexican Government; but Great Britain and Spain soon withdrew, owing to ulterior French designs concerning the internal affairs of Mexico. The fortunes of the French and of the Emperor Maximilian in Mexico and the intervention of the United States are related in a previous volume of this *History.* Porfirio Díaz, in a published account of his political life, couples the two foreign invasions of Mexico, speaking of *la guerre d'émancipation et celles des invasions nord-Américaine et française.* The later external difficulties of Mexico have chiefly been questions with the United States about acts of violence committed on both sides of the frontier. In 1869, a mixed commission met to adjust these claims and finished its work, after many interruptions, in 1876. Meanwhile, the complaints of the United States continued; in 1877, United States troops crossed the frontier, and the two republics were on the verge of war. In 1882 it was agreed that troops of either State might cross the frontier to pursue Indians.

Porfirio Díaz, who has practically ruled Mexico since 1877, served as a youth against the invasion of 1847. From 1852 to 1861 he served Juárez with distinction in civil war; then, after an interval of political life, he raised troops against Maximilian, and commanded the Republican army which recovered the capital. In 1871 he led or joined a revolt against Juárez. On the death of Juárez in 1872, Díaz " pronounced" against his successor, and by the usual mode of successful rebellion became the most prominent and most indispensable man in the country. In 1877 he became President; for four years (1881–5) he held a subordinate post; but, since 1885, he has on each occasion been reelected President. He at once completed the anti-clerical work of Juárez by abolishing nunneries. Then, with stern but beneficent resolution, he closed the long era of rebellions and revolutions, and suppressed disorder by means of an improved police, inflicting summary retribution without excessive recourse to tribunals. In fact, his methods of thwarting attacks on his power have not differed from those employed by other American autocrats. The difference lies in character and intention, and of him it may be said, as Bacon said of Henry VII, that " he drew blood, as physicians do, rather to save life than to spill it." Thus, though disorder and revolt are repressed by terror, his authority rests not upon terror, but upon a general loyalty which seems to approach enthusiasm. Whether he is training the heterogeneous population, largely Indian and half-caste, for a more constitutional system, or whether an autocratic successor will have to be found, is a matter for conjecture.

Chile has a distinct history. Her civil wars have been short, definite in aim, and conclusive in results. The Constitution of 1833 has been more than a mere form, although parliamentary institutions have generally been used and guided by an official oligarchy surrounding the President. After the Liberal insurrections of 1851 and 1858, this system was modified in a constitutional direction. Then came the dispute with Bolivia and Peru; but the reform and anti-clerical movement was growing and achieved some triumphs after the Peace of 1883. At last, in 1886, a coalition of Liberal groups raised to the Presidency a vigorous and capable reformer, José Manuel Balmaceda, who (ten years earlier) had formulated a programme of electoral liberty, municipal and local independence, and separation of Church from State. Balmaceda proceeded to use his brief opportunity, abandoning part of this progressive programme and exerting all the influence of the presidency to achieve the rest, striving at the same time to weld all the Liberal groups into a party united for his support. The result was a rapid succession of Liberal Cabinets of various complexions, a hostile majority in Congress, an attempt to rule through irresponsible Ministers, and, finally, a split between President and Parliament. Balmaceda observed the letter of the law down to January 5, 1891. Then came an immediate pretext for the revolt which had been long prepared: Congress having refused to vote supply, the President decreed the continuance of taxation. Next day the fleet revolted in support of the Chambers against the President. For six months there was serious fighting, with much bloodshed; the war ended with the victory of Congress, followed by the resignation and suicide of Balmaceda.

Public attention in Europe justly regarded this civil war with unusual interest. The sincerity and public spirit of Balmaceda gave dignity to the contest, and, on the other hand, the struggle was a real war between Congress and President, between an oligarchical parliamentary system and a ruler attempting to extend democracy through autocracy. Profound principles, as well as personal ambitions, were at stake. The result has been that Chile continues to be the most aristocratic and the most tranquil of South American States, possessing a Congress which is a real power and maintaining clearer social distinctions than her neighbours. There has been little European immigration, and the manual labour of the country is done by Chilian peasants, largely of half-Indian origin; but the educated classes received a strong infusion of European blood both before and during the struggle for emancipation, and these classes have aimed, with some success, at a cultured European character, both social and political.

The external relations of Chile are largely concerned with Peru. In 1863 a Spanish squadron, claiming reparation for injured Spaniards in Peru, occupied the Chincha Islands. Peru, after some negotiations and an internal revolution, made an offensive alliance with Chile, Bolivia, and Ecuador against Spain. The Spanish squadron, having suffered some losses, bombarded the defenceless Chilian port of Valparaiso, but failed in an attack upon Callao. Hostilities then ended; and, some years later, peace was formally concluded by Spain, first with Peru, and then with Chile.

The War with Spain closed for a time the dispute in progress, since 1843, between Chile and Bolivia concerning their frontier in the desert of Atacama, which had proved valuable from its deposits of guano and nitrate. Conventions, concluded in 1866 and 1874, were successively broken by Bolivia, acting with the secret support of Peru.

Finally, in 1879, the outbreak of hostilities between Chile and Bolivia led to a Chilian declaration of war against Peru. This war, which marks an epoch in the use of ironclad ships, opened with a decisive naval victory for the Chilians, followed up by the invasion of Peru. At a conference held in October, 1880, through the good offices of the United States, Peru rejected the Chilian terms. In January, 1881, Chilian troops entered Lima ; but, as in 1821, Peruvian resistance continued in the interior after the fall of the capital and the collapse of regular government; and it was not until October, 1883, that an improvised Peruvian Administration submitted to the demands of the conquerors. By the Peace of Ancón the province of Tarapacá was ceded to Chile, and parts of two other provinces were ceded provisionally for ten years, their ultimate destiny to depend on a *plébiscite* of the inhabitants. These districts have since remained in Chilian hands. The War left Peru in a state of collapse. Bolivia was obliged to accept an arrangement which left her land-locked, Chile occupying her Pacific coast.

An old question concerning the Argentino-Chilian boundary in Tierra del Fuego and the southern end of the Continent was settled, after ten years of dispute, by the Treaty of 1881, which granted to Chile both shores of Magellan Straits, the control of which passage is, in Chilian opinion, hardly less essential to the national security of Chile than is the control of the Isthmus to the United States ; it was stipulated that the Straits should never be fortified and should always be open to ships of all nations. The same Treaty declared that, northwards from latitude 52°, the boundary should "pass along the highest crests of the Cordillera which divide the waters." This settlement was inconclusive, since the watershed does not coincide with the highest peaks. Chile claimed the watershed, which in Patagonia lies far east of the peaks ; Argentina claimed the highest peaks, some of which stand upon Pacific islands. After ten years of exploration and argument, the two republics were on the verge of war in 1895. Again, in 1898, war was imminent owing to a third question, concerning the boundary in the Puno or plateau of Atacama. But the moderation of the two Presidents, Roca and Errazuriz, led to arbitration. The Atacama question was settled by a tribunal sitting in Buenos Aires, consisting of a Chilian, an Argentine, and Buchanan, United States Minister in Buenos Aires. Buchanan solved the difficulty promptly by dividing the disputed line into sections, proposing that a vote should be taken upon each section, and then ensuring a majority upon each section by his own vote. The main question was submitted to the sovereign of Great Britain ; but, as the arbitration tribunal in London was concluding its labours in 1901, both republics resumed warlike preparations. British diplomacy did its utmost to calm animosity, and King Edward VII intimated that, unless these preparations ceased, he must withdraw from the arbitration. The award was given in 1902 and was peaceably accepted.

CH. XXI.

In Argentina, the dictator Rosas (1833–52), reigning through terror in Buenos Aires, dominated the other provinces, claimed ineffectively authority over Paraguay, and, after 1840, strove to reduce to his authority the republic of Uruguay, which had been declared independent by the Argentino-Brazilian Treaty of 1828, concluded through British mediation. These efforts have a double importance : in the first place, they mark the failure of an attempt resembling in some ways (though with differences of motive and character) Bolívar's design to include in one federation a vast group of provinces possessing a certain geographical or historical unity ; in the second place, they constitute a most significant phase in the relations of Latin America with the maritime nations of Europe and with the United States.

In 1838, a French squadron, claiming reparation for the losses of French citizens, blockaded the Argentine coast ; an offer of the United States Minister in Buenos Aires to negotiate a pacification was declined in turn by both sides ; but in 1840 France, occupied with the Egyptian crisis, withdrew the blockade and concluded with the Argentine Confederation a Treaty which bound that Confederation to recognise the independence of Uruguay, as established by the Treaty of 1828. Thus, in 1840, France, in a manner, pledged herself to support Uruguayan independence, as Great Britain had done in 1828. Meanwhile, Oribe, President of Uruguay, having been defeated and replaced in the Presidency by Rivera, a pastoral chief of the old Gaucho type, took refuge with Rosas. Brazil supported Rivera as representing Uruguayan independence, while Rosas, refusing a proffered Anglo-French mediation, proceeded to use the fugitive Oribe as an instrument for the subjection of Uruguay. In December, 1842, Oribe, at the head of an Argentine army, acting professedly as legal President of Uruguay, but in fact as a military lieutenant of Rosas, defeated Rivera, occupied almost all Uruguay except the capital, and began the nine years' siege of Montevideo, which was defended by a "foreign legion" of Frenchmen and Italians, organised by French naval officers. The French and British Ministers in Buenos Aires demanded in vain of Rosas the cessation of war.

In November, 1843, Rosas declared a "modified blockade" of Montevideo, a confused arrangement, easily evaded ; but, in January, 1845, he decreed a "rigorous blockade," which the French Admiral refused to recognise. Thereupon, the United States naval commander, Prendergast, declined to recognise the blockade, unless equally enforced against all nations, whereas Brent, the United States chargé d'affaires in Buenos Aires, recognised it. Two years later, George Bancroft, as Secretary of the United States Navy Board, reprimanded Prendergast for his refusal to recognise the blockade. Prendergast, in his apology, professed himself unable to understand the error of claiming for his own countrymen the exemption which had been claimed for Frenchmen, adding that, at any rate, he had duly recognised the later Anglo-French blockade.

In April, 1845, Gore Ouseley and Baron Deffaudis reached Buenos Aires upon a joint Anglo-French mission to effect a pacification, on the ground that Great Britain and France were pledged by the Treaties of 1828 and 1840 to maintain Uruguayan independence. This mission demanded the recognition of Uruguayan independence, the raising of the blockade of Montevideo, an amnesty to Argentine refugees and (as an immediate preliminary) the withdrawal of Argentine troops from Uruguay. The proffered mediation of Brent, United States chargé d'affaires, was declined by Ouseley. In July Rosas' Foreign Minister, being pressed for cessation of hostilities, refused to withdraw the troops, and demanded, as a preliminary, the participation of Brent in the negotiations, and the recognition of the blockade. Thereupon, Ouseley and Deffaudis withdrew to Montevideo. On July 22, the English and French Admirals seized off Montevideo the Argentine fleet (part of which was added to a defensive Uruguayan flotilla commanded by Garibaldi); and, in September, they declared a blockade of the province of Buenos Aires. Brent, on the part of the United States, refused to recognise this blockade; but Prendergast, the United States naval commander, recognised it as valid. In November an Anglo-French squadron forced, with some loss, the passage of Punto Obligado, a fort commanding the mouth of the Paraná, convoyed a merchant fleet up the river, and aided insurgents against Rosas in Corrientes.

The Anglo-French blockade of Buenos Aires had lasted twenty months —Oribe, meanwhile, continuing the siege of Montevideo—when, in May, 1847, Lord Howden and Baron Walewski arrived on a second Anglo-French mission of pacification. The United States Minister in Buenos Aires gave a banquet in their honour and proposed the toast of speedy success to their mission. An armistice arranged by Howden and Walewski was refused by the Montevidean Government; whereupon Howden raised the blockade of Buenos Aires, so far as England was concerned, and withdrew from all further intervention, on the ground that the Montevideans were "entirely controlled by a foreign garrison," meaning the French legion. The French blockade still continued; but the United States Minister at Rio now wrote to Rosas that Great Britain, Brazil, and the United States ought to cooperate against France, since the armed mediation was unjust and irregular both in policy and in manner.

In April, 1848, a third Anglo-French mission of pacification under Gore Ouseley and Baron Gros also failed; but, in June, 1848, the French in turn raised their blockade of the Argentine coast, only maintaining the blockade of the Uruguayan ports occupied by Oribe. In 1849, Great Britain concluded a treaty of peace with the Argentine Confederation, which undertook to withdraw the Argentine troops from Uruguay so soon as the French Government should disarm the foreign legion defending Montevideo, evacuate both republics, make a treaty of peace and abandon its hostile attitude. Great Britain in turn recognised the

CH. XXI.

Paraná and Uruguay rivers as interior waters. Thus Great Britain dissociated herself from France, recognising the right of Rosas to take his own course in the river Plate, and ceased to consider the struggle as a genuine international war.

Meanwhile, general hatred was preparing the fall of Rosas (all the independent politicians and all the high-spirited youth being in exile at Montevideo); but the immediate cause of his fall was the jealousy of certain provincial Governors, formerly his own creatures. In 1846, Urquiza, Governor of Entre Rios, revolted, allying himself with Brazil and Montevideo. In 1851, in conjunction with a Brazilian army, he defeated Oribe in Uruguay. Then, supported by the Brazilian fleet, he led 24,000 men (the largest army hitherto assembled in South America) against Rosas; who, deserted by half his troops, was beaten at Monte Caseros and spent the remaining five-and-twenty years of his life farming in England.

In December, 1852, President Fillmore, in his message to Congress, stated that, in compliance with the invitation of France and England, negotiations were in progress for a treaty between the United States and the States of the River Plate. Finally, in July, 1853, by identical Treaties signed simultaneously with France and England, the Argentine Republic granted, "of its sovereign rights," the free navigation of the rivers Paraná and Uruguay to the ships of all nations. A fortnight later, a Treaty of friendship, commerce, and navigation was signed with the United States without any mention of the freedom of river navigation, which had already been secured for all the world by Anglo-French force and diplomacy.

This long episode, extending from the Treaty of 1828 to those of 1853, but really introduced by the diplomatic activities of Castlereagh and Canning, is most significant in regard to the external relations of Latin America. England and France played in the river Plate the part taken by the concert of Europe in the Levant. The attitude of the United States was so indeterminate that their envoys on the spot could not use their opportunities: their diplomatic representative and their naval commander took exactly opposite action in 1845, and their Government did not decide between them for two years. The United States Government, indeed, in one despatch to its envoy, hinted at the necessity of opposing any permanent violation of American soil. But its agent heartily welcomed Anglo-French efforts at pacification; and, when England desisted and declared that Montevidean resistance was the work of France, the United States Minister at Rio proposed that the United States should join with Brazil and Great Britain to thwart France and play the part of "European Concert." Then Brazil, a State monarchical but American, having an immediate interest and an undoubted right of intervention, concluded the task which had been dropped by Great Britain and France. Finally, the United States Government in 1852–3, with a public acknowledgment of gratitude, followed the lead of Great Britain and France. The whole episode, if it be compared with simultaneous events in Texas and Mexico (1835–48), illustrates the comparative insignificance of United States interests in the river Plate fifty years ago; indeed, the silence of United States historians regarding these affairs sufficiently indicates that, in the middle of the nineteenth century, the history of their country is not concerned with the southern hemisphere; for the actions of Guizot and Aberdeen are easily ascertained, and Rosas published in English, French, and Spanish a full documentary history of these events down to 1849.

From 1852 to 1860, Urquiza was President of the Argentine Confederation, making his provincial capital, Paraná, the seat of federal government. The province of Buenos Aires, meanwhile, almost formed a separate republic, aiming either at supremacy over the other provinces or at secession. The other provinces would not accept this supremacy and could not permit secession, since Buenos Aires was the channel of nearly all external communication, commercial and diplomatic, and contained nearly one-third of the population.

In 1861, the struggle between "capitalism" and "provincialism" came to a head. General Mitre led a long-prepared revolt of Buenos Aires against the national Government of Urquiza, and was victorious. Buenos Aires became once more the capital, and Mitre, the historian of South American Emancipation, became first " Constitutional President" of the Confederation. But the struggle reopened, and continued down to the " revolution" of 1880, when the province of Buenos Aires was deprived of all chance of supremacy by being separated from the capital. Since that time, the city of Buenos Aires has formed a federal district under national control. This arrangement was largely the work of General Roca, the soldier who had defeated the revolt of 1880. He had distinguished himself in 1878 by leading a successful campaign of conquest or extermination against the Indians, by which the habitable limits and the economic value of the national territory were enormously increased ; and now, assuming the presidency (1880–6), he proved himself the most astute and capable of Argentine politicians and the chief agent in securing a closer union of the provinces through the consolidation of national government. He was President again in 1898–1904, and has been for a generation the strongest force in the country.

But the reactionary government of Roca's successor, Celman (1886–90)—together with a serious financial crisis in 1889—produced, in 1890, another revolt, which, after sanguinary but inconclusive fighting, compelled Celman to resign. There have since been several revolutionary outbreaks in the provinces, sometimes due to the arrogant and lawless attitude of provincial Governors ; but, in a large sense, the national peace has been maintained, and the country has advanced both in an economic and in a political sense. The Argentine plains have attracted an immense European immigration, giving to the country, and especially to the capital, a certain cosmopolitan character which is not unfavourable to the maintenance of public order, although it is hardly favourable to the growth of a healthy civic sentiment pervading the whole community. The capital, with its million of inhabitants, is far the largest city in the southern hemisphere. The large European immigration, the spread of tillage, the advance in material prosperity, the growth of commerce and of wealth, are influences which, making revolution difficult and costly, favour stability and order.

In short, the two most southerly republics have cultivated, not without success, something of a European character. While differing in character from each other, they are no less distinct from their northern neighbours, and may fairly adopt a different attitude in their external relations. A Colombian historian remarks that the attitude of the United States towards their tropical neighbours is due to the fact that these countries are not European communities, whereas the United States are a European community. These conditions do not equally apply in the southern hemisphere.

The chief factors in the external relations of Latin America are the intimate and long-standing connexion of those countries with the Mediterranean lands and with Europe generally, and that statement or tendency of United States policy known as the Monroe Doctrine. With the acquisition of Louisiana and Florida, the United States became the most important Power on the shores of the great inland sea which forms the Mediterranean Sea of the New World. Thus, the interest of the United States in the coasts of the Caribbean Sea has a distinct history of expansion and self-assertion; but her relations with South American States not touching that sea—particularly with those situated in the southern hemisphere—fall into a different category and illustrate the fact that those southern countries have a much closer connexion, racial, historical, and commercial, with Europe than with the United States. In fact the two American Continents, throughout their history, have both usually faced towards Europe and not towards each other. The river Plate is, by sea, geographically as near to Bordeaux or Southampton as to Washington or New York, and in effect much nearer: at the present time, United States diplomatists and officers find that the most convenient route from New York to Buenos Aires is through Southampton. The suggestion that Colombia, Argentina, Paraguay, and Chile, belong to the same political system and must have the same external relations would resemble (so far as geography goes) a suggestion that Morocco, Mozambique, the Transvaal, and Damaraland belong to the same system and must have the same external relations. Whereas the relations of the United States with the countries of the southern hemisphere form a vague, intermittent, and inconclusive diplomatic story, hardly to be traced more than half a century back and showing no clear basis of consistency, on the other hand their relations with the countries touching Caribbean shores form a history of striking events and decisive acts, moved by a fairly continuous and steady policy during a hundred years.

From 1803 to 1821, the acquisitions of the United States were wrung from the Spanish monarchy. But Monroe's message of 1823, which forbade the spread of any European or monarchical system in America, was followed in 1826 by a United States veto on Mexican or Colombian designs for the liberation of Cuba—a veto which forbade the extension of the republican system in America over the dependency of a European monarchy. This is a significant episode in the deliberate and steady expansion of the United States at the cost of Latin America, since already United States policy imposed sacrifices on republics actually existing. Cuba had possessed a close geographical and political connexion with the Mexican viceroyalty, and Cuban emancipation seemed to be the natural corollary of continental emancipation. Thus, this incident of 1826 introduces the series of events whereby, between 1835 and 1848, the United States absorbed more than half the territory of the Mexican Republic.

After the acquisition of California with the Pacific coast in 1848, the security of inter-oceanic communication across the Isthmus became a paramount question for the United States. In 1846, New Granada guaranteed by treaty the right of way across the Isthmus to the United States, which in turn guaranteed to New Granada the neutrality of the Isthmian road and the right of sovereignty and of property. The railway from Colón to Panamá, begun in 1850, was finished in 1855; but, in 1854, the Isthmian road was so insecure that New Granada sanctioned the formation of a guard of foreign residents for the summary removal of criminals. The Territory of Panamá, which had revolted from New Granada in 1830 and was actually detached from that State for a time in 1840–2, was formed in 1855 into a State of the New Granada Confederation, with autonomy and a separate legislature; in 1862 it assumed the style of Sovereign State of Panamá, but did not secede from the Confederation. Disturbances, such as are frequent in tropical America, were not unusual here.

The Isthmian policy of the United States had to reckon with the strong position of Great Britain in that region, and also with the possession of Cuba and Porto Rico by Spain. The British settlement of Belize (British Honduras) was too distant to be dangerous; but the recent British seizure of the Bay Islands, and the British protectorate over the Mosquito Indians, which had been lately strengthened, alarmed the United States. Actual possession placed Great Britain in a strong position for negotiation; but United States diplomatists showed short-sighted haste in the concessions which they granted in the

Clayton-Bulwer Treaty (1850), dealing with "any ship canal which may be constructed...by the way of the river San Juan de Nicaragua." The two Powers bound themselves never to obtain or maintain any exclusive control over the ship canal, never to erect or maintain any fortifications commanding the same or in the vicinity thereof or to colonise or exercise dominion over Nicaragua, Costa Rica, the Mosquito coast, or any part of Central America; and never to make use of any alliance, connexion, or influence with any of these States to obtain any unequal advantages in regard to commerce or navigation through the said canal. It was added that "the United States and Great Britain having not only desired...to accomplish a particular object but also to establish a general principle, they agree to extend their protection...to any other practicable communication...across the Isthmus...and especially to the inter-oceanic communications...which are now proposed to be established by the way of Tehuantepec or Panamá."

By this Treaty the United States tied their own hands for the future, and successive Administrations for fifty years attempted to ignore or modify the Treaty. On the other hand, the interest of Great Britain was to regard the Treaty as a final settlement and ignore the existence of any further question. Moreover, Great Britain unwittingly assumed the position of champion of the sovereign rights of New Granada and (in certain contingencies) possibly of other tropical republics also.

But this Treaty also marks the beginning of a British tendency to recognise the predominant interest of the United States round the Gulf and Caribbean Sea—a tendency which (as the logical result of the events of 1775–83) makes the United States the heir of British interests in those regions as of British predominance in North America. Before 1850, the two Powers had recognised common interests and, upon occasion, had exercised a kind of dual concert for the maintenance of tranquillity. But after 1850, Great Britain began voluntarily to recede from that position. Thus, in the acrimonious disputes whether the stipulations as to acquisitions in Central America were retrospective (as the United States urged) or only prospective (as Great Britain maintained), Great Britain finally gave way, surrendering the Bay Islands to Honduras and the Mosquito coast to Nicaragua by the Dallas-Clarendon Treaty of 1856, which finally took effect in 1860. President Buchanan declared that the United States were satisfied with that adjustment. But, twenty years later, New Granada having granted to a French company for 99 years the exclusive right of making a canal, President Hayes in a special message to Congress stated: "The policy of this country is a canal under American control." Between 1880 and 1883, despatches from Washington to London attempted, first, to ignore the Treaty, then urged that it was a temporary arrangement for a specific object, and that the United States would not perpetuate any treaty "impeaching our right and long-established claim to priority on the American Continent," and cited the Monroe Doctrine against its provisions. Successive British replies, first, pointed to the existence of the Treaty, then to the provisions for its perpetuity, and then to the fact that, in 1850, the United States Government had not considered itself precluded by the utterances of President Monroe from making the Treaty. Yet, in 1895, 1897, and 1899, Congress, ignoring the Treaty, authorised Commissions to enquire concerning the feasibility of a canal and (on the third occasion) to negotiate with Central American countries for control of the land to be traversed by the canal. Finally, Great Britain in 1901 receded from her passive position of adherence to existing engagements by concluding the Pauncefote-Hay Treaty, which abrogated the Clayton-Bulwer Treaty. The deference shown by Great Britain to the United States in the Venezuelan dispute of 1896, and the diplomatic attitude of Great Britain during the Spanish-American War of 1898, are further symptoms of the tendency of her statesmanship to abdicate in favour of the United States her position in those regions.

A long-standing question concerning the boundary between British Guiana and Venezuela became more pressing after 1880. Great Britain repeatedly declined, not indeed the principle of arbitration, but the scope of arbitration proposed by Venezuela. In 1887, President Blanco demanded arbitration concerning everything west of the Essequibo river. Great Britain assented as to part only, alleging the rest to be indisputably British. Thereupon, Blanco broke off diplomatic re-lations. In 1895, an incident in itself insignificant and afterwards separately adjusted, that is to say, the arrest of British officials by the Venezuelan authorities, precipitated the intervention of the United States, upon the implied invitation of Venezuela. A despatch from Secretary Olney to Lord Salisbury declared that "distance and 3000 miles of intervening ocean make any permanent political union between an European and an American State unnatural and inexpedient....The States of America, south as well as north, by geographical proximity, by natural sympathy, by similarity of Governmental Constitutions, are friends and allies of the United States....Today the United States is practically sovereign on this Continent, and its fiat is law upon the subjects to which it confines its interposition....There is a doctrine of American public law...which...requires the United States to treat as an injury to itself the forcible assumption by an European Power of political control over an American State."

Lord Salisbury in reply denied that the Monroe Doctrine was inter-national law or applicable to this particular case. President Cleveland then submitted the correspondence to Congress, with a message which implied that Great Britain by an extension of boundaries was taking "possession of the territory of one of our neighbouring republics." He added the words: "The Monroe Doctrine finds its recognition in those

CH. XXI.

principles of international law which are based upon the theory that every nation shall have its rights protected and its just claims enforced."

The United States Government appointed a Commission to investigate the dispute between Great Britain and Venezuela. This Commission never reported, for Great Britain now concluded at Washington a treaty of arbitration with Venezuela. The Arbitration Court, sitting in Paris, decided generally in favour of Great Britain: but this is an insignificant part of the episode. Its real significance lies in the fact that Great Britain, after denying the right of the United States to intervene, nevertheless accepted their intervention: in fact, the United States assumed, with British consent, a position in the Caribbean lands resembling that claimed in the eastern Mediterranean by the Concert of Europe. Thus both the tendency and the successful assertion of United States policy achieved a novel and striking development, of profound significance for the republics of Latin America. Opinion in those republics universally approved the action of the United States in this instance.

It may be argued that, international engagements alone being binding, diplomatic precedents have no existence; that Cleveland and Olney themselves tacitly dropped their extreme claims; and that any future case must be decided on its merits both by the United States and by any European Power concerned. Nevertheless, the fact remains that the position assumed in this instance has been considerably strengthened by later events, has been not only recognised but actually supported throughout by the attitude of Great Britain, and has never been seriously challenged by any European Power. As Canning foresaw, the destiny of the tropical republics of America depends on the relations between Great Britain and the United States.

The history of the Clayton-Bulwer Treaty and of the Venezuelan dispute illustrates the development of the Monroe Doctrine between 1850 and 1900. An arrangement, concluded " as a matter of principle " by the United States, in 1850, and declared, in 1860, by the President to be satisfactory, was, in 1880, declared by the United States to be inconsistent with " a doctrine which has for many years been asserted by the United States. This sentiment is properly termed a doctrine, as it has no prescribed sanction and its assertion is left to the exigency which may invoke it." This admission by the United States Secretary of State of the development of doctrine does not imply any large inconsistency in foreign policy: it merely signifies that national policy has advanced with changed conditions, and requires restatement, involving diplomatic contradictions for which it is easy to find precedents. But these contradictions preclude any suggestion that this sentiment or doctrine is an immutable principle or even a part of international law. Such a view would give to any nation the power to modify or interpret international law to suit its own emergencies. Thus, the defect indicated by Calvo in the Monroe Doctrine, that it did not forbid the acquisition of American territory by a European Power through war or treaty, was remedied in 1870 by Grant's presidential message: "I now deem it proper to assert the equally important principle that hereafter no territory on the Continent shall be regarded as subject to transfer to a European Power." Grant also officially asserted that "The time is not so far distant when, in the natural course of events, the European political connexion with this Continent will cease." This declaration anticipates the startling restatement of the Monroe Doctrine by Olney in 1895. But, obviously, there is a wide difference between diplomatic representations and historical conclusions. Since United States historians have generally declared the Monroe Doctrine to be a part of national policy, not of international law, it is needless to elaborate this point.

As to the meaning of the Monroe Doctrine for the other American republics, its tendency may be indicated, but not its scope and limitations: for, obviously, every future emergency will require a separate answer to the question whether national policy counsels action or inaction. It is, however, certain that, although the Monroe Doctrine has not protected these republics from American aggression, such as the advance of Chile upon Peru or of the United States upon Mexico, it has protected them from European aggression. On the other hand, the United States have never denied the right of a European State to make war on an American State, and have not always openly opposed even armed coercion, provoked in time of peace by breaches of public engagements. The United States have never claimed that American republics should escape the consequences of disregarding international engagements or international comity; but the question remains doubtful how far in such cases they are to be left directly exposed to European resentment, or how far the protection of weaker States is to involve coercion and police interference on the part of the United States.

(2)

THE INTERNATIONAL POSITION OF THE LATIN AMERICAN RACES.

The battle of Ayacucho (1824) marked the end of Spanish domination in continental America. It lasted eighty minutes, during which the final blow was dealt to the empire reared by Spain in America, which covered an immense territory and had endured for over 300 years. A Spanish victory at Ayacucho might have meant the reconquest of the lost colonies for Spain. The War in Spanish America was a civil war. The Spaniards had many adherents and partisans amongst the natives, and the floating population—indifferent, and so far as it could be, neutral—would have followed in the wake of victory as the waters the sloping ground.

Emancipation thus achieved meant the establishment of numerous sovereign nationalities, shortly thereafter recognised by foreign Powers—in the first place by the United States and by Great Britain. The new States adopted in their Constitutions and their laws the model and the principles of the Constitution and the laws of the United States. On either side of the Atlantic, the friends of liberty built great hopes on the birth and growth of so many new countries devoted to the republican form of government, of which two experiments had been then recently tried: one in the United States, which still flourished and prospered, a sign of hope in the eyes of men; the other in France, which, born in the midst of tempest and uproar, after a short and chequered career, had given place to a military despotism, destined, in its turn, to be superseded by the old monarchical form of government. The success obtained by the United States seemed to justify the hope that the new American republics would, in their turn, follow a similar prosperous and harmonious development in the path of history. Such expectations were not warranted by the circumstances.

The life of the English colonies of New England had prepared them for liberty. The colonial system of Spain had not admitted of the development of any elements of self-government or of civil liberty. Spain herself was an absolute monarchy, and she could not give what she did not possess. The new nationalities, in their recently acquired independence as towards the mother country, very soon belied and disappointed the prophecies and the hopes so fondly entertained at the hour of their struggle for emancipation.

A state of civil strife and revolution, now open and acute, now latent and simmering, prevailed on the Spanish American Continent, with varying degrees of intensity, during the better part of the remaining seventy-five years of the nineteenth century. The era of revolutions seems to have come to a close, or to have greatly abated its manifestations, within the last two decades; yet trouble is always ready to break out, and the tradition of the past still justifies distrust.

Some of the Latin American States have reached a surprising degree of material prosperity, especially Argentina in the southern, and Mexico in the northern, half of the Continent. Chile and Uruguay come next, and the steady prosperity and progress of Chile is more satisfactory and less disquieting than the advance of Argentina, which rather resembles a flood than beneficent irrigation. Peru may be reckoned next, whilst the remaining States—Ecuador, Colombia, Bolivia, Paraguay, Venezuela, and the Central American Republics—must still be counted as more or less doubtful, and as included within the political storm-belt of the American Continent. Revolutions have been far less frequent in Brazil than in other Latin American countries, and the republic has achieved during the last few years a degree of progress and prosperity bidding fair to surpass that reached by Argentina and Mexico.

Count Aranda, one of the Ministers of Charles III of Spain, in a memorial addressed to his master in 1783, foreshadowed, with prophetic insight, the future development of international life on the American Continent, and the hegemony that would be exercised by the United States of America. These are his words:

"This Republic (the United States of America) has been born, as it were, a pygmy; she has needed the help and the assistance of no less than two such powerful States as France and Spain, in order to conquer her independence; but a day will come when she will be a giant, a veritable awe-inspiring colossus in those regions; she will then forget the favours that she has received; she will only think of her own interest and her own convenience.......The first step of the new nation will be to seize Florida, so as to dominate the Gulf of Mexico. She will then conquer New Spain and the vast empire, the defence of which will be rendered impossible to us, as we shall not be able to struggle against a powerful nation, established on the same continent......."

To prevent the dire possibilities so vividly described, Count Aranda proposed the creation of three autonomous kingdoms, into which the Spanish dominions in America should be parcelled, under the sceptre of Princes of the Bourbon family, and linked together under the hegemony of Spain, thus maintaining for Spain and for her people, in Europe and in America, the reward of centuries of endeavour, sacrifice, and heroism, which had been coupled, unfortunately, with blind and irremediable maladministration. Aranda's prophecy has become a living fact, one of the most momentous facts of the world's life in the present and for the future.

Although unrecognised in Europe and in America outside of the United States (for recent explicit recognitions, as that of Brazil, do not imply a general change of ostensible attitude), the Monroe Doctrine has been a paramount and decisive factor in the growth and development of national and international life on the American Continent. It does not signify, nor stand for, a compact between the United States and other nations; it is not an agreement entailing rights and obligations; it is the expression of the will of the people of the United States, and thus subject to modification or expansion. Its importance therefore depends on the power of the United States, which their geographical position and the condition of their neighbours render unassailable by land. The Doctrine has grown in power with the nation itself, and has steadily gained fuller and more conscious acceptance by the American people year by year. Its influence is bound to become more relentless and more neglectful of the claims and the convenience of others, as opposed to those of the United States, than it has been in the past. From the time of its first enunciation, the Doctrine has been a paramount and decisive factor in the development of American nations.

The Spanish American republics, in common with Brazil, share

CH. XXI.

44—2

certain general conditions as to area, population, and national necessities, intimately connected with their political integrity, and their material and moral development. According to the most generous estimates, the total population of continental Latin America does not exceed 70,000,000 inhabitants; these are organised in seventeen different States, all labelled republics. Two or three of these are small in area; all the others own vast territories, and the disparity between their actual population and the population which might live and thrive on their soil is conspicuous. Either Mexico or Colombia, Venezuela, Peru, or Argentina, could alone contain and support the whole of the population now scattered from the northern boundary of Mexico to the extreme southern limit of Patagonia.

The seventeen Latin American nations are sovereign States, recognised as such by the other nations of the world. This recognition, however, is a convention which would not, and could not, stand the stress of the real requirements and ambitions of the powerful. To the more or less congested nations of the Old World, the holding of such vast territories under the dominion of communities lost, so to speak, in their immensity must ever appear as an anomaly, a temptation to conquest. The colonising spirit of Europe has never been so active and aggressive as during the nineteenth century, the very epoch during which the Latin American nations became independent. There is no available corner of land, no matter how remote, in Asia or in Africa, no island however small or insignificant on any ocean, outside the waters of the American Continents, that has not become the possession of a European Power, or has not been brought under a protectorate or into the sphere of influence of one of those Powers. The lands under the political dominion of the Latin American nations may be equalled in fertility, natural wealth, and abundance of mineral deposits elsewhere on the surface of the globe; but they are nowhere surpassed. The coasts on the two oceans are generally provided with numerous safe and commodious ports; in the southern Continent there exist wonderful networks of navigable rivers, facilitating access to the very heart of the Continent, and spreading in all directions to the inviolate forests and boundless prairies. The mountains teem with all the mineral substances known to man; gold, silver and platinum are found in the spurs of the Cordilleras and in the main ranges, and gold, especially, in the low valleys and in the beds of the rivers and streams.

The powerful nations of Europe would naturally aspire to establish in this rich Continent colonies that should be an extension of themselves, and new centres of wealth and prestige. Notwithstanding these powerful motives, no European colony has been established in America since 1823. The weak Latin republics—weak by comparison with their potential aggressors—many of them discredited by constant misrule, and continuous disturbances, hold to this day—save what has been incorporated

by the United States—the same territories as when they became independent nations.   They owe this immunity from European conquest to the
Monroe Doctrine, which, however, has not protected them from the
United States themselves, as Mexico and Colombia know to their sorrow.
The door to the American Continent, or to the American islands, for
purposes of conquest or colonisation, is shut to Europe.   The overwhelmingly superior force of the United States, as compared with the
other nations of the American Continent, makes all resistance impossible.
The special advantages of position and unlimited resources of the
United States, coupled with the rivalries of the European Powers
among themselves, preclude all idea of successful European intervention
against them.   The Monroe declaration, therefore, stands as the supreme
law in international matters on the American Continent, North, Central,
and South.

Since the days of their War of independence with Spain, the people
of Spanish America had looked upon the United States with admiration,
and even with gratitude for the moderate portion of sympathy shown to
them, which did not take official form until 1822, when the struggle had
lasted ten years, and the final victory of the rebellious colonies seemed
assured.   The identity of political ideals, irrespective of the diversity of
conditions, tended to strengthen the bond of sympathy amongst the
Spanish Americans towards the United States; whose institutions were
practically copied, so that the American Constitution was reedited,
with variations according to circumstances, in each one of the Latin
republics.

The political boundaries of the old Spanish administrative sections
were adopted for the new nations that had superseded them.   Owing to
the vastness of the territory, and to the scarcity of population, the exact
boundaries in each case had not been defined with absolute precision ;
furthermore, seeing that, except for Brazil, the demarcations of territory
did not signify difference of political dominion, since everything belonged
to Spain, it is not strange that they should have been somewhat vague
and open to controversy.   In this there lay a source of danger to the
peace of the Continent.   Fortunately, the boundary questions, though
at times they have almost brought about war, have been peacefully
settled, generally by foreign arbitration, and, where they remain still
undecided, there is little doubt that a solution of a similar kind will be
found, as the precedent is too firmly established for any other course to
be deemed possible.

The achievement of emancipation, and the adoption of a constitution
and laws, were but preliminary, though essential, acts in the life of the
new nations.   As already stated, internal affairs did not run smoothly
for a long period of years, nor can it be said that their present course is
unrippled in all Latin American countries.

The republican form of government, " of the people, for the people, by the people," is that established in the letter of the written law, throughout the Latin American Continent; such, doubtless, is the ideal of the people's endeavour; but in practice a great deal is still lacking. Some of the Latin American nations have turned back towards absolutism, without ceasing to call themselves republics. In the countries where such a thing happens, the will of the people is not allowed to find utterance; public power is wielded by one man styled "President," who retains office for life, if he can. No attempt at the establishment of a hereditary dynasty has been made of late years; yet the Presidents of the type described above exercise a more arbitrary power than any European monarch of the present day. In a few instances, these despotisms have brought about an end—at least for the time being— of the former revolutions and disturbances. In Mexico, the material prosperity achieved under this kind of despotism, which is a special product of Latin America, has been so great, that it has blinded the mind of freedom-loving men in other countries to the inherent curse that lies at the root of all despotism—never so baneful as when it masquerades as liberty and democracy.

From the very beginning of their life as independent nations, the Latin countries of America have been borrowers of money. Even before the War with Spain had come to a close, Colombia and the province of Buenos Aires had obtained loans in the London market. Latin America to this day requires foreign capital to develop its natural resources, to build its public works, and, not unfrequently, to supply the requirements of its public treasury, for purposes of administration or of armament. European capital flows, and has flowed, to Latin America since the first loans contracted in 1820, either in the usual commercial and banking form, or under government guarantee, in one form or another. In this latter case, the advances made by a foreign country become a powerful international force, which cannot be ruled out by political declarations or doctrines, even though they be so elastic and uncompromising as the Monroe Doctrine. Thanks to the capital received from abroad, through private enterprise or official guarantee, Latin America, from Mexico down to Argentina and Chile, has constructed its railroads and its ports, its public works of all descriptions, and has developed its industries, agricultural or manufacturing, with a rapidity and to an extent, in some cases, unparalleled in the history of the world. The capital thus employed has been furnished almost exclusively by Europe, with hardly any participation by the United States. The official debt of Latin America to Europe, that is to say, the debt guaranteed by the Governments of the respective countries, amounts today to at least £500,000,000. The capital invested by Europe in private enterprises, mining, agricultural, industrial, of navigation, banking, etc., may be safely reckoned at double that amount.

Failure or loss in private undertakings does not necessarily nor usually entail international political results, when they arise from normal causes; default in or repudiation of public debts may lead to serious international complications, of which instances have already presented themselves; furthermore, such monetary claims against a debtor nation seem to lend themselves conveniently to the disguise of imperialistic endeavours, not openly avowed as such on account of the Monroe Doctrine. In 1903, Germany, Great Britain, and Italy, carried out a naval demonstration along the coasts of Venezuela, in the course of which they exercised acts of warfare, such as the seizure and sinking of ships, the shelling of ports, and the establishment of a general blockade. The alleged reason for such proceedings was the refusal or unwillingness of Venezuela to pay certain pecuniary claims of subjects of the attacking Powers. It would have fared ill with Venezuela if the United States had not intervened, advising the allied Powers that no permanent seizure or occupation of territory in Venezuela would be permitted. Faced by this declaration, and all that it implied, the three Great Powers reluctantly put to sea, and the claims were submitted, under the auspices of the United States, to special International Commissions at Washington, and to the Hague Permanent Court, by which tribunals they were settled in due course.

Two remarks appear pertinent in this case: first, that it may not be altogether wrong to suppose that the collection of debts from Venezuela was the ostensible, but not the real, motive. In all probability, the main and underlying aim was to test the Monroe Doctrine, which, had it proved to be less rigorous, might have opened an era of conquest—or, at least, of colonisation by purchase, or by some other peaceful means—on the American Continent, to those who might consider themselves as left out in the distribution of Asia and Africa. Secondly, that the awards of the arbitrators—the International Commissions and the Hague Court —whose decisions are beyond suspicion of bias in favour of Venezuela, throw a lurid light on the action of the Great Powers; where tens of thousands were asked for, at the cannon's mouth, only hundreds were allotted.

In 1904, the creditors of the republic of Santo Domingo urged the Governments of France and Germany to collect by force the amounts claimed by them from the recalcitrant republic; the United States intervened, and eventually undertook the direct administration of the revenues of the republic, apportioning them between the creditors, and the payment of the expenses of public administration.

In the possible cases of default, or repudiation, of its foreign debt by any Latin American country in the future, and of a declaration by the Government whose subjects the creditors may happen to be, of the intention to collect by force of arms, the two cases just cited may form precedents, extending the Monroe Doctrine far beyond the intentions of its originator. In this, its latest aspect, intimately connected with the ebb and flow of life, economic and fiscal, and with the vicissitudes of commerce and industry, its importance as an international factor greatly surpasses its former possibilities.

Driven from all her possessions, on the American Continent, Spain retained after 1824 the islands of Cuba and Porto Rico. Bolívar, the victorious leader and founder of the republics of Colombia, Peru, and Bolivia—the first of which, in 1832, divided itself into the three republics of New Granada, Ecuador, and Venezuela—conceived the idea, in 1826, of an alliance with Mexico, to wrest from the Spanish mother country the scanty remaining shreds of her once boundless American empire. Preparations for the undertaking had begun, and the project seemed in a fair way of being carried forward, when the President of the United States, Madison, made it known that the American Government would not consent to any attack upon the Spanish posses- sions. The United States policy, it would seem, demanded, at that precise historic moment, the maintenance of things as they were. Three years earlier, no European interference was to be tolerated in favour of Spain; now, it came to be Spain's turn to be protected from her offspring, grown not only independent, but ready to wage against the mother country a new war of exclusion from the American seas.

The spirit of rebellion, ever latent in Cuba, and of which occasional signs had become apparent at different times, culminated in 1868 in an armed insurrection, which carried on war against Spain for ten years of uninterrupted fighting, during which the resources of the capital were severely taxed, and great ruin and misery brought upon the island. The peace restored in 1878 was in reality but a truce, as later events were to show. Public sentiment in the United States was frankly in favour of the rebellious Cubans. Several most delicate incidents ensued during the long years of that insurrectionary movement, when war between the United States and Spain was barely avoided by the most strenuous efforts of the two Governments, which, however, increased the deep-rooted feeling in favour of Cuba's severance from Spain amongst the American people. The sympathies of the Latin American peoples were decidedly with the Cuban rebels. Assistance to their cause was forthcoming in men and money from more than one Spanish American republic, and the Cuban emissaries and agents found a welcome and a refuge in all of them.

In 1895, a new insurrection broke out in Cuba; Spain nerved herself for the struggle, heedless of all sacrifice; in a short time she landed an army of nearly 200,000 men on the island, and her generals adopted measures of the utmost rigour, even towards non-combatants, that tended to intensify the popular feeling against Spain all over the American Continent. On February 15, 1898, the American cruiser *Maine*, anchored in the bay of Havana, was blown into space; about 258 men of her

crew and officers perished.   This terrible disaster, which many people in
the United States did not hesitate to attribute to the direct and wilful
action, if not of the Spanish authorities themselves, at least of Spanish
subjects, made war between the United States and Spain inevitable.   It
was declared by the United States in the month of April of the same
year, and brought to an end by the surrender of the city of Santiago
on July 16, after the total destruction of the Spanish fleet on July 1,
off the entrance to the port.

As a result of the war, the United States acquired the Philippine
Islands on the Great Ocean, and the island of Porto Rico on the
Caribbean Sea; after a few years of occupation by American troops,
during which Cuba was ruled by an American Governor, a Cuban
President, elected by the people, was installed in office, the American
troops returned to their country, and Cuba started on her career as a
free and independent nation, under the paternal guardianship, however,
of the Government of the United States.   The United States own certain
coaling stations on the island, and have the right of interference in the
internal affairs of Cuba in cases of revolution or public disturbances.
In the manner just described, the United States fulfilled their promise,
made at the time of declaring war against Spain, that they would turn
Cuba over to the Cubans, since they were not waging a war of conquest
or of aggrandisement for themselves.   The United States have already
exercised their right of interference.   In September, 1906, President
Estrada Palma, being unable to maintain the public peace, was superseded
by an American Governor, who landed with an army of occupation,
which soon restored peace and order.   This second American occupation
lasted until the beginning of 1909, when a new Cuban President,
popularly elected, assumed the reins of government.   The island of
Porto Rico remains a colony of the United States; in its case there
existed no promise of placing it under native government.

It is evident that Cuba's independence is precarious; if a great war
were to break out, in which the United States might need to use Cuba
as a base, it is certain that they would act as if Cuba were part of
their own territory, regardless of what the Cuban people might have
to say.   Furthermore, it would not be surprising if the efforts of those
who, in the United States, and even in Cuba itself, advocate the annexation of the island to the Union, were to prove successful.   The patent
fact is, that Cuba is a link in the chain of the hegemony of the United
States over the American Continent, available for that purpose as
circumstances may demand, not as her people, but as the Government
of the United States, may desire.

The sympathies of the Latin American nations, as has been stated,
were entirely with the Cuban people in their revolt against Spain;
however, the intervention of the United States, and the War which they
waged, and which ended in the overthrow of Spain, undoubtedly caused a

revulsion of feeling, guided more by sentiment than by reason, in favour of the mother country, which, however, although very widely spread, did not find any official utterance.

In 1846 the republic of New Granada, at the present day called Colombia, signed a treaty of commerce and friendship with the United States by which the latter acquired certain rights, promising in return "to guarantee the rights of sovereignty and ownership which New Granada possessed over the Isthmus of Panamá."

The republic of Colombia considered herself secure in her sovereignty over the isthmus of Panamá under this guarantee and the Clayton-Bulwer Treaty. The idea of constructing a canal across the isthmus was one that easily suggested itself, in view of the narrowness of the strip of land that separates the two oceans at Panamá; the enterprise had frequently been a matter of study, even during the days of Spanish domination, and on more than one occasion it had been the subject of discussion, and even of contract, between different parties and the Government of the republic of Colombia. In 1878 a contract was signed between the Government of Colombia and Bonaparte Wyse, a citizen of France, for the construction of a canal across the isthmus of Panamá; the *concessionaire* was empowered to transfer the rights acquired by him to any company that he might desire, but the canal was to remain under the political dominion of Colombia, subject to her laws, like any other public or private undertaking within her borders. The concession was taken over by a French company, which raised a vast capital, and undertook the work in earnest, with thousands of workmen, and great abundance of costly and ponderous mechanical appliances, starting at the two extremities of the projected canal on the two oceans.

The French Canal Company, after a heavy expenditure of money, and after having built fairly large sections of the canal, at the two extremities as indicated, found itself unable to continue the work through lack of funds; although the time allowed by the concession had lapsed, it had, on two occasions, been extended by the Colombian Government. At one time, it seemed possible to obtain the guarantee of the French Government for the capital required to finish the work of the canal; but this idea was opposed by the Government of the United States, which alleged that it could not consent to an intervention of this kind on the part of a European Government in favour of the French Canal Company. The concession granted by the Colombian Government stipulated that under no circumstances would it be permissible for the *concessionaire*, or for his assigns, to transfer the concession to a foreign Government; and that, should such a transfer ever come to pass, it would, *ipso facto*, render the said concession null and void.

In 1902 the Directors of the French Company came to an agreement

with the Government of the United States for the sale of their concession
for the sum of $40,000,000. The United States, under this agreement,
could not have acquired the rights of political dominion over the canal,
which alone would have satisfied them. The American ideal had changed
materially since 1850, when the Clayton-Bulwer Treaty was signed.
Blaine, Secretary of State in 1881, had declared that any waterway
across the isthmus of Panamá, or of that of Nicaragua, would be the
great highway between the Atlantic and the Pacific States of the Union,
and would thus substantially form a part of the coast line of the United
States, and that its control, therefore, must be in the hands of the
United States. Blaine's utterance expressed the purpose of the American
Government, steadily maintained by the successive administrations, which
culminated in the Pauncefote-Hay Treaty of 1901, by which England
consented to the abrogation of the Clayton-Bulwer Treaty, thus doing
away with the one great obstacle to acquisition by the United States of
political dominion over the isthmus of Panamá; though the sovereignty
of Colombia over that territory still remained, and was guaranteed by
the American Government.

In 1903 an *ad referendum* Treaty was signed in Washington between
the diplomatic representative of Colombia and the Secretary of State,
known as the Herran-Hay Convention, which, in order to become valid,
required the approval of the Colombian Congress; by that agreement,
Colombia leased to the United States a belt of land across the isthmus,
from one ocean to the other, for the construction of the canal, for a
period of one hundred years, renewable indefinitely for similar periods,
at the option of the United States, which, during the time of the lease,
would exercise sovereign rights over that section of the Colombian
territory. The Colombian Senate, to which the Treaty was submitted
for ratification in due course, rejected it; the disguise for the cession
of territory and loss of sovereignty, under the name of "lease," adopted
in the Treaty, was transparent, and the Senate declared that, even if it
were so inclined, it lacked the authority to cede any part of the national
territory, the rights over which rested exclusively with the people, who
would have to be consulted in the instance at issue.

On November 3 a revolution took place in the city of Panamá, and
the independence of the province as towards the republic of Colombia
was proclaimed. American men-of-war had arrived on the Atlantic and
on the Pacific ports of Panamá just a few days before. The Government
of Colombia was informed by the American Government that no landing
of Colombian troops would be allowed. The independence of Panamá
was recognised by the Government of the United States within three
days of the rebellion, and a Treaty with the republic of Panamá for the
construction of the canal, on lines far more favourable for the United
States than those of the Herran-Hay Treaty, was signed a fortnight
after the proclamation of the independence of Panamá. The French

Canal Company received the agreed price of $40,000,000, and Panamá $10,000,000 for the concessions which it granted. During all this time the Treaty between the United States and Colombia of 1846, by which the former guaranteed Colombia's sovereignty over the isthmus of Panamá, remained in existence, and at the time when these lines were written (1909) it had not been cancelled.

The high-handed policy of the United States with reference to Colombia sent a thrill of painful surprise throughout Spanish America; the people in those countries were naturally led to think that, if occasion should arise, the United States would treat them even as Colombia was treated. Officially, however, the independence of Panamá was very soon recognised by all the Latin American nations, with the exception of Ecuador; but, with regard to this recognition, it may be said that, in international matters, Governments very frequently act in open contradiction to the sentiments of the people.

The republic of Panamá is under the protectorate of the United States, which have the right of interference in its internal affairs in cases of disturbance or revolution; Panamá's independence has not been recognised by the republic of Colombia.

In 1889 there met at Washington, convened by the Government of the United States, a Congress or Conference, at which all the States of Latin America were represented. The essential object was to establish a stronger international sympathy between the United States and its southern neighbours, and among the southern States themselves. A second Panamerican Congress met at Mexico in 1901, and a third at Rio Janeiro in 1906. Numerous measures of great importance have been advocated in these Congresses; but, although perhaps they may have contributed to international harmony on the American Continent, through the exchange of ideas, and the better knowledge of one another produced among the several nations by the publicity given to the facts connected with these measures, no very tangible result has as yet been achieved by them. Mention should, however, be made of the practically unanimous acceptance of the principle of arbitration, embodied in numerous treaties between all the Governments of the American Continent, which has been brought about by these Congresses.

On the other hand, the action of the Panamerican Congresses upon actual history in the shape of accomplished facts is necessarily slow. They have in the main resembled a Panamerican debating society, kept in restraint by an overprudent programme which limits the themes for discussion and even the scope within which the themes may be discussed. As an instance of this, it may be noticed that, at the meeting in Rio Janeiro, one of the Latin American delegates set forth what he considered to be the logical completion of the Monroe Doctrine. This Doctrine, he argued, condemns European conquest, and thus, to that extent, guarantees the integrity of the American nations; but conquest is wrong, no matter who the conqueror may be; therefore, by positive enactment all conquest should be henceforth forbidden on the American Continent. This proposal was not only rejected, but it was not allowed to appear on the official records of the Congress. Among the measures that at one time or another have been advocated in the Panamerican Congresses may be cited: treaties of commercial reciprocity, unification of laws and regulations, of monetary systems, navigation, exercise of professions, etc., etc. The Panamerican Congresses may, undoubtedly, render great services in the future; but hitherto their achievement has not been very great.

In 1903, when England, Germany, and Italy were carrying out their naval demonstration against Venezuela for the purpose of collecting certain pecuniary claims from that republic, Drago, Minister of Foreign Affairs for the Argentine Republic, addressed a note to its diplomatic representative at Washington, placing on record the surprise caused to his Government by the action of the three allied Powers, and laying down certain principles as to the inviolable nature of the sovereignty of nations, which have come to be known as the Drago Doctrine. His final words were: "The principle which the Argentine Republic would like to see recognised, is this: that public debts should never bring about any armed intervention, much less the material occupation of the soil of American nations by European Powers."

The proclamation of this principle constituted a protest against the action of the allied Powers, and, if accepted, would preclude in the future any similar occurrences arising from the default in payment of their public debts by Latin American nations. The Drago Doctrine, which found adherents amongst very eminent publicists in the United States and in Europe, was to have been submitted to the Panamerican Congress of Rio Janeiro in 1906; that body, however, decided to leave it to be considered by the Hague Peace Conference, which was to meet in the following year, where creditor as well as debtor nations would be represented.

The Latin American nations were invited to attend the Second Peace Conference at the Hague, to which all of them sent their representatives. The Drago Doctrine was not brought up for consideration; in its stead the Porter Resolution was adopted, which forbids the employment of force for the collection of public debts until the claims shall have been approved of by an arbitration Court, appointed by the creditor and the debtor countries, and the payment thereof shall have been refused, or until the demand for an arbitration shall have been refused or disregarded by a debtor country. By the Porter Resolution the employment of force for the collection of public debts is thus implicitly, though not expressly, accepted.

Mention should also be made of the Permanent Court of Justice of

CH. XXI.

Central America, established in 1908, under the auspices of the United States and of Mexico, for the settlement of all questions of any nature whatsoever that may arise among the five Central American republics themselves. This Court, it is expected, will contribute to permanent political stability in Central America.

Irrespective of political demarcation of the limitations that the ambitions and the aims of the powerful may create, and of the action of the present political sovereigns of the territory, the Latin American Continent is bound to become the scene of important developments in the near future. It contains, within the tropics, a sufficient amount of lands, situated at a high altitude above sea level and thus fit for the habitation of the white races, to provide for a numerous white population, even under the equator. The long years of Spanish domination, the work of which has been continued and developed by the republics that have succeeded Spain, have created, in all parts and sections of the Continent, centres of civilisation, each one of which may form the nucleus of a province or of a nation. The higher classes throughout the whole of Latin America have attained a high degree of culture ; and the practically inexhaustible resources of the land, in the plains, in the forests, and in the mountains, constitute an attraction for the wandering waves of humanity from the congested regions of Europe, more powerful than any barriers or attempts to stem the tide of humanity in accordance with the conventional interests of any given national entity or group of nations.

CHAPTER XXII.

THE MODERN LAW OF NATIONS AND THE PREVENTION OF WAR.

WE are not concerned here with the speculative exactness of any particular description as applicable to the doctrines known as the Law of Nations or International Law. It is enough for our purpose that there is, in fact, a body of rules and usages which among civilised independent States are recognised as binding upon their several Governments in their dealings with one another and with each other's subjects. No such body of rules can be said to have existed before the end of the Middle Ages; there is no doubt that it exists now, or that its extent and importance are increasing. The development of International Law is among the subjects which eminently belong to modern history. Yet it may claim as venerable antiquity for its origins as any branch of jurisprudence. They go back not only to Roman law but to Greek moral philosophy; this twofold ancestry is preserved in the term still current in Scotland, "the law of nature and of nations," though probably very few scholars pause on the words to think of it. For the law of nature, apart from the technical forms of political and theological systems, is the Greek appeal to an ideal rule justifying itself by reason, and the law of nations, in this earlier sense, is the practical Roman recognition of a working standard in the general usage of civilised mankind. Both elements were necessary: *jus naturale* without *jus gentium* would be an unbodied spirit, *jus gentium* without *jus naturale* would be a soulless body. The latter days of the Roman Republic brought an expansion of Roman jurisdiction and law, which called for a doctrinal foundation. Justice had to be done to merchants and other strangers having no part in the domestic rules or the religious sanctions that were applicable to Roman citizens. The Praetor, in default of any more specific precept, fell back upon general custom—for such is really the nearest version of *jus gentium* in modern English—a custom which we may well believe was to be found chiefly in the usages of Mediterranean trade. A generation of learned lawyers trained in Greek philosophy, and holding frequent intercourse with Greek or Greek-speaking scholars, found it easy to identify the principles of cosmopolitan equity, warranted in fact by the consent of all civilised people, with the justice which had been defined as natural (φυσικόν) in the Aristotelian texts, and contrasted with legal or rather conventional rules (νομικόν). The conception of natural law, as early as Aristotle, involved that of rational design. Hence we find not only *jus naturale* or *naturae* but, nearly as often, *lex*, which in classical Latin implies rational design. For almost all practical purposes, *jus gentium* and *jus naturale* were treated as equivalent by the jurists of the Roman Empire, and there is nothing to show that one term is older than the other. Lawyers were aware, indeed, that the common practice of the Mediterranean nations justified some institutions which the better opinion of Aristotle's successors would not undertake to justify on grounds of universal reason. Such an institution was slavery, recognised by general custom as fully as anything could be. We have express admissions that in this point there was a discrepancy between the ideal of enlightened reason and the facts of common usage ; but our materials do not make it clear whether in the classical periods of Roman jurisprudence there was any official or accepted explanation of such discrepancies. Near the beginning of Justinian's *Institutes*, the repugnance of war, captivity, and slavery, to the law of nature is stated plainly enough ; we must accept them, it seems, as necessary evils made inveterate by custom. In the absence of anything to show the contrary, a Roman lawyer, it is conceived, would assume *jus gentium* to follow *jus naturale*, much as an English Court, failing positive authority, declares that rule to be the law which it thinks most reasonable.

Meanwhile the purely ethical tradition of the Greek writers had been invested with an elegant Latin form by Cicero, and acquired all but a definite religious sanction for Christendom by the approval of Fathers venerated in the Church ; and, early in the thirteenth century, the revived study of Aristotle brought the schoolmen back to the fountain-head of all this authority. We must remember that, in every one of its forms, it was little short of sacred. Aristotle was a heathen certainly, but he was "The Philosopher"; and the *Corpus Juris*, though not much of it was originally the work of Christians, claimed submission in the name not of an unconverted Papinian or Gaius but of the orthodox Emperor Justinian. Thus the law of nature presented itself to medieval scholars as the crown of both moral and legal science, a standard of human conduct independent of positive enactment and even of special Divine revelation, binding always and everywhere by virtue of its intrinsic reasonableness. Unhappily the very loftiness and universality of this conception prevented it from having any certain practical operation ; for, although every one was ready to admit that the law of nature was supreme, it was not so easy for persons and bodies whose interests were in conflict to agree what, in any particular circumstances, the dictates of universal natural reason were. Moreover, men thought that an universal rule called for an universal jurisdiction to administer it. Thus, while infinite speculative ingenuity was expended on a secular conflict between the claims of the Empire and the Holy See, very little was done to arrive at a working settlement of rules of conduct between princes.

Meanwhile, the customs and obligations of chivalry were useful, so far as they went. There were courtly ceremonies in peace and knightly customs in war; but their observance was a matter of individual sentiment and honour, and, in a state of society where private war was still possible and not uncommon, it was fortunate that there was any restraint at all. Chivalry, moreover, belonged to the archaic type of customs; it was the rule not of mankind or of a nation but of an order. To have the benefit of its courtesies as of right, a man must be a knight, or at least capable of becoming one, a woman must be in religion or a member of a knightly family. The condition of being an orthodox Christian would have been added by many. Doubtless, the best practice carried the spirit far beyond the letter, while, among the baser sort, even the letter got scant obedience. When all is said, however, the medieval usages were not law in any sense which we can accept at this day, but custom, and only partial custom, tempering the default of law. Greek and early Roman usage in this as in many other matters was nearer to the lines of advance which we have now found profitable; for, so far as it went, it was conceived as having general and equal application: which is a fundamental element in our modern ideas of legal justice.

The cosmopolitan sentiments and practice of chivalry were reinforced by the coextensive jurisdiction and influence of the Church. So far as the common faith of western Christendom strengthened the common tradition of justice handed down through the institutions of the Roman Empire, and never wholly extinguished, it made an effectual contribution to the foundations of International Law. But, in themselves, the claims of the Church, like those of the medieval Empire, were neither national nor international, but supra-national. St Louis of France would not have understood the modern fashion of investing France or England with moral attributes. He conceived his duties as those of a Christian knight with honour to maintain and a Christian man with a soul to be saved—duties magnified no doubt by his exalted office, but still wholly personal. Students of medieval history must determine for themselves how far religion succeeded in mitigating the evils of war. It is certain that the Church could not prevent Christian rulers from making war upon each other, or from appealing to Divine sanction for their opposite causes with an equal appearance of sincerity. The Holy Father himself, as a temporal prince, was often a belligerent, and his adversaries felt no diffidence about invoking their patron saints against him, as when Siena, beset by Clement VII, solemnly renewed her commendation to Our Lady. There is no historical ground for the assumption sometimes made by recent publicists that Christian doctrine, or, to speak more exactly, the teaching of any Church that has ever enjoyed considerable authority, condemns war in itself more than any other of the evils incident to a sinful world. We speak of the Churches as they have actually been since Christianity became the official religion of the Roman Empire; the question whether the Society of Friends be not nearer the mind of the primitive Christian community than the orthodox doctors of eastern or western hierarchies does not require solution here. It is an obvious reflexion that war, whether between Christians or not, is eminently fertile of temptations to almost every mortal sin except heresy; in fact, even the killing of infidels in defence of the Church, or of one's own life, has in strictness the nature of sin, and, according to early medieval authority, must be atoned for by at least nominal penance. Nevertheless, military service under an orthodox prince was esteemed lawful at all times after the conversion of Constantine, and war against infidel enemies not only passed for meritorious but was even, from time to time, urgently recommended with all the influence which the Papacy could bring to bear on temporal politics; and it is plain that this could not be otherwise at seasons when the very existence of Christendom appeared to be and really was in danger. We cannot conceive a Pope who would have refused his blessing to Don John of Austria. The Templars were ultimately condemned; but the shedding of infidel blood was not among their alleged crimes. Besides, it was impracticable to deprive Christian citizens of the right of self-defence merely because their assailants professed the same faith. What was a Bishop of Siena to do when the Florentines were threatening to storm the town and give no quarter? In Italy the spirit of chivalry, Germanic rather than Latin in its origin, was weakest, never having been thoroughly acclimatised, and the Church ought to have been strongest; and in Italy the inhumanity of medieval war, whether conducted by republics or by despots, was at its very worst. As for doctrinal discussion, there was much writing about the righteousness of wars in the Middle Ages; but the problem was to define the conditions for war being just, in the sense that it could be undertaken without sin. One author's opinion might be less favourable to war than another's; but not one appears to have denied that war was sometimes just and necessary.

On the other hand, many prelates and men of religion exerted themselves with good effect on behalf of peace on celebrated occasions, and, we may believe, on as many others now forgotten or obscure. Again, the Church, to her credit, always stood against slavery, and it was never the practice to enslave Christian captives, unless they were heretics. A few customary prohibitions had survived from ancient times and were approved as binding on Christian warriors. We abhor the use of poison in war; but so did the authors, or at any rate the editors, of the Homeric poems. All that the Church can claim here is that she cast her authoritative vote on the right side. Other restrictions which now seem capricious were attempted by a combination of chivalrous and ecclesiastical sentiment. Weapons of precision, such as the cross-bow, and afterwards fire-arms, fell for a time under a ban which might be enforced by refusing quarter.

In the way of prevention, some good was done by the intervention of Popes as mediators or arbitral judges. It would be idle to seek any precise definition of the capacity in which they acted, as we might well find that, in particular cases, the Pope thought himself entitled to judge between Kings as of right, while the parties held themselves bound to fulfil his award only by reason of voluntary submission. At all events it became more and more apparent that the ideal of universal monarchy was not to be realised in this world; and in this respect the Reformation only hastened an inevitable disillusion. After the Reformation controversies and the Wars of Religion it was plainly impossible to maintain that either the Pope or the Emperor could in fact, even within his own sphere as admitted by all Catholics, exercise the universal jurisdiction which he claimed.

There remained, then, as a check on the greed of rulers and the excesses of their officers, only the persuasive authority of the law of nature, an authority still generally received, although some Protestant controversialists, anxious to restrain Roman interpretation, maintained against the tradition of the schools that the letter of the Scriptures came first—and this afterwards became the orthodox Puritan position. If only something like consent on leading points could be obtained, a real moral weight of opinion would be more effective than a pretended sovereign power which could enforce nothing. We do not mean that the problem was distinctly seen in this light at the time; any such analytical statement can only try to sum up the drift of much speculation and many different endeavours. But. in fact, we find, from and after the early part of the sixteenth century, a series of writers on the law of nature, dealing, it is true, with a wide range of theoretical jurisprudence and ethics, but still trying in the course of their work to find some rule applicable to the relations of States in peace and war. It would be useless for the purpose in hand to dwell upon their arguments, or to enter on the difficult critical task of apportioning their merits. Two of these precursors of Grotius, as they are called, may fitly be commemorated by an English writer: Alberico Gentili, adopted by Oxford, whose treatise is deemed by Professor Holland worthy to be called *juris gentium quod hodie in usu est vera incunabula*; and Richard Hooker, eminent among the English scholars of his time.

Gentili's book *De jure belli* was first published in 1598; it is among the few singled out for commendation by Grotius. We cannot say that Gentili realised the full magnitude of his undertaking. He conceived it as a special problem of applying the law of nature to a class of cases about which hardly anything was to be found in the *Corpus Juris*, the commentators, or even the philosophers. There is nothing revolutionary about his method : he starts from the received identity, for all material purposes, of *jus gentium* and *jus naturae*. The rules of *jus gentium* (still used in its classical sense, as including all kinds of right and duty sanctioned by general observance) are established by the general consent of mankind, *quod successive placere omnibus visum est*; and this, as he justly notes, is the only kind of proof by which unwritten law can ever be established. At the same time, these rules are also binding as being prescribed by absolute and evident reason ; for universal reason is manifested in the consent of reasonable men. Here Gentili seems to be nearer the root of the matter than several much later authors. It is a precept as old as Aristotle to deem that reasonable which appears so to competent persons (in this case civilised governments and their advisers), and it is constantly applied in affairs of internal jurisdiction. Accordingly, princes and rulers are subject in their dealings with one another, even in war, to the rule of natural reason attested by general agreement, which may be called indifferently *jus gentium* when we consider it as customary, or *jus naturae* when we consider it as rational. This law of nature is not only applicable in its broad principles but may be applied to determine specific rules by way of deduction, provided that the case is not covered by any positive ordinance of a competent authority ; such ordinances are binding in cases otherwise doubtful, unless they are manifestly contrary to some precept of universal justice. Gentili is here following the distinction long familiar in the Scholastic system between the " primary" and the "secondary" law of nature ; its practical object was to guard against the law of nature being used as a cloak for frivolous or perverse refusal to obey the law of the land. In the case of dispute between sovereign rulers there is in fact no common positive authority, nor could Gentili, an exile for religion's sake, admit that either the Pope or the Emperor ought of right to have any such authority. Thus we must seek in the law of nature, proceeding by deduction from its general principles, the whole body of rules which, when ascertained, will constitute the *jus belli*. Considering the rudimentary state of European diplomacy at the time, Gentili's confidence in the power of reason was altogether admirable, and the foundation of his doctrine, which Grotius adopted in substance, is in the present writer's opinion quite sound.

Richard Hooker (1554–1600) was born some years later and died several years earlier than Suarez, whose work in this kind is more generally known. The Spanish theologian had a distinct conception of a customary law binding on all nations in their mutual intercourse ; but the value of his insight is somewhat discounted when he adds that the rules under this head are few, simple, and easily deduced from the principles of natural law (*De lege et Deo legislatore*, II. xix. § 9). Hooker, writing not later than 1592, when his *Ecclesiastical Polity* was complete, was much more explicit (*Eccl. Pol.* I. x. 12): "besides that law which simply concerneth men as men, and that which belongeth unto them as they are men linked with others in some form of politic society, there is a third kind of law which toucheth all such several bodies politic, so far forth as one of them hath public commerce with another. And this third is the Law of Nations." There follow some general remarks on the need of "society and fellowship even with all mankind," and the application in this region of the distinction between primary and secondary rules of law, which Hooker uses in a rather forced way to draw the line between rules of peaceful traffic and "laws of arms, which yet are much better known than kept." Hooker then adds, with prudence showing that he was not blind to the magnitude of the subject: "But what matter the Law of Nations doth contain I omit to search." This must have been written or revised about the time when Alberico Gentili was writing or enlarging the dissertations from which his finished treatise was developed. It is tempting to conjecture that the English divine and the Italian civilian may have met and talked over the reformation of European public law. However that may be, Hooker is entitled to stand among the most clear-sighted of the "precursors," and he was the very first writer to use the term "Law of Nations" in English in the specialised sense now so familiar as to be the only one generally understood.

We now turn to the founder of the modern system. Grotius (1583–1645) defines his subject at the outset as *jus illud quod inter populos plures aut populorum rectores intercedit*; and it would be hard to better this in good Latin, for *jus inter gentes* would have conveyed no clear meaning to any Roman jurist; the only Latin terms properly signifying what we now signify by the word State, a nation as a political unit, are *civitas* and *populus*, and *gentes* is not the plural of either, as Grotius very well knew. This by no means diminishes the importance of the fact that "the law regulating the intercourse between distinct States or their governors" is a branch of *jus gentium* in its classical sense, though so individual as to constitute a new head of legal science—a head of which, as Grotius truly said, no one had yet treated fully and systematically, though it nearly concerned the welfare of mankind. More wisely than some later authors, Grotius did not attempt to embody in the definition itself any theory of the origin or sanction of this law, but proceeded to indicate possible origins in the next clause: *sive ab ipsa natura profectum*—the classical law of nature; *aut divinis constitutum legibus*—the precepts of revealed religion, so far as any may be found applicable; *sive moribus et pacto tacito introductum* —custom and implied agreement. All these Grotius recognised as authoritative sources of law; and it was needful for his purposes to rely on all of them. Scholars and philosophers would for the most part accept the law of nature; divines, and especially Protestants (many of whom regarded natural law with suspicion), expected Scriptural warrant;

public men would insist on being assured that the author who called for their attention was walking on the ground of practical affairs and not merely setting up his own opinions as an universal standard. The *Prolegomena* to Grotius' great work, written after its completion, show how clearly he had conceived his undertaking and realised its extent. He had to demonstrate that a common rule of right among States was possible; that it was capable of discovery and exposition; and that it was not confined to peaceful relations but continued to be binding in time of war. With such help as could be derived from earlier very incomplete achievements, he had to establish this rule on foundations of moral and legal justice which learned men would deem sound and men of the world would not think fantastic. Moreover, where existing custom fell short of being tolerably just, he had to propose amendment without assuming to dictate to sovereign princes. This would have been much for a generation of workers to accomplish. Grotius achieved it all himself, and so thoroughly that within half a century his treatise was received as authoritative by the civilised world. How far he was in advance of his fellows is shown by the fact that some of those who came after fell back upon the old lines of composing ambitious systems of natural law with a merely episodic treatment of international relations, and secured European fame and even a passing authority by the solemn exposition of platitudes marshalled after this belated fashion. Other writers, of whom Wicquefort is the best known, confined themselves, so late as the end of the seventeenth century, to the ceremonial side of international usage, the privileges of ambassadors, and the like.

In some ways, we must allow, Grotius' method was exceedingly artificial. He could not expect his own opinions to be received merely on their intrinsic merits, and accordingly he set ancient examples and authorities in array with such abundant pomp and circumstance as are even too formidable for the modern reader. The new law of nations was to march as a conquering host with banners, having enlisted the whole strength of the classical *jus gentium*; we know not whether Grotius foresaw that in the modern tongues the translation of the Latin phrase was to have not only an enlarged but a transformed meaning. Triumphant exhibition of antique authority was not, however, free from drawbacks. The Greek and Roman writers, and even the Scriptures, appeared in many places to permit or encourage such extreme use of a belligerent's rights, especially with regard to the persons and property of conquered enemies, as could not be approved by any one seeking to frame rules of warfare for civilised nations. Nor could Grotius, in the midst of embittered religious wars, have safely taken the position that usage was progressive in its standard of justice and mercy, and had in fact abolished the harsher claims of victors. At the time of the Thirty Years' War, and even later, the tendency of practice was, if anything, retrograde. Moreover, jurists did not habitually, if at all, conceive of *jus gentium* as a living and developing system ; and the law of nature was of course assumed to be immutable even by writers generally rebellious to authority, such as Hobbes.

Grotius solved the problem thus raised by an ingenious device which Whewell, perhaps, stands almost alone in justly commending. He first stated the strict laws of war in the crudest form and with almost ironical exaggeration. Then he proceeded to state under the name of "temperaments" the considerations of natural equity which forbid righteous princes and generals to use their customary rights to the uttermost. Such a conflict between natural justice and legality was in itself already familiar to publicists. Grotius was reproducing, in a novel application, the contrast between *jus naturale* and *jus gentium* which was conspicuous at the head of the *Institutes,* and pleading for the abrogation by improved practice of the harsher rules which, in the case of sovereign princes, had not been made binding by any positive law. Not having any coercive authority to invoke, Grotius trusted to counsels of perfection to be effectual where dogmatic precepts might have failed. An artificial method, certainly ; but amply justified by success. All, and more than all, the "temperaments" of Grotius have long since been assimilated by the ordinary rules of civilised warfare.

The most remarkable omission in Grotius' work, to modern eyes, is that he has next to nothing to say about neutrality considered with regard either to the duties or to the rights of neutral States as against belligerents. In fact, the questions which have been prominent under this head for about a century and a half had then only begun to occur in a sporadic manner and were not ripe for definition. For the rest, Grotius himself wrote, in· his concluding chapter, words of dignified modesty which leave very little to criticism. "I make no claim to have said all that might be said ; but to have said so much as will lay the foundations, whereon if any man will build up a statelier edifice, he shall not find me grudge him aught, but rather shall have my thanks." Others have built, and Grotius would be well pleased in their work. The foundations are still where Grotius laid them.

Official, judicial, and other learned persons who cannot conceive authority divested of official sanction have gravely pointed out that Grotius and his successors, not being legislators, could not make law. More than twenty years ago, Sir Henry Maine gave the right answer : "What we have to notice," he said, "is that the founders of International Law, though they did not create a sanction, created a law-abiding sentiment. They diffused among sovereigns, and the literate classes in communities, a strong repugnance to the neglect or breach of certain rules regulating the relations and actions of States. They did this not by threatening punishments, but by the alternative and older method, long known in Europe and Asia, of creating a strong approval of a certain body of rules." To put it in a slightly different way, they were able to mould the custom of princes and their advisers while it was still plastic; and it took form as a real though imperfect customary law, not a mere assemblage of moral precepts. Ever since the time of Grotius these questions have been treated as belonging to jurisprudence, not to theology or casuistry, and have been handled in the manner of legal argument and not of merely moral persuasion. It may be and often is disputed what is the true rule, or how it is to be applied in particular cases; but the rule, ascertained or not ascertained, is conceived as an ordinance of justice and not a counsel of perfection. Beyond the domain of positive duty there is a region for governments in the society of nations, as for individual citizens within a State, where rights may be exercised in a more or less friendly spirit, with greater or less consideration for the convenience of others, equitably or with insistence on the letter of the bond, stiffly or with readiness to give and take; and no formal ground of complaint is afforded by conduct which, though it may be displeasing or barely civil, is still within the scope of lawful discretion; as in municipal jurisdiction an action will not lie against a man for many things which do not become the character of an amiable neighbour. In this region the skill and tact of diplomatists finds much of its everyday work, and by no means the least important.

Certain writers, again, for the most part in England, have assumed that the law of nations has a merely fictitious existence because it lacks a cosmopolitan judicial Court, with power to decree execution and enforce the decrees. So far as there is anything more in this contention than a dispute about verbal definitions, it seems fit to be considered that in the early history of all systems of law the executive power at the disposal of Courts of justice has been rudimentary. We now understand that civil justice was originally rendered only by virtue of the parties having submitted to be bound by the judgment in the particular case; and, even at a much more advanced stage, we may find Courts which have an elaborate constitution and procedure but no compulsory powers at all. Icelandic society in the early Middle Ages, as the semi-historical sagas describe it (for there is no reason to doubt their substantial truthfulness as a general account of manners and institutions), affords the classical example. It is true that the law of nations is not administered by a Court of universal jurisdiction; the defect has been discussed and lamented ever since Dante wrote his treatise *De Monarchia.* It would be very far from true to say that it is not judicially administered by any Court. Questions of allegiance and territorial jurisdiction, of the existence of war between foreign States or *de facto* Governments, and the consequences thereof, such as blockade with its incidents, and the like, may call and have often called for decision as affecting the rights of suitors in municipal Courts. An English Court had to decide in 1908 whether a warranty against contraband of war in a policy of marine insurance included the transport of belligerent officers in a neutral ship, and decided it in the negative, treating the question as one of international law. Naturally, the lawyers of every country cite their own authorities and writers most; but it is worthy of remark when they cite others at all. More than this, a material part of the law of war, namely the law of prizes, has been administered by Courts of Admiralty, and expressly as an international and not as a local law. Prize Courts have never purported to administer merely municipal law. For Lord Stowell, certainly, the Court of Admiralty was a Court of the law of nations and of the law of nations only : as he said in his well-known judgment in *The Maria,* " the seat of judicial authority is locally here, in the belligerent country, according to the known law and practice of nations, but the law itself has no locality." In this he was only follow-ing the celebrated opinion of the English law officers in the case of the Silesian Loan, an opinion in which Lord Mansfield, then Solicitor-General, took a leading part: "There never existed a case where a Court, judging according to the laws of England only, ever took cognizance of prize...it never was imagined that the property of foreign subjects, taken as prize on the high seas, could be affected by laws peculiar to England." As for the opinion that nations are bound by the law of treaty only, and that there is no other law of nations but that which is derived from positive compact and convention, Lord Stowell rejected it as fit only for Barbary pirates (*The Helena*). It may be said that a national judge may find himself in the position of a judge in his own cause, and that it is hard for him, with the best intentions, to be impartial. This is true ; but it is also true that even in municipal justice this drawback is not always avoidable, and that a judge in his own cause is admitted, at need, as a less evil than total default of justice and judgment. American opinion, it is believed, whether ex-pressed in judicial decisions, in presidential messages and other domestic acts of State, or in diplomatic intercourse, has been invariable in the same sense ever since the United States became a nation.

Regarding the law of nations, then, as a true customary law, though still imperfectly organised, we may say that it is ascertained and developed in three ways: by the authority of writers, by recognition and declara-tion in treaties and other diplomatic acts, and by the embodiment of general opinion in the usage of nations.

The authority of writers on the law of nations is exactly like the authority (as it is often, though according to English professional usage not correctly, called) of private text-writers on municipal law. More or less weight is given to their opinions, according to their reputation and the resulting probability that those opinions correctly represent either the settled consent of civilised Governments or, in questions allowed to be not yet settled, the conclusions in which Governments may be expected to agree. As Grotius himself very wisely said of the School-men's opinions on moral questions : when they agree they are not likely to be wrong. It is absurd to suppose that the law of nations, so far as not expressed in treaties or other authentic acts of State, is nothing but a *cento* of private writers' conjectures for every man to pick and choose from at will. Our highest legal authorities, on the contrary, have fixed the sound doctrine that the writings of experienced and approved publicists are valuable not as mere opinion but as evidence. As the late Justice Gray said in 1899 in the Supreme Court of the United States (*The Paquete Habana*)· "such works are resorted to by judicial tribunals, not for the speculations of their authors concerning what the law ought to be, but for trustworthy evidence of what the law really is." So, a century earlier, Lord Stowell relied on Vattel "not as a lawyer merely delivering an opinion, but as a witness asserting a fact—the fact that such is the existing practice of modern Europe" (*The Maria*). Not that the conclusions of publicists are to be accepted without examination. We have the like right and duty of examining them with regard to the grounds on which they purport to be based that we have in all critical and historical enquiry. But this does not make their testimony worthless, as assumed by a few modern authors and even by some eminent English judges.

Another kind of evidence of the law of nations is afforded by treaties and similar instruments. These, however, must be used with caution. For it is obvious that the terms of an express convention between two or more Powers can of themselves have no binding force upon any other Power which is not a party to it. The parties may happen to recognise a general rule, expressly or by necessary implication, as already settled; or, as is more common, their agreement may be intended to supply the want of any settled rule. In either case the evidence is valuable; but it must not be assumed that a rule which parties think well to establish between themselves is therefore regarded, even by themselves, as fit for general adoption. It is otherwise (and the distinction has in our time become of great importance) where an agreement or declaration is made not by two or three States as a matter of their own private business, but by a considerable proportion, in number and power, of civilised States at large, for the regulation of matters of general and permanent interest. Such acts are the outcome of congresses or conferences held for the purpose, and they are now commonly so framed as to admit of and invite the subsequent adhesion of States which may not have been parties in the first instance. Moreover, it is certain that, when all or most of the Great Powers have deliberately agreed to any rule of general application, their agreement has very great weight even among States whose consent has not been given. Declarations of this kind may, in fact, be expected, in the absence of prompt and effective dissent by some Power of the first rank, to become part of the universally received law of nations before long. As among men, so among nations, the opinions and usage of the leading members in a community tend to form an authoritative example for the whole. A striking proof of this tendency was given in the War of 1898 between Spain and the United States. Neither belligerent was a party to the article of the Declaration of Paris of 1856 against privateering; the United States, indeed, had refused to concur in it. Moreover, the Declaration of Paris was not, in point of form, an instrument of the highest authority. Nevertheless, when the War of 1898 broke out, the United States proclaimed their intention of adhering to the Declaration of Paris, and the rules thereby laid down were, in fact, observed by both belligerents. Great Britain, again, did not accede to the resolution of the Hague Conference of 1899 against the use of expanding bullets, but shortly afterwards acted upon it in the South African War, and formally acceded to it at the Conference of 1907.

The weight of actual usage, and the proof derived from it, remain the most important factors of all; for the final test of validity must in the case of international law, no less than in that of any other customary law, be found in general consent evidenced by conduct. Opinions, even the most plausible, may fail to produce effectual conviction. Solemn declarations may remain a dead letter. Practice alone will show what is really to be expected. Therefore, the opinion in the case of the Silesian Loan already mentioned was careful to state that the law of nations is "founded upon justice, equity, convenience, and the reason of the thing, and confirmed by long usage." Such usage, if uniform or nearly so, is the best evidence of deliberate consent, for discordant opinions as to what is just or convenient could never produce a uniform accepted usage. On the other hand, when we find certain rules generally accepted by independent States, the natural explanation is that all or most of those who are best qualified to judge of "the reason of the thing" believe them to be convenient and just. Thus the elements of custom and reason in the law of nations, so far from being in any normal conflict, are both indispensable and necessary to each other. Not that existing usage is infallible or immutable. There will always be some opinion, sometimes a considerable body of opinion, in advance of the average moral sense of a community, and this no less among nations than among citizens. Its influence will tend to keep usage well up to the mark of average opinion, perhaps a little better. To make it much better is a task that no temporal Government and no spiritual teacher has ever achieved, except in brief seeming and at the price of disastrous reaction. We must aim at that which appears right to the most competent persons, if we can be sure who those are; but, for the time being, we must be content with such working rules as satisfy the majority of wellmeaning and fairly competent persons; and in applying them we must make the best of the universal rule of jurisprudence which prescribes that, in case of doubt, the most reasonable interpretation is to be preferred. It would be idle to complain that Lord Stowell, or any of his predecessors or successors in Admiralty jurisdiction, did not claim

CH. XXII.

supreme authority in matters of faith and morals. Had they done so, they would only have hampered progress by narrow and premature definitions. Nor are we to expect or desire any such jurisdiction to be assumed by any congress or concert of the Powers.

Information as to the development of particular rules in the law of nations is not within our province here, and must be sought in the works of technical writers on the subject. But, within the last half-century, we have seen the beginning of serious and concerted endeavour to make the avoidance of war easier and to mitigate its evils when it occurs. The rate of progress is not yet such as to content enthusiasts for peace, but it appears to be an increasing rate; and if acute disappointment is sometimes felt about failures and shortcomings, as now at the rather small results of the Hague Conference of 1907, it must be remembered that such disappointment, at one stage or another, and probably at more than one, is incident to every movement of reform. For the most part, the reformers have set before themselves the ideal of an international tribunal possessing, if not compulsory jurisdiction, at least such moral weight that resort to its award, except in case of extreme necessity, may become a duty of customary obligation. This is an admirable ideal, and the progress now made towards it is considerable, when we remember how lately the most that seemed practicable was a vague suggestion of appeal to the good offices of some friendly third Power. But we must not forget that arbitration in any form is only an instrument for settling disputes, and is not equally appropriate in all cases. It is not safe to assume that all questions between sovereign States are analogous to those which cause litigation between individuals, and that no difficulty remains in the way of judicial solution if once an adequate judicial authority can be found. This is far from being so.

International controversies may be divided, for the purpose in hand, into four classes. Many particular cases are in fact of a mixed or ambiguous kind; nevertheless one or another of the qualities to be mentioned will mostly be found to prevail in any given example. In the first are such as relate to boundaries and territorial rights, including the construction of any treaties or other authentic documents bearing on such rights. Here we have almost a perfect analogy to cases between private owners. The main problem is to find an arbitrator, board of arbitrators, or standing tribunal, whose decision will command the respect of both parties. More or less trouble may occur in defining the issues to be submitted, and coming to a preliminary understanding upon the extent of the matters that are reasonably open to discussion. These difficulties however are of the kind which with goodwill and good faith can be overcome. In fact, many cases of uncertain boundaries and the like, which in former ages would have led to wars or furnished a convenient pretext for them, have in our own time been peaceably and honourably settled. Moreover, it may be said of these cases, as of similar cases in men's private affairs, that a decision arrived at by competent persons after argument is more likely to be just in itself and, what is more, satisfactory to the parties, than a compromise arrived at by direct negotiation. We may place in the same category with boundary settlements, though in a less important rank, the adjustment of pecuniary claims by subjects of one State against the Government of another, arising out of transactions or events as to which no matter of principle is in dispute. Such claims have often been dealt with by joint Commissions proceeding in a more or less judicial manner, and there is seldom much difficulty about them, though the justice ultimately done is not always prompt. Here there is still a good deal of analogy to the ordinary civil business of municipal Courts.

A second class of controversies turns on alleged breach or non-performance of active obligations arising out of the interpretation of treaties or official declarations, or out of the common customary duty of nations in particular circumstances, as where a breach of neutrality or excess in the exercise of a belligerent's rights against neutrals is complained of. Such cases are less apt than the first class for quasi-judicial treatment. Often it happens that no permanent settlement is possible without laying down regulations for future action which will amount, in effect if not in form, to a new convention. Where this is so, the better way may be to arrange the whole matter by direct negotiation. Even where the settlement has taken the form of arbitration, we shall sometimes find that the real controversy was preliminary and that one or the other party conceded all or most of the substantial points in issue by the form in which it agreed to fix the questions to be referred. A leading example is the *Alabama* dispute between Great Britain and the United States. The rules defined in the Treaty of Washington, when applied to the facts, which were equally notorious to both parties, practically reduced the arbitral tribunal of Geneva to a board for the assessment of damages.

A third class of cases is that which is analogous to civil actions for wrongs. Here, a sovereign State, for the most part representing individual grievances and claims of its subjects, though not always or necessarily so, seeks compensation for harm caused to innocent persons, as owners of property or otherwise, by the incidents of warlike operations or civil disorder within the jurisdiction of the State to which the complaint is addressed; by denial of justice to its subjects in that jurisdiction; by alleged illegal or excessive proceedings of that other State's officers; or by acts done under colour of exercising some international right, but alleged to be a manifest abuse. Arbitral proceedings and awards have been of great use in these cases, but chiefly when the rules to be applied have been already agreed upon by the parties or are otherwise too plain for serious dispute. Very difficult and delicate questions arise when an arbitrator or arbitral commission has to consider whether acts done,

CH. XXII.

perhaps, in a remote quarter of the world and under a foreign system of public law and legislation are to be deemed illegal or in the nature of unfriendly conduct. For such reasons the first King of the Belgians, in 1862, declined to act as arbitrator in a case arising out of the seizure and confiscation of certain American ships by Peru. His reasons for declining were, however, so given as to amount to an informal opinion unfavourable to the claim of the United States, and thereupon the claim was abandoned.

To whatever class a settled claim belonged in its inception, it would not be possible, without enormous labour, to say with any certainty what proportion of such claims have in substance been incident to the working out of former agreements, or otherwise mere items in a series of diplomatic transactions, or what proportion of the residue were in themselves capable of leading to serious trouble between the nations concerned. But it may be observed as to doubts of this kind: first, that accumulation of unsettled differences is a source of risk directly and indirectly, though they may be individually small; secondly, that the prevention of war between powerful States, or the termination of dangerous recrimination and ill-will, is much to have been accomplished even in a few cases. It is true that Governments submit to arbitration only when they do not want to fight; but it is also true that peaceful intentions are not always easy to carry out in the face of excited public opinion, and the existence of a known procedure which provides an honourable way of accommodation may make all the difference. There are moments when any expedient is good if only it serves to gain time.

But the following classification may be useful. Nearly 200 cases of arbitration between 1815 and the end of the nineteenth century are collected in Dr W. Evans Darby's *International Tribunals.* Omitting from the total the cases (nearly 10 per cent.) in which the proceedings were only after hostilities, were not of a judicial character, led to no decision, or were not between independent States, a rough analysis shows the remaining effective arbitrations to fall into the following groups :— questions of title and boundaries, about 30 per cent ; pecuniary claims of citizens in miscellaneous civil matters, about 20 per cent.; construction of treaties (other than boundary), about 10 per cent. ; claims arising out of warlike operations and for alleged illegal proceedings, or denial of justice, about 40 per cent. According to the article on Arbitration in International Law in the *Encyclopaedia of the Law of England*, 2nd edition, Great Britain has been a party to just 50 arbitrations during the nineteenth century and the first few years of the twentieth. Of these, 17 appear to have been on questions of boundaries or territorial rights.

There remains a fourth kind of differences between States, and the most dangerous: those which do not admit of reduction to definite issues at all, or which can be reduced only to the ancient formula of Ennius: "*uter esset induperator.*" Contests for supremacy or predominant influence are not disposed of by argument, in whatever shape they are disguised; indeed, the Powers concerned are usually less willing to invite or tolerate interference in proportion as the formal cause of quarrel is weak. There has seldom been, on paper, a less substantial reason than that which was assigned for the greatest European war remembered by living men. Only one remedy would be quite effectual, namely, that a coalition of Powers of superior collective strength should be prepared to enforce the principles which now stand unanimously acknowledged by the Second Peace Conference of the Hague. A certain number of minor wars have already been prevented, or kept within bounds, by influence of this kind; but the beneficent arts of diplomacy as hitherto practised have certainly not lost their importance in maintaining peace among the Great Powers. It is a grave mistake to depreciate them, as unthinking or ignorant enthusiasts for arbitration have sometimes done. They have probably been successful in our own time oftener and on more critical occasions than the Governments concerned have yet thought it wise to make public. Meanwhile, the frequent repetition of declarations that war ought not to be entered on without a serious attempt at conciliation in some form—a kind of declaration which costs nothing, and which every Power cheerfully makes, but to which no definite interpretation is yet attached—does tend to produce, and may well in time produce, a genuine public opinion capable of affording a considerable moral sanction. Moreover, the existence of a standing quasi-judicial machinery makes it far easier for friendly States to tender their good offices without giving offence to either party.

Broadly speaking, there are two methods of international arbitration, and subdivisions of procedure within each of them. First, the parties may refer the matter in difference to a judge or judges of their own choice, in pursuance of a standing treaty or a special convention for the case in hand. The arbiter may be the ruler of a third State, or a tribunal composed of persons named by the parties directly, or in part by friendly Governments at their joint request. Secondly, the States concerned may prefer to use the machinery provided by a standing international agreement of more general scope.

All the important arbitrations to which Great Britain has been a party have been conducted on the system first mentioned. The reference of the Dogger Bank affair in 1904 to a Commission of enquiry is hardly an exception, for this was not properly an arbitration at all. The other system is that of the permanent Court established after the Hague Conference of 1899. This Court has not yet dealt with any dispute of the first magnitude, or with much European business; but it is hardly the part of those who preach peace and concord to be dissatisfied because nations are less litigious than they expected.

Many more or less ambitious projects of international jurisdiction and tribunals have been put forward in the course of the last two centuries and even earlier. It does not seem useful to describe or enumerate them here; but, before we speak of the Peace Conferences of 1899 and 1907 at the Hague, it may be well to review shortly the procedure actually employed in some of the leading cases of arbitration under conventions limited to the special occasion. We shall not dwell on the causes, particulars, or merits of the disputes which were thus quieted; for such matters belong to general political history, and some of them are dealt with elsewhere in this work.

The Arbitration between Great Britain and the United States on the claims generically known as the *Alabama* claims, for damage done by Confederate cruisers equipped or harboured in British ports during the American Civil War, was provided for by the Treaty of Washington of 1871; the award was made by a composite tribunal sitting at Geneva in 1872. This case is commonly said to have given great encouragement to the promoters of international arbitration, and cited as a kind of prerogative instance. An admirable example was certainly set by the determination of the two Powers to come to an understanding, and by the skill and tact of the diplomatists who settled the Treaty under anything but favourable conditions. There had been many months, it is said twenty, of secret diplomatic correspondence. To judge by the samples now accessible, much of it was, in tone and style, more like the wrangling of country lawyers over a partnership quarrel than the arguments of statesmen. It is hard to say whether Seward's or Lord Russell's temper was worse. If the American's ill-manners were cruder, the Englishman's were more deliberate and had less excuse. Between them, they came very near to involving their nations in a war which the occasion was wholly insufficient to justify. Lord Russell, moreover, showed remarkable ignorance of elementary legal conceptions which really do not go much beyond elementary common sense. He objected to the test of "due diligence" being applied to the conduct of England as a neutral Power, because he imagined that, if an arbitrator found the British Government wanting in due diligence, this finding would be an insult to the national honour as involving a charge of bad faith. If one could not be negligent without bad faith, there would be few honest men indeed in the world. With these unpromising materials, however, a Joint High Commission got to work at Washington in 1871, and settled the rules of a neutral's duty which the contracting parties embodied in the Treaty as the law to be applied to the case. This was done upon suggestions made in the instructions of the British Commissioners; and it was the real central point of the whole business. When these rules were accepted, the office of the formal tribunal constituted under the Treaty was almost confined to defining in detail a liability which, under those rules and on the notorious facts, must to some extent be admitted, and awarding damages accordingly. The immediate effect in England was certainly not to increase the favour in which international arbitration was held; nor could it well be disputed, in the result, that the damages were excessive, since a balance for which no claimants could be found was left in the hands of the United States.

Nevertheless, a fruitful example remained. A dispute between two Powers of the first rank, which, reasonably or not, had in fact become acute and even dangerous, was reduced to terms of judicial compensation without loss of honour on either side. Perfection was not to be looked for in an experiment of such novelty. The transitory details have long ceased to be material, and the precedent has been followed with better success in other cases. It is likewise immaterial, for this purpose, that the rules of the Treaty of Washington have not become part of the general law of nations.

After twenty years, another arbitral tribunal decided another question, that of the Behring Sea seal fishery, between Great Britain and Canada, on the one hand (Canada, whose interests were immediately concerned, having an official and even a leading part in the carriage of the proceedings), and the United States, on the other. The method may be described as that of the Geneva Arbitration, with considerable improvement. There were seven arbitrators: two named by Great Britain, two by the United States, one by the President of the French Republic, one by the King of Italy, and one by the King of Sweden and Norway.

The strictly judicial members of the tribunal were Lord Hannen for England and Justice Harlan of the Supreme Court at Washington for the United States, and the choice could not have been better. A distinct qualification was laid down by the Treaty, which required the arbitrators to be jurists of distinguished reputation, if possible acquainted with the English language. The Treaty also stated the specific questions which the tribunal was to answer. The Court sat in Paris, and made its award in August, 1893, a year and a half after the conclusion of the Treaty. In the result, the claim of the United States to an exclusive jurisdiction beyond the limits of territorial waters was disallowed by a majority of the arbitrators, and the provisions made by the Treaty for eventual further regulation came into play.

The political history of the dispute between Venezuela and Great Britain concerning the boundary of British Guiana, which had lasted for about forty years, has been given in an earlier volume of this *History*. Practically, the case for Venezuela was managed by the United States; it was therefore natural that the Venezuelan representatives on the tribunal were two members of the Supreme Court at Washington (Chief Justice Fuller and Justice Brewer). The British Government, through the Judicial Committee of the Privy Council, named Lord Herschell and

Sir R. Henn (now Lord) Collins. The four members so appointed named a fifth, Professor de Martens, of St Petersburg, who acted as President. There were two remarkable features about this Arbitration. First, the award was unanimous. Secondly, the Court made rules of procedure for itself. The rules were communicated to the Hague Conference of 1899, which was sitting at the time of the award, and adopted by it: and thus the settlement of a controversy which had been magnified far beyond the value of the subject-matter made a contribution of real importance to the formation of a recognised international procedure. A rational and acceptable scheme of procedure is the first condition for anything like a truly judicial handling of international questions.

In 1899 the republics of Chile and Argentina referred a long-pending boundary question to the sole award of the King of England. This was an interesting reversion to the oldest form of international arbitration, and it was justified by complete success. A few years earlier, objections would probably have been raised in the United States to a European monarch being appealed to as arbiter between two South American republics; but the relations between the United States and Great Britain were now cordial, and no such objection was heard of. An advisory Commission was appointed here, composed of Lord Macnaghten, Sir John Ardagh, and Sir Thomas Holdich. Early in 1902 Sir Thomas Holdich undertook in person a survey of the southern Andes for the better information of the commissioners, and in November of the same year the King made his award. The result gave satisfaction, it is believed, to both parties; they were certainly delivered from an excessive burden of warlike expenditure. An incidental consequence was the accession to the British navy of the *Swiftsure* and the *Triumph*, two battleships of original design and of great power for their size, built to the order of Chile and sold to Great Britain after the award. About the same time, a boundary question between Great Britain and Brazil was in like manner referred to the King of Italy alone; but this was so far from being a matter of acute controversy that very few people outside the Foreign Office heard of it.

In the case of the Alaska boundary, as in the Behring Sea case, the question was in the first line of Canadian much more than British interest. A novel experiment was tried in making up the arbitral Commission, which consisted of six members, three named by each party: they all were or ought to have been "impartial jurists of repute"; it is doubtful whether the first epithet fitted more than one of the six, and very doubtful how far the rest of the description, in any ordinary meaning of the words, included some of the others. Following the Behring Sea precedent, the Convention of July, 1903, under which the proceedings took place, laid down the specific questions to be decided.

The decision was on the whole against the Canadian claim of title, and the two Canadian judges who were members of the tribunal handed in separate dissenting opinions. So far as any general inferences can be drawn from this case, they do not seem favourable to the plan of referring questions to a body of arbitrators representing only the parties. It is difficult for such arbitrators, at best, to preserve a judicial balance of mind; the absence of an umpire makes it even more difficult. A better scheme, on similar general lines, had been proposed in an Arbitration Treaty of 1897 between Great Britain and the United States, which failed to take effect in consequence of a division of opinion in the American Senate on a purely domestic question of constitutional usage, namely, whether it did not impair the Senate's treaty-making power by dispensing with the specific consent of that body to every reference of a matter under dispute. But that project is now superseded by a much simpler form of reference to the tribunal of the Hague, to which the Treaty of 1903 between Great Britain and France led the way. We shall mention the recent Conventions after speaking of the Peace Conferences, and it does not appear useful to give the details of a scheme altogether unlikely to be revived or imitated. Enough to say that, in its anxiety to leave no reasonable ground of objection open, it provided three distinct forms of arbitration for different classes of disputes.

Meanwhile the question of permanent provisions for international arbitration had been much discussed, and there had been attempts, as we have noticed, to deal with the problem by treaties. By far the greatest steps in advance, however, have been made by the Peace Conference held at the Hague in 1899, on the invitation of the Emperor of Russia, and the later Conference of 1907, held at the same place and in like manner but with a more numerous attendance. At the Conference of 1899, the delegates of practically all the civilised Powers concurred in establishing a permanent judiciary system ready to be called into action whenever two or more States desire a matter in difference to be settled. After several proposals had been made and discussed, a convention was adopted on July 28, of which the form is understood to have been largely due to the British delegation, and especially to Lord Pauncefote. It provided for the conduct of good offices and mediation; enquiry by mixed commissions into disputed matters of fact; arbitral jurisdiction under agreements of reference; the constitution of a permanent Court, with an international office, at the Hague; and rules of procedure. Recourse to arbitration remains voluntary; but the preliminary friction, incident to choosing the arbitrators or persons who are to nominate them and settling their procedure, is got rid of by providing a standing scheme of regulation to govern all references to the Hague tribunal unless the parties have expressly agreed otherwise. The provision for Commissions of enquiry did good service in the case of the North Sea incident of 1904, during the Russo-Japanese War, when a Russian fleet on its way from the Baltic to the Channel, and ultimately to the Pacific, came upon the Hull fishing fleet off the Dogger Bank on a dark night and, mistaking them for hostile torpedo craft, opened fire. Happily, so far as there could be good fortune in such a conjuncture, the darkness checkered by fitful and crossing search-lights, the confusion of a sudden and vague alarm, want of training, and a rolling sea, conspired to make the Russian gunners' aim as uncertain as their officers' judgment, so that the loss of life was small and the material damage, though considerable, less than might have been expected. One or two detached ships of the Russian squadron itself fared ill enough.

When the matter first became known, public feeling in England had naturally enough run high. The informal good offices of the French Government, in alliance with Russia and on friendly terms with Great Britain, were probably the most important factor in bringing about an amicable settlement; but it would have been much harder, if an appropriate general method of procedure had not been already furnished by the cosmopolitan authority of the Hague Conference. A mixed naval Commission was formed on the model laid down by the Hague Convention, but with enlarged powers of deciding on responsibility as well as finding the facts. The proceedings were carried through with becoming judicial dignity and excellent discretion; due compensation was made; and the honour of the Russian service, which was deemed to have been called in question, was saved without offence to any one. It is doubtful whether a formal tribunal of jurists or diplomatists could have handled this delicate affair so well, if at all; and from this point of view the example is specially instructive.

The Conference of 1899, it must be observed, was not convoked in the first instance to do precisely the work which in the event it accomplished. Another object was put first in the general invitation or "rescript" addressed by the Tsar, through his Foreign Minister, to all the Powers represented at his Court (August 24, 1898): namely, "a possible reduction of the excessive armaments which weigh upon all nations," to be effected by "putting a limit to the progressive development of the present armaments." But it was not found practicable, either in 1899 or in 1907, to achieve anything in this direction beyond echoing the Tsar's pious wishes. In 1907, any serious discussion of the topic was declared impracticable beforehand. Indeed, it seems fairly plain to any one acquainted with the conduct of public business, that any arrangement for the reduction of armaments by mutual agreement among the Powers must involve the settlement of some proportionate scheme founded on considerations not only of the magnitude of the several States concerned but of the character of the interests to be protected and the protection reasonably required; further, that such a scheme cannot be established without some recognised comparative standard of naval and military power; and, moreover, that there are great technical difficulties in fixing such a standard, especially with regard to naval units of widely varying date, design, functions, and efficiency. Then, it seems hard to believe that for the necessary exchange of views on all these details, many of them entangled with confidential matter, an open conference of delegates from all the Governments in the world is the fittest place, or a fit or hopeful place at all. Long and strictly private negotiation, it is submitted, must precede any useful treatment of the disease of excessive armaments at a general conference; and the proper moment for such negotiation to begin, with any good prospect, among the Governments most concerned, will not be accelerated by the rhetorical repetition of commonplaces about the wickedness of war. Within five years, the sovereign who had convened the first Peace Conference was himself involved in war on a great scale by land and sea. Nothing is easier than for irresponsible preachers to point the moral of his ill-fortune. A more sober judgment will note the ironies of history without making haste to condemn their victims.

As the matter stands at present, Great Britain is the only Power that has made any definite overture towards the end which all agree to be desirable. The British Government has declared itself, both in Parliament and at the Hague Conference, ready to concur in an exchange of programmes of naval construction among the Great Powers. It is not known that this offer has met with any acceptance.

In 1907, the Second Peace Conference passed an amended convention for the settlement of international disputes, expressly superseding, as between the contracting Powers, the former convention of 1899, which therefore need not be further considered. By the provisions now in force resort to good offices or mediation is declared to be proper, and the spontaneous offer of such is recommended; offers of this kind cannot be complained of as unfriendly. A special form of mediation through other friendly Powers acting as seconds, and for the time superseding direct negotiation, is also recommended where applicable. The difference between a mediator and an arbitrator is elementary; but we note, for abundant caution, that a mediator's office is to advise without purporting to decide, whereas an arbitrator's is judicial, and he is bound to decide but has no right to advise. Leo XIII mediated with success between Germany and Spain in the matter of the Caroline Islands in 1885. Commissioners of enquiry may regulate their own procedure, and avail themselves of the offices and staff of the permanent Court at the Hague. Practical regulations are laid down to facilitate the collection of evidence, and the division of costs is provided for. As to arbitration, the constitution of the permanent Court of Arbitration is confirmed. Its essential feature is a standing list of qualified arbitrators, not more than four being named by each contracting Power. When a Court has to be made up, each Power concerned in the cause chooses two members from the list,

CH. XXII.

and the arbitrators choose an umpire; there are further and seemingly effectual provisions in case they fail to agree. The *bureau international*, which is the permanent office or chancellery of the Court, is under the direction of a diplomatic board at the Hague. Terms of reference are, as a rule, to be handed in by the parties; but the Court may settle them itself if so requested by both parties, or under certain conditions even if only required by one. Elaborate provisions are made for the conduct of the proceedings. Further, a more summary form of arbitration with two arbitrators and an umpire may be adopted in affairs of less weight. All this appears, from a lawyer's point of view, to be sound and businesslike work. Doubtless, the jurisdiction is voluntary: but so was all jurisdiction in its beginning. As time goes on, it will be less and less reputable among civilised States to talk of going to war without having exhausted the resources of the Hague Convention; and the necessity of any formal international declaration in that behalf may be avoided altogether, if the tribunal acquires by custom, as one hopes it will, a stronger authority than any express form of words would confer. That the time is not now ripe for any such form is shown by the vague and halting recognition "in principle" of a general duty of arbitration which is embodied in the Final Act of the Conference. Nor do we see much reason to regret the failure of an attempt to set up a new tribunal of arbitral justice, with permanent paid judges, which was to be more formal, more continuous, and less dependent on the parties' choice, and, it was hoped, would eventually supersede the existing Court. This scheme was brought forward by the United States. It broke down on the impossibility of agreeing in what manner and proportions judges should be appointed by the several Powers; the recognised equality of all independent States before the law of nations being extended by several members of the Conference, especially the leading South American delegates, to a claim for absolute equality in all political and administrative schemes. This interpretation, we submit, is perverse; but, on more than one occasion, it was among the gravest hindrances to the work of the Conference. In our opinion, however, there were much better reasons for not being in haste to imitate the forms of a Court exercising true federal jurisdiction. What is wanted to promote peace is not the nearest approach to compulsion, nor the most imposing Court, nor the most learned decisions possible, nor yet the speediest (for sometimes delay is rather of advantage), but a working plan for producing, with as little friction as may be, decisions likely to be accepted. This the two Peace Conferences at the Hague have given us, and it is much.

Meanwhile a considerable number of general treaties have been concluded (M. Renault says about sixty down to July, 1908) agreeing to refer differences to the Hague tribunal: the Anglo-French Treaty of 1903 led the way (the text may be seen in the *Law Quarterly Review*, Vol. XXI, p. 114, as well as in the usual official publications) and has served as a pattern. A rather special treaty between Italy and Argentina was communicated to the Hague Conference in September, 1907.

In the course of 1908, several Arbitration Treaties in identical form (closely resembling that of the Treaty between France and Great Britain) were concluded between the United States and other Powers, Great Britain among them. The operative article is as follows:—

> "Differences which may arise of a legal nature or relating to the interpretation of treaties existing between the two Contracting Parties, and which it may not have been possible to settle by diplomacy, shall be referred to the Permanent Court of Arbitration established at The Hague by the Convention of the 29th of July, 1899, provided, nevertheless, that they do not affect the vital interests, the independence, or the honour of the two Contracting States, and do not concern the interests of third Parties."

Due recognition is given to the constitutional position of the Senate in the United States, by requiring in every case a special agreement of reference, to be entered into by the President with the advice and consent of the Senate. The other Powers which are parties to these Conventions, down to July 1, 1908 (so they are officially called, not Treaties), are France, Italy, Japan, Mexico, the Netherlands, Norway, Portugal, Spain, Sweden, and Switzerland. For some reason the Conventions are limited to a period of five years, possibly to make amendments easier if any should be thought of.

A list of the Arbitration Treaties concluded by Great Britain down to July 1, 1909, will be found in the Bibliography to this chapter. Brazil made Arbitration Treaties with many Powers in the spring of 1909.

All or nearly all the above-mentioned Treaties contain, it will be noted, an exception of questions involving the vital interests, independence, or honour of the contracting States. Lord Salisbury wrote, in the course of the negotiations preceding the unratified treaty of 1897 with the United States: "Neither Government is willing to accept arbitration upon issues in which the national honour or integrity is involved." Clearly, no nation will submit to any tribunal the question whether it shall accede to demands which its rulers consider ruinous or humiliating. What arbitrable question was there between Elizabeth of England and Philip of Spain when the Armada was off the Lizard? or, as has been pertinently asked, between Austria and France in 1859, or Russia and Turkey in 1877? Therefore, some such clause of exception appears unavoidable if the good faith of treaties is to be upheld, and we confess that we do not attach much importance to its exact form. It may be said that these exceptions can be used frivolously or in bad faith. But the same drawback exists in the construction and application of all treaties whatever. Well-meant proposals were made at the Hague for settling a list of causes of difference which should not be deemed vital; but the only result that appeared practicable was an

CH. XXII.

enumeration of such matters of current business as have commonly been found well within the resources of diplomacy, and the project was wisely dropped.

We must now say a word of the Concert of Europe, a term so current as to be familiar to every one who has followed the course of affairs during the last generation. An enquirer from another planet, or even a citizen of the New World who had not attended much to recent European history, might be moved to ask : If there is a European Concert, what need is there of Peace Conferences, and why do armaments continue to grow ? The answer is that the Concert of Europe is a name which in modern practice conveniently designates a wholly local and anomalous episode in international politics, and disguises formal irregularities which only necessity has justified. Lord Salisbury thought the name "somewhat absurd." In the earlier part of the nineteenth century the current word appears to have been "system." Ever since the War of Greek Independence the Great Powers of Europe have endeavoured more or less constantly, and with more or less good results, to restrain the chronic elements of disorder in the Balkan peninsula and the eastern Mediterranean, due to the superposition of a dynasty bound by the law and the traditions of Islam on a mixed population of Christians agreeing in nothing but that name, and at feud with one another no less than with their nominal rulers. The Concert, such as it was, was far from harmonious in the days of Mehemet Ali's revolt, failed to prevent the Crimean War in 1853–4, and the Russo-Turkish War in 1877, and was impotent to deal with Egypt. That country has come practically under British protection by a series of accidents, makeshifts, and fictions whose outcome, now legitimate by the consent of the Powers, is the despair of legal and political definition. On the other hand the European Concert, in 1897, though unable to prevent war between Greece and Turkey, reduced it to comparatively trifling dimensions; and, better still, it pacified Crete, with much trouble, indeed, and in a clumsy fashion. Whether the international situation of Crete be more or less anomalous than that of Egypt is a question few publicists care to discuss if they can avoid it. One thing is certain, that in point of form the acts of interference in Crete undertaken by the Powers in 1897 and 1898, including a pacific blockade, repeated prevention of Turkish troops from landing, and assumption of administrative and judicial authority, gave the Sultan an excellent cause of war against every one of them ; but there were more excellent reasons against the exercise of his right, and all these acts were, in fact, authorised sooner or later by the more or less willing consent or acquiescence of the Turkish Government.

The endeavours of the Powers to improve the state of Macedonia, which were carried on with indifferent success for some years, were interrupted, and will, one may hope, be superseded by the peaceful revolution of 1908 which restored the Turkish Constitution. The still later events of 1908 and 1909 are too recent to be matter of historical criticism, but they have in any case proved that the Concert of Europe no longer exists.

With regard to the Russian initiative in the matter of peace conferences, it will be remembered that, so early as 1804, the Emperor Alexander I proposed a league of which the principle was to be obligatory mediation, and which should aim, among other objects, at framing a code of the law of nations. In 1818, at the Conference of Aix-la-Chapelle, he spoke of an ideal "system of Europe" in a wider sense than that which the "Concert" has come to bear in later times. It would seem that the formation of any such system can be looked for only when the political institutions and ideas prevailing in the chief nations of the world have become much more nearly uniform than they are; and it is far from clear that the present tendency is to approximation, for the fashion—a passing one, let us hope—is rather to exaggerate national and racial differences.

The Declaration of London, 1909, does not fall within the scope of this chapter, as it is of a technical character, and deals only with questions arising out of an actual state of war. It is, however, an important supplement to the work done by the Hague Conference of 1907. Better definition of the rules governing maritime warfare and the rights and duties of nations in relation thereto will remove occasions of controversy, which have often tended to involve neutral Powers in the quarrels of the original belligerents.

CHAPTER XXIII.

SOCIAL MOVEMENTS.

THE condition of the people in 1842, as seen in the streets of Bolton in Lancashire, was described by Colonel Perronet Thompson (1783–1869) in language that palpitates with anger. "Anything like the squalid misery, the slow, mouldering, putrefying death by which the weak and feeble of the working classes are perishing here, it never befel my eyes to behold nor my imagination to conceive. And the creatures seem to have no idea of resisting or even repining. They sit down with oriental submission, as if it was God and not the landlord that was laying his hand upon them." At the same time the new Boards of Guardians throughout the whole country were employing between forty and fifty thousand adult able-bodied men in oakum-picking, stone-breaking, and bone-crushing, in the "labour yards" attached to the hated "Bastilles of the poor," on pittances of poor relief just sufficient to keep them and their families alive. Of such workers as were fortunate enough to be still in wage-earning employment, men, women, and children, "pent up in a close dusty atmosphere from half-past five or six o'clock in the morning till seven or eight o'clock at night, from week to week, without change, without intermission, it is not to be wondered at," states a contemporary government Report, "that they fly to the spirit and beer-shops and the dancing-house on the Saturday nights to seek those, to them, pleasures and comforts which their own destitute and comfortless homes deny." In the Bolton of the twentieth century, though there is still individual squalor and personal misery to be found, the population—six times as numerous as in 1842—may, taken as a whole, safely be described as prosperous, healthy, intellectually alert, taking plenty of holidays, and almost aggressive in its independent self-reliance. So great a change, to be paralleled in many an industrial city of western Europe, demands an explanation.

To some observers of the first half of the nineteenth century—to John Dalton (1766–1844) or Sir Humphry Davy (1778–1829), for instance, or to Michael Faraday (1791–1867) or Sir Charles Lyell

(1797–1875)—it may have seemed, as is still sometimes asserted, that it was to physical or biological science, "far more than to the work of statesmen or to the creation of constitutions, or to the elaboration of social systems or to the study of sociology" that we had to look as "the great ameliorator of the human lot in life." Unfortunately for this view, we must recognise that physical science had already achieved great marvels, and that some of the principal mechanical inventions which transformed English industry and enormously increased the wealth of its wealthy classes were already more than half a century old, when Bolton, and industrial England generally, lay, in 1842, in the lowest trough of its misery. If to ameliorate the human lot in life had been any part of the purpose of the great mechanical inventions, or of the far-reaching discoveries of physical science of the preceding half-century, they must be accounted to have egregiously failed. Since then, we have had to admit, as John Stuart Mill indicated already in 1848, that all the discoveries of physical science and all the mechanical inventions in the world, have not lightened, and by themselves never will lighten, the toil of the wage-earning class. A scientific discovery or a mechanical invention, though it may revolutionise the processes of industry and vastly augment our total productive power, does not in itself affect the terms of the bargain which the employer of labour is able to make with the wage-earner; does not make the profitableness of the "marginal man" to the employer any greater than before; and, accordingly, does not by itself make the working day shorter or the wages greater.

What mechanical, physical, chemical, and biological science has done to enlarge the range of our knowledge and augment our power over the forces of nature will be described in a subsequent chapter. But it is demonstrated by a whole century of experience that, while every advance in our knowledge of the universe increases the potential capacity of those who control affairs, this mere increase of knowledge, as a matter of fact, does nothing in itself to prevent or to diminish the poverty and social wretchedness of those in the rear. These are, indeed, in the procession of civilisation, left all the further behind. The social result of any increased power over nature enjoyed by the community as a whole depends on the use to which the community as a whole chooses to put it. But the ordered sequences of physical and biological phenomena which usually claim the name of science do not exhaust its scope. Of man in society, with all his various groupings and arrangements, as forming part of the universe, we may also increase our knowledge, and thereby increase our power to control phenomena outside the realm of physical or biological science, which are potent in the amelioration of the human lot in life. In short, there may be progress in political science, as well as in the sciences dealing with the non-human part of the universe. What has transformed the Bolton cotton-spinners of 1842 into the Bolton cotton-spinners of the twentieth century—what falls therefore to be described in this chapter—is no mechanical, physical, chemical, or biological discovery, but a certain subtle revolution in the ideas of men; a certain advance in our acquaintance with those social laws which, to use Montesquieu's pregnant phrase, "are the necessary relations derived from the nature of things"; and, therewith, a certain increase of power to influence social phenomena. This power to influence social phenomena has taken shape in specific social movements associated with such appellations as municipal action and cooperation, factory legislation and trade unionism, sanitation and education, the Poor Law and the collective provision for the orphans, the sick, and the aged, and all that vaguely defined social force commonly designated socialism. These social movements, while the chemists and physicists have been at work in their laboratories, have resulted in the development of new social tissue; have been, in short, gradually transforming human society itself.

The revolution of the last three-quarters of the nineteenth century in men's ideas about social arrangements, and the consequent changes in social tissue which those ideas have been causing, may be described in many different ways. We may first notice, partly as cause and partly as effect, a certain shifting of the very basis of the local organisation of the community. In the manor, in all the varieties of the manorial borough, in the gild, and in the unreformed municipal corporation, men had for centuries unconsciously grouped themselves on the basis of their occupations as producers. Whatever else these social groupings may have been, on the economic side the manor was, at the outset, a group of agricultural tenants, the gild a group of craftsmen or traders, even the borough corporation a group of burgage occupiers whose economic interests were similar. These groups of tenants, craftsmen, or burghers—at no time coextensive with the whole of the local residents—had, by their very nature, a tendency to exclusiveness, and inevitably became small oligarchies in the midst of an unprivileged population, losing whatever sense they may once have had of fulfilling the communal needs, and expressing only their own members' separate and exclusive interests. Thus it was, throughout western Europe, the organisation of local administration on this old basis, which was essentially that of associations of producers, that long stood in the way of social reform. We see in England the slow beginnings of a different grouping in the gradual rise during the seventeenth and eighteenth centuries of the parish vestries and the various bodies of road or harbour or town Improvement Commissioners, the latter as yet unnoticed by historians, which began to provide for the needs, and to act in the name, not of this or that exclusive group, but of all the local residents. And, as all the local residents necessarily used or enjoyed the benefits of the roads, the harbours, the lighted pavements, the cleansed streets, the improved thoroughfares, and the organisations for the protection of life and property, which these new local governing bodies, by the opening of the nineteenth century, were beginning to develop, we may properly regard them as associations of consumers.

This was the real import of the revolution effected in England and Wales by the Municipal Corporations Act of 1835. It substituted, in the structure of English local government, for the associations which, in their economic aspect, had originated as associations of producers, with their exclusive interests and tendencies, an organisation of the residents of each locality, for the purpose of satisfying their common needs. The Act was incomplete, and in many ways imperfect. It took three-quarters of a century for the principles then adopted to be carried into every part of English local government. The municipal history of the nineteenth century, all-important as it has been to the life of the nation, has found, as yet, no historian. Of the steps in the structural development we need only mention, so far as England is concerned, the gradual absorption, between 1840 and 1870, of nearly all the old bodies of Town Improvement Commissioners, and the concentration in the Town Council of practically all the functions of municipal government; the admission, between 1835 and the present day, of a hundred-and-fifty new and growing towns to full municipal privileges; the gradual democratisation, between 1867 and 1885, of the municipal councils by various changes in franchise and qualification (including the removal of all property qualification, and the acceptance, as electors, of the dwellers in single rooms and of independent women occupiers); the extension to growing urban communities, from 1848 onwards, under the Public Health Acts, of what were practically municipal powers of self-government under other names; the organisation, in 1888, of the local government of the whole metropolitan area and of the rural districts on what was virtually the same municipal basis; and the establishment, in 1894, of Parish Councils in the villages.

In 1870, as the result of changes made while the Education Bill of that year was under consideration by the House of Commons, there was a temporary reversion to the eighteenth century type of local organisation, separately elected School Boards being established independently of the general local governing body of the locality. In 1902 and 1903 these were all abolished, their duties being transferred to the general governing body of the Borough or County. Of the separately elected local governing bodies there remains, in 1910, only the Board of Guardians, which had been established under the Act of 1834 to administer the public provision for the relief of the poor; and, in 1909, a Royal Commission, appointed to overhaul the whole Poor Law administration, recommended the immediate abolition of this separate authority, and the transfer of its duties to the Borough and County Councils. With the exception of the management of some of the great rivers and ports, which does not logically come within the functions to be entrusted to the ratepayers of a particular urban area, and for which accordingly there are often separately appointed trusts or commissions, the whole of England and Wales may be said to be now under democratic municipal government, on the lines advocated by Jeremy Bentham, adopted for the Boroughs by Lord Melbourne in 1835 and for London and the rural counties by the Ministry of Lord Salisbury in 1888. To the local Council of citizens, elected by ballot, annually or triennially, by the resident occupiers of house, office, or room, without qualification or restriction, is accorded a practically unlimited freedom, within the sphere allotted to it by law, to spend as it pleases, without any effective government control, the compulsory levies which, practically without legal limit, it is empowered, by mere majority vote, to make upon all the occupiers of land or houses within its area. It has taken more than a couple of generations for the local government of the rural districts, as well as that of the towns, to become (as Francis Place predicted in 1835) in this way "municipalised"; and (as may now be added) for this democratic organisation on the basis of the association of consumers for the supply of their own needs to be recognised as "Municipal Socialism."

Of the development of local government in western Europe and the United States—in its collective performance for the community of services formerly left to individual enterprise, essentially similar to that in the United Kingdom—space does not permit us to treat. The number and variety of services performed by the local governing bodies of France and Switzerland, Germany and Austria, Belgium and Denmark, Italy and Holland, like that of the local governments of New Zealand and the Argentine Republic, is often greater than in English or American municipalities. The municipal expenditure of New York and Paris exceeds even that of London.

However we may regard it, to this local collective activity, in its numerous and varied manifestations, is to be attributed a large share of the social transformation of all the cities of the civilised world, during the last three-quarters of the nineteenth century. We naturally see this transformation most clearly at what may be termed the nodal points of society, the urban centres where men are most thickly clustered together. The rapid development and multiplication of these nodal points is at once a cause and a result of the transformation. Throughout western Europe, the United States, Australasia, and South Africa (and, in fact, throughout the civilised world) the number and proportion of the dwellers in towns has increased, and is increasing, out of all proportion to the rural population; so that in many countries one-half, and in the most developed countries three-fourths, of all the inhabitants are now to be found in urban communities. In place of a world in which the towns were but exceptions in the common range of rural life, we have a world of towns, between which there are still to be found interstices of country. These urban communities have left behind them, once for all, the ideal of a society of independent, self-sufficing households, each producing for its own needs. Instead, they take on the character, gradually, and at first without social self-consciousness, of cooperative communities, based upon the obligatory membership of municipal citizenship, in which one function after another is organised and fulfilled for the common benefit by the collective forces of the social group. Thus, we see throughout western Europe, and particularly in the England of the latter half of the nineteenth century, the municipal governments administering on a communal basis such services, once entirely a matter for individual self-provision by each household, as paving, lighting, and cleansing the streets; the prevention of assault, theft, and damage by flood or fire; the removal of faecal matter and garbage; the public supply and distribution on a large scale of the primary needs of existence, such as water, housing, milk, and now, in one place or another, even other food; the communal provision of artificial light, of certain forms of fuel, and of hydraulic or electric power; the provision of the means of transport and of intercommunication; the collective production, in public forests or on drainage farms, or in connexion with other municipal departments or institutions, of all sorts of agricultural products, and of this or that manufacture; the complete and minutely detailed care of the orphans, the sick, the blind, the deaf and dumb, the crippled, the mentally defective, the infirm and the aged; elaborate provision for the special needs connected with maternity, infancy, childhood, and the disposal of the dead; the provision of schools for children and of opportunities of instruction for adolescents and adults, as well as of libraries, museums, and art galleries; the organisation of apprenticeship, technical education, artistic production, and scientific research; the public organisation of the labour market; the prevention and treatment of destitution and distress caused by unemployment or misfortune; and the provision, for all classes and all ages, of music and other means of recreation, including the regulation of amusement and even its organisation. Among the tens of thousands of urban communities, in which more than half the population of western Europe and Australasia and an equally rapidly increasing proportion of the United States are now to be found, we see today an infinite variety in the extent, the manner, and the results of this collective organisation. What is universal and ubiquitous is a steady and continuous growth in the volume and the range of collective activity.

In the reorganisation of society which is thus everywhere proceeding, one important element in the consciousness of personal freedom, on the one hand, and in the efficiency of the social service, on the other, is the relation that exists between the local administrative bodies and the national Government. Here we may distinguish three main types. In France and Germany, the local administration, which is largely entrusted

CH. XXIII.

to salaried officials of high professional qualifications, is, broadly speaking, closely supervised by and completely subordinate to the various departments of the executive Government of the State. The functions and powers of the local councils of elected representatives are narrowly limited; and their actual interferences with the local administration are, in almost all cases, subject to the control and approval of the central executive departments. In sharpest contrast stand the local governing bodies of the United States, which are, broadly speaking, wholly autonomous corporations, subject only to the State Legislature, to which the State executive departments are also subject, and which is itself limited in its powers by the State Constitution, to be changed only, after more or less elaborate precautions, by the electorate of the State as a whole. The result is that the administration of the local governing bodies of the United States is, broadly speaking, subject to no external supervision or control other than that of the ratepaying and voting electorates of their several localities.

In the United Kingdom, a middle course has been pursued. Prior to the Reform Act of 1832, there was virtually no connexion between the executive departments of the national Government and such local governing bodies as existed, which were accordingly, within the ample scope of the powers conferred on them by the law of the land, in practice as completely autonomous as those of the United States have remained. Nor did any supervision or control by the national Government enter into Lord Melbourne's plan of 1835. Gradually, however, it was perceived that it was essential that there should be, at any rate, some external audit of local government accounts; and that some external approval should be required before the local governing body was permitted, not merely to spend the rates paid by those who elected it, but also to embark on enterprises to be incurred out of loans mortgaging the future. Presently, it was realised that the government of a town was not merely a matter of interest to the inhabitants of that town, and that, whether in respect of roads and bridges, or in respect of infectious disease, whether in the health or in the education of its citizens, the nation as a whole had something at stake. The central executive departments had, moreover, at their command, a wider experience and a greater knowledge than any local body could possess. The difficulty was how to secure national inspection and audit, and national supervision and control, without offending the susceptibilities of local autonomy on the one hand, and without, on the other, losing the advantages of local initiative and freedom. The problem has been solved in the United Kingdom by the expedient of the grant in aid. The national Government, in the past three-quarters of a century, has successively "bought" the rights of inspection, audit, supervision, initiative, criticism, and control, in respect of one local service after another, and of one kind of local governing body after another, by the grant, in aid of the local finances, and therefore of the local ratepayers, of annual subventions from the national revenue. These subventions have often been demanded by local governing bodies, and sometimes ignorantly accorded by complacent Ministries, as mere "doles" in relief of local burdens. Their actual function is, in fact, seldom explicitly realised. The bulk of the various grants in aid are now given conditionally on particular services being conducted in general accord with regulations framed for the purpose, and designed to secure a certain prescribed minimum of efficiency. The executive department necessarily assumes the duty of supervision and inspection, in order to see that the conditions are complied with. Since the amount of the grant may be reduced in default of such compliance, the criticisms and suggestions of the executive department, accompanied as they may be by a warning, come with authoritative force. They are not, as they are in France and Germany, mandatory injunctions, leaving nothing to local initiative and local discretion. The local governing body may grumble and dispute the accuracy or the cogency of the inspector's criticisms, or the value of his suggestions. Gradually, however, in one way or another, these well-informed criticisms and suggestions are attended to, at the instance of the local governing body itself, and in its own way. By this process, and with the aid of government grants, such local services as police and education have, without loss of consciousness of local autonomy, gradually been levelled up to a high minimum of efficiency. The process with regard to public health and the local provision for the invalidated has only just begun.

In the relations in which, with regard to the several services that it renders, the municipal association of consumers stands to its individual members, we see a wide variety. Consumption or use of the services may be legally compulsory, or may be left optional. It may be effectively voluntary, or virtually obligatory. Sometimes, the services are supplied to the individual users or consumers on payment of the whole or part of the average cost, in proportion to the amount supplied, as with gas and electricity; sometimes, in return for payment at generalised rates per unit irrespective of cost, as with road or bridge or ferry tolls, or the postal and tramway services; sometimes, for payments which purport to be made for the service, but are actually computed on some basis of fiscal ability, irrespective of the amount of service enjoyed, as is usual with water supply. Most commonly, however, the services are furnished on a frankly communistic basis, that is to say gratuitously, or at a nominal charge, with or without restriction or limit of user, the cost being defrayed from the communal property of the inhabitants, or levied upon them, according to their presumed ability, by means of taxation. So rapid, so unselfconscious, and so ubiquitous has been this development of municipal services that no complete statistical or descriptive survey of it has yet been made; and there is, as yet, no scientific study of its fiscal processes, and especially none of its "special assessments," or charges on the individual for special services rendered. All that can be predicated of western Europe as a whole is that the extent, the variety, and the success of these communal enterprises, is, decade by decade, rapidly increasing. In England, the total capital under communal administration of this sort now amounts to more than a thousand millions sterling (or over £22 per head of population of the whole country)—a total that probably exceeds the entire capital of the England of Elizabeth, of the England of Cromwell, and even of the England of Sir Robert Walpole. To estimate how much this development of municipal services has meant in the amelioration of the human lot in life, let anyone consider how potent, how continuous and, in the crowded city life, how all-pervading, is the efficacy, in preventing suffering, degradation, and demoralisation among the masses, of the schoolmaster and the policeman, of the public doctor and the hospital, of the care of the orphans and the aged, of the systems of drainage and water supply, of the provision of parks and libraries. It is these things—not the discovery of radium or of the origin of species or the latest advances in spectrum analysis—that stand between the great urban aggregations of the twentieth century and the brutality and misery of barbarism. The typical figure of the England of the Middle Ages was the lord of the manor; the dominant types of the England of a century ago were the improving landlord and the capitalist mill-owner; the most characteristic personages of the England of the twentieth century are the elected councillor, the elementary schoolmaster, the school-doctor, and the borough engineer.

We see an essentially similar development of associations of consumers in another direction, specially characteristic of the latter part of the nineteenth century, differing from municipal government in resting on the basis of voluntary membership. What is known as the cooperative movement, the beginnings of which are to be found in the eighteenth century, has assumed different forms in different countries and in different decades. At the outset, it often took the shape of associations of producers, little communities of agriculturists or craftsmen, seeking themselves to own and to direct the instruments of their joint industry, and to share its product among their own members. These early cooperative experiments in agriculture and manufactures, sometimes limited in their aims, sometimes passing into communistic settlements—though taken up with fervent belief and potent driving force by Robert Owen (1771–1858), and frequently repeated by different groups of enthusiasts for half a century—failed to secure a permanent footing, and were one by one abandoned. Without realising how great was the discovery that they had made, the twenty-eight weavers of Rochdale in 1844 formed their little cooperative society in a new way, on the basis of the association of consumers. It was in the desire to organise jointly the supply of their own needs and to combine for the more advantageous expenditure of their own incomes—

not in the aspiration, which was one of the common forms of the time, towards cooperation as producers—that "the Rochdale Pioneers" inaugurated, and within half a century created, what has been aptly described as a State within the State.

Obtaining the necessary capital by their members' own savings, fed from the ever-growing profits of their enterprises, the Cooperators have spread from town to town throughout the United Kingdom, and advanced from success to success. Their two-and-three-quarter million members, mostly of the wage-earning class, and representing probably one-fifth of the whole population, are now aggregated in about 1500 separate societies, which are themselves united in several great federations. Among them they carry on every kind of business (except only the provision of alcoholic drinks), from agriculture and manufacture to transport and banking; they have their own arable, pasture, and fruit farms, and their own creameries, butter and bacon and biscuit works, cocoa and jam and sauce and pickle factories; their own flour-mills and bakeries; their own dressmaking and shirtmaking and tailoring work-shops, and even a corset factory; their own cotton-mills and clothing factories; their own hide and skin and boot and shoe and brush and mat and soap and lard and candle and furniture works; their own tinplate works and metal ware and crockery factories; their own printing establishments and their own newspapers; their own tea estates in Ceylon; their own buyers in foreign countries and their own ships on the sea; their own thousands of distributive stores, their own arrangements for insurance, their own banks, and even their own common libraries. Today, in the United Kingdom, the amount of the trade thus done by the two-and-three-quarter millions of Cooperative families with their fifty-five millions sterling of capital—the aggregate amount of the commodities and services thus supplied by themselves to themselves by the agency of their little army of 50,000 salaried officials, of the work thus performed for the common benefit without the supposed indispensable incentive of individual profit-making, and yet without any of the im-practicabilities of communism—exceeds one hundred and twenty millions sterling annually; or more than the aggregate receipts from all sources of the municipalities and county councils and the other local governing bodies put together.

The two movements of municipalisation and cooperation have, in fact, been in the United Kingdom the complements of each other, and have as yet scarcely overlapped. Both represent an application of democracy to the supply of the wants of the household. The universal and compulsory cooperation of the citizens, embodied in municipal government, has developed so far mainly in the provision, by the agency of a salaried municipal staff, of gratuitous or nearly gratuitous services, or of such fundamental common necessities as water, light, transport, and housing. The bringing under democratic control of the manufacture and distribution of the thousand and one commodities of food, clothing, and furniture that each household also requires has been undertaken, in the main, by the Cooperative Society formed on a voluntary basis and acting through its own salaried staff of officials. Together, as the result of the growth of the latter half of the nineteenth century these two movements in the United Kingdom have brought under collective control the supply of commodities and services representing an annual expenditure of something like two hundred millions sterling, or approximately one-eighth of the whole personal expenditure of the United Kingdom.

So great a shifting of the control and management of the production and distribution of the commodities by which we live could not fail to produce far-reaching social changes; changes which are all the greater in that they have taken place largely in the range of the life of the manual workers, and are, indeed, as yet scarcely known or appreciated by the middle and upper classes.

While the cooperative movement has, since its new birth in 1844, had enthusiastic prophets from other social classes—prophets and propagandists like Frederick Denison Maurice (1805–72), Thomas Hughes (1822–96), and Vansittart Neale (1810–92)—it has been essentially a working class movement. Moreover, it has been a movement without great intellectual personalities, in which integrity, prudence, and a certain gift among the thousands of committee-men of patient unselfish service in humdrum duties have counted for more than genius, though the historian must record the lifelong propaganda of George Jacob Holyoake (1817–1906). It is, in fact, in its intellectual and moral influence upon its members and the education of character, even more than the financial savings that it effects and encourages, that the cooperative movement has wrought a beneficent revolution among tens of thousands of working class families in the mining and manufacturing centres, and has contributed so largely to the social transformation of Great Britain. Each of the fifteen hundred cooperative societies, administering its own tens of thousands of pounds' worth of capital, engaging in an innumerable variety of enterprises, manufacturing as well as distributive, and sharing in the wider life of the federated movement as a whole, is managed by little committees of almost exclusively working class representatives, democratically elected by all the members, and accounting for their action at quarterly public meetings where all the affairs of the society are discussed. The largest society, the federal organisation known as the Cooperative Wholesale Society, wielding six millions of capital, doing twenty-five million pounds a year of business, employing nearly 20,000 hands, in a hundred different trades, at a hundred-and-fifty separate establishments, in ten different counties, is all managed by a committee of thirty-two ex-workmen, elected annually by the two million members. To the half-century of training in public administration and in the working of representative institutions, which the cooperative movement has provided in nearly all the English and Scottish mining and manufacturing centres, the British working class owes much of its political education. A similar educational effect is to be seen in Ireland, where the cooperative movement, established practically by the patient service of Sir Horace Plunkett, is scarcely twenty years old. Here, the prominent type is that of the cooperative creamery or butter factory, established by a group of peasant farmers or small holders for the better disposal of the milk of their cows. The cooperative creamery is managed by a committee of the contributing members, and the profits are shared among them in proportion to the quantity and quality of the milk supplied by each. Beginning with a common enterprise of this sort, the small holders of many localities have learnt to combine and to work together for other purposes in which they have a common interest.

The cooperative movement is often ignorantly described as having succeeded in distribution and failed in production. Yet, beginning first with distribution, the fifteen hundred cooperative societies in Great Britain have built up a large number of manufacturing enterprises of the most varied kind and not a few of agricultural character, especially in dairy products. Their creameries and their manufacturing enterprises enjoy a permanent and ever-growing success. Five of the largest flour-mills in England, producing annually food for two million persons, and the most extensive boot and shoe factory in the United Kingdom, turning out more than a million pairs a year, are both owned and managed by the federated two millions of cooperators. It is, however, true that another type of cooperative society, founded on the diametrically opposite principle of the association of producers, has always languished, and has never attained any great measure of success. Taken up by the Christian Socialists of 1848, the ideal of the " self-governing workshop," in which the wage system would be superseded by groups of craftsmen, themselves owning the capital with which they worked, and selling the common product for the common benefit, long continued to captivate successive generations of idealistic workmen and philanthropists. But innumerable experiments have demonstrated that this organisation, though it may live for a time, and even for a long time in particular industries, is not usually compatible with the discipline, the concentration of managerial capacity, and the accumulation of capital, required by modern competitive industry. Cooperative societies of this kind, generally confining themselves to industries of low capitalisation in proportion to the number employed, either fail altogether, or else depart from the " self-governing workshop " ideal—mostly coming, in fact, to consist, in large proportion, of investing members who are not workers, and who appoint a manager to direct wage-workers who are not members. The modern form in which the idea of the

CH. XXIII.

association of producers now finds embodiment is that of profit-sharing, often termed industrial copartnership, or the concession by the owners of the capital of a bonus over and above wages, combined, if possible, with some representation of the manual workers in the council of partners or directors by which the business is directed. This, though in practice little more than a philanthropic modification of joint-stock capitalism, has in certain cases had a great result in stimulating saving among the best of the workmen, and in enabling them to join the class of small investors.

On the Continent of Europe, the cooperative movement took at first other forms. In Germany, the most prominent for a long time was that of the cooperative loan society, where the joint savings or the corporate borrowings of the members constituted a fund from which loans could be made to such of their own number as required capital, a system of mutual guarantee and neighbourly supervision enabling this credit to be given safely to individual borrowers without means. We need not here distinguish between the Schulze-Delitzsch banks, started about 1850 by Hermann Schulze, burgomaster of Delitzsch, specially adapted to urban circumstances, and spreading mainly in the towns; and the Raiffeisen banks, begun about the same time by Friedrich Wilhelm Raiffeisen, burgomaster of a district near Neuwied, designed to meet the needs of agriculturists, and spreading chiefly in the country. The Schulze-Delitzsch banks, of which there have come to be over a thousand, with over half a million members, and loan transactions of a hundred and fifty million pounds sterling annually, are individually larger institutions than the majority of the Raiffeisen banks, of which there are now no fewer than 13,000 with a million and a half members, and loan transactions approaching two hundred million pounds sterling annually. In this form, cooperation, while bringing under collective control the banking services needed by its members, and, so to speak, "democratising" the moneylender, is so far from aiming at superseding individual profit-making enterprise, that it has come to the aid of the *petite industrie*, alike in manufacture and in agriculture. Among the small masters and jobbing handicraftsmen, by whom so much of German industry is still carried on, and especially among the peasant proprietors and small holders who contribute so large a proportion of its agriculture, this popular cooperation to supersede the individual banker or usurer—to perform collectively for the common good what would otherwise be done individually for private profit—has wrought marvels of prosperity.

In France, the most prominent part in the cooperative movement was long played by small cooperative societies engaged in manufacturing industry, in which many of the workers were members. But, with increasing international intercourse, all forms of cooperation are now to be found in all the countries of western Europe; the largest part being now played by the Cooperative Societies of the nature of associations of consumers, who combine in order, by their own salaried agents, to provide for themselves collectively, whether in agriculture, manufacturing, banking, transport, or retail distribution, without the intervention of any profit-maker, what they and their households individually require.

Such a shifting as we have described of the very basis of social organisation from producers to consumers in the development of municipal government and the cooperative movement, could not fail, even though largely without consciousness of itself, to influence the politics and the legislation of the time.   In the United Kingdom in particular, the whole movement for freedom of trade, whether it took the form of abolition of gild and apprenticeship restrictions, or removing the customs barriers between nations, obtained its popular support and its far-reaching influence largely from the claim of the consumer to free the products he needed or desired, from the bonds and fetters of custom or law or tax.   The English manufacturer of the early part of the nineteenth century may have desired Free Trade as a means of growing rich beyond the dreams of avarice; but Peel and Gladstone opened the ports because it was felt that the claims of the consumer could no longer be denied.   Other countries followed the lead thus given by the United Kingdom.   The last remnants of gild ordinance and customary regulations hampering free competition passed rapidly away, and " Cobden Treaties" and "most favoured nation clauses" seemed, by the end of the third quarter of the nineteenth century, destined at no distant date to remove all "artificial" obstacles, and to attain the " Early Victorian " economic ideal of that perfect freedom of competition in which the consumer finds all the economic processes of the world conducted in obsequious obedience to his taste or whim, at the lowest possible cost of production.

But it gradually appeared that, in this apotheosis of the consumer, there were certain adverse features.   The "industrial revolution," as it is called, which took place in England in the eighteenth century and on the Continent of Europe and in the United States at various dates in the nineteenth century, had resulted in all forms of industry, whether mining or manufacturing, transport or retail distribution, and even the greater part of agriculture, being organised on a capitalist basis.   Especially in manufacturing industry, and in the towns, the typical figure ceased to be that of the master craftsman, himself a manual worker, who, in his family group of journeymen and apprentice, owned his industrial plant and the commodity that he produced, and sold that commodity for his own profit.   In his place, we have the capitalist *entrepreneur*, using his capital to hire large numbers of lifelong wage-earners, entirely divorced from any economic interest either in the plant with which they work or the product which the associated labour of the factory or mine turns out for the profit of the proprietor.   The forge of the village blacksmith has been superseded by the iron foundry, employing scores or hundreds

CH. XXIII.

of "hands." The latter part of the nineteenth century witnessed a continuous and almost ubiquitous tendency towards the consolidation of industrial enterprises into larger and larger aggregates, in the twentieth century sometimes amounting to as many as fifty thousand workmen in a single capitalist enterprise; though this tendency is far less marked in agriculture than in other forms of enterprise. The result has been, throughout the whole of the nineteenth century, that the proportion of the workers who owned the product of their labour, or who participated in the profit derived from its sale, has steadily diminished; while the proportion of recipients of a mere wage or salary has steadily increased. The opening of the twentieth century finds, except in the agricultural small holdings of certain countries, and in a few surviving handicrafts, nearly the whole manual-working class divorced from the soil and from the ownership of the capital with which it works; dependent (apart from its relatively small invested savings) exclusively on wages; and constituting, in all advanced industrial nations, from two-thirds to four-fifths of the entire population. The nations have become, not democracies of independent producers such as Rousseau and Jefferson and Franklin contemplated, but "democracies of hired men," whose economic interests are primarily not in the amount of their product, of which they enjoy no share, but in the conditions of employment that "freedom of competition" accords to them.

It is the growing popular appreciation of this fact, long unseen either by the economists or by the capitalist class, which has, in the main, produced the social movements of the past three-quarters of a century. It seemed of small advantage to the Lancashire coal-miner of 1842 that he might get his clothes cheaper by means of perfect freedom of competition, if this meant also that he found himself driven to work excessive hours under insanitary conditions, in mines where precautions against accidents were omitted because they were expensive to the employer, and for wages which the employer's superiority in economic strength inevitably reduced to the barest subsistence level. It was a poor consolation to the Bolton cotton-spinner of 1842 that he could buy more cheaply the coal used by his wretched household, when the cotton-mill (equipped with the latest mechanical inventions for diminishing human toil) was compelling him and his wife and his little children to labour for twelve or fifteen hours a day, under revolting sanitary conditions, amid dangerous machinery left unfenced for the sake of economy, and in an atmosphere deliberately made unhealthy by gas and steam, in order that there might be fewer threads broken in the yarn that he was making. When the results of unrestrained competition in the employment of labour were gradually, and very slowly, perceived by the philanthropists, and made known by Robert Owen (1771–1858) and Lord Shaftesbury (1801–85), the statesmen found that they had no answer. The Free Trade economists of the first half of the nineteenth century—

and indeed, all who, consciously or unconsciously, were basing human society upon the needs and desires of the consumers—had learnt only half their lesson. They had been so much taken up with the idea of removing barriers and obstacles to have failed to realise that they had also to get rid of those illegitimate profits, involving a drain on the national life. M'Culloch and Nassau Senior, Cobden and Bright, understood that the grant of money aid to a particular industry out of the rates and taxes enabled that industry to expand, and to secure more of the nation's brains and capital, and more of the world's trade than was economically advantageous. They even recognised that the use of unpaid slave labour constituted an illegitimate drain on the national resources quite as much. But they never comprehended that to set the employer free to make exactly what arrangements he chose for his work, and to conclude exactly what bargains he chose with his individual operatives, inevitably meant, because of his superiority in economic strength, the reduction of wages for mere " common labour " to the worth of the marginal man—to a point, in fact, which experience proved to be even below what was physiologically necessary for subsistence—the exaction of hours of daily labour far in excess of what was compatible with healthy existence; the harnessing to the mill of the pregnant woman, of the nursing mother, of the immature youth, even of the child; the subjection of them all, in the attempt to reduce expenses to a minimum, to brutalising and insanitary conditions, and even to incessant risk of accident, for lack of the necessary expensive precautions; and, actually, when it was found to facilitate the manufacture, to the deliberate use of deleterious substances and the deliberate vitiation of the atmosphere by artificial heat and moisture to the ruin of the operatives' health.

All this meant, by the using up of successive supplies of human labour, each in turn to be prematurely flung on the rubbish heap of charity and the Poor Law, a subsidy to particular industries, not less inimical to the objects of Free Trade than if it had been granted from the taxes. But because it came as a drain on the vitality of the nation as a whole, paid in the first instance by the manual workers themselves, whose blood was thus coined for drachmas, the economic nature of the arrangement was long unrecognised. Not until the latter part of the century was it perceived that, if the object of Free Trade was to promote such a distribution of capital, brains, and labour as would result in the greatest possible satisfaction of human needs, with the least expenditure of human efforts and sacrifices, the limitation of the autocracy of the employer—the enforcement with regard to the conditions of work of the will of the many instead of the will of the one—was not only a necessary extension of democracy, but also as indispensable a part of the Free Trade movement, considered as an assertion of the real interests of the consumer, as the tariff reforms of Cobden and Bright. " During that

CH. XXIII.

period," wrote the Duke of Argyll (1823–1900), "two great discoveries have been made in the Science of Government; the one is the immense advantage of abolishing restrictions on trade; the other is the absolute necessity of imposing restrictions on labour....And so the Factory Acts, instead of being excused as exceptional, and pleaded for as justifiable only under extraordinary conditions, ought to be recognised as in truth the first legislative recognition of a great National Law, quite as important as Freedom of Trade, and...like this last...destined to claim for itself wider and wider application."

We see this revolt against sacrificing everything to cheapness, which unrestricted freedom of enterprise was supposed to produce, leading gradually to factory legislation. The first hesitating steps in the legislative regulation of the conditions of employment, beginning with the Factory Acts of 1802, 1819, 1825 and 1833, and the Mines Regulation Act of 1842, were taken merely empirically, with the object of remedying patent abuses, and of giving to specific classes of wage-earners, by the strong arm of the law, that protection against ill-usage which they had been unable to obtain for themselves. Step by step this legislative protection has been extended, from trade to trade, from one class of workers to another, and from one element in industrial life to another. The Mines Regulation Act of 1842 was followed by successive statutes, steadily increasing the extent and minuteness of the precautions required against accidents, of the provisions for safeguarding the workers against being cheated in their wages, of the regulation of the work of women and boys, of the limitation of the hours of labour even of adult men, and, generally, of the supervision of the methods of working. By the Merchant Shipping Acts a similar legislative protection was extended to the seamen, and all others employed on ships. By the Regulation of Railways Acts of 1889 and 1893, the Board of Trade was charged with the prevention of excessive hours of labour among railway servants, and was enabled to insist on a reduction in the hours in all cases in which this was deemed necessary. By successive Truck Acts, Factory and Workshop Acts, and Shop Hours Acts, practically all manufacturing industries and nearly all retail shops employing female or youthful assistants have similarly been brought under regulation and inspection. "We have today," as the biographer of Richard Cobden enthusiastically recounts, "a complete, minute, and voluminous code for the protection of labour; buildings must be kept pure of effluvia; dangerous machinery must be fenced, children and young persons must not clean it whilst in motion; their hours are not only limited but fixed; continuous employment must not exceed a given number of hours, varying with the trade, but prescribed by the law in given cases; a statutable number of holidays is imposed; the children must go to school, and the employer must every week have a certificate to that effect; if an accident happens, notice must be sent to the proper authorities; special provisions are made for bake-houses, for lace-making, for collieries, and for a whole schedule of other specified callings; for the due enforcement and vigilant supervision of this immense host of minute prescriptions, there is an immense host of inspectors, certifying surgeons, and other authorities, whose business it is ' to speed and post o'er land and ocean' in restless guardianship of every kind of labour, from that of the woman who plaits straw at her cottage door, to the miner who descends into the bowels of the earth, and the seaman who conveys the fruits and materials of universal industry to and fro between the remotest parts of the globe."

From England, factory legislation spread successively to France, Switzerland, and Germany; to Austria and Italy; to all but the more backward southern States of the United States of America; to the principal British colonies and to India; and even to Holland and Belgium, which long remained behind the other industrial countries. Taking the subject as a whole, and regarding administration as well as legislation, the United Kingdom still keeps the lead. But in many details other nations have improved on the lessons they have learnt from England. Especially in such matters as the minimum age at which children may be employed in the factory, the provision for continuation of their school education, the prevention of street trading by children and young persons, the protection of the workers from deleterious substances, the regulation of the employment of women just before and after child-birth, and the securing of a living wage in the "sweated" trades, Switzerland or Bavaria, France or New Zealand, Massachusetts or Victoria, have here and there gone ahead of British legislation. A voluntary association, the International Union for Labour Legislation, with its seat at Basel, now seeks to systematise and render identical or equivalent the " Labour Codes" of the civilised world.

The general acceptance and wide extension of factory legislation is, however, of very recent date. During the first half of the nineteenth century any interference with individual bargaining between employer and workmen found, as a principle, no favour with the enlightened classes; and the workers, despairing of parliamentary help, sought to protect themselves by voluntary associations. It is, indeed, a feature of the typical nineteenth century development of the substitution of collective for individual control that voluntary association and government action have always gone on side by side, the one apparently always inspiring, facilitating, and procuring successive developments of the other. Just as the progress of the collective control of the conditions of life in the form of municipal government has been paralleled by the growth of collective control over the household supplies in the form of the cooperative movement, so the progress of legislative regulation of the conditions of labour in the factory and the mine has been paralleled by the advance of analogous regulation by means of Trade Unionism.

CH. XXIII.

Beginning, apparently, at the end of the seventeenth century, but not for over a hundred years making any great headway, the operatives in particular industries have combined in order to maintain their standard of life. Their instrument was, essentially, that eventually adopted by Parliament in the Factory Acts, namely, the substitution, for the terms that the individual employer was able to impose on the individual wage-earner, of common rules for the trade as a whole, embodying a minimum standard below which no employer and no operative was allowed to descend. Parliament began with common rules as to sanitation, protection against accidents, and the hours of labour of children. The Trade Unions began with common rules about rates of wages and methods of remuneration and the normal working day. Parliament enforced the common rules by official inspection and criminal prosecutions. The Trade Union developed only slowly a staff of salaried officials, and these had no right of entry to the employers' premises; and the only instrument on which it could rely to secure conformity with the common rules laid down for the trade was the strike.

We need not repeat the nineteenth century story of English Trade Unionism—how by the aid of Francis Place (1771–1854) and Joseph Hume (1777–1855) it was grudgingly legalised in 1824–5; how it got caught up in 1830–5 in one of the many phases of Owenism, and nearly became entangled, in 1842–8, in the political movement of Chartism; how it gained a new start, on more sober lines, in 1846–51, and developed on the more solid financial basis of an industrial insurance association; how these changes led to renewed parliamentary recognition of Trade Unionism in 1871 and 1875; how the movement, which had sunk into a somnolent acquiescence in industrial conditions, became reinvigorated in the last decade of the century, as the result of awakening "class consciousness" among the labourers; how, in 1903, in the "Taff Vale Railway case," the judges once more reversed the intention which Parliament had imperfectly expressed in its statute, and made the Trade Union (though denied the rights of a corporate body) liable for pecuniary damages as if it were a corporate body; how, in consequence of this decision, the Trade Unions swung their whole force into the rising "Labour party," and extorted from an unwilling Legislature, in 1906, a new Statute specifically conceding the inviolability of their corporate funds. Nor is it pertinent to recall the various pitched battles which, over the establishment of the common rules that we have described, the Trade Unions have fought with the employers, in the form of long and embittered strikes and lockouts, from which no decade has been free. It must suffice to record that, at the beginning of the twentieth century, the Trade Unions of the United Kingdom number over two and a quarter million members, enjoy an annual revenue of more than three million pounds, and possess accumulated corporate funds exceeding six millions sterling. In many great industries—as it significantly happens, exactly those in which British industry has been most successful in holding its own against foreign competition—such as cotton-spinning and weaving, ship-building, and coal-mining, practically every workman belongs to his Union.

Trade Unionism, like factory legislation, has spread to all industrial nations, adopting practically the same devices to secure its ends. Beginning, usually, with attempts at restricting the numbers of the trade, by limitation of apprentices or other barriers to entrance, as was natural with what, after all, was an association of producers, though of wage-earning producers only, and occasionally vainly seeking to adopt such typical employers' devices as restricting output and regulating prices, the organised workmen are seen everywhere settling down, as they acquire experience of the practical economics of the labour question, into the one device of the common rule, overriding where necessary all individual bargaining. Just as factory legislation, on the points with which it deals, lays down common rules in the form of prescribed minima, below which no employer and no workman is permitted to descend, so the Trade Union of workmen seeks, in treaty with the associated employers, to enact for the trade similar common rules, prescribing minima on other matters. These common rules everywhere include a standard minimum rate of remuneration, whether by time or (as an actual majority of Trade Unionists desire) more commonly by the piece ; usually, also a normal day, or standard minimum of leisure ; and, in the most advanced trades, also standard conditions relating to the sanitation, the safety, and the comfort of the workers. All such common rules the Trade Union seeks to get accepted by the employers, either by the method of collective bargaining, where the workmen as a whole, after more or less of discussion, make a treaty with the employers as a whole ; or, to the extent that the legislature is under popular control, by statutory enactment.

Thus, in the most advanced industrial communities, Trade Unionism and factory legislation share the field between them. The common rules of the one supplement and support the common rules of the other. The cotton mill-owner and the cotton operative—in 1842, in practice almost free to do as they individually chose—find themselves at the beginning of the twentieth century moving in " the higher freedom of collective life." The management of the industry is recognised to be of common concern. No mill-owner and no operative may do " what he likes with his own." The associated employers, the associated workmen, and the community as a whole represented by the factory inspector, are bound together by elaborate codes, partly statutory, and partly the outcome of voluntary treaties, regulating wages, hours, holidays, meal-times, temperature, humidity, sanitary conveniences, the use of machinery, the speed of its working, the character of the material, the duration of engagements, and nearly every detail of the factory life. These codes, which are enforced not by the Government factory inspectors

CH. XXIII.

alone, but also by salaried officials of the Employers' Association and salaried officials of the Trade Union, who enjoy in practice the same right of entry as the factory inspector, impose *minima* only, not *maxima*, and thus leave freely open to individual emulation and competitive enterprise of masters or of workmen the utmost opportunity on the upward way, but rigorously bar, to employer and operative alike, as inevitably leading to a degradation of the standard of life of the whole class, any attempt to pursue the downward way.

Towards the latter part of the nineteenth century, the historian has to record a further development. Men have gradually become aware, dimly and imperfectly, that there is a more fundamental basis for both factory legislation and Trade Unionism than the mere protection of the weak against the personal power which the command of capital gives to the employer. What is now seen to be essential is that, whether the workman be weak or strong in his bargaining power, wise or foolish in his demands, the community must see to it that those conditions which are requisite for social well-being shall not be infringed. This is now accepted, not only as a matter of emulation among nations, but, according to the lessons which Political Economy has learnt from biology and from Darwinism, as a fundamental necessity of national existence. " Every society," said Mr Asquith, " is judged, and survives, according to the material and moral minima which it prescribes to its members." Hence has come the conception of what has been called the " national minimum"; conditions of existence which, because they are deemed indispensable to social health, the State insists on importing into every bargain for the hire of labour, if not also into every act of a man's life.

There is a national minimum of sanitation, including protection against avoidable accidents and preventable diseases. Three-quarters of a century of endeavour, beginning with Robert Owen in 1819 and Sir Edwin Chadwick (1800–90) and Southwood Smith (1788–1861) from 1835 onward, gave us, first the general Public Health Act of 1848, and then the successive extensions of public health activity, by which the death-rate at all ages has been so much diminished. We now insist by law, not only that no factory, but also that no dwelling-house, shall be permitted to fall below the minimum prescribed for health. A new meaning and a new universality is given to the requirement that there shall be proper ventilation and heating of all workshops ; that machinery shall be fenced ; and that the vitiation of the atmosphere of the mill by " steaming " shall be kept within limits. It is this conception of a national minimum of sanitation which inspires and justifies the statutory provisions which now demand that proper water supply, sanitary conveniences, and drainage, shall be everywhere provided ; that houses shall be properly built ; that suburbs shall be properly planned and laid out ; that constantly increasing precautions shall be taken against infectious diseases ; and that, when accidents do happen, or when, in the course of the industry, certain specific diseases are contracted, the medical treatment and maintenance of the injured workman shall be provided for by public hospitals and by a public medical service, as well as by money compensation. All this is not merely the protection of the weak, because it applies equally to the strong, and is enforced even against the wish of those whom it is desired to benefit. It is an assertion of the right and duty of the community as a whole to prescribe in its own interest the minimum conditions of health for every one of its citizens.

There is a similar national minimum of education. For its own sake, the State now insists (though not yet in rural parts of Ireland) that every child from five to thirteen or fourteen shall receive what is deemed proper instruction, and provides (at an expense from public funds in the United Kingdom of £25,000,000 a year) an elaborate array of schools and universities of every kind. There is, though as yet only over a part of the industrial field, a national minimum of leisure, in the legislative prohibition of the employment of persons for more than a specified number of hours in the twenty-four. This enforcement of a national minimum of leisure, applied at first only to parish apprentices, then to children in textile factories, then to women, then to other industries, has now been extended to adult men, imperfectly in the great railway service and in certain dangerous processes, and (in 1908) generally to all coal-miners working underground. Finally, we have in the legislation of New Zealand and Australia—now also partially imitated in the United Kingdom and France—what amounts to a much more important national minimum of subsistence than was afforded in England by its Poor Law. In the "determinations" of the Wages Boards of Victoria, and in the "awards" of the compulsory Arbitration Tribunals of New Zealand and New South Wales, and by the Trade Boards of the United Kingdom (1909), we see the imposition on the employers in particular trades of legally enforced common rules as to the minimum rates of wages to be paid in those trades, strictly analogous to the common rules with regard to sanitation and the hours of labour already imposed by the factory legislation which has spread through the whole civilised world. The same conception of a national minimum has lent a new significance also to the intervention by the Government of the State in the duties which have been entrusted to local governing bodies. The opening of the nineteenth century saw each locality free, in practice, to administer its own local affairs in the way that its own inhabitants, or those who acted on their behalf, chose to prefer. The twentieth century finds us recognising that we are members one of another; and that, if any one district permits insanitary conditions to continue, or provides an inadequate police force, or lets its roads fall below the common standard, or starves its educational service, it is not only the local residents who suffer, but the nation as a whole. Hence, in the United Kingdom, the enforcement upon local governing bodies of the national minimum of

CH. XXIII.

efficiency in one service after another is becoming even more insistent and peremptory. Among local authorities, as among individuals, the laggards are being increasingly screwed up. This, indeed, is to some extent the explanation of the persistent rise of local government expenditure, even in the most somnolent districts, and of the ever widening spheres of municipal activity. Thus it is that at the opening of the twentieth century the potent lever of the grant in aid is securing for itself a constantly increasing field of play in English internal administration, and is, in fact, if we consider the actual business of twentieth century government, already the central feature of the real as distinguished from the nominal Constitution of the United Kingdom.

There is, in this development, yet another factor to be mentioned. In addition to many of the services and commodities which the people use or consume being placed under collective control, by municipalisation or cooperation, while many of the conditions of their daily life are subjected to collective regulation, by factory legislation or Trade Unionism, they are found, at the opening of the twentieth century, enjoying elaborately organised collective provision for the special needs of those among them who are unable to provide for themselves. Here again, we have to record the parallel development of the two forms of collective organisation, the one universal and obligatory, the other partial and voluntary. England had had, from the latter part of the sixteenth century, a nationally prescribed public provision for the poor. In 1842, however, this was nothing but the relief of destitution—the bare keeping alive by doles of necessaries those who would otherwise have starved. The actual legal scope of the Poor Law has continued, down to the present day, essentially unaltered. But the second half of the nineteenth century saw the growth of new methods of provision for one class after another, until, by the end of the century, the operations of the Boards of Guardians had come to form only a fraction of what was being done out of the rates and taxes.

For the children, in particular, the local Education Authorities, from 1870 onwards, have provided more and more elaborate education; at first for weekly fees, but after 1890 gratuitously; at first in elementary subjects only, but after 1902 without restriction of subject or grade or limit of age; at first in the form of tuition only, but gradually also in the supply of books and instruments, by school journeys and excursions, and (from 1906 onwards) even medical inspection and medical treatment and school breakfasts and dinners wherever required. With regard to the sick, the local Health Authorities have, from 1848 onwards, been steadily increasing their organisation and their services; until the opening of the twentieth century sees in existence more than seven hundred municipal hospitals, in which treatment and maintenance is provided, irrespective of their personal means, for all who are suffering from any of a constantly growing number of diseases in which the community is specially concerned; and this maintenance and treatment is usually provided gratuitously. In the most highly organised cities, the salaried Medical Officer of Health has now his own extensive staff of assistant doctors, health visitors, and sanitary inspectors who, instead of waiting for requests, make it their business to "search out" disease, and in the public interest practically to press on the sufferers both the medical treatment and the hospital maintenance which they may require. A special staff often visits every house in which there is a birth; a municipal milk dispensary often supplies, either at an unremunerative price or quite gratuitously, the requisite milk for the infant, and keeps it under periodical observation. For the persons of unsound mind, or in any way mentally defective, the local Lunacy Authority provides elaborate asylums, irrespective of their means; built, equipped, and maintained on a scale far above that of even the prosperous wage-earning household. For the aged, following the example of New Zealand and Australia, and, in a sense, also that of Denmark, the Government has provided non-contributory superannuation allowances; and the local Pension Authority began in 1909 to disburse pensions from national funds to 700,000 persons over 70 years of age whose income did not exceed thirty-one pounds ten shillings a year. For the able-bodied men and women in distress from want of employment, local Distress Committees, acting under the Unemployed Workmen Act of 1905, provide assistance deemed more suited to their needs than that of the Poor Law.

Thus, with regard to each section of the pauper army which the Boards of Guardians in 1834 were established to relieve, there has since grown up a new public authority, making other provision deemed more suitable to its peculiar requirements. Meanwhile the administration of the Poor Law has itself been transformed. Instead of giving mere relief, the Boards of Guardians, under the influence of public opinion, have provided elaborate schools for the children, highly equipped hospitals for the sick, with all the services of modern surgery, convalescent homes, etc., and, here and there, even comfortable asylums for the respectable aged, apart from the evils of that general mixed Workhouse, which meets, in the twentieth century, with ever widening condemnation. The result is that, in place of the seven millions sterling that was being annually spent on the poor in 1832, when the well-known Royal Commission was appointed to restrict so terrible a drain on the nation's wealth, the total expenditure from rates and taxes in the first decade of the twentieth century, on the maintenance, education, and medical treatment of the poorer classes, reached, in the United Kingdom, nearly seventy millions sterling annually, of which less than one-third still retains any association with pauperism or the Poor Law.

Side by side with this steadily increasing collective provision for particular classes out of public funds, we see a parallel development of collective provision on voluntary lines. In 1842, when the wage-earner fell ill, or when any of his household fell ill, there was usually no resource on which he could rely, except his individual savings, and the exiguous services contributed by the Poor Law of that period. Gradually and almost silently, there has grown up in the United Kingdom a marvellous network of voluntary Friendly Societies, organised and administered by their members, in which, in the first decade of the twentieth century, no fewer than six or seven millions of the wage-earning and lower middle classes are enrolled. These voluntary organisations, managed almost entirely by working men, or, at all events, by men who have been manual working wage-earners, have learnt, by the hard lessons of experience, how to provide for their members with safety and efficiency a weekly money payment during sickness, the requisite medical attendance, maintenance when necessary during convalescence, and the expenses of burial. These benefits have been gradually developed in such a way as to constitute a rough sort of provision against the premature invalidity of the insured workers. But in thus developing, these voluntary Friendly Societies, unaided by any subvention from public funds, seem to have reached the limit of their power. Their attempts to provide for their members either old age pensions or maintenance during unemployment have not achieved success. The weekly contributions required to provide for the benefits already undertaken appear to be as great as the mass of the wage-earners can be induced to afford—to be, in fact, beyond the means of the millions of the more lowly paid and the more irregularly employed labourers, among whom Friendly Society membership makes no headway. In certain highly organised trades (comprising only 7 per cent. of the adult wage-earners) the Trade Unions add insurance against unemployment to the other benefits. This insurance has, however, not been found possible by two-thirds of the Trade Unionists, and is unknown to the other five-sixths of the adult wage-earners who are outside the Trade Unions, the great majority being engaged in occupations to which Trade Unionism has not yet extended. For old age pensions there is nowhere any extensive collective provision by voluntary organisations. Hence it was that the State stepped in to do what voluntary agencies had failed to provide. In the last quarter of the nineteenth century, the Government of the German Empire built up an enormous scheme of insurance of the wage-earners against sickness, accident, premature invalidity, and super-annuation, under which no less than thirty million pounds sterling are now annually distributed to more than three millions of beneficiaries. But in Germany there existed nothing equivalent to the network of voluntary Friendly Societies that cover the United Kingdom ; and the government scheme had therefore necessarily to include provision for sickness as well as for old age. The funds have been provided partly by a universal and compulsory deduction from wages, partly by an obligatory contribution from all employers of labour, and partly by the State, which itself controls, through a complicated hierarchy of voluntary committees, the elaborate organisation that so great an insurance fund involves. One great drawback of the scheme is that no provision is made for wives or widows who are not themselves wage-earners—a difficulty which no contributory scheme, based on deductions from wages, or on payments in connexion with wages, has yet surmounted.

The peculiar combination of government and voluntary administration, and of the workmen's contributions with state subventions, which the German Empire has created, is slowly being imitated, at the beginning of the twentieth century, in France and Switzerland, Belgium and Norway. In the United Kingdom, as in Australia and New Zealand, the existence of voluntary Friendly Societies on a large scale apparently prevents the Government from following this example. Moreover, in the United Kingdom at any rate, the extensive provision for the hospital treatment of sickness made both by the Public Health and by the Poor Law authorities, and the elaborate system of poor relief to persons incapacitated from going to work, already covers, though in different ways, part of what is done under the German pension scheme. Thus it is that, in the United Kingdom, as in New Zealand and Australia, the government pension scheme has, so far, dealt only with old age, and has proceeded on the lines of exacting no separately earmarked contribution from workmen or employers, but of freely awarding pensions out of the national exchequer to aged persons fulfilling the specified conditions. In one direction, however, the grant of public funds in aid of workmen's collective insurance has spread even more rapidly than government insurance schemes. The first ten years of the twentieth century saw developed, in several continental countries, a plan by which workmen were encouraged and enabled to undertake that collective provision for unemployment which the better paid among the English and American artisans had long made for themselves. Under what is called the Ghent system—instituted at Ghent in 1901, and within seven years adopted by all the other towns of Belgium; imitated in France (1905); at St Gall in Switzerland (1905); at Strassburg (1906); in Norway (1906); and in Denmark (1907)—a contribution from public funds is paid to Trade Unions and other societies giving "out of work pay" to their members when out of employment, amounting to a definite proportion of the sums actually so disbursed in the preceding year. Under this stimulus, there has been in these countries a great development of Trade Union insurance against unemployment. Pressure to join a Trade Union is in this way converted by the public authorities into pressure to insure against future distress from want of work.

Thus, in all directions and throughout the whole civilised world, we may distinguish, as the dominant characteristic of the social movements of the past three-quarters of a century, an ever growing elaboration of organised common action. What was formerly either left to the individual household to provide, or left altogether unprovided, is now, to an ever increasing extent, provided for large numbers of households by some collective administration. This collective administration takes many forms, differing widely from country to country, from service to service, and from decade to decade. Some of it, as we have shown, is on a voluntary basis, and the cooperation is really optional. Much of it, on the other hand, is governmental in its nature, whether municipal or national; though the use of the service is often optional. The common rules may be voluntary in their origin, and yet virtually compulsory; they may, on the other hand, take the form of peremptory laws, which it is left open to particular localities or communities to adopt or not as they choose. With the rapidly growing preponderance and size of town populations, the cooperation tends, however, to become more and more obligatory. Without the common rules that the law lays down and without the services that the municipality supplies, the citizen of the twentieth century would usually find it impossible to live.

But it is not alone the nineteenth century need for collective organisation that has made this so prominent an element in all the social movements of the last seventy-five years. What we see in many directions is the deliberate substitution of collective action, where individual action was still perfectly practicable. Factory Acts and Mines Regulation Acts were not made because the capitalist employers found any difficulty in achieving their ends. A large part of the impulse to this collective organisation, whether in Trade Unionism, or cooperation, factory legislation, or municipal developments, has come from that desire for popular self-government which is the spirit of democracy. But it is democracy in a more extended sphere than that to which the old jurists were accustomed to restrict it. This extension is, however, only one of a long series. When the Commons of England had been granted the right to vote supplies, it must have seemed an unwarrantable extension that they should claim legislation also. When they passed from legislation to the exercise of control over the executive, the constitutional lawyers were aghast at their presumption. The attempt of Parliament to seize the command of the military forces of the nation was the signal for the outbreak of a Civil War. Its authority over foreign policy is only two centuries old. Every one of these developments of the collective authority of the nation over the conditions of its own life was denounced by great authorities as an illegitimate usurpation. Every one of them is still being resisted in countries in the less advanced stages of political development. In Russia the right to refuse supplies is not yet definitely conceded; in Prussia control over the executive is withheld, and throughout the German Empire the control of the army; while in Austria-Hungary, the legislature is still without the power to control the foreign policy of that composite empire. In the United Kingdom, we have been silently extending the power of the people to regulate, by means of their elected representatives, the conditions under which they work and live. To the capitalist, as to the great mass of the middle and upper classes, this extension of collective action has often seemed an infringement of individual liberty. To the mass of the people it has seemed a positive increase in individual liberty, and a necessary application of democracy. Although the power that kept the worker in the unregulated factory for fourteen or fifteen hours, or that subjected him to insanitary conditions, was not the tyranny of king or priest or noble, the wage-earner felt that it was tyranny all the same, and he has sought to curb it, and to enlarge the individual liberty that he enjoyed, by the substitution of collective for individual control. It was not within the minds of Rousseau, Franklin, or Jefferson, or of the leaders of the French Revolution, that the personal power over men's lives, to which they objected when it was exercised from the throne or the castle or the altar, might also come to be exercised in the factory or the mine. But the industrial revolution, which these early democrats did not foresee, brought to the possessors of wealth a huge accession of personal power, which they naturally felt as an increase in personal freedom. To the wage-earner, however, it seemed loss of freedom ; and when at last he learnt to use the device of the common rule, he saw his way to get back, by means of representative institutions, some of the power over his own life of which the industrial revolution had deprived his class. Thus it is the extension of representative self-government from the political to the industrial sphere, and from mere political to industrial and social relationships, which is the dominant feature of the opening of the twentieth century.

We are thus brought round, by our analysis of the different social movements of the past three-quarters of a century, to that which has latterly become the most clamorous of them all, namely socialism itself. For it is just the conscious and deliberate substitution, in industrial as well as in political matters, of the collective self-government of the community as a whole, organised on a democratic basis, for the individual control over other men's lives which the unrestrained private ownership of land and industrial capital inevitably involves, that constitutes the central idea of socialism. The socialist movement, now an intellectual and political force in every country of the civilised world, definitely asserts this as the intellectual master-key of nineteenth century history, and claims that the trend of the changes of the past hundred years, as of the contemporaneous changes in economic thought and political science, is in the direction of substituting for the personal power of the owners of land and industrial capital the collective decision of the nation as a whole. In accordance with the experience of the past, the socialist demands the application of representative democracy to all the industrial conditions of the worker's life. Whatever the historian may think of the socialist movement—and no historian can pretend to be, on such a subject, without bias—he must, at least, admit its persistence, its force, and its ubiquity. It is possible to trace the parentage of the socialist idea, on the one hand to Rousseau, who was hardly conscious of its economic aspect, and on the other to Saint-Simon, who ignored its democratic features. Fichte put much the same idea into philosophy, and Robert Owen, confusedly, into his long-continued propaganda. But not until about 1832 does the name of socialism seem to have been used; and it was then applied most commonly to schemes of more or less communistic settlements, apart from the competitive world, such as those advocated by Robert Owen (1771–1858) and Abraham Combe (1785–1827), François-Marie-Charles Fourier (1772–1837) and Etienne Cabet (1788–1856); or else to schemes of state-aided production by associations of producers, such as Louis Blanc (1813–82) and Ferdinand Lassalle (1825–64) had in view in France and Germany, and such as the Christian Socialists of 1848 may have aspired to in England.

With the publication by Karl Marx (1818–83) in 1848 of the so-called " Communist Manifesto," and its appeal to workers of all countries to unite, the modern movement of organised political socialism may be said to begin. From this time forward, socialism put aside the foundation of Utopias in the form of separate societies or colonies, apart from the competitive world, and definitely insisted on the reorganisation of the existing social and industrial order on the basis of democratic government. We cannot here describe the slowly developing political movement which has, since 1848, spread to all civilised countries; the foundation, in London (1864), of the International Society of Working Men, with its strange combination of Trade Unionists and revolutionaries; of its internal struggles with an "anarchist," or ultra-individualist section under Michael Bakúnin (1814–76); or of its final disappearance, about 1873. Much more important in the story of the socialist movement is the retirement of Marx from other work in order to write his book on Capital, which was published in 1867, and which has furnished inspiration to the socialists of all countries. Not that this book, impressive in its argumentative and rhetorical power, describes any definite scheme of collectivism, which is rather assumed than advocated. But Marx read in the British Museum library the English blue-books, which had led up to the successive Factory Acts, and, on the horrors that they revealed, he constructed a dynamic description of the industrial revolution in England, which, put as the inevitable result of unrestrained private ownership of land and industrial capital, has reverberated round the world. We need not take seriously today the peculiar version of the law of value which Marx had learnt from David Ricardo on the one hand, and Thomas Hodgskin on the other; and which, as explaining the paradox of mere subsistence wages in the midst of ever augmenting wealth-production, was used by Marx with such impressive effect. Formally, this theory of wages is incorrect; and it has gone overboard from the economic ship, along with the wages doctrines of M'Culloch and Ricardo themselves. But, substantially, Marx was, in his analysis of the wage system in modern industry, assuming it to be uncontrolled by Trade Unionism or factory legislation, as right as he was impressive; and it is this analysis, together with that of Friedrich Engels (1820–95), which has indirectly contributed to the widespread contemporary acceptance of Trade Unionism and factory legislation, and of the doctrines of the common rule and the national minimum that we have already described. In England, where the effective socialist movement dates only from 1881, it has been intellectually more influenced by that other derivative from Ricardo, the law of rent, with its corollary of the inevitable appropriation, by the owners of land, of the economic advantage of all but the worst land in use. This doctrine, handed on by John Stuart Mill (1806–73) who in his posthumous *Autobiography* classed himself "decidedly under the general designation of Socialist"—postulating as the necessary basis of the society of the future, "a common ownership in the raw material of the globe, and an equal participation of all in the benefits of combined labour"—was promulgated with great rhetorical power by Henry George (1839–97), who may be said to have thus unwittingly provided the motive force for the rise of an organised socialist party in the United Kingdom.

Translated into terms of practical legislation and administration, the socialist programme, in England as in all other countries, is more and more shaping itself into four several lines of social reform. We see, first, the progressive extension of collective ownership and administration, either national or local, of one form of industrial capital after another, typified by the ever widening government ownership of railways, canals, telegraphs, telephones, postal communications, forests, water power, town sites, and agricultural land; by the municipal ownership and administration of the supply of water, gas, and electricity, of tramways, ferries, and bridges, of sewage farms and water-catchment areas and agricultural settlements of one sort or another; by the provision of houses, baths and wash-houses, parks and open spaces, organised games and free concerts; and, in short, by all the infinite variety of developments which mark the thousands of urban communities of western Europe. We have next the progressive assertion of the paramount control of the community over such land and industrial capital as is still left in individual ownership, in the form of ever increasing regulations, embodied in Factory and Workshop Acts, Mines and Railways Regulation Acts, Merchant Shipping Acts, Truck Acts and Shop Hours Acts, and what not. These regulations—denounced in 1844 as "Jack Cade legislation," because they were held, in effect, to confiscate a portion of the value of the capitalist's

CH. XXIII.

property—are now more and more consciously inspired by the idea of securing, at all hazards, a "national minimum" of education, sanitation, leisure, and subsistence to every citizen, whether he likes it or not. All these developments of collective action cost money; and this fact helps to make increasingly acceptable the third line of socialist progress, namely, that (as Jeremy Bentham long ago advised) the State should use its power of taxation in such a way as partially to redress the inequalities of income that private ownership of the means of production involves; and, in particular, that a steadily increasing proportion of the shares received, irrespective of personal participation in industry, as rent and interest, should be absorbed for the benefit of the national exchequer. Finally, we have the fourth line of the socialist advance, in the constant elaboration of the collective provision, for those unable to provide for themselves, of whatever may be regarded for the time being as the national minimum that the modern State undertakes to secure to every citizen. We need only mention the ever increasing collective expenditure on the infants and the children of school age, on the sick and infirm, on the blind, the deaf, and the crippled, on the mentally defective of all kinds, on the prematurely invalidated and the aged, on the widowed mothers of young children; and now even on the able-bodied man or woman unable, amid the complications and fluctuations of modern industry, to find wage-earning employment.

This fourfold path of collective administration of public services, collective regulation of private industry, collective taxation of unearned income, and collective provision for the dependent sections of the community—and not any excursion in Utopia or "cloud-cuckoo-land"—is the way in which the socialist really invites us to follow. Thus, much of what is claimed as the progress of socialism might be equally well described as a merely empirical development from the principles of Canning, Peel, Bentham, and Gladstone. In short, while it is common ground that much of the legislation of the past quarter of a century, and much of the economic and political writing of the time, in England as in other countries, has been greatly influenced in the directions that we have described, opinions will differ as to how far the world is likely to proceed along such lines; and also as to the extent to which the vociferous efforts of the organised and avowed socialists are a cause, or merely an effect, of the general movement of thought.

The change that has come over the civilised world in the various manifestations that we have described may be summed up in a phrase. What may be called an "atomic" view of human society has been replaced by a more "organic" conception. Three-quarters of a century ago the dominant social philosophy was that of *Laisser faire*. Though in England and some other countries arrangements were made to keep the starving from death, and to prevent actual brigandage and robbery by violence, what little collective action existed was undertaken grudgingly, and by way only of exception. The community as a whole assumed no responsibility for the individual. The pressure upon his will produced by the free competitive struggle would, it was assumed, if only "let alone," result in the utmost possible development of human happiness and human faculty. The current ideal of the social order was that of a congeries of warring atoms, the free competition of which would, it was quite confidently assumed, unconsciously result in the best attainable social state. The unit, it was said, was the family group; by which was meant, in practice, the male head of the family, the wife and children being scarcely recognised by the law as human beings, with rights or interests independent of those of the dominant adult male. By the beginning of the twentieth century we find an altogether different conception of society. The unit is no longer the family group, but the individual human being, whether newly born infant, child, adolescent, adult woman, or male head of the household. And we no longer believe that "beneficent private war" necessarily secures public ends.

The first of these changes in thought, the substitution of the individual human being for the family group, as the unit of the State, has involved the legal protection of the child and the emancipation of the woman, both of them social movements of far-reaching significance which are still in progress. A century ago, in Europe and the United States, as in India and China, children were, in the eye of the law, at the almost unrestrained disposal of their parents, and wives of their husbands. Neither children nor wives could, without elaborate and costly special arrangements, own property, or dispose of their own persons, or invoke the protection of the criminal law as against the dominant male head of the family, for any tyranny, ill-treatment, or cruelty short of actual death, and scarcely even for that. Gradually there is being built up, in one country after another, a legal recognition of what we may call the right of the infant, the child, and the adolescent to maintenance and proper nurture; protection against neglect and cruelty; education; exemption from premature work in industry or agriculture; and even vocational training. It is, however, interesting to notice that this gradual building up of the "children's charter" has been accomplished not so much on the plea of humanity—for so strong was the reluctance to "break up the family" that England began to punish cruelty to animals before it punished the cruelty of parents to their children—as on the ground of the State's paramount interest in the lives and upbringing of its citizens. It has been, on the whole, the latter argument which has led to the successive Public Health and Factory Acts, the Mines and Shipping Acts, the Education Acts and the more recent provisions for feeding children found hungry at school and medically treating those in need—the whole series culminating in the Children Act of 1908, which attempts to secure to every child in the land, from the newly born infant to the adolescent, even against its own father and mother, what may be termed a national minimum of proper upbringing. All the civilised nations of the world exhibit a similar evolution, in different degrees, and in their own way. As with factory legislation, so with the protection of children, some countries (notably some of the New England States and some of the Australasian colonies) have, in certain particulars, gone ahead of the United Kingdom. Others, such as Russia and Austria-Hungary, have as yet made few inroads on the paternal authority. All, however, may be said to have entered on the same course. "It is intolerable," old natives of India complain, "that the law Courts should treat women and children as if they were men."

The emancipation of women has, indeed, become already more general than the legal protection of children. This is entirely a movement of the nineteenth century. *The Vindication of the Rights of Women,* which Mary Wollstonecraft (1759–97) published in 1791, with its demand for equal rights and equal opportunities for all human beings, irrespective of sex, found no substantial support for half a century. The theoretical democrats of the French Revolution definitely excluded women, not only from the political franchise, but even from public meetings and political agitation. There were practically no opportunities for the education of girls beyond the most elementary stage. In the eye of the law the daughter was a household drudge, the wife a chattel. Even in the United States, in 1840, Harriet Martineau found only seven employments practically open to women, as alternatives to marrying for a living, namely, teaching, needlework, keeping boarders, working in cotton-mills, book-binding, typesetting, and household service. About the middle of the nineteenth century, various sporadic demands for greater freedom for women, in the United States and in Great Britain, arrested the attention of John Stuart Mill (1806–73), and led eventually to the publication of his *Subjection of Women,* a plea for complete equality of opportunity for both sexes. From this time onward, the movement went from success to success. Good schools for girls were founded in all the countries of western Europe, and in the United States. The University of Zurich led the way in 1867 in opening university education to women; and Paris followed shortly afterwards. The Universities of Sweden and Finland opened their lectures and their degrees to women in 1870; those of Denmark in 1875; and those of Italy in 1876. The University of London conceded degrees to women in 1878, and that of Dublin in 1879. The Universities of Norway followed in 1884; those of Spain and Roumania in 1888; those of Belgium and Greece in 1890, and those of Scotland in 1892. Meanwhile, as the Universities of Oxford and Cambridge, and those of the eastern part of the United States, failed to provide for women, women's colleges were started (Girton, 1872; Newnham, 1875; Somerville, 1879; Lady Margaret, 1879) in England, and both colleges and universities for women in the United States. In the more recent growth of state universities in western America, and of the

Universities of Manchester, Liverpool, Leeds, Sheffield, Birmingham, Wales and Bristol, women are admitted on practically the same conditions as men.

With the opening of higher education to women, there came naturally a demand for the opening of the brain-working professions. Elizabeth Blackwell got a legal qualification to practise medicine in New York in 1849. Various American States and the Netherlands were admitting women to practise medicine by 1870; England followed in 1876, and has already between five and six hundred female doctors at work; Russia and Belgium in 1890. Here and there, especially in the United States, women are acting as ministers of religion and in some branches of the legal profession. The right of married women to their own property and their own earnings was recognised in Great Britain by the Married Women's Property Acts of 1870 and 1882; and the legal systems of most civilised countries are now arriving in their own ways at approximately the same position. What may, perhaps, be deemed the last phase of this progressive evolution of women into complete social equality with men is that of the civic franchise. Women householders had long voted in the vestries, which administered the civil affairs of the English parishes; and, when local boards of health and town improvement commissioners were established in 1847 and 1848, this franchise was continued to them. It was conceded for English town council elections in 1869; for school boards in 1870; for Scotch town councils in 1881; for county councils throughout the United Kingdom in 1888 and 1889. Between 1861 and 1904, analogous local franchises were conceded to women in twenty-six States of the United States. In four States women possess the full state franchise (Wyoming, 1869; Colorado, 1893; Utah, 1895; and Idaho, 1896). In Australia and New Zealand, women were, between 1867 and 1908, successively admitted to all franchises. In Sweden, Norway, and in Finland, full rights have now been conceded; in the latter country, indeed, nineteen women were, in 1907, elected to the Finnish Diet.

This substitution of the individual human being, whether man or woman, infant or adult, for the family group, as the unit of the social order, has far-reaching consequences. But the disintegration of what we may call the eighteenth century form of *patria potestas*, has gone along not with a more lax, but with a closer, integration of the State. The community as a whole recognises that it has corporate ends, which it must pursue by corporate organisation. Its interests, which are not necessarily those of any individual member of it, loom large before us. We see no guarantee that perfect freedom of competition among individuals will not result in what no one of the competitors is aiming at, or has even in view. We are more and more disposed to believe that the community, which does not, with the aid of the best science of the time, consciously promote its corporate interests, will probably find those corporate interests adversely affected. We can, therefore, no longer afford to "let things alone." The universal maintenance of a definite minimum of civilised life—recognised to be in the interest of the community no less than in that of the individual—becomes the joint responsibility of an indissoluble partnership, in which the State and the individual citizens, men, women, and children, have each their several parts to play. This does not mean that charitable doles and public assistance should be made a substitute for what the individual can effectively procure by his own exertions. Reasonable socialists and reasonable individualists alike recognise that the real test of any proposed change is whether or not it will result, in fact, in stimulating and developing the aggregate of individual faculty and individual responsibility which alone make up the strength and force of the community. This is the potent argument alike for the emancipation of women and for the enforcement of the national minimum. The issue between the parties is, indeed, as regards each successive reform, simply one of fact. What is clear is that, when the community accepts a corporate responsibility, the fulfilment of this responsibility by the device of the universal provision of the necessary common service by the municipality or the State has at any rate the advantage of leaving unimpaired the salutary inequality between the thrifty and the unthrifty, though on a higher level than before. As a matter of fact, the thrifty parent does not find that the universal provision of elementary schooling, and the establishment of a "scholarship ladder" to the University, at all diminish the advantage over his wasteful and extravagant neighbour, with which his thrift and abstinence have endowed him. On the contrary, the more the State and the municipality provide gratuitously for all, the higher are the advantages that prudence and economy open up to the exceptionally provident man.

Not without bearing on this result of collective action is the fact that, as has already been described, in the United Kingdom of the past three-quarters of a century, an increase of governmental action has been invariably accompanied, at a slightly later date, by an increase also in voluntary cooperation in the same sphere. We have seen how the steady development of "municipal collectivism" since 1835 has been accompanied by the growth of the cooperative movement since 1844. The early Factory and Mines Acts of 1802–42 were followed by the great extension of common rules secured by Trade Unionism since 1843. The expansion of the Poor Law into an extensive hospital and domiciliary provision for the sick, the infirm, and the aged, has been at least paralleled by the growth of Friendly Societies. We see here no sign that governmental collective action is inimical to voluntary cooperation in supplement and support of what is done by the State and by the law. It is, moreover, an inevitable complement of the corporate responsibility and the indissoluble partnership, which are the intellectual basis of the twentieth century State and twentieth century citizenship, that new and enlarged obligations, unknown in a *régime* of

Laisser faire, are placed upon the individual citizen, and enforced upon him by the community. The Bolton cotton-spinner of 1842 had no need to keep his children in health, or his house healthy; his wife could with absolute impunity let the babies die; the parents could put their offspring to work at the earliest age; the whole household was free, in fact, to live practically as it chose, even if it infected and demoralised the neighbourhood. Now, the Bolton cotton-spinner lives in a whole atmosphere of new obligations—such as the obligation to keep his family in health, and to send every child between five and thirteen daily to school, properly washed and dressed, and at an appointed hour; and the obligation not to infect his environment, and to submit when required to hospital treatment. While it becomes more and more imperative, in the public interest, to enforce the fulfilment of personal and parental and marital responsibility on every adult, it becomes more and more clear that no such responsibilities can be effectively enforced without at the same time ensuring to every adult the opportunity of fulfilling them. To enforce the fulfilment of these obligations on the negligent and the recalcitrant, the modern State has other expedients than the punishments of the criminal law. What happens is that the collective action of the community, by a series of deliberate experiments on volition, "weights the alternatives" that present themselves to the mind of the ordinary man. He retains as much freedom of choice as before, if not more than before. But he finds it made more easy, by the universal provision of schools, to get his children educated, and more disagreeable to neglect them. By the provision of public baths and cleansing stations, he finds it made more easy for him to keep his family free from vermin, and more disagreeable to let them remain neglected and dirty. By the public provision of hospitals and medical attendance, it is made more easy for parents to keep their dependents in health, and more disagreeable to let them die. The public organisation of the labour market by means of labour exchanges makes it easier for the man out of work to find employment, and enables the State (as the socialists and Trade Unionists are at one with the rest of the world in demanding) to make it more disagreeable for the "work-shy." In every direction, the individual finds himself, in the growing elaboration of organisation of the twentieth century State, face to face with personal obligations unknown to his grandfather, which the development of collective action both enables and virtually compels him to fulfil. The claim is made—in the spirit of the teaching of Thomas Henry Green (1836–82), whose influence on English political thought deserves this recognition—that this new atmosphere of personal obligation results, paradoxically enough, in an actual increase, taking the population as a whole, in the enlargement of individual faculty, and in the opportunity for individual development. In short, in the growing collectivism of the past seventy-five years, law has been the mother of freedom.

CH. XXIII.

CHAPTER XXIV.

THE SCIENTIFIC AGE.

IF the last century may justify Lord Acton's title of the scientific age, the reason is to be sought not merely, or even chiefly, in the rapid growth of our knowledge of Nature. Science is as old as mankind, for in the primitive arts of life we have the application of fragmentary knowledge of the properties of matter, and in early myth and fable we have theories of the origin of nature and of man founded on the evidence then available. But, during the last hundred or hundred-and-fifty years, the whole conception of the natural universe has been changed by the recognition that man, subject as he is to the same physical laws and processes, cannot be considered separately from the world around him, and the assurance that scientific methods of observation and experiment are applicable, not only to the subject-matter of pure science, but to all the many and varied fields of human thought and activity.

In the great inventions of former ages we see the needs of practical life stimulating directly the activities of the craftsman. The need precedes and calls forth the invention, unless the invention be the result of accidental discovery. During the last century, on the other hand, we see scientific investigation in the laboratory preceding and suggesting practical applications and inventions. The invention, when made, opens a new field. Thus, Faraday's electromagnetic researches suggested to others the invention of the dynamo and modern electromagnetic machinery. The discovery of living microscopic organisms as the cause of malaria and other diseases, and the agency of insects in the dissemination of these organisms, have led to the adoption of measures whereby whole districts have been rendered healthy for the habitation of man. Mendel's experiments, in the cloister of Brünn, on the growth of peas have led already to the systematic production of improved types of wheat, and to a knowledge of the principles governing the inheritance of specific qualities which in the future may have incalculable effects on the welfare of the human race. There seems no limit to the extension of sense perception, and to the possibility of improving or modifying the conditions of human existence.

While the great explorers of the past century have brought almost the whole of the terrestrial globe within our ken, in every other direction the world has expanded and new grounds have been opened which lie ready for investigation. There is the correct unravelling of the past history of the earth, its inhabitants, and their civilisation; there is the accurate observation and improvement of the present conditions of existence, social and political; there is the moulding of the future, to which every living soul contributes for good or evil. And, above all, there is the work of ascertaining and making known the great laws in accordance with which the world progresses on its way. Science has now its supreme opportunity. When, from toiling obscurely in the rear of empirical knowledge and practice, science passed over and held up the torch in front, the scientific age may be said to have begun.

In this chapter, it is proposed to illustrate the growth of scientific method by tracing broadly the development of those branches of science which may be classed as physical or biological, and to follow the spread of the ideas so obtained into the general thought of the age.

At the close of the Newtonian epoch, as shown in an earlier volume of this work, the possibility of treating the existing state of the solar system in its mechanical aspect by methods and principles established by terrestrial observation, induction, and deduction, was clear to the leaders of scientific thought. In common parlance, it was felt that the thing might be understood.

Thus the mechanics of the solar system, first put on a sound footing in England by Newton's fundamental discovery of the law of gravitation, were developed and perfected during the latter years of the eighteenth century (1773–87) by the labours of Joseph-Louis Lagrange (1736–1813), and Pierre-Simon Laplace (1749–1827). From Newton's law, that each particle of matter attracts every other particle with a force proportional to the product of the masses and inversely proportional to the square of the distance, these mathematicians explained almost all the details of the complicated planetary motions, and proved the essential stability of the planetary system. During his second great period of activity (1799–1825), Laplace systematised all such knowledge in his monumental treatise *Mécanique Céleste*, which aimed at giving a complete solution of the whole mechanical problem of the solar system, and fell but little short of its aim. At the same time, he carried the perfected Newtonian philosophy into general literature by his *Système du Monde*, thus completing the work begun by Voltaire and the encyclopedists. It was this entrance of contemporary scientific ideas into the general thought of the time that distinguished France in the eighteenth century among the nations of Europe.

The most striking verification of Newton's principles in circumstances which appealed to the popular mind may be said to have been given by John Couch Adams (1819–92) and Urbain-Jean-Joseph Leverrier (1811–77), who, working independently in the countries of Newton and Laplace, predicted the existence of an unknown planet by the perturbations of another planet *Uranus*, of which the motions were not explicable completely by the attractions of known bodies (1845–6). Johann Gottfried Galle (1812–1910), an astronomer of Berlin, turning his telescope to the position assigned by Leverrier, found a new planet to which was given the name *Neptune*. Probably this one discovery had a greater effect in establishing the credibility of scientific method in the civilised world at large than the far more important coordination of observation and hypothesis in the preceding fifty years.

By its success in explaining the planetary motions, the law of inverse squares is verified to a high degree of accuracy; but the mechanism of gravitation, the mode of action of the forces, is still unexplained by any hypothesis generally accepted.

While thus the most important physical property of matter was traced to its ultimate consequences, the interpretation of the chemical composition of matter lagged far behind. The Aristotelian conception of a substance essentially light, embodying the principle of levity, was banished from Mechanics by the classical experiments of Galileo, but chemists, led astray by the phenomena of flame, maintained Stahl's theory of *phlogiston* till 1783. A body while burning lost phlogiston; and, since during the process the balance showed a gain, phlogiston must possess a negative weight. However, in the second half of the eighteenth century, the study of gases brought new facts to light. Although, about 1765, Henry Cavendish showed how to collect and examine gases, the old ideas lasted for some time longer. Even Joseph Priestley (1733–1804), who discovered the gas oxygen, named it dephlogisticated air; and Cavendish, who in 1781 dethroned water from its ancient position as one of the elements, described its newly discovered constituents as phlogiston and dephlogisticated air. But Antoine-Laurent Lavoisier (1743–94), repeating in 1783 Cavendish's experiment, grasped the fact that there was no need to invent a body with strange properties unlike those of the material substances known directly to the senses. He named Cavendish's gases oxygen and hydrogen, and recognised them as ordinary substances possessing mass and weight, though the persistence of the older ideas is shown by the inclusion of "light" and "caloric" with oxygen, azote, and hydrogen among the list of 33 simple substances given in his *Traité élémentaire de Chimie*, published in 1789.

The way was now clear for the detailed study and interpretation of the laws of chemical combination. It was found that elements combined in fixed and definite proportions by weight, while, if two elements combined to form more than one compound, the weight of one element *A* which combined with a certain weight of another *B* in the first compound, bore a simple relation to the weight of *A* combined with that weight of *B* in the second. John Dalton (1766–1844) saw that these phenomena were best explained by a new form of atomic theory, and in 1804 he put forward the view that the ratio of the weights of two elements in their simplest compound measured the relative weights of their respective atoms.

The experiments of Joseph-Louis Gay-Lussac (1778–1850), who showed that gases always combine in volumes which bear simple ratios to each other, led to the generalisation of Americo Avogadro (Conte di Quaregna) (1776–1856), who pointed out that, on Dalton's theory, equal volumes of all gases at the same temperature and pressure must contain numbers of atoms which stand in simple ratios to each other. Further study of the phenomenon of gaseous combination led to the distinction between the physical molecule—the smallest part of an elementary compound which can exist free—and the chemical atom—the smallest part of an element which can enter into chemical combination.

Thus the atomic hypothesis, founded by the metaphysical speculations of the Greeks, took shape in modern guise as a definite quantitative theory framed to explain chemical measurements. But, while the Greeks sought to resolve all matter into a common atomic constituent, Dalton went no further than the specific atom of each chemical element, not to be divided by the processes of Chemistry, and he left unanswered the deeper question of the constitution of the chemical atoms and their possible resolution, by means other than chemical, into more ultimate parts, perhaps identical in all types of matter. But Dalton's theory, unlike that of the ancients, was a living, working hypothesis, necessary to explain the facts and to suggest lines of future experiment and enquiry. By its light, nearly all modern chemical research has been undertaken and interpreted, till in recent years the application of the theory of energy to Chemistry gave a means of coordinating certain phenomena without the aid of atomic and molecular conceptions.

The number of chemical elements has grown from the twenty to which atomic weights were assigned by Dalton, till at the present time some eighty separate chemical individuals are recognised. Each new method of research applied to Chemistry has resulted in a group of new elements. Thus the use of the separating power of the electric current in 1807 gave Sir Humphry Davy (1778–1829) the alkaline metals potassium and sodium; the methods of spectrum analysis in the middle of the nineteenth century disclosed such elements as rubidium, caesium, thallium, and gallium by the quality of the light which they emitted when incandescent; and the phenomena of radio-activity have added to the list bodies like radium, which exist in nature in quantities much too small to be detected even by the delicate means of spectrum analysis. On the other hand, an example of the new results which may be obtained by increasing the accuracy of older methods of research is found in

Lord Rayleigh's investigation of certain minute differences in density which he observed in the gas nitrogen when prepared from different sources. These labours resulted in 1894 in the discovery of the gas argon as an unsuspected constituent of the atmosphere, and led indirectly to the isolation of other new gases, chiefly by Sir William Ramsay.

The work of Dalton and Avogadro enabled chemists to calculate the relative weights of the atoms of the different elements, and in 1869 the Russian Dmitri Iwánowitsch Mendeléeff (1834–1907), systematising the earlier vague speculations of William Prout (1785–1850) and Newlands, showed that, if the elements be arranged in a table in order of ascending atomic weights, we see a striking recurrence of similarity in physical and chemical properties at regular intervals in the table. An evident gap in the table even enabled Mendeléeff to predict the existence and properties of an element then unknown.

This periodic law shows that the physical and chemical properties of the elementary atoms depend on their mass, and suggests irresistibly the conclusion that their differences are due to differences in complexity of structure and arrangement of parts, rather than to any essential distinction in the nature of their ultimate substance. Thus we are again led back to the conception of an identical physical basis for all types of matter, and kept on the watch for evidence in favour of that view of nature.

The comparatively simple compounds formed by most of the chemical elements are unlike the very complex ones built up by the unique substance carbon, which enters into the composition of all organic compounds, from which the bodies of plants and animals are constructed. It was long thought that the processes which occurred in living structures were unlike in kind to those produced artificially in the laboratory. The synthesis of urea, a typical organic body, artificially prepared by Friedrich Wöhler (1800–82) in 1828, did much to shake this belief, while the preparation of sugar from its elements by Emil Fischer and Julius Tafel in 1887 solved a problem which long had baffled the experimenter, and brought another branch of the chemistry of life into the arena of the laboratory.

The success of the Newtonian theory in explaining the existing mechanism of the solar system led inevitably to speculations about the mode of origin of that system. As Mach says: " The French encyclopedists of the eighteenth century imagined that they were not far from a final explanation of the world by physical and mechanical principles; Laplace even conceived a mind competent to foretell the progress of nature for all eternity, if but the masses, their positions, and initial velocities were given." This overestimate of the importance of one particular and limited aspect of nature was the outcome of the striking success of the new mechanical conceptions. Applying the idea to a less ambitious problem, Laplace sought to trace the origin of the existing solar system in its mechanical properties by his famous nebular hypothesis, which pictured the primordial chaos as consisting of a mass of scattered nebulous matter filling the space now occupied by the sun and his attendant planets. Laplace indicated that known dynamical principles might reasonably mould such a system into the revolving spheres familiar to Astronomy. This suggestion, incapable by the nature of the case of direct observational or experimental examination, remains an unverified hypothesis, though the later evidence of the spectroscope has shown that some visible nebulae are giving forth the light characteristic of the glowing vapour which Laplace's hypothesis suggests as the primal state of the solar system. But the importance of the theory lies in the claim it makes for scientific method to explore the depths of the past. Nevertheless, here, as in other fields, speculation overran the true path of advance, which lay, for the time at any rate, in the patient and laborious study of the earth's surface by the methods of Geology—a science which, in the time of Laplace, had barely struggled into being.

Long after dynamical Astronomy had gained freedom from the geocentric theory enforced by the sixteenth century theologians, Geology lay bound in the chains of a too literal interpretation of Biblical cosmogony. Primordial cataclysms or Noachic deluges were invoked to explain the structure of rocks and the presence of marine fossils in the depths of land areas. It was not till James Hutton (1726–97) published his *Theory of the Earth* (1785) that these ideas were questioned seriously. Hutton first appreciated the fact that many processes competent to produce stratified rocks and to embed fossils in them are still going on in the operations of sea, river, and lake. "No powers," he said, "are to be employed that are not natural to the globe, no action to be admitted of except those of which we know the principle." This, the "uniformitarian" theory, lay forgotten for some time while "Neptunists" and "Vulcanists" still quarrelled about the relative importance of water and fire in the cataclysmic origin of the world.

Then came Sir Charles Lyell (1797–1875), who grasped once more the possibilities of the long continued action of existing processes. Astronomy had emancipated itself from the orthodox chronology, and other branches of knowledge were struggling into a position to claim the same licence. Since the days of Hutton the available evidence had been enriched by the new knowledge of Palaeontology. William Smith (1769–1839) had assigned relative ages to rocks by examining their fossil contents; Georges Cuvier (1769–1832) had reconstructed the extinct mammalia of the Paris basin; and Jean-Baptiste de Lamarck (1744–1829) had made an extensive classification of recent and fossilised shells. Thus, not only was Lyell able to bring evidence from all countries to show how the face of the earth is being moulded into new forms by water, volcanoes, and earthquakes, but he was able to explain the sequence of fossil remains by slow secular changes in the forms of animal and vegetable life. Hence it was that the publication of Lyell's *Principles of Geology* in 1830–3 marked the first great epoch in modern geological science. But it was not till 1863 that Lyell considered the evidence clear enough to warrant him in assigning to man a place in the natural series of organic types. The discovery of flint implements, associated with the bones of long extinct animals, at Abbeville and elsewhere, showed that man had existed on the globe for periods compared with which the few thousand years of the accepted chronology were but as a day, and gave to the human race a long pedigree of ancestors slowly rising in the scale of prehistoric civilisation. The work of Thomas Henry Huxley (1825–95) in studying the skulls of prehistoric and primitive types of man was originally undertaken for the purpose of throwing light on the history of the human race; but it proved to be the beginning of the new science of Ethnology.

The principle used by Lyell and the other uniformitarians, that the past must be explained by the present unless good cause can be shown to the contrary, and the fact that, so far as our knowledge goes, no such cause is seen to be operative in the history of the globe, brought once more to the front the old conception of organic evolution. The idea of the origin of all living beings from a few ancestral types was familiar to the Greeks; but it had vanished from the thought of the world during the centuries of theological scholasticism. The work of the geologists forced naturalists to face a question which already had begun again to interest philosophers—in particular, Herbert Spencer (1820–1903), who was advocating a general evolutionary system in almost all branches of human thought. But nearly all competent biologists felt that the evidence was insufficient. No clear cases of transmutation of species could be adduced, and no cause had been suggested sufficient to explain such transmutation. Lamarck, it is true, had put forward the view that the accumulated and inherited effect of use and habit might, in the course of many generations, explain the divergence of existing species; the giraffe, for instance, being supposed to have acquired his long neck by the continued efforts of his ancestors to browse on trees just beyond their reach. But no certain evidence was or is forthcoming of the direct inheritance of acquired characters. In other directions, too, Lamarck's hypothesis was considered insufficient, and till 1858 the weight of biological opinion was overwhelmingly against the idea of transmutation. Even Lyell himself was not then prepared to accept as conclusive the evidence of continuity in the case of organic remains.

In the year 1858 Charles Darwin (1809–82) and, independently, Alfred Russel Wallace published a new theory, fortified, in the case of Darwin, by the results of many years of patient and laborious observation and experiment, which he summarised in 1859 in his great book on *The Origin of Species.* It was known well enough that the different individuals of a species show innate divergences of structure more or less marked; that any one species tends to multiply till it overtakes its means of subsistence and a struggle for life eliminates the weakest; that a certain limited power of adaptation to environment was common to all living beings. But no one previously had understood the true significance of these facts. As Huxley said: "The suggestion that new species may result from the selective action of external conditions upon the variations from the specific type which individuals present— and which we call 'spontaneous' because we are ignorant of their causation—is as wholly unknown to the historian of scientific ideas as it was to biological specialists before 1858. But that suggestion is the central idea of *The Origin of Species,* and contains the quintessence of Darwinism." The selective action is exercised by the pressure of the struggle for life, which favours those individuals which possess variations of direct use to them in their surroundings. Those individuals tend to survive at the expense of the others, and to produce offspring. The new generation shows variation also, and, once more, those individuals which are modified in favourable directions have a better chance of survival. Gradually, differences accumulate, generation after generation, in the descendants of each one of the original offspring, and, in time not one only, but many new species may be formed, as the result of minute accumulated variations. In animals a secondary cause of selection—one by which ornamental variations not of direct utility arise—is the choice of mates, which tends to reproduce variations pleasing to the opposite sex. In plants, the success of flowers in attracting the fertilising insect life is also a factor in the situation.

Darwin's *Origin of Species* was met on its publication by a storm of criticism. Naturalists themselves failed for some time to appreciate the strength of the evidence which Darwin brought forward to support his case. Hence, at first, many were found in opposition, though a few gave in their adhesion—Joseph (now Sir Joseph) Hooker, whom Darwin had consulted throughout in the preparation of his work, Lyell, who expressed his later conversion in the *Antiquity of Man,* and Huxley, from the first the militant champion of Darwin's theory. Huxley's work in popularising the new views in his book *Man's Place in Nature* (1863) and elsewhere can hardly be overestimated; while the progress of general evolutionary philosophy, made easy by Darwin's theory of a possible cause, owed most perhaps to the labours of Herbert Spencer. While the objections of biologists were founded on doubt as to the sufficiency of the evidence for natural selection, the repugnance of others was based on unwillingness to accept the possibility of evolution at all. Like the Copernican system of Astronomy, which threatened to depose the earth from its central position in the Universe, the Darwinian hypothesis was thought to dethrone man from his proper place in the scheme of things, and was seen to be inconsistent with the accepted dogma of the special creation of each distinct species, and the separate and final creation of the human race as a culminating point. Hence, outside the ranks of men of science, the opposition was led by certain theologians who failed to distinguish between the essential and non-essential bulwarks of the faith. In truth they did not appreciate the characters of the men or the nature of the arguments with which they had to deal, and were blind to the fact that scientific methods and evidence had become a dominating factor in the history of general thought. Even men of the world, accustomed to regard themselves as fallen from a higher state, proclaimed with Disraeli that they were " on the side of the angels."

But time brought the inevitable reconciliation. The beginning of better things was marked by the foundation in 1869 of the Metaphysical Society, composed of distinguished men of the most opposite schools of thought, who thus learnt through personal intercourse and private discussion to recognise a unity of purpose and a mutual regard unattainable before. The friendships formed among Darwin, Lyell, Huxley, and Kingsley, Stanley, Colenso, leaders of liberal religious thought, were of great importance in the history of the controversy.

In tracing the result of evolutionary philosophy on religion, the effect of other awakening influences must not be forgotten. The new lights thrown on Biblical history by archaeological work in Mesopotamia, Asia Minor, Egypt, and Palestine; the revision of ideas about the nature of the Bible produced by textual criticism; the comparative study of early religions by anthropologists; and the increased knowledge of the development of Christianity in the first few centuries—all helped to shake the old idea of immutability in religion, and to place the Bible on its true footing as the unique record of the evolution of a nation's moral consciousness. When that idea was grasped thoroughly, there was no need to claim for the Bible, or for religious records generally, any exemption from investigation—new knowledge, from whatever source, could only be welcomed by theologians as an integral part of revelation.

Ideas, like natural species, are subject to variation and a struggle for survival. Age after age, the pressure of the intellectual environment tends to destroy those beliefs unfitted to the general knowledge of the time, and to preserve others in harmony with the mental and moral atmosphere. The necessary variations may arise from the slight changes which an idea undergoes when translated into thoughts and words by different minds, or from the abrupt changes which are made by great reformers and correspond to the "sports" of biological science. Unchanging scientific theories, unchanging social institutions, unchanging religious beliefs, are no more possible than unchanging species. What is living is subject to change; what is stationary has lost the power of adaptation, and, in a changing world, must die.

The comparative study of primitive religions has thrown much light on the intellectual life of man just emerging from the savage state, and has enabled us to trace the development from myth and magic to the elaborate religious systems of Greece and Rome. As the survival of rudimentary organs, now useless to their possessors, has given evidence as to the development of animal and vegetable life, so the survival of primitive religious observances, embedded in medieval Christianity, has shown how Jewish and pagan ideas were absorbed, developed, and used, in the early ages of the Church, and has taught us the continuity of religious systems in their external aspects; while man's essential need of some of the ideas which former ages have considered exclusively Christian has been shown by tracing them in primitive form through early stages of religious development. It is possible that advancing knowledge will go further in this direction: and it is to be hoped that the time has passed when theologians fear the influence of new knowledge. Whether we believe that man is led upward by an intelligent and beneficent Power, or hold that he is struggling onward unaided, the conception of evolution remains helpful, either as illustrating the methods of the Creator, or as pointing out the way in which man has reached his present position, and suggesting the best course for the future.

While religious thought has assimilated to a certain extent the evolutionary view, the trend of modern apologetics also shows the direct influence of experimental and inductive science in general and of the conception of evolution in particular. At the beginning of the period we have under review, Paley's *Evidences of Christianity* (1794) represented the arguments which appealed to the age as confirmatory of Christian doctrine. Now, all leaders of religious thought agree in holding the insufficiency of Paley, and in laying stress on the evidential value of the individual religious consciousness and the various types of individual religious experience. The importance of the latter point of view, from the standpoint of the scientific study of comparative religion, was, perhaps, first emphasised adequately by William James' book, *Some Varieties of Religious Experience*, published in 1904.

This change in mental attitude must be ascribed to the need of the age for observational, if not for experimental, evidence in all subjects. But even more striking examples are seen in the foundation, in 1885, of the Society for Psychical Research to investigate by scientific methods the phenomena of thought transference and human personality, and the work of the various schools of Experimental Psychology in England, the United States, and France.

The conception of evolution once formed and widely disseminated must influence profoundly social and political theories. Instead of the ideal State, absolutely best for all time, sought for by the makers of Utopias, we have, as the object of our endeavour, that State which is best in the conditions of a given period, and at a given stage of intellectual, moral, and political development. No fixed condition can ever be reached, no finality obtained; the existing legal, social, and political institutions must, in a healthy State, be merely one stage in a perennial development.

Room is still left for the ardent reformer and for the convinced reactionary, for every man is free to form an opinion how far the existing State has lagged behind or departed from the best conditions for the given time; but the more temperate discussion of political and social questions during the last quarter of a century is to be traced, partly, to a recognition that no finality can ever be reached, that absolute political truth is unattainable—in fact, does not exist.

As the study of the spectra of different nebulae and stars has given evidence about the mode of formation of suns and worlds, so the study of the social and political condition of the different races now existing in different stages of civilisation has shown how the more advanced peoples must have struggled through earlier times. The scientific value of folklore and tradition, too, has now come to be appreciated as illuminating primitive culture. And, for more advanced periods, it is seen that development need not necessarily proceed along the same lines for different nations even in a high stage of civilisation. It is recognised that different institutions are suited to different peoples: no one would now undertake a crusade to establish the universal sway of one form of government, as did the French republicans of revolutionary times. Those social and political forms are best worthy to survive which best fit the particular environment, and are most capable of adaptation as the environment changes. It is true that in Biology it is doubtful if functional adaptations are transmitted by heredity; but in Sociology no such doubt exists—one age is influenced profoundly by the acquired characteristics of its predecessor.

Since the time of Darwin, all biological research is permeated with the idea of natural selection. Much work has been directed to the elucidation of the phenomena and origin of the variations which are necessary for the play of selection, and to the study of the allied problem of the inheritance of acquired characters. If such characters are not transmitted, no modification of Lamarck's hypothesis can explain evolution, and recent research has done much to emphasise the obvious difficulty of seeing how the essential properties of the germ cells could be affected by habits acquired after their formation. The most important of the new investigations have been inspired by the rediscovery of the forgotten work already referred to on the breeding of peas by Gregor Mendel (1822–84), Abbot of Brünn.

Certain characters both of plants and animals have been found to exist in pairs, so that the absence of one involves the presence of the other. One such case is that of the colours of Blue Andalusian fowls. These birds do not breed "true"; that is, all their offspring are not blue like the parents. On the average of a large number, half the chicks of blue parents are blue, while the other half are divided equally between white and black. Both white and black birds with a mate of their own colour " breed true " and give all white or black chicks. Both white and black are true breeds, which, kept to themselves, retain their characters for an indefinite number of generations. White and black colours are definite Mendelian characters, to which, evidently, something in the germ cells corresponds. Now, a white bird mated with a black produces invariably all blue offspring, which, mated among themselves, reproduce the phenomena described above.

Such facts are explained if we suppose that of the germ cells of the blue birds half bear the black character and half the white. If " white " meets "white" the result is "white"—and so with black. But if "white" meets " black " a mixture, in this case " blue," appears. In other cases the mixed form simulates one of the pure breeds, one of the characters being "dominant" and the other "recessive." But, whether the mixture of breed is apparent outwardly or not, it becomes clear in the character of the next generation, which, unlike the offspring of a pure breed, is not homogeneous.

Mendel's results have removed one of the difficulties of the theory of natural selection. It was not easy, on the old ideas, to see how a favourable variation could avoid being bred out of the race, if its fortunate possessor had to choose a mate from his less gifted con-temporaries. But, if the character exist pure in his germ cells, and is transmitted in right number to the germ cells of his offspring, the chances of its meeting a corresponding character in time are greatly increased.

Already Mendelian principles have been used tentatively by scientific agriculturists, among others by Rowland Biffen in an attempt to produce a new variety of wheat which possesses the combined advantages of free bearing English, and " strong baking " foreign grain, characters hitherto considered to be incompatible with each other. It is clear that such knowledge gives us a power of producing new varieties of plants and animals by the light of intelligible scientific principles, instead of by the empirical and instinctive skill of the individual breeder, on whom we have hitherto relied.

The bearing of these investigations on the problems of human in-heritance is of immense importance to the future well-being of the race. Instead of being formed by a vague mixture of the qualities of all our ancestors, it is possible that we may possess definite characteristics of some of them only, and may transmit to our children characters we do not ourselves manifest. But, whether or not definite Mendelian laws are found to hold good for mankind, the statistical study of the human race gives overwhelming proof of the power of inheritance in transmitting characters both physical and mental. The old theory of leading families, of more than average character, ability, and physical advantages, has been shown by Sir Francis Galton to stand the test of careful examination. Recent work on heredity gives an intelligible reason for such beliefs, and lays stress once more on the importance of the aristocratic theory of the family as against the extreme egalitarian views of the middle-class nineteenth century. Thus we find a scientific justification of the recent revival of interest in family history.

Meanwhile, it is a duty to notice the effects of the diverging birth-rate of different sections of the community. The fact that parents classed as feeble-minded and the lowest grade of casual labourers have more than the average number of children, while parents of the professional and more thrifty artisan classes have less, is of greater significance for the future of the nation than has yet been grasped. Already those who are consulted find that it is difficult to supply men fitted by character and early training, as well as by intellect, to fill the responsible posts which increase in number in proportion to the growth of the nation as a whole. If unchecked, the wrongly directed relative change in the birthrate of different classes may do more harm in the progressive degeneration of the race than all the improved conditions of life can reverse by raising the status of each fleeting generation. We may drain our cities, found hospitals and asylums, maintain open spaces, educate expensively every child; but it is doubtful whether we thus produce any appreciable direct effect on future generations. While, through favourable environment, the indirect effect of promoting the development of the natural qualities of any individual will be immense, it is the innate qualities which we can neither create nor destroy that are of direct and supreme importance. The function of environment can only be to render more available the latent ability of the community. At the same time, it is well to remember that though environment can never improve what does not already exist, it cannot apparently, however unfavourable, destroy utterly the germ of better things. A race may pass through a generation or two of slum existence amid insanitary surroundings and yet retain the power of reverting to the higher type at the first opportunity. Be that as it may, the only sure way to bring about a progressive increase in the beauty, moral character, physical vigour, and mental capacity of the race is to favour in every possible way (some ways that have been suggested are impossible) the reproduction of those elements that are valuable, and to discourage the transmission of ugly, criminal, weak-minded, or feeble-bodied tendencies.

Medicine, and still more Surgery, have shared in the general advance of biological knowledge. The changes which perhaps most affect the bulk of mankind are the introduction of anaesthetics and the recognition of the part played by living micro-organisms in many diseases. The physiological effects of nitrous oxide gas were demonstrated by Davy in 1800, but it was not till 1844 that it was used in dentistry by Horace

Wells of Hartford, Connecticut. Ether was first employed by William Thomas Green Morton (1819–68), of Boston, Massachusetts, in 1846, and adopted in 1847 by Sir James Simpson, of Edinburgh (1811–70), who also introduced the use of chloroform later in the same year. Not only do anaesthetics save an incalculable amount of pain in surgery, but they have made possible difficult and prolonged operations which could not be carried out while patients were conscious.

The germ theory of disease was put on a sound experimental footing by the work of Louis Pasteur (1822–95). About the year 1855, Pasteur showed that alcoholic, acetic, and lactic fermentation were due to the action of three different and specific living microscopic organisms. He also disproved the occurrence of spontaneous generation in any known case, and showed that the growth of bacteria was to be traced in all cases to the entrance of germs from outside, or to the development of those already present.

The analogy of certain diseases with the processes of putrefaction and fermentation was apparent at once. Pasteur himself demonstrated that similar causes were operative in many cases, such as chicken cholera and the silk-worm disease, and reduced enormously the ravages of these two scourges. Moreover, he extended Jenner's principle of vaccination, which till then was an isolated observation. Pasteur discovered that, by growing pure cultures of the germs of certain diseases, he was able to attenuate their malignity. Animals inoculated with the weakened virus suffered little inconvenience, and were thereafter rendered immune for a time at any rate to the attacks of the malignant disease. In the case of rabies he went further, and showed that inoculation after infection was effectual, and thus diminished to about one per cent. the mortality from this previously incurable and most dread disease.

In some cases, part of the life history of the harmful micro-organisms can take place only in another host. Thus the germ of malaria, discovered in 1880 by Laveran, a French army surgeon, requires for its development one particular kind of mosquito. About 1885, Italian observers had, by systematic investigation, found that the infection was given to men through the bites of mosquitoes, and in 1894–7 Sir Patrick Manson and Major Ronald Ross proved that Anopheles mosquitoes were sometimes infested by cells which turned out to be malaria parasites in an early stage of development. These mosquitoes breed in stagnant water, and thus, by draining wet places, or covering stagnant water with a film of paraffin oil, vast areas of malarious ground have been made healthy. Similar methods have been applied with success in the case of yellow fever. Another recent instance of successful preventive measures is to be found in the campaign against Maltese or Mediterranean fever. During the past few years, a committee of the Royal Society has traced this disease to a micro-organism, passing part of its life in goats, which nevertheless remain apparently perfectly healthy. By prohibiting the sale of milk from contaminated goats, by the sterilisation of the milk where the use of goats' milk is inevitable, or by the more satisfactory substitution of condensed milk, the ravages of this disease, formerly so disastrous to residents in Malta and on the Mediterranean shores, and to the detachments of the British Army and Navy stationed in those districts, have been stopped almost entirely.

The process of fermentation has been further elucidated by investigations founded on a discovery by Eduard Buchner, who, in 1897, extracted from the yeast plant a substance solutions of which, though entirely free from living organisms, can convert sugar into alcohol and carbonic acid, just as living yeast cells do. Thus it seems that, in this case, yeast acts on sugar, not because it is alive, but because it contains this substance. Many other such substances, which are known as enzymes, have been discovered in living cells. Some of them, such as those of the digestive secretions, pass from their cells of origin before coming into action. Others, like the ferment of yeast, in natural conditions never leave the cell. But the essential process seems to be the same in both classes, and to be analogous to the physical or chemical action known as catalysis, in which one substance hastens chemical change in another, without itself suffering alteration.

The renown of applying Pasteur's results to Surgery belongs to Joseph (now Lord) Lister. The use of anaesthetics had opened new possibilities of surgical operation, but the potential benefits were almost neutralised by the terrible after-effects of septic poisoning. Hospitals were hotbeds of infection, and the mortality was such that an open wound in hospital was almost a sentence of death. Lister came just in time to save the hospital system. Recognising at once the significance of Pasteur's experiments, he saw that the introduction of putrefactive organisms must be prevented. At first by the employment of strong antiseptic dressings and by spraying the atmosphere with carbolic acid, and later by the more effective method of sterilising all instruments and other objects in the neighbourhood of the patient, Lister in time practically banished septic poisoning. Operations impossible before could now be undertaken with comparative safety, and the lives of countless sufferers have been saved.

The functions of beneficial and of pathogenic bacteria have now come to be better understood. Among other work, that of Elias Mechnikoff stands preeminent. Mechnikoff has traced the destruction of harmful bacteria which enter the healthy body to the action of the colourless corpuscles of the blood, which, in a devoted army, make their way to the infected spot and destroy the enemy at the cost of their own lives. Whether this process is effected by an actual absorption, or by indirect chemical means, is still a subject of controversy.

The knowledge that many diseases are due to specific micro-organisms has had great influence on the development of hygiene or preventive medicine. It is possible to guard against many sources of infection when we know the manner in which the infection is spread, whether by water, air, earth or food. The purity of the water supply is now the object of constant watchfulness on the part of public authorities, while improvements in the methods of disposal of sewage and other waste products are continually being made. Greater care is taken to secure healthy surroundings for the sources of the supplies of milk, bread, and meat, while a knowledge of the importance of abundance of fresh air is producing better ventilation of buildings. The recognition of sources of infection has led to the compulsory notification of certain infectious diseases, and to powers given to local authorities to disinfect houses. The discovery of the germicidal effect of sunlight shows its importance for health, while, above all, the need of scrupulous cleanliness in every department of household management has been proved by science. Some germs may be banished altogether. Others, too ubiquitous to be eliminated entirely, can be reduced in number in all dangerous places. The human body can deal with the attacks of enemies when the invasion is confined within limits depending on the general state of health. It is only when too many pathogenic organisms enter at once that the outer means of defence break down, and the citadel has to stand the dangerous siege of a specific illness.

When it is impossible to feel confident as to the purity of the water supply, as with an army in the field, Pasteur showed that most of the harmful germs may be destroyed by boiling, or treating with certain chemicals, such as bromine. Similar treatment has often been applied to other articles of food and drink. Milk especially is liable to contain tubercle bacilli, but, unless the heating be stopped at about 85° centigrade, a temperature sufficient to kill most dangerous germs, changes may be produced in the substance itself making it less digestible, while the addition in large quantities of germicidal preservatives, such as boracic acid, is a more direct danger to health. Hence the present tendency is to rely more on purity of supply, than on sterilisation after contamination.

The net result of improved Medicine, Surgery, and Hygiene is perhaps best measured by the change in the deathrate of the population. Two centuries ago, the average annual mortality of London was about 80 per thousand; it is now about 15 per thousand. Doubtless, the lowered deathrate is accompanied by an improved state of health in those who survive, though it is less easy to express the change in figures. Whether the change produces on the whole good or evil for the innate qualities of the race, is, as we have said above, a doubtful question.

While Geology and Biology were passing through the changes we have traced, Physical Science underwent an equally great extension.

Newton's preference for the emission or corpuscular theory of light, as against Huygens' undulatory theory, delayed, by the influence of his great name, the advance of Physical Optics. Newton did not see how to explain the rectilinear propagation of light on undulatory principles, though he recognised the advantage of the theory in explaining the fringes of colour seen with thin plates, where two trains of waves may be supposed to coalesce, and, by the local coincidence of motion in opposite directions, produce rest, *i.e.* absence of light of one particular colour. In 1801-3, Thomas Young (1773-1829) revived the wave theory to explain by the interference of two trains of waves his detailed experiments on the fringes of colour which accompany shadows, especially of thin fibres, and the colours of thin plates studied by Newton. But it was not till Augustin-Jean Fresnel (1788-1827) developed Young's views, with the skill and elegance in mathematical analysis characteristic of France, that the theory obtained general acceptance. Fresnel first overcame Newton's chief objection to the theory—the difficulty of explaining the propagation of light in straight lines and the existence of sharp shadows, phenomena unlike those of sound, for which an undulatory theory was accepted. Fresnel showed that such rectilinear propagation would be a property of waves, if the wave-length was minute compared with the size of the obstacles or the other distances concerned. The question of the direction of the vibration which constitutes the wave was also solved by Young, who suggested to Dominique-François Arago (1786-1853) in 1817 that the phenomena of polarisation, whereby rays of light are shown to possess different properties on different sides, must mean that the undulations are transverse to the direction in which the light is travelling.

Having established undulations, natural philosophers proceeded to adopt the old conception of an all-pervading aether, and to use it for supplying what the late Lord Salisbury once called "a nominative case to the verb 'to undulate'." The fortunes of this idea we shall trace later.

The opening years of the nineteenth century saw the triumph of the wave theory of light; the middle of the century was marked by the rise of spectrum analysis. Newton had decomposed white light into its constituent coloured beams by passing it through a prism, and the spectrum so obtained was found to vary with the source of light. Joseph Fraunhofer (1787-1826) had mapped the black lines first noticed by William Hyde Wollaston (1766-1828), crossing the coloured spectrum of sunlight, and the nature of these lines had been explained in his lectures by Sir George Gabriel Stokes (1819-1903). Any mechanical system capable of vibrating will be set into motion if impulses fall on it timed to coincide with its natural period. This principle of resonance is illustrated by the mode of action of a child's swing, and by the sound taken up by piano wires when a note is sung in their neighbourhood. Thus the molecules of the vapours which surround the sun, through which his rays must pass, will absorb those vibrations which they would themselves emit if hotter, and deprive the light which passes on of those constituents. Sunlight will be wanting in rays corresponding with those of the vapours in the solar atmosphere, and the solar spectrum will be crossed by lines that are dark compared with neighbouring regions. If those dark lines correspond with the light lines found in the spectra of terrestrial substances when incandescent, the presence of those substances in the sun is to be inferred. The study of terrestrial spectra had led the German chemists Robert Wilhelm Bunsen (1811–99) and Gustav Robert Kirchhoff (1824–87) to the same conclusion, and in 1860, reviving independently a forgotten experiment which Léon Foucault (1819–68) had made in 1849, they succeeded in producing artificially one of Fraunhofer's lines, by passing the intense white light of the electric arc through the cooler vapour of sodium volatilised in the flame of a spirit lamp. A new branch of chemical analysis—that of the sun and stars—was opened to investigation.

This discovery has put new life into Astronomy, which had come to be concerned mainly with the improvement of gravitational Mathematics. A new science and literature of Astrophysics has arisen. And not only can we study the chemistry of other worlds. An incandescent body approaching rapidly crowds its waves of light together; more waves reach the observer's eye in a second. But the number of impulses in a second determines the colour, and the place of the bright line in the spectrum of the light. Thus a slight displacement of a known line towards the violet end of the spectrum indicates relative approach between the earth and the origin of light, displacement towards the red end indicates retrocession. We can estimate the movements and velocities of stars by studying the light which they emit. The application of photography, too, has done much to increase the delicacy and accuracy of solar and stellar spectroscopy. Visual images persist only for some tenth part of a second. Hence the energy which reaches an eye in that time must be more than a certain minimum or the optic nerve is not affected. But a photographic plate can be exposed to the light of an invisible star for hours, and the long-continued effect eventually may become appreciable.

The origin of photography is to be found in the observations, made about 1780 by Karl Wilhelm Scheele (1742–86), a Swedish chemist, on the darkening action of sunlight on silver chloride. In 1839, after the death of his partner, Joseph Nicéphore Niepce (1765–1833), Daguerre (1789–1851) showed how to fix an image, and about the same time William Henry Fox Talbot (1800–77) also worked out a process. The use of collodion to make a sensitive surface was suggested by Gustave Le Gray in 1850, and the successful application of gelatine emulsions to produce rapid plates is due initially to the work of C. Bennett in 1878. Since that date the use of photography in scientific investigation has developed step by step with its application in other directions.

Besides its help to spectroscopy, mention may be made of the power it gives to the observer of recording automatically the readings of instruments, such as those which measure the magnetic properties of the earth. A beam of light is reflected from a mirror carried on the moving part of the instrument on to a strip of sensitive paper moved forward by clockwork. During the last few years, the old problem of colour-photography has been advanced a measurable distance towards solution.

In the middle years of the nineteenth century a new theory of heat was illuminating all branches of physics—indeed of science. The old idea that heat was an imponderable substance, which bodies gave out as they cooled, had done good work in starting quantitative measurements and in introducing the idea of heat as a definite quantity. But, even when generally accepted as a working hypothesis, this view had often been questioned by the best minds. Its final overthrow is to be traced to the careful and laborious measurements of the heat developed by friction, made, between the years 1840 and 1850, by James Prescott Joule (1818–89). Joule showed that, however work is done, whether against mechanical friction or electrical resistance, the amount of heat produced by the expenditure of a given quantity of work is invariable. Heat is equivalent to work, and appears in equivalent amount when mechanical energy disappears. This definite quantitative result combined with a general sense of coordination, which was arising under the name of " the Correlation of Forces," to give rise to the modern conception of energy as the power of doing work, and as a quantity which remains constant during any series of physical changes.

The principle of the conservation of energy contains the whole theory of the change of work into heat; but, in the converse change, which we see in steam-engines and other heat-engines, further consideration is needed. While the heat which disappears from the whole system is converted into work, much of the heat developed by the fuel simply passes from one part of the system to another, and is useless for purposes of mechanical power. The chief steps in the solution of this problem were as follows. In 1824, Sadi Carnot (1796–1832) pointed out the importance of considering complete cycles of operation before drawing conclusions as to the relation between heat put in from without and work done by the engine. The working substance, steam, air, whatever it may be, must be traced back to its initial state of temperature, volume, and pressure. Otherwise, instead of converting an external supply of heat into work, we may be drawing on the store of internal energy of the working substance—a store which cannot last indefinitely. During the year 1848 and onwards, William Thomson (afterwards Lord Kelvin, 1824–1907), William John Macquorn Rankine (1820–72), and Rudolph Julius Emmanuel Clausius (1822–88), developed rapidly, by the aid of Carnot's cycle, the principles of Thermodynamics. Every heat-engine works with a difference of temperature—possesses a source of heat and a refrigerator. Its efficiency increases as the difference of temperature increases, and the ratio between the quantity of heat absorbed from its source by a theoretically perfect frictionless engine and that given up to the refrigerator may be shown to be independent of the form of the engine or the nature of the working substance. The efficiency depends on the temperatures of the source and refrigerator alone, and thus may be used to compare those temperatures on a true absolute scale which is independent of the properties of any particular substance.

The efficiency of an engine depends on the difference in temperature which the engine can use. But, in nature, differences in temperature are tending continually to diminish owing to conduction of heat, friction, and other leakages. Hence, while the total amount of energy in an isolated system is constant, it tends perpetually to become less and less available for the performance of useful work. This great principle of the " dissipation of energy," or the diminution of its availability, lies at the base of all modern Thermodynamics. It controls the efforts of the engineer, while its consequences have given us a general theory of chemical equilibrium at the hands of Kelvin, Hermann von Helmholtz (1821–94), and Willard Gibbs.

Heat is a form of energy, and strong evidence shows it to be the kinetic energy of the vibratory motion of the molecules of which we suppose matter to be composed. In a gas these motions are most free, and the kinetic theory of gases has been developed during the last half century chiefly by Waterston, Kelvin, Clausius, and James Clerk Maxwell (1831–79). While we consider molecules statistically in great numbers, the law of dissipation of energy holds. But, could we command a daemon with faculties fine enough to control individual molecules, and separate those which by chance collisions had acquired high velocities from those moving slowly, we could reconcentrate the energy of a system. Thus Maxwell showed possible limitations to the continual loss of availability which the energy of an isolated system undergoes.

The statistical method, founded on the theory of chance and proba-bility, and applied to the kinetic problem of gases, has been used extensively in Sociology, and in the practical problems of political administration. While we cannot predict what any one molecule or man will do at a given time, we know within narrow limits the behaviour of a quantity of gas as a whole, the number of persons who will die in a certain year, and the addition to the national drink-bill which will be caused by a rise of five degrees in the average temperature of a summer season. But, unlike molecules, men can be dealt with individually. Whilst, for the purposes of prediction, we must deal with them only in masses, influences of various kinds, personal, philanthropic, religious, as well as the constraints of custom and of legal enactments, may modify the properties of the whole mass by working upon the individual.

Eventually, we may perhaps hope, by segregating the physically and mentally unfit, by encouraging the increase of healthy stock and placing them in the most favourable environment, to assist the relative growth of desirable qualities and thus to improve slowly the whole body of the human race, as Maxwell's imagined daemon could sort out the individual molecules of a mass of gas.

The striking development in electrical theory and practice seen during the period under review began in the year 1800 with Volta's discovery of the galvanic pile or cell, which consists essentially of two plates of unlike metal placed in a solution of an acid or a salt. The older electric machines of the eighteenth century, while they supplied isolated charges of electricity at very high tension, could not yield any great quantity. The electromotive force of the galvanic battery was much lower, but it was capable of giving a continuous current of electricity. The chemical effects of such currents when passed through a solution of an acid or salt were soon noticed; they led almost at once to the technical industry of electroplating, and, in more recent years, have cheapened and simplified, or even rendered possible, many chemical manufactures and metallurgical processes such as the extraction of pure metals from their ores.

In 1820 Hans Christian Oersted (1777–1851) discovered that a wire carrying an electric current deflected a magnetic needle to which it was parallel, and this magnetic force was soon used as a measure of the intensity of the current, which was shown by Georg Simon Ohm (1789–1854) in 1827 to be proportional to the electromotive force driving it. In 1831 Michael Faraday (1791–1867) demonstrated the momentary induction of a current in one circuit, when another current was made or broken in another circuit, or when a magnet was brought near or taken away. This induction of electric currents by a change in the magnetic force through the circuit is the principle of the dynamo and of the transformer, while the converse phenomenon gives us the electric motor. Few single experiments have led to greater industrial developments than this observation of a momentary electric current, barely perceptible by means of the instruments of its discoverer.

If Faraday's discovery has greater direct industrial applications, Oersted's original observation of the deflexion of a magnetic needle by a current has had a deeper influence on the intellectual history of the world, for it led directly to the invention of a practical form of electric telegraph. The rate of propagation of an electric disturbance along a wire is so great that it may be considered instantaneous. The first devices for electric signalling employed frictional electricity, but the earliest application of the voltaic cell to a practical telegraph was made about 1837 by Sir Charles Wheatstone (1802–75). Long submarine cables have a very great electric capacity, which means that they will also absorb a large quantity of electricity before the further end is raised to a potential high enough to affect the needle of an ordinary recording instrument. This absorption takes an appreciable time, and thus submarine telegraphy over great distances presents special problems of its own, which were overcome by Lord Kelvin, who invented very delicate galvanometers, when the laying of the first successful Atlantic cable in 1858 had shown the need for improved apparatus.

The locomotive engine, invented without much help from theoretical science, and the electric telegraph, the direct consequence of laboratory discoveries, effected the great industrial and social revolution of the middle of the nineteenth century. Together they did more to change the mode of life of the average man than any other development since the invention of printing.

The acceptance of the undulatory theory of light demanded, as we have seen, a medium to undulate. In 1865 Clerk Maxwell, developing mathematically the ideas which Faraday with instinctive genius had put forward thirty years earlier, showed that, to explain the properties of the electromagnetic field, it was necessary again to imagine a medium, and a medium which possessed properties identical with those required to explain the propagation of light. Maxwell proved mathematically that the velocity of an electromagnetic wave through the medium determined the relative magnitudes of certain electric units, so that, by comparing the values of the units, the velocity could be calculated. Experiment on the units showed that the velocity was the same as that of light— about 186,000 miles a second. The waves which constitute light, it may be inferred, are of an electromagnetic character. In view of recent work, it should be noted that it is not necessary to imagine the medium to be continuous; it may possibly be fibrous in structure, and the propagation of light and other electric disturbances may be more analogous to the running of tremors along wires than to the spreading of waves over a continuous medium like water.

In 1888 Heinrich Hertz demonstrated the passage through space of an electromagnetic wave produced by the oscillatory discharge of an electrified system. He measured the wave-length, and showed that the waves possessed many of the properties which waves of light would exhibit were their wave-length magnified some million times. Improvements in detail in the method of producing, and still more of detecting, these waves have been made by Sir Oliver Lodge, Guglielmo Marconi, and others, and have rendered possible the various systems of wireless telegraphy which are now extending rapidly. Wireless telegraphy must affect profoundly the art of naval warfare, while, from the point of view of science, one of its chief uses will be the extension of the area of the meteorological observations of western Europe over the Atlantic Ocean.

The chemical effects of the voltaic current were among the earliest scientific observations of the nineteenth century. When a current is passed, for instance, through the solution of a metallic salt, the metal appears at one terminal, and the acid at the other. About 1830, Faraday studied this process in detail, and showed that the amount of chemical change was strictly proportional to the quantity of electricity which had passed. To explain the appearance of the products of the chemical decomposition at the terminals only, it was necessary to suppose that the opposite parts of the salt moved in opposite directions through the liquid. Hence, Faraday termed these parts " ions," and explained the passage of the current as the movement of discrete charges of electricity carried by the moving atoms or groups of atoms of the salt. The theory of ions has been developed successfully to explain many of the physical and chemical properties of solutions, and has been applied also to elucidate the phenomena of electric conduction through gases.

When a gas is rarefied by an air-pump till the pressure is very low, the negative ions, then called " cathode rays," where they strike solid objects give rise to the so-called X rays, discovered accidentally by Conrad Wilhelm Röntgen in 1895. Röntgen rays traverse many substances opaque to light, and cause phosphorescent and photographic effects on properly prepared screens. Hence the bones in the living body may be seen as shadows on a phosphorescent screen, or photographed on a sensitive plate. The application of this discovery to surgery in general, and to gun-shot wounds in particular, is well known.

If Röntgen rays are of practical importance, the cathode rays from which they arise are of greater theoretical interest. They were found to consist of a stream of projected particles carrying negative electric charges. In the year 1897 Sir Joseph John Thomson measured the velocity of these particles and also the ratio of their mass to the electric charge they carried. This he did by determining the deflexion of the rays in a magnetic and also in an electric field. The deflexions are greater, the greater is the ratio of the charge to the mass and the less is the velocity. The velocity was proved to be about one-tenth that of light. Soon afterwards, Thomson and other physicists showed that the charge on each single cathode ray particle is identical with the charge on a negative ion in liquid electrolysis, and determined its absolute value. The mass of the particle was then calculated from the former experiments, and found to be about the eight-hundredth part of the mass of the smallest chemical atom known—that of hydrogen.

The charge and the mass were found to be identical whatever the nature of the residual gas in the tube, and whatever metal was used for the electrodes. Thus these cathode ray particles were seen to be contained in many different kinds of matter, and the charge with which they are associated appears to be a true fundamental electric unit.

At this point of the enquiry, evidence from another side became applicable. Light, as we have seen, is an electromagnetic phenomenon, and the electromagnetic waves which constitute light must arise from minute electric charges in a state of vibration, just as the long waves used in wireless telegraphy are started by the oscillations of electricity on large systems. Thus every substance must contain electric charges capable of emitting electromagnetic waves when the substance is raised to incandescence. Led by such reasoning, Hendrik Antoon Lorentz and Sir Joseph Larmor put forward an electronic theory of matter, and imagined that the basis of the various atoms was to be sought in differing arrangements of the fundamental electric units or electrons. It is natural to identify this conception with that of the minute material particles or corpuscles suggested by the phenomena of cathode rays. Moreover, an electrified body when in motion carries electromagnetic energy with it through the surrounding space. Hence, the space contains momentum, and the body behaves as though its mass were increased. Thus a moving electric charge possesses properties similar to the inertia of moving matter. It may be that the properties we associate with matter are the effects of the electrical elements of which that matter is composed.

On this view, matter is resolved into electricity, or electricity into matter: it is impossible to say that one of these conceptions is more fundamental than the other. Owing to its effect on our muscular sense, matter, and the system of mechanics associated with it, may seem more familiar, but, had we a special electric sense, we might be more ready to "explain" matter in terms of electricity than electricity in terms of matter.

The luminous effects caused by the incidence of Röntgen rays on phosphorescent and fluorescent substances led to the idea that such substances might themselves emit rays. A search for such phenomena led to a discovery of a different nature. In 1896 Henri Becquerel found that compounds of the metal uranium, whether phosphorescent or not, and independently of any excitation by light, emitted rays which affected a photographic plate through opaque screens, and made the air through which they passed a conductor of electricity.

Pierre (d. 1906) and Mme Marie Curie, continuing Becquerel's search, observed a greater activity in the mineral pitchblende than its contents of uranium warranted. Led by the gradually increasing intensity of its electrical effects as it was concentrated into a smaller mass of material, they separated chemically, by a long series of operations, a new element of transcendent radiating properties, to which they gave the name of radium.

At least three different types of radiation, differing in their penetrative properties, are emitted by these active substances. The energy associated with the rays is considerable, and capable, in the case of radium, of producing a marked evolution of heat. At the same time, new kinds of matter appear. Thus radium, as an accompaniment of its radioactivity, produces a radio-active gas or emanation, which, while itself emitting radiation, gives rise to a solid deposit on the containing vessel. The deposit also has radio-active properties, and passes successively into several new types of radio-active solid matter. Such changes have been studied and elucidated, especially by Ernest Rutherford, who, in conjunction with Frederick Soddy, put forward, in 1903, a theory which has successfully coordinated and explained all the radio-active phenomena hitherto observed.

In Rutherford's view, the energy of radio-activity is liberated by internal changes in single radio-active atoms as a result of their explosive disintegration. In a mass of radium, only about one atom in some millions breaks up in any given hour; but in this way gradually the radium would, as radium, disappear. The less penetrative type of radiation, known as α rays, behaves in electric and magnetic fields as would a stream of positively electrified particles of about the mass of helium atoms, and the actual growth of helium has been detected spectroscopically by Sir William Ramsay in a minute volume of radium emanation. Helium seems to be a general product of radio-active change, and has been found in proportionate quantity by Robert John Strutt in radio-active minerals. Moreover, the amount of radium in such minerals has been shown also to bear a constant ratio to their contents of uranium, and this result suggested that radium was derived from uranium. The evolution of a radio-active emanation gives an extremely delicate test for the presence of radium, but attempts thus to trace the growth of radium in solutions of uranium salts failed. But Bertram Borden Boltwood showed that radium was slowly produced from actinium, another radio-active constituent of uranium minerals—a constituent, too, which exists in such minerals in amounts proportional to their contents of uranium. By such means a probable pedigree of some fifteen generations has been traced for the radio-active family of elements containing uranium and radium and their products.

The importance of the results attained by recent physical research marks an epoch in the history of natural science. The minute corpuscle of the cathode ray stream is identical with the β particle of the more penetrating radio-active rays and with the negative ion of gases at low pressures and high temperatures. It enters into the composition of all matter, and seems to be one of the basic constituents from which, by differences in order and arrangement, the elementary atoms are made. Till we know more about the nature of positive electricity, a complete theory of atomic structure is impossible, but already some tentative hypotheses have been made by Sir Joseph John Thomson, and suggest in a remarkable manner the periodic properties of the chemical elements when arranged in Mendeléeff's table.

We have found by experiment one common basis, perhaps an electrical basis, for matter, and the phenomena of radio-activity have shown that the process of everlasting change, characteristic of organic evolution and of the growth of the earth and of the solar system, is found again in the successive types of matter which appear in radio-active transformation.

Whether such changes go on in all matter is still undetermined, but it is impossible any longer to say that all chemical atoms are immutable, indestructible, eternal.

This sketch of the development of scientific method and knowledge during the last century may serve to indicate the ground won by science for the use and benefit of mankind. Perhaps the most striking feature of the more recent discoveries has been their cumulative effect. A new branch of Physics at once bears chemical fruit, while knowledge gained in Physical Chemistry is applied alike by physicists, chemists, and physiologists. Archaeology throws light on Anthropology, and Anthropology on the Comparative History of Religion. Academic study of the problems of heredity has immediate bearing on Agriculture and Sociology, while the mechanical arts are lying in wait for the results of research in the laboratory, and in using extend them. We understand at last that knowledge is one, and that only for convenience sake has it been divided into subjects and sections along lines determined by historical reasons.

About the future of science it is difficult to speculate. The rate of advance is never uniform; the stream broadens or contracts, runs first fast and then slow. Periods of quiescence allow one branch and then another to take stock of possessions recently acquired. It may be that the mind of man itself is changing and developing, and in time may come to possess faculties as yet undreamed of or only dimly foreshadowed. But, on the other hand, it may be that the power of the human intellect to probe the deeper mysteries of nature is limited, and our age and perhaps the succeeding century may stand for all time marked as that period of history in which the greatest advance in theoretical science was made. However this may be, it is much less doubtful that the practical applications of scientific knowledge will go on extending, and that future ages will see no limit to the growth of man's power over the resources of nature, and of his intelligent use of them for the welfare of his race.

CHAPTER XXV.

MODERN EXPLORATIONS.

ASIA.

DURING the last two centuries, Asiatic explorers have not discovered new kingdoms or new rivers or new courses of old rivers—if minor discoveries may be ignored; and the discoveries, during the last fifty years, of new mountain systems hundreds of miles long and with summits over 20,000 feet high in western China, Tibet, and Chinese Turkestan, of secluded lakes in Tibet and unknown buried cities in Turkestan, and of the ruins of Karakorum, once the capital of Mongolia, have not affected history. But the opening or reopening, by white men, of inter-course by land between furthest West and furthest East is an event of first-rate historical moment. This the explorers have achieved or brought about; and, although the work is but begun, it has already brought the land frontiers of Russia, England, France, and China into contact over a considerable area. Consequently, a modern history of Asiatic explorations will deal principally with Asiatic trade-routes, in so far as they have been developed by European explorers.

In the sixteenth century the new ocean way to India and China superseded the old Asiatic through-routes, which were subsequently reopened, added to, and adapted to European uses, by the efforts of explorers. At least four through-routes have been opened or reopened. The first is the north-east passage along the Arctic Ocean. The second is the great straight Russian post-road through Omsk, Tomsk, Irkutsk, and Nerchinsk, which lies mostly between 55° and 50° N. lat., but has three crooked endings: one, turning south-east beyond Irkutsk to Kiachta and crossing the desert of Gobi from Urga to Kwei-hwa-cheng, Kalgan, and Peking, which became a Russian post-route in 1860 and was the route of the motor race from Peking to Paris (1907); a second, turning south-east near Nerchinsk and crossing Manchuria to the Gulf of Pe-chi-li—which became a railroad (1904) before it was a road; thirdly, the Russian post-road, often only a river track, down the Amur and up the Ussuri and so to Vladivostók, which was begun in 1860 and which

Charles Wenyon was the last to follow and describe (1895). The third
through-way consists of the caravan-routes between 45° and 40° N. lat.,
from the Caspian by Khiva or Merv and Bokhara or Balkh to the
mountain belt which joins the Himalayas, Hindu Kush, and Pamirs, to
the Tian Shan and Alatau, and almost joins the Alatau to the Tarbagatai
and Altai mountains, and thence, either by Kashgar and Lob-nor to
Su-chau in Kan-su (Marco Polo's route), or by Guchen and Hami, or by
Suok, Kobdo, and Uliassutai, either to Su-chau or to Kalgan and so
to eastern China. The fourth and last is formed by the caravan-routes
from the Bosporus by Teheran, Meshed, Herat, and Kabul, or Kandahar,
or else by Bagdad, southern Persia, and the Mekran, to India, and
beyond India by some half-known jungles and mountains, from Sadiya
(Assam), Bhamo, or Mandalay (Burma) to Atuntse (Szech'uan), Momein,
or Ta-li-fu (Yunnan), and so to eastern China.

These through-ways are not mutually exclusive; but there are connexions and combinations and compromises between them. Thus, the
first, third, and fourth routes were associated in their origin, and the
northernmost variants of the third and fourth routes are used more
often than not in conjunction with the southernmost variants of the
second and third routes respectively; and at Kashgar there is a favourite
junction, so to speak, for Yarkand, Kashmir, and India. Along the
Arctic Ocean way great men, elsewhere wars and treaties, provided the
stimulus and opportunity for exploration, and knowledge of the Continent
was won by sufferings inflicted less by nature than by man. The first
way was achieved by international effort, the second by Russian effort,
the third by competitive English and Russian efforts, and the fourth by
English effort; but here too there were exceptions, and of late years
representatives of all the Great European Powers have devoted themselves
to China, and Tibet has been trodden by men of many nations, though
this was only the case when victory was within sight.

The north-east passage was first essayed by Sir Hugh Willoughby,
who discovered Novaia Zemlia and perished, and by his companion,
Richard Chancellor, who stopped at the White Sea, swerved southward,
ascended the Dwina, and arrived at Moscow, the capital of Ivan the
Terrible (1553–4). Anglo-Russian commerce began by this way, and
Sir Anthony Jenkinson, who followed in Chancellor's footsteps so far
as Moscow, went still further southward, descended the Volga, with a
Cossack escort, crossed the Caspian, which he was the first Englishman
to see, and then visited Khiva and Bokhara (1557–8), whence he
brought back ambassadors to the Tsar, and afterwards Derbent, the
Caucasus, and Persia (1561). The first search for the first through-way
to the East resulted in a through-journey from the Arctic Ocean almost
to the Tropic of Cancer, and led to the unlocking, not only of the
first, but of the third and fourth doors to the East. The second door was
forced open a few years later, and Ivan the Terrible was again the cause.

Ivan's Treaties with a Siberian chief, whom Tatars subsequently attacked, and Ivan's wars against rebel Cossacks, induced Ermak Timotheevich, one of these Cossacks, to attack the offending Tatars and to occupy Siberia, in order to regain Ivan's favour (1581–4). Siberia then meant the triangle of rivers of which the apex is the junction of the Tobol and Irtish at Tobolsk ; and Ermak entered Siberia, almost where the present post-road from Perm to Vladivostók enters, by the Tura, which is an affluent of the Tobol, which is an affluent of the Irtish, which is an affluent of the Ob. His followers settled upon their conquests, and proceeded, in small parties, to discover, trade in, plunder, or subdue the lands situated on the middle Ob, Yenisei, and Lena. The process sometimes bore the character of exploration or trade, and sometimes of robbery or conquest, but was invariably a process of colonisation. Settlements and forts were established wherever the Cossacks went and their zig-zag course was marked by the foundation of Tiumen (1586), Tobolsk (1587), Beresoff (1593), and Tomsk (1604) on the Ob and its affluents the Tura, Tobol, and Irtish, and of Krasnoiarsk and Yeniseisk on the Yenisei, and of Yakutsk on the Lena (between 1607 and 1632); and of Verchni Udinsk (1648) east, and Irkutsk (1652) west of Lake Baikal. Four bye-routes were taken from Yakutsk : to the Yana, Indigirka, and Kolima on the Arctic Ocean ; up the Aldan, which is a tributary of the Lena, and down the Ulya to Okhotsk on the Pacific Ocean ; from the Kolima by sea through Behring Strait, which Vitus Behring rediscovered (1728), to the mouth of the Anadyr on the Pacific (1648); and up the Aldan and down the Zeia and Amur into the Pacific and back by the second bye-route (1643–5). A fifth bye-route led up to the sources of the Ob, Irtish, and Yenisei in the Altai mountains, where Raskolnik heretics settled (1719 *sqq.*), and the Government built forts (1718–59) and opened mines (1747), and Russia approached Chinese Turkestan. Great navigable rivers are the key to northern Asia, as they are to North America ; and, when the first four bye-routes had been followed, every important river of northern Asia was known, and Siberia, which now meant northern Asia, ceased to be a region for the mere explorer. Thus Lieutenant John Cochrane went from end to end of Siberia mostly on foot (1821–3), while John Ledyard, with ten guineas in his pocket, travelled to Yakutsk (1787), and Lieutenant James Holman, though blind and alone, travelled to Lake Baikal without difficulty (1822–4). After 1860, free colonists poured into Siberia at an increasing pace, and the rate now exceeds 200,000 per annum. On and near the Siberian through-way, colonists and tourists followed the explorers, whose efforts were now diverted to the northernmost through-way to the East.

The first four bye-routes from Yakutsk supplied essential links for the discovery of the north-east passage, which, although known in 1740, was only accomplished in 1878–9. Sir Hugh Willoughby's voyage to the Kara Sea was repeated by Arthur Pet and Charles Jackman (1580) and by a Dutchman named William Barents (1594–6), who, availing himself of Pet and Jackman's journals, explored Novaia Zemlia and discovered Spitzbergen. Between 1734 and 1740, a combined national effort was made to connect the eastern discoveries of the Cossacks with the western discoveries of the English and Dutch navigators. Accordingly, Lieutenants Muravieff, Malygin, and Skuratoff, sailed from the White Sea to the Ob, and Ivan Kosheloff from the mouth of the Ob to the Yenisei (1734–8), and Fedor Minin from the mouth of the Yenisei to the Pyasina and back (1738). About the same time, Pronchisheff and his wife sailed from the mouth of the Lena westward almost to the Taimur or to the Pyasina, and returned to die (1736), and Khariton Laptieff, who took over their task, actually reached the Pyasina, but travelled the last part of the way by land (1739). Meanwhile, doubts had arisen as to whether men had actually sailed from the Lena to the Kolima, and Dmitri Laptieff tried to do so and reached the Kolima, but he also travelled part of the way by land (1739–40). Then, the Government desisted, and a private merchant named Shalavroff tried again and went the whole way by sea (1761–2). The whole northern passage was known in 1740; and in 1762 all of it had been traversed by sea except a small section east of the Pyasina. Early in the nineteenth century, the search for the north-east passage was resumed by many nations with ocean-going ships, and Hedenström and Jacob Sannikof discovered the New Siberia Islands from Siberia. Sir Henry Kellett, R.N., sighted (1849), and Lieutenant Berry, U.S.N. (1881), explored Wrangel Island from the Pacific, and an Austrian named Julius Payer discovered Franz Josef Land from the Atlantic (1872). Economic as well as international forces came into play. Norse walrus-hunters invaded the Kara Sea (1869 *sqq.*), an English trader named Joseph Wiggins reached the Ob, and a Swede named Adolf Nordenskjöld reached the Yenisei from the Atlantic (1875); and, in 1878–9, Nordenskjöld sailed from the Atlantic through the Arctic to the Pacific Ocean in one ship, one of his companions ascending the Lena to Yakutsk by the way. Some trade grew up between the Atlantic, the Ob, and the Yenisei, and in 1904 munitions of war were taken by water from the Atlantic to Krasnoiarsk. The islands have chiefly been used as bases for attempts on the North Pole, Spitzbergen being S. A. Andrée's base (1897), Franz Josef Land the Duke of Abruzzi's base (1899–1900), and the New Siberia Islands Fridtjof Nansen's base (1893–6).

The completion of the second through-way to the East was attended by diplomatic complications which affected the history of the third and fourth through-ways. Under the Treaty of Nerchinsk (1689), the Russians retired from the Amur below the Shilka, and trade between Russia and China was after a time limited to Kiachta and the Urga-Kalgan route. More than twelve hundred miles to the west of the

Urga-Kalgan route, Russia advanced to Lepsinsky (1855), and Russian factories and consuls were authorised at Chuguchak and Kuldja (1851); so that Russia now faced and touched extramural China in Turkestan as well as in Mongolia.

Immediately after the Crimean War came to an end (1856), Russia, England and France applied pressure to China from different sides, for different reasons and by different methods. An Anglo-French naval expedition occupied Canton, Taku (1858), and Peking (1860); and, by the Treaties of Aigun and Tientsin (1858) and Peking (1860) between Russia and China, a postal service was established between Urga and Kalgan under Russian supervision. The left bank of the Amur, the Ussuri, and Vladivostók were ceded to Russia, who immediately completed her post-road beyond Nerchinsk to Vladivostók; and Kashgar shared the fate of Kuldja. By the Treaties of Tientsin between China, France, and England, new Treaty Ports were opened, and China permitted British and French travellers and missionaries to travel inland with passports signed by their consuls and countersigned by the local authorities (1858, 1860)—a privilege which was shortly afterwards extended to other Europeans; and, after 1877, the Treaty Ports began to include inland towns upon the middle Yang-tsze-kiang. The unveiling of China began (1860). Till then, but for Marco Polo and a few missionaries in past centuries and Earl Macartney's political mission, which went by the grand canal from Peking to Canton (1793), the interior of China had been a sealed book.

Immediately after 1860, Captain Thomas Blakiston surveyed the Yang-tsze-kiang from Shanghai and Nanking up to Ping-shan, a town 1760 miles from its mouth and reached by H.M.S. *Woodcock* in 1902. In 1866–8 Lieutenant François Garnier ascended or marched up by the Mekong from Saigon in Cambodia towards Yunnan; proved that the Mekong is not the Menam; reached Ta-li-fu foodless, bootless, and ragged, and returned by the Yang-tsze-kiang from Ping-shan to Shanghai. Next, Thomas Cooper, "pioneer of commerce in pig-tail and petticoats," as he called himself, ascended the Yang-tsze-kiang and reached Batang in Szech'uan on his way to Sadiya in Assam (1868), and afterwards reached the Mishmee hills from Sadiya on his way to Batang (1869); and Augustus Margary passed by Ta-li-fu and Momein to Bhamo on an official commercial mission, but was murdered in Yunnan on his way back (1874–5). Long afterwards, Prince Henry of Orleans passed from Hanoi to Ta-li-fu, Batang, and Atuntse, and from Atuntse, somewhat north of Cooper's proposed route, through wild tribes and jungles to Sadiya (1895–6): otherwise Cooper's through-way has been of little use as yet. On the other hand, Margary's route, which was followed by an English mission to enquire into his murder, Archibald Colquhoun's variant of Margary's route, which started from Canton up the Si-kiang (1881–2), and Captain Alfred Wingate's *via media* between Margary's and Colquhoun's routes (1898–9) are now often traversed. Serious exploration of the Red river of Tonkin began with Dupuis and Millot (1872), and of the Menam, "which is the Nile of Siam," with Holt Hallett and McCarthy (1881–7), and both these rivers led towards Ta-li-fu. From east, south-east, and south, at first by the rivers of Nanking and Cambodia, then by the rivers of Canton, Tonkin, and Siam, explorers poured inland. The movement began in the early sixties, immediately after the opening of China, and culminated 30 or 40 years later, when empire followed exploration, and a succession of treaties (1893–1904) necessitated the appointment of Frontier Commissioners, who were explorers and something more. Every exploration on the great rivers converged on Yunnan and Szech'uan in western China, where the Mekong, the Salwin, and the many-branched Yang-tsze-kiang run parallel and close together between lofty mountain ridges, and was undertaken in the interests of Anglo-Indian, Indo-Chinese, Anglo-Malay, and Siamese trade.

Other motives for exploration reinforced these influences. In 1860 a Prussian geographer, Ferdinand von Richthofen, sailed for China, imbued with the ideas of Alexander von Humboldt and in order to pursue the interests of science. When at last he set to work (1868), he, among other things, journeyed from Canton to Peking almost wholly on the same meridian and partly on what is now the Hankow and Peking line of railway, and from Cheng-tu-fu in Szech'uan by Si-nan-fu to Peking (1868–72): but he was little in Szech'uan, and neither in Yunnan nor Kan-su. The earliest effectual exploration of these three western provinces must be credited to the French missionaries, who also arrived in China in 1860 under Abbé Desgodins in order to pass on to Tibet, and have ever since been waiting on the western frontier of China, although they still regard Tibet as their destination. These men laid the foundations of that knowledge about western China which Colborne Baber, who passed through Szech'uan for 2–300 miles from Ta-chien-lu in the north to Hui-li-chau in the south (1877–8), and many others, have extended but not completed.

While the door of China was ajar and invited religious, scientific, political, and commercial explorers, that of Tibet was double-locked and tantalised them. Jesuit and Franciscan missionaries had penetrated Lhassa in Tibet from India and Peking in the seventeenth and eighteenth centuries; but in the nineteenth century only one missionary journey was made to Lhassa. In 1845–7 two Lazarist fathers, Évariste Huc and Joseph Gabet, went from Peking by Ning-hia-fu (on the Hoang-ho) and Koko-nor to Lhassa, returning by Batang, Cheng-tu-fu, and the Yang-tsze-kiang. Abbé Huc's geography was vague; but his vivid accounts of monasteries with 10,000 monks apiece, of courtiers putting out their tongues by way of salutation, of *yaks* frozen while swimming and preserved like flies in amber, of valleys all of which were over

12,000 feet high, of prayer-mills and prayer-barrels, touched the imagination, so that Tibet began to lure the adventurous.

Tibet was assailed from all sides and first from the south. From India, Warren Hastings' emissaries, George Bogle (1774–5) and Samuel Turner (1783–4), had visited southern Tibet, reaching the San-po and Namling or Shigatse, but not Lhassa, by a pass just east of Sikkhim : and Thomas Manning, a friend of Charles Lamb, had reached Lhassa (1811–12) by the same pass. In 1865 Colonel Thomas George Montgomerie, having educated native Indians as surveyors, sent them forth by this and other routes, arrayed as Buddhist pilgrims with prayer-barrel (in which compasses and field-books were hidden) and with rosary (in order that they might count their paces); and they on three occasions visited Lhassa and perambulated Tibet (1865–82). But since Manning no white visitor reached Tibet by this route, nor did any white visitor, except Huc and Gabet, ever reach Lhassa by this or any other route, until Sir Francis Younghusband marched from Sikkhim to Lhassa, at the head of 3000 soldiers (1904).

Four hundred miles west of Sikkhim, William Moorcroft, a horse-dealer, crossed the Himalayas to Lake Manasarowar in Tibet, which is the intermittent source of the Sutlej and lies close to the source of the San-po (1812); after the First Sikh War Henry and Richard Strachey visited the lake from the same quarter (1846–7); Arnold Landor was there (1897); some officers of Sir Frank Younghusband's army were sent home up the San-po to Lake Manasarowar and the upper Sutlej (1904), mapping the trans-Himalayan range as they went; and Sven Hedin also was there, after exploring the trans-Himalayas (1907–8). Besides these, there was no one to solve the secular puzzle whether the lake is or is not connected with the Sutlej, sometimes or always. But Tibet is prolific of puzzles and no one has yet traced the San-po into the Brahmaputra ; so that some people, doubtless, still identify the San-po with the Salwin or Irrawaddy.

Tibet was also approached from the north-east. First, Nicolai Prjevalsky went from Peking by Ding-hu (on the Hoang-ho) to Koko-nor and the uppermost Yang-tsze-kiang in Tibet. Part of his route coincided with Marco Polo's route between Europe and China, and part of it with Abbé Huc's route to Lhassa; but the coincidences were not exact, and Prjevalsky returned to a point 60 miles west of Ning-hia-fu, whence he struck, by a new route, due north by Borston Well to Urga across 700 miles of desert (1870–2). This Russian example inspired an Englishman, Ney Elias, who with one Chinese servant went from Peking and Kwei-hwa-cheng by Uliassutai, Kobdo, and Suok over the spurs of the Altai mountains to Russia (1872–3). He was the first white through-traveller on the central Asiatic through-way since the Middle Ages. And the English example was imitated by a Russian, who accomplished a second through-route from east to west. Hardly had

Ney Elias returned home, when Colonel Sosnofski journeyed from Peking, in order to open up what he declared to be the best commercial route between Russia and western China, crossing by Su-chau, Hami, Barkul, and Guchen to the low-lying slit between the Alatau and Tarbagatai mountains and to Lake Zaisan. The stimulus which Prjevalsky's first journey imparted to the development of the central Asiatic route was strong, but soon spent itself. After 1875, there was a lull in eastward and westward movements; and men's minds and efforts were diverted southward, to Tibet. This diversion was mainly due to the subsequent journeys of Prjevalsky, who started from points nearer to Tibet, accompanied by an escort of ten or twenty Cossacks " on a war footing, rifles slung, revolvers in their belts, watches kept night and day," and who said that he expected to find somewhere in northern Tibet " a second California."

In 1876–8, starting from Kuldja, he went south-east by Karashahr and Kurla to the strange migratory lake Lob-nor, which he rediscovered; and he tried but failed to go on towards Lhassa, due south of Lob-nor across the Altyn Tagh range, which he discovered. In three subsequent journeys (1879–88) he repeated these efforts. In 1879, he went from Lake Zaisan, at the foot of the Altai mountains, by Uliungur south-south-east to Barkul, Hami, Sa-chu, and across the Altyn Tagh to the headwaters of the Yang-tsze-kiang, where he had been in 1871, and then to within 200 miles of Lhassa. In 1883–5, he went from Urga by Koko-nor to the sources of the Hoang-ho, which he determined; then, crossing the Altyn Tagh by another pass, he followed its northern base from Lob-nor to Cherchen, Keria and Khoten, whence he struck north across the desert to Aksu, and Issik Kul in the Alatau mountains, and the neighbourhood of Kuldja. In 1888, when about to repeat his journey of 1885 to Keria, with variations, and to make a last attempt on Lhassa from the north, he died. These three last journeys, taken together with each other or with one or other of his earlier journeys, involved a circuitous east to west traverse from China to western Asia; but his principal new routes across Chinese Turkestan were from north to south, or from south to north.

After his death, in 1888, Pievtsoff (1889 *sqq.*) and P. K. Kozloff (1899–1901; 1901 *sqq.*), who succeeded him, perfected the survey of these and other routes from the southern frontier of Russian territory to the northern frontier of Tibet, as though their goal had been in southern, not in eastern Asia. The line of advance of Prjevalsky and his successors intersected the east and west trade-route at innumerable points; but the trade-route itself was never followed for long. Except for these implied or composite traverses from east to west by Prjevalsky, there were no recorded traverses by other through-travellers between 1875 and 1887. Prjevalsky's interest in Tibet was one cause of this abstention, but other causes were at work. In the middle seventies, two new factors entered into the situation. Ladakh in north-east Kashmir became a western base, not for a through-route, but for local excursions to Tibet and to Khoten, Yarkand, and Kashgar, in Chinese Turkestan, and to the Pamir plateau; and the Pamir plateau presented a potent counter-attraction to through-routes and even to Tibet.

But, in order to understand why travellers went from all sides to the Pamirs, travellers' routes to the west and north-west of India along the western half of the central Asiatic through-way must be discussed. These routes were traversed partly by officials on official business, partly by private adventurers, and partly by officials bent on private adventure.

In 1783 George Forster, an Indian civilian, "out of curiosity and pleasure" went home from India through Kabul, Kandahar, Herat, Toorsheez, Sharud, Barfrush, and Russia. In the early nineteenth century, France and England sent to Persia rival ambassadors, through whose narratives Persia once more became known, and by whose followers the ways to Persia from east and west were explored. The diplomatic suite of Sir Harford Jones, one of these ambassadors, included James Morier, who went on an official mission by land from Ispahan by Teheran, Kazvin, Tabriz, Erzerum, and Amasia, to the Bosporus (1809); and the suite of another, Sir John Malcolm, included Charles Christie and Henry Pottinger, who went from India overland by Khelat—the one by Surhud, Bumm, and Kirman, and the other by Seistan, Furrah, and Herat (1810), to join their chief at Yezd and Ispahan. These three diplomats, between them, accomplished a through-route from India to Constantinople along the branches of the great southern through-route (1809–10). After diplomats we come to a horse-dealer. In 1824–5 William Moorcroft went to buy horses, passing from India by Kabul, Bamian, Khulm, Kunduz, and Balkh, to Bokhara and Andkhui, where he died, having met with little inconvenience except from the ingrained inability of Orientals to distinguish between traders, ambassadors, and prisoners of State. Next, Captain Arthur Conolly (1829–30), like Forster, went overland from England to India on his way to rejoin his regiment, and some French officers did the same from Persia to the Punjab. These tours led to political missions.

In 1832 Alexander Burnes went, like Moorcroft, by Kabul, Bamian, Khulm, Kunduz, and Balkh to Bokhara—on the pretence of travelling homeward like Conolly, but in reality upon a vague political mission. In 1836 a definite political mission was sent to Afghanistan, with which Burnes, Conolly, Charles Stoddart, James Abbott, Richmond Shakespear, and John Wood were associated. Of these, Abbott (1839), Shakespear (1840), and Conolly (1841) were sent on to Khiva, on political business, the former two continuing their journey to Russia and England; John Wood (1837–8) was sent with Dr Lord to Kunduz, and, while Dr Lord was treating patients, amused himself by tracing the Oxus to the Pamirs, which he was the first white man to visit since Benedict Goez (1603), and where he discovered one of the sources of the Oxus in Victoria Lake; and Stoddart (1838) and Conolly (1841) were sent to Bokhara, where both were murdered together with their would-be rescuer Lieutenant Wyburd (1842). Russian embassies also reached Khiva (1819), Bokhara (1820, 1842), Herat, and Kabul (1837); so that Russians and Englishmen were now in close contact at three points in west central Asia, and it might seem that there was no more° work for explorers to do here. But these murders set the clock back: and then two of the strangest explorers that ever were seen went wandering through the land. First, arrayed in black gown and red doctor's hood and with open Bible in his hand, Dr Joseph Wolff went to Bokhara from the Euxine in order to ask what had become of Stoddart and Conolly, learned their fate, and, still more wonderful to relate, returned safely (1844). Secondly, in 1863, a Hungarian philologer, Arminius Vambéry, dressed as a Dervish, and yelling *Ya hoo Ya hakk* "2000 times," entered Khiva and saw human heads rolled out of sacks "like potatoes" as the price of robes of honour, and grey-beards lying eight in a row and having their eyes gouged out. His genius for language saved him there, and at Bokhara, Samarkand, Andkhui, and Herat, which he visited. Wolff and Vambéry were the last of the explorers who travelled through these parts with their lives in their hands. War came and swept the pestilential slave markets of Khiva and Bokhara clean: the visits of MacGahan (1874) and Frederick Burnaby (1875–6) to Khiva ushered in an era of holiday tourists, and a railway was built from Krasnovodsk on the east coast of the Caspian to Kizil-Arvat, Bokhara, and Samarkand (1888), and thence to the foot of the mountains between Russian Turkestan and Kashgar.

Of all the routes followed in 1838–42, John Wood's was the only pure explorer's route and the only one which bore fruit in discoveries. War made west central Asia too dangerous or too safe for exploration; in Persia, English officials, such as Sir Henry Rawlinson (1833 *sqq.*) and Molesworth Sykes (1893 *sqq.*), and, on the Persian, Afghan, and Baluch frontiers, Russo-Persian (1882), Russo-Afghan-English (1885), and Perso-Afghan-English (1872, 1895–7, 1905) Frontier Commissioners performed the functions of explorers. Politics ousted travel, except, it would seem, on the Pamir plateau, towards which men streamed, but not from the side of Badakshan.

Ladakh, which became the starting-point for the Pamirs, had been one of Moorcroft's bases for horse-dealing in central Asia, and W. H. Johnson, of the Indian Survey, crossed the Karakorum pass thence to Khoten, which no European had visited for 260 years and where he heard of cities buried in the sand (1865). This date was also immediately after the date of the opening of China, which is the one and only critical date in the modern history of Asiatic explorations. In 1868 Robert Shaw, an Indian tea-planter, went by the same pass to Yarkand and Kashgar simultaneously with an English geographer, the illfated George

Hayward, and with a Russian officer, Captain Rheinthal.   These
expeditions led to two official English missions under the leadership of
Sir Douglas Forsyth (1870–4) and to two official Russian missions under
the leadership of Generals Alexander Kaulbars and Kuropatkin; and,
during the second English mission, English surveyors on the Pamirs came
into touch with the Russian Survey from the north.   New sources of the
Oxus were descried and stimulated geographical inquisitiveness; and
the ultimate source of the Oxus became the question of the hour, until
Henri Dauvergne, a trader in Kashmir, finally solved it (1889).   Sport,
also, made the Pamirs popular; and then clouds began to darken the
place where three empires—Russia, England, and China—had at last
met; until in 1895 Commissioners of these three Powers delimited their
frontiers here.   Travel merged in politics, and geography in history.

Ladakh was also a base for Tibet and Chinese Turkestan; and,
after the Forsyth mission (1874), Kashgar, and in the late eighties
Gilgit and Chitral, were in touch with Ladakh.   In 1885, Arthur
Carey, an Indian civil servant, pioneered a circular trip through
northern Tibet and Chinese Turkestan from and to Ladakh.   In
Chinese Turkestan, his route touched Prjevalsky's routes at Khoten,
Kurla, and Karashahr: he was the first European to follow the Tarim
from the confluence of the Yarkand and Khoten to its end in Lob-nor;
and he was the second—Alexander Regel was the first (1879)—who
visited Turfan after Goez (1603), although Turfan lies on one of the
historic highways between east and west.   Carey's routes in northern
Tibet resembled those of Prjevalsky, although they were not the same;
his entry into Tibet being from Lob-nor, and his exit from Tibet being
into Sa-chu.   Shortly after Carey's return, while geographical interest
was on the wane, and before politics intervened on the Pamirs, English
and other travellers once more pressed from west to east or east to west,
and interest in historic through-ways was revived.   Gilgit and Kashgar
became starting-points or goals for the journey to or from Peking.   In
1887, Sir Frank Younghusband traversed the whole historic trade-route
from Peking and Kalgan by Borston Well, Hami, Turfan, Karashahr,
Kurla, and Aksu, to Kashgar; returning to India by the Mustagh glacier
pass (west of the Karakorum and east of the Pamirs) and by Gilgit.
A third route was thus recovered by European for European.   In the
same year, Mark Bell started from Peking and, like Sosnofski, crossed
from Lan-chau-fu by Su-chau to Hami, Barkul, and Guchen and then
turned south by Urumtsi to Karashahr and, like Younghusband, west
by Kurla and Aksu to Kashgar.   Bell's route may be described as a
combination of the second and third recovered routes.   A fifth route
was recovered in 1893–4 by St George Littledale and his wife, who
reached Samarkand from the Caspian by railway, crossed the central
mountain belt of Asia to Kashgar, and passed thence by Aksu and Kurla
to Lob-nor, crossed the Gobi by a track which Marco Polo, the last

European who used it, described as haunted by goblin voices, reached Sa-chu, Koko-nor, and Lan-chau-fu, drifted down the Hoang-ho to its northernmost reaches, and drove thence to Peking.

By this time, the central Asiatic routes between the outposts of Europe and the Pacific Ocean began to be used by tourists, such as the two American bicyclists who retraced Sosnofski's route from Kuldja to Peking (1894); by archaeologists, like Marc Aurel Stein (1900 *sqq.*); by "geologic and physiographic" investigators, like the American professor Ellsworth Huntington (1905–6), and by historical pilgrims, like Major Clarence Bruce, who traced Marco Polo's footsteps from Keria 1300 miles eastward (1905–6); and they ceased to be an arena for explorers pure and simple.

In the nineties—while through-routes were passing from the region of poetry to that of prose—Tibet was once more explored, not as an end in itself, but to provide an alternative through-route which had not yet lost its atmosphere of romance. In 1889–90, Gabriel Bonvalot and Prince Henry of Orleans went from Kuldja to Karashahr and thence to Keria. Then, they swooped down like Prjevalsky from Keria towards Lhassa, were diverted eastward by the stubborn obstruction of Tibet, emerged, like Abbé Huc, at Batang and Ta-chien-lu in western China, and continued their journey through Yunnan to Tonkin. Then a French *mission scientifique* under Dutreuil de Rhins (1890–5) followed the through-route by Bokhara, Kashgar, and Keria as far as Cherchen, and, making the usual dash towards Lhassa and suffering the inevitable diversion to the east, reached Peking by nearly the same road that Abbé Huc had trodden in the reverse direction. All attempts on Lhassa from the north failed as they had failed under Prjevalsky's guidance; crooked through-ways partly due south and partly due east were useless; but at last, when Younghusband penetrated Tibet and Lhassa from the south (1904), a French expedition under Comte de Lesdain (1904–5) went straight from Ngan-si-chau by the sources of the Yang-tsze-kiang, and by Shigatse (but not by Lhassa) to Sikkhim. Northern India and Mongolia were united, so far as one white explorer could unite them, through Tibet. Here, at last, descents into Tibet from the north yielded a historical result.

During the nineties, western China and north-western India were also put in communication with one another by many European explorers travelling through northern Tibet.

In 1891, Captain Hamilton Bower traversed Tibet from Ladakh to Batang and Ta-chien-lu in China between north latitude 33° and 30°; the country through which he passed had neither tree nor shrub, and the traveller, during five months' travel, never slept below an elevation of 15,000 ft. above the sea; and similarly, in 1896, Captain Montagu Wellby traversed Tibet from Ladakh, between north latitude 35° and 36°, to the sources of the Yang-tsze-kiang, which he determined, and thence by

Koko-nor, Si-ning-fu, and Lan-chau-fu to Peking; and he too was for four months in a desolate stony country which averaged 16,000 ft. above the sea. Similar traverses between east and west have also been assisted by Captain Henry Deasy's (1896) and Captain Cecil Rawling's (1903) round trips from end to end of northern Tibet from and to Ladakh, and by Woodville Rockhill's circular trip into Tibet by Koko-nor and out of it by Batang (1891–2), which began and ended in Peking, where he was attached to the American embassy, and by a somewhat similar round trip by Miss Annie Taylor (1892–3), and by Sven Hedin's three monumental journeys in Chinese Turkestan and Tibet (1893–7, 1899–1902, 1906–8).

In the last of these journeys, Sven Hedin reexamined the valley and the mountains which border the valley of the San-po between Shigatse and the source of the San-po—members of Sir Frank Younghusband's expedition to Lhassa having examined both valley and mountains cursorily (1904–5)—and it would seem that by far the best east and west traverse of Tibet from Ladakh lies along this valley to the neighbourhood of Lhassa, and thence by the two pilgrim routes which Abbé Huc followed to China. Perhaps this through-way is destined to become an important part of the chain with many links which joins Europe to China. Not only this journey, but every other journey made by Sven Hedin, covers as much new ground as those of any three of his fellow-travellers; but his discoveries lie so close to those which have already been described and are on so many routes that they cannot be discussed here. He has fulfilled and completed the tasks of other men.

In 1860, between the Urga-Kalgan route and the Tian Shan and allied mountains lay 2000 miles of country, inhabited by Chinese Turki (as they used to be called) or traversed in every direction by Mongolians, but of which, so far as we know, Europeans knew nothing at first hand except from medieval writers. Between Chinese Turkestan or Mongolia and India lay Tibet, larger and less known than Greenland at that date, yet annually traversed by tens of thousands of coloured pilgrims from time immemorial. Nowadays, white travellers' tracks form an intricate network over Chinese Turkestan, Mongolia, and Tibet, and virgin soil is scarce.

But, in Asia, virgin soil means tracts open to certain Orientals and closed to every white man. With the opening up of such tracts secluded nations begin to have external relations and a common share in one world-history. Exploration is the pacific method by which nations which loiter in some back-water are enticed into the main stream of world-politics and commerce. But the process is slow; frontier-treaties can be made in a day, but it takes many white travellers to overcome prejudices of more than a thousand years. The travellers' triumphs of which mention has been made are only the prelude of the inevitable social, political, and commercial change, and there are still vacant spots in Asia which no white traveller has reached : for instance, near the sources of the Irrawaddy between Assam, Burma, and Szech'uan, in the western valleys of Kafiristan, near Telu Dagh and the Dersim in Kurdistan, and in the south Arabian desert of Rub-el-Khali, 850 miles long by 650 miles broad in parts : that desert, however, is probably a real desert, not a labyrinth of passages for Asiatics like the desert of Gobi, but an uninhabitable void, as its name denotes.

AFRICA.

In the late eighteenth century nothing was known at first hand of any part of the interior of Africa, nor was any lake known except Lake Tsana in Abyssinia, nor any mountain except the Mount Atlas of tradition and Ptolemy's mythical Mountains of the Moon, nor the source of any river except that of the Blue Nile : and there were rumours of a river which Pliny called the Niger, and which was supposed to run nearly or quite across Africa along the 15th parallel of north latitude or thereabouts : yet no white man had ever seen it, and, as in the case of the Murray of Australia, its mouth was destined to be discovered from its headwaters, students identifying it in the meantime with the Gambia, the Senegal, or some affluent of the upper Nile or with both. If one-half of these rumours were true, the Nile and Niger were to Africa what the Ganges and Indus were to India ; and the Niger and its fabulous city of Timbuktu began to perplex the intellect and dazzle the imagination of Europe.

In 1769–71, while James Cook, accompanied by Sir Joseph Banks, was discovering or rediscovering Australasia, James Bruce, who had gone out of pure love of travel and at his own cost by Massowah to Abyssinia, was musing over the sources of the Blue Nile—which a Portuguese Jesuit, Pedro Paez, had also seen (1615)—and was watching Abyssinians eating live cows raw, and was wandering from Gondar, the capital, by the sources of the Atbara to Sennar, Shendy, Berber, and thence across the desert to Assuan and Cairo. Charles Poncet, a French doctor, had already gone from Assiout by Sheb, Selimé, Dongola, Korti, Derreira (near Metemma), and Sennar to Gondar and returned by Massowah many years before (1698 *sqq.*) : so that Bruce's feat was not so new as his information, which provoked equal mirth and unbelief throughout the whole of western Europe. In 1793 a second unofficial traveller, William George Browne, went from Assiout by Sheb, Selimé, and Ein Aga, to Kobé, the capital of Darfur, wishing to pass thence either westward to Pliny's Niger, or southward to the unknown sources of the White Nile, or eastward to Sennar and Gondar, but returning after three years' captivity by the way which he alone of white men has ever trodden.

In 1788, the African Association, of which Sir Joseph Banks was the moving spirit, began to send forth " geographical missionaries " towards the supposed course of the Niger. The Association was formed in the year after William Wilberforce began his crusade against slavery ; but it had no direct connexion with philanthropy, its objects being austerely scientific. Its first emissaries from Egypt and Tripoli were John Ledyard (1788), who had been a comrade of Captain Cook, and William Lucas (1789), but both died almost before they began their work ; and, when England was at war, German and Swiss emissaries were selected in the respective persons of Friedrich Hornemann and John Burckhardt. Hornemann went west from Cairo by Siwah and Augila to Murzuk in Fezzan, where he heard that.the Niger flowed eastward into a lake named Lake Chad (1799) and further eastward towards the Nile; so, after a journey to Tripoli and back, he started south (1800) and vanished somewhere, it was said, in Nupé on the Niger. John Burckhardt was to follow him : and by way of practice travelled, " nearly in the same route by which Bruce returned," as far as Berber and Shendy, and thence to Suakin and Mecca and back to Cairo ; but, when about to start in Hornemann's tracks, he also died (1817). Then the sceptre passed from the African Association to private initiative and to the British Government. Private initiative was represented by Wilhelm Eduard Rüppell, who went from Debbeh across the desert to El Obeid in Kordofan, where he was the first white visitor (1825); so that explorers' tracks now furrowed the deserts between Egypt and the Red Sea, Abyssinia, Sennar, Kordofan, Darfur, and Fezzan. The British Government succeeded to the tasks of western as well as to those of eastern and northern adventurers.

In the far west, the ground had been prepared by French and English colonists, and more than prepared by the African Association. André Brue ascended the Senegal (16° N. lat.) to its confluence with the Salemé (1698 *sqq.*), and two wrecked mariners, Saugnier (1784) and Pierre de Brisson (1785), were enslaved by Arabs and taken from Cape Blanco or somewhere near it through deserts to Morocco. There were also English factories on the Gambia (14° N. lat.) at Pisania, and news brought to the Senegal and Gambia invested Timbuktu and the Niger with the halo of an Arabian Night's Entertainment.

Daniel Houghton (1790), the first emissary of the African Association, ascended the Gambia and reached the upper Senegal at a point beyond that which French enterprise had attained. There he was murdered. Mungo Park (1795–7), his successor, started the same way, and was the first white man to see the Niger. He noted that it flowed eastward, and followed it to Silla, 800 miles due east of his starting-place and 200 miles south-west of Timbuktu. He was robbed, enslaved, and feverstricken, and paid for his board by writing "charms" which his hosts instead of reading licked up. He returned, convinced that the Niger was the Congo, and bent on renewing his quest.

In 1801 Sir Joseph Banks persuaded the Government to despatch Park on a new expedition; and Park started in 1805 with 44 doomed companions, mostly British soldiers, to follow, more or less, his old tracks. A small remnant of sick survivors reached Sansanding on the Niger where they embarked on boats, and their leader wrote: " Though I were myself half dead I would still persevere, and if I could not succeed in the object of my journey I would at last die on the Niger." Six years later, natives brought news that the white boatmen had drifted past the port of Timbuktu to Bussa, 1000 miles away, where they perished one and all.

It was about now that two geographers, Reichard (1808) and James McQueen (1816), suggested the true theory of the position of the Niger's mouth; but the Government, spurning theorists, wavered only between the views of practical men like Hornemann and Mungo Park, and, in the year after Waterloo, sent James Tuckie to the Congo, Major Peddie to the Nunez (10° N. lat.), and Joseph Ritchie and George Lyon (1818) to Tripoli, of whom all except Lyon perished without adding to knowledge: and Lyon only went to Tegerrie, or a little further than Murzuk where Hornemann was in 1799. At the same time, Thomas Bowdich went on a political mission from Cape Coast Castle inland to Kumassi, which he was the first white man to see. Thus the first combined assault failed. A second combined assault followed.

In 1822, the colony of Sierra Leone sent Alexander Laing inland to the sources of the Rokelle, whence he saw the hills where the Niger rose, and returned. In the same year, the British Government sent Dixon Denham and Hugh Clapperton to Tripoli, whence they crossed the whole desert of Sahara from north to south. Their route lay by Murzuk, Tegerrie, Bilma, and Agadem, over wastes strewn with the skeletons of slaves to Kukawa on Lake Chad, which they discovered. Starting from Lake Chad, Denham examined its north and south shores and discovered the Shari, which is the chief feeder of the lake, and travelled with raiders south but not quite so far as the Benue, returning to the lake with the loss of all his clothes; while Clapperton travelled west along what is now the border of northern Nigeria to Kano and Sokoto, without quite reaching the main stream of the Niger. The two leaders returned from Kukawa by the way they came; and the belief now prevailed that the Niger emptied itself into the Gulf of Guinea at Volta or elsewhere, and also, by its Chadda or Benue branch, which no one had yet seen, through the Shari into Lake Chad.

The third and last triple effort took place under the auspices of the British Government in 1825. Dickson went from Whydah, east of the Volta, overland to Abomey, the capital of Dahomey, and died an unknown death between Abomey and Youri on the Niger; a little further east, Hugh Clapperton, Richard Lander, and others went overland from Badagry by Katunga and Bussa, where Park perished, to Sokoto and Kano, meaning to go east to Lake Chad and the Nile; but all the leaders died, except Lander, who then turned due south and, when

CH. XXV.

almost within sight of the Benue, was forced to retrace his footsteps
to Kano and Badagry. Alexander Laing, in the meantime, went south
from Tripoli to Murzuk, north-north-west to Ghadames, and south-
south-west across the Sahara through Ensalah, Tanezruft, and Mukhtar
to Timbuktu, where he remained five weeks. Timbuktu, the goal of so
many seekers, was at last won, and the winner was murdered three days
after he quitted it. These cruel victories had two sequels: René Caillié,
a French adventurer, is said to have reached Timbuktu by a variant of
Park's route (1828) and to have crossed the Sahara, west of Laing's
route, by El Aruan, El Trab, and Tafilet, to Fez in Morocco. Richard
and John Lander crossed once more from Badagry to Bussa (1830),
went upstream to Youri, and downstream past the Benue, which proved
to be an affluent not an effluent of the Niger, to the delta of the Niger,
where they were robbed and held to ransom. The story of their sudden
disaster and of their strange rescue by a sea captain is one of the most
surprising in the record of African adventure, coming as it did at the
last moment of a cloudless voyage. The secret of the Niger was now
divulged. The Sahara had been crossed in three places, or, if we count
Saugnier and de Brisson, in five: and the crucial riddle of northern
and north-western Africa was read. Commercial, philanthropical and
political events began when the age of romance and enquiry ended: and
romance and enquiry flitted to southern Africa, to which we now turn.

In 1840, the year in which Abbé Huc and other French Lazarists
arrived in China, David Livingstone, a missionary of the London
Missionary Society, arrived in South Africa and travelled from Algoa
bay 500 miles due north to the mission-post established by Robert
Moffat at Kuruman, on the threshold of the northern wilderness. In
1849 he crossed the Kalahari desert, on a visit to some Bechuana
living 500 miles north of Kuruman on or near Lake Ngami, which he
discovered. There were now three known lakes in Africa, Lakes Tsana,
Chad, and Ngami. Thence he passed to the Makilolo, who lived on a
branch of the upper Zambesi (Linyanti), and for and with whom he
travelled up the Zambesi by Lake Dilolo (which is one of its sources)
and Kassange to Loanda on the Atlantic, and back again to Linyanti;
and then to Quilimane on the Indian Ocean (1853–6). The upper
Zambesi, Lake Dilolo, and the Victoria Falls of the Zambesi were
discovered, and Africa was at last crossed by a white man. What he
did was great; but what he read and heard of and had left undone
seemed greater to his imagination and lured him still further north.
He read that, when England took over Cape Colony, the Portuguese of
Angola and Quilimane tried to join hands: that they went on embassies
to Kazembe and Muata Yánvo north of his route; and that they sent
men, whom the Governor of Angola called "slaves," by Muata Yánvo,
from one colony to the other: and now he conversed with natives of

Muata Yánvo, with Portuguese who had been not only at Kazembe but at a lake named Lake Nyassa, out of which the Shiré flowed, and, strangest of all, with Arab slave-traders who had reached the Makilolo for the first time at the same moment as he, and who told him of a lake named Tanganyika and of a river, the Lualaba, rising in some other lake.

When Livingstone returned home (1856), the Crimean War was just over and great schemes of exploration were in the air. Two Church of England missionaries who had been planted at Mombasa (1842 *sqq.*) —Krapf and Rebmann by name—saw Mounts Kenia and Kilimanjaro (1848–9) with their snowy crests, and heard of vast inland seas. Memories of the snow mountains and the lakes to which men traced the Nile in the days of Herodotus recurred ; and Richard Burton and John Speke were sent to Zanzibar, whence both discovered Lake Tanganyika, and Speke discovered the southern shore of Victoria Nyanza (1856–9). In 1860–3, John Speke sailed once more to Zanzibar with James Grant, and went thence by Karagué and Uganda to where the Nile issues from Victoria Nyanza, and thence, more or less by the valley of the Nile, to Gondokoro and so to Cairo. At Gondokoro they met Sir Samuel and Lady Baker, who had come on an independent expedition, and who now followed the Nile to the Albert Nyanza, of which they were the discoverers. The Nile was traced to its two reservoirs, Lakes Victoria and Albert Nyanza, and, in the language of the day, the problem which had baffled men's minds ever since Israel went down into Egypt was solved.

While Burton, Speke, Grant, and Baker were busy on the Nile, Livingstone ascended the Shiré, discovered Lake Shirwa, and explored, and perhaps discovered, Lake Nyassa while in governmental employ ; for he had now changed from a travelling teacher to a teaching traveller. The Universities' Mission on Lake Nyassa immediately followed and failed ; and his attempts to reach Lake Bangweolo near Kazembe were for a time unsuccessful (1858–64).

Livingstone's third expedition was made under similar government auspices in 1865. His course lay up the Rovuma to Lake Nyassa ; and from the south of that lake to Lake Tanganyika ; and from the south of that lake to Lake Moero north of Kazembe and to Lake Bangweolo 100 miles south ; and from the west of Lake Tanganyika with Arab help to Nyangwé, 450 miles north by west of Lake Moero. At, above, and below Bangweolo, Moero, and Nyangwé, he saw the great river Lualaba, which was the greatest of his discoveries. During this period, Henry Stanley, then in the employ of the *New York Herald*, discovered and relieved Livingstone at Ujiji on Lake Tanganyika (1871) ; and after a few months' travel together they parted. Livingstone, who was as old as Franklin when Franklin went to the north-west, hoping to crown his life by tracing the inscrutable Lualaba in its downward course, returned inland and died on the threshold of his great enterprise at Lake Bangweolo (1873) ; and Captain Verney Cameron, who had been sent to

help or succeed him, went westward by Lake Tanganyika whose outflow
to the Lualaba he discovered, to Nyangwé, where he failed to get boats,
then southward to Kikemba and the western Lualaba, which he discovered; then westward along the Zambesi-Congo watershed to Bihé and
Benguela on the Atlantic coast (1873–5). His was the second traverse
of the Continent between east and west. Stanley, hearing of Livingstone's
death, started once more, with the assistance of the *Daily Telegraph*
and the *New York Herald.* He circumnavigated Victoria Nyanza, which
sceptics had hitherto believed to be a constellation of little lakes;
persuaded the King of Uganda to accept British missionaries; saw a new
lake afterwards called Lake Albert Edward Nyanza; reached Nyangwé
much as Livingstone and Cameron had reached it, and embarked upon
the Lualaba, wondering as he did so whether it would prove to be the
Benue-Niger, the Nile, the Congo, or haply the Shari or Ogowé. Thence,
after fighting thirty-two battles, passing forty rapids, and traversing
1700 miles of river, "through an Odyssey of wandering and an Iliad
of conflict," he reached the mouth of the Congo (1874–7)—an exploit to
which La Salle's descent of the Mississippi (1682) is the only parallel.
In 1879 Stanley was sent out by an international committee, over which
the King of the Belgians presided, to found a new, non-political, philanthropic State, afterwards known as the Congo Free State, intended to
control the river area of 900,000 square miles which Livingstone and he
had opened up to the European world. It was as though a new country
ten times as large as Great Britain had suddenly arisen from the sea.
Two travellers, Livingstone and Stanley, wrought this miracle, and the
spirit which moved them was of missionary origin. Meanwhile, other
forces were already at work elsewhere.

The first force was the pure passion for knowledge, which, since
Rüppell, became more and more German. In 1849 the British Govern-
ment organised an expedition, modelled on Denham's expedition to the
Niger from the north; and, Englishmen being engaged elsewhere, in the
Second Sikh War and on the search for Franklin, it employed amongst
others Heinrich Barth (1849–55) and Eduard Vogel (1853–5). James
Richardson, the leader, having died (1850), Barth became leader. The
southward route from Tripoli lay through Asiu, Asben, and Agades to
Katséna; and Kukawa on Lake Chad was Barth's, as it had been
Denham's centre, from which a southward trip took him to Yola on the
other side of the upper Benue, which he was the first to see: an eastward
trip took him to Masena in Baghirmi, and a westward to Timbuktu, and
he, too, went sometimes with raiders. Eduard Vogel's southward trip
from Lake Chad reached the same point on the Benue which William
Baikie had just reached by boat from the confluence of the Niger and
Benue, while his eastward trip took him to Wara in Wadai, where he
was murdered. Wadai was hitherto virgin soil to Europeans, and
patriotic efforts were made in Germany to ascertain Vogel's fate or to

continue what he had begun.   Fired with the same zeal for knowledge,
Moriz von Beuermann from the north (1862–3), Theodor von Heuglin
and Hermann Steudner (1861–4) from the south-east, or from what was
then known as the Bahr-el-Gazal province of Egypt, only added to the
roll of scientific martyrs.   Gerhard Rohlfs traversed Africa from Tripoli
by Lake Chad to Lagos on the Gulf of Guinea (1865–7), and Gustav
Nachtigal went from Tripoli and Murzuk to the Tibesti mountains,
which he was the first to see, and by Denham's route to Lake Chad, and
from Lake Chad to Borku, Abeshr (Wadai), Kibet, Darfur, El Obeid,
Khartum, and Egypt (1869–74).   Nachtigal's traverse, occurring as it did
before the Egyptian conquest of Darfur, was at that date unique, and
brought together Barth's, Vogel's, Browne's, and Rüppell's discoveries.
Pellegrino Manteucci (1880–1) afterwards made a similar but a longer
traverse from furthest east to furthest west, going from Suakin by
Khartum, El Obeid, Darfur, Abeshr, and Lake Chad, to the mouth
of the Niger, and died immediately after his return.   Meanwhile the
Bahr-el-Gazal province, which had already been explored in part by an
English consul, John Petherick (1856 *sqq.*), a French trader, Jules Poncet
(1857–9), a rich Dutch lady, Alexine Tinné (1863), a poor Italian, Carlo
Piaggia (1863–5), and a Greek doctor, Papagiotis Potagos (1876–7),
was put under the searchlights of science by two German enthusiasts,
Georg Schweinfurth of Riga (1868–70) and Wilhelm Junker of Moscow
(1877–86).   Schweinfurth's discovery of the westward-flowing river
Welle, south of the Bahr-el-Gazal basin (1870), was almost as sensational as Park's discovery of the eastward-flowing Niger, or Lander's
of the westward-flowing Benue.   Could this river be the Shari, or the
Benue ?   If it was the Benue, then what the ancients said was true, and
the Niger did all but join the Nile with the Atlantic.   Junker, who
carried on Schweinfurth's work, and Stanley (1878) held that it was an
affluent of the Congo : and George Grenfell, who first ascended the
Ubanghi affluent of the Congo (1884), and officials of the Congo Free
State (1887–90), eventually proved the identity of the Ubanghi and
Welle.   Except for these German expeditions and for some others
between Angola and the Congo, German enterprise in Africa became
commercial and political shortly after 1871, and science was subordinated
to other ends.

It is not proposed in this chapter to follow the footsteps of German
or any other explorers within the spheres of influence assigned to Germany
or other nations in 1878 or 1884.   Between 1878 and 1908, the whole
interior of Africa except Abyssinia and Morocco was actually or virtually
annexed by European nations, and exploration became an incident of
energetic colonial administration.   Serpa Pinto, Hermann von Wissmann,
Sir Frederick Lugard, Sir Frederick Cardew, Sir Harry Johnston, and
Sir Alfred Sharpe, explored because they administered, and administered
because they explored, and their exploits belong to the history of

particular colonies. But there were still some few explorations which, although national in object and method, resembled those explorations of earlier ages which were either disinterested or which preceded colonial history.

Joseph Thomson's discovery (1883–4) of the route, which is now a railway route, from Mombasa to Victoria Nyanza, made a British protectorate of Uganda and the union of the Egyptian Sudan with south-east Africa (which was General Gordon's dream), or even with South Africa (which was Cecil Rhodes' dream), possible. Henry Stanley's journey to Lake Albert Nyanza (1887–9) through the primeval forests of the upper Aruwhimi, in order to take Emin Pasha, the last and latest left of General Gordon's lieutenants, to Zanzibar, brought to light the original forest home of the Homeric pygmies, Mount Ruwenzori (16,800 ft.) or those very Mountains of the Moon which, according to Ptolemy, fed the Nile with their snows, and which recent geographers had ridiculed, and Lake Albert Edward Nyanza, which was now traced by the Semliki river into Lake Albert Nyanza, and was thus proved to be the ultimate western source of the Nile. French advance during this period showed the far reach and nice sense of symmetry which distinguished her great Canadian adventurers; but the story is somewhat long. In south-west French Africa Paul du Chaillu, an American of French origin, discovered gorillas, dwarfs, and, last but not least, the mouths and upper reaches of the Ogowé (1857–65). French administrators developed the Ogowé, and a French officer, Pietro Savorgnan de Brazza, thinking the Ogowé was Livingstone's Lualaba, ascended it, found its source (1878), and descended the Alima to Stanley Pool on the Congo (1880). Next Casimir Maistre, among others, pushed up the Ubanghi to the Shari (1891–3), where Émil Gentil launched a steamer with which he reached Lake Chad (1897). Wherever Frenchmen went they established posts; but the effective occupation of Lake Chad was, through accidents of war, postponed until 1899. Meanwhile, Captain Louis Binger discovered the kingdom of Kong behind Sierra Leone (1887–90), treaties were made, and the French colonies on the coast were connected by a common hinterland; Timbuktu was occupied (1893–4); and an expedition from Senegal arrived at Lake Chad in 1899, just a year later than had been intended. Again, in 1899–1900, Fernand Foureau arrived at Lake Chad from Algiers, having traversed the Sahara by a route which had not been trodden by Europeans before or since Barth (1849); and he too was a year late. Gentil from 1200 miles south, the Senegalese from 2000 miles west, and Foureau from 1700 miles north, met in Denham's and Barth's temporary centre: and Lake Chad became a permanent base for further advances up the Shari towards the Bahr-el-Gazal affluent of the Nile. At the same time Jean-Baptiste Marchand went from French south-west Africa to the Congo, and up the Ubanghi to a point reached by Junker from the east and de La Kéthulle from the west; and crossed to the Suet, an affluent of the Bahr-el-Gazal, which he descended to Fashoda on the Nile (1896–8). Had not Gentil, Foureau, and the rest been a year behind time, Marchand would now have been almost in touch with them. England too was in the way: for 1898 was the year of the Anglo-Egyptian reconquest of the Sudan, and the Nile and Bahr-el-Gazal were restored by right of reconquest to Egypt and England. In 1899, Marchand resumed his journey up the Sobat and Baro to a spot reached by Christian de Bonchamps from Jibuti in the Gulf of Aden a year earlier, and thence by de Bonchamps' route to Jibuti, having accomplished his immense new traverse of 3000 miles over what was almost all well-worn ground. As with the advance of the Cossacks, it is difficult to know whether to regard these exploits as the exploits of travellers simultaneously meeting around Lake Chad, or as a magnificent political concentration around the new hub of a continental empire, like that which France once built in Louisiana, with means equally slender and over distances equally vast, in order to confine her rivals to the west Atlantic shores. Organised persistent travel and conquest were almost synonymous in three-fourths of Africa as well as in North America, and the French reading of African destiny was nearly right; but French aspirations were not completely fulfilled. Since 1900, Lake Chad has been the centre of a French dependency, vast but not so vast nor yet so exclusive as some Frenchmen designed, because a year or two later the English and German centres of gravity shifted somewhat from the Atlantic shores inland, and round this lake three empires met. In 1902 the Governors of British Nigeria and the German Cameroons established effective British and German rule on its west and south shores, and Lake Chad began to combine the physical eccentricities of Lob-nor with the political interest of the Pamirs.

Few parts of Africa are unknown. Since 1884 traverses between German or British East Africa and the mouth of the Congo or Angola, and since 1899 traverses from the Cape to Cairo, and across the Sahara, have been frequent. Somaliland and south-western Abyssinia were for a long time almost blanks on the map, before the travels of Frank James (1885), Samuel Teleki (1887–8), the Hungarian who discovered Lake Rudolf, Luigi Robecchi (1888), and Donaldson Smith, the American who discovered Lake Abaya and the northern route to Lake Rudolf (1894–5), induced travellers to scour these lands from end to end. Yet there is not one protectorate which has not many dark corners still. In the Libyan desert, the through-route to Darfur from the north has only been trod by Browne, although Sheb, Selimé, and Ein Aga on the way between Egypt and Darfur were visited a year or two ago; and Kufara has only once been reached, by Gerhard Rohlfs from the north (1878–9); so that but for him it is an unknown island surrounded by a sea of ignorance three-hundred miles wide.

POLAR EXPLORATION.

Outside Asia and Africa, there are large unexplored regions in Dutch New Guinea, Kimberley District (Australia), the basin of the upper Amazon, Alaska, and the regions round the North Pole, and South Pole. Immediately after the Wars with France ended in the Peace of Paris (1763), James Cook's three voyages (1768–71, 1772–5, 1776–9) laid the foundation upon which every British colony in the Pacific, including British Columbia, was built; accordingly these voyages belong to colonial history. But they also belong to Polar history. In the second voyage Cook reached 71° 10′ S. lat. while searching for an Antarctic Continent; and in the third voyage he passed through Behring Strait and reached 70° 20′ N. lat. in Alaska while searching for a north-west passage from the west of North America. Immediately after the Napoleonic Wars, North Polar expeditions recommenced with the new search for a north-west passage, from the point on the east of North America reached by William Baffin and John Davys two centuries earlier. Sir John Ross inaugurated the new departure in 1818, and Sir William Edward Parry in 1819–20, both going to Baffin Bay; Parry arriving through Lancaster Sound at Melville Island (1819–20) and Regent Inlet (1824–5); and Ross and his nephew, Sir James Ross, arriving through Lancaster Sound and Regent Inlet at the magnetic North Pole and at King William Island (1829–33). Meanwhile, Sir John Franklin (1819–22, 1825–7) journeyed to the north coast of Canada by land, and explored it on foot and by boat in the neighbourhood of the mouths of the Coppermine river, which Samuel Hearne saw in 1771, and of the Mackenzie river, which Sir Alexander Mackenzie discovered in 1789; and ships were sent to Behring Strait, in order if necessary to cooperate with Franklin in his second expedition. Owing to these combined efforts and to further work from the land side by Franklin's successors nearly all the whole north coast of Canada, from the neighbourhood of King William Island to Behring Strait, became known before 1845.

In 1845 the Admiralty made its final effort. Sir John Franklin volunteered for the command, and, when it was objected that he was sixty years old, replied indignantly " No ! no ! only fifty-nine." This was Franklin's last voyage. After passing through Lancaster Sound (1845), he and all his crew perished on or near King William Island (1847–8). Relief parties swept the sea in summer, and skimmed over ice and snow both in winter and in summer, searching for news of those who were lost. But the search only succeeded partially in 1854, and completely in 1857, many years after the last survivor had died. One of the searchers, Sir Robert Maclure, made the north-west passage from Behring Strait by sea along the south of Melville Island, but lost his ship on the way (1854). As a result of the search for Franklin, the whole northern coast and northern archipelago of Canada became known (1845–57);

and the search for the north-west passage was abandoned and almost forgotten, until people read one day that a Norseman, Captain Roald Amundsen, had made the north-west passage by sea in one ship from Lancaster Sound by King William Island to Behring Strait, that is to say, by Franklin's attempted route (1903–6). Meanwhile, before the last voyage of Franklin, Parry started towards the North Pole and James Ross towards the South Pole, James Ross discovering Victoria land and a mountain which he called Mount Erebus (1839–43), and there the history of Antarctic exploration rested until the close of the century, when the nations of Europe organised new Polar expeditions.

In the course of the Antarctic expeditions which ensued, Captain Robert Scott reached Victoria land and started overland from near Mount Erebus and then over glaciers to 82° 17′ S. lat. (1902–4); and, afterwards, Lieutenant (now Sir) Ernest Shackleton adopted the same base and similar methods, and reached the magnetic South Pole and a point 88° 23′ S. lat., that is to say, 97 miles from the terrestrial Pole (1907–9). The whole country was a glaciated tableland rising higher and higher to over 10,000 feet above the sea and without any living thing. The North Polar region had hitherto been only penetrated to within 206 miles of the terrestrial Pole by the Duke of Abruzzi (1900) and within 225 miles by Fridtjof Nansen (1895) from the Asiatic side. More continuous and successful efforts have been made from the side of Smith Sound between the continent of Greenland and Ellesmere land on the west of Greenland. Charles Hall and some other Americans of the United States were the pioneers (1860 *sqq.*) of this route and Sir George Nares, Sir Lewis Beaumont, and others, who derived their inspiration and experience from the Franklin relief expeditions, followed in their train (1875 *sqq.*). Their most important achievement was to trace the north coast of Ellesmere land and Greenland, which Lieutenant Robert Peary, U.S.A. since 1886 has made his base for several polar expeditions, in the last of which he reached the North Pole (1909). He started, also, from this base on inland expeditions into Greenland. In 1888, Fridtjof Nansen made the first traverse of south Greenland from east to west; later, Peary traversed north Greenland and rounded the northernmost point of Greenland from the west (1901), and a Danish expedition under Mylius Erichsen, coming from the east, explored the last unknown north-eastern strip of the coasts of Greenland (1906–8). Thus, one continental tableland 10,000 feet above the sea, almost as high as Tibet and quite as high and almost as barren as Victoria land, was dragged out of darkness into light; and exploration of the earth arrived at its climax, here as elsewhere, in the early years of the twentieth century. The South Pole remains unconquered: but it now seems that the conquest of the Poles is not likely to yield anything historically new, beyond completing the results of previous discoveries which possessed some scientific but little historical significance.

CHAPTER XXVI.

THE GROWTH OF HISTORICAL SCIENCE.

HISTORICAL study begins with the humanists of the Italian and German Renaissance. In the Middle Ages printing was unknown, books were rare, and credulity was universal. The revival of classical learning revealed a new world of experience and ideas, and coincided with a quickened interest in the history of man. For a brief period the European mind devoted itself to secular learning; but the Renaissance was destroyed by the Reformation. History became the expression of confessional animosities, and remained enveloped in an ecclesiastical atmosphere till the opening of the eighteenth century. In this long struggle there is little to choose between Protestant and Catholic controversialists, but in its course many documents were brought to light and valuable materials were accumulated. Thus the Annals which Baronius compiled from the Vatican archives in answer to Flacius are still indispensable to the documentary study of Church history. In the seventeenth century sectarian violence somewhat abated, and useful work was accomplished by the schools of Anglican and Gallican divines, whose position between the Protestant and the Ultramontane camps was favourable to moderate views. Of still greater value was the work of Mabillon and his fellow Benedictines of St Maur. Nearly every historical scholar, however, regarded ecclesiastical history as the highest object of study, and men of the first rank like Scaliger, Camden, and Conring, who devoted themselves to secular research, were few in number, except in Holland.

With the approach of the eighteenth century the study of secular history became more general. The accumulation of material was carried on by Muratori and Leibniz, Madox and Hearne, Eckhel and other mighty scholars, whose erudition has never been surpassed and whose works remain an inexhaustible quarry for later generations. In the next place, the critical treatment of authorities began. Mabillon created the science of diplomatic; Bentley exposed the forgery of Phalaris; Père Simon began the critical study of the Old Testament, Reimarus and Semler of the New; Astruc established the composite nature of the Pentateuch;

Perizonius and Pouilly, Beaufort and Vico, anticipated Niebuhr's destructive criticism of early Roman history. Throughout the century the *Académie des Inscriptions* played an active part as an organiser of disinterested discussion and research. Another class of writers approached history from a philosophical point of view. Vico first treated it as the subject of a special science. Montesquieu investigated the origin and effects of laws and institutions. Adam Smith analysed the causes of national prosperity and decay, and Malthus sought for the laws of population. The conception of progress, which is lacking in Montesquieu, was clearly enunciated by Leibniz, related to history in Lessing's brief but pregnant essay on the *Education of the Human Race*, and received its fullest development in Turgot's *Discourse at the Sorbonne*. The conception of the organic nature of civilisation, of the unity of humanity, of the debt of every age to its predecessors, was applied by Burke and Herder; but it found no place in Voltaire or Condorcet, who despised the past, nor in Rousseau, who hated the present. Though the attempts to construct imposing philosophical edifices on a basis of historical generalisation were for the most part premature, fruitful ideas were thrown into circulation, and the conception of history was enriched and widened. Finally, historical narrative itself reached a high standard. National histories were for the first time written in literary form in England by Hume, in France by Hénault, in Switzerland by Johannes Müller, in Germany by Mascov and Schmidt. The first scholarly and comprehensive Church history was composed by Mosheim, the first history of classical art by Winckelmann. Schlözer, Spittler, Pütter, Gatterer, and Heeren made Göttingen the centre of historic study in Germany and produced useful historical narratives and handbooks. Voltaire founded a new genre by his *Essai sur les Mœurs*, and Robertson reconstructed the age of Charles V. Above all, Gibbon constructed a bridge from the old world to the new which is still the highway of nations, and stands erect long after every other structure of the time has fallen into ruins.

Although work of the greatest value was thus accomplished, the spirit of the time, its absolute standard, its self-sufficiency, its conviction that the past was an old almanack, a world both dark and dead, were fatal to patient and methodical enquiry. One result was that writers were apt to content themselves with very superficial study. Another was that the medieval world was never really understood. Voltaire maintained that the early Middle Ages were no more deserving of study than wolves and bears; and Gibbon's contempt for religious feeling and belief rendered him blind to the meaning of many objects which he passed during his long journey. A second general weakness was the lack of critical faculty in dealing with authorities. To Johannes Müller all chronicles and charters, so long as they were old, were of equal value. Rollin and Hooke simply transcribed the legends of Livy. Scepticism itself was as uncritical as was credulity, for Hardouin believed many of the Latin classics to have been written by medieval monks. Archives were guarded with a jealousy appropriate to the custody of crown jewels. The conditions which rendered it possible to set forth the truth without fear or favour were as rare as was the determination to learn what the truth actually was, and what was the critical equipment required for finding it.

The years that immediately preceded and followed the opening of the nineteenth century witnessed a revolt against the superficial rationalism of the eighteenth century and the emergence of forces that rendered possible the birth of historical science. The most powerful factor in this change of standpoint, which was felt all over Europe but found its earliest and strongest expression in Germany, was the Romantic movement. The seed sown by Herder germinated in a passionate love for the past, for the exotic, for the marvellous and picturesque, for distant lands and literatures, for strange modes of thought and utterance. During the first decade of the century August Wilhelm von Schlegel lectured on the origins of German literature; Tieck edited the *Minnelieder*; Arnim and Brentano collected early German songs and ballads; Friedrich von Schlegel directed attention to the thought of the East; Boisserée revived interest in medieval art. The Eddas and the Nibelungen were in all hands. The ages of belief and imagination were vindicated against the age of reason. Despite their lack of critical instinct and their fantastic taste, the Romanticists made it possible to understand and appreciate things which rationalism had contemptuously dismissed, and widened the intellectual horizon of Europe.

A second factor that prepared the ground for historical science was the birth of nationalism. The eighteenth century was cosmopolitan, and the political organisation of Germany seemed fitted to render every idea of a common fatherland impossible. But the battle of Jena and Napoleon's violent reconstruction of the map of Europe led to a pride and interest in national history and tradition, to a new and thrilling national consciousness. The lectures of Fichte, the songs of Arndt and Körner, the speeches of *Tell* put into words the inarticulate emotions of millions of Germans. The name of France, lately the standard of taste and manners, became an offence, and "Father" Jahn taught the young men of Germany to worship their own country. By the end of the War, Germany had outgrown the eighteenth century. Sensationalism had yielded to idealism, the rule of reason to deep religious feeling, cosmopolitanism to nationalism. On every side was heard the demand for reconstruction, for the rebuilding and strengthening of the national life.

The change is apparent in the birth of a historical school of jurisprudence. Herder had declared that law sprang from the spirit of a nation, and Gustav Hugo maintained that it must be followed to its sources and could only be understood historically. This fruitful conception was illustrated in 1808, when Karl Friedrich Eichhorn published the

first volume of a history of German institutions, based on study
of the sources and prefaced by a declaration that his desire to understand the legal conceptions and practice of the present had led him
irresistibly to the study of the past. While Eichhorn was calling
attention to the indestructible value of German law and its place in
the development of national life, his friend Savigny published an essay
in which the main principles of the historical school were fully explained.
The obvious merits of the French Code, which parts of Germany had
experienced, led to a demand for a similar codification, which was
forcibly stated by the distinguished jurist Thibaut. To this challenge
Savigny replied in his *Vocation of our Time for Legislation and Jurisprudence*, opposing not only the project under discussion, but any and
every codification. To codify was to paralyse. With Montesquieu, he
declared that institutions must not be judged *à priori*, and, with Burke,
that the history and nature of a people forbade sudden and violent
changes. Law was a living thing, like language, growing out of the
life of the people and expressing itself spontaneously in the institutions
of the country, not the creation of legislation and edicts. Its origin
was custom, springing from the fundamental instincts of a nation, and
developing unconsciously and without effort. In a word, law was a
historical not a philosophical science. The project was deferred ; but
the lasting influence of Savigny's essay, both for good and evil, was far
more important than its immediate success. He did not realise that
civilised nations accumulate an ever increasing stock of common notions,
and he was unjust not only to the French but also to the German codes
already in existence. He was blind to the immense practical utility
of occasionally sweeping away legal rubbish, of simplifying, defining,
and coordinating. Again, though pronouncing the people to be the
legislators, he forbids them to legislate. In the early life of a nation
law is largely an unconscious growth; but in its maturity the people
legislates by a conscious act of will. But, though hostile to political
liberty, Savigny's teaching gave an incalculable impetus to historical
study. His evolutionary manifesto popularised the conception of organic
development, emphasised the continuity of history, and shifted attention
from the play of events on the surface to the underlying moral and
intellectual influences and the abiding institutions of national life.

A final factor that stimulated critical investigation was the publication of Friedrich August Wolf's *Prolegomena to Homer* in 1795, which
exerted a profound influence on every branch of research. The method
that appeared to give such startling results could obviously be applied
to other writings, sacred and profane. That the sources of history
themselves must be analysed and subjected to internal and external
criticism was the principle which Wolf contributed to the growth of
historic study in the nineteenth century.

All these influences were combined in Niebuhr, the first great

German historian. Though by no means a Romanticist, he shared the Romanticist dislike of the rationalism of the eighteenth century. He had studied history with passion from his earliest years, and agreed with Savigny and Eichhorn that the present could only be understood from the past. He was, in the next place, an accomplished classical scholar and had assimilated the critical method of Wolf. Finally, he was deeply interested in politics, and had joined Stein in regenerating Prussia after the battle of Jena. After the foundation of the University of Berlin in 1809, he delivered lectures on Roman History which appeared in book form in 1811. At the close of the War he accepted the post of Prussian Minister to the Holy See, but during his residence in Rome he did little historical work beyond aiding Bunsen in his labours on the archaeology of the city. On settling in Bonn in 1824, he began to recast his History, of which he published two volumes, and at his death he left a third ready for press.

In his prefaces, his letters, and in his conversations recorded by Lieber, Niebuhr repeatedly indicated the conditions of his success. He had learned from his own public career to conceive of the history of Rome as a living reality, and to interpret its problems in the light of modern equivalents. In a well-known passage he relates how, in the time of Prussia's humiliation, he went back to the study of a great people to strengthen his mind and that of his hearers. In the next place, he declared that he could not have understood Roman history without an intimate acquaintance with the constitutional struggles that had taken place in England. His third qualification was his critical method. He compared himself to an anatomist, dissecting words instead of bodies, and defined a historian as one who could construct a complete picture from fragments of the design, a complete figure from a torso. When his unsurpassed knowledge of the literary sources of Roman history could add no more, the faculty of intuition was brought into play to determine the value of unsupported evidence.

Niebuhr was the first to make ancient Rome a living political organism and to illustrate Roman and universal history by one another. He was also the first to collect and discuss the whole of the available literary evidence, and to steer a middle course between blind acceptance of Livy's narrative and wholesale scepticism. To these immense merits Niebuhr owes his unassailable position as the principal author of the great revolution in historical study effected in the opening years of the nineteenth century. Goethe expressed a wish that all history might be treated in a similar manner, and Savigny declared that the mere existence of such a work was an encouragement to him in the composition of his *History of Roman Law in the Middle Ages*. Böckh dedicated his first book to Niebuhr, and the English translation of the *Roman History* dominated Oxford and Cambridge for a generation. There are good reasons, however, why his fame has proved more enduring than his writings. No historian of the front rank has possessed so little skill in presenting his knowledge to the world. His work bristles with technical discussions that interrupt the narrative and with parentheses that break the thread of thought. But there is a graver fault than lack of lucidity and literary skill. The method of divination which he believed would be the main pillar of his fame is radically unsound. In hands less skilled than his it could only lead to disaster, and his own use of it was in the highest degree arbitrary. The extravagances into which it led him were pointed out with ruthless vigour by Cornewall Lewis and corrected in a kindlier spirit by Schwegler. The impetus to historical research was given by Niebuhr; but the edifice had to be erected on surer foundations.

Between the first and second editions of Niebuhr's work, Böckh's *Domestic Economy of Athens,* published in 1817, applied the historic method to Greek study. He declared that there was no philology that was not history, and he realised the programme of Wolf by seizing the life of the ancients as a whole. For the first time, the daily life of the Greeks was portrayed, their legislation, administration, finance, trade, industry, their human reality, brought home to the modern world. The book inspired the Prussian Academy of Sciences to entrust its author with the task of collecting and editing Greek inscriptions. Bekker and other scholars were despatched in search of material, and the first volume appeared in 1824. Though the information was often fragmentary, it was highly important, and the *Corpus Inscriptionum Graecarum* laid one of the foundation stones of the study of Greek history.

Böckh's lectures at Berlin were of scarcely less importance than his writings; and one of his earliest pupils shares with him the honour of being the founder of the historical study of Greek life. Otfried Müller won distinction with his doctor's thesis, and quickly poured forth a series of works which illumined almost every department of the Greek world. Böckh foretold that his brilliant pupil would leave him far behind. Müller was not greater than his master; but he was more original and imaginative, and his range was wider. His studies of the Greek races, his *Prolegomena to a Science of Mythology* and *Handbook of Archaeology,* opened up new paths through the forest. As he grew older he turned more and more to art, and insisted on exact knowledge of the country and its monuments. Leake had recently called attention to the wealth of material that lay scattered over the surface of the peninsula. Müller foresaw the necessity of excavations and realised that the country itself was one of the chief documents of the historian. His early death during his visit to the land of his dreams in 1840 was an irreparable blow to science; but the cause for which he had fought had already triumphed. The great work of Creuzer on the symbolism of the ancients, a book of wide and curious learning, had been sharply criticised by the older school of philologists which looked to Gottfried Hermann of Leipzig as its leader; and, though the methods of Böckh and Müller were utterly different from those of Creuzer, they were attacked by Hermann with equal bitterness for decoying students from the textual study of Greek literature. But it was beyond the power even of Hermann to forbid the entrance of the historical method into classical studies. The art, literature, and religion of Greece were simultaneously studied by Welcker, her philosophy by Ritter and Brandis, and the mysteries were explored by Lobeck.

While Niebuhr and Böckh were revealing the ancient world, the study of early Germany was gradually taking shape. The Romanticists had unlocked a rich storehouse of treasures; but their philological equipment was too scanty to estimate its value. From their midst appeared a man who possessed the critical insight and the patient industry that they lacked. Though Jacob Grimm was the intimate friend of Brentano and Arnim, he traced his inspiration to Savigny, whose lectures he attended at Marburg. During a visit to Paris in company with Savigny, Grimm undertook investigations which led him to dedicate himself to the study of German origins. On his return from France he began to pour forth the flood of essays and dissertations which only ceased with his death, and in 1812, with the aid of his brother Wilhelm, produced a work which made his name a household word throughout Germany. What Arnim and Brentano had done for the ballads of the German Middle Ages was done by the Grimms for the fairy tales. From the legends Grimm passed to the structure and development of the language itself. Comparative philology had already won notable triumphs. Bopp had established the connexion between Sanskrit and the languages of Europe; Wilhelm von Humboldt's Essay on the Basques had explained the principles of philological investigation; and Rask's *Icelandic Grammar* provided new material for a study of the Teutonic tongues. With these guides Grimm produced the first volume of his *German Grammar* in 1819, which brought life and law into the development of language, established the connexion between speech and the stages of civilisation, and served as a model for the Romance and Celtic grammars of Diez and Zeuss. In 1828, he broke new ground in his *German Legal Antiquities,* in which he detected the living voice of the people. In 1835, he in his *German Mythology* collected and explained the old sagas and cosmologies, and traced their persistence under Christian disguises. The latter years of his life witnessed the production of a *History of the German Language* and the beginning of a great *German Dictionary* under his direction.

Jacob Grimm was not the first to love German origins; but he was the first to study them critically and to make them intelligible. While Wilhelm worked with exquisite refinement and scholarship in comparatively narrow fields, Jacob's genius lay in bringing order and meaning into vast territories hitherto almost unexplored. The unifying principle of his work was his conviction that speech, mythology, law, and literature alike revealed the soul of his race. But this fruitful conception was accompanied by a certain limitation of vision. He resembled Savigny in his preference of unconscious to conscious production, of folk-songs to the works of individual poets, of nature to culture. In another direction also his work needed supplementing. His main interest lay in penetrating to the thought behind the word; but to place the mechanical part of philology on a secure basis there was need of a cooler and less imaginative mind. If Grimm is the founder of the study of German origins, Lachmann's position is at his side. Trained in the excellent school of Benecke at Göttingen, Lachmann began his career in 1816 by his investigations into the origin of the *Nibelungenlied*, applying the method of Wolf and decomposing the cycle into independent songs. Confining himself to the formal side of philology, Lachmann devoted himself to penetrating the exact meaning of literary monuments, establishing their chronology, discovering the laws of metre, restoring, punctuating, and elucidating the texts. His inspiration is seen in the work of his friends Moritz Haupt and Müllenhoff.

The interest of Grimm lay chiefly in the literature, language, and beliefs of his Teutonic forefathers. It was appropriate that the stimulus to a knowledge of their political life and fortunes should come from the greatest German statesman of his age. In the peaceful years of his retirement Stein planned an edition of the sources of German history in the Middle Ages, "to create a taste for German history, to make its systematic study easier, and thus to contribute to the maintenance of a love for the common fatherland and the memory of our great ancestors." In 1819, a Society for ancient German History was formed; in 1820, a review was founded to discuss and make preparation for the work, and Pertz, a pupil of Heeren, was invited to direct the enterprise. In 1824 it was announced that the work would consist of five parts: Writers, Laws, Imperial Acts, Letters, Antiquities. In 1826, the first volume of the *Scriptores* appeared, and the series of stately volumes, now under the direction of the Berlin Academy of Sciences and supported by ample subsidies, is still unfinished. Pertz' chief colleague was Böhmer, who independently collected and arranged the Imperial Acts, the first volume of which appeared in 1831. He believed that history could only be securely written by getting behind chronicles and biographies to the words of the actors themselves, and his volumes are of enduring value owing to the mass of new material of the highest importance contained in them, and to the stimulus they gave to the formation of similar collections. The *Regesta* were printed by Böhmer without much attempt to ensure their authenticity; but his critical power improved in later volumes, and Jaffé, Ficker, and Sickel, with whom the editing of *Regesta* has reached perfection, built upon his foundations. These publications mark a turning-point in medieval study. Wilken's *History of the*

Crusades, Sartorius' book on the Hanseatic League, Voigt's volumes on Gregory VII and the Teutonic Order, Luden's *History of the German People*, had been useful and learned works; but their treatment of sources was not equal to their industry in collecting them. The most popular production of the pre-critical era, Raumer's *History of the Hohenstaufen*, made no pretence to exact research. The volumes were fresh, clear, and lively, and became the source of innumerable dramas and romances; but they were neither strong nor deep, and they do not compare with Stenzel's scholarly work on the Franconian Emperors.

A still more powerful influence now began to be felt in every department of historical study. Leopold von Ranke had been deeply impressed by Niebuhr's history while a student at Leipzig, and by the works of Böckh and Otfried Müller while teaching at Frankfort-on-the-Oder. In a reminiscence dictated at the age of ninety, he recalled that he had been struck by the difference in the portraits of Charles the Bold and Louis XI in *Quentin Durward* and the pages of Commines, and had determined to hold fast to facts. The fruits of this resolution appeared in 1824 in his work on the *Romance and Germanic Peoples, 1494–1514*. The preface announced the aim of the author to be to relate events "as they actually happened." The office of judging the past and instructing the future, said Ranke, had been attributed to history; but his volume made no attempt to perform such lofty tasks. The historian must approach his subject without presuppositions, and write history for its own sake. The promise of complete objectivity was abundantly fulfilled, and a lengthy supplement examined the sources on which the narrative rested. He traced the statements of the famous chroniclers to their source, estimated their opportunity of knowledge, and analysed the influence of their opinions and surroundings on their writings. The work founded the science of evidence, and the modern historical method is generally held to date from its publication.

The success of the book secured the author's summons to Berlin, where he quickly disinterred a large collection of *Relazioni* by Venetian and other Italian ambassadors. With the aid of this material, Ranke produced his *Princes and Peoples of Southern Europe*, a masterly survey of the constitution, army, finances, and policy of the Turkish monarchy and of the several provinces and dependencies of Spain in the sixteenth and seventeenth centuries. He now fully realised the importance of manuscripts, and obtained leave to set out on a prolonged tour of discovery. In Vienna he composed a history of Servia, which Niebuhr, shortly before his death, pronounced to be the best historical work in German literature. Venice and Florence supplied him with abundant material, and in Rome he delved deeply in the archives of the great families. On his return to Berlin, after an absence of over three years, he possessed a clearer insight into the development and relations of the States of modern Europe than any living writer.

The *History of the Popes* was published in 1834–6. The Counter-Reformation and the fortunes of the Papal States in modern times had never been comprehensively treated; and now there appeared a luminous survey, resting on profound research, presented in a clear and attractive style, and dealing with the most controversial questions in a purely scientific spirit. Ranke declared with pride that no one could say that his book was written by a friend or a foe of the Papacy. The work at once became an European classic; but its successor represented a further advance in Ranke's art. He determined to reply to the critics who asserted that he had not done justice to the moral superiority of German Protestantism. For this purpose the story of the strife of dogmas was widened into a narrative of the life of the German nation during the Reformation. In the preface to the first volume, which appeared in 1839, Ranke expressed his conviction that modern history could no longer be written from the reports of contemporary historians, still less from the narratives derived from them, but must rest on manuscript sources and the evidence of eye-witnesses and of the actors themselves. At Frankfort he found detailed reports of the Diets from which he reconstructed the machinery of the Empire, while extensive discoveries at Weimar, Dresden, and Brussels enabled him to see the events of the time through the eyes of its principal figures. He was not strong in theology; but the work presented for the first time a picture of the Reformation as a great national movement. Ranke's art underwent no further development, and during the next twenty years he applied it successively to Prussia, France, and England. His closing years were devoted chiefly to the eighteenth century and to the composition of his *Universal History*.

Ranke was beyond comparison the greatest historical writer of modern times, not only because he founded the scientific study of materials and possessed in an unrivalled degree the judicial temper and sobriety of judgment at which every historian professes to aim, but because his powers of work and length of life enabled him to produce a larger number of first-rate works than any historian who ever lived. He laid the foundation of our knowledge of modern political history, and he was congratulated by Arneth on having given a masterpiece to every country. Döllinger called him *Praeceptor Germaniae*, and Thiers hailed him as the first of European historians. His style is clear and flowing, and his books are intelligible to any cultivated reader. Though he deemed it the duty of the historian to keep himself out of sight, he declared that his first qualification was to have a real interest in humanity, and that the supreme purpose of history was to mark the place of men and nations in the development of civilisation. But, though Ranke's work was perfect in its way, it was not complete. When the history of States has been written and the development of the European system has been made clear, the life of the people and the ideas that underlie and explain action have still to be described. In the second place, his tranquil, harmonious nature made him to some extent blind to great tides of emotion and great outbursts of passion, to the heroism and tragedy in the life of men. The *History of England* excels in explaining the relation of English and European politics, but fails to penetrate the inner meaning of Puritanism. The *Reformation* conveys little idea of the wild exaltation of the time, and loses its sureness of touch when it reaches the Peasants' Revolt. It was well that Ranke did not carry out his plan of a history of the French Revolution. In dealing with individuals and nations alike he was most at home in the middle regions of human experience.

Ranke's impersonal attitude towards history provoked widespread opposition. When he began to write, Rotteck's *Universal History*, which presented a monotonous spectacle of tyrannised peoples and depicted the Middle Ages as a period of barbarism and darkness, was the bible of south German Liberalism. Rotteck's star paled with great rapidity; but the view that history was much more than a search for truth was represented by two men of far greater ability. The most influential historical teacher when Ranke began to write was Schlosser. In his two greatest works, the *Universal History* and the *History of the Eighteenth Century*, he judges from the standpoint of the strictest Kantian morality. Though he was weak in politics, law, and economics, he had a wide knowledge of the history of culture; but the conception of growth, of the change in standards and ideals, was unknown to him. He was a thorough *bourgeois* and treated nobles and rulers with a severity equal to Rotteck's. Schlosser made no secret of his distaste for Ranke's colourless pictures and of his contempt for his minute industry. But the manifesto of the Schlosser school against Ranke was composed by the greatest and most faithful of its members. In Gervinus' study of his beloved teacher, Ranke is charged with finding the principal charm of his calling in the discovery of the unknown, however unimportant it be, and is sharply censured for the mildness of his judgments. Though more objective in judgment than his master, Gervinus continued the traditions of the hanging judge, and his histories of German poetry and of the nineteenth century, though works of real learning and merit, are disfigured by their censorious tone. A more powerful attack was made from a widely different standpoint. The chorus of praise that greeted Ranke's first work was marred by the voice of Leo, who belittled his critical achievements and declared that his objective method robbed history of all value and meaning. Leo was the child of Haller and Adam Müller, the colleague of Stahl and Gerlach in the Conservative reaction that overtook Germany in the second quarter of the century. His *History of the Italian States* possessed considerable merit; but his *Universal History*, which appeared in the years 1835–44 and enjoyed immense popularity, records his furious hatreds and his blind partialities, his adoration of the Middle Ages and, though a Protestant, his hatred for the Reformation, the *Aufklärung*, and the Revolution.

While Ranke was thus censured for his reserve by the schools of Schlosser and Leo, he was also subjected to attack on the score of want of patriotism by those who saw in the increase of the might of Prussia the salvation of German politics. The *Prussian History* which he published on completing the *Reformation* caused disappointment, and in many quarters indignation, by its cool tones and its calculated reticence. Despite these criticisms, his fame and influence steadily increased. Though fault has been found with his critical work by Bergenroth, Gindely, and others, and though every book he wrote has been modified or supplemented by later research, it was he who made German historical scholarship supreme in Europe. As a lecturer he could not compare with Savigny, Droysen, or Häusser; but in his *Seminar* he was in the highest degree stimulating. The *Yearbooks of the German Kingdom*, compiled by his pupils in the thirties, applied his methods to medieval study; while the foundation of the *Historische Zeitschrift*, under the editorship of Sybel, twenty years later, and the creation of the Historical Commission of the Bavarian Academy by his friend and pupil King Maximilian marked the triumph of his school.

Of the three most distinguished of Ranke's pupils the eldest two, Waitz and Giesebrecht, devoted the greater part of their lives to the study of the Middle Ages. After beginning his literary career by a monograph on Henry I in Ranke's *Yearbooks*, Waitz joined the staff of the *Monumenta* and remained Pertz' most valued assistant till he succeeded him as Director forty years later. In 1844 appeared the first volume of his *German Constitutional History*, which founded the scientific study of medieval institutions. Of even greater importance for medieval scholarship was the *Seminar* at Göttingen, in which he taught generations of eager students the principles of criticism which he had learned from Ranke. Beginning, like Waitz, with a volume in Ranke's *Yearbooks*, Giesebrecht devoted his long life to the composition of a single work. The first volume of the *History of the Medieval Empire* appeared in 1855. He combined a perfect knowledge of sources and an unsurpassed mastery of critical method with a style of rare charm and power, and his picture of the Empire, painted in the years of mingled depression and hope between Olmütz and Sedan, took Germany by storm. Though a less romantic view of the Holy Roman Empire now prevails, his great achievement is to have created a national interest in the eventful centuries that stretch from the rise of the Saxon Emperors to the tragic end of the Hohenstaufen. Though Giesebrecht's explicit purpose of national instruction and edification carries us some distance beyond the cosmopolitanism and Olympian detachment of his master, it was left to the youngest of Ranke's three great pupils to break completely away from the Berlin tradition and to share in the foundation of the "Prussian" school of historians. After applying the critical method with brilliant success to the First Crusade, Sybel entered political life, as an adversary of Ultramontanism, feudalism, and radicalism. The events of 1848 turned his attention to the French Revolution, which occupied him for thirty years. Devoting special attention to economic conditions and international relations, Sybel at the same time made his book the vehicle of a vigorous polemic against the doctrines of the Revolution. His closing years were devoted to a massive *History of the Founding of the German Empire*, for which Bismarck not only opened the archives of State but himself supplied information.

While Sybel's devotion to Prussia did not forbid sharp criticism of Prussian policy, Droysen and Treitschke devoted themselves to the glorification of the Hohenzollern. After producing important works on Alexander and his successors, Droysen turned to modern history, and in his *Lectures on the Wars of Liberation* and his biography of York gave the first living picture of the heroic age of Prussia. He took an active part in the Frankfort Parliament and devoted the last thirty years of his life to a *History of Prussian Policy*, which he traced in fourteen volumes to Frederick the Great. The work is of enduring value, owing to its precious freight of documents; but its contention that the Hohenzollern had always been the conscious exponents of a national German policy has made few converts. The most striking personality and the most eloquent writer of the school was Treitschke, the Macaulay of Germany. Beginning his literary career with patriotic poetry, he devoted his immense powers as writer and professor before 1870 to an attack on the *Bund* and to a passionate demand for a national political life based on the ejection of Austria and the forcible incorporation of the smaller German States in the Prussian monarchy. Though Germany, when united, remained a federal State, Treitschke's demand for a powerful empire was met, and he was satisfied. He had planned a history of modern Germany when a young man; but the first volume did not appear till 1876. With the possible exception of Mommsen's *Roman History*, Treitschke's *Germany in the Nineteenth Century* is the most brilliant historical work in the language. Every side of national life and thought is treated with a knowledge, vigour, and eloquence that have made the book a national possession. But its faults are as conspicuous as its merits. It is written throughout from a Prussian standpoint, with a pronounced antipathy to the smaller States and without comprehension for the men and movements that opposed the military and bureaucratic *régime* of the Hohenzollern. Treitschke was the last and greatest of the Prussian school, which arose in the years of depression and contributed powerfully to prepare the soil in which Bismarck worked. Its inspiration was political rather than scientific, and it disappeared with the realisation of its ideals. Their successors write national history with greater fairness and tranquillity; and Moriz Ritter on the Counter-Reformation and the Thirty Years'

War, Erdmannsdörffer on the Great Elector, Koser on Frederick the Great, Max Lehmann on the Wars of Liberation, Erich Marcks on the unification of Germany, and Riezler on the evolution of Bavaria, are safer if less brilliant guides.

In German Austria historical production is of recent date. The long rule of Metternich was unfavourable to intellectual activity, the censorship was active, and the archives were only opened to men such as Bucholtz, Chmel and Hurter, whose dynastic and religious orthodoxy was beyond question. Hammer-Purgstall's *History of the Ottomans,* the most valuable work of the period, was based chiefly on material collected beyond the borders of the State. It was not till Arneth became Director of the Archives that a more enlightened policy prevailed and a flourishing school of historians arose. Arneth himself, the greatest of them, undertook the life of Maria Theresa; Beer, Helfert, Zeissberg, Krones, Huber, Schlitter, and Wertheimer assisted in exploring and defending Habsburg policy; and Friedjung has lately given the Austrian side of the struggle which ended at Sadowa. Medieval studies began with the foundation of the Historical Institute in 1854 on the model of the *École des Chartes,* and reached a high standard under the guidance of Sickel and Mühlbacher.

The period which elapsed in France between the fall and the restoration of the Bourbons was unfavourable to historical composition. The Revolution contemptuously dismissed the past as the age of monarchy, feudalism, and monasticism. The two chief groups of historical workers, the religious Orders and the Academies, were swept away. The situation remained unchanged when Napoleon seized the helm; for, though he appointed Daunou to the control of the archives, he had no intention of rendering them more accessible. In 1808, Abbé Halma, librarian to the Empress, asked for permission to continue Velly and Hénault. The Emperor replied that it would be most useful to continue these works; but the author must be attached to the existing Government. When his narrative appeared, no one would have the wish or the patience to write another, especially as it would be discouraged by the police. This characteristic document explains why histories of France did not appear till after the fall of Napoleon. A few works dealing with safe subjects were written by men who were on good terms with the Emperor. Daru produced a prolix and uncritical history of Venice, Michaud defended the Crusades against the depreciation of the eighteenth century, and Raynouard and Fauriel began the study of Provençal literature.

During this period of despotism and confusion Chateaubriand's writings were setting free the springs of emotion and stimulating the historical imagination, and, when the iron hand of Napoleon was removed, the archives were thrown open. Assisted by the Academy of Inscriptions, Daunou resumed the Benedictine *Histoire littéraire de la France*, which had been suspended for a generation. It was not, however, till 1820, when Augustin Thierry, inspired by *Ivanhoe* and *Les Martyrs*, issued a series of *Letters on the History of France*, that the historical movement really began. Indignant at the contrast between the chronicles and their modern commentators, he resolved to reproduce the freshness and vitality of the sources and to reconstruct the Middle Ages. In 1825 appeared the first volume of the *Conquest of England by the Normans*, by universal testimony the revelation of a new art. His peculiar power lay in his intuition of the sentiments and passions of the past. Thierry was a man of deep feeling and an incomparable artist; but, like a thorough child of the Romanticists, he was stronger in imagination than in criticism. Further, his exaggeration of the factor of race and his burning sympathy with the defeated led him to explain the two centuries that followed the conquest by the continuing strife of Saxons and Normans. But these faults are outweighed by the impetus he gave to historic study by his contagious love for the past, his devotion to the life of the people, and his exquisite literary art.

The standard of historical reform which Thierry had raised was quickly joined by eager volunteers. His brother Amédée devoted to the Gauls a series of works which, though not strictly critical in method, obtained immense popularity. But his most famous colleague was Barante, who prefaced his great work on the Dukes of Burgundy with Quintilian's words, " *Historia scribitur ad narrandum non ad probandum.*" He proposed nothing beyond a paraphrase of his sources. He takes no side in the Burgundian struggle, for history appeared to him a theatre, not a court of law. Barante indeed carried the objective ideal to the point of absurdity. His work is artificial and lifeless, because it is utterly impersonal. He is an annalist, not a historian; yet he was eagerly read, and it was to him that France owed her introduction to Froissart, Monstrelet, and Commines. At the same time the first attempt at a complete history of France was made by Sismondi, who had earned reputation by a voluminous history of the Italian republics. His work, which appeared during the years 1821 to 1844 in 31 volumes, presented the first tolerable account of the decline of Roman power, of the German invasions, of feudalism, of the growth of towns, of economic changes and their influence. For the first time Frenchmen could read a full, connected, and scholarly account of their national life. But the work lacked movement and colour, was weak in synthesis and the development of ideas, and was disfigured by its censorious tone. He had loved the Italian republics as Grote loved Athens; but, tried by the high standard of a Protestant moralist and a republican, French history assumed a gloomy air of tyranny and ignorance.

Of a widely different character was the second attempt at a history of France. After a boyhood spent in the utmost penury, Michelet sprang into fame in 1827 as the author of a handbook of modern history. Four

years later, his *Introduction to Universal History* revealed his passion for
liberty, the course of which he traced in the growing mastery of man
over nature, in science, religion, and industry.   In 1833 he began his
History of France, which he brought down to the death of Louis XI, in
six volumes, and which occupies a unique place in historical literature.   He
declared, with entire truth, that his life had passed into the book.   With
Thierry's love of the Middle Ages and power of visualising the past
Michelet combined an intensity of feeling and a moral passion that were his
own.   Thierry was a superb narrator; Michelet was, in addition, a poet and
preacher.   On such congenial themes as St Louis and Gothic architecture
he lavishes all the colours of his palette, and the picture of Joan of Arc,
in which history and legend are mixed, is one of the imperishable masterpieces of literature.   His imagination was of the heart rather than of
the eyes; but his heart was too full, his emotions too little under control,
for a perfect student.   Taine has compared him to Doré and Delacroix,
Monod to a great musician.   He had not the patience to enter deeply
into a problem.   His pages swarm with errors.   In later volumes his
faults grew upon him.   He developed an intense hatred for the Church,
and his dislike of Kings and Courts became a passion.   His *History of
the French Revolution*, which he wrote between the earlier and later parts
of his *History of France*, is a hymn of praise to the people entering
on the scene after centuries of oppression.   Michelet was a magician,
a Prospero calling up visions of dazzling beauty.   His two great books
possess all the qualities of inspiration—movement, colour, passion,
eloquence, but none of the qualities of science—clearness, justice,
measure, authority.   They are rhapsodies on the theme of France, paeans
to her humble and nameless children.

The method of history which first emerged, which was founded by
Thierry, reached its supreme development in Michelet, and inspired
the historical novels of Victor Hugo and Alfred de Vigny, may be called
the artistic or narrative school.   By its side arose a group of writers
whose object was rather to explain than to recount, to teach lessons
than to paint pictures, to whom the individual was of less interest than
the collective life, the anatomy and physiology of history of greater
importance than its outward form or colour.   Its founder, Guizot, had
lectured on the origins of representative government and published the
first volumes of a valuable though colourless work on the English
Revolution; but it was not till his appointment to the Sorbonne in
1828 and the delivery of his lectures on *Civilisation in Europe* that he
became the founder of scientific history in France.   This masterly course
still remains the most thoughtful introduction to the study of European
history.   Though he lacked narrative and descriptive power, Guizot possessed the accuracy, insight, and elevation of thought that were needed for
such a task.   He was not an artist but a thinker, and he had a marvellous
power of seizing and revealing the internal concatenation of events and

the ideas that underlie them. On the completion of the course, he turned to the history of France. His method was to dissect the political, economic, and intellectual structure of society, to lay bare its elements and forces, separately and in connexion. He has been blamed for presenting laws instead of life, abstractions in place of men and women. A juster censor would perhaps contend that he makes history appear more orderly and rational than it really is, and allows too little place to the will and the passions, the follies and the failures, of individual men.

In the early years of the Restoration two young Provençals, Thiers and Mignet, came to Paris, linked in intimate friendship and inspired with the same ideas and ambitions. Their task was to overthrow the Bourbons. The direct method of attack was by journalism; but they believed that a blow might also be struck by writing histories of the French Revolution. They enjoyed the acquaintance of Talleyrand, and they met many of the surviving actors at the houses of Manuel and Laffitte. Thiers' work, which began to appear in 1823, was a rapid, eloquent, vivid narrative, neither learned nor profound. Its success encouraged him to go deeper into his subject, and the later volumes show a marked improvement. It was the first account of the Revolution written by one who was not himself an actor or a contemporary, and Sainte-Beuve testifies that it had the effect of a *Marseillaise*. It condemned the Terror; but the plain lesson of the book was that the Revolution had been checked in mid-career and clamoured for completion. The *History of the Consulate and the Empire* which followed revealed a remarkable talent for describing finance and military operations. The method is that of the well-informed reporter, who achieves his effects by accumulation of detail. He boasted that he had not scrupled to give the price of bread, soap, and candles, the depth of snow on the passes, and the number of ammunition carts. He belongs neither to the artistic nor to the philosophic school. He is weak in psychology and blind to the forces that move below the surface. His works were not so much achievements in historical science as political events.

A far higher place in the hierarchy of historians is occupied by Thiers' lifelong friend. Mignet's sketch of the French Revolution appeared in 1824, and, like that of Thiers, led up to the logical and political necessity of completing the Revolution by a constitutional monarchy; but the work was far more than a political pamphlet. He had studied as little as Thiers, and he lacked the pictorial style and the robust prolixity of his friend. His strength lay in his power of establishing the connexion of events, of tracing the thread of progress through the maze of war and faction. So rare is this power that the book, though never revised, still maintains its authority. In Thiers we meet the man of action, in Mignet the thinker, liberal in maxims and sparing of anecdotes. It is true that Mignet was by temperament unable to enter into the deeper and wilder passions of the time; but his complete self-possession enabled him to estimate its actual results more calmly and clearly than those who were dazzled or scorched by the blaze. After the Revolution of 1830, he became Director of the Archives, and in 1835 published the documents relative to the War of the Spanish Succession, with an introduction unsurpassed for insight, judgment, and power of condensation. His later works, dealing with the international history of the sixteenth century, above all his *Rivalry of Charles V and Francis I,* were the fruit of prolonged research, perfect in form and arrangement, and scrupulously impersonal. In another department his fame is equally secure. In 1837 he became Perpetual Secretary of the Academy of Moral and Political Sciences, and in this capacity produced a series of memorial addresses which gave the *éloge* a new life and a classic form, and present an incomparable gallery of portraits illustrating political and intellectual movements from 1789 till the Third Republic. Mignet's output was relatively small; but his work is of the finest quality.

Equally judicial, though more conservative in temperament, was Tocqueville, the success of whose book on the United States inspired him with the determination to study the origins of democracy in France. After several years of research, the thin volume on the *Ancien Régime* appeared. In brief but pregnant chapters, Tocqueville explained the nature of the central and provincial government and administration of France in the eighteenth century and analysed the economic conditions and intellectual atmosphere on the eve of the Revolution. Though a premature death prevented him from dealing with the Revolution itself, his book contributed more to its elucidation than the works of Thiers and Mignet, Michelet and Louis Blanc, Lamartine and Quinet.

Tocqueville's work was taken up, nearly twenty years later, by Taine, whom the horrors of the Commune led to search for the causes of the instability of French institutions. His *Origines de la France Contemporaine* began in 1875 with the *Ancien Régime,* in which, while recognising the faults of the old monarchy, he described with marked hostility the growth of revolutionary ideas. The volumes which followed on the Revolution exhibited an intense dislike of its doctrines and leaders. The attack on Jacobinism, written, as his letters reveal, in a spirit of profound pessimism, was greeted with delight by the monarchists of France; but its scientific pretensions have been challenged by Aulard. Taine's knowledge of the period was inadequate, his use of sources in the highest degree arbitrary. His explanation of the course of the Revolution by a political theory, and his omission of such vital factors as the intrigues of the Court and the danger on the frontier go far to render his book rather a brilliant polemic than a solid contribution to history. Of far greater sanity and historical value is the work in which Sorel exhibited the Revolution, not as an outbreak of Jacobin madness, but as the culminating point in the series of intellectual and political changes that had been in progress throughout the eighteenth century, and pointed out that in its foreign policy it was continuing the tradition of the monarchy. Still more important has been the work of Aulard, the greatest living authority on the Revolution, to whom we owe the publication of the records of the Jacobin Club and the Committee of Public Safety.

Napoleon has been studied at least as eagerly as the Revolution, and has been the chosen theme of some of the ablest of French historians. Lanfrey replied effectively to Thiers, and Taine described Napoleon as a *condottiere* born out of due time. His personal life has been minutely explored by Chuquet and Masson, his policy by Sorel and Vandal, his fall by Houssaye. An admirable account of the Second Empire has been written by La Gorce. The period of the Monarchy has been illuminated by the Duc de Broglie's studies of the diplomacy of Louis XV, by Boislisle's edition of *Saint-Simon*, by Hanotaux' masterly fragment on Richelieu, and the Duc d'Aumale's history of the House of Condé. Delisle, Monod, Molinier, Luchaire, and other medievalists trained in the *École des Chartes*, have produced work surpassed by no other country. The most celebrated book on the Middle Ages written during the Third Republic was Fustel de Coulanges' *History of the Institutions of Ancient France*. Fustel believed that by mastering every scrap of written evidence for the centuries concerned he could reconstruct without fear of error. He collected a mass of evidence to show that the institutions of ancient France were Roman, not German, and that the Franks brought little but barbarism with them. His researches threw a flood of light on the structure and development of medieval society; but he is a dangerous guide and his results are nowhere accepted in their entirety. The most eminent of his pupils, Camille Jullian, is at work on a monumental *History of Gaul*.

While in Germany and France historical studies grew to a large extent out of the Romantic movement, in England the earlier Romanticists found their inspiration less in the past than in nature and in the emotions of the human heart. Scott's novels appeared only in the second generation of romanticism, and, though they aroused widespread interest in history, exerted far less influence on English than on continental writers. At the opening of the century historical study was at its lowest ebb. The professors at Oxford and Cambridge rarely delivered lectures or wrote books, and the national records were allowed to rest in peace. It was not till the appearance in 1817 of Hallam's *State of Europe in the Middle Ages* that the modern English historical school was founded. The book was rather descriptive and explanatory than antiquarian. The preface announced that attention would be chiefly devoted to laws and modes of government; and, indeed, Hallam's legal training, his calm, judicial mind, and his intimate acquaintance with public men and the problems of State fitted him to deal with institutions rather than with men or ideas. The work lacked colour and movement;

but as a first attempt to carve tracks through the forest it was of inestimable value, and its obvious power and measured style, sometimes rising to a grave eloquence, secured it instant recognition.

The study of medieval England progressed rapidly during the following years. Editions of early texts were published by Ellis and Madden, Harris Nicolas, Thorpe, and Duffus Hardy. The first Record Commission had been appointed in 1800, and the Surtees, Camden, Parker, Chetham, and other learned societies were founded in rapid succession. A first attempt to utilise part of this wealth of new matter was made by Palgrave in his *Rise and Progress of the English Commonwealth*, published in 1832. The impetus given by Savigny to the historical study of law and institutions had resulted in the formation of two schools, called Germanist and Romanist according to their estimate of the influence of Rome. In this controversy Palgrave took his stand with the Romanists. He explained medieval England by the blending of the monarchical powers inherited from Rome with Teutonic freedom, issuing in a State with an absolute king and a large measure of local independence. Social conditions, he maintained, were little changed by the Anglo-Saxon, and still less by the Danish and Norman, conquests, the indestructible elements remaining throughout Roman. The work was learned and ingenious, but arbitrary and fanciful; and his neglect of Teutonic influences was a grave fault. It was to this neglected Germanic factor that attention was called by Kemble, whose great collection of charters was the result of prolonged search in cathedral, collegiate, and other libraries, and whose volumes on *The Saxons in England*, in which he summarised his discoveries, founded the scientific study of early English institutions and remained supreme till the advent of Stubbs. While recognising that the Britons were not annihilated in any part of the country, he pronounced the character of the Anglo-Saxon period to be entirely Teutonic, neither Celtic nor Roman elements exerting the slightest influence. The research of Seebohm and other investigators has profoundly modified Kemble's view of the so-called mark; but his contention that Saxon England was essentially Germanic, not Roman, is now generally accepted.

During the same period the exploration of the ancient world was commenced. Niebuhr's *History of Rome*, which was translated as it appeared in its final form, scared certain theological circles by its free handling of authorities. To Arnold, on the other hand, "it opened a new world"; and on Niebuhr's death he determined to continue his work. Arnold possessed gifts denied to Niebuhr, among them a clear and noble style, and his narrative of the greater moments of his story, such as the invasion of Hannibal, is incomparable; but he accepted too much on Niebuhr's authority and did little to advance the critical study of Roman history.

The progress of Greek studies was far more rapid. In 1784, Mitford, a Tory squire and member of Parliament, had begun the publication of a *History of Greece*, which was not completed till 1818. Though his learning was considerable, he made his work the vehicle of his political prejudices, rating the Athenian democrats as the prototypes of the hated Whigs. Of far greater value were the chronological investigations of Fynes Clinton. Aided by these works and trained in the methods of Niebuhr, whose work he had helped to translate, Thirlwall compiled the first scholarly history of Greece in any language. A moderate Liberal of the school of Hallam, Thirlwall exposed Mitford's mistakes and perversions and painted the main events and figures of Greek history in their true colours. Though he lacked the power of picturesque style and arresting phrase, his work ranks among the greatest productions of English scholarship for its learning, conspicuous fairness, and critical power. That it never received the recognition that it deserved was due to the simultaneous appearance of a more brilliant handling of the same theme. Grote had planned a history of Greece as early as 1822; but his entry into political life deferred its realisation, and it was not till 1846 that the first of the twelve volumes appeared. Grote had never visited the country nor asked himself how nature affected the development of the drama. Greece was simply the scene of certain political events. The standpoint, too, was Athenian, not Hellenic, and the early and later stages suffer in consequence. The ethnological section inspired him with little interest, and the closing scenes are marred by his maltreatment of the Macedonian destroyer of his idol. On the other hand, he carried forward the criticism of the sources. While Thirlwall had rejected secondary authorities, Grote tested Thucydides and other witnesses in the light of his own judgment and political experience. Above all, he was the first European writer to make the politics of Greece a real and living thing. His work has never been surpassed in its force and vividness and, despite its democratic bias, has done more than any other to bring the life of Greece into general knowledge.

A bias of a different character made itself apparent in the treatment of modern themes. No serious attempt had been made to describe English conquests in the East, still less to discuss the problems which it involved, before the appearance of Mill's *History of British India* in 1818. The style was bad, and the judgment both of Hindu civilisation and of the East India Company unduly severe; but it contained valuable information, and its power of generalisation was highly stimulating. A second work which challenged current opinions was the first comprehensive history of England since Hume. Its author, Lingard, had transcribed a large number of documents at the Vatican during a visit to Rome, and in 1819 began the publication of his history. Protestants were surprised at its temperate tone; but it was unmistakably the work of a Catholic, and the picture of the Reformation presented that movement in a new light. Subsequent editions were improved as they were called for, and the book is not even now altogether superseded.

The most widely read works, however, were those which represented conflicting political interests. In the preface to his voluminous *History of Europe* Alison frankly confesses that his purpose is to warn his fellow-countrymen against the perils of change. The work became canonical with the dominant political party; but with the downfall of the older Toryism after the Reform Bill it lost much of its authority. If Alison found in the history of the French Revolution and the Napoleonic wars the most suitable text for his sermon, the seventeenth and eighteenth centuries lay ready to hand as the chosen ground of the Whig retort. The authoritative Whig presentation of modern English history was given in 1827 in Hallam's *Constitutional History*, which immediately took its place as a text-book in the Universities and a classic of political literature. The part which has least stood the test of time, though it won the greatest applause at the moment of its appearance, is that devoted to the first two Stewarts.

Among those who hailed the *Constitutional History* with delight was a writer in the *Edinburgh Review*, who was to eclipse Hallam as the mouthpiece of the Whigs. Macaulay had won reputation at a bound by his article on Milton in 1824; but it was in the lengthy review of Hallam that he first fully expressed his attitude towards the modern history of England. He found the historical essay rudimentary and left it alive and complete, and his articles glitter like gems in the dusty pages of the *Edinburgh Review*. Passing rapidly from the work to its subject, he paints a character or a period in a few strong, broad strokes. It has been truly said that Macaulay did for English history in the seventeenth and eighteenth centuries what Shakespeare's historical plays accomplished for earlier times. Some essays, such as those on Temple and Chatham, are masterpieces. The style is simple and rapid, the picture glows with colour, the past lives again. On the other hand the essays as a whole suffer from serious limitations. Macaulay's knowledge, though vast, was confined to certain periods, and he knew little of the Middle Ages or even of English history before Elizabeth. Again, the essays formed part of the campaign against Toryism. Macaulay was the greatest of party writers; but his trenchant judgments and unsparing condemnations are now out of date. Thirdly, he lacked insight into the complexities of character, and had no grasp of religious or philosophical problems. The article on Bacon is fatal to his fame as a serious thinker, and his treatment of George Fox betrays his narrow emotional limits. The *History of England* is far more mature and satisfactory. There is more knowledge and self-control, and the subject lends itself to dramatic treatment. He had declared that the fragment of Mackintosh on the Revolution combined the accuracy and judgment of Hallam with the vivacity and colouring of Southey, and maintained that a history of England written in this manner would be the most fascinating book in the language. Such a book he set himself in his later years to write. Though his William, his Marlborough, and his Penn require qualification, the work is full of imperishable scenes and remains the most magnificent torso in historical literature.

A writer who stood ostentatiously aloof from the party cries of his day, but whose attitude to history was no less determined by his personal convictions, possessed in a conspicuous degree some of the qualifications that Macaulay lacked. Carlyle's main interest was in the moral world. His early essays defined history as the essence of innumerable biographies, and the realisation of a divine plan. In 1837, after numerous studies of France in the eighteenth century, appeared the *History of the French Revolution*, "hot out of my soul, born in blackness, whirlwind and sorrow." First of all writers and more successfully than any save Michelet, he revealed the human and personal interest of the drama, its tragedy, its pathos, its exaltation. But it is a superb prose epic, not a history. Carlyle does not realise that the destructive work of the Revolution was merely the completion of a process begun long before; and its constructive work escapes him altogether. He was interested in the individual soul, and had no real conception of the continuity of humanity or of the collective life in a people. For this reason he was unable to grasp the significance of his subject in relation to the history of the world. In regard to details the book is as faulty as it is in its general conception. He exaggerated the heaviness of the feudal burdens, the degradation of the clergy and noblesse, the desire of the people for the complete upheaval that actually occurred. On the other hand he excels in portraits, and the King, the Queen, Lafayette, Mirabeau, Danton, Robespierre are still what he left them.

The *French Revolution* was followed by the *Lectures on Heroes and Hero Worship*, which contain the fullest statement of Carlyle's attitude towards history. Men being mostly foolish, their wisest course was to follow great leaders. Mohammad, Luther, Cromwell, and Napoleon were passed in review; but the supreme illustration of the doctrine appeared in *Cromwell's Letters and Speeches*. One of the greatest figures in European history was disinterred from a load of calumny and allowed to speak for himself. Even while Carlyle was at work, Forster had once again drawn the familiar portrait of the renegade republican. The *Letters and Speeches* convinced all reasonable men, Forster among them, not only of Cromwell's transcendent greatness but of his sincerity. By the side of this immense achievement the faults of the book appear almost insignificant. Yet they are grave enough, and further illustrate the weakness of Carlyle's method. His work is an epic, a Cromwelliad, in which the opponents and critics of the hero are branded as fools or knaves. In the second place, Puritanism is represented as a struggle of light against darkness, isolated from the religious and social movements of preceding generations and perishing with the Protector. Finally, the political ideas of Cromwell himself are misunderstood. The discovery of the *Clarke Papers* has revealed the conservatism and the hesitations of the man whom Carlyle pictures as sharing his own contempt for Parliament and advancing with unfaltering strides towards dictatorship.

Carlyle founded no school; but his main ideas were accepted by Froude, and set forth in his brilliant narrative of the revolt of England against Rome. Though the fruit of prolonged labour and containing a mass of new material, the book suffers from faults which exclude it from the first rank. His hatred of Catholicism was such that he turned a blind eye to the failings of the champions of the Reformation and made Henry VIII into something like a national hero. The volumes on Edward, Mary and Elizabeth are of greater value; but inaccuracies of transcription and quotation are common, and his personal likes and dislikes are violent and arbitrary. Nothing is too good to believe of the Regent Murray, while the Casket letters are accepted *en bloc* in the indictment of Mary Stewart. The same faults occur in his other works; and *The English in Ireland* is marred by unconcealed animosity against the Irish Catholics. His style is unsurpassed; but his statements need to be checked and his judgments controlled.

Meanwhile a more exact school was forming at Oxford, the greatest figure of which was Stubbs, the English Waitz, who made his name by editing Hoveden and other early chroniclers for the Rolls Series, and especially by his introductions to these editions. Succeeding Goldwin Smith as Regius Professor of Modern History at Oxford, he began in 1874 to publish his *Constitutional History*, one of the two greatest works of English historical scholarship of the last half-century. To a knowledge of the sources which no one had ever possessed and a complete acquaintance with German research on Teutonic institutions Stubbs joined a rare critical acumen and an almost infallible judgment. He succeeded not only in reconstructing the main lines of English constitutional development, but in giving the first authoritative account of English history till the coming of the Tudors. The first volume is now partially antiquated; but the second and third volumes are still our best guides to the later Middle Ages. Stubbs was a master of pregnant and weighty phrase. His character studies are often models of portraiture, and the survey of England at the close of the Middle Ages, which fills the last half of the third volume, is a masterpiece of lightly borne learning and artistic presentation. His friend and fellow-worker, Freeman, differed widely from him in temperament and outlook. Stubbs was reserved and concise; Freeman was a hero-worshipper and propagandist and dragged every detail on which he could lay hands into his pages. Equally different was their sphere of work. While Stubbs spent his life in studying medieval England, Freeman preached the unity of history and was equally at home in Athens and Rome, Aachen and

Constantinople.   His output was enormous and no part of it is without
value.   The *Federal Government* and the *History of Sicily* are imposing
fragments, and the *Historical Essays* are vigorous and erudite.   The
Norman Conquest, with its pendant *William Rufus*, is the crown of
Freeman's life.   Prolix though it is, disfigured by prejudices and preferences, weak on its legal and institutional side and neglectful of
unprinted sources, it is nevertheless a noble monument of historical
research, full of sound learning and brilliant writing.   The third member
of the Oxford school belonged to a younger generation than those whom,
in a famous dedication, he saluted as his masters, and died before them.
Though the historical essays of Green's earlier life are often models of
delicate grace and his later works are solid contributions to a knowledge
of early England, it is the *Short History* which has immortalised his
name.   The hero of his story was the English people; only thus, he
taught, could English history be conceived as a whole and properly
understood.   His enunciation of what has now become a commonplace
was a landmark in historic study.   Not less admirable than the design
was its execution.   By skilful grouping of periods and omission of
unessential detail, by a vivid style and sympathy with every aspect of
national life, social, literary, religious, artistic, no less than political, he
succeeded in giving a living picture of the development of England
within the compass of a single volume.   The difficulties of such a task
are indicated by the fact that no one but Green has accomplished it in
England or elsewhere.

The exact methods of the Oxford school reappear in Gardiner's
monumental work on the Puritan Revolution.   To the detachment of
Guizot and Ranke he added an immensely greater acquaintance with the
sources, and for the first time narrated the most critical years of English
history with full knowledge and unerring judgment.   If it be one of the
sovereign duties of the historian to make the standpoint and personalities
of rival factions intelligible, Gardiner is one of the greatest of historians.
His knowledge and catholicity of temper enabled him to understand men
who could never understand one another.   He sees the grandeur of the
political ideal of Bacon as clearly as he sees that of Coke and Pym, and
makes his readers feel how much each side has contributed to the making
of England.   Though of inferior merit to Gardiner's magnificent achievement, Lecky's history of the eighteenth century is a work of considerable
importance.   The volumes on England are rather in the nature of a
commentary on certain aspects of national life than a narrative of events,
and in no way supersede the meritorious work of Lord Stanhope.   Of
far greater value are the Irish volumes, which gave the first full and
impartial account of the Grattan Parliament and the Union and corrected
the innumerable errors of fact and judgment into which Froude had
fallen.

A new vein of historical study was opened up by Seeley.   Confining

himself in the main to the modern world, defining history as the life of
States and keeping ever in view their international relationships, Seeley's
knowledge of the diplomatic history of modern Europe was wide and
deep.   His *Life of Stein* introduced English readers to a new aspect of
the Napoleonic era.   His *Expansion of England* explained with extraordinary clearness the relation between the foundation of the British
Empire and the struggle with France.   Finally, the posthumous volumes
on *British Policy* traced with masterly skill the influence of the religious
and dynastic struggles of the Continent on foreign policy from Elizabeth
to William of Orange.   Though his view of history was exclusively
political, Seeley was an inspiring writer and teacher, and his work,
though small in bulk, is of high quality.   Several other considerable
works were written during the last decades of the century.   In *Italy
and her Invaders* Hodgkin produced one of the most fascinating
among recent historical works.   Creighton portrayed the Papacy of the
fifteenth and sixteenth centuries in the detached and reticent manner of
Ranke.   English history in the nineteenth century has been impartially
related in a series of works by Spencer Walpole.   Among writings of
smaller dimensions may be mentioned Bryce's *Holy Roman Empire*,
Brewer's volumes on Wolsey, Trevelyan's *Early Life of Charles James
Fox*, and Church's *History of the Oxford Movement*.   This brief
summary may be closed with the names of two men whose loss the world
of scholars is still mourning—Maitland, whose studies of the early
history of English law and society are equally remarkable for their
learning, originality and charm, and Lord Acton, who, though he never
wrote a book, inspired the writing of many books, left behind him
valuable essays and fragments, and by his universal knowledge, many-
sided personality, and enthusiasm for freedom, broadened and deepened
the conception of history.

In the New World the first notable historian was Bancroft, whose
History of the United States began to appear in 1834.   It reflected the
spirit of Jacksonian democracy, exuberant, self-satisfied, uncritical.   It
immediately became canonical, and it is only in quite recent years that
a more critical scholarship has challenged its dominion.   A similar
tendency to the idealisation of his countrymen disfigured Palfrey's
important work on New England.   While men of all parties agreed in
praise of the colonial period, differences of opinion manifested themselves
when the history of the early Presidents came to be narrated.   Thus a
strong Federalist bias disfigures the valuable work of Hildreth.   This
weakness has now been largely overcome, and we may trust Henry
Adams for the period of Jefferson and Madison, and Rhodes for the
story of the slavery struggle.   American historians, however, have
achieved their greatest triumph outside the borders of their country.
Parkman described the struggle of France and England for Canada in a
series of brilliant monographs.   Prescott wrote the story of Spain in the

days of her glory and of her conquests in the New World. Motley studied the Dutch War of Independence in works of extraordinary power and wide research, marred by excessive partiality for his heroes, William the Silent and Barneveldt. More recently, Captain Mahan has illuminated history by directing attention to the part played by sea power in the fortunes of modern States, and founded a school of naval historians in both hemispheres.

Historical research has been actively pursued in Italy. Mai discovered and gave to the world many of the treasures of the Vatican Library; Visconti and Borghesi devoted their unique gifts to archaeology and epigraphy; Troya presented the first detailed view of the invasions; Cesare Cantu brought together much information relating to literature and culture in his *History of Italy*. Litta's studies on the Great Families of Italy, and Sclopis' *History of Legislation*, are of permanent value. Recent events were described in Colletta's narrative of the chequered fortunes of Naples, Botta's survey of the Napoleonic period, Coppi's continuation of the annals of Muratori, and Farini's *History of the Papal States*. Historical studies in Tuscany were fostered by the wealth and zeal of Gino Capponi, the historian of Florence, to whom the formation of the *Archivio Storico*, the first Italian historical review, was chiefly due. In the latter half of the century Ferrari produced a brilliant narrative of the Revolutions of Italy, Romanin wrote the first adequate history of Venice, Amari related the fortunes of the Mussulmans in Sicily, Villari won European reputation by his biographies of Machiavelli and Savonarola and his studies of the early history of Florence, and Pais is at work on a comprehensive history of early Italy. In Spain Llorente compiled his attack on the Inquisition, and the national annals were recorded in the interminable volumes of Lafuente. Of far higher merit is the cooperative history edited by Cánovas for the Spanish Academy. In Danvila y Collado, Menéndez y Pelayo, and Altamira, Spain possesses historical scholars of the first rank. Sweden has been provided with a national history by Geijer, Hungary by Mailáth, Greece by Paparrigopoulo. The archives of Belgium and Holland have yielded a rich harvest to the labours of Gachard and Frédéricq, Fruin and Blok.

The Slavonic countries have shared in the general movement. Karamsin and Solovieff have written the history of Russia, and Bilbassoff's *Catharine II* has become a classic. Lelewel, the Polish Michelet, employed his exile in compiling a work on medieval Poland. It is in Bohemia, however, that the growth of historical studies has been most closely related to the national life. Since the battle of the White Hill Bohemian culture had ceased to exist; but in the early years of the nineteenth century the national consciousness was reawakened by the writings of Kollár, Šafařík, and Palacký, who was appointed by the Diet to write the history of the nation. The most important part of the work, the magnificent treatment of Hus, was denounced by the censor; but though Palacký cancelled certain passages and inserted others, he lived long enough to witness the abolition of the censorship and to reinsert the original words. The book was not only a historical masterpiece but also a political event, a revelation to a down-trodden people of the glory of their past, and a trumpet-call to play their part in the world once more. The critical study of history, however, has also led to the destruction of many cherished patriotic beliefs. In Switzerland the legend of Tell and others that Johannes Müller had unsuspectingly accepted were ruthlessly destroyed by Kopp. When Herculano de Carvalho's great *History of Portugal* began to appear it was so fiercely denounced that after describing a single century the author thought well to desist.

Historical science is becoming increasingly international, and the remainder of the field may be surveyed without regard to national boundaries.

The history of Roman studies since Niebuhr is largely the record of the activity of a single man. While Mommsen was growing up, little work of outstanding importance appeared except Drumann's biographies of Caesar and his contemporaries and Rubino's constitutional studies. After publishing his first work on Roman Associations in 1843, he visited Italy, where he founded the scientific study of early Italian dialects and ethnography. He then turned to Latin epigraphy. Borghesi had made large collections for a *Corpus* and was hoping for aid from Paris; but, as aid did not arrive, Mommsen began the work single-handed, and edited the Samnite and Neapolitan inscriptions. Shortly afterwards, the Berlin Academy undertook the task and entrusted the direction to Mommsen. The *Corpus Inscriptionum Latinarum*, the greatest historical undertaking of the century, was the main occupation and the most important monument of his life. Liberally supported by the Academy and aided by the Archaeological Institute in Rome, Mommsen produced the first volume in 1863, and lived to see the appearance of nearly twenty volumes, half of which he edited himself. The *Corpus* has recovered for the world large tracts of Roman history and forms one of the main sources of Mommsen's own writings.

In productive power Mommsen equalled Ranke, and surpassed all other historians of the first rank. The most popular and personal of his works, the greatest effort of his genius though not of his scholarship, was the *Roman History*, which appeared in three volumes, in 1854–6. Written for a series in which the results, not the processes, of learning were demanded, the work differed fundamentally from Niebuhr's, and from the valuable volumes in which Schwegler was in the same years testing Niebuhr's results. Legendary matter was simply omitted, the opinions of the author boldly advanced without proof. The work vibrates with power, passion, genius. Niebuhr had reconstructed the institutions of ancient Rome; Mommsen revealed its life. The third volume was the climax of the whole. The great events and personalities of the closing days of the Republic, the lyrical enthusiasm for Caesar, the fiery attack on Pompey and Cicero, the consummate style, the epigrams and allusions, render it perhaps the most striking single volume in historical literature. Despite well-grounded criticisms of its political morality, the book remains without a rival. Mommsen next turned to special departments of research and published the *Chronology* in 1858, the *Coinage* in 1860, and the *Digest* during the years 1868–70. He then began his largest and, in his own opinion, most important work, the *Staatsrecht*, one of the greatest constitutional treatises in historical literature. In this he broke new ground, extending his survey to the Empire and explaining the nature and evolution of the Principate. Before the *Staatsrecht* was finished, the world was surprised by a massive survey of the *Provinces of the Roman Empire*, based on the inscriptions, explaining for the first time the character and achievements of the imperial administration, and disposing for ever of the notion that the Empire was merely an age of despotism and decay. The book was described as the fifth volume of the *Roman History*; but the projected fourth volume, on the Empire itself, was, unhappily, never written. The closing years of his life were mainly devoted to a gigantic treatise on Roman Criminal Law and to editions of Jordanes, Cassiodorus, Nennius, the *Liber Pontificalis*, and the Theodosian Code, thus extending the sphere of his studies till Rome was swallowed up in the Middle Ages. His publications extended over sixty years. There is no immaturity in his early works and no decline in the later. The imaginative and critical faculties met and balanced the large vision and the genius for detail. The complete assimilation and reproduction of a classical civilisation for which scholars have struggled ever since Scaliger has been achieved by Mommsen alone. Rome before him was like modern Europe before Ranke. He was, too, more than a man of learning. He had championed Schleswig-Holstein, had lost his professorship at Leipzig during the reaction, had withstood Bismarck in the plenitude of his power, and aided the movement for intellectual and artistic liberty. His works are alive, and however remote the subject we feel that we are dealing with living men.

When Otfried Müller explored Greece in 1840 he was accompanied by Ernst Curtius, and the period which opened with his death is chiefly associated with the name of his greatest pupil. The collection of inscriptions has gone rapidly forward, and Böckh's *Corpus* has been broken up into geographical sections; but Greek history has gained even more from the spade. After winning his spurs with a work on the Peloponnesus he published the first volume of his *Greek History* in 1861, in which he incorporated the latest researches of himself and others in Greece and Asia Minor. Though greatly inferior to Grote in his handling of politics, Curtius for the first time connected Greek history with topography and dealt fully with the aesthetic side of Greek civilisation. The work makes an impression rather of charm than of power, and the enthusiasm of the discoverer has led to a somewhat idealised reconstruction of Hellenic culture; but it widened the conception of Greek history and still retains a certain authority.

Curtius' volumes were scarcely completed when Schliemann's excavations in Troy, Mycenae and Tiryns opened up prehistoric Hellas. The results were marvellous; but the methods were crude and unscholarly. Having spent his life in business, Schliemann brought an untrained mind to his task, embraced baseless hypotheses, and in the process of excavation seriously damaged some of the remains. Much of his work has had to be done over again by Dörpfeld. A more perfect technique has been shown in the excavations of Olympia by the Germans, of Delphi by the French, and in those now being carried on by the British School at Sparta. The new material which has been gathered in such bewildering quantity has been reduced to narrative form by Busolt, Beloch, Holm, Eduard Meyer, and Bury. The economic side of Greek history has been explored by Pöhlmann, and the discovery of the *Constitution of Athens* has been utilised in Wilamowitz' classical work on Athenian institutions. Droysen's labours on the Hellenistic era have been resumed by Kärst and Niese, Mahaffy, Bouché-Leclercq, and Bevan; and Freeman devoted his closing years to the history of Greek Sicily. The intellectual and artistic life of Greece has been illustrated by Zeller, Gomperz, Brunn, and innumerable other workers; but the problem of the Homeric poems remains as inscrutable as ever. The history of medieval Greece and of the Byzantine Empire, the services of which to civilisation Gibbon never appreciated, has been reconstructed by the solid researches of Hopf and Finlay, Rambaud and Diehl, Schlumberger, Bury, Sathas, and Lambros. Its literature has been surveyed by Krumbacher, its law by Zachariä von Lingenthal, and its contribution to art assessed in the brilliant studies of Strzygowski.

One of the most notable achievements of nineteenth century scholarship was the opening up of the East by comparative philology and archaeology. The relationship between Sanskrit and the languages of Europe that had been established by Sir William Jones, Colebrooke, and Friedrich Schlegel was proved in detail by Bopp in 1817. Twenty years later, Burnouf used the Pali manuscripts discovered by Bryan Hodgson in Nepal to reveal Buddhism to the West, and Lassen began his encyclopaedic survey of ancient India. The key to hieratic Egyptian was discovered by Young and Champollion, and the cuneiform inscriptions of Assyria were deciphered by the combined labours of Grotefend, Burnouf, Lassen, Hincks, Oppert and Rawlinson. Hittite, like Etruscan, still awaits a key. In the middle of the century systematic excavations and surveys were commenced. Lepsius was sent to Egypt by the King of Prussia, and his work of revelation has been continued by Brugsch, Mariette, Maspero, and Flinders Petrie. The spades of Botta and Layard brought Assyria to light, and Lycia was revealed by Fellows. Semitic studies were systematically inaugurated by Sylvestre de Sacy and his pupils, and have profited by Renan's *Corpus* of Inscriptions. The first critical account of Mohammad and the early Caliphs was given by Weil in 1843, and Dozy brought order into the chaotic and legendary history of the Moors in Spain. Almost every province of the history of antiquity has benefited by the encyclopaedic knowledge of Gutschmid. The researches into the ancient East were first coordinated and popularised in Duncker's *History of Antiquity*. But Duncker's knowledge was second-hand, and his work is now largely antiquated. The gigantic task of writing the history of antiquity from the original sources is now being carried out with incomparable learning and power by Eduard Meyer. The horizon is still rapidly widening. The history of civilisation is being pushed steadily back, and the recent sensational discoveries of the Tel-el-Amarna tablets and the Oxyrhynchus papyri, of Arthur Evans at Cnossus, de Sarzec at Tello, de Morgan at Susa, and Hilprecht at Nippur, open up boundless vistas and counsel arrest of judgment.

The revelation of the ancient East has owed and contributed much to the critical study of the Old Testament, and many of the essential problems of Jewish history have been rescued from controversy. Before the century opened, Eichhorn had adopted the principle of regarding the books of the Old Testament as oriental writings, to be interpreted in accordance with Semitic habits of thought. In the second and third decades Gesenius and Ewald laid the foundations of exact Semitic philology, and the latter's *History of Israel*, a work unsurpassed for literary power, skilful arrangement, and freshness of treatment, brought the Jews definitely within the circle of historic studies. In 1836, Vatke introduced order into the books and recovered the stages of religious development, by showing that the Law was later than the Prophets and the Psalms later than both. His work was confirmed and continued by Reuss and Graf, and in the hands of Kuenen and Wellhausen became the basis of a revised narrative. Jewish history has benefited comparatively little by excavations but largely by the light thrown on Semitic habits of thought by such scholars as Lagarde, Nöldeke, and Robertson Smith.

The Christian Church stood equally in need of objective treatment. The school of Spittler and Planck rejected a mass of legendary detail ; but they were not yet imbued with the historical spirit. A new era opened in 1826 with the first volume of Neander's *History of the Church.* Neander's temperament was that of a Pietist. He failed to appreciate the political, the national, the institutional side of Church history, and he judged men by the measure of their edification. In critical questions he shared the weakness of the Romanticists, relying on the commonly accepted sources, not all of them authentic, and adding little that was new. As a guide, despite his massive learning, he was less useful than his contemporary Gieseler. His mission was to show the reality and beauty of the religious life throughout Christian history. At the opposite pole of thought stood Baur. Neander represented the new historic movement by his passionate interest in the past, the Tübingen professor by his application of critical methods to sacred history. His supreme achievement was to declare that the writings of the Old and New Testaments and the events of Jewish and Christian history must be studied in exactly the same way as other writings and events. His second great merit was the introduction of the idea of law and growth into the region of dogma and institutions. He had learned from Hegel to regard history as the development of spirit, each phase necessitating its successor; but this attitude led him, as it had led Hegel, to undervalue the influence of individuals. In their detailed critical work, again, Baur and his school committed serious errors, and their chronology of the Canon, their exaggeration of the differences between Peter and Paul, above all, their neglect of the personality of Christ in their explanations of the foundation of Christianity, have been rejected by subsequent research.

Since the decline of the Tübingen school, the study of Church history has made immense progress. The opening of the Vatican archives in 1881 has rendered possible the documentary study of the Papacy. Light has been thrown on the atmosphere out of which Christianity grew by the researches of Schürer, Hausrath and Pfleiderer. The constitution of the early Church has been recovered by Lightfoot, Hatch, and Weiszäcker, the life of its members revealed by Rossi's labours in the Roman Catacombs, and its fortunes related in Renan's brilliant volumes on the *Origins of Christianity*. Ramsay has reconstructed the history of the Church in Asia Minor from inscriptions and monuments. The evolution of dogma has been traced by Dorner and Harnack, of Canon Law by Richter and Hinschius. Large tracts of ecclesiastical thought and practice have been lit up by the life-long labours of Karl Hase, by Ritschl's profound studies of Pietism, and by the massive monographs of Henry Charles Lea, the Nestor of American historians. It is at last becoming possible to treat Church history objectively. Harnack and Duchesne touch at many points in the history of the early Church. Creighton and Pastor do not seriously disagree about the Popes of the Renaissance. Kawerau's works on the Reformation approach very closely to the ideal of historical justice, and some advance has been made on the Catholic side. The best account of Calvin is by Kampschulte, and the legend of Luther's suicide has been finally exploded by Nicholas Paulus.

Though the progress of historical science has been for the most part the work of Protestants, important contributions have been made by Catholic scholars. The renaissance of historical studies began in the second quarter of the century. In France Montalembert and Ozanam painted some rose-coloured pictures of monastic and medieval life; but the centre of the revival was Munich. Möhler's famous *Symbolik* revived the methods of Bossuet's attack on the Reformation. Görres studied the Mystics in a spirit of Catholic romanticism. Phillips, Schulte, and Maassen explored the history of Canon Law. Döllinger earned the applause of his Church by his massive attack on the Reformation. Hefele began his classical *History of the Councils*; Hergenröther published his profoundly learned study of Photius; and Pichler related the separation of the Eastern and Western Churches.

The growth of Ultramontanism under Pius IX divided Catholic scholarship into two camps. Döllinger and his pupils not only rejected the definitions of the Vatican Council, but proceeded to submit the entire history of the Church to a critical if not a hostile examination. Döllinger himself denounced the papal claims in *Janus*; Friedrich wrote a damaging history of the Council and of the growth of Ultramontanism which preceded it; Reusch compiled a work of colossal erudition on the *Index* of forbidden books. Schulte, the greatest of Canonists, gave the history of the Old Catholic movement, and Langen traced the history of the Church to Innocent III. The Ultramontanes have been no less active and have carried the war into the enemy's camp. Hergenröther, the most learned of them all, replied to *Janus*; Janssen's famous *History of the German People from the close of the Middle Ages*, the most successful of all Catholic histories, proved that the eve of the Reformation was less dark, and the intellectual, social, and moral confusion that accompanied it were greater, than had been supposed. Denifle threw a flood of light on the philosophy and education of the Middle Ages, and ended his life by a violent attack on the character of Luther. Pastor is relating the history of the Papacy from the middle of the fifteenth century with the aid of the Vatican archives. Gasquet has explained the methods by which the English monasteries were dissolved by Henry VIII. Onno Klopp, the author of the monumental *Fall of the House of Stewart*, has explained the policy of the Habsburgs in their struggle with Louis XIV, and Kervyn de Lettenhove has defended the Catholic side in the Dutch War of Independence. The Görres and Leo Societies have formed convenient centres for Ultramontane scholarship. In addition to the foes and friends of the Vatican Decrees, there have been several historians who, though remaining within the fold, have had little liking for Ultramontanism and have come into collision with authority. Kraus, after reluctantly consenting to mutilate his valuable handbook of Church history, turned to less directly controversial topics and produced a work of enduring value on Christian art. Acton, after rendering yeoman's service to Döllinger during the Council and publishing outspoken pamphlets and letters on the Papacy, withdrew from the fray and turned to the wider aspects of history. Among other scholars of this class, Ehrhard, Batiffol, Loisy, and above all Duchesne, have won an acknowledged position in patristic study and in the history of the early Church.

Increasing attention has been paid to *Kulturgeschichte*, which may roughly be defined as embracing the non-political aspects of civilisation. The founder of the genre was Voltaire, whose *Essai sur les Mœurs* is the parent of innumerable studies of the civilisation and social life of nations. The *Volksseele* was discovered by Herder, the Romanticists, and Jacob Grimm, and intellectual developments were included in the surveys of Guizot and Schlosser. It was not, however, till the middle of the nineteenth century that it obtained an assured position owing to the simultaneous activity of three distinguished writers. The Revolution of 1848 was one of the influences that led Riehl to devote his life to the study of German civilisation, the influence of natural conditions, the psychology of classes, the circumstances, habits, and thoughts of the mass of the people. By his *Natural History of the German People*, his monograph on the Palatinate, and other works published during the fifties, Riehl contributed more than anyone else to elucidate the influences that have determined German life. While Riehl was busy with the elaboration of an historical sociology, Gustav Freytag produced a survey of the life of the German people. His *Pictures from the Past* are the nearest equivalent in historical literature to Green's *Short History*, and enjoy equal popularity. Freytag brought to his task wide knowledge, a rare skill in the selection of illustrative material, and an absorbing interest in the minutest manifestations of the life and character of his countrymen. Though he was not a trained historian, his book contains much information not easily found elsewhere and forms the best introduction to the study of German history. The greatest of the triumvirate was Jacob Burckhardt. His *Age of Constantine* gave a vivid picture of the intellectual and religious atmosphere of the fourth century; but it was by his incomparable *Civilisation of the Renaissance*, published in 1860, that he won his position as the greatest historian of culture. For the first time the manifold aspects and activities of the Renaissance were studied separately and in combination, and the seed-time of the modern world presented as a living whole. Of scarcely inferior merit to Burckhardt's masterpiece is Friedländer's picture of the life and thought of the Roman Empire, which closely followed it in time of publication. Gregorovius' *City of Rome in the Middle Ages*, Sainte-Beuve's *History of Port Royal*, Lecky's volumes on *Rationalism* and *European Morals*, Symonds' *Renaissance in Italy*, Dill's pictures of Roman society, are other well-known examples of a class of works which have thrown light on problems with which the purely political historian cannot deal. The value of *Kulturgeschichte* lies in its synthetic treatment of human development, and no one would now venture to contend that history is merely past politics. Its danger is that in its reaction against a purely political treatment of history it may underestimate the importance of the State, and in its preoccupation with the life of the people may overlook the work of individuals. That these dangers are not imaginary has been shown in the heated controversy produced by Lamprecht's remarkable *German History*.

Since the middle of the century the study of institutions has become one of the main tasks of the historian. The outstanding works of Waitz and Stubbs, Fustel de Coulanges, and Mommsen have already been mentioned. Maine's *Ancient Law* and Fustel's *La Cité Antique* interested wide circles in the conceptions underlying Greek and Roman life. Maurer and Ficker, Brunner and Gierke have explored the law and institutions of medieval Germany, Viollet and Luchaire those of France, Gneist, Maitland, Seebohm, Liebermann, and Vinogradoff those of England. Karl Hegel spent a long life in studying the evolution of towns. Economic and social conditions have also been subjected to minute scrutiny. In the middle of the century Knies and Roscher drew attention to the relativity of economic principles and appealed to history as a guide and a test. Shortly afterwards, Nitzsch and Inama-Sternegg wrote the economic history of the German people, Thorold Rogers reconstructed the economic life of England from manorial registers and prices, and Levasseur narrated the history of the labouring classes of France. Above all, the writings of Schmoller and his pupils have enriched history with innumerable studies of the economic life of the past.

Finally primitive civilisation has been brought within the circle of historical study. The discoveries of Boucher des Perthes, Pitt-Rivers, and their successors, have thrown back the opening of the human drama thousands of years, and we recreate prehistoric man from language and legend, skull and weapon. Anthropology has become a science and the habits and beliefs of our savage ancestors have been made intelligible.

While historical science is thus extending its conquests in every direction, the philosophy of history lags behind. It helps us little to have been told by Hegel that the spirit of man is progressively reaching the consciousness of its own freedom. We should allow their due value to the efforts of Herder and Ritter, of Buckle and Ratzel, towards measuring the influence of geographical and natural conditions on human development and even to Comte's attempted formulation of the laws of mental and social evolution. But, though the day may not yet have dawned when for working hypotheses shall be substituted a philosophy of history, defining and explaining the purpose and the plan of human evolution, every true historian contributes, equally with the students of physical science and of psychology, to the progress of our knowledge of man.

CHAPTER I.

MODERN EUROPE.

Langlois, C. V. Bibliographie Historique. 2 vols. Paris. 1904.
Stein, H. Bibliographie générale. Paris. 1897.

Annual Register. 1868–1909.
Bourgeois, E. Manuel historique de politique étrangère. Vol. III. (1830–78.)
    Paris. 1905.
Bulle, E. Geschichte der neuesten Zeit. 1815–85. 4 vols. Leipzig. 1888.
Débidour, A. Histoire diplomatique de l'Europe Contemporaine. 1814–78. 2 vols.
    Paris. 1891.
Fyffe, C. A. History of Modern Europe. Vol. III. 1848–78. 1895.
Gooch, G. P. Annals of Politics and Culture (to 1899). Cambridge. 1901.
Hertslet, Sir E. History of Europe by Treaty (with maps). Vol. IV. 1875–91.
    1891.
Hertslet, L. and Sir E. Treaties and Conventions between Great Britain and
    Foreign Powers relating to Commerce, etc. 20 vols. 1827–95.
Irving, J. Annals of our Time (1837–91). Last part 1892.
Lavisse, E. and Rambaud, A. Histoire générale. Vol. XII. 1870–1900. Paris.
    1901.
Phillips, A. Modern Europe, 1815–99. 1901.
Rose, J. H. Development of European nations (1870–1900). 1905.
Schiemann, T. Deutschland und die grosse Politik, 1901, etc. Berlin, 1902, etc.
Schulthess, H. Europäischer Geschichtskalender (yearly). Munich. 1861–.
Seignobos, C. Histoire politique de l'Europe Contemporaine. 1815–96. Paris.
    1897.
Shadwell, A. Industrial efficiency; a comparative study of industrial life in
    England, Germany, and America. 2 vols. 1906.

CHAPTER II.

FOREIGN RELATIONS OF THE UNITED STATES DURING THE CIVIL WAR.

Government, Parliamentary and Congressional publications of Great Britain and the United States.

Annuaire de l'Institut de Droit International. Paris, etc. Vol. I, 1877, pp. 108–14, 139–40 (the Three Rules of Washington); Vol. xv, 1896, pp. 231, 232 (transport of persons by sea).

Bancroft, F. Life of. By W. H. Seward. 2 vols. New York and London. 1900.

Bernard, M. A Historical Account of the Neutrality of Great Britain during the American Civil War. 1870.

Calvo, C. Le Droit International Théorique et Pratique. Paris. 3rd edn. 1880. (Vol. I, pp. 204–9, §§ 81–5: recognition of belligerency; Vol. III, pp. 410–36, §§ 2263–92: treatment of ships and *Alabama* question; Vol. IV, pp. 72–90, §§ 2533–47: *Trent* case.)

Cushing, C. The Treaty of Washington. New York. 1873.

Davis, J. C. Bancroft. Mr Fish and the *Alabama* claims. Boston and New York. 1893.

Geffcken, F. H. In Holtzendorff's Handbuch des Völkerrechts. Vol. IV, pp. 702–9 (*Alabama* question), and pp. 735–8 (*Trent* case). Berlin, 1885–90.

Moore, J. B. A Digest of International Law, as embodied in [public documents, especially of the United States] and the writings of jurists. 8 vols. Washington. 1906. (The *Trent* case is treated in Vol. VII, pp. 763–79, and the French intervention in Mexico in Vol. VI, pp. 488–507.)

—— History and Digest of the International Arbitrations to which the United States has been a party. 6 vols. Washington. 1898. (See Vol. I, pp. 495–682, and Vol. IV, pp. 4057–178.)

CHAPTER III.

GREAT BRITAIN.

I. PERIODICAL LITERATURE.

Fletcher, W. I. and Poole, W. F.   Index to periodical literature.   Abridged Edition. 1815–99.

II. OFFICIAL PAPERS.

Parliamentary papers.   Reports of Royal Commissions and other public enquiries. [A brief summary of some of the more important of these papers in appendix to Low and Sanders' Political History of England (see below).] Hansard's Debates.

III. HISTORIES.

Bardoux, J.   Essai d'une psychologie du peuple anglais.   2 vols.   Paris.   1906–7.
Bright, J. F.   History of England.   Vol. v.   1880–1901.   1904.
Clayden, P. W.   England under Beaconsfield, 1873–80.   1880.
—— England under the Coalition, 1885–92.   1892.
Geffcken, F. H.   The British Empire.   E. Tr. by J. F. Macmullan.   1898.
Griffith-Boscawen, A. S. T.   Fourteen years in Parliament.   1907.
Low, Sidney, and Sanders, L. C.   Political History of England.   Vol. xii.   1837–1901.   With Bibliography.   1907.
McCarthy, J.   History of our own Times, 1837–1901.   7 vols.   1879–1905.
Paul, H.   History of Modern England (to 1895).   5 vols.   1904–6.
Ward, T. H.   Reign of Queen Victoria.   2 vols.   1887.
Whates, H.   Third Salisbury Administration, 1895–1900.   1901.
Whitmore, C. A.   Six years of Unionist Government, 1886–92.   1892.

IV. BIOGRAPHIES, MEMOIRS, ETC.

Dictionary of National Biography.   63 vols.   1885–1900.

Arch, Joseph.   His life, by himself.   1898.
Argyll, G. D. Campbell, Duke of.   Autobiography.   2 vols.   1896.
Beaconsfield, Lord.   By J. A. Froude.   1890.
Beaconsfield, Lord, and other Tory memories.   By T. E. Kebbel.   1907.
Benson, Archbishop, Life of.   By A. C. Benson.   2 vols.   1899.
Bradlaugh, Charles.   Life and work.   By H. B. Bonner.   2 vols.   1894.

Bright, John.   Life and speeches.   By G. B. Smith.   1881.
Cambridge, George, Duke of.   Military life, by W. W. C. Verrer.   1905.
—— Private life, based on journals and correspondence.   By E. Sheppard.   2 vols.
   1906.
Cardwell, Lord, at the War Office.   By Sir Robert Biddulph.   1904.
Chamberlain, Joseph, Life of.   By L. Creswicke.   4 vols.   1904.
—— By S. H. Jeyes.   2 vols.   1903.
Childers, Hugh C. E., Life of.   By Lieut.-Col. S. Childers.   2 vols.   1901.
Churchill, Lord Randolph, Life of.   By W. S. Churchill.   1907.
Colley, Sir George, Life of.   By Sir W. F. Butler.   1899.
Creighton, M., Bishop of London, Life of.   By Mrs Creighton.   1904.
Dufferin, Lord, Life of.   By Sir A. Lyall.   2 vols.   1905.
Fawcett, Henry, Life of.   By Leslie Stephen.   1885.
Forster, William Edward, Life of.   By Sir T. Wemyss Reid.   2 vols.   1888.
Frere, Sir Bartle, Life and correspondence of.   By J. Martineau.   2 vols.   1895.
Gladstone, William Ewart, Life of.   By John Morley (Lord Morley of Blackburn).
   3 vols.   1904.
—— Life of.   By G. W. E. Russell.   1891.
Gordon, General C. G., Life of.   By D. C. Boulger.   4th edn.   1900.
Granville, Earl, Life of.   By Lord E. Fitzmaurice.   2 vols.   1905.
Holyoake, G. J.   Sixty years of an agitator's life.   2 vols.   1892.
Hornby, Admiral Sir G. P.   By Mrs Fred Egerton.   1896.
Loftus, Lord Augustus.   Diplomatic Reminiscences.   4 vols.   1892–4.
Malmesbury, J. H. Harris, third Earl of.   Memoirs of an ex-Minister.   2 vols.
   1884.
Northcote, Sir Stafford, first Earl of Iddesleigh.   Life, Letters, and Diaries.   By
   Andrew Lang.   2 vols.   Edinburgh.   1891.
Rumbold, Sir H.   Recollections of a Diplomatist.   5 vols.   1902–5.
Russell, G. W. E.   Collections and recollections.   1898.
Rylands, P.   Correspondence and speeches.   With sketch of his career.   By
   L. G. Rylands.   2 vols.   Manchester.   1890.
Salisbury, Marquis of, Life of.   By H. D. Traill.   1890.
Selborne, R. P. Earl.   Memorials.   4 vols.   1896–8.
Shaftesbury, Seventh Earl of, Life of.   By E. Hodder.   3 vols.   1886.
Sherbrooke, Viscount, Life and Letters of.   By A. P. Martin.   2 vols.   1893.
Smith, William Henry, Life and times of.   By Sir H. Maxwell.   Edinburgh and
   London.   1894.
Tait, Archibald Campbell, Archbishop of Canterbury, Life of.   By R. T. Davidson
   and W. Benham.   1891.
Temple, Frederick, Archbishop of Canterbury, Memoirs of.   Edited by Archdeacon
   Sandford.   2 vols.   1906.
Victoria, Queen, Life of.   By Sidney Lee.   1904.
Wolseley, G. J. W., Viscount, Memoir of.   By C. R. Low.   2 vols.   1878.
—— Story of a soldier's life.   Westminster.   1903.

V.   COLLECTIONS OF SPEECHES, ETC.

Beaconsfield, Earl of.   Selected Speeches.   Ed. T. E. Kebbel.   2 vols.   1882.
Bright, John.   Speeches.   Ed. E. T. Rogers.   1879, 1892.
—— Public letters.   Coll. by H. J. Leech.   1885.
Chamberlain, Joseph.   Speeches.   Ed. H. W. Lucy.   1885.
—— Foreign and Colonial Speeches.   1897.
Gladstone, William Ewart.   Speeches and public addresses.   Vols. ix and x only
   published.   Ed. A. W. Hutton and H. J. Cohen.   1892–4.

VI. TREATISES.

Anson, Sir W. R.   Law and Custom of the Constitution.   2 vols.   Oxford. 1886–92.

Arnold-Forster, H. O.   The Army in 1906.   1906.

—— Military needs and military policy.   1909.

Booth, Charles.   Life and Labour of the people in London.   17 vols.   1889–1903.

Craik, Sir H.   The State in relation to education.   1896.

Dicey, A. V.   Law of the Constitution.   7th edn.   1908.

Giffen, Sir R.   Essays in finance.   2 vols.   1880–6.

—— The growth of capital.   1889.

—— Progress of the working classes.   1884.

Low, Sidney.   The governance of England.   1904.

Lowell, A. L.   The Government of England.   2 vols.   New York.   1903.

Williams, W. M. J.   The King's Revenue.   1908.

(See also Bibliographies to Chapters I, IV, XV, XVI, XX, XXIII.)

CHAPTER IV.

IRELAND.

Argyll, Duke of. The Bessborough Commission. 1881.
—— Irish Nationalism : an Appeal to History. 1893.
B., H. Letters from Ireland (reprinted from the New Ireland Review). Dublin.
    1902.
B., J. H. An Address to the Members of the Established Church in Ireland.
    1867.
Bagenal, P. H. Parnellism Unveiled. 1880.
—— Crime in Ireland. Dublin. 1882.
—— The American-Irish and their influence on Irish Politics. 1882.
—— The Priest in Politics. 1893.
Bailey, W. F. Ireland since the Famine. 1903.
Baldwin, Prof. Suggestions on the State of Ireland. Dublin. 1883.
Balfour, A. J.—Mr Balfour's tours in Connemara and Donegal. Dublin. 1890.
Ball, J. T. The Reformed Church of Ireland (1537–1889). Dublin. 1892.
Bateman, J. The great landowners of Great Britain and Ireland. 1878.
Baxter, R. Irish Tenant Right Question. 1869.
Becker, B. H. Disturbed Ireland (1880–1). 1881.
Blennerhasset, Sir R. Ireland 1837–87. In Ward, T. H., Reign of Victoria.
    Vol. II. 1887.
Bloodhound, the, our best ally in Ireland. 1882.
Bombay Civilian, a. The Land Question in Ireland viewed from an Indian Stand-
    point. 1870.
Bonn, M. J. Die englische Kolonisation in Irland. 2 vols. Berlin. 1906.
—— Modern Ireland and her agrarian Problem. (E. Tr.) 1906.
Bovet, M. A. de. Lettres d'Irlande. Paris. 1889.
—— Trois mois en Irlande. Paris, 1891. (E. Tr.) 1891.
Brabourne, Lord. Facts and fictions in Irish History. Edinburgh. 1886.
Brady, W. M. Essays on the English State Church in Ireland. 1869.
Bright, J. Letters on Home Rule. Birmingham. 1892.
Brodrick, G. C. The Irish Land Question : Past and Present. 1880.
Bullock-Hall, W. H. Gleanings in Ireland. 1883.
—— Gleanings in Ireland after the Land Acts. 1886.
Butt, I. Protection to Home Industry. Dublin. 1846.
—— The transfer of land by means of a judicial assurance. Dublin. 1857.
—— Fixity of Tenure : Heads of a suggested legislative enactment. Dublin. 1866.
—— The Irish People and the Irish Land. Dublin. 1867.
—— The Problem of Irish Education. 1875.
Buxton, S. C. The Irish Land Bill of 1870. 1881.
Caird, J. The Irish Land Question. 1869.
Cairnes, J. E. Political Essays. 1873.

Cant-Well, E. (pseud.). Ireland under the Land Act. 1882.

Carr, E. An Eviction in Ireland. Dublin. 1881.

Cavour, C. Benso di Count. Thoughts on Ireland (trans.). 1863.

Chamberlain, Joseph. Home Rule and the Irish Question. 1887.

—— Speeches on the Irish Question, 1887–90. 1890.

Clancy, J. J. A year of "Unionist" coercion. 1888.

Condon, E. O'M. The Irish in America. New York. 1887.

Cosby, D. S. A. The Irish Land Problem, and how to solve it. Dublin. 1901.

Coulter, H. West of Ireland. Dublin. 1862.

Couper, C. T. Trial of the Dynamitards, Dec. 1883. Edinburgh. 1884.

[Coyne, W. P.] Ireland industrial and agricultural. Dublin. 1902.

Craig, E. T. The Irish Land and Labour Question. 1882.

—— J. D. Real Pictures of Clerical Life in Ireland. 1903.

Daryl, P. Ireland's Disease. 1888.

Daunt, W. J. O'Neill. Eighty-five years of Irish History. 2 vols. 1886.

—— Essays on Ireland. Dublin. 1886.

Davitt, M. Leaves from a Prison Diary. 1883.

—— The Fall of Feudalism in Ireland, etc. 1904.

De-la-Poer-Beresford, J. H. The Beresford Commission. 1881.

Dennis, R. Industrial Ireland. 1887.

Devoy, J. The Land of Eire: the Irish Land League. 3 pts. New York. 1882.

Dicey, A. V. England's Case against Home Rule. 1886.

—— Letters on Unionist Delusions. 1887.

—— Why England maintains the Union. 1887.

—— A Leap in the Dark. 1893.

Dickinson, E. M. A Patriot's Mistake: personal recollections of the Parnell family. Dublin. 1905.

Disestablishment and Disendowment the first steps towards Revolution, etc. 1869.

Donegal, The Condition of (reprinted from the Times). 1889.

Doyle, J. P. Old Ireland made New Ireland. 1881.

Dublin Review, the. Dublin. 1863–1905.

Dufferin, Lord (Marquis of Dufferin and Ava). Irish Emigration and the Tenure of Land in Ireland. 1867.

Duffy, Sir C. G. How Ireland ought to receive the Land Act. Dublin. 1881.

—— League of North and South 1850–4. 1886.

—— The revival of Irish Literature. 1894.

Dun, F. Landlords and tenants in Ireland. 1881.

English Liberal. The Truth about Ireland. 1884.

Essays on the Irish Church. By Clergymen of the Established Church in Ireland (J. Byrne, A. W. Edwards, W. Anderson, A. T. Lee). Oxford and London. 1866.

Ferguson, W. D. The Tenure and Improvement of Land in Ireland. Dublin. 1851.

Fitzgibbon, G. The Land difficulty in Ireland. 1869.

Floredice, W. H. A Month among the mere Irish. 1881.

Forty years in the Church of Ireland; or the Pastor, the Parish and its People from 1840–80. 1882.

Fournier, P. La Question agraire en Irlande. Paris. 1882.

Fox, J. A. Reports on the condition of the peasantry of Mayo during the Famine Crisis of 1880. Dublin. 1880.

Freeman's Journal, the. Dublin. 1863–1905.

—— Church Commission. Dublin. 1868.

[Gamble, Judge.] "Political Economy"—The Irish Landlord and his Accusers. Dublin. 1882.

George, H. The Irish Land Question. New York. 1881.

Gibbs, F. W.   English Law and Irish Tenure.   1870.

Gladstone, W. E.   Chapter of Autobiography.   1868.

Goddard, E.   Dreams for Ireland.   Dublin.   1903.

Godkin, J.   Ireland and her Churches.   1867.

—— The Land War in Ireland.   1870.

—— Education in Ireland.   Dublin.   1862.

Green, J. B.   Notes on Ireland.   1886.

Gregg, J., Bishop of Cork.   Charge to the Clergy of Cork, Cloyne and Ross. Dublin.   1867.

Gregory, Lady.   Ideals in Ireland.   1901.

Grey, Earl.   Ireland : Causes of its present condition.   1888.

Griersen, F.   The Celtic Temperament and other Essays.   Dublin.   1901.

Grimshaw, T. W.   Facts and Figures about Ireland.   2 pts.   Dublin.   1893.

Guilbaud de Lavergne, L. G. L.   Essai sur l'économie rurale de l'Irlande.   Paris. 1882.

Gwynn, S. L.   To-day and to-morrow in Ireland.   Dublin.   1903.

H.   The new "Pacata Hibernia," etc.   1881.

H., W. T.   The Encumbered Estates of Ireland.   1850.

Hamilton, J.   Sixty years' experience as an Irish landlord.   1894.

Harris, A.   Revival of industries in Ireland.   1888.

Hart, Mrs E. A.   Cottage Industries of Ireland.   1887.

Healy, T. M.   Why there is an Irish Land Question.   Dublin.   1881.

Hector, J.   Redemption of the Land.   1881.

Hervé, E.   La Crise irlandaise.   Paris.   1885.

Hill, Lord G. A.   Facts from Gweedore.   1887.

Hodgkin, H.   Irish Land Legislation and the Royal Commission.   1881.

Hogan, J. F.   The Irish in Australia.   1887.

Holmes, F. M.   History of the Irish Land League.   1882.

Hopkins, T.   Kilmainham Memories.   1896.

Houston, E. C.   "Number One's" (i.e. P. J. P. Tynan's) Book.   1894.

Hurlbert, W. H.   Ireland under Coercion.   2 vols.   Edinburgh.   1888.

Hussey, S. M.   The Reminiscences of an Irish Land Agent.   1904.

Ireland and the English Catholics...with some account of...the appointment of Monsignor Persico (reprinted from the Freeman's Journal).   1887.

Ireland and the Irish.   By a member of the University of Dublin.   Dublin.   1881.

Ireland and the Holy See: a Retrospect 1866–83.   Rome.   1883.

Ireland from one or two neglected points of view.   1888.

Ireland.   The Land Question.   Dublin.   1880–1.   [Pamphlets issued by the Irish Land Committee.]

Ireland, What she once was and what she might be yet.   1887.

Irish Churchman.   The Church Establishment in Ireland.   1868.

Irish Landlord.   Ireland : her landlords, her people and their homes.   Dublin. 1860.

Irish Land Question, the, impartially considered.   1870.

Irish Mechanic.   My Country and her Cause.   Belfast.   1882.

Irish Merchant.   The Present and Future of Ireland as the Cattle Farm of England. Dublin.   1865.

Irish Nationality in 1870.   By a Protestant Celt.   Dublin.   1870.

Irish Problem, the, and England's Difficulty.   A history of the great Irish Question.   1886.

Irish Problem, the, and how to solve it.   An historical and critical review, etc. 1881.

Irish Problem, the, as viewed by a Citizen of the Empire.   1887.

Irish Question, the.   [Pamphlets issued by the Irish Press Agency.]   1886, etc.

Irish Seditions 1793–1830. 1883.

Irish Times, the. Dublin. 1868–1905.

Irish Unionist Alliance publications. Dublin. 1891, etc.

James, H. (Lord James of Hereford). The Work of the Irish League. 1890.

Jephson, H. L. Notes on Irish Questions. Dublin. 1870.

Keans, H. S. W. B. Yeats and the Irish Literary Revival. (Contemp. Men of Letters Series.) 1904.

Kennedy, T. History of the Irish Protest against over-taxation 1853–97. Dublin. 1897.

Kervyn de Volkakesbeke, P. A. C. La Lutte de l'Irlande. Lille. 1891.

Killen, J. B. The Irish Question as viewed by one hundred eminent statesmen. New York. 1886.

—— W. D. Ecclesiastical History of Ireland. 1875.

Kinahan, G. H. A Handbook on the reclamation of waste lands in Ireland. Dublin. 1882.

—— Economic Geology of Ireland. Dublin. 1889.

King, D. B. The Irish Question. New York. 1882.

Kinnear, J. B. Ireland in 1881. 1881.

[Lambert, H.] A Memoir of Ireland in 1850. Dublin. 1851.

Landlordism in Ireland, with its difficulties, etc. 1853.

Lavelle, Rev. P. The Irish Landlord since the Revolution. Dublin. 1870.

Le Caron, H. Twenty-five years in the Secret Service. 1892.

Lecky, W. E. H. Democracy and Liberty. 2 vols. 1896.

Lee, A. T. Facts respecting the present state of the Church in Ireland. 1868.

Leech, H. B. 1848 and 1887: Continuity of the Irish revolutionary movement. 1887.

Le Fanu, W. R. Seventy years of Irish Life. 1896.

Lefevre, G. J. S. English and Irish Land questions. 1881.

—— Incidents of Coercion 1882 and 1888. 1888.

—— Irish Members and English gaolers. 1889.

—— Combination and Coercion in Ireland. 1890.

Letters from Donegal 1886. 1886.

Letters from Ireland 1886. By the Special Correspondent of the Times. 1887.

Lloyd, C. D. C. Ireland under the Land League. Edinburgh. 1892.

Locker-Lampson, G. A consideration of the State of Ireland in the Nineteenth Century. 1907.

London Clergyman. The Church in Ireland. 1869.

Longfield, M. (Judge). Land tenure in Ireland. (Cobden Club.) 1870–81.

Lough, T. England's Wealth Ireland's Poverty. 1897.

Lucy, H. W. A Diary of two Parliaments. 1886.

—— Diary of the Home Rule Parliament 1892–5. 1896.

Mabelan, D. Home Rule and Imperial Unity. 1886.

Macaulay, J. Ireland in 1872. 1873.

MacCarthy, J. G. Irish Land Question plainly stated and answered. 1870.

—— A Plea for the Home Government of Ireland. 1871.

—— Five years in Ireland: 1895–1900. Dublin. 1903.

—— J. H. Ireland since the Union. 1887.

—— M. J. F. Mr Balfour's rule in Ireland. Dublin. 1891.

—— Priests and People in Ireland. Dublin. 1901.

MacDowall, A. B. Facts about Ireland. 1888.

MacKnight, T. Ulster as it is; or 28 years' experience as an Irish Editor. 1896

Maguire, J. F. The Irish in America. 1868.

—— T. Reasons why Britons should oppose Home Rule. Dublin. 1886.

—— England's Duty to Ireland. Dublin. 1886.

Mahoney, J. S. C. S. Parnell and what he has achieved. New York. 1886.

Malone, S. Tenant Wrong illustrated in a Nutshell. 1867.

Maudet-Grancey, E. de. Chez Paddy. Paris. 1887.

McCann, J. Some Facts, Figures and Factors in the Economic and Financial Problem of Ireland to-day. Dublin. 1902.

—— The Irish Problem. Some Pleas for the preservation of the Irish Peasantry. Dublin. 1902.

McGrath, T. Pictures from Ireland, chiefly on the Landlord Question. 1880.

Mill, J. S. England and Ireland. 1868.

—— Chapters and Speeches on the Irish Land Question. 1870.

Modern Ireland : its vital questions, etc. By an Ulsterman. 1868.

Molinari, G. de. L'Irlande. La Canada. Jersey. Paris. 1881.

Moore, G. Parnell and his Island. 1887.

Moran, Cardinal P. F. The Pastoral Letters and other writings of Cardinal Cullen. 3 vols. Dublin. 1882.

Morison, J. Cotter. Irish Grievances. 1868.

Morley, J. Ireland's Rights and England's Duties. 1868.

—— Life of Gladstone. 3 vols. 1903.

Morris, W. O'Connor. Letters on the Land Question of Ireland (reprinted from the Times). 1870.

—— Memories and Thoughts of a Life. 1895.

—— Ireland 1798–1898. 1898.

—— Present Irish Question. 1901.

Muddick, J. E. The Crime of the Century. The life-story of R. Pigott. 1904.

Murphy, J. N. Ireland : Industrial, Political and Social. 1870.

Murray, A. E. History of the Commercial and Financial Relations between England and Ireland. 1903.

Mysteries of Ireland (The), giving an…account of Irish Secret Societies from…1798 to…1883, etc. 1884.

Nemours-Godré, L. La Bataille du Home Rule. Paris. 1892.

Norman, H. Bodyke : chapter in the history of Irish landlordism. 1887.

O'Brien, J. T. (Bishop of Ossory). The Church in Ireland. 1866.

—— The Case of the Established Church in Ireland. 1868.

—— The Disestablishment and Disendowment of the Irish Church…considered. 1869.

—— R. B. The parliamentary history of the Irish Land Question. 1880.

—— The Irish Land Question and English public opinion. 1881.

—— Fifty years of Concessions to Ireland 1831–81. 1883.

—— Irish Wrongs and English Remedies. 1887.

—— The Home Ruler's Manual. 1890.

—— Life of Charles Stewart Parnell. 2 vols. 1898.

—— Life of Lord Russell of Killowen. 1901.

—— Irish Memories. 1904.

—— W. P. The Great Famine in Ireland and a retrospect of the fifty years 1845–95. 1896.

O'Connor, T. P. Gladstone, Parnell and the Irish Struggle. Philadelphia. 1888.

—— The Parnell Movement. 1889.

O'Donnell, F. H. Parnellism and Crime (reprints from the Times). 1888.

—— The Ruin of Education in Ireland. 1902.

—— History of the Irish Parliamentary party. 1910.

O'Gara, A. P. A. The Green Republic. 1902.

O'Leary, J. Recollections of Fenians and Fenianism. 1896.

Oliver, R. Unnoticed Analogies. A talk on the Irish Question. 1888.

O'Reilly, B. Life of Archbishop MacHale. 2 vols. New York. 1890.

O'Shaugnessy, R. Local Government and taxation in Ireland. (Cobden Club.) 1882.

Oulton, R. The Repeal of the Union. 1868.

Over-Taxation, the, of Ireland : a record of the financial relations between Great Britain and Ireland. Dublin. 1897.

Parnellite Split, the. (Reprinted from the Times.) 1891.

Particulars and conditions of the sales by public auction of estates in Ireland pursuant to the orders of the Court...for the sale of Incumbered Estates, etc. 154 vols. Dublin. 1851–76.

Pascal, G. de. La Question irlandaise. 2 pts. Lyons. 1889.

Past, the, and the Future of Ireland, indicated by its educational history, etc. 1850.

Paterson, R. Mercantile Ireland *versus* Home Rule. Belfast. 1888.

Peasant Proprietors in Ireland.... By the Times Commissioner. 1888.

Peel, Sir Robert. Papers. Ed. C. S. Parker. 3 vols. 1889.

Pfister, H. von. England und Irland. Berlin. 1886.

Philp, K. "Boycotting," or avenging Ireland's wrongs. New York. 1881.

Pigott, R. Personal Recollections of an Irish Journalist. Dublin. 1882.

Pim, J. Ireland and the Imperial Parliament. Dublin. 1871.

Plunkett, H. C. Help for self-help in Ireland. Dublin. 1898.

—— The New Movement in Ireland. Dublin. 1898.

—— Ireland in the New Century. 1903.

Politikos (pseudon.). La Fine di un Agitatore irlandese, C. S. Parnell. Rome. 1891.

Powell, Sir G. S. Baden. The Truth about Home Rule. Edinburgh. 1888.

—— The saving of Ireland, industrial and financial. Edinburgh. 1898.

Pressensé, F. de. L'Irlande et l'Angleterre depuis l'acte d'union 1800–88. Paris. 1889.

Proceedings of the Dublin Mansion House Relief Committee, 1880. Dublin. 1881.

Protestant Celt. A scheme of University Education in Ireland. 1872.

Queen's Enemies, the, in America at Chicago. 1886.

Radical Cure, the, for Ireland...a new Plantation. Edinburgh and London. 1890.

Redmond, J. E. Historical and Political Addresses 1883–97. Dublin. 1898.

Report of H.M.'s Commissioners of the Revenues and Condition of the Established Church of Ireland. Dublin. 1868.

Rome and Fenianism : the Pope's anti-Parnellite Circular. 1883.

Russell, C. (Lord). New Views on Ireland. Dublin. 1880.

—— T. W. Ireland and the Empire. A Review 1800–1900. 1901.

—— England's Opportunity in Ireland. Dublin. 1902.

Rutherford, J. The Fenian Conspiracy. 2 vols. 1877.

Ryan, W. P. The Irish Literary revival. 1894.

S., T. E. The Rights of Ireland to political freedom, etc. 1879.

Saint-Thomas, H. Le Rêve de Paddy. Paris. 1886.

Schindler, D. En Irlande. Paris. 1903.

Scully, V. Occupying ownership in Ireland. 1881.

Shaw, Sir C. The abuses of the Irish Church verified by historical records. 1866.

Simond, C. Parnell et l'Irlande. Paris. 1891.

Smith, G. B. Life and Speeches of John Bright. 2 vols. 1881.

—— R. J. Ireland's Renaissance. Dublin. 1903.

Special Commission, Report of the Proceedings of the. 4 vols. 1890.

Stead, W. T. The discrowned King of Ireland, C. S. Parnell. 1891.

Stein, L. von. Die drei Fragen des Grundbesitzes. Die irische Frage. Stuttgart. 1881.

Sullivan, A. M. New Ireland : Political Sketches, etc. Glasgow. 1882.

—— T. D. Speeches from the clock. Dublin. 1887.

Sullivan, T. D.   Recollections of troubled Times 1848–1903.   Dublin.   1905.

Thébaud, A. J.   Ireland past and present.   New York.   1901.

Thornton, W. T.   Plea for Peasant Proprietors with the outlines of a plan for their establishment in Ireland.   1848.   Reprinted.   1874.

Trench, R. C., Archbishop of Dublin.   Letters and Memorials.   2 vols   1888.

Trevelyan, C. E.   The Irish Crisis.   1880.

Tuke, J. H.   Irish Distress and its Remedies.   1880.

Two Centuries of Irish History 1691–1870.   1888.   2nd edn. enlarged.   1907.

Tynan, P. J. P.   Irish national Invincibles.   New York.   1894.

United Irishman, the.   Dublin.   1868–1905.

Verschoyle, H.   A charge delivered to the clergy of the united Diocese of Kilmore, Elphin and Ardagh.   1867.

W., G.   Letters from a stranger in Ireland.   1885.

Walpole, Sir Spencer.   The History of Twenty-five Years.   Vols. i and ii (1856–70).   1904.

Walsh, J., Archbishop.   The Irish University Question.   Dublin.   1897.

—— R. F.   Memorial volume to C. S. Parnell.   3 pts.   New York.   1892.

Westcombe, W. H.   The Irish Question.   1886.

Young, F.   Ireland at the Cross Roads.   1904.

CHAPTER V.

THE THIRD REPUBLIC.

I. DOCUMENTS.

A. Collections of Documents, Speeches, etc.

Almanach national. Annuaire de la République française. From 1871.
Bulletin des lois.
Crisenoy, J. de. Annales des assemblées départementales. 20 vols. Paris. From 1887.
Journal officiel de la République française. (Comptes Rendus of the Assemblies, and Reports.)

Bert, P. Discours parlementaires, 1872–81. Paris. 1881.
Challemel-Lacour, P. Œuvres oratoires. Ed. J. Reinach. Paris. 1897.
Daniel, Lebon André. L'Année Politique. Paris. From 1874.
Ferry, J. Discours et opinions. Ed. P. Robiquet. Paris. 1893–8.
Floquet, C. Discours et opinions. Paris. 1896.
Gambetta, L. Discours et plaidoyers politiques. Ed. J. Reinach. 11 vols. Paris. 1881–5.
Hélie, F. Les Constitutions de la France. Paris. 1879.
Jaurès, J. Discours parlementaires. Paris. 1903.
Mathiez and Cahen. Les lois françaises, avec documents politiques. Paris. 1906.
Monnier, H. and Duguit. Les Constitutions françaises depuis 1789. 2nd edn. Paris. 1907.
Mun, Comte A. de. Discours et écrits divers. Ed. J. Grandmaison. 5 vols. Paris. 1898.
Thiers, L. A. Discours parlementaires. Ed. M. Calmon. 16 vols. Paris. 1879–89.
Vialatte, A. La vie politique dans les Deux Mondes. 2 vols. Paris. 1908, etc.
Waldeck Rousseau, P. M. R. Discours parlementaires et politiques. 2 vols. Paris. 1879–99.
Wallier, R. Le Vingtième siècle politique. Paris. 1901, etc.

Principal Journals.—Monarchist: le Français, l'Univers, la Gazette de France, le Petit moniteur universel, le Soleil, le Gaulois; Catholic: la Libre Parole, l'Éclair, la Croix; Republican, Left Centre or Opportunist: Journal des Débats, le Temps, la République Française, le Figaro, le xixe Siècle; Radical and Socialist-Radical: le Siècle, le Rappel, l'Aurore, le Radical, la Lanterne, l'Action; Bonapartist or Nationalist: le Pays, la Patrie, la Presse, l'Écho de Paris; Popular or for news only: le Petit Journal, le Petit Parisien, le Matin, le Journal; Socialist: la Petite République, l'Humanité, le Cri du peuple, la Guerre sociale. (See Avenel. Annuaire de la Presse française.)

Reviews : des Deux Mondes, de Paris, Revue Bleue, Revue politique et Parlementaire, Nouvelle Revue, Grande Revue, le Correspondant, la Revue hebdomadaire, Revue Socialiste.

B. LETTERS AND MEMOIRS.

Bardoux, A. Dix années de vie politique. Paris. 1882.

Blanc, L. La Constitution de 1875. Paris. 1883.

Brisson, H. Souvenirs. Paris. 1908.

Callet, A., Membre de l'Assemblée nationale. Les origines de la Troisième République. Paris. 1889.

—— Les responsabilités. Paris. 1895.

Cassagnac, P. de. Histoire de la Troisième République. Paris. 1875.

Chambord, Comte de. Écrits politiques et correspondance, de 1841 à 1879. Paris. 1880.

Chesnelong, P. C. La campagne monarchiste d'octobre 1873. Paris. 1895.

Clamageran, J. J. Correspondance. Paris. 1906.

Delafosse, J. Vingt ans au Parlement. Paris. 1899.

Delpit, M. Journal et correspondance. Paris. 1897.

Denormandie, E. Notes et Souvenirs. Paris. 1896.

Dreux Brézé, Marquis de. Notes et Souvenirs pour servir à l'histoire du Parti royaliste. 4th edn. Paris. 1899.

Du Barail, General F. C. Mes Souvenirs. 3 vols. Paris. 1905.

Ducrot, General. Mémoires sur les projets de Restauration monarchique. Paris. 1909.

Falloux, Comte F. A. P. de. Mémoires d'un royaliste. 2 vols. Paris. 1888.

Fidus (Eugène Balleyguier dit Loudun). Journal. 4 vols. Paris. 1888, 1890.

—— La mort du Prince Impérial. Paris. 1887.

Gambetta, L. Souvenirs publiés par Bertol-Graivil. Paris. 1883.

—— Lettres ; in Revue de Paris. December, 1906 and January, 1907.

Gontaut-Biron, Vicomte E. de. Mémoires. 2 vols. Ed. A. Dreux. Paris. 1906, 1907.

Harcourt, Emmanuel de. Souvenirs inédits.

Lamy, É. Quatre ans de provisoire de 1871 à 1875. Paris. 1876.

Lefèvre, Pontalis, A. L'Assemblée nationale et M. Thiers. In the Correspondant, 1879.

Lenglé, P. Le neveu de Bonaparte, ou le parti bonapartiste et le prince Napoléon, de 1879 à 1893. Paris. 1893.

Littré, F. L'établissement de la Troisième République. Paris. 1880.

Marcère, E. de. Entretiens et Souvenirs Politiques. 2 vols. Paris. 1894.

—— Le seize mai et la fin du Septennat. Paris. 1900.

—— L'assemblée nationale, le gouvernement de Thiers. Paris. 1904.

Margerie, de. Pages d'Histoire Contemporaine. Paris. 1873.

Meaux, Vicomte C. de. Souvenirs Politiques. Paris. 1904.

Périn, G. Discours Politiques et Notes de Voyage. Paris. 1907.

Richard, R. Le bonapartisme sous la troisième République. Paris.

Simon, J. Le gouvernement de M. Thiers. 2 vols. Paris. 1878.

—— Le soir de ma journée. Paris. 1895.

Taine, H. Correspondance. Vols. III and IV. Paris. 1905.

Target, P. L. Dix ans de République. Paris. 1889.

Thiers, A. Notes et Souvenirs de 1870 à 1873. Paris. 1903.

—— Occupation et libération du territoire. (Correspondance.) 2 vols. Paris. 1903.

Vinols de Montfleury, Baron J. G. Mémoires d'un Membre de l'assemblée nationale. Paris. 1883.

II. GENERAL HISTORIES.

Benoit, L. E.   Histoire de quinze ans, 1870–85.   Paris.   1886.
Berthezène, A.   Histoire de cent ans.   La Basse République, 1870–90.   Paris.   1900.
Coubertin, P. de.   L'évolution française sous la Troisième République.   1896.   Eng.
    trans. by T. Hapgood, with preface by Albert Shaw.   London.   1898.
Courcelle-Seneuil, J. G.   La Société moderne.   Paris.   1892.
Denis, S.   Histoire contemporaine.   4 vols.   Paris.   1902.
Duret, C.   Histoire de France de 1870 à 1873.   2 vols.   Paris.   1901.
Ferry, J.   La Troisième République.   In Rev. de Paris, 1897, p. 1.
Goyau, G.   Patriotisme et humanitarisme.   Essai d'histoire contemporaine.   Paris.
    1901.
Guillon, E.   Quatre-vingt ans d'Histoire nationale.   Paris.   1891.
Hanotaux, G.   Histoire de la France contemporaine.   4 vols.   Eng. trans. by
    C. Tarver.   Westminster.   1903.
Latimer, E.   France in the xixth Century, 1830–90.   1906.
Lavisse, E. and Rambaud, A.   Histoire Générale.   T. xii (France).   1898.
Martin, H.   Histoire contemporaine de la France.   Paris.   1885.
Muel, Léon.   Gouvernements, ministères et constitutions de la France jusqu'en 1890.
    Paris.   1890.
——   Précis historique des assemblées parlementaires jusqu'en 1895.   Paris.   1896.
Rambaud, A.   Histoire de la civilisation contemporaine en France.   1888.
Teste, L.   Les monarchistes sous la Troisième République.   Paris.   1891.
Vogel, K.   Die dritte französische Republik bis 1895.   Stuttgart.   1895.
Weill, G.   Histoire du parti républicain en France.   Paris.   1900.
Zevort, E.   La France sous le régime du Suffrage Universel.   Paris.   1894.
——   Histoire de la Troisième République.   To the death of President Carnot.
    4 vols.   Paris.   1901.

III. BIOGRAPHIES.

Aumale, Duc de.   By E. Daudet.   Paris.   1898.
Chambord, Comte de.   By Dubosc de Pesquidoux.   Paris.   1887.
——   ou Henri de France.   By H. de Pène.   Paris.   1884.
——   Histoire d'Henri V.   By A. de Saint-Albin.   Paris.   1874.
Dufaure, sa vie et ses discours.   By G. Picot.   Paris.   1883.
Ferry, Jules.   By A. Rambaud.   Paris.   1903.
Gambetta.   Sa vie, ses idées politiques.   By Neucastel.   Paris.   1885.
——   à l'Assemblée.   By E. de Pressensé.   In Revue Bleue.   1883.
——   By Joseph Reinach.   Paris.   1885.
——   Souvenirs anecdotiques.   By A. Tournier.   1893.
——   inconnu.   By A. Lavertujon.   Paris.   1909.
Grèvy, Jules.   By Barboux.   Paris.
Paris, Comte de.   By le Marquis de Flers.   Paris.   1888.
Say, Léon.   Sa vie, ses œuvres.   By Michel.   2 vols.   Paris.   1899.
Simon, Jules.   By Léon Séché.   Paris.   1887.
Thiers, M., ou cinquante années d'Histoire contemporaine.   By C. de Mazade.   Paris.
    1884.
——   A.   By P. de Rémusat.   Paris.   1889.
Waldeck-Rousseau.   By E. Charles.   Paris.   1902.
——   By H. Leyret.   2 vols.   Paris.   1906.

IV. SPECIAL WORKS.

A. Political.

Broglie, Albert Duc de.   Histoire et Politique: Étude sur la Constitution de 1875.
Paris.   1897.

Castellane, Marquis de.   Le Dernier Essai de restauration monarchique de 1873.
In the Nouvelle Revue.   1895.

Daudet, E.   Souvenirs de la Présidence du Maréchal MacMahon.   Paris.   1879.
—— La vérité sur l'essai de Restauration monarchiste en 1873.   Paris.   1873.

Doniol, H.   La libération du territoire.   Paris.   1897.

Dufeuille, E.   Les monarchistes et la République.   In the Correspondant, 1883,
1884.

Duguet, E.   Les députés et les cahiers électoraux de 1889.   Paris.   1890.

Favre, L.   Histoire politique de l'année 1877.   2 vols.   Paris.   1880.

Germain-Cornille, R.   Les cahiers électoraux de 1881.   Paris.   1882.

Grenville Murray, E. C.   The men of the Septennat.   1876.

Hippeau, E.   Histoire diplomatique de la Troisième République.   Paris.   1888.

Lucas, A.   Précis historique de l'affaire du Panama.   Paris.   1893.

Mermeix, G. T.   Les Coulisses du Boulangisme.   Paris.   1890.

Procès du Général Boulanger devant la Haute Cour.   Paris.   1889.

Reinach, J.   Le Ministère Gambetta.   Paris.   1884.
—— La Politique opportuniste.   Paris.   1890.
—— Histoire de l'affaire Dreyfus.   6 vols.   Paris.   1902–8.

Verly, A.   Le général Boulanger et la Conspiration monarchique.   Paris.   1893.

B. Social.

Associations professionnelles ouvrières, publiés par l'Office du travail.   Vol. I.   1899.

Bourdeau, J.   L'évolution du Socialisme.   Paris.   1901.

Chailley-Bert, J. and Fontaine, A.   Lois Sociales, 1895 to 1909.   Paris.   1909.

Eichthal, E. de.   Socialisme, communisme, et collectivisme.   2nd edn.   1901.

Guesde, J.   Quatre ans de lutte de Classe à la Chambre.   Paris.   1901.

Halévy, D.   Essai sur le mouvement ouvrier français.   Paris.   1901.

Jaurès, J.   Études Socialistes.   Paris.   1901.

Lagardelle.   L'évolution des syndicats ouvriers en France.   Paris.   1901.

Lavy, A.   L'œuvre de Millerand.   Paris.   1902.

Louis, P.   Histoire du Socialisme français.   Paris.   1901.
—— Les étapes du Socialisme.   Paris.   1904.

Pelloutier, F. L. E.   Histoire des Bourses du travail.   Paris.   1902.

Seilhac, L. de.   Le monde socialiste.   Paris.   1904.
—— Les congrès ouvriers en France, 1876–97.   Paris.   1899.

Skarzinski, Count L.   Le progrès social à la fin du XIXe siècle.   Paris.   1901.

Waldeck-Rousseau, P. M.   Questions Sociales.   Paris.   1900.

Weill, G.   Histoire du Mouvement Social en France.   Paris.   1904.

C. Religious Affairs.

Debidour, A.   L'Église catholique et l'État de 1870 à 1906.   2 vols.   Paris.   1906.
(Based upon the French Archives and containing a very complete bibliography.)

Doumergue, É.   Essai sur l'histoire du culte réformé.   Paris.   1890.

Felice, G. de, and Bonifas, F.   Histoire des protestants de France.   6th edn.
Toulouse.   1875.

Législation des cultes protestants, 1787–1887.   Paris.   1887.

Mater, A.   La politique religieuse de la République française.   Paris.   1909.
—— Les textes de la politique française en matière ecclésiastique, 1905–8.   Paris.
    1909.

D.   Finances.

Amagat, A. L.   Les finances françaises sous l'Assemblée nationale et les Chambres
    républicaines, 1883 et 1889.   2 vols.   Paris.
Bodet, M.   Les finances françaises de 1870 à 1878.   2 vols.   Paris.   1881.
Chirac, A.   L'agiotage de 1870 à 1886.   Paris.   1887.
Clarigny, A. C.   Les finances de la France de 1870 à 1890.   Paris.   1890.
Nicolas, C.   Les budgets de la France depuis le commencement du xixe siècle.
    Tableaux.   Paris.   1883.
Sudre, C.   Les finances de la France au xixe siècle.   2 vols.   Paris.   1883.
Wührer.   Histoire de la Dette publique en France.   2 vols.   Paris.   1886.

E.   Education and Public Instruction.

Beauchamp, A. de.   Recueil des lois et règlements sur l'Enseignement Supérieur,
    1789–1898.   5 vols.   Paris.   1898.
Bourgeois, É.   L'enseignement secondaire et le vœu de la France.   Paris.   1900.
Duplan, E.   L'enseignement primaire public, 1877–88.   2 vols.   Paris.   1891.
Durand, A.   La législation des écoles maternelles et des écoles primaires.   Paris.
    1882.
Duruy, A.   L'instruction publique et la démocratie, 1879–86.   Paris.   1889.
Gréard, V. C. O.   La législation de l'Enseignement primaire en France depuis 1789.
    7 vols.   Paris.   1890–1902.
Liard, L.   L'Enseignement Supérieur en France de 1789 à 1893.   2 vols.   Paris.
    1889–94.
Macé, V.   La ligue de l'Enseignement.   Paris.   1890.
Spuller, S. E.   Au ministère de l'Instruction Publique, 1887 et 1893.   2 vols.   Paris.
    1888, 1895.

F.   Economic Development.

Annuaire Statistique de la France.   Yearly.   Paris.
Statistique agricole de la France de 1892.   Paris.   1897.
Résultats statistiques du recensement de la population de 1901.   1906.
Résultats statistiques du recensement des industries et professions du 29 mars, 1896.
    Paris.   1901.

Baudrillart, H. J. L.   Les populations agricoles de la France.   3 vols.   1885, 1891.
Henry, A. and de Lavergne.   La richesse de la France.   Paris.   1909.
Léon, P.   Fleuves, canaux, chemins de fer.   Paris.   1903.
Les forces productives de la France.   Ouvrage collectif.   Paris.   1908.
Levasseur, E.   La population française depuis 1789.   3 vols.   Paris.   1889–92.
—— Questions ouvrières et industrielles sous la Troisième République.   Paris.   1906.
Luçay, Comte H. de.   Les vœux des agriculteurs de France, 1868–94.
Noel, O.   Histoire du commerce extérieur de la France depuis la Révolution.
    Paris.   1879.
—— La Banque de France.   Paris.   1891.

Picard, A. Les chemins de fer français. 6 vols. Paris. 1883–4.
—— Rapport général sur l'Exposition de 1889. 10 vols. Followed by the reports of the Jury of the same Exhibition. 19 vols. 1890.
—— le Bilan d'un Siècle. General report on the Exhibition of 1900. Followed by the reports of the Jury of the Exhibition of 1900. Paris. 1902.
Roux, C. Notre Marine Marchande. Paris. 1901.
Viger, L. Deux années au Ministère de l'Agriculture. Paris. 1895.
Zolla, D. La crise agricole. Paris. 1902.

G. Colonies.

Statistiques coloniales, published yearly by the Colonial Ministry.
Publications of the Ministry on the occasion of the Exposition universelle of 1900.

Amand, A. A. and Méray, H. Organisation administrative, politique et judiciaire des colonies. Paris. 1900.
Chailley-Bert, J. Dix ans de politique coloniale. Paris. 1902.
Dorvault, F. and Imbart de La Tour, J. La propriété et la main d'œuvre aux colonies. Paris. 1900.
Dubois, M. and Ferrier, A. Un Siècle d'Expansion coloniale. Paris. 1900.
Froidevaux, H. L'Instruction Publique aux colonies.
Guy, C. Mise en valeur du domaine colonial. Paris. 1900.
Lecomte, H. Agriculture aux colonies. Paris. 1900.
Les colonies françaises. Encyclopédie sous la direction de Maxime Petit. 2 vols. Paris. 1903. (With the most complete bibliography of the subject.)
Lorin, H. La France, puissance coloniale. Paris. 1906.
Rouard de Card, E. Les territoires africains et les conventions franco-anglaises de 1783 à 1899. Paris. 1901.

CHAPTER VI.

THE GERMAN EMPIRE.

I. BIBLIOGRAPHIES.

Allgemeine Deutsche Biographie, hrsg. von der Historischen Kommission bei der K. Akademie der Wissenschaften zu München. Ed. by R. von Liliencron and F. X. von Wegele. Vols. I–LV. Supplements, to 1899. Leipzig. 1875–1910.

Biographisches Jahrbuch und Deutscher Nekrolog, hrsg. von A. Bettelheim. (Periodical.) Vols. I–XII. Berlin. 1898 sqq.

Brase, M. Die deutsche Koloniallitteratur von 1884–95. Berlin. 1897. Supplements every year in Zeitschrift für Kolonialpolitik.

Dahlmann-Waitz. Quellenkunde der deutschen Geschichte. 7th edn., by E. Brandenburg. Leipzig. 1906.

Jahresberichte der Geschichtswissenschaft. (From 1878.) (Periodical.) Vols. I–XXX. Berlin. 1880 sqq.

Singer, A. Bismarck in der Litteratur. Würzburg. 1909.

II. CONTEMPORARY AUTHORITIES.

Aegidi, L. K. and Klauhold, A. Das Staatsarchiv. Sammlung der officiellen Aktenstücke zur Geschichte der Gegenwart. (Periodical.) Hamburg and Leipzig. 1861 sqq.

Annalen des Deutschen Reiches für Gesetzgebung, Verwaltung und Statistik, herausgegeben von G. Hirth und M. von Seydel. (Periodical.) Leipzig. 1871–81. Munich. 1882 sqq.

Dokumente zur Geschichte der Wirtschaftspolitik in Preussen und im Deutschen Reich. 5 vols. Berlin. 1889-91. (Vols. I, III, V: H. von Poschinger, Fürst Bismarck als Volkswirt. Vols. II, IV: Aktenstücke zur Wirtschaftspolitik des Fürsten Bismarck.)

Schulthess, H. Europäischer Geschichtskalender. Jahrgang 1–49. (Periodical.) From 1897, by G. Roloff. Nördlingen, Munich. 1861 sqq.

Specht, F. and P. Schwabe. Die Reichstagswahlen 1867-1903. Eine Statistik nebst den Programmen der Parteien. 2nd edn. Berlin. 1904.

Statistik des Deutschen Reichs. Herausgegeben vom kaiserlichen statistischen Amt. Vols. I–LXIII. Berlin. 1873–83. New series. Vols. I–CLVII. Berlin. 1884 sqq.

Stenographische Berichte über die Verhandlungen des deutschen Reichstages, nebst Sammlung sämtlicher Drucksachen des Deutschen Reichstages. Berlin. 1871 sqq.

Wippermann, K. Deutscher Geschichtskalender für 1885 sqq. Leipzig. 1886 sqq.

BISMARCK.

Bismarck, Fürst Otto von. Gedanken und Erinnerungen. 2 vols. Stuttgart. 1898. Pop. edn. 1905. Anhang zu den Gedanken und Erinnerungen. (i, Kaiser Wilhelm und Bismarck. ii, Aus Bismarcks Briefwechsel.) 2 vols. Stuttgart. 1901.

Busch, M. Bismarck. Some secret pages of his history. Being a diary kept during 25 years...intercourse with the great chancellor. 3 vols. London. 1898. German edn. Tagebuchblätter. 5 vols. Leipzig. 1899.

Kohl, H. Bismarck-Briefe 1836–73. 7th edn. Bielefeld. 1898.

—— Bismarck-Jahrbuch. 6 vols. Berlin. 1894–9.

—— Fürst Bismarck. Regesten zu einer wissenschaftlichen Biographie des ersten Deutschen Reichskanzlers. 2 vols. (1815–90.) Leipzig. 1891–2.

Mittnacht, Frhr. von. Erinnerungen an Bismarck. 2 vols. Stuttgart. 1904–5.

Penzler, J. Bismarck nach seiner Entlassung. 7 vols. Leipzig. 1897–8.

Politische Reden, die, des Fürsten von Bismarck. Historisch-kritische Gesamtausgabe, besorgt von H. Kohl. 14 vols. Stuttgart. 1892–1904.

Poschinger, H. von. Fürst Bismarck und die Parlamentarier. 3 vols. Breslau. 1894–5.

—— Fürst Bismarck und der Bundesrat (1867–90). 5 vols. Stuttgart and Leipzig. 1896–1901.

—— Fürst Bismarck und die Diplomaten 1852–90. Hamburg. 1900.

Tiedemann, C. von. Sechs Jahre Chef der Reichskanzlei unter dem Fürsten Bismarck. Leipzig. 1909.

Whitman, S. Personal reminiscences of prince Bismarck. London. 1902.

Wilmowski, G. von. Meine Erinnerungen an Bismarck. Ed. by M. von Wilmowski. Breslau. 1899.

Bülow, Graf. Reden ; nebst urkundlichen Beiträgen zu seiner Politik, hrsg. von J. Penzler. Leipzig. 1903.

Caprivi, Graf von. Reden im Deutschen Reichstage, Preussischen Landtage und bei besonderen Anlässen 1883–93. Mit der Biographie, hrsg. von R. Arndt. Berlin. 1894.

William I.—Wilhelms des Grossen Briefe, Reden und Schriften, hrsg. von E. Berner. 2 vols. Berlin. 1906.

William II.—Kaiserreden. Reden, Erlasse, Briefe, Telegramme Kaiser Wilhelms II, hrsg. von A. O. Klaussmann. Leipzig. 1902.

—— Kaiser Wilhelms II Reden 1896–1900, hrsg. von J. Penzler. Leipzig. 1904.

III. GENERAL WORKS.

Blum, H. Das deutsche Reich zur Zeit Bismarcks. Politische Geschichte von 1871 bis 1890. Leipzig. 1893.

—— Fürst Bismarck und seine Zeit. 6 vols. Munich. 1895. Register. 1898.

Egelhaaf, G. Geschichte der neuesten Zeit vom Frankfurter Frieden bis zur Gegenwart. Stuttgart. 1908. 2nd edn. 1909.

Hahn, L. Fürst Bismarck. Sein politisches Leben und Wirken urkundlich in Tatsachen und des Fürsten eigenen Kundgebungen dargestellt. 5 vols. (Vol. v, by K. Wippermann.) Berlin. 1878–91.

Hintzpeter, G. Kaiser Wilhelm II. Eine Skizze nach der Natur gezeichnet. Bielefeld. 1888.

Klein-Hattingen, O. Bismarck und seine Welt. Grundlegung einer psychologischen Biographie. 3 vols. Berlin. 1902–4.

Kohl, H. Dreissig Jahre Preussisch-Deutscher Geschichte 1858 bis 1888 in amtlichen Kundgebungen. Giessen. 1888.

Lamprecht, K. Deutsche Geschichte. Supplement: Zur jüngsten deutschen Vergangenheit. 2 vols. 1904–5. Vols. viii–xii: Neueste Zeit. Berlin. 1906–9.

Lavisse, E. Trois empereurs de l'Allemagne. Paris. 1888.

Lenz, M. Geschichte Bismarcks. Leipzig. 1902.

Lichtenberger, H. L'Allemagne moderne: son évolution. Paris. 1907.

Lowe, C. The German Emperor William II. 1896.

Marcks, E. Kaiser Wilhelm I. 5th edn. Leipzig. 1905.

Matter, P. Bismarck et son temps. Vol. iii. 1870–98. Paris. 1908.

Mehring, F. Die deutsche Sozialdemokratie. 3rd edn. Bremen. 1879.

—— Geschichte der deutschen Sozialdemokratie. 2nd edn. 4 vols. Stuttgart. 1903.

Oncken, W. Unser Heldenkaiser. Berlin. 1897.

Parisius, L. Deutschlands politische Parteien und das Ministerium Bismarck. Vol. i. Berlin. 1878.

Philippson, M. Das Leben Kaiser Friedrichs III. Wiesbaden. 1900.

Poschinger, H. von. Kaiser Friedrich. 3 vols. Berlin. 1898–1900.

Whitman, Sidney. Imperial Germany. London. 1888. German edn. Berlin. 1889.

IV. SPECIAL WORKS.

Foreign Affairs.

Geffcken, F. H. Frankreich, Russland und der Dreibund. Berlin. 1904.

Gontaut-Biron, Vicomte F. de. Mon ambassade en Allemagne. Paris. 1906.

Guarini, G. B. La Germania e la questione d' Oriente fino al congresso di Berlino. Part ii. Rome. 1898.

Handbuch des Deutschtums im Auslande, nebst einem Adressbuch der deutschen Auslandsschulen. 2nd edn. Berlin. 1906.

Klaczko, T. Zwei Kanzler. Fürst Gortschakow und Fürst Bismarck. Basel. 1877.

May, G. Le traité de Francfort. Étude d'histoire diplomatique et de droit international. Paris. 1910.

Meynier, V. France and Germany from the peace of Francfort in 1871 to the peace of Algeciras in 1906. London. 1908.

Nauticus. Jahrbuch für Deutschlands Seeinteressen. (Periodical.) Berlin. 1899 sqq.

Rohrbach, P. Deutschland unter den Weltvölkern. Materialien zur auswärtigen Politik. Berlin. 1908.

Schiemann, T. Deutschland und die grosse Politik. Annual. Berlin. 1902 sqq.

Tardieu, A. La France et les alliances. Paris. 1909.

Army and Navy.

Binder-Krieglstein, Baron E. von. Die Kämpfe des deutschen Expeditionskorps in China und ihre militärischen Leistungen. Berlin. 1902.

Kaiserliche Marine, die, während der Wirren in China 1900–1. Herausgegeben vom Admiralstab der Marine. Berlin. 1903.

Kämpfe, die, der deutschen Truppen in Südwestafrika. Herausgegeben vom Grossen Generalstabe. I. Der Feldzug gegen die Hereros. II. Hottentottenkrieg. 2 vols. Berlin, 1907.

Schwabe, K. Der Krieg in Deutsch-Südwestafrika 1904–6. Berlin. 1907.

CONSTITUTIONAL HISTORY.

Hue de Grais. Handbuch der Verfassung und Verwaltung in Preussen und dem Deutschen Reiche. 11th edn. Berlin. 1896.

Kloeppel, P. Dreissig Jahre Deutscher Verfassungsgeschichte. Vol. I. (1867–77.) Leipzig. 1900.

Laband, P. Das Staatsrecht des Deutschen Reiches. 4th edn. 4 vols. Tübingen. 1901.

—— Deutsches Reichsstaatsrecht. Tübingen. 1907.

Meyer, G. Lehrbuch des deutschen Staatsrechtes. 6th edn. (Ed. by G. Anschütz.) Leipzig. 1905.

Seydel, M. von. Verfassungsurkunde für das deutsche Reich. 2nd edn. Freiburg. 1897.

—— Bayrisches Staatsrecht. 7 vols. Munich and Freiburg. 1884–94.

Zorn, P. Das Staatsrecht des deutschen Reichs. 2 vols. 2nd edn. Berlin, Leipzig. 1895–7.

ECONOMY AND FINANCES.

Ashley, W. T. The progress of the German working classes in the last quarter of a century. London. 1904. German trans. Tübingen. 1906.

Blondel, G. Études sur les populations rurales d'Allemagne et la crise agraire. Paris. 1897.

—— L'essor industriel et commerciel du peuple allemand. Paris. 1898.

Cohn, S. Die Finanzen des deutschen Reiches seit seiner Begründung. Berlin. 1899.

Eheberg, K. T. Die industrielle Entwicklung Bayerns seit 1800. Erlangen. 1898.

Freytag, C. F. Die Entwicklung des Hamburgischen Warenhandels 1870–1900. Berlin. 1908.

Goltz, Frhr. F. A. G. L. von der. Geschichte der deutschen Landwirtschaft. 2 vols. Stuttgart and Berlin. 1902–3.

Gothein, E. Die geschichtliche Entwicklung der Rheinschiffahrt im 19. Jahrhundert. Leipzig. 1903.

Handbuch der Wirtschaftskunde. Herausgegeben im Auftrage des Deutschen Verbandes für das kaufmännische Unterrichtswesen. 4 vols. Leipzig. 1901–4.

Heitz, E. Die sozialpolitische Bewegung in Deutschland 1863 bis 90. Stuttgart. 1891.

Helfferich, K. Die Reform des deutschen Geldwesens nach der Gründung des Reiches. 2 vols. Leipzig. 1898.

Hübener, E. Die deutsche Wirtschaftskrisis von 1873. Berlin. 1905.

Jung, J. Die Entwickelung des Deutschen Post- und Telegraphenwesens in den letzten 25 Jahren. 3rd edn. Leipzig. 1893.

Loewe, C. Geschichte des Nordostseekanals. Berlin. 1895.

Lotz, W. Verkehrsentwicklung in Deutschland 1800–1900. Leipzig. 1900.

Mayer, A. von. Geschichte und Geographie der deutschen Eisenbahnen von ihrer Entwicklung bis auf die Gegenwart. 2 vols. Berlin. 1891.

Peters, M. Die Entwickelung der deutschen Rhederei seit Beginn des 19. Jahrhunderts. 2 vols. Jena. 1899–1905.

Reichsbank, die, 1876–1900. Jena. 1901.

Rheinisch-Westfälischen Steinkohlen-Bergbaus, die wirtschaftliche Entwicklung des, in der zweiten Hälfte des 19. Jahrhunderts. 3 vols. Berlin. 1904.

Riesser, F. Zur Entwicklungsgeschichte der deutschen Grossbanken mit besonderer Rücksicht auf die Konzentrationsbestrebungen. 3rd edn. Jena. 1910.

Schmoller, G. Vier Briefe über Bismarcks volkswirtschaftliche und sozialpolitische Stellung und Bedeutung. (Soziale Praxis. 1908.)

Schwabe, H. Die Entwicklung des deutschen Binnenschiffahrt bis zum Ende des 19. Jahrhunderts. Berlin. 1899.

Soetbeer, A. Die fünf Milliarden. Betrachtungen über die Folgen der grossen Kriegsentschädigung. Berlin. 1877.

Sombart, W. Die Deutsche Volkswirtschaft des 19. Jahrhunderts. Berlin. 1903.

Zedlitz-Neukirch, Frhr. von. Dreissig Jahre Preussischer Finanz- und Steuerpolitik. Berlin. 1901.

Zimmermann, A. Die Handelspolitik des Deutschen Reiches vom Frankfurter Frieden bis zur Gegenwart. 2nd edn. Berlin. 1900.

COLONIES.

Dove, K. Die deutschen Kolonien. I. Leipzig. 1909.

Fabri, F. Fünf Jahre deutscher Kolonialpolitik. Gotha. 1889.

Gareis, C. Deutsches Kolonialrecht. 2nd edn. Giessen. 1902.

Hassert, K. Deutschlands Kolonien. Erwerbungs- und Entwicklungsgeschichte, Landes- und Volkskunde und wirtschaftliche Bedeutung unserer Schutzgebiete. Leipzig. 1899. Nachtrag. Leipzig. 1903.

Herrfurth, K. Fürst Bismarck und die Kolonialpolitik. Berlin. 1909.

Kiepert, R. Deutscher Kolonial-Atlas für den amtlichen Gebrauch in den Schutzgebieten. (Text by I. Partsch.) Berlin. 1893.

Koebner, O. Einführung in die Kolonialpolitik. Jena. 1908.

Kolonialgesetzgebung, die deutsche. Sammlung der auf die deutschen Schutzgebiete bezüglichen Gesetze, Verordnungen, Erlasse und internationalen Vereinbarungen. Vol. I by Riebow (1893), II–V by Zimmermann (1897–1901), VI–IX by Schmidt-Dargitz and Koebner (1903–6), X, XI by Koebner and Gerstmeyer (1907–10).

Koschitzky, M. von. Deutsche Kolonialgeschichte. 2 vols. Berlin. 1888.

Külz, W. Deutsch-Südafrika im 25. Jahre deutscher Schutzherrschaft. Berlin. 1909.

Leutwein, T. Elf Jahre Gouverneur in Deutsch-Südwestafrika. Berlin. 1906.

Meyer, H. Das deutsche Kolonialreich. Eine Länderkunde der deutschen Schutzgebiete. Vol. I. Ostafrika (by H. Meyer) und Kamerun (by S. Passarge). Leipzig. 1909.

Perbandt, C. von, G. Richelmann and R. Schmidt. H. von Wissmann. Deutschlands grösster Afrikaner. Berlin. 1906.

Peters, C. Das Deutsch-Ostafrikanische Schutzgebiet. Munich and Leipzig. 1895.

—— Die Gründung von Deutsch-Ostafrika. Berlin. 1906.

—— Die deutsche Emin Pascha-Expedition. Munich. 1891.

Pfeil, Graf J. von. Zur Erwerbung von Deutsch-Ostafrika. Berlin. 1907.

Schnee. Unsere Kolonien. Leipzig. 1908.

Weissenborn, W. Sechs Jahre deutscher Kolonialpolitik. Berlin. 1890.

CHURCHES.

Brück, H. Geschichte der Katholischen Kirche im 19. Jahrhundert. 4 vols. Mainz. 1887–1900. Vols. I–III. 2nd edn. 1902.

—— Die Kulturkampfbewegung in Deutschland 1872 bis 1900. Mainz. 1901.

Döllinger, I. von. Das Papsttum. (New edn. of Janus. Der Papst und das Konzil. 1869.) Ed. by T. Friedrich. Munich. 1892.

Goyau, G. L'Allemagne religieuse. Le Protestantisme. Paris. 1898.

Hahn, L. Geschichte des "Kulturkampfes" in Preussen. In Aktenstücken dargestellt. Berlin. 1881.

Hergenröther, J. Anti-Janus. Freiburg. 1870.

Hinschius, P. Die preussischen Kirchengesetze des Jahres 1873. (Fortsetzungen 1874, 1875, 1880, 1886.) 5 vols. Berlin. 1873–86.

Lefèbre de Béhaine, Comte E. Léon XIII et le prince de Bismarck. Fragments d'histoire diplomatique avec pièces justificatives. Paris. 1898.

Majunke, P. Geschichte des Kulturkampfes in Preussen-Deutschland. Paderborn. 1876–88.

Nippold, Fr. Handbuch der neuesten Kirchengeschichte seit der Restauration von 1814. 5 vols. 3rd edn. Berlin. 1889–1904.

—— Ursprung, Umfang, Hemmnisse und Aussichten der altkatholischen Bewegung. Berlin. 1873.

Schulte, J. F. von. Der Altkatholizismus. Geschichte seiner Entwicklung, innern Gestaltung und rechtlichen Stellung in Deutschland. Giessen. 1887.

Seeberg, R. Die Kirche Deutschlands im 19. Jahrhundert. Leipzig. 1903–4.

Werckshagen, C. Der Protestantismus am Ende des 19. Jahrhunderts in Wort und Bild. 2 vols. Leipzig. 1901.

PHILOSOPHY, ART AND LITERATURE.

Bartels, A. Die deutsche Dichtung der Gegenwart. Die Alten und die Jungen. 6th edn. Leipzig. 1904.

Busse, C. Geschichte der deutschen Dichtung im 19. Jahrhundert. Berlin. 1901.

Chamberlain, H. St. Die Grundlagen des 19. Jahrhunderts. 2 vols. 4th edn. 1903.

—— Die ersten zwanzig Jahre der Bayreuther Bühnenfestspiele. Bayreuth. 1896.

Francke, K. Glimpses of modern German culture. New York. 1908.

Guilland, A. L'Allemagne nouvelle et ses historiens. Paris. 1899.

Gurlitt, E. Die deutsche Kunst des 19. Jahrhunderts. Berlin. 1899.

Hanstein, A. von. Das jüngste Deutschland. Zwei Jahrzehnte miterlebter Literaturgeschichte. Leipzig. 1900.

Hinneberg, P. (and others). Die Kultur der Gegenwart. Ihre Entwicklung und ihre Ziele. Berlin and Leipzig. 1906 sqq.

Litzmann, B. Das deutsche Drama in den literarischen Bewegungen der Gegenwart. 4th edn. Hamburg. 1897.

Meier-Graefe, J. Geschichte der deutschen Kunst im 19. Jahrhundert. Stuttgart. 1904.

Meyer, R. M. Die deutsche Litteratur des 19. Jahrhunderts. 3rd edn. Berlin. 1906.

Rethwisch, C. Deutschlands höheres Schulwesen im 19. Jahrhundert. Berlin. 1893.

Riemann, H. Geschichte der Musik seit Beethoven 1806–1900. Berlin and Stuttgart. 1901.

Stern, A. Die Deutsche Nationallitteratur vom Tode Goethes bis zur Gegenwart. 5th edn. Marburg, Leipzig. 1905.

Windelband, W. Die Philosophie im Beginn des 20. Jahrhunderts. Festschrift für Kuno Fischer. Heidelberg. 1907.

Ziegler, Th. Die geistigen und sozialen Strömungen des 19. Jahrhunderts. Berlin. 1898. 3rd edn. 1910.

V. BIOGRAPHIES AND MEMOIRS.

Aus Ed. Laskers Nachlass. Ed. by W. Cahn. Part ɪ: Fünfzehn Jahre parlamen-
tarischer Geschichte 1866–80. Berlin. 1902.

Bigge, W. Feldmarschall Graf Moltke. 2 vols. Munich. 1900.

Chamberlain, H. St. Richard Wagner. 4th edn. Munich. 1907.

Denkwürdigkeiten des Fürsten Chlodwig zu Hohenlohe-Schillingsfürst. Ed. by
F. Curtius. 2 vols. Stuttgart and Leipzig. 1907. Eng. trans. London. 1907.

Finck, W. Wagner and his work. 2 vols. London. 1893.

Förster-Nietzsche, E. Das Leben Friedrich Nietzsches. 2 vols. Leipzig. 1895
–1904.

Friedrich, J. Ignaz von Döllinger. 3 vols. Munich. 1899–1901.

Frobenius, H. Alfred Krupp. Dresden. 1898.

Gerlach, E. L. von. Aufzeichnungen aus seinem Leben und Wirken 1795–1877.
(Ed. by Jakob von Gerlach.) 2 vols. Schwerin. 1903.

Glasenapp, H. Das Leben Richard Wagners. 6 vols. 4th edn. Leipzig. 1906-7.

Goltz, Frhr. F. von der. Moltke. Berlin. 1903.

Hansen, J. Gustav von Mevissen. Ein rheinisches Lebensbild 1815–99. 2 vols.
Berlin. 1906.

Hassel, P. Aus dem Leben des Königs Albert von Sachsen. 2 vols. (–1873.)
Berlin. 1898, 1900.

Hüsgen, E. Ludwig Windthorst. Cologne. 1907.

Jähns, M. Feldmarschall Moltke. 2 vols. Berlin. 1894–1900.

Knopp, I. N. Ludwig Windthorst. Dresden. 1898.

Kock, H. H. Das Leben des Generalfeldmarschalls Edwin von Manteuffel. Bielefeld
and Leipzig. 1890.

Krickeberg, E. Heinrich von Stephan. Dresden. 1907.

Leuss, W. Wilhelm Freiherr von Hammerstein, 1881–1895, Chefredacteur der
Kreuzzeitung. Berlin. 1905.

Oncken, H. Rudolf von Bennigsen. Ein deutscher liberaler Politiker. Nach
seinen Briefen und hinterlassenen Papieren. Vol. ɪ: –1866; Vol. ɪɪ: 1866–
1902. 2 vols. Stuttgart and Leipzig. 1910.

Parisius, L. Leopold Freiherr von Hoverbeck. 2 vols. Berlin. 1897–1900.

Pastor, L. August Reichensperger 1808–95. 2 vols. Freiburg i. Br. 1899.

Petersdorff, H. von. Kleist-Retzow. Ein Lebensbild. Stuttgart. 1907.

Pfülf, O. Hermann von Mallinckrodt: die Geschichte seines Lebens. Freiburg.
1892.

Philippson, M. Max von Forckenbeck. Dresden. 1898.

Puttkamer, A. and M. von. Die Aera Manteuffel. Federzeichnungen aus Elsass-
Lothringen. Stuttgart. 1904.

Richter, Eugen. Im alten Reichstag. Erinnerungen. 2 vols. Berlin. 1895.

Riehl, A. Friedrich Nietzsche, der Künstler und Denker. Stuttgart. 1901.

Roon, Count von. Denkwürdigkeiten aus dem Leben des Generalfeldmarschalls
Grafen v. Roon. 5th edn. 3 vols. 1905.

Rust, H. Reichskanzler Fürst Chlodwig zu Hohenlohe-Schillingsfürst und seine
Brüder. Düsseldorf. 1897.

Schäffle, A. E. F. Aus meinem Leben. 2 vols. Berlin. 1905.

Schlenther, P. Gerhart Hauptmann. Berlin. 1898.

Schneegans, A. Memoiren (1835–98). Ein Beitrag zur Geschichte des Elsasses in
der Übergangszeit. Ed. by H. Schneegans. Berlin. 1904.

Spahn, M. Ernst Lieber als Parlamentarier. Gotha. 1906.

Wagener, H. Erlebtes. Meine Memoiren aus der Zeit von 1848 bis 1866 und von
1873 bis jetzt. Berlin. 1883–4.

CHAPTER VII.

AUSTRIA-HUNGARY.

I. BIBLIOGRAPHIES.

A. Austria.

Bibliografie české historie (Bibliogr. of the History of Bohemia). Annual supplement to the Český časopis historický (Historical Review of Bohemia). Prague. 1904 sqq.

Dahlmann-Waitz. Quellenkunde der deutschen Geschichte. 7th edn., by E. Brandenburg. Leipzig. 1906. Ergänzungsband. Leipzig. 1907.

Krones, Ritter von Marchland, F. Grundriss der Oesterreichischen Geschichte mit besonderer Rücksicht auf Quellen- und Literaturkunde. Vienna. 1882.

Masslow, O. Bibliographie zur deutschen Geschichte. Historische Vierteljahrschrift of Gerhard Seeliger. Leipzig. 1898, etc.

B. Hungary.

Mangold, L. Történeti bibliografia. In the historical review Századok, Budapest.

II. DOCUMENTS.

A. Legal and Statistical Documents.

(1) *Collections of laws.*

a. Official collections. A. Austria : Reichsgesetzblatt. B. Hungary : Törvénytár. [Begins with the laws of the Diet 1865–7 ; published in Magyar and translated into the other languages used in the State.]

b. Private collections. A. Austria : Manzsche Taschenausgabe der österreichischen Gesetze. Vienna. Among these, the Staatsgrundgesetze contain, as an appendix, the constitutional laws of Hungary. B. Hungary : Darday, S., Közigazgatási törvénytár.

(2) *Reports of parliamentary proceedings.*

a. Official records of parliamentary proceedings. Austria : Stenographische Protokolle, Abgeordnetenhaus and Herrenhaus (minutes of the Diets). Hungary : Förendiházi napló, and képviselöházi napló.

b. Private summaries or reproductions. Austria : Verhandlungen des österreichischen verstärkten Reichsrathes, 1860. 2 vols. Vienna. 1860. Die neue Gesetzgebung Oesterreichs, erläutert aus den Reichsraths-Verhandlungen. I. Die Verfassungsgesetze und die Gesetze über den finanziellen Ausgleich mit Ungarn. Vienna. 1868. Hungary : Der ungarische Reichstag. 3 vols. Budapest. 1861.

c. Statistics. Austrian: Statistisches Jahrbuch. Vienna. 1861–81. Statistisches Handbuch, 1882 sqq. Oesterreichische Statistik. Vienna. 1882 sqq. Mitteilungen aus dem Gebiete der Statistik ; since 1875 Statistische Monatsschrift. [These four publications are directed by the Statistische Centralcommission at Vienna.] Hungarian : A magyar Királyi kormány...évi muködéséröl és az ország közállapotairól szóló jelentés és sztatisztikai évkönyv. (Report of the Royal Hungarian Government on its work during the year and on the position of the country, with statistical summary.) Budapest. 1899 sqq. Ungarisches statistisches Jahrbuch. Budapest. 1872 sqq. Hivatalos sztatisztikai közlemények. Budapest. 1868 sqq.

(3) *Private collections of documents.*

Černý, J. Boj za právo (the struggle for rights). Prague. 1893.

Fischel, A. Das österreichische Sprachenrecht. Eine Quellensammlung. Brünn. 1901.

—— Materialien zur Sprachenfrage in Oesterreich. Brünn. 1902.

Kolmer, G. Parlament und Verfassung in Oesterreich. Vols. i–iv. Vienna. 1902 sqq. *In course of publication.*

Ungarische Verfassungsstreit, der, urkundlich dargestellt. In Das Staatsarchiv. Sammlung der officiellen Aktenstücke zur Geschichte der Gegenwart. Herausgegeben von L. K. Aegidi u. A. Klauhold. Hamburg. 1862.

(4) *Periodicals.*

Only the most important Austrian and Hungarian Journals and Reviews are indicated here.

Journals : (*a*) Vienna: Presse, Neue Freie Presse, Zeit, Vaterland, Arbeiter-Zeitung ; Prague : Politik (since 1907, Union); Čas, Národní Listy ; Cracow : Czas. (β) Budapest: Pesti Napló, Pester Lloyd, Budapesti Hirlap, Neues Pester Journal.

Reviews : (*a*) Vienna : Oesterreichisch-ungarische Revue, Die Zeit, Oesterreichische Rundschau, Der Kampf, Zeitschrift für Volkswirtschaft, Sozialpolitik u. Verwaltung ; Prague : Osvěta (Light), Naše Doba (Our Time), Česká Revue (Bohemian Review), Deutsche Arbeit, Pokroková Revue (Progressist Review). (β) Budapest : Budapesti Szemle (Review of Budapest), Hungarian Review.

B. Memoirs, Correspondence, Speeches, and Polemical Writings.

Acht Jahre Amtsleben in Ungarn. Von einem k. k. Stuhlrichter in Disponibilität. Leipzig. 1861.

Andrássy, Count J.—Speeches of Count J. Andrássy, edited by B. Lederer. 2 vols. Budapest. 1891–3.

—— Die Einheit der österreichisch-ungarischen Armee. Rede, gehalten im ungarischen Magnatenhause am 5. April 1889. Vienna. 1889. Translated from the Magyar.

Andreas Memor (Visy Imre). Tiz év története (History of ten years). Budapest. 1885.

Andrian-Warburg, Frhr. J. von. Denkschrift über die Verfassungs- und Verwaltungsfrage in Oesterreich. Leipzig. 1859.

Apponyi, Count Albert. Speeches, 1872–95. 2 vols. Budapest. 1897.

Arneth, Ritter A. von. Aus meinem Leben. 2 vols. Stuttgart. 1893.

Ausgleich und Verfassungstreue. 2nd edn. Leipzig. 1873.

Baernreither, J. M. Bosnische Eindrücke. Vienna. 1908.

Belcredi, Count L. Fragmente aus dem Nachlasse des ehemaligen Staatsministers Grafen Richard Belcredi, in the Review Kultur. (Vienna, 1905 and 1906.)

Beust, Count F. F. von. Aus drei Vierteljahrhunderten. Erinnerungen und Aufzeichnungen. 2 vols. Stuttgart. 1887.

Bismarck, Prince O. von. Gedanken u. Erinnerungen. 2 vols. Stuttgart. 1898.

Briefwechsel zwischen Anastasius Grün und L. A. Frankl. Berlin. 1897.

Busbach, P. Az utolsó öt év. (The five last years.) Budapest. 1893.

—— Egy viharos emberöltö. (A troubled period.) 2 vols. Budapest. 1897–9.

Déak, Francis.—Ferencz beszédei. Összegyüjtötte Kónyi Manó (Speeches of F. Déak, collected by Emm. Kónyi). 6 vols. Budapest. i–iii. 2nd edn. 1903. iv–vi. 1897–8.

—— Levelek (correspondence). Budapest. 1890.

—— Ein Beitrag zum ungarischen Staatsrecht. Bemerkungen über W. Lustkandl's Ungarisch-österreichisches Staatsrecht. Budapest. 1865. Translated from the Magyar. The originals appeared in the Budapesti Szemle.

Drei Jahre Verfassungsstreit. Beiträge zur jüngsten Geschichte Oesterreichs. Von einem Ungar. Leipzig. 1864.

Dreissig Jahre aus dem Leben eines Journalisten. 3 vols. Vienna. 1894–8.

Eim, G. Politické úvahy (Political reflexions). Prague. 1898.

Emléklapok Vajai baró Vay Miklós életéből (Recollections of the life of Baron Nicolas Vay de Vaja). Budapest. 1889.

Empire, The Austro-Hungarian, and the policy of Count Beust. London. 1870.

Eötvös, Baron J. Die Garantien der Macht und Einheit Oesterreichs. Leipzig. 1859.

—— Die Sonderstellung Ungarns vom Standpunkte der Einheit Deutschlands. Budapest. 1861.

—— Die Nationalitätenfrage. Budapest. 1865.

Fischhof, A. Ein Blick auf Oesterreichs Lage. Vienna. 1866.

—— Oesterreich und die Bürgschaften seines Bestandes. Vienna. 1869.

—— and Unger. Zur Lösung der ungarischen Frage. Vienna. 1861.

Fořt, J. Ven z přitmí (Towards full light). Prague. 1905.

Fournier, A. Wie wir zu Bosnien kamen. Vienna. 1909.

Friedjung, H. Der Ausgleich mit Ungarn. Leipzig. 1877.

Friedmann, B. Zehn Jahre österreichischer Politik. i. Vienna. 1879.

Fröbel, J. Ein Lebenslauf. 2 vols. Stuttgart. 1890–1.

Georgewitsch, V. Die serbische Frage. Stuttgart. 1909.

Györffy, G., beszédei (speeches) 1884–94. Budapest. 1894.

—— tiz év a magyar parlament történetéből (Ten years of the history of the Hungarian Parliament) 1895–1905. Budapest. 1905.

Hasner, L. von. Denkwürdigkeiten. Stuttgart. 1892.

Helfert, Frhr. J. A. von. Meine persönlichen Beziehungen mit Palacký. In Pamatník na oslavu stych narozenin F. Palackého. (Memoir for the hundredth anniversary of the birth of F. Palacky.) Prague. 1898.

—— Revision des ungarischen Ausgleichs. 2 parts. Vienna. 1876.

Kákay Aranyos (pseudonym of Kecskeméthy). Orszaggyűlési arny- és fényképek (parliamentary portraits). Budapest. 1861.

—— Újabb arny- és fényképek (new portraits). Budapest. 1866.

—— A mi nagy férfiaink (Our great men). Budapest. 1874.

Kákay Aranyos II (Cornel Ábrányi the younger). Újabb orszaggyűlési arny- és fényképek (new parliamentary portraits). Budapest. 1877.

—— Tisza Kálman, Politikai élet- és jellemrajz (C. Tisza, biography and political portrait). 3rd edn. Budapest. 1878.

—— Grof Andrássy Gyula. Politikai élet- és jellemrajz. Budapest. 1878.

Kecskeméthy, A. von. Ein Jahr aus der Geschichte Ungarns. Vienna. 1862.

Kossuth, L. Meine Schriften aus der Emigration. 3 vols. Pressburg and Leipzig. 1880–2.

Kramář, K. Anmerkungen zur böhmischen Politik. Vienna. 1906.

Lustkandl, W. Das ungarisch-österreichische Staatsrecht, zur Lösung der Verfassungsfrage historisch und dogmatisch dargestellt. Vienna. 1863.

Masaryk, T. G. Českáo ázka (The Čech question). Prague. 1895.

—— Naše nynější krise (Our present crisis). Prague. 1895.

Meyer, B. R. von. Erlebnisse. Vienna and Budapest. 1875.

Mollinary, Frhr A. von. 46 Jahre im österreichisch-ungarischen Heere. 2 vols. Zurich. 1906.

Nalžov, Aus dem politischen Nachlass des Grafen Taaffe, in Politik, 1904, Nos. 335–42, 349–56.

Oláh, G. A fuzió (1875) (Fusion). Budapest. 1909.

Palacký, F. Gedenkblätter. Auswahl von Denkschriften, Aufsätzen und Briefen aus den letzten fünfzig Jahren. Prague. 1874.

—— Spisy drobné. I. Spisy a řeči z oboru politiky (Essays: I. Political essays and speeches). Prague. 1898.

Perthaler, H. von. Neun Briefe über Verfassungsreformen in Oesterreich. Leipzig. 1860.

—— Palingenesis. Denkschrift über Verwaltungsreformen in Oesterreich. Leipzig. 1860.

—— Vier Fragen. Vienna. 1861.

Rieger, F. L.—Řeči dra F. L. Riegra a jeho jednání v zakonodárných sborech (Speeches of F. L. Rieger and his parts in the legislative assemblies). Prague. 1888.

—— Z vlastních pamětí F. L. Riegra. II. Za Belcrediho az do vitězštví Beustova (Fragment of the memoirs of F. L. Rieger, from the time of Belcredi up to the victory of Beust). In Osvěta. Prague. 1906.

Schäffle, A. E. Aus meinem Leben. 2 vols. Berlin. 1904.

Siebenbürgen und die österreichische Regierung in den letzten vier Jahren. Leipzig. 1865.

Szilágyi Dezső beszédei. Vol. I. Közös ügyek. (Speeches. Vol. I. Common affairs.) Budapest. 1906.

Tomek, V. V. Styky mé s Palackým do roku 1862 (My relations with Palacký up to 1862). In Pamatník. (See above under Helfert, Frhr. J. A. von.)

Várady, G. Hulló levelek (Falling leaves). Maramaros Sziget. 1895.

Zeithammer, A. O. Zur Vorgeschichte der Fundamentalartikel. In Politik-Union, 1907, No. 359; 1908, Nos. 1, 5–11.

Zwölf Artikel über die ungarische Frage. Reprint from the Wanderer. Vienna. 1862.

III. LATER WORKS.

A. General.

Andrássy, Count J.   Ungarns Ausgleich mit Oesterreich von Jahre 1867.   (Translated from the Magyar.)   Leipzig.   1897.

Beksics, G.   Der Dualismus.   In Zeitschrift für ungarisches öffentliches und Privatrecht.   i.   Budapest.   1895.

Chéradame, A.   La question d'Autriche-Hongrie au commencement du xxème siècle.   Paris.   1901.

Colquhoun, A.   The Whirlpool of Europe.   London.   1907.

Denis, E.   La Bohême depuis la Montagne Blanche.   2 vols.   Paris.   1903.

Eisenmann, L.   Le Compromis austro-hongrois.   Paris.   1904.

Friedjung, H.   Der Kampf um die Vorherrschaft in Deutschland.   2 vols.   Stuttgart.   7th edn.   1907.

Henry, R.   Des monts de Bohême au golfe Persique.   Paris.   1908.

Horn, G.   Le Compromis de 1868 entre la Croatie et la Hongrie.   Paris.   1907.

Kaizl, J.   Vyrovnaní s Uhry r. 1867 a 1877.   Historickým úvodem opatřil A. Rezek (The compromise with Hungary 1867 and 1877, with a historical introduction by A. Rezek).   Prague.   1866.

Knatchbull-Hugessen, C. M.   Political evolution of the Hungarian Nation.   2 vols.   1908.

Leger, L.   Histoire de l'Autriche-Hongrie.   Paris.

Loiseau, C.   Le Balkan slave et la crise autrichienne.   Paris.   1900.

Luschin von Ebengreuth, A.   Oesterreichische Reichsgeschichte.   Bamberg.   1896.

Marczali, H.   A legújabb kor története (Contemporary History).   Budapest.   1892.

——— A magyar nemzet története (History of the Hungarian Nation).   Vol. x.   Budapest.   1898.

Oesterreichisches Staatswörterbuch.   Published by E. Mischler and J. Ulbrich.   2nd edn.   Vienna.   1908.

Popovici, A.   Die vereinigten Staaten von Grossoesterreich.   Leipzig.   1906.

Rogge, W.   Oesterreich, von Világos bis zur Gegenwart.   3 vols.   Leipzig.   1872–3.

——— Oesterreich seit der Katastrophe Hohenwart-Beust.   2 vols.   Leipzig.   1879.

Scotus Viator.   The future of Austria-Hungary and the policy of the great powers.   1907.

Springer, R. (pseudonym of Renner, K.).   Grundlagen und Entwicklungsziele der österreichisch-ungarischen Monarchie.   Vienna.   1906.

——— Der Kampf der österreichischen Nationen um den Staat.   i.   Vienna.   1902.

Srb, A.   Politické dějiny národa českého od roku 1861 (Political history of the Čech people since 1861).   2 vols.   Prague.   1899–1901.

Sybel, H. von.   Die Begründung des deutschen Reichs durch Wilhelm I.   3rd and 4th edns.   7 vols.   Munich.   1890–4.

Tezner, F.   Der österreichische Kaisertitel, das ungarische Staatsrecht und die ungarische Publizistik.   Vienna.   1899.

——— Die Wandlungen der oesterreichischen Reichsidee.   Vienna.   1905.

Zwiedineck-Südenhorst, H. von.   Deutsche Geschichte 1806–71.   3 vols.   Stuttgart.   1897–1904.

B. Treatises on Constitutional and Political Questions.

Adler, V.   Das allgemeine, gleiche und geheime Wahlrecht und das Wahlunrecht in Oesterreich.   Vienna.   1893.

Apponyi, Count A. La constitution et le parlementarisme hongrois, in Annuaire du Parlement. Paris. 1902.

—— The juridical nature of the relations between Austria and Hungary. An address delivered at the Arts and Science Congress, held at St Louis in 1904.

Austerlitz. Das neue Wahlrecht. Vienna. 1907.

Bernatzik, E. Die österreichischen Verfassungsgesetze. Leipzig. 1906.

Charmatz, R. Deutsch-österreichische Politik. Leipzig. 1907.

Eisenmann, L. Le régime des cultes en Autriche et en Hongrie, in Bulletin de la Société de Législation comparée. Paris. 1906–8.

Glückmann, J. Das Heerwesen der österreichisch-ungarischen Monarchie. 4th edn. Vienna. 1895.

Gumplowicz, L. Das Recht der Nationalitäten und Sprachen in Oesterreich-Ungarn. Innsbruck. 1879.

Hongrie, la, contemporaine et le suffrage universel. Paris. 1909.

Kmety, K. A magyar közjog tankönyve (Treatise of Hungarian constitutional law). 3rd edn. Budapest. 1907.

Kremer, A. von. Die Nationalitätsidee und der Staat. Vienna. 1885.

Madeyski, S. von. Die deutsche Staatssprache, oder Oesterreich ein deutscher Staat. Vienna. 1884.

Miklós Ödön. Összegyüjtött munkai (complete works). 2 vols. Budapest. 1906.

Móricz, P. A magyar orszaggyűlési partok küzdelmei a koronázástól a Déak- és balközép partok egybeolvadásaig (the struggles of political parties in Hungary from the coronation to the fusion of the parties of Déak and the Left Centre). Budapest. 1902.

Pražák, J. Rakouské právo ustavní (Austrian constitutional law). 4 vols. 2nd edn. Prague. 1901–3.

Reichsratswahlen in Ostgalizien 1897, die. Vienna. 1898.

Rieger, B. Ustavní dějiny Rakouska (Constitutional History of Austria). Reprint from Slovník naučný (Encyclopaedia) of Otto. Prague. 1903.

Ulbrich, J. Lehrbuch des österreichischen Staatsrechts. Vienna. 1883.

C. Treatises on the Questions of Nationalities.

Auerbach, B. Les races et les nationalités en Autriche-Hongrie. Paris. 1898.

Bauer, O. Die Nationalitätenfrage und die Sozialdemokratie. Vienna. 1907.

Bertha, A. de. Magyars et Roumains devant l'histoire. Paris. 1899.

Brote, E. Die rumänische Frage in Siebenbürgen und Ungarn. Vienna. 1895.

Hainisch, M. Die Zukunft der Deutsch-Oesterreicher. Vienna. 1892.

Hermann von Herrnritt, R. Die Nationalität als Rechtsbegriff. In Grünhut, Zeitschrift für das Privat- und öffentliche Recht der Gegenwart. xxvi. Vienna. 1874.

Menger, M. Der böhmische Ausgleich. Stuttgart. 1891.

Rauchberg, H. Der nationale Besitzstand in Böhmen. 3 vols. Prague. 1905.

Scotus Viator. Racial problems in Hungary. London. 1909.

D. Treatises on Economic and Social Questions.

Bazant, J. von. Die Handelspolitik Oesterreich Ungarns 1875 bis 1892. Leipzig. 1894.

Beer, A. Die Finanzen Oesterreichs im xix Jahrhundert. Prague. 1877.

—— Die österreichische Handelspolitik im xix Jahrhundert. Vienna. 1891.

Fiedler, F. Rakousko-uherska vyrovnání po roce 1878 (The Austro-Hungarian compromises since 1878). Prague. 1903.

Gärtner, F. Der österreichisch-ungarische Ausgleich. In Archiv für Sozial-
wissenschaft und Sozialpolitik. xxv. Tübingen. 1905.

Gonnard, R. L'émigration européenne au xixème siècle. Paris. 1906.

—— La Hongrie au xxème siècle, étude économique et sociale. Paris. 1908.

Louis-Jaray, G. La question sociale et le Socialisme en Hongrie. Paris. 1909.

Majláth, Comte J. La Hongrie rurale, sociale et politique. Paris. 1909.

Matlekovits, A. von. Das Königreich Ungarn, volkswirtschaftlich und statistisch
dargestellt. 2 vols. Leipzig. 1900.

Rauchberg, H. Die Bevölkerung Oesterreichs, auf Grund der Ergebnisse der
Volkszählung vom 31 Dezember 1890. Vienna. 1895.

Steinitzer, E. Die jüngsten Reformen der veranlagten Steuern in Oesterreich.
Leipzig. 1905.

Waentig, H. Gewerbliche Mittelstandspolitik. Leipzig. 1898.

E. BIOGRAPHIES.

Arnold-Foster, F. Deák, a memoir. London. 1880.

Beksics, G. Kemény Zsigmond. A forradalom és a kiegyezés (Sigismond Kemény.
The Revolution and the Compromise). 2nd edn. Budapest. 1883.

Ebeling, E. F. F. Graf von Beust. 2 vols. Leipzig. 1870–1.

Ferenczi, Z. Deák élete (Life of Deák). 3 vols. Budapest. 1904.

Friedjung, H. Graf Kalnoky. In Biographisches Jahrbuch und deutscher Nekrolog.
Vol. iii. Berlin. 1897, etc.

Goll, J. František Palacky. Prague. 1898.

Jahn, J. F. L. Rieger. Prague. 1889.

Krones, F. von. M. v. Kaiserfeld. Leipzig. 1888.

Mayr, A. Hans von Perthalers auserlesene Schriften (with biography). Vienna.
1883.

Thalloczy, L. von. Graf Anton Szécsen (in Oesterreichisch-Ungarische Revue,
xxix). Vienna. 1902–3.

Wolfsgruber, C. J. O. Kardinal Rauscher. 2 vols. Freiburg. 1888.

CHAPTER VIII.

ITALY.

I. PUBLISHED DOCUMENTS.

Actes de S. S. Pie X. Encycliques, Motu Proprio, Brefs et Allocutions. Original texts and French translations. 2 vols. Paris. 1905–8.

Foreign Office. Miscellaneous Series. Report on Amount of Private Wealth in Italy as compared with that of other Countries in Europe. No. 205. London. 1891.

—— Diplomatic and Consular Reports. Italy. Nos. 3744, 3778, 3795, 3799, 3902, 3912. London. 1907. Nos. 3959, 4037. London. 1908.

Lettres Apostoliques, etc. de S. S. Leon XIII. 7 vols. Paris. 1903–4.

Libro Verde. Avvenimenti d'Africa. N. xxiii. N. xxiii bis. N. xxiii ter. N. xxiii quater. Rome. 1896. Trattato di Pace. N. x. Rome. 1897. Missione Antonelli in Etiopia. N. xvii. Rome. 1891.

Livre Jaune. Affaires d'Orient. Congrès de Berlin. Paris. 1878.

Livre Jaune. Affaires de Tunisie : Annexes à la Correspondance Diplomatique sur les Affaires de Tunis. Paris. 1881.

State Papers. Turkey (Treaty of Berlin). No. 44. (1878.) London. 1878. Egypt. Nos. 11, 15, 17, 18. (1882.) London. 1882. Egypt. No. 1. (1883.) London. 1883. Egypt. Nos. 14 and 16. (1885.) London. 1885. Italy. Law Respecting Papal Guarantees. No. 1. (1892.) London. 1892.

II. STATISTICS. ECONOMIC CONDITIONS.

Alongi, G. La Maffia : La Camorra. Biblioteca Antropologica Giuridica. Serie ii. Vols. x and xiii. Turin. 1887 and 1890.

Atti della Giunta per la Inchiesta Agraria. 22 vols. Rome. 1881–6.

Banca Popolare di Milano. Memoria per la Esposizione di Milano, 1906. Milan. 1906.

—— Resoconto dell' Assemblea generale dei Soci tenutasi il giorno 24 febbraio, 1907. Milan. 1907.

Banca Popolare di Credito in Bologna. Resoconto dell' anno 1907 e Atti dell' Assemblea generale dei Soci tenuta il 9 febbraio 1908. Bologna. 1908.

Bodio, L. Di Alcuni Indici Misuratori del Movimento Economico in Italia. 2nd edn. Rome. 1891.

Bruni, E. Codice Doganale Italiano. Milan. 1894.

Congresso vii° delle Banche Popolari Italiane ; Cremona, 19–21 settembre, 1907. Relazioni. Rome. 1907.

Credito e Cooperazione. Anno xix. Rome. 1907.

Fischer, P. D.   Italien und die Italiener am Schlusse des Neunzehnten Jahrhunderts.   Berlin.   1899.

Franchi, L.   Codici e leggi del Regno d'Italia.   2nd edn.   4 vols.   Milan.   1902–4.

Martinengo-Cesaresco, Countess E.   Lombard Agriculture (in Lombard Studies).   London.   1902.

Mazzoccolo, E.   La Nuova Legge Comunale e Provinciale.   5th edn.   1905.

Ministero di Agricoltura.   Annuario Statistico Italiano, 1904.   Rome.   1904.

——   Annuario Statistico Italiano, 1905–7.   Fascicolo Primo.   Rome.   1907.

——   1905–7.   Fascicolo Secondo.   Rome.   1908.

——   Emigrazione e Colonie.   Rome.   1906.

——   Statistica dei Debiti Comunali e Provinciali.   Rome.   1905.

——   Movimento delle Popolazioni nell' Anno 1906.   Rome.   1908.

——   Statistica Industriale.   Rome.   1905–6.

——   Statistica Emigrazione per l'Esterno.   Rome.   1906.

——   Notizie sull' Agricoltura in Italia.   Rome.   1900.

——   Notizie sull' Istruzione Agraria in Italia.   Rome.   1900.

Mosca, G.   Che Cosa è la Mafia?   Bologna.   1900.

Nathan, E.   Vent' Anni di Vita Italiana.   Rome and Turin.   1906.

Nitti, Prof. F. S.   L'Emigrazione Italiana e i suoi Avversari.   Turin.   1888.

——   Scienza delle Finanze.   Naples.   1903.

——   The Wealth of Italy.   Rome.   1907.

Noseda, E.   Lavoro delle Donne e dei Fanciulli : Nuova Legge e Regolamento.   Milan.   1903.

Papafava, F.   La Questura di Napoli Alleata della Camorra.   Giornale degli Economisti.   July, 1907.   Rome.   1907.

Perdoni, T.   Le Forze Idrauliche dell' Italia e il loro Impiego.   Milan.   1902.

Salvatore, A.   Leggi e Regolamenti sugli Infortuni degli Operai sul Lavoro.   Milan.   1900.

Statistics of Italy : Journal of Royal Statistical Society.   Vol. LXVI.   Pt II.   London.   1903.

Virgilii, F.   Cooperazione nella Sociologia e nella Legislazione.   Milan.   1900.

——   Il Problema Agricolo e l'Avvenire Sociale.   Milan.   1900.

III. HISTORIES.

Billot, A.   La France et l'Italie.   Histoire des Années Troubles, 1881–99.   Paris.   1905.

Gori, A.   Il Regno d'Italia, 1860–1900.   (Storia Politica d'Italia.)   Milan.   1904.

King, B. and Okey, T.   Italy to-day.   1901.

——   L'Italia d'Oggi.   2nd edn.   Bari.   1904.

King, B.   A History of Italian Unity.   2 vols.   1899.

Orsi, P.   Italia Moderna.   2nd edn.   Milan.   1902.

Stillman, W. J.   The Union of Italy, 1815–95.   1898.

——   Francesco Crispi.   1899.

IV. SPECIAL TREATISES.

Arbib, E.   Cinquant' Anni di Storia Parlamentare.   Vol. IV.   1870–80.   Rome.   1907.

Chiala, L.   Pagine di Storia Contemporanea de 1858 al 1892.   3 vols.   Turin and Rome.   1892–3.

——   La Spedizione di Massowa.   Turin and Naples.   1888.

——   Tunisi.   Turin.   1895.

——   La Triplice e la Duplice Alleanza.   Turin.   1898.

Colajanni, N.   Banche e Parlamento.   3rd edn.   Milan.   1893.
—— Gli Avvenimenti di Sicilia e le loro Cause.   2nd edn.   Palermo.   1896.
—— L'Italia nel 1898.   Milan.   1899.
D'Avril, A.   Négociations relatives au Traité de Berlin.   Paris.   1887.
Jonquière, C. E. L. M. T. de la.   Les Italiens en Erythrée.   Quinze ans de Politique Coloniale.   Paris.   1897.
Loiseau, C.   L'Équilibre Adriatique.   Paris.   1901.
Lyde, L. W. and Mockler-Ferryman, A. F.   A Military Geography of the Balkan Peninsula.   1905.
Mantegazza, V.   Guerra in Africa : Appendice, Il Trattato di Ucialli.   Florence.   1896.
—— L'Altra Sponda.   Milan.   1905.
Morandi, L.   Come fu educato Vittorio Emanuele III.   Turin.   1903.
Morelli, G.   Vittorio Emanuele II dai Documenti di sua Vita e Morte.   Milan.   1903.
Orero, General B.   Ricordi d'Africa.   Nuova Antologia.   Jan. 16, Feb. 1 and 16.   Rome.   1901.
Pinon, R.   L'Empire de la Méditerranée.   Paris.   1904.
Schulthess, H.   Europäischer Geschichtskalender : Italien ; Die Römische Kurie.   Nördlingen and Munich.   1871–1907.
Villari, L.   Italian life in Town and Country.   1902.
—— (Ed. by).   The Balkan Question.   1905.

V. THE CATHOLICS : MODERNISM.

Anon.   Le Idee di un Vescovo sul Non Expedit ; documenti inediti.   Rassegna Nazionale, January 16, 1904.   Florence.   1904.
Anon.   I Deputati Cattolici alla Camera : Parole di un Vescovo.   Ibid.   November.   1904.   Florence.   1904.
Barzellotti, Prof. G.   L'Italia e il Papato.   Nuova Antologia, March 1, 1904.   Rome.   1904.
Documenti Pontifici contro il Modernismo.   Rome.   1908.
Eufrasio.   Il Non Expedit.   Nuova Antologia, September 1, 1904.   Rome.   1904.
Houtin, A.   L'Américanisme.   Paris.   1904.
Lebreton, I.   The Encyclical and Modernist Theology.   Tr. by Alban Goodwin, S. J.   London.   1908.
Loisy, A. F.   Études bibliques.   Paris.   1903.
—— Études évangéliques.   Paris.   1902.   And other works.
Murri, Don R.   L'Enciclica "Pascendi" e la Filosofia Moderna.   Il Rinnovamento, November—December, 1907.   Milan.   1907.
Programma dei Modernisti.   Lettera Enciclica della Santità di nostro Signore Papa Pio X a tutti i Vescovi dell' Orbe Cattolico.   Rome.   1908.   Tr. by A. L. Lilley.   1908.
Rickaby, Jos., S. J.   The Modernist.   Catholic Truth Society.   1908.
Sabatier, P.   Modernism.   London and Leipzig.   1908.
Scotti, F. T. G.   La Fine della Cultura Sociale.   Rassegna Nazionale, July 1, 1906.   Florence.   1906.
—— Il Primo Congresso della Lega Democratica Nazionale.   Ibid.   Oct. 16, 1906.   Florence.   1906.
S.F.S.   The Encyclical "Pascendi Gregis."   The Month.   Nov. 1907.
Tyrrell, G.   A much abused letter.   1906.
—— Mediaevalism.   1908.
Un Cattolico Italiano.   La Dissoluzione delle Associazioni Cattoliche.   Nuova Antologia, August 16, 1898.   Rome.   1898.

VI. SOCIALISM.

Atti del Partito Socialista Italiano. IX Congresso Nazionale, Roma, 7—10 ott. 1906. Resoconto Stenografico. Rome. 1907.

Bissolati, L. Il Congresso Socialista Italiano. Nuova Antologia. October 1, 1906. Rome. 1906.

Chiappelli, A. Il Socialismo e il Pensiero Moderno. 2nd edn. Florence. 1899.

Gatti, G. Agricoltura e Socialismo. Milan. 1900.

Magri, F. Riformisti e Rivoluzionari nel Partito Socialista Italiano. Pt 1. Rassegna Nazionale, November 16, 1906. Florence. 1906.

—— Pt 2. Ibid. April 1, 1907. Florence. 1907.

Soldi, R. Le Varie Correnti nel Partito Socialista Italiano. Giornale degli Economisti, June, 1903. Rome. 1903.

Sombart, W. Sozialismus und Soziale Bewegung. 6th edn. Jena. 1908.

Villari, Prof. P. Scritti sulla Questione Sociale in Italia. Florence. 1902.

VII. NORTH AND SOUTH.

Bosco, A. L'Emigrazione dal Mezzogiorno. Giornale degli Economisti, April. Bologna. 1906.

De Viti de Marco, A. Trattati di Commercio e Interessi Meridionali. Ibid. July, 1903. Rome. 1903.

Munthe, A. Letters from a Mourning City : Naples, 1884. Translated from the Swedish by M. V. White. 1887.

Niceforo, A. Italia Barbara Contemporanea. Milan. 1898.

—— La Delinquenza in Sardegna. Palermo. 1897.

—— Nord e Sud. Turin. 1900.

—— Provvedimenti per il Mezzogiorno. Discorso alla Camera. Turin. 1906.

Papafava, F. La Legge per la Basilicata. Giornale degli Economisti, March, 1904. Rome. 1904.

—— Il Disegno di Legge per Napoli. Ibid. April and May, 1904. Rome. 1904.

Prato, G. Emigrazione della Fame in Basilicata. Rassegna Nazionale, May 1, 1903. Florence. 1903.

Renda, A. La Questione Meridionale : Inchiesta con Risposte di C. Lombroso, A. Loria, G. Ferrero, N. Colajanni, F. Squillace, etc. etc. Milan and Palermo. 1900.

VIII. CONTEMPORARY CRITICISM.

Arbib, E. La Questione d'Africa alla Camera Italiana. Nuova Antologia. Rome. January 16 and February 1, 1896.

—— L'Africa nei Libri Verdi. Ibid. February 16, March 1, and May 16, 1896.

—— Vittorie e Sconfitte. Milan. 1894.

Branzoli-Zappi, E. Il Bilancio dello Stato e la Funzione Ispettiva del Parlamento. Giornale degli Economisti. Rome. August, 1903.

Cesaro, Duca di. I Contadini in Sicilia. Rassegna Nazionale. Florence. December, 1905.

Dragoni, C. La Camera dei Deputati e l'Ispettorato del Lavoro. Giornale degli Economisti. Rome. April, 1906.

Fante, General C.   A Proposito dei nostri Ordinamenti Militari.   Nuova Antologia.
  Rome.   February 16, 1903.
Ferraris, M.   Le Nuove Spese Straordinarie per la Marina di Guerra.   Ibid.   June 1,
  1905.
—— Lo Sfacelo Ferroviario in Italia.   Ibid.   Jan. 16, 1906.
Ferrero, G.   Il Fenomeno Crispi e la Crise Italiana.   Turin.   1895.
Florio, F.   La Conversione del Consolidato Italiano.   Giornale degli Economisti.
  Rome.   July, 1906.
Ghersi, L.   Il Problema Militare.   Nuova Antologia.   Rome.   August 16, 1904.
Giretti, E.   La Società dei Terni, il Governo ed il "Trust" Metallurgico.   Giornale
  degli Economisti.   Rome.   Oct. and Nov. 1903.
Johannis, A. I. de.   Finanze, Sgravi, Riforma Tributaria.   Pt I.   Rassegna Nazionale.
  Florence.   December 1, 1905.
—— Pt 2.   Ibid.   January 16, 1906.
Luzzatti, L.   La Conversione della Rendita Italiana.   Nuova Antologia.   Rome.
  October 16, 1906.
Manassei, P.   Le Crisi Agrarie e le Imposte Fondiarie.   Rassegna Nazionale.
  Florence.   November 16, 1903.
Nitti, Prof. F. S.   Il Partito Radicale.   Turin and Rome.   1907.
Papafava, Count F.   L'Aquedotto delle Puglie.   Giornale degli Economisti.
  Rome.   August, 1902.
Persico, T.   Perche Abbiamo Pochi Uomini di Stato?   Rassegna Nazionale.
  Florence.   January 16, 1906.
Sonnino, Baron S.   Quid Agendum?   Nuova Antologia.   Rome.   September 16,
  1900.
Un Ex-Deputato.   Dove Andiamo a Finire?   Rassegna Nazionale.   Florence.
  January 1, 1904.

CHAPTER IX.

THE LOW COUNTRIES.

A. THE NETHERLANDS (HOLLAND).

(1) HISTORY OF THE PERIOD (1870–1905).

Blok, P. J.   Geschiedenis van het Nederlandsche Volk.   Vol. VIII.   Leyden.   1908.

Bruyne, J. A.   Geschiedenis van Nederland in onzen tijd.   5 vols.   Schiedam. 1889–1906.

Eeuw, Een halve, 1848–98.   Nederland onder de regeering van Koning Willem III en het regentschap van Koningin Emma door Nederlanders.   Geschreven onder redactie van P. H. Ritter.   2 vols.   Amsterdam.   1898.

Houten, S. van.   Vijf en twintig Jaar in de Kamer, 1869–94.   Haarlem.   1905.

Kemper, J. de Bosch.   Staatkundige Geschiedenis van Nederland na 1830.   Met letterkundige aanteekeningen en onuitgegevene stukken.   5 vols.   Amsterdam. 1873–82.

Kepper, G. L.   De Regeering van Koning Willem III.   Groningen.   1887.

—— Het Regentschap van Koningin Emma.   The Hague.   1895.

Nuyens, W. J. E.   Geschiedenis van het Nederlandsche Volk van 1815 tot op onze dagen.   4 vols.   Amsterdam.   1883–6.

Rengers, W. J. van Walderen.   Schets eener parlementaire Geschiedenis van Nederland sedert 1849.   The Hague.   1889.

Rijsens, F. van.   Geschiedenis van ons Vaderland.   Groningen.   1904.

Woff, N. H.   De Regeering van Koningin Wilhelmina.   Rotterdam.   1901.

(2) BIOGRAPHICAL AND GENERAL.

Deschamps, P.   La reine Wilhelmine.   Paris.   1901.

De Vries, M.   Handleiding tot de kennis van het leven en de werken van Mr G. Groen v. Prinsterer.   The Hague.   1895.

Fruin, J. A.   De Nederlandsche Wetboeken tot 1876.   Utrecht.   1831.

Heemskerk Az, J.   De Practijk onzer Grondwet.   Utrecht.   1881.

Houten, S.   Staatkundige brieven.   Haarlem.   1886.

—— Nieuwe Staatkundige brieven.   The Hague.   1909.

Huet, C. Busken.   Brieven.   2 vols.   Haarlem.   1890.

Husen, R.   Het leven van Koning Willem III.   Heusden.   1889.

Lohman, A. F. de Savornin.   Onze Constitutie.   Utrecht.   1907.

—— De Pacificatie.   Amsterdam.   1889.

Marius, G. Hermine.   Dutch Painting in the nineteenth century (trans. by de Mattos).   London.   1908.

Nippold, F.   Die Römische Katholische Kirche im Königreich der Niederlande Leipzig.   1877.

Painting, Modern Dutch. Edinburgh Review. July, 1909.

Pierson, Allard. Onze Tijdgenooten. Amsterdam. 1898.

—— N. G. Verspreide Geschriften. 3 vols. The Hague. 1901–6.

Renan, E. La Reine Sophie de Hollande. Rev. d. Deux Mondes. xxi, 952. Paris. 1877.

Versluys, J. Het Kiesrecht van Mr Tak van Poortvliet. Amsterdam. 1892.

Vos, A. J. de. Groen van Prinsterer en zijn tijd. Dordrecht. 1886.

Thijm, J. A. Alberdingk. By A. J. Amsterdam. 1893.

Willem III, Guillaume III, Roi de Hollande. By F. Loliée. Nouvelle Revue. Paris. 1890.

(3) The Dutch Indies.

Boys, H. Scott. Some Notes on Java and its administration by the Dutch. Allahabad. 1892.

Day, C. The policy and administration of the Dutch in Java. New York. 1904.

Deventer, M. L. van. Geschiedenis der Nederlanders op Java. 2 vols. Haarlem. 1887–95.

Gerlach, A. J. A. Nederlandische Oost-Indië. The Hague. 1874.

Kleyn, R. H. Het gewestelijk bestuur op Java. Leyden. 1889.

Perelaer, M. T. H. Nederlandische Indië. 4 vols. Leyden. 1881–3.

Pierson, N. G. Koloniale Politiek. Amsterdam. 1877.

Verslag van het beheer en der Staat der Nederl. bezittingen in Oost- en West-Indië en ter Kust van Guinea. 44 vols. The Hague. 1849–96.

B. BELGIUM.

(1) History of the period (1870–1905).

Balau, Abbé Sylvain. Soixante-dix ans d'histoire contemporaine. Brussels. 1890.

Bertrand, L. Histoire de la Démocratie et du Socialisme en Belgique dépuis 1860. Brussels. 1906.

—— Léopold II et son règne. Brussels. 1890.

Cinquante ans de la liberté. 4 vols. Brussels. 1880.

Dujardin-Beaumetz, J. F. P. Histoire graphique de l'industrie houillère en Belgique. Paris. 1888.

Hoorebeke, Ladislas van. Quatre ans d'évolution, 1890–4. Ghent. 1894.

Hymans, L. La Belgique contemporaine. Mons. 1880.

—— Histoire parlementaire de la Belgique. 6 vols. Brussels. 1878–80.

Juste, T. Léopold I et Léopold II, leur vie et leur règne. Brussels. 1877.

MacDonnell, J. de C. King Leopold II. His rule in Belgium and the Congo. 1905.

Olschewky, S. Léopold II, roi des Belges, sa vie et son règne, 1865–1905. Brussels. 1905.

(2) Biographical and General.

Conscience, Hendrik. Zijn leven en zijne werken. Haarlem. 1883.

Flandin, É. Institutions politiques de l'Europe contemporaine. Belgique. Tom. i, pp. 160–307. Paris. 1907.

Frère-Orban, W. La Belgique et le Vatican. 3 vols. Brussels. 1880–1.

Giron, A. Droit publique de la Belgique. Brussels. 1884.

—— Droit administratif. 2 vols. Brussels. 1881.

Guilléry, J. Les Sociétés commerciales en Belgique. 3 vols. Brussels. 1883.

Huët, C. Busken. Het Land van Rubens. Belgische reisherinneringen. Amsterdam. 1879.

Lauer, M. Entwickelung und Gestaltung der Belgischen Volksschulwesen. Berlin. 1885.

Laveleye, E. de. Le parti clérical en Belgique. Paris. 1874.

Lebeau, J. Souvenirs personnels. Brussels. 1883.

Patria Belgica. 3 vols. Brussels. 1883.

Thonissen, J. J. La Constitution Belge annotée. Brussels. 1879.

Wilmotte, Maurice. La Belgique, morale et politique, 1830–90. Brussels. 1902.

Woeste, Charles. Vingt ans de polémique. 2 vols. Brussels. 1885.

—— Échos des luttes contemporaines. 2 vols. Brussels. 1906.

(3) The Congo.

Castelein, A. L'État du Congo, ses droits et ses devoirs. Brussels. 1907.

Congo. La vérité sur le Congo. Bulletin Mensuel. Brussels. 1903, etc.

Congo Reform Association Official Organ. Liverpool. 1905.

Congo Commission of Enquiry, Evidence laid before. Liverpool. 1905.

Deschamps, E. L'Afrique Nouvelle. Essai sur l'état civilisateur des Pays Neufs et sur la Fondation, l'Organisation et le Gouvernement de l'État Indépendant du Congo. Brussels. 1903.

Morel, E. D. The Congo Slave State. Liverpool. 1903.

—— King Leopold's Rule in Africa. 1904.

—— Great Britain and the Congo. 1909.

Nys, E. L'État Indépendant du Congo et le droit international. Brussels. 1903.

Rapport des Secrétaires Généraux au Roi Souverain. Bulletin officiel. Brussels. 1907.

CHAPTER X.

THE IBERIAN PENINSULA.

I. SPAIN.

A. BIBLIOGRAPHY.

Hartzenbusch, E.   Apuntes para un catálogo de periodicos madrileños.   Madrid. 1894.

Torres Campos, M.   Bibliografia contemporanea del derecho y de la politica. Madrid. 1883. See also White, G. F., under E.

B. PUBLISHED DOCUMENTS.

Derecho parlamentario Español.   Madrid. 1885.
Diario de las Sesiones de Cortes.   Madrid.
Muro Martinez, J.   Constituciones en España.   Madrid. 1881.
Sancho de los Santos, Modesto.   Las Cortes Españolas de 1907.   Madrid.   1908.
Tetuan, L. O'Donnell, duque de.   Apuntes del ex-Ministro de Estado.   Madrid. 1902.

C. BIOGRAPHIES.

Amadeus, King of Spain.   Whitehouse, H. R.   New York. 1897.
Cánovas del Castillo, Antonio.   El Solitario y su tiempo.   Madrid. 1883.
——   Life of.   Creux, V. C.   Paris. 1897.
——   Life of.   Pons y Umbert A.   Madrid. 1901.
Castelar, Emilio.   Dario, R.   Madrid. 1899.
——   González Araco, M.   Su vida y muerte.   Madrid. 1900.
——   Grimaldi, A. L. E.   Semblanza moral, intelectual y politica.   Cadiz.   1868.
——   Sandoval, F. de.   Coup d'œil sur sa vie.   Paris. 1886.
Ruiz Zorrilla, M. R. E. M.   Historia de.   Madrid. 1885.

D. MEMOIRS AND TRAVELS.

Diercks, Gustav.   Das Moderne Giestesleben Spaniens.   Leipzig. 1886.
Echegaray, J.   Recuerdos.   Madrid.
Mesonero Romanos, R. de.   Memorias de un Sotentrion.   Madrid. 1881.
Valero de Tornos, J.   Crónias retrospectivas.   Recuerdos de la Segunda Mitad del Siglo xix por un portero del observatorio.   Con un prólogo de Jacinto Octavio Picon.   Madrid. 1901.
Villalba Hervas, M.   De Alcolea á Sagunto 1868–74.   Madrid. 1899.
Zorrilla, J.   Recuerdos del tiempo viejo.   Barcelona. 1880–3.

E.　GENERAL HISTORIES AND TREATISES.

Aguilar, F. de A.　El Pase Regio.　Madrid.　1875.

Becker, J.　España y Marruecos.　Relaciones diplomaticos durante el Siglo xix.　Madrid.　1903.

Bermejo, I. A.　Historia de la intermidad y de la última Guerra Civil.　Madrid.　1876.

Borrego, A.　La Revolucion, la intermidad y el advenimiento de la Restauracion.　Madrid.　1875.

—— Historia de la Revolucion.　Madrid.　1877.

Calvo, M. M.　Regimen parlamentario en España.　Madrid.　1883.

Casas, J. B.　La Guerra Separatista de Cuba.

Castelar, E.　Discursos parlamentarios y politicos.　Madrid.　1885.

Castillo, D. J.　Politica de España en Filipinas.

Cherbuliez, V.　L'Espagne Politique, 1868–74.　Paris.　1874.

Clarke, H. Butler.　Modern Spain.　1815–98.　Cambridge.　1906.

Concas y Palau, V.　La Escuadra del Almirante Cervera.　Madrid.　1900.

Costa, J.　Oligarquia y Caciquismo como la forma actual del Gobierno en España.　Madrid.　1903.

Fabie, A. M.　Ensayo de la legislacion Española, en sus estados de ultramar.　Madrid.　1896.

Gimenez, E. S.　Secretos é intimidades del Campo Carlista en la pasada guerra civil.　Barcelona.　1896.

Guytot, Y.　L'évolution politique et Sociale de l'Espagne.　Paris.　1899.

Houghton, A.　Les origines de la Restauration des Bourbons en Espagne.　Paris.　1890.

Latimer, E. W.　Spain in the nineteenth century.　Chicago.　1898.

Lauser, W.　Geschichte Spaniens von dem Sturze Isabellas (1868–75).　Leipzig.　1877.

Lopez Dominguez, General José.　Operaciones del Ejercito del Nodé.　Madrid.　1876.

—— Comentarios sobre el sitio de Cartagena.　Madrid.　1877.

Lowell, J. R.　Impressions of Spain.　1900.

Mañe y Flaquer Maz.　La Paz y los Fueros.　Barcelona.　1876.

Molins, J. E. de.　La Crisis en España.　Parte agrícola.　Barcelona.　1904.

Narracion Militar de la Guerra Carlista 1869–76.　Madrid.　1883–9.

Palacio y Garcia de Velasio, F. X.　Conde de las Almenas.　La politica de la Regencia.　Madrid.　1886.

Pirala, A.　Historia de la Guerra de Cuba.　Madrid.　1895, 1898.

—— Historia Contemporánea.　Madrid.　1900.

—— España y la Regencia.　Madrid.　1904.

Polavieja, General.　Mi mando en Cuba.　Madrid.　1896.

Reig y Casanova, E.　Presente y Porvenir Economico de la Iglesia en España.　Madrid.　1908.

Retana, W. E.　Folletos Filipinos.　Madrid.　1892.

Reynald, H.　Histoire d'Espagne depuis la Mort de Charles III.　Paris.　1873.

Rodríguez Solis, E.　Historia del partido republicano español.　Madrid.　1893.

Salmeron, N.　Discursos parlamentarios.　Madrid.　1881.

Tarrida del Marmol, F.　Les Inquisiteurs de l'Espagne.　Paris.　1897.

White, G. F.　A Century of Spain and Portugal (1786–1898).　1909.　[Contains a full bibliography.]

II. PORTUGAL.

Adam, Mme J.   La patrie portugaise.   Paris.   1896.

Andrade Corvo, J. de.   Estudios sobre as provincias ultramarinas.   4 vols.   Lisbon.   1883–7.

Carvalho Soveral, A. de.   Breve estudio sobre a ilha de Moçambique.   Oporto.   1887.

Delannoy, C.   L'Angola et la colonisation portugaise.   Soc. Belg. de Géographie.   Bulletin annual.   Brussels.   1895.

Diario das Cortes Geraes e Extraordinarias.   Lisbon.

Documentos para a historia das Cortes Geraes da Naçao Portugueza.   Lisbon.   1889–91.

Franca, B. da.   Sabsidios para a historia de Macau.   Lisbon.   1888.

Gremieux, C.   Possessions portugaises dans l'extrême orient.   Paris.   1883.

Iseghem, A. van.   Les Îles portugaises de l'Afrique.   Brussels.   1897.

Kutschera, M.   Macau der erste Stutzpunkt europäischen Handels in China.   Vienna.   1900.

Le Grand, M.   Le Portugal.   Notice historique au point de vue du développement de ses relations avec la France.   Fécamp.   1895.

Oliveira Martins, J. P.   Historia de Portugal.   Lisbon.   1896.

—— Portugal contemporaneo.   Lisbon.   1895.

—— Portugal em Africa.   Oporto.   1891.

Pimheiro, C. M.   Os Colonias portuguezas no secolo xix.   Lisbon.   1890.

Salisbury, W. A.   Portugal and its people.   Lisbon.   1893.

Santo Luiz, Cardinal F. de.   Os Portuguezes na Africa, Asia, America e Oceania.   Lisbon.   1890.

Tavares de Medeiros, J. J.   Das Staatsrecht Portugals.   4 vols.   Freiburg and Tübingen.   1892.

Ternant, V. de.   Les Colonies portugaises.   Paris.   1890.

Thael, G. N.   The Portuguese in South Africa.   1896.

Worsfold, W. B.   Portuguese Nyassaland.   1899.

CHAPTER XI.

SCANDINAVIA.

I. SWEDEN AND NORWAY.

A. Documents and Memoirs.

Protokoll, Första och Andra Kammarens, med Bihang. 909 vols. Stockholm. 1872–1905.

Storthingsforhandlinger, 1872–1905. 359 vols. Christiania. 1872–1905.

Affaires de Norvège. Documents officiels concernant la dissolution de l'union entre la Norvège et la Suède et la constitution du royaume de Norvège. 1903–5. Documents officiels communiqués par le Gouvernement Norvégien en 1907. Archives diplomatiques. T. ci. Paris. 1907.

Aktstykker vedkommende Spörgsmaalet om diplomatiske Sagers Behandling 1885–91. Udgivet af de konservative Foreningers Centralstyrelse. Christiania. 1891.

De Geer, L. Minnen. 2 vols. Stockholm. 1892. 2nd edn. Stockholm. 1906.

Författningssamling, Svensk. 1872–1905. Stockholm. 1872–1905.

Förhandlingarna i konsulatfrågan. [Protokoll d. 5 april 1905 i sammansatt svenskt och norskt statsråd.] Stockholm. 1905.

Ibsen, S. Da unionen lösnede. i–v. Samtiden. Christiania. 1906.

I den unionella frågan. [Protokoll d. 5 april 1905 i sammansatt svenskt och norskt statsråd.] Stockholm. 1905.

I den unionella frågan. Utdrag af Post- och Inrikes Tidningar för den 13 och den 20 juni 1905. Stockholm. 1905.

Knudsen, C. Spredte Minder fra 1905. Christiania. 1906.

Motzfeldt, K. Dagböger 1854–89. Ed. E. Motzfeldt. Med Forfattarens Portræt og Biografi. Christiania and Copenhagen. 1908.

Oplösning, Unionens. En Dagbog. Med illustr. Særaftryk af "Aftenposten." 2nd edn. Christiania. 1905.

—— ——, 1905. Officielle aktstykker vedrörende unionskrisen og Norges gjenreisning som helt suveræn stat. Med talrige facsimiler og billeder. Ed. J. V. Heiberg. Christiania. 1906.

Ord, Sveriges, i unionskonflikten. Svenska riksdagens skrifvelse till K. M:t den 28 juli 1905. Stockholm. 1905. English translation: The union between Sweden and Norway. The address presented to the King by the Swedish parliament. Stockholm. 1905.

Traktater, Sverges, med främmande makter. Vol. 12: 1868–77. Ed. O. Alin. 13: 1: 1878–85. Ed. C. Sandgren. 13: 2: 1885–90. Ed. C. Sandgren. Stockholm. 1900–5.

Vogt, J. Statsraad Colletts Hus og hans Samtid. Erindringer 1814–89. Christiania. 1903.

Yttrande, Underdånigt, af den för utarbetande af förslag till ändrade bestämmelser angående Sveriges och Norges förening af Kongl. Maj:t den 13 november 1895 i nåder förordnade komité jämte förslag af komiténs särskilda ledamöter. Stockholm. 1898.

B. Historical Works.

Alin, O. Unionskommitténs resultat. Några betraktelser. Svenska National-föreningens skrifter. 13. Stockholm. 1898.

Arcadius, C. O. Louis De Geer. Svenskt Folkbibliotek. 3: 11. Stockholm. 1906.

Aschehoug, T. H. Norges offentlige Ret. Part 2: Norges nuvarende Statsfor-fatning. Vols. I–III. Christiania. 1874–81.

Aubert, L. M. B. La Norvège devant le droit international. Repr. from Revue de droit international et de Législation comparée. Brussels. 1896.

[Bergstrand, W.] Bidrag till den skandinaviska unionens historia efter 1814, by Marcellus. Stockholm. 1885.

—— Norska riksrättstragedien och unionen, by Marcellus. Stockholm. 1884.

Berner, H. E. Norsk eller fælles Udenrigsminister. Christiania. 1891.

Beyer-Boppard, C. Ein Senior von Europiens Monarchen. Grundriss zu einem biographischen Denkmal für König Oscar II von Schweden und Norwegen. Leipzig. 1901.

Bugge, S. Samhold i Norden. Populær-Videnskabelige Foredrag. Efterladte Arbeider. Christiania. 1907.

Clason, S. Historisk redogörelse för unionsfrågans tidigare skeden. Stockholm. 1898.

Diplomaticus. I Sverige 1905. Erindringer og Optegnelser. Christiania. 1906.

Edén, N. Det svenska programmet i unionskrisen. Upsala and Stockholm. 1905. English translation: Sweden for peace. The programme of Sweden in the union crisis. Stockholm. 1905.

Engeström, J. O. Th. Norge. Dess ekonomi och finanser. 2nd edn. Upsala. 1906.

Flodström, T. Sveriges och Norges utrikes styrelse. Stockholm. 1903.

Forssell, H. Uttalanden i konsulatfrågan. Ed. H. Hjärne. Stockholm. 1905.

Getz, B. Norges folkeretslige Stilling og Statsforfatning. Norge i det nittende Aarhundrede. Vol. I. Christiania. 1901.

—— Die schwedisch-norwegische Union. Die Zukunft. Vol. VIII. Berlin. 1894.

Haralds, Hj. E. G. Boström. Svenskar. 2. Stockholm. 1907.

Hasselgren, A. Oscar II. En lefnadsteckning. Stockholm. 1908.

Hedin, A. Tal och skrifter. Ed. V. Spångberg. Stockholm. 1904–5.

Historia, Sveriges, intill tjugonde seklet. Ed. E. Hildebrand. Part 10: A. Ryd-fors, Sveriges historia, 1859–1900–[07]. Stockholm. 1902, 1909.

Historie, Norges. Fremstillet for det norske folk, by A. Bugge, E. Hertzberg, J. E. Sars. Vol. VI: J. E. Sars, Tidsrummet 1814–1905. Christiania. 1908. (*In progress.*)

Hjärne, H. King Oscar of Sweden and Norway. The Forum. Vol. III. New York and London. 1896.

Ibsen, S. Spörgsmaalet om et særskilt norsk konsulatvæsens forh. til det fælles diplomati og det fælles udenrigsstyre. Christiania. 1901.

Kjellén, R. Den tredje stora unionskommittén. Ett stycke unionshistoria. Stats-vetenskaplig Tidskrift. Vol. I. Upsala. 1898.

—— 1866–1909. Historiska randanmärkningar till den svenska rösträttsfrågans lösning. Historiska studier tillägnade H. Hjärne. Upsala and Stockholm. 1908.

Kjellén, R. Unionen sådan den skapades och sådan den blifvit. 1. Den ursprungliga unionen. 2. Unionens historia (1814–91). 3. Den nuvarande unionen. Föreningen Heimdals folkskrifter. 1, 14, 15, 18, 19. Stockholm. 1893, 1894.

Land och folk, Sveriges. Historisk-statistisk handbok på offentligt uppdrag utgifven af G. Sundbärg. Stockholm. 1901. English translation: Sweden. Its people and its industry. Historical and statistical handbook. Published by order of the government. Stockholm. 1904.

Linck, J. Konung Oscar II. Biografisk skildring. Stockholm. 1897.

Maricourt, Réné de, baron de Moncz. Oscar II intime. Paris. 1906.

Mohn, A. Une page d'histoire de la civilisation. La Suède et la révolution Norvégienne. Geneva and Paris. 1906.

Morgenstierne, B. Den unionelle Ret. Repr. from Forelæsninger over den norske Statsforfatningsret.

Nansen, Fr. Norge og Foreningen med Sverige. Christiania. 1905. English translation: Norway and the union with Sweden. Christiania. 1905.

Nielsen, J. Norge i 1905. Med en inledande Oversigt over Unionshistoriens niti Aar. Horten. 1906.

Nordlund, K. Den svensk-norska krisen. Aktstycken jämte historik. Upsala and Stockholm. 1905. English translation: The Swedish-Norwegian crisis. A history with documents. Upsala and Stockholm. 1905.

Norge i det nittende aarhundrede. Tekst og billeder af norske forfattare og kunstnere. Ed. W. C. Brögger. 2 vols. Christiania. 1901–2.

Norway. Official publication for the Paris exhibition. Publ. by S. Konow. Christiania. 1900.

Oscar II, Sveriges konung 1872–1907. En minnesskrift åren 1829–96 bearbetning efter J. Linck, åren 1897–1907 af H. A. Ring. Jämte en bilaga af O. Hellkvist. Stockholm. 1908.

Ræder, O. Munch. Unionen og egen Udenrigsminister. Christiania. 1893.

R[euterskiöld], C. A. Om de ministeriella ärendena och formerna för deras behandling i Sverige-Norge. Upsala. 1891.

Rinman, E. B. Fiction and fact about the Scandinavian crisis. Stockholm. 1905.

Rydfors, A. Konung Oscar II och Sveriges folk. Stockholm. 1897.

Rydin, H. L. Anteckningar om den norska vensterns unionspolitik och dennas statsrättsliga karaktär under åren 1891–1902. Upsala. 1902.

—— Unionen och konungens sanktionsrätt i norska grundlagsfrågor. Stockholm. 1883.

Sars, J. E. Norges politiske Historie, 1815–85. Med Tillægsafhandlinger angaaende Norge i det nittende Aarhundrede, by Chr. Collin, L. A. Havstad, O. Holm, Ragna Nielsen. Christiania. 1899–1904.

—— Unionsspörgsmaalet. Nyt Tidsskrift. Christiania. 1892–3.

Spångberg, V. Adolf Hedin, väktaren och förgångsmannen. En politisk studie. Verdandis småskrifter. 100. Stockholm. 1901.

Staaff, K. The grounds of Sweden's protest. North American Review. Vol. CLXXXI. New York. 1905.

Svensén, E. Karl Ifvarsson och landtmannapartiet. Verdandis småskrifter. XXIV. Stockholm. 1890.

Utheim, J. Grundloven om Norges Udenrigsstyre. Bibl. for de tusen hjem. Christiania. 1894.

Varenius, O. Konsulatfrågan. Upsala. 1893.

—— Nyare unionell litteratur och olika unionella rättsåskådningar. Kritisk framställning. I–III. Upsala. 1893.

[——] Den svensk-norska unionen och dess rättsliga grund. I–III. Nya Dagligt Allehanda. Stockholm. 1893. [Has been translated into French and German.]

Varenius, O. Den gemensamme utrikesministern och likställigheten. Upsala. 1893.
Vullum, E. Unionen og dens Fremtid. Bergen. 1894.
Wrangel, F. U. Redogörelse för konung Oscar II's 25-åriga regeringsjubileum. Stockholm. 1898.
Överland, O. A. Norges historie, 1814–1902. Med et omrids af Sveriges og Danmarks historie i det 19de aarhundrede. Christiania. 1902.

II. DENMARK.

A. Documents.

Rigsdagstidende, 1864–5 to 1904–5. 265 vols. Copenhagen. 1864–1905.

B. Historical Works.

Barfod, H. P. B. Hans Majestæt Kong Christian IX. Spredte Træk til et Livsbillede. Copenhagen. 1888.
Clausen, H. Nordslesvig, 1863–93. Den nationale stilling på landet. Sönderjydske Aarböger. Flensburg. 1894.
Hansted, B. Om Betingelserne for Afslutning af vor politiske Strid. Et Udkast. Copenhagen. 1894.
Hegermann-Lindencrona, C. Betragtninger i Anledning af D. G. Monrads politiske Breve. Copenhagen. 1875.
Holm, H. Forligets förste Rigsdagssamling 1894–5. En Redegörelse. Copenhagen. 1895.
—— Kampen om Ministeriet Reedtz-Thott. En Redegörelse for Rigsdagssamlingen 1896–7. Copenhagen. 1897.
Jörgensen, A. D. Historiske afhandlinger. Ed. C. F. Bricka. Vol. iv. Afhandlinger vedrörende Danmarks nyeste historie og nutidsforhold. Copenhagen. 1899.
Matzen, H. Grundloven og Folkets Selvstyrelse. Copenhagen. 1873.
Monrad, D. G. Politiske Breve. Parts i–xix. Copenhagen. 1874–82.
Neergaard, N. Danmarks Riges Historie siden 1852. Copenhagen. 1909. (Vol. vi of Danmarks Riges, Joh. Steenstrup, K. Erslev, A. Heise, etc.)
Scavenius, J. F. Om Forliget og dets Betingelser. Copenhagen. 1893.
Schleisner, P. A. Til Belysning af Dagshistorien efter Frederik den Syvendes Död. Copenhagen. 1889.
Thorsöe, Alex. Kong Christian den Niende. Et historisk Tilbageblik i Anledning af Hans Majestæts 87-aarige Födselsdag den 8 April 1905. Copenhagen. 1905.
Troels-Lund, T. F. De tre nordiske Brödrefolk. Copenhagen. 1906.

CHAPTERS XII AND XIII.

RUSSIA.

I. FOR GENERAL REFERENCE.

Brockhaus and Ephron. Otděl'noe izdanie stateĭ o Rossii iz Encyklopediskago Slovaría Brokhausa i Ephrona. (Separate edition of the articles on Russia from the Encyclopaedia of Brockhaus and Ephron.) St Petersburg. 1900. [Invaluable.]

Derĭužinskiĭ, V. T. Policeĭskoe pravo. (Police Law.) Posobie dlĭa studentov. 2nd edn. St Petersburg. 1908.

Istoričeskiĭ obzor děĭatel'nosti Komiteta Ministrov. (Historical Review of the Work of the Committee of Ministers.) Vols. i–iv. Sostavlen S. M. Seredoninym i I. I. Ixorževskim, pod glavn. red. Stats-Sekretaría Kulomzina. Kanceliarii k–teta Ministrov (K stolětiĭu K-ta Ministrov 1802–1902). St Petersburg. 1902. [Official.]

Ivanoff-Razumnik. Istoriĭa russkoĭ obščestvennoĭ mysli. (A History of Russian Social Thought.) Individualism i měščanstvo v russkoĭ Literaturiě i žizni xix v. Vols. i and ii. 2nd edn. St Petersburg. 1908. [Very suggestive.]

Ivanovskiĭ, V. V. Učebnik administrativnago prava. (Text-Book of Administrative Law.) (Policeĭskoe pravo. Pravo vnutrenníago upravleniĭa.) Kazan. 1904.

Korkunoff, N. M. Russkoe gosudarstvennoe pravo. Posobie k lekciĭam. Vols. i and ii. 5th edn. St Petersburg. (Russian State Law.) 1904–5. [A standard work.]

Le-Roy-Beaulieu, A. L'Empire des Tsars et les Russes. 3 vols. Paris. 1897–8. [A most valuable study of Russian life and institutions.]

Rambaud, A. Histoire de la Russie. 5th edn., revised and completed to 1900. Paris. 1900.

Sergěevskiĭ, N. D. Russkoe ugolovnoe pravo. (Russian Criminal Law.) Posobie k lekciĭam. Čast obščaiĭa. 6th edn. St Petersburg. 1905.

Šerševenič, G. Ph. Učebnik russkago graždanskago prava. (Hand-book of Russian Civil Law.) 6th edn. St Petersburg. 1907.

Suvoroff, N. Učebnik Cerkovnago Prava. (Text-Book of Church Law.) 2nd edn. Moscow. 1902.

Svatikoff, S. G. Obščestvennoe dviženie v Rossii (The movement in Russia), 1700–1895. Publ. by N. Paramonoff. Rostoff na Donu. 1905. [Lacking in perspective, but useful.]

Věstnik Evropy. St Petersburg. 1868–1910. [The most solid of Russian Monthlies.]

Wallace, Sir D. M. Russia. 2 vols. London. 1905. [The best English study of Russian life and institutions.]

II. REIGN OF ALEXANDER II. 1861-81.

Bakunin, M. Bog i gosudarstvo. (God and the State.) In Ravenstvo. Moscow. 1906. [An exposition of the views of the leading Anarchist.]

Baturinskiĭ, V. P. A. I. Hertzen ego družʹia i znakomye. (A. I. Hertzen, his friends and acquaintances.) Materialy dlïa istorii obščestvennago dviženiĭa v Rossii. Vol. i. Publ. by G. T. Lʹvovič. St Petersburg. 1904.

Černyševskiĭ, N. G. Čto dělatʹ? (What is to be done?) St Petersburg. 1909. [A novel by a Socialist leader.]

Debogoriĭ-Mokrievič, V. Vospominaniĭa. (Reminiscences.) Publ. in Svobodnyĭ trud by A. I. Mukova and M. A. Poluboĭarova. St Petersburg. 1906. [A charming and most instructive sketch of the Revolutionaries, 1866–78.]

Džanšieff, G. Osnovy sudebnoĭ reformy. (The Principles of the Reform of the Law-Courts.) (K 25^{ti} -lětiĭu novago suda.) Istorikoĭuridičeskie etĭudy. Moscow. 1891.

Golovačeff, A. A. Desĭatʹ lět reform. (Ten years of Reforms.) 1861–71. In Věstn. Evropy. St Petersburg. 1872.

Hertzen, A. I. Byloe i dumy. (Polnoe sobranie sočineniĭ. Vols. ii and iii.) Pub. by Ph. Pavlenkoff. St Petersburg. 1905.

Kolĭupanoff, N. Biografiĭa Aleksandra Ivanoviča Košeleva. (The Biography of A. I. Košeleff.) Vol. i, Parts 1 and 2; ii. Publ. by Košeleva. Moscow. 1889–92. [A Moderate Reformer.]

Kolokol. 1857–64. London. 1864–7. Geneva. [The organ of A. I. Hertzen.]

Korniloff, A. A. Obščestvennoe dviženie pri Aleksandre II (1855–81). Istoričeskie očerki. Moscow. 1909. [A very valuable sketch.]

Kropotkin, Prince P. A. Memoirs of a Revolutionist. London. 1907. [From the point of view of an independent Revolutionary: important.]

Lavroff, P. L. (P. Mirtoff). Istoričeskiĭa pisʹma. (Historical Letters.) 4th edn. "Russkoe Bogatstvo." St Petersburg. 1906. [This work helped to found a school of Russian socialism.]

Lemke, M. Epoxa cenzurnyx reform 1859–65 godov. (The Epoch of Reforms in the Censorship (1859–65).) Publ. by M. V. Pirožkoff. Istorič. Otd. n°. 3. St Petersburg. 1904.

Na slavnom Postu (1860–1900). Literaturnyĭ sbornik, posvěščennyĭ N. K. Mixaĭlovskomu. 2nd edn. St Petersburg. 1906. [Records of Revolutionaries.]

Nevěděnskiĭ, S. Katkoff i ego vremĭa. (Katkoff and his Times.) St Petersburg. 1888.

Nikitenko, A. V. Zapiski i dnevnik (1826–77). Vols. i–iii. Moĭa pověstʹ o samom sebě i o tom "čemu svidětelʹ v žizni byl." St Petersburg. 1893. [A very valuable running commentary by a Liberal censor.]

Perepiska, Ĭu. T. Samarina s baronessoĭu. E. T. Raden (1861–76). Moscow. 1893. [Correspondence of the Slavophil thinker.]

Pharesoff, A. I. Semidesĭatniki. (The Men of the Seventies.) Očerki umstvennyx i političeskix dviženiĭ v Rossii. St Petersburg. 1905.

Tatiščeff, S. S. Imperator Aleksandr II ego žiznʹ i carstvovanie. Vols. i and ii. Publ. by A. Suvorin. St Petersburg. 1903. [The standard history of this reign.]

Tun, A. Istoriĭa revolĭucionnago dviženiĭa v Rossii. (History of the Revolutionary movement in Russia.) Perevod s německago, pod redakcieĭ i s priměčaniĭami L. E. Šiško. St Petersburg. [The notes are valuable.]

III. RUSSIFICATION AND EXPANSION OF THE EMPIRE. REACTION. 1882–1904.

Arsen'eff, K. K. Zakonodatel'stvo o pečati. (Velikiĭa reformy 60-x gg. v ix prošlom i nastoĭašćem. Pod. red I. V. Hessena i A. I. Kaminka.) Publ. by P. P. Geršunin and Co. St Petersburg. 1903. [A series of valuable articles on the Press.]

Berg. Zemskoe Xozĭaĭstvo pribaltiĭskago kraĭa. (State of Agriculture in the Baltic Provinces.) St Petersburg.

Dmowski, R. La Question Polonaise. Transl. by V. Gasztowtt. Paris. 1909. [The writer was leader of the National Democrats: a suggestive publicistic work.]

Fisher, J. R. Finland and the Tsars. 1809–99. London. 1899.

Hessen, I. V. Sudebnaĭa reforma (Velikiĭa reformy 60-x godov v ix prošlom i nastoĭašćem pod red. I. V. Hessena i A. I. Kaminka). Publ. by P. P. Geršunin and Co. St Petersburg. 1905. [A one-sided review of the history of the Law Courts.]

Ĭacimirskiĭ, A. I. Novĕĭšaĭa pol'skaĭa literatura. (Recent Polish Literature.) Ot Vozstaniĭa 1863 goda do našix dneĭ. Vols. i and ii. Publ. by O. N. Popova. St Petersburg. 1908.

Koulomzine, A. N. de. Le Transsibérien. Paris. 1904.

Kouropatkine, Colonel. Les confins anglo-russes. Transl. by G. le Marchand. Paris. 1879.

Mel'gunoff, S. Cerkov' i gosudarstvo v Rossii. (Church and State in Russia.) (K voprosu o svobodĕ sovĕsti.) Sbornik Stateĭ. Vols. i and ii. Moscow. 1907–9.

Pobedonosceff, K. P. Reflections of a Russian Statesman. Transl. by R. C. Long. 1898.

Prugavin, A. S. Zakony i spravočnyĭa svĕdĕniĭa po načal'nomu narodnomu obrazovaniĭu. (The Laws, etc. concerning elementary education.) 2nd edn. St Petersburg. 1904.

Samarin, Ĭu. T. Okraĭny Rossii. (The Outskirts of Russia.) Sobr. sočin. Vols. viii–x. Moscow. 1890–8. [The Slavophil view: chiefly concerning the Baltic Provinces.]

Skrine, F. H. and Ross, E. D. The Heart of Asia. Part ii. Philadelphia. 1899.

Slĭuzberg, G. B. Pravovoe i ekonomičeskoe položenie evreev v Rossii. (Iz materialov po evreĭskomu voprosu.) St Petersburg. 1907. [Accounted the best exposition of the Jewish view.]

Solov'eff, V. Nacional'nyĭ vopros v Rossii. (The National question in Russia.) Vols. i and ii. 3rd edn. St Petersburg. 1891. [Solov'eff is known as the most eminent of modern Russian philosophers.]

Uxtomskiĭ, Prince E. E. Putešestvie na Vostok Ego Imperatorskago Vysočestva Gosudarĭa Naslĕdnika Cesareviča 1890–1. (Journey of His Imperial Highness the Cesarevich to the East.) St Petersburg. 1893–7. [Contains an exposition of the Far East policy by one of its chief supporters.] French transl. by L. Leger: Voyage en Orient de S.A.I. le Césarévitch. 2 vols. Paris. 1893–8.

IV. THE ZEMSTVA. 1866–1904.

Aksakoff, I. S. Gosudarstvennyĭ i zemskiĭ Vopros. Stat'i o někotoryx istoričeskix sobytiĭax. 1860–86. Stat'i iz "Dnĭa," "Moskvy," "Moskviča," i "Rusi." Polnoe Sobranie sočineniĭ. Vol. v. Moscow. 1886. [A Slavophil view of Zemstvo questions.]

Golubeff, A. Knĭaz' Aleksandr Illarionovič Vasilčikoff. Biografičeskiĭ očerk. St Petersburg. 1882.

Melkaĭa Zemskaĭa Edinica. Sbornik stateĭ. 2nd edn. Kn. P. D. Dolgorukova i Kn. D. I. Šaxovskago pri učastii red. gaz. "Pravo." St Petersburg. [The Liberal view on the need of a smaller unit of local government.]

Pazuxin, A. Sovremennoe sostoĭanie Rossii i soslovnyĭ vopros. Moscow. 1886. [The Reactionary view on the Zemstvo: it became the basis of the Law of 1890.]

Skalon, V. Ĭ. Zemskie voprosy. Očerki i obozreniĭa. Publ. by the Zemstvo Gazette. Moscow. 1882. [The best writer on Zemstvo questions.]

—— Zemskiĭe vzglĭady na reformu městnago upravleniĭa. Obzor zemskix otzyvov i proektov. Moscow. 1884. [Views of Zemstvo men on local government.]

Schreider, G. I. Naše gorodskoe obščestvennoe upravlenie. Etĭudy očerki i zamětki. Vol. i. St Petersburg. 1902. [On self-government in towns.]

Tixonoff, T. I. Zemstvo v Rossii i na okrainax. (The Zemstvo in Russia and in the Borderlands.) St Petersburg. 1907.

Vasil'čikoff, A. K. O samoupravlenii. Sravniteľnyĭ obzor russkix i inostrannyx zemskix i obščestvennyx učreždeniĭ. Vols. i–iii. 3rd edn. St Petersburg. 1872. [A respected public man on self-government.]

Veselovskiĭ, B. Istoriĭa zemstva za sorok lět. Publ. by O. N. Popova. St Petersburg. 1909. [A good history of the Zemstvo.]

Witte, Count S. Ĭu. Samoderžavie i Zemstvo—Zapiska. Predislovie Čerevanina. (Autocracy and the Zemstvo. A Memorandum for official circles.) St Petersburg. 1908.

V. FINANCIAL POLICY: MINISTRY OF COUNT WITTE. 1892–1903.

Bextěeff, S. S. Xozĭaĭstvennye itogi istekšago sorokapĭatilětiĭa. Vols. i and ii St Petersburg. 1902–6. [Economic figures of the last forty years.]

Bliox, I. S. Finansy Rossii xix stolětiĭa. Istoriĭa-statistika. (Finances of Russia in the nineteenth century: history and statistics.) Vols. i–iv. St Petersburg. 1882. [Valuable.]

Brandt, V. F. Inostrannye Kapitaly: ix vliĭanie na ękonomičeskoe razvitie strany. (Foreign capital in Russia.) 3 vols. St Petersburg. 1898–1901. [Valuable.]

Kovalevskiĭ, V. I. Rossiĭa v koncě xixago vieka. Ministerstvo Finansov. St Petersburg. 1900. [An economic sketch by the Assistant Minister of Finance.]

Mendelěeff, D. K poznaniĭu Rossii s priloženiem Karty Rossii. 2nd edn. A. Suvorin. St Petersburg. 1906. Dopolnenie St Petersburg. 1907. [Suggestive notes of great value.]

Migulin, P. P. Russkiĭ gosudarstvennyĭ kredit (1769–1899). Opyt istoriko-kritičeskago obzora. Vols. i–iii. Charkoff. 1899–1904. [A very substantial study.]

—— Reforma denežnago obraščenia v Rossii i promyšlennyĭ Krizis (1893–1902). Charkoff. 1902. [On the reform of the currency; valuable.]

Migulin, P. P.   Naša novĕĭšaĭa želĕznodorožnaĭa politika i Želĕznodorožnye zaimy (1893–1902).   Charkoff.   1905.   [On recent railway policy; valuable.]

Ministerstvo finansov 1802–1902 časti I–II.   St Petersburg.   1902.   [An official history of the Ministry of Finance.]

Nikolaĭ-On   Očerki našego poreformennago obščestvennago xozaĭstva.   St Petersburg.   1893.   [An important exposition from the anti-western school of popular thought.]

Ozeroff, I. X.   Ękonomičeskaĭa Rossiĭa i eĭa finansovaĭa politika na isxodĕ XIX i v načalĕ XX vĕka.   Publ. by D. S. Gorškoff.   Moscow.   1905.   [An able but tendentious economist on financial policy.]

Vliĭanie urožaev i xlĕbnyx cĕn na nĕkotoryĭa storony russkago narodnago xozaĭstva.   (The Influence of crops and grain prices on certain sides of Russian Economy.)   Stat'i.   Vols. I and II.   Ed. by A. I. Čuproff and A. S. Posnikoff.   St Petersburg.   1897.

Voroncoff, V.   Sud'by kapitalizma v Rossii.   St Petersburg.   1882.   [A partisan but important book from the anti-western school of popular thought.]

VI. THE PEASANT QUESTION.   1861–1904.

Astyreff, N. M.   V volostnyx pisarĭax.   Očerki krest'ĭanskago samoupravleniĭa. 3rd edn.   Mag. Knižnoe Dĕlo.   Moscow.   [An informing record of life among the peasants.]

Družinin, N.   Ĭuridičeskoe položenie krest'ĭan.   Izslĕdovanie.   Ed. Knižn. Mag. N. Martynova.   St Petersburg.   1897.   [On the legal position of the Peasants.]

Ĭanson, Ĭ.   Opyt statističeskago izslĕdovaniĭa o krest'ĭanskix nadĕlax i platežaz. 2nd edn.   St Petersburg.   1881.   [Statistics on peasant holdings and dues.]

Ivanĭukoff, I.   Padenie krĕpostnogo prava v Rossii.   2nd edn.   "Obščestven. Pol'za."   St Petersburg.   1903.   [On the fall of serfdom: very valuable.]

Korniloff, A. A.   Krest'ĭanskaĭa reforma.   (Velikiĭa reformy 60-x gg. v ix prošlom i nastoĭaščem.)   Edd. I. V. Hessen and A. I. Kaminko.   Publ. by P. P. Geršunin and Co.   St Petersburg.   1905.   [A short but useful sketch of the history of the Peasant Question.]

—— Sem' mĕsĭacev sredi golodaĭuščix krest'ĭan.   Otčet o pomošči goladavšim nĕkotoryx mĕstnosteĭ Moršanskago i Kirsanovskago uĕzdov Tambovskoĭ gub. v. 1891–2.   Moscow.   1893.   [Notes on the famines of 1891–2 in central Russia.]

Loxtin, P.   Bezzemel'nyĭ proletariat v Rossii.   Opyt opredĕleniĭa količestva bezzemel'nago proletariata, sozdannago suščestvuĭuščimi sposobami krest'ĭanskago zemlevladĕniĭa.   Moscow.   1905.   [On the landless peasants.]

—— Sostoĭanie sel'skago xozĭaĭstva v Rossii sravnitel'no s drugimi stranami. Itogi k XX-mu vĕku.   St Petersburg.   1901.   [A comparative survey of Russian agriculture.]

Migulin, P. P.   Vykupnye plateži k voprosu o ix poniženii.   Charkoff.   1904.   [A study of the redemption dues.]

Nuždy derevni po rabotam komitetov o nuždax sel'skoxozĭaĭstvennoĭ promyšlennosti.   Sbornik stateĭ.   Vols. I and II.   Ed. N. N. L'vova i A. A. Staxoviča pri učastii red. gaz. Pravo.   St Petersburg.   1904.   [The Liberal view of agricultural distress.]

Polĕnoff, A. D.   Izslĕdovanie ękonomičeskago položeniĭa central'nočernozemnyx guberniĭ.   (Records of a Commission on the central Provinces.)   Trudy osobago sovĕščaniĭa 1899–1901 g.   Moscow.   1901.

Posnikoff, A.   Obščinnoe Zemlevladĕnie   Vols. I and II.   2nd edn.   B-ki A. Bortnevskago.   Odessa.   1878.   [On communal land tenure.]

Postnikoff, V. E. Iužnorusskoe krest'ianskoe xoziaĭstvo. 2nd edn. Moscow.
1907. [On peasant agriculture in southern Russia.]
Priležaeff, A. V. Čto takoe kustarnoe proizvodstvo? St Petersburg. 1882.
[On cottage industries.]
Rittix, A. A. Krest'ianskiĭ pravoporiadok. Svod trudov městnyx komitetov po
49 guberniam. St Petersburg. 1904. [Records of official local committees
on the legal position of the peasants.]
Šaxovskoĭ, Kn. N. V. Otxožie sel'sko-xoziaĭstvennye promysly. St Petersburg.
1895. [Trades of emigrant peasants (the "Go-aways").]
Sbornik uzakoneniĭ i rasporiaženiĭ pravitel'stva kasaiuščixsia krest'ianskago zemleu-
stroĭstva i zemlepol'zovaniia. Zemskiĭ Otděl Ministerstva Vnutrennix Děl.
St Petersburg. 1907. [The laws on peasant land tenure; official.]
Witte, Count S. Iu. Zapiska po krest'ianskomu dělu. St Petersburg. 1904.
[A suggestive memorandum.]

VII. RUSSIAN INDUSTRY: THE SOCIAL-DEMOCRATS. 1861-1904.

Akimoff, V. M. Očerk razvitiia socialdemokratii v Rossii. Socialdemokratičeskiĭ
Otděl. Publ. by O. N. Popova. St Petersburg. 1906. [The best history of
Social Democracy in Russia.]
Ianžul, I. I. Fabričnyĭ byt Moskovskoĭ gubernii. (Memoirs of a factory inspector
in the Moscow province.) Otčet za 1882–3 g. fabričnago inspektora nad
zaniatiiami maloletnix rabočix Moskovskago okruga. St Petersburg. 1884.
Iskra. Za dva goda. 2 vols. St Petersburg. 1906. [A publication of the Social
Democratic organ (the Majority Men).]
Pažitnoff, K. A. Položenie rabočago klassa v Rossii. 2nd edn. St Petersburg.
1908. [On the condition of the working-class.]
Plexanoff, G. Zamětki Publicista. Novyia pis'ma o taktikě i beztaktnosti. Publ. by
N. Glagoleff. St Petersburg. [The most authoritative Social Democratic
publicist.]
Pogožeff, A. V. Učet Čislennosti i sostava rabočix v Rossii. Materialy po statistikě
truda. Publ. by Imper. Akad. Nauk. St Petersburg. 1906. [Statistics on
factory workers.]
Struve, P. Kritičeskiia Zamětki k voprosu ob ękonomičeskom razvitii Rossii.
Vol. I. St Petersburg. 1894. [A striking application of the ideas of Karl
Marx to Russia.]
Tugan-Baranovskiĭ, M. Russkaia fabrika v prošlom i nastoiaščem. Istoriko-
ękonomičeskoe izslědovanie. 3rd edn. Kniž. Mag. Naša Žizn'. St Petersburg.
1907. [A valuable history of Russian industry.]

VIII. THE REFORM MOVEMENT. 1904-9.

Baring, M. A Year in Russia. 1907.
Briančaninoff, A. I. Meždudum'ie. Vol. I. St Petersburg. 1907. [Records of
the interval between the First and Second Dumas.]
Byloe. Monthly. St Petersburg. 1906–7; and in 1908 continued under the
title Minuvszie Gody. [Important historical articles mostly from the revolu-
tionary standpoint.]
Engel, G. and Goroxoff, V. Iz istorii studenčeskago dviženiia 1899–1906. Ed.
V. Serdakovskago. St Petersburg. [On the movement among the students.]

Materialy k istorii russkoĭ kontr-revolĭucii. Vol. i. Pogromy po official'nym dokumentam. St Petersburg. 1908. [An exposure of the "Pogroms" of 1905, with official documents.]

Milĭukoff, P. N. God Bor'by. Publicističeskaĭa xronika. 1907. St Petersburg. [Publicist articles during 1906.]

—— Russia and its Crisis. Chicago. 1900. [Lectures by the leader of the Cadet Party.]

Osvoboždenie. (Fortnightly.) 1902–4. Stuttgart. 1905. Paris. [The organ (but not authoritative) of the Union of Liberation, ed. by P. B. Struve.]

Pamĭatnik Ępoxi 17ago Oktĭabria. (Sputnik Izbiratelĭa.) St Petersburg. [An elector's handbook of 1906 with surveys and records.]

Pravo. (Weekly.) St Petersburg. 1899–1910. [The leading Liberal weekly.]

Savič, G. G. Novyĭ Gosudarstvennyĭ Stroĭ: spravočnaĭa Kniga. St Petersburg. 1907. [A good handbook of the legislation of the Reform movement.]

Smirnoff, A. Kak prošli vybory vo vtoruĭu gosudar'stvennuĭu Dumu. St Petersburg. 1907. [An interesting analysis of the second electoral campaign.]

Stenografičeskiĭ Otčet Gosudarstvennoĭ Dumy. Pervago sozyva. Vtorago sozyva. Tret'ĭago sozyva. St Petersburg. 1906–9. [Verbatim report of the three Dumas.]

Urusoff, Kn. S. D. Zapiski gubernatora. Kišinev, 1903–4 g. Publ. by V. Sablin. Moscow. 1907. [Memoirs of a Liberal Governor in Kišinev.]

Venožinskiĭ, V. Političeskaĭa Zabastovka v. Spb. Universitetě. Očerk. St Petersburg. 1906. [The Great Strike of 1905 in St Petersburg.]

"Zarnicy" Sbornik. Vol. i. St Petersburg. 1907. [The article on the Union of Liberation is the one authoritative record (by Prince D. I. Šaxovskoĭ).]

Zemleustroitel'nyx Kommisiĭ, Obzor Děĭatel'nosti Uězdnyx (1907–8). St Petersburg. 1909. [Official review : of the land settlement : very important.]

CHAPTER XIV.

THE OTTOMAN EMPIRE AND THE BALKAN PENINSULA.

1. TURKEY AND THE EASTERN QUESTION GENERALLY.

(A) BIBLIOGRAPHY.

Bengescǔ, G. Essai d'une notice bibliographique sur la Question d'Orient.—
Orient européen, 1821–97. Brussels and Paris. 1897. [Contains only French
and Belgian publications.]
Yovanovitch Voyslav, M. The Near Eastern Question [1481–1906]. Belgrade.
1909. [A comprehensive bibliography.]

(B) DOCUMENTS.

The Parliamentary Papers concerning Turkey are too numerous to mention in
detail—for the crisis of 1876–81 there are 109. They can easily be found with
the aid of the Index. The French Yellow and Italian Green Books, being less
voluminous and unindexed, are set out in full.

Documents Diplomatiques (Livres Jaunes):
    Affaires d'Orient. 1875–6–7.
         ,,   ,,   Congrès de Berlin. 1878.
    Affaires arméniennes. 1893–7. Supplément. 1895.
    Affaires de Crète. June, 1894—February, 1897.
    Autonomie crétoise. May—December, 1897.
    Affaires d'Orient. 1898.
    Affaires de Crète. 1904–5.
    Affaires de Macédoine, 1903–5.
         ,,   ,,   1906–7.
Documenti Diplomatici (Libri Verdi):
    1877. Affari d'Oriente.
    1878.   ,,   ,,
    1889–90. Candia.
    1898–9. Creta.
    1904–9. Macedonia.
Papantonákes. Κρητικά. Canea. 1901. [Documents relating to the Cretan In-
surrection of 1897–8.]

(C) CONTEMPORARY AUTHORITIES.

Abbott, G. F. The Tale of a Tour in Macedonia. 1903.
—— Turkey in transition. 1909.
Abd-ur-Rahman Sheref. Tarikh-i-derlet-i-osmainé. 2 vols. Constantinople. 1900.
Amadori-Virgilj, G. La Questione Rumeliota e la Politica Italiana. Vol. I. Bitonto.
1908.
Avril, Baron A. d'. Négociations relatives au traité de Berlin et aux arrangements
qui ont suivi. Paris. 1887.
Baker, Col. G. Turkey in Europe. 1877.

Baker Pasha, Lt-General V.   The War in Bulgaria.   1879.

Bamberg, F.   Geschichte der Orientalischen Angelegenheit im Zeitraume des Pariser und des Berliner Friedens (Allg. Gesch. in Einzeldarstellungen).   iv, 5. Berlin.   1892.

Barbarich, E.   Albania.   Monografia.   Rome.   1905.

Beaman, A. H.   Twenty Years in the Near East.   1898.

Bérard, V.   La Turquie et l'Hellénisme contemporain.   5th edn.   Paris.   1904.

——   La Politique du Sultan.   4th edn.   Paris.   1900.

——   La Macédoine.   2nd edn.   Paris.   1900.

——   Les Affaires de Crète.   2nd edn.   Paris.   1900.

——   Pro Macedonia.   Paris.   1904.

——   Le Sultan, l'Islam, et les Puissances.   Paris.   1907.

——   La Révolution turque.   Paris.   1909.

Bliss, E. M.   Turkey and the Armenian atrocities.   1896.

Bonghi, R.   Il Congresso di Berlino e la Crisi d'Oriente.   2nd edn.   Milan.   1885.

Brailsford, H. N.   Macedonia : its races and their future.   1906.

Brancoff, D. M.   La Macédoine et sa population chrétienne.   Paris.   1905.

Bryce, J.   Transcaucasia.   With Supplement on the Armenian Question.   1896.

Buxton, C. R.   Turkey in revolution.   1909.

Buxton, N.   Europe and the Turks.   1907.

Chlumecky, Baron L. von.   Oesterreich-Ungarn und Italien.   Das westbalkanische Problem und Italiens Kampf um die Vorherrschaft in der Adria.   Leipzig.   1907.

Choublier, M.   La Question d'Orient depuis le traité de Berlin.   Paris.   1897.

Consul's Daughter, A.   (Lady Blunt.)   The peoples of Turkey.   1878.

Daily News Correspondence of the War of 1877–8.   1878.

Draganof.   La Macédoine et les réformes.   Paris.   1906.

Driault, E.   La Question d'Orient depuis ses origines jusqu'à nos jours.   3rd edn.   Paris.   1905.

Durham, M. E.   The Burden of the Balkans.   1905.

——   High Albania.   1909.

Edwards, H. S.   Sir W. White, Ambassador at Constantinople, 1885–91.   1902.

Eliot, Sir C. N. E. ("Odysseus").   Turkey in Europe.   2nd edn.   1908.

Galanti, A.   L'Albania.   Rome.   1901.

Gladstone, W. E.   The Bulgarian Horrors and the Question of the East.   1876.

——   The Armenian Question.   1905.

Gopčević, Sp.   Oberalbanien und seine Liga.   Leipzig.   1881.

——   Makedonien und Alt-Serbien.   Vienna.   1889.

Greene, F. V.   The Russian Army and its campaign in Turkey in 1877–8.   1880.

——   The Campaign in Bulgaria, 1877–8.   1903.

Halid, Halil.   The Diary of a Turk.   1903.

Halil Ganem.   Les Sultans Ottomans.   2 vols.   Paris.   1902.

Hecquard, C.   La Turquie sous Abdul-Hamid II : Exposé fidèle de la gérance d'un Empire pendant un quart de siècle (31e août 1876—1er septembre 1900). Brussels.   1901.

Herbert, W. V.   The Defence of Plevna, 1877.   1895.

——   The Chronicles of a Virgin Fortress [Vidin].   1896.

Holland, T. E.   The European Concert in the Eastern Question.   Oxford.   1885.

King-Lewis, G.   Critical Times in Turkey.   1904.

Knight, E. F.   The awakening of Turkey.   1909.

Krahmer, Major-General.   Geschichte des russisch-türkischen Kriegs auf der Balkan-Halbinsel, 1877–8.   Berlin.   1902.

La Jonquière, Vicomte A. de.   Histoire de l'Empire Ottoman.   Paris.   1881.

Lavaleye, E. de.   La Péninsule des Balkans.   2 vols.   Brussels.   1886.   [English translation.   1887.]

Leger, L.   La Save, le Danube, et le Balkan.   2nd edn.   Paris.   1889.

Leger, L. Russes et Slaves. 2 vols. Paris. 1890–6.

Loiseau, C. Le Balkan Slave et la Crise autrichienne. Paris. 1898.

—— L'Équilibre adriatique : l'Italie et la Question d'Orient. Paris. 1901.

Lyde, L. W. and Mockler-Ferryman, A. F. Military Geography of the Balkan Peninsula. 1905.

Lynch, H. F. B. Armenia : Travels and Studies. 2 vols. 1901.

Mantegazza, V. L'Altra Sponda. Italia e Austria nell' Adriatico. Milan. 1905.

Maurice, Major F. The Russo-Turkish War, 1877. 1905.

Midhat Bey, Ali Haydar. The Life of Midhat Pasha. 1903.

Miller, W. The Balkans. (Story of the Nations.) 2nd edn. With new chapter (1896–1908). 1908.

—— Travels and Politics in the Near East. 1898.

—— Three Years of the Eastern Question [1898–1901]. In Gentleman's Magazine, November 1901.

—— The Macedonian Claimants. In Contemporary Review, March 1903.

Minchin, J. G. C. The Growth of Freedom in the Balkan Peninsula. 1886.

Nicolaides, C. La Macédoine. Berlin. 1899.

Percy, Earl. Highlands of Asiatic Turkey. 1901.

—— (Lord Warkworth.) Notes from a Diary in Asiatic Turkey. 1898.

Roth, K. Geschichte der christlichen Balkanstaaten. Leipzig. 1907.

Thompson, G. C. Public opinion and Lord Beaconsfield, 1875–80. 2 vols. 1886.

Vandal, A. Les Arméniens et la réforme de la Turquie. Paris. 1897.

Villari, L. (editor). The Balkan Question : the present condition of the Balkans. 1904.

Voïnov, I. F. La Question macédonienne et les réformes en Turquie. Paris. 1905.

Ward, Capt. M. C. P. Handbook of the Armies of the Balkan States. 1900.

Wyon, R. The Balkans from within. 1904.

2. GREECE.

(A) DOCUMENTS.

Parliamentary Papers :

    1878. c. 1974. Vol. LXXX. c. 1968, 1969. Vol. LXXXII.

    1878–9. c. 2330. Vol. LXXVII.

    1880. c. 2633. Vol. LXXVIII. c. 2637. Vol. LXXXI. c. 2705. Vol. LXXXII.

    1881. c. 2912, 2940. Vol. XCVIII. c. 2759. Vol. C.

    1886. c. 4731, 4732, 4765. Vol. LXXIV.

    1898. c. 8664. Vol. CVI. c. 8778, 8818, 8849, 8851. Vol. CVII.

Documents Diplomatiques (Livres Jaunes) :

    Négociations relatives à la rectification des frontières de la Grece. 2 vols. 1879–80.

    Affaires de Grèce. 2 parts. 1880–1.

    Affaires de Roumélie et de Grèce. 1885–6.

    Conflit gréco-turc. February—May 1897.

    Arrangement financier avec la Grèce. 1898.

Documenti Diplomatici (Libri Verdi) :

    1880–2. Vol. I, pp. 725—903. Rettificazione della frontiera turco-ellenica.

       ,,   Vol. II. Conferenza di Berlino per la questione turco-ellenica. (1880.)

       ,,   Vol. III. Questione turco-ellenica. (1881.)

    1882–6. Vol. II. Questione turco-ellenica. (1882.)

Documents Diplomatiques (Livre blanc hellénique).
    Conflit gréco-turc.   April—September 1897.   Athens.   1897.
Hellenic White Books:
    Ἔγγραφα κατατεθέντα εἰς τὴν Βουλὴν περὶ τῶν ἐκβολάδων καὶ σκωριῶν Λαυρίου
        1872–3.   Athens.   1873.
    Διπλωματικὰ ἔγγραφα περὶ τοῦ Ἑλληνικοῦ ζητήματος, κατατεθέντα ἐν τῇ Βουλῇ
        τῶν Ἑλλήνων ὑπὸ τοῦ ἐπὶ τῶν Ἐξωτερικῶν Ὑπουργοῦ.   Athens.   1878.
    Μετατροπὴ τῶν δανείων τοῦ 1824 καὶ 1825, ἀδείᾳ τοῦ ἐπὶ τῶν Οἰκονομικῶν
        Ὑπουργείου.   Athens.   1879.
    Διπλωματικὰ ἔγγραφα ἀφορῶντα εἰς τὸ μεθοριακὸν ζήτημα.   Athens.   1882.
    Διπλωματικὰ ἔγγραφα κατατεθέντα εἰς τὴν Βουλὴν ὑπὸ τοῦ ἐπὶ τῶν Ἐξωτερικῶν
        Ὑπουργοῦ περὶ τοῦ Ἀποκλεισμοῦ.   Athens.   1886.
    Διπλωματικὰ ἔγγραφα περὶ σταφίδος (Διαπραγματεύσεις μετὰ τῆς Ἀγγλικῆς
        Κυβερνήσεως).   Athens.   1889.
    Ἔγγραφα περὶ τῆς Ὑποθέσεως Ζάππα, 1863–92.   Athens.   1892.
    Διπλωματικὰ ἔγγραφα ἀφορῶντα εἰς τὸν ἑλληνοτουρκικὸν πόλεμον τοῦ 1897.
        Athens.   1897.
    Μετάφρασις τῶν κυριωτέρων ὑπομνημάτων, δι᾿ ὧν ἡ Ἑλληνικὴ Κυβέρνησις προσ-
        έφυγεν εἰς τὴν διαιτησίαν τῶν ἐν Κων/πόλει πρεσβευτῶν τῶν 6 Μ. Δυνάμεων.
        Athens.   1901.
    Ἔγγραφα Ἑλληνορρουμανικῆς διαφορᾶς.   Athens.   1906.

(B) CONTEMPORARY AUTHORITIES

Becker, G.   La Guerre contemporaine dans les Balkans, 1897.   Paris.   1899.
Bickford-Smith, R. A. H.   Greece under King George.   1893.
Bigham, C.   With the Turkish Army in Thessaly.   1897.
Constantine, Crown Prince.   Ἔκθεσις τῆς Α. Β. Ὑψηλότητος τοῦ Διαδόχου ἐπὶ τῶν
    πεπραγμένων τοῦ στρατοῦ Θεσσαλίας κατὰ τὴν ἐκστρατείαν 1897.   Athens.   1898.
Evangelídes, T. E.   Κωνσταντῖνος Σμολένσκης.   Βιογραφικὸν Δοκίμιον.   Athens.   1897.
German Staff Officer, A.   The Greco-Turkish War of 1897.   1898.
Gladstone, W. E.   The Hellenic factor in the Eastern Problem.   In Con-
    temporary Review for December 1876.   Reprinted in Gleanings from Past
    Years.   Vol. iv, 259–304.   1879.
Goltz, Baron C. v. der.   Der thessalische Krieg und die türkische Armee.   Berlin.
    1898.
Idroménos, A. M.   Τὸ Σύνταγμα τῆς Ἑλλάδος.   Athens.   1908.
Kyriakídes, E. K.   Ἱστορία τοῦ συγχρόνου Ἑλληνισμοῦ, 1832–92.   Vol. ii.   Athens.
    1894.
Miller, W.   Greek Life in Town and Country.   1905.
Nevinson, H. W.   Scenes in the Thirty Days War between Greece and Turkey,
    1897.   1898.   [The Campaign in Epiros.   The author was correspondent of
    the Daily Chronicle.]
Philáretos, G. N.   Σύνταγμα τῆς Ἑλλάδος.   Athens.   1889.
Rose, W. K.   With the Greeks in Thessaly.   1897.   [The author was Reuter's
    correspondent.]
Rumbold, Sir H.   Final Recollections of a Diplomatist.   1905.
Samuelson, J.   Greece; her present condition.   1894.   [Deals with Greek finance.]
Sergeant, L.   Greece in the Nineteenth Century, 1821–97.   1897.
[A lifelike picture of the war of 1897 may be found in Mr H. N. Brailsford's
    novel, The Broom of the War-god.   1898.   The author was a volunteer.]

3. ROUMANIA.

(A) BIBLIOGRAPHY.

Bengescŭ, G. Bibliographie franco-roumaine du XIXe siècle. Vol. I. Brussels. 1895.

Damé, F. (cf. infra) has bibliographies, especially for the Jewish question. Cf. also Revue historique, vol. LXXIII, pp. 366–9; vol. XCVI, pp. 80 sqq. for Roumanian publications between 1894 and 1907.

(B) DOCUMENTS.

Parliamentary Papers:
  1878. c. 2007. Vol. LXXXII.
  1880. c. 2554. Vol. LXXIX.

Documents Diplomatiques (Livres Jaunes):
  Question de la reconnaissance de la Roumanie. 2 vols. 1879–80.
  Commission technique européenne. 1880. (Delimitation of Roumano-Bulgarian frontier near Silistria.)

Livre vert roumain:
  La question du Danube. Bucharest. 1881.

Kogălniceanu, V. M. Acte si documente din corespondenţa diplomatică a lui Mihail Kogălniceanu, 1877–8. [Documents regarding the War of those years.] Vol. I. Bucharest. 1893.

Roumanian Academy, Trei-Ḍeci de Ani de Domnie aĭ Regului Carol I, 1866–96. 2 vols. Bucharest. 1897.

Sturdza, D. A. Charles Ier, Roi de Roumanie: Chronique, Actes, Documents [1866–77]. 2 vols. Bucharest. 1899–1904.

(C) CONTEMPORARY AUTHORITIES.

Aus dem Leben König Karls von Rumänien. Aufzeichnungen eines Augenzeugen. Vols. II–IV. Stuttgart. 1900. Reaches to 1881. A summary, Reminiscences of the King of Roumania, has been published by S. Whitman. London and New York. 1899.

Bellessort, A. La Roumanie contemporaine. Paris. 1905.

Bibesco, G. Histoire d'une frontière. La Roumanie sur la rive droite du Danube. Paris. 1883.

Boteanu, G. Memoriu din resboiul de la 1877–8. [The war of those years.] Bucharest. 1895.

Colescu, L. Progrès économiques de la Roumanie, réalisés sous le règne de S. M. le Roi Carol I. Bucharest. 1907.

Damé, F. Histoire de la Roumanie contemporaine depuis l'avènement des Princes indigènes jusqu'à nos jours, 1822–1900. Paris. 1900.

Eliade, P. Histoire de l'esprit public en Roumanie au XIXme siècle. Paris. 1905.

Gubernatis, Count A. de. La Roumanie et les Roumains. Florence. 1898.

Samuelson, J. Roumania Past and Present. 1882.

Sincerus, E. Les Juifs en Roumanie depuis le traité de Berlin jusqu'à ce jour. 1901.

Witte, Baron J. de. Quinze ans d'histoire: 1866–81. Paris. 1905.

4. BULGARIA AND EASTERN ROUMELIA.

(A) DOCUMENTS.

Parliamentary Papers:
1880. c. 2634, 2636. Vol. LXXXI.
1881. c. 2992. Vol. XCVIII.
1886. c. 4612, 4767. Vol. LXXV.
1887. c. 4933-4. Vol. XCI.
1888. c. 5370. Vol. CIX.
Documents Diplomatiques (Livres Jaunes):
Affaires de Roumélie et de Grèce. 1885-6.
Documenti Diplomatici (Libri Verdi):
1882-6. Vol. IV. Rumelia Orientale. Ser. 1 and 2.
1886-7. Rumelia Orientale e Grecia. Ser. 3.—Bulgaria.
1889-90. Bulgaria.
Léonoff, R. Documents secrets de la politique russe en Orient, 1881-90. Berlin and Leipzig. 1893.

(B) CONTEMPORARY AUTHORITIES.

Bath, Marquis of. Observations on Bulgarian Affairs. 1880.
Beaman, A. H. M. Stambuloff. 1895.
Becker, G. La Guerre contemporaine dans les Balkans, 1885. Paris. 1899.
Bilimek, H. Der bulgarisch-serbische Krieg, 1885. Vienna. 1886.
Cholet, Count A. P. de. Étude sur la Guerre bulgaro-serbe. Paris. 1891.
Dicey, E. The Peasant State. 1894.
Drandar, A. G. Cinq ans de règne. Le Prince Alexandre de Battenberg en Bulgarie. Paris. 1884.
—— Les Évènements politiques en Bulgarie depuis 1876 jusqu'à nos jours. Brussels. 1896.
Dupuy-Péyou, L. La Bulgarie aux Bulgares. Paris and Brussels. 1896.
Golovin, A. F. Fürst Alexander I von Bulgarien, 1879-86. Vienna. 1896.
Gopčević, Sp. Bulgarien und Ostrumelien, mit besonderer Berücksichtigung des Zeitraums von 1878-86. Leipzig. 1886.
Huhn, Major A. von. Der Kampf der Bulgaren um ihre Nationaleinheit. Leipzig. 1886. Eng. tr.: The Struggle of the Bulgarians for National Independence. 1886.
—— The Kidnapping of Prince Alexander. 1887.
Jireček, C. Das Fürstenthum Bulgarien. Vienna. 1891.
—— Geschichte der Bulgaren. Prague. 1876.
Kanitz, F. Donau-Bulgarien und der Balkan. 2nd edn. Leipzig. 1882. Also in French: La Bulgarie danubienne et le Balkan. Paris. 1881.
Koch, A. Mitteilungen aus dem Leben und der Regierung des Fürsten Alexander von Bulgarien. Darmstadt. 1887. Eng. tr.: Prince Alexander of Battenberg. 1887.
Lamouche, L. La Bulgarie dans le passé et le présent. Paris. 1892.
Ministère du Commerce bulgare. La Bulgarie contemporaine. Brussels. 1906. Eng. tr.: Bulgaria of to-day. 1907.
Samuelson, J. Bulgaria Past and Present. 1888.
Sobolev, L. N. Der erste Fürst von Bulgarien. Leipzig. 1886.
Wolff, Sir H. D. Rambling Recollections. Vol. II. 1908. [The author was British delegate on the Eastern Roumelian Commission.]
Cf. also various articles by Mr J. D. Bourchier [Times correspondent at Sofia] in the Fortnightly Review. Vols. L, LV, LX.

5. SERVIA.

(A) BIBLIOGRAPHY.

Royal Servian Academy. Essai de bibliographie française sur les Serbes et les Croates (1554–1900). Belgrade. 1900.

(B) DOCUMENTS.

Parliamentary Papers:
1877. c. 1742. Vol. LXXXIX.

(C) CONTEMPORARY AUTHORITIES.

Boskarc, S. La Mission de Serbie dans la Question d'Orient. Florence. 1887.

Coquelle, P. Le Royaume de Serbie. Paris. 1894.

Cuniberti, F. La Serbia e la Dinastia degli Obrenovitch (1804–93). Turin. 1893.

Durham, M. E. Through the Lands of the Serb. 1904.

État-Major Général de l'Armée Serbe. Guerre de la Serbie contre la Turquie, 1877–8. Paris. 1879. [Translation.]

Georgević, V. Das Ende der Obrenovitch: Beiträge zur Geschichte Serbiens, 1897–1900. Leipzig. 1905. [The author was Prime Minister.]

Gopčević, S. Serbien und die Serben. Leipzig. 1888.

Gubernatis, Count A. de. La Serbie et les Serbes. Florence. 1897.

Hogge, J. La Serbie de nos jours. Brussels. 1900.

Kanitz, F. Das Königreich Serbien und das Serbenvolk von der Römerzeit bis zur Gegenwart. 2 vols. Leipzig. 1904–9.

Lazard, E. and Hogge, J. La Serbie d'aujourd'hui. 2 pts. Gembloux. 1900.

Mallat, J. La Serbie contemporaine. 2 vols. Paris. 1902.

Mijatović, C. Servia and the Servians. 1908.

Pearson, E. M. and McLaughlin, L. E. Service in Servia under the Red Cross. 1877.

Protić, S. The Secret Treaty between Servia and Austria-Hungary. Fort. Review, May, 1909.

Račić, V. Le Royaume de Serbie: Étude d'histoire diplomatique. Paris. 1901.

Ristić, J. Дипломатска историја Србије. (Diplomatic History of Servia.) 1875–8. 2 vols. Belgrade. 1896–8.

Salusbury, P. H. B. Two Months with Tchernaieff in Servia. 1877.

Stead, A. (ed.). Servia by the Servians. London. 1909. [The official view.]

Sydačkoff, Bressnitz von. Die Geschichte Serbiens vom Jahre 1868 bis auf den heutigen Tag unter den Königen Milan und Alexander. Berlin and Leipzig. 1895–6. Das Ende der Dynastie Obrenović. Leipzig. 1900. [*Chronique scandaleuse.*]

Vivian, H. Servia, the Poor Man's Paradise. 1897.

—— The Servian Tragedy. 1904.

6. MONTENEGRO.

(A) BIBLIOGRAPHY.

Tenneroni, A. Per la bibliografia del Montenegro. 2nd edn. Rome. 1896.

Tondini, C. Notice sur la bibliographie du Monténégro. Paris. 1889.

(B) DOCUMENTS.

Parliamentary Papers :
  Correspondence respecting the Montenegrin frontier, and Further Correspondence. Turkey. No. 22. (1880.) c. 2711. Vol. LXXXII. Turkey. Nos. 1, 2. (1881.) c. 2752, 2758. Vol. c.
Documents Diplomatiques (Livres Jaunes):
  Affaires du Monténégro. 2 vols. Paris. 1880.
Documenti Diplomatici (Libri Verdi):
  1880-2. Vol. I, pp. 553—723.
Diplomatic and Consular Reports on Trade and Finance:
  Nos. 95 (1888), 1761 (1896), 1884 (1897), 2114 (1898). [None published since 1898.]

(C) CONTEMPORARY AUTHORITIES.

Chiudina, G. Storia del Montenero (Crnagora) da' tempi antichi fino ai nostri. Spalato. 1880.
Coquelle, P. Histoire du Monténégro et de la Bosnie depuis les origines. Paris. 1895.
Denton, W. Montenegro—its people and their history. 1877.
Gladstone, W. E. Montenegro or Tsernagora. A Sketch. In Nineteenth Century, May 1877. Reprinted in "Gleanings from Past Years." Vol. IV. 1879.
Gopčević, S. Der türko-montenegrinischer Krieg, 1876-8. Vienna. 1876-9.
Maton, E. Histoire du Monténégro ou Tsernagore. Paris. 1881.
Miller, W. The Montenegrin Bicentenary. In Gentleman's Magazine, October 1896.
—— The Montenegrin Jubilee. In Macmillan's Magazine, September 1901.
Wyon, R. and Prance, G. The Land of the Black Mountain. 1903.

(A number of compilations and pamphlets of small value were published in Italy on the occasion of the Montenegrin wedding in 1896.)

7. BOSNIA AND THE HERZEGOVINA.

Anonymous. Der Aufstand in der Hercegovina und Süd-Bosnien. Vienna. 1883.
Barre, A. La Bosnie-Herzégovine, Administration Autrichienne (1878-1907).
Cvijic, I. L'Annexion de Bosnie et la Question Serbe. Paris. 1909.
Drage, G. Austria-Hungary. 1909. (Chapters XIV sqq.)
Evans, A. J. Through Bosnia and the Herzegovina on foot. 1876.
—— Illyrian Letters. 1878.
Fournier, A. Wie wir zu Bosnien kamen—eine historische Studie. Vienna. 1909.
Haardt, V. von. Die Occupation Bosniens und der Herzegovina. Vienna. 1878.
Hercalović, T. Vorgeschichte der Occupation Bosniens und der Herzegovina. Agram. 1906.
Koetschet. "Aus Bosniens letzter Türkenzeit."
Mackenzie, G. M. and Irby, A. P. Travels in the Slavonic Provinces of Turkey-in-Europe. 3rd edn. [Vol. I, chapters i–iii relate to Bosnia at this period.] 1877.
Occupation, die, Bosniens und der Hercegovina. (Generalstabswerk.) Vienna. 1879-80.
Saix, Vicomte de. Les Pays sud-Slaves de l'Autriche-Hongrie.
Spalaïkovitch, M. J. La Bosnie et l'Herzégovine. Étude d'histoire diplomatique de droit international. Paris. 1899.
Stillman, W. J. Herzegovina and the late Uprising. 1877.
Thomson, H. C. The Outgoing Turk. 1897.

CHAPTER XV.

EGYPT AND THE EGYPTIAN SUDAN.

I. BIBLIOGRAPHY.

Ilbrahim Hilmy, H.H. Prince. The Literature of Egypt and the Sudan from the earliest times to the year 1886 inclusive. 2 vols. London. 1886-7.

II. REPORTS, SPEECHES, ETC.

Blue Books on Egypt, including Lord Cromer's Annual Reports.
Hansard's Parliamentary Debates.

III. HISTORIES, TREATISES, ETC.

Cameron, D. A. Egypt in the 19th century, or Mehemet Ali and his Successors until the British occupation in 1882. 1898.
Colville, Colonel H. E. History of the Sudan Campaign. In two parts, with a case of maps. 1889.
Colvin, Sir A. The Making of Modern Egypt. 1906.
Cromer, Earl of. Modern Egypt. 2 vols. 1908.
Dicey, E. The story of the Khedivate. 1902.
Fitzgerald, P. H. The Great Canal at Suez, its political, engineering and financial history. 2 vols. 1876.
Freycinet, C. de. La Question d'Égypte. Paris. 1905.
Jerrold, B. The Belgium of the East. 1882.
Lesseps, F. de. Le Canal de Suez. 8 vols. Paris. 1875.
Milner, A. England in Egypt. 1892. 6th edn. 1899.
Mouriez, P. Histoire de Méhémet Ali, Vice-Roi d'Égypte. 4 vols. Paris. 1857.
Royle, C. Egyptian Campaigns. 1882-99. 1900.
Vyse, G. W. Egypt: Political, Financial and Strategical. 1900.
Wingate, Major Sir F. R. Mahdism and the Egyptian Sudan, being an account of the rise and progress of Mahdism and of subsequent events in the Sudan to the present time. 1891.

IV. BIOGRAPHIES, MEMOIRS, ETC.

Butler, Lt.-Gen. Sir W. F. Charles George Gordon. 1904.
Guizot, F. P. G. Mémoires pour servir à l'histoire de mon temps. 8 vols. Paris. 1858-67.

Hake, A. E.   The Story of Chinese Gordon.   1884.
——   The Journals of Major-Gen. Gordon at Kartoum.   1885.
Hill, G. B.   Gordon in Central Africa, 1874–9.   1899.
Malet, Sir E.   Egypt 1879–83.   1909.
Murray, Sir C. A.   A short Memoir of Mohammed Ali.   1898.
——   T. D. and White, A. S.   Sir Samuel Baker.   1895.
Vetch, Colonel R. H.   Life, Letters and Diaries of Lieut.-Gen. Sir G. Graham.
    Edinburgh.   1901.
Vingtrinier, A.   Soliman-Pacha (Colonel Sève) Généralissime des Armées Égyptiennes,
    ou, Histoire des Guerres de l'Égypte de 1820 à 1860.   Paris.   1886.
Watson, Colonel Sir C. M.   The life of Major-General Sir C. W. Wilson.   1909.

V.   TREATISES AND MONOGRAPHS.

Baker, Sir S. W.   The Albert N'yanza, Great basin of the Nile, and Explorations
    of the Nile sources.   2 vols.   1867.
——   Ismailia, a Narrative of the Expedition to Central Africa for the suppression
    of the slave-trade, organised by Ismail, Khedive of Egypt.   2 vols.   1874.
Brackenbury, Major-General Sir H.   The River Column.   Edinburgh.   1885.
Broadley, A. M.   How we defended Arabi and his friends.   A story of Egypt and
    the Egyptians.   1884.
Burton, R. F.   The Nile Basin.   1864.
Butler, A. J.   Court Life in Egypt.   1887.
Casati, Major G.   Ten years in Equatoria and the return with Emin Pasha.   2 vols.
    1891.
Dicey, E.   England and Egypt.   1881.
Knight, E. F.   Letters from the Sudan.   1897.
Leon, E. de.   Egypt under its Khedives, or The old house of bondage under new
    masters.   1864.
McCoan, J. C.   Egypt as it is.   1877.
Portal, G. H.   An Account of the English Mission to King Johannis of Abyssinia
    in 1887.   Winchester.   1888.
Sandwith, F. M.   The Cairo Lunatic Asylum 1888.   Journal of Mental Science.
    Jan. 1889.
——   The History of Kasr el Ainy A.D. 1466–1901.   Records of the Egyptian
    Govt. School of Medicine.   Cairo.   1901.
Slatin, R. C.   Fire and Sword in the Sudan, a personal narrative of fighting and
    serving the Derwishes 1879–95.   1896.
Speke, Captain J. H.   Journal of the Discovery of the Source of the Nile.
    Edinburgh.   1863.
Steevens, G. W.   With Kitchener to Khartum.   1898.
Urquhart, A. R. and Tuke, W. S.   Two visits to the Cairo Asylum, 1877–8.
    Journal of Mental Science.   April, 1879.
Verner, Captain W. W. C.   Sketches in the Sudan.   1885.
Wallace, Sir D. M.   Egypt and the Egyptian Question.   1883.
Willcocks, W.   Egyptian Irrigation.   2nd edn.   1899.

CHAPTER XVI.

INDIA.

I. OFFICIAL PUBLICATIONS.

Parliamentary Papers relating to the East Indies, 1869-1908.

The mere catalogue of these fills 77 folio pages of print in the Annual Lists and General Index of the Parliamentary Papers relating to the East Indies. The most important for the period (1869–1909) are:—Correspondence respecting the relations between the British Government and that of Afghanistan since the accession of the Ameer Shere Ali Khan, 1878. Further Papers relating to the affairs of Afghanistan published in 1878, 1879, 1881 and subsequent dates. Reports of the Indian Famine Commissions in 1880, 1898, and 1902. Reports of the Indian Finance Committee, 1886, of the Indian Currency Committees in 1893, 1899, and of the Royal Commission on the Administration of the Expenditure of India, 1900. Reports of the Indian Education Commission, 1883, and of the Indian Universities Commission, 1902. Reports of the Royal Commission on Opium, 1893. Papers regarding British relations with the neighbouring tribes on the North-west Frontier of India and the military operations undertaken against them, 1898. North-west Frontier and Punjab Frontier administration: correspondence (1897–1901), 1901. Report of the Plague Commission, 1902. Correspondence on Army Administration, 1905. Papers relating to the Reconstitution of the Provinces of Bengal and Assam, 1905–6. Papers relating to the Imperial Advisory Council and Provincial Advisory Councils, the enlargement of the Legislative Councils, and the discussion of the Budget, 1907–9. Memorandum on some of the Results of Indian Administration during the past fifty years, 1909. Reports on the Moral and Material Progress and condition of India, published annually.

II. SECONDARY WORKS.

A. General.

Boulger, D. C. India in the Nineteenth Century. 1901.
Chesney, Sir George. Indian Polity, a view of the System of Administration in India. 1894.
Cotton, Sir H. J. S. New India, or India in transition. 1907.
Cunningham, Sir H. S. British India and its rulers. 1882.
Dictionary of National Biography. 63 vols. 1885–1900.
Dutt, R. C. India in the Victorian Age. 1904.
—— The economic history of India in the Victorian Age. 1906.

Hunter, Sir W. W. The Indian Empire. 1893.
—— The India of the Queen and other Essays. 1903.
Ilbert, Sir C. P. The government of India. Oxford. 1907.
Imperial Gazetteer, the, of India. 26 vols. Oxford. 1907-8.
Lee-Warner, Sir W. The Protected Princes of India. 1894.
Lilly, W. S. India and its problems. 1902.
Lyall, Sir A. C. The Rise and Expansion of the British Dominion in India. 1907.
Morison, Sir Theodore. Imperial rule in India. Westminster. 1899.
Strachey, Sir John. India, its administration and progress. 1903.
Townsend, M. Asia and Europe. 1905.
Trotter, L. J. History of India under Queen Victoria. 2 vols. 1886.
Tupper, Sir C. L. Our Indian Protectorate. 1893.

B. Biographies, Memoirs, Speeches.

Aitchison, Sir C. Lord Lawrence. (Rulers of India.) Oxford. 1892.
Balfour, Lady Betty. The History of Lord Lytton's Indian Administration. 1899.
Black, C. E. D. The Marquess of Dufferin and Ava. 1903.
Curzon of Kedleston, Viscount. Indian Speeches, compiled by S. C. Surha. 4 vols. Calcutta. 1900-6.
—— Lord Curzon in India, being a selection from his speeches as Viceroy and Governor-General of India. 1898-1905. Ed. Sir Thomas Raleigh. 1906.
Dufferin and Ava, Marquis of. Speeches delivered in India. 1890.
Forrest, G. W. The Administration of the Marquis of Lansdowne. Calcutta. 1894.
Lyall, Sir A. C. The Life of the Marquis of Dufferin and Ava. 2 vols. 1905.
Mallet, B. Thomas George, Earl of Northbrook. 1908.
Martineau, J. The Life and Correspondence of Sir Bartle Frere. 2 vols. 1895.
Roberts, Earl. Forty-one years in India. 2 vols. 1897.
Smith, R. Bosworth. The Life of Lord Lawrence. 2 vols. 1883.
Temple, Sir Richard. The Story of my Life. 2 vols. 1896.
—— Men and events of my time in India. 1882.
Thornton, T. H. Sir Richard Meade and the Feudatory States of Central and Southern India. 1898.

C. The North-western Frontier and Afghanistan.

Abdur Rahman Khan, The Life of. Ed. Mir Munshi Sultan Mohammad Khan. 2 vols. 1900.
Adye, Sir John. Indian Frontier Policy. An historical sketch. 1897.
Churchill, W. L. S. The story of the Malakand Field Force. 1898.
Durand, A. The making of a Frontier. 1899.
Hanna, H. B. The Second Afghan War, its causes, its conduct, and its consequences. Westminster. 1899 (vol. i). 1904 (vol. ii).
Hensman, Howard. The Afghan War of 1879-80. 1881.
Holdich, Sir T. H. The Indian Borderland, 1880-1900. 1901.
Hutchinson, H. D. The Campaign in Tirah, 1897-8. 1898.
James, L. The Indian Frontier War, being an Account of the Mohmund and Tirah Expeditions. 1898.
Noyce, F. England, India, and Afghanistan. 1902.
Robertson, Sir G. S. Chitral, the Story of a Minor Siege. 1898.
Warburton, Sir R. Eighteen Years in the Khyber, 1879-98. 1900.

D. The Central Asian Question, Persia and Tibet.

Candler, E. The unveiling of Lhasa. 1905.

Chirol, V. The Middle Eastern Question, or some political problems of Indian defence. 1903.

Colquhoun, A. R. Russia against India. The struggle for Asia. 1900.

Crosby, O. T. Tibet and Turkestan. 1905.

Curzon, G. N. (Viscount Curzon of Kedleston). The Pamirs and the source of the Oxus. 1897.

—— Persia and the Persian Question. 2 vols. 1892.

Forsyth, Sir T. D. Report of a Mission to Yarkand in 1873. Calcutta. 1875.

Gordon, Sir T. E. Persia Revisited. 1896.

Knight, E. F. Where three Empires meet. 1893.

Landon, P. Lhasa. 2 vols. 1905.

CHAPTER XVII.

THE FAR EAST.

CHINA.

Angier, A. G.   The Far East Revisited.   1908.

Ball, J. O.   Things Chinese.   1900.

Boulger, D.   A History of China.   3 vols.   1881.

Brinkley, F.   Japan and China: their History, Arts, and Literature.   12 vols.
    London and Edinburgh.   1903–4.

Chirol, M. V.   The Far Eastern Question.   1896.

Colquhoun, A. R.   China in Transformation.   London and New York.   1898.

——— English Policy in the Far East.   1885.

Cordier, H.   La France en Chine au dix-huitième siècle.   Paris.   1883.

Curzon, Lord (Viscount Curzon of Kedleston).   Problems of the Far East.
    Westminster.   1896.

Davis, Sir J. F.   The Chinese.   3 vols.   1844–5.

Douglas, Sir R. K.   China (Story of the Nations).   New York and London.   1899.

Du Halde, P.   General History of China...done from the French of P. du H. by
    J. Brookes.   4 vols.   1736.

Gundry, R. S.   China and her neighbours.   1893.

Hart, Sir R.   These from the Land of Sinim.   2nd edn.   1903.

Hertslet, Sir E.   Treaties, etc. between Great Britain and China; and between
    China and Foreign Powers...in force on the 1st Jan. 1896.   2 vols.   1896.

Loch, Lord.   Personal narrative of occurrences during Lord Elgin's Second Embassy
    to China in 1860.   1900.

Morrison, G. E.   An Australian in China.   1895.

Oliphant, Lawrence.   Narrative of the Earl of Elgin's Mission to China and Japan
    in the years 1857, 1858, 1859.   2 vols.   Edinburgh and London.   1859.

Poole, S. L., and Dickins, F. V.   Life of Sir Harry Parkes.   2 vols.   1894.

Smith, A. H.   Chinese Characteristics.   Edinburgh.   1900.

——— S. P.   China from Within; or the Story of the Chinese Crisis.   1900.

The Anti-foreign riots in China in 1891.   Shanghai.   1892.

The Englishman in China during the Victorian Era, as illustrated in the Career of
    Sir Rutherford Alcock.   2 vols.   Edinburgh and London.   1900.

Translations of the Peking Gazette.   1872, etc.

Weale, B. L. P.   Manchu and Muscovite.   1904.

Williams, S. W.   The Middle Kingdom.   Revised edn.   2 vols.   1883.

ANNAM AND TONQUIN.

Annales impériales de l'Annam, Fonds de Hué. Paris. 1889, etc.

Billot, M. L'Affaire du Tonkin. Histoire diplomatique de notre protectorat sur l'Annam et de notre conflit avec la Chine. Par un diplomate (M.B.). Paris. 1888.

Chailley-Bert, J. Paul Bert au Tonkin. Paris. 1887.

Colquhoun, A. R. The Truth about Tonquin. 1884.

Devéria, P. Relations de la Chine avec l'Annam. Paris. 1885.

Dubois, R. Le Tonkin en 1900. Paris. 1900.

Garnier, F. Rapport au ministre de la marine sur la mission. Paris. 1875.

Lanessan, J. L. de. L'Empire d'Annam. Paris. 1889.

Michelle, P. L. L'Amiral Courbet au Tonkin. Tours. 1887.

Norman, C. B. Tonkin; or France in the Far East. 1884.

Philastre, P.-L. Code Annamite. 2 vols. Paris. 1876.

Scott, J. G. France and Tongking. 1885.

SIAM.

Anderson, J. English intercourse with Siam in the 17th century. 1890.

Bowring, Sir J. The Kingdom and People of Siam; with a Narrative of the Mission to that country in 1855. 2 vols. London. 1857.

Calendar of State Papers. Colonial Series, preserved in H.M.S. Record Office and elsewhere. 4 vols. From 1513–1629.

Crawfurd, J. Journal of an Embassy from the Governor General of India to the Courts of Siam and Cochinchina. 1830.

English Governess, the, at the Siamese Court; being recollections of six years in the Royal Palace at Bangkok. Boston. 1870.

Finlayson, G. The Mission to Siam and Hué the capital of Cochinchina in the years 1821–2. From the Journal of the late G. F. Esq. 1827.

Malloch, D. E. Siam. Calcutta. 1842.

Pallegoix, Mgr. Description du Royaume Thai ou Siam. 2 vols. Paris. 1854.

Smith, W. H. Five Years in Siam. 1891–6. 2 vols. 1898.

Somerville, M. Siam; on the Meinam from the Gulf to Ayuthia. 1897.

MALAY PENINSULA.

Belfield, H. C. Handbook of the Malay States. 1904.

Bird (afterwards Bishop), Isabella L. The Golden Chersonese. 1883.

Clifford, Sir H. In Court and Rampong; sketches of native life in the Malay Peninsula. 1897.

—— In a Corner of Asia: impressions of men and things in the Malay Peninsula. The Oversea Library, No. 5. 1899.

—— Further India; the story of exploration in Burma, Malaya, etc. 1904.

Dennys, N. B. Descriptive Dictionary of British Malaya. 1894.

Ireland, A. The Far Eastern Tropics. Administration of tropical dependencies. Westminster. 1905.

MacLarty, F. M. Affairs of the Colony; history of the Straits Settlements and British Protected States of the Malay Peninsula. Penang. 1893.

Sherborn, C. D. Bibliography of Malaya, 1888–90. London and Edinburgh. 1890. Straits Asiatic Society Journal, No. 22.

Skeat, W. W.   Malay Magic: an introduction to the folklore and popular religion of the Malay Peninsula.   1900.
—— Wild Tribes of the Malay Peninsula.   Washington.   1903.
Straits Settlement.   Précis concerning the Straits Settlements and the Native States of the Malay Peninsula.   1892.
Swettenham, Sir F. A.   Malay Sketches.   1895.
—— The Real Malay.   Pen Pictures.   1900.
—— British Malaya.   An Account of the Origin and Progress of British Influence in Malaya.   1907.
Wallace, A. R.   The Malay Archipelago.   1890.

PHILIPPINE ISLANDS.

Atkinson, F. W.   The Philippine Islands.   Boston.   1805.
Blair, E. H. and Robertson, J. A.   Philippine Islands.   1493–1803.   Cleveland.   1903.
Brown, A. J.   The New Era in the Philippines.   New York.   1903.
Butterworth, H.   The Story of Magellan and the Discovery of the Philippines.   New York.   1899.
Caro y Mora, J.   Ataque de Li-ma-hong à Manila en 1574.   Manila.   1898.
Combés, F.   Historia de Mindanao y Joló.   Obra publicada 1667.   Madrid.   1897.
Foradada, F.   La Soberania de España en Filipinas.   Barcelona.   1897.
Govantes, F. M. de.   Episodios historicas de Filipinas.   Manila.   1881.
Le Roy, J. A.   Philippine Life in town and country.   New York.   1905.
March, A.   History of the Philippines.   New York.   1899.
Medina, J. T.   Bibliografiá española de las Islas Filipinas 1523–1810.   Santiago.   1897.
—— El Tribunal de la Inquisición en las Filipinas.   Santiago.   1899.
Meyer, A. B. and Schabenberg, A.   Die Philippinen, 1890, etc.   Publ. des K. Ethnographischen Museum in Dresden, No. 8.   Leipzig.   1881, etc.
—— The Distribution of the Negritos in the Philippine Islands.   Dresden.   1899.
Montero y Vidal, J.   Historia de Filipinas.   Madrid.   1887, etc.
—— El Archipiélago filipino.   Madrid.   1886.
Morris, C.   Our Island Empire.   Handbook of the Philippine Islands, etc.   Philadelphia.   1899.
Pardo de Tavera, J. H.   Biblioteca Filipina.   Washington.   1903.
Potter, H. C.   The East of to-day and to-morrow.   New York.   1902.
Retana, W. E.   Catálogo de la biblioteca filipina de W. E. Retana.   Madrid.   1898.
Robinson, A. G.   The Philippines: The war and the people.   New York.   1901.
Sawyer, F. H.   The Inhabitants of the Philippines.   1900.
Stephens, J. E.   Yesterdays in the Philippines.   1898.
Willis, H. P.   Our Philippine Problem.   New York.   1905.
Worcester, D. C.   The Philippine Islands and their people.   New York.   1893.
Younghusband, G.   The Philippines and round about.   1899.

CHAPTER XVIII.

JAPAN.

I. HISTORIES AND OTHER TREATISES.

Adams, F. O. History of Japan. 2 vols. 1874.

Alcock, Sir Rutherford, K.C.B. Capital of the Tycoon. 2 vols. 1863.

Black, J. R. Young Japan. 2 vols. 1881.

Brinkley, F. R. Japan and China. 12 vols. London and Edinburgh. 1903–4.

—— (translated by). History of the Empire of Japan. Compiled by the Japanese Commissioners to the Chicago Exhibition. Tokio. 1893.

Chamberlain, B. H. Handbook to Japan. (Murray's Series.) Tokio. 1907.

—— Things Japanese. 5th edn. 1905.

Colquhoun, A. R. The Mastery of the Pacific. 1902.

Couvant, M. Okorobo. Paris.

Dickins, F. V. Life of Sir Harry Parkes. Vol. II. Japan. 2 vols. 1894.

Dyer, H. Dai Nippon. 1904.

Griffis, W. E. The Mikado's Empire. 2 vols. 11th edn. 1906.

Guillemard, F. H. H. The Cruise of the Marchesa. 2 vols. Vol. I. Formosa and Liukiu. 1886.

House, E. H. Japanese Expedition to Formosa in 1874. Tokio. 1875.

Iyenaga, T., Ph.D. The Constitutional Development of Japan, 1853–91. Baltimore. 1891.

Kaempfer, Englebert, M.D. History of Japan. First published in 1727. Reprinted in three volumes. Glasgow. 1906.

Kanagawa Prefecture. The Peruvian Bark "Maria Luz." Yokohama. 1874.

Lanman, C. Japan and its Leading Men. Boston. 1885.

Mazelière, M. de la. Le Japon—Histoire et Civilisation. 3 vols. Paris. 1907.

Mitford, A. B. (Lord Redesdale). Tales of Old Japan. 2 vols. 1871.

Mounsey, A. H. The Satsuma Rebellion. 1879.

Murray, D. The Story of Japan, with Supplementary Chapter by J. H. Longford. 1904.

Norman, H. Real Japan. 1904.

Okakura, Y. The Spirit of the East. 1905.

Palmer, Major General H. S., R.E. Letters from the Land of the Rising Sun. Correspondence contributed to the Times, 1886–92. Yokohama. 1894.

Ransome, S. Japan in Transition. 1902.

Rathgen, K. Japan's Volkswirtschaft und Staatshaushalt. Leipzig. 1891.

CH. XVIII.

Rein, J. J.　Japan nach Reisen und Studien.　Leipzig.　1905.
Siebold, Frhr. A. von.　Der Eintritt Japans in das Europäische Volksrecht.　Berlin.
　　1900.　English translation.　1905.
Suyematsu, Baron.　The Risen Sun.　1905.

Encyclopaedia Britannica.　Ninth and Tenth Editions.
　　Japan.　Vol. 13.　By T. R. H. McClatchie.
　　Japan.　Vol. 29.　By F. R. Brinkley.
　　Korea.　Vol. 30.　By F. R. Brinkley.
　　Formosa.　Vol. 28.　By F. R. Brinkley.

II.　OFFICIAL AND OTHER PUBLICATIONS.

Parliamentary Papers.
　　Japan No. 3.　1870.　Correspondence respecting Affairs in Japan, 1868–70.
　　Japan No. 1.　1876.　Correspondence respecting the Treaty between Japan
　　　　and Korea.
　　Japan No. 1.　1894.　Correspondence respecting the Revision of the Treaty.
Treaties and Conventions between the Empire of Japan and other Powers, 1854–84.
　　Foreign Office.　Tokio.　1884.
The Japan Weekly Mail.　Yokohama.　1870–1907.　1870–6.　Ed. W. G. Howell.
　　1882–1907.　Ed. F. R. Brinkley.
Transactions of the Asiatic Society of Japan.　Tokio.　1874–1905.
　　Vol. I.　Russian Descents in Saghalin and Iturup in 1806 and 1807.　By
　　　　W. G. Aston.
　　Vol. II.　The Sword of Japan.　By T. R. H. McClatchie.
　　Vol. III.　The Legacy of Iyeyasu.　By W. E. Grigsby.
　　Vol. V.　Japanese Heraldry.　By T. R. H. McClatchie.
　　Vol. V.　The Japanese Penal Codes.　By J. H. Longford.
　　Vol. VI.　Hideyoshi's Invasion of Korea.　By W. G. Aston.
　　Vol. VI.　Review of the Introduction of Christianity into China and Japan.
　　　　By J. H. Gubbins.
　　Vol. VIII.　Hideyoshi and the Satsuma Clan in the Sixteenth Century.　By
　　　　J. H. Gubbins.
　　Vol. IX.　Hideyoshi's Invasion of Korea.　Chapter II—The Retreat.　Chap-
　　　　ter III—Negotiation.　By W. G. Aston.
　　Vol. XI.　Hideyoshi's Invasion of Korea.　By W. G. Aston.
　　Vol. XV.　The Feudal System in Japan under the Tokugawa Shoguns.　By
　　　　J. H. Gubbins.
　　Vol. XXIII.　Comparison of the Japanese and Liukiuan languages.　By B. H.
　　　　Chamberlain.
　　Vol. XXIV.　Review of the History of Formosa.　By J. W. Davidson.
　　Vol. XXVI.　Laws of the Tokugawa Period.　By J. H. Gubbins.
　　Vol. XXX.　History of the Rise of Political Parties in Japan.　By A. H. Lay.

III.　UNTRANSLATED JAPANESE WORKS.

Chōsen jijō.　Korean Affairs.　By Yenomoto Muyo.　Tokio.　1882.
Chōsen Kinkiō Kibun.　Report on the Present Condition of Korea (1882).　Com-
　　piled by the General Staff Department of the War Office.
Kaikoku go jiu nen shi.　Fifty Years History of the Opened Country, 1859–1909.
　　By various writers, including Princes Ito and Yamagata, Marquis Matsugata,
　　Counts Okuma and Yamamoto, Viscount Inouye and many others.　2 vols.
　　Tokio.　1909.

Kizokuin Giji Sokkiroku. Stenographic Reports of the Proceedings in the House of Peers. Tokio. 1890 and following years. (*In progress.*)

Nihon Saikiō Shi. A History of Western Doctrine (i.e. Christianity) in Japan. Published by the Privy Council. Tokio. 1876.

Sensen Kōkwa Chōsen Ronshiu. The Reasons for War or Peace with Korea. By Kishijima Shiutarō. Tokio. 1882.

Shiugiin Giji Sokkiroku. Stenographic Reports of the Proceedings in the House of Commons. Tokio. 1890 and following years. (*In progress.*)

Taiwan Sōtoku Fu Hōki Teiyō. Compendium of the Laws and Regulations of the Government General of Formosa. Published by the Section of Correspondence of the Civil Branch of the Government General of Formosa, 1882.

IV. RELIGION.

Aston, W. G. Shinto, the way of the Gods. 1905.

Fujishama, R. Le Bouddhisme Japonais. Paris. Angers. 1889.

Griffis, W. E. The Religions of Japan. 1895.

Haas, H. Annalen des Japanischen Buddhismus. Deutsche Gesellschaft für Natur- und Völkerkunde Ostasiens. Yokohama. 1908.

Lloyd, A. Developments of Japanese Buddhism. Asiatic Society of Japan. Yokohama. 1874.

Revon, M. Le Shinntoisme. Paris. 1907.

CHAPTER XIX.

RUSSO-JAPANESE WAR.

I. BIBLIOGRAPHIES.

No bibliography has yet been published. "Recent publications of Military Interest," issued quarterly by the General Staff, War Office, contains the names of the chief books and articles, dealing with the War, published since the first number appeared in April 1907. The half-yearly supplement to the Militär-Wochenblatt, published in Berlin in January and July of each year since 1904 and entitled Uebersicht über die periodische Militär-Literatur des In- und Auslandes, also contains much useful information. Aubert, Der russisch-japanische Krieg 1904–5, Berlin. 1909. [Contains a list of works.]

II. MANUSCRIPTS.

The most important documents connected with the naval and military operations have been collected at St Petersburg and Tokio by the General Staffs of Russia and Japan respectively. Access to them can only be obtained through diplomatic channels.

III. OFFICIAL PUBLICATIONS.

These have been compiled in the War Departments of the several Governments and are based, for the most part, upon the reports of military attachés who had special facilities for observation. They contain the most reliable information published at the present time.

The Russo-Japanese War. Compiled by the General Staff, War Office. Part I. Causes of the War. Opening events up to and including the battle of the Yalu. 1906.

—— Part II. From the battle of the Yalu to Liao-yang exclusive. 1908. [Other parts will follow; the maps are good and complete.]

Reports from British Officers attached to the Japanese and Russian forces in the Field. Compiled by the General Staff, War Office. 3 vols. with 2 cases of maps. 1909.

Medical and Sanitary Reports from Officers attached to the Japanese and Russian Forces in the Field. Compiled by the General Staff, War Office. 1908.

Kriegsgeschichtliche Einzelschriften, Erfahrungen aussereuropäischer Kriege neuester Zeit. II. Aus dem russisch-japanischen Kriege 1904 bis 1905. Prepared by the German General Staff.

Heft 37, 38. 1. Port Arthur. Berlin. 1906.
Heft 39, 40. 2. Yalu. Berlin. 1907.
Heft 41, 42. 3. Wafangou und Vorkämpfe von Liaoyan. Berlin. 1908.
Heft 43, 44. 4. Die Schlacht bei Liaoyan. Berlin. 1908.

[The maps in this series are good and complete.]

Mitteilungen des Ingenieur-Komitee. Heft 40. Ein Beitrag zur Beurteilung des Kampfes um Port Arthur. Berlin. 1905.

Einzelschriften über den Russisch-Japanischen Krieg. 10 parts. Vienna. 1905–6. [Based on materials supplied by the Austro-Hungarian General Staff.]

Fernandez de Cordova. Campano Russo-Japanese. Madrid. 1908. [Official report of the Spanish Military Attaché to his General Staff.]

Military Information Division. Reports of the Military Observers attached to the Armies in Manchuria during the Russo-Japanese War. Parts i–v. Washington. 1906–9.

La Guerra tra la Russia e il Giappone, 1904–5. Vol. i. Rome. 1908. Prepared by the Italian General Staff.

Русско-Японская война въ сообщеніяхъ Николаевской Академіи Генеральнаго Штаба. (The Russo-Japanese War. Lectures given at the Nicholas Academy [Russian Staff College].) 3 parts. St Petersburg. 1906–8. French translation : Conférences sur la guerre Russo-Japonaise faites à l'Académie d'État-Major Nicolas. 3 parts. Paris. 1907–9.

Kinai, M. The Russo-Japanese War (Official Reports). 2 vols. Tokio. 1905–7. London. 1907. [An English translation of the Japanese official reports.]

Schönmeyer, Major Don Alfredo. Informe sobre la Guerra Ruso-Japonesa. Report of the Chilian Military Attaché to the Russian Army. Santiago de Chile. 1906.

Ariga, Nagao. La guerre Russo-Japonaise au point de vue continental et le droit international d'après les documents officiels du grand état-major japonais. Paris. 1908.

IV.   ACCOUNTS BY EYE-WITNESSES.

Apushkin, V. A. Дѣло о Сдачѣ Крѣпости Портъ-Артуръ. (The trial of officers concerned in the surrender of Port Arthur.) St Petersburg. 1908.

Baring, M. With the Russians in Manchuria. 1905.

Bartlett, Ashmead. Port Arthur. The Siege and the Capitulation. 1906.

Bazini, L. La battaglia di Mukden. Milan. 1907.

Brooke, Lord. An eye-witness in Manchuria. 1905.

Burleigh, Bennet. The Empire of the Far East or Japan and Russia at War. 1906.

Camperio. Al Campo Russo in Manciuria. Milan. 1907.

Gädke, Oberst. Kriegsbriefe aus der Mandschurei. Berlin. 1905.

Gertsch, Colonel F. Vom russisch-japanischen Kriege. 2 parts. Bern. 1907, 1909.

Hamilton, Sir Ian, K.C.B., D.S.O. A Staff-officer's Scrap-book during the Russo-Japanese War. 2 vols. 1905–7.

Klado, Captain. The Battle of the Sea of Japan. 1906.

Kostyenko, Major-General. Осада и сдача крѣпости Портъ-Артуръ. (The siege and surrender of Port Arthur.) Kieff. 1906.

Kuropatkin, General. The Russian Army and the Japanese War. 1909.

Kvitka, Colonel A. Journal d'un Cosaque du Trans-baïkal. Paris. 1908.

Martinov, E. Унастіе Зарайцевъ въ бою дри Ляньдянсанѣ. (The Zaraisk Regiment at Lang-tzu-shan.) St Petersburg. 1908.

Nojine, E. K. The Truth about Port Arthur. 1908.

Nottbeck, von. Erlebnisse und Erinnerungen aus dem russisch-japanischen Kriege. Berlin. 1907.

Novitski, Colonel. Сандепу. (Sandepu.) St Petersburg. 1907.

Politovsky, E. S. From Libau to Tsushima. 1908.

Romanovski, Yu and Schwarz, A. von. Оборона Портъ-Артура. (The defence of Port Arthur.) St Petersburg. 1908.

Russisch-japanische Krieg, der. Urteile und Beobachtungen von Mitkämpfern. Vienna. 1906.

Sakurai, Tadayoshi. Human bullets. A Soldier's Story of Port Arthur. 1908.

Schellendorf, Major Bronsart von. Sechs Monate beim japanischen Feldheer. Berlin. 1906.

Schwartz, Oscar von. Zehn Monate Kriegskorrespondent beim Heere Kuropatkin. Berlin. 1906.

Schwarz, Lt-Col. A. von. De l'influence des combats livrés sous Port-Arthur sur la construction des forts. Paris. 1908.

Semenov, Vladimir. The battle of Tsushima. 1906.

—— Ras plata. Diary during the blockade of Port Arthur and the voyage of Admiral Rodjestvensky's Fleet. 1909.

Smith, W. Richmond. The siege and fall of Port Arthur. 1905.

Spaits, Rittmeister. Mit Kosaken durch die Mandschurei. Vienna. 1907.

Svyechin, Captain. Въ Восточномъ отрядѣ отъ Ляояна къ Тюренчену и обратно. (With the Eastern force from Liao-yang to the Yalu and back.) Warsaw. 1908.

Svyeshnikov, Colonel. Набѣгъ на Инкоу. (The raid on Yingkou.) St Petersburg. 1906.

Tettau, Major Freiherr von. Achtzehn Monate mit Russlands Heeren in der Mandschurei. 2 vols. Berlin. 1907–8.

Thomas, V. Trois mois avec Kuroki. Paris. 1905.

Villétard de Laguérie, R. Trois mois avec le Maréchal Oyama. Paris. 1905.

V. OTHER WORKS.

Asakawa, K. I. The Russo-japanese conflict, its causes and issues. 1904.

Aubert, Captain. Der russisch-japanische Krieg. Berlin. 1909.

Bardonnant, Lt-Colonel. Du Yalou à Liao-yang. Paris. 1908.

Bujac, Colonel E. La guerre Russo-japonaise. Paris. 1908.

Cherenisov, Colonel. Русско-Японская война 1904–5 года. (The Russo-Japanese War of 1904–5.) Kieff. 1907.

Grandprey, Colonel C. de. Le siège de Port Arthur. Paris. 1906.

Guionic, Lt-Colonel G. Réflexions sur la Guerre de Mandchourie. Paris. 1907.

Immanuel, Captain F. Der russisch-japanische Krieg. 6 parts. Berlin. 1904–6.

Janson, Lt-General von. Das Zusammenwirken von Heer und Flotte im russisch-japanischen Kriege. Berlin. 1905.

Japan-Russian War, the. The Yusakusha Publishers. Tokio. 1904.

Lignitz, General V. F. W. A. von. Der japanisch-russische Krieg. 2 parts. Berlin. 1908. (*In progress.*)

Löffler, Major. Der russisch-japanische Krieg. 2 vols. Berlin. 1905.

Lüttwitz, Freiherr R. A. von. Das Angriffsverfahren der Japaner im Ost-Asiatischen Kriege 1904–5. Berlin. 1906.

Meunier, Major R. La guerre Russo-japonaise. Paris. 1906.

Russo-Japanese War, the. The Kinknodo Company. 10 vols. Tokio. 1904 5.

Schlacht am Schaho, die. Supplement to the Militär-Wochenblatt. Berlin. 1906.

Schlacht von Mukden, die. Supplement to Militär-Wochenblatt. Berlin. 1905.

War in the Far East, the. By the Military Correspondent of the "Times." 1905.

CHAPTER XX.

THE EUROPEAN COLONIES.
(1870—1907.)

I. BIBLIOGRAPHIES.

1. GENERAL.

Fortescue, G. K. Subject-Index of the Modern Works added to the Library of the British Museum in the years 1831–1900, edited by. 3 vols. 1902–3. In the years 1901–5. 1906. *See under names of Colonies and Countries.*

2. THE BRITISH EMPIRE.

(a) General.

Catalogue of the Royal Colonial Institute arranged in chronological order under the names of the various Colonies, includes books, pamphlets and magazines: separate catalogues of State Papers (Imperial and Colonial) and maps.

(b) Africa (South).

See Vol. XI. Bibliography of ch. 27 (3) 1. A.

Amery, L. S. The "Times" History of the War in South Africa. Vol. VII. (Contains a list of books on South African History.)

(c) Australasia.

See Vol. XI. Bibliography of ch. 27 (4) 1. A.

(d) Canada.

See Vol. X. Bibliography of ch. 21. 1.

(e) West Indies.

Cundall, F. Bibliography of the West Indies (excluding Jamaica). Kingston. 1909.
—— Bibliographia Jamaicensis. Kingston. 1902. With Supplement. 1908.
Larned, J. N. Literature of American History. 1902. (Contains a short bibliography.)

3. DUTCH COLONISATION.

Catalogus van de Boeken en Kaarten uitmakende de Bibliotheëk van het Departement van Koloniën. The Hague. 1898.
Nijhoff, M. List of the best books relating to Dutch East India. The Hague. 1902.
Repertorium of de Litteratur betreffende de Nederlandsche Koloniën. Vol. I, 1866–93. Vol. II, 1894–1900. The Hague. 1895, 1901.

CH. XX.

4. German Colonisation.

Brose, M. Repertorium der Deutsch-Kolonialen Litteratur von 1834–95. Berlin. 1897. (Continued annually under the same title.)

Decharme, P. Bibliographie critique de la colonisation allemande. Paris. 1900.

Hassert, K. Deutschlands Kolonien. Leipzig. 1898. (Contains a list of books relating to German colonisation.)

5. The Congo State.

Wauters, A. J. Bibliographie du Congo, 1880–95. Brussels. 1895.

—— L'État indépendant du Congo. Brussels. 1899. (Contains short lists of books under the various headings of the subject-matter.)

II. GENERAL WORKS ON EUROPEAN COLONISATION.

Leroy Beaulieu, P. De la colonisation chez les peuples modernes. 2 vols. 5th edn. Paris. 1902.

Zimmerman, A. Die europäischen Kolonien. 5 vols. Berlin. 1896–1903.

III. THE BRITISH EMPIRE.

A. General.

(1) *Official Publications, Compilations of Statistical and other information.*

Abstract, Statistical, for the Colonial and other Possessions of the United Kingdom. Annual.

Bedwell, C. E. A. The Legislation of the Empire, 1898–1907. Edited under the direction of the Society of Comparative Legislation. 4 vols. 1909.

Colonial Office List, The. Annual.

Parliamentary Papers. (A selected list will be found under the names of the various colonies and subjects in Messrs P. S. King and Co's Catalogue of Imperial Parliamentary Papers. 1801–1900. A fuller list coming down to the present time will be found in the Catalogue (Parliamentary Papers. United Kingdom) of the Royal Colonial Institute. A few only of the more important are separately mentioned under the various headings in this bibliography.)

Annual Reports made to the Secretary of State by the Governors of the Colonies, 1870–86. 34 vols. 1872–87. From 1887 the Report on each colony is published separately.

Proceedings of the Colonial Conference 1887. Vol. i. Proceedings C. 5091. Vol. ii. Appendix of Papers C. 5091. 1.

Constitution of the Executive and of the Legislative Assemblies of the British Colonies. 2 parts. 1889–90. 194.

Earl of Jersey's Report on the Colonial Conference at Ottawa 1894, with Proceedings of the Conference 1894. C. 7553.

Names of Bills passed in colonies possessing responsible government to which Her Majesty has not given her assent. 1894. 196.

Proceedings of the Colonial Conference 1897. C. 8596.

Disabilities or Restrictions on British Indian subjects in British Colonies and Dependencies. 1900. 383, Sess. 2.

Papers relating to the Colonial Conference 1902. Cd. 1299.

Resolutions of Colonial Legislatures since 1890 in favour of preferential trade with the United Kingdom. 1905. Cd. 2326.

Census of the British Empire, 1901. 1906. Cd. 2660.

Minutes of Proceedings of Colonial Conference 1907. Cd. 3523.
Papers laid before the Colonial Conference 1907. Cd. 3524.
Provisions in colonial laws conferring powers of local option in regard to
  licences for the sale of intoxicating liquors. 1907. 47.
Piggott, F. T. Imperial Statutes applicable to the Colonies. 2 vols. 1902.
Proceedings of the Royal Colonial Institute. 1869-.
Year-Book. The British Empire. 1903.
—— Colonial. London. 1890-.
—— of the Imperial Institute. 3rd issue. 1894.
—— The Statesman's. A statistical and historical annual of the States of the
  world and their colonies.

(2) *Other Works.*

Bowen, Sir G. F. Thirty Years of Colonial Government (1859-88). Edited by
  Stanley Lane Poole. 2 vols. 1889.
Brassey, T. A. Problems of Empire. 1904.
Carnarvon, Fourth Earl of. A selection from the letters and speeches of, entitled
  The Defence of the Empire. Edited by Sir G. S. Clarke. 1897.
Century and the Empire, The. A series of Essays on Imperial Problems by various
  writers. 1905.
Chalmers, R. A History of Currency in the British Colonies. 1893.
Dilke, Sir C. W. Problems of Greater Britain. 2 vols. 1890.
—— British Empire. 1899.
Egerton, H. E A short History of British Colonial Policy. 2nd edn. 1905.
Freeman, E. A. Greater Greece and Greater Britain. 1886.
Fuchs, C. J. The Trade Policy of Great Britain and her Colonies since 1860.
  Translated by C. H. M. Archibald. 1905.
Greswell, W. P. The Growth and Administration of the British Colonies. 1837-
  97. 1898.
Jebb, R. Studies in Colonial Nationalism. 1905.
Jenkyns, Sir H. British Rule and Jurisdiction beyond the Seas. Oxford. 1902.
Jose, A. W. The Growth of the Empire. 1905.
Keith, A. B. Responsible Government in the Dominions. 1909.
—— The development of Colonial Self-Government in the 19th century. Journal
  of the Royal Society of Arts. No. 2883. Vol. LVI.
Knight, E. F. Over-Sea Britain. A descriptive record of the Empire. 1907.
Labillière, F. P. de. Federal Britain. 1894.
Leroy Beaulieu, P. Les nouvelles Sociétés Anglo-Saxonnes, Australie, Nouvelle-
  Zélande, Afrique du Sud. Paris. 1901.
Markham, V. R. Factory and Shop Acts of the British Dominions. 1908.
Parkin, G. R. Imperial Federation. 1892.
Payne, E. J. Colonies and Colonial Federations. 1904.
Pollard, A. F. The British Empire, edited by. 1909.
Root, J. W. Colonial Tariffs. Liverpool. 1906.
—— Trade Relations of the British Empire. 2nd edn. Liverpool. 1904.
Shortt, A. Imperial Preferential Trade from a Canadian Point of View. Toronto.
  1904.
Snow, A. H. The Administration of Dependencies. New York and London. 1902.
Tarring, C. J. Chapters on the Law relating to the Colonies. 3rd edn. 1906.
Todd, A. Parliamentary Government in the British Colonies. 2nd edn. 1894.
Trotter, W. F. The Government of Greater Britain. (Temple Primers.) 1905.
Whates, H. R. The Third Salisbury Administration, 1895-1900. 1900.
Wolseley, Viscount. The Story of a Soldier's Life. 2 vols. 1903.

B. AFRICA (EXCEPTING SOUTH AFRICA AND EGYPT).

(1) *Official Publications, Compilations of Statistical and other information.*

For fuller information reference should be made to the Catalogue of the Royal Colonial Institute, Parliamentary Papers (Colonies).

British East Africa and Uganda. Official Gazette of the East African and Uganda Protectorate. 1901–.
—— Official Orders in force in the East African Protectorate on Jan. 1, 1903. (For the period 1876–1902.)
Gambia. Laws and Ordinances, 1843–67. Blue Book. 1898–.
Gold Coast. Ordinances. 1888–. Blue Book. 1883–.
Sierra Leone. Ordinances and Orders in Council. 1875–. Blue Book. 1893.
Revised edition of the Ordinances of Sierra Leone, by E. T. Packard and D. F. Wilbraham with appendix containing Orders in Council, etc., 1811–1908. 4 vols. 1908–9.
Southern Nigeria. Ordinances. 1894–.
—— Blue Book. Lagos. 1885–.

Parliamentary Papers (Imperial).
Report on the condition of the settlements on the West Coast of Africa, with Maps. 2 parts. 1865. 412, 412 I.
Correspondence respecting affairs in the Cameroons, 1885, with Map. Africa, No. 1. 1885. C. 4279.
Report relating to Uganda by Sir Gerald Portal, 1894. Africa, No. 2. 1894. C. 7303.
Report on the condition and progress of the East Africa Protectorate from its establishment to July 20, 1897, by Sir A. Hardinge, with Map. Africa, No. 7. 1897. C. 8683.
Papers relative to the liquor trade in West Africa. 2 parts. 1897. C. 8480, 205.
Royal Niger Company. Revocation of Charter. Balance Sheets of Company, 1887–98. Revenue and Expenditure of Niger Government, 1887–98. 1899. C. 9372.
Convention of 1898 between England and France delimiting possessions and spheres of influence East and West of the River Niger, 1899. Maps, Treaty Series, No. 15. 1899. C. 9334.
Convention between England and France respecting Newfoundland and West and Central Africa, 1904. Treaty Series, No. 5. 1905. Cd. 2383.

Archer, F. B. The Gambia Colony and Protectorate. An official Handbook. Part i is a history of the colony. 1906.
Collection of Treaties with Native Chiefs on the West Coast of Africa. African (West), No. 411. 1892. (Printed for the use of the Colonial Office.)
Handbook of British East Africa. Prepared in the Intelligence Division, War Office. 1893.
Somaliland. Official history of the operations in 1901–4. General Staff, War Office. 2 vols. 1907.
Year-Book, the West African. 1901–.

(2) *Other Works.*

(*a*) General.

Sanderson, E. Great Britain in Modern Africa. 1907.
Stanley, D. (editor). The Autobiography of Sir H. M. Stanley. 1909.
Wiart, W. E. C. de. Les grandes compagnies coloniales anglaises au xixe siècle. Paris. 1899. (British South Africa, East Africa, and Royal Niger Companies.)

(*See also VII, the Partition of Africa.*)

(*b*) Central Africa.

Johnston, Sir H. H. Livingstone and the exploration of Central Africa. 1891.
—— British Central Africa. 1897.

(*c*) East Africa.

Eliot, Sir C. The East Africa Protectorate. 1905.
Gregory, J. W. Foundation of British East Africa. 1901.
Hindlip, Lord. British East Africa. Past, present and future. 1905.
Johnston, Sir H. H. The Uganda Protectorate. 2 vols. 1902.
Lucas, C. P. Geography of South and East Africa, revised by H. E. Egerton. Part II of Vol. IV of the Historical Geography of the British Colonies. Oxford. 1904.
Lugard, Sir F. Rise of our East African Empire. 2 vols. Edinburgh. 1893.
Lyne, R. N. Zanzibar in contemporary times. 1905. (Contains a list of official papers relating to Zanzibar.)
McDermott, P. L. British East Africa. 1893.
Portal, Sir G. The British Mission to Uganda in 1893, edited by R. Rodd. 1894.
Worsfold, W. B. Portuguese Nyassaland. 1899.

(*d*) West Africa.

Burleigh, B. Two Campaigns, Madagascar and Ashantee. 1896.
Crooks, J. J. History of Sierra Leone. 1903.
Ellis, A. B. History of the Gold Coast. 1893.
Ferryman, A. F. Mockler. British Nigeria. 1902.
Fitzgerald, C. The Gambia and its proposed cession to France. 1875.
George, C. The Rise of British West Africa. 1903.
Kingsley, M. H. West African Studies. 1899.
Lucas, C. P. West Africa. (Vol. III of the Historical Geography of the British Colonies.) 2nd edn. Oxford. 1900.
Macdonald, G. The Gold Coast past and present. 1898.
Morel, E. D. Affairs of West Africa. 1902.
Reade, W. The Ashantee Campaign. 1874.
Richardson, R. Story of the Niger. 1888.
Septans, Lieut.-Col. A. Les expéditions anglaises en Afrique, 1873–96. Paris. 1896.
Shaw, F. L. (Lady Lugard). A Tropical Dependency, Western Soudan and Northern Nigeria. 1905.
Wallis, C. B. The Advance of our West African Empire. 1903.

C. South Africa.

(1) *Official Publications, Compilations of Statistical and other information.*

Cape of Good Hope.

Votes and Proceedings of the Parliament. 1870–.
Debates in the House of Assembly. 1892–.
Debates in the Legislative Council. 1892–.
Statutes of the Cape of Good Hope, 1652–1901. Edited by H. Tennant and E. M. Jackson. 4 vols. 1895–1904.
Results of a Census taken 1875.
Results of a Census taken 1891.
Blue Book. 1873–85.
Report of the Commission upon the Railways of the Colony. 1878.

Natives. Report and Proceedings of the Government Commission on Native Laws and Customs. Cape Town. 1883.
South African Native Affairs Commission, 1903–5. Vol. I, Report of the Commission. Cape Town. 1905. Vol. II, Minutes of Evidence, Cape Colony. Cape Town. 1904. Vol. III, Minutes of Evidence, Natal. Cape Town. 1904. Vol. IV, Minutes of Evidence, Rhodesia, Bechuanaland Protectorate, British Bechuanaland (Cape Colony), Orange River Colony, Basutoland, Transvaal Colony and again in the Cape Colony. Cape Town. 1904. Vol. V, Index and Annexures. Cape Town. 1905.

Frere, Sir Bartle. Correspondence relating to the recall of. Edited by Sir B. Frere. London. 1880.
Noble, J. Descriptive Handbook of the Cape Colony. 1875.
—— Official Handbook of the Cape of Good Hope. Cape Town. 1886.

Natal (Parliamentary Papers).

Votes and Proceedings of the Legislative Council to 1893.
Sessional Papers of the Legislative Council to 1892.
Votes and Proceedings of the Legislative Assembly, 1893–.
Sessional Papers of the Legislative Assembly, 1893–.
Laws of Natal, 1875–.
Debates of the Legislative Council, 1879–93.
Debates of the Legislative Assembly, 1893–.
Blue Book of Natal to 1893.
Statistical Year-Book of Natal, 1894–.
Statutes of Natal. A compilation of the Statutes 1845–99. Compiled and edited by R. L. Hitchins. 3 vols. 1900–2.

Orange River Colony.

Debates of the Legislative Council, 1903–.
Minutes of Proceedings of the Legislative Council, 1906–7.
Ordinances, 1902–.
Statute Law of the Orange River Colony. Translated by C. L. Botha. Translation revised by S. H. Barber and J. H. L. Findlay. 1901.

Transvaal.

Votes and Proceedings of the Legislative Council, 1903–8.
Reports of Select Committees of the Legislative Council, 1903–8.
Statute Law of the Transvaal. Translated by S. H. Barber, W. A. Macfadyen, and J. H. L. Findlay. 1901.

Laws, Volksraad Resolutions, Proclamations, etc., in the Transvaal. Translated
·by S. H. Barber, W. A. Macfadyen, and J. H. L. Findlay. 1901.
Political Laws of the South African Republic, with Appendix containing the
Constitution of the Orange Free State. Translated by W. A. Macfadyen.
1896.

Parliamentary Papers (Imperial).

Delagoa Bay Correspondence respecting the claims of Her Majesty's Govern-
ment. 1875. With Maps. Portugal No. 1 (1875). C. 1361.
Proposal for Conference of Delegates from the Colonies and States of South
Africa. 1875. C. 1244.
Correspondence respecting proposed Conference. 2 parts. 1876–7. C. 1399,
C. 1732.
Convention of settlement of Transvaal Territory. 1881. C. 2998.
Report of the Transvaal Royal Commission. 2 parts. 1882. C. 3114,
C. 3219.
Convention between Her Majesty and the South African Republic. 1884.
C. 3914.
Correspondence respecting the Convention of 1884. With Map. 1884. C. 3947.
Correspondence respecting the Conference of Delegates from the Orange Free
State, the Cape of Good Hope and Natal on the question of Customs Union
and Railway Extension. 1888. C. 5390.
Correspondence respecting the action of Portugal in Mashonaland 1890. Africa,
No. 2. 1890. C. 5904.
Correspondence relating to the proposal to establish responsible government in
Natal. 2 parts. 1891, 1893. C. 6487, 216.
Correspondence relating to the British South Africa Company in Mashonaland,
Matabeleland and Bechuanaland. 4 parts. 1893. C. 7171, 7190, 7196,
7290.
Petition from British subjects resident in the South African Republic presented
to Sir H. B. Loch at Pretoria. 1894. C. 7554.
Correspondence respecting the number of British subjects. 1895. C. 7633.
Correspondence on the subject of recent disturbances in the South African
Republic. 1896. C. 7933.
Report from the Select Committee appointed to enquire into the circumstances
of the incursion into the South African Republic 1897 (64). Second
Report with Proceedings, Evidence, etc., 1897 (311).
Report of the Committee of the Cape of Good Hope House of Assembly on the
Jameson Raid. 1897. C. 8380.
Correspondence on the proposed changes in the Administration of the British
South Africa Company's territories. (Charter of Company, 1889. Orders
in Council, 1891, 1894.) 2 parts. 1898. C. 8732, 8773.
Papers relating to the Complaints of British subjects in the South African
Republic. 1899. C. 9345.
Correspondence relating to the Bloemfontein Conference. 1899. C. 9404.
Correspondence respecting terms of surrender of the Boer forces in the field.
1902. Cd. 1096.
Report of His Majesty's Commissioners on the War in South Africa. London.
1903. Cd. 1789.
Census Returns of British South Africa. 1904. Cd. 2103.
Report of South African Native Affairs Commission, 1903–5. 1905. Cd. 2399.
Report of Transvaal Labour Commission and Minutes of Evidence. 2 parts.
1904. Cd. 1896–7.
Transvaal Constitution, 1906. Letters Patent and Instructions. Cd. 3250.

CH. XX.

Report of the Natal Native Affairs Commission, 1906–7.　1908.　Cd. 3889.

Letters Patent and Instructions relating to the Orange River Colony.　1907
Cd. 3256.

Papers relating to a federation of the South African Colonies.　1907.　Cd. 3564.

Report of the Delegates to the South African Convention 1908–9, with copy of
Draft South African Constitution Bill.　1909.　Cd. 4525.

Second Report with copy of Bill as finally passed by the Convention.　1909.
Cd. 4721.

Year-Book, the South African.　1902–.

(2)　*Other Works.*

(a)　Political and General History.

Ashmead Bartlett, Sir E.　The Transvaal Crisis.　The Case for the British (Uit-
lander) Residents.　1896.

Baden Powell, R. S. S.　The Matabele Campaign.　1901.

Bosman, W.　The Natal Rebellion of 1906.　1907.

Bourne, H. R. Fox.　Blacks and Whites in South Africa.　2nd edn.　1900.

Brand, Hon. R. H.　The Union of South Africa.　Oxford.　1909.

Bryce, J.　Impressions of South Africa.　1899.

Bryden, H. A.　A history of South Africa, 1652–1903.　Edinburgh.　1904.

—— The Victorian Era in South Africa.　1897.

Cana, F. R.　South Africa from the Great Trek to the Union.　1909.

Carnarvon, Earl of.　The Cape in 1888.　(Fortnightly Review, June.)　1888.

Colquhoun, A. R.　Renascence of South Africa.　1900.

—— Africander Land.　1906.

Fitzpatrick, J. P.　The Transvaal from within.　1900.

Fremantle, H. E. S.　The New Nation.　1909.

Frere, Sir Bartle.　The Union of the various portions of South Africa.　1881.

—— Afghanistan and South Africa.　A Letter to the Right Hon. W. E. Gladstone.
1881.

Froude, J. A.　Two Lectures on South Africa (delivered in 1880).　1880.　2nd edn.
1900.

Garrett, F. E. and Edwards, E. J.　The Story of a South African Crisis.　1897.

Greswell, W. P.　Our South African Empire.　2 vols.　1885.

—— Geography of Africa south of the Zambesi.　Oxford.　1892.

Hyatt, S. P.　The Northward Trek.　1909.

Iwan-Müller, E. B.　Lord Milner and South Africa.　1902.

Kidd, Dudley.　Kafir Socialism.　1908.

Leroy-Beaulieu, P. P.　Les nouvelles sociétés anglo-saxonnes.　Afrique du Sud.
Paris.　1901.

Lucas, C. P.　A Historical Geography of the British Colonies.　Vol. iv.　South
and East Africa.　Part i, Historical.　Oxford.　1898.

MacKenzie, J.　Austral Africa.　2 vols.　1887.

—— W. D.　South Africa.　1900.

Marindin, G. E.　Letters of Lord Blachford.　1896.

Markham, V. R.　New Era in South Africa.　1904.

—— South Africa Past and Present.　1900.

Mermeix, M.　Le Transvaal et La Chartered.　Paris.　1897.

Molteno, P. A.　A Federal South Africa.　1896.

Moodie, D. C. F.　History of the Battles and Adventures of the British, Boers and
Zulus in Southern Africa to 1880.　Vol. ii.　Cape Town.　1888.

Natives of South Africa, the.　Edited by The South African Native Races Committee.　1901.

Rose, E. B. The Truth about the Transvaal. 1902.
Statham, F. R. South Africa as it is. 1897.
Streatfield, F. N. Kafirland, a ten months Campaign, 1878. 1879.
Theal, G. McC. History of South Africa since 1795. Vol. v. 1854-72. 2nd edn.
    1900.
—— Progress of South Africa in the Century. (Nineteenth Century Series.)
    1902.
—— South Africa (Story of the Nations). 5th edn. 1899.
—— Beginning of South African History. 1902.
—— Portuguese in South Africa. Cape Town and London. 1896.
Wills, W. A. and Collingridge, L. T. The Downfall of Lobengula. 1894.
Wilmot, A. Manual of South African History. 1901.
—— Expansion of Southern Africa. 1894.
Wilson, D. M. Behind the Scenes in the Transvaal. 1901.
Worsfold, W. B. South Africa. 2nd edn. 1897.
—— History of South Africa. (Temple Primers.) 1900.

(b) The Zulu War and the first annexation of the Transvaal.

Ashe, W. and Wyatt Edgell, E. V. The story of the Zulu Campaign. 1880.
Carter, T. F. A Narrative of the Boer War. 1883. 2nd edn. 1896.
Colenso, F. E. and Durnford, E. History of the Zulu War. 1880.
—— The Ruin of Zululand. 2 vols. 1884-5.
Farrer, J. A. Zululand and the Zulus. 1879.
Leyds, W. J. The first annexation of the Transvaal. 1906.
MacKinnon, J. P. and Shadbolt, S. The South African Campaign, 1879. 1880.
Moodie, D. C. F. History of the Battles and Adventures of British, Boers and
    Zulus in Southern Africa to 1880. 2 vols. Cape Town. 1888.
Septans, Lieut.-Col. (*See under West Africa.*)
Wilmot, A. History of the Zulu War. 1880.

(c) The South African War, 1899-1902.

Amery, L. S. The "Times" history of the War in South Africa, 1899-1902. 7 vols.
    (Vol. vii contains a bibliography.) 1900-9.
Buchan, J. The African Colony. Studies in Reconstruction. Edinburgh and
    London. 1903.
Erwin, F. Der Südafricanische Krieg von 1899-1902. Berlin. 1903.
German Official Account of the War in South Africa, Oct. 1899 to Feb. 1900.
    Translated by W. H. H. Waters. 1904. March 1900 to September 1900.
    Translated by H. du Cane. 1906.
Goodman, C. S. With General French and the Cavalry in South Africa. 1902.
Mahan, A. T. The War in South Africa, 1899-1900. 1900.
Maurice, Sir F. History of the War in South Africa. Compiled by direction of
    His Majesty's Government, edited by. 3 vols. 1906-8. Vol. iv. Edited by
    Capt. M. H. Grant. 1910.
Wet, C. R. de. Three Years' War, 1899-1902. 1902.

(d) Works relating to single Colonies.

Boon, M. J. History of the Orange Free State. 1885.
Darwin, L. Short History of Basutoland. Prepared in the Intelligence Branch,
    War Office. 1886.
Hensman, H. History of Rhodesia. 1900.

CH. XX.

Hone, P. F.   Southern Rhodesia. 1909.
Keane, A. H.   The Boer States. 1900.
Lagden, Sir G.   The Basutos. 2 vols. 1909.
Newman, C. L. N.   Matabeleland. 1895.
Nixon, J.   Complete story of the Transvaal. 1885.
Thomson, H. C.   Rhodesia and its Government. 1898.

(e) Biographies.

Butler, L.   Sir Redvers Buller. 1909.
Butler, Sir W. F.   Life of Sir G. Pomeroy Colley. 1899.
Cox, Sir G. W.   Life of J. W. Colenso. 2 vols. 1888.
Fuller, Sir T. E.   Cecil John Rhodes. 1910.
Hensman, H.   Cecil Rhodes.   Edinburgh and London. 1901.
Kruger, Paul.   The Memoirs of, told by himself. 2 vols.   With Appendices
    containing a few documents. 1902.
Little, H. W.   H. M. Stanley. 1890.
MacKenzie, W. D.   John MacKenzie. 1902.
Martineau, J.   Life of Sir Bartle Frere. 2 vols. 1895.
Molteno, P. A.   Life and Times of Sir J. C. Molteno. 2 vols. 1900.
Morley, J.   Life of W. E. Gladstone. 1903.
Statham, F. R.   Paul Kruger and his Times. 1898.
Vindex.   Cecil Rhodes.   His Political Life and Speeches, 1881–1900. 1900.
Wood, Sir H. E.   From Midshipman to Field Marshal. 2 vols. 1906.
Worsfold, L. B.   Lord Milner's Work in South Africa. 1906.

D. Australasia.

(1) *Official Publications, Compilations of Statistical and other information.*

Reference should be made to the bibliography of Australasia in Vol. xi, ch. 27
(A), (2).

The chief official publications of the Commonwealth and the various States or
Colonies are :

Commonwealth.

Journals of the Senate together with Sessional Papers, Reports of Committees, etc.,
    1901–; House of Representatives, Votes and Proceedings, Reports of Com-
    mittees, etc., 1901–; Parliamentary Papers, General, 1901–; Parliamentary
    Debates, 1901–; Acts of Parliament, 1901–; Index of General Papers of both
    Houses, 1901–7. 1907.
Official Year Book of Commonwealth of Australia, containing authoritative statistics
    for 1901–7, corrected statistics for 1788–1900.   No. 1, 1908, by G. H. Knibbs.
    Melbourne. 1908.

New South Wales.

Votes and Proceedings of the Legislative Assembly ; Journals of the Legislative
    Council ; Debates of the Legislative Assembly and the Legislative Council;
    Statutes of New South Wales; Statutes of New South Wales to 1894, con-
    taining all Acts of practical utility still in force.   Index by H. M. Cockshott
    and S. E. Lamb.   Sydney. 1904.   For 1894–1906.   Sydney. 1898–1907.

New Zealand.

Journals of the House of Representatives; Appendices to Journals; Journals and
    Appendices of the Legislative Council; Statutes; Debates; Year Book, Official,
    Annual.   1891–; Statistics of New Zealand, Official, Annual.

Queensland

Votes and Proceedings of the Legislative Assembly; Journals of the Legislative Council; Statutes of Queensland; Parliamentary Debates; Census of Queensland, 1876, 1881, 1886, 1891. Published 1877, 1881, 1887, 1891.

South Australia.

Proceedings of the Parliament; Acts of Parliament; Debates of the Houses of Legislature.

Tasmania.

Journals of the House of Assembly to 1883; Journals of the Legislative Council to 1883; Journals and Papers of Parliament, 1884; Statutes of Tasmania, 1826–82. 4 vols. 1883; Census, 1881. 1893.

Victoria.

Papers presented to both Houses of Parliament; Votes and Proceedings of the Legislative Assembly; Votes and Proceedings of the Legislative Council; Consolidated Statutes. 7 vols. 1890; Acts of Parliament; Parliamentary Debates; Census of Victoria, 1871, 1881, 1891, 1901.

Western Australia.

Votes and Proceedings of the Legislative Council; Minutes, Votes and Proceedings of the Parliament, 1890–; Parliamentary Debates, 1876–; Acts of Parliament; Census, 1870, 1881, 1891, 1901; Report of the Aborigines Department, 1906.

Fiji.

Minutes and Proceedings of the Legislative Council, 1884–; Ordinances, 1884–; Blue Book, 1891–.

New Guinea.

Annual Report on, 1886–.

Parliamentary Papers (Imperial).

Correspondence with the Australian Colonies with reference to proposals for Intercolonial Tariff arrangements, 1872. C. 576.

Correspondence respecting differences on constitutional points between the two Houses of the Legislature of Victoria. 5 parts. 1878–9. C. 1982, C. 1985, C. 2173, C. 2217, C. 2339.

Correspondence relating to Chinese Immigration into the Australian Colonies with Acts passed by Legislatures of these Colonies and Canada and British Columbia on the subject, 1888. C. 5448.

Report of Committee on the Western Australia Constitution Bill, 1890. Cd. 160.

Correspondence relating to the Federation Conference in Australia, 1890. C. 6025.

Official Record of the Proceedings and Debates of the National Australian Convention held in Sydney 1891. C. 6466.

Papers relating to the federation of the Australian Colonies. 2 parts. 1900. Cd. 124 and 158.

Coghlan, T. A. Statistical Summary of the Seven Colonies of Australasia. Sydney. 1902.

CH. XX.

Coghlan, T. A. Wealth and Progress of New South Wales. 1886–. Annual.
    Sydney. 1887–.
Johnston, R. M. Tasmanian Official Record, 1890–2. Hobart. 1890–2.
—— Handbook of Tasmania for 1902–3. Hobart. 1892 and 1894.
Vogel, J. Official Handbook of New Zealand. 1875.

(2) *Other Works.*

(a) Constitutional History.

Blackmore, E. G. Law of the Constitution of South Australia. Adelaide. 1894.
Jenks, E. Government of Victoria. 1891.
Moore, W. H. The Constitution of the Commonwealth of Australia. 1902.
Parkes, Sir H. Federal Government of Australia. Speeches, 1889–90. Sydney.
    1890.
Quick, J. and Garran, R. R. Annotated Constitution of the Australian Common-
    wealth. Sydney. 1901.

(b) Economic History.

Broadhead, H. State Regulation of Labour and Labour Disputes in New Zealand.
    Christchurch, N. Z. 1908.
Chomley, C. H. Protection in Canada and Australia. 1904.
Clark, V. S. The Labour Movement in Australasia. 1906.
Epps, W. The land systems of Australasia. London. 1894.
Lloyd, H. D. A Country without strikes. New York and London. 1900.
Lyne, C. The Industries of New South Wales. Sydney. 1882.
Métin, A. Le Socialisme sans doctrines. Paris. 1901.
—— Législation ouvrière et sociale en Australie et Nouvelle-Zélande. Paris. 1901.
Reeves, W. P. State Experiments in Australia and New Zealand. 2 vols. 1902.
St Ledger, A. Australian Socialism. 1909.
Vigouroux, L. L'Évolution sociale en Australasie. Paris. 1902.
Wawn, W. T. South Sea Islanders and the Queensland Labour Trade. 1893.

(c) Political and General History.

Calvert, A. F. Exploration of Australia, 1844–96. 1896.
Cockburn, Sir J. A. Australian Federation. 1901.
Coghlan, T. A. and Ewing, T. T. Progress of Australasia in the Nineteenth Century.
    (Nineteenth Century Series.) 1903.
Colquhoun, A. R. The Mastery of the Pacific. 1902.
Favenc, E. History of Australian Explorations, 1788–1888. 2 vols. Sydney. 1888.
Galloway, W. J. Advanced Australia. 1899.
Grey, J. G. Australia Old and New. 1901.
Guillemard, F. H. H. Australasia. Vol. II. Malaysia and the Pacific Archi-
    pelagoes. Revised by A. H. Keane. (Stanford's Compendium of Geography.)
    2nd edn. 1908.
Jenks, E. History of the Australasian Colonies to 1893. (Cambridge Historical
    Series.) Cambridge. 1896.
Laurie, J. S. The Story of Australasia. 1896.
Leroy Beaulieu, P. P. Les nouvelles Sociétés Anglo-saxonnes, Australie, etc. Paris.
    1901.
Lyne, C. New Guinea. An account of the establishment of the British Protectorate.
    1885.

Rogers, J. D.   Australasia.   In the Historical Geography of the British Colonies.
    Edited by C. P. Lucas.   Vol. vi.   Part i, Historical.   Part ii, Geographical.
    Oxford.   1907.
Rusden, G. W.   History of Australia.   2nd edn.   Vol. iii.   Melbourne.   1897.
Tregarthen, G.   Australian Commonwealth.   (Story of the Nations.)   1893.
Walker, H. de R.   Australasian Democracy.   1897.
Westgarth, W.   Half a Century of Australasian Progress.   1889.
Wise, B. R.   The Commonwealth of Australia.   1909.

(d) Works relating to single Colonies.

Bonwick, J.   The Resources of Queensland.   1880.
Bradshaw, J.   New Zealand of to-day, 1884–7.   1888.
Buller, J.   Forty Years in New Zealand.   1878.
Calvert, A. F.   Western Australia.   1894.
Cooper, H. S.   Our New Colony Fiji.   1882.
Fenton, J.   History of Tasmania to 1884.   Hobart.   1884.
Hodder, E.   History of South Australia.   Vol. ii.   1893.
Irvine, R. J. and Alpers, O. T. J.   Progress of New Zealand in the Century.
    (Nineteenth Century Series.)   London and Edinburgh.   1902.
Meston, A.   Geographical History of Queensland.   Brisbane.   1895.
Parkes, Sir H.   Speeches connected with the public affairs of New South Wales,
    1848–74.   Melbourne.   1876.
Reeves, W. P.   Long White Cloud.   1898.
—— New Zealand.   New York.   1908.
Rusden, G. W.   History of New Zealand.   Vol. iii.   2nd edn.   London and
    Melbourne.   1895.
Siegfried, A.   La Démocratie en Nouvelle-Zélande.   Paris.   1904.   (Contains a
    short bibliography.)
Stout, Hon. R.   Progress of New Zealand, 1864–84.   Wellington.   1886.
Thomson, B.   The Fijians.   1908.
Turner, H. G.   History of Victoria.   Vol. ii.   1904.
Vogel, J.   New Zealand and the South Sea Islands.   1878.
Wakefield, E.   New Zealand after fifty years.   1889.

(e) Biographies.

Des Voeux, Sir G. W.   My Colonial Service.   Vol. ii.   1903.
Drummond, J.   Life of R. J. Seddon.   1907.
Duffy, Sir C. G.   My life in two Hemispheres.   Vol. ii.   1898.
Gisborne, W.   New Zealand Rulers and Statesmen, 1840–97.   2nd edn.   1897.
Henderson, G. C.   Sir George Grey.   1907.
Lyne, C. E.   Life of Sir H. Parkes.   1897.
Mennell, P.   Dictionary of Australasian Biography (1855–92).   1892.
Morris, E. E.   Memoir of G. Higinbotham.   1895.
Parkes, Sir H.   Fifty Years in the making of Australian History.   2 vols.   1892.
Stebbing, W.   C. H. Pearson.   Education Minister in Victoria.   1900.
St John, Sir S.   Rajah Brooke.   1899.

E. Canada and Newfoundland.

(1) *Official Publications, Compilations of Statistical and other information.*

Alaska Boundary.
    British Case. (Printed at the Foreign Office.) 1903.
    Appendix to British Case. 3 vols. Vols. ii and iii, Maps. 1903.
    Case of the United States. Washington. Government Printing Office. 1903.
    Counter Case of the United States. Washington. Government Printing Office. 1903.
    Argument of the United States. Washington. Government Printing Office. 1903.
Census of Canada, 1870–1. 5 vols. Ottawa. 1873–8, 1880–1. 4 vols. Ottawa. 1882–5, 1890–1. 4 vols. Ottawa. 1893–7, 1900–1. 4 vols. Ottawa. 1903–6.
Census of the...North West Territories, 1884–5. Ottawa. 1886. Census of the... North West Provinces, Population and Agriculture, 1906. Ottawa. 1907.
Coghlan, T. A. Report on Immigration with special reference to Canada. Intelligence Department. New South Wales. Bulletin No. 13. Sydney. 1905.
Coté, N. O. Political Appointments, Parliaments...in the Dominion of Canada, 1867–95. Ottawa. 1896.
Debates of the Dominion House of Commons. Ottawa. 1870–2, 1875–. The continuous series begins with 1875. Debates of the Senate. Ottawa. 1876–.
Halifax Commission, 1877. Documents and Proceedings of. 3 vols. Washington. 1878.
Houston, W. Documents illustrative of the Canadian Constitution. Toronto. 1891.
Journals of the Dominion House of Commons. Ottawa. 1867–; Journals of the Dominion Senate. Ottawa. 1867–; General Index to the Journals of the House and the Sessional Papers, 1867–90. 2 vols. Ottawa. 1880–91.
    Journals of the Legislative Assemblies of all the provinces and of Newfoundland, as well as the Journals of the Legislative Council of Quebec, Nova Scotia, New Brunswick (to 1892), Prince Edward's Isle (to 1893), British Columbia, North West Territories, and Newfoundland are also published.
Papers in reference to the Manitoba School Case, Sessional Papers. Ottawa. 1895.
Parliamentary Papers (Imperial).
    Correspondence respecting the Alaska Boundary and Map. 1904. Cd. 1877, 8.
    Correspondence respecting the Case of Monsieur Letellier. 1879. C. 2445.
    Report to the Board of Trade on the North West of Canada. By J. Mavor. 1904.
    Report to the Minister of Agriculture in Canada on the alleged emigration from Canada to the United States. 1882. 383.
Report of the Royal Commission on Chinese and Japanese Immigration, 1902. Sessional Paper, No. 54. Ottawa. 1902.
Sessional Papers of the Parliaments of the Dominion. Ottawa. 1867–. Sessional Papers of the Assemblies of Ontario, Quebec, British Columbia, Manitoba are also published.
Statutes of the Dominion of Canada. Ottawa. 1867–. The Statutes of all the provinces and of Newfoundland and the Ordinances of the North West Territories are also published. The Dominion Law Index, 1867–97, by H. H. Bligh and W. Todd. 2nd edn. Toronto. 1898.
Year-Book of Canada, Statistical, Annual, 1885–1905, followed by the Canada Year-Book. Annual. 1906–. Ottawa.

(2) *Other Works.*

(*a*) Constitutional History.

Bourinot, Sir **J. G.** Canadian Studies in Comparative Politics. Montreal. 1890.
—— Constitutional History of Canada. Montreal. 1888. Toronto. 1901.
—— Federal Government in Canada. (Johns Hopkins University Studies.) Baltimore. 1889.
—— How Canada is governed. Toronto. 1895.
—— Parliamentary Government in Canada. (From the Annual Report of the American Historical Association for 1891.) Washington. 1892.
Clement, W. H. P. The Law of the Canadian Constitution. Toronto. 1892.
Lefroy, A. H. F. The Law of Legislative Power in Canada. Toronto. 1897.
Munro, J. E. C. Constitution of Canada. Cambridge. 1889.
Teece, R. C. A Comparison between the Federal Constitutions of Canada and Australia. Sydney. 1902.
Wheeler, E. J. Confederation Law of Canada. Privy Council Cases on the British North America Act, 1867. 1896.

(*b*) Economic History.

Breckenridge, R. M. The Canadian Banking System, 1817–90. New York. 1895.
Chomley, C. H. Protection in Canada and Australia. (Protection in various countries.) 1904.
Economics, Canadian Papers prepared for reading before the Economical Section of the British Association. Montreal Meeting, 1884. Montreal. 1885.
Fleming, Sir S. The Intercolonial. Montreal. 1876.
Jeans, J. S. Canada's Resources and Possibilities. 1904.
Keefer, T. C. The Canals of Canada. Montreal. 1894.
MacLean, S. J. Tariff History of Canada. University of Toronto Studies in Political Science. No. 4. Toronto. 1895.
Manufactures of Ontario and Quebec, Guide to. Montreal. 1870.
National Policy, Canada under the, Arts and Manufactures. Montreal. 1883.
Perry, J. R. Public Debts in Canada. University of Toronto Studies in History and Economics. Vol. I. Toronto. 1901.
Porritt, E. Sixty Years of Protection in Canada, 1846–1907. 1908.
Shortt, A. Imperial Preferential Trade. Toronto. 1904.
Trout, J. M. and E. The Railways of Canada for 1870–1. Toronto. 1871.
Walker, B. E. A History of Banking in Canada. In the History of Banking in all Nations. Vol. III. 1896.

(*c*) Political and General History.

Balch, T. W. The Alaska Canadian Frontier. Philadelphia. 1902. (Reprinted from the Journal of the Franklin Institute. March, 1902.)
Bourinot, Sir J. G. Canada, 1760–1900. (Cambridge Historical Series.) Cambridge. 1900.
—— Intellectual Development of the Canadian people. Toronto. 1881.
—— Our intellectual strength and weakness. (Royal Society of Canada Series.) Montreal and London. 1893.
Bradley, A. G. Canada in the Twentieth Century. 1903.
Bryce, G. Short History of Canadian People. 1887.
Cockburn, A. P. Political Annals of Canada. 1909.

Collins, J. E.　Canada under the Administration of Lord Lorne.　Toronto.　1884.

Dent, J. C.　The Last Fifty Years.　Canada since the Union of 1841.　Vol. ii. Toronto.　1881.

Ewart, J. S.　The Manitoba School Question.　Toronto.　1894.

Hodgins, T.　British and American Diplomacy affecting Canada, 1782–1899. Toronto.　1900.

Hopkins, J. C.　The Story of the Dominion.　Toronto.　1901.

—— Morang's Annual Register of Canadian affairs for 1901.　Toronto.　1902.

—— The Canadian Annual Review of Public Affairs, 1902.　Toronto.　1903–.

—— Encyclopaedia of Canada.　6 vols.　Toronto.　1898–1900.

Lareau, E.　Histoire du Droit Canadien.　Vol. ii.　Montreal.　1889.

Leggo, W.　History of the Administration of the Earl of Dufferin.　Montreal.　1878.

Montagu, E. S. and Herbert, B.　Canada and the Empire.　1904.

Morgan, H. J.　The Dominion Annual Register and Review.　8 vols.　1878, 1879, 1880–1, 1882, 1883, 1884, 1885, 1886, published at Montreal 1879, Ottawa 1880, Montreal 1882, Toronto 1883–6, Montreal 1887.

Morris, A.　Treaties of Canada with the Indians of Manitoba and the North West Territories.　Toronto.　1880.

Municipal Government in Canada.　University of Toronto Studies in History and Economics.　Vol. ii.　Nos. 1, 2, 3.　Toronto.　1902–4.

Parkin, G. R.　The Great Dominion.　1895.

Prowse, D. W.　History of Newfoundland.　2nd edn.　1896.

Roberts, C. G. D.　History of Canada.　1898, 1904.

Royal Society of Canada.　Proceedings and Transactions of.　First Series, 1882–94. Second Series, 1895–1906.　Third Series, 1907–.　Ottawa.　General Index to. Ottawa.　Toronto.　London.　1908.

Siegfried, A.　Le Canada, les deux races.　Paris.　1906.　English Translation. London.　1907.

Smith, Goldwin.　Canada and the Canadian Question.　1891.

Stewart, G.　Canada under the Administration of the Earl of Dufferin.　1878.

Tracy, F. B.　Tercentenary History of Canada.　Vol. iii.　New York.　1908.

Whates, H. R.　Canada, the new nation.　1906.

Withrow, W. H.　Popular History of the Dominion of Canada.　Toronto.　1893.

(d) Provincial History.

Adam, G. M.　The Canadian North West.　Toronto.　1885.

Bancroft, H. H.　History of British Columbia, 1792–1887.　San Francisco.　1887. (Vol. xxxii of Bancroft's Works.)

Begg, A.　History of the North West.　3 vols.　Toronto.　1894–5.

—— History of British Columbia.　London.　1894.　Toronto.　1896.

Boulton, Major.　Reminiscences of the North West Rebellions.　Toronto.　1886.

Bryce, G.　Manitoba.　1882.

Gosnell, R. E.　Year-Book of British Columbia, 1897, 1903.　Annual. Victoria, B. C.

Haultain, T. A.　A History of Riel's Second Rebellion.　Toronto.　1885.

Macdonell, J. P.　The Ontario Boundary Controversy.　Proceedings before the Privy Council, edited by.　Toronto.　1896.

Métin, A.　La Colombie Britannique.　Paris.　1908.　(Contains a bibliography.)

Osborne, E. B.　Greater Canada.　1900.

(*e*) Biographies.

Adam, G. M. Sir John A. Macdonald. Toronto and London. 1891.
Biggar, C. R. W. Sir Oliver Mowat. 2 vols. Toronto. 1905.
Black, C. E. D. Marquess of Dufferin and Ava. 2nd edn. 1903.
Coats, R. H. and Gosnell, R. E. Sir James Douglas. (Makers of Canada.) Toronto. 1908.
Collins, J. E. Life and Times of Sir John Macdonald. Toronto. 1883.
Dent, J. C. The Canadian Portrait Gallery. 4 vols. Toronto. 1880-1.
Dictionary, The Canadian Biographical, Ontario Volume. Toronto, Chicago and New York. 1880.
Gosnell, R. E. and Coats, R. H. Sir James Douglas. (Makers of Canada.) 1908.
Grant, W. L. and Hamilton, F. George Monro Grant. Edinburgh and Toronto 1905.
Hannay, J. Life and Times of Sir Leonard Tilley. St John, N. B. 1897.
—— Wilmot and Tilley. (Makers of Canada.) Toronto. 1907.
Hopkins, J. C. Life and Work of Sir John Thompson. Brantford. Ontario. 1895.
Lyall, Sir A. The Life of the Marquis of Dufferin and Ava. Vol. I. 1905.
Mackenzie, A. Life and Speeches of Hon. G. Brown. Toronto. 1882.
Macpherson, J. P. Life of Sir John A. Macdonald. 2 vols. St John, N. B. 1891.
Moreau, H. Sir Wilfrid Laurier. Paris. 1902.
Parkin, G. R. Sir John A. Macdonald. (Makers of Canada.) Toronto. 1908.
Pope, J. Memoirs of Sir J. A. Macdonald. 2 vols. Ottawa and London. 1894.
Willison, J. S. Sir Wilfrid Laurier and the Liberal Party. 2 vols. 1903.
Willson, Beckles. Lord Strathcona. 1902.

F. West Indies.

(1) *Official Publications, etc.*

Leeward Islands. (*a*) General.

Minutes of the General Legislative Council. Acts of the General Legislature. Blue Book.

(*b*) Antigua

Minutes of Legislative Council. Acts of Local Legislature.

(*c*) Dominica.

Minutes of Legislative Assembly.

Windward Islands. (*a*) Grenada.

Minutes of House of Assembly. Minutes of Legislative Council.

(*b*) St Vincent.

Minutes of the Legislative Council.

(*c*) St Lucia.

Ordinances of the Legislative Council.

Jamaica.

Minutes of the Legislative Council. Journal of the Legislative Council. Laws. Blue Book.

CH. XX.

Trinidad and Tobago.

Minutes of Legislative Council and Council Papers. Ordinances, 1855–82, 1884. Blue Book. Debates of Legislative Council of Trinidad and Tobago, 1900–6.

Barbados.

Minutes of the Proceedings of the Legislative Council and Assembly. Laws of Barbados. Blue Book.

British Guiana.

Minutes of the Combined Court. Minutes of the Court of Policy. Ordinances. Blue Book. Laws of British Guiana. Sir T. C. Rayner. 5 vols. 1905.

British Honduras.

Minutes of the Legislative Council. Acts.

Bahamas

Votes of the House of Assembly. Votes of the Legislative Council.

Parliamentary Papers (Imperial). *See for a full list:* F. Cundall. Bibliography of West Indies. Kingston. 1909.

> Report of Royal Commission on the Public Revenues, Expenditure, Debts and Liabilities of the West Indian Islands. 4 parts, with Maps. 1884. C. 3840, —I, —II, —III.
> Petition from the inhabitants of Jamaica for a change in the Constitution of the Colony and Further Correspondence respecting the constitution of the Legislative Council. 2 parts. 1884. C. 3854, C. 4140.
> Documents and Correspondence. Venezuela-British Guiana Boundary Question. Venezuela. 5 parts, with Maps. 1896. C. 7972, 8106, 8194, 8195, 7972-1, United States. 2 parts. C. 7926, 8105.
> Report by Sir David Barbour on the Finances of Jamaica. 1899. C. 9412.
> Report of the West Indian Royal Commission. 5 vols. With Maps and Diagrams. 1897–8. C. 8655, 8656, 8657, 8669, 8799.

(2) *Other Works.*

Aimes, H. H. S. A History of Slavery in Cuba, 1511 to 1868. Contains a bibliography. New York and London. 1907.
Beeton, M. M. The Foreign Sugar Bounties. 1898.
Bodu, J. M. Trinidadiana. A chronological review of events. Port of Spain. 1890.
Callahan, J. M. Cuba and International Relations. Baltimore and London. 1899.
Colquhoun, A. R. Greater America. London and New York. 1904.
Davey, R. Cuba, Past and Present. 1898.
Des Voeux, Sir G. W. My Colonial Service. Vol. I. 1903.
Eves, C. Washington. The West Indies. 4th edn. 1897.
Fiske, A. K. The West Indies. New York and London. 1899.
Froude, J. A. The English in the West Indies. 1888.
Gallenga, A. L. The Pearl of the Antilles. 1873.
Gardner, W. J. A History of Jamaica. 1873 and 1909.
Grey, Earl. Colonial Policy of Lord John Russell's Administration. Vol. I. 2nd edn. 1853.
Hill, R. T. Cuba and Porto Rico, with the other islands of the West Indies. 1898.

Kirke, H.   Twenty-five years in British Guiana.   1898.
Lee Warner, Sir W.   Memoirs of Field Marshal Sir H. W. Norman (Governor of Jamaica, 1883–8).   1908.
Leger, J. N.   Haiti, her history and her detractors.   New York.   1907.
—— La Politique extérieure d'Haïti.   Paris.   1886.
Livingstone, W. P.   Black Jamaica.   1899.
Lucas, C. P.   The West Indies.   Vol. II of the Historical Geography of the British Colonies.   2nd edn.   Oxford.   1905.
Morales, Y. and V.   Iniciadores y Primeros Mártires de la Revolución Cubana   Havana.   1901.
Oliver, V. L.   History of Antigua.   3 vols.   1894–9.
Olivier, Sir S.   White Capital and Coloured Labour.   1906.
Phillippo, J. M.   Past and Present State of Jamaica.   1843.
Rodway, J.   West Indies.   1896.
—— History of British Guiana.   Vol. III.   1833–93.   Georgetown.   1894.
Root, J. W.   The British West Indies and the Sugar Industry.   Liverpool.   1899.
Salmon, C. S.   The Caribbean Confederation.   1888.
St John, Sir S.   Hayti or the Black Republic.   2nd edn.   1889.
Walker, H. de R.   West Indies and the Empire.   1901.

IV.   DUTCH COLONISATION.

(1) *Periodical Publications, Official Publications, etc.*

Jaarcijfers Koloniale.   The Hague.
Louter, J. de.   Handleiding tot de Kennis van het Staats en Administratief Recht van Nederlandsch-Indië.   4th edn.   The Hague.   1895.
Regeeringsalmanak voor Nederlandsch-Indië.   Batavia.
Staatsblad van Nederlandsch-Indië.   Batavia.
Verslag Koloniaal.   Verslag van het beheer en den staat der Nederlandsche bezittingen en Oost- en West-Indië en ter kuste van Guinea, 1849–1901.   Hague.   1850–1901.

(2) *Other Works.*

Reference should be made to the bibliography of Ch. 23, Vol. XI, I. C.

Chailley, Bert J.   Java et ses habitants.   Paris.   1900.
Day, C.   Dutch in Java.   New York.   1904.
Encyclopaedie van Nederlandsch-Indië.   The Hague.
Gonnaud, P.   La Colonisation hollandaise à Java.   Paris.   1905.
Hooyer, G. B.   Krijgsgeschiednis van Nederlandsch-Indië, 1811–94.   3 vols.   Batavia.   1895.

V.   FRENCH COLONISATION.

(1) *Periodical Publications.*

Année Coloniale, la.   Paris.   1900–.
Annuaire Coloniale.   Annuaire agricole, commercial et industriel des colonies Françaises.   Paris.   1888–.
Annuaire du Ministère des Colonies.   Paris.   1898–.
Quinzaine Coloniale, la.   Organe de l'Union Coloniale Française.   Paris.   1897–.

Also the Annuaire and the Journal Officiel published by the Governments of the respective colonies.

(2) *Other Works.*

Alcindor, É.   Les Antilles Françaises, leur assimilation politique à la métropole. Paris. 1899.

Ballet, J.   La Guadeloupe. Renseignements sur l'histoire, etc. 3 vols. Basse Terre. 1894–1902.

Barrett, P.   L'Afrique Occidentale. Sénégambie et Guinée. 2 vols. Paris. 1888.

Boizard, E. and Tardieu, H.   Histoire de la législation des sucres, 1664–1891. Paris. 1891.

Brunet, L.   L'œuvre de la France à Madagascar. Paris. 1903.

Chailley-Bert, J.   Dix années de politique coloniale. Paris. 1902.

Darcy, J.   France et Angleterre. Cent années de rivalité coloniale en Afrique. Paris. 1904.

Davillé, E.   La Colonisation Française aux Nouvelles Hébrides. Paris. 1895.

Dubois, M. and Terrier, A.   Un siècle d'expansion coloniale. Paris. 1902.

Ferry, E.   La France en Afrique. Paris. 1905.

Lanessan, J. L.   L'Expansion coloniale de la France. Paris. 1886.

Lebon, A.   La Politique de la France en Afrique, 1896–8. Paris. 1901.

Le Brun-Renaud, C.   Les possessions Françaises de l'Afrique occidentale. Paris. 1886.

Legendre, P.   La Conquête de la France Africaine. Paris.   1904.

——— Notre Epopée coloniale. Paris. 1901.

L. C. L.   Saint-Pierre, Martinique, 1635–1902. Annales des Antilles françaises. Paris. 1905.

Lorin, H.   La France, puissance coloniale. Paris. 1906.

Mattei, Commandant.   Bas Niger, Bénoué, Dahomey. Paris. 1895.

Norman, C. B.   Colonial France. 1886.

Petit, E.   Organisation des Colonies Françaises. 2 vols. Paris. 1894.

Philebert, C.   La Conquête pacifique de l'intérieur africain. Paris. 1889.

Rambaud, A.   La France Coloniale. 6th edn. Paris. 1893.

Rouard de Card, E.   Les Traités de Protectorat conclus par la France en Afrique, 1870–95. Paris. 1897.

——— Les territoires africains et les conventions franco-anglaises. Paris. 1901.

VI.   GERMAN COLONISATION.

(1) *Documents, Official Publications, Compilations of Statistical and other Information.*

Documents relating to the German Colonies are contained in the Library of the Ministry of Foreign Affairs, of the Seminary of Oriental Languages and of the German Colonial Society.

Debates of the Reichstag.

German White Books.

Deutsche Kolonialpolitik, die. Aktenstücke. Leipzig. 1885. Since 1885 published as Jahrbuch der deutschen Kolonialpolitik. Leipzig. 1889–.

Deutsche Kolonialzeitung. Organ des deutschen Kolonialgesellschaft. Berlin.

Deutsches Kolonialblatt, published twice monthly, since April, 1890. Berlin.

Fitzner, R. Deutsches Kolonial Handbuch. Berlin. 1896–.

Meinecke, G. Koloniales Jahrbuch. First year, 1888. Berlin. 1889–.

Riebow. Deutsche Kolonial-Gesetzgebung to 1892. Berlin. 1893. Continued to 1899 by A. Zimmermann, since published annually.

Zimmermann, A. Deutsche Kolonial-Gesetzgebung, 1893–7. Berlin. 1898.

(2) *Other Works.*

Baumgarten, J.   Ostafrica, Der Sudan und das Seengebiet.   Gotha.   1890.
Bülow, H. von.   Deutschlands Kolonien und Kolonialkriege.   Dresden.   1900.
Chéradame, A.   La Colonisation et les Colonies allemandes.   Paris.   1905.
Das Überseeische Deutschland; die deutschen Kolonien in Wort und Bild.   Berlin.
    1903.
Dawson, W. H.   The evolution of modern Germany.   1908.
Decharme, P.   Compagnies et Sociétés coloniales allemandes.   Paris.   1903.
Fabri, F.   Fünf Jahre deutscher Kolonialpolitik.   Gotha.   1889.
Hassert, K.   Deutschlands Kolonien.   Leipzig.   1898.
Klose, H.   Togo unter deutscher Flagge.   Berlin.   1899.
Peters, K.   Das Deutsch-Ostafrikanische Schutzgebiet.   Munich.   1895.
Treitschke, H. von.   Die ersten Versuche deutscher Kolonialpolitik.   Preussische
    Jahrbücher.   Band 54.

VII.   PARTITION OF AFRICA.

(*See also under headings British Africa, French Colonisation, German Colonisation.*)

(1) *Documents.*

Ortroy, F. van.   Conventions internationales définissant les limites actuelles des
    possessions en Afrique.   Brussels.   1898.
Parliamentary Papers (Imperial).
    Protocols and General Act of the West African Conference, 1885.   Africa.
        No. 4.   1885.   C. 4361.
    General Act of the Berlin Conference, 1885.   Africa.   No. 3.   1886.   C. 4739.

(2) *Other Works.*

Banning, E.   Le partage politique de l'Afrique.   Brussels.   1888.
Bonnefon, E. L.   L'Afrique politique en 1900.   Paris.   1900.
Brown, R.   The story of Africa and its explorers.   4 vols.   1896–8.
Canuti, G.   L' Italia in Africa e le guerre con l' Abissinia.   Florence.   1899.
Chatelain, C. A.   L'Afrique et l'expansion coloniale.   Paris.   1901.
Deville, E.   Le partage de l'Afrique.   Paris.   1898.
Fitzmaurice, Lord E.   Earl Granville.   Vol. II.   1905.
Hertslet, Sir E.   The Map of Africa by Treaty.   3 vols.   3rd edn.   1909.
Johnston, Sir H. H.   Colonization of Africa.   (Camb. Hist. Series.)   Cambridge.
    1905.
Keltie, J. Scott.   The Partition of Africa.   2nd edn.   1895.
Kidd, B.   The Control of the Tropics.   New York.   1898.
Lorin, H.   L'Afrique à l'entrée du vingtième siècle.   Paris.   1901.
Reparáz, G.   España en Africa y otros estudios de política colonial.   Madrid.   1891.
Rose, J. H.   Political Development of Modern Europe, 1870–1900.   1908.
White, A. S.   The Development of Africa.   1892.

VIII. THE CONGO STATE.

(1) *Official Publications, Periodicals, etc.*

Annuaire de l'État indépendant du Congo. Brussels. 1903–.
Belgique Coloniale, la. Brussels. 1895–.
Bulletin officiel de l'État indépendant du Congo. Brussels. 1885–.
Mouvement Geographique, le. Brussels. 1884–.
Parliamentary Papers (Imperial).
> Correspondence and Report from His Majesty's Consul at Boma respecting the administration of the Congo State. Africa. No. 1. 1904. Cd. 1933.
> Protocols and General Act of the West African Conference 1885. Africa. No. 4. 1885. C. 4361.
> General Act of the Berlin Conference, 1885. Africa. No. 3. 1886. C. 4739.

Rapport de la Commission d'enquête au Roi de la Belgique. Printed in the Bulletin Officiel of the Congo State, Sept., Oct., 1905. Brussels. 1905. Abstract of the Report. By G. W. Macalpine. 1906.
Report of the Vice-Governor-General to the Secretary of State. Printed in the Bulletin Officiel of the Congo State. July. 1904.

(2) *Other Works.*

Bentley, W. H. Pioneering on the Congo. 2 vols. 1900.
Boulger, D. C. The Congo State. 1898.
Bourne, H. R. Fox. Civilization in Congoland. 1903.
Castelein, A. The Congo State, its origin, rights and duties. 1908.
Cattier, F. Droit et Administration de l'État indépendant du Congo. Brussels. 1898.
—— Étude sur la situation de l'État indépendant du Congo. 2nd edn. Brussels. 1906.
Chapaux, A. Le Congo historique, diplomatique, etc. Maps. Brussels. 1894.
Descamps, E. L'Afrique nouvelle. Paris. 1903.
Droogmans, H. Le Congo. Quatre Conférences publiques. Brussels. 1895.
Hinde, S. L. The fall of the Congo Arabs. 1897.
Johnston, Sir H. H. George Grenfell and the Congo. 2 vols. 1908.
Macdonell, J. de C. King Leopold II, his rule in Belgium and the Congo. 1905.
Morel, E. D. Affairs of West Africa. 1902.
—— King Leopold's Rule in Africa. 1904.
Mountmorres, Viscount. The Congo independent State. 1906.
Stanley, Sir H. M. The Congo and the founding of its Free State. 2 vols. 1885.
Truth about the Civilization in England, by a Belgian. 1903.
Vandervelde, E. Les derniers jours de l'État du Congo. Journal de Voyage. Juillet—octobre, 1908. Paris. 1909.
Wack, H. W. The Story of the Congo Free State. New York. 1905.
Wauters, A. J. L'État indépendant du Congo. Brussels. 1899.

CHAPTER XXI.

THE REPUBLICS OF LATIN AMERICA.

A complete bibliography of the subject is impossible: long lists could be compiled concerning single episodes, such as the Venezuelan frontier question or the frontier dispute between Chile and the Argentine Republic. Moreover, almost every State preserves pamphlets and official publications in large numbers, besides historical and illustrative literature. Official publications are omitted in the present bibliography, except when distinctly historical in character; but the most useful may be indicated here. Every State publishes its written Constitution, sometimes also an official translation in French or English; the legal codes, civil and criminal, are also published: in most of the capitals an official gazette is issued, and there is usually an official or semi-official description or survey, mainly statistical and geographical, but sometimes including also a historical sketch. Such publications could probably be obtained through the legations or consulates of the several republics. The library of the Bureau of American Republics at Washington contains a comprehensive collection of these official publications, besides historical and illustrative works; and the periodical Bulletin of that Bureau supplies much statistical information. *The Statesman's Year-book* contains short bibliographies of official and other publications. For the relations between the United States and Spanish America reference may be made to the bibliography of Vol. VII, chapters XI, XX and XXI.

In using the present bibliography, it should be noted that Spaniards and Spanish-Americans use the words "America" and "American" (*Americano*) in their widest sense, as corresponding to "European" or "Asiatic"; but unless some qualification is added (as *América* or *Americanos del Norte*) the words may be always taken as applying to Spanish America.

I. GENERAL.

Akers, C. E. History of South America, 1854–1904. 1904.
Altamira, R. Cuestiones Hispano-Americanas. Madrid. 1900.
Arosemena, J. Constituciones políticas de la América Meridional. Paris. 1878.
Barral-Montferrat, Marquis de. De Monroe à Roosevelt. Paris. 1903.
Barros Arana, D. Histoire de la guerre du Pacifique. 2 vols. Paris. 1881.
Beltran y Rozpide, R. Los Pueblos Hispano-Americanos en el siglo XX. Madrid. 1904.
Bulletin of Bureau of American Republics. Washington. 1891–. (*In progress.*)
Bunge, C. O. Nuestra América. Barcelona. 1903.
Callahan, J. M. Cuba and International Relations. Baltimore. 1899.
Calvo, C. Colección completa de los tratados de la América Latina. 16 vols. Paris. 1862–7.

CH. XXI.

Clowes, Sir W. Laird. Four Modern Naval Campaigns (including the Chileno-Peruvian war of 1879–81, the Chilian Civil war of 1891, the Brazilian Civil war of 1893–6). 1902.

Conferences:

International American Conference. Minutes (English and Spanish). Washington. 1890.

Segunda Conferencia Internacional Americana. Recomendaciones, resoluciones... (Spanish, English, French). Mexico. 1902.

Several treatises and pamphlets were published in Mexico in 1901–2 under the title *Conferencia Internacional Americana.*

Third International American Conference. Minutes (English and Spanish). Rio. 1907.

Congreso social y económico Hispano-Americano, reunido en Madrid el año 1900. 2 vols. Madrid. 1902.

Coolidge, A. C. The United States as a World Power. New York. 1908.

Dawson, T. C. The South American Republics. 2 vols. New York. 1903–4.

Deberle, A. Histoire de l'Amérique du Sud. Paris. 1897.

Drago, L. M. La República Argentina y la cuestión Venezolana. Buenos Aires. 1903.

Edgington, T. B. The Monroe Doctrine. Boston. 1905.

Enock, C. R. The Great Pacific Coast. 1910.

Hart, A. B. Foundations of American Foreign Politics (with bibliography). New York. 1901.

Herndon, W. L. (Lieutenant U.S. Navy). Exploration of the Valley of the Amazon (by order of U.S. Government). 2 vols. Washington. 1854.

Holdich, Sir T. H. The Countries of the King's award (Chile and Argentine Republic). 1904.

Kasson, J. A. Evolution of the Constitution of the United States. Boston. 1904.

Kirkpatrick, F. A. South America and the War. (Introduction—General Conditions in Latin America.) 1918.

Latané, J. H. Diplomatic Relations of the United States and Spanish America. Baltimore. 1900.

Noel, J. V. History of the Second Pan-American Congress. Baltimore. 1902.

Pérez Triana, S. Informes y Notas de la delegación de Colombia en la segunda Conferencia de la Paz de la Haya. Rotterdam. 1908.

—— La doctrina Drago: colección de documentos, con una advertencia preliminar de S. Pérez Triana y una introducción de W. T. Stead. 1908.

Phelps, E. J. The Monroe Doctrine. New York. 1896.

Quesada, V. G. La política Americana y las tendencias Yankees. Buenos Aires. 1887

Reddaway, W. F. The Monroe Doctrine. Cambridge. 1898.

Robinson, A. G. Cuba and the Intervention. New York. 1905.

South-American Journal, the. (Published weekly in London.)

South-American edition of The Times, the (English and Spanish). December 23rd, 1909.

Wallace, E. The Constitutions of the Argentine Republic and of the United States of Brazil, translated from the Spanish. Chicago. 1894.

II. SEPARATE STATES.

A. The River Plate (Argentine Republic, Uruguay, Paraguay).

Argentine Republic. Registro oficial. Buenos Aires. 1879–99.

—— Map of Argentine Republic: with a short description. Argentine Government Information Office.

—— Colección de tratados celebrados por la Republica Argentina con las naciones estrangeras. Buenos Aires. 1870 (?).

Argentine Republic.   Correspondencia entre el gobierno de Buenos Aires y Juan B. Nicholson.   Buenos Aires.   1839.

—— Affaires de la Plata.   Petitions et documents.   Paris.   1844.

—— Colección de documentos sobre la misión de los ministros de S. M. B. y de S. M. el rey de los Franceses.   Buenos Aires.   1845.

—— Correspondencia con los ministros de Inglaterra y de Francia.   Buenos Aires.   1846.

—— Archivo Americano: nueva serie (documents concerning the Anglo-French intervention).   3 vols.   Buenos Aires.   1847–8.

   The last three collections are printed in Spanish, French and English.

Bruyssel, E. van.   La République du Paraguay.   Brussels.   1893.

Carbajal, L. D.   La Patagonia: studi generali.   4 vols.   Turin.   1889–1900.

Dardye, E. de B. la.   Paraguay: the land and the people.   1892.

Dominguez, L. L.   Historia Argentina.   Buenos Aires.   1870.

Garibaldi, G.   Autobiography, first volume (English translation).   3 vols.   1889.

Hirst, W. A.   Argentina; its...history, political conditions, resources...and general development.   1910.

Jourdan, E. C.   Guerra do Paraguay.   Rio.   1890.

Kennedy, A. J.   La Plata, Brazil and Paraguay during the war.   1869.

Kirkpatrick, F. A.   Rosas (in Cornhill Magazine, November, 1899).

Koebel, W. H.   Modern Argentina.   1907.

Marbais du Graty, A.   La Confédération Argentine.   Paris.   1858.

Masterman, G. F.   Seven eventful years in Paraguay.   1869.

Mulhall, M. G.   Handbook of the River Plate.   1892.

Page, Commander T. G.   La Plata...Narrative of exploration of Tributaries of the River La Plata and adjoining countries during 1853–6, under orders of the U.S. Government.

Paraguay: Concise History of its rise...and causes of the present war with Brazil. 1867.

Paraguay and the war in La Plata.   1865.

Saldías, A.   La Epoca de Rozas (Rosas).   5 vols.   Buenos Aires.   1892.

Sprague, M. A.   History of the Argentine Republic.   Chicago.

Thompson, G.   The Paraguayan war.   1869.

Washburn, C. A.   History of Paraguay.   2 vols.   Boston.   1871.

Zeballos, E. de.   Descripción amena de la República Argentina.   3 vols.   Buenos Aires.   1881.

B.   Brazil.

Abreu and Cabral.   Brazil geográfico-histórico.   Rio.   1884.

Canstatt, O.   Das republikanische Brazilien in Vergangenheit und Gegenwart. Leipzig.   1898.

Constitution des États-Unis du Brésil.   Paris.   1891.

Fialho, A.   Historia da Fundação da República.   Rio.   1891.

Lamberg, M.   Brasilien, Land und Leute.   Leipzig.   1899.

Mossé, B.   Dom Pedro II, Empereur du Brésil.   Paris.   1889.

Mulhall, M. G.   Rio Grande do Sul and its German Colonies.   1873.

Redmont, J. C. and Curtis, W. E.   History of Brazil.   Chicago.

Wright, M. R.   The New Brazil.   Philadelphia.   1901.

C.   Chile.

Chile.   Recopilación de tratados...celebrados entre la República de Chile y las potencias extranjeras.   Edited by A. Bascuñan Montes.   Santiago.   1894.

—— Le Chile et L'Espagne.   Paris.   1865.

Echevarrea y Reyes, A. Geografía Política de Chile. 2 vols. Santiago. 1888.
Elliot, G. F. Scott. Chile: its history and development. 1907.
Figueroa, P. P. Diccionario Biográfico general de Chile (1550–1889). Santiago. 1889.
Fitzgerald, E. A. The Highest Andes (containing a summary of the frontier dispute). 1899.
Hancock, A. V. History of Chile (with bibliography). Chicago. 1893.
Hervey, M. H. Dark Days in Chile, an account of the Revolution of 1891. 1891–2.
Smith, W. A. Temperate Chile. 1900.
Wright, M. H. The Republic of Chile. 1905.

D. Mexico.

Bancroft, H. H. History of Mexico (last 3 vols.). 6 vols. San Francisco. 1883....
—— Popular History of the Mexican people. 1894.
Bonaparte, Prince Roland, and others. Le Mexique au début du xxe siècle. Paris. 1904.
Brocklehurst, T. V. Mexico of to-day. 1883.
Burke, V. R. Life of Benito Juarez. 1894.
Diaz, P. Rapport du Général Porfirio Diaz...sur les actes de son administration entre 1884 et 1896. Paris. 1897.
Enock, C. R. Mexico: its...civilisation, history, political conditions...resources... and general development. 1907.
George, P. Das heutige Mexico und seine Kulturfortschritte. Jena. 1906.
Godoy, J. F. Porfirio Diaz (a biography in English). New York. 1910.
Kozhevar, E. Report on the Republic of Mexico. 1886.
La Bédollière, E. G. de. Histoire de la guerre du Mexique. Paris. 1866.
Martin, P. F. Mexico of the Twentieth Century. 2 vols. 1907.
Moses, B. Constitution of the United States of Mexico. Philadelphia. 1899.
Romero, M. Mexico and the United States. New York. 1898.
Sierra, J. Mexico ; its Social Evolution. 3 vols. (English translation.) Mexico. 1905.
Zamacois, N. Historia de Méjico. Vols. xiii—xix. Barcelona. 1888.

E. The Northern Republics (Venezuela and Colombia, including Panama).

Abbot, H. L. Problems of the Panamá Canal. 1905.
Arbitration between Governments of H. B. M. and the United States of Venezuela. Proceedings (blue-book). 1899.
Benedetti, C. Histoire de Colombia. Paris. 1887.
Borda, J. J. Compendio de historia de Colombia. Bogotá. 1890.
Colombia. Anales diplomáticos y consulares. Edited by A. T. Uribe. Bogotá. 1900–1.
—— Descripción histórica, geográfica y política de la República de Colombia. Bogotá. 1887.
Documents regarding the frontier of British Guiana and Venezuela : with maps (blue-book). 1896.
Esguerra, J. Diccionario geográfico de los Estados Unidos de Colombia. Bogotá. 1878.
Landaeta Rosales, M. Gobiernos de Venezuela, 1810–1905. Caraccas. 1905.
Moses, B. Constitution of Colombia (translation of text). Philadelphia. 1898.
Pensa, H. La République et le Canal de Panamá. Paris. 1906. [A diplomatic history, with an essay on the Monroe Doctrine.]
Pereira, R. S. Les États-Unis de Colombia ; précis d'histoire et de géographie. Paris. 1883.

Pérez, F.   Geografía general, física y política de los Estados Unidos de Colombia.
    Bogotá.   1883.
Petre, F. L.   The Republic of Colombia.   1906.
Scruggs, W. L.   The Colombian and Venezuelan Republics.   2 vols.   Boston.
    1905.
Triana, S. P.   Down the Orinoco in a canoe.   1902.
Veloz Goiticoa, N.   Venezuela, Geografía, Recursos..., Legislación....   Caraccas.
    1904.

F.   PERU.

Enock, C. R.   Peru : its...civilisation, history, political conditions...resources...
    and general development (with bibliography).   1907.
Markham, Sir C. R.   The war between Peru and Chile.   1883.
——— History of Peru (with bibliography).   Chicago.   1892.
Maurtua, V. M.   The question of the Pacific.   Translated from the Spanish by
    F. A. Pezet.   Philadelphia.   1901.   [A Peruvian statement of the case.]
Middendorf, E. W.   Peru : Beobachtungen und Studien über das Land und seine
    Bewohner.   Berlin.   1893.
Paz Soldán, M. F.   Narración de la guerra de Chile contra Perú y Bolivia.   La Paz.
    1884.

G.   ECUADOR.

Berthe, A.   García Moreno, Président de l'Équateur.   Paris.   1888.
Cancio, A. Z. de.   Vida de...García Moreno.   Madrid.   1899.
Domecq, J. B.   García Moreno, Président...de l'Équateur.   Tours.   1896.
Grandin, L.   García Moreno.   In Biographies du xixe siècle.   Paris.   1888.
Josefa, M. T.   García Moreno.   Paris.   1892.
Kaufmann, A. G.   García Moreno.
Lambel, A. P. F. de.   García Moreno.   Paris.   1891.

H.   BOLIVIA.

Anderson, T. H.   History of Bolivia.   Chicago.
Ford, J. N.   Tropical America.   1893.
Wright, M. R.   Bolivia.   Philadelphia.   1907.

I.   THE REPUBLICS OF CENTRAL AMERICA.

Bancroft, H. H.   History of Central America.   3 vols.   San Francisco.   1883-.
    (Vol. III.)
Barrantes, E. M.   Elementos de historia de Costa Rica.   San José.   1892.
Biolley, P.   Costa Rica and her Future.   Translated from the Spanish.   Washington.
    1899.
Pector, D.   Étude économique sur la République de Nicaragua.   Neuchatel.   1893.
Squier, E. G.   Honduras ; Descriptive, Historical and Statistical.   1870.

J.   THE ANTILLES.

Bonneau, A.   Haïti, ses progrès, son avenir.   Paris.   1862.
Hazard, S.   Santo Domingo, past and present ; with a glance at Haiti.   1873.
Justin, J.   Études sur les institutions Haïtiennes.   Paris.   1894.
Léger, J. N.   Haiti, her history and detractors.   New York.   1907.
Porter, R. P.   Industrial Cuba.   New York.   1899.
Preiss, E. G.   Cuba unter Spanischer Regierung.   New York.   1897.
Pritchard, H.   Where Black rules White.   1900.
St John, Sir S.   Haiti or the Black Republic.   1899.
Tippenhauer, L. G.   Die Insel Haïti.   2 vols.   Leipzig.   1893.

CHAPTER XXII.

HISTORY OF THE LAW OF NATIONS.

There are not many works formally treating of this topic. On the other hand, the regular text-books of international law contain historical matter which is more or less copious and accurate, according to the writer's predilection and scholarship. A list of such books would be out of place here, but we may refer to the Marquis de Olivart's Bibliographie du droit international, Paris, 1905 and 1907 (two parts published, a final one promised). This purports to note only works in the author's own library, but we know of nothing approaching it in completeness.

A concise bibliography is appended to the article on International Law in the Encyclopaedia of the Laws of England, 2nd edn., 1907.

The following are (in order of publication) the only considerable works known to the writer which treat expressly of the origin and history of the law of nations, as distinct from its doctrinal exposition.

Balch, T. W. L'évolution de l'arbitrage international. (Reprint from the Revue de droit international et de législation comparée.) Philadelphia, 1908. [An English version of this work is promised.]

Holland, T. E. Studies in International Law. Oxford, 1898. [Contains among other profitable matter the fullest account of Alberico Gentili and his work.]

Hosack, J. The rise and growth of the law of nations, as established by general usage and by treaties. 1882. [A narrative purporting only "to describe generally the actual practice and usages of nations" down to the Treaty of Utrecht and deliberately excluding any reference to the growth of ideas, doctrine, and literature. The name of Grotius is not in the index.]

Lapradelle, A. de, and Politis, N. Recueil des arbitrages internationaux. Préface de Louis Renault. Vol. i, 1798–1855. Paris. 1905.

Moore, J. B. History and digest of the international arbitrations to which the United States has been a party. 6 vols. (Vol. vi consists of maps). Washington, D. C. 1898. [A most valuable repertory of facts and documents.]

Nys, E. Les origines du droit international. Brussels and Paris. 1894.

Walker, T. A. A history of the law of nations. Cambridge. 1899. Vol. i. (All published.)

Ward, Robert. An enquiry into the foundation and history of the law of nations in Europe from the time of the Greeks and Romans to the age of Grotius. 1795. 2 vols. [Rather a rambling anecdotal collection of notes than a history.]

Wheaton, H. History of the Law of Nations in Europe and America from the earliest times to the Treaty of Washington, 1842. New York. 1845.

I. FIRST PEACE CONFERENCE, 1899.

The proceedings of the Hague Conference of 1899 were published officially by the Belgian Government:

Conférence internationale de la paix: La Haye, 18 mai—29 juillet 1899. Ministère des affaires étrangères. The Hague. 1899. [Four parts separately paged. A list of arbitration Treaties and arbitration clauses in other Treaties in force in 1899 is given in Part IV, pp. 228–39.]

The preliminary correspondence is published by the British Government, Russia, No. 1 (1899), C. 9090, and the proceedings, or the greater part of them, in a continuation, Misc. No. 1 (1899), C. 9534, but in the inconvenient form of enclosures interpolated in correspondence.

General accounts of the Conference, and reprints of the principal conventions and declarations in French or English, may be found in several recent works on international law and arbitration: the full text of the conventions is given in a useful form in Whittuck, E. A., International Documents, noted below under the head of the Second Peace Conference.

COMMISSION OF INQUIRY ON THE NORTH SEA INCIDENT.

There is an apparently official report printed at Paris [1905]: Commission internationale d'Enquête constituée en vertu de la Déclaration du 12/25 novembre 1904, échangée à Saint-Pétersbourg entre les Gouvernements de Grande-Bretagne et de Russie. The Commission purported to be "réunie conformément aux articles 9–14 de la Convention de la Haye du 17 (29) juillet 1899, pour le règlement pacifique des conflits internationaux," but was charged not only to ascertain the facts but to report on the question of responsibility.

The British official papers contain the declaration constituting the Commission; the preliminary correspondence, Russia, No. 2, 1905; the report of the Commissioners, Russia, No. 3, 1905 (all these in Parl. Papers 1905, Vol. CIII); and a special Board of Trade Report in Vol. LXIV, which, however, is now of lesser importance. The evidence does not seem to have been officially published in England.

II. SECOND PEACE CONFERENCE, 1907.

Charteris, A. H. The Second Peace Conference. In Juridical Review. Edinburgh and London, for Oct. 1907 and Jan. 1908. [An accurate general account, and the fullest, so far, produced in English.]

Deuxième conférence internationale de la paix. La Haye 15 juin—18 octobre 1907. Actes et documents. The Hague. 1907. 3 vols. [The uniform date notwithstanding, the volumes were issued at different times in 1908-9.]

Higgins, A. P. The Hague Peace Conferences and other international conferences concerning the laws and usages of war. Texts of conventions with commentaries. Cambridge. 1909. [Includes the London Naval Conference of 1909.]

International Documents, etc. Ed. E. A. Whittuck. 1908. [Text of general conventions as to war and arbitration, including the acts of both the first and the second Hague Conference.]

Lémonon, E. La deuxième Conférence de la Paix. Préface de M. Léon Bourgeois. Paris. 1908.

Parliamentary Papers. Miscellaneous, No. 1 (1908), Cd. 3857. [Contains preliminary correspondence, instructions to British delegates, Sir E. Fry's report on the results, text of Final Act and Conventions in French and English.]

—— Misc. No. 4 (1908), Cd. 4081. Protocols of the eleven plenary meetings of the Second Peace Conference held at The Hague in 1907, with the annexes to the protocols. 545 pp. [French text only. The annexes, which form the greater part of the volume, from p. 87 to the end, consist of reports and documents made or transmitted by the standing Committees to the Conference in plenary meeting. Annexe 66, p. 529, gives a list of arbitration treaties and treaties containing arbitration clauses to which Italy has become a party since 1899; most but not all of them provide for reference to the Hague tribunal.]

A note of the final reservations and abstentions from signature of particular Powers appeared in the Times and other public prints of July 2, 1908.

Renault, L. La conférence de La Haye en 1907. In Séances et Travaux de l'Académie des sciences morales et politiques. Paris. 1908. (P. 438.)

—— L'œuvre de la Haye, 1899 et 1907. Conférence faite à l'École libre des sciences politiques le 5 juin 1908. In Annales des sciences politiques, 15 July 1908. Paris.

Scott, J. B. The Hague Peace Conference of 1899 and 1907. Baltimore. 1909. 2 vols. [Contains American documents not published in Europe.]

Westlake, J. The Hague Conference. In Quarterly Review for Jan. 1908 (No. 414). (See also list of works at head of article.)

THE EUROPEAN CONCERT.

Crete, 1897–9. For full accounts see the Parliamentary Papers of those years. [It would be useless to give specific references here, as they are more readily found by means of the index in any library where the papers are accessible.]

III. PERMANENT ARBITRATION TREATIES CONCLUDED BY GREAT BRITAIN WITH FOREIGN POWERS.

Austria-Hungary : January 11, 1905.

Colombia : December 30, 1908.

Denmark : October 25, 1905.

France : October 14, 1903. (Prolonged by Exchange of Notes of October 14, 1908.)

Germany : July 12, 1904. (Renewed for one year July 1909; prolonged by exchange of Notes of Dec. 7, 1909. As to the latest exchange of notes with Germany, see Treaty Series, no. 36 (1909), Cd. 4968.)

Italy : February 1, 1904. (Prolonged by Exchange of Notes of January 4, 1909.)

Netherlands : February 15, 1905.

Norway : See Sweden and Norway.

Portugal : November 16, 1904.

Spain : February 27, 1904. (Prolonged by Exchange of Notes of January 11, 1909.)

Sweden and Norway : August 11, 1904.

Switzerland : November 16, 1904.

United States : April 4, 1908.

(All these agreements were concluded for a period of five years in the first instance. The Treaty with the United States contains a special provision as to the consent of the Senate of the United States and of any self-governing Dominion of the British Empire whose interests may be affected.)

The foregoing particulars were prepared, by the courtesy of the Foreign Office, before the publication of a parliamentary paper, Miscellaneous, no. 9 (1909), Cd. 4870, in which they may now be verified.

CHAPTER XXIII.

SOCIAL MOVEMENTS.

I. LOCAL GOVERNMENT.

A. The United Kingdom.

The Annual Reports of the Local Government Boards for England, Scotland and Ireland; the Local Taxation Accounts; and the annual returns as to tramways, gas, and electricity, supply official records. The Municipal Year-Book and the London Manual (annual) give convenient descriptions. An extensive collection of documents (reports, accounts, proceedings, etc.) of local governing bodies in all the principal countries is to be found at the British Library of Political Science in connection with the London School of Economics. The Bibliography of British Municipal History, by G. Gross (1897), and the bibliographies given in English Local Government, by Sidney and Beatrice Webb (1904 and 1908), mention practically all the works, large and small, bearing on the history of particular towns.

Arminjon, P. L'Administration Locale en Angleterre. Paris. 1895.

Ashley, P. W. L. Local and Central Government in England, France, Prussia and United States. 1906.

Atkinson, C. J. F. Concise Handbook of Provincial Local Government Law. Leeds. 1902.

—— M. Local Government in Scotland. Edinburgh. 1904.

Bertolini, P. Il Governo locale inglese e le sue relazione con la vita nazionale. Turin. 1899.

Blunden, G. H. Local Taxation and Finance. 1895.

Boverat, R. Le Socialisme Municipal en Angleterre. Paris. 1907.

Cannan, E. History of Local Rates in England. 1896.

Chapman, S. J. Local Government and State Aid. 1899.

Clifford, F. History of Private Bill Legislation. 2 vols. 1885-7.

Darwin, L. Municipal Trade. 1903.

Geddes, P. A Study in City Development. Edinburgh. 1904.

Gneist, R. von. Das Englische Verwaltungsrecht. Berlin. 1884.

—— Self-government, Communalverfassung und Verwaltungsgerichte in England. Berlin. 1871.

Gomme, G. L. The Governance of London. 1907.

—— The Principles of Local Government. 1897.

Graham, J. C. Taxation and Local Government. 1899.

Green, Mrs J. R. Town Life in the Fifteenth Century. 2 vols. 1895.

Grice, J. W. National and Local Finance. 1910.

Hugo, C. Städteverwaltung und Munizipal-Sozialismus in England. Stuttgart. 1897.
Irons, J. E. Burgh Government. Edinburgh, 1905.
Jenks, E. The Outlines of English Local Government. 2nd edn. 1908.
Maitland, F. W. Justice and Police. 1885.
—— Township and Borough. 1898.
Meyer, H. R. Municipal Ownership in Great Britain. 1906.
Montet, E. Étude sur le Socialisme Municipal Anglais. Paris. 1901.
Muir, R. History of Municipal Government in Liverpool to 1835. 1906.
National Civic Federation of New York. Report on Municipal and Private Operation
    of Public Utilities in the United Kingdom. 3 vols. New York. 1907.
Odgers, W. Blake. Local Government. 1907.
O'Meara, J. J. Municipal Taxation at Home and Abroad. 1894.
Porter, R. P. Dangers of Municipal Trading. 1907.
Probyn, J. W. Local Government and Taxation. (Cobden Club Essays.) 1875.
Redlich, J. and Hirst, F. W. Local Government in England. 2 vols. 1903.
Scholefield J. (editor). Encyclopaedia of Local Government Law. 1905.
Shaw, A. Municipal Government in Great Britain. New York. 1895.
—— G. B. The Common Sense of Municipal Trading. 1904.
Simon, Sir John. English Sanitary Institutions. 1890.
Sinzheimer, L. Der Londoner Grafschaftsrat. Vol. I. Stuttgart. 1900.
Smith, Toulmin. The Parish. 1857.
Suthers, R. B. Mind Your Own Business: the Case for Municipal Management.
    1905.
Vauthier, M. Le Gouvernement Local de l'Angleterre. Brussels. 1895.
Vine, Sir J. R. Somers. English Municipal Institutions, 1835-79. 1879.
Webb, Sidney. The London Programme. 1891.
Webb, Sidney and Beatrice. English Local Government from the Revolution to
    the Municipal Corporations Act, Vol. I. : The Parish and the County. 1904.
    Vols. II, III : The Manor and the Borough. 1908.
—— History of Liquor Licensing. 1904.
—— The Break Up of the Poor Law. 1909.
—— The Public Organisation of the Labour Market. 1909.

B. The United States.

Allinson, T. and Penrose, J. Philadelphia, 1681-1887. Philadelphia. 1887.
Bemis, E. W. Local Government in the South and South-west. Baltimore. 1893.
Champernowne, H. The Boss. New York. 1894.
Conkling, A. B. City Government in the United States. New York. 1894.
Devlin, T. C. Municipal Reform. New York. 1896.
Eaton, A. M. Origin of Municipal Incorporation in England and the United States.
    New York. 1902.
—— The Government of Municipalities. New York. 1899.
Goodnow, F. J. Comparative Administrative Law. New York. 1903.
—— Municipal Problems. New York. 1897.
—— Municipal Home Rule. New York. 1895.
—— City Government in the United States. New York. 1904.
Gould, E. R. L. Local Government in Pennsylvania. Baltimore. 1883.
Hatton, A. R. Digest of City Charters. Chicago. 1906.
Holcomb, W. P. Pennsylvanian Boroughs. Philadelphia. 1886.
Hollander, J. H. Financial History of Baltimore, 1729-1898. Baltimore. 1899.
Hosmer, J. K. South Adams Town Meeting. New York. 1884.
Howe, F. C. The City the Hope of Democracy. 1908.

Levermore, C. H. Republic of New Haven. New York. 1886.
Maclear, A. B. Early New England Towns. New York. 1908.
Robinson, C. M. The Improvement of Towns. New York. 1901.
—— Modern Civic Art. New York. 1903.
Rowe, L. S. Problems of City Government. New York. 1909.
Steffens, L. The Shame of the Cities. New York. 1904.
Wilcox, Delos F. The American City. New York. 1904.
—— The Study of City Government. New York. 1897.
Williamson, C. C. Finances of Cleveland. New York. 1907.
Zueblin, C. American Municipal Progress. New York. 1902.

C. The European Continent.

Acollas, P. A. R. P. E. Les Finances Communales. *s.l.* 1898.
Arias, G. Il Sistema della costituzione economica e sociale italiana. Turin. 1905.
Barbieri, A. Lo Stato ed il comune. Bologna. 1886.
Bellangé, C. Le Gouvernement Local en France. Paris. 1900.
Benz, R. von. Autonomie und Centralismus in der Gemeinde. Innsbruck. 1895.
Bernimouin, E. Les Institutions Provinciales et Communales de la Belgique. Brussels. 1891–2.
Blodig, H. Die Selbstverwaltung als Rechtsbegriff. Vienna. 1894.
Borioni, L. La vita della Provincia italiana. Rome. 1893.
Colajanni, N. Le Istituzione Municipale. Turin. 1883.
Deschanel, P. La Décentralisation. Paris. 1885.
Dresden. Die Deutschen Städte. Geschildert nach den Ergebnissen der ersten deutschen Städteaustellung zu Dresden, 1903. Leipzig. 1904.
Dubois, P. Le Budget Départemental.
—— Essai sur les Finances Communales. Paris. 1898.
Eiben, H. Die Ortspolizei. Cologne. 1908.
Ferron, H. de. Institutions municipales et provinciales comparées. Paris. 1884.
Gerstfeldt, P. Städtefinanzen in Preussen. Berlin. 1882.
Giron, Alfred. Essai sur le Droit Communal de la Belgique. Brussels. 1868.
Giulini, P. Il Decentramento dello Stato e la dislocazione delle imposte. Milan. 1892.
Grais, H. de. Handbuch der Verfassung und Verwaltung. Berlin. 1902.
Guignard, A. Le Self-Government ou la Décentralisation. Paris. 1897.
Hartman, H. G. Administratie de Gemeenten in Nederland. The Hague. 1891.
Helm, G. L. van den. De Gemeente-Administratie. The Hague. 1882.
Hugo, C. Arbeiterpolitik in der deutschen Städteverwaltung. Stuttgart. 1904.
—— Die Deutsche Städteverwaltung. Stuttgart. 1901.
Kaufmann, R. von. Kommunales Finanzwesen. Berlin. 1906.
Kinne, H. Die Autonomie der Communalverbände in Preussen. Berlin. 1908.
Laufer, F. Unser Polizeiwesen. Bibliothek der Rechts und Staats-Kunde, Vol. xxii. Stuttgart. 1905.
Leroy Beaulieu, P. L'Administration Locale en France et en Angleterre. Paris. 1872.
Lindemann, H. and Südekum, A. Kommunales Jahrbuch. 2 vols. Jena (annual).
Luçay, Count H. de. La Décentralisation. Paris. 1895.
Magne, E. L'esthétique des Villes. Paris. 1908.
Manzoni, L. Bibliografia dei Municipii. Rome. 1876–92.
Marcère, E. de. La Décentralisation. Paris. 1895.
Marie, J. De l'administration départementale. Paris. 1882.

Mercier, P.　Les Exploitations Municipales en France.　Évreux.　1905.

Meuriot, P.　Les agglomérations urbaines de l'Europe contemporaine.　Paris. 1898.

Mombert, P. ˙ Die deutschen Stadtgemeinden und ihre Arbeiter.　Munich.　1902.

Morgand, L.　La Loi Municipale.　Paris.　1902.

Morier, Sir R. B. D.　Local Government in England and Germany.　London. 1888.

Most, O.　Die Schuldenwirtschaft der deutschen Städte.　Jena.　1909.

Mounet, E.　Histoire de l'administration provinciale en France.　Paris.　1885.

Munro, W. B.　The Government of European Cities.　New York.　1909.

Preuss, H.　Das Städtische Amtsrecht in Preussen.　Berlin.　1902.

Redlich, J.　Das Wesen des österreichischen Kommunalverfassung.　**Leipzig.** 1910.

Richald, L.　Les Finances Communales en Belgique.　Brussels.　1892.

Romera, E.　Administracion local.　Almazan.　1896.

Schön, P.　Das Recht der Kommunalverbände in Preussen.　Leipzig.　1897.

Shaw, A.　Municipal Government in Continental Europe.　New York.　1901.

Sidenbladh, C.　Sveriges Kommuner i administrativt, judicielt och echlesiastikt häusiende.　Stockholm.　1898.

Silbergleit, H.　Preussens Städte.　Berlin.　1908.

Simonet, J. B.　Traité élémentaire de Droit Public et Administratif.　**Paris.**　1902.

Statistisches Jahrbuch Deutscher Städte.　Berlin (annual).

Stern, M.　Geschichten von Deutschen Städten.　New York.　1902.

Turquey, E.　Les Octrois Municipaux.　Paris.　1899.

Wagener, A.　Die Kommunalsteuerfrage.　Berlin.

Weber, A.　Die Grossstadt und ihre socialen Probleme.　Leipzig.　1908.

Zadek, J.　Hygiene der Städte.　Berlin.　1909.

Zadow, F.　Der ausserordentliche Finanzbedarf der Städte.　Jena.　1909.

II.　FACTORY LEGISLATION.

Ansiaux, M.　Heures de Travail et Salaires.　Paris.　1896.

Anton, G. K.　Geschichte der preussischen Fabrikgesetzgebung.　1891.　Staats- und socialwissenschaftliche Forschungen.　Ed. G. Schmoller.　Leipzig.　1878-.

Arlidge, J. T.　The Diseases of Occupations.　1892.

Bouquet, L.　Le Travail des enfants, des filles, etc.　Paris.　1893.

Brauts, V. L. J. L.　Législation du Travail Comparée et internationale.　Louvain. 1903.

Brentano, L.　Hours and Wages in relation to production.　1894.

Conférence Internationale du règlement du travail, Reports of.　1890.

Deutschen Handwerker und Arbeiter-Schutzgesetze.　Berlin.　1901.

Durand, E.　L'inspection du Travail en France de 1841 à 1902.　Paris.　1902.

France, Ministère du Commerce.　Législation Ouvrière et sociale en Australie et Nouvelle-Zélande.　Paris.　1901.

Grillet, L.　La Réglementation du Travail.　Encyclopédie scientifique des aide-mémoires.　Paris.　1892-.

Hodder, E.　Life of the seventh Earl of Shaftesbury.　1886.

Hutchins, B. L. and Harrison, A.　History of [English] Factory Legislation. 1903.

Jäger, E.　Geschichte und Literatur des Normalarbeitstages.　Stuttgart.　1892.

Jeans, V.　Factory Act Legislation.　Manchester.　1892.

Jones, Lloyd.　Life and Times of Robert Owen.　1889.

Kydd ("Alfred"), S.　History of the Factory Movement.　2 vols.　1857.

Landmann, J.   Die Arbeiterschutzgesetzgebung der Schweiz.   Basel.   1904.
Lohmann, T.   Die Fabrikgesetzgebungen der Staaten des Europäischen Continents.
    Berlin.   1878.
Louis, J.   L'Ouvrier devant l'État.   Histoire comparée des lois du travail.   Paris.
    1904.
Marx, Karl.   Das Kapital.   1867.
Oliver, Sir T.   Dangerous Trades.   1902.
Owen, Robert.   Observations on the Manufacturing System.   1815.
Plener, E. von.   English Factory Legislation.   1873.
Podmore, F.   Life of Robert Owen.   1908.
Rae, J.   Eight Hours for Work.   1894.
Reeves, W. P.   State Experiments in Australia and New Zealand.   1906.
Schäffle, A.   The Theory and Policy of Labour Protection.   1893.
Taylor, R. W. C.   Introduction to History of the Factory System.   1886.
——   The Modern Factory System.   1891.
——   The Factory System and the Factory Acts.   1894.
Webb, Mrs S. (and others).   The Case for the Factory Acts.   1901.
——   ——   ——   Socialism and National Minimum.   1908.
Webb, S. and Cox, H.   The Eight Hours Day.   1891.
Weyer, O.   Die Englische Fabrikinspection.   Tübingen.   1888.
Willoughby, W. F.   Foreign Labour Laws.   Washington.   1899.

III.   TRADE UNIONISM.

There is an extensive collection of Reports and ms. material in the British
Library of Political Science, at the London School of Economics.   S. and B. Webb's
History of Trade Unionism and Industrial Democracy contain elaborate biblio-
graphical lists.   Isabel Taylor's Bibliography of Unemployment and the Unemployed,
1909, supplements these from another standpoint.

Barnett, G. E.   Bibliography of American Trade Union publications.   Baltimore.
    2nd edn.   1909.
——   The Printers: a Study in American Trade Unionism.   Cambridge.   1906.
Beveridge, W. H.   Unemployment.   1909.
Brentano, L.   On the History of Gilds and Origin of Trade Unions.   1870.
——   Zur Kritik der Englischen Gewerbvereine.   Leipzig.   1872.
Bureau, P.   Le Contrat de Travail: le rôle des syndicats professionnels.   Paris.
    1902.
Commons, J. R.   Trade Unionism and Labour Problems.   New York.   1905.
Dechesne, L.   Les Syndicats Ouvriers belges.   Brussels.   1906.
Deffiennes, M.   La Coalition Ouvrière et la Grève, 1789–1884.   Paris.   1903.
Dubois, E.   Les Trade Unions et les Associations Professionnels en Belgique.
    Brussels.   1894.
Ely, R. T.   Labor Movement in America.   1890.
Georgi, E.   Theorie und Praxis des Generalstreiks in der modernen Arbeiter-
    bewegung.   Jena.   1908.
Halévy, D.   Essais sur le Mouvement ouvrier en France.   Paris.   1901.
Hermans, H.   Handboek voor de moderne vakvereeniging.   Maestricht.   1908.
Hollander, J. and Barnett, G. E.   Studies in American Trade Unionism.   Baltimore.
    1906.
Howell, G.   Conflicts of Capital and Labour.   1890.
——   Trade Unionism, New and Old.   1891.
Hudig, D.   De Vakbeweging in Nederland, 1866–78.   Amsterdam.   1904.
Jeauneney, J.   Associations et Syndicats de fonctionnaires.   Paris.   1908.

Kennedy, J. B. Beneficiary Features of American Trade Unions. Baltimore.
    1908.
Kessler, G. Die deutschen Arbeitgeberverbände. Leipzig. 1907.
Kirk, W. National Labor Federations in the United States. Baltimore. 1907.
Kritsky, Mdlle. L'évolution du Syndicalisme en France. Paris. 1908.
Labriola, A. (and others). Syndicalisme et Socialisme. Paris. 1908.
Levasseur, E. Histoire des classes ouvrières et de l'industrie en France de 1789 à
    1870. Paris. 1903.
Motley, J. M. Apprenticeship in American Trade Unions. Baltimore. 1901.
Mueller, O. Die Christliche Gewerkschaftsbewegung Deutschlands. 1905.
Powderly, T. V. Thirty Years of Labor, 1859–89. Columbus. 1889.
Pratt, E. A. Trade Unionism and British Industry. 1904.
Raynaud, B. Le Contrat Collectif de travail. Paris. 1901.
Saint-Léon, E. Martin. Le Compagnonnage: son histoire. Paris. 1901.
Sakolski, A. M. The Finances of American Trade Unions. Baltimore. 1909.
Schulze-Gaevernitz, G. von. Social Peace. 1893.
Thorndike, A. Zur Rechtsfähigkeit der deutschen Arbeitsberufvereine. Tübingen.
    1908.
Vandervelde, E. Enquête sur les associations professionnelles d'artisans et ouvriers
    en Belgique. Brussels. 1891.
Webb, Sidney and Beatrice. History of Trade Unionism. 1907.
—— Industrial Democracy. 1907.
—— Problems of Modern Industry. 1907.

IV. FRIENDLY SOCIETIES AND GOVERNMENTAL INSURANCE.

Arboux, J. La Mutualité Française. Paris. 1907.
Baernreither, J. M. English Associations of Working Men. 1889.
Bödiker, T. Reichs-Versicherungsgesetzgebung. Berlin. 1906.
—— Die Arbeiterversicherung in den europäischen Staaten. Berlin. 1895.
Brabrook, Sir E. W. Provident Societies and Industrial Welfare. 1898.
Brooks, J. G. Compulsory Insurance in Germany. Washington. 1895.
Derijean, G. L'assurance contre le chômage. Paris. 1899.
Gotze, E. and Schindler, O. Jahrbuch der Arbeiterversicherung. 2 vols. Berlin
    (annual).
Guillot, P. Les Assurances Ouvrières. Paris. 1897.
Hasbach, W. Englische Arbeiterversicherung. Berlin. 1883.
Jenny, O. H. Englisches Hülfskassenwesen. Berlin. 1905.
Lefort, J. Caisses de retraites ouvrières. Paris. 1906.
Leyers, Franz. Die Hülfskassen in Gegenwart und in der Zukunft. Tübingen.
    1908.
Lohmar, Paul. Die Deutsche Arbeiterversicherung. Berlin. 1907.
Schloss, D. F. Insurance against Unemployment. 1909.
Schmidt, C. Aufgaben der deutschen Invalidenversicherungsanstalten. Berlin.
    1905.
Schmitz, J. Arbeiterversicherung. Berlin. 1888.
Sutherland, W. Old Age Pensions. 1907.
Tessiore, E. L' assicurazione e gli infortuni. Milan. 1899.
Wilkinson, J. F. Mutual Thrift. 1892.
—— The Friendly Society Movement. 1886.
Willoughby, W. F. Workingmen's Insurance. Washington. 1898.
Zacher, G. Arbeiterversicherung im Auslande. 5 vols. Gross-Lichterfelde.
    1900–8.

V. COOPERATION.

The largest collections of reports, MS. and other unpublished material, so far as concerns the United Kingdom, are at the offices of the Cooperative Union, Nicholas Hey, Manchester, and at the British Library of Political Science, in the London School of Economics, London.

The International Cooperative Bibliography (270 pp.) issued by the International Cooperative Alliance in 1906, supplies an extensive list of works. Fay's Cooperation at Home and Abroad, 1908, gives a convenient select bibliography.

The yearly reports of the Cooperative Union, the Cooperative Wholesale Society, the Scottish Cooperative Wholesale Society, the Labour Copartnership Association, and the International Cooperative Alliance afford the latest available information.

A. The United Kingdom.

Acland, A. H. Dyke and Jones, B. Working Men Cooperators. Manchester. 1908.

Aves, Ernest. Cooperative Industry. 1907.

Cernesson, J. Les Sociétés Coopératives Anglaises. Paris. 1905.

Faux, H. Les Sociétés Coopératives de Consommation en Angleterre. Rennes. 1905.

Fay, C. R. Cooperation at Home and Abroad. 1908.

Holyoake, G. J. The History of the Rochdale Pioneers. Last edn. 1900.

—— The Cooperative Movement To-day. 1903.

—— The History of Cooperation, revised and completed. 2 vols. 1908.

Jones, B. Cooperative Production. Oxford. 1894.

Lloyd, H. D. Labour Copartnership. 1898.

Pitman, H. Memorial of E. V. Neale. Manchester. 1894.

Plunkett, Sir Horace. Ireland in the New Century. 1905.

Potter, Beatrice (Mrs Sidney Webb). The Cooperative Movement in Great Britain. 1892.

Schloss, D. F. Methods of Industrial Remuneration. 1907.

—— Report on Profit Sharing. 1894.

Valleroux, P. Hubert. La Coopération. Paris. 1904.

Webb, Catherine. Industrial Cooperation. Manchester. 1904.

Wolff, H. W. Cooperative Banking. 1907.

—— People's Banks. Last edn. 1910.

B. France.

Almanach de la Coopération Française. Paris (annual).

Berget, A. La Coopération dans la Viticulture Européenne. Lille. 1902.

Castlenau, E. Des Associations de vente de vin dans le Midi de la France. Paris. 1907.

Corréard, J. Les Sociétés coopératives de consommation. Paris. 1908.

Coulet, E. Le Mouvement Syndical et coopératif dans l'Agriculture française. Montpellier. 1898.

Fagneux, L. La Caisse de crédit Raiffeisen et le Raiffeisenisme en France. Paris. 1908.

Fontaine, A. Les Associations Ouvrières de Production. Office du Travail. Paris. 1897.

Gide, C. Les Sociétés Coopératives de la Consommation. Paris. 1904.

Gide, C. L'Économie Sociale. Paris. 1907.

Godin, J. B. A. Mutualité sociale et Association du capital et du travail. Paris. 1881.

—— Documents pour une biographie de. By M. A. Godin. Paris. 1901.

Hubert-Valleroux, P. Les Associations Coopératives. Paris. 1884.

Lucas, L. Des Coopératives Agricoles en France. Bordeaux. 1908.

Ministère de l'Agriculture. Enquête sur les Sociétés de Coopération. Paris. 1866.

Ministère du Travail. Statistique de la Coopération Industrielle et Commerciale en France. Paris. 1907.

Protopopescco, I. Coopération et Sociétés Coopératives. Paris. 1908.

Rieu, F. La Coopération ouvrière à travers les âges. Paris. 1898.

Rivet, H. Les Boulangeries Coopératives en France. Paris. 1904.

Rocquigny de Farel, Comte H. M. R. de. Les Syndicats Agricoles et leur œuvre. Paris. 1906.

Seilhac, L. de. La Verrerie Ouvrière d'Albi. Paris. 1901.

Taton, G. La Coopération dans l'Industrie Beurrière. Paris. 1908.

Tiefaine, P. Les Laiteries Coopératives en France. Paris. 1901.

Williams, A. Twenty years of Copartnership at Guise. London. 1903.

C. Germany.

Jahrbuch der Erwerbs- und Wirtschaftsgenossenschaften im Deutschen Reiche. Berlin (annual).

—— des Zentralverbandes deutscher Konsumvereine. Berlin (annual).

Kaufmann, H. Geschichte des Konsumgenossenschaftlichen Grosseinkaufes in Deutschland. Hamburg. 1904.

—— Die Lohn- und Arbeitsverhältnisse genossenschaftlicher Angestellter und Arbeiter. Hamburg. 1906.

Krüger, H. Die Deutsche Genossenschaftsgesetzgebung. Leipzig. 1908.

—— Vorschuss- und Kredit-Vereine als Volksbanken. Berlin. 1904.

Lindecke, O. Das Genossenschaftswesen in Deutschland. Leipzig. 1908.

Müller, F. Die geschichtliche Entwicklung des landwirthschaftlichen Genossenschaftswesens in Deutschland. Leipzig. 1901.

Oppenheimer, F. Die Siedlungsgenossenschaft. Leipzig. 1898.

Riehn, R. Das Konsumvereinswesen in Deutschland. Stuttgart. 1902.

Schneider, F. Baugenossenschaften, Bau- und Sparvereine. Berlin. 1899.

—— Konsumvereine. Berlin. 1904.

D. Belgium.

Annuaire de la Coopération Ouvrière belge. Brussels (annual).

Bertrand, L. Histoire de la Coopération en Belgique. Brussels. 1903.

Heldt, B. H. Instellingen op social en cooperatief gebiet in Belgie. Leeuwarden. 1892.

Léger, M. A. Les Coopératives et l'organisation Socialiste en Belgique. Brussels. 1899.

Malherbe, G. Les Fromageries ou Fruitières Coopératives. Brussels. 1899.

Resteau, C. Traité des Sociétés Coopératives. Brussels. 1906.

Rowntree, B. S. Life and Labour : Lessons from Belgium. 1910.

Trigaut, J. and Miserez, H. Les Machines Agricoles Syndicales. Brussels. 1901.

Turmann, M. Les Associations Agricoles en Belgique. Paris. 1903.

E. Switzerland.

Jahrbuch des Verbandes schweizerischer Konsumvereine. Basel (annual).
Jahresbericht über den schweizerischen Raiffeisenverband. Frauenfeld (annual).
Müller, Dr Hans. Die schweizerischen Konsumgenossenschaften. Basel. 1896.
Schweizerischer Genossenschafts-Kalender. (Annual.)

F. Italy.

Bassi, E. Le Latterie Sociali in Italia. Milan. 1900.
Ficcarelli, R. A. Manuale per le piccole cooperative di consumo. Milan. 1904.
Ligue Nationale, la, des Sociétés Coopératives Italiennes depuis 1866 jusqu'à 1906. Milan. 1907.
Maffi, A. Manuale per le Società cooperative di produzione e agricole. Milan. 1908.
Niccoli, V. Cooperative rurali, di credito, di assicurazione, di mutuo soccorso, di consumo, di acquisto, di materie prime, di vendita di prodotti agrari. Milan. 1908.
Pellegrini, U. La Cassa Rurale in Italia. Udine. 1906.
Pizzamiglio, L. Distributing Cooperative Societies. 1891.
Rabbeno, U. Societe Cooperativi di produzione. Milan. 1889.
——— La Cooperazione in Italia. Milan. 1886.
Reggiani, E. La Produzione del latte e le latterie sociali cooperative. Milan. 1908.
Società Umanitaria, la. L' opera della Società Umanitaria della sua fondazione. Milan. 1906.

G. Other Countries.

Apostol, P. L'artèle et la coopération. 1899. [Russia.]
Bancel, A. D. Kooperatyzin. Warsaw. 1908. [Russia.]
Bemis, E. W. Cooperation in New England. Baltimore. 1888.
——— Cooperation in the Middle States. Baltimore. 1888.
Bois, W. E. du. Economic Cooperation among Negro Americans. Atlanta. 1908. [United States.]
Chambres Consultatives des Associations ouvrières de Production. La Coopération de Production dans les Colonies françaises. Paris. 1904.
Chaves, Arias L. Las cajas rurales de credito del sistema de Raiffeisen. Zamora. 1907. [Spain.]
Marken, J. C. van. L'organisation sociale dans l'industrie; les sociétés industrielles de Hof van Delft. Delft. 1900. [Holland.]
Medina, F. Las Sociedades cooperativas. Buenos Aires. 1887.
Meijers, E. M. Landbancc-operatie in Nederland. Amsterdam. 1908.
Valentiner, J. Études sur les Associations de crédit hypothécaire en Danemark. 1902.

VI. EMANCIPATION OF WOMEN.

Anthony, C. Social and Political Dependence of Women. 1880.
Bebel, A. Die Frau. Engl. transl. by H. B. A. Walther: Women in the Past, Present and Future. 1894.
Blackburn, H. Handbook for Women. 1895.

Blackburn, H.   Women's Suffrage: a Record of the Suffrage movement in the British Isles.   1901.

Blackwell, E.   Pioneer Work in the Medical Profession.   1895.

Boston Public Library.   Bibliography of Higher Education of Women.   Boston. 1897.

Braun, L.   Die Frauenfrage.   Berlin.   1901.

Coit, Stanton D.   Women in Church and State.   1908.

Dicey, A. V.   Letters on Votes for Women.   1909.

Gilman, C. P. S.   Women and Economics.   1905.

Gnauck-Kuhne, E.   Die Frauenbewegung.   1908.

Godwin, M. W.   Vindication of the Rights of Women.   1792.

International Congress of Women, Reports of.   7 vols.   1900.

Jenks, E.   Husband and Wife in the Law.   1909.

Lange, H. and Baumer, G.   Handbuch der Frauenbewegung.   5 vols.   Berlin. 1901–5.

Lawrence, W. P.   Women's Fight for the Vote.   1909.

Lesueur, D.   L'Évolution féminine.   Paris.   1905.

Loria, A.   Le Féminisme au point de vue sociologique.   1907.

McLaren, Lady.   The Women's Charter.   1910.

Mathew, A. H.   Woman's Suffrage.   1909.

Mill, J. S.   The Subjection of Women.   1867.

Ostrogorski, M.   La Femme au point de vue du droit public.   Paris.   1892.

Rosler, A.   Die Frauenfrage.   1907.

Stanton, E. C. (and others).   History of Woman's Suffrage.   4 vols.   New York. 1881–1902.

Stopes, C. C.   British Freewomen.   1890.

Villiers, Brougham.   The Case for Women's Suffrage.   1909.

Wegener, M. (editor).   Merkbuch der Frauenbewegung.   Leipzig.   1908.

CHAPTER XXIV.

For this chapter it seemed beyond its purpose to supply a bibliography.

CHAPTER XXV.

MODERN EXPLORATIONS.

I. BIBLIOGRAPHICAL.

Boucher de la Richarderie, B.   Bibliothèque universelle des Voyages...classés par ordre de pays dans leur série chronologique.   6 vols.   Paris.   1808.

Fortescue, G. K.   Subject Index of modern works added to the Library of the British Museum 1881–1900 (s. v. Asia, Africa, China, etc.).   3 vols.   1902. Ditto, 1900–5.   1907.

Royal Asiatic Society of London.   Catalogue.   1893.

Royal Geographical Society of London.   Catalogue by H. R. Mill.   1895.   [Appendix I gives contents of Collections of Voyages by Hakluyt, Pinkerton, etc. Appendix II enumerates official publications classified by subjects, e.g. Asia, Africa, etc.]

Studii biografici e bibliografici sulla Storia della Geografia in Italia.   2 vols.   Rome. 1882.

II. ORIGINAL AUTHORITIES.

A.   ASIA AND AFRICA.

Mittheilungen aus Justus Perthes geographischer Anstalt.   By A. Petermann. With separate decennial indexes (Inhalts-Verzeichnisse) and Supplements (Ergänzungsbände) to the above.   Gotha.   1855 sqq.   (In progress.)

Royal Geographical Society of London.

Journal.   50 vols.   1832–80.   With separate decennial Indices, 1844, 1853, 1867, 1881, 1884.

Proceedings.   22 vols.   1855–78.   New Series.   14 vols.   1879–92.

Journal, including Proceedings.   1893 sqq.   With separate index to first 20 vols.   1906.   (In progress.)

Supplementary Papers to the above.   1832 sqq.   (In progress.)

Société de Géographie.   Paris.

Bulletins.   134 vols.   1822–99.   Separate indexes to the Bulletins, 1822–1900. 3 vols.   1845, 1866, 1900.

Comptes rendus.   17 vols.   1883–1900.

La Géographie (continues Comptes rendus and Bulletins).   1900 sqq.   (In progress.)

Société géographique impériale de Russie.   Comptes rendus.   St Petersburg. 1851 sqq.   (In progress.)

Società geografica Italiana.   Bollettini.   With separate index, 1865–75, and after this date separate decennial indices.   Florence and Rome.   1868 sqq.   (In progress.)

CH. XXV.

B. Asia.

(1) *Principal works.*

Abbott, J. Herat, Khiva, etc. 2 vols. 1856.
Anderson, J. Mandalay to Momien. 1876.
Bellew, H. W. Kashmir and Kashgar. Edinburgh. 1875.
Bishop, Isabella. Journeys in Persia and Kurdistan. 2 vols. 1891.
—— Korea and her neighbours. 2 vols. 1898.
—— Yang-Tse Valley and beyond. 2 vols. 1899.
Bruce, James. Travels to discover the Source of the Nile. 5 vols. Edinburgh.
    1790.
Burnes, Sir Alexander. Travels into Bokhara. 3 vols. 1835.
Burton, Sir Richard. Pilgrimage to El Medinah and Mecca. 3 vols. 1855–6.
Capus, G. À travers le Royaume de Tamerlane. Paris. 1892.
Curzon of Kedleston, G. N., Viscount. Russia in Central Asia. 1889.
—— Persia. 2 vols. 1892.
—— Problems of the far East, Japan, Korea, China. 1894. 2nd edn. 1896.
Dutreuil de Rhins, J. L. L'Asie Centrale. Paris. 1889.
—— Mission Scientifique. 3 vols. Paris. 1897–8.
Freshfield, Douglas W. Travels in Central Caucasus. 1869.
Gill, W. River of Golden Sand. 2 vols. 1880.
Hakluyt Society Publications. Vols. LXXII, LXXIII: Early Voyages to Russia and
    Persia. 2 vols. 1886.
Hedin, Sven. Through Asia. 2 vols. 1898.
—— Scientific Results of a Journey in Central Asia. 1899–1902. Stockholm.
    1904–. (*In progress.*)
Holdich, Sir T. Tibet the Mysterious. 1906.
—— Indian Borderland. 2nd edn. 1909.
Hosie, A. Three Years in Western China. 2nd edn. 1897.
Huc, É. Souvenirs d'un voyage dans la Tartarie. 2 vols. Paris. 1850.
Huntington, E. Geologic and Physiographic Reconnaissance in Central Turkestan.
    Washington. 1905–.
—— Pulse of Asia. Boston. 1907.
Palgrave, W. G. Narrative of a Year's Journey through Central and Eastern
    Arabia. 3rd edn. 2 vols. London and Cambridge. 1865.
Prjevalsky, N. Mongolia. Transl. E. D. Morgan. 1876.
—— From Kulja across the Tian Shan to Lob Nor. Transl. E. D. Morgan.
    1879.
Shaw, R. Visits to High Tartary. 1871.
Sherring, C. A. Western Tibet. 1906.
Sykes, P. M. Ten Thousand Miles in Persia. 1902.
Wellby, M. S. Through Unknown Tibet. 1898.
Younghusband, Sir F. The Heart of a Continent. 1896. 2nd edn. 1904.

(2) *Books by travellers.*

The following travellers have described their Asiatic travels in books with
various titles:

Abbott, J.; Allen, T. G.; Baber, E. Colborne; Barzini, L.*‡; Bellew, H. H.;
Bishop, Isabella; Blakiston, T.; Bogle, G.; Bonvalot, G.*†; Bower, Hamilton;

* Engl. or Engl. transl.   † French or French transl.   ‡ Italian.

Bruce, C. D.; Burnaby, Fred; Burnes, Alexander; Capus, G. †; Colquhoun, A.; Conolly, A.; Cooper, T.; Crosby, O. T.; Deasy, H. H. P.; Desgodins, C. H.; Dutreuil de Rhins, J. L.; Ferrier, J. P.*; Forsyth, Sir T. Douglas; Futterer, C. §; Garnier, M J. F.†; Goldsmid, Sir F. J.; Hallett, Holt; Hedin, Sven*; Prince Henri d'Orléans†; Hosie, A.; Huc, Évariste*†; Huntington, Ellsworth; Jack, R. Logan; Jones, Sir Harford; Knight, E. F.; Landor, A. Savage; Lesdain, Comte de*†; Little, A. J.; Littledale, St G.; MacCarthy, J.; MacGahan, J.; Malcolm, Sir John; Manning, Thomas; Margary, A.; Masson, C.; Moorcroft, W ; Morier, J.; Nordenskjöld, Adolf*; Payer, Julius* §; Potagos, Papagiotis †; Pottinger, Sir H.; Prjevalsky, N.*; Rawling, C. J.; Rawlinson, Sir Henry; Richthofen, Ferdinand von §; Rockhill, W. Woodville; Shaw, R.; Stein, M. A.; Sykes, P. Molesworth; Tavernier, J. B.*†; Taylor, Annie; Turner, S.; Vambéry, Arminius*; Vigne, G. T.*; Wellby, M. S.; Wenyon, C.; Wiggins, J.; Wolff, Joseph; Wood, J.

(3) *Notes by travellers.*

Records or authoritative notices:

Carey, A. D. In Royal Geogr. Soc. Proceedings. 1887. [Pp. 731 sqq.] And Supplementary Papers. Vol. III. 1890.
Elias, N. In Geogr. Journal. 1873.
Hayward, G. In Geogr. Journal. 1870.
Moorcroft, W. In Asiatic Researches. Vol. XII. Calcutta.
Prjevalsky, N. In Royal Geogr. Soc. Proc. 1887.
Rheinthal, Captain. In R. Michell's Account of a Russian Mission. 1870.
Shakespear, Sir R. In Blackwood's Magazine. Edinburgh. 1842.
Siberian Explorers, Map of. In E. Reclus, Nouv. Géogr. Universelle (*see below* under III *A*). Vol. v, p. 579.
Strachey, H. Journal of Asiatic Society of Bengal. Calcutta. 1848.
—— Geogr. Journal. Vol. XIX, p. lxvii. 1849.
—— Sir R. Geographical Journal (New Series). Vol. xv, pp. 150 sqq. 1900.

C. Africa.

(1) *Principal works.*

African Association, Proceedings of. 2 vols. 1790–1902.
Arnot, F. S. From the Zambesi to Benguella. Glasgow. 1883.
Barth, H. Travels in North and Central Africa. 5 vols. 1857–8.
Burton, Sir Richard. Lake Regions of Central Africa. 2 vols. 1860.
—— Wanderings in West Africa. 2 vols. 1863.
—— Lands of Cazembe (Lacerda, Monteiro, Graça, etc.). 1873.
Duveyrier, Henri. Sahara algérien et tunisien. Paris. 1905.
Grant, Col. J. A. A Walk across Africa. 1864.
Johnston, Sir H. H. The Uganda Protectorate. 2 vols. 1902.
—— George Grenfell and the Congo. 2 vols. 1908.
Junker, W. Travels in Africa. 1875–86. 3 vols. 1890–2.
Livingstone, D. Missionary Travels. 1857. Ed. F. S. Arnot. 1899.
—— Expedition to the Zambesi. 1865.
—— Last Journals. 2 vols. 1874.

* Engl. or Engl. transl.   † French or French transl.
§ German.

Lugard, Sir F. J. D. The Rise of our East African Empire. 2 vols. Edinburgh.
    1893.
Nachtigal, Gustav. Sahara und Sudan. 3 vols. Berlin. 1879–89.
Schweinfurth, G. The Heart of Africa. 2 vols. 1873.
Société de Géographie. Documents scientifiques de la Mission Saharienne (Mission
    Foureau-Lamy). 2 vols. Paris. 1905.
Speke, John M. Journal of the Discovery of the source of the Nile. 1864.
Stanley, Sir H. M. How I found Livingstone. 1872.
—— Through the Dark Continent. 2 vols. 1878.
—— The Congo and the Founding of its Free State. 2 vols. 1885.
—— In Darkest Africa. 2 vols. 1890.

(2) *Books by travellers.*

The following travellers have described their African travels in books with
various titles:

Andersson, C. J.; Baikie, W.; Baker, Sir Samuel; Barth, H.*; Bonchamps,
C. de†; Bóttego, V.‡; Bowdich, T.; Browne, W. G.; Bruce, James; Burckhardt,
John; Caillié, R.; Cameron, Verney; Capello, H.*‖; Cecchi, A.; Chaillu, P. du*;
Denham, Dixon; Duveyrier, Henri†; Emin Pasha*§; Foureau, Fernand; Galton,
Francis; Gentil, Émil†; Gordon, Charles G.; Grant, James; Grenfell, George;
Hornemann, F.*; Krapf, J.*; James, Frank; Johnston, Sir H. H.; Junker, W.*§;
Laing, A. G.; Lander, R.; Lugard, Sir F.; Lyon, G.; Maistre, C.†; Moffatt, Robert;
Nachtigal, G.§; Paez, Pedro‡; Park, Mungo; Peters, Carl*§; Petherick, John;
Piaggia, C.‡; Pinto, A. de Serpa*; Poncet, Charles*†; Potagos, Papagiotis†;
Richardson, J.; Robecchi-Brichetti, L.‡; Rohlfs, Gerard*§; Rüppell, W. E.;
Schweinfurth, Georg*§; Speke, John; Stanley, Sir H. M.; Teleki, Count S.*;
Thomson, Joseph; Wellby, Montagu S.; Wissmann, H. von*§.

(3) *Notes by travellers.*

Records or authoritative notices:
Laing, Alexander G. In Quarterly Review. 1830.
Marchand, J. B. In J. Poirier. De L'Oubanghi à Fachoda. Paris. 1900.
Paez, Pedro. In C. Beccari. Rerum Aethiopicarum Scriptores. Vol. ii. Rome.
    1902 sqq.
Tinné, A. In W. Wells. Alexandrine Tinné. New York. 1871.
Vogl, E. In E. and C. H. Schauenburg. Reisen in Central Africa. 3 vols. Lahr.
    1859–67. (Vol. i, pp. 493 sqq.)

D. Parliamentary Papers and other Official Documents.

Papers connected with the Development of trade between British Burma and
    Western China and with the Mission to Yün-nan of 1874–5. 1876. C. 1456.
Reports:

(1) By Mr Baber on the route followed by Mr Grosvenor's Mission. 1878.
        C. 1994.
(2) By Mr Baber of his Journey to Ta-chien-lu. 1878–9. C. 2393.
(3) By A. Hosie of a Journey through Kwei-chau and Yün-nan. 1833.
(4) By F. S. A. Bourne of a Journey in South-Western China. 1888.

* English or Engl. transl.   † French or French transl.
‡ Italian.   § German.   ‖ Portuguese.

(5) By C. W. Campbell, H. M.'s Consul, on a Journey in Mongolia. 1904. Cd. 1874.

(6) By George Kidston on a Journey in Mongolia. 1904. Cd. 1954. 1904. Cd. 2096.

(7) By Act. Cos. Litton on a Journey in North West Yün-nan. 1904. Cd. 1836.

(8) By Consul-Gen. Hosie on Se-chuan. 1905. Cd. 2247.

(9) By Consul-Gen. Hosie on a Journey to the Eastern frontier of Tibet. 1905. Cd. 2586.

(10) By W. J. Clenell, H. M.'s Consul, on a Journey in Kiang-si. 1906. Cd. 2762.

Papers relating to Tibet. 1904. Cd. 1920. Cd. 2054. 1905. Cd. 2370.

Hertslet, Sir E. Map of Africa by Treaty. 3 vols. 1896.
—— Treaties between Great Britain, etc. with China. 2 vols. 3rd edn. 1908.

III. SECONDARY AUTHORITIES.

A. Asia and Africa.

Cooley, W. D. History of Maritime and Inland Discovery. 3 vols. 1830–1.

Keltie, J. S. The World's Great Explorers. 7 vols. 1889–92.
—— The Story of Exploration. (*In progress.*) London. 1903 sqq.

Murray, H. Historical Account of Discoveries in Africa. 2 vols. Edinburgh. 1818.
—— Historical Account of Discoveries in Asia. 3 vols. Edinburgh. 1820.

Pinkerton, J. Collection of Voyages. 17 vols. 1804–14.

Reclus, E. Nouvelle Géographie Universelle. 19 vols. (separate). (*In progress.*) Paris. 1876 sqq.

Stanford, E. Compendium of Geography and Travel:
—— Asia. 2 vols. 1906–9.
—— Africa. 2 vols. 1904–7.
—— North America. 2 vols. 1897–8.
—— Central and South America. 2 vols. 1901.
—— Australasia. 2 vols. 1907–8.

B. Asia.

Hellwald, F. von. Russians in Central Asia. 1874.

Krahmer, G. Russland in Asien. Berlin. 1905. (*In progress.*)

Markham, Sir Clements R. Memoir of the Indian Surveys. 1871. 2nd edn. 1878.
—— Narratives of the Mission of C. Bogle to Tibet and of the Journey of T. Manning, with notes, etc. 1876.

Michell, J. and R. Russians in Central Asia. 1865.

Skrine, F. H. B. Heart of Asia. A History of Russian Turkestan. 1899.

Yule, Sir H. Cathay and the Way thither. 2 vols. 1866.

C. Africa.

Keltie, J. S. Partition of Africa. 1895.

Monteiro, J. J. Angola and the River Congo. 2 vols. 1875.

CHAPTER XXVI.

THE GROWTH OF HISTORICAL SCIENCE.

I. GENERAL WORKS.

Acton, Lord. A Lecture on the study of history. Cambridge. 1895.

Adams, C. K. Manual of Historical Literature. New York. 1888.

Altamira, R. La Enseñanza de la Historia. Madrid. 1895.

Barth, P. Die Philosophie der Geschichte als Soziologie. Leipzig. 1897.

Bauer, A. Die Forschungen zur griechischen Geschichte, 1888–93. Munich. 1899.

Baur, F. C. Die Epochen der Kirchlichen Geschichtschreibung. Tübingen. 1852.

Bernheim, E. Lehrbuch der Historischen Methode. Leipzig. 1908.

Bethge, R. Ergebnisse der Germanistischen Wissenschaft im letzten Vierteljahrhundert. Leipzig. 1902.

Bury, J. B. Introduction to Gibbon's Decline and Fall of the Roman Empire.
1896.

—— An inaugural lecture. Cambridge. 1903.

Cheyne, T. K. Founders of Old Testament Criticism. 1893.

Döllinger, I. Akademische Reden. Vol. II. Nördlingen. 1889.

Flint, R. The philosophy of history in France and Germany. Edinburgh and
London. 1874.

Freeman, E. A. Methods of Historical Study. 1886.

—— The unity of history. (Rede Lecture.) 1872.

Häusser, L. Gesammelte Schriften. 2 vols. Berlin. 1869–70.

Hilprecht, H. Explorations in Bible Lands. Edinburgh. 1903.

Jahresbericht der Geschichtswissenschaft. Berlin. 1878–.

Jodl, F. Die Culturgeschichtschreibung. Halle. 1878.

Kroll, W. Die Altertumswissenschaft im letzten Vierteljahrhundert. Leipzig.
1905.

Langlois, C. Manuel de Bibliographie historique. 2 vols. Paris. 1895, 1904.

Langlois, C. and Seignobos, C. Introduction to the Study of History. 1898.

Michaelis, A. A Century of Archaeological Discoveries. 1908.

Mohl, J. Vingt-sept Ans d'Histoire des Études Orientales. 2 vols. Paris.
1879–80.

Rosenmund, R. Die Fortschritte der Diplomatik seit Mabillon. Munich. 1897.

Sandys, J. E. A History of Classical Scholarship. Vols. II and III. Cambridge.
1908.

Schweitzer, A. The Quest of the Historical Jesus. 1910.

Wachler, L. Geschichte der historischen Forschung und Kunst. 2 vols. Göttingen. 1812, 1816.

Wolf, G. Einführung in das Studium der neueren Geschichte. Berlin. 1910.

Year's Work, The, in Classical Studies. 1906 sqq.

II. GERMANY, AUSTRIA AND SWITZERLAND.

(a) GENERAL WORKS.

Acton, Lord. German Schools of History. In Historical Essays and Studies. 1907.

Benfey, T. Geschichte der Sprachwissenschaft und orientalischen Philologie. Munich. 1869.

Bursian, C. Geschichte der classischen Philologie. Munich. 1883.

Cardauns, H. Die Görres-Gesellschaft, 1876–1901. Cologne. 1901.

Curtius, E. Alterthum und Gegenwart. Vols. II and III. Berlin. 1882, 1889.

Dove, A. Ausgewählte Schriften. Leipzig. 1898.

Gierke, O. Die historische Rechtsschule und die Germanisten. Berlin. 1903.

Goldfriedrich, J. Die historische Ideenlehre in Deutschland. Berlin. 1902.

Göttinger Professoren. Gotha. 1871.

Grimm, J. Kleine Schriften. Vol. I. Berlin. 1864.

Harnack, A. Geschichte der Preussischen Akademie der Wissenschaften. Berlin. 1901.

Haym, R. Die Romantische Schule. Berlin. 1870.

Historische Commission, Die, 1858–83. Munich. 1883.

Kluckhohn, A. Vorträge und Aufsätze. Munich. 1894.

Lexis, W. Die deutschen Universitäten. 2 vols. Berlin. 1893.

Lorenz, O. Die Geschichtswissenschaft. Berlin. 1886.

Michaelis, A. Geschichte des deutschen Archäologischen Instituts. Berlin. 1879.

Ranke, L. von. Reden. Sämmtliche Werke, Vols. LI and LII. Leipzig.

Raumer, R. von. Geschichte der Germanischen Philologie. Munich. 1870.

Ritter, M. Ueber die Gründung, Leistungen und Aufgaben der Historischen Commission. Sybel's Historische Zeitschrift, Vol. CIII. Munich and Leipzig.

Schaumkell, F. Geschichte der deutschen Kulturgeschichtschreibung. Leipzig. 1905.

Sybel, H. von. Vorträge und Abhandlungen. Munich. 1897.

Treitschke, H. von. Deutsche Geschichte im 19ten Jahrhundert. 5 vols. Leipzig. 1879–94.

Wegele, F. Geschichte der deutschen Historiographie. Munich. 1885.

(b) MONOGRAPHS.

Acton, Lord. Döllinger's Historical Work. In History of Freedom and other Essays. London. 1907.

Arneth, A. von. Aus meinem Leben. 2 vols. Stuttgart. 1893.

Barth, P. Geschichtsphilosophie Hegels. Leipzig. 1890.

Bürkner, R. Karl von Hase. Leipzig. 1900.

Classen, J. B. G. Niebuhr. Gotha. 1876.

Curtius, F. Ernst Curtius. Ein Lebensbild in Briefen. Berlin. 1903.

Dilthey, Karl. Otfried Müller. Göttingen. 1898.

Dörfel, J. Gervinus als historischer Denker. Gotha. 1904.

Droysen, G. J. G. Droysen. Vol. I. Leipzig. 1910.

Duncker, M. Droysen. In Abhandlungen. Leipzig. 1887.

Ebers, G. Richard Lepsius. New York. 1887.

Ennecerus, L. Savigny. Marburg. 1879.

Erben, W. Sickel. In Historische Vierteljahrsschrift. Vol. XI.

Eyssenhardt, F. B. G. Niebuhr. Gotha. 1886.

Friedrich, J. Ignaz von Döllinger. 3 vols. Munich. 1899–1901.

Gervinus, G. Leben, von ihm selbst. Leipzig. 1893.

Gierke, O. Rudolf von Gneist. Berlin. 1896.

Goetz, L.　F. H. Reusch.　Gotha.　1901.
Grabmann, M.　Heinrich Denifle.　Mainz.　1905.
Guglia, E.　Leopold von Ranke.　Leipzig.　1893.
Harnack, A.　Neander.　In Reden und Aufsätze.　Vol. i.　Giessen.　1904.
Hartmann, L.　Mommsen.　Gotha.　1908.
Hausrath, A.　Zur Erinnerung an Treitschke.　Leipzig.　1901.
Hauviller, M.　F. X. Kraus.　Colmar.　1904.
Hermann, F.　Die Geschichtsauffassung Ludens.　Gotha.　1904.
Hertz, M.　Karl Lachmann.　Berlin.　1851.
Hoffmann, Max.　August Böckh.　Leipzig.　1901.
Hüffer, H.　Alfred von Reumont.　Cologne.　1904.
Janssen, J.　J. F. Böhmer's Leben.　3 vols.　Freiburg i. B.　1868.
Jung, J.　Julius Ficker.　Innsbruck.　1907.
Kekulé, R.　Das Leben F. G. Welcker's.　Leipzig.　1880.
Kittel, O.　W. von Humboldt's Geschichtliche Weltanschauung.　Leipzig.　1901.
Klopp, W.　Onno Klopp.　Ein Lebenslauf.　Osnabrück.　1907.
Lamprecht, K.　Ranke's Ideenlehre.　In Alte und Neue Richtungen.　Berlin.　1896.
Lieber, F.　Reminiscences of Niebuhr.　London.　1835.
Lorenz, O.　L. von Ranke.　Berlin.　1891.
Lutolf, A.　J. E. Kopp.　3 vols.　Lucerne.　1868.
Marcks, E.　Biographie Baumgarten's.　In Baumgarten's Aufsätze und Reden.　Strassburg.　1894.
——　H. von Treitschke.　Heidelberg.　1906.
Meyer, E. H.　J. M. Lappenberg.　Hamburg.　1867.
Nalbandian, W.　Ranke's Bildungsjahre.　Leipzig.　1902.
Niebuhr, B. G.　Life and Letters of.　3 vols.　London.　1852.
Pastor, L.　Johannes Janssen.　Freiburg i. B.　1894.
Ranke, L. von.　Zur eigenen Lebensgeschichte.　Leipzig.　1890.
Schaff, P.　Neander.　Gotha.　1886.
Scherer, W.　Jacob Grimm.　Berlin.　1885.
Schiemann, T.　Treitschke's Lehr- und Wanderjahre, 1834–67.　Munich.　1898.
Schuchhardt, C.　Schliemann's Excavations.　London.　1891.
Schulte, J. von.　K. F. Eichhorn.　Stuttgart.　1884.
Sepp, H.　Görres und seine Zeitgenossen.　Nördlingen.　1877.
Simonsfeld, H.　W. H. Riehl.　Munich.　1898.
Springer, A.　F. C. Dahlmann.　2 vols.　Leipzig.　1870.
Stenzel, K.　G. Stenzel's Leben.　Gotha.　1897.
Stoll, A.　Friedrich Wilken.　Cassel.　1896.
Trog, H.　Jakob Burckhardt.　Basel.　1898.
Weber, G.　F. C. Schlosser.　Leipzig.　1876.
Zeller, E.　(Baur. Die Tübinger historische Schule.)　In Vorträge und Abhandlungen.　Vol. i.　Leipzig.　1875.

III.　FRANCE.

Aulard, A.　Taine, historien de la Révolution française.　Paris.　1907.
Bardoux, M.　Guizot.　Paris.　1894.
Boutmy, E.　Taine, Scherer, Laboulaye.　Paris.　1901.
——　A. Sorel.　In Études politiques.　Paris.　1907.
Caron, P. and Sagnac, P.　L'État actuel des Études d'Histoire moderne en France.　Paris.　1902.
Charmes, Xavier.　Le Comité des Travaux historiques.　3 vols.　Paris.　1886.
Darmesteter, J.　Notice sur la Vie et l'Œuvre de Renan.　Paris.　1893.
Diehl, C.　Les Études Byzantines en France.　Byz. Zeitschrift.　Leipzig.　1900.
Fagniez, G.　Le Duc de Broglie.　Paris.　1902.

Faguet, E.   Politiques et Moralistes.   3 vols.   Paris.   1891–8.
Flint, R.   Historical Philosophy in France.   Edinburgh.   1893.
Galley, J. B.   Claude Fauriel.   Saint-Étienne.   1909.
Giraud, V.   Essai sur Taine.   Paris.   1902.
Guérard, B.   Notice sur Daunou.   Paris.   1855.
Guiraud, P.   Fustel de Coulanges.   Paris.   1896.
Guizot, F.   De Barante.   London.   1867.
Hanotaux, G.   H. Martin.   Paris.   1885.
Hartleben, H.   Champollion.   2 vols.   Berlin.   1906.
Jullian, C.   Extraits des historiens français au 19ème siècle.   Paris.   1897.
Livret de l'École des Chartes, 1821–91.   Paris.   1891.
Maigron, L.   Le roman historique.   Paris.   1898.
Margerie, A. de.   Taine.   Paris.   1894.
Maury, A.   L'ancienne Académie des Inscriptions et Belles-Lettres.   Paris.   1864.
Mazade, C. de.   Thiers.   Paris.   1884.
Merlet, G.   Tableau de la Littérature française, 1800–15.   Vol. ii.   Paris.   1883.
Mignet, F.   Portraits et Notices.   Vol. ii.   Paris.   1852.
——   Éloges historiques.   Paris.   1864.
——   Nouveaux Éloges historiques.   Paris.   1877.
Molinier, A.   Les Sources de l'histoire de France.   Vol. v.   Introduction Générale.
      Paris.   1904.
Monod, G.   Taine, Renan, Michelet.   Paris.   1896.
——   Jules Michelet.   Paris.   1905.
Oliphant, M.   Count Montalembert.   2 vols.   1872.
Petit, E.   François Mignet.   Paris.   1889.
Petit de Julleville, L.   Histoire de la Langue et de la Littérature française.
      8 vols.   Paris.   1896–1900.
Picot, G.   Le Duc d'Aumale.   Paris.   1898.
Quinet, Mme Edgar.   Quinet.   2 vols.   Paris.   1888–9.
——   Cinquante Ans d'Amitié.   Michelet and Quinet.   Paris.   1903.
Rapport sur les Progrès des Études relatives à l'Égypte et à l'Orient.   Paris.   1867.
Renan, E.   Essais de Morale et de Critique.   (Augustin Thierry.)   Paris.   1859.
Sainte-Beuve, C. A.   Portraits Contemporains.   Causeries du Lundi.   Derniers
      Lundis.   Paris.
Saint-Hilaire, B.   Victor Cousin.   3 vols.   Paris.   1895.
Séché, L.   Sainte-Beuve.   2 vols.   Paris.   1904.
Simon, J.   Thiers, Guizot, Rémusat.   Paris.   1885.
——   Mignet, Michelet, Henri Martin.   Paris.   1890.
Sonolet, L.   Henry Houssaye.   Paris.   1905.
Sorel, A.   Notes et Portraits.   Paris.   1909.
Taine, H.   Life and Letters.   3 vols.   1902–8.
Thienot, J.   Rapport sur les Études historiques.   Paris.   1867.
Tocqueville, A. de.   Memoir, Letters and Remains.   2 vols.   1861.
Wailly, N. de.   Notice sur Guérard.   Paris.   1855.
Wallon, H.   Éloges Académiques.   2 vols.   Paris.   1882.

IV. GREAT BRITAIN AND AMERICA.

Alison, A.   Autobiography.   2 vols.   Edinburgh.   1883.
Bain, A.   Character and Writings of Grote.   In Grote's Minor Works.   1873.
Bryce, J.   Studies in Contemporary Biography.   1902.
Clark, J. W.   V. Thirlwall.   In Old Friends at Cambridge and elsewhere.   1900.
Creighton, L.   Life and Letters of M. Creighton.   2 vols.   1904.
Elton, O.   Memoir and Letters of York Powell.   Oxford.   1906.

Firth, C. H. Introduction to Cromwell's Letters and Speeches. Ed. S. Lomas. 1904.

Fisher, H. A. L. F. W. Maitland. Cambridge. 1910.

Freeman, E. A. Grote and Thirlwall. In Historical Essays. Second Series. 1889.

Froude, J. A. Carlyle's Life. 4 vols. 1890.

Gardiner, S. R. and Mullinger, J. B. Introduction to English History. 3rd edn. 1894.

Gasquet, F. A. Lord Acton and his circle. 1903.

Green, J. R. Letters. Ed. L. Stephen. 1901.

Grote, Mrs. The personal Life of George Grote. 1873.

Howe, A. Life and Letters of George Bancroft. 2 vols. 1908.

Huth, A. H. Life and Writings of Buckle. 2 vols. 1880.

Jameson, J. F. History of Historical Writing in America. Boston. 1891.

Lecky, W. E. H. Memoir of. By his wife. 1909.

Mignet, F. Hallam. In Éloges historiques. Paris. 1864.

Milman, A. Memoir of H. H. Milman. 1900.

Morison, J. C. Macaulay. 1882.

Motley, J. M. Correspondence. 2 vols. 1889.

Paul, Herbert. Memoir of Lord Acton, in Letters to Mary Gladstone. 1904.

—— Life of Froude. 1905.

Rawlinson, G. Life of Sir H. Rawlinson. 1898.

Robertson, J. M. Buckle and his Critics. 1895.

Smith, A. L. F. W. Maitland. Oxford. 1908.

Stanley, A. P. Life of Arnold. 2 vols. 1844.

Stephens, W. Life and Letters of E. A. Freeman. 2 vols. 1895.

Stubbs, W. Letters. Edited by W. H. Hutton. 1904.

Ticknor, G. Life of Prescott. 1864.

Trevelyan, Sir G. O. Life of Macaulay. 2 vols. 1875.

Vinogradoff, P. Villainage in England, Introduction. Oxford. 1892.

Wace, H. Memoir of J. S. Brewer. In English Studies. 1881.

Walker, Hugh. Victorian Literature. Cambridge. 1910.

V. OTHER COUNTRIES.

Baldasseroni, F. Pasquale Villari. Florence. 1907.

Blok, P. J. Fruin. In Verspreide Studien. Groningen. 1903.

Döllinger, I. Herculano da Carvalho. In Akademische Reden. Vol. II. Nördlingen. 1889.

Frédéricq, P. The Study of History in Holland and Belgium. Baltimore. 1890.

Guerrier, W. Solovieff. In Sybel's Historische Zeitschrift. Vol. XLV. Munich and Leipzig.

Guiraud, J. De Rossi. In Revue Historique. Vol. LVIII.

Luchaire, J. Essai sur l'Évolution intellectuelle de l'Italie, 1815-30. Paris. 1906.

Lützow, Count. Lectures on the Historians of Bohemia. 1905.

Nielsen, J. Erik Geijer. Odense. 1902.

Potvin, C. Cinquante Ans de Liberté. Vol. IV. Brussels. 1882.

Reumont, A. von. Gino Capponi. Gotha. 1880.

Steenstrup, J. Historieskrivningen i Danmark i det 19de Aarhundrede. Copenhagen. 1889.

Stephens, H. M. Modern Historians and their Influence on small Nationalities. Contemporary Review. July 1887.

Tommasini, O. Amari. In Scritti di Storia e critica. Rome. 1891.

CHRONOLOGICAL TABLE

OF

PRINCIPAL EVENTS MENTIONED IN THIS VOLUME.

1867 Karl Marx' *Das Capital.*
 Fenian outrages at Manchester and Clerkenwell.
1868 Revolution in Spain: insurrection in Cuba.
 Feb.–Dec. Disraeli prime Minister.
 British Abyssinian expedition: Magdala stormed.
 December. Gladstone prime Minister.
1869-77 Mexican Boundary Commission.
1869 Union-Pacific railway completed.
 November. Suez Canal opened.
1870-89 Guzmán Blanco dictator in Venezuela.
1870-2 Cardwell's Army reforms.
1870 Franco-German War.
 Great Britain guarantees neutrality and independence of Belgium.
 Vatican decrees announce Papal Infallibility.
 October. Russia denounces Treaty of Paris (1856).
 Treaty of Versailles: William I of Prussia becomes German Emperor.
 Irish Land Act and Coercion Act.
 Forster's Elementary Education Act establishes school boards.
 Irish Home Government (Home Rule) Association formed.
1871 January. Conference of London partly abrogates Treaty of Paris (1856).
 February. French National Assembly at Bordeaux.
 ,, Peace preliminaries between France and Germany signed.
 March. Commune in Paris.
 ,, Bulgarian Exarchate created.
 May. Peace of Frankfort.
 ,, Treaty of Washington submits *Alabama* claims to arbitration.
 August. Thiers President of the French Republic.
 September. First Old-Catholic Congress at Munich.
 Amadeus of Savoy King of Spain.
 Return of the religious Orders to France.
 Fundamental Articles announced in Bohemia.
 Law of Guarantees in Italy.
 Completion of the Japanese revolution.
1872 January. Comte de Chambord's Declaration from Antwerp.
 July. French Committee of Defence adopts compulsory military service.
 September. Agreement between the three Emperors (*Dreikaiserbund*).
 ,, Geneva award on *Alabama* claims announced.
 November. Thiers demands Commission to draw up a Constitution.
 First rebellion against Spain in the Philippine Islands.
 Self-government instituted in Cape Colony.
 Death of Charles XV of Sweden: Oscar II.
1873 Abolition of the Statholdership in Norway.
 Abdication of Amadeus in Spain: Spanish Republic proclaimed.
 Anti-ecclesiastical legislation in Prussia (*Kulturkampf*).
 May. Resignation of Thiers: Macmahon President.
 July. Final evacuation of France by German troops.
 October. Comte de Chambord's Frohsdorf Letter.
 British Residents placed in the Malay States.
 Dutch begin the war of Achin.
 Uniform monetary system in the German empire.
1874 February. Disraeli (Beaconsfield) prime Minister.
 Russo-German treaty.
 December. Alfonso XII King of Spain.
 Stubbs' *Constitutional History of England.*

1875 Final establishment of the Constitution of the French Republic.
March.   Crisis in the relations between France and Germany.
   „   Papal Bull *Quod nunquam.*
May.   Further anti-ecclesiastical legislation in Prussia.
Great Britain purchases the Khedive's shares in the Suez Canal.
The Herzegovina in insurrection.
Great Britain annexes the Fiji Isles.
Russia secures Saghalín.
Treaty between Japan and Korea.
1876 May.   Bulgarian massacres.
   „   British fleet sent to Besika bay.
   „   Abd-ul-Aziz deposed : Murad V.
June.   Servia and Bulgaria declare war on Turkey.
August.   Murad V deposed : Abd-ul-Hamid II.
November.   Russian troops reach Turkish frontier.
December.   Conference of Constantinople.
Establishment in Egypt of the Commission of the Public Debt.
1877 April.   War breaks out between Russia and Turkey.
Roumanian independence declared.
Siege of Plevna (surrendered December).
Montenegrins take Nikshich.
Gordon governor-general of the Sudan (resigned 1880).
Transvaal annexed by Great Britain.
Permissive Federation Act for British South African Colonies.
Parnell leader of Irish party : organised obstruction in the House of
   Commons.
Satsuma rebellion in Japan.
Porfirio Díaz President of Mexico.
1878 January.   Death of Victor Emmanuel II.   Accession of Humbert I.
   „   Russians take Adrianople and Montenegrins Spizza, Antivari, and
      Dulcigno.
February.   Death of Pius IX.   Election of Leo XIII.
   „   British fleet sent to Constantinople.
   „   Austria occupies Bosnia and the Herzegovina.
March.   Treaty of San Stefano between Russia and Turkey.
June–July.   Berlin Conference : Treaty of Berlin.
June.   Cyprus Convention.
   „   International Exhibition at Paris.
September.   British envoy sent to Afghanistan.
October.   Pact of Halepa (Crete).
Colombia grants concession for French construction of Panamá Canal.
Congress of Zemstva at Kieff.
1879 January.   Zulu War ; battle of Isandhlwana ; defence of Rorke's Drift.
May.   Yakub Khan signs Treaty of Gandamak.
July.   Battle of Ulundi.
   „   Taaffe president of ministry in Austria (till 1893) and Tisza in Hungary.
September.   Cavagnari murdered : second invasion of Afghanistan.
Defensive alliance of Austria and Germany.
Acute agricultural depression begins in Great Britain.
1880 April.   Gladstone becomes prime Minister.
   „   Great Britain recognises Abdurrahman in Afghanistan.
July.   Battle of Maiwand.
   „   Battle of Kandahar.
August.   Turkey cedes part of Thessaly to Greece.

1880 November. Montenegro obtains Dulcigno.
  December. Boer revolt in the Transvaal.
  Jesuits expelled from France: Congregations required to obtain a license.
  Party of *Socialist Workers* formed in France.
  Ismaïl deposed in Egypt: Tewfik Khedive.
1881 February. Battle of Majuba Hill.
  March. Murder of Tsar Alexander II. Alexander III Tsar.
  May. Treaty of Bardo: France occupies Tunis.
  June. France establishes free primary education.
    „ Labour Congress at Reims.
  August. Pretoria Convention restores independence to the Transvaal.
    „ Gladstone's Irish Land Act.
  September. Murder of President Garfield.
  November. Gambetta Minister in France (till January, 1882).
  Roumania declares itself a kingdom.
  Rising of the Mahdi in the Sudan.
  French protectorate on Upper Niger established.
  British North Borneo Company chartered.
  Chilian troops take Lima: Treaty between Chile and Argentina.
1882 Triple Alliance of Austria, Germany and Italy.
  Servia declares itself a kingdom.
  War between Servia and Bulgaria.
  May. Phoenix Park murders: Prevention of Crimes (Ireland) Act.
    „ *Temporary Rules* in Russia enacted against Jews.
    „ Arabi Pasha Minister in Egypt.
  June. Outrages in Alexandria: British fleet bombards fortifications.
  August. Battle of Tel-el-Kebir.
  Africander Bond formed in Cape Colony.
  German Colonial Society formed.
  First Conference at Tōkiō.
1883 Egyptian army under Hicks destroyed near El Obeïd.
  August. French protectorate over Annam established.
  Great Britain repudiates Queensland's annexations in New Guinea.
  First General Congress of Mutual Aid Societies at Lyons.
  Germany begins system of workmen's insurance.
1884 Congress of Berlin recognises French Congo and the Congo Free State
    under Leopold II.
  Renewed alliance of the three Emperors.
  Secret neutrality treaty (*reinsurance*) between Germany and Russia.
  October. Afghan Boundary Commission meets.
  Gordon sent to Khartum.
  Wolseley's attempt to relieve Khartum.
  Russia annexes Merv.
  Germany establishes protectorate over Angra Pequeña.
  German and British annexations in New Guinea.
  Fournier Convention. French military intervention in Tonkin.
  Convention of London between Great Britain and the Transvaal.
  Right of Association recognised in France.
  Great Boer *treks* in South Africa.
  Japanese intervention in Korea.
1885 January. Fall of Khartum: Sudan evacuated.
  March. France adopts a protective tariff.
  May. Collision between Afghans and Russians at Penjdeh.
  June. Salisbury prime Minister.

1885 June. Treaty of Tientsin between France and China.
      September. Union of the two Bulgarias.
      November. Death of Alfonso XII of Spain. Regency of Maria Cristina.
      Italy occupies Massowah.
      Ashbourne Irish Land Act.
      Canadian Pacific railway completed.
      Australian Federal Council attempted.
      British annexation of southern Bechuanaland.
      German East Africa Company formed.
      British East Africa Company formed (chartered 1888).
      Forcible Russianisation of Esthonia and Livonia begins.
1886 January. Gladstone prime Minister.
      May. Birth of Alfonso XIII.
      June. First Home Rule Bill.
      July. Salisbury prime Minister.
      October. O'Brien's *Plan of Campaign*.
      Treaty of Bucharest.
      Alexander of Bulgaria kidnapped, restored, and resigns.
      British annexation of Upper Burma.
      British Royal Niger Company chartered.
      Anglo-German Agreement delimits spheres of East African companies.
      Gold rush to the Transvaal.
      Polish League formed.
      Balmaceda President of Chile.
1887 First jubilee of Queen Victoria.
      First British Colonial Conference.
      Ferdinand of Saxe-Coburg becomes Prince of Bulgaria.
      Treaty between France and China.
      April. Boulanger's plot in France.
      Drummond Wolff's mission to Teheran.
      Joint control of Great Britain and France in New Hebrides.
1888 March. Death of William I of Germany ; Frederick III Emperor.
      June. Death of Frederick III ; William II Emperor.
      British protectorate over North Borneo, Brunei, and Sarawak established.
      Russian railway reaches Samarkand.
      Treaty between Russia and Korea.
      Conversion of British National Debt.
      Local Government Act.
      Parnell Commission.
1889 Milan of Servia abdicates : Alexander succeeds.
      Young Čech party becomes prominent in Bohemia.
      Franco-Russian *entente*.
      British South Africa Company formed.
      Pedro II deposed in Brazil.
      Panamerican conference at Washington.
      China gives permission for railway construction.
      Treaty of Accialli between Italy and Abyssinia.
1890 Death of William III of Holland. Wilhelmina Queen.
      March. Fall of Bismarck.
      Fall of Tisza in Hungary.
      July. Heligoland ceded to Germany by Great Britain.
      British protectorate over Zanzibar recognised by Germany.
      French protectorate over Madagascar recognised.
      Anglo-French treaty delimits boundaries by Lake Chad.

1890 Balfour's Congested Districts Boards and light railways in Ireland.
General strikes in Australia begin.
First Japanese parliament.

1891 Anglo-Portuguese Agreement delimits Zambesi territories.
Trans-Siberian railway begun.
Three years' famine in Russia begins.
Ravachol Anarchist outrages in Paris: strike at Fourmies.
German general insurance system completed.
Great strike and financial crisis in Australia.
Close of Chilian civil war.

1892 January. Death of Tewfik Pasha: Abbas II Khedive. Anti-British
agitation begins in Egypt.
  „   Méline Customs tariff in France.
Reconciliation between Leo XIII and France.
France attacks Dahomey and annexes the Ivory Coast.
Cross' Indian Councils Act.
August. Gladstone prime Minister.
Witte's financial reforms in Russia begin.
National Union formed on the Witwatersrand.

1893 Shipóff president of the Moscow Zemstvo.
Polish *Workmen's Union* forms a socialist party.
Matabele war in British South Africa.
Responsible government granted to Natal.
September. Gladstone's second Home Rule Bill rejected.
New Zealand extends the franchise to women.
Arbitration at Paris on Behring Sea fisheries concluded.
Brazilian civil War begins.

1894 Death of Tsar Alexander III. Nicholas II.
March. Gladstone resigns. Rosebery prime Minister.
June. Murder of President Carnot in France.
December. Trial and condemnation of Captain Dreyfus.
Armenian massacres.
War between Japan and China.
Treaty between Great Britain and Japan.
Commercial treaty for ten years between Germany and Russia.
British protectorate over Uganda declared.
French take Timbuktu.
New Zealand Factory Act for inspection of all workshops.
Harcourt's death-duties budget.

1895 Franco-Russian alliance.
June. Salisbury prime Minister.
August. British occupation of Chitral.
October. Murder of the Queen of Korea.
December. Jameson raid into the Transvaal.
Murder of Stambuloff: Ferdinand of Bulgaria recognised by Russia.
Further Armenian massacres.
Polish National League reorganised.
Close of war between Japan and China.
France, Germany, and Russia intervene between Japan and China.
Secret Russo-Chinese Treaty.
The Transvaal violates the Convention of London: British ultimatum.
Brazilian civil War ends.
Cuban rebellion renewed.
Great opening of mines and factories in southern Russia.

1895 Röntgen discovers X-rays.
1896 President Cleveland's Venezuelan message.
Franco-British treaty secures integrity of Siam.
Annexation of Madagascar by France.
Defeat of Italian troops at Adowah.
Egyptian army occupies Dongola.
Massacre of Armenians at Constantinople.
Victoria (Australia) Factory Act establishes Wages Boards.
First outbreak of plague in India.
1897 Second jubilee of Queen Victoria.
Massacre at Canea: the five admirals occupy Crete.
War between Greece and Turkey.
Germany leases Kiaochow from China.
Afridi and Mohmand tribes rise on Indian frontier.
Renewed revolt of the Philippine Islands against Spain.
Murder of Cánovas.
Linguistic decrees for Bohemia announced.
Employers' Liability Act.
Dreyfus agitation begins.
1898 February. Destruction of the *Maine* in Havana bay.
April. The United States declare war on Spain; Santiago taken.
July. Cuba separates from Spain.
September. The Egyptian army takes Omdurman and the Sudan.
    „   Marchand's expedition reaches Fashoda.
October. Storming of Dargai: peace restored on Indian frontier.
December. Treaty of Paris between Spain and the United States.
Peace conference invited by the Tsar of Russia.
Bóbrikoff governor of Finland.
Russia leases Port Arthur from China.
Great Britain leases Wei-Hai-Wei from China.
France leases Kwang Chow Wan from China.
The Emperor of China resigns to the Dowager Empress.
Boxer movement begins in China.
The United States take Manila and annex the Philippine Islands.
The United States annex Hawaii.
Commercial war between France and Italy ended.
Prince George of Greece Commissioner in Crete.
Milan riots.
Plunkett's Agricultural Society in Ireland founded.
Irish Local Government Act.
1899 Death of Luiz I of Portugal. Carlos I King.
Peace conference at the Hague.
Constitution of Finland abrogated.
Boulanger plot defeated in France.
Dreyfus affair concluded.
Macedonian Committee at Sofia demands autonomy for Macedonia.
The Transvaal and the Orange Free State declare war on Great Britain.
Sieges of Ladysmith, Kimberley, and Mafeking.
British-Egyptian agreement regulates the Sudan.
Germany and the United States divide Samoa Isles.
Conclusion of Venezuelan boundary arbitration.
Gold rush to Klondyke.
November. Battle of Modder river.
December. Battles of Magersfontein and of the Tugela.

1899 O'Brien's United Irish League.
1900 Murder of Humbert I : Victor Emmanuel III.
    February. Battle of Paardeberg, capture of Bloemfontein, relief of Ladysmith.
    May. Relief of Mafeking.
    ,,   Annexation of Orange Free State.
    June. Battle of Diamond Hill.
    September. Annexation of the Transvaal by Great Britain.
    Royal Niger Company surrenders to the Crown.
    British protectorate over Lagos and Nigeria established.
    Boxers attack the Legations at Peking.
    Joint column enters Peking.
    Treaty between France and Italy.
    Australian Federation Act creates Commonwealth of Australia.
    Legal uniformity within the German empire completed.
1901 January. Death of Queen Victoria. Edward VII.
    Triple Alliance renewed.
    Trans-Siberian railway opened.
    July. French treaty with Morocco.
    Habibulla Amir of Afghanistan.
    Australia excludes Asiatics and all coloured labour.
1902 Anglo-Japanese alliance.
    Russo-Chinese treaty.
    Peace of Vereeniging accepted by the Boers.
    French Panamá Company cedes its concession to the United States.
    Balfour's Education Act for England and Wales.
    Irish Land Conference.
    Witte's Agricultural Committees formed in Russia.
    Russian strikes.
1903 March. General abolition of sugar bounties.
    Death of Leo XIII. Pius X Pope.
    Murder of Alexander of Servia : Peter I (Karageorgevich).
    Austria and Russia announce the Mürzsteg Programme for Macedonia.
    April. Russian troops reach the Yalu.
    Polish League issues its Programme.
    Pogróms on Jews in Russia.
    Great strikes at Baku.
    Chamberlain leaves the ministry in order to advocate Imperial preference.
    Irish Land Purchase Act.
    Native rising in British Somaliland.
    Great Britain, Germany, and Italy make naval demonstration against Venezuela.
    United States recognise independence of Panamá and obtain lease of Canal district.
1904 February. War breaks out between Russia and Japan.
    ,,   Siege of Port Arthur begins.
    April. Pius X breaks with the French Government.
    ,,   Anglo-French agreement.
    August. Treaty of London between Great Britain and France.
    October. Franco-Spanish agreement upon Morocco.
    ,,   Battles of Liaoyang and the Sha-ho.
    ,,   Dogger Bank incident.
    General strike in Italy.
    British march to Lhassa.

1904 Herrero revolt against German rule begins in East Africa.
1905 January. Fall of Port Arthur.
    February. Battle of Mukden.
    May. Battle of Tsushima.
    June. Japanese take Saghalín.
      ,, Germany requires dismissal of M. Delcassé.
    August. Peace of Portsmouth between Russia and Japan.
      ,, Anglo-Japanese alliance renewed.
      ,, Norway dissolves Union with Sweden: Haakon VII King of Norway.
    September. Algeciras Conference.
      ,, International fleet occupies harbour of Mitylene.
      ,, Unions formed in Russia: Union of Unions meets.
      ,, Strikes and *pogróms* in Russia: liberties promised to Finland.
    October. Tsar's manifesto.
    Zemstvo Congress in Moscow.
    Campbell-Bannerman prime Minister.
1906 Self-government conferred on the Transvaal.
    Imperial Conference of British Colonial delegates.
    Murder of the Grand Duke Sergius in Russia.
    First Russian Duma meets.
    Separation Law of Church and State in France.
    Third Panamerican Congress meets at Rio Janeiro.
1907 Anglo-Russian Convention settles spheres of influence in Persia.
    Austro-Hungarian *Compromise* renewed.
    Second and third Russian Dumas.
    Second Hague Conference.
    Immigration agreement between Canada and Japan.
1908 Jubilee of Emperor Francis Joseph.
    Murder of Carlos of Portugal: accession of Manuel.
    Baltic and North Sea Conventions.
    Young Turk revolution at Constantinople.
    Austria annexes Bosnia and the Herzegovina.
    Crete demands union with Greece.
    Bulgaria proclaims her independence.
    Mr Asquith prime Minister.
1909 Death of Leopold II: Belgium annexes Congo State.
    Abd-ul-Hamid II deposed: Mohammad V Sultan.
    Federation of British South Africa.
    Declaration of London.
    Germany recognises French sphere of influence in Morocco.
    Peary reaches the North Pole.
1910 Death of Edward VII. Accession of George V.

INDEX OF NAMES

CAMBRIDGE: PRINTED BY J. B. PEACE, M.A., AT THE UNIVERSITY PRESS.